The Oxford Handbook of
Quantitative Methods

OXFORD LIBRARY OF PSYCHOLOGY

EDITOR-IN-CHIEF

Peter E. Nathan

AREA EDITORS:

Clinical Psychology
David H. Barlow

Cognitive Neuroscience
Kevin N. Ochsner and Stephen M. Kosslyn

Cognitive Psychology
Daniel Reisberg

Counseling Psychology
Elizabeth M. Altmaier and Jo-Ida C. Hansen

Developmental Psychology
Philip David Zelazo

Health Psychology
Howard S. Friedman

History of Psychology
David B. Baker

Methods and Measurement
Todd D. Little

Neuropsychology
Kenneth M. Adams

Organizational Psychology
Steve W. J. Kozlowski

Personality and Social Psychology
Kay Deaux and Mark Snyder

OXFORD LIBRARY OF PSYCHOLOGY

Editor-in-Chief PETER E. NATHAN

The Oxford Handbook of Quantitative Methods

Edited by
Todd D. Little

VOLUME 2: STATISTICAL ANALYSIS

OXFORD
UNIVERSITY PRESS

OXFORD
UNIVERSITY PRESS

Oxford University Press is a department of the University of Oxford.
It furthers the University's objective of excellence in research, scholarship,
and education by publishing worldwide.

Oxford   New York
Auckland   Cape Town   Dar es Salaam   Hong Kong   Karachi
Kuala Lumpur   Madrid   Melbourne   Mexico City   Nairobi
New Delhi   Shanghai   Taipei   Toronto

With offices in
Argentina   Austria   Brazil   Chile   Czech Republic   France   Greece
Guatemala   Hungary   Italy   Japan   Poland   Portugal   Singapore
South Korea   Switzerland   Thailand   Turkey   Ukraine   Vietnam

Oxford is a registered trademark of Oxford University Press in the UK and certain other
countries.

Published in the United States of America by
Oxford University Press
198 Madison Avenue, New York, NY 10016

© Oxford University Press 2013

First issued as an Oxford University Press paperback, 2014.

All rights reserved. No part of this publication may be reproduced, stored in a
retrieval system, or transmitted, in any form or by any means, without the prior
permission in writing of Oxford University Press, or as expressly permitted by law,
by license, or under terms agreed with the appropriate reproduction rights organization.
Inquiries concerning reproduction outside the scope of the above should be sent to the
Rights Department, Oxford University Press, at the address above.

You must not circulate this work in any other form
and you must impose this same condition on any acquirer.

Library of Congress Cataloging-in-Publication Data
The Oxford handbook of quantitative methods / edited by Todd D. Little.
    v. cm. – (Oxford library of psychology)
ISBN 978–0–993487–4 (hardcover); 978–0–19–937015–3 (paperback)
ISBN 978–0–993489–8 (hardcover); 978–0–19–937016–0 (paperback)
1. Psychology–Statistical methods.   2. Psychology–Mathematical models.   I. Little, Todd D.
BF39.O927 2012
150.72′1—dc23
2012015005

9 8 7 6 5 4 3 2
Printed in the United States of America
on acid-free paper

SHORT CONTENTS

Oxford Library of Psychology   vii

About the Editor   ix

Contributors   xi

Table of Contents   xvii

Chapters   1–758

Index   759

OXFORD LIBRARY OF PSYCHOLOGY

The *Oxford Library of Psychology*, a landmark series of handbooks, is published by Oxford University Press, one of the world's oldest and most highly respected publishers, with a tradition of publishing significant books in psychology. The ambitious goal of the *Oxford Library of Psychology* is nothing less than to span a vibrant, wide-ranging field and, in so doing, to fill a clear market need.

Encompassing a comprehensive set of handbooks, organized hierarchically, the *Library* incorporates volumes at different levels, each designed to meet a distinct need. At one level are a set of handbooks designed broadly to survey the major subfields of psychology; at another are numerous handbooks that cover important current focal research and scholarly areas of psychology in depth and detail. Planned as a reflection of the dynamism of psychology, the *Library* will grow and expand as psychology itself develops, thereby highlighting significant new research that will impact on the field. Adding to its accessibility and ease of use, the *Library* will be published in print and, later on, electronically.

The *Library* surveys psychology's principal subfields with a set of handbooks that capture the current status and future prospects of those major subdisciplines. This initial set includes handbooks of social and personality psychology, clinical psychology, counseling psychology, school psychology, educational psychology, industrial and organizational psychology, cognitive psychology, cognitive neuroscience, methods and measurements, history, neuropsychology, personality assessment, developmental psychology, and more. Each handbook undertakes to review one of psychology's major subdisciplines with breadth, comprehensiveness, and exemplary scholarship. In addition to these broadly conceived volumes, the *Library* also includes a large number of handbooks designed to explore in depth more specialized areas of scholarship and research, such as stress, health and coping, anxiety and related disorders, cognitive development, or child and adolescent assessment. In contrast to the broad coverage of the subfield handbooks, each of these latter volumes focuses on an especially productive, more highly focused line of scholarship and research. Whether at the broadest or most specific level, however, all of the *Library* handbooks offer synthetic coverage that reviews and evaluates the relevant past and present research and anticipates research in the future. Each handbook in the *Library* includes introductory and concluding chapters written by its editor to provide a roadmap to the handbook's table of contents and to offer informed anticipations of significant future developments in that field.

An undertaking of this scope calls for handbook editors and chapter authors who are established scholars in the areas about which they write. Many of the nation's and world's most productive and best-respected psychologists have agreed to edit *Library* handbooks or write authoritative chapters in their areas of expertise.

For whom has the *Oxford Library of Psychology* been written? Because of its breadth, depth, and accessibility, the *Library* serves a diverse audience, including graduate students in psychology and their faculty mentors, scholars, researchers, and practitioners in psychology and related fields. Each will find in the *Library* the information they seek on the subfield or focal area of psychology in which they work or are interested.

Befitting its commitment to accessibility, each handbook includes a comprehensive index, as well as extensive references to help guide research. And because the *Library* was designed from its inception as an online as well as a print resource, its structure and contents will be readily and rationally searchable online. Further, once the *Library* is released online, the handbooks will be regularly and thoroughly updated.

In summary, the *Oxford Library of Psychology* will grow organically to provide a thoroughly informed perspective on the field of psychology—one that reflects both psychology's dynamism and its increasing interdisciplinarity. Once published electronically, the *Library* is also destined to become a uniquely valuable interactive tool, with extended search and browsing capabilities. As you begin to consult this handbook, we sincerely hope you will share our enthusiasm for the more than 500-year tradition of Oxford University Press for excellence, innovation, and quality, as exemplified by the *Oxford Library of Psychology.*

Peter E. Nathan
Editor-in-Chief
Oxford Library of Psychology

ABOUT THE EDITOR

Todd D. Little
Todd D. Little, Ph.D, is a Professor of Educational Psychology and Director of Texas Tech University Research Institute. Little is internationally recognized for his quantitative work on various aspects of applied SEM (e.g., indicator selection, parceling, modeling developmental processes) as well as his substantive developmental research (e.g., action-control processes and motivation, coping, and self-regulation). In 2001, Little was elected to membership in the Society for Multivariate Experimental Psychology. In 2009, he was elected President of APA's Division 5 (Evaluation, Measurement, and Statistics) and in 2010 was elected Fellow of the division. In 2012, he was elected Fellow in the Association for Psychological Science. He founded, organizes, and teaches in the internationally renowned KU "Stats Camps" each June (see crmda.KU.edu for details of the summer training programs). Little has edited five books related to methodology including *The Oxford Handbook of Quantitative Methods* and the *Guilford Handbook of Developmental Research Methods* (with Brett Laursen and Noel Card). Little has been principal investigator or co-principal investigator on more than 15 grants and contracts, statistical consultant on more than 60 grants and he has guided the development of more than 10 different measurement tools.

CONTRIBUTORS

Leona S. Aiken
Department of Psychology
Arizona State University
Tempe, AZ

Rawni A. Anderson
Center for Research Methods
and Data Analysis
University of Kansas
Lawrence, KS

Luc Anselin
GeoDa Center for Geospatial Analysis
and Computation
School of Geographical Sciences and
Urban Planning
Arizona State University
Tempe, AZ

Amanda N. Baraldi
Department of Psychology
Arizona State University
Tempe, AZ

David E. Bard
Department of Pediatrics
University of Oklahoma Health Sciences
Center
Oklahoma City, OK

Theodore P. Beauchaine
Department of Psychology
Washington State University
Pullman, WA

Gabriëlla A.M. Blokland
Genetic Epidemiology Laboratory
Queensland Institute of
Medical Research
School of Psychology and Centre
for Advanced Imaging
University of Queensland
Brisbane, Australia

Annette Brose
Max Plank Institute for Human
Development
Berlin, Germany
Max Plank Institute for Human Cognitive
and Brain Sciences

Timothy A. Brown
Department of Psychology
Boston University
Boston, MA

Trent D. Buskirk
Department of Community Health-
Biostatistics Division
Saint Louis University
Saint Louis, MO

Noel A. Card
Family Studies and Human Development
University of Arizona
Tucson, AZ

Deborah M. Casper
Family Studies and Human Development
University of Arizona
Tucson, AZ

Daniel R. Cavagnaro
Department of Psychology
The Ohio State University
Columbus, OH

Rand D. Conger
Department of Human and Community
Development
University of California at Davis
Davis, CA

David Cook
Abt Associates Inc.

Thomas D. Cook
Institute for Policy Research
Northwestern University
Evanston, IL

Stefany Coxe
Department of Psychology
Arizona State University
Tempe, AZ

R.J. de Ayala
Department of Educational
Psychology
University of Nebraska Lincoln
Lincoln, NE

Pascal R. Deboeck
  Department of Psychology
  University of Kansas
  Lawrence, KS

Sarah Depaoli
  Department of Educational Psychology
  University of Wisconsin Madison
  Madison, WI

Cody S. Ding
  College of Education
  University of Missouri-Saint Louis
  Saint Louis, MO

M. Brent Donnellan
  Department of Psychology
  Michigan State University
  East Lansing, MI

Dawnté R. Early
  Department of Human and Community Development
  University of California at Davis
  Davis, CA

Craig K. Enders
  Department of Psychology
  Arizona State University
  Tempe, AZ

David M. Erceg-Hurn
  School of Psychology
  University of Western Australia
  Crawley, WA, Australia

Aurelio José Figueredo
  Department of Psychology
  School of Mind, Brain, & Behavior
  Division of Family Studies and Human Development
  College of Agriculture and Life Sciences
  University of Arizona
  Tucson, AZ

Rafael Antonio Garcia
  Department of Psychology
  School of Mind, Brain, & Behavior
  University of Arizona
  Tucson, AZ

Amanda C. Gottschall
  Department of Psychology
  Arizona State University
  Tempe, AZ

Michael J. Greenacre
  Department of Economics and Business
  Universitat Pompeu Fabra, Barcelona
  Barcelona, Spain

Brian D. Haig
  Department of Psychology
  University of Canterbury
  Canterbury, New Zealand

Kelly Hallberg
  Institute for Policy Research
  Northwestern University
  Evanston, IL

Lisa L. Harlow
  Department of Psychology
  University of Rhode Island
  Kingston, RI

Emily J. Hart
  Department of Psychology
  University at Buffalo
  The State University of New York
  Buffalo, NY

Kit-Tai Hau
  The Chinese University of Hong Kong
  Hong Kong

Joop J. Hox
  Department of Methodology and Statistics
  Utrecht University
  Utrecht, The Netherlands

James Jaccard
  Department of Psychology
  Florida International University
  Boca Raton, FL

Paul E. Johnson
  Department of Political Science
  Kansas University
  Lawrence, KS

Kelly M. Kadlec
  Department of Psychology
  University of Southern California
  Los Angeles, CA

David Kaplan
  Department of Educational Psychology
  University of Wisconsin-Madison
  Madison, WI

Ken Kelley
  Department of Management
  University of Notre Dame
  Notre Dame, IN

Harvey J. Keselman
  Department of Psychology
  University of Manitoba
  Winnipeg, Canada

Neal M. Kingston
  School of Education
  University of Kansas
  Lawrence, KS
Yasemin Kisbu-Sakarya
  Department of Psychology
  Arizona State University
  Tempe, AZ
Laura B. Kramer
  School of Education
  University of Kansas
  Lawrence, KS
Todd D. Little
  Director, Texas Tech University
    Research Institute
  Professor, Educational Psychology,
    College of Education
  Texas Tech University
  Lubbock, TX
Richard E. Lucas
  Department of Psychology
  Michigan State University
  East Lansing, MI
David P. MacKinnon
  Department of Psychology
  Arizona State University
  Tempe, AZ
Patrick Mair
  Institute for Statistics and Mathematics
  Vienna University of Economics
    and Business
  Vienna, Austria
Herbert W. Marsh
  Department of Education
  University of Oxford
  Oxford, UK
Katherine E. Masyn
  Graduate School of Education
  Harvard University
  Cambridge, MA
John J. McArdle
  Department of Psychology
  University of Southern California
  Los Angeles, CA
Roderick P. McDonald[†]
  Sydney University
  Sydney, Australia
  Professor Emeritus
  University of Illinois
    at Urbana-Champaign
  Professor Emeritus
  Macquarie University
  [†]April 16, 1928 – October, 29, 2011
Sarah E. Medland
  Genetic Epidemiology Laboratory
  Queensland Institute of Medical Research
  School of Psychology
  University of Queensland
  Brisbane, Australia
Peter C. M. Molenaar
  Department of Human Development
    and Family Studies
  Pennsylvania State University
  University Park, PA
Alexandre J.S. Morin
  Department of Psychology
  University of Sherbrooke
  Sherbrooke, Quebec, Canada
Miriam A. Mosing
  Genetic Epidemiology Laboratory
  Queensland Institute of Medical Research
  School of Psychology
  University of Queensland
  Brisbane, Australia
Keith E. Muller
  Department of Health Outcomes
    and Policy
  University of Florida
  Gainesville, FL
Eun-Young Mun
  Center of Alcohol Studies
  Rutgers University
  Piscataway, NJ
Alan T. Murray
  GeoDa Center for Geospatial Analysis
    and Computation
  School of Geographical Sciences
    and Urban Planning
  Arizona State University
  Tempe, AZ
Jay I. Myung
  Department of Psychology
  The Ohio State University
  Columbus, OH
Benjamin Nagengast
  Department of Education
  Oxford University
  Oxford, UK

Sally Gayle Olderbak
　Department of Psychology
　School of Mind, Brain, & Behavior
　University of Arizona
　Tucson, AZ

Jamie M. Ostrov
　Department of Psychology
　University at Buffalo
　The State University of New York
　Buffalo, NY

Trond Peterson
　Department of Sociology
　University of California-Berkeley
　Berkeley, CA

Mark A. Pitt
　Department of Psychology
　The Ohio State University
　Columbus, OH

Larry R. Price
　College of Education and College of Science
　Texas State University-San Marcos
　San Marcos, TX

Nilam Ram
　Department of Human Development and Family Studies
　Pennsylvania State University
　University Park, PA
　Max Plank Institute for Human Development
　Berlin, Germany

Sergio J. Rey
　GeoDa Center for Geospatial Analysis and Computation
　School of Geographical Sciences and Urban Planning
　Arizona State University
　Tempe, AZ

Joseph L. Rodgers
　Department of Psychology
　University of Oklahoma
　Norman, OK

Robert Rosenthal
　Department of Psychology
　University of California, Riverside
　Riverside, CA

Ralph L. Rosnow
　Department of Psychology
　Temple University
　Philadelphia, PA

André A. Rupp
　Department of Measurement, Statistics, and Evaluation (EDMS)
　University of Maryland
　College Park, MD

Gabriel Lee Schlomer
　Division of Family Studies and Human Development
　College of Agriculture and Life Sciences
　University of Arizona
　Tucson, AZ

Christof Schuster
　Department of Psychology
　Justus-Liebig-Unversitat Giessen
　Giessen, Germany

James P. Selig
　Department of Psychology
　University of New Mexico
　Albuquerque, NM

Paul E. Spector
　Department of Psychology
　University of South Florida
　Tampa, FL

Peter M. Steiner
　Department of Educational Psychology
　University of Wisconsin-Madison
　Madison, WI

Carolin Strobl
　Ludwig-Maximilians-Universität München Faculty of Mathematics, Informatics and Statistics Institute of Statistics
　Munich, Germany

Bruce Thompson
　Baylor College of Medicine
　Austin, TX

Terry T. Tomazic
　Department of Sociology and Criminal Justice
　Saint Louis University
　Saint Louis, MO

James T. Townsend
　Department of Psychological and Brain Sciences
　Indiana University
　Bloomington, IN

Trisha Van Zandt
　Department of Psychology
　The Ohio State University
　Columbus, OH

Alexander von Eye
  Departments of Psychology
  Michigan State University
  East Lansing, MI
  University of Vienna
  Vienna, Austria

Stefan von Weber
  Department of Mechanical Engineering
  Hochschule Furtwangen University
  Furtwangen im Schwarzwald, Germany

Karin J.H. Verweij
  Genetic Epidemiology Laboratory
  Queensland Institute of Medical Research
  School of Psychology
  University of Queensland
  Brisbane, Australia

Theodore A. Walls
  Department of Behavioral Science
  University of Rhode Island
  Kingston, RI

Lihshing Leigh Wang
  Educational Studies Program
  University of Cincinnati
  Cincinnati, OH

Amber S. Watts
  Center for Research Methods and Data Analysis and
  Lifespan Institute, Gerontology Center
  University of Kansas
  Lawrence, KS

William W.S. Wei
  Department of Statistics
  Temple University
  Philadelphia, PA

Zhonglin Wen
  South China Normal University

Stephen G. West
  Department of Psychology
  Arizona State University
  Tempe, AZ

Keith F. Widaman
  Department of Psychology
  University of California at Davis
  Davis, CA

Rand R. Wilcox
  Department of Psychology
  University of Southern California
  Los Angeles, CA

Lisa M. Willoughby
  Department of Psychology
  Saint Louis University
  Saint Louis, MO

Coady Wing
  Institute for Policy Research
  Northwestern University
  Evanston, IL

Pedro Sofio Abril Wolf
  Department of Psychology
  University of Cape Town
  Cape Town, South Africa

Vivian Wong
  School of Education and Social Policy
  Northwestern University
  Evanston, IL

Carol M. Woods
  Center for Research Methods and Data Analysis and
  Department of Psychology
  University of Kansas
  Lawrence, KS

Wei Wu
  Center for Research Methods and Data Analysis and
  Department of Psychology
  University of Kansas
  Lawrence, KS

Ke-Hai Yuan
  Department of Psychology
  University of Notre Dame
  Notre Dame, IN

CONTENTS

1. Introduction 1
   Todd D. Little
2. Overview of Traditional/Classical Statistical Approaches 7
   Bruce Thompson
3. Generalized Linear Models 26
   Stefany Coxe, Stephen G. West, and *Leona S. Aiken*
4. Categorical Methods 52
   Carol M. Woods
5. Configural Frequency Analysis 74
   Alexander von Eye, Eun-Young Mun, Patrick Mair, and *Stefan von Weber*
6. Nonparametric Statistical Techniques 106
   Trent D. Buskirk, Lisa M. Willoughby, and *Terry J. Tomazic*
7. Correspondence Analysis 142
   Michael J. Greenacre
8. Spatial Analysis 154
   Luc Anselin, Alan T. Murray, and *Sergio J. Rey*
9. Analysis of Imaging Data 175
   Larry R. Price
10. Twin Studies and Behavior Genetics 198
    Gabriëlla A. M. Blokland, Miriam A. Mosing, Karin J. H. Verweij, and *Sarah E. Medland*
11. Quantitative Analysis of Genes 219
    Sarah E. Medland
12. Multidimensional Scaling 235
    Cody S. Ding
13. Latent Variable Measurement Models 257
    Timothy A. Brown
14. Multilevel Regression and Multilevel Structural Equation Modeling 281
    Joop J. Hox
15. Structural Equation Models 295
    John J. McArdle and *Kelly M. Kadlec*

16. Developments in Mediation Analysis   338
    David P. MacKinnon, Yasemin Kisbu-Sakarya, and *Amanda C. Gottschall*
17. Moderation   361
    Herbert W. Marsh, Kit-Tai Hau, Zhonglin Wen, Benjamin Nagengast, and *Alexandre J.S. Morin*
18. Longitudinal Data Analysis   387
    Wei Wu, James P. Selig, and *Todd D. Little*
19. Dynamical Systems and Models of Continuous Time   411
    Pascal R. Deboeck
20. Intensive Longitudinal Data   432
    Theodore A. Walls
21. Dynamic Factor Analysis: Modeling Person-Specific Process   441
    Nilam Ram, Annette Brose, and *Peter C. M. Molenaar*
22. Time Series Analysis   458
    William W.S. Wei
23. Analyzing Event History Data   486
    Trond Petersen
24. Clustering and Classification   517
    André A. Rupp
25. Latent Class Analysis and Finite Mixture Modeling   551
    Katherine E. Masyn
26. Taxometrics   612
    Theodore P. Beauchaine
27. Missing Data Methods   635
    Amanda N. Baraldi and *Craig K. Enders*
28. Secondary Data Analysis   665
    M. Brent Donnellan and *Richard E. Lucas*
29. Data Mining   678
    Carolin Strobl
30. Meta-Analysis and Quantitative Research Synthesis   701
    Noel A. Card and *Deborah M. Casper*
31. Common Fallacies in Quantitative Research Methodology   718
    Lihshing Leigh Wang, Amber S. Watts, Rawni A. Anderson, and *Todd D. Little*

Index   759

CHAPTER
1 Introduction

Todd D. Little

> **Abstract**
>
> In this introductory chapter to *The Oxford Handbook of Quantitative Methods*, I provide an overview of the two volumes. More specifically, I describe the rationale and motivation for the selected topics that are presented in the volumes. I also list out my instructions to the chapter authors and then describe how the chapters fit together into thematic groupings. I also extend my sincerest gratitude to the persons who assisted me along the way, as no work this comprehensive can be done without the considerable help and assistance of many persons. I conclude with how pleased I am with the quality and comprehensiveness of the chapters that are included.
>
> **Key Words:** Overview; Quantitative Methods; Methodology; Statistics

Oxford Introduction

Handbooks provide a crucial venue to communicate the current state of the field. They also provide a one-stop source for learning and reviewing current best practices in a field. *The Oxford Handbook of Quantitative Methods* serves both of these functions. The field of quantitative methods is quite broad, as you can probably imagine. I have tried to be thorough in my selection of topics to be covered. As with any handbook of this magnitude, some topics were all set to have a contribution submitted, only to have some unforeseen hindrance preclude its inclusion at the last minute (e.g., graphical representations of data, ecological inference, history of quantitative methods). Some topics overlap with others and may not have found their way to become a separate chapter, but their fundamental elements are found in parts of other chapters.

This handbook is one of many that Oxford University Press (OUP) is assembling but will be the capstone methodology handbook. As many of you know, OUP is building a comprehensive and synthetic Library of Handbooks covering the field of psychology (the Editor-in-Chief of the library is Peter Nathan, University of Iowa Foundation Distinguished Professor of Psychology and Public Health). The library comprises handbooks in the truest sense of the word: books that summarize and synthesize a topic, define the current scholarship, and set the agenda for future research. Each handbook is published as a bound book, and it will also be developed for electronic delivery. In this format, the content will be integrated across topics and available as a fully integrated electronic library. I think the idea of a comprehensive electronic library is very forward-thinking. This format is a very attractive opportunity to have a fully comprehensive and up-to-date handbook of methods in our field. Hence, I agreed to take on the role of editor of *The Oxford Handbook of Quantitative Methods*.

I am very pleased with the quality of the work that each author provided. As per my request to the contributing authors, each chapter is meant to be both accessible and comprehensive; nearly all the authors were very responsive to my requests. The guidelines I asked authors to consider were:

• Handbook chapters should be comprehensive and authoritative; readers will rely heavily on these chapters, particularly when they move to the online format.

• Handbook chapters should present not only the strengths of the topic covered but also any limitations.

• Handbook chapters should make all assumptions underlying the topic explicit.

• Regarding citations, handbook chapters should cover the historical origins as well as the recent renditions of a given key topic.

• Handbook chapters should not present one-sided views on any debate; rather, they should report the issues and present the arguments—both pro and con. Authors can direct readers to other platforms where a position piece is presented.

• To facilitate the online linkages, handbook chapters should point to other online resources related to the topic presented.

• Every element of every formula presented must be explicitly explained; assume no knowledge of how to read formulae.

• Examples, examples, examples, and, when in doubt, provide an example! Concrete examples are absolutely critical to communicate quantitative content.

• Avoid jargon and acronyms. Please spell out acronyms, and if you use jargon, please remind the reader of the meaning or definition of the jargon every three to four times it is used; similarly, if you use an acronym, then remind the reader of what it means every three to four times it is used.

• Use active voice, and do not shy away from the use of I/me or we/us. Channel how you lecture on the topic. It will create a crisp and enjoyable read.

• Do not start a sentence with "This" followed by a verb. The referent to "this" must be restated because of the ambiguity this creates. This *general guideline* should be followed as a rule!

Authors, like editors, have preferences and habits, so you will find places, chapters, and so on where some of my admonitions were not followed. But the quality of the product that each chapter provides is nonetheless uncompromised. We have established a Wiki-based resource page for the handbook, which can be found at crmda.KU.edu/oxford. Each author has been asked to maintain and upload materials to support his or her chapter contribution. At the top of that page is a link that encourages you to offer comments and suggestions on the topics and coverage of the handbook. These comments will be reviewed and integrated into future editions of this handbook. I encourage you, therefore, to take advantage of this opportunity to help shape the directions and content coverage of this handbook.

Statistical software has blossomed with the advent of hardware that provides the necessary speed and memory and programming languages coupled with numerical algorithms that are more efficient and optimized than yesteryear. These software advances have allowed many of the advances in modern statistics to become accessible to the typical end-user. Modern missing data algorithms and Bayesian estimation procedures, for example, have been the beneficiaries of these advances. Of course, some of the software developments have included simplified interfaces with slick graphic user interfaces. The critical options are usually prefilled with default settings. These latter two aspects of advancing software are unfortunate because they lead to mindless applications of the statistical techniques. I would prefer that options not be set as default but, rather, have the software prompt the user to make a choice (and give good help for what each choice means). I would prefer that a complete script of the GUI choices and the order in which steps were taken be automatically saved and displayed.

I have organized the handbook by starting with some basics. It begins with the philosophical underpinnings associated with science and quantitative methods (Haig, Chapter 2, Volume 1) followed by a discussion of how to construct theories and models so that they can be tested empirically and the best model selected (Jaccard, Chapter 5, Volume 1). I then turn to an enlightened discussion of ethics in the conduct of quantitative research (Rosnow & Rosenbloom, Chapter 3, Volume 1) and related issues when quantitative methods are applied in special populations (Widaman, Early, & Conger, Chapter 4, Volume 1). Harlow (Chapter 6, Volume 1) follows with an encompassing and impassioned discussion of teaching quantitative methods.

The theme in the next grouping of chapters centers on measurement issues. First, the late McDonald (Chapter 7, Volume 1) provides a thorough overview of Modern Test Theory.[1] Ayala (Chapter 8, Volume 1) adds a detailed discussion of Item Response Theory as an essential measurement and analysis tool. After these principles of measurement are discussed, the principles and practices surrounding survey design and measure development are presented (Spector, Chapter 9, Volume 1). Kingston and Kramer (Chapter 10, Volume 1) further this discussion in the context of high-stakes testing.

A next grouping of chapters covers various design issues. Kelley (Chapter 11, Volume 1) begins this section by covering issues of power, effect size, and sample size planning. Hallberg, Wing, Wong, and Cook (Chapter 12, Volume 1) then address key experimental designs for causal inference: the gold standard randomized clinical trials (RCT) design and the underutilized regression discontinuity design. Some key quasi-experimental procedures for comparing groups are discussed in Steiner and Cooks' (Chapter 13, Volume 1) chapter on using matching and propensity scores. Finally, Van Zandt and Townsend (Chapter 14, Volume 1) provide a detailed discussion of the designs for and analyses of response time experiments. I put observational methods (Ostrov & Hart, Chapter 15, Volume 1), epidemiological methods (Bard, Rodgers, & Mueller, Chapter 16, Volume 1), and program evaluation (Figueredo, Olderbak, Schlomer, Garcia, & Wolf, Chapter 17, Volume 1) in with these chapters because they address more collection and design issues, although the discussion of program evaluation also addresses the unique analysis and presentation issues.

I have a stellar group of chapters related to estimation issues. Yuan and Schuster (Chapter 18, Volume 1) provide an overview of statistical estimation method; Erceg-Hurn, Wilcox, and Keselman (Chapter 19, Volume 1) provide a nice complement with a focus on robust estimation techniques. Bayesian statistical estimation methods are thoroughly reviewed in the Kaplan and Depaoli (Chapter 20, Volume 1) contribution. The details of mathematical modeling are synthesized in this section by Cavagnara, Myung, and Pitt (Chapter 21, Volume 1). This section is completed by Johnson (Chapter 22, Volume 1), who discusses the many issues and nuances involved in conducting Monte Carlo simulations to address the what-would-happen-if questions that we often need to answer.

The foundational techniques for the statistical analysis of quantitative data start with a detailed overview of the traditional methods that have marked social and behavioral sciences (i.e., the General Linear Model; Thompson, Chapter 2, Volume 2). Coxe, West, and Aiken (Chapter 3, Volume 2) then extend the General Linear Model to discuss the Generalized Linear Model. This discussion is easily followed by Woods (Chapter 4, Volume 2), who synthesizes the various techniques of analyzing categorical data. After the chapter on configural frequency analysis by Von Eye, Mun, Mair and von Weber (Chapter 5, Volume 2), I then segway into nonparametric techniques (Buskirk, Tomazic, & Willoughby, Chapter 6, Volume 2) and the more specialized techniques of correspondence analysis (Greenacre, Chapter 7, Volume 2) and spatial analysis (Anselin, Murry, & Rey, Chapter 8, Volume 2). This section is capped with chapters dedicated to special areas of research—namely, techniques and issues related to the analysis of imaging data (e.g., fMRI; Price, Chapter 9, Volume 2). The closely aligned worlds of behavior genetics (i.e., twin studies; Blokland, Mosing, Verweij, & Medland, Chapter 11, Volume 2) and genes (Medland, Chapter 10, Volume 2) follows.

The foundations of multivariate techniques are grouped beginning with Ding's (Chapter 12, Volume 2) presentation of multidimensional scaling and Brown's (Chapter 13, Volume 2) summary of the foundations of latent variable measurement models. Hox (Chapter 14, Volume 2) layers in the multilevel issues as handled in both the manifest regression framework and the latent variable work of structural equation modeling. McArdle and Kadlec (Chapter 15, Volume 2) detail, in broad terms, different structural equation models and their utility. MacKinnon, Kisbu-Sakarya, and Gottschall (Chapter 16, Volume 2) address the many new developments in mediation analysis, while Marsh, Hau, Wen, and Nagengast (Chapter 17, Volume 2) do the same for analyses of moderation.

The next group of chapters focuses on repeated measures and longitudinal designs. It begins with a chapter I co-wrote with Wu and Selig and provides a general overview of longitudinal models (Wu, Selig, & Little, Chapter 18, Volume 2). Deboeck (Chapter 19, Volume 2) takes things further into the burgeoning world of dynamical systems and continuous-time models for longitudinal data. Relatedly, Walls (Chapter 20, Volume 2) provides an overview of designs for doing intensive longitudinal collection and analysis designs. The wonderful world of dynamic-factor models (a multivariate model for single-subject data) is presented by Ram, Brose, and Molenaar (Chapter 21, Volume 2). Wei (Chapter 22, Volume 2) covers all the issues of traditional time-series models and Peterson (Chapter 23, Volume 2) rounds out this section with a thorough coverage of event history models.

The volume finishes with two small sections. The first focuses on techniques dedicated to finding heterogeneous subgroups in one's data. Rupp (Chapter 24, Volume 2) covers tradition clustering and classification procedures. Katherine E. Masyn (Chapter 25, Volume 2) cover the model-based approaches encompassed under the umbrella of mixture modeling. Beauchaine (Chapter 26, Volume 2) completes this first group with his coverage of the nuances of taxometrics. The second of the final group of chapters covers issues related to secondary analyses of extant data. I put the chapter on missing data in here because it generally is applied after data collection occurs, but it is also a little out of order here because of the terrific and powerful features of planned missing data designs. In this regard, Baraldi and Enders (Chapter 27, Volume 2) could have gone into the design section. Donnellan and Lucas (Chapter 28, Volume 2) cover the issues associated with analyzing the large-scale archival data sets that are available via federal funding agencies such as NCES, NIH, NSF, and the like. Data mining can also be classified as a set of secondary modeling procedures, and Strobl's (Chapter 29, Volume 2) chapter covers the techniques and issues in this emerging field of methodology. Card and Casper (Chapter 30, Volume 2) covers the still advancing world of meta-analysis and current best practices in quantitative synthesis of published studies. The final chapter of *The Oxford Handbook of Quantitative Methods* is one I co-authored with Wang, Watts, and Anderson (Wang, Watts, Anderson, & Little, Chapter 31, Volume 2). In this capstone chapter, we address the many pervasive fallacies that still permeate the world of quantitative methodology.

A venture such as this does involve the generous and essential contributions of expert reviewers. Many of the chapter authors also served as reviewers for other chapters, and I won't mention them by name here. I do want to express gratitude to a number of *ad hoc* reviewers who assisted me along the way (in arbitrary order): Steve Lee, Kris Preacher, Mijke Rhemtulla, Chantelle Dowsett, Jason Lee, Michael Edwards, David Johnson (I apologize now if I have forgotten that you reviewed a chapter for me!). I also owe a debt of gratitude to Chad Zimmerman at OUP, who was relentless in guiding us through the incremental steps needed to herd us all to a final and prideworthy end product and to Anne Dellinger who was instrumental in bringing closure to this mammoth project.

Author Note

Partial support for this project was provided by grant NSF 1053160 (Todd D. Little & Wei Wu, co-PIs) and by the Center for Research Methods and Data Analysis at the University of Kansas (Todd D. Little, director). Correspondence concerning this work should be addressed to Todd D. Little, Center for Research Methods and Data Analysis, University of Kansas, 1425 Jayhawk Blvd. Watson Library, 470. Lawrence, KS 66045. E-mail: yhat@ku.edu. Web: crmda.ku.edu.

Note

1. This chapter was completed shortly before Rod's unexpected passing. His legacy and commitment to quantitative methods was uncompromising and we will miss his voice of wisdom and his piercing intellect; *R.I.P.*, Rod McDonald and, as you once said, *pervixi…* .

References

Anselin, L., Murry, A. T., & Rey, S. J. (2012). Spatial analysis. In T. D. Little (Ed.), *The Oxford Handbook of Quantitative Methods* (Vol. 2, pp. 154–174). New York: Oxford University Press.

Baraldi, A. N. & Enders, C. K. (2012). Missing data methods. In T. D. Little (Ed.), *The Oxford Handbook of Quantitative Methods* (Vol. 2, pp. 635–664). New York: Oxford University Press.

Bard, D. E., Rodgers, J. L., & Muller, K. E. (2012). A primer of epidemiology methods with applications in psychology. In T. D. Little (Ed.), *The Oxford Handbook of Quantitative Methods* (Vol. 1, pp. 305–349). New York: Oxford University Press.

Beauchaine, T. P. (2012). Taxometrics. In T. D. Little (Ed.), *The Oxford Handbook of Quantitative Methods* (Vol. 2, pp. 612–634). New York: Oxford University Press.

Brown, T. A. (2012). Latent variable measurement models. In T. D. Little (Ed.), *The Oxford Handbook of Quantitative Methods* (Vol. 2, pp. 257–280). New York: Oxford University Press.

Buskirk, T. D., Tomazic, T. T., & Willoughbby, L. (2012). Nonparametric statistical techniques. In T. D. Little (Ed.), *The Oxford Handbook of Quantitative Methods* (Vol. 2, pp. 106–141). New York: Oxford University Press.

Card, N. A. & Casper, D. M. (2012). Meta-analysis and quantitative research synthesis. In T. D. Little (Ed.), *The Oxford Handbook of Quantitative Methods* (Vol. 2, pp. 701–717). New York: Oxford University Press.

Cavagnaro, D. R., Myung, J. I., & Pitt, M. A. (2012). Mathematical modeling. In T. D. Little (Ed.), *The Oxford Handbook of Quantitative Methods* (Vol. 1, pp. 438–453). New York: Oxford University Press.

Coxe, S., West, S. G., & Aiken, L. S. (2012). Generalized linear models. In T. D. Little (Ed.), *The Oxford Handbook of Quantitative Methods* (Vol. 2, pp. 26–51). New York: Oxford University Press.

De Ayala, R. J. (2012). The IRT tradition and its applications. In T. D. Little (Ed.), *The Oxford Handbook of Quantitative Methods* (Vol. 1, pp. 144–169). New York: Oxford University Press.

Deboeck, P. R. (2012). Dynamical systems and models of continuous time. In T. D. Little (Ed.), *The Oxford Handbook of Quantitative Methods* (Vol. 2, pp. 411–431). New York: Oxford University Press.

Ding, C. S. (2012). Multidimensional scaling. In T. D. Little (Ed.), *The Oxford Handbook of Quantitative Methods* (Vol. 2, pp. 7–25). New York: Oxford University Press.

Donnellan, M. B. & Lucas, R. E. (2012). Secondary data analysis. In T. D. Little (Ed.), *The Oxford Handbook of Quantitative Methods* (Vol. 2, pp. 665–677). New York: Oxford University Press.

Erceg-Hurn, D. M., Wilcox, R. R., & Keselman, H. H. (2012). Robust statistical estimation. In T. D. Little (Ed.), *The Oxford Handbook of Quantitative Methods* (Vol. 1, pp. 388–406). New York: Oxford University Press.

Figueredo, A. J., Olderbak, S. G., & Schlomer, G. L. (2012) Program evaluation: Principles, procedures, and practices. In T. D. Little (Ed.), *The Oxford Handbook of Quantitative Methods* (Vol. 1, pp. 332–360). New York: Oxford University Press.

Greenacre, M. J. (2012). Correspondence analysis. In T. D. Little (Ed.), *The Oxford Handbook of Quantitative Methods* (Vol. 2, pp. 142–153). New York: Oxford University Press.

Haig, B. D. (2012). The philosophy of quantitative methods. In T. D. Little (Ed.), *The Oxford Handbook of Quantitative Methods* (Vol. 1, pp. 7–31). New York: Oxford University Press.

Hallberg, K., Wing, C., Wong, V., & Cook, T. D. (2012). Experimental design for causal inference: Clinical trials and regression discontinuity designs. In T. D. Little (Ed.), *The Oxford Handbook of Quantitative Methods* (Vol. 1, pp. 223–236). New York: Oxford University Press.

Harlow, L. (2012). Teaching quantitative psychology. In T. D. Little (Ed.), *The Oxford Handbook of Quantitative Methods* (Vol. 1, pp. 105–117). New York: Oxford University Press.

Hox, J. J., (2012). Multilevel regression and multilevel structural equation modeling In T. D. Little (Ed.), *The Oxford Handbook of Quantitative Methods* (Vol. 2, pp. 281–294). New York: Oxford University Press.

Jaccard, J. (2012). Theory construction, model building, and model selection. In T. D. Little (Ed.), *The Oxford Handbook of Quantitative Methods* (Vol. 1, pp. 82–104). New York: Oxford University Press.

Johnson, P. E. (2012). Monte Carlo analysis in academic research. In T. D. Little (Ed.), *The Oxford Handbook of Quantitative Methods* (Vol. 1, pp. 454–479). New York: Oxford University Press.

Kaplan, D. & Depaoli, S. (2012). Bayesian statistical methods. In T. D. Little (Ed.), *The Oxford Handbook of Quantitative Methods* (Vol. 1, pp. 407–437). New York: Oxford University Press.

Kelley, K. (2012). Effect size and sample size planning. In T. D. Little (Ed.), *The Oxford Handbook of Quantitative Methods* (Vol. 1, pp. 206–222). New York: Oxford University Press.

Kingston, N. M. & Kramer, L. B. (2012). High stakes test construction and test use. In T. D. Little (Ed.), *The Oxford Handbook of Quantitative Methods* (Vol. 1, pp. 189–205). New York: Oxford University Press.

MacKinnon, D. P., Kisbu-Sakarya, Y., & Gottschall, A. C. (2012). Developments in mediation analysis. In T. D. Little (Ed.), *The Oxford Handbook of Quantitative Methods* (Vol. 2, pp. 338–360). New York: Oxford University Press.

Marsh, H. W., Hau, K-T., Wen, Z., & Nagengast, B. (2012). Moderation. In T. D. Little (Ed.), *The Oxford Handbook of Quantitative Methods* (Vol. 2, pp. 361–386). New York: Oxford University Press.

Masyn, K. E. & Nylund-Gibson, K. (2012). Mixture modeling. In T. D. Little (Ed.), *The Oxford Handbook of Quantitative Methods* (Vol. 2, pp. 551–611). New York: Oxford University Press.

McArdle, J. J. & Kadlec, K. M. (2012). Structural equation models. In T. D. Little (Ed.), *The Oxford Handbook of Quantitative Methods* (Vol. 2, pp. 295–337). New York: Oxford University Press.

McDonald, R. P. (2012). Modern test theory. In T. D. Little (Ed.), *The Oxford Handbook of Quantitative Methods* (Vol. 1, pp. 118–143). New York: Oxford University Press.

Medland, S. E. (2012). Quantitative analysis of genes. In T. D. Little (Ed.), *The Oxford Handbook of Quantitative Methods* (Vol. 2, pp. 219–234). New York: Oxford University Press.

Ostrov, J. M. & Hart, E. J. (2012). Observational methods. In T. D. Little (Ed.), *The Oxford Handbook of Quantitative Methods* (Vol. 1, pp. 286–304). New York: Oxford University Press.

Peterson, T. (2012) Analyzing event history data. In T. D. Little (Ed.), *The Oxford Handbook of Quantitative Methods* (Vol. 2, pp. 486–516). New York: Oxford University Press.

Price, L. R. (2012). Analysis of imaging data. In T. D. Little (Ed.), *The Oxford Handbook of Quantitative Methods* (Vol. 2, pp. 175–197). New York: Oxford University Press.

Ram, N., Brose, A., & Molenaar, P. C. M. (2012). Dynamic factor analysis: Modeling person-specific process. In T. D. Little (Ed.), *The Oxford Handbook of Quantitative Methods* (Vol. 2, pp. 441–457). New York: Oxford University Press.

Rosnow, R. L. & Rosenthal, R. (2012). Quantitative methods and ethics. In T. D. Little (Ed.), *The Oxford Handbook of Quantitative Methods* (Vol. 1, pp. 32–54). New York: Oxford University Press.

Rupp, A. A. (2012). Clustering and classification. In T. D. Little (Ed.), *The Oxford Handbook of Quantitative Methods* (Vol. 2, pp. 517–611). New York: Oxford University Press.

Spector, P. E. (2012). Survey design and measure development. In T. D. Little (Ed.), *The Oxford Handbook of Quantitative Methods* (Vol. 1, pp. 170–188). New York: Oxford University Press.

Steiner, P. M. & Cook, D. (2012). Matching and Propensity Scores. In T. D. Little (Ed.), *The Oxford Handbook of Quantitative Methods* (Vol. 1, pp. 237–259). New York: Oxford University Press.

Strobl, C. (2012). Data mining. In T. D. Little (Ed.), *The Oxford Handbook of Quantitative Methods* (Vol. 2, pp. 678–700). New York: Oxford University Press.

Thompson, B. (2012). Overview of traditional/classical statistical approaches. In T. D. Little (Ed.), *The Oxford Handbook of Quantitative Methods* (Vol. 2, pp. 7–25). New York: Oxford University Press.

Van Zandt, T., & Townsend, J. T. (2012). Designs for and analyses of response time experiments. In T. D. Little (Ed.), *The Oxford Handbook of Quantitative Methods* (Vol. 1, pp. 260–285). New York: Oxford University Press.

von Eye, A., Mun, E. U., Mair, P., & von Weber, S. Configural frequency analysis. In T. D. Little (Ed.), *The Oxford Handbook of Quantitative Methods* (Vol. 2, pp. 73–105). New York: Oxford University Press.

Walls, T. A. (2012). Intensive longitudinal data. In T. D. Little (Ed.), *The Oxford Handbook of Quantitative Methods* (Vol. 2, pp. 432–440). New York: Oxford University Press.

Wang, L. L., Watts, A. S., Anderson, R. A., & Little, T. D. (2012). Common fallacies in quantitative research methodology. In T. D. Little (Ed.), *The Oxford Handbook of Quantitative Methods* (Vol. 2, pp. 718–758). New York: Oxford University Press.

Wei. W. W. S. (2012). Time series analysis. In T. D. Little (Ed.), *The Oxford Handbook of Quantitative Methods* (Vol. 2, pp. 458–485). New York: Oxford University Press.

Widaman, K. F., Early, D. R., & Conger, R. D. (2012). Special populations. In T. D. Little (Ed.), *The Oxford Handbook of Quantitative Methods* (Vol. 1, pp. 55–81). New York: Oxford University Press.

Woods, C. M. (2012). Categorical methods. In T. D. Little (Ed.), *The Oxford Handbook of Quantitative Methods* (Vol. 2, pp. 52–73). New York: Oxford University Press.

Wu, W., Selig, J. P., & Little, T. D. (2012). Longitudinal data analysis. In T. D. Little (Ed.), *The Oxford Handbook of Quantitative Methods* (Vol. 2, pp. 387–410). New York: Oxford University Press.

Yuan, K-H., & Schuster, C. (2012). Overview of statistical estimation methods. In T. D. Little (Ed.), *The Oxford Handbook of Quantitative Methods*. (Vol. 1, pp. 361–387). New York: Oxford University Press.

CHAPTER 2

Overview of Traditional/Classical Statistical Approaches

Bruce Thompson

Abstract

The chapter presents the basic concepts underlying "traditional/classical" statistics (i.e., the univariate *t*-test, ANOVA, ANCOVA, Pearson's *r*, Spearman *rho*, *phi*, and multiple regression; the multivariate Hotelling's T^2, MANOVA, MANCOVA, descriptive discriminant analysis, and canonical correlation analysis), laying these concepts out within an historical context, and emphasizing the interrelatedness of these methods as part of a single general linear model (GLM). Similarities and differences in analyzing data with univariate as opposed to multivariate methods are detailed. Some specific practice guidelines for a GLM interpretation rubric are offered.

Key Words: statistical significance, null hypothesis tests, *p*-values, test statistics, sampling error, effect sizes, standardized differences, corrected effect sizes, practical significance, effect size benchmarks

---

"Traditional" or "classical" statistics are the quantitative methods developed in the first decades, roughly 1890 until 1940, of the existence of psychology as a discipline. Included are those analyses that dominated quantitative reports until roughly 1980: univariate methods (the *t*-test, ANOVA, ANCOVA, Pearson's *r*, Spearman's *rho*, and multiple regression) and multivariate generalizations (Hotelling's T^2, MANOVA, MANCOVA, descriptive discriminant analysis [DDA], and canonical correlation analysis [CCA]).

Although these analyses were developed at different times over a period of decades (David, 1995), the methods share many features in common and indeed together constitute a single analytic family called the general linear model (GLM; Cohen, 1968; Knapp, 1978). First, quantitative analyses can be used to compute the probabilities of the sample results, $p_{CALCULATED}$, assuming that the sample came from a population where the null hypothesis being tested is true (e.g., H_0: $\mu_1=\mu_2=\mu_2$, or $r^2 = 0$), and given the sample size (Cohen, 1994; Thompson, 1996). The computation and interpretation of $p_{CALCULATED}$ values is referred to as statistical significance testing. Second, quantitative analyses can be used to compute indices of experimental effect or relationship strength, called *effect sizes*, which can be used to inform judgment regarding the practical significance of study results (Kirk, 1996; Thompson, 2002a).

Traditional/classical statistics can be used only for the first purpose, only for the second purpose, or for both purposes. Indeed, from roughly 1900 until 1990, and especially from 1950 until 1990 (Hubbard & Ryan, 2000), psychologists tended to use these analyses to focus on statistical significance, but more recently psychologists have begun to focus on practical significance.

Purposes of the Chapter

The chapter, first, provides a brief historical background on the development of traditional/classical statistics. Second, the chapter elaborates the basic ideas of the general linear model (GLM), which itself serves as a framework for understanding traditional/classical statistics. Third, the chapter details how variance partitioning is a fundamental commonality within the GLM, by considering how traditional/classical *univariate* statistics partition variance, and then uses these partitions to (1) conduct statistical significance tests; (2) compute univariate effect size statistics to inform judgments about practical significance; and/or (3) conduct statistical analyses to evaluate whether results are, in fact, replicable. Fourth, the parallel processes of variance partitioning are then explained in the context of *multivariate* analyses (i.e., traditional/classical statistics used in the presence of two or more outcome variables). Fifth, the comparability of univariate versus multivariate results for data involving multiple outcome variables is explored. Finally, a generic rubric with some specific practical guidelines for interpreting traditional/classical statistical results is presented.

Brief History of Traditional/Classical Statistics
Statistical Significance: $p_{CALCULATED}$ Values

"Traditional" or "classical" statistics have an old, well-documented history (cf. Hald, 1990, 1998; Huberty, 1993; Stigler, 1986). In his accessible chapter-length treatment, Huberty (1999) noted some of the major milestones:

- In 1885, English economist and mathematician Francis Y. Edgeworth conducted a study of wasp traffic in the morning versus at noon, and first used the term "significant" with respect to the differences tested using probabilities (David, 1995).
- In 1908, William S. Gossett, a worker in the Dublin brewery, Guinness, published the one-sample t-test, which can be used to compute the probabilities that means from two samples came from populations with equal means.
- In 1918, English eugenicist Ronald A. Fisher published the basic concepts of the analysis of variance (ANOVA); in 1934, Iowa State University statistician George W. Snedecor published the ANOVA test statistic, F, which he named in Fisher's honor and can be used to compute the probabilities that means for two, or more than two, groups came from populations with equal means.

However, statistical significance p-values have not been uniformly used throughout their history. When Karl (born Carl) Pearson retired at University College in London in 1933, his department was divided into a statistics department headed by his son, Egon S. Pearson, and a eugenics department headed by Ronald A. Fisher. In 1934, Jerzy Neyman was appointed to the faculty in Egon Pearson's department. These scholars ultimately divided themselves into philosophical schools, and they bitterly debated their differences from the mid-1930s until Fisher died in Adelaide, Australia in 1962.

The Neyman-Pearson school focuses on both a null hypothesis and an alternative hypothesis and uses a rigidly fixed cutoff α to reject or not reject the null hypothesis. This school considers two types of decision errors: (1) Type I error, or the rejection of a null hypothesis that is true in the population, having an associated probability α, and (2) Type II error, or the failure to reject a null hypothesis that is false in the population, having an associated probability β.

The Fisherian school, on the other hand, only considers the null hypothesis. Within this school, one only rejects or fails to reject the null and is not concerned with an alternative hypothesis as a rival to the null hypothesis. The focus is on determining whether there is an effect when no effect is expected. Fisher did not view the resulting p-values as actual probabilities about the real world but, rather, hypothetical values that nevertheless have some utility. Fisher also viewed statistical significance tests as making only weak arguments versus alternative statistical analyses and inferences.

Mulaik, Raju, and Harshman (1997) provided an excellent summary of the views in these two schools in the appendix to their chapter in the book, *What if There Were No Significance Tests?* In some sense, the battles between the two schools were never fought to a definitive conclusion. Indeed, many scholars may be unaware of the existence of the two schools. Today, the social sciences, for better or for worse, seemingly have adopted a random mish-mash of these competing views.

Thus, applications of p-values have a long history. However, the full, widespread reliance on p-values in the social sciences did not occur until the 1950s (Hubbard & Ryan, 2000). And the physical sciences never experienced an uptake of a focus on p-values and, rather, focus on the replicability of results across repeated experiments.

Practical Significance: Effect Sizes

Even early on, some scholars voiced concerns about overemphasizing *p*-values or "statistical significance" rather than "practical significance," as reflected in the title of Boring's (1919) article, "Mathematical vs. scientific importance." Effect sizes (e.g., Cohen's *d*, Glass' delta, r^2, the regression R^2, the canonical correlation R_C^2, the ANOVA/MANOVA η^2, the ANOVA ω^2) inform judgments about practical significance by quantifying the magnitude of experimental effect of a given intervention or the strength of relationship between variables (*see* Grissom & Kim, 2011; Thompson, 2006b, 2007).

Like *p*-values and various statistical significance tests, effect sizes also have a long history and are thus necessarily part of "traditional/classical statistical approaches" (*see* Huberty, 2002). For example, in 1924 Sir Ronald Fisher derived the η^2 effect size in the ANOVA context, and in 1935 Truman L. Kelley proposed an "adjusted" or "corrected" η^2 that he named ε^2. Some milestones in the movement toward greater emphasis on effect sizes include:

1988 First social science journal, *Measurement and Evaluation in Counseling and Development*, requires effect size reporting.

1994 Second social science journal, *Educational and Psychological Measurement*, requires effect size reporting; the American Psychological Association *Publication Manual*, used by more than 1,000 journals, first mentions effect sizes, and effect size reporting is "encouraged" (p. 18).

1996 The APA appoints Task Force on Statistical Inference to make recommendations on whether statistical significance tests should be banned from APA journals.

1999 Wilkinson and APA Task Force on Statistical Inference (1999) publish their recommendations in the *American Psychologist*, the APA flagship journal.

2006 The American Educational Research Association (AERA, 2006) speaks to the importance of effect sizes by promulgating its "Standards for Reporting on Empirical Social Science Research in AERA Publications."

The fact that all traditional/classical statistics can be used to compute effect sizes is one of the commonalities that joins these methods into the GLM.

General Linear Model

The GLM is the concept that "all analytic methods are correlational ... and yield variance-accounted-for effect sizes analogous to r^2 (e.g., R^2, η^2, ω^2)" (Thompson, 2000, p. 263). All the GLM methods apply weights (e.g., regression β-weights, factor pattern coefficients) to the measured/observed variables to estimate scores on composite/latent/synthetic variables (e.g., regression $\hat{Y}$, factor scores). As Graham (2008) explained,

> The vast majority of parametric statistical procedures in common use are part of [a single analytic family called] the General Linear Model (GLM), including the *t* test, analysis of variance (ANOVA), multiple regression, descriptive discriminant analysis (DDA), multivariate analysis of variance (MANOVA), canonical correlation analysis (CCA), and structural equation modeling (SEM). Moreover, these procedures are *hierarchical* [italics added], in that some procedures are special cases of others. (p. 485)

In 1968, Cohen proved that multiple regression analysis subsumes all univariate parametric statistical analyses as special cases. For example, you can obtain ANOVA *p*-values and effect sizes by running a multiple regression computer program, but not vice versa.

Ten years later, Knapp (1978) showed that all commonly utilized univariate *and* multivariate analyses are special cases of canonical correlation analysis. Later, Bagozzi, Fornell and Larcker (1981) demonstrated that structural equation modeling (SEM) is an even more general case of the GLM.

All the statistical methods considered in the present chapter are part of a single analytic family in which members have more similarities than differences with each other (Zientek & Thompson, 2009). Thus, broad statements and principles can be stated that generalize across all the methods within the GLM. One fundamental principle is that traditional/classical statistical analyses partition the variances on outcome variables into subcomponents and also focus on computing ratios of the variance partitions to the total observed variances of the outcome variables.

Variance Partitions and Their Ratios: Univariate Statistics

Within one meaning for *univariate statistics*, univariate statistics are conducted when a single outcome/dependent/criterion variable is predicted or explained by one or more independent/predictor variable(s). For example, the Pearson *r* correlation coefficient is a univariate statistic under this one (of several) definition of univariate statistics. Similarly, a factorial 3 × 2 (3 teaching methods by 2 flavors of human gender) ANOVA of knowledge posttest scores is a univariate analysis under this definition.

The basic statistic in all univariate analyses (e.g., t-test, ANOVA, ANCOVA, Pearson r) is the sum-of-squares (SS) of the dependent variable (e.g., Y). The importance of the SS_Y (or SS_{TOTAL}) is reflected in Thompson's (2006a) definition: the SS_Y is *"information about both the amount and the origins of individual differences"* (p. 60).

The importance of the SS_Y becomes clear when we consider how psychologists think about people. Psychologists posit that people are individual. Everybody is weird in at least some ways (i.e., an outlier), and some people are way weird! In fact, it is exactly these idiosyncracies that we are interested in understanding or explaining via our studies.

Statistics are located in either of two "worlds": (a) the unsquared, score world, or (b) the squared, area world. Statistics in the area world, some of which have explicit exponents of 2, include SS_Y, the variance, the Pearson r^2, and Cronbach's α reliability statistic. The score world actually has two subcomponents: (a1) the unstandardized score world with the statistics still in the same metric as the scores (e.g., the mean, the median, the standard deviation), and (a2) the standardized score world, in which the scaling or standard deviation (SD) has been removed from the statistic by dividing by SD (e.g., the Pearson r, z scores).

Although the mathematics of computing SS_Y are not as important as the conceptual definition of SS_Y, these computations will be briefly reviewed here. Presume that we have collected scores on a brief cognitive test, Y_i, from $n = 4$ individuals randomly sampled from the population of students attending the hypothetical Farnsworth School, as presented in Table 2.1. Note that deviation scores for each individual are represented by lowercase letters (e.g., y_i) and are computed by subtracting the group mean from each individual's Y_i score (i.e., $y_i = Y_i − M_Y$).

Table 2.1 also illustrates the computation of SS_Y for the measured/observed variable Y. Because for our data $SS_Y = 20.00$, we have information about individual differences in the knowledge of the four students. If SS_Y had equaled 0.0, then we would have had zero information about individual differences in the knowledge of the students, and thus would have been rendered completely unable to explore or understand their knowledge differences.

Table 2.1. Hypothetical Dataset #1 Illustrating Computation of SS_Y

Person	Y_i	$-M_Y = y_i$	y_i^2
Geri	2	−5.00 = −3.00	9.00
Murray	4	−5.00 = −1.00	1.00
Wendy	6	−5.00 = 1.00	1.00
Deborah	8	−5.00 = 3.00	9.00
M_Y	5.00		
Sum (SS_Y)			20.00

It is also clear that the students do not contribute equally to our information about their individual differences. We have more (and equal) information about the individual differences of Geri and Deborah and less (but equal) information about Murray and Wendy. Also, every one of the four students contributed some information about individual differences, because $y_i \neq 0.0$ for any of the students.

We will now turn briefly to the univariate variance partitioning process in two commonly used traditional/classical statistics: first, the Pearson's r, and second, the ANOVA test of mean differences across groups. We will also briefly discuss the statistical estimation theory, called *ordinary least squares* (OLS), commonly used in traditional/classical univariate statistics.

Pearson's r Computations

Presume that we want to determine whether there is a relationship between performance on the cognitive test and whether the students have recently had major surgery (coded 0 = "no"; 1 = "yes"). Geri and Murray have not had recent surgery, but Wendy and Deborah have.

As reported in Table 2.2, the SS_X for our second measured variable is 1.00. We can compute the unstandardized correlation between Y and X, or the covariance (COV_{YX}), using the formula $COV_{YX} = \Sigma yx_i/(n − 1)$. For our data, as reported in Table 2.2, $\Sigma yx_i = 4.00$, so we have $COV_{YX} = 4.00/(4 − 1) = 4.00/3 = 1.33$.

We can compute the standardized covariance, the Pearson's r, by removing from our estimate via division both SD_Y and SD_X. For our data, $SD_Y = (SS_Y/[n − 1])^{.5} = (20.00/[4 − 1])^{.5} = (20.00/3)^{.5} = 6.67^{.5} = 2.58$, and $SD_X = (SS_X/[n − 1])^{.5} = (1.00/[4 − 1])^{.5} = (1.00/3)^{.5} = 0.33^{.5} = 0.58$. The Pearson's $r = COV_{YX}/(SD_Y * SD_X) = 1.33/(2.58 * 0.58) = 1.33/1.49 = 0.89$. The coefficient of

Table 2.2. Statistics Needed to Compute the Pearson's r

		SS_X computations		Cross-products Computations		
Person	X_i	$-M_X = x_i$	x_i^2	x_i	y_i	yx_i
Geri	0	$-0.50 = -0.50$	0.25	-0.50	-3.00	1.50
Murray	0	$-0.50 = -0.50$	0.25	-0.50	-1.00	0.50
Wendy	1	$-0.50 = 0.50$	0.25	0.50	1.00	0.50
Deborah	1	$-0.50 = 0.50$	0.25	0.50	3.00	1.50
M_X	0.50					
Sum			1.00			4.00

determination, r^2, is $0.89^2 = 0.80$. We can always express this ratio as a percentage (i.e., $0.80 \times 100 = 80.0\%$), which inherently reminds us that the result is a ratio, and also helps us remember that this ratio is an area-world, rather than a score-world, statistic. The result tells us that with knowledge of whether the students had undergone recent major surgery, we could explain or predict 80.0% of the individual differences (i.e., the variability) in their cognitive test scores. Our predictor variable seems to work relatively well, given that $r^2 = 80.0\%$ and the r^2 has a mathematical limit of 100%.

We can also compute a regression equation with weights to be applied to scores on the predictor variable that we can use with people other than Geri, Murray, Wendy, and Deborah to predict how well they would do on the cognitive test, if we knew whether the new people had undergone major surgery. The prediction would work roughly as well with new participants, as long as the new people were similar to the people in our original sample. The regression equation to obtain the predicted Y_i scores on composite/latent/synthetic variable $\hat{Y}_i$ is:

$$\hat{Y}_i = a + b(X_i).$$

We can compute a multiplicative constant, b, for scores of new people on X_i, using the formula $b = r(SD_Y/SD_X) = 0.89 (2.58/0.58) = 0.89 * 4.47 = 4.00$ (see Thompson, 2006a). We can compute an additive constant, a, for scores of new people on X_i, using the formula $a = M_Y - b(M_X) = 5.00 - 4.00(0.50) = 5.00 - 2.00 = 3.00$ (again, see Thompson, 2006a).

We can also apply these constants to the X_i scores of the four students for whom we already know their Y_i scores. In practice, this may not be a useful exercise, because why would we want to predict what the scores on Y_i will be, using $\hat{Y}_i$ scores, when we already know these Y_i scores. However, we can obtain some further insight into the GLM by computing the $\hat{Y}_i$ scores for Geri, Murray, Wendy, and Deborah.

Participant	$a + (b * X_i)$	$= a + b * X_i = \hat{Y}_i$
Geri	$3.00 + (4.00 * 0)$	$= 3.00 + 0.00 = 3.00$
Murray	$3.00 + (4.00 * 0)$	$= 3.00 + 0.00 = 3.00$
Wendy	$3.00 + (4.00 * 1)$	$= 3.00 + 4.00 = 7.00$
Deborah	$3.00 + (4.00 * 1)$	$= 3.00 + 4.00 = 7.00$

And we can compute the scores of the four students on a second composite/latent/synthetic variable, e_i, defined as $e_i = Y_i - \hat{Y}_i$. For our data, we have:

Participant	$Y_i - \hat{Y}_i$	$= e_i$
Geri	$2 - 3.00$	$= -1.00$
Murray	$4 - 3.00$	$= 1.00$
Wendy	$6 - 7.00$	$= -1.00$
Deborah	$8 - 7.00$	$= 1.00$

So, we have four variables in the analysis: Y_i, X_i, $\hat{Y}_i$, and e_i. We have already computed SS_Y and SS_X. We can also compute SS_{YHAT} and SS_e, using the same formula for the sum of squares for all four SS calculations. This yields:

Participant	$\hat{Y}_i - M_{YHAT} = yhat_i$		$yhat_i^2$
Geri	$3.00 - 5.00$	$= -2.00$	4.00
Murray	$3.00 - 5.00$	$= -2.00$	4.00
Wendy	$7.00 - 5.00$	$= 2.00$	4.00
Deborah	$7.00 - 5.00$	$= 2.00$	4.00
Sum			16.00

Thus, for our data, $SS_{YHAT} = 16.00$ and:

Participant	$e_i - M_e = e_i$		e_i^2
Geri	$-1.00 - 0.00 = -1.00$		1.00
Murray	$1.00 - 0.00 = 1.00$		1.00
Wendy	$-1.00 - 0.00 = -1.00$		1.00
Deborah	$1.00 - 0.00 = 1.00$		1.00
Sum			4.00

Thus, $SS_e = 4.00$.

Key Concepts

In every analysis within the GLM, we are partitioning the total variance of the variable(s) we care about (i.e., the dependent variable[s]) into parts. In the present example, there are two partitions. The first partition of SS_Y is the part of SS_Y that we can explain/predict if we have knowledge of the scores on X_i. For our data, this $SS_{EXPLAINED/REGRESSION/MODEL/BETWEEN} = 16.00$. The second partition of SS_Y is the part of SS_Y that we can*not* explain/predict if we have knowledge only of the scores on X_i. For our data, this $SS_{UNEXPLAINED/RESIDUAL/ERROR/WITHIN} = 4.00$.

Logically, the explained and the unexplained partitions of the SS_Y information about individual differences on the outcome variable are inherently nonoverlapping, and sum to equal SS_Y (i.e., $[SS_{YHAT} = 16.00 + SS_e = 4.00] = SS_Y = 20.00$). Equally important, we can see that $r^2 = SS_{EXPLAINED/REGRESSION/MODEL/BETWEEN}/SS_Y = 16.00/20.00 = 80.0\%$. This kind of ratio (i.e., the ratio of explained to total variance) is used throughout the GLM to compute various effect sizes analogous to r^2 (e.g., the regression R^2, the CCA R_C^2, the ANOVA/MANOVA/DDA η^2).

ANOVA Computations

We can also conceptualize our heuristic example as an ANOVA problem in which we want to test the null hypothesis that the two group test means ($M_{NO\ SURGERY} = 3.00$; $M_{SURGERY} = 7.00$) are equal. Recall that the SS_{TOTAL} (or SS_Y) is computed as the sum of the squared deviations of (#1) the *individual scores* from the (#3) *grand mean* (i.e., $M_Y = 5.00$). The SS_{TOTAL} for the ANOVA, of course, remains equal to the 20.00, because the Y_i scores are unchanged by running a different analysis of the same data.

The ANOVA $SS_{EXPLAINED/REGRESSION/MODEL/BETWEEN}$ is computed as the sum of the squared deviations of (#2) the *group means* (i.e., 3.00 and 7.00, respectively) from the (#3) *grand mean* (i.e., $M_Y = 5.00$). For our data, we have:

$$[n_0 * (M_0 - M_Y)^2] + [n_1 * (M_1 - M_Y)^2]$$
$$[2 * (3.00 - 5.00)^2] + [2 * (7.00 - 5.00)^2]$$
$$[2 * (-2.00)^2] + [2 * (2.00)^2]$$
$$[2 * 4.00] + [2 * 4.00]$$
$$8.00 + 8.00 = 16.00$$

The ANOVA $SS_{UNEXPLAINED/RESIDUAL/ERROR/WITHIN}$ is computed as the sum of the squared deviations of (#1) the *individual scores* from the (#2) the *group means* (i.e., 3.00 and 7.00, respectively), computed separately, and then "pooled" together. For our data, we have for the nonsurgery group:

$Y_i - M_0 = \quad y_i \quad y_i^2$

$2 - 3.00 = -1.00 \quad 1.00$

$4 - 3.00 = \quad 1.00 \quad 1.00$

Sum $\quad\quad\quad\quad\quad\quad 2.00$

And for the surgery group we have:

$Y_i - M_1 = \quad y_i \quad y_i^2$

$6 - 7.00 = -1.00 \quad 1.00$

$8 - 7.00 = \quad 1.00 \quad 1.00$

Sum $\quad\quad\quad\quad\quad\quad 2.00$

Thus, the $SS_{UNEXPLAINED/RESIDUAL/ERROR/WITHIN}$ for our ANOVA equals $2.00 + 2.00 = 4.00$.

The ANOVA η^2 effect size tells us how much of the variability in the outcome variable scores we can explain or predict with knowledge of to what groups our four participants belonged. For our data, the $\eta^2 = SS_{EXPLAINED/REGRESSION/MODEL/BETWEEN}/SS_{TOTAL}$

$$16.00/20.00 = 80.0\%$$

The reader will have noticed that regression r^2 and the ANOVA η^2 are equal. More importantly, the fact that the formulas for computing these effects are the same suggests the omnipresence of the GLM. Indeed, the same formula for this ratio of explained-to-total-variance is used throughout the GLM. For example, when we use multiple regression to predict Y_i scores using multiple predictor variables, $R^2 = SS_{EXPLAINED/REGRESSION/MODEL/BETWEEN}/SS_{TOTAL}$.

Statistical Estimation Theory

Everywhere in the GLM, we apply weights to the measured/observed variables to estimate scores on composite/latent/synthetic variables. For example, our weights in our prediction equation were $a = 3.00$ and $b = 4.00$. Additive and multiplicative constants such as these have the properties that they:

1. maximize the $SS_{EXPLAINED/REGRESSION/MODEL/BETWEEN}$;
2. minimize the $SS_{UNEXPLAINED/RESIDUAL/ERROR/WITHIN}$; and

3. maximize the ratio of explained-to-total-variance (e.g., η^2, r^2, the regression R^2, the CCA R_C^2).

Because all the analysis within "traditional/ classical analyses" that are part of the GLM (e.g., t-tests, ANOVA, ANCOVA, Pearson's r, regression, MANOVA, MANCOVA, DDA, CCA) have these three properties, all these methods are called *ordinary least squares* (OLS) analyses. That is, the parameters (e.g., the weights) estimated in these models optimize the fit of the sample statistics to the sample data.

Although OLS analyses have been widely used for more than a century, other statistical estimation theories are also available. For example, "maximum likelihood" is another estimation theory first discussed by Sir Ronald Fisher in 1922. Maximum likelihood methods optimize the fit of models or parameters, not to the sample data in hand but, rather, to the population data. This seems a very appealing feature of maximum likelihood estimation, because usually we care most about the population and only care about the sample to the extent that the sample informs our inferences about the population.

One reason why OLS methods have remained popular is that OLS estimation is hugely less computationally intensive than maximum likelihood estimation. Computational simplicity was particularly important in the era preceding the 1970s, because computers and statistical software only became widely available around the 1970s. Prior to the 1970s, when computation were frequently done by hands-on mechanical calculators, computations not only had to be done by hand but by convention were done repeatedly (e.g., 8 times, 15 times) until any two sets of results matched, so that the possibility of human error could be ruled out and confidence could be vested in the results!

Three Classes of General Linear Model Statistics

Throughout the GLM, including traditional/ classical univariate statistics, statistical results can be sorted into three classes. These are (1) effect sizes used to inform judgments about practical significance, (2) $p_{CALCULATED}$ and related results used to test statistical significance, and (3) statistical analyses used to inform judgments about the replicability of results.

Practical Significance: Effect Sizes

As noted previously, effect sizes quantify the magnitudes of intervention effects or variable relationships (Grissom & Kim, 2011; Thompson, 2006b, 2007). More detailed treatment of effect sizes is presented in the encyclopedia chapter on meta-analysis, but some discussion of effect sizes is warranted here because effect sizes are a key commonality that joins traditional/classical statistics together into a single GLM.

One extremely powerful way to think about effect sizes is to think of these as model fit statistics. Every analysis (e.g., t-test, ANOVA, DDA, CCA) fits a model to our data. As Thompson (2006a) explained, "As the effect size (e.g., R^2) approaches mathematical limits, or takes on large values, there is evidence that the correct variables and the correct analysis has been used, and that the model is *one* plausible model that fits the data" (p. 251).

However, using effect size as indices of model fit presumes that the model is "falsifiable" given the research situation. As explained in more detail elsewhere, "Some analyses inevitably generate perfect (or near perfect) fit if the degrees of freedom error is (or approaches) zero. *Every* model with $df_{ERROR} = 0$ will perfectly fit the data, and yield an R^2 of 100%, regardless of what the measured variables are. Thus, large effect sizes provide stronger evidence of model fit when the degrees of freedom error is larger" (Thompson, 2006a, p. 251).

Kirk (1996) catalogued more than three dozen effect sizes, and the number is growing. More exotic, but promising, effect sizes include Huberty's group overlap index (I; Hess, Olejnik & Huberty, 2001; Huberty & Holmes, 1983; Natesan & Thompson, 2007) and Grissom's (1994) "probability of superiority." Here, only the most frequently reported effect sizes, grouped into three categories, will be considered.

Standardized Differences. In medicine, where single, meaningful metrics of measurement tend to be used universally (e.g., deaths per 1,000 patients, milligrams of cholesterol per deciliter of blood), effect sizes are computed simply as mean differences:

$$\text{Unstandardized } d = M_{EXPERIMENTAL} - M_{CONTROL}$$

However, in psychology we use different measures of constructs, which each may have different standard deviations. So, to compare effects across measures across studies in a given literature, if, but only if, we believe that outcome measures truly have different metrics, we must standardize the effect size by removing the *SD* by division for each prior study. Our goal is to standardize with our best estimate of the population σ_Y. The result is a standardized score-world statistic.

Glass' delta is one option. Glass reasoned that an intervention may impact not only the outcome variable means but might also affect the dispersion of the outcome variable scores in the intervention group. Therefore, he suggested standardization using only the *SD* of the control group as the best population parameter estimate:

$$\text{Glass' delta} = (M_{\text{EXPERIMENTAL}} - M_{\text{CONTROL}}) / SD_{\text{CONTROL}}$$

For example, if $M_{\text{EXPERIMENTAL}} = 110.0$, $SD_{\text{EXPERIMENTAL}} = 10.0$, $n_{\text{EXPERIMENTAL}} = 10$, $M_{\text{CONTROL}} = 100.0$, $SD_{\text{CONTROL}} = 15.0$, $n_{\text{CONTROL}} = 15$, we have:

$$(110.0 - 100.0)/15.0 = 10.0/15.0 = 0.67$$

Cohen's *d* is a second choice. Cohen reasoned that not all interventions impact dependent variable dispersion and that a more precise estimate of the population σ_Y may occur if we use outcome variable scores from both groups, thus yielding an estimate based on a larger sample size. This estimate is computed as:

$$\text{Cohen's } d = (M_E - M_C)/[\{(SD_E^2 * n_E)$$
$$+ (SD_C^2 * n_C)\}/(n_E + n_C)]^{0.5}$$
$$(110.0 - 100.0)/[\{(10.0^2 * 10)$$
$$+ (15.0^2 * 15)\}/(10 + 15)]^{0.5}$$
$$10.0/[\{(100.0 * 10) + (225.0 * 15)\}/(10 + 15)]^{0.5}$$
$$10.0/[\{1000.0 + 3375.0\}/25]^{0.5}$$
$$10.0/[4375.0/25]^{0.5}$$
$$10.0/175.0^{0.5}$$
$$10.0/13.23 = 0.76$$

Of course, we can also compute standardized differences using other location statistics, such as medians, winsorized means, or trimmed means. Means can be unduly influenced by outlying scores. Thus, as Grissom and Kim (2005) noted, sometimes "A *sample's* [italics added] median can provide a more accurate estimate of the mean of the *population* [italics added] than does the mean of that sample" (p. 40).

Variance-Accounted-For Statistics. Because all the traditional/classical statistics that we are considering are correlational, all analyses yield r^2-type effect sizes. Because r^2 (and R^2 and R_C^2) and η^2 all quantify how far sample results diverged from the null hypothesis expectation of a zero effect, these statistics are also all area-world effect sizes.

Corrected/Adjusted Effects. No sample perfectly represents the population from which the sample was drawn. Any deviation of sample from population features is called "sampling error." Thus, samples are like people: Every sample is unique as against every other sample, and every sample is somewhat weird, and some samples are way weird.

Sampling error causes problems in all our statistical estimates, including effect sizes, because our calculations cannot distinguish between sampling error variance and sample variance that accurately represents the population. This may be particularly problematic when we are using OLS as our statistical estimation theory, because OLS estimation is particularly insensitive to these distinctions. The result is that "uncorrected" or "unadjusted" effect sizes (e.g., η^2, r^2, the regression R^2, the CCA R_C^2) tend to overestimate population effect sizes.

Fortunately, because we know what causes sampling error, we theoretically can develop formulas to "correct" or "adjust" the effect estimates. Three sample features tend to influence sampling error. First, our samples tend to be less representative of the population, and thus have *more* sampling error, as sample size gets *smaller*.

Second, we tend to have *more* sampling error as studies include *more* measured/observed variables. This second dynamic occurs because of the influence of outliers. Outliers are *not* evil, horrible people whose anomalous scores distort all statistics for all variables. Obviously, each of us is very good at some things and very bad at other things, and so we are all outliers on at least some variables! Therefore, for a fixed *n* of people, as we sample across more and more measured variables, we afford increased opportunities for the weirdness of at least some of the people to be manifested.

Third, we tend to have *more* sampling error as the population effect size gets *smaller*. This dynamic is less obvious. Thompson (2002a) suggested thinking about the dynamic in the context of a population for a bivariate scattergram for a billion people when the population $r = +1.00$. This means that in the population scattergram, all the 1 billion asterisks sit on a single regression line. Thompson (2002a) noted,

> In this instance, even if the researcher draws ridiculously small samples, such as $n = 2$ or $n = 3$,

and no matter which participants are drawn, we simply cannot incorrectly estimate the variance-accounted-for effect size. That is, *any* two or three or four people will always define a straight line in the sample scattergram, and thus [sample] r^2 will always be 1.0. (p. 68)

One correction formula was developed by Ezekiel (1929) for the regression R^2 but arguably also can be applied both with the Pearson's r^2 and the CCA R_C^2 (Thompson, 1990; Wang & Thompson, 2007). The corrected R^2, R^2*, can be computed as:

$$R^2* = 1 - [(n-1)/(n-v-1)][1 - R^2], \quad (5)$$

where v is the number of predictor variables. For example, for $r^2 = 5.0\%$ and $n = 10$, we have:

$$1 - [(10-1)/(10-1-1)][1 - 0.05]$$
$$1 - [9/8][0.95]$$
$$1 - [1.12][0.95]$$
$$1 - 1.07$$
$$r^2* = -6.9\%$$

In our example, the negative corrected variance-accounted-for effect size for a squared, area-world statistic is troubling and indicates that all the originally detected effect and, more, is an artifact of sampling error variance. Put differently, in a sense, with knowledge of our predictor variable X_i scores, we know less than if we had no predictor variable.

For ANOVA, we can compute Hays' (1981) ω^2 as the adjustment to the η^2:

$$\omega^2 = [SS_{BETWEEN} - (k-1)MS_{WITHIN}]/$$
$$[SS_Y + MS_{WITHIN}],$$

where k is the number of levels in the ANOVA way, and $MS_{WITHIN} = SS_{WITHIN}/(n-1-[k-1])$. For example, for our ANOVA of the Table 2.1 data, for which $\eta^2 = 80.0\%$ and $MS_{WITHIN} = 4.0/(4-1-[2-1]) = 4.0/2.0 = 2.0$, we have:

$$\omega^2 = [16.0 - (2-1)2.0]/[20.0 + 2.0]$$
$$[16.0 - (1)2.0]/[20.0 + 2.0]$$
$$[16.0 - 2.0]/[20.0 + 2.0]$$
$$14.0/[20.0 + 2.0]$$
$$14.0/22.0 = 63.6\%$$

Notice that the "shrunken" r^2* and ω^2 values (–6.9% and 63.6%, respectively) are smaller than the uncorrected r^2 and η^2 values (5.0% and 80.0%, respectively).

Statistical Significance

Once we have computed an effect size (e.g., the regression R^2, the CCA R_C^2, the ANOVA/MANOVA/DDA η^2), we may want to determine the likelihood of our sample results, under certain assumptions. A $p_{CALCULATED}$ can be derived for this purpose. Like all proportions, p-values range from 0.0 to 1.0. A $p_{CALCULATED}$ value tells us the *probability of obtaining our effect size, or one larger, assuming that the sample came from a population described by the null hypothesis (i.e., the population effect size is zero) and given our sample size*. For a fixed non-zero effect size, $p_{CALCULATED}$ will get *smaller* as (1) sample size (n) gets *larger* or (2) the sample effect size gets *larger*.

Of course, we must take n into account when deriving $p_{CALCULATED}$, because n impacts sampling error. If we draw a sample of IQ scores from a population in which $\mu = 100.0$, and $\sigma = 15.0$, when sample size is small, there necessarily is a greater probability (i.e., $p_{CALCULATED}$) of obtaining a sample mean that differs markedly from 100.0 than for samples larger in size.

Less obvious is why we must assume that the null hypothesis exactly describes the population from which we have drawn our sample. Thompson (1996) explained:

> Why *must* the researcher assume that the sample comes from a population in which H_0 [e.g., H_0: $M_{MEN}=M_{WOMEN}$] is true? Well, *something* must be assumed, or there would be infinitely many equally plausible (i.e., indeterminate) answers to the question of what is the probability of the sample statistics. For example, sample statistics of standard deviations of 3 and 5 would be most likely (highest $p_{CALCULATED}$) if the population parameter standard deviations were 3 and 5, would be slightly less likely if the population standard deviations were 3.3 and 4.7, and would be less likely still (an even smaller $p_{CALCULATED}$) if the parameters were standard deviations of 4 and 4. (p. 27)

We can compute $p_{CALCULATED}$ and use the result to inform our subjective judgment about what our results mean. Alternatively, we can compare our $p_{CALCULATED}$ against an *a priori* $p_{CRITICAL}$ (α) value and reject our null hypothesis and describe our results as being "statistically significant," *iff* (if and only if) $p_{CALCULATED} < \alpha$. For questions with which to self-assess conceptual mastery of $p_{CALCULATED}$, *see* Thompson (2006a, pp. 180–181).

Sampling Distribution. Statistical significance testing is only relevant when we have sample data. If we have population data, then no statistical inference is necessary. We know the exact population parameter values (e.g., μ, σ, ρ).

If instead we have sample data, and we want to derive $p_{CALCULATED}$, either for subjective descriptive purposes, or to decide whether to reject a null hypothesis (H_0), then we also require a "sampling distribution," or some related distribution (i.e., a test statistic distribution, such as t or F). One use of the sampling distribution is to obtain $p_{CALCULATED}$. So, understanding of the sampling distribution is important to understanding of traditional/classical statistics, because traditional/classical statistics have long been used to conduct statistical significance testing using $p_{CALCULATED}$. But understanding of the sampling distribution is also important even if statistical significance is not being conducted, because the sampling distribution also has a role in evaluating practical significance.

The distinctions between the population, the sample, and the sampling distribution are clear.

1. Populations contain *scores* of N people. The population is the group about which we would like to generalize. For example, if a researcher only cared about the scores of four women, and did not wish to generalize beyond these four women, then those scores would be a population. The quantitative characterizations of the scores computed in the population are "parameters" (e.g., μ, σ, ρ).

2. Samples contain *scores* of n people sampled from a larger population. The quantitative characterizations of the scores computed in the sample are "statistics" (e.g., M, SD, r).

3. Sampling distributions contain all the *statistics* that can be computed for all the possible samples of a given size n for a given statistic. For example, for the sampling distribution of the mean, there are different sampling distributions for $n = 5$, $n = 6$, and $n = 7$. Also, even for a fixed $n = 50$, there are different sampling distributions for the statistic mean, the statistic SD, and the statistic coefficient of kurtosis.

In practice, most researchers are extremely ambitious, and want to generalize their findings to all people for all time. For such researchers, the population is infinitely large. And infinitely many sample statistics for samples of a given size n can be drawn from infinitely large populations. In such cases, the sampling distribution must be derived theoretically.

However, in some cases the population is finite, and thus sampling distributions are finite. And in any case, working with finite populations facilitates concrete understanding of what sampling distributions are and what some of the properties of sampling distributions are.

Let's treat the Table 2.1 scores as if they constituted a population, so that we have both a finite population and a finite sampling distribution. We will also focus on only one statistic: the mean. The mean has some positive and some negative features as a statistic (e.g., sensitivity to outliers) but at least is a very familiar statistic.

For our finite population, the sampling distribution for M for $n = 1$ would be:

Sampling Distribution for M for $n = 1$

	Score(s)	M	
Sample #1	2	2.0	
Sample #2	4	4.0	* * * *
Sample #3	6	6.0	_____
Sample #4	8	8.0	0 2 4 6 8

Note that for the sampling distribution for the mean, and (only) at $n = 1$, the population distribution and the sampling distribution would be identical, and all numerical characterizations of the two distributions would be equal. Thus, the means of the population distribution and the sampling distribution would be identical, and the standard deviations of the population distribution and the sampling distribution would be identical.

For our finite population, the sampling distribution for M for $n = 2$ would be:

Sampling Distribution for M for $n = 2$

	Score(s)	M	
Sample #1	2, 4	3.0	
Sample #2	2, 6	4.0	
Sample #3	2, 8	5.0	*
Sample #4	4, 6	5.0	* * * * *
Sample #5	4, 8	6.0	_____
Sample #6	6, 8	7.0	0 2 4 6 8

And for our finite population, the sampling distribution for M for $n = 3$ would be:

Sampling Distribution for M for $n = 3$

	Score(s)	M	
Sample #1	2, 4, 6	4.0	
Sample #2	2, 4, 8	4.7	* * * *
Sample #3	2, 6, 8	5.3	_____
Sample #4	4, 6, 8	6.0	0 2 4 6 8

From the forgoing examples, we can deduce that the sampling distribution gets *narrower* (i.e., more homogeneous) as n get *larger*. This dynamic merely reflects the reality that our sample statistics better estimate population parameters as sample size increases, because larger sample size implies smaller sampling error.

Indeed, one might reasonably compute the *SD* of the sampling distribution as a way to quantify the expected precision of our statistical estimates of population parameters. This *SD* (i.e., the *SD* of the sampling distribution) is *extremely* important in statistics. Rather than name the *SD* of the sampling distribution "the *SD* of the sampling distribution," we instead label this statistic the "standard error of the statistic" (e.g., SE_M, SE_r).

One use of the *SE* is to help us decide how risky it will be for us to fall in love with our statistic—for example, in one study, possibly $M_Y = 105.0$ and $SE_M = 40.0$, whereas in a second study $M_Y = 105.0$ and $SE_M = 5.0$. In both studies the mean is estimated to be 105.0, but the larger SE_M in the first study suggests caution in relying on the estimate of the mean, given that the estimate is expected to fluctuate considerably across all the equally likely samples that can be drawn at the given sample size from the population.

Statistics, like love, involves making some difficult on-balance decisions. In love, a given person may say, "This will be the most dangerous thing I have ever done, but the payoffs may be worth the potential risks, and I'm going to allow myself to love." A different person confronted with the same potential risks and rewards may say, "Not in a million years." Similarly, in statistics, we must decide how trustworthy is our given point estimate, such as a mean. The *SE* helps inform our subjective choices of whether to fall in love with our point estimate by quantifying the danger involved in judging the point estimate to be reasonably trustworthy.

Obtaining $p_{CALCULATED}$. The sampling distribution (or some related distribution) must be used to obtain $p_{CALCULATED}$. In Thompson (2006a, pp. 136–140), I provided a concrete example of this process. The process assumed that the New Orleans Saints questioned whether the coin the referee was flipping at the beginning of each game to decide who would kick the football first was a fair coin. It was presumed that the Saints' captain and the referee agreed to draw a sample of $n = 10$ flips of the suspect coin. They agreed to reject the null hypothesis that the suspect coin was fair if the suspect coin had a number of heads for which $p_{CALCULATED}$ was less than 5.0%.

In the example, a sampling distribution was created by asking each of 80,000 fans in the stadium to flip coins from their pockets, each assumed to be fair, exactly 10 times. The numbers of heads were then recorded in a sampling distribution consisting of 80,000 statistics. In the example, the following results were obtained for the extremes of the sampling distribution:

Number of heads	Number of samples	Percentage	Cumulative % from sampling space ends
0	78	0.10%	0.1%
1	781	0.98%	1.1%
2	3,516	4.40%	5.4%
...			
8	3,516	4.40%	5.4%
9	781	0.98%	1.1%
10	78	0.10%	0.1%

In this scenario, the null that the suspect coin is fair will be rejected either if there are too few heads or too many heads. The likely rule will be that the null will be rejected if there are very few heads, and the probability of the small number of heads is less than 0.05 in 2, or 2.5%. The null will also be rejected if there are way too many heads, and the probability of the large number of heads is less than 0.05 in 2, or 2.5%. For our example, because 1.1% is less than 2.5%, the null hypothesis will be rejected *iff* the sample of 10 flips of the suspect coin yields 0, 1, 9, or 10 heads.

Let's assume that the trial of 10 flips yields 2 heads. The probability of obtaining exactly 2 heads is 4.4%, but the probability of obtaining 2 or fewer heads yields the $p_{CALCULATED}$ value of 5.4%, which is greater than 2.5%. Because $p_{CALCULATED} = 5.4\% > p_{CRITICAL} = 2.5\%$, the result is not statistically significant, and we fail to reject the null hypothesis that the coin is fair.

Test Statistics. Sampling distributions can be quite difficult to estimate. Fortunately, years ago statisticians realized that related distributions, called *test distributions* (e.g., t, F, χ^2), could more easily be derived for sampling distributions and that a comparison of the test statistic calculated ($TS_{CALCULATED}$, e.g., $t_{CALCULATED}$, $F_{CALCULATED}$) with a $TS_{CRITICAL}$ always yields the same decision about rejecting or not rejecting the null, as does a comparison of a $p_{CALCULATED}$

Table 2.3. Hypothetical Dataset #2 for the MANOVA/DDA Example

Participant	X	Y	Group	DDA function scores
Kathy	3	0	0	−1.799
Peggy	12	12	0	−0.554
Carol	13	11	0	−3.004
Catherine	22	23	0	−1.759
Jill	2	2	1	1.759
Camie	11	14	1	3.004
Donna	12	13	1	0.554
Shawn	21	25	1	1.799

with a $p_{CRITICAL}$ (i.e., α). The only difference in using TS versus p is that with p-values, we reject if $p_{CALCULATED} < p_{CRITICAL}$, but with test statistics we reject if $TS_{CALCULATED} > TS_{CRITICAL}$.

To illustrate these computations, and later to draw linkages between ANOVAs versus MANOVA/DDA of the same data, we will presume that another $n = 8$ students from the hypothetical Farnsworth School are randomly selected for an experiment investigating the effectiveness of two different teaching methods. Four of the students are randomly selected to be taught all their courses using traditional lecture methods (coded Group = "0"), whereas four students are selected to be taught all their courses using an inquiry approach in which students are exposed to puzzlements that force them to discover underlying principles (coded Group = "1"). Table 2.3 presents their end-of-year posttest scores on mathematics (X) and writing (Y) tests.

For our ANOVAs of the Table 2.3 data, we can test the statistical significance of the means on the measured/observed variables by computing the F ratios, which are area-world ratios of the variances sometimes called *mean squares* (i.e., $MS_{EXPLAINED/REGRESSION/MODEL/BETWEEN}$, $MS_{UNEXPLAINED/RESIDUAL/ERROR/WITHIN}$). The $MS_{BETWEEN} = SS_{BETWEEN}/df_{BETWEEN}$, where $df_{BETWEEN}$ = the number of groups minus one. The $MS_{WITHIN} = SS_{WITHIN}/df_{WITHIN}$, where $df_{WITHIN} = n$ minus one minus $df_{BETWEEN}$.

For our data, for X we have:

$$F_{CALCULATED} = [2.0/(2-1)]/$$
$$[362.0/(8-1-1)]$$
$$[2.0/1]/[362.0/6]$$
$$2.0/60.3 = 0.03$$

For Y we have:

$$F_{CALCULATED} = [8.0/(2-1)]/$$
$$[530.0/(8-1-1)]$$
$$[8.0/1]/[530.0/6]$$
$$8.0/88.3 = 0.09$$

We can obtain the $F_{CRITICAL}$ value at $\alpha = 0.05$ for $df_{BETWEEN} = 1$ and $df_{WITHIN} = 6$ degrees of freedom using the Excel statistical function FINV. For our data, entering "= FINV(0.05,1,6)" yields 5.99. Because 0.03 < 5.99 and 0.09 < 5.99, we fail to reject the null hypotheses that the outcome variable means are different across the two groups (i.e., major surgery vs. no major surgery).

The basic test statistic is t, which is sometimes also referred to as the "critical ratio" or the Wald statistic. This test statistic can be computed as:

$$t = \text{parameter estimate}/SE_{PARAMETER}$$

The various test statistics (e.g., z, t, F, χ^2) are, in fact, all related to each other. For example, "a chi-square variable is formed by summing squared, unit normal z-scores; in turn, chi-square variables are combined to form F-variables" (Glass & Hopkins, 1984, p. 269).

The $t_{CRITICAL}$ tends to not change much as sample size increases once n is around 30 or so. For example, for $\alpha = 0.05$, we can see that the $t_{CRITICAL}$ is approximately |2.0| at various samples sizes:

t	n
2.26	10
2.04	30
2.01	50
1.99	70
1.99	90

Replicability

Replicability "is almost universally accepted as *the most important criterion* [emphasis added] of genuine scientific knowledge" (Rosenthal & Rosnow, 1984, p. 9). Similarly, Cohen (1994) noted the problems with overreliance on $p_{CALCULATED}$ values and argued that "given the problems on statistical induction, we must finally rely, as have the older sciences, on replication" (p. 1002).

Scientists want to discover important study results that are real and thus replicate. Scientists do not want to discover phenomena that are ephemeral. However, $p_{CALCULATED}$ values do *not* evaluate replicability (Cumming, 2008; Cumming & Maillardet,

2006). This is because $p_{CALCULATED}$ assumes the null hypothesis perfectly describes the population and then estimates the likelihood of the sample coming from this population. In other words, $p_{CALCULATED}$ is the probability of the sample given the population ($S|P$), and not the probability of ($P|S$) (Cohen, 1994).

If $p_{CALCULATED}$ was about ($P|S$), then the $p_{CALCULATED}$ would bear upon result replicability, because knowing the probability of the population parameters would also inform us about what statistics would likely occur in future samples (Thompson, 1996). But as Cohen (1994) so poignantly noted in his seminal article, "The Earth is round ($p < .05$)," the statistical significance test "does not tell us what we want to know, and we so much want to know what we want to know that, out of desperation, we nevertheless believe that it does!" (p. 997). Because $p_{CALCULATED}$ is not helpful in evaluating result replicability, but replicability is important, scholars use two other classes of methods to evaluate likely result replicability: internal replicability analyses and external replicability analyses (Thompson, 1996, 2006a, pp. 254–266).

External Replicability Analyses. In a recent U.S. Supreme Court case, Chief Justice John Roberts, Jr. opined that "The way to stop discrimination on the basis of race is to stop discriminating on the basis of race." In a similar vein, if a researcher wants to know if results replicate, then the logical analytic choice is to collect data in a new, independent sample and determine whether the same results are obtained. Unfortunately, requiring faculty seeking tenure or students seeking PhD degrees to replicate all their studies would be unrealistic and probably would lead to unacceptably high faculty unemployment and numerous student divorces.

Internal Replicability Analyses. Only true external replication provides direct evidence about whether results will replicate. However, internal replicability analyses, which use the original sample data to address replicability concerns, are the next-best alternative.

The most difficult challenge to replicability in the social sciences is that people are so individual and idiosyncratic. As Thompson (2006a) noted:

> Physical scientists do not have to confront these differences ... For example, a physicist who is observing the interaction patterns of atomic particles does not have to make generalizations such as, "Quarks and neutrinos repel each other, unless the quarks in gestation had poor nutrition or in childhood received poor education." Internal replicability analyses seek partially to overcome these challenges by mixing up the participants in different ways in an effort to evaluate whether results are *robust across the combinations of different idiosyncracies.* (p. 254)

Of course, internal replicability analyses are never as conclusive as external replicability analyses, but they do have the benefit of being superior to the replicability analyses most common in the literature: $p_{CALCULATED}$ (i.e., nothing).

There are three primary internal replicability analyses: (1) cross-validation, (2) the jackknife, or (3) the bootstrap (Thompson, 1994). The jackknife and the bootstrap are computer-intensive methods and historically were not used with traditional/classical statistics. But free bootstrap software, for example, has been written for use in conducting numerous analyses, including the traditional/classical statistics considered here. Space limitations preclude anything but a cursory overview of these methods.

In *cross-validation*, the sample is randomly split into subsamples, and the primary analysis is repeated in each subsample. The weights (e.g., regression β weights, factor pattern coefficients, CCA function coefficients) from each subsample are then employed with the alternative subsample to compute latent variable scores and to determine whether the effect size is replicated.

In the *jackknife*, as conceptualized by Tukey, the analysis is conducted repeatedly, each time dropping a subset of k participants, where k most often is each participant one at a time. Then some additional computations are typically performed to characterize the overall stability of the estimates.

In the *bootstrap*, as conceptualized by Efron, repeated "resamples," each of size n, are drawn randomly *with replacement* from the original sample of n participants. For example, if the original sample size was $n = 100$, in the first resample consisting of 100 rows of peoples' scores being drawn, Tom's row of scores might be drawn three times, Dick's row of scores might be drawn twice, and Harry's row of scores might be drawn not at all. In the second resample, Tom and Harry's rows of scores might not be drawn at all, but the row of data (i.e., scores of on all the measured variables) of Dick might be drawn five times.

Typically, 1,000 to 5,000 resamples are drawn. Then the statistics computed across all the resamples are averaged. And the *SD* of each resampled statistic (e.g., 5,000 M_Xs) is computed. In effect, this *SD* is actually an *empirically estimated* standard error (*SE*) for a given statistic on a given variable. This *SE* can be used either *descriptively*, to inform a personal judgment about how much confidence to vest in a given statistic (i.e., more confidence when then *SE* is closer to zero), or *inferentially*, to compute a *t*-test for a given statistic, or to empirically estimate confidence intervals for point estimates. Diaconis and Efron (1983) provide an accessible brief explanation of the concepts underlying the bootstrap.

Variance Partitions and Their Ratios: Multivariate Statistics

A multivariate analysis is computed in the presence of two or more outcome variables when all the measured/observed variables are considered simultaneously. As noted by Zientek and Thompson (2009):

> Multivariate analyses are consistent with a worldview that (a) most effects are multiply caused (e.g., reading curricula may impact reading achievement, but so may free lunch programs), and conversely, (b) most interventions have multiple effects (e.g., successful reading interventions may impact reading achievement, but children who read better also may develop more positive self-concepts, and more positive attitudes toward schooling). (p. 345)

Consequently, the use of multiple outcome variables in a single psychology study is quite common, and statistical analyses that simultaneously consider all the variables in the study are important because such analyses honor the fact that the variables coexist in reality.

Common traditional/classical multivariate statistics within the traditional/classical statistics venue are T^2, MANOVA, MANCOVA, descriptive discriminant analysis (DDA), and canonical correlation analysis (CCA). Our goal now is to illustrate the computations in traditional/classical multivariate analyses and especially to draw linkages between the computations in univariate and multivariate GLM analyses.

Here we will test group differences using MANOVA/DDA (*see* Huberty, 1994) of the Table 2.3 data. Again, we must partition information about total variability (e.g., *SS*, variance) into two components: (1) explained/regression/model/between and (2) unexplained/residual/error/within. Because we are simultaneously considering the scores on both outcome variables within a single analysis, we will use matrices containing multiple statistics, rather than only three single numbers (i.e., $SS_{BETWEEN}$, SS_{WITHIN}, SS_{TOTAL}) for a single outcome variable.

Our three matrices containing *SS* and sums of cross-products of deviation scores (e.g., Σyx_i) statistics for these data are:

$$\begin{array}{cc} & X \quad Y \\ B = X & 2.0 \quad -4.0 \\ Y & -4.0 \quad 8.0 \end{array} \quad \begin{array}{cc} & X \quad Y \\ W = X & 362.0 \quad 436.0 \\ Y & 436.0 \quad 530.0 \end{array} \quad \begin{array}{cc} & X \quad Y \\ T = X & 364.0 \quad 432.0 \\ Y & 432.0 \quad 538.0 \end{array}$$

We can see the linkages of the univariate methods and multivariate methods in the fact that the diagonal entries in the **B**, **W**, and **T** matrices are the univariate *SS* values for the *X* and *Y* variables (i.e., $_X SS_{BETWEEN} = 2.0$, $_X SS_{WITHIN} = 362.0$, $_X SS_{TOTAL} = 364.0$, $_Y SS_{BETWEEN} = 8.0$, $_Y SS_{WITHIN} = 530.0$, $_Y SS_{TOTAL} = 538.0$). If we conducted two ANOVAs of these data, then we would obtain η^2 values of $2.0/364.0 = 0.5\%$ and $8.0/538.0 = 1.5\%$, respectively.

We can convert our $F_{CALCULATED}$ values into $p_{CALCULATED}$ values using the Excel FDIST statistical function. For our data, "= FDIST(0.03, 2 – 1, 8 – 1 – 1)" yields $p_{CALCULATED} = 0.86$, and "= FDIST(0.02, 1, 6)" yields $p_{CALCULATED} = 0.77$. Thus, neither of the two sets of differences in the two means are statistically significant, and the related effect sizes are small.

However, in multivariate analyses we also simultaneously consider how the outcome variables are related to or interact with each other. The off-diagonal entries containing the sums of cross-products of deviation scores (i.e., –4.0, 436.0, and 432.0) are where we model these relationships.

In traditional/classical multivariate statistics, as in traditional/classical univariate statistics, we can compute a test statistic (e.g., $F_{CALCULATED}$) by dividing a between-variance partition by a within-variance partition. However, we must use matrices in the multivariate analyses, rather than the single numbers we would use in a univariate analysis. And things are a bit different in matrix algebra than in the algebra that is more familiar to most of us.

One difference between matrix algebra and regular algebra is that (1) in regular algebra we *can* divide by multiplying a number by the reciprocal of the number with which we are dividing (e.g., $20/5 = 20 * (1/5) = 4$), but (2) in matrix algebra we *must* divide by multiplying by a special reciprocal matrix called an "inverse" matrix, which is symbolized by a –1 superscript. We can solve for the inverse of the

W matrix by first specifying an "identity" matrix, **I** (so called because any matrix times **I** yields the initial matrix, unchanged). The **I** matrix must have the same "rank" (i.e., number of rows and columns) as the matrix we are inverting (i.e., **W**, because we want to divide by the within-variance partition, just as we do in ANOVA), and for our data we have:

$$\mathbf{I} = \begin{matrix} 1.0 & 0.0 \\ 0.0 & 1.0 \end{matrix}$$

To solve for $\mathbf{W}^{-1}$, we use the equation:

$$\mathbf{W}_{2\times 2} * \mathbf{W}_{2\times 2}^{-1} = \mathbf{I}_{2\times 2}$$

where $\mathbf{W}_{2\times 2}$ and $\mathbf{I}_{2\times 2}$ are already known.

In practice, we can solve for $\mathbf{W}^{-1}$ using the statistical function INV that is part of the SPSS MATRIX syntax. For our data,

$$\mathbf{W}^{-1} = \begin{matrix} 0.3005 & -0.2472 \\ -0.2472 & 0.2052 \end{matrix}$$

We then solve for $\mathbf{B}_{2\times 2} * \mathbf{W}_{2\times 2}^{-1}$ (again using SPSS MATRIX syntax commands), and we obtain:

$$\mathbf{H} = \begin{matrix} 1.5896 & -1.3152 \\ -3.1791 & 2.6304 \end{matrix}$$

Eigenvalues

The key statistics in univariate analyses are area-world *SS* values of different kinds (i.e., between, within, total). In multivariate analyses, the key statistics are called "eigenvalues" (i.e., λ_j, also synonymously called "characteristic roots"), which like *SS* values are in an area-world squared metric. In some traditional/classical multivariate analyses, eigenvalues are also multivariate squared correlation coefficients (e.g., the R_C^2 in CCA).

The number of eigenvalues of the **H** matrix (which is, remember, effectively **B** divided by **W**) is equal to the number of dependent variables in the analysis (here, 2). However, the number of non-zero eigenvalues in MANOVA/DAA equals the smaller of (1) the number of dependent variables or (2) the number of groups (k) minus one. For our data, we have two dependent variables, and $k - 1 = 1$. Thus, because $1 < 2$, we will obtain only one non-zero eigenvalue for our Table 2.3 data.

Computing eigenvalues in matrix algebra is quite complicated but is not quite so difficult when the dimensionality of the matrix for which we want to solve for the eigenvalues is 2 × 2, as is our $\mathbf{H}_{2\times 2}$. First, we label the cells of **H** as follows: $A = 1.5896$, $B = -1.3152$, $C = -3.1791$; $D = 2.6304$.

Each of the $j = 2$ eigenvalues will equal:

$$\lambda_j = [(A + D)/2] +/- Q$$

For our data, the leftmost portion of the equation equals:

$$(1.5896 + 2.6304)/2$$
$$4.22/2 = 2.11$$

We solve for Q as follows:

$$Q = [\{(4 * B * C) + [(A - D)^2]\}^{0.5}]/2$$
$$[\{(4 * -1.3152 * -3.1791)$$
$$+ [(1.5896 - 2.6304)^2]\}^{0.5}]/2$$
$$[\{(4 * 4.1812) + [(1.5896 - 2.6304)^2]\}^{0.5}]/2$$
$$[\{16.7246 + [(1.5896 - 2.6304)^2]\}^{0.5}]/2$$
$$[\{16.7246 + [-1.0408^2]\}^{0.5}]/2$$
$$[\{16.7246 + 1.0833\}^{0.5}]/2$$
$$[17.8079^{0.5}]/2$$
$$4.2199/2 = 2.11$$

So, for our data $\lambda_1 = 2.11 + 2.11 = 4.22$, and $\lambda_2 = 2.11 - 2.11 = 0.00$.

In traditional/classical multivariate statistics, unlike in traditional/classical univariate statistics where there is only one way to test statistical significance, there are four different ways to test null hypotheses: (1) the Wilks test, which involves multiplying a function of the eigenvalues of $\mathbf{B}^*\mathbf{W}^{-1}$ times each other; (2) the Roy test, which involves only the largest eigenvalue of $\mathbf{B}^*\mathbf{W}^{-1}$; (3) the Hotelling-Lawley test, which involves summing the eigenvalues of $\mathbf{B}^*\mathbf{W}^{-1}$; and (4) the Pillai-Bartlett test, which involves summing the eigenvalues of $\mathbf{B}^*\mathbf{T}^{-1}$ (see Stevens, 2009). The $p_{\text{CALCULATED}}$ results of these four tests for a given data set will be identical if the number of groups is two, as is the case for our MANOVA/DDA. Here, given space limitations, we will illustrate only the Wilks test.

Wilks proposed computing a statistic he labeled Wilks' Λ, which equals:

$$[1/(1 + \lambda_1)] * [1/(1 + \lambda_2)] * ...[1/(1 + \lambda_j)]$$

For our data,

$$\Lambda = [1/(1 + 4.22)]$$
$$[1/5.22] = 0.19$$

We can then use formulas suggested by Rao (*see* Table 4.2 in Tatsuoka, 1971) to convert the Wilks' Λ

into an $F_{CALCULATED}$. The formulas differ depending on how many k groups and how many p outcome variables we have. For our data,

$F_{CALCULATED} = [(1 - \Lambda)/\Lambda] * [(n - p - 1)/p]$

$[(1 - 0.192)/0.192] * [(8 - 2 - 1)/2]$

$[0.808/0.192] * [(8 - 2 - 1)/2]$

$4.22 * [(8 - 2 - 1)/2]$

$4.22 * [5/2]$

$4.22 * 2.50 = 10.55$

Now we can use the EXCEL statistical function

$= FDIST(10.55, 2, 8 - 2 - 1)$

to obtain the $p_{CALCULATED}$ value, which for our data equals 0.02.

An appealing feature of Wilks' Λ is that the statistic can also be used to compute multivariate η^2:

multivariate $\eta^2 = 1 - \Lambda$

For our data, multivariate $\eta^2 = 1 - 0.19 = 81.0\%$. This means that with knowledge of group membership, we can predict or explain 81.0% of the variability in the multivariate latent variables being analyzed (*see* Zientek & Thompson, 2009).

Multivariate versus Univariate Analyses

A comparison of the ANOVAs of the Table 2.3 data as against the MANOVA/DDA of the same data is quite instructive. For our data, we obtained:

ANOVA	MANOVA
X $p_{CALCULATED} = 0.86$	$p_{CALCULATED} = 0.02$
$\eta^2 = 0.5\%$	
Y $p_{CALCULATED} = 0.77$	multivariate
$\eta^2 = 1.5\%$	$\eta^2 = 81.0\%$

Obviously, the univariate and the multivariate analyses of the same data yield night-versus-day differences with respect to both statistical significance and effect size. These differences suggest a number of very important questions and very important conclusions.

Why Do the Univariate and the Multivariate Results Differ? The univariate ANOVAs analyze how different the means on the observed/measured variables X and Y were from each other (i.e., 12.5 vs. 11.5 for X, and 11.5 vs. 13.5 for Y). The MANOVA/DDA, on the other hand, does *not* test differences on the observed/measured variables. Rather, MANOVA/DDA creates composite/latent/synthetic variables scores directly analogous to the $\hat{Y}$ scores in regression by applying weights to the measured outcome variables. The DDA standardized weights for our data were −10.41 and 10.42, respectively, as can be confirmed by an SPSS MANOVA or DDA analysis of the Table 2.3 data.

Table 2.3 lists these latent outcome variable scores in the right-most column. For heuristic purposes, the reader is encouraged to run an ANOVA of these DDA function scores. Doing so will yield an ANOVA $\eta^2 = 25.32/31.32 = 80.8\%$.

Which Results are Most Ecologically Valid? Only the multivariate analyses simultaneously consider all the variables and all their relationships. The unique feature of the multivariate results is computing the off-diagonal sums-of-cross-products terms in the various matrices, which are not computed or considered within ANOVA. As Zientek and Thompson (2009) argued, "[O]nly the multivariate analyses take into account all possible simultaneous relationships among the variables, and thus honor the ecological reality that the variables in reality coexist" (p. 347). Thus, when univariate and multivariate results differ for a given data set, arguably it is the multivariate results that are ecologically valid.

Can ANOVAs Reasonably be Used Post Hoc *to MANOVA/DDA?* In ANOVA, *post hoc* tests are necessary *iff* both (1) a way or factor has more than two levels and (2) the omnibus null hypothesis is rejected. If one is testing mean differences on an outcome variable across boys versus girls, and there are statistically significant differences, then these two outcome variable means were different. But if the ANOVA way or factor had three or more levels (e.g., freshman, sophomores, juniors, seniors), and the omnibus null hypothesis is rejected, the question that then arises is which group means differed.

In a one-way MANOVA, even if the MANOVA way has only two levels, when the omnibus null hypothesis is rejected, *post hoc* tests are needed to address the question as to on what variables the groups differed. And if there are three or more levels in the way or factor, and the omnibus null hypothesis is rejected, then *post hoc* tests are needed to address two questions: (1) Which groups differ? and (2) On what variables do the groups differ?

Surprisingly, about three-fourths of published MANOVA articles incorrectly report *post hoc* ANOVAs (Kieffer, Reese, & Thompson, 2001), although the use of ANOVAs *post hoc* to finding statistically significant MANOVA effects is completely illogical, given that the two analyses address different research questions and also focus on different variables (i.e., measured vs. latent). Thus, Tatsuoka

(1971) admonished that "one would usually be well advised to follow up a significant multivariate test with a [descriptive] discriminant function analysis in order to study the nature of the group differences more closely" (p. 50). And Borgen and Seling (1978) argued:

> When data truly are multivariate, as implied by the application of MANOVA, a multivariate follow-up technique seems necessary to "discover" the complexity of the data. [Descriptive] discriminant analysis is multivariate; univariate ANOVA is not. (p. 696)

Interpretation Rubric: Specific Recommendations for Best Practice

A reasonable rubric for interpreting results within the GLM poses two questions: (1) Do I have anything? and (2) Only if I have something, from where does my something originate? The latter question typically involves interpretation of (1) the GLM weights (e.g., regression β weights, factor pattern coefficients) and (2) the structure coefficients (*see* Courville & Thompson, 2001). Some additional comments on the three types of evidence bearing on the first question may be helpful, especially with respect to specific practical recommendations for best interpretation practices.

Statistical Significance

Scholars have increasingly recognized the limits of statistical significance testing. Two main limitations can be highlighted. First, statistical significance has nothing to do with result importance. A valid deductive argument simply cannot contain in its conclusions any information not present in its premises. As Thompson (1993) explained, "If the computer package did not ask you your values prior to its analysis, it could not have considered your value system in calculating p's, and so p's cannot be blithely used to infer the value of research results" (p. 365).

Second, p-values are a confounded joint function of both sample size and effect size. This implies that $p_{CALCULATED}$ cannot reasonably be used an index solely of effect size:

> Because p values are confounded indices, in theory 100 studies with varying sample sizes and 100 different effect sizes could each have the same single $p_{CALCULATED}$, and 100 studies with the same single effect size could each have 100 different values for $p_{CALCULATED}$. (Thompson, 1999, pp. 169–170)

In some respects, $p_{CALCULATED}$ is a test of the sample size, which the researcher already knows prior to conducting the test. And the result of the statistical significance test is potentially less interesting because every non-zero effect size will be statistically significant at some sample size (Thompson, 2006a). In the words of Kirk (2003), the

> ... practice of focusing exclusively on a dichotomous reject-nonreject decision strategy of null hypothesis testing can actually *impede scientific progress* ... In fact, focusing on p values and rejecting null hypotheses actually *distracts us from our real goals*: deciding whether data support our scientific hypotheses and are practically significant. The focus of research should be on our scientific hypotheses, what data tell us about the magnitude of effects, the practical significance of effects, and the steady accumulation of knowledge. (p. 100, italics added)

Effect Sizes

In his various books on power analysis, Cohen proposed some benchmarks for "small," "medium," and "large" effects. These can be applied across many effect size choices (e.g., d, η^2, R^2), because formulas can be used to convert most effect sizes into each others' metrics. However, the view taken here is that Cohen's benchmarks should *not* be used in result interpretation, except in areas of new or original inquiry in which little or nothing is known about the typical effects in a given literature.

Cohen (1988) himself intended these benchmarks only as general guidelines, and he emphasized:

> [T]hese proposed conventions were set forth throughout with much diffidence, qualifications, *and invitations not to employ them if possible* [italics added] ... They were offered as conventions because they were needed in a research climate characterized by a neglect of attention to issues of [effect size] magnitude. (p. 532)

At least in established areas of research, "there is no wisdom whatsoever in attempting to associate regions of the effect-size metric with descriptive adjectives such as 'small,' 'moderate,' 'large,' and the like" (Glass, McGaw & Smith, 1981, p. 104). As noted elsewhere, "if people interpreted effect sizes [using fixed benchmarks] with the same rigidity that $\alpha = .05$ has been used in statistical testing, we would merely be being stupid in another metric" (Thompson, 2001, pp. 82–83).

The context of the study *must* be considered when evaluating study effects. As Thompson (2006b) noted, small effects may be noteworthy if:

1. the outcome variable is very important, such as human longevity;
2. the outcome variable is particularly resistant to intervention;
3. small effects generated over time cumulate into large effects; or
4. outcomes have multiple causes such that one or a few interventions inherently have limited impact, as is so often the case in educational research. (cited references omitted, p. 595)

For example, the η^2 for smoking or not on longevity or for taking a daily aspirin or not on heart attack incidence (at least for men) are both about 1%. These effects may be small, but the outcome is highly valued, and the effect is consistently replicated time after time.

Result Replicability

Even results from single studies ought to be interpreted within a meta-analytic perspective, using "meta-analytic thinking" (cf. Cumming & Finch, 2001). Thompson (2002b) defined meta-analytic thinking as "both (a) the prospective formulation of study expectations and design by explicitly invoking prior effect sizes and (b) the retrospective interpretation of new results, once they are in hand, via *explicit, direct* comparison with the prior effect sizes in the related literature" (p. 28, emphasis added). These comparisons will be facilitated once effect size reporting becomes ubiquitous.

Author Note

Bruce Thompson, Texas A&M University and Baylor College of Medicine (Houston).

References

American Educational Research Association. (2006). Standards for reporting on empirical social science research in AERA publications. *Educational Researcher, 35*(6), 33–40.

Bagozzi, R.P., Fornell, C., & Larcker, D.F. (1981). Canonical correlation analysis as a special case of a structural relations model. *Multivariate Behavioral Research, 16*, 437–454.

Borgen, F.H., & Seling, M.J. (1978). Uses of discriminant analysis following MANOVA: Multivariate statistics for multivariate purposes. *Journal of Applied Psychology, 63*, 689–697.

Boring, E. G. (1919). Mathematical vs. scientific importance. *Psychological Bulletin, 16*, 335–338.

Cohen, J. (1968). Multiple regression as a general data-analytic system. *Psychological Bulletin, 70*, 426–433.

Cohen, J. (1988). *Statistical power analysis for the behavioral sciences* (2nd ed.). Hillsdale, NJ: Erlbaum.

Cohen, J. (1994). The Earth is round ($p < .05$). *American Psychologist, 49*, 997–1003.

Courville, T. & Thompson, B. (2001). Use of structure coefficients in published multiple regression articles: β is not enough. *Educational and Psychological Measurement, 61*, 229–248.

Cumming, G. (2008). Replication and *p* values predict the future only vaguely, but confidence intervals do much better. *Perspectives on Psychological Science, 3*, 286–300.

Cumming, G., & Finch, S. (2001). A primer on the understanding, use and calculation of confidence intervals that are based on central and noncentral distributions. *Educational and Psychological Measurement, 61*, 532–575.

Cumming, G., & Maillardet, R. (2006). Confidence intervals and replication: Where will the next mean fall? *Psychological Methods, 11*, 217–227.

David, H. A. (1995). First (?) occurrence of common terms in mathematical statistics. *The American Statistician, 49*, 121–133.

Diaconis, P., & Efron, B. (1983). Computerintensive methods in statistics. *Scientific American, 248*(5), 116–130.

Ezekiel, M. (1929). The application of the theory of error to multiple and curvilinear correlation. *American Statistical Association Journal (Proceedings Supplement), 24*, 99–104.

Glass, G.V, & Hopkins, K. (1984). *Statistical methods in education and in psychology* (2nd ed.). Englewood Cliffs, NJ: Prentice-Hall.

Glass, G.V, McGaw, B., & Smith, M.L. (1981). *Meta-analysis in social research*. Beverly Hills, CA: Sage.

Graham, J. M. (2008). The General Linear Model as structural equation modeling. *Journal of Educational and Behavioral Statistics, 33*, 485–506.

Grissom, R. J. (1994). Probability of the superior outcome of one treatment over another. *Journal of Applied Psychology, 79*, 314–316.

Grissom, R. J. & Kim, J.J. (2011). *Effect sizes for research: Univariate and multivariate applications*. (2nd ed.). New York: Routledge.

Grissom, R., & Kim, J.J. (2005). *Effect sizes for research: A broad practical approach*. Mahwah, NJ: Erlbaum.

Hald, A. (1990). *A history of probability and statistics and their applications before 1750*. New York: Wiley.

Hald, A. (1998). *A history of mathematical statistics from 1750 to 1930*. New York: Wiley.

Hays, W. L. (1981). *Statistics* (3rd ed.). New York: Holt, Rinehart and Winston.

Hess, B., Olejnik, S., & Huberty, C.J (2001). The efficacy of two Improvement-over-chance effect sizes for two-group univariate comparisons under variance heterogeneity and nonnormality. *Educational and Psychological Measurement, 61*, 909–936.

Hubbard, R., & Ryan, P. A. (2000). The historical growth of statistical significance testing in psychology—and its future prospects. *Educational and Psychological Measurement, 60*, 661–681.

Huberty, C.J (1993). Historical origins of statistical testing practices: The treatment of Fisher versus Neyman-Pearson views in textbooks. *Journal of Experimental Education, 61*, 317–333.

Huberty, C.J (1994). *Applied discriminant analysis*. New York: Wiley and Sons.

Huberty, C.J (1999). On some history regarding statistical testing. In B. Thompson (Ed.), *Advances in social science methodology* (Vol. 5, pp. 1–23). Stamford, CT: JAI Press.

Huberty, C.J (2002). A history of effect size indices. *Educational and Psychological Measurement, 62*, 227–240.

Huberty, C.J & Holmes, S.E. (1983). Two-group comparisons and univariate classification. *Educational and Psychological Measurement, 43*, 15–26.

Kieffer, K.M., Reese, R.J., & Thompson, B. (2001). Statistical techniques employed in *AERJ* and *JCP* articles from 1988 to 1997: A methodological review. *Journal of Experimental Education, 69*, 280–309.

Kirk, R. E. (1996). Practical significance: A concept whose time has come. *Educational and Psychological Measurement, 56*, 746–759.

Kirk, R. E. (2003). The importance of effect magnitude. In S. F. Davis (Ed.), *Handbook of research methods in experimental psychology* (pp. 83–105). Oxford, UK: Blackwell.

Knapp, T. R. (1978). Canonical correlation analysis: A general parametric significance testing system. *Psychological Bulletin, 85*, 410–416.

Mulaik, S. A., Raju, N. S., & Harshman, R. A. (1997). Appendix to "There is a time and place for significance testing." In L. L. Harlow, S. A. Mulaik & J.H. Steiger (Eds.), *What if there were no significance tests?* (pp. 103–115). Mahwah, NJ: Erlbaum.

Natesan, P. & Thompson, B. (2007). Extending Improvement-over-chance *I*-index effect size simulation studies to cover some small-sample cases. *Educational and Psychological Measurement, 67*, 59–72.

Rosenthal, R., & Rosnow, R.L. (1984). *Essentials of behavioral research: Methods and data analysis*. New York: McGrawHill.

Stevens, J. (2009). *Applied multivariate statistics for the social sciences* (5th ed.). London: Routledge.

Stigler, S.M. (1986). *The history of statistics*. Cambridge, MA: Belknap.

Tatsuoka, M. M. (1971). *Significance tests: Univariate and multivariate*. Champaign, IL: Institute for Personality and Ability Testing.

Thompson, B. (1990). Finding a correction for the sampling error in multivariate measures of relationship: A Monte Carlo study. *Educational and Psychological Measurement, 50*, 15–31.

Thompson, B. (1993). The use of statistical significance tests in research: Bootstrap and other alternatives. *Journal of Experimental Education, 61*, 361–377.

Thompson, B. (1994). The pivotal role of replication in psychological research: Empirically evaluating the replicability of sample results. *Journal of Personality, 62*, 157–176.

Thompson, B. (1996). AERA editorial policies regarding statistical significance testing: Three suggested reforms. *Educational Researcher, 25*(2), 26–30.

Thompson, B. (1999). If statistical significance tests are broken/misused, what practices should supplement or replace them?. *Theory & Psychology, 9*, 165–181.

Thompson, B. (2000). Ten commandments of structural equation modeling. In L. Grimm & P. Yarnold (Eds.), *Reading and understanding more multivariate statistics* (pp. 261–284). Washington, DC: American Psychological Association.

Thompson, B. (2001). Significance, effect sizes, stepwise methods, and other issues: Strong arguments move the field. *Journal of Experimental Education, 70*, 80–93.

Thompson, B. (2002a). "Statistical," "practical," and "clinical": How many kinds of significance do counselors need to consider? *Journal of Counseling and Development, 80*, 64–71.

Thompson, B. (2002b). What future quantitative social science research could look like: Confidence intervals for effect sizes. *Educational Researcher, 31*(3), 24–31.

Thompson, B. (2006a). *Foundations of behavioral statistics: An insight-based approach*. New York: Guilford.

Thompson, B. (2006b). Research synthesis: Effect sizes. In J. Green, G. Camilli, & P.B. Elmore (Eds.), *Handbook of complementary methods in education research* (pp. 583–603). Washington, DC: American Educational Research Association.

Thompson, B. (2007). Effect sizes, confidence intervals, and confidence intervals for effect sizes. *Psychology in the Schools, 44*, 423–432.

Wang, Z., & Thompson, B. (2007). Is the Pearson r^2 biased, and if so, what is the best correction formula? *Journal of Experimental Education, 75*, 109–125.

Wilkinson, L., & APA Task Force on Statistical Inference. (1999). Statistical methods in psychology journals: Guidelines and explanations. *American Psychologist, 54*, 594–604.

Zientek, L.R., & Thompson, B. (2009). Matrix summaries improve research reports: Secondary analyses using published literature. *Educational Researcher, 38*, 343–352.

CHAPTER 3

Generalized Linear Models

Stefany Coxe, Stephen G. West, *and* Leona S. Aiken

Abstract

The general linear model (GLM), which includes multiple regression and analysis of variance, has become psychology's data analytic workhorse. The GLM can flexibly represent and test a wide variety of relationships between independent variables and a single continuous outcome variable. When the outcome variable takes on other forms (e.g., binary, ordered and unordered categories, counts), GLM may give nonoptimal performance. The generalized linear model (GLiM) extends the well-developed GLM approach to address these types of outcome variables. We describe the basic framework of GLiM and discuss several commonly used exemplars: logistic regression for binary outcomes, multinomial logistic regression for unordered categories, ordinal logistic regression for ordered categories, and Poisson regression for count outcomes. We also consider hurdle and zero-inflated Poisson regression models for data sets in which zero has a special status. Finally, we discuss model estimation, significance testing, measures of model fit, model diagnostics, and residual checking. With the increasing availability of user-friendly software to perform GLiM analyses, we expect the use of these models in psychology will increase dramatically in the coming years.

Key Words: Multiple regression, generalized linear model, logistic regression, ordinal regression, Poisson regression, counts, link function, conditional distribution, zero-inflated Poisson, diagnostics

Introduction: From the General to the Generalized Linear Model

The starting point for generalized linear models is the familiar *general linear model* (GLM), the most widely taught and used method of data analysis in psychology and the behavioral sciences today. The GLM is comprised of both multiple regression and analysis of variance. Multiple regression and analysis of variance allow researchers to study the relationships between one or more independent variables and a single continuous dependent variable. In multiple regression, the independent variables may be continuous or categorical; in analysis of variance, the independent variables are categorical, so that it can be considered a special case of multiple regression (Cohen, 1968). The form of the relationship between each independent variable and the dependent variable can be linear or curvilinear. These relationships can be general or conditional, potentially involving interactions between two or more independent variables. The generality and flexibility of the GLM in representing and testing hypotheses about a wide variety of relationships between independent variables and a dependent variable are among its important strengths (Cohen, Cohen, West, & Aiken, 2003). A further strength is that when its assumptions are met, the GLM provides unbiased estimates of its parameters and standard errors. No other approach can have greater statistical power. These strengths and the wide usage of the GLM have led it to be characterized as "everyday data analysis" and the "data analytic workhorse."

Hidden within the previous paragraph are important, often overlooked caveats: the outcome (dependent) variable is assumed to be continuous and unbounded (range from $-\infty$ to $+\infty$); the assumptions of the GLM are met. Although the GLM is relatively robust to many problems, *funny dependent variables* (variables other than unbounded continuous variables, also referred to as *limited dependent variables*) can produce serious violations of GLM assumptions, leading to biased parameter estimates and nonoptimal hypothesis tests. This chapter focuses on the *generalized linear model* (GLiM), a general approach for overcoming these problems. The GLiM takes the well-understood approach and machinery of the GLM and applies it to the prediction of funny dependent variables to provide proper parameter estimates and hypothesis tests.

We begin with a brief review of ordinary least squares (OLS) regression basics, noting that these basics also apply to analysis of variance as a special case with categorical independent variables. We then develop the key new ideas of GLiM that permit its extension to dependent variables that are not continuous. We consider in detail the specific GLiM models that permit analysis of types of funny dependent variables encountered with some frequency: binary responses (e.g., case, noncase in health or mental health), unordered categories (e.g., political party: Democrat, Republican, Independent), ordered categories (e.g., "none," "a little," "a lot" categories on a children's response scale), and counts (e.g., number of alcoholic beverages consumed in a day). We then consider issues of assessing fit and model diagnostics in GLiM. Finally, we briefly point to new developments in which ideas from GLiM are being incorporated in other areas such as multilevel modeling, growth curve modeling, and structural equation modeling.

Multiple Regression

Multiple regression predicts a single continuous outcome variable as a linear function of any combination of continuous and/or categorical predictor variables. In its standard algebraic form, the general expression for a regression equation is given by:

$$Y = b_0 + b_1 X_1 + b_2 X_2 + \cdots + b_p X_p + e \quad (1)$$

where Y is the observed value of the outcome variable, b_0 is the intercept, b_1 to b_p are the regression coefficients for the p predictor variables X_1 to X_p, respectively, and e is the error of prediction (residual). Other terms representing interactions (e.g., $X_1 X_2$), higher-order polynomial effects (e.g., X_1^2), or other functions of the predictors (e.g., $\log(X_2)$) can be included in the equation if dictated by the research problem.

Multiple regression can also be expressed in matrix form. The regression equation represented by Equation 1 with n participants, p regression coefficients for the p predictors plus a separate intercept, $\mathbf{Y} = \mathbf{XB} + \mathbf{b}_0 + \mathbf{e}$, where $\mathbf{Y}$ is the $n \times 1$ vector of observed outcome values, $\mathbf{X}$ is the $n \times p$ matrix of predictors, $\mathbf{B}$ is the $p \times 1$ vector of estimated regression coefficients, $\mathbf{b}_0$ is the $n \times 1$ intercept vector in which the entries are identical for each participant, and $\mathbf{e}$ is the $n \times 1$ vector of unobserved errors.

Assumptions

Ordinary least squares is commonly used to estimate multiple regression equations. Assumptions that are directly related to the predictors in multiple regression are minimal and will not be our focus here. Independent variables are assumed to be measured without error and each predictor is typically assumed to be fixed, that is, the values of each independent variable are specifically chosen by the experimenter rather than sampled from all possible values of the predictor. However, there are additional assumptions of multiple regression that can be violated by funny dependent variables; these assumptions are related to the errors and can be much more problematic.

The Gauss-Markov Theorem (Kutner, Nachtsheim, & Neter, 2004) states that, in order for least-squares estimates to be the best linear unbiased estimates (BLUE) of the population regression coefficients, three assumptions about the errors of prediction must be met. First, the conditional expected value of the errors must be equal to 0. That is, for any value of the predictors $\mathbf{X}$, the expected value of the errors is 0:

$$E(e_i | \mathbf{X}) = 0. \quad (A1)$$

Second, the errors must have constant and finite conditional variance, σ^2, a property known as homoscedasticity. That is, for any value of the predictors $\mathbf{X}$, the variance of the errors is a single constant value σ^2.

$$Var(e_i | \mathbf{X}) = \sigma^2, \text{ where } \sigma^2 < \infty. \quad (A2)$$

Third, errors for individual cases must be uncorrelated:

$$Cov(e_i, e_j) = 0, \text{ where } i \neq j. \quad (A3)$$

These three assumptions (A1 to A3) are necessary to ensure that the estimates of the regression coefficients are unbiased and have the smallest possible standard errors (i.e., they are BLUE).

To make valid statistical inferences about the regression coefficients, one additional assumption must be made about the errors. Tests of significance and confidence intervals for regression coefficients assume that the errors are normally distributed. Together with assumptions A1 and A2 above, this implies that the errors are assumed to be conditionally normally distributed with a mean of 0 and constant variance σ^2:

$$e_i|\mathbf{X} \sim N(0, \sigma^2). \quad (A4)$$

This additional assumption A4 leads to the replacement of assumption A3 with the stronger assumption that individual errors are independent (Kutner et al., 2004).

Funny Dependent Variables and Violations of Assumptions

Funny (limited) dependent variables can be found in many substantive research areas. Common types of funny dependent variables are categorical variables and counts. Categorical dependent variables include binary variables, unordered categories, and ordered categories. An example of a naturally categorical variable is pregnancy—a woman may be classified as either pregnant or not pregnant. In some disciplines, continuous variables are sometimes partitioned into categories. In clinical research using the Beck depression inventory, an individual with a score of less than 20 might be classified as nondepressed and an individual with a score of 20 or more as depressed. In health research, an individual with a systolic blood pressure reading of less than 140 millimeters may be classified as normal, an individual with a reading of 140 to 159 millimeters as hypertension stage 1, and an individual with a reading of over 160 millimeters as hypertension stage 2. Count variables can only take on discrete, positive values (0, 1, 2, 3, etc.) and so they may not be a good approximation to a continuous variable. Examples include the number of aggressive acts committed by a child in an observation session, a woman's number of lifetime pregnancies, or a person's number of traffic accidents. When categorical variables or counts with low mean values serve as dependent variables, the assumptions of OLS regression are frequently violated.

HETEROSCEDASTICITY

The errors of the linear regression model will be *heteroscedastic*; that is, the variance of the errors will not be constant across all values of the predicted dependent variable. For example, the error variance of binary (and count) variables is dependent on the predicted score. The error variance of a binary variable is largest at a predicted probability value $= 0.5$ and decreases as the predicted probability value approaches 0 or 1; the error variance of a count variable often increases as the predicted value increases. A consequence of heteroscedasticity is biased standard errors. Conditional standard errors may be larger or smaller (depending on the situation) than those in the constant variance case assumed by OLS regression. Incorrect standard errors result in biased hypothesis tests because z-tests and t-tests of parameter estimates involve dividing the parameter estimate by the standard error of the parameter estimate.

NON-NORMALITY

The errors will not be normally distributed because of the limited number of observed values that a categorical or count dependent variable may take on. For example, when the observed criterion is binary, taking on only values of 0 or 1, the error value for a predicted value $\widehat{\pi}$ is also binary; the error for that predicted score can only take on values of $(1 - \widehat{\pi})$ or $(0 - \widehat{\pi})$. In this case, the errors are conditionally discrete. A discrete variable cannot be normally distributed, so the errors cannot be normally distributed, making the typical statistical tests and confidence intervals on the regression coefficients invalid.

LINEARITY

Multiple regression assumes a model that is both linear in the parameters and linear in the variables (Cohen, Cohen, West, & Aiken, 2003, pp. 193–195). Linear in the parameters indicates that the predicted score is obtained by multiplying each predictor by its associated regression coefficient and then summing across all predictors. A relationship that is linear in the parameters is exemplified by the linear regression Equation 1 presented previously.

Linear in the variables indicates that the relation between the predictor and the outcome is linear. In other words, a plot of the relation between the predictor X and the outcome is approximated by a straight line. As noted earlier, linear regression can also accommodate some types of nonlinear relations. For example, a quadratic relation between the predictor X and the outcome can be incorporated into a linear regression by including X^2 as a predictor. If the relation between X and the outcome is quadratic, the relation between X^2 and the outcome with X partialed out will be linear, so the model will still be linear in the variables.

If the relationship between predictors and the outcome is nonlinear and is not accommodated by powers of the predictors, estimates of the linear regression coefficients and the standard errors will be biased (Cohen et al., 2003, p. 118). In this case, linear regression is *not* the appropriate analytic approach. Nonlinear relations between predictors and the outcome are common for discrete and categorical outcome variables. For example, consider an economist who is attempting to predict a binary outcome, the probability of purchasing a new car versus a used car as a function of household income. An increase in income of $ 20,000 will increase the likelihood of purchasing a new car a great deal for households with an income of $ 50,000, but probably has little effect on the likelihood of purchasing a new car for a household with an income of $ 500,000. If the relationship between the predictors and the dependent variable is not linear, the linear regression model will be misspecified because the form of the relation is misspecified.

For outcome variables with upper bounds, lower bounds, or both, another consequence of using a linear model when the relationships between the predictors and the outcome are nonlinear is that predicted criterion scores may fall outside the range of the observed scores. This problem is common with bounded variables, which are often undefined and not interpretable outside their observed limits. For example, when the outcome variable is binary, predicted scores are probabilities and can only range from 0 to 1. Predicted values that are less than 0 or greater than 1 cannot be interpreted as probabilities. For a model of count data, predicted values less than 0 are not interpretable because an event cannot occur a negative number of times.

Generalized Linear Models

Given that OLS regression cannot easily accommodate funny dependent variables without producing potentially severe violations of assumptions, there is a clear need for a more general statistical model that can be applied to a wider range of outcome variables. The generalized linear model (GLiM), developed by Nelder & Wedderburn (1972) and expanded by McCullagh and Nelder (1983, 1989), extends linear regression to a broader family of outcome variables. The GLiM incorporates the basic structure of linear regression equations, but introduces two major additions to the framework. First, it accommodates typically nonlinear relationships of predictors to the criterion through transformation of the predicted score to a form that is linearly related to the predictors; a *link function* relates predicted to observed criterion scores. Second, the GLiM allows a variety of *error structures* (i.e., conditional distributions of outcome variance) beyond the normally distributed error structure of linear regression.

Three Components of a GLiM

There are three components to the generalized linear model: the systematic portion, the random portion, and the link function. The systematic portion of the model parallels the model for the predicted value in OLS regression. It defines the relation between η, which is some function of the expected value of Y, and the independent variables in the model. This relationship is defined as linear in the variables,

$$\eta = b_0 + b_1 X_1 + b_2 X_2 + \cdots + b_p X_p. \quad (2)$$

Thus, the regression coefficients can be interpreted identically to those in linear regression: a 1-unit change in X_1 results in a b_1-unit change in η, holding all other variables constant.

The random portion of the model defines the error distribution of the outcome variable. The error distribution of the outcome variable refers to the conditional distribution of the outcome given a set of specified values on the predictors. The GLiM allows any discrete or continuous probability distribution in the exponential family. Each of the members of this family have a probability density function (or probability mass function if the distribution is discrete) that can be written in a form that includes the natural logarithm e raised to a power that is a function of the parameters[1]. The most familiar member of this family is the normal distribution,

$$f(Y|\mu, \sigma^2) = \frac{1}{\sqrt{2\pi\sigma^2}} e^{\left(-\frac{(Y-\mu)^2}{2\sigma^2}\right)}, \quad (3)$$

in which the height of the normal curve is a function of two independent parameters, the population mean (μ) and variance (σ^2). Other distributions in the exponential family that are commonly used in GLiMs are the binomial, multinomial, Poisson, exponential, gamma, and beta distributions. Other distributions exist in the exponential family, but are less commonly used in GLiMs.

The link function relates the conditional mean of Y, also known as the expected value of Y, $E(Y|X)$, or μ, to the linear combination of predictors η defined by Equation 2. The link function allows for nonlinear relations between the predictors and the predicted outcome; the link function transforms the *predicted value of the dependent variable* to a new form that has a linear relationship with the predictors. Several link functions are possible, but each error distribution has an associated special link function known as its *canonical link*. The canonical link satisfies special properties of the model, makes estimation simpler, and is the most commonly used link function. To cite three examples we will discuss in detail later in this chapter, the natural log (ln) link function is the canonical link for a conditional Poisson distribution. The logit or log-odds is the canonical link for a conditional binomial distribution, resulting in logistic regression. The canonical link for the normal error distribution is identity (i.e., a 1.0 or no transformation) resulting in linear regression.

In this framework, linear regression becomes just a special case of the GLiM: the error distribution for linear regression is a normal distribution and the link function is identity. A wide variety of generalized linear models are possible, depending on the proposed conditional distribution of the outcome variable. Table 3.1 shows the error distributions and their associated canonical links for several of the models within the GLiM framework.

Maximum Likelihood Estimation

Parameter estimation for GLiMs employs maximum likelihood (ML) methods. With ML, iterative numeric methods are used to find estimates of the population parameters that are most likely to have produced the observed data. There is no closed form or algebraic solution as in OLS regression. Conceptually, ML estimation works by considering many different parameter values and assessing the likelihood that the observed data came from a population with those parameters. The parameter estimates that yield the largest likelihood of producing the sample are chosen as estimates for the model. The likelihood function is based on the assumed distribution of the errors or residuals. For example, the errors in linear regression are assumed to be normally distributed, so the likelihood function is based on the normal distribution (*see* Equation 3). The probability density function shows the value of a normally distributed variable, Y, as a function of μ and σ^2. The likelihood function for the outcome, Y, of an individual case in linear regression is denoted by ℓ and is given by

$$\ell(Y|\mu,\sigma^2) = \frac{1}{\sqrt{2\pi}} e^{\left(-\frac{(Y-\mu)^2}{2\sigma^2}\right)}. \quad (4)$$

For linear regression, the mean structure of the model is given by the regression equation $b_0 + b_1X_1 + b_2X_2 + \cdots + b_pX_p$ and the variance is constant and equal to σ^2. The likelihood function for the outcome of an individual case becomes

$$\ell(Y|b_0 + b_1X_1 + b_2X_2 + \cdots + b_pX_p, \sigma^2)$$
$$= \frac{1}{\sqrt{2\pi}} e^{\left(-\frac{(Y-(b_0+b_1X_1+b_2X_2+\cdots+b_pX_p))^2}{2\sigma^2}\right)}. \quad (5)$$

Generalized linear models assume that all cases are mutually independent (i.e., there is no clustering of the data), so the likelihood of the entire sample of n cases (denoted by L) is found by multiplying together each of the individual likelihood functions:

$$L(Y|b_0 + b_1X_1 + b_2X_2 + \cdots + b_pX_p, \sigma^2)$$
$$= \prod_{j=1}^{n} \frac{1}{\sqrt{2\pi}} e^{\left(-\frac{(Y-(b_0+b_1X_1+b_2X_2+\cdots+b_pX_p))^2}{2\sigma^2}\right)}, \quad (6)$$

where $\prod$ indicates that all n values should be multiplied together. The goal of ML estimation is to find the parameter estimates that maximize the likelihood of the observed sample values, shown in Equation 6. However, because likelihoods are values less than 1 and multiplying many of these values together can result in extremely small values and error caused by rounding, a transformation of the likelihood function is used instead.

The natural logarithm of the likelihood function, or the log-likelihood, is the transformation used. The natural logarithm has two effects that make it a good choice for a transformation. First, it converts the multiplication in Equation 6 into addition, making calculation easier. Second, the natural logarithm transforms the very small positive *likelihood values* into larger-magnitude *log-likelihood values*, minimizing rounding error. Taking the natural logarithm of the sample likelihood function results in the log-likelihood function:

$$\ln L(Y|b_0 + b_1X_1 + b_2X_2 + \cdots + b_pX_p, \sigma^2)$$
$$= \sum_{j=1}^{n} \ln \left(\frac{1}{\sqrt{2\pi}} e^{\left(-\frac{(Y-(b_0+b_1X_1+b_2X_2+\cdots+b_pX_p))^2}{2\sigma^2}\right)} \right).$$
$$(7)$$

Table 3.1. Error distributions, canonical link functions, means, and variances for some common GLiMs.

Model	Error distribution	Link function	Mean	Variance
Linear regression	$f(Y\|\mu, \sigma^2) = \frac{1}{\sqrt{2\pi\sigma^2}} e^{\left(-\frac{(Y-\mu)^2}{2\sigma^2}\right)}$	$\eta = \mu$	μ	σ^2
Logistic regression	$P(Y = y\|n, \pi) = \frac{n!}{y!(n-y)!} \pi^y (1-\pi)^{n-y}$	$\eta = \ln\left(\frac{\hat{\pi}}{1-\hat{\pi}}\right)$	$n\pi$	$n\pi(1-\pi)$
Multinomial logistic regression	$P(Y_1 = y_1, \ldots, Y_k = y_k\|n, \pi_1, \ldots, \pi_k) = \frac{n!}{y_1! \cdots y_k!} \pi_1 \cdots \pi_k$	$\eta = \ln\left(\frac{\hat{\pi}}{1-\hat{\pi}}\right)$	$n\pi$	$n\pi(1-\pi)$
Ordinal logistic regression	$P(Y = y\|n, \pi) = \frac{n!}{y!(n-y)!} \pi^y (1-\pi)^{n-y}$	$\eta = \ln\left(\frac{\hat{\pi}}{1-\hat{\pi}}\right)$	$n\pi$	$n\pi(1-\pi)$
Poisson regression	$P(Y = y\|\mu) = \frac{\mu^y}{y!} e^{-\mu}$	$\eta = \ln(\mu)$	μ	μ
Beta regression	$f(Y\|a, b) = \frac{\Gamma(a+b)}{\Gamma(a)\Gamma(b)} y^{a-1}(1-y)^{b-1}$	$\eta = \ln\left(\frac{\hat{\pi}}{1-\hat{\pi}}\right)$, $\eta = \ln(\mu)$	$\frac{a}{a+b}$	$\frac{ab}{(a+b)^2(a+b+1)}$
Gamma regression	$P(Y = y\|k, \theta) = \frac{y^{k-1} e^{-y/\theta}}{\theta^k \Gamma(k)}$	$\eta = 1/\mu$	$k\theta$	$k\theta^2$
Negative binomial	$P(Y = y\|r, \pi) = \binom{y-1}{r-1} \pi^r (1-\pi)^{y-r}$	$\eta = \ln(\mu)$	μ	$\mu + \alpha\mu^2$

This function is $(p + 2)$-dimensional, where p is the number of terms in the regression equation (not including the intercept); the additional dimensions represent the intercept and the likelihood. For example, if a linear regression model included only the intercept, then $p = 0$ and the log-likelihood function would be represented by a parabola in a two-dimensional plane. If a linear regression model included the intercept and one predictor, then $p = 1$ and the log-likelihood function would be a three-dimensional paraboloid surface.

Consider a linear regression model with an intercept and single predictor, estimated with ML. The two horizontal axes represent values of b_0 and b_1, respectively. The vertical axis represents values of the log-likelihood function. The three-dimensional surface of the log-likelihood function resembles a mountain. The peak of the mountain is the largest or maximum value of the log-likelihood function. The values of b_0 and b_1 corresponding to this maximum value of the log-likelihood function are the ML estimates of b_0 and b_1; they are the parameter estimates of b_0 and b_1 which make the observed sample most likely. For linear regression, the least-squares estimation solution corresponds to the ML estimation solution.

Maximum likelihood estimation is used for all GLiMs, but the likelihood functions differ for different GLiMs. The error structure of the GLiM being used dictates the probability distribution used as a basis for the likelihood function. For the linear regression model estimated with maximum likelihood, the likelihood function is based on the normal distribution because linear regression assumes a normally distributed error structure. If a Poisson regression model were being used, a Poisson distribution error structure would be assumed, so the likelihood function for ML estimation would be based on the Poisson probability distribution.

DEVIANCE FOR MAXIMUM LIKELIHOOD ESTIMATION

One consequence of the parameters of GLiMs being estimated using ML is that GLiMs lack the familiar sums of squares from linear regression. Ordinary least squares estimation is based on the variation in the outcome variable, also called the total sum of squares (SS). Variation in the outcome is the sum of the squared deviations of the scores on the dependent variable around their mean, $\sum (Y_i - \bar{Y})^2$. Ordinary least squares estimation completely partitions the total SS into a portion that is explained by the regression model (explained SS, $\sum (\hat{Y}_i - \bar{Y})^2$) and a portion that remains unexplained (residual SS, $\sum (Y_i - \hat{Y}_i)^2$). The total SS is completely partitioned into two nonoverlapping parts, the explained SS and the residual SS, so

$$\sum (Y_i - \bar{Y})^2 = \sum (\hat{Y}_i - \bar{Y})^2 + \sum (Y_i - \hat{Y}_i)^2. \quad (8)$$

The residual SS is minimized in the OLS procedure, resulting in regression coefficients that maximize the explained SS. The squared multiple correlation, or $R^2_{multiple}$, measures the proportion of variation in the outcome that is accounted for by the predictors. The proportion of variation that is accounted for by the predictors is the explained SS and the total variation is the total SS, so

$$R^2_{multiple} = \frac{SS_{explained}}{SS_{total}}. \quad (9)$$

For linear regression, the $R^2_{multiple}$ can be equivalently calculated as 1 minus the proportion of variation that is not accounted for by the model, or

$$R^2_{multiple} = 1 - \frac{SS_{residual}}{SS_{total}}. \quad (10)$$

Calculating $R^2_{multiple}$ for GLiMs in the same manner as for linear regression is problematic for several reasons. First, the total variation in the outcome cannot be partitioned into two *orthogonal* components reflecting explained and unexplained variation. In linear regression, the relationship between the observed outcome value, Y_i, and the predicted value, $\hat{Y}_i$, is linear. This linear relationship means that the residuals, $Y_i - \hat{Y}_i$, are uncorrelated with the observed outcome value, Y_i. In GLiMs, the relationship between the observed outcome value, Y_i, and the predicted value, $\hat{Y}_i$, may be nonlinear. This nonlinear relationship leads to a covariance between the residual term, $Y_i - \hat{Y}_i$, and the observed outcome, Y_i (Cameron & Trivedi, 1998, p. 144), resulting in an additional term in the partitioning of the total SS (Cameron & Trivedi, 1998, p. 153):

$$\sum (Y_i - \bar{Y})^2 = \sum (\hat{Y}_i - \bar{Y})^2 + \sum (Y_i - \hat{Y}_i)^2 \\ + 2 \sum (\hat{Y}_i - \bar{Y})(Y_i - \hat{Y}_i). \quad (11)$$

This additional term in the partitioning of the total SS means that different methods of calculating $R^2_{multiple}$ shown in Equations 9 and 10 will *not* be equivalent for GLiMs as they are in linear regression. Second, the ML estimation method used in GLiMs does not minimize the residual SS, so calculating

$R^2_{multiple}$ for GLiMs can result in out-of-bounds values (i.e., $R^2_{multiple} > 1$ or $R^2_{multiple} < 0$). Finally, GLiMs typically display heteroscedasticity of variance, that is, the variance of the predicted values is dependent on the value of the predictors. How one interprets a single $R^2_{multiple}$ value is unclear when the variance explained may vary as a function of the value of the predictors.

Any model estimated with ML methods will produce a *deviance* value for the model, which can be used to assess fit of the model. For the special case of linear regression model with normal errors, the deviance is equal to the residual SS (Cameron & Trivedi, 1998, p. 153), so some authors consider the deviance to be roughly analogous to the residual SS in other GLiMs. However, since there are not analogues to total SS and explained SS for GLiMs, the deviance value differs from the residual SS. The residual SS value can be used to calculate a measure of absolute fit for the linear regression model ($R^2_{multiple}$) without reference to other models. In contrast, the deviance is a *relative* measure, so it can only be interpreted in relation to another model. In fact, the deviance for a model is actually calculated in reference to another model, the so-called "full model" or "fully saturated model," which has one parameter for each observation and can perfectly reproduce the observed data (Long, 1997, p. 94).

The deviance for a model of interest, $D(M_\beta)$, is calculated as a function of the log-likelihoods of the full model and the model of interest. The deviance of the model is:

$$D(M_\beta) = -2\ln L(M_\beta) - (-2\ln L(M_F))$$
$$= 2\ln L(M_F) - 2\ln L(M_\beta), \quad (12)$$

where M_β is the model of interest and M_F is the full model. The likelihood of the full model is defined as 1 (i.e., the probability of the full model having produced the observed data is 1.0, since we know that the full model perfectly reproduces the observed data). The natural log of 1 is equal to 0, so the log-likelihood of the full model is 0. Equation 12 above then becomes

$$D(M_\beta) = -2\ln L(M_\beta), \quad (13)$$

and we can see that the deviance of a model is simply -2 times the log-likelihood of that model. The deviance for a model can be used to calculate analogues to the linear regression $R^2_{multiple}$; these are discussed in a later section.

Common Generalized Linear Models
BINARY LOGISTIC REGRESSION

Binary logistic regression (Agresti, 2002, 2007; DeMaris, 2004; Fahrmeir & Tutz, 2001; Hosmer & Lemeshow, 2000) is a commonly used and appropriate analysis when the outcome variable is binary, meaning that the outcome takes on one of two mutually exclusive values. Examples of common binary outcome variables are alive or dead in health research, and pass or fail in educational research. Binomial logistic regression is a GLiM with binomial distribution error structure and logit link function. The probability mass function for the binomial distribution,

$$P(Y = y|n, \pi) = \frac{n!}{y!(n-y)!}\pi^y(1-\pi)^{n-y}, \quad (14)$$

gives the probability of observing a given value, y, of variable Y that is distributed as a binomial distribution with parameters n and π. Consider a binary variable that has two mutually exclusive values; one of these values is the outcome value of interest, often called a "success" or "case," and it occurs with probability π. The binomial distribution gives the probability of a specific number of successes, y, in a set of n independent trials, where each success occurs with probability π and each failure with probability $(1-\pi)$. For example, if we wanted to know the probability of obtaining a specific number of heads from 10 flips of a fair coin, we would use the binomial distribution with $n = 10$ and $\pi = 0.5$. The mean of this distribution is $n\pi$ and the variance is $n\pi(1-\pi)$. In 10 flips of a fair coin, the mean number of heads is $10 \times 0.5 = 5$ heads with variance equal to $10 \times 0.5 \times 0.5 = 2.5$ heads.

Note that unlike the normal distribution, for which the mean and variance are independent of one another, the variance of the binomial distribution is dependent on the mean. Additionally, the variance of the distribution is dependent on the probability of a success; this dependency will be important for interpreting the model. When n is very large and π is near 0.5, the binomial distribution resembles a normal distribution; it is bell-shaped and symmetric, though it is still a discrete distribution.

The canonical link function for the binomial distribution is the logit. The logit is a mathematically convenient function that allows the logistic regression model to have a linear form. The *logit* is defined as the natural log of the odds, where the *odds* is the probability of an event occurring divided by the probability of the event not occurring. The formula

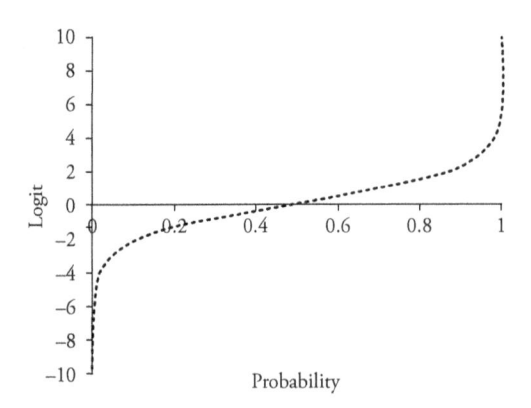

Figure 3.1 Relationship between probability and logit.

for the logit is

$$\text{logit} = \ln\left(\frac{\hat{\pi}}{1-\hat{\pi}}\right), \quad (15)$$

where $\hat{\pi}$ is the predicted probability of an event occurring. An advantage of GLiM is that it allows a nonlinear relation between predicted values and predictors. Figure 3.1 illustrates the nonlinear relation between probability and the logit.

For binary logistic regression, observed outcome values are typically coded 1 (case or success) or 0 (noncase or failure), but predicted values are in the form of a predicted probability. Probabilities are continuous but bounded by 0 and 1. Probabilities can also be algebraically converted to odds, that is, the probability of an event occurring divided by the probability of the event not occurring. For example, if the probability of being a case is 0.75, the probability of being a noncase is 0.25, so the odds of being a case is 0.75/0.25 = 3; an individual is three times more likely to be a case than a noncase. Applying Equation 15 to compute the logit, we find

$$\text{logit} = \ln\left(\frac{\hat{\pi}}{1-\hat{\pi}}\right) = \ln\left(\frac{0.75}{0.25}\right) = 1.099,$$

where $\hat{\pi}$ is the predicted probability of being a case.

Coefficient interpretation

The linear form of the binary logistic regression model is of the following form:

$$\text{logit} = \ln\left(\frac{\hat{\pi}}{1-\hat{\pi}}\right) = \eta$$
$$= b_0 + b_1 X_1 + b_2 X_2 + \cdots + b_p X_p. \quad (16)$$

Equation 16 shows why binary logistic regression is often referred to as being "linear in the logit." The logit is equal to the linear combination of regression coefficients and predictors on the right ride of Equation 16. A plot of Equation 16 is a straight line, similar to linear regression. One interpretation of the regression coefficients is in terms of the logit and is identical to that of linear regression. A 1-unit increase in X_1 results in a b_1-unit increase in the logit, holding all other variables constant. This interpretation is straightforward, but the logit is a mathematically convenient function, not a natural unit of interpretation for most researchers.

Two more interpretable forms of the binary logistic regression model are available: one in terms of the odds of being a case and one in terms of the probability of being a case. These forms can be obtained following some algebraic manipulation of Equation 16. Raising both sides of Equation 16 to the power of e results in:

$$e^{\ln\left(\frac{\hat{\pi}}{1-\hat{\pi}}\right)} = e^{b_0 + b_1 X_1 + b_2 X_2 + \cdots + b_p X_p}. \quad (17)$$

Note that performing the same operation on both sides of an equation does not change the equation. A property of e and the natural log is that $e^{\ln(x)} = x$, so the left side of the equation can be simplified, resulting in:

$$\text{odds} = \left(\frac{\hat{\pi}}{1-\hat{\pi}}\right) = e^{b_0 + b_1 X_1 + b_2 X_2 + \cdots + b_p X_p} \quad (18)$$

Equation 18 shows the effect of the predictors on the predicted odds, but it is not obvious how each of the predictors contributes to the odds. A property of exponents is that $x^{a+b+c} = x^a x^b x^c$, so the single term on the right side of Equation 18 can be broken up into several smaller parts, resulting in:

$$\text{odds} = \left(\frac{\hat{\pi}}{1-\hat{\pi}}\right) = e^{b_0} e^{b_1 X_1} e^{b_2 X_2} \cdots e^{b_p X_p}. \quad (19)$$

Now we can see that changes in a predictor result in multiplicative changes in the predicted odds. To further clarify the interpretation, we can look at a term for a single predictor, such as X_1 (i.e., $e^{b_1 X_1}$). Using the property of exponents shown above, we can examine the effect of a 1-unit change in X_1 on the odds:

$$e^{b_1(X_1+1)} = e^{b_1 X_1 + b_1} = e^{b_1 X_1} e^{b_1}. \quad (20)$$

The e^{b_1} term above is known as the odds ratio. It is the effect of a 1-unit change in X_1 on the odds of being a case. For a 1-unit increase in X_1, the odds of being a case is multiplied by e^{b_1}, holding all other variables constant.

The odds ratio is particularly useful when interpreting the effect of categorical predictors and is commonly used in health research. Consider using gender to predict whether the binary outcome occurs,

$$\ln\left(\frac{\hat{\pi}}{1-\hat{\pi}}\right) = \eta = b_0 + b_1(gender), \qquad (21)$$

where gender is dummy-coded such that male = 1 and female = 0. The exponentiation of the regression coefficient for gender, e^{b_1}, is the odds that a male (coded 1 on gender) will be a case divided by the odds that a female (coded 0 on gender) will be a case. This odds ratio, which ranges from 0 to positive infinity, will be equal to 1 if there is no difference in the outcome across genders. An odds ratio greater than 1 means that men (coded 1) are more likely to be a case than women (coded 0). An odds ratio less than 1 means that men are less likely to be a case than women.

Further algebraic manipulation of Equation 19 will lead to interpretation of regression coefficients in terms of the probability of being a case:

$$(1 - \hat{\pi}) \times \text{odds} = \hat{\pi}, \qquad (22)$$

$$\text{odds} - \hat{\pi} \times \text{odds} = \hat{\pi}, \qquad (23)$$

$$\text{odds} = \hat{\pi} + \hat{\pi} \times \text{odds}, \qquad (24)$$

$$\text{odds} = \hat{\pi} \times (1 + \text{odds}), \qquad (25)$$

$$\hat{\pi} = \frac{\text{odds}}{1 + \text{odds}}. \qquad (26)$$

The probability of being a case is equivalent to the odds of being a case divided by 1 plus the odds of being a case. Substituting the equation for the odds from Equation 19 into Equation 26 produces the predicted probability of being a case:

$$\hat{\pi} = \frac{e^{b_0} e^{b_1 X_1} e^{b_2 X_2} \ldots e^{b_p X_p}}{1 + (e^{b_0} e^{b_1 X_1} e^{b_2 X_2} \ldots e^{b_p X_p})}. \qquad (27)$$

The relationship between probability and the logit is an S-shaped curve, shown in Figure 3.1. This nonlinear relationship and the fact that the logistic regression model is "linear in the logit" means that the relationship between a predictor and the predicted probability will also be nonlinear. A plot of Equation 27 with a single predictor is an S-shaped curve bounded at 0 and 1, the defined limits of probability. Given this nonlinear relation between the predictors and the probability, it is not possible to specify in a simple manner the change in probability for a 1-unit change in a predictor, as was shown above for the logit and odds metrics; the change in probability is different depending on the value of the predictor. The probability metric is, however, useful for calculating the probability of being a case for specific values of the predictors. For example, if the predictor is age, one can calculate the probability of being a case for participants of age 5, age 10, age 15, or any other value.

Latent variable interpretation

Logistic regression and other binary outcome GLiMs can also be interpreted in a latent variable framework (Long, 1997). In this framework, the observed binary outcome is a discrete manifestation of an underlying continuous latent variable. The continuous latent variable is not observed directly, but the binary outcome that results from the continuous variable is observed. A common example of a latent variable conceptualization of a binary outcome is mental illness diagnosis. Some clinical psychologists would assume that depression follows a continuum in which individuals can display gradations in symptoms. While recognizing that depression follows such a continuum, many researchers and clinicians are interested in diagnosis; that is, do individuals exhibit a sufficient number or extremity of symptoms to classify them as affected by this mental illness or not? This diagnosis of depression is a binary variable that reflects the underlying continuum of depressive symptoms. There is a cut point (threshold) in the continuous depression variable above which individuals are classified as "depressed," whereas all those below the cut point are classified as "not depressed."

The latent variable interpretation of binary outcome models is not appropriate in all situations (e.g., pregnant versus not pregnant), but some common binary outcomes, such as mental illness or disease diagnosis (e.g., hypertension) and passing or failing an exam, lend themselves to this interpretation. The latent variable interpretation of a binary outcome GLiM is no different from the standard logistic regression model described above, except that the predicted probabilities can also be thought of as an ordering of individuals on the continuous latent variable.

Alternative models for binary outcomes

Logistic regression is not the only appropriate option for analyzing binary outcomes. Two other commonly used GLiMs for binary outcomes are the probit model and the complementary log-log (or clog-log) model. Like the logistic regression model, both the probit and clog-log models relate the predictors to the predicted probability with an S-shaped curve. These two alternative models have different link functions and error distributions than logistic regression (Agresti, 2002; Allison, 1999).

The *probit model* uses a normal error distribution. The probability density function for the normal distribution is shown in Equation 3. Probit regression is named for its link function, the inverse cumulative normal link function, also known as the probit. The probit function of a probability results in the z-value on the standard normal distribution that is associated with that probability. For example, probit(0.025) = −1.96, probit(0.5) = 0, and probit(0.975) = 1.96. Note that, like the logit, the probit function is symmetric around a probability of 0.5. The regression equation for probit regression is:

$$\text{probit}(\hat{\pi}) = b_0 + b_1 X_1 + b_2 X_2 + \cdots + b_p X_p. \quad (28)$$

This linear form of the probit model depicts changes in the probit, as in Equation 16 of the logistic model. Probit regression coefficients can also be interpreted in the probability metric, as in Equation 27 of the logistic model. This metric depicts nonlinear changes in the probability of an event occurring. The probit model is often used in structural equation models when the outcome variable is binary because it is desirable to have the interpretation of a normally distributed latent variable. However, the probit model is less useful than the logit model in some cases; for example, the probit model does not yield the odds-ratio interpretation of the logit model, so all interpretation must occur in the probit metric or the nonlinear probability metric.

The *clog-log model* uses a double-exponential error distribution. The probability density function for the double-exponential distribution is

$$f(Y|\mu, b) = \frac{e^{-\left(\frac{|y-\mu|}{b}\right)}}{2b}, \quad (29)$$

where μ is the mean parameter and b is the scale parameter. The link function for the clog-log model is the complementary log-log link function, $\ln(-\ln(1-\hat{\pi}))$. For example, clog-log(0.025) = −3.68, clog-log(0.5) = −0.37, and clog-log(0.975) = 1.31. Note that the clog-log function produces an asymmetric S-shaped curve; the increase in probability for low values of a predictor occurs more slowly than the increase in probability for high values of a predictor. The clog-log model is often used in epidemiological and dose-response models (Piegorsch, 1992), where an asymmetric response is expected. The clog-log model is also used when the binary outcome reflects whether an event has occurred in a certain period of time (Allison, 1999, pp. 73–75). For example, the clog-log model is often used in toxicology studies where the binary outcome reflects whether an organism died in a 1-hour period after administration of a substance.

Overdispersion

Several GLiMs have error structures based on distributions in which the variance is a function of the mean. Logistic regression is one of these; the binomial distribution has mean = $n\pi$ and variance = $n\pi(1-\pi)$. This condition is known as *equidispersion*. The implication of the mean and variance of the error structure distribution being dependent is that the conditional mean and conditional variance of the errors will also be dependent.

Actual data are commonly overdispersed, that is, the conditional variance of the errors is larger than the value implied by the error distribution. It is also possible for the conditional variance to be smaller than the value implied by the error distribution, but underdispersion is rarely encountered in practice with data in the social and behavioral sciences. If overdispersion is not accounted for, estimates of the standard errors will be too small, test statistics for the parameter estimates will be too large, the level of statistical significance will be overestimated, and confidence limits will be too small (Cox & Snell, 1989). Overdispersion can occur in GLiMs in which the conditional variance is a function of the predicted mean. The issue of overdispersion is not present in linear regression, because the normal distribution has two *independent* parameters, one defining the mean and one defining the variance or dispersion of the distribution.

The overdispersed logistic regression model includes an additional parameter that is used in the estimation of the conditional variance, known as the *overdispersion scaling parameter*, φ. The model estimated with this correction now essentially assumes an error distribution that is binomial with mean $n\pi$ and variance $\varphi n\pi(1-\pi)$. The scaling parameter φ will be greater than 1 if overdispersion is present in the data, equal to 1 if there is equidispersion, less than 1 if there is underdispersion. The amount of dispersion in the model is typically estimated using the Pearson chi-square goodness-of-fit statistic (McCullagh & Nelder, 1989), which is a measure of the overall fit of the model. Most popular statistical packages produce both this Pearson chi-square and a deviance chi-square. The calculation of the scaling parameter is given by

$$\varphi = \frac{\chi^2_{Pearson}}{df}. \quad (30)$$

The overdispersed model allows the conditional variance to be larger than the conditional variance implied by the conditional mean so that the standard errors (which are based on the conditional variance) will be larger than the standard errors in the standard binary logistic regression model by a factor of $\sqrt{\varphi}$. Interpretation of coefficients for the overdispersed binary logistic regression model is identical to that of the standard binary logistic regression model. The deviance for this model also must be adjusted by the scaling factor; the deviance for the overdispersed binary logistic regression model is equal to the deviance for the standard binary logistic regression model divided by φ. The smaller deviance of this model indicates better fit.

The likelihood ratio test (Chernoff, 1954; Wilks, 1938) or the Score test (Cook & Weisberg, 1983; a.k.a., Lagrange multiplier [LM] test) may be used to assess whether significant overdispersion is present in the data. These two tests are asymptotically equivalent, meaning that they will produce the same result with very large sample sizes. The likelihood ratio test is a nested model test that compares the deviance of Model 1 in which the scaling parameter (φ) has been fixed to a specific value (typically 1) to the deviance of Model 2 in which the scaling parameter is estimated. For logistic regression, φ can be 1 for a standard binary logistic regression model (Model 1) or estimated for an overdispersed binary logistic regression model (Model 2). The difference in deviances for the two models, $D(Model1) - D(Model2)$, follows a χ^2 distribution with 1 degree of freedom. If the test exceeds the critical value of 3.84 for α = .05, the model with a freely estimated scaling parameter (i.e., the overdispersed model) fits the data better than the model in which the scaling parameter is fixed to 1. The Score test takes an alternative approach involving the slope of the likelihood function; the Score test produces results that are asymptotically identical to the likelihood ratio test but may be less accurate than the likelihood ratio test in small samples.

MULTINOMIAL LOGISTIC REGRESSION

Multinomial logistic regression is the generalization of logistic regression to outcome variables that have three or more *unordered* categories. An example of a categorical outcome variable with three unordered categories is political affiliation: Democrat, Republican, and Independent. The three options for the outcome variable are distinct, but have no inherent ordering. The multinomial logistic regression model is a GLiM with a multinomial error distribution and the logit link function; the multinomial error distribution simplifies to the binomial distribution when there are only two outcome options. Multinomial models are often used to predict individuals' preferences among choice alternatives, for example, in consumer research.

The multinomial logistic regression model is estimated by $(a - 1)$ simultaneously solved binary logistic regression equations, where a is the number of categories in the outcome variable. When estimating multinomial logistic regression models, one of the outcome categories is chosen as a reference category. For the example above, suppose that Democrats are coded 1, Republicans are coded 2, and Independents are coded 3. Using category 3, Independent, as the reference category, we would estimate the following two equations:

$$\ln\left(\frac{\hat{\pi}_1}{\hat{\pi}_3}\right) = b_{0,1.3} + b_{1,1.3}X_1 + b_{2,1.3}X_2 + \cdots$$
$$+ b_{p,1.3}X_p \quad \text{and} \quad (31)$$

$$\ln\left(\frac{\hat{\pi}_2}{\hat{\pi}_3}\right) = b_{0,2.3} + b_{1,2.3}X_1 + b_{2,2.3}X_2 + \cdots$$
$$+ b_{p,2.3}X_p. \quad (32)$$

The third equation,

$$\ln\left(\frac{\hat{\pi}_1}{\hat{\pi}_2}\right) = b_{0,1.2} + b_{1,1.2}X_1 + b_{2,1.2}X_2 + \cdots + b_{p,1.2}X_p, \quad (33)$$

is completely redundant with the previous two equations, and so is not necessary for model estimation. (The regression coefficients in this third equation are discussed below.) The value π_1 represents the probability of an outcome in category 1, π_2 represents the probability of an outcome in category 2, and π_3 represents the probability of an outcome in category 3. Note that $\pi_1 + \pi_2 + \pi_3 = 1$ because these three categories are mutually exclusive, exhaustive and represent all possible options for the variable. Note also that there are different regression coefficients for the same predictor, the two equations, for example, $b_{1,1.3}$ for X_1 in the first equation and $b_{1,2.3}$ for X_1 in the second equation. This means that the same predictor may have a different effect on the likelihood of being in category 1 versus 3 as opposed to category 2 versus 3.

Coefficient interpretation

Interpretation of the regression coefficients in this model follows from the interpretation of logistic regression coefficients. The important difference here is that each regression coefficient specifies the effect of a predictor for a *specific outcome comparison*. For example, consider using gender (X_1) and age (X_2) to predict political party affiliation. Gender is dummy-coded such that male = 1 and female = 0. Using the first equation above,

$$\ln\left(\frac{\hat{\pi}_1}{\hat{\pi}_3}\right) = b_{intercept,1.3} + b_{gender,1.3}(gender) + b_{age,1.3}(age), \quad (34)$$

for interpretation, we would compare the effects of gender and age on the likelihood of being a Democrat (category 1) versus the reference category Independent (category 3). The exponentiation of the regression coefficient for gender, $e^{b_{gender,1.3}}$, represents the odds that a male will be a Democrat rather than an Independent divided by the odds that a female will be a Democrat rather than an Independent, holding age constant. The Republican and Independent outcomes can be similarly compared using Equation 32.

Comparison between categories 1 and 2 is not directly given by either of the two estimated equations, but they are theoretically obtainable from Equations 31 and 32 because of the relationship $\pi_1 + \pi_2 + \pi_3 = 1$ (Allison, 1999, pp. 113–114). The regression coefficients for the comparison between outcome categories 1 and 2 are the difference between the corresponding regression coefficients from Equations 31 and 32. For instance, in the example described above with gender and age as predictors, the regression coefficient for gender that compares outcome categories 1 and 2 is:

$$b_{gender,1.2} = b_{gender,1.3} - b_{gender,2.3}. \quad (35)$$

Regression coefficients for the comparison between outcome categories 1 and 2 for the other predictors can be obtained in a similar manner. Alternatively, the outcome variable can be recoded and another category (e.g., category 1) involved in the comparison of interest can be specified as the reference category.

ORDINAL LOGISTIC REGRESSION

The ordinal logistic regression model (Agresti, 2002, 2010; Fahrmeir & Tutz, 2001; Hosmer & Lemeshow, 2000; Allison, 1999) generalizes binomial logistic regression to outcome variables that have three or more *ordered* categories. For example, educational attainment is an ordered outcome, with outcome choices of completion of high school, college, or post-graduate degrees. These three options for the outcome variable are distinct and have an inherent ordering. Researchers in the social sciences sometimes use single item Likert-type scales containing ordered categories, such as "strongly agree," "agree," "neutral," "disagree," and "strongly disagree." Self-report measures for children often contain ordered categories such as "none," "a little," and "a lot."

Like multinomial logistic regression, the ordinal logistic regression model is a GLiM with a multinomial error distribution and logit link function that is estimated using $(a - 1)$ binary logistic regression equations. However, the ordinal logistic regression model differs from the multinomial logistic regression model in several key ways that often make it a better model choice. Specifically, if the outcome options are ordered and certain assumptions are met, the ordinal logistic regression model is easier to interpret and has more statistical power than the multinomial logistic regression model.

First, the ordinal logistic regression model uses a different transformation of the outcome probabilities than the multinomial model. The ordinal logistic regression model takes into account the fact that the outcome has a specific ordering. Therefore, rather than modeling every distinct comparison between categories, the ordinal logistic regression model characterizes the cumulative probability of an individual being in a certain category *or a higher category*. For example, if the outcome has five categories, such as the Likert scale described above, there would be four equations estimated. For each equation, the predicted outcome would be the natural log of the probability of belonging to *a specific category or higher* divided by the probability of belonging to all lower categories. If one considers that the categories are ordered from "strongly disagree" (lowest) to "strongly agree" (highest), the four predicted outcomes would be:

$$\ln\left(\frac{\hat{\pi}_{disagree} + \hat{\pi}_{neutral} + \hat{\pi}_{agree} + \hat{\pi}_{stronglyagree}}{\hat{\pi}_{stronglydisagree}}\right), \quad (36)$$

$$\ln\left(\frac{\hat{\pi}_{neutral} + \hat{\pi}_{agree} + \hat{\pi}_{stronglyagree}}{\hat{\pi}_{stronglydisagree} + \hat{\pi}_{disagree}}\right), \quad (37)$$

$$\ln\left(\frac{\hat{\pi}_{agree} + \hat{\pi}_{stronglyagree}}{\hat{\pi}_{stronglydisagree} + \hat{\pi}_{disagree} + \hat{\pi}_{neutral}}\right), \text{ and} \quad (38)$$

$$\ln\left(\frac{\hat{\pi}_{stronglyagree}}{\hat{\pi}_{stronglydisagree} + \hat{\pi}_{disagree} + \hat{\pi}_{neutral} + \hat{\pi}_{agree}}\right). \quad (39)$$

Equation 36 compares strongly disagree to the four higher categories, Equation 37 compares strongly disagree and disagree to the three higher categories, Equation 38 compares strongly disagree, disagree and neutral to the two higher categories, and Equation 39 compares strongly disagree, disagree, neutral, and agree to strongly agree.

Second, the ordinal logistic regression model makes a key additional assumption known as the *proportional odds* or *parallel regressions assumption*. Recall that the multinomial logistic regression model is estimated with ($a - 1$) regression equations, each of which has a different regression coefficient for each predictor; for example, the predictor X_1 has the regression coefficient $b_{1,1,3}$ in Equation 31 but the regression coefficient $b_{1,2,3}$ in Equation 32. The proportional odds assumption states the all ($a - 1$) equations share the same regression coefficient for the same predictor; the corresponding regression coefficients are constrained to be equal across equations. Constraining the regression coefficients to be equal implies that a predictor variable has the same effect on *moving up a category*, regardless of the category's location in the ordered set. Different intercepts for each equation allow for the fact that different proportions of the sample will be in each outcome category. The ordinal logistic regression model for an outcome with three outcome options, ordered 1 (lowest) to 3 (highest), would be estimated by the following two equations:

$$\ln\left(\frac{\hat{\pi}_3}{\hat{\pi}_1 + \hat{\pi}_2}\right) = b_{0,3} + b_1 X_1 + b_2 X_2 + \cdots$$
$$+ b_p X_p \quad \text{and} \quad (40)$$
$$\ln\left(\frac{\hat{\pi}_2 + \hat{\pi}_3}{\hat{\pi}_1}\right) = b_{0,23} + b_1 X_1 + b_2 X_2 + \cdots$$
$$+ b_p X_p. \quad (41)$$

Note that the nonintercept regression coefficients are the same in both equations. The effect of X_1 is specified by the same regression coefficient (b_1) in both equations. When this assumption is met, it simplifies the interpretation of the results and leads to increased statistical power of hypothesis tests.

Coefficient interpretation

For each of the ($a - 1$) equations used to estimate the ordinal logistic regression model, the regression coefficients can be interpreted in a manner similar to that of binary logistic regression. Consider an example in which age and gender are used to predict choice on a three-category ordered variable from "disagree" (low), to "neutral," to "agree" (high). The equations to estimate this model would be:

$$\ln\left(\frac{\hat{\pi}_{agree}}{\hat{\pi}_{disagree} + \hat{\pi}_{neutral}}\right)$$
$$= b_{0,agree} + b_1(gender) + b_2(age) \quad \text{and} \quad (42)$$
$$\ln\left(\frac{\hat{\pi}_{neutral} + \hat{\pi}_{agree}}{\hat{\pi}_{disagree}}\right)$$
$$= b_{0,neutral,agree} + b_1(gender) + b_2(age). \quad (43)$$

The regression coefficients for age and gender, respectively, are the same in both equations. That is, the effect of age on choosing "agree" instead of "neutral" or "disagree" is the same as the effect of age on choosing "neutral" or "agree" instead of "disagree": age has the same effect on *moving up a category*, regardless of location in the ordering of categories. The proportional odds assumption can be tested in common software packages using a χ^2 test which compares the deviance from Model 1 in which the corresponding regression coefficients are constrained to be equal across the equations (as shown above in Equations 40 and 41) to the deviance from Model 2 in which they are permitted to differ.

As in binary logistic regression, these equations can be interpreted in terms of the logit, odds, or probability. For the logit interpretation, a 1-unit increase in age results in a b_1-unit increase in the logit of "'agree' versus lower categories," holding all other variables constant. (The proportional odds assumption means that a 1-unit increase in age also results in a b_1-unit increase in the logit of "'neutral' or 'agree' versus lower categories," holding all other variables constant.) For the odds interpretation, a 1-unit increase in age results in a multiplicative e^{b_1}-unit increase in the odds of choosing "agree" versus a lower category, holding all other variables constant. An interpretation in terms of probability is, as in the case of binary logistic regression, complicated by the nonlinear relation between the predictors and the predicted probability. The change in probability is not a constant function of the predictors; the amount of change in probability depends on the value of the predictor.

POISSON REGRESSION

Poisson regression (Cameron & Trivedi, 1998; Coxe, West, & Aiken, 2009; Long, 1997) is an appropriate analysis when the outcome variable is a count of the number of events in a fixed period of time. Outcome measures such as the number of alcoholic beverages consumed in a day or the number of school absences for a child during a semester are examples of variables involving counts.

The probability mass function for the Poisson distribution,

$$P(Y = y|\mu) = \frac{\mu^y}{y!}e^{-\mu}, \qquad (44)$$

gives the probability of observing a given value, y, of outcome variable Y that is distributed as a Poisson distribution with parameter μ. For the count variable Y, μ is the arithmetic mean number of events that occur in a specified time interval; the Poisson distribution would yield the probability of 0, 1, 2, ...K events, given the mean μ of the distribution. The Poisson distribution differs from the normal distribution used in linear regression in several ways that make the Poisson more attractive for representing the properties of count data. First, the Poisson distribution is a discrete distribution that takes on a probability value only for non-negative integers. In contrast, the normal distribution is continuous and takes on all possible values from negative infinity to positive infinity. Second, count outcomes typically display increasing variance with increases in the mean. This property is a violation of the previously mentioned constant variance (homoscedasticity) assumption of linear regression; such violations can severely bias standard error estimates in OLS regression. The Poisson distribution is specified by only one parameter, μ, which defines *both* the mean and the variance of the distribution. In contrast, the normal distribution requires two independent parameters to be identified: the mean parameter, μ, and the variance parameter, σ^2. The fact that the mean and variance of the Poisson distribution are completely dependent on one another can be useful in modeling count outcomes.

A Poisson distribution with a high expected value (as a rule of thumb, greater than 10) begins to roughly resemble a normal distribution in shape and symmetry. However, the Poisson distribution is still discrete and has identical values for the mean and variance. Figure 3.2 shows the probability of each number of events for several different values of μ. Notice how the distributions with very low means are right skewed and asymmetric; the distribution with a mean of 10 appears roughly symmetric. The variances of distributions with higher means are larger.

Poisson regression is a GLiM with Poisson distribution error structure and the natural log (ln) link function. The Poisson regression model can be expressed as:

$$\ln(\hat{\mu}) = b_0 + b_1 X_1 + b_2 X_2 + \cdots + b_p X_p, \qquad (45)$$

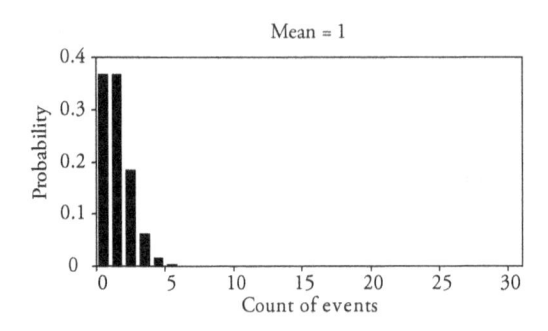

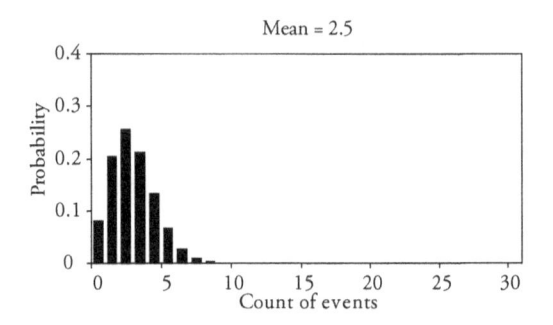

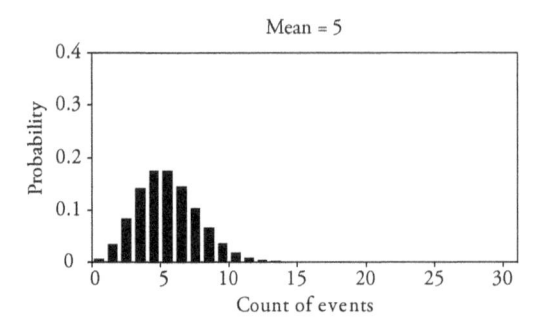

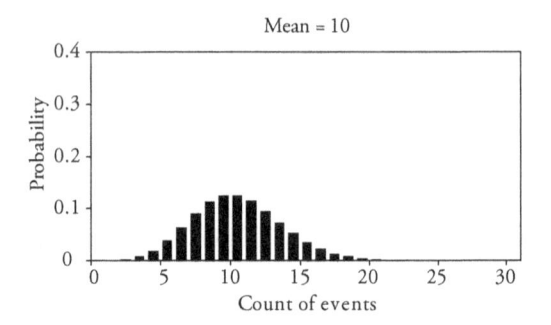

Figure 3.2 Poisson distributions with different values of the mean parameter.

where $\hat{\mu}$ is the predicted count on the outcome variable, given the specific values on the predictors $X_1, X_2, \ldots, X_p$.

Assuming a conditionally Poisson error distribution also means that the residuals of a Poisson regression model are assumed to be *conditionally* Poisson distributed, rather than normally distributed as in linear regression. A discrete distribution such as the Poisson distribution will represent the discrete nature of the residuals that must occur with a discrete outcome. Otherwise stated, because the observed values are counts and can therefore only assume nonnegative integer values, the residuals take on only a limited set of values.

Coefficient interpretation

Recall that the linear form of the Poisson regression model is of the following form: $\ln(\hat{\mu}) = b_0 + b_1 X_1 + b_2 X_2 + \cdots + b_p X_p$. One interpretation of the regression coefficients is in terms of $\ln(\hat{\mu})$ and is identical to that of linear regression. A 1-unit increase in X_1 results in a b_1-unit increase in $\ln(\hat{\mu})$, holding all other variables constant. This interpretation is straightforward, but has the disadvantage of interpreting the change in the units of a *transformation* of the outcome (i.e., the natural logarithm of the predicted count). This interpretation may be of minimal interest when the counts on an outcome reflect a meaningful scale. The researcher would prefer to characterize how the predictors are expected to affect *the number of times the event occurs*. A second interpretation in terms of the count variable can be obtained following some algebraic manipulation of the regression equation. Raising both sides of Equation to the power of e results in:

$$e^{\ln(\hat{\mu})} = e^{(b_0 + b_1 X_1 + b_2 X_2 + \cdots + b_p X_p)}. \quad (46)$$

Once again, note that performing the same operation on both sides of an equation does not change the equation. We again use the property of e and the natural log that $e^{\ln(x)} = x$, so the left side of the above equation can be simplified, resulting in:

$$\hat{\mu} = e^{(b_0 + b_1 X_1 + b_2 X_2 + \cdots + b_p X_p)}. \quad (47)$$

Now we have an equation that shows the effect of the predictors on the actual predicted count, but it is not yet obvious how each of the predictors contributes to the expected count. Again we draw on the property of exponents that $x^{a+b+c} = x^a x^b x^c$, so the single term on the right side of the equation can be broken up into several smaller parts, resulting in an equivalent equation:

$$\hat{\mu} = e^{b_0} e^{b_1 X_1} e^{b_2 X_2} \cdots e^{b_p X_p}. \quad (48)$$

Now we can see that change in the value of a predictor results in a *multiplicative* change in the predicted count. This type of change contrasts with linear regression, in which changes in the predictor result in *additive* changes in the predicted value. To further clarify the interpretation, we can look at the term for a single predictor, such as X_1 (i.e., $e^{b_1 X_1}$). Using the property of exponents shown above, we can examine the effect of a 1-unit change in X_1 on the outcome:

$$e^{b_1 (X_1 + 1)} = e^{b_1 X_1 + b_1} = e^{b_1 X_1} e^{b_1}. \quad (49)$$

The e^{b_1} term is the effect of a 1-unit change in X_1 on the outcome. For a 1-unit increase in X_1, the predicted count ($\hat{\mu}$) is *multiplied by* e^{b_1}, holding all other variables constant.

Overdispersion

As discussed in the context of logistic regression, overdispersion may be an issue for GLiMs with dependent conditional mean and variance. Poisson regression assumes *equidispersion*, that is, the conditional mean and conditional variance are assumed to be equal. For each combination of the values of the predictors, $X_1, X_2, \ldots, X_p$, the conditional mean is equal to the conditional variance. However, as was the case with logistic regression, actual data can be overdispersed; the conditional variance of the residuals is larger than the conditional mean. Ignoring overdispersion results in underestimation of standard errors, which results in overestimation of significance. Two models that are typically used to account for overdispersion in count data are the overdispersed Poisson regression model and the negative binomial model.

Overdispersion occurs for two primary reasons in cross-sectional data. First, there may be individual differences in responses that are not accounted for by the model. This problem commonly occurs if an important predictor is omitted from the model; the variance in the outcome that would have been explained by the omitted predictor is considered unexplained heterogeneity. Unexplained heterogeneity can occur in GLiMs besides Poisson regression and is similar to the heterogeneity of variance that may occur in linear regression when an important predictor is omitted. Second, models of counts such as Poisson regression assume that each event that occurs for an individual is an independent event, which may not be the case. For example, the probability of consuming a first alcoholic drink may not be equal to the probability of consuming a second alcoholic drink given that the individual has consumed the first. This situation in which counts for an individual are not independent of one another is known as *contagion* or *state dependence*.

Overdispersed Poisson regression

The simplest adjustment for overdispersion is the overdispersed Poisson model (Gardner, Mulvey, & Shaw, 1995; Land, McCall, & Nagin, 1996; Long, 1997). Like the overdispersed binary logistic regression model, the overdispersed Poisson regression model includes an additional parameter that is used in the estimation of the conditional variance known as the *overdispersion scaling parameter*, φ. The model estimated with this correction now essentially assumes a Poisson error distribution with mean μ and variance $\varphi\mu$. The scaling parameter φ will be greater than 1 if there is overdispersion in the data, equal to 1 if there is equidispersion (equivalent to the standard Poisson model), and less than 1 if the data are underdispersed. As in logistic regression, the amount of dispersion in the model is typically determined by the Pearson chi-square goodness-of-fit statistic (McCullagh & Nelder, 1989), which is a measure of the overall fit of the model. The scaling parameter is calculated as:

$$\varphi = \frac{\chi^2_{Pearson}}{df}. \qquad (50)$$

The overdispersed model allows the conditional variances to be larger than their corresponding conditional means so that the standard errors (which are based on the conditional variances) will be larger than the standard errors in the standard Poisson model by a factor of $\sqrt{\varphi}$. The coefficients for the overdispersed Poisson model are interpreted identically to those of the standard Poisson model. The deviance and standard errors for this model are also adjusted by the scaling factor; the deviance for the overdispersed Poisson model is equal to the deviance for the standard Poisson model divided by φ. The smaller deviance of this model indicates better fit.

Negative binomial regression

A second common method to account for overdispersion is the negative binomial model (Gardner, Mulvey, & Shaw, 1995; Hilbe, 2007; Land, McCall, & Nagin, 1996; Long, 1997). One shortcoming of the Poisson regression model is that it does not contain an error (disturbance) term that fully parallels the error term found in linear regression. The standard Poisson model does not allow for heterogeneity among individuals. Often there is additional heterogeneity between individuals that is not accounted for by the predictors in the model and the Poisson error function alone, which results in overdispersion. The negative binomial model accounts for overdispersion by assuming there is unexplained variability among individuals who have the same predicted value. Compared to the Poisson distribution, this additional unexplained variability among individuals leads to larger variance in the outcome distribution but has no effect on the mean.

To illustrate, consider a study in which two variables, gender and age, predict a count outcome. The standard Poisson model assumes that the outcomes for all individuals with the same values of the predictors are samples from a *single* Poisson distribution with a given mean. In other words, the subset of women who are 30 years old are treated as being alike and modeled by a Poisson distribution with the same mean parameter. The negative binomial model, however, allows the observations of individuals with the same values on the predictors to be modeled by Poisson distributions with different mean parameters. Here, for example, one 30-year-old woman may be modeled with a Poisson distribution with a mean of μ_1, whereas another 30-year-old woman is modeled with a Poisson distribution with a mean of μ_2.

Note that the data are still modeled using Poisson distributions, but each individual may be represented by a Poisson distribution with a different mean parameter. The variation in individual mean parameters for individuals with the same values on the predictors must be assumed to follow a probability distribution. The negative binomial model uses another standard (though less familiar) probability distribution in the exponential family, the gamma distribution (Freund & Walpole, 1980, pp. 196–197), to represent the distribution of means. In the negative binomial model the error function is a mixture of two different probability distributions, the Poisson and gamma distributions. The mixture of a Poisson distribution and a gamma distribution in this manner results in the negative binomial distribution. The probability mass function for the negative binomial distribution,

$$P(Y = y|r, \pi) = \frac{(y-1)!}{(r-1)!(y-r)!}\pi^r(1-\pi)^{y-r}, \qquad (51)$$

gives the probability of observing a given value, y, of variable Y which is distributed as a negative binomial variable with parameters r and π. The negative binomial distribution gives the probability of requiring y independent binary trials, each occurring with probability π, to achieve r successes. For example, if we wanted to know the probability of requiring y coin flips from a fair coin to obtain exactly three heads, we would use the negative binomial distribution with $r = 3$ and $\pi = 0.5$. The mean of this distribution is $r(1 - \pi)/\pi = 3$ and the variance is $r(1 - \pi)/\pi^2 = 6$ (Ross, 2006, pp. 177–178).

The conditional mean of the outcome, given the values of the predictors, is identical for the standard Poisson model and the negative binomial model. In contrast, the conditional variance of the outcome will be larger in the negative binomial model than in the standard Poisson model. The variance for the negative binomial model is given by $\mu + \alpha\mu^2$ rather than μ as in Poisson regression. The α parameter is estimated by ML along with the other model parameters. If $\alpha = 0$, there is no overdispersion, and the negative binomial model reduces to standard Poisson. An α parameter greater than 0 indicates that overdispersion is present; larger values indicate more overdispersion. The regression coefficients for the negative binomial model are interpreted identically to those for the standard Poisson model. The unexplained heterogeneity (between-individual variation) underlying the overdispersion is partialed out of the effects.

Comparison of count models

Comparisons among the Poisson regression model, the overdispersed Poisson regression, and the negative binomial regression model are common (e.g., Berk & MacDonald, 2008; Gardner, Mulvey, & Shaw, 1995; Land, McCall, & Nagin, 1996). Standard Poisson regression is the most basic analysis for count data and is relatively easy to interpret. However, a failing of Poisson regression is that its assumption of equidispersion is often unreasonable with real data. The overdispersed Poisson regression model is also fairly easy to interpret; it is a better choice than the Poisson regression model when the data are overdispersed and the research question involves the regression coefficients and their significance (Gardner, Mulvey, & Shaw, 1995). Negative binomial regression is more general and likewise more complex than either of the Poisson regression models, but is useful when the probability distributions of counts for an individual case are of most interest. For example, Gardner, Mulvey, and Shaw (1995) suggest that because the negative binomial model can more closely follow individual conditional counts, it is more appropriate than Poisson regression when future prediction for an individual is of interest. However, Berk and MacDonald (2008) warn that using the negative binomial regression model is not a fix for all modeling problems. If the model is misspecified (e.g., by omitting important predictors), using the negative binomial model will give a "false sense of security when the fundamental errors in the model remain" (p. 283).

Excess zeros

An additional issue that is unique to models of count outcome such as Poisson regression is the concept of so-called excess zeros. *Excess zeros* refers to a situation in which the number of "0" responses observed exceeds the number of "0" responses predicted by the model. Overdispersed data can occasionally give an illusion of excess zeros. In this case, the appearance of excess zeros can be remedied by using a model that accommodates overdispersion (e.g., overdispersed Poisson or negative binomial).

More commonly in many areas of behavioral research, excess zeros occur for important theoretical reasons. Often, excess zeros occur because values in the sample are coming from different groups. One theoretical context in which excess zeros occur is hurdle models in which all zeros come from one group, whereas all positive counts (i.e., > 0) come from a second group. A second context in which excess zeros are modeled is in zero-inflated Poisson models. As in the hurdle model, some zeros come from a group that has no probability of displaying the behavior of interest and therefore always responds with a "0." These zeros that must always occur are termed *structural zeros*. However, in zero-inflated Poisson models, some zeros may come from a group that produces zeros with some probability (e.g., occasional drinkers).

To address excess zeros, it is important to determine whether structural zeros are part of the research question. For example, consider a study of alcohol consumption by college students. Some students may never drink alcohol for health, religious, or legal reasons; these students would produce structural zeros if included in the sample. If the investigator is interested only in the behavior of students who would *ever* consume alcohol, the nondrinkers who produce structural zeros should be screened out of the sample. This screening is an issue of study design; information must be collected to help distinguish between structural zeros and nonstructural zeros.

However, if the research question involves all individuals (in this example, "ever drinkers" and "never drinkers"), appropriate statistical models must be used to correctly estimate model parameters for all individuals. Excess zeros that remain in the model can result in distorted estimates of the mean and variance of the outcome. Models to address this issue are discussed in the section on two-part models.

Truncated zeros

A less common problem involving zeros is the absence of zeros in the sample. Typically, this results from the sampling plan of the study. For example, if data are collected from a hospital, the sample for a study of medical visits will only include individuals who have visited the hospital at least once. No one in the sample can have a value of "0" for number of visits. Long (1997) describes several models that can account for these "missing" zeros. The general approach is to modify the Poisson or negative binomial model to model the probability of a given count on the outcome variable, *given that the count is greater than zero* during the observation period.

TWO-PART MODELS

Two-part models or joint models are an expansion of GLiMs that can be used when a single outcome variable has multiple facets that are modeled simultaneously or when multiple outcome variables are conceptually closely related. One example of an outcome variable that is amenable to joint modeling is the number of cigarettes smoked in a day. This type of count outcome gives two pieces of information: (1) whether the person has smoked or not and, (2) if they have smoked, how many cigarettes they have smoked. The outcomes modeled in two-part models are most commonly binary and count, but researchers have also jointly modeled binary and time-to-event data (e.g., delay after awakening until first cigarette is smoked; Rizopoulos, Verbeke, Lesaffre, & Vanrenterghem, 2008; Song, Davidian, & Tsiatis, 2002).

A major application of two-part models is in the analysis of count outcomes that have excess zeros. These two-part excess-zeros models work under the premise that the observed counts are generated by two different processes. There are two major types of these two-part models for excess zeros: hurdle and zero-inflated regression models. They differ in how zeros in the sample are proposed to be generated.

Hurdle regression models

Hurdle regression models (Long, 1997; Mullahy, 1986) are often used to model human decision-making processes. For example, Liu and Cela (2008) offer a hurdle model for number of visits to a doctor. The initial visit is motivated by the patient, while subsequent visits may be influenced by the doctor's suggestions; one process determines whether an initial visit occurs, but another process determines the number of follow-up visits. The zero versus nonzero portion of the model is typically modeled by a logistic or probit regression. Modeling of the nonzero counts is conducted with a truncated Poisson model (introduced above) or truncated negative binomial model; this part predicts the probability of a count, given that the count is greater than zero. In these models, different predictor variables can be used in the binary and positive counts portions of the model, reflecting the fact that different variables may be influencing the two processes involved.

For the simplest hurdle regression model in which the zero/non-zero distinction is modeled with logistic regression and the positive count portion is modeled with a truncated Poisson regression, the probability mass function is a function of two parameters: the proportion of zeros in the sample, θ, and the expected value of the Poisson count portion of the model, μ. The probability mass function is given by

$$P(Y = y|\theta, \mu) = \theta \text{ for } Y = 0 \text{ and by} \quad (52)$$

$$P(Y = y|\theta, \mu) = \frac{e^{-\mu}\mu^y(1-\theta)}{(1-e^{-\mu})y!} \quad (53)$$

when Y takes on integer values greater than 0. The log-likelihood contribution for an individual with a value of 0 on the outcome is derived from the probability function in Equation 52. The log-likelihood contribution for an individual with a positive value on the outcome is derived from the probability function in Equation 53. The total log-likelihood for the model is the sum of each of these individual log-likelihoods.

Hurdle regression models can be evaluated using advanced SAS procedures including PROC NLMIXED and PROC NLIN, M*plus*, and with hplogit in STATA. These software packages produce two sets of regression coefficients, one for each portion of the model, as well as various fit statistics, such as the deviance (-2LL). Each set of regression coefficients can be interpreted according to the corresponding model. For example, in the logit-Poisson hurdle regression model just discussed, the binary portion of the model is estimated with logistic regression and the count portion of the model is estimated with a truncated Poisson model. The regression coefficients for the binary portion of the model can be interpreted as they are in standard binary logistic regression: e^{b_j} is the multiplicative effect of predictor j on the odds of being a case. In this situation, the probability of being a "case" is the probability of having a positive-count outcome value rather than a zero-outcome value.

One test of whether there are "excess" zeros in the sample is derived from the fact that the standard Poisson regression model is nested within the logit-Poisson hurdle regression model (Liu & Cela, 2008). A likelihood ratio test comparing the two models, paralleling model comparison procedures to test for overdispersion, can be used to determine whether the fit of the two-part hurdle regression model is significantly better than that of the standard Poisson regression model. A significant likelihood ratio test indicates that zeros in the sample are better accounted for by the hurdle regression model than by a standard Poisson regression model. The negative binomial regression model is not nested within the hurdle regression model, so a likelihood ratio test cannot be used to compare these models; the Akaike Information Criterion (AIC; Akaike, 1974), Bayesian Information Criterion (BIC; Schwarz, 1978), or Vuong test for non-nested models (Greene, 1994) can be used to compare them.

Zero-inflated regression models

Zero-inflated regression models (Greene, 1994; Hall & Zhengang, 2004; Lambert, 1992; Long, 1997) are often used when the sample is thought to be composed of individuals from two different populations: those who have no probability of displaying the behavior of interest and therefore always respond with a zero, and those who produce zeros with some probability. In the alcohol example discussed above, some of the zeros will come from individuals who never drink for religious, health, or other reasons and thereby produce structural zeros that must always occur. Other zero values will come from individuals who have some probability of consuming alcoholic beverages but did not consume any on the day in question. The structural zero versus nonstructural zero and positive count portion of the model is typically modeled by a logistic or probit regression. Modeling of the nonstructural zeros and positive counts is conducted with a Poisson model, overdispersed Poisson model, or negative binomial model. As in hurdle regression models, different predictor variables can be used in the binary and positive counts portions of the zero-inflated model, reflecting the fact that different variables may be influencing the two processes involved.

For a standard zero-inflated Poisson model, the probability mass function is a function of two parameters: the estimated proportion of cases that are structural zeros, ω, and the expected value of the Poisson count portion of the model, μ. The probability mass function is given by

$$P(Y = y|\omega, \mu) = \omega + e^{-\mu}(1 - \omega) \text{ for } Y = 0, \text{ and by} \quad (54)$$

$$P(Y = y|\omega, \mu) = \frac{e^{-\mu}\mu^y(1-\omega)}{y!} \quad (55)$$

for values of Y greater than 0. As in hurdle regression, the log-likelihood for the model sums the corresponding probability function for each individual.

Zero-inflated count outcome models can be estimated in SAS, STATA and M*plus*. When the same predictors are used for both portions of the model, the zero-inflated Poisson (ZIP) model is referred to as the ZIP(tau) model, which can be estimated using SAS PROC NLMIXED. These software packages produce two sets of regression coefficients, one for each portion of the model, as well as various fit statistics, such as the deviance (-2LL). Each set of regression coefficients can be interpreted according to the corresponding model. For example, in the zero-inflated Poisson model, the structural zero versus nonstructural zero portion of the model is estimated with logistic regression and the count portion of the model is estimated with a standard Poisson model. The regression coefficients for the binary portion of the model can be interpreted as they are in standard binary logistic regression: e^{b_k} is the multiplicative effect of predictor k on the odds of being a case. In this situation, the probability of being a "case" is the probability of belonging to the group that produces both *non*structural zeros and positive counts.

Poisson regression, overdispersed Poisson regression, and negative binomial models are not nested within zero-inflated count models. Thus, likelihood ratio tests cannot be used to compare these models. The Vuong (1989) test, proposed by Greene (1994) for zero-inflated count models, can be used to compare zero-inflated count models and hurdle regression models to Poisson, overdispersed Poisson, and negative binomial models. For each of the two models being compared, the probability of the observed outcome value given the observed predictor values is calculated; these values are given by $P_1(Y_i|X_i)$ and $P_2(Y_i|X_i)$, where P_1 is the probability for the zero-inflated or hurdle model and P_2 is the probability for the Poisson, overdispersed Poisson, or negative binomial regression model. A quantity,

m_i, is calculated for each case i, where

$$m_i = \log\left(\frac{P_1(Y_i|X_i)}{P_2(Y_i|X_i)}\right). \quad (56)$$

The Vuong test statistic,

$$V = \frac{\sqrt{n}\left(\frac{1}{n}\sum_{i=1}^{n} m_i\right)}{\sqrt{\frac{1}{n}\sum_{i=1}^{n}(m_i - \bar{m})^2}}, \quad (57)$$

has a null hypothesis that the expected value of m_i is equal to 0—that is, that the probability of the observed outcome value is the same for both models. The Vuong test statistic is normally distributed. Values of V greater than 1.96 indicate that Model 1 is preferred, while values less than –1.96 indicate that Model 2 is preferred; values between –1.96 and 1.96 indicate that the models are not statistically different. Liu and Cela (2008) provide SAS syntax to calculate the Vuong statistic comparing Poisson regression to zero-inflated Poisson regression.

OTHER GLIMS

Generalized linear models are very versatile and our focus has been on those models for which clear applications exist or have begun to be developed for behavioral science data. Many other models can potentially be developed within the GLiM family that might have broad application. Space limitations preclude coverage in this chapter of even the full set of most common GLiMs described by statisticians (*see* Table 3.1). Some of those not presented here may have important potential applications in the behavioral sciences. For example, beta regression (Kieschnick & McCullough, 2003; Paolino, 2001; Smithson & Verkuilen, 2006) expands GLiMs by jointly modeling the mean and variance of an outcome. These joint models may potentially have separate link functions and predictors for the conditional mean and variance, with a single error structure subsuming both. Smithson and Verkuilen (2006) have pointed out that beta regression may be useful for a wide variety of outcome variables that are not necessarily discrete, but also do not meet the assumptions of multiple regression. These outcome variables include ones that have upper or lower bounds, excessive skew, or excessive heteroscedasticity. Examples include proportions or the individual's mean score on a set of Likert-type items (e.g., bounded by a lower score of 1 and an upper score of 5) that are highly non-normally distributed, even U-shaped.

Pseudo-R-Squared Measures of Fit

The $R^2_{multiple}$ is a familiar measure of fit for a linear regression model. It conveys important information in a simple way; it is a single number that summarizes the overall fit of the model. As discussed previously, calculation of $R^2_{multiple}$ as in linear regression is not appropriate for GLiMs. Several methods of creating analogues to $R^2_{multiple}$ have been developed for GLiMs in general and for specific models (e.g., logistic regression).

Most R^2 analogues are developed by following the same logic used for developing the R^2 measure itself in regression. The key feature is that in linear regression there are multiple, equivalent definitions of R^2. To name three, R^2 is simultaneously: (1) the proportion of variation in the outcome variable that is explained by the predictors, (2) the ratio of the variation of the predicted outcome scores to the variation of the observed outcome scores, and (3) a transformation of the likelihood ratio for the model. Still other definitions are possible. Many of the R^2 analogues for GLiMs fall into one of these three categories. In linear regression, these three methods will produce identical values of R^2; this is not the case for GLiMs (West, Aiken, & Kwok, 2003).

McFadden (1973) suggested using the likelihoods of the model of interest ($L(M_\beta)$) and of a model with an intercept only ($L(M_\alpha)$) to calculate an R^2 measure similar to Equation 10. Here, the likelihood of the model with no predictors is considered analogous to a measure of the total SS. McFadden's (1973) measure is

$$R^2_{McFadden} = 1 - \frac{\ln\{L(M_\beta)\}}{\ln\{L(M_\alpha)\}}. \quad (58)$$

This measure will equal zero if the likelihoods of the two models are identical; it can only equal 1 when the model of interest is a fully saturated model (in which the Likelihood = 1 and $\ln(L) = 0$). Menard (2000) asserts that $R^2_{McFadden}$ is the best measure for logistic regression because it is interpretable as the proportion reduction in error and because it is relatively independent of the base rate of cases in the outcome variable. Cameron and Windmeijer (1997) suggest a similar measure of R^2 for the Poisson regression model, defined in terms of model deviance (-2LL). The *deviance* R^2 is defined as

$$R^2_{deviance} = 1 - \frac{D(M_\beta)}{D(M_\alpha)}. \quad (59)$$

Like McFadden's measure and $R^2_{multiple}$ from linear regression, the deviance R^2 is theoretically bounded by 0 and 1. This measure will equal 0 only if the deviance of the model of interest (M_β) is the same as the deviance of the intercept-only model (M_α); that is, the measure is 0 if the predictors do not have predictive value.

A second type of R^2 analog uses the ratio of the variance of the predicted outcome to the variance of the observed outcome. McKelvery and Zavoina (1975) suggested this measure for models that have a latent variable interpretation (i.e., appropriate for some logistic regression, probit regression, and ordinal logistic regression models); for this measure, the variances are of the latent variable outcome. The formula for this measure is

$$R^2_{M\&Z} = \frac{Var(\hat{Y}^*)}{Var(Y^*)} = \left(\frac{Var(\hat{Y}^*)}{Var(Y^*) + Var(e)}\right), \quad (60)$$

where $Var(Y^*)$ is the estimated variance of the latent outcome variable, $Var(\hat{Y}^*)$ is the variance of the predicted latent outcome variable, and $Var(e)$ is the residual error variance of the latent outcome variable. For logistic regression, $Var(e)$ (the residual or error variance) is fixed to $\pi^2/3$; for probit regression, it is fixed to 1 (Winship & Mare, 1984). Simulation studies have shown that this measure is closest to the $R^2_{multiple}$ for linear regression when a continuous underlying latent variable is divided into two discrete categories (e.g., DeMaris, 2002; Hagle & Mitchell, 1992; Windmeijer, 1995).

A third type of R^2 analog relies on a transformation of the likelihood ratio for the model of interest. Recall that linear regression is equivalent to a GLiM with an identity link function and normally distributed errors. The $R^2_{multiple}$ for the linear regression model is equivalent to the R^2 based on ML estimation of the linear regression model,

$$R^2_{ML} = 1 - \left[\frac{L(M_\alpha)}{L(M_\beta)}\right]^{\frac{2}{n}}, \quad (61)$$

where $L(M_\alpha)$ is the likelihood of the model with only an intercept, $L(M_\beta)$ is the likelihood of the model of interest, and n is the number of observations in the analysis. Equation 61 can be applied to any GLiM to obtain an R^2 analog measure based on the likelihood of the model. Cox and Snell (1989) developed this measure for logistic regression; however, like McFadden's (1973) measure, this R^2 can never achieve a maximum value of 1. Nagelkerke (1991) rescaled Cox and Snell's (1989) measure to have a maximum value of 1 by dividing by the maximum value possible, $1 - (L(M_\alpha))^{2/n}$.

Diagnostics
MODEL DIAGNOSTICS

Checking model assumptions is an important part of assessing model adequacy. Examining the residuals of the model serves as a method for checking the assumptions regarding the error structure. In linear regression, a typical graphical method used to assess model adequacy is to plot the raw residuals against the observed predictor values. This plot should show no relationship between the observed value of the predictor and the mean of the respective residuals. Additionally, the plot should show constant variance of the residuals across all values of the observed value (homogeneity). If there are multiple predictors, the residuals should also be plotted against the predicted value, $\hat{Y}$ (Cohen et al., 2003, Chapter 4).

This method of model assessment is *not* appropriate for GLiMs. For GLiMs, there is a nonlinear relationship between the observed value and the predicted value, which leads to a correlation between the residual term, $Y_i - \hat{Y}_i$, and the observed value, Y_i. Additionally, many GLiMs display heteroscedasticity in the error variance (e.g., logistic regression and Poisson regression). For all error structures discussed in this chapter (with the exception of the normal distribution for linear regression), the distribution mean and variance share parameters; for example, the mean and variance of the binomial distribution share the n and π parameters and the mean and variance of the Poisson distribution share the μ parameter.

Given that the raw residuals for most GLiMs are heteroscedastic and asymmetric (Cameron & Trivedi, 1998, p. 141; Fox, 2008, Chapter 15), alternative types of residuals must be used to assess model adequacy. Pierce and Schafer (1986) suggested that deviance residuals are the best choice for GLiMs. Deviance residuals measure the contribution of an individual's observation to the overall model deviance; deviance residuals are a function of the individual likelihoods for each observation. Individual deviance residuals are summed to form the model deviance. For a GLiM that is correctly specified, there should be no relationship (i.e., regression line with slope approximately 0) between the deviance residuals and the predicted value; there should also be roughly constant variance across all values of the predicted values.

CASE DIAGNOSTICS

Regression diagnostics are a group of statistics that focus on individual cases in the sample to help a researcher detect outliers, poorly fitting cases, and especially cases that exert excessive influence on the values of parameter estimates. For linear regression, regression diagnostics are well-developed and understood, with three main types of diagnostic statistics: *leverage statistics* detect cases that are extreme on the predictors, *distance statistics* detect cases that have large discrepancies between the observed and predicted values on the outcome variable, and *influence statistics* detect cases that have a large influence on the regression coefficients. The diagnostics for distance and influence are based on the key idea of case deletion: the same regression model is estimated with all cases included and then one specific case (case i) is deleted and the results are compared. Conceptually, this would be done n times, once for each case in the data set. For linear regression, simple relationships exist that allow the full set of diagnostic statistics to be quickly and exactly calculated in a single computer run. Authors have offered conventions for values on the diagnostic statistics that call for further study of the case and its influence. Cohen et al. (2003, Chapter 10) present a full discussion of these issues. However, in GLiMs, the calculation of diagnostic statistics becomes more complicated, and clear conventions for their interpretation have not yet been offered.

Leverage

In linear regression, leverage measures assess how extreme an observation is only on the predictors; the outcome, Y, is ignored completely. Formally, leverage measures indicate the discrepancy of a case on the set of predictors $(X_1, X_2, ..., X_p)$ from the centroid of the predictor space, the point representing the means on all predictors $(\bar{X}_1, \bar{X}_2, ..., \bar{X}_p)$. Leverage statistics in linear regression are calculated from the Hat matrix, $\mathbf{H}$, which is a function of only the predictors:

$$\mathbf{H} = \mathbf{X}\left(\mathbf{X}'\mathbf{X}\right)^{-1}\mathbf{X}', \qquad (62)$$

where $\mathbf{X}$ is the $n \times p$ matrix of observed predictors. For a single predictor for an individual case i, leverage is the ith diagonal element of the Hat matrix, which is a function of only the predictors and sample size:

$$h_{ii} = \frac{1}{n} + \frac{(X_i - \bar{X})^2}{\sum_{i=1}^{n}(X_i - \bar{X})^2}. \qquad (63)$$

In GLiMs, leverage measures are more difficult to interpret. The Hat matrix in GLiMs is not solely a function of the predictors:

$$\mathbf{H} = \mathbf{W}^{1/2}\mathbf{X}\left(\mathbf{X}'\mathbf{W}\mathbf{X}\right)^{-1}\mathbf{X}'\mathbf{W}^{1/2}, \qquad (64)$$

where $\mathbf{W}$ is a function of the predicted score, the regression coefficients, the observed predictors, and the variance of the observed outcome variable. The Hat matrix for GLiMs reflects both the outcome variable and the predicted outcome scores, so the "leverage" measures for GLiMs do not have the same meaning as they do in linear regression. Hoaglin and Welsch (1978) and Cameron and Trivedi (1998) suggest a cut-off score of $2p/n$ for leverage scores for GLiMs, where p is the number of predictors and n is the sample size. The mean value of the leverage scores, h_{ii}, will be p/n so the cut-off reflects a score twice as large as the average expected leverage value.

Distance

Distance measures assess the discrepancy between the observed outcome value and the predicted outcome value; all distance measures are based on the residuals, $\left(Y_i - \hat{Y}_i\right)$. In linear regression, the optimal measure for assessing distance for case i is the externally Studentized residual, a type of standardized residual. In linear regression, the externally Studentized residual for case i is

$$t_i = \frac{\left(Y_i - \hat{Y}_{i(i)}\right)}{\sqrt{MS_{residual(i)}(1 - h_{ii})}}, \qquad (65)$$

where h_{ii} is the ith diagonal element of the Hat matrix, $\hat{Y}_{i(i)}$ is the predicted score for case i based on a regression model in which case i was excluded, and $MS_{residual(i)}$ is the mean square residual for a regression model in which case i was excluded. These externally Studentized residuals can be calculated for all cases in a linear regression analysis simultaneously. In contrast, Fox (2008) notes that in GLiMs, exact calculation of externally Studentized residuals requires fitting the regression model to n data sets in which each case, in turn, has been deleted; each of the n deviances would be compared to the deviance of the full model. Various simpler procedures that approximate the Studentized residual have been suggested. Cameron and Trivedi (1998) suggest estimating the externally Studentized residuals for Poisson regression as

$$d_i^* = \frac{d_i}{\sqrt{1 - h_{ii}}}, \qquad (66)$$

where d_i is the deviance residual for case i, and h_{ii} is the ith diagonal element of the Hat matrix. Externally Studentized residuals in GLiMs can be interpreted in a similar to way to linear regression; they signal cases that may be responsible for increased standard errors and reduced statistical power for tests of significance of individual coefficients.

Influence

Influence measures assess how much the deletion of a particular case will actually change the values of predicted scores and regression coefficients; that is, whether the case affects the results and conclusions from the regression analysis. Linear regression has both global and specific measures of influence. *DFFITS* and Cook's *D* assess overall change in the predicted scores from deleting a specific case. For example, *DFFITS* indexes the number of standard deviations by which a case changes its own predicted score when the case is included in versus deleted from the analysis. In linear regression, *DFFITS* for case *i* is given by

$$DFFITS_i = t_i \sqrt{\frac{h_{ii}}{1 - h_{ii}}}, \quad (67)$$

where t_i is the externally Studentized residual for case *i*, and h_{ii} is the *i*th diagonal element of the Hat matrix (Cohen et al., 2003).

In addition, linear regression includes measures of influence on the individual regression coefficients. *DFBETAS*, one for each regression coefficient for each case, assess the number of standard deviations by which an individual case changes each regression coefficient. In linear regression, *DFBETAS* for case *i* and regression coefficient *j* is given by:

$$DFBETAS_{ij} = \frac{b_j - b_{j(i)}}{\text{standard error}(b_{j(i)})}, \quad (68)$$

where b_j is the *j*th regression coefficient and $b_{j(i)}$ is the *j*th regression coefficient in a regression model in which case *i* was excluded.

For GLiMs, calculating exact estimates is not computationally feasible in very large samples, so procedures that provide approximations to *DFFITS*, Cook's *D*, and *DFBETAS* have been offered. Fox (2008) suggests an approximation to Cook's *D* of

$$D_i = \frac{R_{Pi}^2}{\tilde{\varphi} \times p} \times \frac{h_{ii}}{1 - h_{ii}}, \quad (69)$$

where R_{Pi}^2 is the squared Pearson residual for case *i*, $\tilde{\varphi}$ is the estimated dispersion parameter for the model, *p* is the number of predictors on the model (including the intercept), and h_{ii} is the *i*th diagonal element of the Hat matrix.

As noted above, clear conventions for interpreting diagnostic statistics do *not* currently exist in GLiM, and the different approximations used in their calculation may place their values in different metrics. With the exception of leverage, there are no recommended cut-off scores for diagnostics in GLiMs as there are for diagnostics in linear regression. One straightforward graphical way to interpret these statistics is to plot a frequency distribution or histogram of the diagnostic statistic values and examine the figure for a conspicuous high value. Another method is to construct index plots in which case number is on the *X*-axis and the value of the diagnostic statistic is on the *Y*-axis. In this way, cases that are very discrepant on one of the diagnostic statistics will "pop out" in the plot, allowing the researcher to easily identify them. Separate index plots are constructed for leverage, distance, global influence, and the measure of specific influence for each predictor. Cases with scores that are high in magnitude *relative* to other cases in the data set deserve careful scrutiny. Cohen et al. (2003, pp. 391–419) describe in detail the application of these procedures to linear regression, and Fox (2008, pp. 412–415) describes their extension to GLiM.

Summary and Conclusion

Linear regression is an adaptable system for relating one or more predictors to a single continuous outcome variable. However, linear regression makes strong assumptions regarding the distribution of the model errors; the errors are assumed to be conditionally normal with constant variance. Many commonly studied types of outcome variables result in violations of the error assumptions of linear regression. Violation of the assumptions with regard to the error distribution results in biased standard errors and biased tests of significance.

The GLiM is an appropriate alternative to linear regression when these assumptions are violated. Generalized linear models can be used for a wide variety of categorical and limited dependent variables that are common in the behavioral sciences. Commonly used models within the GLiM framework include logistic regression for binary outcomes, multinomial regression for three or more unordered categories, ordinal logistic regression for ordered categories, and Poisson regression for count outcomes. Two-part hurdle and zero-inflated Poisson regression models address cases in which two groups may be included in the data, one of which always produces an observed response of zero and which may be censored. Other models within the GLiM framework not discussed here permit researchers to address a wide variety of traditionally problematic forms of data including outcome variables with upper and lower bounds, excessive kurtosis, excessive skewness, or even U-shaped distributions. Measures of effect size and regression diagnostics for the model and for individual cases have been proposed for GLiMs and continue to be refined.

The basic theoretical work on GLiMs was carried out in statistics, and many of the early applications of these models occurred in other disciplines, including medicine, epidemiology, sociology, and economics. With the increasing availability of user-friendly software to perform many of the common GLiMs, we expect these models to increase in utilization across psychology and the behavioral sciences. Successful applications with problematic data sets will further expand the use of GLiMs and extend the range of problems to which they are applied.

Funny dependent variables can also cause problems of biased estimates of coefficients and inappropriate standard errors in more advanced statistical procedures. New developments in statistical theory now extend the ideas underlying the GLiM to structural equation modeling, growth curve modeling, multilevel modeling, and survival analysis (Raudenbush & Bryk, 2002; Skrondal & Rabe-Hesketh, 2004). These procedures are already being incorporated into statistical packages such as HLM, M*plus*, and Stata. Our hope is that this chapter will serve as a useful introduction to these procedures and will help awaken researchers to their possibilities and overcome the problematic results that may be produced by funny dependent variables.

Author Note

Stephen G. West was supported by a Forschungspreis from the Alexander von Humboldt Foundation at the Arbeitsbereich Methoden und Evaluation at the Freie Universität Berlin, Germany during the writing of this proposal. Correspondence should be directed to Stefany Coxe, Psychology Department, Florida International University, Miami, FL 33199, USA. E-mail: stefany.coxe@fiu.edu

Notes

1. Probability density and probability mass functions describe the relative likelihood of a random variable taking on specific values or ranges of values. For some probability mass distributions for categorical variables, the distribution is commonly written in a simpler form so that this characteristic may not be immediately apparent. These functions are important in developing appropriate hypothesis tests.

References

Agresti, A. (2002). *Categorical data analysis* (2nd ed.). New York: Wiley.

Agresti, A. (2007). *An introduction to categorical data analysis* (2nd ed.). New York: Wiley.

Agresti, A. (2010). *Analysis of ordinal categorical data* (2nd ed.). New York: Wiley.

Akaike, H. (1974). A new look at the statistical model identification. *IEEE Transactions on Automatic Control, 19,* 716–723.

Allison, P. D. (1999). *Logistic regression using the SAS system: Theory & application.* Cary, NC: SAS Institute.

Berk, R., & MacDonald, J. M. (2008). Overdispersion and Poisson regression. *Journal of Quantitative Criminology, 24,* 269–284.

Cameron, A. C., & Trivedi, P. K. (1998). *Regression analysis of count data.* New York: Cambridge.

Cameron, A. C., & Windmeijer, F. A. G. (1997). An R-squared measure of goodness of fit for some common nonlinear regression models. *Journal of Econometrics, 77,* 329–342.

Chernoff, H. (1954). On the distribution of the likelihood ratio. *Annals of Mathematical Statistics, 25,* 573–578.

Cohen, J. (1968). Multiple regression as a general data-analytic system. *Psychological Bulletin, 70,* 426–443.

Cohen, J., Cohen, P., West, S., & Aiken, L. (2003). *Applied multiple regression/correlation analysis for the behavioral sciences* (3rd ed.). Mahwah, NJ: L. Erlbaum Associates.

Cook, R. D., & Weisberg, S. (1983). Diagnostics for heteroscedasticity in regression. *Biometrika, 70,* 1–10.

Cox, D. R., & Snell, E. J. (1989). *Analysis of binary data* (2nd ed.). New York: Chapman and Hall.

Coxe, S., West, S. G., & Aiken, L. S. (2009). The analysis of count data: A gentle introduction to Poisson regression and its alternatives. *Journal of Personality Assessment, 91,* 121–136.

DeMaris, A. (2002). Explained variance in logistic regression: A Monte Carlo study of proposed measures. *Sociological Methods and Research, 31,* 27–74.

DeMaris, A. (2004). *Regression with social data: Modeling continuous and limited response variables.* Hoboken, NJ: Wiley.

Fahrmeir, L., & Tutz, G. (2001). *Multivariate statistical modeling based on generalized linear models* (2nd ed.). New York: Springer.

Fox, J. (2008). *Applied regression analysis and generalized linear models* (2nd ed.). Thousand Oaks, CA: Sage.

Freund, J. E., & Walpole, R. E. (1980). *Mathematical statistics* (3rd ed.). Englewood Cliffs, NJ: Prentice-Hall.

Gardner, W., Mulvey, E. P., & Shaw, E. C. (1995). Regression analyses of counts and rates: Poisson, overdispersed Poisson, and negative binomial models. *Psychological Bulletin, 118,* 392–404.

Greene, W. H. (1994, March). *Accounting for excess zeros and sample selection in Poisson and negative binomial regression models.* Working paper No. EC-94-10, Department of Economics, New York University.

Hagle, T. M., & Mitchell, G. E. (1992). Goodness-of-fit measures for probit and logit. *American Journal of Political Science, 36,* 762–784.

Hall, D. B. & Zhengang, Z. (2004). Marginal models for zero-inflated clustered data. *Statistical Modelling, 4,* 161–180.

Hilbe, J. (2007). *Negative binomial regression*. New York: Cambridge University Press.

Hoaglin, D. C., & Welsch, R. E. (1978). Hat matrix in regression and ANOVA. *American Statistician, 32*, 17–22.

Hosmer, D. W., & Lemeshow, S. (2000). *Applied logistic regression* (2nd ed.). New York: Wiley.

Kieschnick, R., & McCullough, B. D. (2003). Regression analysis of variates observed on (0,1): Percentages, proportions, and fractions. *Statistical Modeling, 3*, 193–213.

Kutner, M. H., Nachtsheim, C. J., & Neter, J. (2004). Applied linear regression models (4th ed.). New York: McGraw-Hill.

Lambert, D. (1992). Zero-inflated Poisson regression, with an application to defects in manufacturing. *Technometrics, 34*, 1–14.

Land, K. C., McCall, P. L., & Nagin, D. S. (1996). A comparison of Poisson, negative binomial, and semiparametric mixed Poisson regression models: With empirical applications to criminal careers data. *Sociological Methods and Research, 24*, 387–442.

Liu, W., & Cela, J. (2008). Count data models in SAS. *SAS Global Forum 2008*, Paper 371-2008.

Long, J. S. (1997). *Regression models for categorical and limited dependent variables*. Thousand Oaks, CA: Sage Publications.

McCullagh, P., & Nelder, J. A. (1983). *Generalized linear models*. New York: Chapman and Hall.

McCullagh, P., & Nelder, J. A., (1989). *Generalized linear models* (2nd ed.). New York: Chapman and Hall.

McFadden, D. (1973). Conditional logit analysis of qualitative choice behavior. In P. Zarembka (Ed.), *Frontiers of econometrics* (pp. 105–142). New York: Academic Press.

McKelvery, R. D., & Zavoina, W. (1975). A statistical model for the analysis of ordinal dependent variables. *Journal of Mathematical Sociology, 4*, 103–120.

Menard, S. (2000). Coefficients of determination for multiple logistic regression analysis. *American Statistician, 54*, 17–24.

Mullahy, J. (1986). Specification and testing of some modified count data models. *Journal of Econometrics, 33*, 341–365.

Nagelkerke, N. J. D. (1991). A note on a general definition of the coefficient of determination. *Biometrika, 78*, 691–692.

Nelder, J. A., & Wedderburn, R. W. (1972). Generalized linear models. *Journal of the Royal Statistical Society A, 135*, 370–384.

Paolino, P. (2001). Maximum likelihood estimation of models with beta-distributed dependent variables. *Political Analysis, 9*, 325–346.

Piegorsch, W. W. (1992). Complementary log regression for generalized linear models. *American Statistician, 46*, 94–99.

Pierce, D. A., & Schafer, D. W. (1986). Residuals in generalized linear models. *Journal of the American Statistical Association, 81*, 977–986.

Raudenbush, S. W., & Bryk, A. S. (2002). *Hierarchical linear models* (2nd ed.). Thousand Oaks: Sage Publications.

Rizopoulos, D., Verbeke, G., Lesaffre, E., & Vanrenterghem, Y. (2008). A two-part joint model for the analysis of survival and longitudinal binary data with excess zeros. *Biometrics, 64*, 611–619.

Ross, S. M. (2006). *A first course in probability* (7th ed.). Upper Saddle River, NJ: Pearson Prentice Hall.

Schwarz, G. (1978). Estimating the dimension of a model. *Annals of Statistics, 6*, 461–464.

Skrondal, A., & Rabe-Hesketh, S. (2004). *Generalized latent variable modeling: Multilevel, longitudinal and structural equation models*. Boca Raton, FL: Chapman & Hall/CRC.

Smithson, M., & Verkuilen, J. (2006). A better lemon squeezer? Maximum-likelihood regression with beta-distributed dependent variables. *Psychological Methods, 11*, 54–71.

Song, X., Davidian, M., & Tsiatis, A. A. (2002). A semiparametric likelihood approach to joint modeling of longitudinal and time-to-event data. *Biometrics, 58*, 742–753.

Vuong, Q. H. (1989). Likelihood ratio tests for model selection and non-nested hypotheses. *Econometrica, 57*, 307–333.

West, S. G., Aiken, L. S., & Kwok, O. (2003, August). *Hierarchical and generalized linear models: What multiple regression didn't tell us*. Address to the American Psychological Association, Toronto, Ontario, Canada.

Wilks, S. S. (1938). The large-sample distribution of the likelihood ratio for testing composite hypotheses. *Annals of Mathematical Statistics, 9*, 60–62.

Windmeijer, F. A. (1995). Goodness-of-fit measures in binary choice models. *Econometric Reviews, 14*, 101–116.

Winship, C., & Mare, R. D. (1984). Regression models with ordinal variables. *American Sociological Review, 49*, 512–525.

CHAPTER 4

Categorical Methods

Carol M. Woods

Abstract

Categorical methods refer to statistical procedures for analyzing data when the outcome variable is binary, nominal, or ordinal, according to Stevens' (1946) popular taxonomy of scale types. Myriad such methods exist. This chapter is focused specifically on methods for a single binary or ordinal outcome. The methods addressed are: the Pearson χ^2 statistic, the mean score statistic, the correlation statistic, midrank scores, odds ratios, differences between proportions, the γ-family measures of ordinal association, the Mantel-Haenszel test, the Mantel test, average conditional effect sizes, the Breslow-Day-Tarone test, binary logistic regression, and the proportional odds logistic regression model.

Key Words: Discrete, binary, ordinal, Likert-type, chi-square, logistic, Mantel-Haenszel

Introduction

Categorical methods refer to statistical procedures for analyzing data when the outcome variable is binary, nominal, or ordinal, according to Stevens' (1946) popular taxonomy of scale types. A chapter of this length could not begin to address all methods that have been developed for such data, so it is useful to first clarify the scope. This chapter focuses on methods for assessing relationships among observed variables, when the observations are independent, and there is a single outcome variable. Therefore, methods involving latent variables, multiple outcomes, or dependency in the data caused by matched pairs, clustering, or repeated measurements over time, are not addressed here. Emphasis is placed on binary and ordinal variables because these seem to be more popular outcomes in psychology than nominal variables.

The methods to be addressed are: (1) χ^2 tests for bivariate association, including a control variable; (2) effect sizes for pairs of binary or ordinal variables (with and without a control variable); (3) binary logistic regression; and (4) the proportional odds logistic regression model (for an ordinal outcome). Tables 4.1 and 4.2 provide definitions of symbols and key terms, respectively, for the entire chapter.

Testing for Significant Association Between Two Categorical Variables

The classic Pearson χ^2 statistic is applicable for testing whether there is a significant association between two binary or nominal variables. (It does not violate statistical properties of the test to apply the classic χ^2 to ordinal variables, but the variables are treated as nominal, which reduces power and ignores information, so other tests are preferable.) For example, following a treatment outcome study for depression, was outcome (favorable vs. unfavorable) significantly associated with (treatment vs. placebo) group? Table 4.3 provides example data from such a study. They are provided in the form of a contingency table. By convention, the independent variable is placed on the rows, and the outcome variable is placed on the columns.

Table 4.1. List of Symbols Used in This Chapter

a_j	midrank score; $\left[\sum_{l<j} n_{+l}\right] + \dfrac{(n_{+j}+1)}{2}$	
b	GLM parameter (appears with a subscript)	
BD	$\sum_{h=1}^{q} \dfrac{\left[n_{h11} - E\left(n_{h11}\vert\hat{\psi}_{MH}\right)\right]^2}{var\left(n_{h11}\vert\hat{\psi}_{MH}\right)}$, Breslow-Day statistic	
C	total number or concordant pairs	
D	total number of discordant pairs	
df	degrees of freedom	
E	Expected frequency for use in Q_{HL}	
$E(\ )$	Expected value	
$\bar{f}_i$	$\sum_{j=1}^{J} \dfrac{a_j n_{ij}}{n_{i+}}$, mean (over columns) for row i	
$g(\ )$	GLM link function	
G	$\sum_{i=1}^{I}\sum_{j=1}^{J} \dfrac{\left(n_{ij} - m_{ij}\right)^2}{m_{ij}}$, classic Pearson χ^2	
h	counter for strata, $h = 1, 2, 3, \ldots q$	
ℓ	optimized log of the likelihood function	
log	Natural log function	
m_{ij}	$\dfrac{n_{i+}n_{+j}}{N}$, expected value of n_{ij} under the null hypothesis	
M^2	$(N-1)r^2$, correlation statistic	
n_{ij}	observed frequency in the ij cell	
n_{hij}	observed frequency in the ij cell of stratum h	
n_{i+}	marginal frequency for row i	
n_{+j}	marginal frequency for column j	
n_h	total sample size for stratum h	
N	total sample size	
O	observed frequency for use in Q_{HL}	
p_1	$\dfrac{n_{11}}{n_{1+}}$, proportion of participants with outcome 1 for group 1	
p_2	$\dfrac{n_{21}}{n_{2+}}$, proportional of participants with outcome 1 for group 2	
p_{1i}	model predicted probability of responding in category 1	
p_{2i}	model predicted probability of responding in category 2	

Table 4.1. Continued

p_{3i}	model predicted probability of responding in category 3
$p_{[1 \text{ or } 2]i}$	model predicted probability of responding in category 1 or 2
Q_{HL}	$\displaystyle\sum_{\text{all O-E pairs}} \frac{(O-E)^2}{E}$, Hosmer-Lemeshow fit statistic
Q_{Mantel}	$\displaystyle\frac{\left(\sum_{h=0}^{q} T_h - \sum_{h=0}^{q} E(T_h)\right)^2}{\sum_{h=0}^{q} \sigma_{T_h}^2}$, Mantel statistic; $T_h = \displaystyle\sum_{i=1}^{I}\sum_{j=1}^{J} u_i v_j n_{hij}$ $$E(T_h) = \frac{\left[\sum_{i=1}^{I} u_i n_{hi+}\right]\left[\sum_{j=1}^{J} v_j n_{h+j}\right]}{n_h}$$ $$\sigma_{T_h}^2 = \frac{1}{n_h - 1}\left[\sum_{i=1}^{I} u_i^2 n_{hi+} - \frac{\left(\sum_{i=1}^{I} u_i n_{hi+}\right)^2}{n_h}\right]\left[\sum_{j=1}^{J} v_j^2 n_{h+j} - \frac{\left(\sum_{j=1}^{J} v_j n_{h+j}\right)^2}{n_h}\right]$$
Q_{MH}	$\displaystyle\frac{\left[\sum_{h=1}^{q}(n_{h11} - E(n_{h11}))\right]^2}{\sum_{h=1}^{q} var(n_{h11})}$, Mantel Haenszel statistic; $E(n_{h11}) = \dfrac{n_{h1+}n_{h+1}}{n_h} \quad var(n_{h11}) = \dfrac{n_{h1+}n_{h2+}n_{h+1}n_{h+2}}{n_h^2(n_h - 1)}$
Q_s	$\displaystyle\frac{(N-1)\sum_{i=1}^{I} n_{i+}(\bar{f}_i - \mu)^2}{Nv}$, mean score statistic
SE	standard error
u_i	scores on row variable used for Q_{Mantel} formula
v_j	scores on column variable used for Q_{Mantel} formula
$var_{p_1 - p_2}$	$\dfrac{p_1(1-p_1)}{n_{1+}} + \dfrac{p_2(1-p_2)}{n_{2+}}$
x	predictor in GLM (appears with subscript)
X	row variable (may be predictor)
Y	column variable (may be outcome)
z	deviate of the standard normal distribution
μ	An expected value. (1) Context of Q_s: $\displaystyle\sum_{j=1}^{J} \frac{a_j n_{+j}}{N}$, expected value of $\bar{f}_i$ under H$_o$ or (2) Context of GLM: expected value of y (the outcome variable)

Table 4.1. Continued

φ	odds ratio
$\hat{\varphi}_{LA}$	$\dfrac{\sum_{h=1}^{q} \dfrac{1}{n_h} \sum_{j=1}^{c-1} A_{hj} D_{hj}}{\sum_{h=1}^{q} \dfrac{1}{n_h} \sum_{j=1}^{c-1} B_{hj} C_{hj}}$, Liu-Agresti (1996) cumulative average conditional odds ratio estimator
$\hat{\psi}_{MH}$	$\dfrac{\sum_{h=1}^{q} \dfrac{n_{h11} n_{h22}}{n_h}}{\sum_{h=1}^{q} \dfrac{n_{h12} n_{h21}}{n_h}}$, Mantel-Haenszel estimator of the average conditional odds ratio
v	$\sum_{j=1}^{J} \left(a_j - \mu \right)^2 \left(\dfrac{n_{+j}}{N} \right)$, variance of $\bar{f}_i$

Note. Gamma-family measures of ordinal association are defined in Table 6.

Table 4.2. Key Terms Used in This Chapter

Concordant pair: An X – Y pairing such that when there is an increase in two values of X ($x_i > x_j$), the corresponding two values of Y also increase ($y_i > y_j$). Or the pairs may both decrease (i.e., $x_i < x_j$ and $y_i < y_j$).

Consistent: as the sample size increases, the probability that a consistent estimate differs from the true value by a small amount goes to 0

Continuity correction: modification to a statistic to improve the approximation of a discrete distribution by a continuous distribution.

Differential item functioning: when an item has different measurement properties for one group versus another group irrespective of true mean differences on the construct.

Discordant pair: An X – Y pairing such that when there is an increase in two values of X ($x_i > x_j$), the corresponding two values of Y decrease ($y_i < y_j$), or vice versa (i.e., $x_i < x_j$ and $y_i > y_j$).

Efficient: among consistent estimators, this estimator has the smallest variance

Link function: in a generalized linear model, the function that specifies how the outcome variable relates to the predictors.

Logit: natural log of the odds

Marginal: frequency obtained by summing across either rows or columns of a contingency table

Midranks: rank scores computed such that individuals in each columnwise category are assigned the mean of the ranks that would apply for a complete ranking of everyone in the whole sample.

Monotonic association: degree to which larger X-values are associated with larger Y-values (and vice versa).

Standard normal deviate: number that takes on values of the standard normal distribution

Stratification variable: control variable. Levels are strata (one level is a stratum).

Tied pair: A pair is tied if they have the same value on the variable (i.e., $x_i = x_j$, $y_i = y_j$, or both).

Table 4.3. Example Data: Treatment Outcome Study for Depression (Hypothetical)

	Favorable	Unfavorable	
Treatment	55	15	70
Placebo	30	50	80
	85	65	150

The Pearson χ^2 is equal to the difference between observed and expected frequencies, squared, divided by the expected frequency, summed over all of the cells in the table: $G = \sum_{i=1}^{I}\sum_{j=1}^{J}\frac{(n_{ij}-m_{ij})^2}{m_{ij}}$, where $i = 1, 2, 3, ..., I$ counts rows of a contingency table, or levels of the independent variable (e.g., treatment groups), $j = 1, 2, 3, ..., J$ counts columns or levels of the outcome variable (e.g., outcomes); n_{ij} = observed frequency in the ij cell of the data table; m_{ij} = expected value of n_{ij} under Ho: rows and columns are independent; and $m_{ij} = \frac{n_{i+}n_{+j}}{N}$. Frequencies with "+" are marginals ("+" refers to summation over the missing index), and N is the total sample size. When the expected frequencies are adequate (e.g., at least about five per cell), G follows a χ^2 distribution with $df = (I-1)(J-1)$.

For the example data in Table 4.3, $m_{11} = \frac{(70)(85)}{150} = 39.67$, $m_{12} = \frac{(70)(65)}{150} = 30.33$, $m_{21} = \frac{(80)(85)}{150} 45.33$, and $m_{22} = \frac{(80)(65)}{150} = 34.67$. With frequencies from Table 4.3 plugged in, $G = \frac{(55-39.67)^2}{39.67} + \frac{(15-30.33)^2}{30.33} + \frac{(30-45.33)^2}{45.33} + \frac{(50-34.67)^2}{34.67} = 25.63$, and $df = 1$. Because 25.63 is much larger than 1, it is clear that we reject Ho with any reasonable α level and conclude that there is a significant association between treatment group and treatment outcome.

The Pearson χ^2 generalizes for variables with more than two levels (i.e., nominal variables), it just becomes more tedious to compute by hand. It is widely implemented in statistical software packages. A couple of other χ^2-distributed tests also test bivariate association for binary and nominal variables: the Randomization χ^2, and the Likelihood ratio χ^2. These statistics are also implemented in popular software programs (e.g., SAS). The three tests are asymptotically equivalent, and I am not aware of any reason to prefer either of these two over the classic Pearson χ^2.

When at least one of the variables is ordinal, power for testing whether there is an association between two variables is greater if the ordinality of the variable(s) is considered. Valid application of these tests requires the assignment of scores, usually rank scores, to the ordinal variable before the χ^2 statistic is computed. A popular type of rank score is the midrank. Midranks are computed according to the following formula:

$$a_j = \left[\sum_{l<j} n_{+l}\right] + \frac{(n_{+j}+1)}{2}, \quad (1)$$

where n_{+j} is the marginal column frequency. For the most part, a midrank is the column marginal with 1 added to it and 2 divided from it. The term in brackets in Equation 1 indicates that the marginal frequency for the column previous to the one of interest is added in as well. By this formula, individuals in each columnwise category are assigned the mean of the ranks that would apply for a complete ranking of everyone in the whole sample. Consider the example data in the upper panel of Table 4.4. Interest lies in testing whether there is a significant association between nominal treatment group and ordinally rated improvement in symptoms. The midrank scores are computed in the lower panel of Table 4.4.

When one variable is ordinal, a statistic that tests H_a: the mean of the ordinal variable is not equal for all rows, is the mean score statistic:

$$Q_s = \frac{(N-1)\sum_{i=1}^{I} n_{i+}(\bar{f}_i-\mu)^2}{Nv},$$

where N = total sample size, n_{i+} = row marginal, $\bar{f}_i$ = mean (over columns) for row i, μ = expected value of $\bar{f}_i$ under H_o: rows and columns are independent (assumed constant over rows), and v = variance of $\bar{f}_i$ (assumed constant over rows). Row means are computed by weighting midranks by cell frequencies: $\bar{f}_i = \sum_{j=1}^{J}\frac{a_j n_{ij}}{n_{i+}}$, where a_j is a midrank score as given in Equation 1. The expected value is a grand mean, or the mean of the outcome variable averaging over levels of the row variable:

$$\mu = \sum_{j=1}^{J}\frac{a_j n_{+j}}{N}, \text{ and } v = \sum_{j=1}^{J}(a_j - \mu)^2 \left(\frac{n_{+j}}{N}\right)^2.$$

Continuing the example from Table 4.4, calculations are:

$$\bar{f}_A = \sum_{j=1}^{J}\frac{a_j n_{1j}}{n_{1+}}$$

$$= \frac{55.5(20) + 145.5(40) + 240.5(40)}{100}$$

Table 4.4. Example Data: Hypothetical Treatment Study

Treatment	Improvement none	some	marked	
A	20	40	40	100
B	20	10	70	100
placebo	70	20	10	100
	110	70	120	300

Midrank scores:

group	$\left[\sum_{l<j} n_{+l}\right]$	$\frac{(n_{+j}+1)}{2}$	a_j
none	0	$\frac{(110+1)}{2} = 55.5$	55.5
some	110	$\frac{(70+1)}{2} = 35.5$	145.5
marked	110 + 70	$\frac{(120+1)}{2} = 60.5$	240.5

$$= 165.5$$

$$\bar{f}_B = \sum_{j=1}^{J} \frac{a_j n_{2j}}{n_{2+}}$$

$$= \frac{55.5(20) + 145.5(10) + 240.5(70)}{100}$$

$$= 194$$

$$\bar{f}_{placebo} = \sum_{j=1}^{J} \frac{a_j n_{3j}}{n_{3+}}$$

$$= \frac{55.5(70) + 145.5(20) + 240.5(10)}{100}$$

$$= 92$$

$$\mu = \sum_{j=1}^{J} \frac{a_j n_{+j}}{N}$$

$$= \frac{55.5(110) + 145.5(70) + 240.5(120)}{300}$$

$$= 150.5, \text{ and}$$

$$v = \sum_{j=1}^{J} (a_j - \mu)^2 \left(\frac{n_{+j}}{N}\right) = (55.5 - 150.5)^2$$

$$\left(\frac{110}{300}\right) = (240.5 - 150.5)^2 \left(\frac{120}{300}\right)$$

$$= 6555. \text{ Thus,}$$

$$Q_s = \frac{(299)\begin{bmatrix} 100(165.5 - 150.5)^2 + \\ 100(194 - 150.5)^2 \\ + 100(92 - 150.5)^2 \end{bmatrix}}{300(6555)}$$

$$= 84.23.$$

When the sample size is adequate (explained below), Q_s is χ^2-distributed with $I - 1$ *df* (I = total number of rows). Here *df* = 2 and H₀ is rejected with any reasonable α level. In this example, the mean improvement is statistically significantly different for different treatment groups, and we can see from the $\bar{f}_i$ that the mean improvement is largest for group B, followed by group A, followed by placebo. If researchers desire *post hoc* statistical comparisons between the groups following a significant omnibus Q_s test, Mann-Whitney U tests could be carried out, probably with an α correction for multiple testing, which is particularly important if many groups are compared. A Mann-Whitney U test (*see*, e.g., Higgins, 2004) is an alternative to an independent samples *t*-test when normality is violated, as is necessarily true for binary and ordinal data.

A rule of thumb sample size guideline for Q_s is to perform the following using the data in contingency table form: select any column other than the first or last to use as the cut-point column, k, and

Table 4.5. Hypothetical Data: Relating Responses to Two Questionnaire Items

	Item 2			
Item 1	Not at all	Somewhat	A great deal	
Strongly agree	32	14	4	50
Agree	28	12	5	45
Disagree	15	21	8	44
Strongly disagree	10	10	28	48
	85	57	45	187

add together all frequencies in columns before and including the cut-point (1st through kth column) and then add together all frequencies in columns after the cut-point ($[k+1]$th through Jth column). The sample is probably sufficient if all sums are about 5 or greater (Stokes, Davis, & Koch, 2000, p. 69).

If both variables are ordinal, then numerous options are available for testing whether there is an association between them. Here, I discuss a χ^2 statistic designed for this purpose; alternative strategies are given subsequently. If midrank scores are first assigned to each ordinal variable, then it is applicable to test for monotonic association using the correlation statistic: $M^2 = (N-1)r^2$ with $df = 1$, where N = total sample size, and r = Pearson product moment correlation between the row and column variables. Monotonic association is the degree to which larger X values are associated with larger Y values (and vice versa). Monotonicity is less restrictive than linearity; curvilinear associations can be monotonic. Note that when Pearson's r is computed with rank scores, it is Spearman's rank correlation.

Consider the example in Table 4.5, where interest lies in relating the ordinal responses given to two questionnaire items. Midrank scores are computed for both the row and column variables, as illustrated in the previous example, and the Pearson (Spearman) correlation is 0.4335. Thus, $M^2 = (187-1)(0.4335)^2 = 34.95$ with $df = 1$, and we conclude that there is a significant positive monotonic association between the item scores. Remember that the sample size must be adequate to validly treat M^2 as χ^2. Some rules of thumb for "adequate" are: (1) $N \geq$ about 20, and (2) if you collapse the contingency table (summing cell counts) into all possible 2 × 2 tables, all cell counts should be about greater than or equal to 5 (Stokes et al., 2000, p. 104).

One limitation of χ^2 tests is that there is no measure of effect size. If the sample is large enough, then the test is significant, but there is no indication about the degree to which the relation between variables might be practically meaningful. Thus, it is useful to use significance tests in combination with one or more measures of effect size. The next section is focused on measures of effect size for relationships between categorical variables.

Measuring Strength of Association Between Two Categorical Variables
Two Binary Variables

When both variables are binary, two popular methods for measuring the strength of their association are a comparison of proportions and an odds ratio. A proportion is our best estimate of the population probability and takes on values between 0 and 1 (thus, the difference between two proportions takes values between –1 and 1). Considering the data in Table 4.3 as an example, our best guesses of the probability that participants in the treatment and placebo groups (respectively) will have favorable outcome are $55/70 = 0.786$ and $30/80 = 0.375$. The general formulas for these proportions are: $p_1 = \frac{n_{11}}{n_{1+}}$, $p_2 = \frac{n_{21}}{n_{2+}}$. The proportion of participants with favorable outcome is much larger for the treatment group than the placebo group.

A confidence interval (CI) for the difference between proportions can be computed as: $p_1 - p_2 \pm \left\{ z\left(\sqrt{var_{p_1-p_2}}\right) + \frac{1}{2}\left(\frac{1}{n_{1+}} + \frac{1}{n_{2+}}\right) \right\}$, where z is a standard normal deviate such as 1.96 for a 95% CI, and $var_{p_1-p_2} = \frac{p_1(1-p_1)}{n_{1+}} + \frac{p_2(1-p_2)}{n_{2+}}$ (Fleiss, Levin, & Paik, 2003, p. 60). For the data in Table 4.3, $var_{p_1-p_2} = \frac{0.786(0.214)}{70} + \frac{0.375(0.625)}{80} = 0.00533$ and $0.411 \pm \left\{ 1.96\left(\sqrt{0.00533}\right) + \frac{1}{2}\left(\frac{1}{70} + \frac{1}{80}\right) \right\}$. To facilitate interpretation, the proportions can be subtracted in whichever order renders the result positive. The 95% CI for the treatment outcome example is (0.255, 0.567). Plausible values for the true difference in proportion of favorable outcome for the treatment and placebo groups range from 0.255 to 0.567.

The odds ratio is a function of proportions (because proportions estimate probabilities). When we have two mutually exclusive, exhaustive events like favorable versus unfavorable outcome (for each group), the ratio of the probabilities is the odds. For the data in Table 4.3, the odds of favorable outcome for the treatment group are: $Odds = \frac{p_1}{1-p_1} = \frac{0.7857}{0.2143} = 3.666$ and the odds of favorable outcome for the placebo group are: $Odds = \frac{p_2}{1-p_2} = \frac{0.375}{0.625} = 0.600$. A comparison of these odds is their ratio: $\varphi = \frac{\frac{p_1}{1-p_1}}{\frac{p_2}{1-p_2}} = \frac{3.666}{0.600} = 6.111$. The odds of favorable outcome for the treatment group are 6.111 times the odds of favorable outcome for the placebo group.

Notice that the odds ratio may also be computed using the frequencies directly:

$$\varphi = \frac{\frac{p_1}{1-p_1}}{\frac{p_2}{1-p_2}} = \frac{\frac{n_{11}}{n_{1+}}\left(\frac{n_{1+}}{n_{12}}\right)}{\frac{n_{21}}{n_{2+}}\left(\frac{n_{2+}}{n_{22}}\right)} = \frac{\frac{n_{11}}{n_{12}}}{\frac{n_{21}}{n_{22}}} = \frac{n_{11}n_{22}}{n_{12}n_{21}}. \quad (2)$$

For the data in Table 4.3, $\varphi = \frac{n_{11}n_{22}}{n_{12}n_{21}} = \frac{55(50)}{15(30)} = 6.111$. Odds ratios can take on values between 0 to $+\infty$, and notice that $\varphi = 1$ indicates that the odds are equivalent for the two groups. As with other effect sizes, values of φ considered large or important depend on norms and how the numbers relate to real-world outcomes for a particular research area.

Two Ordinal Variables

When both variables are ordinal (a binary variable can be considered ordinal), many researchers have been taught to use Spearman's (1904) rank correlation, r_s (see Lovie, 1995, for a historical account of this coefficient, which is not unilaterally due to Spearman). It can be produced by applying the well-known formula for Pearson's r to ranked data (thus scores on both X and Y are equally spaced integers from 1 to N). The mean rank (i.e., midrank) is usually assigned for ties.

Although r_s is well known and simple to compute, Freeman (1986) points out that its computation presumes more than just ordinality for the data. Empirical evidence of this is apparent in the fact that r_s can be non-zero even when the total number of concordant (C) and discordant (D) pairs are equal. C and D (defined below) are the building blocks of effect sizes that do consider only ordinality; these indices are always 0 when C and D are equal. The majority of authors who specialize in ordinal effect sizes have rejected r_s for one reason or another, and given modern computing power, we can do better.

The γ (Goodman & Kruskal, 1954) family of effect sizes are often a good choice for quantifying the strength of monotonic association between ordinal row and column variables. The indices compare pairs of observations on X (e.g., row variable) and pairs of observations on Y (e.g., column variable). If an increase in X occurs with an increase in Y (i.e., $x_i > x_j$ and $y_i > y_j$), or if both X and Y decrease (i.e., $x_i < x_j$ and $y_i < y_j$), then the X-Y pair is *concordant* (x_i and x_j are two different realizations of variable X, and y_i and y_j are defined analogously). If X and Y change in opposite directions (i.e., $x_i > x_j$ and $y_i < y_j$ or $x_i < x_j$ and $y_i > y_j$), then the pair is *discordant*. The pair is tied if they have the same value on the variable (i.e., $x_i = x_j, y_i = y_j$, or both). For all i and j, the total number of concordant pairs is C, and the total number of discordant pairs is D. The number of pairs tied on only X, only Y, or both X and Y is T_x, T_y, and T_{xy}, respectively. The sum of C, D, T_x, T_y, and T_{xy} is the total number of nonredundant pairings.

Table 4.6 lists 10 indices in the γ family identified by Woods (2007; *see also* Woods, 2008); they form a family because they all reduce to γ in the absence of ties. All indices in Table 4.6 are a function of the difference between C and D and (theoretically) range from –1 (perfect negative association) to 1 (perfect positive association), with values farther from 0 indicating stronger association. If X and Y are independent, then all indices are 0, but 0 does not necessarily imply independence because an index can be 0 when X and Y are associated non-monotonically (e.g., by a U-shaped relation; Agresti, 1984, p. 160). It can be useful to plot X and Y to check for non-monotonicity.

Perhaps the two most well-known members of the gamma family are γ (Goodman & Kruskal, 1954; Yule, 1900) and τ_a (Kendall, 1938). All tied pairs are excluded from γ, whereas all pairs are included in τ_a. In the presence of ties, the (absolute) upper limit of τ_a is the proportion of pairs untied on either variable, rather than 1. An alternative, τ_b, was proposed to correct τ_a for ties (Daniels, 1944; Kendall, 1945). Wilson (1974) also proposed a modified version of τ_a that excludes T_{xy} from the denominator (*see* Table 4.6).

A limitation of τ_a, τ_b, and Wilson's e is that the theoretical bounds cannot be reached when the number of categories for X and Y are unequal

Table 4.6. Gamma-Family Indices of Ordinal Association

Index	Reference
$\gamma = \dfrac{C-D}{C+D}$	Goodman & Kruskal (1954)
	Yule (1990)
$\tau_a = \dfrac{C-D}{\frac{1}{2}N(N-1)} = \dfrac{C-D}{C+D+T_x+T_y+T_{xy}}$	Kendall (1938)
$\tau_b = \dfrac{C-D}{\sqrt{(C+D+T_x)(C+D+T_y)}}$	Daniels (1944)
	Kendall (1945)
$e = \dfrac{C-D}{C+D+T_x+T_y}$	Wilson (1974)
$\tau_c = \dfrac{C-D}{\frac{1}{2}N^2 \dfrac{(m-1)}{m}}$	Stuart (1953)
$d_{yx} = \dfrac{C-D}{C+D+T_y} = d^K_{xy}, \quad d_{xy} = \dfrac{C-D}{C+D+T_x} = d^K_{yx}$	Somers (1962a)
	Kim (1971)
$d^{LG}_{yx} = \dfrac{C-D}{C+D+2T_y}, \quad d^{LG}_{xy} = \dfrac{C-D}{C+D+2T_x}$	Leik & Gove (1969)
$d^K = \dfrac{C-D}{C+D+\left(\frac{1}{2}T_x\right)+\left(\frac{1}{2}T_y\right)}$	Kim (1971)

Note. C = number of concordant pairs, D = number of discordant pairs, N = sample size, m = the smaller number of categories, T_x = number of pairs tied on X but not on Y, T_y = number of pairs tied on Y but not on X, T_{xy} = number of pairs tied on both X and Y.

(Agresti, 1976; Liebetrau, 1983; Stuart, 1953). This limitation is not a weakness if a one-to-one monotonic relationship is of interest, because such a relation can exist only when categories of X and Y are equal (*see* Freeman, 1986). Nevertheless, Stuart (1953) introduced τ_c to correct for this attenuation by dividing $C - D$ by the maximum value it can attain with unequal levels of X and Y.

Three asymmetric ordinal indices, Somers' (1962a) d_{yx}, Leik and Gove's (1969) d^{LG}_{yx}, and Kim's (1971) d^K_{yx}, were developed to focus on predictive relationships. The subscript "yx" specifies Y as the dependent variable (DV) and X as the independent variable (IV); "xy" refers to the opposite assignment. Somers' (1962a) and Leik and Gove's (1969) measures ignore ties on the IV, whereas Kim's measures ignore ties on the DV. Notice that $d^K_{yx} = d_{xy}$ and $d^K_{xy} = d_{yx}$. Kim (1971) also presented a symmetric index, d^K, which is a weighted sum of d^K_{yx} and d^K_{xy}, with weights proportional to the number of ties on each variable.

Substantial commentary is published on interpretational differences among the ordinal measures (Costner, 1965, 1968; Freeman, 1986; Gonzalez & Nelson, 1996; Kim, 1971; Leik & Gove, 1969, 1971; Somers, 1962a, 1962b, 1968; Wilson, 1969, 1971, 1974). Criteria suggested for evaluating and comparing them include simple interpretation, interpretation in terms of proportional reduction in error, known upper and lower bounds, and simplicity (or availability) of sampling theory. Liebetrau (1983) recommends that investigators "choose a measure that can assume its extreme values for the type of association" considered important (p. 88). Readers wishing to select an ordinal measure for a particular application are encouraged to consult this literature, especially Freeman (1986).

Confidence intervals are available for the γ family indices. In simulations, Woods (2007) found that CIs using the "consistent" standard error (SE) formula derived by Cliff and Charlin (1991), along with a deviate of the t ($df = N- 2$) distribution performed the best (compared to alternative CIs computed differently) for τ_a, τ_b and Somers' d_{yx} (or d_{xy}). At that time, the best-performing Cliff and Charlin consistent (CC) SEs were not available for the other γ family indices. Woods (2009a) derived CC SEs for γ, Wilson's e, τ_c, d_{yx}^{LG} (or d_{xy}^{LG}), and d^K and similarly found support for the superiority of the CC CIs. Based on accuracy of the CC CIs in research by Woods (2007, 2009a), τ_a τ_b, e, τ_c, and d^K seem to be the best choices in the γ family for four- and five-category variables and small N (i.e., $25 < N < 100$).

Association With a Control Variable
Significance Testing

Simple methods requiring few assumptions also may be used to test for a significant association between the row (X) and column (Y) variables, controlling for a third variable. For the methods discussed here, statistical control refers to averaging over levels of the variable. The control variable is sometimes called a stratification variable, with levels referred to as strata, and an individual level a stratum. With a control variable, there are sets of tables, one table for every stratum. A variable is statistically controlled in the context of categorical analysis for some of the same reasons this is done with continuous data: to control possible confounding variables, increase power, and find effects that might not otherwise be found. The control variable may be continuous or categorical.

To validly apply the methods, it is necessary for the effects to be in the same direction (e.g., odds ratios all greater than 1 or all less than 1) across tables, because effects in opposite directions reduce power or cancel out completely, making it appear as though there is no relationship between X and Y. If there is a possibility that the effect changes direction over tables, then individual tables should be examined before the more omnibus statistic is applied. If the effects vary much over tables, then this is moderation (the same phenomenon as when there is a significant interaction in a regression model) and the omnibus test should not be used. Individual tables could be analyzed, conditional on stratum, with methods described above if the number of strata is small. Or if assumptions are justifiable, then a regression model for a categorical outcome (e.g., logistic regression) with an interaction term could be used instead.

Mantel and Haenszel (1959) introduced a test of significance for 2×2 tables:

$$Q_{MH} = \frac{\left[\sum_{h=1}^{q}(n_{h11} - E(n_{h11}))\right]^2}{\sum_{h=1}^{q} \text{var}(n_{h11})}, \quad (3)$$

where $h = 1, 2, 3, ..., q$ counts strata; n_{m11} is the observed frequency in the row 1 column 1 cell for statum h; E and var are the expected value and variance under the null hypothesis of independence: $E(n_{h11}) = \frac{n_{h1+}n_{h+1}}{n_h}$, $var(n_{h11}) = \frac{n_{h1+}n_{h2+}n_{h+1}n_{h+2}}{n_h^2(n_h-1)}$; and n_h is the stratum specific sample size. For a single stratum (i.e., no control variable), Q_{MH} is equal to the randomization χ^2 referred to above.

The statistic can be computed with a continuity correction, by replacing the numerator in Equation 3 with: $\left[\left|\sum_{h=1}^{q}(n_{h11} - E(n_{h11}))\right| - \frac{1}{2}\right]^2$ (where the vertical bars indicate absolute value). The correction improves the approximation of the discrete data to the continuous χ^2 distribution. With the correction, the p-value better approximates an exact conditional test, but it tends to be conservative (Agresti, 2002, p. 232). Under the null hypothesis, when row and column marginal totals are assumed fixed, and the sample size is sufficient, Q_{MH} is distributed $\chi^2(df = 1)$. Mantel and Fleiss (1980) have provided a rule of thumb for determining whether a small sample is adequate for Q_{MH} to be $\chi^2(1)$ that generalizes the rule for a single 2×2 table that each expected frequency should be at least 5.

For sets of 2×2 tables, a significance test may be used for the homogeneity assumption. Jones, O'Gorman, Lemke, and Woolson, (1989) studied seven tests for homogeneity of odds ratios in sets of 2×2 tables and recommended the Breslow-Day (BD) test (Breslow & Day, 1980, p. 142) for general use when the data are not sparse.

The BD statistic is:

$$BD = \sum_{h=1}^{q} \frac{\left[n_{h11} - E\left(n_{h11}|\hat{\psi}_{MH}\right)\right]^2}{\text{var}\left(n_{h11}|\hat{\psi}_{MH}\right)}, \quad (4)$$

where n_{h11} is the frequency in the row-1, column-1 cell, and the expected value and variance are functions of the average conditional odds ratio, $\hat{\psi}_{MH}$

Table 4.7. Hypothetical Data: Treatment Outcome Controlling Center

Center	Treatment	Improvement Yes No	Total
1	Test	28 16	44
1	Placebo	14 31	45
	Total	42 47	89
2	Test	37 8	45
2	Placebo	24 21	45
	Total	61 29	90

(see Equation 6), and computed under the null hypothesis of homogeneity of odds ratios. Under the null hypothesis of homogeneity, BD is distributed approximately asymptotically χ^2 with $df = q-1$.

Breslow (1996) subsequently realized that the BD test is "asymptotically invalid." Tarone (1985) first identified a problem related to the fact that BD is a function of $\hat{\psi}_{MH}$ and provided a corrected version of the BD test. A correction term is needed because $\hat{\psi}_{MH}$ is not efficient, in the sense of having the smallest variance among consistent estimators (Breslow, 1996; Tarone, 1985). However, because $\hat{\psi}_{MH}$ is close to efficient, the correction term is usually very small; as shown in simulations by Jones et al. (1989), there may often be little practical difference between the BD test and Tarone's corrected version. When Tarone's test is readily available, it is preferred, but it is unlikely to reverse the conclusion about homogeneity obtained from the BD test.

Example

Consider an example where we are interested in the association between binary improvement following treatment or placebo, controlling for center. Table 4.7 displays the data. This example happens to have only two centers, but there could be many centers (i.e., many levels of the stratification variable). A test of the homogeneity assumption should be carried out first. Tarone's correction results in a rather complicated statistic so it is preferable to avoid carrying out the Breslow-Day-Tarone test by hand. Here, SAS (version 9.2) was used, which produced the following output:

Breslow-Day-Tarone Test for Homogeneity of the Odds Ratios

Chi-Square	0.0043
DF	1
Pr > ChiSq	0.9480

Total Sample Size = 179

The nonsignificant result indicates no evidence of heterogeneity so we proceed under the assumption that odds ratios are homogeneous over strata.

Expected frequencies for the strata are: $m_{111} = \frac{n_{11+}n_{1+1}}{n_1} = \frac{(44)(42)}{89} = 20.76$ and $m_{211} = \frac{n_{21+}n_{2+1}}{n_2} = \frac{(45)(61)}{90} = 30.5$. Variances are $v_{111} = \frac{n_{11+}n_{12+}n_{1+1}n_{1+2}}{n_1^2(n_1-1)} = \frac{(44)(45)(42)(47)}{89^2(88)} = 5.607$ and $v_{211} = \frac{n_{21+}n_{22+}n_{2+1}n_{2+2}}{n_2^2(n_2-1)} = \frac{(45)(45)(61)(29)}{90^2(89)} = 4.969$. Therefore, the test statistic is, $Q_{MH} = \frac{[(n_{111}-m_{111})+(n_{211}-m_{211})]^2}{v_{111}+v_{211}} = \frac{[(28-20.76)+(37-30.5)]^2}{5.607+4.969} = \frac{(7.24+6.5)^2}{10.576} \approx 17.84$. This value of 17.84 is much larger than the $df = 1$; thus, it is significant at any reasonable α level, and we reject the null hypothesis of independence in favor of the conclusion that there is a significant association between treatment group and outcome, controlling for center.

Mantel (1963) described an extension of the Q_{MH} (which reduces to Q_{MH} for sets of 2 × 2 tables) for ordinal X and Y. The Mantel statistic is:

$$Q_{Mantel} = \frac{\left(\sum_{h=0}^{q} T_h - \sum_{h=0}^{q} E(T_h)\right)^2}{\sum_{h=0}^{q} \sigma_{T_h}^2}, \quad (5)$$

where h counts strata (1, 2, ..., q). X and Y should be assigned scores appropriate for ordinal data, such as midranks described in an earlier section of this chapter. $T_h = \sum_{i=1}^{I}\sum_{j=1}^{J} u_i v_j n_{hij}$, where u_i and v_j are scores on X and Y, respectively, and n_{hij} is a frequency for stratum h. $E(T_h)$ is the value expected if X and Y are independent: $E(T_h) = \frac{\left[\sum_{i=1}^{I} u_i n_{hi+}\right]\left[\sum_{j=1}^{J} v_j n_{h+j}\right]}{n_h}$. The variance is equal to the reciprocal of the within-strata sample size (less 1) multiplied by a term representing row variability and a term representing column variability: $\sigma_{T_h}^2 = \frac{1}{n_h-1}\left[\sum_{i=1}^{I} u_i^2 n_{hi+} - \frac{\left(\sum_{i=1}^{I} u_i n_{hi+}\right)^2}{n_h}\right]$

$\left[\sum_{j=1}^{J} v_j^2 n_{h+j} - \frac{\left(\sum_{j=1}^{J} v_j n_{h+j}\right)^2}{n_h}\right]$. Under the null hypothesis of independence, the Mantel statistic is distributed χ^2 ($df = 1$).

Table 4.8. Dumping Syndrome Data

Hospital 3:

Tissue removal	none	slight	moderate	Total	Midrank Score
0%	8	6	3	17	9
25%	12	4	4	20	27.5
50%	11	6	2	19	47
75%	7	7	4	18	65.5
Total	38	23	13	74	
Midrank Score	19.5	50	68		

Hospital 4:

Tissue removal	none	slight	moderate	Total	Midrank Score
0%	12	9	1	22	11.5
25%	15	3	2	20	32.5
50%	14	8	3	25	55
75%	13	6	4	23	79
Total	54	26	10	90	
Midrank Score	27.5	67.5	85.5		

Table 4.8 provides an example where we are interested in evaluating whether there is a significant relationship between the severity of dumping syndrome (i.e., severe ulcers) and the amount of stomach tissue removed in surgery, controlling for hospital. The data are (a subset of) the dumping syndrome data, which first appeared in Grizzle, Starmer, and Koch (1969), obtained for this chapter from Stokes et al. (2000). For manageability in illustrating computations, there are only two hospitals (i.e., two strata), but the methodology does well with many-valued stratification variables. Midrank scores (computed as described earlier) are also given in Table 4.8 and used to compute Q_{Mantel}.

For the third hospital,

$$T_1 = \sum_{i=1}^{I}\sum_{j=1}^{J} u_i v_j n_{1ij} = (9)(19.5)(4)$$
$$+ (9)(50)(6) + \cdots + (65.5)(68)(4)$$
$$= 105610.3,$$

$$E(T_1) = \frac{\left[\sum_{i=1}^{I} u_i n_{1i+}\right]\left[\sum_{j=1}^{J} v_j n_{1+j}\right]}{n_1}$$
$$= \frac{[(9)(32) + \cdots][(19.5)(38) + \cdots]}{74}$$
$$= 104062.5$$

and

$$\sigma_{T_1}^2 = \frac{1}{n_1 - 1}\left[\sum_{i=1}^{I} u_i^2 n_{1i+} - \frac{\left(\sum_{i=1}^{I} u_i n_{1i+}\right)^2}{n_1}\right]$$
$$\times \left[\sum_{j=1}^{J} v_j^2 n_{1+j} - \frac{\left(\sum_{j=1}^{J} v_j n_{1+j}\right)^2}{n_1}\right] =$$

$$\frac{1}{73}\left[((9^2)(17)+\cdots)-\frac{(2775)^2}{74}\right]$$
$$\times\left[((19.5^2)(38)+\cdots)-\frac{(2775)^2}{74}\right]$$
$$=12133539.$$

For the fourth hospital, $T_2 = 189,547.5$, $E(T_2) = \frac{(4095)(4095)}{90} = 186322.5$, and $\sigma_{T_2}^2 = 29,449,780$. Summing over hospitals, $Q_{Mantel} = \frac{[(105610.3+189547.5)-(104062.5+186322.5)]^2}{12133539+29449780} = 0.548$. Given $df = 1$, $p = 0.459$ and the conclusion is that controlling for hospital, the relationship between severity and percentage of tissue removed is not statistically significant.

Effect Sizes

Many of the same effect sizes discussed above for contingency tables are used for sets of contingency tables, except that they must now be computed in average conditional form. To compute an average conditional effect size, the bivariate index is computed between X and Y at each value of Z (where Z is the control variable), and the mean is taken over all levels of Z. The index must be presumed homogenous over strata, otherwise it is misleading to average over strata.

Along with Q_{MH}, Mantel and Haenszel (1959) introduced an estimator of the average conditional odds ratio:

$$\hat{\psi}_{MH} = \frac{\sum_{h=1}^{q}\frac{n_{h11}n_{h22}}{n_h}}{\sum_{h=1}^{q}\frac{n_{h12}n_{h21}}{n_h}}, \quad (6)$$

which ranges from 0 to $+\infty$ and is consistent (i.e., goes to 0 as sample size increases) but not efficient unless the odds ratio is exactly 1 (Tarone, Gart, & Hauck, 1983). This formula is intuitive when one considers Equation 2 for the odds ratio; here, we just incorporate the within-strata sample size (n_h), and sum over strata ($h = 1, 2, ..., q$).

For the example in Table 4.7, odds ratios for the individual centers are: $\frac{n_{11}n_{22}}{n_{12}n_{21}} = \frac{28(31)}{16(14)} = 3.875$ and $\frac{n_{11}n_{22}}{n_{12}n_{21}} = \frac{37(21)}{8(24)} = 4.047$. An average conditional estimator should equal approximately the average of these two values, which are relatively close to one another, justifying the homogeneity assumption. The MH estimator gives:

$$\hat{\psi}_{MH} = \frac{\sum_{h=1}^{q}\frac{n_{h11}n_{h22}}{n_h}}{\sum_{h=1}^{q}\frac{n_{h12}n_{h21}}{n_h}} = \frac{\frac{28(31)}{89}+\frac{37(21)}{90}}{\frac{16(14)}{89}+\frac{8(24)}{90}} = 3.95.$$

With center held constant, the odds of improvement for the treatment group are 3.95 times the odds of improvement for the placebo group.

For ordinal variables, all of the effect sizes in the γ family (discussed earlier in this chapter) may be computed in average conditional (ACO) form. An index such as $\gamma = \frac{C-D}{C+D}$ is computed for every I × J table, and the values from individual tables are averaged, possibly with weights. The indices are useful for descriptive purposes, but it is also useful to have an SE for them to use for confidence intervals and significance tests. Inference is not readily available for the ACO versions of all measures in the γ family. However, Quade (1974, building on the work of Davis, 1967) introduced an asymptotic SE that applies to a subset of ACO γ family measures. These five indices (ACO γ, τ_a, Wilson e, d_{yx}, d_{xy}) will be referred to as Quade-family indices.

An index is a member of the Quade (1974) family if it can be written in the form:

$$\frac{C_M - D_M}{R} = \frac{\sum_i(C_{Mi} - D_{Mi})}{\sum_i R_i} = \frac{\sum_i W_{Mi}}{\sum_i R_i}, \quad (7)$$

where C_M and D_M are the number of pairs matched on Z that are also concordant or discordant (respectively) with respect to X and Y. R is the number of relevant pairs, or those that could have been classified as concordant or discordant. For example, R for ACO γ is the number of pairs matched on Z but not tied on X or on Y. A "matched" pair may be defined differently for different problems. Quade (1974) presented the idea of matching pairs using tolerance (ε), which is the maximum discrepancy permitted between two observations before they are considered unmatched. When $\varepsilon = 0$, "matched" is the same as "tied" and $\varepsilon = 0$ is often the best choice, but realize that $\varepsilon > 0$ is possible and could be useful for some circumstances. Considering all matched pairs $i = 1, 2, ..., N_M$, R_i is the number of relevant pairs that include observation i, and $\sum_i R_i = 2R$. Of these, C_{Mi} is the number of concordant pairs that include observation i, D_{Mi} is the analogous quantity for discordant pairs, and W_{Mi} is the difference: $\sum_i W_{Mi} = 2(C_M - D_M)$.

Quade's (1974) asymptotic SE for indices in the form of Equation 7 is:

$$\sigma = \frac{2}{\left(\sum_i R_i\right)^2}$$

$$\times \sqrt{\left(\sum_i R_i\right)^2 \sum_i W_{Mi}^2 - 2\sum_i R_i \sum_i W_{Mi} \sum_i R_i W_{Mi} + \left(\sum_i W_{Mi}\right)^2 \sum_i R_i^2},$$

(8)

where summation is over all matched pairs. Confidence intervals and significance tests are carried out by treating the ratio of Equation 7 to Equation 8 as a deviate of the standard normal distribution.

I am not aware that popular computer software implements Quade family SEs at this time, but Woods (2009a) published code for the R program (R Development Core Team, 2005) that computes ACO indices in the Quade family, and their SEs. For the example in Table 4.8, this R code produces the following output.

Quade's (1974) Family of Average Conditional Ordinal Measures, with Asymptotic SEs:

Goodman & Kruskal's gamma = 0.1210495
SE: 0.1343878
Kendall's tau-a = 0.02872100 SE: 0.03183665
Wilson's e = 0.03877746 SE: 0.04281531
Somers' dyx = 0.06638326 SE: 0.07353472
Somers' dxy = 0.05267255 SE: 0.05816601

The interpretation of, for example, Wilson's *e* is: Controlling for hospital, the association between symptom severity and tissue removal is about 0.04, which is quite small. The asymptotic SE can be used for a 95% CI: 0.039 ± (0.043*1.96) = [–0.045, 0.123], which gives a plausible range of values for the index and shows that it is not significantly different from 0 (with $\alpha = 0.05$).

An additional effect size option with ordinal data is a cumulative average conditional odds ratio developed by Liu and Agresti (1996). Their estimator, $\hat{\varphi}_{LA}$, is the sum of all possible odds ratios computed for individual 2 × 2 tables constructed by collapsing categories at all possible places that preserve ordering. It requires assuming that the cumulative log-odds ratio is constant over categories.

The estimator is,

$$\hat{\varphi}_{LA} = \frac{\sum_{h=1}^{q} \frac{1}{n_h} \sum_{j=1}^{c-1} A_{hj} D_{hj}}{\sum_{h=1}^{q} \frac{1}{n_h} \sum_{j=1}^{c-1} B_{hj} C_{hj}},$$

(9)

where *h* counts strata, n_h is the within-strata sample size, and A_{hj}, B_{hj}, C_{hj}, and D_{hj} refer to frequencies in a 2 × 2 table constructed by collapsing response categories such that the response is either $\leq j$ or $> j$. For two binary variables, $\hat{\varphi}_{LA}$ reduces to $\hat{\psi}_{MH}$. Liu and Agresti (1996) derived a rather complicated variance estimator for $\hat{\varphi}_{LA}$ (given on p. 1225 of their article), which is not invariant to reversing the order of response categories. I am not aware that $\hat{\varphi}_{LA}$ is implemented in general purpose statistical software at this time; however, it is implemented in specialized software used in psychometrics for identifying differential item functioning (DIF, defined in the next section) written by Penfield (DIFAS, 2005), which is freely available.

Application to Differential Item Functioning

Q_{MH} and related methods have historically been more popular in medical contexts than in psychology; however, there are many uses for them in psychology. For example, Holland and Thayer (1988) described how Q_{MH} can be used to test for DIF. Differential item functioning occurs when an item on a test or questionnaire has different measurement properties for one group of people versus another, irrespective of mean differences on the construct. Test administrators seek to avoid bias in testing by identifying items that may be biased toward certain groups based on characteristics that covary with group membership (e.g., gender or ethnicity). The bias becomes particularly vital for high-stakes tests used to influence personnel selection or admission to training programs.

Q_{MH}-related methods (including χ^2_{Mantel}, the generalized Mantel Haenszel [MH] statistic [Somes, 1986] that handles nominal variables, effect sizes, and methodological refinements in this area) have become some of the most widely used tools for testing DIF. For many years, MH-related statistics were the dominant methodology used by the Educational Testing Service for DIF testing, and many psychometricians consider MH statistics gold standards against which new DIF methodologies must be evaluated.

To apply Q_{MH} to a DIF context, X is group membership (e.g., male/female or urban/rural region), Y is the binary item response (e.g., right/wrong, or true/false), and Z is a summed score (i.e., sum of all items on the test) used to match the two groups on the construct. A separate test is run for every item. If the test is significant, then there is an association between group and item response controlling for proficiency (as measured by summed scores), which is interpreted as DIF. Effect sizes provide information about the magnitude of DIF in addition to the binary result of a significance test. Kreiner and Christensen (2002, 2004) suggested using ACO γ for DIF testing, and Woods (2009b) presented and carried out simulations to test the Quade (1974) family of ACO measures for DIF testing.

Many methodological details about DIF testing with MH-type methods have been described and evaluated in the psychometric literature, and interested readers are urged to consult this literature before applying MH methods for DIF. For example, it is usually recommended that the matching criterion is purified so that it consists of only DIF-free items (not all items on the test), but it should always include the item being tested for DIF (Su & Wang, 2005; Wang & Su, 2004; Zwick et al., 1993).

Mantel Haenszel approaches do not model measurement error (there are no latent variables) and detect only one type of DIF (with respect to item difficulty, not other item characteristics such as discrimination). Nevertheless, they are worth having in the DIF toolkit because they are easy to implement, make few assumptions, are unlikely to have estimation difficulties, and may produce good answers with smaller sample sizes than the more advanced approaches that use latent variables and require more statistical assumptions.

All methods discussed so far are limited to, at most, three variables, which keeps things simple, but there are often more than two predictors of interest in our studies. We move now to models for one binary or ordinal response variable, which may include as many predictor variables as the sample size will support.

Logistic Regression

Logistic regression is one type of generalized linear model (Nelder & Wedderburn, 1972)—a class of models that generalizes the general linear model (GLM; i.e., the regression/ANOVA model) for use with a categorical outcome. For the linear regression model (for one person, thus subscripts on the xs for people are omitted for simplicity), $g[E(y|x)] = E(y|x) = \mu = b_o + b_1x_1 + b_2x_2 + \cdots b_kx_k$, ($k$ = total number of predictors). The outcome (y) conditional on the predictor (x) is assumed normally distributed (i.e., the error is normally distributed), and the link function does nothing. A link function specifies how the outcome relates to the predictors. A conditional mean defined by the normal distribution is shown above as μ, and a link function that does nothing is the identity link. Key differences between linear regression and logistic regression are in the link function and the distribution assumed for the errors (i.e., the mean of the outcome variable conditional on all predictors).

Because of these differences from regression/ANOVA, maximum likelihood (ML) is used instead of ordinary least-squares estimation for parameter estimates of generalized linear models. The regression parameters are ML estimates; thus, when there is adequate sample size, they are consistent, efficient, and normally distributed. Of course, the interpretation of the parameter estimates is also different for logistic regression than for linear regression—from logistic regression, parameters are usually converted to odds ratios or predicted probabilities (as elaborated below). We focus here on evaluation of model fit and interpretation of parameter estimates.

Binary Response

Binary logistic regression is specifically for an outcome that has only two levels. In the binary logistic regression model (omitting person specific subscripts), $g[E(y|x)] = \log\left(\frac{E(y|x)}{1-E(y|x)}\right) = \log\left(\frac{p}{1-p}\right) = b_o + b_1x_1 + b_2x_2 + \cdots b_kx_k$, the error is assumed distributed binomial so that the conditional mean is defined as the binomial probability parameter, p, and the link function is the logistic function shown above. Error is not shown because the expected value of the model has been taken, and it is a fundamental assumption of all GLMs that the expected value of the error is 0.

MODEL FIT

If all predictors are categorical and the sample size is adequate, then the fit of a logistic regression model is evaluated with a χ^2 test, such as Pearson's or the Likelihood Ratio χ^2 (H$_o$: model-predicted counts are equal to observed counts; H$_a$: model-predicted counts are not equal to observed counts). For good model fit, we wish to *fail to* reject H$_o$. Some guidelines to help decide whether the sample size is adequate for the χ^2 model fit test are: (1) each unique group defined by settings for the predictors should have at least about 10 observations; (2) 80% of predicted counts should be at least about 5; and (3) all other predicted counts should be greater than 2, with essentially no 0 counts (Stokes et al., 2000). Also, the Pearson and Likelihood Ratio χ^2 values should not differ very much because they are asymptotically equivalent and usually similar in samples that are large enough for either one to be validly applied.

When there is at least one continuous predictor, the sample size requirement for the χ^2 test is almost never met. In this case, a variation of the χ^2 model fit test described by Hosmer and Lemeshow (1980) can be used. The Hosmer-Lemeshow test is a way of grouping the data before applying the Pearson χ^2 model fit test. The sample size for the statistic is the number of groups defined by settings on the predictors. About 10 groups of about the same size are formed, based on the magnitude of the model-predicted probabilities (observations with similar probabilities are grouped together). The expected frequency (E) for the group is the sum of the predicted probabilities for all the individuals in the group. The E is compared to the observed frequency (O) for the group (i.e., a count of the number of individuals in the group for which the event of interest was actually observed). The χ^2 is computed analogously to the formula given previously, with summation over all O–E pairs: $Q_{HL} = \sum_{\text{all O-E pairs}} \frac{(O-E)^2}{E}$, and df = number of groups minus 2.

An example application of the Hosmer-Lemeshow test is provided next. The model predicts the presence of coronary artery disease (CAD) from age ($N = 78$); estimated parameters are: $g[E(y|x)] = -3.643 + 0.080x_1$. Age ranges from 28 to 63 years, and every age has model-predicted probabilities of having CAD (CAD = 1; p_1) and not having CAD (CAD = 0; p_0). For a 28-year-old, $p_1 = \frac{\exp[-3.6431+(0.0801)28]}{1+\exp[-3.6431+(0.0801)28]} = 0.1977$ and $p_0 = 1 - 0.1977 = 0.8023$; whereas for a 63-year-old, $p_1 = \frac{\exp[-3.6431+(0.0801)63]}{1+\exp[-3.6431+(0.0801)63]} = 0.8023$ and $p_0 = 0.1977$. Observations are grouped by the magnitude of p_1, so 28-year-olds are in group 1 and 63-year-olds are in group 9 (there are a total of 9 groups for this example).

Members of group 1 are shown in Table 4.9. E for CAD = 1 is the sum of the p_1 values: $0.1977 + 0.2244 + 0.2535 + \cdots + 0.3016 = 2.37$, and E for CAD = 0 is the sum of p_0 values: $0.8022 + 0.7756 + 0.7465 + \cdots + 0.6984 = 6.63$. Observed frequencies (O) are just the counts in this group: O = 1 for CAD = 1 and O = 8 for CAD = 0. The E and O for each group are given in Table 4.10; these 18 pairs are used to compute $Q_{HL} = \sum_{\text{all O-E pairs}} \frac{(O-E)^2}{E} = 10.451$ with $df = 7$; $p = 0.164$. Recall that for good model fit, we wish

Table 4.9. One of Nine Groups Used to Compute Example Hosmer-Lemeshow Fit Statistic

	Members of Group 1			
Obs	CAD	age	p_1	p_0
1	0	28	0.19777	0.80223
2	0	30	0.22442	0.77558
3	0	32	0.25352	0.74648
4	1	32	0.25352	0.74648
5	0	33	0.26898	0.73102
6	0	34	0.28502	0.71498
7	0	34	0.28502	0.71498
8	0	35	0.30162	0.69838
9	0	35	0.30162	0.69838

Note: Obs = observation number, CAD = coronary artery disease (0 = no, 1 = yes), p_1 = probability of CAD = 1, p_0 = probability of CAD = 0

to *fail to* reject H$_0$. Here, we get our wish. The test fails to reject the hypothesis that the model fits.

A limitation of χ^2 model fit tests is that they are sensitive to sample size: No model fits perfectly, so if the sample is very large, then even good models will be rejected. An examination of residuals can be helpful along with the χ^2 test for this reason and also because residuals reflect more specific versus global aspects of model fit. Collett (2003) provides a detailed treatment of different types of residuals and other diagnostics for binary logistic regression.

Models also can be compared to others as a way to evaluate fit. The likelihood ratio test for comparing nested models is valid many times, even when the sample size requirement is not met for a χ^2 test of absolute fit. A smaller model is nested within a larger model if it can be obtained by removing parameters from the larger model. Information criteria (e.g., Akaike's information criterion, AIC; Bayesian information criterion, BIC), which are a function of the optimized log likelihood with a penalty, can be used to compare either nested or non-nested models (smaller is better fit). The AIC is $-2\ell + 2k$, and the BIC is $-2\ell + k \log(N)$, where ℓ = log of the optimized likelihood, k = number of parameters, and N = sample size.

Table 4.10. Summary of all Groups Used to Compute Example Hosmer-Lemeshow Fit Statistic

Group	Total	CAD = 1 Observed	CAD = 1 Expected	CAD = 0 Observed	CAD = 0 Expected
1	9	1	2.37	8	6.63
2	9	5	3.15	4	5.85
3	8	5	3.44	3	4.56
4	8	5	3.86	3	4.14
5	7	3	3.61	4	3.39
6	8	3	4.46	5	3.54
7	9	3	5.57	6	3.43
8	9	6	6.23	3	2.77
9	11	10	8.31	1	2.69

Note: CAD = coronary artery disease (0 = no, 1 = yes), Total = count of people in this group; Observed = count of people who actually gave this response; Expected = count of people expected by the model to give this response

PARAMETER INTERPRETATION

Regression parameters are not readily interpretable when the model is in the linear-logit form (logit = log odds): $\log\left(\frac{p_i}{1-p_i}\right) = b_o + b_1 x_{1i}$, so for interpretation, we exponentiate both sides of the model which removes the log: $\left(\frac{p_i}{1-p_i}\right) = \exp(b_o + b_1 x_{1i})$. The exponential function (rewritten for brevity as e with arguments raised to a power) is a linear operator, so $\exp(b_o + b_1 x_i) = e^{(b_o + b_1 x_i)} = e^{b_o} e^{b_1 x_i} = e^{b_o}\left(e^{b_1}\right)^{x_i}$. Now, if x_1 differs for one observation versus another by 1 unit, then $\left(\frac{p_i}{1-p_i}\right) = e^{b_o}\left(e^{b_1}\right)^{x_i+1} = e^{b_o}\left(e^{b_1}\right)^{x_i}\left(e^{b_1}\right)^1$. So, with every 1-unit difference in x, multiply the odds that the response = 1 by e^{b_1}. This interpretation differs from linear regression because the relationship is multiplicative, and of course, we are talking about odds.

The exponentiated regression parameters from logistic regression are odds ratios. Suppose we predict the presence of CAD from gender (male = 1, female = 0) ($N = 78$), parameter estimates are $\log\left(\frac{p_i}{1-p_i}\right) = -0.56 + 1.25\,(sex_i)$, and the gender difference is significant (SE for $b_1 = 0.48$; $z = 2.607$; $p = .0009$). If we exponentiate both sides of the model, we get the odds of CAD: $\left(\frac{p_i}{1-p_i}\right) = 0.57\,(3.5)^{(sex_i)}$, so that when gender = 1 (male), the odds are 2.00 and when gender = 0 (female), the odds are 0.57. The ratio of odds for men versus women is: $\frac{\left(\frac{p_1}{1-p_1}\right)}{\left(\frac{p_0}{1-p_0}\right)} = \frac{e^{-0.56}(e^{1.25})}{e^{-0.56}} = e^{1.25} = 3.5 = \frac{2.00}{0.57}$. The explanation above is a long way of explaining why the correct way to interpret a logistic regression parameter is to (1) exponentiate and (2) interpret as an odds ratio. For this example, the odds of men having CAD are 3.5 times the odds of women having coronary artery disease.

When there is more than one predictor in a logistic regression model, the exponentiated parameters are partial odds ratios but are otherwise interpreted as in the previous example. Nominal predictors require coding just as in GLMs. With continuous predictors, it is important to remember the multiplicative relationship illustrated above. Reconsidering the example above, age significantly predicts the presence of CAD ($b_1 = 0.0801$, SE = 0.03, $z = 2.67$; $p = 0.008$). To interpret this regression slope, first exponentiate, $\exp(0.0801) = 1.08$, then for every additional 1 year of age, multiply the odds by 1.08. Alternatively, the odds of having CAD increase by (1.08 – 1.0 =) 0.08 for every additional year of age. One is subtracted from the odds ratio because this is the value that the ratio would take if the odds were the same for both groups.

Sometimes it is desirable to discuss what happens to the odds with an increase of several years (e.g., 5 or 10). To do this, always multiply the constant (5 or 10) by the regression coefficient in raw form, not exponentiated form, and then exponentiate second. For example, 0.08(5) = 0.4 and exp(0.4) = 1.49. For every 5 years that age increases, multiply the odds by 1.49. The odds of CAD increase by 0.49 for every 5 years that age increases.

As with other GLMs, it is useful to evaluate interactions among predictors in logistic models. Consider predicting whether an athlete takes creatine monohydrate (a supplement that can enhance athletic performance) from gender (female = 1, male = 0) and whether they live in the United States (coded 1) versus the United Kingdom (coded 0). The interaction between predictors is significant (b_3 = −2.339, SE = 0.76, z = 3.06, p = 0.002), meaning the odds of yes for United States versus United Kingdom are not the same for the gender groups. The coefficient for the interaction term does not have a useful interpretation (even when exponentiated). This parameter is tested for significance, but further exploration is required to understand the nature of the interaction.

To interpret the interaction, we can hold constant gender and examine United States versus United Kingdom differences, hold constant country and examine gender differences, or both. To form the correct ratios, it is useful to write out the expression for the odds for each group defined by settings on the predictors. The full model is:

$$\left(\frac{p}{1-p}\right) = \exp\left[b_o + b_1 gender + b_2 country + b_3 (interaction)\right],$$

and both predictors are coded 0 (U.K. and male) or 1 (U.S. and female). Thus, the expressions for the odds are:

U.S., female: $\exp(b_o + b_1 + b_2 + b_3)$
U.S., male: $\exp(b_o + b_2)$
U.K., female: $\exp(b_o + b_1)$, and
U.K., male: $\exp(b_o)$.

Next, we form ratios of odds. The odds of yes for United States versus United Kingdom are:

$\frac{e^{b_o} e^{b_2}}{e^{b_o}} = e^{b_2} = \exp(1.339) = 3.82$ for males, and $\frac{e^{b_o} e^{b_1} e^{b_2} e^{b_3}}{e^{b_o} e^{b_1}} = e^{b_2} e^{b_3} = \exp(1.339 - 2.339) = 0.37$ for females. So we can see how incorrect it would be to have treated these ratios as homogeneous (i.e., to have ignored the interaction). The odds of taking creatine for men in the United States are 3.82 times the odds for men in the United Kingdom, but the odds of taking creatine for women in the United States are 0.37 times the odds for women in the United Kingdom.

Another way to look at the results is to divide the groups by country and look at gender differences. The odds of yes for female versus male are $\frac{e^{b_o} e^{b_1} e^{b_2} e^{b_3}}{e^{b_o} e^{b_2}} = e^{b_1} e^{b_3} = \exp(-0.426 - 2.339) = 0.06$ for the United States, and $\frac{e^{b_o} e^{b_1}}{e^{b_o}} = e^{b_1} = \exp(-0.426) = 0.65$ for the United Kingdom.

Thus, for the United States, the odds of a woman taking creatine are 0.06 times the odds for a man, whereas for the United Kingdom, the odds of a woman taking creatine are 0.65 times the odds for a man.

Proportional Odds Model

A popular logistic regression model for an ordinal outcome is the proportional odds model (McCullagh, 1980). This model handles ordering of the response through the use of cumulative logits. Consider an outcome with three ordered categories. There is a probability corresponding to each outcome: 1 (p_1), 2 (p_2), and 3 (p_3). The cumulative logits, $\log\left(\frac{p_{1i}}{p_{2i}+p_{3i}}\right)$ and $\log\left(\frac{p_{1i}+p_{2i}}{p_{3i}}\right)$, together refer to the log odds of a lower versus higher response. The proportional odds model is a multivariate extension of a GLM wherein the parameters for the cumulative logits are estimated simultaneously and the regression slope(s) for all logits are constrained to be equivalent. This constraint is the proportional odds assumption (which can be tested).

For three categories and one predictor, the model is:

$$\log\left(\frac{p_{1i}}{p_{2i}+p_{3i}}\right) = b_{01} + b_1 x_{1i}$$

$$\log\left(\frac{p_{1i}+p_{2i}}{p_{3i}}\right) = b_{02} + b_1 x_{1i}.$$

The intercept is different for every logit, whereas the regression parameters for all predictors are the same for all logits. These ideas generalize for more outcome categories and more predictors. As with the model for a binary outcome, the exponentiated regression parameters are interpreted as odds ratios. Model fit is evaluated using the same statistics described in earlier sections for the binary logistic regression model.

We will examine Allison's (2003) data, with an outcome that is the answer to the question, "If you found a wallet on the street, would you: (1) keep the wallet and the money, (2) keep the money and return the wallet, or (3) return both the money and the wallet?" The responses are ordered from least (1) to most (3) ethical. A simple model predicts this outcome from gender (male = 1, female = 0) and whether parents explained why when they were punished as a child (1 = almost always, 0 = sometimes or never). The deviance and Pearson χ^2 are similar to one another (5.34 and 5.35, respectively, $df = 4$) and both are nonsignificant ($p = 0.25$), suggesting adequate model fit.

Another aspect of model fit is the evaluation of the proportional odds assumption. This assumption can be tested by comparing two nested models with the likelihood ratio test. One model has regression coefficients equal for each logit, and one model has coefficients estimated separately for each logit. A nonsignificant difference between the models indicates that separate slopes for each logit are not needed so we have justification to proceed in constraining them equal across logits. For the stolen wallet example, this model comparison is, in fact, nonsignificant ($\chi^2 = 2.064$, $df = 2$, $p = 0.356$). If the assumption had been violated, options would include fitting separate binary logistic regression models for each logit (with the outcome variable recoded), fitting a different ordinal-response model such as the adjacent categories model, or treating the categories as unordered with the baseline category logits (also called nominal logistic or generalized logits) model. Agresti (2002) is a good reference for both of these models.

The ML estimates are:

$$\log\left(\frac{p_{1i}}{p_{2i}+p_{3i}}\right) = -1.88 + 1.148 gender_i$$
$$- 1.289 explain_i$$

$$\log\left(\frac{p_{1i}+p_{2i}}{p_{3i}}\right) = -0.23 + 1.148 gender_i$$
$$- 1.289 explain_i.$$

Gender significantly predicts response (SE = 0.31, z = 3.68, $p < 0.001$), as does the explaining punishment variable (SE = 0.32, z = 4.03, $p < 0.001$). Holding constant the explaining variable, the odds of a less ethical response are exp(1.148) = 3.15 times greater for men than for women. Holding gender constant, the odds of a less ethical response from someone whose parents explained punishments are exp(−1.289) = 0.28 times the odds for someone whose parents did not explain punishments.

We might also be interested in calculating the model-predicted probabilities of each response. The probability of responding "1" can be obtained from the first logit, $\left(\frac{p_{1i}}{p_{2i}+p_{3i}}\right) = \left(\frac{p_{1i}}{1-p_{1i}}\right) = \exp(b_{o1} + b_1 x_{1i} + \cdots + b_k x_{ki})$, by solving for p_1: $p_{1i} = \frac{\exp(b_{o1}+b_1 x_{1i}+\cdots+b_k x_{ki})}{1+\exp(b_{o1}+b_1 x_{1i}+\cdots+b_k x_{ki})}$. The second logit, $\left(\frac{p_{1i}+p_{2i}}{p_{3i}}\right) = \left(\frac{p_{[1\ or\ 2]i}}{1-p_{[1\ or\ 2]i}}\right) = \exp(b_{o2} + b_1 x_{1i} + \cdots + b_k x_{ki})$, can be solved for the probability of responding "1" or "2": $p_{[1\ or\ 2]i} = \frac{\exp(b_{o2}+b_1 x_{1i}+\cdots+b_k x_{ki})}{1+\exp(b_{o2}+b_1 x_{1i}+\cdots+b_k x_{ki})}$. The probability of responding "2" is: $p_{2i} = p_{[1\ or\ 2]i} - p_{1i} = \frac{\exp(b_{o2}+b_1 x_{1i}+\cdots+b_k x_{ki})}{1+\exp(b_{o2}+b_1 x_{1i}+\cdots+b_k x_{ki})} - \frac{\exp(b_{o1}+b_1 x_{1i}+\cdots+b_k x_{ki})}{1+\exp(b_{o1}+b_1 x_{1i}+\cdots+b_k x_{ki})}$.

Finally, because the response categories are mutually exclusive and exhaustive, the probability of responding "3" is $p_{3i} = 1 - p_{i[1\ or\ 2]} = 1 - \frac{\exp(b_{o2}+b_1 x_{1i}+\cdots+b_k x_{ki})}{1+\exp(b_{o2}+b_1 x_{1i}+\cdots+b_k x_{ki})}$.

For the stolen wallet example, the predicted probabilities for each group and each logit are given in Table 4.11. Then p_2 is obtained by subtraction for each group:

$$p_{[2or1]1} - p_{11} = 0.4093 - 0.1171$$
$$= 0.2922 \text{ (male, explained)}$$

$$p_{[2or1]2} - p_{12} = 0.7154 - 0.3248$$
$$= 0.3906 \text{ (male, not explained)}$$

$$p_{[2or1]3} - p_{13} = 0.1802 - 0.0404$$
$$= 0.1398 \text{ (female, explained), and}$$

$$p_{[2or1]4} - p_{14} = 0.4437 - 0.1324$$
$$= 0.311 \text{ (female, not explained)}.$$

Subtraction is also the most convenient way to calculate p_3 for each group:

$$p_{31} = 1 - p_{[2or1]1} = 1 - 0.4093$$
$$= 0.5907 \text{ (male, explained)},$$

$$p_{32} = 1 - p_{[2or1]2} = 1 - 0.7154$$
$$= 0.2846 \text{ (male, not explained)},$$

$$p_{33} = 1 - p_{[2or1]3} = 1 - 0.1802$$
$$= 0.8198 \text{ (female, explained), and}$$

$$p_{34} = 1 - p_{[2or1]4} = 1 - 0.4437$$
$$= 0.5563 \text{ (female, not explained)}.$$

Table 4.12 summarizes the information gained from interpreting the results this way. Some readers find it more intuitive to understand probabilities and how their magnitude differs for different groups, rather than odds ratios.

Table 4.11. Model Predicted Probabilities for the Stolen Wallet Example

Group	Model predicted probability
	Logit 1
Male, explained	$p_{11} = \dfrac{\exp(-1.8801 + 1.14881 - 1.2886)}{1 + \exp(-1.8801 + 1.14881 - 1.2886)} = 0.1171$
Male, not explained	$p_{12} = \dfrac{\exp(-1.8801 + 1.14881)}{1 + \exp(-1.8801 + 1.14881)} = 0.3248$
Female, explained	$p_{13} = \dfrac{\exp(-1.8801 - 1.2886)}{1 + \exp(-1.8801 - 1.2886)} = 0.0404$
Female, not explained	$p_{14} = \dfrac{\exp(-1.8801)}{1 + \exp(-1.8801)} = 0.1324$
	Logit 2
Male, explained	$p_{[2or1]1} = \dfrac{\exp(-0.2263 + 1.14881 - 1.2886)}{1 + \exp(-0.2263 + 1.14881 - 1.2886)} = 0.4093$
Male, not explained	$p_{[2or1]2} = \dfrac{\exp(-0.2263 + 1.14881)}{1 + \exp(-0.2263 + 1.14881)} = 0.7154$
Female, explained	$p_{[2or1]3} = \dfrac{\exp(-0.2263 - 1.2886)}{1 + \exp(-0.2263 - 1.2886)} = 0.1802$
Female, not explained	$p_{[2or1]4} = \dfrac{\exp(-0.2263)}{1 + \exp(-0.2263)} = 0.4437$

Table 4.12. Summary of Predicted Probabilities for the Stolen Wallet Example

	Response		
Group	1	2	3
Male, explained	0.12	0.29	0.59
Male, not explained	0.32	0.39	0.28
Female, explained	0.04	0.14	0.82
Female, not explained	0.13	0.31	0.56

Note: 1 = keep the wallet and the money (least ethical), 2 = keep the money and return the wallet (middle), and 3 = return both the money and the wallet (most ethical).

Binary logistic regression and the proportional odds model are used for many purposes in psychology and other disciplines. Because I discussed the application of Q_{MH} (and related effect sizes) for tests of DIF, I should also note that there is a large body of research on the use of various logistic regression models for this purpose (*see*, e.g., Rogers & Swaminathan, 1993; Swaminathan & Rogers, 1990).

Conclusion

This chapter described a few multipurpose methods that can be used to analyze relationships among variables when there is a single binary or ordinal outcome and the observations are independent. Please be aware that many more methods exist for analyzing categorical outcomes, and almost anything that can be done with continuous data can be done (with some modification) with categorical data. Results of data analysis should be most accurate when statistical assumptions are as accurate as possible; thus, it is important to pay attention to the level of measurement of the data and to find (or create) appropriate methods for handling them.

Future Directions

For those learning about extant methods for handling categorical outcomes, methods to pursue next might include the nominal logistic (also called baseline category or generalized logits) model and ordinal multiple regression (OMR; Cliff, 1994,

1996; Long, 1999, 2005). Cliff introduced OMR to answer questions about ordinal relationships between one ordinal outcome and one or more ordinal predictors, and Long developed inference (1999, 2005). Ordinal multiple regression is a linear model estimated with ordinary least-squares estimation, but it is not a GLM; it is based on a matrix of Kendall's τ_a coefficients rather than Pearson correlations.

References

Agresti, A. (1976). The effect of category choice on some ordinal measures of association. *Journal of the American Statistical Association, 71,* 49–55.

Agresti, A. (1984). *Analysis of ordinal categorical data.* New York: Wiley.

Agresti, A. (2002). *Categorical data analysis* (2nd edition). Hoboken, NJ: Wiley & Sons.

Allison, P. (2003). *Logistic regression using the SAS system: Theory and Application.* Cary, NC: SAS Institute.

Breslow, N. E. (1996). Statistics in epidemiology: The case control study. *Journal of the American Statistical Association, 91,* 14–28.

Breslow, N. E. & Day, N. E. (1980). *Statistical methods in cancer research: Volume 1—The analysis of case-control studies.* Lyon, France: International Agency for Research on Cancer.

Cliff, N. (1994). Predicting ordinal relations. *British Journal of Mathematical and Statistical Psychology, 47,* 127–150.

Cliff, N. (1996). *Ordinal methods for behavioral data analysis.* Mahwah, NJ: Lawrence Erlbaum.

Cliff, N., & Charlin, V. (1991). Variances and covariances of Kendall's tau and their estimation. *Multivariate Behavioral Research, 26,* 693–707.

Collett, D. (2003). *Modeling binary data,* (2nd edition). Boca Raton, FL: Chapman & Hall.

Costner, H. L. (1965). Criteria for measures of association. *American Sociological Review, 30,* 341–353.

Costner, H. L. (1968). Reply to Somers. *American Sociological Review, 33,* 292.

Daniels, H. E. (1944). The relation between measures of correlation in the universe of sample permutations. *Biometrika, 33,* 129–135.

Davis, J. A. (1967). A partial coefficient for Goodman and Kruskal's gamma. *Journal of the American Statistical Association, 62,* 189–193.

Fleiss, J. L., Levin, B., & Paik, M. C. (2003). *Statistical methods for rates and proportions,* (3rd edition). Hoboken, NJ: Wiley & Sons.

Freeman, L. C. (1986). Order-based statistics and monotonicity: A family of ordinal measures of association. *Journal of Mathematical Sociology, 12,* 49–69.

Gonzalez, R., & Nelson, T. O. (1996). Measuring ordinal association in situations that contain tied scores. *Psychological Bulletin, 119,* 159–165.

Goodman, L. A., & Kruskal, W. H. (1954). Measures of association for cross classifications. *Journal of the American Statistical Association, 49,* 732–764.

Grizzle, J. E., Starmer, C. F., & Koch, G. G. (1969). Analysis of categorical data by linear models. *Biometrics, 25,* 489–504.

Higgins, J. J. (2004). *Introduction to modern nonparametric statistics.* Pacific Grove, CA: Brooks/Cole-Thomson Learning.

Holland, P. W., & Thayer, D. T. (1988). Differential item performance and the Mantel-Haenszel procedure. In H. Wainer, & H. I. Braun (Eds.), *Test validity* (pp. 129–145). Hillsdale, NJ: Lawrence Erlbaum.

Hosmer, D. W., & Lemeshow, S. (1980). A goodness-of-fit test for the multiple logistic regression model. *Communications in Statistics, A10,* 1043–1069.

Jones, M. P., O'Gorman, T. W., Lemke, J. H., & Woolson, R. F. (1989). A Monte Carlo investigation of homogeneity tests of the odds ratio under various sample size configurations. *Biometrics, 45,* 171–181.

Kendall, M. G. (1938). A new measure of rank correlation. *Biometrika, 30,* 81–93.

Kendall, M. G. (1945). The treatment of ties in ranking problems. *Biometrika, 33,* 239–251.

Kim, J. (1971). Predictive measures of ordinal association. *American Journal of Sociology, 76,* 891–907.

Kreiner, S., & Christensen, K. B. (2002). Graphical Rasch models. In M. Mesbah, B. F. Cole, & M. T., Lee (Eds.), *Statistical methods for quality of life studies* (pp. 187–203). Dordrecht, Netherlands: Kluwer Academic Publisher.

Kreiner, S., & Christensen, K. B. (2004). Analysis of local dependence and multidimensionality in graphical loglinear Rasch models. *Communications in Statistics, 6,* 1239–1276.

Leik, R. K., & Gove, W. R. (1969). The conception and measurement of asymmetric monotonic relationships in sociology. *American Journal of Sociology, 74,* 696-709.

Leik, R. K., & Gove, W. R. (1971). Integrated approach to measuring association. *Sociological Methodology, 3,* 279–301.

Liebetrau, A. M. (1983). *Measures of association* (Sage University Paper Series on Quantitative Applications in the Social Sciences, series no. 07-032). Newbury Park, CA: Sage.

Liu, I-M., & Agresti, A. (1996). Mantel-Haenszel-type inference for cumulative odds ratios with a stratified ordinal response. *Biometrics, 52,* 1223–1234.

Long, J. D. (1999). A confidence interval for ordinal multiple regression weights. *Psychological Methods, 4,* 315–330.

Long, J. D. (2005). Omnibus hypothesis testing in dominance based ordinal multiple regression. *Psychological Methods, 10,* 329–351.

Lovie, A. D. (1995). Who discovered Spearman's rank correlation? *British Journal of Mathematical and Statistical Psychology, 48,* 255–269.

Mantel, N. (1963). Chi-square tests with one degree of freedom: Extensions of the Mantel-Haenszel procedure. *Journal of the American Statistical Association, 58,* 690–700.

Mantel, N. & Fleiss, J. (1980). Minimum expected cell size requirements for the Mantel-Haenszel one-degree of freedom chi-square test and related rapid procedure. *American Journal of Epidemiology, 112,* 129–143.

Mantel, N., & Haenszel, W. (1959). Statistical aspects of the analysis of data from retrospective studies of disease. *Journal of the National Cancer Institute, 22,* 719–748.

McCullagh, P. (1980). Regression models for ordinal data (with discussion). *Journal of the Royal Statistical Society, Series B, 42,* 109–142.

Nelder, J., & Wedderburn, R. W. M. (1972). Generalized linear models. *Journal of the Royal Statistical Society, Series A, 135,* 370–384.

Penfield, R. D. (2005). DIFAS: Differential item functioning analysis system. *Applied Psychological Measurement, 29,* 150–151.

Quade, D. (1974). Nonparametric partial correlation. In H. M. Blalock (Ed.), *Measurement in the social sciences: Theories and strategies* (pp. 369–398). Chicago: Aldine Publishing Company.

R Development Core Team (2005). R: A language and environment for statistical computing. R Foundation for Statistical Computing, Vienna, Austria. ISBN 3-900051-07-0, URL http://www.R-project.org.

Rogers, H. J., & Swaminathan, H. (1993). A comparison of logistic regression and Mantel-Haenszel procedures for detecting differential item functioning. *Applied Psychological Measurement, 17*, 105–116.

SAS Institute Inc., SAS 9.2. Cary, NC: SAS Institute Inc., 2002–2008.

Somers, R. H. (1962a). A new asymmetric measure of association for ordinal variables. *American Sociological Review, 27*, 799–811.

Somers, R. H. (1962b). A similarity between Goodman and Kruskal's tau and Kendall's tau with a partial interpretation of the latter. *Journal of the American Statistical Association, 57*, 804–812.

Somers, R. H. (1968). On the measurement of association. *American Sociological Review, 33*, 291–292.

Somes, G. W. (1986). The generalized Mantel-Haenszel statistic. *The American Statistician, 40*, 106–108.

Spearman, C. S. (1904). The proof and measurement of association between two things. *American Journal of Psychology, 15*, 72–101.

Su, Y. & Wang, W. (2005). Efficiency of the Mantel, generalized Mantel-Haenszel, and logistic discriminant function analysis methods in detecting differential item functioning for polytomous items. *Applied Measurement in Education, 18*, 313–350.

Stevens, S. S. (1946). On the theory of scales of measurement. *Science, 103*, 677–680.

Stokes, M. E., Davis, C. S., & Koch, G. G. (2000). *Categorical data analysis using the SAS system,* (2nd edition). Cary, NC: SAS Institute.

Stuart, A. (1953). The estimation and comparison of strengths of association in contingency tables. *Biometrika, 40*, 105–110.

Swaminathan, H., Rogers, H. J. (1990). Detecting differential item functioning using logistic regression procedures. *Journal of Educational Measurement, 27*, 361–370.

Tarone, R. E. (1985). On heterogeneity tests based on efficient scores. *Biometrika, 72*, 91–95.

Tarone, R. E., Gart, J. J., & Hauck, W. W. (1983). On the asymptotic inefficiency of certain noniterative estimators of a common relative risk or odds ratio. *Biometrika, 70*, 519–522.

Wang, W., & Su, Y. (2004). Factors influencing the Mantel and generalized Mantel-Haenszel methods for the assessment of differential item functioning in polytomous items. *Applied Psychological Measurement, 28*, 450–480.

Wilson, T. P. (1969). A proportional-reduction-in-error interpretation for Kendall's tau-b. *Social Forces, 47*, 340–342.

Wilson, T. P. (1971). A critique of ordinal variables. *Social Forces, 49*, 432–344.

Wilson, T. P. (1974). Measures of association for bivariate ordinal hypotheses. In H. M. Blalock, (Ed.), *Measurement in the social sciences: Theories and strategies* (pp. 327–342). Chicago: Aldine Publishing Company.

Woods, C. M. (2007). Confidence intervals for gamma-family measures of ordinal association. *Psychological Methods, 12*, 185–204.

Woods, C. M. (2008). Correction to results about confidence intervals for Spearman's r_s. *Psychological Methods, 13*, 72–73.

Woods, C. M. (2009a). Consistent small-sample variances for six gamma-family measures of ordinal association. *Multivariate Behavioral Research, 44*, 525–551.

Woods, C. M. (2009b). Testing for differential item functioning with measures of partial association. *Applied Psychological Measurement, 33*, 538–554.

Yule, G. U. (1900). On the association of attributes in statistics: With illustrations from the material of the childhood society. *Philosophical Transactions of the Royal Society of London, Series A, 194*, 257–319.

Zwick, R., Donoghue, J., & Grima, A. (1993). Assessment of differential item functioning for performance tasks. *Journal of Educational Measurement, 30*, 233–251.

CHAPTER 5

Configural Frequency Analysis

Alexander von Eye, Eun-Young Mun, Patrick Mair, *and* Stefan von Weber

Abstract

Statistical data analysis routinely expresses results in terms of main effects and interactions at the level of variables. The implicit assumption of this routine is that the observed relationships are valid across the entire range of admissible scores. In contrast, applications of configural frequency analysis (CFA) proceed from the assumption that main effects and interactions reflect local relationships among variables. In other words, effects can be identified for some categories of variables but not for others. In this chapter, an introduction to CFA is provided in three sections. The first section covers sample questions that can be answered with CFA. These questions illustrate the range of CFA application, and they show that CFA focuses on local effects. The second section presents technical elements of CFA, including the CFA base model, the CFA null hypothesis, significance tests used in CFA, and methods of α protection. The third section provides sample base models of CFA and data applications. The sample base models cover Prediction CFA, two-Group CFA, CFA methods for the predictions of endpoints and for the analysis of the relationships between series of measures, and CFA methods for the analysis of mediator hypotheses.

Key words: configural frequency analysis (CFA), local effects, longitudinal CFA, two-Group CFA, mediatior CFA, moderator CFA

According to Goodman (1984), cross-classifications of categorical variables can be analyzed with the goals of examining (1) the joint distribution of the variables that span the cross-classification; (2) the association structure of these variables; and (3) the dependency structure of these variables. *Configural frequency analysis* (CFA; Lienert & Krauth, 1975; von Eye, & Gutiérrez Peña, 2004; von Eye, Mair, & Mun, 2010) adds a fourth perspective. Configural frequency analysis allows researchers to answer questions in terms of deviations from expectation and in terms of odds in multivariate cross-classifications of categorical variables. Specifically, CFA asks whether individual cells or groups of cells in a table deviate from expectancy that is specified in terms of a probability model. Consider the following examples.

The effects of Aspirin are well known. The drug was developed as an non-steroidal analgesic—that is, a pain killer. Other common applications use Aspirin as an antipyretic to reduce fever and as an anti-inflammatory medication. Because of its antiplatelet effect, the drug is popular as a preventive measure against heart attacks. Additional uses of Aspirin focus on reducing acute rheumatic fever, Kawasaki disease (even in children under age 16 years), pericarditis, coronary artery disease, and acute myocardial infarction. Undesired side effects include increased risks of gastrointestinal ulcers, gastric mucosal injury, gastrointestinal hemorrhage (bleeding), tinnitus, and Reye's syndrome.

New medicinal uses of Aspirin are constantly being discovered. Recent results suggest that Aspirin can be effective in the reduction of risk of a number of cancers, including, for example, colon cancer, and it seems to reduce the risk of death from overall as well as from various types of cancer, including colorectal and breast cancer. In addition, Aspirin seems to help diabetics keep their blood sugar at desired levels.

Desired and undesired effects of drugs and treatment in general are evaluated with respect to expectations. The bases for specifying expectations are theory and earlier experience. It is well known that spontaneous recovery rates of many health conditions are high. For example, it is assumed that late-stage spontaneous remissions of cancer do occur but rarely so. However, spontaneous remissions of early stage microscopic cancers may be common but underestimated in frequency. Similarly, neurotic behaviors are known to have quite high rates of spontaneous recovery. When it comes to evaluating their efficacy, a new drug or therapy has to show better rates of success than one would expect from treatment as usual or spontaneous recovery without treatment. This applies accordingly when the rates of undesired side effects are weighed. Both the desired effects and the side effects are formulated in terms of probability statements. There are portions of the population who do not show these effects.

From a data analysis perspective, the results of analyses of the desired and undesired effects of treatments can rarely be meaningfully expressed in terms of correlations or regression coefficients. More appropriate methods focus on (1) local or conditional relationships among variables, (2) odds and odds ratios, and (3) discrepancies from expectation. An example of a local or conditional statement is that the effects of Aspirin only apply to individuals older than age 16 years, because the drug is, with just a few exceptions, almost never administered to children. An example of a statement expressed in units of odds is that 38 ± 12 vascular events per 1,000 diabetic patients—that is, almost 5%—could be prevented, were the patients treated with Aspirin in the context of secondary prevention. This result seems to apply equally well to males and females. Similarly, the risk of gastrointestinal problems from Aspirin is 7% as compared to 8% from a placebo.

In a different domain, an example of a statement expressed in terms of discrepancies from expectation is that 54% of the children who had been exposed to domestic violence maintained positive adaptation and were characterized by easy temperament compared to their nonresilient counterparts (Martinez-Torteya, Bogat, von Eye, & Levendosky, 2009).

This chapter provides an overview of CFA. First, it presents sample questions that can be answered with CFA. Second, technical elements of CFA are introduced, focusing on the CFA base model, null hypothesis, significance tests, and α protection. Third, sample models are presented and applied to empirical data. This chapter focuses on frequentist approaches to CFA (for Bayesian approaches, *see* Gutiérrez Peña, & von Eye, 2000) and on log-linear base models (for base models that are not log-linear, *see* von Eye, 2004).

Sample Questions That Can Be Answered With Configural Frequency Analysis

This section presents three sample questions that can be answered with CFA. The selection of questions is representative but not exhaustive. Additional questions are discussed by von Eye, Mair, and Mun (2010), and new possibilities keep emerging as new methods and models of CFA are being developed. Before discussing the questions that can be answered with CFA, we introduce the term *configuration*. Cells in a cross-classification can be labeled by the categories of the variables that span the cross-classification. The pattern of labels is termed *configuration*.

CFA Sample Question 1: Do different numbers of cases than expected show a particular configuration? This is the fundamental question asked in every CFA application. To answer this question, the researcher needs to determine the expected frequency for the configuration under study. This can be accomplished by either creating an estimated frequency or by using the *a priori* known probability for this configuration. The latter knowledge rarely exists. Therefore, most CFA applications estimate configural frequencies from data using a chance probability model, also called the *CFA base model*. In the second section of this chapter, CFA base models are defined and examples are given. The statistical comparison of an observed cell frequency with an expected cell frequency is performed under the null hypothesis that there is no difference. The comparison can lead to either one of two results. First, it can be that the null hypothesis prevails for a particular configuration. Whenever this is the case, researchers move on and test the CFA null hypothesis for other cells. If, however, the null hypothesis is rejected for a configuration, then this configuration is, then, considered *rogue, outstanding, outlandish, extreme,* or *deviating from expectation.* There can be two reasons why the null hypothesis is rejected. First, the observed frequency can be greater than the expected frequency. If this is the case, then the configuration under study is said to *constitute a CFA type.* Second, the observed frequency can be smaller than the expected frequency. In this case, the configuration under study is said to *constitute a CFA antitype.*

CFA Sample Question 1 shows that CFA results in statements about individual cells (or groups of cells) rather than statements about variables and their interrelationships. Therefore, CFA is considered one of the prime methods of *person-oriented research* (Bergman & Magnusson, 1997; Bergman, von Eye, & Magnusson, 2006; von Eye & Bergman, 2003).

To enable a CFA type/antitype decision, three conditions must be fulfilled. First, the base model must be specified such that there is a unique interpretation of the meaning of the types or antitypes. Second, the base model must be specified such that the sampling scheme is taken into account. Third, the significance threshold must be protected to accommodate the increased risks that come with multiple significance tests. The section regarding Technical Elements of CFA covers all three of these issues.

CFA Sample Question 2: Are there relationships between groups of variables at the level of configurations? There are many methods that can be used for the analysis of relationships among groups of variables. Examples include MANOVA, canonical correlation analysis, principal component analysis, log-linear modeling, correspondence analysis, and structural equations modeling (SEM). Each of these methods creates descriptions of relationships between groups of variables at the level of variables. In contrast, CFA captures relationships at the level of configurations. Specifically, a type describes a pattern of variable categories in one group of variables that co-occurs more often than expected with a pattern of variable categories in another group of variables. If no causal or predictive relationship is implied (as is often the case in applications of factor analysis or correspondence analysis), then this variant of CFA is called *interaction structure analysis (ISA)*. If causal or predictive relationships are implied, then this variant of CFA is called *prediction CFA (P-CFA)*.

In longitudinal research, a number of special cases of P-CFA has been discussed. These cases include CFA models for the prediction of trajectories, the prediction of endpoints, or the relationships among longitudinal series of scores (von Eye, Mair, & Mun, 2010).

CFA Sample Question 3. Can mediating relationships be established at the level of configurations? In mediator models, researchers examine the relationships among a predictor variable, an outcome, and a mediator.

In standard mediation analysis (Baron & Kenny, 1986; MacKinnon, Kisbu–Sakarya, & Gottschall, Chapter 16, this volume; MacKinnon, Fairchild, & Fritz, 2007) regression analysis or structural modeling are used to establish mediation. However, in many research contexts, the variables involved in a mediation process are categorical. In those cases, one can ask whether mediation exists in general—that is, for all categories of the variables used to describe the mediation process, or in particular for selected configurations of variable categories. If researchers entertain the hypothesis that mediation exists only for selected variable categories, then CFA is the method of choice to determine which configurations carry the mediation process (von Eye, Mair, & Mun, 2010; von Eye, Mun, & Mair, 2009). One interesting possible outcome is that, within the same table, processes of partial, full, or even no mediation may co-exist. In the section Mediator Configural Frequency Analysis we present configural mediation models and application examples.

Technical Elements of Configural Frequency Analysis

In this section, it is first shown how a CFA base model can be specified. Second, the CFA null hypothesis is presented, along with a selection of significance tests. This is followed by a discussion of α protection and methods that are used to reduce the risk of committing an α error. The third part of this section covers sampling schemes and their implications for the specification of CFA base models. The fourth part of this section summarizes the steps that are performed when applying CFA.

We begin this section by showing a data example (cf. von Eye, Mun, & Mair, 2009). We use data from the Overcoming The Odds (OTO) project (Taylor, Lerner, et al., 2002). The OTO is a longitudinal project that was conducted to study positive development in African-American male youth. The assumption that underlies this study is that every youth possesses assets that can open the doors to positive development. The OTO project studied the role that individual and ecological assets play in this development. The youth who participated in this study were either gang members ($n = 45$; average

age at the beginning of the study = 15.82 years) or members of community-based organizations (CBO; $n = 50$; average age at the beginning of the study = 16.31 years). The participants indicated in interviews whether they had been sexually active in the past year. The variables were coded as 1 = *sexually active* and 2 = *not active*, and 1 = *gang member* and 2 = *CBO member*. In the following data example, we ask whether sexual activity at Time 1 (Sex 1), sexual activity at Time 2 (Sex 2), and group membership (Gang or CBO member; in the following passages, group membership is abbreviated by "Gang;" the two categories of this variable are still Gang vs CBO member) are related to each other. First, we fit a log-linear model that allows us to describe the 2 × 2 × 2 (Sex 1 × Gang × Sex 2) cross-tabulation at the level of variable relationships. Second, we perform a preliminary CFA in which we ask whether the relationships among the three variables are carried by particular configurations that stand out as type- or antitype-constituting. Table 5.1 displays the cross-classification along with CFA results.

Log-linear analysis shows that two interactions are sufficient to explain the frequency distribution in Table 5.1. Specifically, the hierarchical model that includes the interactions between Gang Membership and sexual activity at Time 1 as well as between sexual activity at Time 1 and Time 2 comes with a LR-X^2 (likelihood ratio X^2) = 1.28 ($df = 2$; $p = 0.53$). We conclude that this model fits very well. Neither of the two interactions comes as a surprise. In particular, the sexual activity at Time 1 x Time 2 interaction was expected, as auto-associations are often the strongest terms in models of repeated observations.

Although this model describes the data well, the results do not tell us where, exactly, in the table the activity is. In different words, the interaction terms do not tell us whether each cell that could be involved in is indeed involved in and makes a contribution to the interactions. In the present example, this would involve testing all eight cells. Therefore, we perform a CFA that allows us to determine for each cell whether it deviates from a base model (*see* Table 5.1 for results). The base model that we use here includes only the main effects of the variables that span the table. This model is called the first order CFA base model. If a cell makes a contribution to the interactions that are needed to explain the data then it will contain more (types) or fewer (antitypes) cases than estimated by the base model. We use the z-test to perform the cell-wise CFA tests, and the Bonferroni procedure for the protection of α (*see* the Protecting [α] section for more detail on testing in CFA). For the base model, we obtain a LR-X^2 = 103.66, which suggests significant model–data discrepancies ($df = 4$; $p < 0.01$). We, therefore, expect types and antitypes to emerge.

Table 5.1 shows that CFA identified two types and three antitypes. The first type is constituted by Configuration 1 1 1. It suggests that more gang members than expected indicated that they had been sexually active at both time-points. Twenty-one respondents showed this profile, but fewer than 4 had been expected. The second type has just

Table 5.1. First Order CFA of the Cross-Classification of Sex1, Gang, and Sex 2

Configuration Sex 1 Gang Sex 2	m	$\hat{m}$	z	p	Type/Antitype
111	21.00	3.630	9.1170	0.000000	Type
112	2.00	9.633	−2.4594	0.006959	
121	4.00	4.033	−0.0166	0.493397	
122	1.00	10.704	−2.9660	0.001509	Antitype
211	0.00	8.686	−2.9472	0.001603	Antitype
212	22.00	23.051	−0.2189	0.413364	
221	1.00	9.651	−2.7847	0.002679	Antitype
222	44.00	25.612	3.6333	0.000140	Type

the opposite profile, 2 2 2. These are CBO members who indicated that they had not been sexually active at either point in time. Forty-four respondents showed this profile, but only 25.6 had been expected.

The first antitype, constituted by Configuration 1 2 2, describes CBO members who indicated that they had been sexually active at the first but inactive at the second point in time. One respondent showed this profile, but almost 11 had been expected. Not a single respondent showed profile 2 1 1, but almost 9 had been expected. Thus, it also constitutes an antitype. These are gang members who said that at the first point in time, they had not been sexually active, but became active in the year before the second interview. The third antitype is constituted by Configuration 2 2 1. One CBO member said that he had been sexually inactive during the year before the first interview but active during the year before the second interview. About 10 had been expected to show this response pattern.

These results show some of the characteristics that are typical of CFA results (von Eye, Mair, & Mun, 2010). Specifically:

1. CFA results are interpreted, in virtually all cases, only after the base model is rejected. Rejection of the base model does not necessarily result in types and antitypes. However, if the base model describes the data well, significant discrepancies between model and data do not exist, and there is no need to search for types and antitypes.

2. Typically, only a selection of cells (configurations) emerges as type- and antitype-constituting. The remaining cells do not deviate from the base model. Types and antitypes, therefore, indicate where, in the table, the action is. In Table 5.1, three of the eight cells did not contradict the base model. These cells indicate where the three variables are independent of one another. The type and antitype cells show the locations of the model–data discrepancies that carry the interactions needed to explain the data.

3. Although, in Table 5.1, two of the largest cells constitute types, and the smallest cell constitutes an antitype, this is not always the case. It is not a surprise when a relatively small cell constitutes a type or a relatively large cell constitutes an antitype. The main reason for this characteristic of CFA is that it focuses on *discrepancies from expectation* rather than sheer size (zero-order CFA being the only exception; *see* von Eye, 2002).

The Configural Frquency Analysis Base Model

Configural Frquency Analysis base models are of utmost importance in CFA applications. The base model determines the interpretation of types and antitypes. The CFA base model is a chance model that contains all effects and terms in which the researcher is NOT interested in. By implication, at least some of the terms and effects in which the researcher is interested in must exist for the base model to be rejected. Based on the information that is used to specify a base model, four groups of base models can be distinguished. These are (1) log-linear models, (2) models based on population parameters, (3) models with *a priori* determined probabilities, and (4) models based on distributional assumptions (von Eye, 2004). Every CFA base model must meet the following three criteria (von Eye & Schuster, 1998):

1. *Uniqueness of interpretation of types and antitypes.* There must be only one reason for discrepancies between observed and expected cell frequencies. Examples of such reasons include the presence of higher order interactions and predictor–criterion relationships.

2. *Parsimony.* Base models must be as simple as possible. That is, base models must include as few terms as possible and terms of the lowest possible order. Methods have been proposed to simplify CFA base models (Schuster & von Eye, 2000).

3. *Consideration of sampling scheme.* The sampling scheme of all variables must be considered. Particular sampling schemes can limit the selection of base models. For example, if a categorical variable is observed under product-multinomial sampling, then base models must take into account the main effects of this variable.

Of the four groups of base models, log-linear models are the most popular base models, by a wide margin. Therefore, this chapter focuses on log-linear base models (for CFA base models that are not log-linear, *see* von Eye, 2002). Two groups of log-linear base models have been defined. The first group includes *global models*. These models assign the same status to all variables. Therefore, there is no distinction between, for example, predictors and criteria or independent and dependent variables. The second group includes *regional CFA base models*. These models are suitable when variables differ in status. We first introduce readers to global base models.

GLOBAL CONFIGURAL FREQUENCY ANALYSIS BASE MODELS

Within the group of global models, there exists a hierarchy. At the bottom of this hierarchy, there is the base model of *zero-order CFA*. This model reflects the assumption that the explanation of the frequency distribution under study requires no effects whatsoever. The resulting expected frequencies are thus uniformly distributed. Types and antitypes can emerge if any effects exist. In log-linear modeling terms, the base model of zero-order CFA assumes the form $\log \hat{m}_i = \lambda$, where $\hat{m}_i$ is the estimated expected frequency for Cell i, λ is the constant (intercept), and i goes over all cells in the cross-classification. If the base model of zero-order CFA (essentially a null model) is rejected, then any effect, including main effects and interactions can be the cause for types and antitypes to emerge. Types from zero-order CFA indicate agglomerations in the data space, and antitypes indicate sparsely populated sectors of the data space. Therefore, zero-order CFA has also been called *configural cluster analysis*.

On the second level of the hierarchy of global CFA models, we find *first order CFA*. This CFA model uses the base model that proposes main effects but no associations among variables. This model is also called the *model of variable independence* or the *base model of classical CFA*. Types and antitypes will emerge only if variable associations exist. As was shown with the example in Table 5.1, usually only a selection of cells stands out as types or antitypes. In other words, deviations from independence will be found only locally. Therefore, types and antitypes from first order CFA are said to reflect *local associations*.

Suppose a cross-classification is spanned by the four variables A, B, C, and D. Then, the log-linear base model of first order CFA is

$$\log \hat{m}_i = \lambda + \lambda^A + \lambda^B + \lambda^C + \lambda^D,$$

where the superscripts indicate the variables that span the table. If this base model is rejected, effects must exist that are of higher order than main effects—that is, interactions.

At the following higher levels, increasingly higher order interactions are taken into account. Types and antitypes emerge if associations exist at the levels not considered in the base model. For d variables, the highest possible order of a base model takes the $d-1^{st}$ order interactions into account. Types and antitypes can then emerge only if interactions of the dth order exist. In different words, under a CFA base model of the highest possible order, types and antitypes emerge only if a saturated hierarchical log-linear model is needed to provide a satisfactory description of the observed frequency distribution.

To give an example of a higher order CFA base model, we use second order CFA. This model assumes that first order interactions exist. For the four variables A, B, C, and D, the second order CFA base model is

$$\log \hat{m}_i = \lambda + \lambda^A + \lambda^B + \lambda^C + \lambda^D + \lambda^{AB} + \lambda^{AC} + \lambda^{AD} + \lambda^{BC} + \lambda^{BD} + \lambda^{CD},$$

where the double superscripts indicate two-way interactions. This model can be rejected only if second (i.e., three-way interactions) or higher order interactions exist that, then, can manifest in the form of types and antitypes.

REGIONAL CONFIGURAL FREQUENCY ANALYSIS BASE MODELS

Regional CFA models group variables. Examples of such models include P-CFA (von Eye & Rovine, 1994; von Eye, Mair, & Bogat, 2005), which distinguishes between predictors and criteria, ISA (Lienert & Krauth, 1973), which distinguishes between two groups of variables of equal status, and *k*-group CFA, which includes one or more classification variables and one or more variables that are used to distinguish among these groups. Models of CFA that distinguish among more than two groups of variables have been discussed (Lienert & von Eye, 1988), but have found limited application.

For the purposes of this chapter, we present the log-linear base models for P-CFA and two-group CFA. We use the four variables A, B, C, and D again. For P-CFA, we consider A and B predictors and C and D criterion variables. The P-CFA base model takes the following effects into account:

1. all main effects;
2. all possible interactions on the predictor side (the model is thus saturated in the predictors);
3. all possible interactions on the criterion side (the model is thus saturated in the criteria).

The model is thus

$$\log \hat{m}_i = \lambda + \lambda^A_j + \lambda^B_k + \lambda^C_l + \lambda^D_m + \lambda^{AB}_{jk} + \lambda^{CD}_{lm},$$

where the superscripts indicate the variables, the subscripts on the right-hand side of the equation indicate the parameters that are estimated for the main effects and interactions, and i goes over the cells of the table. Of all possible interactions, the following ones are not part of this P-CFA base model: [A, C], [A, D], [B, C], [B, D], [A, B, C], [A, B,

D], [A, C, D], [B, C, D], and [A, B, C, D]. Each of these interactions involves at least one predictor and at least one criterion variable. Therefore, the P-CFA base model can be rejected only if one or more of those interactions exist that establish predictor–criterion relationships. Prediction CFA types and antitypes reflect, by necessity, such relationships. A data example of P-CFA is given in the Prediction Configural Frequency Analysis section.

We now use the four variables A, B, C, and D to exemplify a two-group CFA base model. For this example, we consider D the classification variable and A, B, and C the variables used to discriminate between the groups indicated by D. The two-group CFA base model takes the following effects into account:

1. all main effects;
2. all possible interactions on the side of the discrimination variables; the model is thus saturated in the discrimination variables.

Because, in this example, there is only one variable that indicates group membership, there is no need to consider interactions with this variable. However, if there are two or more such grouping variables (e.g., gender or employment status), the interactions among these variables need to be taken into account also. In the present example, the model is

$$\log \hat{m}_i = \lambda + \lambda_j^A + \lambda_k^B + \lambda_l^C + \lambda_m^D \\ + \lambda_{jk}^{AB} + \lambda_{jl}^{AC} + \lambda_{kl}^{BC} + \lambda_{jkl}^{ABC}.$$

Of all possible interactions, the following ones are not part of this two-group CFA base model: [A, D], [B, D], [C, D], [A, B, D], [A, C, D], [B, C, D], and [A, B, C, D]. Each of these interactions involves at least one discrimination variable and D, the grouping variable. Therefore, the two-group CFA base model can be rejected only if one or more of those interactions exist that establish group differences. two-group CFA types and antitypes reflect, by necessity, such differences. A data example for two-group CFA follows the 2-Group CFA Analysis section.

The Configural Frequency Analysis Null Hypothesis

Among the main differences between log-linear modeling and CFA is the goal of analysis. Using log-linear modeling, researchers attempt to find a model that describes the data well. In contrast, using CFA, researchers try to specify a meaningful base model in the hope that it can be rejected. If it is rejected, then types and antitypes are bound to emerge. These types and antitypes tell the researchers where, in the cross-classification, the targeted effects are strongest.

Using the notation of von Eye and Gutiérrez Peña (2004; cf. von Eye, Mair, & Mun, 2010), we consider d variables, $X_1, ..., X_d$. Crossed, these variables form a contingency table with $R = \prod_{i=1}^d c_i$ cells, where c_i is the number of categories of the ith variable. The probability of Cell r is π_r, with $r = 1, ..., R$. The frequency with which Cell r was observed, is m_r. The probabilities of the R frequencies depend on the sampling scheme of the data collection (von Eye & Schuster, 1998; von Eye, Schuster, & Gutiérrez Peña, 2000; see the Sampling Schemes and Their Implications for the Specification of CFA Base Models section). Typically, sampling is multinomial and we obtain

$$P(M_1 = m_1, ..., M_R = m_R | N, \pi_1, ..., \pi_R)$$
$$= \frac{N!}{m_1! ... m_R!} \prod_{r=1}^R \pi_r^{m_r},$$

with $\Sigma_r p_r = 1$ and $\Sigma_r m_r = N$, the sample size. It follows that M_r is binomially distributed with

$$P(M_r = m_r | N, \pi_r)$$
$$= \frac{N!}{m_r!(N - m_r)!} \pi_r^{m_r}(1 - \pi_r)^{N-m_r}.$$

To test hypotheses about particular cells, one can use the binomial distribution, and one obtains

$$B_{N,p}(x) = \sum_{j=0}^x \frac{N!}{j!(N-j)!} p^j (1-p)^{N-j},$$

with $0 \leq x \leq N$. A number of alternative tests has been proposed (more detail on tests follows in the Significance Tests for Configural Frequency Analysis section).

As was discussed in the context of the example in Table 5.1, Configural frequency analysis tests are performed to make decisions concerning the presence of CFA *types* and *antitypes*. Types suggest that more cases were observed than expected with reference to a base model. Antitypes suggest that fewer cases were observed than expected with reference to the base model. In the testing procedure, we use the CFA null hypothesis H_0: $E[m_r] = \hat{m}_r$, or, in words, that Cell r does not constitute a type or an antitype, where $\hat{m}_r$ is the expected frequency under the base model. If a cell constitutes a type, this null hypothesis is rejected because

$$B_{N, \pi_r}(m_r - 1) \geq 1 - \alpha.$$

Accordingly, if a configuration constitutes an antitype, the null hypothesis for this configuration is rejected because

$$B_{N,\pi_r}(m_r) \leq \alpha.$$

In *exploratory CFA*, each of the R cells of a cross-classification is subjected to a CFA test. In *confirmatory CFA*, the focus is on a selection of $R' < R$ cells.

Significance Tests for CFA

In the previous section, we described the binomial test for the cell-wise search for CFA types and antitypes and, in Table 5.1, we used the z-test. If $Np \geq 10$ (Osterkorn, 1975), then the z statistic

$$z_r = \frac{m_r - Np_r}{\sqrt{Np_r q_r}}$$

is a good approximation of the normal distribution, where p_r is the estimate of π_r, $q_r = 1 - p_r$, and r indicates that the test is being performed for the rth cell. p_r is usually estimated from the data as $p_r = \hat{m}_r/N$. Other tests that are popular in CFA applications include the X^2 and the Freeman-Tukey deviate.

These tests are all applicable under any sampling scheme. In contrast, Lehmacher's (1981) approximative hypergeometric test can only be used when sampling is product-multinomial. This test starts from the relation

$$X_r = \frac{m_r - \hat{m}_r}{\sqrt{\hat{m}_r}} \approx N(0, \sigma),$$

for $df = 1$. When the model fits, $\sigma^2 < 1$ (Christensen, 1997; Haberman, 1973). To obtain a better estimator for the standard error in the denominator, Lehmacher derived the exact variance,

$$\sigma_r^2 = Np_r[(1 - p_r - (N-1)(p_r - \tilde{p}_r)],$$

where p_r is as before. Lehmacher's test requires that p_r be estimated based on a base model that takes the product-multinomial sampling into account. To illustrate the estimation of $\tilde{p}$, we use the example of a table that is spanned by $d = 3$ variables. For this case, the estimate is

$$\tilde{p}_{ijk} = \frac{(m_{i..} - 1)(m_{.j.} - 1)(m_{..k} - 1)}{(m-1)^d},$$

where i, j, and k index the categories of the three variables that span the table. Using the exact variance, X_r can be replaced by the statistic

$$z_{L,r} = \frac{m_r - \hat{m}_r}{\sigma_r}.$$

Because $p > \tilde{p}$, Lehmacher's $z_{L,r}$ will always be larger than X_r and, therefore, have more power. To prevent non-conservative decisions, Küchenhoff (1986) suggested using a continuity correction.

A residual measure that was proposed for use in CFA (von Eye & Mair, 2008) is the *Standardized Pearson Residual*, r_i,

$$r_i = \frac{m_i - \hat{m}_i}{\sqrt{\hat{m}_i(1 - h_i)}},$$

where i goes over all cells of the table and h_i is the ith diagonal element of the well-known *hat matrix*,

$$H = W^{1/2}X(X'WX)^{-1}X'W^{1/2},$$

where X is the design matrix for the base model. The elements w_{ii}—that is, the elements of the diagonal matrix W—are the estimated expected cell frequencies, $\hat{m}_i$. The standardized Pearson residual r_i has the interesting characteristic that when one of the variables is dichotomous, corresponding cells can come with exactly the same standardized Pearson residual.

The statistic r_i is about as powerful as Lehmacher's test. It may be preferable to Lehmacher's z because it can be applied under any sampling scheme.

Protecting α

In both exploratory and confirmatory application, CFA involves multiple null hypothesis testing. It is well known that multiple significance tests on the same data can cause problems. Two issues stand out. The first is *capitalizing on chance*, the second concerns the *dependency of tests*. Only the first of a series of tests on the same data is performed at the *a priori* specified α level. When more than one test is performed, the risk of committing α errors increases, even if the tests are independent. To give an example, consider the situation in which the 27 cells of a $3 \times 3 \times 3$ table are examined under $\alpha = 0.05$. In this situation, the probability of falsely rejecting the null hypothesis twice is 0.24. The researcher who performs many tests on the same sample thus capitalizes on chance or, in different words, faces a dramatically increased risk of committing an α error if no measures are taken to protect α.

This risk becomes even greater when tests are dependent. Von Weber, Lautsch, and von Eye (2003) showed that, if the expected cell frequencies are estimated under a log-linear main effect model, the outcomes of the second, third, and fourth CFA tests in a 2×2 table are completely dependent upon the outcome of the first test. Krauth (2003) showed that the number of possible patterns of types and antitypes increases as the size of a table increases.

However, the tests of CFA never become completely independent. To illustrate this point (*see also* Krauth, 2003; von Eye & Gutiérrez Peña, 2004), let the outcome of a CFA test be T (a type was found), A (an antipype was found), or O (the null hypothesis prevailed). Let R be the number of cells in a cross-classification. Then, the maximum number of (T, A, O) patterns is $M = 3^R$. In the case of a 2×2 table, this number would be $M_{2 \times 2} = 3^4 = 81$. The dependency of the test outcomes, however, leads to only three possible patterns: T, A, A, T; A, T, T, A; and O, O, O, O, where the order of outcomes is for the order of cells 1 1, 1 2, 2 1, and 2 2.

In more general terms, let c_i be the number of categories of variable i, and $s_i = R/c_i$ the number of configurations (cells) that contain category j_i, with $1 \leq j_i \leq c_i$. If we select from the c_i categories $(c_i - 1)$ categories, then the number of configurations containing these categories is $(c_i - 1)s_i$. Now, Krauth (2003) showed that the a lower bound of number of possible (T, A, O) patterns for these configurations is $(3^{s_i} - 2^{s_i+1} + 2)^{c_i-1}$. For r_i that can differ in value, the lower bound can be given as

$$L_P = \max(3^{s_i} - 2^{s_i+1} + 2)^{c_i-1}, \quad \text{for } 1 \leq i \leq d.$$

The upper bound of the number of (T, A, O) patterns is

$$U_P = \min(3^{s_i} - 2^{s_i+1} + 2)^{c_i}, \quad \text{for } 1 \leq i \leq d.$$

Obviously, the number of possible (T, A, O) patterns is always smaller than R. Therefore, the existence of particular types and antitypes may affect (cause) the existence of other types and antitypes in the same table.

A number of procedures have been proposed for the *protection of* α. The most conservative of these is the *Bonferroni procedure*. This procedure requires (1) that the sum of all adjusted significance levels not exceed the nominal α, or $\Sigma_r \alpha_r \leq \alpha$, where r goes over all cells of the cross-classification that are being examined; and (2) that the significance threshold be the same for each test, or $\alpha_r = \alpha^*$, for all r, where α^* is the adjusted threshold. The value of α^* that fulfills both of these conditions is $\alpha* = \alpha/R$.

Holm's procedure (1979) does not require the latter condition. Rather, it takes the number of tests into account that was performed before the current one. This results in the protected

$$\alpha_r^* = \frac{\alpha}{R - i + 1},$$

where i numbers the tests, and $i = 1, \ldots, R$. This procedure requires the test statistics to be ranked in descending order. The CFA tests are then performed in order. As soon as the first null hypothesis prevails, the procedure stops. The first α^* is the same under the Bonferroni and the Holm procedures. Beginning with the second test, Holm's procedure is less conservative than the Bonferroni procedure. For the last—that is, the Rth test—the Holm-protected $\alpha^* = \alpha$.

As another alternative to Holm's procedure, Holland and Copenhaver (1987) proposed

$$\alpha_r^* = 1 - (1 - \alpha)^{\frac{1}{R-i+1}}.$$

This procedure is even less conservative than Holm's procedure, but only slightly so.

Other procedures have been proposed (e.g., Hommel, 1988, 1989; Hommel, Lehmacher, & Perli, 1985). For more general procedures, *see*, for example, Keselman, Cribbie, and Holland (2002).

Sampling Schemes and Their Implications for the Specification of Configural Frequency Analysis Base Models

The best known and most frequently employed approaches to the collection of categorical data are the *multinomial* and the *product multinomial sampling schemes* (Christensen, 1997; Jobson, 1992). These two schemes are discussed in the present section. It is important to note that employing either of the two sampling schemes does not impact the usefulness of log-linear base models for analyzing the data. Specifically, parameter estimates will stay the same and so will overall goodness-of-fit values of CFA base models and log-linear models in general. However, the selection of possible CFA base models may be limited by the use of particular sampling schemes (von Eye, 2002; von Eye & Schuster, 1998).

Multinomial Sampling. Multinomial sampling is performed when a random sample of observations is randomly placed into the cells of a cross-classification, with no constraints as to where the observation can be placed. When there is only one categorical variable such as gender or disease type, the sampling is termed *multinomial*. When the classification categories result from crossing two or more variables, the sampling is termed *cross-classified multinomial*. In the following sections, we consider only cross-classified multinomial sampling, because CFA is almost always used to analyze cross-classifications of two or more variables. Cross-classified multinomial sampling allows for random assignment of individuals to cells of the entire cross-classification. Consider a two-dimensional table with R rows and C columns, and $i = 1, \ldots, R$ and $j = 1, \ldots, C$. Then the joint density of the sample cell frequencies is

$$f(N_{11}, N_{12}, \ldots, N_{RC})$$
$$= \frac{N!}{\prod_{i=1}^{R} \prod_{j=1}^{C} N_{ij}!} \prod_{i=1}^{R} \prod_{j=1}^{C} \pi_{ij}^{N_{ij}},$$

where π_{ij} indicates the probability for Cell ij, $\sum_{i=1}^{R} \sum_{j=1}^{C} \pi_{ij} = 1$, and $\sum_{i=1}^{R} \sum_{j=1}^{C} = N_{ij}$. The expectancies of the N_{ij} are $E[N_{ij}] = N\pi_{ij}$. The variances of the N_{ij} are $V[N_{ij}] = N\pi_{ij}(1 - \pi_{ij})$ for $i = 1, \ldots, R$ and $j = 1, \ldots, C$. The covariances are $Cov[N_{ij}, N_{kl}] = N\pi_{ij}\pi_{kl}$, for $i \neq k$; $j \neq l$; $i, k = 1, \ldots, R$; and $j, l = 1, \ldots, C$. Because the assignment of cases is made to any of the cells in the table, there is no constraint on the expected frequencies other than $\sum_i \sum_j N_{ij} = N$.

Product multinomial sampling. The product multinomial distribution describes the joint distribution of two or more independent multinomial distributions. Consider the $R \times C$ cross-classification with *fixed row marginals* $N_{i.}$ for $i = 1, \ldots, R$. Row marginals are considered fixed when the number of cases in the rows is determined *a priori*. This can be the case by design, or when individuals in each row represent sub-populations—for example, females and males, or alcoholics and non-alcoholics. The joint density of the R rows results from multiplying the row-specific multinomial probabilities. In an $R \times C$ table, this product is

$$f(N_{11}, N_{12}, \ldots, N_{RC})$$
$$= \prod_{i=1}^{R} \left[\frac{N_{i.}!}{\prod_{j=1}^{C} N_{ij}!} \prod_{j=1}^{C} \left[\frac{\pi_{ij}}{\pi_{i.}} \right]^{N_{ij}} \right].$$

This product indicates that the probability of observing the contingency table with cell frequencies $N_{11}, N_{12}, \ldots, N_{RC}$ is given as the product of probabilities of the R independent vectors of row probabilities $(N_{11}, \ldots, N_{1C}), \ldots, (N_{R1}, \ldots, N_{RC})$. This applies accordingly if column marginals are fixed, or if the marginals are fixed for more than one variable (*cross-classified product-multinomial sampling*).

Although the estimation of parameters is the same for these two sampling schemes, the type and number of CFA models that can be considered, can differ. Consider a study on the effects of drinking in which the researchers include two independent classification variables, Drinking (D; yes/no) and Gender (G; female/male), and one dependent variable,

Liver Cancer (C; shows signs of liver cancer/does not show signs of liver cancer; see von Eye & Schuster, 1998). Together, these three variables form a $2 \times 2 \times 2$ cross-classification with Drinking and Gender as the independent variables, and Liver Cancer the dependent variable. Now, the researchers decide to fix the margins of the two independent variables. Specifically, they determine the number of drinkers and nondrinkers to be included in the sample a priori, and they also determine the number of male and female respondents a priori. In addition, the numbers of drinkers and nondrinkers are the same, per gender. Therefore, any model analyzing these three variables must reproduce the bivariate Gender–Drinking marginals, $m_{ij.}$. All models that include the (hierarchical) term $D \times G$—that is, [D, G]—fulfill this condition. These are the five models that include the terms [D, C, G]; [D, G], [D, C], [G, C]; [D, G], [D, C]; [D, G], [G, C]; and [D, G], [C] (models separated by semi colons). All models without the $D \times G$ term are not admissible. The inadmissible models include, for example, the classical CFA base model of variable independence with the terms [D], [G], [C], and the model [D, C], [G, C].

Sampling Schemes and Their Implications for Configural Frequency Analysis. The standard, "classical" CFA base model implies variable independence. The sampling scheme for this model can be cross-classified multinomial but not cross-classified product-multinomial. The reason for this condition is that cross-classified product-multinomial sampling creates two-, three-, or higher-dimensional marginal probabilities that must be reproduced by the base model. The base model of variable independence does not automatically reproduce these marginal probabilities.

To illustrate, consider the following two examples (von Eye, 2002; von Eye & Schuster, 1998). First, 50 female and 50 male smokers participate in a study on responses to physical exercise. Each of the two samples is subdivided in groups of 25 based on the rigor of exercise. The design for this study can be depicted as in Table 5.2.

This table displays four cells with 25 respondents each. If Gender and Rigor of Exercise are crossed with one or more response variables, then the cells in Table 2 turn into the bivariate marginals of a larger design. If data from this design are analyzed using the main effect-only base model, then the expected cell frequencies may not sum up to 25 for the four bivariate marginals. This would be incorrect, and types and antitypes could emerge just because of this

Table 5.2. Design for Gender and Rigor of Exercise in Smokers Study

		Gender	
		Female	Male
Exercise	Rigorous	25	25
	Less rigorous	25	25

error. These types and antitypes would not reflect local associations.

In the following, second example, we use a real data example, and we illustrate the effects of selecting a wrong base model. In the 1999 indictment, 100 senators, 55 Republicans, and 45 Democrats voted on whether President Clinton was guilty of perjury and obstruction of justice. Sixty-two of the 100 senators had been senators for two or more terms, and 38 senators had been in their first term. On both charges, the voting categories were *guilty* or *not guilty*. The four variables under study can be crossed to form the 2 × 2 × 2 × 2 cross-classification of the variables Party Membership (M; 1 = *Democrat*, 2 = *Republican*), Number of Terms (T; 1 = *two or more terms*, 2 = *first term*), judgement on Perjury (P; 1 = *not guilty*, 2 = *guilty*), and judgement on Obstruction of Justice (O; 1 = *not guilty*, 2 = *guilty*). Table 5.3 displays this cross-classification, along with results from standard CFA under the base model of variable independence. The standard normal z-test was used along with the Bonferroni-protected significance level $\alpha* = 0.003125$.

The results in Table 5.3 suggest the existence of four types and two antitypes. The first type is constituted by Configuration 1 1 1 1. It suggests that more seasoned Democrat senators than expected from the base model voted not guilty on both accounts. The second type, 1 2 1 1, suggests that more first-term Democrat senators than expected from the base model voted not guilty on both accounts. The third type, 2 1 2 2, indicates that more seasoned Republican senators than expected from the base model voted guilty on both accounts, and the fourth type, constituted by Configuration 2 2 2 2, suggests that more first-term Republicans than expected voted guilty on both accounts.

The two antitypes can be interpreted as follows. The first antitype is constituted by Configuration 1 1 1 2. It suggests that fewer seasoned Democrats than expected voted not guilty on the Perjury account but guilty on the Obstruction of Justice account. The second antitype, 2 1 2 1, indicates that fewer seasoned Republicans than expected voted guilty on the Perjury account but not guilty on the Obstruction of Justice account.

These results seem to describe the voting according to party lines nicely. They do not describe 10 Republicans who jumped the party lines (*see* Configurations 2 1 1 1, 2 1 1 2, 2 2 1 1, and 2 2 1 2, for which no antitypes could be established for lack of statistical power). However, the interpretation of the types and antitypes shown in Table 5.3 is highly problematic because they are based on an inadmissible base model, and are therefore not valid. The reason why the base model of variable independence is, in this case, inadmissible is that the $M \times T \times P \times O$ cross-classification contains two cross-classified variables that were sampled according to a bivariate product-multinomial sampling scheme. These are the variables Party Membership (M) and Number of Terms (T). In addition, the number of first-term senators per party is also fixed as subgroups of known size. The $M \times T$ bivariate marginals of this design must be reproduced by the expected frequencies. The main effect-only base model that was used for Table 5.3 is unable to achieve this.

For example, the base model of variable independence estimates that 17.1 first-term Democrats were members of the U.S. Senate in 1999. However, there were 13. Therefore, types and antitypes can emerge because of this mis-specification alone. Such types and antitypes may reflect the specification error rather than data characteristics. To determine, whether the pattern of types and antitypes in Table 5.3 changes when the base model is correctly specified, we re-calculate the CFA under a different base model. For the results in Table 5.3 the base model was

$$\log \hat{m} = \lambda_0 + \lambda_i^M + \lambda_j^T + \lambda_k^P + \lambda_l^O,$$

that is, the main effects model. We now recalculate this analysis under the base model

$$\log \hat{m} = \lambda_0 + \lambda_i^M + \lambda_j^T + \lambda_k^P + \lambda_l^O + \lambda_{ij}^{MT}$$

This model considers the interaction between Number of Terms and Party Membership. The results from this new base model appear in Table 5.4. To obtain results that are comparable to the ones presented in Table 5.3, we protected α using the Bonferroni procedure, and used the z-test.

Table 5.4 suggests that taking the bivariate product-multinomial nature of the variables Party Membership and Number of Terms into account changes the resulting pattern of antitypes. Configuration 2 1 2 1 no longer constitutes an antitype.

Table 5.3. CFA of the Variables Party Membership (M), Number of Terms (T), Judgement on Perjury (P), and Judgment on Obstruction of Justice (O) (Base Model of Variable Independence)

Configurations MTPO	Frequencies m	$\hat{m}$	Statistics z	$p(z)$	Type/Antitype?
1111	32	7.67	8.78	$<\alpha^*$	T
1112	0	7.67	−2.77	0.0028	A
1121	0	6.28	−2.51	0.0061	
1122	0	6.28	−2.51	0.0061	
1211	13	4.70	3.83	$<\alpha^*$	T
1212	0	4.70	−2.17	0.0151	
1221	0	3.85	−1.96	0.0249	
1222	0	3.85	−1.96	0.0249	
2111	3	9.38	−2.08	0.0186	
2112	4	9.38	−1.76	0.0395	
2121	0	7.67	−2.77	0.0028	A
2122	23	7.67	5.53	$<\alpha^*$	T
2211	2	5.75	−1.56	0.0590	
2212	1	5.75	−1.98	0.0238	
2221	0	4.70	−2.17	0.0151	
2222	22	4.70	7.98	$<\alpha^*$	T

[a] $<\alpha^*$ indicates that the tail probability is smaller than can be expressed with 4 decimal places.

The knowledge concerning the number of terms of the senators in both parties now allows one to expect that a smaller number of first-term Republican senator votes guilty on the Perjury and not guilty on the Obstruction of Justice charges than based on the main effect model. As a result, the observed zero for Configuration 2 1 2 1 is not significantly different than the expected frequency of 6.75[1]. In general, none of the expected cell frequencies is the same under both models.

The main issue of this comparison of results from two different base models is that the expected cell frequencies in Table 5.4 now add up to the correct uni- and bivariate marginal frequencies. For example, summing the first four expected frequencies in Table 5.4 yields $N_{11.} = 32$. This is exactly the required value; it reproduces the *a priori* known marginal.

This example illustrates that mis-specification of the base model can result in (1) patterns of types and antitypes that reflect discrepancies from the design and sampling characteristics that should have been considered in the base model, and (2) mis-estimation of uni-, bi-, or multivariate marginal frequencies. In sum, we state that

(1) when variables are observed under a product-multinomial sampling scheme, their marginals must be exactly reproduced. The CFA base model must therefore include the main effects of these variables.

(2) When variables are observed under a cross-classified product-multinomial sampling scheme, their bivariate or multivariate marginals must also be exactly reproduced. The CFA base

Table 5.4. CFA of the Cross-classification of Party Membership (*M*), Number of Terms (*T*), Judgment on Perjury (*P*), and Judgement on Obstruction of Justice (*O*)

Configurations MTPO	Frequencies m	$\hat{m}$	Statistics z	$p(z)$	Type/Antitype?
1111	32	8.80	7.82	$<\alpha^*$	T
1112	0	8.80	−2.97	0.0015	A
1121	0	7.20	−2.68	0.0036	
1122	0	7.20	−2.68	0.0036	
1211	13	3.58	4.96	$<\alpha^*$	T
1212	0	3.58	−1.89	0.0293	
1221	0	2.93	−1.71	0.0436	
1222	0	2.93	−1.71	0.0436	
2111	3	8.25	−1.83	0.0338	
2112	4	8.25	−1.48	0.0694	
2121	0	6.75	−2.60	0.0047	
2122	23	6.75	6.26	$<\alpha^*$	T
2211	2	6.88	−1.86	0.0315	
2212	1	6.88	−2.24	0.0125	
2221	0	5.63	−2.37	0.0088	
2222	22	5.63	6.90	$<\alpha^*$	T

[a] $<\alpha^*$ indicates that the tail probability is smaller than can be expressed with four decimal places.

model must therefore include the main effects and the interactions of these variables. In general, the CFA base model must be saturated in the variables that are cross-classified product-multinomial.

The Six Steps of Configural Frequency Analysis

In this section, we describe the six steps researchers take when applying CFA (von Eye, 2002). We first list the steps and then explicate them in more detail. The six steps are:

(1) Decision concerning type of CFA to perform: frequentist or Bayesian CFA

(2) Specification of a CFA base model and estimation of expected cell frequencies

(3) Selection of a concept of deviation from independence

(4) Selection of a significance test

(5) Application of significance tests and identification of configurations that constitute types or antitypes

(6) Interpretation of types and antitypes.

The following paragraphs give an overview of these six steps. The following sections provide details, illustrations, and examples. Readers already conversant with CFA will notice the many new facets that have been developed to increase the number of models and options of CFA. Readers new to CFA will realize the multifaceted nature of the method.

SELECTION OF FREQUENTIST OR BAYESIAN CONFIGURAL FREQUENCY ANALYSIS

The first models of CFA were formulated from a frequentist perspective (Lienert, 1969). This is no surprise considering that Bayesian statistics was less well developed in the 1960s. In the meantime, however, Bayesian statistics that used to be computationally challenging has developed to be a formidable methodology for which computer programs are available.

Various approaches to Bayesian variants of CFA exist (Wood, Sher, & von Eye, 1994; Gutiérrez-Peña & von Eye, 2000, 2004; von Eye, Schuster, & Gutiérrez-Peña, 2000). Bayesian CFA has been shown to be practical in the sense that it can be performed using standard statistical software. In this chapter, we focus on frequentist CFA. However, to provide an idea of *Bayesian CFA*, consider the *Bayes Theorem*:

$$\Pr(B_j|A) = \frac{\Pr(A|B_j)\Pr(B_j)}{\sum_j \Pr(A|B_j)\Pr(B_j)},$$

where $Pr(A|B_j)$ is the conditional probability of event A, given event B_j. The theorem gives the probabilities for B_j when the event A is known and has occurred. $Pr(B_j)$ is known as the *prior probability*, and $Pr(B_j|A)$ is the posterior probability. $Pr(A|B_j)$ is the normalized *likelihood*. The events $B_1, \ldots, B_J$ are mutually exclusive and exhaustive.

Bayesian inference is based on Bayes' Theorem and involves four principal steps (Everitt, 1998; Gelman, Carlin, Stern, & Rubin, 1995):

(1) Calculating the likelihood, $f(x|\theta)$, that describes the data X in terms of the unknown parameters θ;

(2) Calculating the prior distribution, $f(\theta)$, which reflects knowledge about θ that existed prior to the collection of data;

(3) Employing the Bayes Theorem to calculate the *posterior distribution*, $f(\theta|x)$, which reflects knowledge about θ after having observed the data; this step implies that the distribution $f(\theta|x)$ can be updated each time new data come in; and

(4) Deriving inference statements and making statistical decisions based on the posterior distribution.

One of the fundamental differences between Bayesian and frequentist null hypothesis testing concerns the *prior distribution*. Frequentist statistics does not use the prior distribution. It only uses the likelihood. Stated differently, the likelihood and the prior distribution that contains the researcher's knowledge or beliefs about the parameters make Bayesian analysis unique and different from frequentist analysis. Applied in the context of CFA, Bayesian inference allows one to describe the probability density of the observed—that is, the posterior distribution—based on some prior distribution. In Bayesian CFA, the prior distribution reflects the CFA base model and, possibly, additional knowledge about the process that generated the data.

The decision concerning the selection of frequentist or Bayesian CFA can be guided by the existence of prior knowledge. If prior knowledge exists, for example, in the form of prior results or theoretical assumptions concerning the data generating process, then Bayesian CFA may be the method of choice. If, however, no such knowledge exists, then standard frequentist CFA may be preferable.

SELECTION OF A CONFIGURAL FREQUENCY ANALYSIS BASE MODEL AND ESTIMATION OF EXPECTED CELL FREQUENCIES

Expected cell frequencies for most CFA models (for exceptions, *see*, for example, von Eye & Mun, 2007; von Eye & Niedermeier, 1999) are estimated using the log-frequency model $\log \hat{m} = X\lambda$, where $\hat{m}$ is the array of model frequencies—that is, frequencies that conform to the model specifications—X is the *design matrix*. Its vectors reflect the CFA base model under study. λ is the vector of model parameters. These parameters are not in the center of interest in frequentist CFA. Instead, CFA focuses on the discrepancies between the expected and the observed cell frequencies. Configural frequency analysis is applied with the anticipation that the base model, which takes into account all effects that are NOT of interest to the researchers, fails to describe the data well. If types and antitypes emerge, then they indicate (1) where the most prominent discrepancies between the base model and the data are, and (2) that the effects of interest exist. For an example, consider the base model of P-CFA discussed above (von Eye & Rovine, 1994; von Eye, Mair, & Bogat, 2005).

SELECTION OF A CONCEPT OF DEVIATION FROM INDEPENDENCE

In CFA application, types and antitypes emerge when the discrepancy between observed and expected cell frequencies is statistically significant. Interestingly, the measures that are available to describe the discrepancies use different definitions of deviation, and they differ in the assumptions that must be made for proper application. For example, the χ^2-based measures assess the magnitude of the discrepancy relative to the expected frequency. This group of measures differs mostly in statistical power and can be employed under any sampling scheme. The hypergeometric test and the binomial test also assess the magnitude of the discrepancy, but they presuppose product-multinomial sampling. The relative risk, RR_i, defined as the ratio N_i/E_i where i indexes the configurations, indicates the frequency with which an event was observed, relative to the frequency with which it was expected. RR_i is a descriptive measure (cf. DuMouchel, 1999). RR_i is also applicable under any sampling scheme. Similarly, the measure log P (for a formal definition, see DuMouchel, 1999) has been used both descriptively and to test CFA null hypotheses. If used for statistical inference, the measure is similar to the binomial and other tests used in CFA, although the rank order of the assessed extremity of the discrepancy between the observed and the expected cell frequencies can differ dramatically. Some CFA software packages include log P as a descriptive measure (von Eye, 2007).

Two-group CFA compares two groups of respondents. The comparison uses information from two sources. The first source consists of the frequencies with which particular configurations were observed in the comparison groups. The second source consists of the sizes of the comparison groups. The statistics on which the decisions concerning group differences are based can be distinguished based on whether they are *marginal-dependent* or *marginal-free*. Marginal-dependent measures indicate the magnitude of an association under consideration of the marginal distribution of responses. Marginal-free measures only consider the association. It is easy to show that marginal-dependent tests can suggest different appraisals of data than marginal-free tests (von Eye, Spiel, & Rovine, 1995).

Marginal-free measures have been discussed mostly in the context of two-group CFA. Well-known marginal-free measures include the odds ratio and the log-linear interaction. Marginal-dependent measures include the Φ-coefficient and the correlation ρ.

SELECTION OF SIGNIFICANCE TEST

Three arguments can be used to guide the selection of measures for CFA: *exact versus approximative* test, *statistical power*, and *sampling scheme*. In addition, the tests employed in CFA differ in their sensitivity to types and antitypes. For example, the Pearson X^2-test is the least sensitive to antitypes. In comparison, all other tests are more sensitive to antitypes. If samples are very large, all tests identify types and antitypes at about equal rates. Anscombe's (1953) z-approximation occupies the other end of the spectrum. In particular, when samples are small, it tends to over-emphasize antitypes.

PERFORMING SIGNIFICANCE TESTS AND IDENTIFYING CONFIGURATIONS AS CONSTITUTING TYPES OR ANTITYPES

Based on the cell-wise significance tests, one determines whether a configuration constitutes a type, an antitype, or supports the null hypothesis. It is important to keep in mind that exploratory CFA usually involves employing significance tests to each cell in a cross-classification. This procedure comes with the risk of an inflated α error. The inflation is caused by capitalizing on chance and dependence of CFA tests. In large tables, the increased risk can result in large numbers of possibly wrong conclusions about the existence of types and antitypes. Therefore, before labeling configurations as type/antitype-constituting, measures must be taken to protect the test-wise α. A selection of such measures was presented earlier.

INTERPRETATION OF TYPES AND ANTITYPES

The interpretation of types and antitypes uses five kinds of information. The first is the *meaning of the configuration* itself. The meaning of a configuration is given by the definition of the categories of the variables that span the cross-classification under study. The meaning of a type or antitype can often be seen in tandem with the meaning of the configuration. For example, it may not be a surprise that there exist no cars with built-in shoe-shining machines (Elvis Presley's car might be the sole exception). Therefore, in the space of cars, cars with built-in shoe shining machines may meaningfully define an antitype. In contrast, one may entertain the hypothesis that couples that voluntarily stay together for a long time are happy. Thus, in the space of couples, happy, long-lasting relationships may form a type.

The second source of information is the *CFA base model*. The base model determines nature and interpretation of types and antitypes. Consider, for example, the CFA model of variable independence. If this model yields types or antitypes, then they can be interpreted as reflecting local associations (Havránek & Lienert, 1984). Another example is P-CFA. As was explained above, the base model of P-CFA is saturated in both the predictors and the criteria. The relationships among predictors and criteria are not taken into account, because they may lead to the formation of types and antitypes. If P-CFA yields types or antitypes, then they are reflective of predictive local relationships among predictors and criteria, not just of associations among predictors and criteria in general.

The third kind of information is the *sampling scheme*. In multinomial sampling, types and antitypes reflect characteristics of the entire population from which the sample was drawn. In product-multinomial sampling, types and antitypes reflect characteristics of the particular sub-population in which they were found. Consider the type that may emerge for men who own sport utility vehicles and drive them more than 20,000 miles a year. This type may describe the male but not the female population, or the human population in general.

The fourth kind of information is the *nature of the statistical measure* that was employed for the search for types and antitypes. As was indicated above, different measures can yield different patterns of types and antitypes. Therefore, interpretation needs to consider the nature of the measure, and results from different studies can be compared only if the same measures were employed.

The fifth kind of information is external in the sense of *external validity*. Often, researchers ask whether types and antitypes also differ in other variables than the ones used in CFA. Methods of discriminant analysis, logistic regression, MANOVA, or CFA can be used to compare configurations in other variables (for examples, *see*, von Eye, Mair, & Mun, 2010).

Sample Models and Applications of Configural Frequency Analysis

In the following sections, we present sample CFA models and applications. The original CFA base model, that of variable independence, was already introduced in the context of Table 5.3. Therefore, this model will not be repeated here. Instead, we begin, in the Prediction CFA Analysis and 2-Group CFA section, with an application of P-CFA and a special case of P-CFA: two-group CFA. In the Models for Longitudinal CFA Analysis, we discuss examples of longitudinal CFA, and in the Mediator CFA Analysis section, we discuss Mediator CFA.

Prediction Configural Frequency Analysis and 2-Group CFA

In this section, we first discuss Prediction CFA (P-CFA), and then a formally equivalent special case: two-group CFA.

PREDICTION CONFIGURAL FREQUENCY ANALYSIS

As was discussed in the section with sample questions above, P-CFA does not ask whether variables can be predicted from one another. Rather, P-CFA asks whether a particular pattern of categories of predictor variables allows one to predict an above or below expectancy occurrence rate of a particular pattern of criterion variables. The base model of all P-CFA models (the original P-CFA was proposed by Heilmann, Lienert, & Maly, 1979) has the following characteristics:

1. It is *saturated in the predictors*. Because of this characteristic, it is guaranteed that types and antitypes cannot emerge just because associations among predictors exist.

2. It is *saturated in the criteria*. Because of this characteristic, it is guaranteed that types and antitypes cannot emerge just because associations among criterion variables exist.

3. It proposes *independence among predictors and criteria*.

Because types and antitypes cannot result from associations among the predictors or associations among the criteria, P-CFA types and antitypes necessarily indicate predictor – criteria relationships at the level of patterns of variable categories. If the null hypothesis for Cell r can be rejected, then Cell r constitutes a *prediction type*, if $m_r > \hat{m}$, and a *prediction antitype*, if $m_r < \hat{m}$. In other words, if, for the pattern of predictor and criterion variables in Cell r, more cases are found than expected, then the predictor pattern of Cell r predicts the above expectancy-occurrence of the criterion pattern of Cell r. If fewer cases are found than expected, then the predictor pattern of Cell r predicts the below-expectancy-occurrence of the criterion pattern of Cell r. Given the right conditions (e.g., non-confounding), prediction types can be interpreted as causal—for example, by stating that a particular predictor pattern causes a particular criterion pattern to occur. Similarly, antitypes may be interpreted as causal as well—for example, by saying that a particular predictor pattern prevents a particular criterion pattern from occurring.

von Eye, Mair, and Bogat (2005) discuss the following data example. The New York Times published on January 8, 2003, a cross-classification of the three variables Race of Victim (V), Race of Defendant (D), and Penalty Issued (P) for 1,311 death penalty-eligible murder cases in Maryland that had been recorded from 1978 to 1999[2]. For the present purposes, we code the two race variables as 1 = *Black*, and 2 = *White*, and the Penalty variable as 1 = *death penalty not issued* and 2 = *death penalty issued*. In the following application of P-CFA, we ask whether patterns of the two race variables allow one to predict the penalty issued. We use the P-CFA base model

$$\log \hat{m} = \lambda + \lambda^V + \lambda^D + \lambda^P + \lambda^{VD}$$

This model takes all three main effects into account as well as the association between Race of Defendant and Race of Victim, and it proposes that these two variables are unrelated to the penalty issued. For the cell-wise CFA tests, we use the z-test and protect α using the Bonferroni procedure, which results in the protected $\alpha* = 0.00625$. Table 5.5 presents results of P-CFA.

The goodness-of-fit likelihood ratio X^2 for the CFA base model is 35.34. This value suggests significant data–model discrepancies ($df = 3; p < 0.01$). Therefore, we expect types and antitypes to emerge. P-CFA suggests that one type and one antitype exist. The antitype, constituted by Configuration 1 1 2, indicates that the pattern Black defendant–black victim is less likely to result in the death penalty than one would expect under the assumptions specified in the P-CFA base model. The type is constituted by Configuration 1 2 2. It indicates that the pattern White defendant–black victim is more likely to result in the death penalty than expected.

Comparing Logistic Regression With Prediction CFA. For a comparison with P-CFA, von Eye, Mair, and Bogat (2005) also estimated a logistic regression model of the data in Table 5.5. The Hosmer and Lemeshow goodness-of-fit $X^2 = 0.88$ suggests that the model–data discrepancies are non-significant ($df = 1; p = 0.35$). The logistic regression model fits and it can be concluded that the two predictors, Race of Defendant and Race of Victim, are predictive of the Penalty issued for murder. The significance tests for the parameters show that Race of Defendant is the only significant predictor. Both predictors had been entered simultaneously.

From a model comparison perspective, an interesting question is whether the results from P-CFA and logistic regression are the same, just disguised differently. To answer this question, we compare the statistical models used for the estimation of parameters and expected cell frequencies. The P-CFA base model was defined above. Models of logistic regression with one dependent measure have the following characteristics:

(1) They are saturated in the predictors; and
(2) They contain the terms that relate individual predictors and, possibly, their interactions to the criteria.

In the present data example, the logistic regression model is

$$\log \hat{m} = \lambda + \lambda^V + \lambda^D + \lambda^P + \lambda^{VD} + \lambda^{VP} + \lambda^{DP}$$

(Note that logistic regression models can always equivalently be expressed in terms of log-linear models, but not the other way around; *see* Table 5.6). As the P-CFA base model, the logistic regression model is saturated in the predictors, because it contains the main effects and the interaction between the two predictors, V and D. Another similarity is

Table 5.5. PCFA of the predictors Race of Victim (V), Race of Defendant (D) and the Criterion Penalty (P)

Configuration VDP	m	$\hat{m}$	z	p	Type/antitype?
111	593	570.094	0.959	0.169	
112	14	36.906	−3.770	0.000	Antitype
121	7284	302.422	−1.059	0.145	
122	38	19.578	4.164	0.000	Type
211	25	24.419	0.118	0.453	
212	1	1.581	−0.462	0.322	
221	272	277.064	−0.304	0.380	
222	23	17.936	1.196	0.116	

Table 5.6. Logistic Regression Models and Corresponding P-CFA Base Models

Model in hierarchy	Log-linear representation	Corresponding Logit model	Corresponding P-CFA base model	Terms not part of P-CFA base model[a]
1	[VD][P]	α	[VD][P]	[VP][DP][VDP]
2a	[VD][VP]	$\alpha + \beta_i^V$	[VD][DP]	[VP][VDP]
2b	[VD][DP]	$\alpha + \beta_j^D$	[VD][VP]	[DP][VDP]
3	[VD][VP][DP]	$\alpha + \beta_i^V + \beta_j^D$	[VD][P]	[VP][DP][VDP]
4	[VDP]	$\alpha + \beta_i^V + \beta_j^D + \beta_{ij}^{VD}$	[VD][P]	[VP][DP][VDP]

[a]In this column, the redundant lower order terms are included in addition to the higher order terms; this was done to illustrate the predictor–criterion relationships not included in the P-CFA base models.

that neither model contains the three-way interaction among all three variables. The logistic regression model differs from the P-CFA base model in that it contains all bivariate predictor–criterion relationships. Including the three-way interaction would render this model (but not the P-CFA base model) saturated.

Other models are conceivable. Table 5.6 summarizes a selection of logistic regression and the corresponding P-CFA base models for the three variables in the present example. Each of the base models can be expressed in terms of a hierarchical log-linear model (for notation, see Agresti, 2002).

The first model in Table 5.6 proposes that V and D cannot be used to predict P. Model 2a proposes that, of the two potential predictors, only V can be used to predict P. Model 2b proposes that only D can be used to predict P. The third model is the standard logistic regression model. It includes both predictors. The fourth model is saturated. It includes the three-way interaction of D, V, and P.

Table 5.6 shows that from a P-CFA perspective, Models 1 and 3 in the hierarchy are equivalent. The first model states that neither predictor is related to the criterion. The third model states that both predictors are related to the criterion. The P-CFA base model for both states that neither predictor is related to the criterion. Both models can be contradicted only if predictor–criterion relationships exist. Therefore, if either model is contradicted, then types and antitypes suggest that, at least locally, the predictors and the criterion are related to each other.

TWO-GROUP CFA

Two-group CFA allows researchers to ask whether two (or more) groups differ in configurations of variables. In this respect, two-group CFA is comparable to discriminant analysis and logistic regression. However, as in all comparisons of CFA with other methods of statistics, two-group CFA expresses results in terms of configurations in which the groups differ rather then variables in which the groups differ (Lienert, 1971; von Eye, 2002; von Eye, Spiel, & Rovine, 1995).

Two-group CFA allows researchers to answer the question whether and where the two groups differ in the distribution of the configurations. The null hypothesis is that no differences exist between the two groups in the configurations. This null hypothesis is tested locally—that is, for each configuration. The base model for two-group CFA:

(1) is saturated in the variables used to compare the two groups; and

(2) proposes independence between the grouping variable(s) and the comparison (also called discriminant) variables.

(3) If two or more variables are used to specify the groups, then the model is also saturated in these variables.

Types can emerge from this base model only if a relationship exists between the discriminant and the grouping variables. This characteristic is shared by two-group CFA and P-CFA. A type in two-group CFA suggests that in one of the two groups, a particular configuration was observed more often than expected based on the base model. In two-group CFA, there is no need to distinguish between types and antitypes. If one group was observed exhibiting a particular configuration more often than the other group, then, one can conclude that both a type and an antitype were identified. Therefore, two-group CFA identifies *discrimination*

Table 5.7. 2 × 2 × 2 Cross-Classification for Two-Group CFA

Configurations $P_1 P_2^a$	Groups A	B	Row totals
11	m_{11A}	m_{11B}	$m_{11.}$
12	m_{12A}	m_{22B}	$m_{12.}$
21	m_{21A}	m_{21B}	$m_{21.}$
22	m_{22A}	m_{21B}	$m_{22.}$
Column totals	$m_{..A}$	$m_{..B}$	m

[a] P_1 and P_2 are the discriminant variables, A and B are categories of the grouping variable

types. These are type-antitype pairs that co-occur by necessity.

For an illustration of two-group CFA, consider a 2 × 2 × 2 cross-classification where the last variable indicates group membership. Table 5.7 displays the arrangement of this cross-classification.

Two-group CFA compares the two groups in each configuration. This comparison implies forming a 2 × 2 cross-classification that contains the target configuration in its first row and the aggregated remaining configurations in its second row. Table 5.8 provides a scheme for the resulting 2 × 2 cross-classification.

To test the null hypothesis of no association between discriminant configuration ij and the grouping variable, a number of tests has been proposed. A selection of these tests is presented here (for more tests, *see* von Eye, 2002).

The first test for two-group CFA to be presented here is Fisher's exact test, which gives the probability of cell frequency as a

$$p(a) = \frac{A!B!C!D!}{N!a!b!c!d!},$$

where A, B, C, and D are defined as in Table 5.8. Fisher's test has the virtue of being exact. No assumptions need to be made concerning the characteristics of an approximation of some test statistic to some sampling distribution. However, the test can be numerically intensive to calculate—particularly when samples are large. Therefore, it appears only rarely as an option in CFA programs.

The following test is approximative. It is best applied when samples are large. It is the X^2,

$$X^2 = \frac{N(|a \cdot d - b \cdot c| - 0.5 \cdot N)^2}{ABCD}.$$

This X^2 statistic is approximately distributed as χ^2 with $df = 1$.

Alternative tests that have been proposed include the *odds ratio* and the *correlation coefficient*. For the 2 × 2 tables that we study in two-group CFA, the odds ratio is

$$\theta = \frac{p_{11}/p_{21}}{p_{12}/p_{22}}.$$

The correlation coefficient is

$$\rho = \frac{p_{11}p_{22} - p_{12}p_{21}}{\sqrt{p_{.1}p_{.2}p_{.1}p_{.2}}}.$$

The correlation coefficient ρ is identical to Pearson's ϕ coefficient.

The odds ratio is the only test in this group that is marginal-free (Goodman, 1991). All other tests are marginal-dependent. The results of two-group CFA can vary depending on the data characteristics to which the selected test is sensitive to (in addition to differences in power).

Data Example. For the following data example, we use data from a study on the development of aggressive behaviors in adolescents (Finkelstein, von Eye, & Preece, 1994). The authors asked adolescents to indicate whether they perpetrated physically aggressive acts against their peers. Data were collected in the years 1983, 1985, and 1987. One hundred fourteen adolescents participated (67 females).

Table 5.8. 2 × 2 Cross-Classification for Two-Group CFA Testing

Configurations $P_1 P_2$	Groups A	B	Row totals
ij	$a = m_{ijA}$	$b = m_{ijB}$	$m_{ij.}$
all others combined	$c = m_{..A} - m_{ijA}$	$d = m_{..B} - m_{ijB}$	$m - m_{ij.}$
Column totals	$m_{..A}$	$m_{..B}$	m

To illustrate the use of two-group CFA, we ask whether the developmental trajectories of physical aggression against peers are gender-specific. For the present purposes, we dichotomized the responses at the grand mean. Three variables resulted, P83, P85, and P87, coded as 1 = *below* and 2 = *above average*. Gender was coded as 1 = *female* and 2 = *male*. We employed the normal approximation of the binomial test and protected α using the Holland-Copenhaver procedure.

The base model for this analysis takes into account:

1. The main effects of all four variables in the analysis; and

2. All first and second order associations among the three physical aggression variables.

The base model is thus saturated in the physical aggression variables, and discrimination types cannot emerge just because of the autocorrelations among the repeatedly observed variables. In addition, this base model implies independence between Gender and the three physical aggression variables. Table 5.9 displays results from two-group CFA.

The overall goodness-of-fit LR-X^2 = 24.65 suggests that the base model fails to describe the data well ($df = 7$; $p = 0.001$). Accordingly, Table 5.9 suggests that three discrimination types exist. The first is constituted by the Configuration pair 1 1 1 1 and 1 1 1 2. It shows that the trajectory of consistently below average physical aggression is observed more often in girls than in boys. The second discrimination type pair, 2 2 1 1 and 2 2 1 2 suggests that the trajectory of above-average physical aggression over the first two observation periods that is followed by below-average physical aggression over the third period is also observed more often in girls than in boys. The third discrimination type pair, 2 2 2 1 and 2 2 2 2, suggests that the trajectory of consistently above average physical aggression against peers is found more often in boys than in girls.

Using the odds ratio—that is, the marginal-free measure of interaction in a 2 × 2 table—the first and the last discrimination types emerge also. The second discrimination type pair, 2 2 1 1 and 2 2 1 2, does not surface again. It is important to note that this difference does not necessarily reflect a difference in power between the z-test and θ. It may also reflect the difference between marginal-free and marginal-dependent measures of interaction.

A comparison of these results with those obtained from log-linear modeling illustrates the differences in focus: variable relationships versus configurations. One fitting log-linear model includes the two-way interactions [G, P83], [G, P85], [P83, P85], [P83, P87], and [P85, P87]. For this model, the overall goodness-of-fit LR-X^2 is 7.09 ($df = 6$; $p = 0.31$). This model suggests that time-adjacent associations (parallel to autocorrelations in continuous data) are needed to explain the data in Table 5.9 as well as the associations between Gender and Physical Aggression during the first two observation periods. These results certainly are plausible and interpretable. However, the results from two-group CFA tell us precisely where in the table the gender differences can be found. In all other configurations, there are no gender differences.

Models for Longitudinal CFA

A large number of CFA models for longitudinal data has been proposed (von Eye, 2002; von Eye, Mair, & Mun, 2010). For example, the following questions can be answered using CFA of longitudinal data:

1. Is the distribution of differences between time-adjacent observations different than expected, is it related to other variables, or can it be predicted from other variables?

2. Is the distribution of second or higher-order differences (differences between lower-order differences) distributed as expected, is it related to other variables, or can it be predicted from other variables?

3. Do shifts from one category to another occur at unexpected rates, and can these shifts be predicted from other variables?

4. Are trends and location of scores related to each other or to other variables? Here, in Questions 1 through 3, and in the following questions, the "other variables" can be time-varying but also time-invariant covariates.

5. Are the (categorized) coefficients of polynomials that describe series of scores distributed as expected, are they related to other variables, or can they be predicted from other variables?

6. Are characteristics of series of scores that differ in length related to or predictable from other variables?

7. How do outcomes in control groups compare to outcomes in treatment groups?

8. Are there CFA-detectable patterns of correlation or distance sequences over time?

Table 5.9. Two-Group CFA of Developmental Trajectories of Physical Aggression Against Peers

Configuration P83 P85 P87 G	m	z	p	Type?
1111	32.00			
1112	10.00	2.886	0.001953	Discrimination type
1121	2.00			
1122	0.00	1.195	0.116042	
1211	3.00			
1212	3.00	−0.448	0.326908	
1221	4.00			
1222	1.00	0.986	0.162024	
2111	12.00			
2112	6.00	0.741	0.229196	
2121	5.00			
2122	2.00	0.702	0.241284	
2211	5.00			
2212	12.00	−2.666	0.003837	Discrimination type
2221	4.00			
2222	13.00	−3.200	0.000687	Discrimination type

9. Are there extreme patterns of development in within-individual series of scores?

10. Can patterns of endpoints of development be predicted from prior development?

11. Can patterns of series of scores be predicted from starting points?

12. Can trajectories of repeated observations be predicted from other variables (see the example in Table 5.9)?

13. Are trajectories related to each other at the level of configurations?

14. Are the relationships among trajectories moderated by other variables?

In the following sections, we present two examples of longitudinal CFA. The first concerns the prediction of endpoints or outcomes, the second concerns the study of relationships between two or more series of scores.

PREDICTING ENDPOINTS OF DEVELOPMENT

Predicting endpoints or outcome of development is important in a large number of contexts. Examples include the prediction of the endpoint of the development of adolescent drug use, the endpoint of a period of domestic violence, the outcome of training efforts, the outcome of therapy, or the outcome of incarceration. In each case, a series of events that occur before the endpoint is used to predict a particular endpoint or outcome. In most instances, the endpoint or outcome is defined as a variable category, a particular state, or a particular event. Therefore, CFA is a method of interest when endpoints are to be predicted.

The base model for CFA of predicting endpoints takes the following effects into account (see von Eye, Mair, & Mun, 2010):

1. Main effects of all variables.
2. Interactions of every order among the variables observed before the predicted event. This base model is thus saturated in the observations made before the predicted event.

The base model of CFA of predicting endpoints assumes that the predicted endpoint is unrelated to the observations made prior to the endpoint. It thus can be rejected only if relationships between the prior events and the endpoint exist.

Data Example. To illustrate the application of CFA of predicting endpoints, we use the Finkelstein, von Eye, and Preece (1994) data on the development of aggression in adolescence again. We ask whether earlier observations of Physical Aggression Against Peers in 1983 and 1985 ($P83$ and $P85$) are predictive of above- versus below-average Physical Aggression Against Peers in 1987 (*P*87). The base model for this analysis is

$$\log \hat{m} = \lambda + \lambda^{P83} + \lambda^{P85} + \lambda^{P87} + \lambda^{P83,P85}.$$

There are only three interactions that could possibly be included in this log-linear model in addition to the ones included already in the base model. These are the interactions [*P*83, *P*87], [*P*85, *P*87], and [*P*83, *P*85, *P*87]. Each of these interactions links an earlier observation with the endpoint. Therefore, if the base model is rejected, then at least one of these three interactions must exist, and one can conclude that the endpoint can be predicted from the earlier observations. For the following CFA, we use the *z*-test and protect α using the Holland and Copenhaver procedure. Table 5.10 displays CFA results.

The overall goodness-of-fit of the base model LR-X^2 is 25.21 ($df = 3$; $p < 0.01$). The model is thus rejected and we anticipate that types and antitypes emerge. Indeed, Table 5.10 shows that CFA identified one type and one antitype. The antitype is constituted by Configuration 1 1 2. It suggests that it is particularly unlikely that an adolescent turns out above-average in Physical Aggression Against Peers in 1987 when he/she showed below average scores in both 1983 and 1985. The type, constituted by Configuration 2 2 2, suggests that adolescents who showed above average aggression in both 1983 and 1985 are more likely than chance to show aggression above the average in 1987. All other trajectories do not occur more or less likely than expected under the assumption of independence of the 1983–1985 trajectory from the 1987 observation.

This result shows that CFA identifies those trajectory–outcome patterns that occur at unexpected rates. Table 5.10 shows, in addition, that these are not necessarily the most frequent patterns. The most frequent pattern is Configuration 1 1 1. However, this pattern occurs at a rate that conforms to the one predicted from the independence assumption.

RELATING SERIES OF MEASURES TO EACH OTHER

One of the more interesting yet under-researched questions in longitudinal studies concerns the relationship of two or more series of measures to each other. From a CFA perspective, types and antitypes that indicate relationships between series of measures can emerge if the base model with the following characteristics is rejected:

1. The main effects of all variables are taken into account.
2. Interactions of every order among the measures of the first series are taken into account.
3. Interactions of every order among the measures of the second series are taken into account.

In general, interactions of any order are taken into account within each comparison series of measures, and independence of the series is assumed. If this model is rejected, one or more of the interactions must exist that link series to one another.

Table 5.10. Predicting Physical Aggression Against Peers from Earlier Developmental Trajectories of Physical Aggression Against Peers

Configuration P83 P85 P87	*m*	$\hat{m}$	*z*	*p*	Type/antitype?
111	42.00	32.035	1.7606	0.039153	
112	2.00	11.965	−2.8808	0.001983	Antitype
121	6.00	8.009	−0.7098	0.238908	
122	5.00	2.991	1.1615	0.122727	
211	18.00	18.202	−0.0473	0.481141	
212	7.00	6.798	0.0774	0.469161	
221	17.00	24.754	−1.5586	0.059551	
222	17.00	9.246	2.5502	0.005383	Type

Data Example. To illustrate the CFA approach to the study of relationships among series of measures, we use the Finkelstein, von Eye, and Preece (1994) data on the development of aggression in adolescence again. We ask whether the series of two observations of Physical Aggression Against Peers in 1983 and 1987 (P83 and P87) is related to the series of two observations of Aggressive Impulses, that were observed at the same points in time (AI83 and AI87). The base model for this question is

$$\log \hat{m} = \lambda + \lambda^{P83} + \lambda^{P87} + \lambda^{P83,P87} + \lambda^{AI83} + \lambda^{AI87} + \lambda^{AI83,AI87}.$$

The following interactions are not part of this base model: [P83, AI83], [P83, AI87], [P87, AI83], [P87, AI87], [P83, AI83, AI87], [P87, AI83, AI87], [P83, P87, AI83], [P83, P87, AI87], and [P81, P87, AI83, AI87]. Each of these interactions involves at least one observation from both series of scores. Therefore, if the base model is rejected, then at least one of the interactions must exist that relates the two series to each other. This can result in the emergence of types and antitypes. Table 5.11 displays results from CFA. We used the z-test and Perli, Hommel, and Lehmacher's (1987) procedure to protect α.

The overall goodness-of-fit of the base model LR-X^2 is 28.46 ($df = 9$; $p < 0.01$). The model is thus rejected and we anticipate that types and antitypes emerge. The first type that is shown in Table 5.11, constituted by Configuration 1 1 – 1 1, suggests that consistently below average Physical Aggression Against Peers goes hand-in-hand with consistently below-average Aggressive Impulses. The largest number of respondents show this pattern. The second largest number shows Pattern 2 2 – 2 2. These are the respondents who show consistently above-average Physical Aggression Against Peers that goes hand-in-hand with consistently above-average

Table 5.11. Relating the Series of Measures of Physical Aggression Against Peers (*P*83 and *P*87) to the Series of Measures of Aggressive Impulses (*AI*83, *AI*87)

Configuration P83 P87 AI83 AI87	m	$\hat{m}$	z	p	Type/antitype?
1111	24.00	16.000	2.0000	0.022750	Type
1112	5.00	6.316	−0.5236	0.300290	
1121	10.00	10.526	−0.1622	0.435566	
1122	9.00	15.158	−1.5817	0.056864	
1211	1.00	2.333	−0.8729	0.191367	
1212	4.00	0.921	3.2082	0.000668	Type
1221	1.00	1.535	−0.4319	0.332916	
1222	1.00	2.211	−0.8142	0.207768	
2111	9.00	11.667	−0.7807	0.217484	
2112	3.00	4.605	−0.7480	0.227221	
2121	12.00	7.675	1.5610	0.059267	
2122	11.00	11.053	−0.0158	0.493685	
2211	4.00	8.000	−1.4142	0.078650	
2212	3.00	3.158	−0.0889	0.464600	
2221	2.00	5.263	−1.4224	0.077458	
2222	15.00	7.579	2.6956	0.003513	Type

Aggressive Impulses. One of the smaller cells also constitutes a type. This is Cell 1 2 – 1 2. It describes those respondents who increase their Physical Aggression Against Peers in parallel with an increase in Aggressive Impulses. All other cells support the null hypothesis, according to which the two series of measures are unrelated to each other, at the level of configurations.

Mediatior Configural Frequency Analysis

The process of mediation has found a considerable amount of interest in theories according to which effects are not necessarily direct such that only two variables are linked to each other. For methods of analysis of mediation hypotheses from a variable-oriented perspective, we refer the reader to the literature—particularly MacKinnon (Chapter 16, this volume; see also Baron & Kenny, 1986; MacKinnon, Fairchild, & Fritz, 2007; cf. von Eye, Mun, & Mair, 2009).

Mediation analysis with categorical variables that is undertaken in the context of person-oriented research aims at testing mediation hypotheses for particular patterns of variable categories rather than entire variables. This strategy has three characteristics (von Eye, Mun, & Mair, 2009):

1. Processes of mediation are not described at the level of variables but at the level of patterns of variable categories.
2. It can be expected that, in the same frequency table, some category patterns support mediation hypotheses, but others may not.
3. It is conceivable that, in the same frequency table, some of those patterns that support mediation hypotheses support hypotheses of full mediation, but others support hypotheses of partial mediation.

In the following sections, we describe the CFA approach to mediation analysis (*Configural Mediation Analysis*). The description is based on the approach proposed by von Eye, Mun, and Mair (2009). We begin with a definition of *configural mediation models*:

A *configural mediation model* is defined by three elements:

1. Types and antitypes that reflect the associations among predictors, mediators, and criteria;
2. Rules to make a decision about the existence of mediation

3. Rules to make a decision about the nature of mediation as either partial or full.

The rules under 2 and 3 are applied at the level of configurations instead of variables.

Configural mediation analysis can be performed in two ways (von Eye, Mair, & Mun, 2010). The first way involves (1) estimating a logit model, and (2) using CFA to determine the configurations that reflect mediation. The second way uses CFA methods throughout. In this chapter, we use only CFA methods.

This second approach to configural mediation analysis proceeds in two phases that are interwoven. The first phase involves performing a series of four CFA analyses. In these analyses, the relationships discussed in Baron and Kenny's (1986) procedure are examined. If types and antitypes result in the first phase, then the second phase can start. In this phase, comparisons of the type and antitype patterns from the analyses in the first phase are performed. These comparisons lead to decisions about the nature of mediation in a configuration.

PHASE I: FOUR BASE MODELS FOR CONFIGURAL MEDIATION ANALYSIS

In the first phase of configural mediation analysis, we estimate four base models to examine the relationships among the Predictor, P, the Mediator, M, and the outcome variable, O.

Model 1: Base Model of Variable Independence. The first of the four models is a standard, first order CFA—that is, the main effect model $[P], [M], [O]$. This analysis is needed for three reasons. First, it serves to determine whether types and antitypes exist at all. Only if this is the case can mediation hypotheses can be supported, in principle, at the level of individual configurations. If no types or antitypes emerge, then the analysis can stop after Model 1. However, if types and antitypes do emerge, then hypotheses of mediation can be entertained, and the following three models are estimated. Types and antitypes from Model 1 are a necessary condition for mediation to exist at the level of configurations. Second, the results from this model will, in the second phase, be compared with those from other models. Third, the results from the base model of variable independence are the ones that will be interpreted if mediation hypotheses prevail.

Model 2: Predicting the Outcome from Predictor and Mediator. Performing a CFA under Base Model 2 corresponds to estimating the second of the above regression equations. This base model includes $[P, M], [O]$, which is a CFA multiple regression model (*see* the Technical Elements of CFA Analysis section of this chapter). This model can lead to one of the following two conclusions. If a type or antitype from Model 1 disappears from Model 2, then the Predictor is related to the Mediator. If, however, a type or antitype from Model 1 remains, then the Predictor is unrelated to the Mediator, and the analysis comes, for this configuration, to an end. New types or antitypes from Model 2 suggest that the Predictor, the Mediator, or both are related to the Outcome. The following models need to be estimated to determine the characteristics of possibly existing mediator relationships.

Model 3: *Predicting the Outcome from the Mediator*. The third base model is also a configural prediction model. It relates the Predictor and the Mediator and also the Predictor and the Outcome to each other. The base model that accomplishes this task is [*P, M*][*P, O*]. If types and antitypes from Model 2 disappear under Model 3, then the relationship between the Predictor and the Outcome exists, for these configurations (cf. Steps 2 and 3 in Baron and Kenny's procedure; Kenny 2005). If new types and antitypes emerge from Model 3, then the relationship between the Mediator and the Outcome exists. The relationship between Mediator and Outcome is a necessary condition for mediation to exist.

Model 4: *Predicting the Outcome from the Predictor*. The fourth base model is another configural prediction model, parallel to the third. The Mediator is related to both the Predictor and the Outcome. The base model here is [*P, M*], [*M, O*]. If types and antitypes from Model 2 disappear under this base model, then the Mediator is directly related to the Outcome. If new types or antitypes appear under Model 4, then the direct relationship between the Predictor and the Outcome exists. This is required for partial mediation (see Kenny, 2005). If, under this model, types and antitypes do not disappear, then a fully mediated relationship can still exist.

In brief, the types and antitypes from these four CFA base models indicate whether

1. the variables *P, M*, and *O* are related at all (Model 1);
2. Predictor, Mediator, or both are related to the Outcome (Model 2);
3. the Mediator is related to the Outcome (Model 3); and
4. the Predictor is related to the Outcome (Model 4).

Table 5.12 recapitulates the four base models.

Table 5.12. CFA Base Models for Configural Mediation Analysis of Variables *P*, *M*, and *O*

Step	CFA base model	Types and antitypes can be caused by
1	[*P*], [*M*], [*O*]	[*P, M*], [*P, O*], [*M, O*], [*P, M, O*]
2	[*P, M*], [*O*]	[*M, O*], [*P, O*], [*P, M, O*]
3	[*P, M*], [*P, O*]	[*M, O*], [*P, M, O*]
4	[*P, M*], [*M, O*]	[*P, O*], [*P, M, O*]

Interestingly, Table 5.12 indicates that, in each model, types and antitypes can result from the three-way interaction between *P*, *M*, and *O*—that is, [*P, M, O*]. This interaction can be the cause for types and antitypes to emerge either by itself or in combination with any of the other effects listed in the right hand column of Table 5.12. von Eye, Mun, and Mair (2009) discuss methods for exploring the role that this three-way interaction plays in mediation analysis. The one recommended for most applications involves ignoring the three-way interaction. This decision can be justified with reference to the *Effect Sparsity Principle* (Box & Meyer, 1986; von Eye, 2008; Wu & Hamada, 2009). This principle suggests that as the order of interactions increases, they become increasingly less important. In a way related to the *Pareto Principle*, the Effect Sparsity Principle focuses on the "vital few" instead of the "trivial many."

PHASE II: DECISIONS CONCERNING THE TYPE OF MEDIATION

The conclusion from the results from the four base models in Table 5.12 concerns the existence of mediation. In other words, the existence of relationships is necessary for mediation, among the three variables *P*, *M*, and *O*, at the level of configurations. The specific nature of mediation as not existing, full, or partial is unknown at this point. To determine the nature of mediation, a series of comparisons can be performed. The result of these comparisons is a decision concerning the kind of mediation. This decision describes the nature of mediation for particular types and antitypes.

In configural mediation analysis, each configuration is examined with the goal of determining whether it supports a hypothesis of full or partial mediation. Based on the series of comparisons, it can occur that, in the same table, one group of configurations conforms with the base model, because mediation hypotheses are not supported. A second group of configurations may support the hypothesis of full mediation, and a third group of configurations may support the hypothesis of partial mediation.

We now describe the comparisons, with a focus on individual types and antitypes.

Six possible outcomes are of interest.

1. If Model 1 (standard, first order CFA) results in no types and no antitypes, or if none of the Models 2, 3, or 4 results in types or antitypes then there is no mediation because the variables P, M, and O are unrelated to one another at the level of individual configurations. In this case, the following comparisons of configural mediation analysis are not needed.

2. If a type or an antitype from Model 1 also appears under each of the Models 2, 3, and 4 then none of the bivariate relationships between the three variables P, M, and O exists. Therefore, types and antitypes with this characteristic do not suggest mediation.

3. If a type or an antitype from Model 1 disappears in Model 2, then the path from P to M exists, for this particular configuration. Both full and partial mediation are still possible. The information generated in the following comparisons is needed to make a decision about type of mediation.

4. If a type or an antitype from Model 2 disappears in Model 3, then the path from P to O exists, for this particular configuration. Both forms of mediation and the direct-effects-only model are still options. The following comparisons result in decisions about type of relationships among P, M, and O.

5. If a type or an antitype from Model 3 disappears in Model 4, then the path from M to O exists. Both forms of mediation are still options.

6. If a type or an antitype from Model 1 disappears in all three Models 2, 3, and 4, then it is unclear whether its disappearance results because the path from P to M exists (Outcome 2) or whether other paths exist. In this case, additional models may need to be estimated to determine the role played by the other paths.

Data Example. For the example, we use data from the OTO study (Lerner, Taylor, & von Eye, 2002; Taylor et al., 2002) again. The OTO is a longitudinal study of the development of positive functioning, and the role that individual and ecological assets play in this functioning, in African-American male youth. The youth who participated in this study were either gang members ($n = 45$; average age at the beginning of the study $= 15.82$ years) or members of CBO ($n = 50$; average age at the beginning of the study $= 16.31$ years). The participants indicated in interviews whether they had been sexually active in the last calendar year. The variables were scored as $1 = $ *sexually active* and $2 = $ *not active*; $1 = $ *gang member*; $2 = $ *CBO member*; and $1 = $ *below average number of assets* and $2 = $ *above average number of assets*. In the following analyses, we explore the mediation hypothesis that the link between Assets at Time 1 (A) and sexual activity at Time 1 (S) is mediated by group membership (Gang or CBO member; G). The analyses are exploratory in the sense that we do not specify configuration-specific hypotheses about which type of mediation will result. It should also be noted that there is no causal implication in the mediation hypotheses in this data example. We do not propose that assets at Time 1 prevent sexual activity at Time 1 in either Gangs or CBO groups. However, we do assume that the probability of sexual activity may be lower for those respondents who have more assets, in particular for CBO members.

The following four CFA models are estimated:

Model 1: $\log \hat{m} = \lambda + \lambda_i^{Assets\ 1} + \lambda_j^{Gang} + \lambda_k^{Sex\ 1}$,

Model 2: $\log \hat{m} = \lambda + \lambda_i^{Assets\ 1} + \lambda_j^{Gang} + \lambda_k^{Sex\ 1} + \lambda_{ij}^{Assets\ 1,\ Gang}$,

Model 3: $\log \hat{m} = \lambda + \lambda_i^{Assets\ 1} + \lambda_j^{Gang} + \lambda_k^{Sex\ 1} + \lambda_{ij}^{Assets\ 1,\ Gang} + \lambda_{ik}^{Assets\ 1,\ Sex\ 1}$,

Model 4: $\log \hat{m} = \lambda + \lambda_i^{Assets\ 1} + \lambda_j^{Gang} + \lambda_{ij}^{Assets\ 1,\ Gang} + \lambda_{ik}^{Gang,\ Sex\ 1}$.

In addition, the model that includes all two-way interaction terms is estimated—that is, the model

$$\log \hat{m} = \lambda + \lambda_i^{Assets\ 1} + \lambda_j^{Gang} + \lambda_k^{Sex\ 1},$$
$$+ \lambda_{ij}^{Assets\ 1\ Gang} + \lambda_j^{Assets\ 1,\ Sex\ 1}$$
$$+ \lambda_{jk}^{Gang,\ Sex\ 1}$$

This model corresponds to a second order CFA. It was estimated to determine whether the three-way interaction [Asset 1, Gang, Sex 1] can be a cause for the emergence of types and antitypes.

Table 5.13 presents the results of Model 1, that is, a CFA of variable independence. The z-test and the Holland-Copenhaver procedure for the protection of α were used.

Table 5.13. First Order CFA of the Cross-Classification of Assets 1, Gang, and Sex 1

Configuration GSA	m	$\hat{m}$	z	p	Type/antitype?
111	22.00	5.584	6.9464	0.000000	Type
112	1.00	7.679	−2.4102	0.007973	Antitype
121	6.00	13.363	−2.0142	0.021995	
122	16.00	18.374	−0.5538	0.289849	
211	3.00	6.205	−1.2866	0.099111	
212	2.00	8.532	−2.2362	0.012669	
221	9.00	14.848	−1.5176	0.064560	
222	36.00	20.416	3.4492	0.000281	Type

The base model of variable independence comes with a LR-X^2 of 63.88 ($df = 4$; $p < 0.01$). This value indicates that significant model – data discrepancies exist. We, therefore, anticipate that types and antitypes exist. Table 5.13 shows that CFA identified two types and one antitype. We ask whether each of these three "outlandish cells" supports mediation hypotheses. To prepare conclusions about the nature of the two types and the antitype in the context of mediation hypotheses, we estimate CFA base models 2, 3, and 4. The results from these analyses are summarized in Table 5.14, along with a summary of the results from Table 5.13 (Model 1).

In the following paragraphs, we perform the comparisons that prepare the conclusions about mediation. These steps need to be performed separately, for each model and for each type and antitype. To illustrate the comparisons and the conclusions, we perform these steps for Types 1 1 1 and 2 2 2. We begin with Configuration 1 1 1.

1. Model 1 did result in two types and one antitype. Therefore, mediation can exist.

2. None of the types and antitypes remains unchanged over all four models. Therefore, at least some of the bivariate relationships among Assets, Gang, and Sex at Time 1 must exist. These two results apply for the entire table. Therefore, Steps 1 and 2 do not need to be repeated for Configuration 1 2 2.

3. Type 1 1 1 emerges from Model 1 and remains in Models 2 and 4. We conclude that the path from Gang to Sex 1 does not exist. Mediation is, already at this point, no longer an option for Configuration 1 1 1.

4. Type 1 1 1 from Models 1 and 2 disappears in Model 3. We conclude that the direct path from Assets to Sex at Time 1 exists.

5. Type 1 1 1 from Models 1 and 2 re-emerges in Model 4. We also conclude that the path from Gang to Sex at Time 1 does not exist.

Before making the conclusion that, for Type 1 1 1, mediation is not supported, we need to determine the role played by the three-way interaction [Assets, Gang, Sex at Time 1]. This interaction could be the cause for this type to exist. To answer this question, we perform a second order CFA of the data in Table 5.13. The LR-$X^2 = 2.48$ ($df = 1$; $p = 0.12$) for this model indicates that the frequency distribution in Tables 5.13 and 5.14 is close to perfectly explained when all 2-way interactions are taken into account. The X^2 is so small that it is impossible for a configuration to constitute a type or an antitype. Stated differently, the three two-way interactions explain the data so well that there is no room for the three-way interaction to improve the model. We conclude that the three-way interaction cannot be the cause for Type 1 1 1 (or the other type or the antitype) to emerge.

We now are ready to interpret the type that is constituted by Configuration 1 1 1. Type 1 1 1 describes male African-Americans who, at the first interview (age 16 years), were gang members and reported sexual activities as well as below numbers of assets. For these respondents, the null hypothesis

Table 5.14. Configural Mediation Analysis of the Cross-Classification of Assets 1, Gang, and Sex 1

Configuration GSA	m	Base model Model 1 [G], [S], [A]	Model 2 [A, G], [S]	Model 3 [A, G], [A, S]	Model 4 [A, G], [G, S]
111	22	Type	Type		Type
112	1	Antitype			Antitype
121	6		Antitype		Antitype
122	16				Type
211	3				
212	2		Antitype		
221	9			Type	
222	36	Type			
LR-X^2 (df)		63.88 (4)	49.35 (3)	10.34 (2)	29.00 (2)

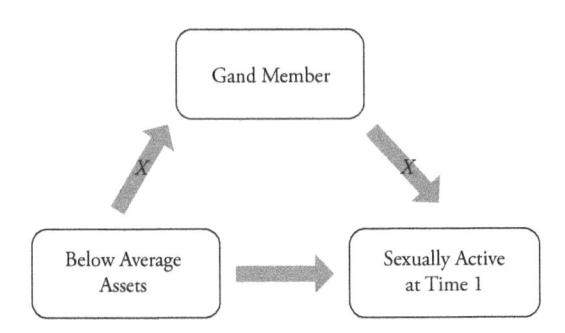

Figure 5.1 Testing a Configural Mediation Hypothesis for Type 1 1 1 (an X indicates that a path does not exist for this configuration)

that Gang membership does not play the role of mediator for the developmental path from assets to sexual activity is confirmed. In different words, the prediction of Sexual Activity at Time 1 from Assets at the same point time is not mediated by Gang Membership. Figure 5.1 depicts the relationship found for Configuration 1 1 1.

The second sample configuration that we explain in detail is 2 2 2. It also constitutes a type in Model 1. As was explained above, there is no need to repeat the first two steps of analysis, and we can directly proceed to Step 3.

3. Type 2 2 2 disappears in Model 2. We conclude that the path from above average Assets to CBO exists. Both forms of mediation are still options.

4. Type 2 2 2 also disappears in Model 3. We might conclude that the path from CBO Membership to no Sex at Time 1 may exist. However, this type might have disappeared because Models 2 and 3 both contain the [P, M] interaction. Either way, both forms of mediation are still options.

5. Type 2 2 2 also disappears in Model 4. We conclude that the path from CBO Membership to Sex at Time 1 does exist. This path is a necessary condition for mediation.

We are now ready to interpret the type that is constituted by Configuration 2 2 2. Type 2 2 2 describes male African-Americans who, at the first interview (age 16 years) were CBO members and reported above average numbers of assets, but no sexual activities. Because there are connections between Assets and CBO Membership as well as between Gang Membership and Sex at Time 1, mediation exists for this configuration. In other words, the configuration in which lack of Sexual Activity at Time 1 is predictable from above average numbers of assets and mediated by Gang Membership constitutes a CFA mediation type. Mediation is partial because the direct path from Assets to no

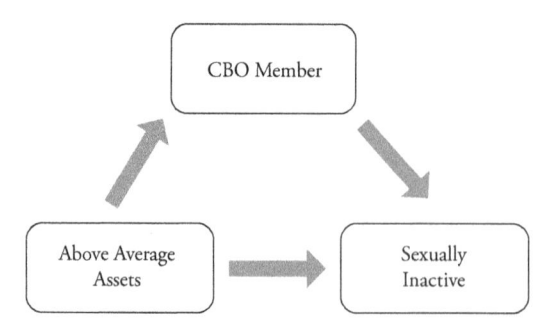

Figure 5.2 Testing a Configural Mediation Hypothesis for Type 2 2 2

Sexual Activity exists in addition to the mediated paths. Figure 5.2 displays the results of configural mediation testing for Configuration 2 2 2.

In sum, whereas the type that is constituted by Configuration 1 1 1 contradicts the hypothesis that Gang/CBO Membership mediates the relationship between the number of assets and sexual activity at age 16 years, in African-American male adolescents, the type that is constituted by Configuration 2 2 2 supports the hypothesis of a partially mediated relationship.

Future Directions

Three current lines of development of CFA can be made out. The first is pursued to increase and enrich the number of scholarly questions that can be answered with CFA. Examples of such questions include mediator CFA, moderator CFA, or new models of longitudinal CFA (von Eye, Mair, & Mun, 2010). The second line involves the embedding of CFA into the arsenal of existing methods of statistical analysis. Examples of such efforts include von Eye and Mair's (2008) attempt at using log-linear modeling to explain the types and antitypes that are found by a CFA. The third line involves developing methods of CFA that allow researchers to use more variables or continuous variables.

Each of these lines will be pursued in the future. The third line in particular is of importance. Using design planning methods such as the ones discussed by Wu and Hamada (2009), data collection can be structured based on optimal designs that are amenable to configural analysis. First approaches to devising such designs exist (von Eye, Mair, & Mun, 2010), but much work remains to be done. Similarly, first steps have been taken to specify configural methods that use search routines that identify sectors in the space of continuous variables that contain types and antitypes (von Eye, 2009). Here also, much work is left to be done to make these methods more user friendly. In general, CFA is in the process of being developed as a method of statistical analysis that has very broad appeal, is easy to use, and allows researchers to answer a large number of questions from a person-oriented research perspective.

Already, researchers realize that, whenever effects of intervention, dosage of drugs, treatment, policy changes, training, life events, climate changes, development, or, in general, relationships among variables are studied, general statements that are expressed in terms of correlations, or covariance structures are rarely of use. Effects are rarely the same for everybody, even under same conditions. Configural frequency analysis is a method that allows researchers and interventionists to identify those sectors in multivariate spaces that stand out because more or fewer cases can be found than one would expect with reference to a base model. These sectors constitute the CFA types and antitypes. These types and antitypes reflect where exactly the effects of interest translate into changes in probability distributions.

Configural frequency analysis makes it easy for researchers to locate not only those sectors in the data space that show the effects of intervention but also those sectors that are of interest when lack of results or effects are of interest (e.g., when side effects of treatment are studied). More generally, CFA is the method of choice when researchers focus on those sectors in the data space that carry the effects of interest.

Author Note

Alexander von Eye, Michigan State University, Department of Psychology, voneye@msu.edu. No grants, no acknowledgements for this chapter.

Notes

1. From a model-fitting perspective, the added M × T interaction resulted in a significantly improved, yet still not satisfactory model fit. The Pearson goodness-of-fit for the main effect model in Table 5.3 was $X^2 = 244.81$ ($df = 11$; $p < 0.01$). The Pearson goodness-of-fit for the model in Table 5.4 was $X^2 = 231.81$ ($df = 10$; $p < 0.01$). The difference between these two nested models was significant ($\Delta X^2 = 13.0$; $\Delta df = 1$; $p < 0.01$).

2. The frequencies in the following analyses sum to 1250. This discrepancy to the sample size reported in the New York Times is the result of rounding (the paper reported % values), and the newspaper's exclusion of 5% of cases that did not fall in the above eight patterns (mostly other-race cases) from analysis.

Appendix Table 1. Symbols and Definitions

Symbol	Definition
T	Type - A cell that contains statistically significantly more cases than expected based on a base model
A	Antitype - A cell that contains statistically significantly fewer cases than expected based on a base model
m	Observed cell frequencies
$E(m_r)$	Expectation of observed cell frequency for cell r
$\hat{m}$	Expected cell frequencies
p_r	Sample proportion for cell r
m_r	Observed frequency for cell r
π_r	Cell probability for cell r
P	Multinomial probability of sampling a case
B	Binomial probability
H	Hat matrix
$\log \hat{m}_i$	Logarithm of the expected cell frequency for cell i
λ	Log-linear model terms to denote main effects and interaction effects
$[A]$	Log-linear main effect term for a variable A
$[A, B]$ or $[AB]$	Log-linear interaction effect term between variables A and B
α^*	Protected α
$z_{L,r}$	Lehmacher's test statistic
z_r	z test for cell r
r_i	Standardized Pearson residual for cell i

References

Agresti, A. (2002). *Categorical data analysis* (2nd ed.). New York: Wiley.

Anscombe, F. J. (1953). Contribution of discussion of paper by H. Hotelling 'New light on the correlation coefficient and its transform'. *Journal of the Royal Statistical Society,* 15(B), 229–230.

Baron, R.M., & Kenny, D.A. (1986). The moderator–mediator variable distinction in social psychological research: conceptual, strategic, and statistical considerations. *Journal of Personality and Social Psychology,* 51, 1256–1258.

Bergman, L.R., & Magnusson, D. (1997). A person-oriented approach in research on developmental psychopathology. *Development and Psychopathology,* 9, 291–319.

Bergman, L.R., von Eye, A., & Magnusson, D. (2006). Person-oriented research strategies in developmental psychopathology. In D. Cicchetti, & Cohen, D.J. (Eds.), *Developmental Psychopathology* (2nd ed., pp. 850–888). London, UK: Wiley.

Box, G., & Meyer, R.D. (1986). Dispersion effects from fractional designs. *Technometrics,* 28, 19–27.

DuMouchel, W. (1999). Bayesian data mining in large frequency tables, with an application to the FDA spontaneous reporting system. *The American Statistician,* 53, 177–190.

Christensen, R. (1997). *Log-linear models and logistic regression* (2nd ed.). New York: Springer.

Everitt, B. S. (1998). *The Cambridge dictionary of statistics.* Cambridge, UK: Cambridge University Press.

Finkelstein, J., von Eye, A., & Preece, M. A. (1994). The relationship between aggressive behavior and puberty in normal adolescents: a longitudinal study. *Journal of Adolescent Health,* 15, 319–326.

Gelman, A., Carlin, J.B., Stern, H.S., & Rubin, D.B. (1995). *Bayesian data analysis.* London: Chapman & Hall.

Goodman, L. A. (1984). *The analysis of cross-classified data having ordered categories.* Cambridge, MA: Harvard University Press.

Goodman, L.A. (1991). Measures, models, and graphical displays in the analysis of cross-classified data. *Journal of the American Statistical Association,* 86, 1085–1111.

Gutiérrez-Peña, E., & von Eye, A. (2000). A Bayesian approach to Configural Frequency Analysis. *Journal of Mathematical Sociology*, 24, 151–174.

Haberman, S. J. (1973). The analysis of residuals in cross-classified tables. *Biometrics*, 29, 205–220.

Havránek, T., & Lienert, G. A. (1984). Local and regional versus global contingency testing. *Biometrical Journal*, 26, 483–494.

Heilmann, W.-R., Lienert, G. A., & Maly, V. (1979). Prediction models in configural frequency analysis. *Biometrical Journal*, 21, 79–86.

Holland, B. S., & Copenhaver, M. D. (1987). An improved sequentially rejective Bonferroni test procedure. *Biometrics*, 43, 417–423.

Holm, S. (1979). A simple sequentially rejective multiple test procedure. *Scandinavian Journal of Statistics*, 6, 65–70.

Hommel, G. (1988). A stagewise rejective multiple test procedure based on a modified Bonferroni test. *Biometrika*, 75, 383–386.

Hommel, G. (1989). A comparison of two modified Bonferroni procedures. *Biometrika*, 76, 624–625.

Hommel, G., Lehmacher, W., & Perli, H.-G. (1985). Residuenanalyse des Unabhängigkeits modells zweier kategorialer Variablen [residual analysis of the model of independence for two categorical variables]. In J. Jesdinsky & J. Trampisch (Eds.) *Prognose- und Entscheidungsfindung in der Medizin* (pp. 494–503). Berlin: Springer.

Jobson, J. D. (1992). *Applied multivariate data analysis. Volume II: Categorical and multivariate methods*. New York: Springer..

Kenny, D.A. (2005). Mediation. In B.S. Everitt, & D.C. Howell (Eds.), *Encyclopedia of Statistics in Behavioral Science* (pp. 1194–1198). Chichester, UK: Wiley.

Keselman H.J., Cribbie R., & Holland B. (2002). Controlling the rate of Type I error over a large set of statistical tests. *British Journal of Mathematical and Statistical Psychology*, 55, 27–39.

Krause, B., & Metzler, P. (1984). *Angewandte Statistik [Applied Statistics]*. Berlin, Germany: VEB Deutscher Verlag der Wissenschaften.

Krauth, J. (2003). Type structures in CFA. *Psychology Science*, 45, 217–222.

Küchenhoff, H. (1986). A note on a continuity correction for testing in three-dimensional configural frequency analysis. *Biometrical Journal*, 28, 465–468.

Lehmacher, W. (1981). A more powerful simultaneous test procedure in Configural Frequency Analysis. *Biometrical Journal*, 23, 429–436.

Lerner, R.M., Taylor, C.S., & von Eye, A. (Eds.)(2002). *Pathways to positive youth development among diverse youth*. San Francisco: Jossey-Bass.

Lienert, G.A. (1969). Die "Konfigurationsfrequenzanalyse" als Klassifikationsmethode in der klinischen Psychologie ["Configurable Frequency Analysis" as a classification method for clinical Psychology]. In M. Irle, (Ed.), *Bericht über den 16. Kongreß der Deutschen Gesellschaft für Psychologie in Tübingen 1968* (pp. 244–255). Göttingen: Hogrefe.

Lienert, G. A. (1971). Die Konfigurationsfrequenzanalyse III. Zwei- und Mehrstichproben KFA in Diagnostik und Differentialdiagnostik. *Zeitschrift für Klinische Psychologie und Psychotherapie*, 19, 291–300.

Lienert, G.A., & Krauth, J. (1973). Die Konfigurationsfrequenzanalyse. V. Kontingenz- und Interaktionsstrukturanalyse multinär skalierter Merkmale [Configural Frequency Analysis. V. Contingency- and interaction structure analysis of polytomous variables]. *Zeitschrift für Klinische Psychologie und Psychotherapie*, 21, 26–39.

Lienert, G.A., & Krauth, J. (1975). Configural Frequency Analysis as a statistical tool for defining types. *Educational and Psychological Measurement*, 35, 231–238.

Lienert, G. A., & von Eye, A. (1988). Syndromaufklärung mittels generalisierter ISA [explaining syndromes using generalized interaction structure analysis]. *Zeitschrift für Klinische Psychologie, Psychopathologie, und Psychotherapie*, 36, 25–33.

MacKinnon, D. P., Kisbu–Sakarya, Y., & Gottschall, A. C. (2012). Developments in mediation analysis. In T. D. Little (Ed.), *The Oxford Handbook of Quantitative Methods, Vol. 2* (pp. xxx–xxx). New York: Oxford University Press.

MacKinnon, D. P., Fairchild, A. J., & Fritz, M. S. (2007). Mediation analysis. *Annual Review of Psychology*, 58, 593–614.

Martinez-Torteya, C., Bogat, G.A., von Eye, A., & Levendosky, A.A. (2009). Resilience among children exposed to domestic violence: the role of protective and vulnerability factors. *Child Development*, 80, 562–577.

Osterkorn, K. (1975). Wann kann die Binomial- und Poissonverteilung hinreichend genau durch die Normalverteilung ersetzt werden [when can one substitute the binomial and the Poisson distribution sufficiently exactly by the normal distribution]? *Biometrische Zeitschrift*, 17, 33–34.

Perli, H.-G., Hommel, G., & Lehmacher, W. (1987). Test procedures in configural frequency analysis. *Biometrical Journal*, 27, 885–893.

Schuster, C., & von Eye, A. (2000). Using log-linear modeling to increase power in two-sample Configural Frequency Analysis. *Psychologische Beiträge*, 42, 273–284.

Taylor, C.S., Lerner, R.M., von Eye, A., Bilalbegoviè Balsano, Dowling, E.M., Anderson, P.M., Bobek, D.L., & Bjelobrk, D. (2002). Individual and ecological assets and positive developmental trajectories among gang and community-based organization youth. *New Directions for Youth Development*, 95, 57–72.

von Eye, A. (2002). *Configural Frequency Analysis–Methods, Models, and Applications*. Mahwah, NJ: Lawrence Erlbaum.

von Eye, A. (2004). Base models for Configural Frequency Analysis. *Psychology Science*, 46, 150–170.

von Eye, A. (2007). Configural Frequency Analysis. *Methodology*, 3, 170–172.

von Eye, A. (2008). Fractional factorial designs in the analysis of categorical data. InterStat, http://interstat.statjournals.net/YEAR/2008/articles/0804003.pdf

von Eye, A. (2009). *Configural Frequency Analysis of Continuous Variables: Considering Data Generation Processes*. Paper presented at the Fourth Statistics Days, University of Luxembourg, Luxembourg.

von Eye, A., & Bergman, L.R. (2003). Research strategies in developmental psychopathology: Dimensional identity and the person-oriented approach. *Development and Psychopathology*, 15, 553–580.

von Eye, A., & Gutiérrez Peña, E. (2004). Configural Frequency Analysis–the search for extreme cells. *Journal of Applied Statistics*, 31, 981–997.

von Eye, A., & Mair, P. (2008). A functional approach to Configural Frequency Analysis. *Austrian Journal of Statistics*, 37, 161–173.

von Eye, A., Mair, P., & Bogat, G.A. (2005). Prediction models for Configural Frequency Analysis. *Psychology Science*, 47, 342–355.

von Eye, A., Mair, P., & Mun, E.Y. (2010). *Advances in Configural Frequency Analysis*. New York: Guilford Press.

von Eye, A., & Mun, E.-Y. (2007). A note on the analysis of difference patterns–structural zeros by design. *Psychology Science*, 49, 14–25.

von Eye, A., Mun, E. Y., & Mair, P. (2009). What carries a mediation process? Configural analysis of mediation. *Integrative Psychological and Behavioral Science*, 43, 228–247.

von Eye, A., & Niedermeier, K.E. (1999). *Statistical analysis of longitudinal categorical data–An introduction with computer illustrations*. Mahwah, NJ: Lawrence Erlbaum.

von Eye, A., & Rovine, M. J. (1994). Non-standard log-linear models for orthogonal prediction Configural Frequency Analysis. *Biometrical Journal*, 36, 177–184.

von Eye, A., & Schuster, C. (1998). On the specification of models for Configural Frequency Analysis–Sampling schemes in Prediction CFA. *Methods of Psychological Research–online*, 3, 55–73.

von Eye, A., Schuster, C., & Gutiérrez-Peña, E. (2000). Configural Frequency Analysis under retrospective and prospective sampling schemes–frequentist and Bayesian approaches. *Psychologische Beiträge*, 42, 428–447.

von Eye, A., Spiel, C., & Rovine, M. J. (1995). Concepts of nonindependence in Configural Frequency Analysis. *Journal of Mathematical Sociology*, 20, 41–54.

von Weber, S., Lautsch, E., & von Eye, A. (2003). On the limits of Configural Frequency Analysis: Analyzing small tables. *Psychology Science*, 45, 339–354.

Wood, P.K., Sher, K., & von Eye, A. (1994). Conjugate methods in Configural Frequency Analysis. *Biometrical Journal*, 36, 387–410.

Wu, C.F.J., & Hamada, M.S. (2009). *Experiments. Planning, analysis, and optimization* (2nd ed.). Hoboken, NJ: Wiley.

CHAPTER 6

Nonparametric Statistical Techniques

Trent D. Buskirk, Lisa M. Willoughby, *and* Terry J. Tomazic

> **Abstract**
>
> The use of parametric or nonparametric approaches when analyzing data is a major decision that investigators often confront. Although this decision may impact the validity of the conclusions that investigators might draw, the decision to use nonparametric approaches is often overlooked as a viable option for a variety of reasons. The intent of this chapter is to help guide researchers on the application of both classical and modern, computationally intensive, nonparametric techniques for investigating hypotheses of interest. Demonstrations are offered using nonparametric and parametric techniques to highlight the differences in how statistical estimates and inferential results may differ between these methodologies.
>
> **Key Words:** Nonparametric, statistical software, permutation tests, resampling, bootstrap, kernel smoothing, exact tests

Introduction

A study was conducted to estimate the proportion of the population that has a family history of Alzheimer's disease. Researchers also wanted to know whether there were differences between males and females in their family history of Alzheimer's disease. A related research study asked whether there were differences in depression severity across those individuals who received medication and those who did not. A tertiary research question for this study involved estimating the relationship between depression severity and total number of comorbid health conditions. A fourth question sought to quantify the number of "blue days" as a function of age, sex, and medication status. A final research question asked participants to rank on a four-point scale how useful a series of daily activities were for relieving stress with the final goal of understanding the mechanisms for coping that people were using in practice.

Any researcher who has taken introductory and intermediate level statistics courses would probably assert that the first question might be explored by using proportions and base a confidence interval on a normal approximation to the binomial distribution, provided there was a large enough sample size. The second question might readily be explored by conducting a two-sample *t*-test or an analysis of variance with the assumption of normality of depression scores across groups. The third question might be explored by using a linear regression model where the distribution of severity is assumed to be normally distributed for each level of comorbid condition. If depression is skewed with fewer subjects expected to have larger severity scores, then the researcher might use a logarithmic (or other suitable) transformation. Linear regression procedures using the transformed data and interpretations are provided in the context of the transformed scale. The fourth question might be explored by using a Poisson regression model that assumes the count of depression blue days is a function of the covariates of interest. In this model, the total number of blue days per combination of the predictors is not normally distributed but rather, is distributed as a Poisson or as count data. The final question regarding stress relief ratings might be explored by looking at the distribution of people providing the highest ranks versus lower ranks for each question or some other clustering technique applied to the rankings to determine whether participants had similar ratings across activities. Depending on the covariates collected, it may also be possible and appropriate to apply some type of ordinal regression modeling to explore the ratings data.

In the analysis of each of these research questions, a statistical modeling/estimation technique was identified as a viable approach to evaluating the hypothesis at hand. Each of these parametric statistical techniques makes assumptions about the distribution of the outcome variable, specifies the nature of the parameters for that distribution (i.e. parameters are linear), and computes estimates of population properties, such as the mean. These assumptions are needed as the basis of valid inference, and in practice, larger sample sizes can be helpful for creating reasonable approximations to the sampling distribution of test statistics that are implied by these assumptions. In some cases, transformations of the outcome (or predictors) may be applied, but their use trades satisfying assumptions for possible complications in interpretation (e.g., depression on the log scale may not be clinically interpretable). When sample sizes are small, or uncertainty surrounds the choice of the type of distribution that may be appropriate for the data collected, then the analyst may want to consider a statistical technique that is more robust to such assumptions—that is, a nonparametric technique. These techniques are a collection of statistical methods that require minimal assumptions about the underlying distribution generating the observed data and generally do not specify *a priori* its functional form (e.g., normally distributed).

The intent of this chapter is to help guide researchers on the application of nonparametric techniques for investigating hypotheses of interest. This is not a comprehensive treatment of computational formulas or theoretical principals. There are many publications that provide excellent instruction on this matter (e.g., Corder & Foreman, 2009; Daniel, 1990; Higgins, 2004; Pett, 1997; Siegel & Castellan, 1988). Rather, we hope to provide an overview of classical and modern nonparametric techniques and, where appropriate, compare these methods to their parametric counterparts. Many of the nonparametric techniques discussed in this chapter are illustrated using data from the 18 to 30-year-olds in the Washington, D.C. subset of the 2008 *Behavioral Risk Factor Surveillance System Survey* (BRFSS) (CDC, 2008). Generally in the analysis of survey data, it is recommended that one use methods that incorporate both the sampling weights and the sampling design into the analysis. For ease of illustration, we have ignored these features of the BRFSS sample data in the analyses presented throughout the chapter. In each case, attempts are made to explain differences in implementing each method as well as how the inferential results from a particular nonparametric method may differ from its parametric analog. The computer syntax/code used to generate these analyses using SAS, SPSS, or R is included in a technical appendix located on the internet at www.compappdx.com. Armed with such information, it is hoped that investigators will become informed decision-makers when choosing statistical approaches for their analyses and can expand their statistical tool kit to include applications of nonparametric techniques.

A Closer Look at Nonparametric Methods

Nonparametric statistical methods represent a class of techniques that do not make assumptions about the population from which the data are sampled. In contrast, parametric methods rely on such assumptions, and most require interval level data that adequately represent specific properties, such as normality or equal variance. Another term for nonparametric statistics is *distribution-free statistics*, which primarily references these techniques in the context where interval-level data do not meet the distributional requirements of parametric tests. For nonparametric techniques, the test statistic is distributed according to a reference distribution that does not rely on population distribution information. For example, there are some nonparametric tests that are based on ranks, and the resulting reference distributions are functions of known sample sizes. Whenever the population distribution is unknown or sample size is too small to invoke a large sample approximation to normality, nonparametric methods may be viable alternatives to maximizing power and preserving Type I error rate. Some nonparametric statistical techniques, however, are not completely distribution-free in that they assume a specific continuous distribution underlies the data. In such instances, normal distribution of the data is neither required nor assumed.

Both parametric and nonparametric statistical tests generally operate within a framework that controls Type I error rate while maximizing power. In some instances, these tests are considered exact, meaning the actual Type I error rate is equal to the stated level of significance. Not all hypothesis tests are exact, especially if they rely on large sample properties of test statistics. For example, a one-sample test for a population mean based on the t-distribution may have an actual Type I error rate that is substantially different from the specified significance level if the sample is drawn from a population that is normally distributed (Ernst, 2004).

In some instances, nonparametric tests will be more powerful than their parametric counterparts, especially if sample sizes are small or assumptions for parametric procedures are not satisfied. Relative efficiency and asymptotic relative efficiency are two quantities that are used to summarize the power/sample size of a nonparametric test compared to its parametric analog. In this case, relative efficiency refers to the relative sample size needed for the parametric test to achieve the same power as the nonparametric test. Asymptotic relative efficiency can be defined as the limiting value of relative efficiency as the overall size of the sample increases without limit (Daniel, 1990). Values less than 1 indicate that the parametric method is more efficient (i.e., requires a smaller sample size for the same power) than the nonparametric method, whereas values exceeding 1 indicate greater efficiency for the nonparametric method.

Classical Nonparametric Methods

Classical nonparametric approaches are the techniques usually covered in most introductory statistics textbooks and include tests that historically have been used to investigate one-, two-, or multiple-population problems. Most of these techniques are readily available in common statistical software and/or have widely available reference tables for determining critical values and computing p-values. In this section, we will describe some of the commonly used nonparametric techniques applied to one-, two-, and multiple-sample scenarios.

Nonparametric Methods Based on a Single Sample: The Binomial Test

The binomial test is useful when one is interested in comparing the proportion of an event or characteristic in one sample to that of another. There are no parametric analogs to this test, but it is a useful technique for a variety of instances, such as the case where an investigator may wish to support that the proportion of a particular sample characteristic (e.g., presence of females) is greater than a population reference value. Data for the binomial test must be dichotomous, with a coding of 1 traditionally representing the presence of a characteristic and 0 representing the absence. Statistical inference proceeds by computing a p-value defined as the probability of observing values equal to or more extreme (e.g., as determined by the alternative hypothesis) than what is observed in the sample as specified in the equation (Siegel & Castellan, 1988):

$$P[Y = k] = \binom{N}{k} p^k q^{N-k}, \text{ where } \binom{N}{k} = \frac{N!}{(k!)(N-k)!}.$$

Here, p equals the test proportion (i.e., the proportion we want to compare against), q represents $1-p$, k represents the number of cases with the characteristic, and N the total sample size.

Using a small sample example, assume that you have obtained a sample of 10 students and want to know the proportion of those who will have exercised at least three times in the past week. You suspect that the true percentage is 60% but think it could be less. From your sample you find that only 4 students (40%) actually exercised at least three times in the past week. To investigate this hypothesis, a large sample or a parametric version of the one-sample proportion test is not appropriate, so we calculate exact probabilities directly from the binomial distribution using the equations provided above. To compute the left-tailed p-value, we determine the probability of observing four or fewer students who exercised in the past week, assuming that the true proportion is actually 0.6 (i.e., $P[Y \leq 4]$). Using the equations above, we find that $P[Y = 4]] = 0.1115$, $P[Y = 3] = 0.0425$, $P[Y = 2] = 0.0106$, $P[Y = 1] = 0.0016$, and $P[Y = 0] = 0.0001$. Summing these values reveals an exact p-value of 0.1663, suggesting that we are unable to reject the null hypothesis at the 0.05 level. Thus, the true proportion of students exercising at least three times in the previous week is not significantly less than 0.6. When the hypothesized probability is 0.5, then the binomial distribution is symmetric. Using the small sample example, if our test probability is 0.5, then $P[Y \leq 4] = P[Y \geq 6] = 0.3770$.

Although the binomial probabilities can be computed using online calculators or tables for various sample sizes, these probabilities are typically approximated using a standard normal distribution. Equations, both without and with correction for continuity to improve the normal approximation, are shown (adapted from Siegel & Castellan, 1988) below: $z = \frac{Y-Np}{\sqrt{Npq}}$ and with the continuity correction $z = \frac{(Y\pm.5)-Np}{\sqrt{Npq}}$.

In the equations above, Y represents the observed frequency, N is the total sample size, p represents the expected or test proportion, and q represents $1 - p$. For the continuity correction, when Y is less than Np (i.e., the mean), then 0.5 is added to Y, and when Y is greater than Np then 0.5 is subtracted from Y. Applying the binomial test to the large sample WASHDC data set, we now wish to determine the probability that the proportion of female respondents (277/441 = 0.63) in the sample reflects the actual proportion of females in the population (here, assume this parameter to be 0.5 for illustration). We are specifically interested in determining the probability of obtaining 277 or more female respondents (of a total of 441), or $P[Y \geq 277]$. Using the equations above, we find that Y = 277 and Np = 220.5. Because we are looking at a "right-tailed" probability the correct continuity correction factor is –0.5. Completing the calculations, we find that z equals 0.5714 with a corresponding p-value of 0.28385, which was obtained from a standard z-table. There is an excellent online calculator for computing exact p-values based directly on the binomial distribution (rather than the large sample normal approximation) located at http://faculty.vassar.edu/lowry/binomialX.html. Using this tool, the "exact" p-value was computed to be 0.28388 (virtually the same as was obtained using the normal approximation, resulting partly from the large sample size and the hypothesized proportion being near or exactly 0.5).

Nonparametric Methods for Comparing Two Independent Samples: The Wilcoxon Mann Whitney Test

When one chooses to compare two groups on a continuous outcome, such as the weight of males to that of females, the standard (parametric) statistical approach is the independent samples t-test. This test has several major assumptions that should be met to ensure proper inference: independence of observations, equal variance within each of the groups, and normally distributed outcomes in each group. In the event that equal variance cannot be assumed, then options, including Welch's correction, may be applied. However, when the assumption of normality is violated or the measurement is made on an ordinal scale, or the sample size is too small to reasonably rely on approximations afforded by the Central Limit Theorem, then alternative approaches, such as the Wilcoxon rank-sum or the Mann Whitney tests, should be considered. The Wilcoxon rank-sum, W_s, and the Mann Whitney, U, statistics are mathematically equivalent techniques shown as this equation adapted from Higgins (2004) $W_s = \frac{n_1(n_1+1)}{2} + U$, where n_1 is the smaller of the two sample sizes. From this point forward, this technique generally will be described as the Wilcoxon Mann Whitney (WMW) test. The WMW test is regarded as the nonparametric analog to the independent samples t-test. Rather than specifically testing the equality of two means, the WMW tests the hypothesis that two distributions are equivalent and appropriate hypotheses may be expressed in terms of the medians or, more generally, order-based statistics (i.e., statistics based on ranks). Whereas some of the assumptions for the WMW are less restrictive than the two-sample t-test, some are similar and include (1) that the outcome variable is measured on at least an ordinal scale; (2) that observations are independent and randomly selected from the population; and (3) that the distribution of scores is similar between the two groups (Pett, 1997). One of the most common applications of the WMW test is in the determination of whether the distribution of outcomes from one group is shifted (upward or downward) from the distribution of outcomes in the second group. Under this framework, the WMW can be considered a test for differences in medians, and the use of the Hodges-Lehmann estimator (median of differences) may be appropriate. The assumptions of normality and equal variance are not required for appropriately conducting the WMW test.

The WMW belongs to a class of rank-based statistics and thus treats the data in ranked form so that the relative ordering of the scores, not the magnitude, is considered in the test statistic. For a small sample, using the Wilcoxon rank-sum form of the WMW test, the equation simply requires that we order all of the data from both groups (taken together as one data set) from smallest to largest and then assign the ranks. The test statistic, W_s, is the sum of the ranks, usually for the group with the smaller sample size. In instances where there are multiple observations having the same value (i.e., tied scores), then the average ranks of the tied scores are typically used.

To illustrate the WMW, we consider the weight (in pounds) for a random sample of six males and

Table 6.1. Data for a Comparison of Weights for a Small Hypothetical Sample of Men and Women

Gender	F	F	F	F	M	M	M	M	M	F	M
Rank order	1	2	3	4	5	6	7	8	9	10	11
Weight (in pounds)	120	125	130	135	140	145	150	155	165	190	225

Table 6.2. Summary Statistics for Male and Female Weights Based on the WASHDC Data Set

Group	N	Mean	Standard deviation	Median	Summed rank	Mean rank
Males	159	181.22	35.71	172	44,361	279
Females	265	152.14	35.50	140	45,739	172.6

five females. The data are ordered, ranked, and displayed in Table 6.1. The W_s value is 20, based on the sum of ranks from the female sample (i.e., $1 + 2 + 3 + 4 + 10$). Using the appropriate table (in this case, Appendix J from Siegel & Castellan [1988] or an online calculator such as at http://elegans.swmed.edu/~leon/stats/utest.html), this statistic yields a two-tailed p-value of 0.082, indicating that the null hypothesis, rather than the two-tailed alternative, would be retained. By comparison, a two-tailed t-test yields a $t(9) = -1.28$, p-value $= 0.233$, and a $CI_{95} = (-64.64, 17.97)$. Again, the statistical decision to retain the null would be made based on these results.

With small sample sizes, the tables used to establish exact probabilities are based on permutation procedures, which will be described in greater detail later in this chapter. With larger sample sizes, however, the sampling distribution of the WMW approximates a normal distribution, and thus approximate p-values based on the normal distribution may be applied (Siegel & Castellan, 1988). The mean and variance that are used in the large sample normal approximation may be derived using the equations (adapted from Siegel & Castellan, 1988) shown as: $Mean = \frac{n_1(n_1+n_2+1)}{2}$ and $Variance = \frac{n_1 n_2(n_1+n_2+1)}{12}$.

In the equation above, n_1 usually represents the smaller sample size of the two groups but this convention varies by statistical packages (see computer appendix, www.compappdx.com), so care should be exercised when interpreting the results. The computed mean and variance values are then used in the following equation to derive a z-statistic, where W_s is the Wilcoxon statistic: $z = \frac{W_s \pm .5 - Mean}{\sqrt{variance}}$.

In the equation, the continuity correction factor (± 0.5) is used when probabilities of the left tail

Table 6.3. Comparison of (Asymptotic) Test Statistics and p-Values Using WMW and Two-Sample t-Tests With and Without the Equal Variance Assumption.

Test	Test statistic (asymptotic)	p-Value
Wilcoxon-Mann-Whitney	−8.663	<0.0001
t-test (equal variance)	8.148	<0.0001
t-test (unequal variance)	8.136	<0.0001

(+0.5) or the right tail (−0.5) are of interest. Most statistical packages include the continuity correction factor when computing approximate p-values for the WMW test to take into account the discrete nature of the rank values. To illustrate, we will use the WASHDC data set to compare the weights of females and males. Table 6.2 presents summary statistics.

Applying the appropriate equations with males representing n_1, we find that the corresponding z-statistic is 8.66, with an asymptotic significance (P) value less than 0.001. The conclusion from this analysis is similar to that derived from the t-test, where $t(422) = 8.15$, P < 0.0001, $CI_{95} = (22.06, 36.09)$ indicates differences in the distributions of weights for males and females (see Table 6.3).

Nonparametric Methods for Two Dependent Samples: The Wilcoxon Signed Rank Test, Sign Test, and McNemar's Test

If an investigator is interested in comparing the weight of subjects from 1 year to the weight of the same subjects from the next year, then the paired samples t-test may be an appropriate option. The

Table 6.4. LDL Cholesterol Measures and Signed Ranks for a Hypothetical Sample of Eight Students Enrolled in a 1-Year Tracking Study

Subject	1	2	3	4	5	6	7	8
LDL cholesterol (baseline)	140	153	148	144	150	146	151	147
LDL cholesterol (1-year later)	142	143	141	138	151	143	142	139
Absolute value of the difference (Baseline: 1 year later)	2	10	7	6	1	3	9	8
Signed ranks	−2	+8	+5	+4	−1	+3	+7	+6

paired samples t-test is a parametric test used when analyzing two related samples, such as in matched samples or repeated measures designs. As with the independent samples t-test, the assumptions for the paired samples t-test include that the data are drawn from a normally distributed population and homogeneity of variance is observed. In the event that the data are not normal or the sample is too small to derive appropriate parameter estimates, then the Wilcoxon signed ranks test (Wilcoxon, 1945) may be considered. The Wilcoxon signed ranks test, not to be confused with the Wilcoxon rank-sum test described in the previous section, is the nonparametric analog to the paired samples t-test. The hypotheses examine whether two samples were drawn from the same populations, with the null hypothesis being that there is symmetry among the difference scores. As with the paired t-test, hypotheses may take on directional or nondirectional forms. Assumptions for the Wilcoxon signed ranks test include that the data are either matched pairs or repeated measures on the same sample, the data are at least ordinal in scaling, the difference scores represent continuous data, and that the difference scores are symmetric about the true (population) median (Pett, 1997).

The basis for the Wilcoxon signed ranks test is the ranks of the non-zero differences between paired scores, with a correction to the variance for ties available. For small samples, the computation of the test statistic, T, is straightforward. The absolute values of the difference scores between pairs are ordered, assigned ranks with the appropriate signs to show directionality, and then summed, producing a negative and a positive summed ranks value. Note that cases with difference scores of zero will be eliminated from the analysis and will result in loss of information in the analysis.

To illustrate with a small sample, consider the low-density lipoprotein (LDL; i.e., "bad") cholesterol levels measured in mg/dL for eight individuals taken at baseline (time 1) and again after 1 year. The difference scores represent the baseline triglyceride measurement through 1-year triglyceride measurement so that positive differences indicate a reduction in LDL cholesterol levels and negative values indicate an increase in LDL cholesterol over the 1-year study period. Using the information in Table 6.4, the sum of the negative ranks (T^-) is 3 and the sum of the positive ranks (T^+) is 33. Depending on the tables, you may use the smaller or the larger of the two values. In our example, we used T^+ (33) and Table H from Siegel and Castellan (1988) and obtained a one-tailed p-value of 0.0195, which corresponds to a two-tailed p-value of 0.039. This indicates that a significant reduction in LDL cholesterol levels occurred over the 1-year follow-up period.

As with the WMW test, the sum of the ranks approximates a normal distribution with larger sample sizes, and thus a normal approximation is appropriate. The mean and standard error are required and the equations are as follows (adapted from Siegel & Castellan, 1988): Mean $= \frac{n(n+1)}{4}$ and Variance $= \frac{n(n+1)(2n+1)}{24}$. These values are then used in the following equation to derive a z-statistic, where T is the Wilcoxon T statistic (i.e., sum of positive ranks): $z = \frac{T - \text{Mean}}{\sqrt{\text{variance}}}$

To illustrate the use of these asymptotic approximations, we again turn our attention to the WASHDC data set to compare self-reported current weight and weight 1 year prior among 18 to 30-year-olds. Of the 409 cases who reported weights for both variables (current and 1 year prior), 163 resulted in no change, and thus the sample size for consideration in the Wilcoxon signed ranks test was 246 because we are using the "rank without zeros" method for handling these ties (Higgins, 2004). Applying a nondirectional (two-tailed) test and the equations noted above with the sum of positive ranks

Table 6.5. Results for Testing the Difference in Current Weight and Weight 1 Year Ago Based on the WASHDC Data Set

Test	Test statistic	p-Value
Wilcoxon signed ranks	z = 1.96	0.0497
Paired test	t = 0.93	0.3554

as the test statistic ($T = 13,004$), corresponding to a p-value of 0.0497 suggests a (median) weight change that is significantly different statistically from zero. In contrast, the p-value from the paired t-test was 0.3554, suggesting no significant differences between current weight and weight from 1 year ago, on average (see Table 6.5 for summary results of these two tests). The different interpretations from these two tests could, in part, be attributed to the presence of two large outliers (i.e., a large positive score and another large negative score), which increased the standard error and reduced the overall test statistic.

Tied ranks will reduce the variance within the data set. To account for tied ranks, the variance correction factor noted in the equation $Variance(ties) = \frac{1}{24}\left(n(n + 1)(2n + 1) - \frac{1}{2}\sum_{j=1}^{g} t_j(t_j - 1)(t_j + 1)\right)$ may be used, where t_j represents the number of ties in a particular grouping, g of ties (adapted from Siegel & Castellan, 1988). Another approach to addressing tied ranks is to break ties using random values that make the test more conservative (e.g., favors change in the direction opposite from what you would have predicted) or are arbitrary but do not affect the results. It is recommended that the results with and without correction for ties be examined no matter how a researcher decides to resolve ties.

The Wilcoxon signed ranks test is regarded as a powerful nonparametric technique. Indeed, when sample sizes are small, power efficiency has been cited as being approximately 95% (Siegel & Castellan, 1988), and under certain circumstances, the power advantage of the Wilcoxon signed ranks test is suggested to be greater than the paired t-test (Blair & Higgins, 1985). It is worth pointing out that although the Wilcoxon rank sums test is generally considered the nonparametric analog to the paired t-test, the sign test may also be a viable option when the directionality of change in paired samples is of interest. The sign test applies the one-sample binomial test to difference scores that retain their positive or negative signs. Applying the sign test to the small sample described above, we find the one-tailed p-value to be 0.145 (the null hypothesis is that the true proportion is 0.5, so two tailed p-values are computed by doubling the one-tailed p-value).

There may be scenarios where comparisons for dichotomous data measured in two dependent samples, such as with a pretest/posttest design, may be of interest. For example, a researcher may wish to compare binge drinking measured as a dichotomous yes–no variable in a group of students before and sometime after an educational intervention. The Wilcoxon signed ranks test would not be an appropriate treatment of binary outcomes. Rather, McNemar's test may be suitable and rests on a comparison of changes that occur in either direction. Keeping the previous example in mind, students who engaged in binge drinking prior to the intervention will subsequently continue to binge drink or stop. Similarly, those who did not engage in binge drinking prior to the intervention may continue to not binge drink or begin to binge drink afterward. As illustrated in the example, two of the four outcomes are indicative of change in different directions, and this is the basis for McNemar's test. Specifically, the null hypothesis of McNemar's test would be that the number of cases that change in one direction (e.g., binge drinker to non-binge drinker) and the number of cases that change in the other direction (e.g., non-binge drinker to binge drinker) is equivalent. To put it another way, the number of individuals who change in either direction is presumed to be equal under the null hypothesis.

To illustrate computation using McNemar's test, suppose we have a small sample of students (N = 20) who participated in an educational intervention that emphasized the health consequences of binge drinking. Fourteen indicated that they were binge drinkers prior to the intervention. Of these individuals, 10 indicated they were not binge drinkers at 6 months post-intervention. Of the six non-binge drinkers prior to the intervention, two indicated that they were binge drinkers at 6 months post-intervention. A total of 12 individuals "changed" in this study, and if one were to predict that the number of individuals who changed in either direction would be the same (i.e., the null), then one would predict that six individuals became non-binge drinkers and six became binge drinkers (i.e., the expected frequencies would be equivalent between groups). However, this is not what we observed, and we wish to test this.

Our example includes a small expected frequency and thus a binomial test (described in General Permutations Tests section) may be used. With the binomial application for McNemar's test, we would use a test probability of 0.5. As a shortcut, we may use an appropriate table, such as Table D from Siegel and Castellan (1988), where we would find the two-tailed probability to be 0.019 × 2 = 0.038, which provides supportive evidence that the intervention had an effect on binge drinking.

If number of expected frequencies were large, then a normal approximation may be used. Assume we conducted a similar study with 120 students and we found that following the intervention, 55 students who were formerly binge drinkers became non-binge drinkers and 13 non-binge drinkers subsequently became binge drinkers. This information can now be used to determine a chi-square statistic using the following equation (adapted from Pett, 1997):

$$\chi^2 = \frac{[A-(A+D)/2]^2}{(A+D)/2} + \frac{[D-(A+D)/2]^2}{(A+D)/2}.$$

In this equation, A represents the number of cases that changed from a yes to a no, and D represents the number of cases that changed from a no to a yes. From these equations, one can clearly see that the frequency of A and D are being contrasted with the hypothesis and that the expected frequency for either A and D are equivalent (i.e., $(A+D)/2$). Through simple algebra, we can derive the following simplified equation to yield the same results: $\chi^2 = \frac{(A-D)^2}{A+D}$.

One may also choose to include correction for continuity to improve the normal approximation by subtracting 1 in the numerator, as in the following equation (adapted from Siegel & Castellan, 1988):

$$\chi^2 = \frac{(|A-D|-1)^2}{A+D}.$$

In our example, the X^2 value would be 25.94 or 24.72, with or without the continuity correction, respectively. This statistic is evaluated with 1 degree of freedom. Using a standard chi-square table with alpha at 0.05, we find that the critical value is 3.84, and thus the results are statistically significant, favoring the hypothesis that the educational intervention was effective in reducing binge drinking.

Nonparametric Methods for Comparing More Than Two Samples

COMPARING MORE THAN TWO INDEPENDENT SAMPLES: THE KRUSKAL-WALLIS TEST

We have described scenarios where a nonparametric test would be more suitable than a parametric test in comparing two independent samples. When more than two groups are compared on a continuous variable, then it is possible that a one-way between-groups analysis of variance (ANOVA)—a parametric test—is appropriate. For example, comparing the weight of adults at different levels of monthly alcohol consumption (e.g., <1 drink, 1–10 drinks, 11–49 drinks, or 50 or more drinks). Like the t-test, it is presumed that the scores are normally distributed, the data are continuous, and that the observations are independent. Now imagine that the data are skewed or that the sample sizes are small. Although ANOVA is generally considered robust to the violations of the parametric assumptions, the levels at which the violations are tolerable are unclear. In the event that ANOVA assumptions are violated in a manner that is suggestive of an alternative technique, the Kruskal-Wallis test is the nonparametric analog that could be considered.

Like the WMW test, the Kruskal-Wallis test is based on ranked data. The assumptions include that the scores from each group are similar in shape of the distribution, cases and groups are independent, and the data are measured on at least an ordinal scale (Pett, 1997). Hypothesis testing for the Kruskal-Wallis test may be expressed with medians, and rejecting the null would indicate that the population medians differ between at least one pair of groups.

Computation of the Kruskal-Wallis test involves arranging the scores from all the groups in order and assigning ranked scores. The sum of ranks is computed for each group and used in the equation below to determine whether there are group differences in the ranks (equation adapted from Siegel & Castellan, 1988):

$$KW = \left[\frac{12}{N(N+1)} \sum_{i=1}^{k} n_i \bar{R}_i^2 \right] - 3(N+1)$$

In the above equation, k represents the number of groups, n_i represents the number of cases in the ith group, $\bar{R}_i$ is the mean rank from the ith group, and N represents the total sample size. When there are more than three groups with more than five observations per group, then the sampling distribution of the Kruskal-Wallis test approximates the chi-square distribution (Siegel & Castellan, 1988) and so the

Table 6.6. Hypothetical Sample of Weights (In Pounds) of 12 Subjects Grouped According to the Level of Alcoholic Beverages Consumed (4 Groupings)

Group 1 ID Weight Rank	Group 2 ID Weight Rank	Group 3 ID Weight Rank	Group 4 ID Weight Rank
1 142 7	4 143 8	7 127 2	10 122 1
2 145 9	5 150 10	8 133 4	11 130 3
3 155 12	6 151 11	9 141 6	12 135 5
$R_1 = 9.33$	$R_1 = 9.67$	$R_1 = 4.00$	$R_1 = 3.00$

Table 6.7. Comparison of the Kruskal-Wallis Method With a One-Way ANOVA Model Comparing Weight By a Categorical Measure of Magnitude of Alcoholic Beverages Consumed in 1-Month Using the WASHDC Data Set

Test	Test statistic	p-Value
Kruskal-Wallis	$X^2(3) = 2.12$	0.55
One-way between-groups ANOVA	$F(3,410) = 0.35$	0.79

test statistic can be compared against the chi-square distribution with $k-1$ degrees of freedom, where k represents the number of groups. With smaller sample sizes, specialized tables may be referenced for specific probability levels. In our hypothetical small sample example, participants were grouped according to the amount of alcoholic beverages consumed per month in the following manner: Group 1 (<1 drink), Group 2 (1–10 drinks), Group 3 (11–49 drinks), and Group 4 (50 or more drinks), and their weights (measured in pounds and shown in Table 6.6) were compared. Using the equations above, we find that KW equals 8.436. Using a table of critical values for the Kruskal-Wallis test for small samples (e.g. Table N of Neave and Worthington, 1988), we find that the obtained KW value is greater than the critical value when alpha is at the 0.05 level (critical value = 5.60), and thus we can conclude that there is a statistically significant difference among the groups. Many software packages will reference chi-square values, and thus when we compare our value against a standard chi-square table with alpha at 0.05 and 3 degrees of freedom, we find that the critical chi-square value is 7.82, also indicating that the differences across the groups are significant at the 0.05 level.

When scores are tied, then a variance correction factor may be applied using the equation below (adapted from Siegel & Castellan, 1988). In this equation, g represents the number of groups of tied ranks, t_i represents the number of tied ranks in the ith group, and N represents the total sample size: $Variance(ties) = 1 - \frac{\left[\sum_{i=1}^{g}(t_i^3 - t_i)\right]}{N^3 - N}$. Turning our attention to the WASHDC data set, we compared the weight of respondents across different levels of monthly alcoholic beverage consumption. Using the same groups as our small sample example, respondents were categorized as Group 1 (<1 drink), Group 2 (1–10 drinks), Group 3 (11–49 drinks), and Group 4 (50 or more drinks). In this particular data set, more than 90% of the scores were tied with at least one other score, suggesting that a correction for ties is necessary, as the correction factor may result in an important difference in the associated probabilities. When the analyses are conducted, we find that the KW chi-square statistic is 2.12, and with 3 degrees of freedom and an alpha of 0.05, this value is smaller than the critical value of 7.82, suggesting that the null hypothesis cannot be rejected (the probability is identified as being greater than 0.5 but less than 0.7). These results concur with the one-way between groups ANOVA results (Table 6.7).

When the overall test of the hypothesis of equivalence across groups is rejected by an ANOVA model, researchers often explore where such differences exist using *post hoc* procedures to protect error rates, like Bonferonni or Tukey's HSD. The only difference in nonparametric applications is the type and availability of *post hoc* procedure used to follow up a significant finding of differences (in medians) across the groups. The number of *post hoc* procedures available and the ease of execution of such methods in modern statistical software are not consistent between parametric and nonparametric methods. Generally, there are more parametric alternatives that are easily implemented in current software packages. Nevertheless, there are several *post hoc* options for the Kruskal-Wallis test (that can be computed manually via summary statistics); we describe a few of the more common approaches. One such *post hoc* option is Dunn's multiple comparisons procedure, which examines the differences in mean ranks (Dunn, 1964). Although the calculations for this procedure are simple, it has been noted as a conservative *post hoc* approach (*see* Pett, 1997 for a brief discussion). Other options include conducting multiple paired comparisons using the WMW test with some sort of correction for Type I error;

one-step procedures, such as the Bonferroni procedure; or step down procedures, such as the Holm's step down (*see* Ludbrook, 1998, for a discussion of these procedures).

Compared with between-groups one-way ANOVA, the reported asymptotic efficiency of the Kruskal-Wallis test is 95.5 when parametric assumptions have been met (Siegel & Castellan, 1988). This result implies that the Kruskal-Wallis approach is nearly as powerful as the ANOVA model whenever the parametric assumptions are met. If such assumptions are not met (such as skewness of the outcome variable), then the Kruskal-Wallis test may in fact be a more powerful alternative (Pett, 1997) than ANOVA, despite the robustness of the ANOVA model.

NONPARAMETRIC METHODS FOR REPEATED MEASURES DATA: FRIEDMAN'S TEST AND COCHRAN'S Q

Often, a study design will involve more than two repeated measurements on the same subject or more than two matched samples. For example, what if an investigator wanted to compare depression and anxiety scores from individuals who were followed for 3 years? When assumptions are met, it is possible to conduct a repeated measure ANOVA to compare the measurements from years 1, 2, and 3. Major assumptions for the repeated measure ANOVA include normally distributed scores, continuous data are analyzed, and sphericity must be met. The sphericity assumption is often difficult to meet, but fortunately statistical packages often will provide alternative interpretation of the test statistic via adjustment to the degrees of freedom (e.g., Greenhouse-Geisser or Huynh-Feldt) or multivariate approach. In the event that the data are skewed or were scaled on an ordinal scale (e.g., little to no depression, mild depression, and high depression), then the Friedman's test, a nonparametric analog to the repeated measures ANOVA, would be the more appropriate statistical test.

The Friedman's test is another approach that examines data based on its rank properties. Just like the analysis of variance test generalizes the two-independent samples t-test to more than two samples, Friedman's test generalizes the sign test to more than two samples. As with the other rank-based tests described thus far, hypothesis testing for the Friedman's test may be expressed by the medians or the average ranks. Assumptions for the Friedman's test include that the data are continuous and at least ordinal in measurement and that there is independence between the cases or relevant analytic units (e.g., families or matched groups) (Pett, 1997). Because of the presence of a repeated measure, ranks are assigned to scores within each case (i.e., row), as opposed to between cases. In the event of tied scores, the mean rank is assigned to each, and correction procedures, to account for the loss of variability, should be applied. To compute the Friedman statistic, Fr, the following formula is used (Siegel & Castellan, 1988):

$$Fr = \left[\frac{12}{Nk(k+1)}\sum_{j=1}^{k} R_j^2\right] - 3N(k+1).$$

In the equation above, k represents the number of conditions (i.e., time point), N represents the total number of cases (i.e. rows), and R_j is the sum of the ranks from the jth repeated measure (i.e., time point). Like the Kruskal-Wallis test, determination of statistical significance may be based on tables with Friedman test-specific critical values for smaller samples or on the chi-square distribution with larger samples. When the chi-square distribution is used, the degrees of freedom will equal $k - 1$, where k represents the number of repeated conditions. The computation to correct for ties is extremely cumbersome, but it can be done and is certainly implemented in modern statistical software. Tied ranks are first resolved by assigning the mean rank and then applying a modified version of the Fr statistic (adapted from Neave & Worthington, 1988):

$$Fr(ties) = \frac{12\sum_{j=1}^{k} R_j^2 - 3N^2 k(k+1)^2}{Nk(k+1) + \frac{\sum_{i=1}^{N}(t_i^3 - t_i)}{(k-1)}}.$$

In this equation, t_i represents the number of observations involved in a tie for the ith case (or row). Note that for Friedman's test, t_i could range from 0 (i.e., all observed outcomes for a case are distinct) to k = number of repeated measures (i.e., all observed outcomes for a case are equal).

Computation of Friedman's statistic (non-tied version) can be demonstrated with a small hypothetical sample of four depressed adults being treated for mild depression over a 2-year period. Negative attitudes about the future were assessed at baseline, and at the end of years 1 and 2 using Beck's Hopelessness Scale (BHS) (Beck, Steer, Beck, & Newman, 1993). Scores on the BHS range from 0 to 20 and are shown in Table 6.8 for this hypothetical sample along with ranks that are assigned within each

Table 6.8. Beck Hopelessness Scale for Four Depression Patients Followed Over a 2-Year Period

	Pretest		Year 1 Posttest		Year 2 Posttest	
ID	BHS score	Rank	BHS score	Rank	BHS score	Rank
1	18	3	12	2	11	1
2	13	2	15	3	9	1
3	14	3	9	2	7	1
4	16	3	15	2	12	1
		$R1 = 11$		$R2 = 9$		$R3 = 4$

Table 6.9. Comparison of Test Results for the Analysis of the Beck Hopelessness Scale Data Given in Table 6.8

Test	Test statistic	p-Value
Friedman's test	$X^2(2) = 6.50$	0.04
One-way repeated measures ANOVA (sphericity assumed)	$F(3,410) = 8.53$	0.02
One-way repeated measures ANOVA (Greenhouse-Geisser)	$F(1.07, 3.21) = 8.53$	0.06

Table 6.10. Comparison of Nonparametric and Parametric Analyses of the Drinks per Week Data Set Simulated Using the Total Drinks Consumed in the Last Month From the WASHDC Data Set

Test	Test statistic	p-Value
Friedman's test	$X2(3) = 214.60$	<0.001
One-way repeated measures ANOVA (sphericity assumed)	$F(3,1290) = 42.52$	<0.001
One-way repeated measures ANOVA (Greenhouse-Geisser)	$F(1.34, 575.87)$	<0.001

patient (i.e., within the repeated factor). Using the equation above, Fr equals 6.50 for our small data set. At the 0.05 level of significance, we find that the critical value is 6.5 (see Table M in Siegel & Castellan, 1988) and thus we find evidence favoring differences in hopelessness scores over time (i.e., we reject the null hypothesis).

Like the Kruskal-Wallis, it is common for software packages to evaluate *Fr* using the chi-square distribution, and thus to illustrate with our example, we would find the chi-square critical value, with 2 degrees of freedom and α of 0.05, to be 5.99. Our obtained value exceeds the critical value and the null may be rejected. As shown in Table 6.9, these results correspond with those of the one-way repeated measures ANOVA. Because of the severe violation of sphericity, we also report the Greenhouse-Geisser corrected statistic for reference, although this statistic is not reliable when computed from small samples.

The WASHDC data set does not include more than two dependent samples for the Friedman's test, so we simulated the weekly alcoholic beverage consumption based on the total drinks consumed in 1 month that is included in the WASHDC data set. As shown in Table 6.10, Friedman's test and both parametric repeated measures ANOVA models indicated the presence of at least one statistically significant difference in drinks consumed per week across the 4 weeks. This data set contained ties within some of the respondents (e.g., same number of drinks consumed for week 1 and 2), so the computed test statistic relies on the tied version of *Fr* (ties).

Because of the fact that the Friedman's test, like ANOVA, indicates the existence of differences but does not specify which pair(s) of conditions, time points, or matched samples differ, *post hoc* testing is warranted. Like the Kruskal-Wallis test, options for follow-up analyses to the Friedman's test with software packages are not always widely available or easily implemented. One option is the Nemenyi procedure that can be conceptualized as a nonparametric version of Tukey's HSD (see Heiman, 1996, for a discussion) and involves computing a critical difference value and comparing the mean rank differences to this value. Other options include conducting a procedure where one comparison group is contrasted against the other groups (Siegel & Castellan, 1988) or multiple paired dependent samples test (i.e., the Wilcoxon signed ranks) with the results qualified with Type I error correction techniques, such as the Bonferroni or a step-down procedure (Pett, 1997).

Compared with the repeated measures ANOVA applied to data that are normally distributed, the estimated power efficiency of the Friedman's test is $2/\pi = 0.64$ when there are two related samples and 0.87 with 10 related samples (Siegel & Castellan, 1988). In practice, the number of repeated measures are likely to be less than 10, so if power is the primary concern, then Friedman's test may not be preferred for repeated measures analysis when the normality assumption is met.

In this section, we have described a nonparametric alternative for data that are treated in ranked form. However, it may be of interest to compare dichotomous data across more than two dependent samples or across more than two time points. The Cochran's Q would serve this purpose and is regarded as an extension of McNemar's test (*see* Nonparametric Methods for Two Dependent Samples section above) to examine differences in frequencies over time. For example, this test may be suitable if one were interested in determining whether a sample of cancer-free 40-year-old men received a prostate cancer screening exam at baseline, within the next 5 years, and again within the following 5 years (i.e., 10 years from baseline). Study subjects will have either received a prostate screening exam (or not) at each of the three time points (baseline, +5 years, and +10 years). The computation for the Cochran's Q is slightly more involved and follows this equation (from Siegel & Castellan, 1988):

$$Q = \frac{(k-1)\left[k\sum_{j=1}^{k} G_j^2 - \left(\sum_{j=1}^{k} G_j\right)^2\right]}{k\sum_{i=1}^{N} L_i - \sum_{i=1}^{N} L_i^2},$$

where k represents the number of repeated measurements, N is the number of cases, G_j is the number of positive characteristics (e.g., 1s) in a given column, and L_i is the number of positive characteristics (e.g., 1s) in a given row. This statistic is evaluated using a chi-square table with $k - 1$ degrees of freedom. Hypothetical data for a sample size of four along

Table 6.11. Data From a Hypothetical Prospective Study of Four 40-Year-Old Men Tracking Prostate Cancer Screening Exam Activity Over Two 5-Year Periods Beyond the Baseline

	Prostate cancer screening exam conducted			
Case	Baseline	5 years later	10 years later	L_i
1	1	1	1	3
2	0	1	0	1
3	1	0	0	1
4	1	0	0	1
	$G1 = 3$	$G2 = 2$	$G3 = 1$	

In this table, a value of 1 indicates that prostate screening was conducted at that time-point.

with the computed components of this equation are shown in Table 6.11. Using the $L_i's$ and $G_i's$ from Table 6.11 along with $N = 4$ and $k = 3$, we compute Cochran's Q = 2.00. Comparing this statistic to the chi-square distribution with 2 degrees of freedom, we find our results are not significant at the 0.05 level. Thus, the results are inconclusive and we are unable to reject the hypothesis that the frequencies of "screenings" does not differ across time.

Nonparametric Correlation Coefficients: Spearman's ρ and Kendall's τ

Thus far we have only examined nonparametric alternatives for testing group differences. The strength of linear association (i.e., correlation) between two variables, such as body mass index (BMI) and the maximum number of drinks consumed on any one occasion in the past month, could also be interesting. In such cases, a viable parametric approach would be to apply the Pearson's Correlation Coefficient r. The assumptions for Pearson's r include that the relationship between the variables is linear and the data are continuous and normally distributed. In the event that the data are not normal or are ordinal in nature, then the Pearson's correlation would not be appropriate. Moreover, Pearson's correlation coefficient is extremely sensitive to outlying observations for either of the two variables of interest. Fortunately, several nonparametric alternatives exist, and we will briefly address two of the more common procedures: Spearman's ρ and Kendall's τ.

Spearman's ρ, often called the Spearman's rank order correlation coefficient, is directly related to the Pearson's correlation coefficient—in particular, when the data reflect ranks, the two statistics will produce equivalent values. Assumptions for the Spearman's ρ are similar to other nonparametric methods in that the data must be continuous in nature, measured on at least an ordinal scale, and represent paired observations. To compute Spearman's ρ the data are separately ordered and ranked for each variable. Differences (d_i) in the variable rankings are computed for each of the N data pairs, and these values are directly incorporated into the computation as follows:

$$\rho = 1 - \frac{6\sum_{i=1}^{N} d_i^2}{N(N^2 - 1)}.$$

Statistical significance may be determined by using tables with ρ critical values for small sample sizes or based on the standard normal approximation for larger sample sizes given by: $z = \rho\sqrt{N-1}$.

Procedures for correcting for ties may be applied separately for each variable (x and y). In the equations below, g represents the number of different sets of ties that exist in the x (or y) rankings and t_i represents the actual number of observations that are included in the ith tie set. Again, computations of g and corresponding t_i-values are computed separately for each variable, X and Y (adapted from Pett, 1997): $\rho(ties) = 1 - \frac{(N^3-N)-6\Sigma d^2-(T_x+T_y)/2}{\sqrt{(N^3-N)^2-[(T_x+T_y)(N^3-N)]+T_xT_y}}$, where $T_x = \sum_{i=1}^{g}(t_i^3 - t_i)$ and $T_y = \sum_{i=1}^{g}(t_i^3 - t_i)$.

For example, consider a hypothetical sample of eight graduate students selected to explore the correlation between BMI and the maximum number of drinks consumed on any drinking occasion in the past month. The data for each variable are ranked separately, and then differences are computed and squared as shown in Table 6.12. Using the non-ties version of Spearman's ρ, we find that $\rho = -0.762$. Using appropriate tables (e.g., Table L of Neave & Worthington, 1988), we find the absolute value of ρ exceeds the critical value of 0.738 for a two-tailed test with α at 0.05. This indicates a significant correlation between BMI and the maximum number of drinks on any one occasion in the past month (and appears to be in a negative, albeit counterintuitive, direction as seen by the sign of the estimate). Incidentally, for these data Pearson's $r = -0.635$, p-value $= 0.091$. The difference in these two results is due in part the large (potentially outlying) BMI observation for case 5 (BMI = 33).

With the WASHDC data set, we use Spearman's ρ to estimate the correlation between BMI and number of days associated with a lack of sleep. Using the equation with ties, we find an extremely weak relationship between these variables ($\rho = 0.027$). Because of the large sample size (i.e., $N = 427$), evaluation of the null hypothesis of no correlation between these variables versus the two-tailed alternative of some correlation was based on the normal approximation. The computed z-score was found to be 0.55, and the corresponding p-value based on the standard normal distribution is 0.58. This result indicates that the correlation between BMI and lack of sleep as measured with the WASHDC data is not significantly different from zero.

Often, the interplay between variables involves more than simple bivariate analyses, and it may be preferable to examine partial correlations. Kendall's τ (another nonparametric correlation statistic) may be generalized to partial correlations and thus may be of interest. Computation procedures for Kendall's τ are very involved, and details may be found, for example, in Pett (1997) or Siegel and Castellan (1988). Briefly, Kendall's τ is based on ranks, and its value is computed by comparing each pair of data points (X_i, Y_i) with (X_j, Y_j) (for $i \neq j$) to determine the number of concordant (X and Y from one data point are either both smaller or both larger than the corresponding value in the other data point) and discordant pairs (i.e., not concordant). As with other statistical procedures, ties are considered and the coefficient may be referred to as Kendall's τ-b. Although most software packages include Kendall's τ for bivariate association, the partial correlation generalization of Kendall's coefficient is not readily available. The Kendall's τ-based partial correlation coefficient is computed as (adapted from Siegel & Castellan, 1988):

$$T_{xy.z} = \frac{T_{xy} - T_{xz}T_{yz}}{\sqrt{(1 - T_{xz}^2)(1 - T_{yz}^2)}},$$

where T_{xy} represents the bivariate Kendall's coefficient for the correlation between, for example, variables "x" and "y."

Using the WASHDC data set, we may be interested in controlling for the effects of another variable, such as age (Z), when examining the correlation between BMI (X) and the number of days in the past month the respondent had a Lack of Sleep

Table 6.12. Hypothetical Body Mass Index and Maximum Number of Drinks (Per Drinking Occasions in the Past Month) Data for Eight Subjects to Illustrate Computation of Spearman's ρ Statistic

Subject	BMI Actual value Rank	Max drinks Actual value Rank	BMI Rank – Max Drinks Rank,	d_i^2
1	22 2	128	−6	36
2	21 1	107	−6	36
3	29 7	22	5	25
4	23 3	96	−3	9
5	33 8	64	4	16
6	24 4	75	−1	1
7	26 5	11	4	16
8	28 6	43	3	9

Table 6.13. Kendal's τ Correlation Statistics Among BMI, AGE, and Lack of Sleep Variables Computed Using the WASHDC Data Set

	BMI (X)	Lack of sleep (Y)
BMI (X)	—	—
Lack of sleep (Y)	0.017	—
AGE (Z)	0.025	−0.0220

Table 6.14. Comparison of Parametric and Nonparametric Correlation Measures Between BMI and Lack of Sleep Using the WASHDC Data Set

Correlation Measure	Statistical Estimate	p-value
Pearson's r	0.087	0.07
Spearman's ρ	0.023	0.58
Kendall's τ	0.017	0.62

(Y). To do so, we would first compute the Kendall's τ coefficient for each pair of variables (see Table 6.13 below). Using the equation above, we find that the partial correlation coefficient is $T_{xy.z} = 0.0171$, which is not substantially different than 0.0170 (i.e., the unpartialled correlation).

The decision to use Spearman's ρ or Kendall's τ with bivariate correlations usually rests with one's own preference (Neave & Worthington, 1988). These techniques are similar in power, so when compared with the Pearson's r and when parametric assumptions are met, the efficiency is approximately 91% (Siegel & Castellan, 1988). If we examine the three methods for quantifying the simple bivariate relationships between BMI and lack of sleep in the WASHDC data set, we find that the data are somewhat consistent, with the lowest p-values associated with the Pearson's r (Table 6.14), which may be caused by the presence of a few larger BMI values.

Nonparametric Analysis of Nominal Data: Chi-Square and Fisher's Exact Tests

Kendall's τ and Spearman's ρ represent nonparametric alternatives to measuring correlation between two variables that are either continuously measured or on the continuous scale but represented as ordinal categorical variables. In this case, the data represent frequencies, or counts, and the degree of relationship between two such nominal variables is quantified as "association" rather than correlation or other statistical measures—including, for example, differences of means or medians. The chi-square test of association (also called the chi-square test of independence) is the most common omnibus method for determining whether overall associations exist between two nominal variables. The actual test uses the chi-square distribution (with (rows-1)*(columns-1) degrees of freedom) to derive inference for the null hypothesis of no association (or that the variables are independent) versus the general multitailed hypothesis of

Table 6.15a. Contingency Table of Visit Recency by Smoking Status Based on WASHDC Data Set

		Smoking status (computed)				
		Current smoker (daily)	Current smoker (some days)	Former smoker	Never smoked	Total
Doctor visit recency	Within past year	18	17	41	223	299
	Within past 2 years	5	5	3	44	57
	Within past 5 years	6	4	11	29	50
	>5 years	2	3	6	9	20
	Never	0	0	1	3	4
	Total	31	29	62	308	430

Table 6.15b. Chi-Square Test of Association Results Derived From the Data Depicted in Table 6.14 (i). Chi-Square Tests

	Value	df	Asymp. sig. (two-sided)
Pearson chi-square	19.110[a]	12	0.086
Likelihood ratio	19.182	12	0.084
Linear-by-linear association	6.474	1	0.011
N of valid cases	430		

a. 11 cells (55.0%) have expected count less than 5. The minimum expected count is 0.27.

some association between the two variables of interest. The utility of the chi-square test as the basis of such inference rests on a few key assumptions of the test, including (1) levels/categories of each variable represent mutually exclusive categories; (2) no cell in the contingency table formed by cross classifying the levels of each variable has a frequency less than 1; and (3) no more than 20% of the cells have an expected frequency of less than 5.

To illustrate the chi-square test, we examine the association between the recency of doctor visits and smoking status. In Table 6.15 (a) we display the 5 × 4 contingency table of counts for doctor visit recency by computed smoking status for the WASHDC data set. The sparseness in the later categories of the doctor recency across all levels of smoking status creates the "warning" footnote that is displayed beneath Table 6.15 (b), which remarks that a large percentage of expected cell counts are below 5.

In practice, a warning message like the one depicted in note a of Table 6.15 (b) is to be expected if the sample size is small relative to the total number of cells formed by cross-classifying one variable by a second, third, fourth, or more. Generally, this message implies that the use of the chi-square distribution as the approximate sampling distribution of the test statistic based on scaled squared differences between observed and expected counts is not adequate. If a researcher chooses to ignore the warning altogether, inference derived from interpreting the stated two-sided p-value (asymptotic) may be in error—that is, the risk of Type I or Type II error may be inflated beyond the specified tolerable limits (Neave & Worthington, 1988). We note that the warning message issued in this example occurs in the context of a sample size of 430 total cases, which generally would not be considered a small sample size. The warning should not be ignored and is not erroneous because the adequacy of the chi-square approximation for the chi-square test of association depends on both the total sample size and the per-cell expected cell sizes.

So what does a researcher who is concerned with making correct inference do in this situation? One possible solution involves combining categories (usually adjacent) of one or more variables to increase the total sample size for the appropriate row or column (e.g., "Never" row in Table 6.15 (a)) and then re-running the chi-square test. This approach potentially implies a slightly different interpretation, based on the combined levels of each variable, which may or may not be acceptable or appropriate. It may also be necessary to combine several categories into one to obtain adequate row/column totals to imply that no more than 20% of the expected cell counts are less than 5. If this approach is neither sufficient nor acceptable, then the researcher may choose to invoke Fisher's exact test.

Fisher's exact test is perhaps the most well-known nonparametric exact test and is most often applied to a pair of dichotomous (i.e., two-level) nominal variables but can be extended to nominal variables that are jointly represented more broadly by an "R-by-C contingency table." Fisher's test treats the marginal row and column count totals as fixed and assigns every possible 2 × 2 table (or R-by-C table), having those same marginal totals, a probability based on the hypergeometric distribution (i.e., a probability distribution that counts the "successes" in a finite sample when the sampling is conducted without replacement). Fisher's test is exact because the p-value is computed directly as the sum of the assigned probabilities from tables that have at least as large of an association as the observed table. No large sample approximations are required in conducting this test (or in the computation of the p-value). However, as the number of categories extends beyond two for either of the two categorical variables, computation of Fisher's exact test becomes too computer-intensive to be practical. Fisher's exact test computed using SAS Version 9.2 for the doctor visit and smoking data depicted in Table 6.15 (a) produced a warning message in the log file stating that there was insufficient memory to perform the exact test calculations. This complication partly results from the moderate sample size in addition to the large number of cells included in Table 6.15 (a). In these instances, an exact test is difficult—if not impossible or impractical—to obtain. A more practical and easily implemented solution would be to base inference on an approximation to the exact test distribution based on Monte Carlo sampling from the collection of all possible R-by-C contingency tables having the observed row and column totals. In this case, the approximate test statistic and p-value based on 10,000 Monte Carlo samples were 19.11 and 0.0955, respectively. A 99% confidence interval for the true p-value can be obtained as a byproduct of Monte Carlo methods and in this case was computed to be (0.08793, 0.1031). Based on this confidence interval, one may be hesitant to reject the null hypothesis of no association between the recency of doctor visits and smoking status with a Type I error rate of 10% but would reject such a hypothesis in favor of a significant association when using the chi-square test (i.e., ignoring the warning).

Monte Carlo and Fisher's exact tests for variables with more than two levels each are not readily available in all statistical software packages; however, both options are available in R and StatXact and are discussed in the computer appendix (www.compappdx.com). Fisher's exact tests are automatically generated in recent versions of SPSS whenever both variables being "cross-tabulated" are dichotomous. Most statistical software tools offer Yates' continuity correction to the chi-square test statistic for tests of association between two dichotomous variables. Although this correction usually improves the chi-square approximation for such a test (Neave & Worthington, 1988), it is generally not preferred to Fisher's exact test because the latter is more readily available in most software packages.

Both Spearman's ρ and Kendall's τ statistics are the basis for tests of correlation between two variables that are minimally at the ordinal level, but they are also nonparametric measures of the magnitude of the correlation. Both the chi-square test and Fisher's exact test provide an overall test of independence (i.e., association) for two nominal variables but do not provide an actual measure of the magnitude of the association. For example, a researcher may want to know (1) whether marital status and smoking are independent, and (2) what is the strength of the association if one exists?

The φ coefficient provides a measure of the strength of association that is appropriate for tests between two dichotomous variables. Because the φ coefficient is derived from the chi-square statistic, assumptions associated with a 2 × 2 chi-square test must be observed (i.e., cell sizes are sufficiently large, etc.). The φ coefficient has a direct relationship with Pearson's r, so the interpretation of the strength of association is straightforward. Although the φ coefficient can be computed for larger contingency tables, it is not suitable because the interpretability of the coefficient is compromised (i.e., values may become larger than 1). In these more general cases, the strength of associations for two variables that form an R-by-C contingency table may be measured using Cramer's V statistic. Like the φ coefficient, Cramer's V may be computed using the chi-square statistic, and thus the appropriate assumptions must be observed. Cramer's V and the φ coefficient are equivalent when both variables are dichotomous. Although Cramer's V is regarded as an appropriate measure of strength of association in more general R-by-C contingency tables, it is somewhat difficult to interpret because it has no direct relationship to the Pearson's r (Pett, 1997). In particular, a Cramer's V value of 1 computed for an R-by-C contingency table when $R \neq C$ (e.g., 4 × 6) does not indicate a perfect correlation. If the overall sample size is small or if the expected cell counts are too small to make the chi-square approximation reasonable, then one may use a nonparametric resampling method that calculates the Cramer's V statistic (or the φ coefficient) repeatedly for each of many R-by-C contingency tables obtained via resampling from the observed data. Resulting measures of the strength of association based on this statistic can then be quantified by using the empirical distribution obtained via resampling. More details about specific nonparametric resampling methods are provided in the next subsection.

Modern Resampling-Based Nonparametric Methods

Generally speaking, modern resampling techniques are computer-intensive nonparametric techniques that generate inference based on resampling from the observed data set or observed marginal distributions. In this way, modern resampling techniques allow the data to speak for themselves by using the particular sample to generate (repeated) estimates of the parameter of interest. Rather than using calculations that are based primarily on an assumed theoretical distribution of the statistic based on the data, resampling methods use the distribution derived from the resamples as the basis of statistical inference. Cirincione and Gurrieri (1997) have provided a broad overview of some of the more commonly applied resampling techniques including permutation testing and bootstrapping with applications in the social sciences. In the following subsections, we will focus primarily on general permutation tests followed by an introductory overview of bootstrap methods.

General Permutation Tests

Permutation tests rely on generating inference from the distribution of a statistic that is computed for each possible sample selected without replacement from the observed data. Samples generated without replacement are also referred to as permutations or re-orderings of the observed data and the distribution of the statistic computed for each possible permutation sample is called the *permutation distribution*. Statistical significance is then determined by comparing the value of the test statistic computed from the original data to the values obtained from the permutation distribution of the same statistic. To derive proper inference, the permutations of the original data must mimic the original data collection procedure/design in a way that is consistent with the null hypothesis under consideration (e.g., null hypothesis of no difference across groups). Generally speaking, permutation-based nonparametric methods are considered exact methods in that they achieve the specified Type I error rate, but in cases where the observed sample is moderate to large, a random subset of all such possible permutations may serve as an approximation to the permutation distribution (i.e., Monte Carlo sampling from the set of all possible permutations). In most cases, using a large Monte Carlo subsample of all possible permutations generally produces near exact inference (Ernst, 2004; Edgington, 1995).

Permutation tests can be applied to the analysis of one, two, or multiple groups. Outcomes can be either univariate or multivariate in nature and may be on any level of scale. LaFleur and Greevy (2009) and Berger (2006) have illustrated applications of permutation tests to ANOVA and logistic regression, while Kennedy and Cade (1996) have evaluated various permutation tests applied to multiple regression. Although permutation tests can be generally applied, their most common use involves comparisons across two independent samples (Efron & Tibshirani, 1993). In the literature there has been some discussion of both *randomization tests* and *permutation tests* applied to the two-sample scenario. Technically, these two approaches are not the same, but in practice the analysis proceeds in a similar manner. More specifically, if a study is based on an experiment that randomizes a collection of patients to one of two treatment groups, then technically the randomization tests are applied to analyze differences across these two groups and inference from these models does not usually apply beyond the particular sample. If, however, there are two populations (i.e., strata) and samples are randomly selected from each population, then a test of the differences is conducted using a permutation test. Inference in this case is usually made to the larger populations from which the samples were drawn. Because the process of conducting the randomization and permutation tests for the two sample problem is essentially the same, we do not make further distinction between them and refer more generally to the common approach as the two-sample permutation test. Interested readers can find more details regarding the nuances between randomization and permutation tests in Ludbrook and Dudley (1998) or Ernst (2004).

Application of Permutation Tests to One Sample

To illustrate the permutation testing method, we begin with a hypothetical one-sample study seeking to evaluate the effectiveness of a new intervention using Internet videos to help relieve anxiety and depression for newly diagnosed cancer patients. Three cancer patients were randomly selected to receive the module in a pretest/posttest design that used the Hospital Anxiety and Depression Scale (HADS) (Zigmond & Snaith, 1983) as the primary outcome measure. A paired *t*-test is the obvious parametric choice for conducting the evaluation; however, the size of this "pilot" study precludes its use unless the differences in HADS scores are exactly normally distributed. Because HADS scores range from 0 to 21, with higher scores indicating more depression/anxiety, positive difference scores (pretest/posttest) indicate reductions in depression and anxiety, negative difference scores indicate increases in anxiety and depression, and difference scores near zero indicate little change. The permutation test may be applied directly to the change scores, which is similar to applying a one-sample *t*-test to the difference scores. Here the fundamental assumption of the one-sample permutation test is that the pre- and post-HADS scores are "exchangeable" under the null hypothesis of no change in HADS scores. A subject's pre-HADS score could just as likely have been that subject's post-HADS score and vice versa.

Observed data from three subjects for our hypothetical one-sample study are presented as permutation 1 in Table 6.16. The one-sample permutation test in this case will enumerate all possible resamples, without replacement, of the original sample, taking into account that resampling must be done within each person consistent with the pretest/posttest, within-person design. The test statistic for each resample will be the average of the recomputed difference scores, and these quantities form the basis of the permutation distribution. Because there are two permutations of the data that can be conducted for each subject (i.e., swap the pre- and post-HADS scores or keep them as they are), there are a total of $2^3 = 8$ total permutation samples that will constitute the sampling distribution. This number will always include the original, observed sample. The set of permutation samples and test statistics for our one-sample permutation test is shown in Table 6.16.

The *p*-value for a two-tailed one-sample permutation test is computed to be the fraction of the total number of permutation samples that produced an average difference statistic as extreme or more when compared with the test statistic computed from the original sample, which in this case is 3. The phrase "as extreme or more" is interpreted in both the positive and negative direction where the absolute values of test statistics are at least as large as the absolute value of the test statistic computed from the original sample. In our example, only one permutation sample on the positive side (sample #3) and two on the negative side (samples #6 and #8) produce a test statistic with an absolute value that is equal to or greater than the observed test statistic. Thus, the *p*-value from this one-sample permutation test is simply $p-value = \frac{4}{8} = 0.5$. The null hypothesis of no-change is not rejected in this case, and the evidence suggests that the average change in depression and anxiety is not significantly different from zero. Incidentally, the computed *p*-value for a paired *t*-test would have been 0.36.

Permutation Tests Applied to Two Samples

As mentioned earlier, the main application of permutation tests comes in the two-independent sample scenario. Like the two-independent samples *t*-test, the two-sample permutation test seeks to examine hypotheses regarding similarities and differences between two populations or groups. However, the two-sample permutation test requires fewer assumptions and seeks to investigate a more general null hypothesis positing that the two populations are the same. The permutation test makes no assumptions about the shape of the underlying distributions of the outcome variable and allows the analyst flexibility in determining the test statistic that is used as the basis of the test (i.e., comparisons can be based on differences of means, medians, standardized means, etc.).

Similarly to the one-sample counterpart, the two-sample permutation test assumes that data are exchangeable under the null hypothesis, and an outcome is as likely to be observed from one group as the other. A two-sample permutation test regards the sample sizes from each of the two populations as fixed and preserves these sizes in forming the permutation samples. The value of the chosen test statistic is computed for each permutation sample and the collection of these values forms the distribution that is used as the basis of the *p*-value computation.

Suppose that a researcher is interested in comparing the effectiveness of a new marketing campaign for promoting the use of healthy lifestyle mobile phone software applications (apps). In the study, 15 subjects were randomly assigned to receive promotional materials, including specific tutorials on how to download and use healthy lifestyle mobile

Table 6.16. Full Enumeration of Eight Permutation Samples Based on a Fictitious Pretest/Posttest of an Intervention Measured by the HADS Score Using a Sample of Three Subjects

Permutation number	Subject	Pre-HADS	Post-HADS	Difference score	Permutation number	Subject	Pre-HADS	Post-HADS	Difference score
1 - Original sample	1	18	12	6	5	1	12	18	-6
	2	13	15	-2		2	15	13	2
	3	14	9	5		3	14	9	5
	Average difference statistic			3.00		Average difference statistic			0.33
2	1	12	18	-6	6	1	12	18	-6
	2	13	15	-2		2	13	15	-2
	3	14	9	5		3	9	14	-5
	Average difference statistic			-1.00		Average difference statistic			-4.33
3	1	18	12	6	7	1	18	12	6
	2	15	13	2		2	15	13	2
	3	14	9	5		3	9	14	-5
	Average difference statistic			4.33		Average difference statistic			1.00
4	1	18	12	6	8	1	12	18	-6
	2	13	15	-2		2	15	13	13
	3	9	14	-5		3	9	14	-5
	Average difference statistic			-0.33		Average difference statistic			-3.00

Table 6.17a. Data for the Two-Sample Study of the Use of Healthy Lifestyle Mobile Phone Apps

Group	Number of healthy lifestyle mobile phone apps downloaded
Placebo	4 6 3 6 3 6 2 6 5 7
Intervention	7 4 8 7 9 9 5 6 9 2 7 5 7 7 6

Table 6.17b. Summary Statistics for the Downloaded Apps for Each of the Two Groups

	GROUP	N	Mean	Std. deviation
Downloaded APPS	Placebo	10	4.80	1.687
	Treatment	15	6.53	1.959

phone apps, and 10 subjects were randomized to the control group (i.e., no additional information). The number of healthy lifestyle apps downloaded during the 2-week study period is the primary outcome of interest. Table 6.17 (a) provides example data and Table 6.17 (b) summary statistics.

Applying the two-independent sample t-test (assuming equal variances) generates a test-statistic of 2.286 with 23 degrees of freedom and a p-value of 0.032. Thus, this test suggests a significant difference in the mean number of apps downloaded between these two groups. However, should we trust the parametric result in this case? The problems are that the sample sizes in each group are small, the number of possible apps for each group is discrete, and count data are bounded on the lower end by 0. A histogram (Fig. 6.1) of these data suggests possible departures from normality.

One possible nonparametric technique for analyzing these data is the WMW test. As previously described, this test will compare whether the population distribution of scores is equivalent across these two groups. If the distribution of the number of healthy apps has the same shape and dispersion for each of the groups, then the WMW test would be testing the equivalence of medians across the two groups. Furthermore, if the distributions were also symmetric, then this test would be testing the equivalence of means across the two groups. In this case, however, the assumptions about the shape and dispersion or, in particular, the normality of the apps variable for each of these groups are in question. Our interest in comparing these two groups persists, and the standardized mean difference is still of interest. This value is simply the t-statistic, but rather than comparing it to the reference t-distribution, it is compared with a permutation distribution that is based on randomly permuting the group assignment of 25 subjects into 10 placebo and 15 treatment observations, resulting in a total of $\binom{25}{10} = 3,268,760$ (subsamples of 25 of size 10, taken without replacement). Thus, a permutation sample consists of randomly permuting the observed data points to either the treatment or placebo groups—the data values shuffle around but the total sample sizes per group are retained for each permutation sample. Even with modern technology, computing the exact full permutation distribution may not be feasible, especially as the sample size and number of groups increase so a test statistic based on an asymptotic approximation may be used instead (Higgins, 2004). For example, the total number of permutations increases to 3,169,870,830,126 if the group sizes are each increased by 10. Asymptotic approximation is obtained by selecting a large Monte Carlo sample of all possible permutations and statistical inference is made using this "approximate" permutation distribution. The precision on the p-value estimate can be improved by choosing a larger number of permutations as described in Ernst (2004) and LaFleur and Greevy (2009). Applying this approach with 10,000 permutation samples using R, we generated a two-permutation test p-value of 0.0375, which provides a similar interpretation—obtaining a value equal to or more than the observed standardized difference in the number of downloaded apps between the two groups appears unlikely (less than 4% chance) if, in fact, there is no difference between the treatment and placebo groups. Monte Carlo sample sizes can be selected to ensure that the p-values are estimated to within tolerable limits as described by Ernst (2004).

The two-sample permutation test does not rely on assumptions regarding the specific shape of the underlying distribution but under the null hypothesis assumes that the two populations are

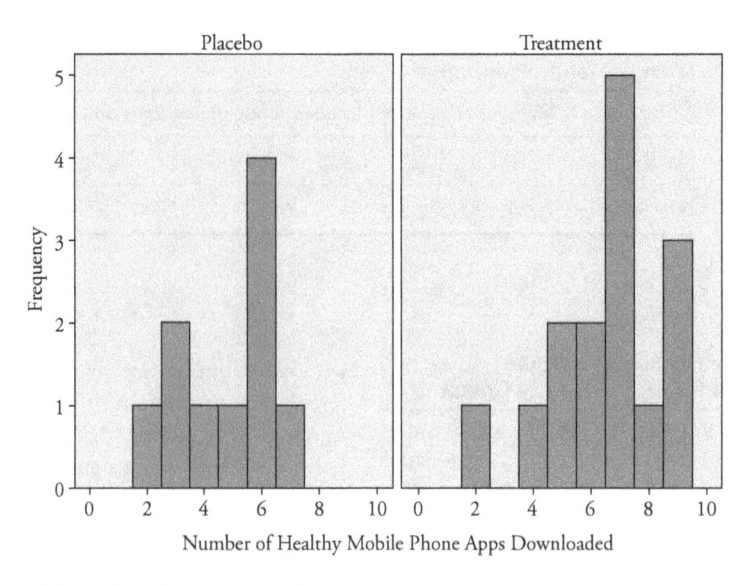

Figure 6.1 Histogram of the number of apps downloaded by treatment group.

equal. Like most other nonparametric techniques, the two-sample permutation test is not as sensitive to outliers as the independent samples t-test. To illustrate this property, assume that the first observation in Table 6.16 (a) for the intervention group was 19 rather than 7, a value that provides even more evidence in favor of greater app downloads between the two groups. Rerunning the two-independent samples t-test however yields a test-statistic of 1.984 and a p-value of 0.059. The corresponding p-value based on 10,000 samples from the permutation distribution yields a p-value of 0.0363. The permutation test suggests that differences in the app download distribution exists between the two groups, whereas the two-sample t-test provides a more ambiguous finding, caused in part by the impact of the outlier on the pooled variance and the overall test-statistic. The impact of extreme scores is mitigated in the permutation test because such values may be assigned to either group in any given permutation sample, and results are averaged out across this distribution.

When parametric assumptions are satisfied, the relative efficiency of permutation-based methods is just below 1, indicating that the nonparametric technique may be slightly underpowered when compared to the parametric technique for the given sample size. However, if parametric assumptions are not satisfied, then the permutation test is more efficient (Keller-McNulty & Higgins, 1987; Tomkins, 2006). Confidence intervals based on the permutation distribution or on Monte Carlo sampling from this distribution can be computed but are generally not reported because the primary emphasis of this technique lies in hypothesis testing. More specific information on confidence intervals derived using the permutation distribution can be found in LaFleur and Greevy (2009), Ernst (2004) or Good (2004). On the other hand, the bootstrap resampling technique focuses on population parameter estimates and their standard errors, thus making confidence interval estimates a natural byproduct. We can now turn our focus to these methods.

Nonparametric Bootstrap Methods Described

Like permutation tests, nonparametric bootstrap methods (henceforth referred to as bootstrap methods) rely on resampling from the observed data to derive statistical inference. Unlike permutation methods, bootstrap methods form bootstrap samples by randomly selecting *with* replacement a sample of the *same size* as the observed data set. Because sampling is with replacement and the sample is the same size as the original data set, it is possible for any given bootstrap sample to contain one or many duplicated data values and also possible that some data values are excluded from one or more of these bootstrap samples. The usual goal of a bootstrap analysis is estimation of a population parameter using an interval estimate that is formed from a statistic point estimate accompanied by an estimate of the standard error of the statistic. The name of the method comes from the idea of pulling oneself up by the bootstraps and was originally proposed in the late 1970s (Efron, 1979).

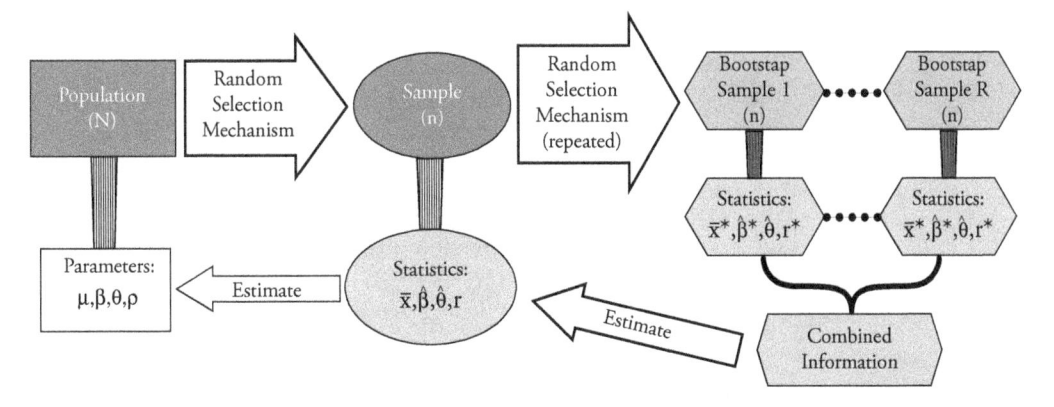

Figure 6.2 Visual depiction of the bootstrap resampling framework.

The bootstrap principle posits that information about the relationship between the parameter and the statistic computed from the observed sample (left side of Fig. 6.2) can be gleaned by analogy from the relationship between the observed sample and recomputed versions of the same statistic obtained from the bootstrap resamples (right side of Fig. 6.2). In essence, the sampling distribution of the statistic can be approximated using subsamples taken from the observed data itself. If the original sample is a fair representation of the population and the number of bootstrap samples is adequately large, then interval estimates of the population parameter can be obtained that contain a point estimate along with some measure of precision.

As illustrated in Figure 6.2, the bootstrap method first computes the pertinent statistic for the observed data set ($\hat{\theta}$) and then computes the statistic for each bootstrap sample ($\theta_1^*, \theta_2^*, K, \theta_R^*$). These recomputed statistics form the basis of the bootstrap sampling distribution that is used for estimation and inference. The standard deviation of these values forms the estimate of the standard error of $\hat{\theta}$ and the difference between the mean of the recomputed values ($\hat{\theta}_1^*, \hat{\theta}_2^*, \ldots, \hat{\theta}_R^*$) and $\hat{\theta}$ is an estimate of the bias in $\hat{\theta}$ for estimating the parameter of interest (θ). Because the bootstrap method estimates the variability and bias in an estimator, it provides an estimate of the mean squared error of the statistic.

There are parametric bootstrap methods that also estimate parameters by using base resamples on random values drawn from a specified parametric distribution whose parameters are estimated from the observed sample. We focus here on the non-parametric version of the bootstrap and make no assumption as to which parametric distribution is appropriate for the data. More information about the parametric bootstrap can be found in Davison and Hinkley (1997). The jackknife method—specifically, the "delete-one jackknife" (*see* Bissell, 1975, or Hinkley, 1983) —is another resampling technique that has been specifically applied to estimating the bias of an estimator. Although the jackknife method is less computationally intensive than the bootstrap, in some simulation studies it has been shown to be slightly inferior (Efron & Gong, 1983).

The number of resamples, R, to use in an application of the bootstrap method is generally driven by the type of parameter being estimated and can range from 50 to more than 10,000 (Efron & Tibshirani, 1993). A small number of bootstrap samples are typically sufficient for estimating means, but a larger number is generally necessary for estimating extreme percentiles (e.g., 95th percentile) of a highly skewed distribution and to produce accurate confidence interval estimates (DiCiccio & Efron, 1996). Although the number of bootstrap resamples is important, the size of the original sample is closely associated with the variation in the bootstrap distribution (Hesterberg, Moore, Monaghan, Clipson, & Epstein, 2003) and coverage error of resulting bootstrap confidence intervals (i.e., a 95% confidence interval may actually be a 90% confidence interval) (Carpenter & Bithell, 2000; Higgins, 2004). Additionally, proper implementation of the bootstrap method requires special attention to ensure that the bootstrap samples are drawn with replacement in a manner consistent with the original sampling design and randomization scheme (Carpenter & Bithell, 2000).

Regardless of the form of the parameter being estimated, there are several types of bootstrap confidence intervals, ranging from the intuitively straightforward percentile method to the more complex, bias-adjusted and accelerated methods. As previously mentioned, bootstrap methods for generating confidence intervals may be prone to coverage error, thus methods for deriving intervals with lower levels of coverage error that also preserve transformations have emerged. DiCiccio and Efron (1996) provide both a technical overview and theoretical justification for four of the common bootstrap confidence interval methods, whereas Carpenter and Bithell (2000) provide a fairly readable and comprehensive comparison of a broader set of the most widely used and available bootstrap-based confidence intervals. A more comprehensive treatment of various bootstrap confidence interval methods can be found in Efron and Tibshirani (1993). Hesterberg et al. (2003) provide a more intuitive discussion with worked examples for three commonly used bootstrap interval methods. Here, we briefly describe four main methods of constructing confidence intervals based on the bootstrap distribution.

The most straightforward and easily implemented bootstrap confidence interval method is the percentile method. A $(1 - 2\alpha) * 100\%$ bootstrap percentile interval spans from the $100*\alpha^{th}$ percentile to the $100*(1-\alpha)^{th}$ percentile of the bootstrap sampling distribution. So, for example, if 1000 bootstrap samples were used, then a 95% bootstrap percentile interval has as its lower endpoint the 25th largest bootstrap estimate and as its upper endpoint the 975th largest bootstrap estimate. The percentile method is simple to implement in practice—namely, it involves locating specific values (i.e., percentiles) from the statistics computed in the bootstrap samples ordered from smallest to largest. This method does not require an estimate of the standard error of the statistic of interest and the endpoints of the generated intervals are within the proper boundaries (i.e., for estimating correlations, these bounds will be no less than −1 and no greater than 1). The percentile method also respects (monotonic) transformations of a given statistic to another scale. The coverage error of the percentile method can be substantial, especially if the true sampling distribution of the statistic of interest (i.e., $\hat{\theta}$) is not symmetric.

A related method that is based on centered bootstrap values (i.e., pivots) is the basic or residual method. Similarly the percentile method, the $(1 - 2\alpha) * 100\%$ basic or residual bootstrap confidence intervals, is based on the $100*\alpha^{th}$ and $100*(1-\alpha)^{th}$ percentiles of the bootstrap distribution of residuals formed by subtracting the statistical estimate from the original sample taken from each estimate derived from subsequent bootstrap samples ($w^* = \hat{\theta}^* - \hat{\theta}$). The specific form of the $(1 - 2\alpha) * 100\%$ basic or residual bootstrap interval is then computed as: $\left(2 * \hat{\theta} - w^*_{(1-\alpha)}, 2\hat{\theta} + w^*_\alpha\right)$, where w^*_α represents the $100*\alpha^{th}$ percentile of the bootstrap residual distribution (i.e., using 1000 bootstrap samples and a $(1 - 2*0.05)*100\%$ or 90% confidence interval, $w^*_{.05}$ represents the 5th largest w^* value when the w^*'s are ordered from smallest to largest). Like the percentile intervals, the residual bootstrap confidence intervals are simple to calculate and can often provide accurate confidence intervals for estimating a population median (Carpenter & Bithell, 2000). The coverage error for these intervals may be substantial when the true sampling distribution of the residuals differs from the bootstrapped estimate. Moreover, it is possible for the residual method to produce confidence interval estimates that are out of practical or natural boundaries (i.e., a negative variance estimate).

One method that improves on the residual method by standardizing the residuals with the estimated standard error of the statistic is the bootstrap t-method. The bootstrap-t interval is computed similarly to a confidence interval based on the t-distribution, except that a nonparametric estimate derived from the bootstrap distribution of t-values (pivots): $t^*_i = \frac{\hat{\theta}^* - \hat{\theta}}{se(\hat{\theta}^*)}$ for each bootstrap sample $i = 1, 2, \ldots, R$ is used to determine the appropriate critical value. In essence, the bootstrap t-method avoids assumptions of normality by using observed data to generate a sample-based t-table derived from the bootstrap distribution of t-values. Confidence intervals are then constructed using the critical values from this sample-based t-table. The $(1-2\alpha)*100\%$ bootstrap t-interval is given by:

$$\left(\hat{\theta} - t^*_{(1-\alpha)} \times \widehat{se}(\hat{\theta}), \hat{\theta} - t^*_\alpha \times \widehat{se}(\hat{\theta})\right),$$

where t^*_α represents the αth percentile of the distribution of the t^*_i's and the two critical values may not be equal in absolute value because of possible asymmetry of the distribution. The standard error in the confidence interval formula is estimated using the entire bootstrap distribution of $\hat{\theta}^*$'s. Just like its parametric counterpart, the bootstrap-t confidence interval is sensitive to outlying observations and may provide unpredictably large endpoints in nonparametric estimation applications. This method tends to work well for location statistics such as mean, median, or other quantiles of a distribution.

If the standard error of the statistic is not known (i.e., no functional formula like $\sigma/\sqrt{n}$ for the sample mean $\bar{x}$), then this method usually employs an iterative application of bootstrap resampling (i.e., double bootstrap), which increases the computational intensity. Like the residual/basic intervals, bootstrap t-intervals can produce bounds that are not realistic or feasible (e.g., a correlation coefficient that is greater than one).

The bias corrected and accelerated (BCa) method for calculating confidence intervals improves on the methods previously listed by correcting the interval for possible biases and for the fact that the shape or skewness of the sampling distribution of the statistic may be affected by the parameter being estimated. The BCa method is the most technically rigorous of those presented in this chapter in that it requires an estimate of both the bias correction and the acceleration, which measures the degree to which the standard error of the statistic varies as a function of the true parameter value. The acceleration can be estimated using the jackknife method previously mentioned in this section, and the bias correction can be estimated as a function of the fraction of bootstrap sample values of the statistic that are less than the observed statistic. Compared with the percentile and basic methods, the BCa method generally has smaller coverage error and tends to perform better when the sampling distribution of the statistic is highly skewed. Like any bootstrap confidence interval method, the BCa does not perform well with very small samples, but is generally the preferred nonparametric method for small to large samples (Efron & Tibshirani, 1993; Hesterberg et al., 2003).

Application and Comparison of Nonparametric Bootstrap Confidence Interval Methods

To illustrate the bootstrap method, suppose a researcher is planning a clinical trial to test a new alcohol consumption intervention and in the process needs to understand the distribution of the number of drinks consumed in a 1-month period for adult youth younger than age 30 years. The researcher is not sure what types of distributions are likely, although a plausible distribution would be the Poisson because count data are involved. However, the Poisson distribution assumes that the mean and variance are the same, and the researcher has a keen interest in evaluating possible overdispersion, where the variability might be higher than expected. A useful statistic that quantifies overdispersion for a given sample is the dispersion index defined by $DI = \frac{s^2}{\bar{x}}$. A 95% confidence interval for the true dispersion is needed for planning the clinical trial. Dispersion quantities must be positive, and interest is specifically given to determining whether the dispersion is different from 1. Assuming a normal distribution with a mean of 1 is not appropriate here because dispersion values must not fall below zero and may be arbitrarily large. The left panel of Figure 6.3 provides a histogram for the "number of alcoholic drinks consumed in the last 30 days" variable from the WASHDC data set.

Clearly the underlying distribution seems highly positively skewed, so without other prior information, the actual shape of the DI statistic distribution that would be implied by the non-normally distributed alcoholic drinks data seems uncertain. Confidence intervals based on the (parametric) standard normal or t-distributions may not be as appropriate, in this case, as those derived using the bootstrap method. We applied the bootstrap method using 1000 bootstrap samples to estimate the sampling distribution of the DI index (displayed in the right half of Fig. 6.3) as well as to derive a 95% confidence interval for the true population DI based on the four methods previously described (displayed in Table 6.18). The bias in using the dispersion index statistic in estimating the true dispersion was estimated to be –0.729 drinks/month.

It is clear from the information provided in Table 6.18 that the normal and basic intervals are slightly shifted to the left of the other intervals. The percentile, bootstrap-t, and BCa methods produced intervals that are shifted more toward the right to compensate for the negative bias, or underestimate, resulting from the bootstrap procedure. The near consistency across the intervals resulted in part from the small amount of skewness of the bootstrap distribution, as displayed in Figure 6.3b. The bootstrap t-interval used an iterative bootstrap approach that estimated the standard error of the dispersion index based on a second set of 100 bootstrap subsamples taken from each of the 1000 initial bootstrap samples. As mentioned in Efron and Tibshirani (1993), the bootstrap t-interval may not be the most suitable application for nonparametric estimation problems such as the one posed here. From Table 6.18, one easily sees that the bootstrap t-interval provides a much higher upper bound compared to the other intervals—partly because of a few outlying values for the number of drinks in the past 30 days depicted in the far right tail of the histogram in Figure 6.3a.

Table 6.18. Comparison of 95% Bootstrap Confidence Intervals Estimating the True Dispersion Index for Amount of Alcoholic Drinks Consumed in 30 Days Using Four Methods

Bootstrap confidence interval method	95% Confidence interval for dispersion index
Normal approximation	(25.68, 60.25)
Basic/Residual	(24.15, 59.11)
Percentile	(26.83, 61.78)
Bootstrap t-interval	(28.71, 105.23)
Bias Corrected and accelerated (BCa)	(30.69, 75.52)

The normal approximation is also included for reference.

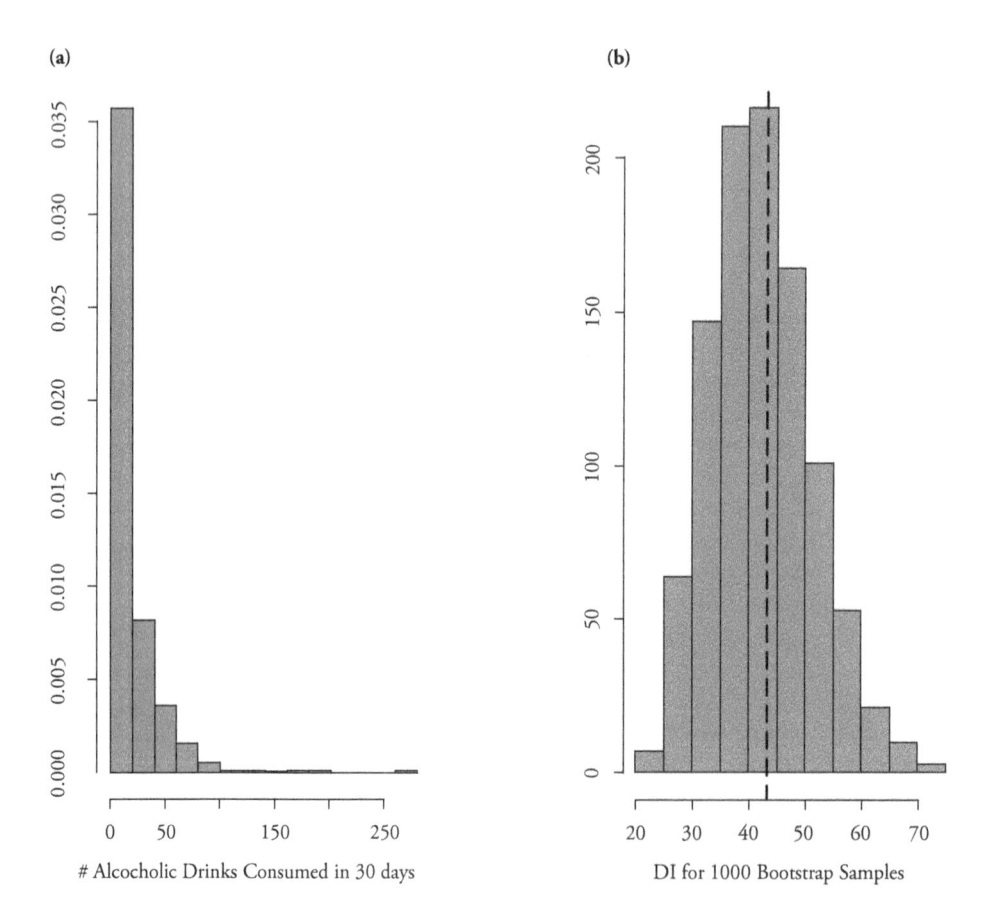

Figure 6.3 (a) Histogram of the Number of Alcoholic Drinks Consumed in the Past 30 Days based on the WASHDC data set (unweighted). (b) Bootstrap distribution of the DI index based on 1000 bootstrap samples drawn from the WASHDC data set. The DI for the observed data set was computed to be just under 43 and is depicted in the histogram as a dashed vertical line.

Other Applications of Bootstrap Methods

One of the main advantages in using bootstrap methods lies in its flexibility to accommodate various forms of parameters, including—but certainly not limited to—means, correlations, medians, trimmed means, regression coefficients, and ratio estimates. Using bootstrap methods to estimate a particular parameter would generally follow a similar procedure as illustrated by the previous example. A more detailed explanation and example of how bootstrap methods can be used to estimate a difference in medians has been provided by Berger (2006).

Similarly, Hesterberg et al. (2003) described how to use the bootstrap method for estimating the correlation coefficient. Bootstrap estimation can also be applied to the regression context; however, care must be taken when determining how bootstrap samples are generated. Fox (2002) has described both the fixed and random x-resampling approaches for generating such samples and outlines how estimates of regression parameters are derived from the resulting bootstrap distribution. More recent applications of the bootstrap have been used to estimate more complicated parameters, such as percentiles of residual distributions. In particular, Colugnati et al. (2005) applied the bootstrap to estimate the fatness cut-off points for childhood obesity that were based on the distribution of studentized regression residuals from sex-specific models that predicted body fat percentage from age.

The bootstrap method is especially useful when the form of the standard error of a statistic is unknown or difficult to estimate (as is the case for differences in medians from two samples) and when an interval estimate is desired. Inference and hypothesis testing using bootstrap methods are generally derived from information obtained from the resulting confidence intervals by determining whether the hypothesized null value of the parameter is included in the bootstrap confidence interval. In fact, under assumptions of similarly shaped distributions, the WMW test provides a nonparametric test of the equality of medians but does not provide an interval estimate of the possible magnitude of this difference. So in this case, the bootstrap confidence interval can provide additional information. Applications of bootstrap methods for testing one-tailed hypotheses are not as common in the literature.

Bootstrap Methods and Permutation Tests

Permutation tests are generally more powerful than an analogous test based on the bootstrap approach, but the inference decision using permutation and bootstrap methods will generally be consistent (LaFleur & Greevy, 2009). Bootstrap hypothesis testing methods are, however, more flexible than permutation tests in relaxing the null hypothesis of completely equal distributions to tests about specific aspects of those distributions (i.e., equality of means and variances or equality of means and unequal variances), but they are generally not exact tests and are usually less accurate (Efron & Tibshirani, 1993).

There are, however, situations where application of permutation tests are not appropriate and where parametric methods are not readily available. For example, if one wanted to test the multimodality of a distribution of a continuous variable such as quality of life from a sample of cancer survivors to understand whether the number of modes in the distribution might coincide with a subset of cancer types, then the test of interest is not the equality of distributions but, rather, a test for the number of modes (i.e., one vs. a number greater than one). Currently there are no parametric tests readily available to test modality, as described in this example, but Efron and Tibshirani (1993) describe a technique for applying the bootstrap method using data based on a nonparametric kernel density estimator of the true outcome variable distribution. Nonparametric kernel density estimation and more general nonparametric curve estimation techniques are described next.

Nonparametric Curve Estimation Methods

Interest in how predictor variables relate to a primary outcome is a common aim in many research studies. For example, a researcher might want to understand the influence of age, level of education, employment status, and sex on monthly alcohol consumption. The birth weight of a newborn infant may be influenced by the weight of the mother, but researchers might ponder whether this relationship is linear or is consistent across several races. In the parametric approaches to modeling and estimating curves, or more generally, response surfaces, a specific distribution for the outcome variable is required for model fitting. In the general linear model framework, the outcome variable is considered to be normally distributed for each combination of the predictor variables. The generalized linear modeling framework allows a broader collection of parametric distributions to be used as the basis of model/curve estimation, including among others, the Poisson, binomial, log-normal or gamma. If neither the data nor transformation of the outcome variable is adequately described by one of these distributions, then a researcher should consider a nonparametric approach to model/curve estimation. In this section we describe nonparametric methods for univariate, bivariate, and multivariate curve/model estimation.

Nonparametric Density Estimation: The One-Variable Case

The decision to apply a nonparametric or parametric method for exploring a research question of interest hinges not only on the sample size but also on the underlying distribution of the data. Although there are formal statistical tests for assessing normality such as the Kolmogorov-Smirnov goodness-of-fit test, other graphical techniques are often used as a first step into exploring the shape of the underlying distribution. For example, the quantile-quantile (Q-Q) plot is a graphical technique that explores the degree to which the distribution veers from normality (or other distributions). Classical parametric approaches to analysis assume some type of underlying distribution of the collected data. Parametric approaches to estimating such distributions often begin with an assumption of the general functional form based on either historical knowledge or the plausibility that the chosen distribution could be a best guess or best approximation to the actual distribution of the outcome (e.g., normal, Poisson, or gamma). Once a functional form of the density has been specified, then the parameters of the specified distribution can be estimated from the collected data and inference can proceed from there. However, if no prior knowledge about the shape of the distribution is available or if prior knowledge indicates that the data may not be adequately represented using a particular distribution, then a nonparametric approach to estimating the distribution may be prudent. Nonparametric estimation of the distribution does not rely on such an *a priori* specification of a distribution but does assume that the data are a random sample from the distribution to be estimated. The target parameter in nonparametric distribution estimation is the probability density function for the outcome variable of interest.

Researchers who have the excellent habit of exploring data visually prior to analyses have been implementing one of the most basic forms of nonparametric density estimation by using a histogram. Although these histograms are conceptually simple, there are technical complexities of the nonparametric technique surrounding the choice of an optimal bin-width, as discussed by both Scott (1979) and Wand (1995). Selecting a bin-width that is too large can create a rather uninteresting depiction of the data distribution that is likely to be uninformative, whereas choosing a bin-width that is too narrow results in a depiction that may be too noisy. As an illustration of applying the default "Sturges" method (*see* Scott, 2010) for determining the optimal number of bins, Figure 6.4 plots a histogram of the 1-year change in weight for males ages 18 to 30 years from the WASHDC data set.

Because the target parameter of interest is a continuous probability density of the outcome variable,

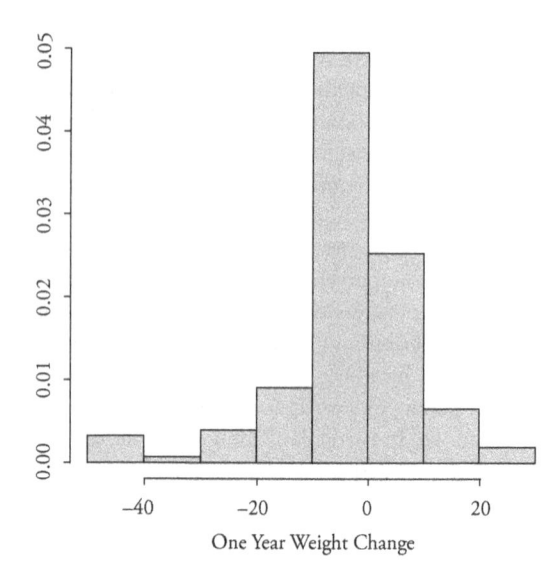

Figure 6.4 Histogram of the 1-year weight loss for 154 males ages 18 to 30 years derived using the WASHDC data. The optimal number of bins was determined using the classical Sturges method, which indicates that a total of $1 + log_2(154) = 8.27$ bins be used to construct the histogram (here, $n = 154$).

the histogram may not be the most visually satisfying because it provides a very "discrete" estimate of this density as evidenced by the large "steps" in the figure. Although the histogram gives a rough sense of the shape of the distribution, it may not be adequate for examining tail behavior or modality in detail. The nonparametric density estimation method extends the graphical depiction afforded by histograms and provides a smoother, continuous estimate of the underlying probability density function of the outcome of interest.

Nonparametric kernel density estimation is commonly used to display the shape of a data set without relying on a parametric model. Rosenblatt (1956) and Parzen (1962) provided early results on kernel density estimation; since then, much research has been done in the area and has been summarized by Wand and Jones (1995). The most common application of nonparametric density estimation assumes that all observations from the outcome of interest (i.e. $Y_1, \ldots, Y_n$) are independent of one another and come from the same continuous distribution (with density function, f). Using a kernel function, K and a positive bandwidth, b, $f(x)$ is estimated by $\hat{f}(x; b) = (bn)^{-1} \sum_{i=1}^{n} K\left(\frac{x-Y_i}{b}\right)$. The statistic of interest actually represents a collection of statistics— estimated heights of the density function of the outcome evaluated over a range of possible values, x.

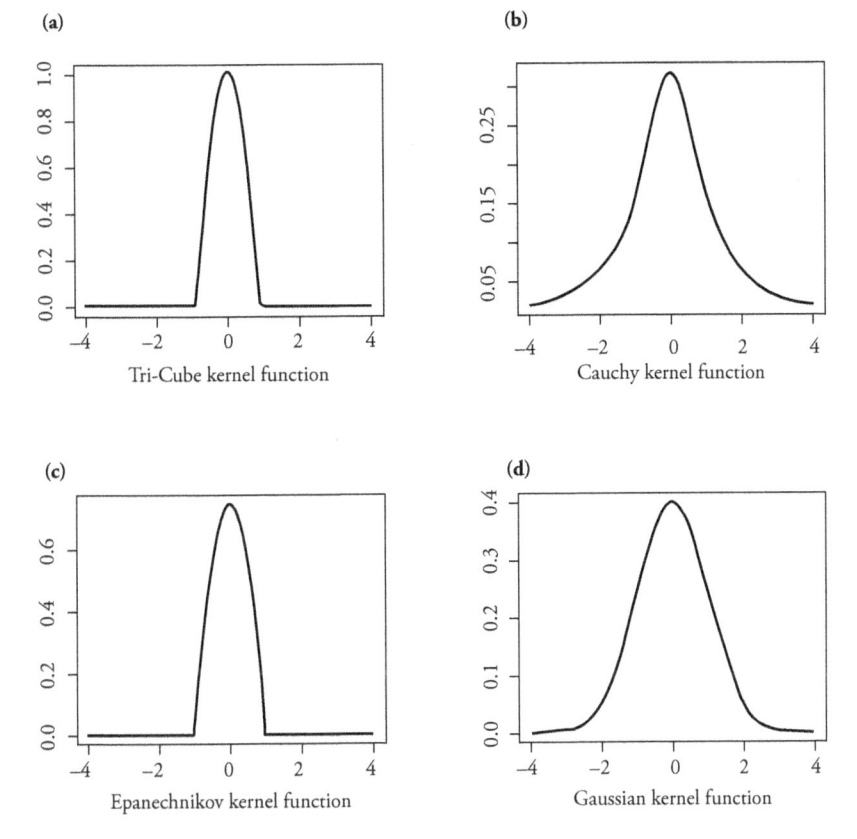

Figure 6.5 Plots of the Tri-Cube (a), Cauchy (b), Epanechnikov (c) and Gaussian (d) kernel density functions. The Epanechnikov and Tri-Cube kernel functions have positive height only for values between −1 and 1, whereas the Gaussian and Cauchy kernel functions have positive height across the continuum of real numbers. Notice that the Tri-Cube kernel gives the largest possible weight (i.e., *y*-axis value) for points near the center point—0.

At each x-point (akin to a bin in a histogram), the height estimate is a weighted average of the difference between the observed data (y's) and the particular x-point, with larger weights being given to observed values that are closer to the particular x-point. The weights are generated using a kernel function, K, which is a probability density function like the standard normal. The bandwidth, b, is akin to the bin-width in a histogram and essentially controls the number of observed y-values that will be used in the estimate of the height of density function at a particular x-point. The process of estimating the height is repeated beginning at the smallest x-point and continued to the largest x-point in a specified range. The observed y-values, or fraction of them depending on the bandwidth and kernel selected, are used in each x-point height computation. For most kernel functions, observations more than b units away from the x-point receive either a zero weight or a very small weight, depending on the type of kernel function used for the calculation. This process is nonparametric because it only estimates the density curve, or shape, and assumes no specific form of the distribution. The kernel density function that is often the default in many modern statistical packages is the Epanechnikov kernel function, but others such as the Gaussian, triweight, and Cauchy may also be available. Figure 6.5 provides a plot of these four particular kernel functions, for reference.

The estimate of the density function for an outcome variable of interest, such as quality-of-life index or intelligence quotient, depends more directly on the *bandwidth* than on the *type of kernel function* chosen to compute the estimate. As is the case with histograms, larger bandwidths result in smoother estimates that in some cases can be too smooth to be informative. Conversely, a bandwidth that is too small will result in an estimate that is too jittery or sensitive to the data at hand. Generally, an optimal bandwidth for each point, or one that can be used globally, seeks to balance these two extremes and is akin to the optimal number of bins used in creating a histogram, which is typically done automatically by default in many software packages. Similarly to the work of Wand (1995) and Scott (1979 and 2010) on optimal bin-width for histograms, optimal bandwidths and methods for estimating the bandwidth for nonparametric density estimates have been reported in the literature by Park and Marron (1990) and by Jones et al. (1996). The issue of bandwidth selection in nonparametric density estimation is akin to bin-width selection for histograms. The theory and approaches to optimal bandwidth estimation are highly technical and beyond the scope of this chapter, but we note that although kernel function choice rarely changes the overall nonparametric density estimate to a great degree, the optimal bandwidth quantity is a function of the type of kernel function used in the estimation process. So the optimal bandwidth to be applied using the Epanechnikov kernel will be slightly different compared to one that is derived for estimates based on the Gaussian kernel function, regardless of the bandwidth estimation technique used in practice. Interested readers are encouraged to explore some of the current methods, such as a smoothed version of the bootstrap applied to the mean integrated squared error statistic or least squares cross-validation techniques that involve multiple stages of estimation discussed in Park and Marron (1990) or Jones et al. (1996). Others (e.g., Fox, 2002) have suggested a more empirical approach to bandwidth selection that is based on visual trial-and-error. Bandwidth values that produce plots that are too smooth would be too large, and those that produce very "choppy" or rough pictures would be too small. The main idea of visually estimating an optimal bandwidth is to select the *smallest* possible value that provides a smooth fit.

To illustrate the dependence of the nonparametric kernel density estimate on the bandwidth, as well as the robustness to the choice of kernel function, the 1-year change in weight distribution for males ages 18 to 30 years was estimated using the WASHDC data set with an Epanechnikov and a Gaussian kernel using a 2- and 5-pound bandwidth (*see* Fig. 6.6). We note that these values are slightly larger than optimal but were chosen as practical and clinically meaningful values taken for illustration. Note that positive quantities indicate weight gain

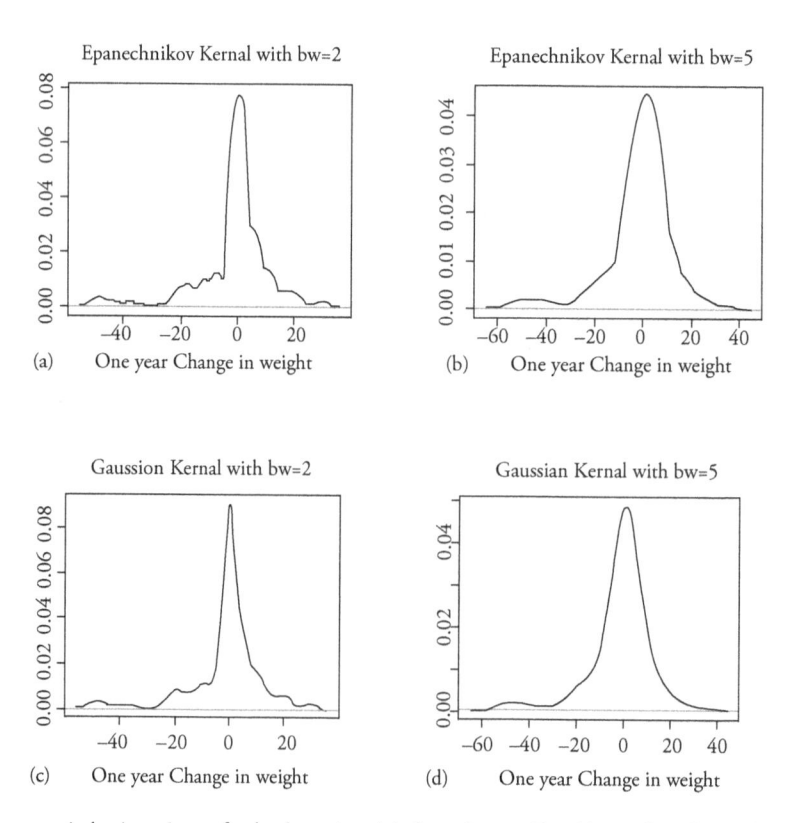

Figure 6.6 Nonparametric density estimates for the change in weight for males ages 18 to 30 years from the WASHDC data set using a 2-pound bandwidth in panels (**a**) and (**c**) for the Epanechnikov and Gaussian kernel functions, respectively, and a 5-pound bandwidth in panels (**b**) and (**d**).

over the past year, whereas negative quantities indicate weight loss. From the figure, it is easy to see that some asymmetry is suggested with slightly longer and heavier tails toward the weight loss end of the range (i.e., distribution appears to be slightly negatively skewed). The estimates have similar shape at each bandwidth, and the smaller 2-pound bandwidth estimates are more jagged compared to the possibly oversmoothed estimates generated using a 5-pound bandwidth.

Simple Nonparametric Regression: Scatterplot Smoothing

In the simple linear regression modeling framework, a two-dimensional scatterplot of the Y-outcome variable versus the X-predictor can be plotted along with an estimate of the least-squares best-fitting regression line. Such an approach assumes independent and identically distributed outcome data that are conditionally normally distributed at each level of the predictor variable with a presumed constant error variance. The model also assumes that the relationship between outcome and predictor can best be described via a straight line. In some instances, the assumptions surrounding normality or equal variance can be remedied by using a transformation (e.g., natural log or arcsine) for the outcome (or predictor) variables. However, in these cases, interpretation of the regression lies on the transformed scale and may not always have an appropriate or meaningful interpretation. And yet, in other instances, a straight line may not be the best geometric depiction of the relationship between the two variables. For example, second test performance may increase rapidly for those students with lower test one scores and more gradually for students with higher test one scores. In these situations, an investigator may be advised to consider nonparametric regression as a viable alternative.

Just like kernel density estimates provide a smoothed version of a single-variable histogram, simple nonparametric regression methods (applied to a single outcome variable, Y and a single predictor, X) such as kernel regression, nearest neighbor regression, smoothing splines, and LOESS provide a smoothed version of the relationship between two variables as depicted in a simple two-dimensional scatterplot that does not assume an *a priori* functional form such as a line or quadratic curve. For this reason, many simple nonparametric regression methods and their extensions to the two-predictor variable setting are referred to as scatterplot smoothing methods. Altman (1992) has given a brief, readable introduction to kernel and nearest neighbor nonparametric regression, and Faraway (2006) has provided an exposition of both kernel and smoothing spline methods. Here, we will focus on the LOESS method (or LOWESS), which is the most popular simple nonparametric scatterplot smoothing method applied to the two-variable scenario, where there is a single outcome variable, Y, and a single predictor, X. The LOESS procedure or, more formally, locally weighted (polynomial) regression (Fox, 2002; Jacoby, 2000) involves repeatedly fitting local weighted polynomial regressions $y_i = \alpha + \beta_1(x_i - x_0) + \beta_2(x_i - x_0)^2 + \cdots + \beta_p(x_i - x_0)^p + \epsilon_i$ using a subset of the observed data over a series of x_0 values in the range of the predictor variable. The weights are determined by a kernel density function that generally assigns greater weight to data points (x_i's) that are closer to the local value of interest x_0 and less weight to data points that are farther away. At each local point, the LOESS estimate of the outcome is $\widehat{y_0} = \widehat{\alpha_0}$ and the estimated intercept from the weighted polynomial regression fitted around x_0. LOESS estimates are produced for a series of local points across the range of the X-predictor variable and are combined to produce a smoothed estimate of the relationship between the outcome and predictor variables.

Although LOESS is a nonparametric curve fitting procedure, there are a few inputs that need to be supplied by the user to obtain the estimated curve: a smoothing parameter, the degree of the LOESS polynomial, and the weighting function. The smoothing parameter determines the percentage of original data that are used as the subset for computing the weighted polynomial regression at each of a series of local points. As is the case in nonparametric density estimation, the LOESS smoothing parameter, or span, should be chosen to generate a nonparametric fit that is neither too smooth, where the span is too large, nor too rough, where the span is too small. The resulting curve should be as simple as possible yet represent the salient features in the relationship between the two variables (Fox, 2002; Jacoby, 2000). Optimal values for the span could depend on the actual application but typical values used in practice range from 0.4 to 0.8. Fox (2002) suggests selecting the smoothing span parameter using cross-validation procedures by omitting each predictor variable data point and iterating the fit consecutively through the data set. Cohen (1999) suggests using a bias-corrected version of the Akaike information criterion (AIC) plotted against candidate smoothing span values in a screen-type plot and identifying the smoothing parameter value corresponding to the lowest trough in the plot. Jacoby (2000) suggests yet another method that is based on plotting residuals versus predictor values for a series of LOESS models fit, using various smoothing parameter values. Choice of optimal span is indicated by the corresponding residual plot with a LOESS line that is closest to a horizontal line at zero. Research on estimating optimal bandwidths is ongoing, especially for the case of multiple nonparametric regression where there is more than one predictor.

The degree of the polynomial used in the LOESS method represents the amount of curvature that is permitted in the LOESS estimates for each local fit. First degree polynomials, or simply straight lines, are recommended whenever the scatterplot suggests a monotonic trend in either direction between the two variables. For scatterplots that represent more curvature or fluctuations in inflection, a second degree polynomial (i.e., the quadratic function) can be used. Higher order polynomials allow greater flexibility in the resultant estimate but come with the price of less precise estimates. Fox (2002) suggests odd-order degrees are more advantageous than even-ordered degrees. In many software applications, the default degree is one.

Finally, the kernel function that is specified in the LOESS method is usually the tri-cube function depicted in Figure 6.5a; however, the user may opt for another kernel function. As in nonparametric kernel density estimates, the LOESS estimates are not as sensitive to choice of kernel function as they are to the smoothing parameter. The bandwidth, h, for the chosen kernel function will vary for each local point (x_0) and will be solely determined by the span/smoothing parameter specified for the LOESS method.

Because the LOESS procedure relies on neighborhoods of observed data to generate point estimates to produce a smoothed curve along a reasonable range of the predictor variable, the observed data for the predictor variable should be densely situated across this range. Otherwise, the stability of the LOESS estimator will be less than optimal. As the size of the data set increases, the LOESS method will become computationally demanding. This concern should pose no real problem in today's computing environments. Sensitivity to outliers is a concern that LOESS shares with its parametric linear regression counterpart, and there is a robust version of the LOESS procedure that further downweights outlying observations with large residuals in an iterative process to obtain a smoothed estimate (see Cleveland, 1979). Although both parametric and nonparametric simple linear regression methods can produce visual estimates, nonparametric methods, including LOESS, do not provide regression estimates. Although statistical inference using the results from the LOESS procedure can be obtained (as described by Jacoby, 2000, and Fox, 2002), it is generally not the main emphasis of these methods.

To illustrate the LOESS method, we examine the relationship between the number of binge-drinking occasions (defined as at least four or five drinks on any single occasion for women and men, respectively) among those who reported any binge-drinking behavior versus the number of days a respondent drank alcohol in the past month using data from the WASHDC data set. In the scatterplot depicted in Figure 6.7, we plot a least-squares regression line (solid), as well as a LOESS curve using first-order polynomials with a span of 50% (thick gray, dashed curve) and a tri-cube kernel function. Because of the two outlying binge observations, we also plot a robust version of the LOESS estimate using the same degree and span (short dashed black curve). From the scatterplot, it seems rather reasonable to concentrate on locally linear fits (degree = 1) because there is a general monotonic trend between binge occasions and number of days on which alcohol was consumed. Note that the influence of outliers is not significant in the LOESS estimate, as evidenced by the high degree of overlap between the two dashed curves in the figure. The prominent "bump" at 12 days of alcohol consumption for the LOESS curve is undoubtedly driven by the observation with 20 binge-drinking occasions. Notice also that both of the LOESS curves generally convey that the relationship between binges and days drinks consumed is very slight for those who drink less than half the month, with a very slightly sloped line. However, binge drinking tended to rise more rapidly for those who drank on more than 15 days in the past month, and this is visually depicted in the figure as an increased steepness in the second half of the LOESS curve. The linear regression estimate overestimates the trend for respondents who drank on fewer than 15 days and underestimates the trend for respondents who drank on a majority of days.

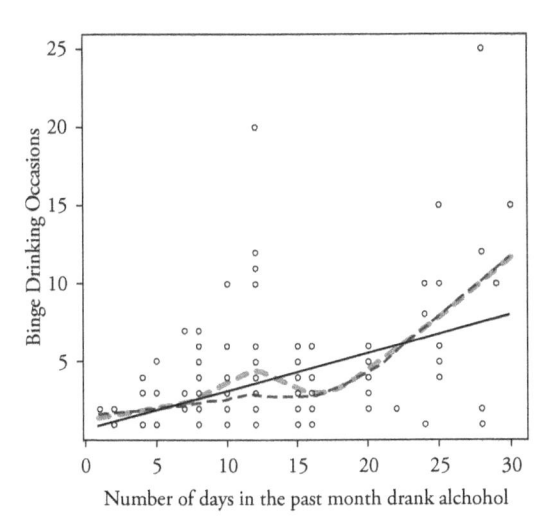

Figure 6.7 Scatterplot of binge-drinking episodes versus number of days on which alcohol was consumed in the past month for those respondents who reported at least one binge-drinking episode using the WASHDC data set. The thick grey, dashed curve represents first degree polynomial with 50% span LOESS fit. The short dashed black curve represents the robust LOESS estimate using the same degree and span. The solid black line is the least squares regression estimate.

Extensions to Nonparametric Multiple Regression

The LOESS procedure generates a curve that visually smoothes a scatterplot, and thus it is best applied to either a two- or three-variable scenario. Extensions of nonparametric regression methods, like LOESS, to the multiple regression context are not as straightforward as in parametric multiple regression. For example, there are several ways to measure distance between predictor variables when trying to determine which subset of predictors are included in each "local" fit. Further, the decision to use univariate and multivariate kernel functions for weighting must also be made in the multiple predictor variable contexts. Broadly speaking, there are two main strategies for extending nonparametric regression from the single- to the multiple-predictor scenario, including general multiple nonparametric regression and additive models. The general nonparametric multiple regression model allows the researcher to examine an outcome as a function of several predictor variables without having to specify the particular form of that function. Although this method is very general, it usually becomes difficult to incorporate many variables at a time, in part because of issues of dimensionality and the fact that in multiple dimensions, data are more sparsely populated in neighborhoods of local fitting points (Fox, 2002). Additive regression is an alternative method that models an outcome as the sum of functions defined separately for each predictor variable. Additive models proceed by estimating a series of partial regression models for the outcome and each predictor, separately, and these estimates can be based on scatterplot smoothing methods such as LOESS or splines. More technical details for additive models and general nonparametric regression can be found in Faraway (2006).

Statistical Software for Conducting Nonparametric Techniques

In the computer appendix of this chapter located at www.compappdx.com, we have included SAS, SPSS, and R code for the classical nonparametric techniques and either SAS or R code for some of the modern techniques applied in this chapter. There are many other computing resources that are available to assist researchers in applying nonparametric statistical methods. Beyond the three mentioned already, STATA has many utilities for conducting both classical and modern nonparametric techniques, including algorithms for bootstrapping. As for other software packages, StatXact provides an analysis tool kit that includes many classical nonparametric techniques as well as a host of permutation testing options that have both exact and approximate tests based on Monte Carlo sampling. Resampling Stats (http://www.resample.com/index.shtml) provides a Microsoft Excel add-on that can perform both single- and multistage bootstrap sampling methods as well as permutation testing. This website also offers an online introductory textbook that discusses resampling techniques. There are also other applets and freestanding programs available on the web for conducting many classical methods described in this chapter as well as two sample permutation tests. Berger (2006) has described a program for computing bootstrap confidence intervals that is freely available.

Concluding Remarks
Nonparametric or Parametric Methods, or Both?

Nonparametric techniques can often be more efficient, in terms of requiring slightly smaller sizes, compared to analogous parametric techniques whenever the outcome of interest does not have a normal distribution or whenever other parametric assumptions are not satisfied. These methods are also often only slightly less efficient than analogous parametric methods when the outcome is normally distributed or when other parametric assumptions are met. For example, with a large sample of heavily skewed data, a researcher might make the prudent choice of applying the more powerful two-sample permutation test instead of the standard parametric two-independent samples t-test. Nonparametric methods may also be an appropriate first analysis in pilot studies or secondary aims of larger studies that might be parametrically underpowered for substantive comparisons.

Many nonparametric procedures enable the user to obtain an exact test of significance, giving a p-value that is computed directly rather than invoking the Central Limit Theorem or appealing to the normal, or other parametric, distribution assumptions. Additionally, nonparametric procedures tend to be less sensitive to outlying observations than their parametric counterparts and in this way are considered to be more flexible and robust methods. Flexibility is also found in terms of the types of data to which these procedures can be applied, where nonparametric techniques can be used to analyze continuous, ordinal or nominal, or ranked data.

There are some types of tests or nonparametric methods that do not have a parametric counterpart, and in these instances, nonparametric methods extend quantitative analytic capabilities. When both parametric and nonparametric procedures exist for a given application, it may be possible to use both methods in tandem rather than having to choose one or the other. A growing trend in the application of nonparametric techniques comes in the arena of exploring the degree to which parametric assumptions are appropriate for a given analysis. For example, the use of a visualization technique, such as the histogram or smoothed density estimates, provides an exploratory glance at the tenability of distributional assumptions related to normality, skewness, or unimodality. Azzalini et al. (1989) suggested the use of nonparametric regression as a way to check the assumptions of a parametric regression model. If the two methods produce similar inference, then a researcher gains confidence that parametric results were not unduly influenced by possible violations in the assumptions underlying the model. On the other hand, if the methods give rise to discordant inference, then one may consider the extent to which assumptions are violated and proceed to present the nonparametric results (which may indeed be less sensitive to those assumptions). This approach emphasizes the concept that the two sets of methods are really complimentary to one another. In a research setting where the assumptions of a parametric test are generally satisfied and the data are of an appropriate form, then the parametric test should certainly be used because it will be more efficient and powerful. However, in many applied settings, this type of scenario seems the exception, rather than the rule. As such, consideration of nonparametric methods in conjunction with parametric methods will likely be the most reasonable and appropriate approach to statistical analyses.

Future Directions

Applications of nonparametric methods have continued to become more common, especially with the advances in personal computing power and further sophistication in statistical analysis software. New traditional-type and modern nonparametric methods continue to emerge in both the statistics and broader research literature. For example, new rank-based techniques have been developed with applications in statistical genetics (*see* Breitling et al., 2004) and permutation-based methods have been developed for analyzing microarray data (*see* Pan, 2003). Further developments of nonparametric methods applied to statistical genetics and clinical trials (especially adaptive designs) will certainly continue into the future. What is also likely to continue is the adaptation of current nonparametric methods to the analysis of alternative types of data. In the past decade there has been a considerable momentum in the adaptation of modern nonparametric techniques to the analysis of survey data with estimators and tests modified to incorporate the survey weights and design variables. For example, Bellhouse and Stafford (1999) discussed adapting histograms to the survey sampling context, whereas Buskirk and Lohr (2005) explored nonparametric weighted kernel density estimation with complex survey data. Korn and Graubard (1998) suggested nonparametric smoothing as a way to improve bivariate relations from survey data, and Breidt and Opsomer (2000) used nonparametric smoothing with auxiliary information for regression-type estimators of population totals. Lahiri (2003) and Shao (2003) explored various bootstrap methods applied to survey sampling data.

As computer resources continue to expand and become more readily available, nonparametric methods such as resampling-based permutation or bootstrap methods will see even more widespread use. More reliance on data-automated methods of estimation of visualization parameters, such as the bandwidth, will become best-practice approaches. Theoretical developments for inference from nonparametric tests, especially in the area of small samples, will also continue, with possible hybrid approaches that combine classical frequency-based and Bayesian perspectives. The continued use of nonparametric methods as a possible augmentation of parametric procedures will also likely become a standard part of the data exploration and assumption evaluation phases of statistical analysis.

Glossary

Asymptotic relative efficiency	Asymptotic relative efficiency is the ratio of variance estimators to one another.
Binomial test	The binomial test is a procedure for determining the significance of deviation from an expected distribution for dichotomous outcomes.
Bonferroni procedure	Bonferroni is a procedure for adjusting the α level downward to control for Type I error rates.
Confidence interval	A confidence interval is an estimate of a population parameter based around a sample value.
Covariate	A covariate variable is a predictor variable that is not usually of central interest but may be included in a model to adjust the associated variance constant.
Linear regression	Linear regression is a modeling approach to estimating population parameters based on the linear relationship among two or more variables.
Logarithmic transformation	Logarithmic transformation is the application of natural logs to data to stabilize the variance in the data
Nonparametric test	Nonparametric tests are those statistical methods that are generally either distribution-free or do not assume that the structure of the model is fixed *a priori*.
Normality	Normality represents the extent to which the data conform to or approximate a normal curve distribution.
Parametric test	Parametric tests are those statistical methods that generally rely on assumptions about population and probability distributions.
Post hoc procedures	A *post hoc* is procedures used after a significance test is performed to determine patterns among the subgroups.
Power	Power is the ability of a statistic to detect a significant effect when one exists.
Robust	With statistics, a test is robust when it is resistant to errors caused by deviations from the assumptions.
Skewness	Skewness is the measurement of asymmetry in a distribution of any data.
Sphericity	Sphericity is the assumption that the variances of difference scores between the levels of a repeated factor are equivalent.
Standard error	The standard error is the method for measuring or estimating the variability in the sampling distribution.
Statistical power	This is the probability that a hypothesis test is rejected when in fact it is false. Power is 1 minus the Type II error rate.

Glossary (Continued)

t-test	A *t*-test is a hypothesis test procedure based on the student's t probability distribution. It can take the form of a single- or two-sample test.
Type I Error rate	This is the rate at which one would declare a significant result when no actual significant result exists in the population. It is often referred to as the rate of false–positives.
Type II Error rate	This is the probability that the null hypothesis is not rejected when, in fact, it is untrue. The type II error rate is generally denoted as β.

Acknowledgement

We would like to thank our graduate assistant Jacob Henrichs for his assistance with the technical appendix.

Author Note

Trent D. Buskirk, Ph.D., Adjunct Associate Professor of Biostatistics, Saint Louis University and Research Director, The Nielsen Company, tdbuskirk@gmail.com

References

Altman, N. S. (1992). An introduction to kernel and nearest neighbors nonparametric regression. *The American Statistician*, 46, 175–185.

Azzalini, A., Bowman, A.W., & Newman, C.F. (1989). On the use of nonparametric regression for model checking. *Biometrika*, 76(1), 1–11.

Beck, A. T., Steer, R. A., Beck, J. S., & Newman, C. F. (1993). Hopelessness, depression, suicidal ideation, and clinical diagnosis of depression. *Suicide and Life-Threatening Behavior*, 23, 139–145.

Bellhouse, D. & Stafford, J. (1999). Density estimation from complex surveys. *Statistica Sinica*, 9, 407–424.

Berger, D. (2006). *Introduction to Resampling Techniques*. Accessed on August 7, 2010, from http://wise.cgu.edu/downloads/Introduction% 20to% 20Resampling% 20Techniques% 20060420.doc.

Bissell, A. F. (1975). The jackknife toy, tool or two-edged weapon? *The Statistician*, 24, 79–100.

Blair, R. C. & Higgins, J. J. (1985). A Comparison of the Power of the Paired Samples Rank Transform Statistic to that of Wilcoxon's Signed Ranks Statistic. *Journal of Educational and Behavioral Statistics*, 10(4), 368–383.

Breidt, F. J. & Opsomer, J. D. (2000). Local polynomial regression estimators in survey sampling. *Annals of Statistics*, 28, 1026–1053.

Breitling, R., Armengauda, P., Amtmanna, A., & Herzyk, P. (2004) Rank products: a simple, yet powerful, new method to detect differentially regulated genes in replicated microarray experiments, *FEBS Letters*, 573, 83–92.

Buskirk, T.D. & Lohr, S. (2005). Asymptotic properties of kernel density estimation with complex survey data. *Journal of Statistical Planning and Inference*, 128, 165–190.

Carpenter, J. & Bithell, J. (2000). Bootstrap confidence intervals: when, which, what? A practical guide for medical statisticians. *Statistics in Medicine*, 19, 1141–64.

Centers for Disease Control and Prevention (CDC) (2008): *Behavioral Risk Factor Surveillance System Survey Data* 2008.

Cirincione, C. & Gurrieri, G. A. (1997). Research Methodology: Computer-Intensive Methods in the Social Sciences, *Social Science Computer Review*, 15(1), 83–97.

Cleveland, W. S. (1979). Robust Locally Weighted Regression and Smoothing Scatterplots, *Journal of the American Statistical Association*, 74(368), 829–36.

Cohen, R. A. (1999). An introduction to PROC LOESS for Local Regression. (SUGI Proceedings) SAS Institute, Cary, N.C. Accessed on August 25, 2010, from http://www.ats.ucla.edu/stat/SAS/library/.

Colugnati, F.A.B., Louzada-Neto, F., & Taddei, J.A.A.C. (2005). An application of bootstrap resampling method to obtain confidence interval for percentile fatness cutoff points in childhood and adolescent overweight diagnoses, *International Journal of Obesity*, 29, 340–347.

Corder, G. W. & Foreman, D. I. (2009). *Nonparametric Statistics for Non-Statisticians: A Step-by-Step Approach*. Hoboken, NJ: Wiley.

Daniel, W. W. (1990). *Applied Nonparametric Statistics*. 2nd ed. Boston: PWS-Kent.

Davison, A. C. & Hinkley, D. V. (1997). *Bootstrap Methods and their Application*. Cambridge: Cambridge University Press.

Diciccio, T. J. & Efron, B. (1996). Bootstrap confidence intervals, *Statistical Science*, 11(3), 189–228.

Dunn, O. J. (1964). Multiple comparisons using rank sums. *Technometrics*, 6, 241–252.

Edgington, E.S. (1995). *Randomization Tests*, 3rd Ed. New York: Dekker.

Efron, B. (1979). Bootstrap Methods: another look at the jackknife. *Annals of Statistics*, 7, 1–26.

Efron, B. & Gong, G. (1983). A leisurely look at the bootstrap, the jackknife, and cross-validation. *The American Statistician*, 37, 36–48.

Efron, B. & Tibshirani, R. (1993). An Introduction to the Bootstrap. New York: Chapman and Hall.

Ernst, M. D. (2004). Permutation Methods: A Basis for Exact Inference, *Statistical Science*, 19(4), 676–685.

Faraway, J. J. (2006). *Extending the Linear Model with R: Generalized Linear, Mixed Effects and Nonparametric Regression Models*. Boca Raton, FL: Chapman & Hall/CRC Press.

Fox, J. (2002). Nonparametric Regression: Appendix to *An R and S-PLUS Companion to Applied Regression*. Accessed on August

15, 2010, from http://cran.r-project.org/doc/contrib/Fox-Companion/appendix-nonparametric-regression.pdf.

Good, P. (2004). Permutation Tests: A practical guide to resampling methods for testing hypotheses (2nd Ed.), New York: Springer-Verlag.

Heiman, G. W. (1996). *Basic Statistics for the Behavioral Sciences, 2nd edition*. Boston: Houghton Mifflin Company.

Hesterberg, T., Moore, D. S., Monaghan, S., Clipson, A., & Epstein, R. (2003). *Bootstrap Methods and Permutation Tests*. In Moore, D. S. & McCabe, G.P. (Eds.), *Introduction to the practice of statistics, 5th ed*. Accessed on August 8, 2010, from http://bcs.whfreeman.com/pbs/cat_160/pbs18.pdf.

Higgins, J. J. (2004). *Introduction to Modern Nonparametric Statistics*. Pacific Grove, CA: Duxbury Press.

Hinkley, D. V. (1983). Jackknife methods. In Johnshon, N.L., Kotz, S., & Read, C.B. (Eds.) *Encyclopedia of Statistical Sciences (Vol. 4)* (pp. 280–287). New York: Wiley.

Jacoby, W. G. (2000). LOESS: a nonparametric, graphical tool for depicting relationships between variables. *Electoral Studies*, 19, 577–613.

Jones, M. C., Marron, J. S., & Sheather, S. J. (1996). A Brief Survey of Bandwidth Selection for Density Estimation. *Journal of the American Statistical Association*, 91, 401–407.

Keller-McNulty, S. & Higgins, J. J. (1987). Effect of Tail Weight and Outliers on Power and Type-I Error of Robust Permutation Tests for Location, *Communications in Statistics: Simulation and Computation*, 16(1), 17–36.

Kennedy, P. E. & Cade, B. S. (1996). Randomization Tests for Multiple Regression. *Communications in Statistics: Simulation and Computation*, 25, 923–936.

Korn, E. & Graubard, B. (1998). Scatterplots with survey data. *The American Statistician*, 52, 58–69.

LaFleur, B. J. & Greevy, R. A. (2009). Introduction to permutation and resampling-based hypothesis tests. *Journal of Clinical Child & Adolescent Psychology*, 38, 286–294.

Lahiri, P. (2003). On the impact of bootstrap in survey sampling and small area estimation. *Statistical Science*, 18, 199–210.

Ludbrook, J. (1998). Multiple comparison procedures updated. *Clinical and Experimental Pharmacology and Physiology*, 25, 1032–1037.

Ludbrook, J. & Dudley, H. (1998). Why Permutation Tests are Superior to t and F Tests in Biomedical Research. *The American Statistician*, 52, 127–132.

Neave, H. R. & Worthington, P. L. (1988). Distribution Free Tests, London: Unwin Hyman.

Pan, W. (2003) On the use of permutation in and the performance of a class of nonparametric methods to detect differential gene expression. *Bioinformatics*, 19(11), 1333–1340.

Park, B. U. & Marron, J. S. (1990). Comparison of Data-Driven Bandwidth Selectors. *Journal of the American Statistical Association*, 85, 66–72.

Parzen, E. (1962). On estimation of a probability function and mode, *Annals of Mathematical Statistics*, 33, 1065–1076.

Pett, M. (1997). *Nonparametric statistics for heath care research: statistics for small samples and unusual distributions*. Thousand Oaks, CA: Sage Publications.

Rosenblatt, M. (1956). Remarks on some nonparametric estimates of a density function. *Annals of Mathematical Statistics*, 27, 186–190.

Scott, D. W. (1979). On optimal and data-based histograms. *Biometrika*, 66, 605–610.

Scott, D. W. (2010). Histogram. *Wiley Interdisciplinary Reviews: Computational Statistics*, 2, 44–48.

Shao, J. (2003). Impact of the bootstrap on sample surveys. *Statistical Science*, 18, 191–198.

Siegel, S. & Castellan, N. J. (1988). *Nonparametric statistics for the behavioral sciences, Second edition*. New York: McGraw-Hill.

Tomkins, C. C. (2006).An Introduction to Non-parametric. Statistics for Health Scientists. *University of Alberta Health Sciences Journal*, 3, 20–27.

Wand, M. P. (1995). Data-based choice of histogram bin-width. *The American Statistician*, 51, 59–64.

Wand, M. P. & Jones, M. C. (1995). *Kernel Smoothing*. New York: Chapman & Hall.

Wilcoxon, F. (1945). comparisons by ranking methods. *Biometrics*, 1, 80–83.

Zigmond, A. S., & Snaith, R. P. (1983). The hospital anxiety and depression scale. *Acta Psychiatr Scand*, 67, 361–370.

CHAPTER 7

Correspondence Analysis

Michael J. Greenacre

Abstract

Correspondence analysis is a multivariate statistical technique for visualizing and describing the associations between two or more variables. It is particularly applicable to a table of categorical data— for example, counts or percentages—but can also be used to visualize non-negative data on a common ratio scale, such as a table of measurements all in centimeters or all in euros. Its main objective is to represent the rows and columns of a data matrix as points in a spatial representation, called a map or a biplot according to the coordinates chosen. The positions of the points suggest and facilitate interpretations of the data content. The method resembles principal component analysis but distinguishes itself by the way distances are measured between points, adapted to categorical data, and by the differential weighting of rows and columns proportional to their marginal sums in the table. Extensions of correspondence analysis are multiple correspondence analysis (for multivariate categorical data) and canonical correspondence analysis (when an additional set of external explanatory variables is available).

Key Words: Correspondence analysis, principal component analysis, singular value decomposition, chi-square, biplot, multiple correspondence analysis, canonical correspondence analysis

Introduction

Correspondence analysis (hereafter referred to as CA) is a multivariate statistical method for analyzing tables of categorical data or any data on a common ratio scale. The primary example of a table suitable for CA is a two-way contingency table, but the method is applicable to more general frequency data and compositional data. CA is also extended to a number of different data types such as multivariate categorical data, ratings, and preferences thanks to various recoding schemes that transform the data into a form suitable for the method. The data are required to be non-negative and all on the same measurement scale, and the marginal row and column totals are assumed to be relevant to their importance—for example, in a contingency table the marginal sums are the sample sizes of the corresponding categories. The main objective of the method is to display the rows and columns of the input table as points in a graphical representation that has certain spatial properties and that facilitates the understanding and interpretation of what is otherwise a complex data set.

The method has a long and interesting history, in that its algebraic properties were already recognized early in the twentieth century by two prominent statisticians, H.O. Hartley and R.A. Fisher, as the way of quantifying two categorical variables to maximize their correlation, or alternatively as a form of categorical discriminant analysis (*see* Hirschfeld, 1936 [Hartley's original German name] and Fisher, 1940). Independently at the same time, Louis Guttman paved the way, albeit unidimensionally, for what is now called multiple correspondence analysis (MCA), an extension of CA that analyzes multivariate categorical data in a similar way (*see* Guttman, 1941). Several "schools" of CA developed in the latter half of the twentieth century, the most important being the French school led by Jean-Paul Benzécri (e.g., Benzécri et al., 1973), the Dutch school led by Jan de Leeuw (e.g., Gifi, 1980) and the Japanese school led by Chikio Hayashi (e.g., Hayashi, 1950). Benzécri was the first to recognize the multidimensional geometric interpretation of the CA theory, and this approach led to the method becoming very popular as a visualization method, initially in France in the 1960s and 1970s and then worldwide. Since the 1980s, CA has become available in all the major statistical packages and has found applications in almost every scientific area of research—chiefly the social and environmental sciences but also in fields as diverse as archeology, geology, linguistics, marketing, and bio-informatics. The books by Lebart, Morineau, and Warwick (1984) and Greenacre (1984) popularized the method in the English-speaking world. Three edited volumes (Greenacre & Blasius, 1994; Blasius & Greenacre, 1998; Greenacre & Blasius, 2006) to which more than 100 researchers have contributed, mostly in the social sciences, have marked the pace of recent developments in this field. Le Roux and Rouanet (2004) and Murtagh (2005) have produced English texts giving the essence of the French approach to CA and data analysis in general. Greenacre (2007) has provided a comprehensive practical introduction to CA and its variants, with a supporting website (http://www.carme-n.org) with data sets and R code for the analyses—this book is also available for free download in a Spanish translation (Greenacre, 2008) at http://www.multivariatestatistics.org. Various packages to perform CA in R are available—here, we have used the R package **ca** (Nenadié & Greenacre, 2007).

A Simple Introductory Example

The graphical results of CA will first be illustrated based on the data in Table 7.1, extracted from Mawani and Gilmour (2010). This table is a cross-classification (in thousands) of Canadians in terms of their self-rated mental health (as columns) and several mental health disorders, as diagnosed by the World Mental Health-Composite International Diagnostic Interview, along with a classification based on the K6 measure of psychological distress (as rows). Figure 7.1 demonstrates the CA map of this table, with points seen to be lying in a curved pattern, which often occurs in the results of CA because of its particular geometry.

Our interpretation would be the following:

- The K6 classification follows closely the self-rated categories, as indicated by the trajectories of their connected categories—they are thus highly associated.
- The mental health disorders lie in the direction of the negative ratings of mental health (poor and fair) in three groupings: depression and panic disorders, which are the most in the direction of poor self-rated mental health (and also highest on the K6 distress scale); bipolar and social phobia; and, finally, agoraphobia, which—of the disorders diagnosed here—is the least acute in terms of the self-ratings.
- The quality of the map is almost perfect: the two dimensions explain 94.2% and 5.6%, respectively, of the data variance, which is 99.8% in total.

Principal Component Analysis and Multidimensional Scaling

To understand the mechanics of CA, it is convenient to introduce first some geometric concepts from principal component analysis (PCA) and multidimensional scaling (MDS), because CA can be seen as a variant of either of these. Both PCA and MDS have the same "dimension-reduction" objective, to reduce high-dimensional data to a few so-called "principal" dimensions, to reveal structure in the data, and so to facilitate their interpretation. The difference between the methods is their starting points: In PCA the initial data are in the form of a rectangular data matrix, often a cases-by-variables matrix, whereas MDS starts with a square matrix of distances among the cases or among the variables.

Basic Idea of Principal Component Analysis

In PCA, the rows of the rectangular data matrix are assumed to be vectors in a high-dimensional space. For example, if 10 attributes (as columns) are observed on each (row) case, then the cases would be points in a 10-dimensional space. By default, all cases would be weighted equally in the analysis—that is, if there are N cases, then each case receives a weight of $1/N$. However, it is a simple generalization to weight each case differently, as, for example, is often done in multiple regression. There can be several reasons for introducing different weights for the cases, the most common being that the cases are not representative of the target population,

Table 7.1. Distribution (in thousands) of self-rated mental health groups, by mental morbidity assessments and K-6 psychological distress categories (high: score 13–24, moderate: score 9–12; none: score 0–8), population 15 years or older, Canada, excluding territories, 2002 (Mawani & Gilmour, 2010)

Mental morbidity measure	Self-rated mental health			
	poor	*fair*	*Good*	*very good/excellent*
Depression	81.5	102.0	94.6	24.9
Bipolar	14.4	31.5	24.3	16.0
Panic disorder	38.8	43.6	50.8	28.0
Social phobia	50.0	99.8	108.0	53.1
Agoraphobia	7.1	15.7	23.3	14.3
K-6 high	144.0	210.7	158.5	55.8
K-6 moderate	67.1	326.6	533.5	377.0
K-6 none	78.5	879.9	5786.0	16,276.0

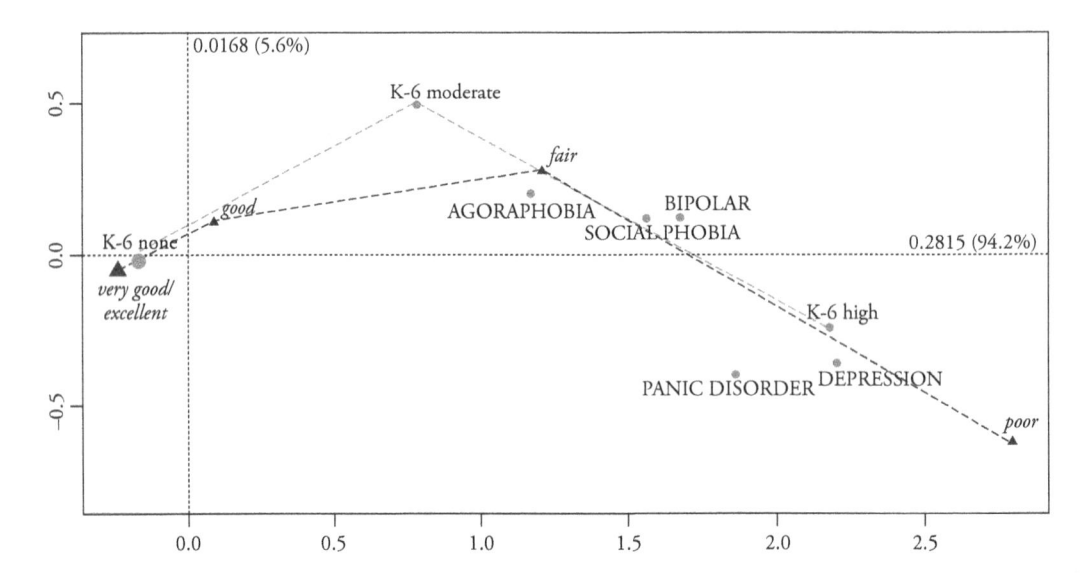

Figure 7.1 CA map of the data in Table 7.1. Both rows and columns are displayed in principal coordinates, showing approximate distances between rows and between columns.

and are thus reweighted to reflect more correctly their importance in the analysis. The objective in PCA is to find a lower-dimensional solution (e.g., a plane) cutting through this high-dimensional space so that the planar version approximates the case points as closely as possible. Fit between the high-dimensional points and the approximating plane (or any other low-dimensional subspace) is usually measured by sum-of-squared distances, as this choice leads to a convenient computational solution, based on matrix decompositions using eigenvalues and eigenvectors, or more elegantly using the singular-value decomposition. This fit is minimized (hence it is a least-squares solution), and the resulting display consists of the cases' projected positions in the best-fitting plane. If this approximate map of the cases is complemented by the projection of the variables onto this plane as well, it is called a *biplot*. This lower dimensional, optimized view of the points is easier to understand and to interpret.

Principal component analysis can be equivalently framed from the point of view of the variables, which is the way Hotelling (1933) defined it in terms of the variables' variance–covariance matrix; this approach can be similarly cast in a geometric framework, where, for example, the variables are points in a high-dimensional space and projected down onto their best-fitting plane. As for the cases, variables could be weighted to reflect their importance in the analysis. When variables are on different scales, the act of standardization is equivalent to a reweighting of the variables to equalize their contributions to total variance of the data.

Measuring Fit

As mentioned above, solutions are found by minimizing sum-of-squared distances from high-dimensional points to their low-dimensional positions. Thanks to the use of squared distances, a simple application of Pythagoras' Theorem shows that there is a decomposition of total (weighted) sum-of-squares, usually referred to as total variance, into a part that is in the solution subspace, called variance explained, and a part that is not in the solution, called unexplained or residual variance. These are usually expressed as percentages of the total, and it is the latter unexplained variance that is minimized by the method, whereas the complementary explained variance is maximized.

Basic Idea of Multidimensional Scaling

Multidimensional scaling (MDS) takes a table of distances between points and represents them optimally in a low-dimensional spatial map. In PCA, a measure of distance is inherently assumed between the cases (as well as between the variables), so the two approaches are essentially the same when that same distance function is used prior to applying MDS. Here, we are glossing over some important technical details, but it suffices to say that the relationship with MDS supports the spatial properties of PCA and the special case—CA.

Correspondence Analysis

Correspondence analysis is a variation of the theme of PCA, applied to non-negative data, all of which should be on the same scale—for example, the table of counts in Table 7.1.

Correspondence analysis treats such a table as a set of rows or a set of columns in an identical way. For example, Table 7.1 can be thought of as a set of rows, the distribution of the mental disorders and K6 groups across the self-rated mental health categories, or as a set of columns, the distribution of the self-rated categories across the row groups.

In CA, it is not the absolute values in the table that are of interest but the relative values. Thus the counts in each row or in each column are considered relative to their respective marginal totals—these sets of relative frequencies are called *profiles*. Then the row and column marginal sums are also considered relative to their totals, which are called the row and column *masses*, respectively, denoted by $r_1, r_2, \ldots$ and $c_1, c_2, \ldots$. These masses will be used as weights for the row profiles and column profiles, respectively. For example, from Table 7.1:

– the row sum of "Depression" is $81.5 + 102.0 + 94.6 + 24.9 = 303.0$
– the row profile of "Depression" is [0.269 0.337 0.312 0.082], where $0.269 = 81.5/303.0$
– the row mass r_1 assigned to "Depression" is $0.0117 = 303.0/25,815.3$, where 25,815.3 is the grand total of the table.
– the column mass c_1 assigned to *"poor"* is $0.0186 = 481.4/25,815.3$, where 481.4 is the marginal total of the first column.

Basic Idea in Correspondence Analysis: The Row Problem

In the row problem of CA, there are three relevant starting entities: (1) the matrix to be visualized, which is the matrix of row profiles, (2) the weights assigned to these profiles, which are the row masses, and (3) the column normalizing factors, which are the inverse square roots of the column masses, as if the column masses were measures of the column variances (thus the row profile elements corresponding to *poor* are divided by $\sqrt{0.0186} = 0.136$). There are several statistical justifications for this last choice—an intuitive reason is that the columns with lower marginal totals generally have lower inherent variances. Further, the choice of these row and column masses implies that the total sum-of-squares of the table being analyzed is proportional to the chi-square statistic χ^2 for the table, which is a well-known measure of association for contingency tables. Specifically, this total variance—called *inertia* in CA—is equal to χ^2/n, where n is the grand total of the table.

Basic Idea in Correspondence Analysis: The Column Problem

The column problem in CA is identical to the row problem applied to the transpose of the original matrix. Then the vectors being visualized are the column profiles, their weights are the column

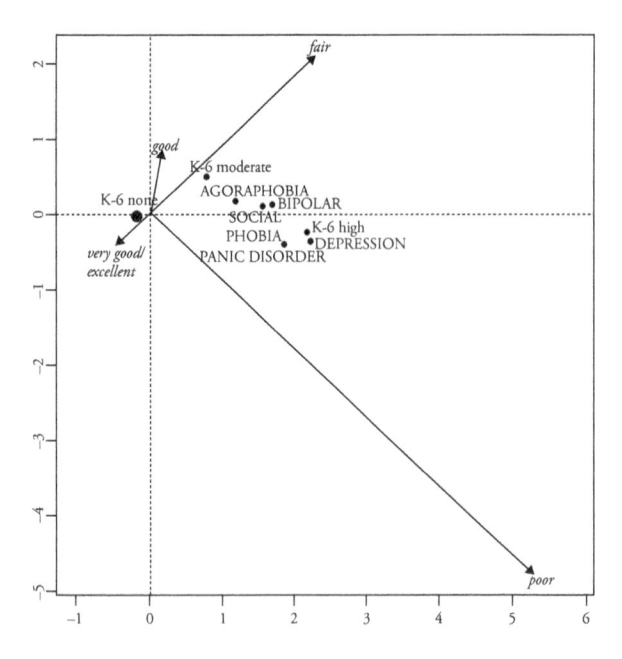

Figure 7.2 CA biplot of the data in Table 7.1, with row profiles in principal coordinates and column points in standard coordinates. The row profiles are at weighted averages of the column points, and the vectors define biplot axes for estimating the profile values.

masses, and their normalizing factors are the inverse square roots of the row masses. Notice how the row and column masses serve different purposes in each problem, as weights on the one hand and as normalizing factors on the other. It turns out that both the row and column problems have the same computational solution, resulting in several equivalences and interesting connections between them (*see*, for example, Greenacre, 2007: Chapter 6).

Correspondence Analysis Displays

Because of a certain liberty in choosing the coordinates of the rows and columns in the final CA display, there are several options for displaying the results—these enrich the visualization possibilities but can also create some confusion for the user. Let us start with the row problem, for example, where the row profiles are optimally visualized by projecting them onto the solution space, usually a two-dimensional plane. The coordinates of the row points are called (row) *principal coordinates*, which are the coordinates used to position the mental disorders in Figure 7.1. The column points (mental health categories) are similarly displayed in principal coordinates in Figure 7.1, giving what is called the *symmetric map*—both the rows and columns have identical weighted sum-of-squares along the two axes of the display, equal to the explained components of explained inertia indicated as 0.2815 on the first (horizontal) axis and 0.0168 on the second (vertical) axis and percentaged out with respect to the total.

Figure 7.2 shows an alternative display option, where the column points are displayed differently, much more spread out—they have been positioned according to their *standard coordinates*. Each column category (the four ratings) can be typified by a row profile called the *unit profile*; for example, "*poor*" can be represented by the profile [1 0 0 0] as if it were a mental disorder where 100% of the respondents with that disorder considered their mental health to be poor. This archetypal extreme disorder is visualized by the point "*poor*" in Figure 7.2, as well as the other extreme unit profiles for "*fair*," "*good*," and "*very good/excellent*." This variant of the CA display has the property that the row points (in principal coordinates) are at weighted averages of the column points (in standard coordinates), using the profile elements as weights. Hence, "depression," with profile [0.269 0.337 0.312 0.082], is at the weighted average position:

$$0.269 \times \text{"poor"} + 0.337 \times \text{"fair"} + 0.312 \times \text{"good"}$$
$$+ 0.082 \times \text{"very good/excellent"} \qquad (1)$$

Figure 7.2 is also a well-defined biplot, which means that lines can be drawn through, or parallel to, the column vectors in Figure 7.2 to give a set of oblique axes for recovering estimates of the row profiles. For example, if the mental disorders are projected onto the axis defined by the vector through "*poor*," where the arrow indicates higher values, the ordering obtained is "depression," "K-6 high," "panic disorder," "bipolar," "social phobia," "agoraphobia," "K-6 moderate," and "K-6 none." In fact,

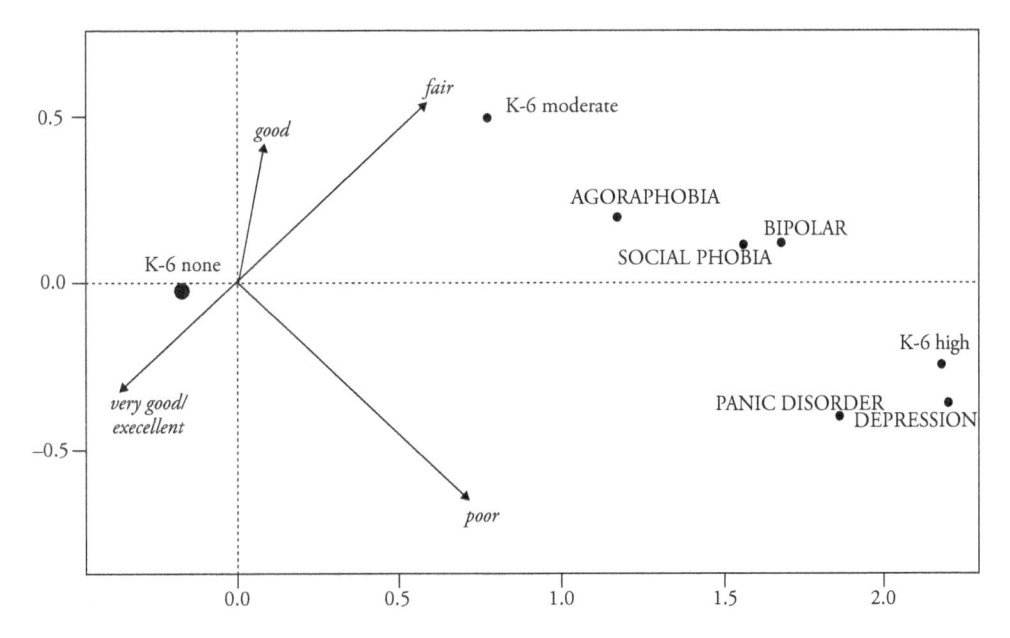

Figure 7.3 CA biplot of the data in Table 7.1, with columns represented in contribution coordinates. The lengths of the arrows are related to the contribution of each column point to the two axes of the solution.

the biplot axis could be linearly calibrated in profile units to obtain numerical estimates of the profile values. The actual profile values on *"poor"* for the above list, ordered from "depression" to "K-6 none," are 0.269, 0.253, 0.241, 0.167, 0.161, 0.118, 0.051, and 0.003, respectively: These agree almost exactly with the placement of the mental disorders on this biplot axis because the inertia explained is almost 100% . Hence, another way of thinking about the analysis is that it finds the configuration of biplot axes for the columns and points for the rows that give an optimal reconstruction of the row profiles.

Figure 7.3 represents another option for scaling the display. The row points are still displayed in principal coordinates, as in Figures 28.1 and 28.2, but the column vectors in standard coordinates in Figure 7.2 have been individually shortened by multiplying them by the respective square roots of their masses—the resultant coordinates are called *contribution coordinates*. The biplot property still holds because the category vectors have the same orientations as in Figure 7.2, and now their lengths on each axis of the display are directly related to their contributions to the solution. Thus *"poor,"* with the highest length in Figure 7.3, is the most important category in the analysis, pulling apart the different disorders and the "K-6 high" versus "K-6 moderate" classifications. Perpendicular to the *"poor"* axis are *"very good/excellent"* and *"fair,"* pointing in opposite directions and together also contributing strongly to the solution. These categories separate the large group "K-6 none" from all the others—if one checks the profile values for *"fair,"* for example, "K-6 none" has a value of 0.038 (i.e., 3.8% of the "K-6 none" group rate their mental health as *"fair"*), whereas for all other rows the profiles values are between 0.25 and 0.37. The category *"good,"* with the shortest length, is the least important one for the interpretation. The contribution biplot functions well in a situation where there are very many column points being considered for the interpretation, because it makes the important contributors stand out from the others.

For an in-depth practical account of the various biplot scalings, *see* Greenacre (2010a).

Multiple Correspondence Analysis

The primary application of CA is to a two-way contingency table—that is, the cross-classification of a set of individuals according to two categorical variables, but the method is still appropriate to frequency tables in general such as Table 7.1, where the same individuals can appear in more than one cell. The extension of CA to more than two categorical variables is called MCA and is most often used to visualize data from sample surveys—hence, the context of the following explanation.

Suppose there are Q questions in a survey and the q-th question has J_q possible categorical responses,

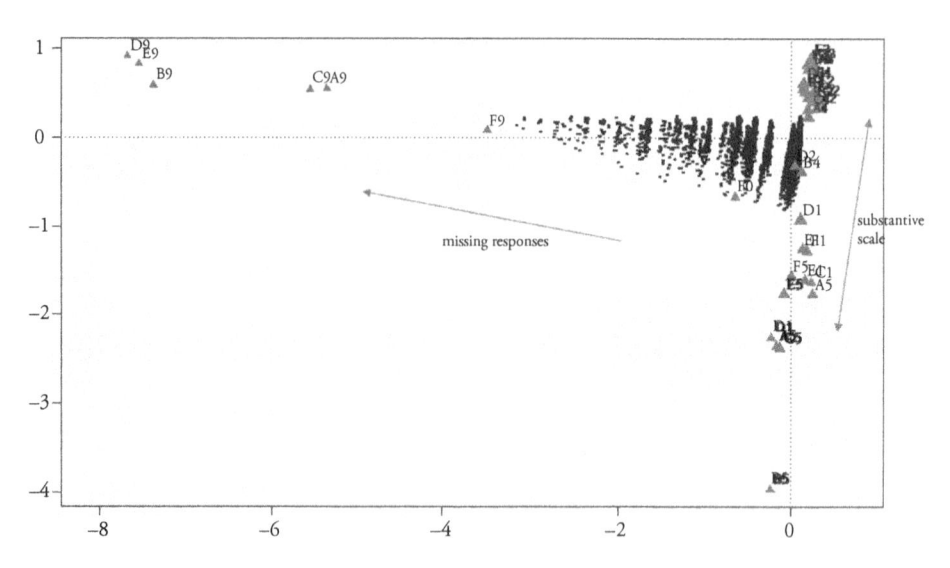

Figure 7.4 MCA biplot of the ISSP leisure time data, with categories in standard coordinates. Each respondent is a dot displayed at the average position of his or her response categories to the six questions. Missing response categories dominate the display.

often including categories for nonresponses such as "don't know" and "no answer/missing value." There are $J = \sum_q J_q$ response categories in total, and a respondent can only be in one category of response for each question. In MCA, every response category generates a zero/one dummy variable, and the original $N \times Q$ matrix of responses is—notionally at least—converted into an $N \times J$ *indicator matrix* **Z**, where the columns are the dummy variables. There are two almost equivalent ways of defining MCA: It is the CA algorithm applied to the matrix **Z** or, alternatively, it is the CA algorithm applied to the cross-product matrix $\mathbf{B} = \mathbf{Z}^T\mathbf{Z}$. **B**, called the *Burt matrix*, is a $J \times J$ symmetric matrix composed of all two-way cross-tabulations of the Q questions with one another.

To illustrate MCA, we use data from the International Social Survey Program (ISSP), a cooperative project between several countries to gather data on the same topic—we use the 2007 survey on "Leisure Time and Sports" (ISSP, 2007) and look specifically at six questions from the survey, denoted here by A through F:

People do different things during their free time. For each of the following, please indicate how often in your free time you:
  A: establish useful contacts?
  B: relax and recover?
  C: learn or develop skills?
  D: feel bored?
  E: feel rushed?
  F: think about work?

The possible responses were: (1) *very often*, (2) *often*, (3) *sometimes*, (4) *seldom*, and (5) *never*. Missing and "don't know" responses were grouped into a category labelled (9). Question F had an additional category (0) *not applicable*. In total, there are six categories for each of the six variables plus the extra one for F, totalling 37 categories. The total sample size was 47,921 from 34 different countries, so the indicator matrix has 47,921 rows and 37 columns for the dummy variables. Each row of the indicator matrix has exactly six 1s indicating the response categories for the particular respondent, and the remainder are 0s. Applying CA to this matrix leads to the MCA biplot of Figure 7.4, where respondent points are in principal coordinates and category points in standard coordinates. With this scaling, each respondent point is positioned at the average of his or her six response categories, because the profile points consist of zeros apart from six values of one-sixth each. The missing responses dominate the first horizontal axis of the display, opposing all the substantive responses that align with the second vertical axis—the cases with various combinations of missing data can be seen extending to the left in bands. This dominance of the missing responses is quite typical for such questionnaire data—although the rate of missing responses is of the order of 3%, the associations between the missing value categories are very

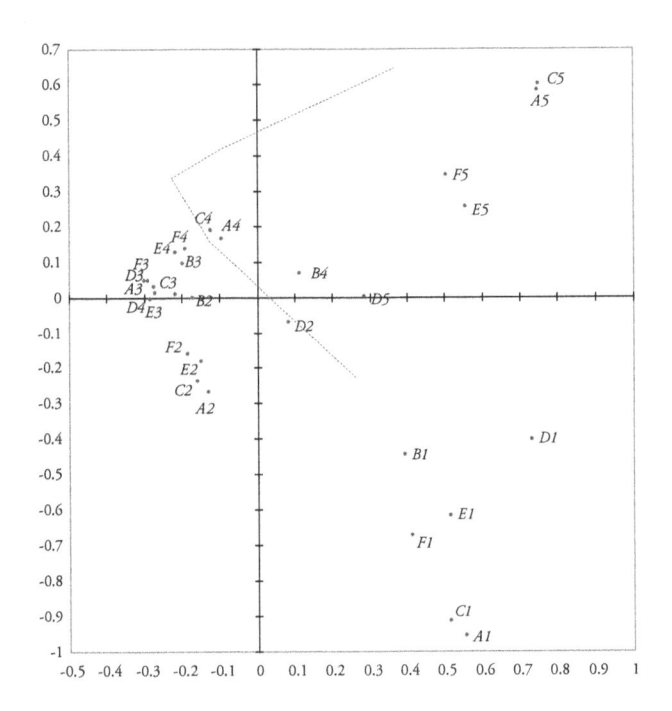

Figure 7.5 Subset MCA map of the substantive categories in the ISSP leisure time data, with categories shown at the average positions of the cases that gave the respective responses. The categories of question *A* are connected from *A*1 (*very often*) to *A*5 (*never*).

strong, often because of response sets. Removing cases with some missing responses would eliminate 9% of the sample. To avoid this depletion of the sample, a variation on MCA called subset MCA analyzes the substantive responses only, ignoring the missing response categories, but maintains the geometry of the original MCA. This attractive feature of analyzing subsets of rows and/or columns in CA and MCA is possible thanks to the fact that each category is a separate variable of the analysis (*see* Greenacre & Pardo, 2006a, 2006b).

Figure 7.5 shows the subset version of the same data set—here we do not show the 47,921 cases but, rather, the average positions of those cases giving the respective responses (e.g., the point *A*1 is the average of the 3,644 cases that gave the response *"very often"* to question *A*). Again we find the categories lying in a curved pattern—for example, the categories from *A*1 to *A*5 are connected, and the pattern is an arch on its side. The arch effect, as it is known, is common in CA and MCA—it can be shown that a strictly unidimensional scale will emerge as a sequence of polynomials on successive axes. In Figure 7.5, the fact that the arch lies on its side means that there is a stronger association between the extremes of the response scales (*"very often"* and *"never"*) and the moderate responses (*"often," "sometimes," "seldom"*). Two variables that follow a very similar trajectory, like *A* (*"establish useful contacts"*) and *C* (*"learn or develop skills"*), are highly associated, whereas the variable *D* (*"feel bored"*) shows a lack of association with the other variables.

An alternative way of thinking about MCA is that it identifies sets of uncorrelated optimal scales in the data. The categories are replaced by quantifications on an interval scale that have optimal properties—for example, the scale values on the first axis lead to quantifications of each variable and summated (or averaged) scores for the respondents that maximize the sum (or average) of the squared correlations between the variables and the scores; or, equivalently, the reliability coefficient Cronbach's alpha is maximized. In homogeneity analysis, which is theoretically equivalent to MCA, a loss function that quantifies the squared differences among the variable quantifications and the score vector is minimized, which is again an equivalent objective to the previous ones (*see* Michailidis & de Leeuw, 1998, for an excellent description of this approach).

What is particularly useful in MCA is to depict additional categorical variables, called supplementary points, on an existing map such as Figure 7.5. We show demographic groups, for example, in the same way as the question category points—as average positions of all those individuals in a particular group. We do not expect these demographic group points to be spread out as widely as the category responses, because the objective of the MCA has

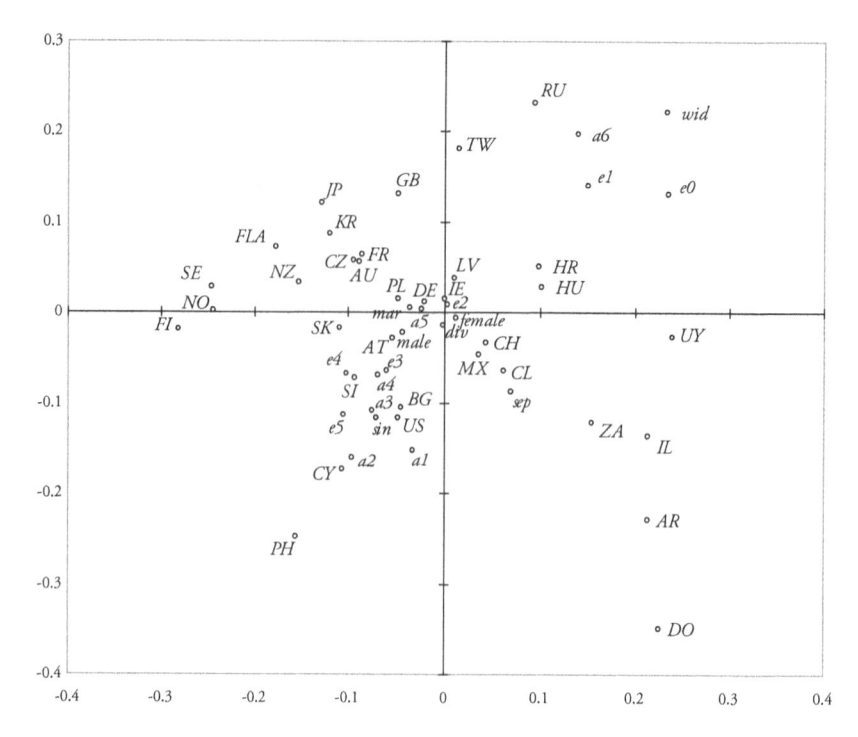

Figure 7.6 Supplementary points for the map of Figure 7.5, showing the following demographic groups: country (34), gender (2), marital status (5), education (6) and age group (6).

been to separate out the respondents in terms of those latter responses, not the demographic categories. Figure 7.6 shows separately the positions of the 34 countries, 2 genders, 7 marital status groups, 6 education, and 6 age groups, with respect to the same planar display as Figure 7.5, with an enlarged scale because of the lower dispersion of the points. Notice the cluster of Norway (NO), Sweden (SE), and Finland (FI) on the left, corresponding to a moderate position on all the questions, with Dominican Republic (DO) and Argentina (AR) responding more than average *"very often"* to the questions, whereas on the *"never"* side, upper right, we find Russia (RU) and Taiwan (TW), as well as oldest age group (a6: 65+ years), widowed (wid), and low education (E0: no formal education, E1: lowest education level).

As mentioned at the start of this section, MCA is often defined as the CA of the Burt matrix, which is composed of all two-way cross-tabulations of the Q variables in a super-matrix. The CA of this $J \times J$ categories-by-categories symmetric matrix leads to exactly the same standard coordinates for the categories, so the positioning of the respondent points in terms of their scores is identical, and so, too, are the positions of the category points and supplementary points. The singular values from the CA of the Burt matrix are the squares of those of the indicator matrix, leading to a disparity in how the percentage of explained inertia is computed, which we clarify now.

Measure of Fit

Greenacre (1988) defined a natural generalization of CA to the multiple case called *joint correspondence analysis* (JCA). The idea in JCA is to explain the inertia in all the pairwise cross-tabulations of the Q variables, excluding the cross-tabulations between a variable and itself that are included in the Burt matrix. For $Q = 2$ variables, JCA is identical to simple CA, as there is only one pairwise table. To come close to the JCA objective using the existing MCA solution, simple adjustments of the total inertia and the inertias on each dimension can be made, leading to a measure of fit that does not depend on whether the indicator or Burt matrix is analyzed. Suppose that the squares of the singular values emanating from the analysis of the Burt matrix are denoted by the eigenvalues λ_k, in other words λ_k are the parts of inertia in the Burt analysis, whereas $\sqrt{\lambda_k}$ are the parts of inertia in the indicator analysis. The adjustment is as follows:

Ajusted eigenvalues: for all $\sqrt{\lambda_k} > 1/Q$,

compute $\left(\dfrac{Q}{Q-1}\right)^2 \left(\sqrt{\lambda_k} - \dfrac{1}{Q}\right)^2 \quad k = 1, 2, \ldots$

Adjusted total inertia: $\left(\dfrac{Q}{Q-1}\right)$

$\left(\sum_k \lambda_k - \dfrac{J-Q}{Q^2}\right),$

where $\sum_k \lambda_k$ is the total inertia of the Burt matrix. The adjusted total inertia (11) is exactly the average inertia in all the $1/2 Q(Q-1)$ pairwise cross-tabulations. The percentages of inertia are then computed by dividing the adjusted eigenvalues by the adjusted total inertia. Only eigenvalues for which $\sqrt{\lambda_k} > 1/Q$ are used in this computation and the percentages computed in this way will add up to less than 100%.

In Figure 7.4 the adjusted percentages are calculated as 60.3% and 14.7%, respectively, thus 75.0% of the inertia is explained in the biplot. In Figure 7.5 the corresponding percentages are 43.1% and 20.6%, respectively, thus 63.7% of the subset inertia is explained in the display.

Application to Other Data Types

Correspondence analysis is regularly applied to data on other measurement scales, thanks to certain data recoding schemes that reduce the data to homogeneous scales that are analogous to count or compositional measurements and thus suitable for CA. So-called "*doubling*" of data is a useful recoding scheme for ratings, preferences, and paired comparisons. For example, a set of objects or attributes is rated, ranked, or compared pairwise by a set of respondents. Then, each object generates two columns of the data, usually tagged by "+" and "–" labels. The columns would be the counts of how many points on the rating scale are above and below the rating given by the respondent or how many objects are preferred and dispreferred, respectively. Each pair of columns sums to a constant, and each object or attribute generates a pair of points in the CA display. The same idea can be used to analyze continuous data on mixed scales, in a kind of nonparametric CA: Each set of observations for a variable is replaced by their ranks, and then the variables are doubled according to the rank-order positions of the respondents on each variable (*see* Greenacre, 2007, p. 183, for an example).

Another option for continuous data is *fuzzy coding*. Continuous data can be categorized into several intervals by cutting up the scale of each variable, but this so-called "*crisp coding*" leads to a large loss of information. Fuzzy coding assigns each measurement to several of the categories at a time using a recoding scheme called membership functions, from the original scale to the categorical scale (*see*, for example, Murtagh, 2005). A continuous measurement to be coded into three categories—for example, low, medium, and high—might be [0 1 0] in the crisp coding but [0.3 0.7 0] in the fuzzy coding to show that it is in the lower region of the variable's range. Fuzzy coded values add up to 1, just like crisp values, and can be returned to the original value of the variable, a process called *defuzzification*, whereas crisply coded values clearly cannot. In addition, the reconstructed data in a low-dimensional solution of a fuzzy coded CA also have the property that they sum to 1 and can be defuzzified to get estimates of the original continuous data (Aºan & Greenacre, 2010). The advantage of fuzzy coded CA is that it can reveal nonlinear relationships among the variables, which is not possible in linear PCA.

Canonical Correspondence Analysis

Canonical correspondence analysis (CCA) applies to situations where additional variables are available for the respondents, cases, or samples that constitute the rows of the data matrix. This situation is common in ecological applications where species abundances are observed at sampling locations and the locations are characterized by environmental parameters. Regular CA of the abundance data would identify the main dimensions that optimally explain those data, and these dimensions might or might not be related to the environmental information. Ecologists are generally more interested in the variance of the abundance data that can be explained by these additional variables, and CCA achieves this objective in a simple way. A restricted form of CA is performed, where the dimensions of the solution are forced to be linearly related to the additional variables. Computationally, the data are first projected onto the subspace defined by the additional variables, and then CA is performed in this restricted subspace. Hence, the total inertia in the abundance data is first split into two parts: inertia in the restricted space and inertia in the rest of the space, or unrestricted space, that is uncorrelated with the additional variables. Dimension reduction is then performed as before, usually in the restricted space, but the variance in the unrestricted space is often of interest as well, when the influence of certain variables is required to be partialled out. As a special case, if there is one external categorical variable (e.g., regions of sampling), CCA is equivalent to aggregating the counts of each species within each region and then performing a regular CA, which amounts to a type of discriminant analysis. Ter Braak (1986) first formulated this method, and it has become extremely popular in the environmental sciences. Greenacre (2010b) shows how CCA can be applied to survey data, like the ISSP data used above, where it serves as an analog to target rotation in factor analysis but for categorical data.

Statistical Inference

In simple CA, when the data form a contingency table based on random sampling, there are certain asymptotic results in the literature, based on the multivariate normal approximation to the multinomial distribution, that permit inference to be made about the parts of inertia explained by each dimension (*see*, for example, Gilula & Haberman, 1986). It is also possible to test whether points differ significantly from the average point at the origin of the map or differ from one another in pairwise tests (Le Roux & Rouanet, 2004). Resampling methods such as the bootstrap and permutation testing prove very useful for estimating confidence regions of points and testing hypotheses in a less model-based way in CA, MCA, and CCA (Greenacre, 2007: Chapter 25).

Conclusion

Correspondence analysis and its extension, MCA, as well as the application to recoded data and the introduction of external explanatory variables in CCA, form a unified set of tools to explore multivariate data—especially categorical data. The basic theory and computations rely on simple matrix decompositions, such as the singular value decomposition, and their properties of least-squares approximation of matrices. Solutions are globally optimal and have the property of nesting—that is, adding further dimensions to the solution merely build on the solutions of lower dimensionality. Few assumptions are made on the input data, apart from the row and column weighting that is generally self-evident, and the underlying philosophy of the approach is to let the data speak for themselves, revealing patterns and structure that may be expected or unexpected.

Note

1. Michael Greenacre's research is sponsored by a collaboration grant of the BBVA Foundation in Madrid. Partial support of Spanish Ministry of Science and Innovation grants MTM2008-00642 and MTM2009-09063 is hereby also acknowledged.

References

Aşan, Z., & Greenacre, M. (2010). Biplots of fuzzy coded data. Conditionally accepted by *Fuzzy Sets and Systems*.

Benzécri, J.-P. et al. (1973). *L'Analyse des données. Tôme II: L'Analyse des correspondances*. Paris: Dunod.

Blasius, J., & Greenacre, M. (Eds.). (1999). *Visualization of categorical data*. New York: Academic Press.

Fisher, R.A. (1940). The precision of discriminant functions. *Annals of Eugenics*, 10, 422–429.

Gifi, A. (1990). *Nonlinear multivariate analysis*. Chichester: Wiley.

Gilula, Z. & Haberman, S. J. (1986). Canonical analysis of contingency tables by maximum likelihood. *Journal of the American Statistical Association 81*, 780–788.

Greenacre, M. (1984). *Theory and applications of correspondence analysis*. London: Academic Press.

Greenacre, M. (1988). Correspondence analysis of multivariate categorical data by weighted least squares. *Biometrika 75*, 457–467.

Greenacre, M. (2007). *Correspondence analysis in practice, second edition*. London: Chapman & Hall/CRC.

Greenacre, M. (2007). *La práctica del análisis de correspondencias*. Madrid: BBVA Foundation. Free download from http://www.multivariatestatistics.org.

Greenacre, M. (2010a). *Biplots in practice*. Madrid: BBVA Foundation. Free download from http://www.multivariatestatistics.org.

Greenacre, M. (2010b). Canonical correspondence analysis in social science research. In: Locarek-Junge, H., & Weihs, C. (Eds.). *Classification as a tool for research* (pp. 279–288). Heidelberg, Berlin: Springer-Verlag.

Greenacre, M., & Blasius, J. (Eds.). (1994). *Correspondence analysis in the social sciences: Recent developments and applications*. London: Academic Press.

Greenacre, M., & Blasius, J. (Eds.). (2006). *Multiple correspondence analysis and related methods*. London: Chapman & Hall/CRC.

Greenacre, M., & Pardo, R. (2006a). Subset correspondence analysis: visualization of selected response categories in a questionnaire survey. *Sociological Methods and Research 35*, 193–218.

Greenacre, M., & Pardo, R. (2006b). Multiple correspondence analysis of subsets of response categories. In Greenacre, M.J., & Blasius, J. (Eds*.) Multiple Correspondence Analysis and Related Methods* (pp. 197–217). London: Chapman & Hall/CRC Press, London.

Guttman, L. (1941). The quantification of a class of attributes: a theory and method of scale construction. In P. Horst (Ed.), *The prediction of personal adjustment* (pp. 321–348). New York: Social Science Research Council.

Hayashi, C. (1950). On the quantification of qualitative data from the mathematico-statistical point of view. *Annals of the Institute of Statistical Mathematics* 2, 35–47.

Hirschfeld, H.O. (1935). A connection between correlation and contingency. *Proceedings of the Cambridge Philosophical Society* 31, 520–524.

ISSP (2007). *International Social Survey Programme : Leisure Time and Sports*. Retrieved August 10, 2010 from http://www.issp.org

Lebart, L., Morineau, A., & Warwick, K. (1984). *Multivariate Descriptive Statistical Analysis*. New York: Wiley.

Le Roux, B., & Rouanet, H. (2004). *Geometric data analysis*. Amsterdam, The Netherlands: Kluwer.

Mawani, F.N., & Gilmour, H. (2010). *Validation of self-rated mental health. Health Reports, 21(3)*. Statistics Canada. Retrieved August 10, 2010 from http://www.statcan.gc.ca/cgi-bin/af-fdr.cgi?l=eng& loc=2010003/article/11288-eng.pdf

Michailidis, G. & de Leeuw, J. (1998). The Gifi system for descriptive multivariate analysis, *Statistical Science* 13, 307–336.

Murtagh, F. (2005). *Correspondence Analysis and Data Coding with R and Java*. London: Chapman & Hall/CRC.

Nenadié, O., & Greenacre, M. (2007). Correspondence analysis in R, with two- and three-dimensional graphics: the ca package. *Journal of Statistical Software 20*. Retrieved August

CHAPTER 8

Spatial Analysis

Luc Anselin, Alan T. Murray, *and* Sergio J. Rey

Abstract

This chapters provides a broad outline of spatial analysis, a collection of methods that share the common characteristic that spatial proximity and relationships matter. We focus on three specific areas: exploratory spatial data analysis, spatial regression and spatial optimization.

Key Words: spatial analysis, geospatial analysis, exploratory spatial data analysis, spatial regression, spatial econometrics, spatial optimization

Introduction

Spatial analysis (now often referred to as *geospatial analysis*) is broadly defined as a "set of methods useful when the data are spatial" (Goodchild and Longley 1999). More specifically, it encompasses a collection of techniques to add value to data contained in a geographic information system (GIS). Such data are *georeferenced*, which means that in addition to value (attribute) the location of the observation is known, typically expressed in a Cartesian coordinate system. As such, spatial analysis forms an important component of the evolving discipline of *Geographic Information Science* (Goodchild 1992). It encompasses many different methodologies that share the common characteristic that spatial proximity and relationships matter. The recent text by de Smith et al. (2007) includes four main components of spatial analysis, in addition to the basic analytic manipulations embedded in most GIS: data exploration and spatial statistics, surface and field analysis, network and location analysis, and geocomputational methods and modeling. In this chapter, we present a slightly different perspective and focus on three broad categories of methodologies: exploratory spatial data analysis, spatial regression analysis and spatial optimization.

An important reason for the growth of geospatial analysis over the past twenty-some years was the realization in the late 1980s that the technology of geographic information systems (and especially desktop systems) provided an excellent opportunity to operationalize and take advantage of the wealth of analytical techniques developed in the quantitative geography literature. In addition, the combination of the computing power in GIS and advanced methods of spatial analysis provided the opportunity to develop integrated systems that contributed not only to practice, but also led to scientific advances and new methods. Early discussions of the integration of spatial analytical methods with GIS can be found in Goodchild (1987), Goodchild et al. (1992), and Anselin and Getis (1992), among others. Goodchild (2010) offers a more recent perspective. An important institutional factor was the establishment in the U.S. of the National Center for Geographic Information and Analysis (Abler 1987), which, through funding from the National Science Foundation provided a major impetus for the development and adoption of spatial analytical methodology. A similar role was played about ten years later by the NSF funded Center for Spatially Integrated Social Science (Goodchild et al. 2000).

Early compilations of methods, applications and software tools for geospatial analysis can be found in Fotheringham and Rogerson (1994), and Fischer and Getis (1997), among others. More recent reviews include Fotheringham and Rogerson (2009), Anselin and Rey (2010), and Fischer and Getis (2010). Extensive technical detail can be found in those references.

In the remainder of this chapter, we provide a concise overview of exploratory spatial data analysis, spatial regression analysis and spatial optimization modeling. We close with some concluding remarks.

Exploratory Spatial Data Analysis

Arguably, one of the first steps in the empirical analysis of any spatially referenced data should be the exploration of the data. This exploration can serve two purposes. First, as part of a model building strategy, application of *Exploratory Spatial Data Analysis* (ESDA) methods to detect any data anomalies, recording errors, or other data related problems can avoid unnecessary work further on the research path where model calibration (see Section 8) and application may have been for naught or misguided were these data problems missed.

While data exploration is good practice in any empirical study, it is particularly critical in the analysis of spatial data as often georeferenced data requires a good deal of preprocessing and data integration, such as georegistration (setting the coordinates for spatial objects), conversion between different data structures (e.g., raster or grid and vector or polygon), and a host of other manipulations often done in the context of a GIS. These manipulations typically involve a chain of sequential steps, each one potentially introducing sources of uncertainty and or error into the derived data.

Closely related to data checking is the use of ESDA methods for model validation and diagnostics. For example, tests for departures from the assumptions underlying model specification in spatial regression analysis rely on methods that are extensions of ESDA.

These two examples of use cases for ESDA methods reflect their *data validation function*. Perhaps the more commonly encountered role for ESDA methods, however, is the *data insight* function these methods provide. In this sense ESDA can be viewed as a special case of exploratory data analysis (EDA), the branch of computational statistics pioneered by John Tukey (Tukey 1977). EDA is a largely model-free set of statistical and graphical methods designed to uncover data errors or anomalies, identify patterns, and generate new insights about the processes under study as reflected in the data that would otherwise have remained hidden. As a result of EDA, new hypotheses about the underlying phenomena may be suggested. The generation of hypotheses stands in marked contrast to a model driven analysis. For the latter, one begins from an initial hypothesis that is used to specify models for calibration, estimation and validation. Indeed the genesis for EDA was the view, held by Tukey, that the classic approach to inference was overly dependent on prior hypothesis and thus restrictive in nature.

When viewed as a branch of EDA, ESDA shares many of EDA's goals and philosophy, as well as a reliance on both numerical and graphical methods. However, the development of ESDA methods has been driven by the recognition that the special nature of spatial data required extension of existing EDA methods as well as the development of entirely new methods. Moreover, some of the methods now widely used and recognized as core components of ESDA actually predate the development of both EDA and ESDA, so the nesting of ESDA inside EDA is not as clean as the above might suggest.

In what follows we first highlight the particular characteristics of spatial data that necessitate ESDA methods. From there we focus on a selection of what we see as the central methods in the ESDA toolkit: spatial autocorrelation analysis; spatial clustering; and extensions for space-time data. We recognize that ESDA is a relatively new and rapidly evolving subfield of spatial analysis and we direct the reader interested in further details to overviews in Anselin et al. (2006), Haining et al. (1998), Unwin and Unwin (1998), Anselin (1999), Bailey and Gatrell (1995).

Spatial Data

Before outlining the main techniques in ESDA it is important to distinguish the three types of spatial data commonly considered in spatial analysis, i.e., point patterns, geostatistical data, and lattice data (Cressie 1991).

Point pattern data takes the form of events recorded within some bounded area or region, such as the location of crimes that occurred within a neighborhood, accidents on a street network or retail outlets within a city. Interest centers on determining whether the points display spatial clustering or some other departure (such as dispersion) from that expected in a completely random spatial process. For overviews of point pattern analysis the reader is directed to Diggle (2003) and the references cited therein.

Geostatistical data are used for phenomena that could conceptually be measured everywhere in space and modeled as a continuous three-dimensional surface, as is commonly encountered in the physical sciences. Examples of such phenomena that are relevant for social sciences would include air temperature and pollution levels in studies of public health. Because it is impossible to in fact measure the phenomena at all locations, often samples are taken at discrete locations and surfaces are constructed for the values of the attribute at other locations using various interpolation methods, such as kriging. Overviews of geostatistical methods can be found in Journel and Huijbregts (1978), Cressie (1991), Chilès and Delfiner (1999) and Rossi et al. (1992), among others.

A final type of spatial data consists of values (attributes) measured for a fixed set of areal units, or so-called *lattice data*. The areal units often are administrative regions such as census tracts/blocks, counties, or states. Here, the focus is on analyzing the variation in the values across the spatial units. Lattice data analysis is distinct from geostatistical data analysis, since in the latter there are an infinite number of locations, while in lattice analysis the number of spatial sunits is fixed and finite (e.g., the number of counties in a state). The focus on attribute variation across the spatial units in lattice data analysis contrasts with the focus on the relative location of events in point pattern analysis. In what follows we limit our focus to the analysis of lattice data.

Spatial Autocorrelation Analysis

A common characteristic of spatially referenced data is to exhibit similar values in nearby locations. This association between value similarity and spatial similarity is known as spatial autocorrelation, and is a reflection of the so-called *first law of geography*:

> "Everything is related to everything else, but near things are more related than distant things" (Tobler 1970).

Spatial autocorrelation can be either positive, reflecting a nonrandom spatial distribution where like values cluster in space, or, less commonly, negative where the autocorrelation reflects nonrandom value dissimilarity in space. In either case the pattern is different from what would be expected if the values were randomly distributed in space.

Spatial autocorrelation can arise in a number of ways. Measurement errors, manipulations such as interpolation (determining values for locations where no observations are available) and problems with the difference between the spatial extent of the process under study and the spatial units at which it is observed are a number of reasons why spatial autocorrelation can be induced in data that was otherwise randomly distributed. With the advent of GIS software, this is an increasingly important concern. Since in this instance the autocorrelation is an artifact of the data construction process, this type of autocorrelation is referred to as *nuisance autocorrelation*. Alternatively, the autocorrelation could reflect the operation of a substantive process, such as in the case of migration or diffusion, interacting agents, or mimicking of nearby behavior by policy making units (such as copy-catting tax rates in adjoining locations), among others. Because the autocorrelation is thus central to an enhanced understanding of the process, it is referred to as *substantive autocorrelation*.

Irrespective of whether the autocorrelation is of a nuisance or substantive nature, spatial autocorrelation has major implications for the statistical analysis of spatially referenced data. Because spatial autocorrelation is a form of statistical dependence, the assumption of random sampling no longer holds. Consequently, carrying out a test for spatial autocorrelation should precede any application of inferential methods to spatially referenced data. Below we outline the main approaches to such testing.

Spatial autocorrelation can also be analyzed from either a global or local perspective. Global autocorrelation is a whole-map property. That is, whether the spatial distribution of attribute values displays clustering or not. Local autocorrelation analysis is relevant when one is interested in detecting departures from the global pattern, or in identifying the specific location of hot (cold) spots that might form individual clusters.

GLOBAL AUTOCORRELATION

The most widely used measure of spatial autocorrelation in an ESDA context is Moran's I (Moran 1948, 1950). For a set of n spatial observations for a variable y, I is given as:

$$I = \frac{n}{S_0} \frac{\sum_{i=1}^{n}\sum_{j=1}^{n} z_i w_{i,j} z_j}{\sum_{i=1}^{n} z_i^2} \quad (1)$$

where the z variable represents the deviation from the mean of the original variable, $z_i = y_i - \bar{y}$. The symbol w_{ij} warrants some special attention. It stands for the so-called spatial weights that define a priori which pairs of locations are likely to interact. The weights are non-zero when two locations i and j are "neighbors," usually determined on the basis of a geographical criterion. The most commonly used criteria are sharing a common border or being within a critical distance of each other. The collected weights are typically referred to as a spatial weights "matrix" $\mathbf{W}$, of the same dimension as the number of observations ($n \times n$) and with zero on the diagonal by convention. The term S_0 is then the sum of all the elements in the weights matrix, or $S_0 = \sum_{i=1}^{n} \sum_{j=1}^{n} w_{i,j}$. Upon closer examination, Moran's I can be seen to be similar to a correlation coefficient, with a measure of spatial covariance in the numerator (the sum of cross-products of neighboring values), with the numerator similar to a measure of variance. This becomes clear when the statistic is rewritten as:

$$I = \frac{\frac{\sum_{i=1}^{n} \sum_{j=1}^{n} z_i w_{i,j} z_j}{S_0}}{\frac{\sum_{i=1}^{n} z_i^2}{n}} \quad (2)$$

Inference on I can be based on a number of different approaches. However, irrespective of which approach is adopted, the null hypothesis is that the y values are randomly distributed in space, in which case the expected value of I is:

$$\mathrm{E}[I] = \frac{-1}{n-1} \quad (3)$$

Note that, unlike the familiar correlation coefficient, this mean is not centered on zero, but slightly to the negative (see Cliff and Ord 1981, for a formal derivation). Since the denominator $n - 1$ becomes larger with n, in large samples, the mean will approach zero.

The variance of the test statistic can be derived analytically under an assumption of normality, or an assumption of non-free sampling (randomization). To evaluate the significance of the statistic, the I value is converted into a so-called z-value which is evaluated as a standard normal variate (for technical details, see, e.g., Cliff and Ord 1981).

An alternative to the analytical approach is to rely on random permutations of the observed values across the spatial units to develop the distribution of I under the null of spatial independence. Such *permutation* tests are quite common in spatial analysis whenever analytical results are difficult (or impossible) to obtain. More specifically, in the case of Moran's I, if the observed value is I_{obs} this is compared to the reference distribution which is constructed from M random permutations (or synthetic maps). For each of these random maps the statistic is recalculated $I_m : m = 1, 2, \cdots, M$. A one-tailed, or directional, pseudo significance level for the statistic can be expressed as:

$$\mathrm{Prob}[I \geq I_{obs} | H_0] = \frac{\Phi + 1}{M + 1} \quad (4)$$

where $\Phi = \sum_{m=1}^{M} \Phi_m$ and:

$$\Phi_m = \begin{cases} 1 & \text{if } I_m \geq I_{obs} \\ 0 & \text{otherwise.} \end{cases} \quad (5)$$

This pseudo significance level consists of the ratio of the number of times the simulated statistic equals or exceeds the observed value I_{obs} plus one (for the observed statistic) over the number or random permutations plus one (again, for the observed statistic). For example, if 4 simulated statistics equal or exceed the observed value in 99 random permutations, the pseudo significance level would be $(4 + 1)/(99 + 1) = 0.05$. For a two-tailed, or non-directional, alternative hypothesis the probability in (4) would have to be multiplied by 2 to obtain the correct pseudo significance level.

The Moran's I statistic can be graphically depicted as the slope of a linear regression fit in a so-called Moran scatterplot (Anselin 1996). This graph uses standardized values of the variable of interest on the x-axis and its spatial lag on the y-axis. The spatial lag consists of a weighted average of the values at neighboring locations (see also Section 8 for further discussion of the spatial lag).

An illustration of Moran's I using OpenGeoDa (Anselin et al. 2006) is displayed in Figure 8.1 where the variable of interest is sudden infant death rates for 1979 (SIDR) in 100 North Carolina counties. The spatial weights matrix is based on contiguity between the counties. Depicted are three graphs. At the top of the figure is a choropleth map for the quintiles of the rates, with the darkest shade corresponding to the highest rates. The data are sorted by magnitude and categorized by quintile, with each quintile corresponding to a different shade. To the left at the bottom of the Figure is a Moran scatter plot. The x-axis shows the SIDS rate in 79 and the y-axis shows its spatial lag, W_SIDR79. The slope of the linear fit to the scatter plot is 0.1666, as listed at the top of the graph. To the right is a histogram of 999 Moran's I values computed from random permutations of the data. The vertical bar to the right corresponds to the observed value I_{obs}. The pseudo significance level is found to be 0.008, as shown at the top left of the graph. Consequently, the null hypothesis of spatial randomness

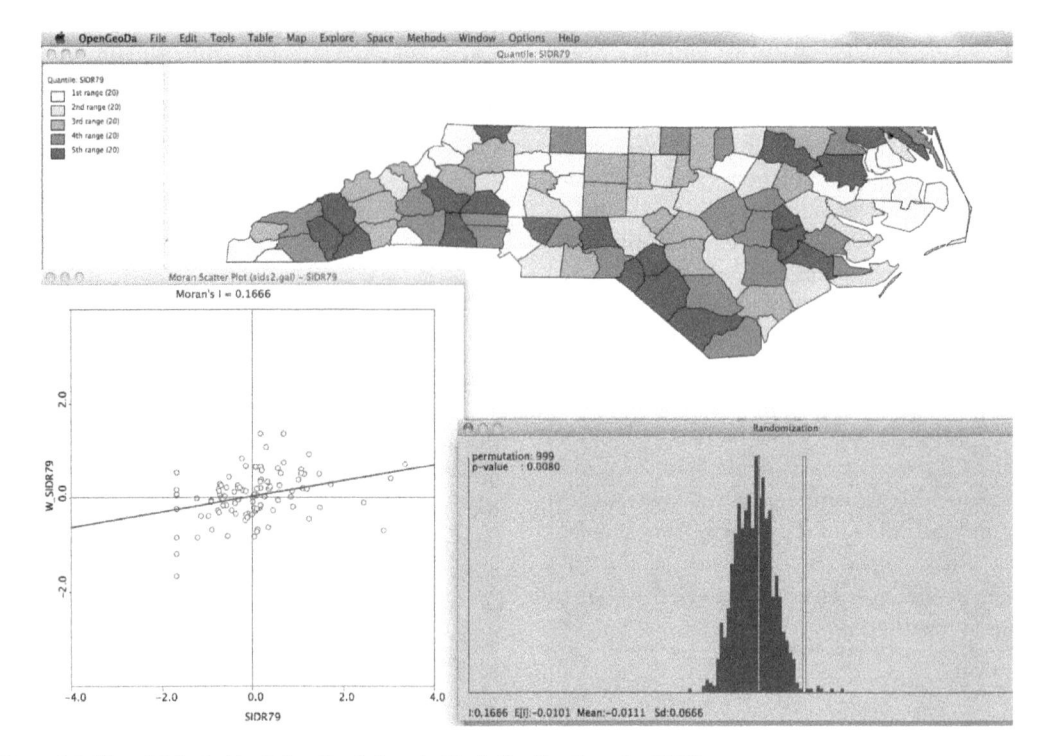

Figure 8.1 Moran's I for Sudden Infant Death Rates in North Carolina Counties (1979)

is rejected. Descriptive statistics for the empirical distribution of the statistics computed from random permutations are listed at the bottom of the graph. These include the analytical mean under the null (−0.0101), the mean of permuted values (−0.0111), and the standard deviation of these values (0.0666).

Moran's I is one of multiple global autocorrelation statistics. For an overview of alternative global autocorrelation statistics see O'Sullivan and Unwin (2003).

LOCAL AUTOCORRELATION

Local autocorrelation statistics are concerned with detecting departures from overall global patterns as well as identifying hot and cold spots, with the latter sometimes referred to as clusters. They do so by developing a measure for each spatial observation that expresses the amount of spatial autocorrelation associated with that observation. Thus, in contrast to the case of global statistics, where there is one value for the entire set of spatial observations, in the local case there are n such measures.

A particular class of local autocorrelation statistics is known as *Local Indicators of Spatial Association* or LISA, suggested by Anselin (1995). To be considered a LISA a local statistic L_i must satisfy two properties:

1. The global autocorrelation statistic must be a function of the local statistics:

$$\sum_{i=1}^{n} L_i = \phi \Gamma \qquad (6)$$

where Γ is the global autocorrelation statistic and ϕ is a scale factor.

2. It is possible to determine the statistical significance of the pattern of spatial association at individual locations $i = 1, 2, \ldots, n$:

$$\text{Prob}[L_i > \delta_i] \leq \alpha_i \qquad (7)$$

where δ_i is a critical value and α_i is a significance level.

One example of a LISA is the local counterpart to Moran's I:

$$I_i = z_i \sum_{j=1}^{n} w_{i,j} z_j, \qquad (8)$$

where the z variable is the same deviation from the mean as in equation 1 and the w_{ij} are the spatial weights.

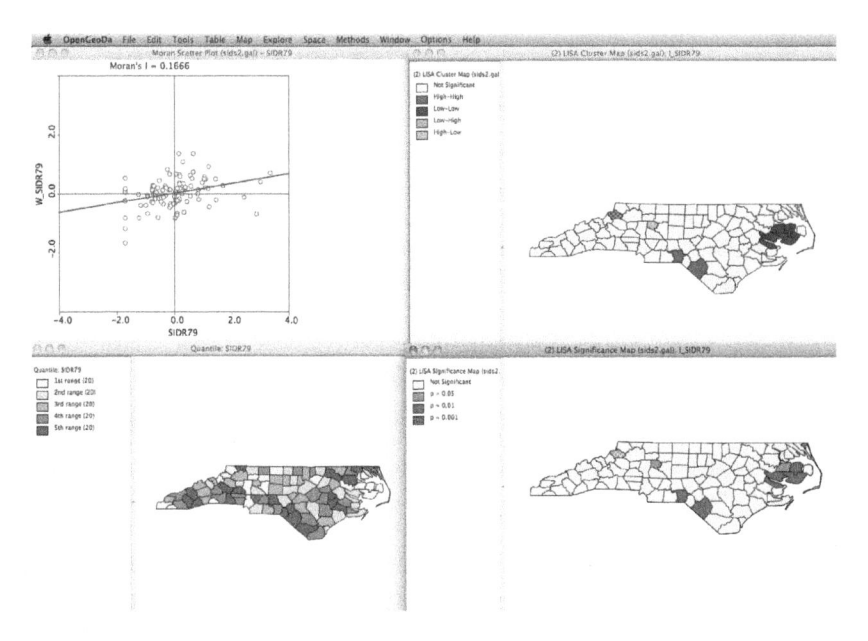

Figure 8.2 Local Statistics for Sudden Infant Death Rates in North Carolina Counties (1979)

Local statistics have seen wide application in recent years, in part driven by their implementation in commercial GIS software and their ability to provide location specific information about spatial autocorrelation which can be then visualized on a map. An illustration using the same North Carolina data as in Figure 8.1 is shown in Figure 8.2. The left part of the figure consists of the Moran scatter plot and the quintile map shown previously. The right part of the figure contains two maps. The bottom map highlights the counties for which the local Moran statistic is significant, with the shading corresponding to the three pseudo p-values of 0.05, 0.01 and 0.001. A darker shading indicates a lower p-value (greater significance). Significance as such does not provide any information as to what type of local spatial association is present (positive or negative). This is obtained by identifying with which quadrant of the Moran scatter plot the significant observations correspond. This allows for the classifications of locations as clusters (high surrounded by high, or low surrounded by low) and spatial outliers (high surrounded by low, or low surrounded by high). A visual representation of the combined classification and significance is illustrated in the top map on the right, a so-called cluster map. Here, the same significant locations as in the bottom map are classified by type, illustrating the presence of high and low clusters as well as some spatial outliers.

Figure 8.2 also illustrates the interactive functionality in OpenGeoDa. The cold-spot county in the northwestern part of the state has been selected on the cluster map, reflected by a cross-hatching in the figure. In turn, the observations associated with this county are then highlighted in the three other views. On the maps, the matching county is also cross-hatched and on the Moran scatter plot the point corresponding to this county is highlighted. This *linking* is one of multiple forms of dynamic graphics that provide powerful mechanisms for the user to explore different dimensions of their data.

While local statistics enjoy much popularity, there are some complications in their interpretation and use. Analytical results for the sampling distribution of the statistics are generally unavailable and, as a result, inference is often based on a conditional randomization of the values surrounding each observation. Given that there are now n tests being carried out the issue of multiple comparisons becomes relevant and several adjustments to the critical values and marginal significance have been suggested in the literature. The n tests will also be dependent since neighboring LISAs will utilize a common subset of observations in their construction. Further discussions of local statistics can be found in de Castro and Singer (2006), Anselin (1995) and Ord and Getis (1995).

Spatial Clustering

As mentioned above, one of the applications of LISAs is to identify clusters within a map pattern. In this regard, the LISA can be seen as a special case of the more general problem of spatial clustering, which is broadly concerned with grouping spatial observations together in such a way that the internal group variance is minimized while the intergroup variance is maximized. Spatial clustering is a large literature with overviews available in Haining (2003, p. 251–265), Lawson and Denison (2002) and Murray and Estivill-Castro (1998).

The variety of spatial clustering methods can be organized into three classes: [1] clustering which is exhaustive and mutually exclusive; [2] clustering which is not exhaustive but is mutually exclusive; and [3] there is a focal point around which one is interested in determining if there is a cluster.

In the first two classes, the number of clusters may or may not be specified *a priori*. If not, then a common strategy is to run a clustering algorithm for different numbers of clusters and select the solution that performs best. Examples of the first class arise in studies of urban neighborhoods and geodemographics (Harris et al. 2005) where there is a need to define a complete partitioning of primitive spatial units such as census blocks or tracts into homogeneous and spatially contiguous neighborhoods or market segments. The second class of clustering methods is widely applied in the analysis of disease and crime rate patterns where the focus is on identifying areas where the rates are elevated. In these cases only a subset of the spatial observations are assigned into clusters. The third class of clustering problems concerns a focal point of interest, such as a noxious facility, so the core of a potential cluster is specified *a priori* which is not the case for the first two sets of clustering methods. The statistical methods to assess whether there is a cluster around the focal point are, however, similar to those applied in the first two cases with unknown cluster locations and generally compare the observed number of events falling within the potential cluster boundary (typically a circle) to what the expected number of such events should be assuming the data generating process is characterized by complete spatial randomness. It is important to adjust the expected counts for spatial variation in the underlying population at risk – so for example in the study of disease cases, spurious clusters, due to population concentrations and uniform risks, are not detected and instead only clusters displaying truly elevated risks are identified.

EXTENSIONS TO SPACE-TIME

With the growing use of geospatial technologies such as global positioning systems there is an increasing amount of data that is not only spatial but also includes a time dimension. An active area of research within ESDA is the development of methods that incorporate this time dimension in a number of different ways. One branch of this research is developing new statistical measures that are designed to characterize the overall spatial dynamics, that is the role of spatial clustering in the evolution of a value distribution over time (Rey 2001, Rey and Anselin 2007). For example, in the literature on regional income convergence and divergence (Rey and Le Gallo 2009) interest has centered on the identification of so called poverty traps or growth clubs consisting of geographically clustered regional economies that display distinct collective income growth patterns over time.

Coupled with these new space-time statistics are a collection of interactive and dynamic graphics that extend the brushing and linking capabilities seen above in the case of OpenGeoDa, to include the temporal dimension. Representative examples of software packages implementing these views are STARS (Rey and Janikas 2006) and CommonGIS (Andrienko and Andrienko 2006).

We illustrate some of these concepts in Figures 8.3 and 8.4, using the STARS software. The variable of interest is the evolution of regional income for states in Mexico over the period 1940–2000. Just like OpenGeoDa, STARS implements the concepts of linking and brushing, connecting all the different views of the data. Figure 8.3 illustrates the situation at the beginning of the period. It contains four graphs. At the top left is a box plot that shows the relative distribution of per capita regional incomes. The three points above the upper bar are outliers, they are more than 1.5 times the interquartile range above the 75-percentile, using the standard approach in EDA. To the right on top is a quintile map of the same variable for the Mexican states. To the left on the bottom is a Moran scatter plot, with the spatial lag of the regional income on the vertical axis and the income on the horizontal axis. This Moran scatter plot pertains to the data for 1940. In the plot on the bottom right of the figure a time series plot is draw that shows the evolution of the Moran's I (the slope in the scatter plot on the left) at the different points in time. The vertical axis represents the magnitude of Moran's I with the time periods on the horizontal axis. In the dynamic version of the graph, the visualization moves through

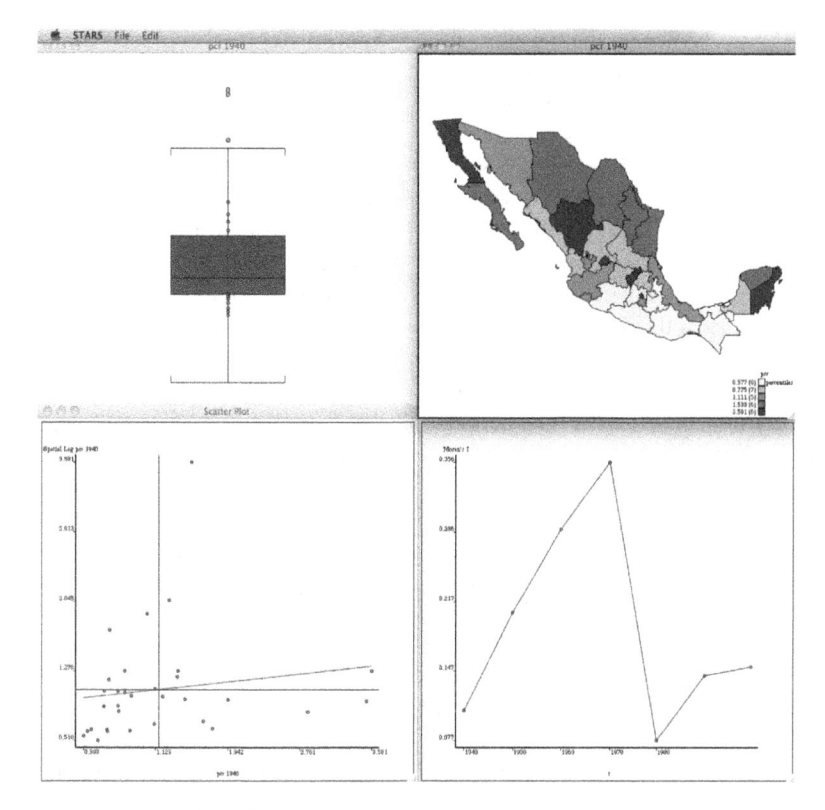

Figure 8.3 Exploratory space-time analysis of Mexican state incomes 1940–2000 using STARS

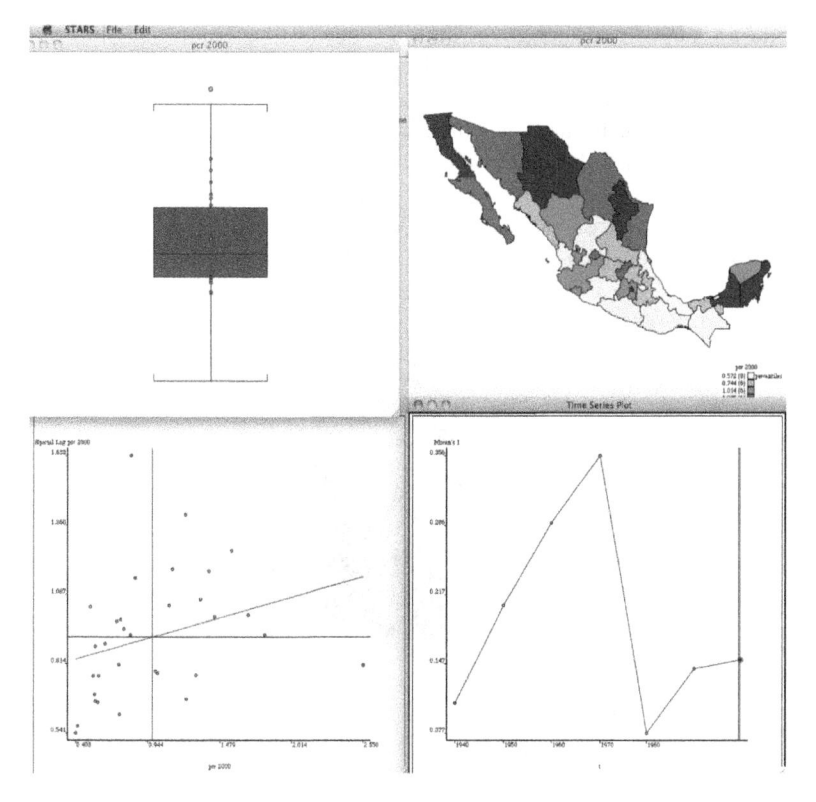

Figure 8.4 Time-sliding as a form of linking

each year in turn, which changes the box plot, the quintile map and the Moran scatter plot. The corresponding Moran's *I* is highlighted as a point on the time series plot. Figure 8.4 shows the situation at the end of the period, in 2000. The time series plot (bottom right) is unchanged, but it now shows a vertical bar at the year 2000. The other three graphs are different, illustrating different outliers (only one state is an outlier in 2000), a different spatial distribution (in the map) and a different Moran's *I* (the slope of the Moran scatter plot). The software allows the user to move the vertical bar, a so-called time slider, interactively over the different time periods. This time sliding allows for the exploration of the dynamics of spatial autocorrelation, since the graphs are updated for each time period.

Extending ESDA to include a temporal dimension opens up the scope of analysis to a wide array of data types. In the case of STARS above, the spatial units are fixed over time while their attribute values change over time. In other cases of space-time data, the location of events may be changing. For example, Figure 8.5 illustrates the origin-destination pattern of convicted sex offenders in relation to the location of schools and the associated spatial restriction zones (Murray et al. 2012). Each arrow shows the residence of the offender at the beginning and at the end of the time period under consideration. The schools are the blue areas surrounded by their spatial restriction zone. The complex patterns generated by such movement data necessitate the development of both new interactive visualization devices as well as exploratory statistics in order to identify interesting structures within this multidimensional data. This remains a very active area of ongoing research.

Spatial Regression Analysis

Spatial regression deals with the specification, estimation, diagnostic checking and prediction of regression models that incorporate spatial effects (e.g., Anselin 2006). In the social sciences literature, it is also often referred to as *spatial econometrics*, a term coined in the early 1970s by the Belgian economist Jean Paelinck (Paelinck and Klaassen 1979). In a regression context, two broad classes of spatial effects may be distinguished, referred to as spatial dependence and spatial heterogeneity (Anselin 1988). In this section, we will focus on how these spatial effects affect regression analysis, with a particular emphasis on the linear regression model, which is the most frequently used in practice.

Early interest in the statistical implications of estimating spatial regression models dates back to the pioneering results of the statisticians Whittle (1954), Besag (1974), Ord (1975) and Ripley (1981). By the late 1980s and early 1990s, several compilations had appeared that included technical reviews of a range of models, estimation methods and diagnostic tests, including Anselin (1988), Griffith (1988) and Haining (1990). Most importantly, with the publication of the text by Cressie (1991), a near-comprehensive technical treatment of the statistical foundations for the analysis of spatial data was provided.

Spatial regression analysis is a core aspect of the *spatial* methodological toolbox and several recent texts covering the state of the art have appeared, including Haining (2003), Waller and Gotway (2004), Banerjee et al. (2004), Fortin and Dale (2005), Schabenberger and Gotway (2005), Arbia (2006), Pfeiffer et al. (2008), Lawson (2009), and LeSage and Pace (2009). Recent surveys of more

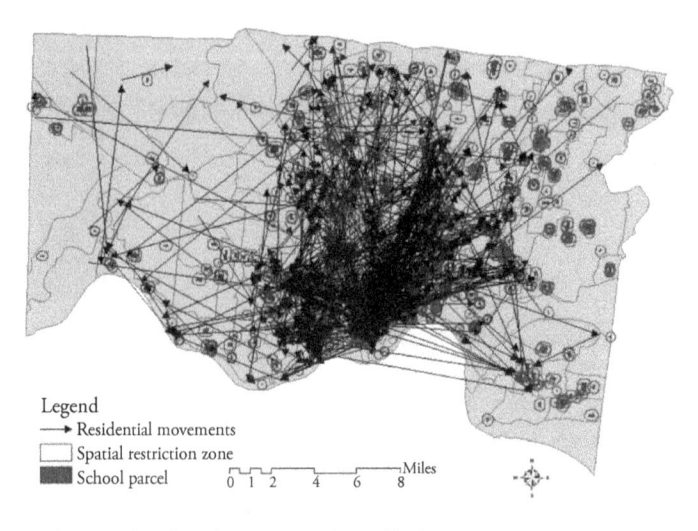

Figure 8.5 Exploratory visualization of residential movements of sex offenders

advanced methodological issues in spatial regression analysis (and spatial econometrics) can be found in Anselin and Bera (1998) and Anselin (2001, 2006, 2010).

In the remainder of this section, we will primarily focus on the various specifications through which spatial effects can be introduced into a regression model. We start with a discussion of the overall problem and then move to spatial dependence and spatial heterogeneity in linear regression models. We close with a brief review of three other spatial models, i.e., specifications of spatial panel data models, spatial latent variable models and Bayesian hierarchical spatial models. Where appropriate, we will address the three other aspects of spatial regression (estimation, specification tests and prediction) with selected references. Due to the highly technical nature of these topics, we will limit ourselves to a review of the main principles and focus primarily on model specification. We refer the interested reader to the review articles cited above and the materials cited in them for technical details and a more in-depth treatment.

Spatial Effects in Regression Specification

In the context of regression analysis, spatial dependence is viewed as a special case of cross-sectional dependence, in the sense that the *structure* of the correlation or covariance between random variables at different locations is derived from a specific ordering, determined by the relative position (distance, spatial arrangement) of the observations in geographic space (or, in general, in network space). While similar to correlation in the time domain, the distinct nature of spatial dependence requires a specialized set of techniques. Importantly, these are *not* a straightforward extension of time series methods to two dimensions.

Spatial heterogeneity is a special case of observed or unobserved heterogeneity, a familiar problem in standard econometrics. In contrast to spatial dependence, tackling spatial heterogeneity does not always require a separate set of methods. The only spatial aspect of the heterogeneity is the additional information that may be provided by spatial structure. For example, the information on spatial structure may inform models for heteroscedasticity, spatially varying coefficients, random coefficients and spatial structural change.

Spatial heterogeneity becomes particularly challenging since it is often difficult to separate from spatial dependence. This difficulty is known in the literature as the inverse problem. It is also related to the impossible distinction between true and apparent contagion. The essence of the problem is that cross-sectional data, while allowing the identification of clusters and patterns, do not provide sufficient information to identify the *processes* that led to the patterns. As a result, it is impossible to distinguish between the case where the cluster is due to structural change (apparent contagion) or follows from a true contagious process. This problem is specific to a pure cross-sectional setting and can be remedied by resorting to observations across space and over time. In a regression context, models for such pooled cross-section and time series data are referred to as spatial panel models.

Spatial Dependence in the Linear Regression Model

The point of departure in our discussion of model specification is the standard linear regression model. To fix notation, we consider, for each observation (location) i, the following linear relationship between a dependent variable y and k explanatory variables x_h:

$$y_i = \sum_{h=1}^{k} x_{hi}\beta_h + \epsilon_i, \qquad (9)$$

where the β_h are the associated regression coefficients and ϵ_i is a random error term.

Spatial dependence is introduced into the regression specification in two fundamentally different ways. In the first, the dependence is conceptualized as following from an interaction process between the observational units. Examples of such interaction processes are externalities, copy catting, peer-effects, etc. This interaction corresponds to the notion of *substantive* spatial dependence introduced in Section 8. In essence, the dependent variable at one location (observation) is specified as a function of its value at neighboring locations. For the sake of simplicity, we consider the linear case only.

The effect of the *neighbors* is encapsulated in a so-called spatially lagged dependent variable, which we will designate as Wy. Technically, an observation on the spatially lagged dependent variable, or spatial lag, is obtained as a weighted average of neighboring values, with the weights specified in a spatial weights matrix, similar to what is necessary for a spatial autocorrelation coefficient (see Section 8). For location i, this becomes:

$$Wy_i = \sum_{j=1}^{n} w_{ij} y_j \qquad (10)$$

with the w_{ij} as the spatial weights. Since the spatial weights are typically row standardized (such that $\sum_j w_{ij} = 1$), the weighted sum in Equation 10 boils down to an averaging of the value of y for the neighboring locations. The operation of creating a new variable as a weighted average of neighboring values is called a *spatial lag operation*. It can be performed on the dependent variable, the explanatory variables, or the error term (for details, see Anselin 2003).

A regression specification that includes a spatially lagged dependent variable is referred to as a mixed regressive, spatial autoregressive model, or *spatial lag* model in short. Conceptually, it is the expression of the equilibrium outcome of a process of social and spatial interaction, although in practice it is often used as a mechanism to filter the dependent variable of the effect of spatial correlation. Formally, the spatial lag model is then:

$$y_i = \rho \sum_{j=1}^{n} w_{ij} y_j + \sum_{h=1}^{k} x_{hi} \beta_h + \epsilon_i, \quad (11)$$

where ρ is the spatial autoregressive coefficient, i.e., the regression coefficient associated with the spatially lagged dependent variable $\sum_{j=1}^{n} w_{ij} y_j$. The rest of Equation 11 is the familiar linear regression specification.

The inclusion of the spatial lag is similar to an autoregressive term in a time series context, hence it is called a spatial autoregressive model, although there is a fundamental difference. Unlike time dependence, dependence in space is multidirectional, implying feedback effects and simultaneity. More precisely, if i and j are neighboring locations, then y_j enters on the right hand side in the equation for y_i, but y_i also enters on the right hand side in the equation for y_j (the neighbor relation is symmetric). The endogeneity implied by this feedback must be accounted for in the estimation process and is qualitatively different from the one-directional dependence in time series.

An important aspect of the spatial lag model is the concept of a spatial multiplier (for details, see Anselin 2003). The multiplier follows from the solution of the model in which all the dependent variables are removed from the right hand side of the equation, the so-called *reduced form*. Using matrix notation, the spatial lag model becomes:

$$\mathbf{y} = \rho \mathbf{W} \mathbf{y} + \mathbf{X} \beta + \epsilon, \quad (12)$$

where $\mathbf{y}$ is now a n by 1 vector of observations on the dependent variables, $\mathbf{W}$ is a n by n spatial weights matrix, $\mathbf{X}$ is a n by k matrix of observations on the explanatory variables, ϵ is a n by 1 vector of error terms, and the coefficients are as before. Solving Equation 12 by means of a matrix inverse operation yields:

$$\mathbf{y} = (\mathbf{I} - \rho \mathbf{W})^{-1} \mathbf{X} \beta + (\mathbf{I} - \rho \mathbf{W})^{-1} \epsilon, \quad (13)$$

with $\mathbf{I}$ as an n by n identity matrix. Equation 13 reveals the spatial multiplier, in the sense that the value of y at any location i is not only determined by the values of x at i, but also of x at all other locations in the system. A simple expansion of the inverse matrix term (for $|\rho| < 1$ and with a row-standardized $\mathbf{W}$), and using the expected value (since the errors all have mean zero) further reveals the structure of the multiplier:

$$E[\mathbf{y}|\mathbf{X}] = \mathbf{X}\beta + \rho \mathbf{W} \mathbf{X} \beta + \rho^2 \mathbf{W}^2 \mathbf{X} \beta + \ldots \quad (14)$$

The powers of ρ matching the powers of the weights matrix (higher orders of neighbors) ensure that a distance decay effect is present.

In the second class of spatial regression model, the spatial dependence does not enter into the substantive part of the regression specification, but affects the covariance structure of the random error terms. The typical motivation for a *spatial error* specification is that there is a mismatch between the scale of observation and the scale at which the phenomenon under study manifests itself. The mismatch implies that neighboring locations share unobserved effects (sometimes called common factors) which results in non-zero off-diagonal elements in the error variance-covariance matrix. The non-spherical error variance-covariance is the expression of *nuisance* spatial autocorrelation (see Section 8).

Spatial error autocorrelation is thus a special case of a non-spherical error covariance matrix, i.e., where $E[\epsilon_i \epsilon_j] \neq 0$, for $i \neq j$, or, in matrix notation, with $E[\epsilon \epsilon'] = \Sigma$. The value and pattern of the non-zero covariances are the outcome of a spatial ordering. In a cross-section, it is impossible to extract this ordering from the data directly, since there are potentially $[n \times (n-1)]/2$ covariance parameters and only n observations to estimate them from. Hence, it is necessary to impose structure.

The spatial covariance structure can be obtained in a number of ways, yielding a wide array of specifications. One of the earliest suggestions was to express the covariance terms as a function of the distance between the observations in question. In this so-called *direct representation*, the covariance between error terms is a function of distance, $E[\epsilon_i \epsilon_j] = \sigma^2 f(d_{ij}, \phi)$, with f as a *proper* function, such that the resulting variance-covariance matrix is positive definite. This approach is most common in the so-called geostatistical literature and provides a way to improve on the precision of spatial prediction, so-called kriging (see Schabenberger and Gotway 2005, for an extensive treatment).

Arguably the most commonly used approach to specify spatial error dependence is to select a spatial stochastic process model for the error term. Typical choices include a spatial autoregressive form (similar to the spatial lag model, but expressed for the error term) and a spatial moving average form. A special case of the spatial autoregressive specification is the conditional autoregressive or CAR model, a common choice as prior in a Bayesian spatial hierarchical model (for reviews, see, e.g. Banerjee et al. 2004).

Specification of Spatial Heterogeneity

A good starting point to discuss the complexities introduced by spatial heterogeneity is to contrast complete homogeneity and extreme structural instability. Under homogeneity, the standard linear regression specification is fixed across observations, the unknown parameter values are constant and the error terms are independent and identically distributed ($i.i.d$). Formally, for each observation i, this is expressed as in equation (9) above. In contrast, in the case of extreme heterogeneity, for each observation, there is potentially a different functional form, encompassing the situation of different parameter values and/or different explanatory variables, and the error is not independent and not identically distributed ($n.i.n.i.d$). Formally, extreme heterogeneity can be expressed as:

$$y_i = f_i \left(\sum_{h=1}^{K_i} x_{ih} \beta_{ih} \right) + \epsilon_i, \qquad (15)$$

where a different functional form f_i pertains to each observations, with a different set of regression coefficients β_{ih} and an error term with a different distribution for each i. This expression suffers from the *incidental parameter* problem, in that there is a different set of parameters for each observation. It is therefore not operational. The number of coefficients to be estimated increases with the number of observations, such that the sample never provides sufficient information to obtain reliable estimates. We solve this problem by imposing structure of a *spatial* form, hence the term spatial heterogeneity.

There are two main approaches to imposing structure. In one, the instability is categorized into a small number of subsets within which the specification is stable. This approach is referred to as *discrete spatial heterogeneity*. The best-known form of this approach is the inclusion of so-called spatial fixed effects in the regression specification. Spatial fixed effects are indicator variables that correspond to a spatial subset of observations, such as all counties within the same state, or blocks within the same census tract. The estimated coefficients of the spatial fixed effects indicate the extent to which individual subregions deviate from the common mean. The notion of a fixed effect applied to the regression intercept can be readily generalized to all the regression coefficients, in a so-called *spatial regimes* model (Anselin 1990). The regression is specified such that different subregions have different coefficient sets, which allows one to test the null hypothesis of regional homogeneity.

The second approach specifies the structural instability in the form of a smooth or continuous variation of the model coefficients, as a special case of varying coefficients. We refer to this approach as *continuous spatial heterogeneity*. An early example of this in the quantitative geography literature is the so-called *spatial expansion* method of Casetti (1972, 1997). In its initial form, the expansion method consisted of fitting a spatial trend surface (a polynomial regression in the coordinates of the observations) to each of the regression coefficients, allowing one to map the *spatial drift* of the estimates. Later, the trend surface was generalized to include any type of expansion variable. In the statistical literature, spatially varying coefficients are viewed as a special case of models in which the coefficients are allowed to vary as smooth functions of other variables (for a general discussion, see Hastie and Tibshirani 1993, among others).

A local form of this principle is reflected in the *geographically weighted regression* or GWR (Fotheringham et al. 1998, 2002). In a GWR, each model coefficient is estimated at each location as a locally weighted (kernel) estimate, using geographically nearby observations as the support. The collection of local coefficients also provides the opportunity to map the spatial variability of each coefficient. The principle behind GWR has been applied to many other estimation contexts besides the linear regression model and continues to be a subject of active research. For example, a recent comparison of the performance of GWR and spatially varying coefficient models in an empirical context is given in Waller et al. (2007).

In spatially varying coefficient models such as the GWR, the continuous heterogeneity is expressed as a function. An alternative that has wide application in Bayesian hierarchical spatial modeling is to specify the variability in the form of a (prior) distribution for the model parameters. This distribution can itself encompass a spatial stochastic process structure, which allows for the spatial variability to be expressed in terms of a small number of parameters. Examples of models with random spatial parameter variation are given in Gelfand et al. (2003) and Assunçao (2003).

Other Spatial Models

The range of possible spatial regression specifications is much greater than the linear spatial lag and spatial error models considered so far. For example, each of these models can be taken in combination with spatial heterogeneity, such as spatial regimes or heteroskedasticity. More fundamentally, there are three broad dimensions in which the spatial specifications can be extended. One consists of introducing spatial dependence and heterogeneity into models that combine observations across space and over time, in so-called spatial panel data models (for recent overviews, see, e.g., Elhorst 2003, Anselin et al. 2008, Lee and Yu 2010). A second considers spatial effects in models with latent variables, such as discrete choice models, which includes as a special case the spatial probit and tobit models (see Fleming 2004). A third direction pertains to the very large volume of Bayesian spatial hierarchical models, which have seen wide application in modern statistics (e.g., Banerjee et al. 2004). In addition to these three broad areas, there is an increasing interest in semi-parametric spatial models (e.g., Pinkse et al. 2002, Basile and Gress 2005, Pinkse and Slade 2010). However, a detailed discussion of semi-parametric models is beyond the current scope.

We next give a brief overview of each class of models (due to space constraints, we direct the interested reader to the references cited for additional examples and technical details). It should be noted that each of these areas are still undergoing very active research and the state of the art is rapidly moving forward.

SPATIAL PANEL REGRESSION MODELS

Spatial dependence of the error or lag form can be introduced into a standard panel model specification in a straightforward manner. The point of departure is the model:

$$y_{it} = \mathbf{x}'_{it}\beta + \epsilon_{it}, \quad (16)$$

where i is an index for the cross-sectional dimension, with $i = 1, \ldots, n$, and t is an index for the time dimension, with $t = 1, \ldots, T$. Using customary notation, y_{it} is an observation on the dependent variable at i and t, $\mathbf{x}_{it}$ a $k \times 1$ vector of observations on the (exogenous) explanatory variables, β a matching $k \times 1$ vector of regression coefficients, and ϵ_{it} an error term. The setting considered here is where the cross-sectional dimension dominates, with $n \gg T$. Also, even though the basic design is referred to as "space" and "time," the second dimension could equally pertain to different cross-sections, such as in a study of industrial sectors or household types. In stacked matrix form, the simple pooled regression then becomes:

$$\mathbf{y} = \mathbf{X}\beta + \epsilon, \quad (17)$$

with $\mathbf{y}$ as a $nT \times 1$ vector, $\mathbf{X}$ as a $nT \times k$ matrix and ϵ as a $nT \times 1$ vector. Note that in order to incorporate spatial effects, the stacking is for a complete cross-section at a time, and not for each individual cross-section over time.

The key to incorporating spatial dependence into this specification is the use of a spatial weights matrix for the panel dimension, by creating a block diagonal $nT \times nT$ matrix with the n-dimensional cross-sectional weights as the diagonal elements, or:

$$\mathbf{W}_{nT} = \mathbf{I}_T \otimes \mathbf{W}_n, \quad (18)$$

where $\mathbf{I}$ is an identity matrix and the subscripts refer to the matrix dimension, with $\otimes$ as the Kronecker product.

A spatial lag model can then be expressed as:

$$\mathbf{y} = \rho(\mathbf{I}_T \otimes \mathbf{W}_n)\mathbf{y} + \mathbf{X}\beta + \epsilon, \quad (19)$$

where ρ is the spatial autoregressive parameter (constant over the time dimension), and the other notation is as before. Similarly, a model with spatial SAR error dependence results in an $nT \times nT$ non-spherical error variance-covariance matrix of the form:

$$\Sigma_{nT} = \sigma_u^2 \left[\mathbf{I}_T \otimes [(\mathbf{I}_n - \lambda \mathbf{W}_n)'(\mathbf{I}_n - \lambda \mathbf{W}_n)]^{-1} \right], \quad (20)$$

where σ_u^2 is a common variance term, and the spatial autoregressive coefficient λ is assumed to be constant over the time dimension. More complex model specifications are reviewed in Anselin et al. (2008).

One class of space-time models has received considerable attention in spatial analysis, particularly in applied economics. In so-called error component models the spatial (and time) dependence is introduced into a classic two-way error component specification (e.g., Baltagi 2001, p. 31). In this model, each error term is decomposed into three terms:

$$\varepsilon_{it} = \alpha_i + \phi_t + u_{it}, \quad (21)$$

where α_i is a cross-sectional unobserved random effect, ϕ_t is a random time effect, and u_{it} is an idiosyncratic component. Spatial dependence can be introduced in the form of a spatial autoregressive process for the idiosyncratic component, but a number of other specifications have been suggested as well (for reviews, see Anselin 1988, Baltagi et al. 2003, 2006, Kapoor et al. 2007). The error component specification is also one of the main ways in which spatial dependence is incorporated in a Bayesian approach (see Section 8).

SPATIAL LATENT VARIABLES

Spatial effects in latent variables models are particularly relevant in applied micro-econometrics, where the observed dependent variable often only takes on discrete values (e.g., a binary dependent variable that takes on values of 0 and 1). Incorporating spatial dependence into these specifications is not straightforward. One common approach (especially in the statistics literature) is to take a Bayesian perspective (see Section 8). Another approach is to specify the dependence for an unobserved latent variable, say y_i^*, which is defined as a linear function of an "index function" and a random error term:

$$y_i^* = \mathbf{x}_i'\beta + \epsilon_i, \tag{22}$$

with $\mathbf{x}_i'\beta$ as the index function, where $\mathbf{x}_i$ is a $k \times 1$ vector of observations on the explanatory variables, and β is a matching vector of coefficients. The observed counterpart of y_i^*, the discrete dependent variable y_i, equals one for $y_i^* > 0$ and zero otherwise. Interest therefore centers on the probability of observing an event, i.e., $P[y_i^* > 0] = P[\mathbf{x}_i'\beta + \epsilon_i > 0]$. By specifying a distribution for the random error term, estimates for β can be obtained. In order to incorporate spatial dependence, the multivariate Gaussian distribution is particularly attractive, which leads to the so-called *spatial probit* model.

The key to modeling spatial dependence in this context is not to express the dependence for the observed variable y_i, but instead to use a spatial model for the latent variable in expression (22). For example, a spatial lag model would be:

$$y_i^* = \rho \sum_j w_{ij} y_j^* + \mathbf{x}_i'\beta + \epsilon_i, \tag{23}$$

or, in matrix notation, using the familiar reduced form:

$$\mathbf{y}^* = (\mathbf{I} - \rho \mathbf{W})^{-1}\mathbf{X}\beta + (I - \rho \mathbf{W})^{-1}\varepsilon. \tag{24}$$

In this *simultaneous* model, the latent variables are jointly determined, both by the values for x at their own location and by the values for x at all other locations, subject to a distance decay effect. One immediate consequence of the simultanelty is that the usual marginal condition $P[y_i^* > 0]$ now pertains to the marginal probability of a (complex) *multivariate* normal distribution with a variance-covariance matrix that includes a spatial parameter. A similar complication occurs for the spatial error specification for a latent variable. As a result, there is no longer an analytical solution to the estimation problem and one typically has to resort to simulation estimators. Overviews of some of the technical issues can be found in Pinkse and Slade (1998), LeSage (2000), Kelejian and Prucha (2001), Fleming (2004), and Beron and Vijverberg (2004), among others.

BAYESIAN HIERARCHICAL SPATIAL MODELS

The application of the Bayesian perspective to spatial regression modeling has seen tremendous growth since the advent of readily available simulation estimators, especially Markov Chain Monte Carlo (MCMC) methods, such as the Gibbs sampler and the Metropolis-Hastings algorithm (see, e.g., Geman and Geman 1984, Gilks et al. 1996). Early applications were severely restricted in terms of the choice of conjugate prior distributions to ensure a proper posterior distribution and an analytical solution to the estimation problem. However, with simulation estimators, increasingly complex specifications can now be analyzed, including complex space-time correlation structures (for a recent review, see Banerjee et al. 2004).

We can make a distinction between Bayesian approaches to the spatial lag and spatial error specifications (as exemplified in the work of LeSage, summarized in LeSage 1997, LeSage and Pace 2009) and models where the spatial effects are introduced in a hierarchical fashion. We focus on the latter.

A major area of application of hierarchical spatial models is the analysis of rates or events as an approach to estimate the underlying risk surface, such as in epidemiology, public health and criminology (Best et al. 1999). The basic principle behind the hierarchical model can be illustrated with a specification for counts of events as a realization of a Poisson distribution with a heterogeneous mean, $y_i \sim Poi(\mu_i)$, where Poi stands for the Poisson distribution and μ_i is a location-specific mean. Standard practice in epidemiology is to express the mean as the product of the "expected count" and the relative risk. The expected count is typically based on a form of standardization and the main interest focuses on the relative risk, i.e., to what extent does the risk at individual locations differ from what should be expected. The model specification thus becomes $y_i|\eta_i \sim Poi(E_i\eta_i)$, with E_i as the expected count and η_i as the relative risk, the parameter of interest.

The hierarchical aspect of this model appears as a random coefficient specification in the form of a distribution for the parameter η_i. Typically, a Gamma distribution is taken as the distribution, itself a function of two parameters, for which prior distributions need to be specified. This is referred to as the Poisson-Gamma model. While it is possible to include spatial effects into this model, this is typically quite complex (Wolpert and Ickstadt 1998).

A simpler approach, which allows for ready inclusion of spatial dependence and spatial heterogeneity, is to take the distribution for the log of the relative risk, $\phi_i = \log \eta_i$, to follow a Gaussian distribution. This approach is referred to as the Poisson-Lognormal model. The conditional distribution of the observed counts, conditional upon the log-relative risk is then $y_i \sim Poi(E_i e^{\phi_i})$. The hierarchical aspect comes in the form of a linear regression specification for the relative risk parameter:

$$\phi_i = \mathbf{x}'_i \beta + \theta_i + \psi_i, \qquad (25)$$

where $\mathbf{x}'_i$ is a vector of variables that explain the heterogeneity of the risk parameter, with an associated coefficient vector β, and θ_i and ψ_i are random components that follow a Gaussian distribution. The first of the random components, θ_i reflects the heterogeneity across space and often takes on a Gaussian prior with a given variance (or, preferably, the inverse of the variance, or precision). The second component incorporates spatial autocorrelation, either in the form of a direct representation (a multivariate Gaussian distribution with a variance-covariance that is a function of inverse distance) or of a CAR process. Estimation of the parameters of the model is carried out by means of MCMC. Both models have seen wide application (see Banerjee et al. 2004, Lawson 2009, for a more extensive discussion and many illustrations).

Bayesian hierarchical spatial modeling continues to be an area of active research.

Spatial Optimization Modeling

There are many ways in which optimization is important in spatial analysis. Murray (2007) discusses a range of contexts, spanning GIS database management, the arrangement and representation of geographic space as well as spatial optimization in planning and decision making. Of course, much of the statistical methods detailed in this chapter rely on optimization to derive best or efficient model parameter estimates. In the remainder of this section we focus on optimization, and spatial optimization modeling more specifically.

Optimization

Optimization is a term that is widely used. Even in basic calculus one encounters functions that can be characterized in terms of local and global optima, with the challenge of identifying such *critical points* and interpreting their significance (see Miller 2000). Of course, local/global optima represent instances of the function that correspond to extreme values, with an economic interpretation of being the most efficient or most profitable when the function describes return on investment, as an example. Optimization is necessarily an area of applied mathematics, but the fields of operations research and management sciences have come to be synonymous with optimization because of their emphasis on identifying, developing and applying optimization based approaches. Therefore, the mathematical view of optimization is that it seeks to obtain values to variables (unknowns) that either maximize or minimize a function subject to constraining conditions (also functions).

A generic optimization problem can be stated as follows:

$$\text{Maximize} \quad f(x) \qquad (26)$$
$$\text{Subject to } g_i(x) \leq \beta_i \; \forall \; i \qquad (27)$$
$$x \geq 0, \qquad (28)$$

where $f(x)$ is a function, x is an $n \times 1$ vector of decision variables, $g_i(x)$ is function i (m in total), and β_i is a coefficient specifying the bound or limit on the value of function i. The objective, (26), represents a function to be optimized. Note that it is also possible to minimize the objective by simply multiplying the associated function by -1. The model constraints are specified in (27), where there are m functions, each bounded by an inequality condition. Finally, decision variable stipulations are given in (28). The idea then is that we need to make decisions on what the best values of the unknown variables should be in order to optimize the objective, but must not violate any of the imposed constraining conditions.

If there are no constraints (27), then from calculus it is theoretically possible to solve this optimization problem by taking the derivative and setting it equal to zero. Unfortunately, in practice it may not be possible to do this. One reason is that the derivative may not exist. Alternatively, it may not be possible to isolate individual variables. Finally, the derivative(s) may simply be too complex/difficult to solve. If there are constraints (27), optimally solving associated problems is all the more challenging. For these reasons, non-linear optimization problems, in general, remain difficult to solve, though many techniques exist for their solution, some available in commercial software.

Many important optimization models involve linear functions in the objective and the constraints. The generic optimization problem can therefore be restated as follows for linear functions:

$$\text{Maximize} \quad \mathbf{cx} \quad (29)$$

$$\text{Subject to} \quad \mathbf{Ax} \leq \mathbf{b} \quad (30)$$

$$\mathbf{x} \geq 0 \quad (31)$$

where $\mathbf{c}$ is a $1 \times n$ vector of benefits, $\mathbf{x}$ is an $n \times 1$ vector of decision variables, $\mathbf{A}$ is a $m \times n$ matrix of constraint coefficients, and $\mathbf{b}$ is a $m \times 1$ vector for right hand side limits. An optimization problem with linear functions is know as a *linear program*, and may be solved using linear programming based methods. There are many commercial software packages for solving linear programs. Further, it is possible to structure linear approximations for many non-linear problems.

Spatial Optimization

With the basics of optimization in hand, we can proceed to discussing its significance in spatial analysis. In general terms, *spatial optimization modeling* extends or applies optimization to a geographic context, focusing on situations where objectives and constraints are inherently defined by space and spatial relationships.

There are three different types of spatial optimization models that have been applied: location models; land use planning models; and, network design and protection models. Much of the current work in these areas makes extensive use of GIS as it enables access to spatial information, provides the capacity to understand, extract and structure spatial relationships, and facilitates the development and solution of model abstractions that reflect the increased reality and complexity faced by planners and decision makers. In the remainder of this section we detail an example of a location model and a land use planning model, focusing on how space is structured mathematically.

LOCATION MODELS

Good overviews of location models can be found in Mirchandani and Francis (1990), Drezner and Hamacher (2002), and Church and Murray (2009). Weber (1909) was an early example of applying spatial optimization, where the interest was finding a location to site a factory in order to minimize transportation costs associated with both raw material inputs and delivery of finished goods to a market. Much location modeling work has followed associated with siting all sorts of public and private sector facilities and services, including libraries, fire stations, telecommunications infrastructure, distribution centers, emergency warning sirens, retail outlets, schools, oil/gas transmission corridors (see Church and Murray 2009). The range of applications and the variety of models are considerable. Given space limitations, it is not possible to review and/or discuss them all here. However, we will detail one model that reflects the significance of geography and spatial relationships in location models, and the inherent challenges of mathematically structuring this.

An important spatial optimization model involves siting a minimal number of facilities in order to ensure that all those areas utilizing the facility are within a maximum service or distance standard. Edmonds (1962) was among the first to discuss this optimization model, the *set covering* problem, but in the context of geographic space Toregas et al. (1971) formulated the problem to locate fire stations such that the every area could be responded to within some maximum time (e.g., 10 minutes). Ando et al. (1998) used the same model to examine species protection through biological reserve siting. While the basic problem remains important and widely applied in practice, the emergence of GIS and more detailed spatial information has led the way to enhanced conceptualization of this problem, involving greater mathematical specification and structure. Murray (2005) formulated and solved a generalization of this problem to site emergency warning sirens in order to cover neighborhood areas (represented as polygons). Consider the following notation:

$i =$ index of areas to be covered;

$j =$ index of potential facility locations;

$l =$ index of coverage levels $(1, 2, 3, \ldots, L)$;

δ_l = minimum acceptable coverage percentage at level l;

Ω_{il} = set of potential facilities j partially covering area i at least δ_l;

α_l = minimum number of facilities needed for complete coverage at level l;

$$x_j = \begin{cases} 1 & \text{if a facility is sited at potential location } j \\ 0 & \text{otherwise} \end{cases}$$

$$y_{il} = \begin{cases} 1 & \text{if area } i \text{ is covered at level } l \\ 0 & \text{otherwise} \end{cases}$$

The basic coverage model suggested by Murray (2005), and detailed in Church and Murray (2009) as well as in Murray et al. (2010), is as follows:

$$\text{Minimize} \quad \sum_j x_j \tag{32}$$

Subject to

$$\sum_{j \in \Omega_{il}} x_j \geq \alpha_l y_{il} \; \forall i, l \tag{33}$$

$$\sum_l y_{il} = 1 \; \forall i \tag{34}$$

$$x_j = \{0, 1\} \; \forall j \tag{35}$$
$$y_{il} = \{0, 1\} \; \forall i, l$$

The objective, (32), is to minimize the number of facilities sited. Constraints (33) relate facility siting to coverage of demand area i, where coverage is not provided until at least α_l facilities are sited that serve the area. Constraints (34) require that coverage must be provided at some level k. Constraints (35) stipulate restrictions on decision variables.

There are two inherent spatial components to this particular model. First, there are the obvious geographic siting decisions, x_j, that indicate where facilities should be placed. Second, there is the tracking of coverage provided to areas by sited facilities, y_{il}. Of course these two components are intimately connected as the siting decisions dictate what will be covered. Beyond this spatial connection, what is significant about this coverage model is that it allows geographic objects in the form of points, lines and areas to be modeled. Thus, the work of Toregas et al. (1971), as an example, is a special case of this approach where the number of coverage levels is one ($L = 1$). In order to address line and area features (e.g., roads and neighborhoods, respectively), however, the model must recognize that complete coverage of an area i may not be possible with only one facility, but rather will require multiple facilities in some cases. The index l therefore represents cases of multiple coverage when l is greater than one. As an example, if $l = 2$ the set Ω_{i2} accounts for those facilities capable of covering area i at least $\delta_2 = 60\%$, but less than 100%. If $\delta_2 = 60\%$, then this set contains all those potential facilities j that cover at least 60% of area i (but less than 100%). As a result, α_2 equal to two in constraint (33) would make sense, as this means that one would need at least two facilities covering area i at least 60% for it to actually be covered. The model therefore incorporates geographic siting decisions as well as tracks which areas are covered by what located facilities, where coverage of an area could be by a single facility, two facilities, three facilities, etc., up to L facilities. The ability both to spatially reference as well derive spatial relationships is critical for applying this coverage model. GIS facilitates both, enabling location models to be structured, as discussed in Murray (2010).

LAND USE PLANNING MODELS

A fundamental land use planning problem involves selecting land to acquire for some purpose. There are many contexts where land acquisition is necessary, such as waste disposal siting, building residential subdivisions, parks and recreation area designation, natural resource management, and establishing nature reserves to protect endangered species. In land acquisition there are many criteria that are important to consider. Among the most critical are often cost and suitability, but shape, area and proximity, among others, can be influential factors in what land should be acquired. The idea is to select land for use, development or preservation, taking into account budgetary and quality issues in the process.

There has been a considerable amount of research devoted to the development and application of a broad range of land acquisition models (see Thompson et al. 1973, Wright et al. 1983, Snyder et al. 1999, Williams 2002, Fischer and Church 2003, Zhang and Wright 2004, Shirabe 2005, Downs et al. 2008). While it is common in the literature to see references to a so called "land acquisition model," there is no one such model. Rather there are a variety of land acquisition models, just as there are numerous location models and many spatial optimization models. Wright et al. (1983) relied on perimeter to define shape in their developed mathematical model. The rationale behind this is that minimizing perimeter necessarily encourages compactness (a circle is the most compact spatial object) and promotes contiguity, or an interconnectivity between acquired land. Others have relied on compactness and perimeter minimization in developed land use planning models, such as Nalle et al. (2002), Fischer and Church (2003), Onal and Briers (2003).

Given that a primary approach for addressing shape is through the use of perimeter, we now formulate a land use planning model based on the work of Wright et al. (1983) that was detailed in Wu and Murray (2007) as well as Church and Murray (2009). Consider the following notation:

i = index of land parcels;

b_i = benefit of acquiring land parcel i;

c_i = cost of acquiring land parcel i;

Φ_i = set of parcels that are adjacent to parcel i;

p_{ij} = edge length between adjacent parcels i and j;

Ψ = set of parcels on region boundary;

ω = importance weight for perimeter minimization;

μ = acquisition budget;

$$x_i = \begin{cases} 1 & \text{if parcel } i \text{ is acquired for a particular land use} \\ 0 & \text{otherwise} \end{cases}$$

$$e_{ij}^+ = \begin{cases} 1 & \text{if } x_i = 1 \text{ and } x_j = 0 \\ 0 & \text{otherwise} \end{cases}$$

$$e_{ij}^- = \begin{cases} 1 & \text{if } x_i = 0 \text{ and } x_j = 1 \\ 0 & \text{otherwise} \end{cases}$$

$$\text{Maximize} (1 - \omega) \sum_i b_i x_i$$

$$- \omega \left[\sum_i \sum_{j \in \Phi_i} p_{ij} \left(e_{ij}^+ + e_{ij}^- \right) + \sum_{i \in \Psi} p_{ii} x_i \right] \quad (36)$$

Subject to

$$\sum_i c_i x_i \leq \mu \quad (37)$$

$$x_i - x_j - e_{ij}^+ + e_{ij}^- = 0 \; \forall i, j \in \Phi_i \quad (38)$$

$$x_i = \{0, 1\} \; \forall i \quad (39)$$

$$e_{ij}^+, e_{ij}^- = \{0, 1\} \; \forall i, j \in \Phi_i \quad (40)$$

The objective, (36), optimizes the weighted combination of benefit and shape. Specifically, the first component represents the maximization of total benefit and the second component minimizes total perimeter in an attempt to encourage compactness and contiguity associated with acquired land. Constraint (38) limits total acquired land by the project budget. Constraints (39) track perimeter resulting from land configuration by accounting for instances where one of two neighboring parcels is selected. Constraints (40) impose integer restrictions on decision variables.

The land use planning model explicitly tracks external edges to account for perimeter. If two neighboring parcels, i and j, are both selected, then $x_i = x_j = 1$. This forces $e_{ij}^+ = e_{ij}^- = 0$ in constraint (39) given the objective component of minimizing external edge in (36). This is what should happen in this case because both parcels are selected and there is no external edge that results between these two parcels. A similar situation occurs when neither are selected. When an external edge is produced (only one of the two neighbors is selected), then the edge must be accounted for. This happens in the model in constraints (39) combined with the minimization objective for total resulting external perimeter. For region boundary parcels, perimeter edge is produced and is accounted for through $\sum_i p_{ii} x_i$.

As with the location model, one facet of the spatial nature of the land use model is that parcels with a specific geographic reference are to be selected. Beyond this, the spatial relationship between neighboring parcels is essential. In this case, the spatial relationship has to do with adjacent parcels, and tracking the resulting perimeter that results from parcel selection. Again, GIS facilitates both aspects of structuring space mathematically.

Conclusion

Spatial analysis techniques have become increasingly accessible to non-specialists, because they have become incorporated into many user friendly software implementations. These include traditional desktop GIS, but also statistical packages and special-purpose software tools. The presence of spatial analytical techniques ranges from software for handheld devices to high performance computing and includes both commercial as well as open source solutions. One particularly exciting recent development is the move towards a cyberinfrastructure for spatial analysis, or cyberGIS (Wang and Armstrong 2009, Wang 2010) which should provide the basis for extensive collaboration across disciplines, using state of the art tools that take into account location, spatial proximity and relationships.

In this chapter, we have attempted to provide a sense of the way in which explicitly accounting for space extends a number of methods. This ranged from data exploration and visualization to regression and optimization. The examples provided are only a small subset of the range of techniques encompassed under the term *spatial analysis*. The references included (as well as references contained in them) should provide an initial guide to the wide range of application of these techniques and their methodological foundations.

Author Note

1. Luc Anselin is Regents' Professor and Walter Isard Chair in the School of Geographical Sciences and Urban Planning and Director of the GeoDa Center for Geospatial Analysis and Computation, Arizona State, Universityluc.anselin@asu.edu

2. Alan T. Murray is Professor in the School of Geographical Sciences and Urban Planning and the GeoDa Center for Geospatial Analysis and Computation, Arizona State University, atmurray@asu.edu

3. Sergio J. Rey is Professor in the School of Geographical Sciences and Urban Planning and the GeoDa Center for Geospatial Analysis and Computation, Arizona State University, srey@asu.edu

References

Abler, R. (1987). The National Science Foundation National Center for Geographic Information and Analysis. *International Journal of Geographical Information Systems*, 1:303–326.

Ando, A., Camm, J., Polasky, S., and Solow, A. (1998). Species distributions, land values, and efficient conservation. *Science*, 279:2126–2168.

Andrienko, N. and Andrienko, G. (2006). *Exploratory Analysis of Spatial and Temporal Data: A Systematic Approach*. Springer Verlag, Heidelberg.

Anselin, L. (1988). *Spatial Econometrics: Methods and Models*. Kluwer Academic Publishers, Dordrecht.

Anselin, L. (1990). Spatial dependence and spatial structural instability in applied regression analysis. *Journal of Regional Science*, 30:185–207.

Anselin, L. (1995). Local indicators of spatial association–LISA. *Geographical Analysis*, 27:93–115.

Anselin, L. (1996). The Moran scatterplot as an ESDA tool to assess local instability in spatial association. In Fischer, M., Scholten, H., and Unwin, D., editors, *Spatial Analytical Perspectives on GIS in Environmental and Socio-Economic Sciences*, pages 111–125. Taylor and Francis, London.

Anselin, L. (1999). Interactive techniques and exploratory spatial data analysis. In Longley, P. A., Goodchild, M. F., Maguire, D. J., and Rhind, D. W., editors, *Geographical Information Systems: Principles, Techniques, Management and Applications*, pages 251–264. John Wiley, New York, NY.

Anselin, L. (2001). Spatial econometrics. In Baltagi, B., editor, *A Companion to Theoretical Econometrics*, pages 310–330. Blackwell, Oxford.

Anselin, L. (2003). Spatial externalities, spatial multipliers and spatial econometrics. *International Regional Science Review*, 26:153–166.

Anselin, L. (2006). Spatial econometrics. In Mills, T. and Patterson, K., editors, *Palgrave Handbook of Econometrics: Volume 1, Econometric Theory*, pages 901–969. Palgrave Macmillan, Basingstoke.

Anselin, L. (2010). Thirty years of spatial econometrics. *Papers in Regional Science*, 89:2–25.

Anselin, L. and Bera, A. (1998). Spatial dependence in linear regression models with an introduction to spatial econometrics. In Ullah, A. and Giles, D. E., editors, *Handbook of Applied Economic Statistics*, pages 237–289. Marcel Dekker, New York, NY.

Anselin, L. and Getis, A. (1992). Spatial statistical analysis and geographic information systems. *The Annals of Regional Science*, 26:19–33.

Anselin, L., Le Gallo, J., and Jayet, H. (2008). Spatial panel econometrics. In Matyas, L. and Sevestre, P., editors, *The Econometrics of Panel Data, Fundamentals and Recent Developments in Theory and Practice (3rd Edition)*, pages 627–662. Springer-Verlag, Berlin.

Anselin, L. and Rey, S. J. (2010). *Perspectives on Spatial Analysis*. Springer-Verlag, Heidelberg.

Anselin, L., Syabri, I., and Kho, Y. (2006). GeoDa, an introduction to spatial data analysis. *Geographical Analysis*, 38:5–22.

Arbia, G. (2006). *Spatial Econometrics: Statistical Foundations and Applications to Regional Convergence*. Springer-Verlag, Berlin.

Assunçao, R. M. (2003). Space varying coefficient models for small area data. *Environmetrics*, 14:453–473.

Bailey, T. C. and Gatrell, A. C. (1995). *Interactive Spatial Data Analysis*. John Wiley and Sons, New York, NY.

Baltagi, B. H. (2001). *Econometric Analysis of Panel Data (Second Edition)*. John Wiley & Sons, Chichester.

Baltagi, B. H., Egger, P., and Pfaffermayr, M. (2006). A generalized spatial panel data model with random effects. Working paper, Syracuse University, Syracuse, NY.

Baltagi, B. H., Song, S. H., and Koh, W. (2003). Testing panel data regression models with spatial error correlation. *Journal of Econometrics*, 117:123–150.

Banerjee, S., Carlin, B. P., and Gelfand, A. E. (2004). *Hierarchical Modeling and Analysis for Spatial Data*. Chapman & Hall/CRC, Boca Raton.

Basile, R. and Gress, B. (2005). Semi-parametric spatial auto-covariance models of regional growth in europe. *Région et Développement*, 21:93–118.

Beron, K. J. and Vijverberg, W. P. (2004). Probit in a spatial context: a Monte Carlo analysis. In Anselin, L., Florax, R. J., and Rey, S. J., editors, *Advances in Spatial Econometrics*, pages 169–195. Springer-Verlag, Heidelberg.

Besag, J. (1974). Spatial interaction and the statistical analysis of lattice systems. *Journal of the Royal Statistical Society B*, 36:192–225.

Best, N. G., Arnold, R. A., Thomas, A., Waller, L. A., and Conlon, E. M. (1999). Bayesian models for spatially correlated disease and exposure data. In Bernardo, J., Berger, J., Dawid, A., and Smith, F., editors, *Bayesian Statistics 6*, pages 131–156. Oxford University Press, New York, NY.

Casetti, E. (1972). Generating models by the expansion method: Applications to geographical research. *Geographical Analysis*, 4:81–91.

Casetti, E. (1997). The expansion method, mathematical modeling, and spatial econometrics. *International Regional Science Review*, 20:9–33.

Chilès, J.-P. and Delfiner, P. (1999). *Geostatistics, Modeling Spatial Uncertainty*. John Wiley & Sons, New York, NY.

Church, R. I. and Murray, A. T. (2009). *Business Site Selection, Location Analysis and GIS*. John Wiley, New York, NY.

Cliff, A. and Ord, J. K. (1981). *Spatial Processes: Models and Applications*. Pion, London.

Cressie, N. (1991). *Statistics for Spatial Data*. Wiley, New York, NY.

de Castro, M. C. and Singer, B. H. (2006). Controlling the false discovery rate: A new application to account for multiple and dependent tests in local statistics of spatial association. *Geographical Analysis*, 38:180–208.

de Smith, M. J., Goodchild, M. F., and Longley, P. A. (2007). *Geospatial Analysis. A Comprehensive Guide to Principles, Techniques and Software Tools (2nd Edition)*. Matador, Leicester.

Diggle, P. J. (2003). *Statistical Analysis of Point Patterns*. Arnold, New York, NY.

Downs, J., Gates, R., and Murray, A. (2008). Estimating carrying capacity for sandhill cranes using habitat suitability and spatial optimization models. *Ecological Modelling*, 214:284–292.

Drezner, Z. and Hamacher, H. (2002). *Facility Location: Applications and Theory*. Springer, Berlin.

Edmonds, J. (1962). Covers and packings in a family of sets. *Bulletin of the American Mathematical Society*, 68:494–499.

Elhorst, J. P. (2003). Specification and estimation of spatial panel data models. *International Regional Science Review*, 26:244–268.

Fischer, D. and Church, R. L. (2003). Clustering and compactness in reserve site selection: an extension of the biodiversity management and selection model. *Forest Science*, 49:555–565.

Fischer, M. M. and Getis, A. (1997). *Recent Developments in Spatial Analysis*. Springer-Verlag, Berlin.

Fischer, M. M. and Getis, A. (2010). *Handbook of Applied Spatial Analysis. Software Tools, Methods and Applications*. Springer-Verlag, Heidelberg.

Fleming, M. (2004). Techniques for estimating spatially dependent discrete choice models. In Anselin, L., Florax, R. J., and Rey, S. J., editors, *Advances in Spatial Econometrics*, pages 145–168. Springer-Verlag, Heidelberg.

Fortin, M.-J. and Dale, M. (2005). *Spatial Analysis: A Guide for Ecologists*. Cambridge University Press, Cambridge.

Fotheringham, A. S., Brundson, C., and Charlton, M. (1998). Geographically weighted regression: A natural evolution of the expansion method for spatial data analysis. *Environment and Planning A*, 30:1905–1927.

Fotheringham, A. S., Brunsdon, C., and Charlton, M. (2002). *Geographically Weighted Regression*. John Wiley, Chichester.

Fotheringham, A. S. and Rogerson, P. (1994). *Spatial Analysis and GIS*. Taylor and Francis, London.

Fotheringham, A. S. and Rogerson, P. (2009). *The SAGE Handbook of Spatial Analysis*. Sage Publications, London.

Gelfand, A. E., Kim, H.-J., Sirmans, C., and Banerjee, S. (2003). Spatial modeling with spatially varying coefficient processes. *Journal of the American Statistical Association*, 98:387–396.

Geman, S. and Geman, D. (1984). Stochastic relaxation, Gibbs distributions, and the Bayesian restoration of images. *IEEE Transactions on Pattern Analysis and Machine Intelligence*, 6:721–741.

Gilks, W., Richardson, S., and Spiegelhalter, D. (1996). *Markov Chain Monte Carlo in Practice*. Chapman and Hall, London.

Goodchild, M. F. (1987). A spatial analytical perspective on geographical information systems. *International Journal of Geographical Information Systems*, 1:31–45.

Goodchild, M. F. (1992). Geographical information science. *International Journal of Geographical Information Systems*, 6:31–45.

Goodchild, M. F. (2010). Whose hand on the tiller? revisiting "spatial statistical analysis and GIS". In Anselin, L. and Rey, S. J., editors, *Perspectives on Spatial Analysis*, pages 49–59. Springer-Verlag, Heidelberg.

Goodchild, M. F., Anselin, L., Appelbaum, R., and Harthorn, B. (2000). Toward spatially integrated social science. *International Regional Science Review*, 23:139–159.

Goodchild, M. F., Haining, R. P., Wise, S., and and others (1992). Integrating GIS and spatial analysis – problems and possibilities. *International Journal of Geographical Information Systems*, 1:407–423.

Goodchild, M. F. and Longley, P. (1999). The future of GIS and spatial analysis. In Longley, P., Goodchild, M. F., Maguire, D. J., and Rhind, D. W., editors, *Geographical Information Systems: Principles, Techniques, Applications and Management*, pages 567–580. Wiley, New York, NY.

Griffith, D. A. (1988). *Advanced Spatial Statistics*. Kluwer, Dordrecht.

Haining, R. (1990). *Spatial Data Analysis in the Social and Environmental Sciences*. Cambridge University Press, Cambridge.

Haining, R. (2003). *Spatial Data Analysis: Theory and Practice*. Cambridge University Press, Cambridge.

Haining, R., Wise, S., and Ma, J. (1998). Exploratory spatial data analysis. *Journal of the Royal Statistical Society: Series D (The Statistician)*, 47:457–469.

Harris, R., Sleight, P., and Webber, R. (2005). *Geodemographics, GIS and Neighborhood Targeting*. John Wiley & Sons Inc, New York, NY.

Hastie, T. and Tibshirani, R. (1993). Varying-coefficient models. *Journal of the Royal Statistical Society B*, 55:757–796.

Journel, A. and Huijbregts, C. (1978). *Mining Geostatistics*. Academic Press, London.

Kapoor, M., Kelejian, H. H., and Prucha, I. (2007). Panel data models with spatially correlated error components. *Journal of Econometrics*, 140:97–130.

Kelejian, H. H. and Prucha, I. (2001). On the asymptotic distribution of the Moran I test statistic with applications. *Journal of Econometrics*, 104:219–257.

Lawson, A. and Denison, D. (2002). *Spatial Cluster Modelling*. CRC Press, Boca Raton, FL.

Lawson, A. B. (2009). *Bayesian Disease Mapping, Hierarchical Modeling in Spatial Epidemiology*. CRC Press, Boca Raton, FL.

Lee, L.-F. and Yu, J. (2010). Some recent developments in spatial panel data models. *Regional Science and Urban Economics*, 40:255–271.

LeSage, J. P. (1997). Bayesian estimation of spatial autoregressive models. *International Regional Science Review*, 20:113–129.

LeSage, J. P. (2000). Bayesian estimation of limited dependent variable spatial autoregressive models. *Geographical Analysis*, 32:19–35.

LeSage, J. P. and Pace, R. K. (2009). *Introduction to Spatial Econometrics*. CRC Press, Boca Raton, FL.

Miller, R. E. (2000). *Optimization*. Wiley, New York, NY.

Mirchandani, P. and Francis, R. (1990). *Discrete Location Theory*. Wiley, New York, NY.

Moran, P. A. P. (1948). The interpretation of statistical maps. *Biometrika*, 35:255–260.

Moran, P. A. P. (1950). Notes on continuous stochastic phenomena. *Biometrika*, 37:17–23.

Murray, A. T. (2005). Geography in coverage modeling: exploiting spatial structure to address complementary partial service of areas. *Annals of the Association of American Geographers*, 95:761–772.

Murray, A. T. (2007). Optimization. In Kemp, K. K., editor, *Encyclopedia of Geographic Information Science*, pages 333–334. Sage, Thousand Oaks, CA.

Murray, A. T. (2010). Advances in location modeling: GIS linkages and contributions. *Journal of Geographical Systems*, 12:335–354.

Murray, A. T. and Estivill-Castro, V. (1998). Cluster discovery techniques for exploratory spatial data analysis. *International Journal of Geographical Information Science*, 12:431–443.

Murray, A. T., Grubesic, T. H., Mack, E. A., Wei, R., Rey, S. J., Anselin, L., and Griffin, M. (2012). Convicted sex offender residential movements. In Leitner, M., editor, *Crime Modeling and Mapping Using Geospatial Technologies*. New York: Springer.

Murray, A. T., Tong, D., and Kim, K. (2010). Enhancing classic coverage location models. *International Regional Science Review*, 33:115–133.

Nalle, D. J., Arthur, J. L., and Sessions, J. (2002). Designing compact and contiguous reserve networks with a hybrid heuristic algorithm. *Forest Science*, 48:59–68.

Onal, H. and Briers, R. A. (2003). Selection of a minimum-boundary reserve network using integer programming. *Proceedings of the Royal Society London B*, 270:1487–1491.

Ord, J. K. (1975). Estimation methods for models of spatial interaction. *Journal of the American Statistical Association*, 70:120–126.

Ord, J. K. and Getis, A. (1995). Local spatial autocorrelation statistics: distributional issues and an application. *Geographical Analysis*, 27:286–306.

O'Sullivan, D. and Unwin, D. (2003). *Geographic Information Analysis*. John Wiley & Sons Inc, Chichester.

Paelinck, J. and Klaassen, L. (1979). *Spatial Econometrics*. Saxon House, Farnborough.

Pfeiffer, D. U., Robinson, T. P., Stevenson, M., Stevens, K. B., Rogers, D. J., and Clemens, A. C. A. (2008). *Spatial Analysis in Epidemiology*. Oxford University Press, Oxford.

Pinkse, J. and Slade, M. E. (1998). Contracting in space: An application of spatial statistics to discrete-choice models. *Journal of Econometrics*, 85:125–154.

Pinkse, J. and Slade, M. E. (2010). The future of spatial econometrics. *Journal of Regional Science*, 50:103–117.

Pinkse, J., Slade, M. E., and Brett, C. (2002). Spatial price competition: A semiparametric approach. *Econometrica*, 70:1111–1153.

Rey, S. J. (2001). Spatial empirics for economic growth and convergence. *Geographical Analysis*, 33:195–214.

Rey, S. J. and Anselin, L. (2007). PySAL: A Python library of spatial analytical methods. *The Review of Regional Studies*, 37:5–27.

Rey, S. J. and Janikas, M. V. (2006). STARS: Space-Time Analysis of Regional Systems. *Geographical Analysis*, 38:67–86.

Rey, S. J. and Le Gallo, J. (2009). Spatial analysis of economic convergence. In Patternson, K. and Mills, T. C., editors, *Palgrave Handbook of Econometrics*, pages 1251–1290. Palgrave, Basingstoke.

Ripley, B. D. (1981). *Spatial Statistics*. Wiley, New York, NY.

Rossi, R., Mulla, D., Journel, A., and Franz, E. (1992). Geostatistical tools for modeling and interpreting ecological spatial dependence. *Ecological Monographs*, 62:277–314.

Schabenberger, O. and Gotway, C. A. (2005). *Statistical Methods for Spatial Data Analysis*. Chapman & Hall/CRC, Boca Raton, FL.

Shirabe, T. (2005). A model of contiguity for spatial unit allocation. *Geographical Analysis*, 37:2–16.

Snyder, S., Tyrrell, L., and Haight, R. (1999). An optimization approach to selecting research natural areas in National Forests. *Forest Science*, 45:458–469.

Thompson, E., Halterman, B., Lyon, T., and Miller, R. (1973). Integrating timber and wildlife management planning. *Forestry Chronicle*, 47:247–250.

Tobler, W. R. (1970). A computer movie simulating urban growth in the Detroit region. *Economic Geography*, 46:234–240.

Toregas, C., Swain, R., ReVelle, C., and Bergman, L. (1971). The location of emergency service facilities. *Operations Research*, 19:1363–1373.

Tukey, J. (1977). *Exploratory Data Analysis*. Addison-Wesley, New York, NY.

Unwin, A. and Unwin, D. (1998). Exploratory spatial data analysis with local statistics. *The Statistician*, 47:415–421.

Waller, L., Zhu, L., Gotway, C., Gorman, D., and Gruenewald, P. (2007). Quantifying geographic variations in associations between alcohol distribution and violence: A comparison of geographically weighted regression and spatially varying coefficient models. *Stochastic Environmental Research and Risk Assessment*, 21:573–588.

Waller, L. A. and Gotway, C. A. (2004). *Applied Spatial Statistics for Public Health Data*. John Wiley, Hoboken, NJ.

Wang, S. (2010). A cyberGIS framework for the synthesis of cyberinfrastructure, GIS, and spatial analysis. *Annals of the Association of American Geographers*, 100:535–557.

Wang, S. and Armstrong, M. P. (2009). A theoretical approach to the use of cyberinfrastructure in geographical analysis. *International Journal of Geographical Information Science*, 23:169–193.

Weber, A. (1909). *Urber den Standort der Industrien(English translation C.J. Friedrich, 1929, Theory of the Location of Industries*. Chicago: University of Chicago Press. Tubingen.

Whittle, P. (1954). On stationary processes in the plane. *Biometrika*, 41:434–449.

Williams, J. (2002). A zero-one programming model for contiguous land acquisition. *Geographical Analysis*, 34:330–349.

Wolpert, R. L. and Ickstadt, K. (1998). Poisson/Gamma random field models for spatial statistics. *Biometrika*, 85:251–267.

Wright, J., ReVelle, C., and Cohon, J. (1983). A multiobjective integer programming model for the land acquisition problem. *Regional Science and Urban Economics*, 13:31–53.

Wu, X. and Murray, A. T. (2007). Spatial contiguity optimization in land acquisition. *Journal of Land Use Science*, 2:243–256.

Zhang, Y. and Wright, J. (2004). Global optimization of combined region aggregation and leveling model. *Journal of Computing in Civil Engineering*, 18:154–161.

CHAPTER 9

Analysis of Imaging Data

Larry R. Price

Abstract

A brief history of imaging neuroscience is presented followed by an introduction to data acquisition using positron emission tomography (PET) and functional magnetic resonance imaging (fMRI). Next, statistical parametric mapping is introduced in conjunction with random field theory as being fundamental to identifying sites of neural activation. The general linear model is discussed as being foundational for all imaging analyses. Finally, methods for studying functional and effective connectivity such as eigenimage analysis, partial least squares, multivariate autoregressive models, structural equation models, and dynamic causal models are reviewed in light of deterministic and stochastic analytic approaches.

Key Words: Functional magnetic resonance imaging (fMRI), positron emission tomography, SPM, Random Field Theory (RFT), Bayesian statistical inference (BSI), multivariate autoregressive models (MAR), multilevel models, structural equation modeling, activation likelihood meta-analysis, general linear model (GLM).

Introduction

Imaging neuroscience has a short history but has evolved rapidly over the past quarter-century. At present, analytic methods in imaging neuroscience consist of a comprehensive epistemological system with the primary goal being the modeling of distributed brain responses. Early analytic approaches in imaging research focused on applying traditional linear models and inferential hypothesis testing (i.e., classical Fisherian statistical methods) of observed voxel-level and/or interregional effects within the brain architecture. For example, researchers were often interested differences between normal and diseased patients specific to the pattern of neural activity modeled via correlations between several areas or regions of the brain. Currently, analytic approaches are exemplified by complex and diverse models of how measurements of evoked neuronal responses are caused. Modeling approaches are classified as either deterministic with simple random components or fully stochastic (i.e., random). In the deterministic approach with simple random effects, observations are composed of a deterministic component plus a random error component attributable to measurement or sampling fluctuations specific to the response or input variable. Stochastic or random models are constructed from fundamental random events to explain dynamic phenomena contemporaneously or temporally. Once a causal model positing how evoked responses occur at a fundamental physiologic level is established (i.e., at level one), such a model can be extended to a second level (e.g., a hierarchical modeling approach) involving relationships between regions in the brain. Today, the focus of imaging analysis is on specifying, fitting, and refining powerful models based on distributed brain responses evolving from the voxel level (where neuronal activity originates) to the

1 Voxel = ~ 60,000 brain cells
3mm
6mm
3mm

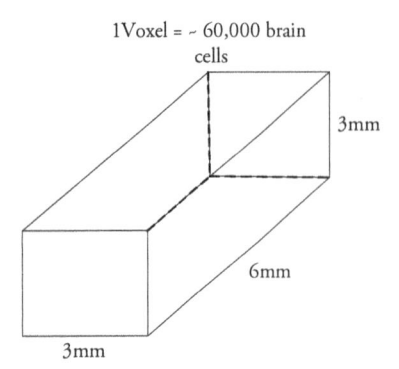

Figure 9.1 Brain neural activation sites by plane and voxel representation.

level of interconnectivity among clusters of voxels represented as regions of activation.

A Brief History of Imaging Methods and Analyses

Initially, research in imaging neuroscience focused on neural activation studies involving changes in regional brain states. For example, in positron emission tomography (PET) imaging, radioactive tracer materials of short half-life and PET are used in a scanning session (Herscovitch, 1983). In PET, neural activation within the brain is measured using radioactively labeled material such as oxygen, fluorine, carbon, and nitrogen human body, either by injection or inhalation, it migrates to areas of the brain actively in use. Upon breakdown, the radioactive material emits a neutron and positron. When a positron collides with an electron, both are destroyed and two γ rays are emitted. Image acquisition proceeds in PET by capturing images of regional brain activity based on neural activation caused by γ ray emission. Next, anatomic regions of interest (ROIs) are constructed manually using anywhere from hundreds to thousands of voxels exhibiting response to stimulus (i.e., 1 voxel is usually a 3mm × 3mm × 6mm volumetric cube of brain anatomy consisting of approximately 60,000 cells; Fig. 9.1). Initial mapping of neural activation within the brain (i.e., activation maps) occurred by Lauter et al. (1985) and Fox et al. (1986).

Early Analytic Approaches Based on the General Linear Model

One shortcoming of the early ROI-constructed approach was the introduction of a substantial degree of imprecision in anatomic validity. Inaccuracies in anatomic validity and the problem of the inseparability of global versus region-specific responses or activations yielded a less-than-optimal analytic approach. Moreover, the ROI analytic approach was limiting because the method was analogous to a fixed-effect or random effects linear model using multivariate analysis of variance (MANOVA) or multivariate analysis of covariance (MANCOVA) corrected for non-sphericity (i.e., correlated errors). In these models, the mean levels of activation within a region of the brain served as dependent measures and the experimental treatment condition served as either a random or fixed effect.

The use of mean regional activity in imaging analyses was eventually viewed as limiting because modeling proceeded from the regional level (where large clusters of voxels displayed activation) downward to the voxel level where neuronal activation originates. Importantly, this downward modeling approach included restrictive assumptions and backward conceptualization. Subsequently, interest in developing a more sophisticated approach originating at the level of the individual voxel (Fig. 9.1) emerged. Neuroscientists quickly realized that by basing analyses at the point where neural activity originated, a forward framework for modeling activation would be possible.

A logical next step was for neuroscientists to develop an approach that allowed for the discrimination between global brain activation effects versus region-specific areas of the brain. An early approach taken was to use a measure of global effect as a covariate in an ANCOVA model, thereby providing a way to separate global versus regional effects at the level of individual voxels (Friston, 2007). However, a problem quickly identified by researchers was that measured hemodynamic responses in one part of the brain were often not the same as in other parts of the brain—"even if the activation stimulus was experimentally controlled to be exactly the same" (Friston, 2007, p. 4). In statistical terms, this finding verified that modeling a region by condition interaction using the ANCOVA approach was ineffective for isolating region specific effects.

Once the need for a voxel-driven modeling approach arose, analytic strategies quickly evolved in diversity and complexity. For example, hierarchical linear and nonlinear models were introduced to improve the accuracy in modeling the variability of neural activation at each level (i.e., at the voxel level and regional level). Building on the hierarchical modeling approach, Bayesian statistical inference was introduced, thereby providing a way to use activation information from one level as hyperparameters (i.e., prior information) to inform the analysis at other levels (Friston & Penny, 2007; Penny & Henson, 2007; Penny et al., 2005). The hierarchical approach provided a substantial gain in precision and flexibility by allowing sites of brain activation to emerge at any given area within the brain. The voxel-driven approach has become synonymous with *statistical parametric mapping* (SPM), a term that subsumes a broad class of imaging modeling and analytic approaches. Plainly speaking, SPM involves specifying continuous statistical processes to test hypotheses about regionally specific effects (Friston, 2007, p. 14; Friston, 1991).

Statistical Parametric Mapping
Positron Emission Tomography and Electroencephalography

The impetus for using statistical parametric mapping as a global phrase was that it provided key terms to cover analytic innovations within imaging neuroscience. As Friston (2007, p. 10) has noted, "SPM acknowledged significance probability mapping work conducted by scientists within the imaging (i.e., PET and fMRI) and electroencephalography (EEG) communities." The focus of significance mapping was to develop maps of probability values (e.g., the likelihood of observing neural activity in specific brain regions) that would formalize spatiotemporal (i.e., existing in space and time) organization arising from evoked electrophysiological responses (Duffy et al., 1981). The probability values derived from significance mapping provided a formal link from evoked neural responses to probability distribution theory. The number and quality of image types acquired using PET technology are varied and include regional cerebral blood flow, oxygen extraction fraction, and oxygen metabolism. Because scan trials in PET are independent of one another, errors within this model may be modeled as stationary (i.e., constant) or follow an autoregressive or correlated structure for different regions of the brain. Finally, one particular convenience of statistical parametric maps is the assumption that the errors of measurement are normally distributed (i.e., a Gaussian process). The Gaussian error model in SPM is a byproduct of image reconstruction, post-processing, smoothing, and experimental design.

Functional Magnetic Resonance Imaging

The introduction of *fMRI* into imaging neuroscience in the last decade of the twentieth century provided the impetus for a new and innovative era. In *fMRI*, hundreds of scans are acquired within a single session, whereas in PET, only a few scans (i.e., one to several) are acquired within a session. Strictly speaking, PET scans are considered to be statistically independent of one another. Functional MRI analyses involve modeling evoked hemodynamic responses in time series consisting of hundreds of repeated scans over a very short time period. Statistically, the time series response vector is realized as a multivariate autoregressive (MAR) model of evoked potential events in combination with a causal model representing hemodynamic response functions (Fig. 9.2). In Figure 9.2, the mechanism of acquisition blood oxygen level dependent measurements (i.e., BOLD) are derived from rCBF and are indirect measures of neural activity. Multivariate time series models allow for variation of hemodynamic response functions within and between brain regions, thereby providing a framework for modeling variability by stimulus or condition, voxel-level, and subject-level effects in a unified analysis. The hemodynamic response occurs by the process of an increased demand for oxygen and the local response to an increase in blood flow to regions of increased neural activity.

A challenge in early *fMRI* work focused on the problem of correlated errors caused by nonindependent repeated *fMRI* scans during image acquisition. The initial solution involved constraining the error structure to a known error covariance structure. Examples of correlated error structures used in fMRI analytic models include stationary or non-stationary (e.g., the error structure changes over the image acquisitions) autoregressive-1 or autoregressive-2 (e.g., the data depend only on the most recent measurement or on the second most recent measurement) covariance structures. Today more rigorous options are available for modeling the error covariance structure in *fMRI* analyses depending on the type of data acquisition and research questions under investigation.

Spatial Normalization and Topological Inference

The process of spatial normalization is defined as aligning brain scan images onto a common anatomic or stereotactic space (Fox et al., 2005) so that meaningful comparisons are able to be made. Spatial normalization is required to provide a common or

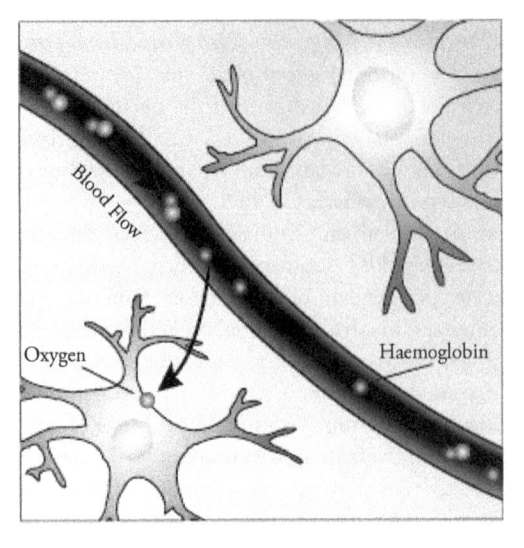

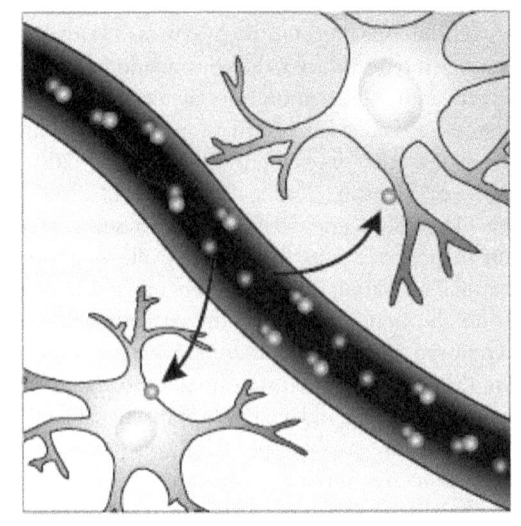

Resting   Activated

Figure 9.2 Origin of the Blood Oxygenation Level Dependent (BOLD) response. Note: Hemoglobin is diamagnetic when oxygenated but paramagnetic when deoxygenated. This difference in magnetic properties leads to small differences in the MR signal of blood depending on the degree of oxygenation. Because blood oxygenation varies according to the levels of neural activity, these differences can be used to detect brain activity. This form of MRI is known as blood oxygenation level dependent (BOLD) imaging. Courtesy of Dr. Stuart Clare, University of Oxford FMRIB Centre, www.fmrib.ox.ac.uk.

universal anatomic metric prior to analyses directed at answering research questions. Fox et al. (1988) initially pioneered a method of spatial normalization that used subtraction or difference maps based on X-rays of the human skull. Recently, Ashburner and Friston (2007) have extended original template- and model-based normalization methods by developing templates that produce subject-specific images. The work of Ashburner and Fristion is an important advance given the wide variation in human brains.

Topology, as a branch of mathematics, is the study of qualitative properties of certain objects that are invariant under certain kind of transformations. The term *qualitative* takes on meaning within brain imaging because the geometric problems specific to neuroscience are independent of the exact shape of the objects involved. Topological spaces show up naturally in brain scans where the goal is to predict the probabilistic behavior of topological shapes within maps representing the three-dimensional architecture of the brain.

Although topological methods provide the foundation for a coherent analytic approach, one problem identified early in using the method was controlling Type I error rate (i.e., false–positive activations) for region-specific effects within certain areas of the brain. For example, the use of unadjusted voxel-based threshold measurements in a large number of statistical tests produced unacceptable Type I error rates. Ultimately, the challenge focused on how to statistically apply contrasts (e.g., traditional Scheffe contrasts or Bonferonni adjustments) between comparisons of unique voxels exhibiting statistically significant versus nonsignificant activation. Critically, unadjusted tests of voxel threshold activations did not account for dependency among neighboring voxels. Random Field Theory (RFT) provided an elegant solution to the problem (Alder & Taylor, 2007; Worsley 2007).

Random Field Theory is the study of random functions defined over a particular geometric or Euclidean space (Alder & Taylor, 2007). Random Field Theory offers a wide array of analytic possibilities for research applications in neuroimaging. Specifically, RFT provides a modeling framework of stochastic (random) processes where problems of continuous three-dimensional image fields are able to be accurately modeled with an optimal level of statistical sensitivity (i.e., control of Type I and Type II error). To understand a random field, consider the dimensional characteristics of a smooth continuous medium such as the ocean's surface. The ocean's surface is visualized as three-dimensional, with two of the points representing the X- and Y-axes in two planes or dimensions (e.g., wave height and length) and the third dimension representing time or movement on the *Z-axis*. Figure 9.3 depicts a random field where peaks and valleys moving in a continuous action are analogous to wave action at the ocean's surface realized as a random pattern over time.

Application of RFT in imaging research proceeds by incorporating a three-dimensional continuous surface or lattice with variable peaks and valleys in three-dimensional space (Fig. 9.3). The functions representing the surface are a stochastic (i.e., random) process defined over a geometric or Euclidean space. Thus, RFT provides a unified framework for modeling stationary and non-stationary covariance structures originating from the voxel level within classic statistical univariate probability methods. Importantly, three-dimensional structural analysis of brain functioning in continuous space and time aligns nicely with *fMRI* scanning methodology. Finally, RFT provides a powerful analytic framework for conducting contrast analyses (i.e., adjusted or corrected *p*-values) between individual RFT peaks within a region of possibly hundreds of voxels in the same anatomic area. Random Field Theory differs from the traditional Bonferonni correction approach, where comparisons are conducted at the voxel level. Because there are always many more voxels in an area of the brain than peaks, lower critical values are used to make RFT tests of significance more powerful (i.e., sensitive in relation to identification of false–positives).

Statistical Parametric Mapping—A Closer Look

Statistical parametric mapping is an analytic framework for (1) identifying regional effects in neuroimaging data, (2) detailing functional anatomy, and (3) identifying and mapping disease-related changes in the brain (Friston et al., 1991; Friston, 2007). According to Friston, the acronym SPM was selected "(a) to acknowledge significance probability mapping as a method for developing pseudo-maps of *p*-values that are in turn used to summarize the analysis of multichannel event related potentials, (b) for consistency with the nomenclature of parametric maps of physiological or physical parameters (i.e., parametric maps of regional cerebral blood flow or volume), and (c) for reference to parametric statistical methods that populate the maps" (2007, p. 15). From a general linear modeling (GLM) perspective, SPM is based on a univariate approach, also known in the neuroimaging community as a massunivariate approach (Friston, 2007, p. 15) caused by the large numbers of voxels under investigation. The univariate approach appears counterintuitive

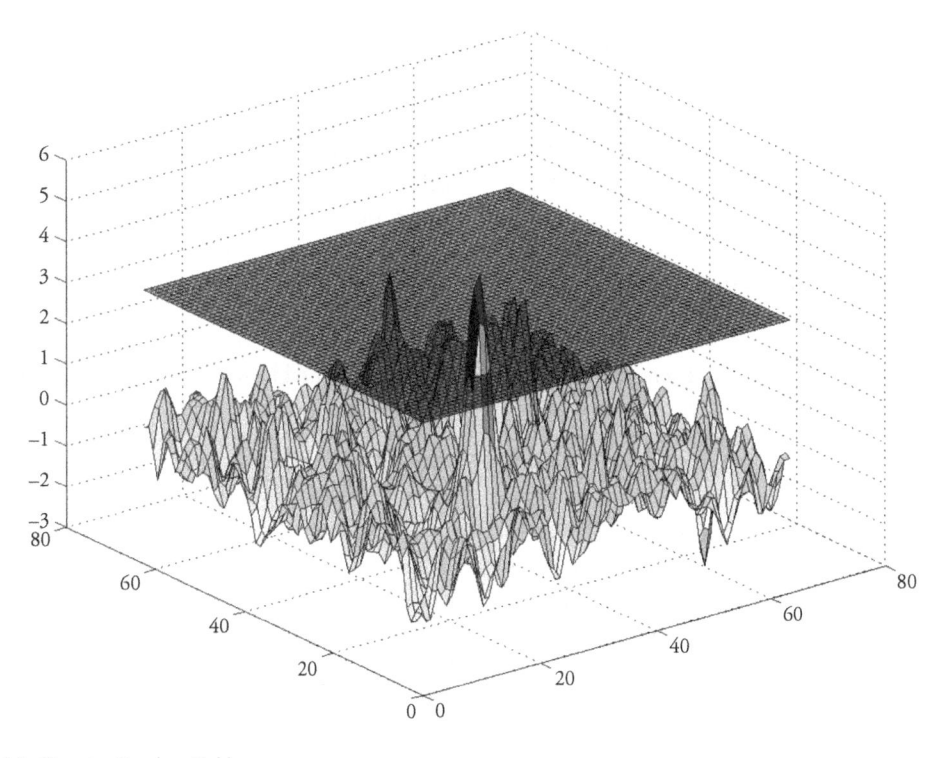

Figure 9.3 Gaussian Random Field

given the multivariate structure of the data acquired in imaging neuroscience where thousands of voxels operate interdependently. However, the measurement, quantity, and type of data acquired in neuroimaging pose unique analytic challenges, yielding traditional multivariate GLM methods less than optimal.

SPM is technically classified as a mass-univariate approach (Friston, 2007, p. 15) conducted on thousands of individual voxels, thus yielding a statistic at every voxel. Friston has argued that the univariate approach is optimal in SPM because of the intractability of the multivariate approach to isolate regionally specific effects at the level of specificity required by researchers. Also, multivariate methods require more scans than voxels—a situation that never occurs in imaging research. Further complicating the issue are spatial correlations in the data and regional shifts in the error variance structure. Because the SPM approach is voxel-driven, the analytic point of origin begins at the most fundamental level activation. Once activation sites are identified using the SPM global or mass-univariate approach, RFT is then used to conduct contrast analyses (i.e., yielding adjusted or corrected p-values) between individual peaks within or between clusters of voxels in the same anatomic area. Random Field Theory accounts or corrects for voxel size differences using resolution information. The Euler characteristic (Worsley, 2007; Alder & Taylor, 2007) is the statistic used to flag the peak or peaks above a particular height or threshold.

Figure 9.4 illustrates the steps involved in using the SPM framework from image acquisition to voxel-based corrected p-values using RFT (Penny, 2003).

Sequential Steps—Image Acquisition to Analysis

Positron emission tomography and fMRI imaging research involves forward or generative modeling strategies in that signals are introduced into anatomical space, then activation measurements reflect how such signals are produced (i.e., how neural activity propagates upward to regional brain activity). The generative modeling paradigm displayed in Figure 9.4 (Penny, 2003) requires the pre-analysis steps of (1) inversion of time series data to remove unwanted variance caused by artifacts (i.e., realignment to ensure accurate within-subject voxel location given a series of scans), and (2) transforming it into standard anatomical space (i.e., spatial normalization). Standard anatomical space templates commonly applied are attributable to Talairach and Tournoux (1988). Next, a research design matrix is created composed of a linear combination of explanatory variables, covariates, or a grouping indicator denoting a specific level of an experimental factor with a specified error component. The design matrix is then subjected to some form of GLM analysis. Random Field Theory is used to detect statistically significant activation sites displayed as the height of a peak(s) in a continuous three-dimensional topological space. Hypothesis tests of regional effects typically proceed within SPM by identifying (1) the number of activated regions accumulated as clusters derived by Euler characteristics (i.e., set-level inferences); (2) cluster-level inferences composed of a collection of voxels exhibiting significance; or (3) statistical inference based on significant effects based on non-redundant contrasts at the level of an individual voxel using contrast-based t- and F-statistics (Friston, 2007; Worsley, 2007). The next section introduces the analytic methods commonly used in the analysis of imaging data after processing.

Analytic Methods
General Linear Modeling—Foundational Issues in Neuroimaging

The GLM is foundational to all imaging analyses. This is true for neuroimaging (i.e., PET and fMRI), electroencephalography (EEG), and magnetoencephalography (MEG) analyses (Kiebel & Holmes, 2007). Differences among analyses are attributable to the type of design matrix specified or the experimental conditions imposed. Typically, analyses follow the classical (i.e., Frequentist) statistical approach and include the following steps in statistical inference—(1) model formulation, (2) parameter estimation, and (3) inference. The classical approach is deterministic (i.e., the fixed-effects GLM), composed of a fixed component plus a normally distributed (Gaussian) random error component attributable to measurement or sampling fluctuations. Prior to statistical analyses, raw data are preprocessed by image reconstruction, normalization, and smoothing. Importantly, the same GLM equation is used at the level of each voxel.

In PET analyses, GLM-based ANOVA analyses are based on directly analyzing measurements acquired from PET scans with no time series component. In fMRI analyses, the voxel-level SPM analyses are precursors to regional analyses and serve as level 1 in hierarchical GLM analyses. Depending on the particular research design, either a one-way ANOVA, factorial ANOVA, or repeated measures

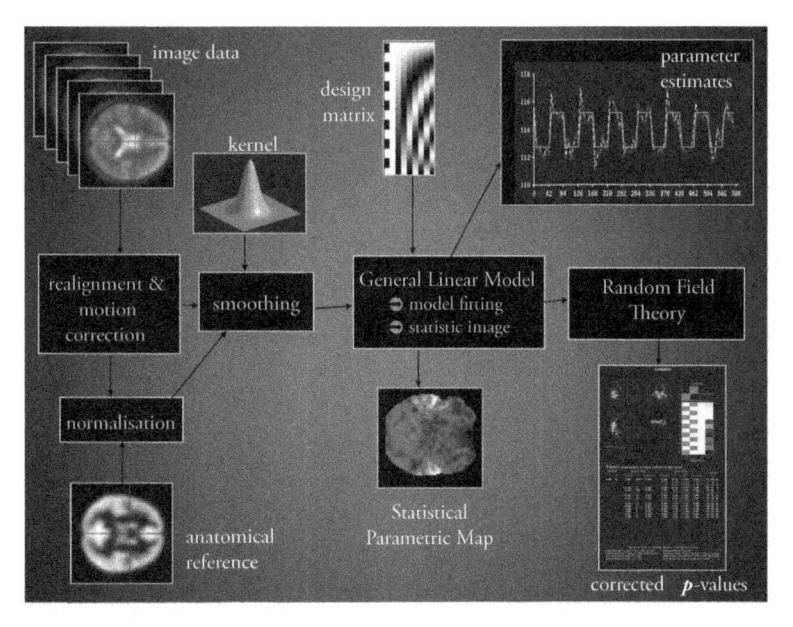

Figure 9.4 Steps in Statistical Parametric Mapping.
Source: W. Penny, 2003 Short Course on SPM

ANOVA (with an appropriate covariance structure for correlated errors) serve as level 2 analytic components. Finally, because of the multivariate nature of neuroimaging data, understanding the mechanics of data analysis from the scalar (individual measurement) level requires a basic understanding of matrix algebra.

Model Basics

The dependent variable measured in *fMRI* analyses is regional cerebral blood flow (rCBF) at the voxel level expressed as a random variable Y_j. Within the model, each observation (i.e., measurement) has an associated explanatory variable or variables denoted as $K(K < J)$ measured with or without error expressed as x_{jk}, where $k = 1, \ldots, K$ indexes the explanatory or predictor variables. Explanatory variables may be categorical or continuous depending on the nature of the research design and experimental conditions. The following Equations 9.1 through 9.4 from Kiebel and Holmes (2007; pp. 101–107) and are given extensive treatment in within the context of imaging analyses. Equation 9.1 illustrates the general linear equation used in the GLM.

EQUATION 9.1. GENERAL LINEAR EQUATION

$$Y_i = x_{j1}\beta_1 + \cdots + x_{jk}\beta_k + \cdots + x_{jk}\beta_K + \epsilon_k$$

- β_k are unknown population parameters corresponding to each predictor or explanatory variable.
- x_j is the explanatory or predictor variable.
- ϵ_k are independently and normally distributed population error components.

To facilitate the multivariate nature of the data, the equivalent matrix form is presented below.

EQUATION 9.2. MATRIX FORMULATION OF THE GENERAL LINEAR EQUATION

$$\begin{pmatrix} Y_1 \\ \vdots \\ Y_j \\ \vdots \\ Y_J \end{pmatrix} = \begin{pmatrix} x_{11} & \cdots & x_{1k} & \cdots & x_{1K} \\ \vdots & \ddots & \vdots & \ddots & \vdots \\ x_{j1} & \cdots & x_{jk} & \cdots & x_{jK} \\ \vdots & \ddots & \vdots & \ddots & \vdots \\ x_{J1} & \cdots & x_{Jk} & \cdots & x_{JK} \end{pmatrix}$$

$$\begin{pmatrix} \beta_1 \\ \vdots \\ \beta_j \\ \vdots \\ \beta_J \end{pmatrix} + \begin{pmatrix} \varepsilon_1 \\ \vdots \\ \varepsilon_j \\ \vdots \\ \varepsilon_J \end{pmatrix}$$

- β_k are unknown population parameters corresponding to each predictor or explanatory variable.
- Y_j are signal measurements expressed as population-level random variables.
- x_j are the explanatory or predictor variables.

- ϵ_k are independently and normally distributed population error components.

The matrix notation for Equation 9.2 is provided in Equation 9.3.

EQUATION 9.3. MATRIX NOTATION OF THE GENERAL LINEAR EQUATION

$$Y = X\beta + \epsilon$$

- Y is the column vector of population measurements or observations.
- β is the column vector of population parameters.
- X is $J \times K$ matrix with jkth element x_{jk} being the design matrix capturing the expectation regarding how the signal was produced.
- ϵ is the column vector of population error terms.

Parameter Estimation

Once data acquisition, smoothing, and normalization are complete, parameter estimation proceeds by the method of maximum likelihood or restricted maximum likelihood. The equation used in the estimation of model parameters is provided in matrix form in Equation 9.4 (Kiebel & Holmes, 2007).

EQUATION 9.4. MATRIX EQUATION FOR LEAST SQUARES ESTIMATES

$$\hat{\beta} = (X^T X)^{-1} X^T Y$$

- X^T is the transpose of X.
- Y is the column vector of response measures.
- X is $J \times K$ matrix from Equation 9.2, with jkth element x_{jk} being the design matrix capturing the expectation regarding how the signal was produced.
- $\hat{\beta}$ are parameter estimates.

Maximum likelihood estimation provides an efficient solution and produces the best linear unbiased estimates (i.e., minimum variance in the sense of least squares estimation) for parameters based on all possible combinations of the data. Frequently in neuroimaging work, the matrix to be used in an analysis is not of full rank (i.e., the matrix is singular because of dependence or high multicollinearity among variables). Matrix singularity occurs when there are an infinite number of solutions for model parameters during the fitting process (Kiebel & Holmes, 2007, p. 104). Critically, data matrices that are rank-deficient yield a singular matrix and are unable to be inverted—a necessary step in manipulating matrices. To overcome the problem of matrix singularity, the Moore-Penrose or generalized inverse (Gentle, 2007) is used to produce estimates based on minimizing sums-of-square error. The resulting parameters obtained using the Moore-Penrose inverse are based on a single set of an infinite number possible. Statistical inference for detecting significant effects at the level of an individual voxel proceeds by using contrast-based t- and/or F-statistics.

Analytic Models and Designs
Positron Emission Tomography

An important aspect regarding research questions in imaging analyses is the separation of global (i.e., whole-brain) effects from regional effects. In the GLM framework, two approaches are used to model parameters relative to the separation of global and regional activation effects—weighted proportional scaling and ANCOVA. In weighted proportional scaling, gain scores and the associated error, which are attributable to the measurement process, are explicitly modeled as a function of neuronal activity at the level of individual voxels. Initially, raw data are transformed to a metric that facilitates interpretation. Once the transformation and rescaling are complete, a diagonal matrix is created incorporating weights on the diagonal of the matrix and zeros elsewhere. The weights on the error covariance matrix diagonal provide a mechanism to apply a weighted regression scheme depicting global activity in the subsequent analysis. The equation used for global normalization, which is attributable to Kiebel and Holmes (2007, p. 109), is provided in Equation 9.5.

EQUATION 9.5. EQUATION FOR GLOBAL NORMALIZATION OF RAW ACTIVATION DATA

$$Y_j^k = \frac{g_j}{50(X\beta^k)_j} + \varepsilon_j'^k$$

- Y_j^k image intensity at voxel $1 \ldots K$ of scan j.
- g_j is the estimated global activity based on the mean of voxel activity or $\sum_{k=1}^{K} \frac{Y_j^k}{K}$.
- 50 is a measure of the global cerebral blood flow per minute.
- X is $J \times K$ matrix, with jkth element x_{jk} being the design matrix capturing the expectation regarding how the signal was produced.
- β^k are unknown population parameters corresponding to each predictor or explanatory variable.

- $\varepsilon_j^{\prime k}$ approximately normally distributed population error covariance with mean 0 and $\sigma_1(k)^2$
- $diag((g1j/50))^{\uparrow}2$
- $Y_j^{\prime k} = \dfrac{50}{g_j\left(Y_j^k\right)}$ is the model-based prediction equation that results in the normalized data.

The ANCOVA is a GLM approach for modeling the effect of regional activity while accounting for global activity. Consider an example of data acquired using PET. Analysis of covariance provides a parsimonious yet powerful approach for modeling change in a single subject's or multiple subjects' global activity that is not attributable to the measurement acquisition process (i.e., a machine-induced change or noise as experienced in *fMRI* data acquisition). Also, in PET the scan trials are independent of one another so there is no requirement for modeling the error structure over different scans at different times.

Following the ANCOVA tradition (Neter et al., 1996), a covariate based on the mean adjusted global activity is included in the model. Moreover, the sum of the regional effects, resulting from experimental manipulation, and global brain activity effects are included in the model. The sum of the effects is allowed to vary over scan trials. The ANCOVA approach includes the assumption that region-specific effects are independent of changes identified related to global activity. However, for this assumption to hold, the dose of radioactive tracer administered to a subject in PET experiments must be constant, otherwise the global gain factor will confound results. Finally, regression slopes are allowed to vary by subjects, conditions, and scan trials if desired. Equation 9.6 (Kiebel & Holmes, 2007, p. 110) illustrates the ANCOVA model.

EQUATION 9.6. ANALYSIS OF COVARIANCE MODEL FOR REGIONAL AND GLOBAL EFFECTS

$$Y_j^k = (X\beta)_j + \lambda^k(g_j - \bar{g}.) + \varepsilon_j^k$$

- Y_j^k image intensity at voxel $1\ldots K$ of scan j.
- g_j is the estimated activity based on voxel specific activity for scan j.
- $\bar{g}.$ is the mean of global activity across all scans.
- X is $J \times K$ matrix with jkth element x_{jk} being the design matrix capturing the expectation regarding how the signal was produced.
- β^k are unknown population parameters corresponding to each predictor or explanatory variable.
- λ^k is the slope parameter for global activity.
- ε_j^k approximately normally distributed population error covariance with mean 0 and $\sigma_k^2 I_j$.

To illustrate an application of the ANCOVA method, consider the following scenario where rCBF denotes regional cerebral blood flow, X is an independent covariate (i.e., a response to a physiological stimulus), and g is the global activity effect. The parameters rCBF, X, and g are to be estimated in the model, with any linear combination serving as a contrast. The null hypothesis of no activation effect for each voxel can be tested against a positive or negative one-sided alternative (Kiebel & Holmes, 2007, p. 111). Equation 9.7 (Kiebel & Holmes, 2007) illustrates the ANCOVA model for analyzing such a design.

EQUATION 9.7. ANALYSIS OF COVARIANCE MODEL FOR REGIONAL AND GLOBAL EFFECTS

$$Y_j^k = \gamma^k(X_j - \bar{X}.)_j + \mu^k + \lambda^k(g_j - \bar{g}.) + \varepsilon_j^k$$

- Y_j^k is the regional intensity at voxel $1\ldots K$ of scan j.
- γ^k is the covariate regression slope for each unique voxel.
- g_j is the estimated activity based on voxel specific activity for scan j.
- $\bar{g}.$ is the mean of global activity across all scans.
- X_j is covariate such as a response to a stimulus.
- μ_k is the constant vector.
- $\bar{X}.$ is the mean covariate effect.
- λ^k is the global activity slope parameter.
- ε_j^k approximately normally distributed error covariance with mean 0 and $\sigma_k^2 I_j$

Equation 9.7 is flexible in that it can be modified to include (1) non-parallel regression slopes or planes; (2) more than a single level of an experimental condition (in either a continuous or discrete metric); (3) factor by condition/subject by condition interactions; (4) a single or multiple subjects (treated as block variable); (5) polynomial regression with specified power functions; and (6) additional covariates (Neter et al., 1996).

fMRI Models

In *fMRI* studies, blood oxygen level-dependent measurements (i.e., BOLD) derived from rCBF are used to indirectly measure neural activity. Recall that this is different than in PET analyses where a radioactive tracer is introduced into the body and the subsequent emission of γ rays serve as dependent measurements. The mass-univariate ANCOVA approach can be extended through the GLM to the analysis of *fMRI* data by including a time series component resulting from multiple scans (i.e., > 150 over a 3- to 5-second period). Therefore, additional analytic details to be addressed in *fMRI* analyses include (1) autocorrelated errors in the data arising from a moderately long series of image acquisitions, and (2) a violation of the homogeneity of covariance structure (i.e., sphericity) assumption specific to repeated measures.

Prior to analyses, *fMRI* images are scaled using proportional scaling or grand mean scaling to normalize intracerebral mean activity intensity. Next, analyses of *fMRI* time series data proceeds by (1) selecting an autocorrelation structure that provides accurate estimates of the serial correlations (and error structure) in the data, (2) temporal filtering, and (3) parameter estimation and inference (Kiebel & Holmes, 2007, pp. 119–120). A time series in *fMRI* is defined as a series of measures of *fMRI* signal intensities over the course of a designed experiment. Typically, *fMRI* data are acquired using a sample time of between 2 and 5 seconds, and in the simplest case, data are acquired on a single subject in a single session. When the goal is to collect data on many subjects, one or more sessions are required for each subject, and the process proceeds with data acquired over several sessions on each subject.

As an example, consider the case where data are captured on a single subject and the goal is to model each voxel using the observed times series vector. Equation 9.8 (Kiebel & Holmes, 2007, p. 118) illustrates the requisite components of the linear time series model composed of deterministic and stochastic parts.

EQUATION 9.8. LINEAR TIME SERIES MODEL FOR *fMRI*

$$Y_s = \beta_l f^1(t_s) + \cdots + \beta_l f^l(t_s) + \cdots + \beta_L f^L(t_s) + e_s$$

- Y_s are the scans serving as observations acquired at one voxel at times t_s where $s = 1 \ldots N$.
- $f^1(.), \cdots, f^L(.)$ are regressors at time-point t covering the possible values of the experiment.
- e_s is the error component.

Equation 9.8 can be expressed in full matrix form, as illustrated in Equation 9.9 (Kiebel & Holmes, 2007, p. 118; Lutkepohl, 2006).

EQUATION 9.9. LINEAR TIME SERIES MODEL FOR *fMRI* EXPRESSED IN MATRIX FORM

$$\begin{pmatrix} Y_1 \\ \vdots \\ Y_s \\ \vdots \\ Y_N \end{pmatrix} = \begin{pmatrix} f^1(t_1) & \cdots & f^l(t_1) & \cdots & f^L(t_1) \\ \vdots & \ddots & \vdots & \ddots & \vdots \\ f^1(t_s) & \cdots & f^l(t_s) & \cdots & f^L(t_s) \\ \vdots & \ddots & \vdots & \ddots & \vdots \\ f^1(t_N) & \cdots & f^l(t_N) & \cdots & f^L(t_N) \end{pmatrix} \begin{pmatrix} \beta_1 \\ \vdots \\ \beta_l \\ \vdots \\ Y_L \end{pmatrix} + \begin{pmatrix} \epsilon_1 \\ \vdots \\ \epsilon_s \\ \vdots \\ \epsilon_N \end{pmatrix}$$

- Y_s are the scans serving as observations acquired.
- at one voxel at times t_s, where $s = 1 \ldots N$.
- $f^1(.), \cdots, f^L(.)$ are regressors at time-point t.
- covering the possible values of the experiment.
- ϵ_s is the normally distributed error component.

Modeling Serial Correlation via the Error Covariance Matrix

Data acquired using *fMRI* exhibit serial correlation between scans resulting in a biased t- or F-test statistic. The serial correlation inflates Type I error of the null hypothesis of no activation. One approach to addressing the serial correlation problem involves (1) de-correlating the data prior to analyses (also known as pre-whitening), or (2) using a design matrix based on generalized least squares parameter estimation with no whitening. A second approach is to correct the degrees of freedom used in the t- or F-tests with an appropriate *post hoc* adjustment such as the GLM univariate Greenhouse-Geisser (1959) correction (Kiebel & Holmes, 2007). Applying the Greenhouse-Geisser method involves a downward adjustment of degrees of freedom (*df*) because in case of uncorrelated errors, *df* are lower. Because the problem lies specifically within the error portion of the general linear equation and not the design matrix, a third approach involves modeling the form of the serial correlations between voxels with a stationary first order autoregressive plus white noise model (AR1 + wn). The first order autoregressive white noise model is the simplest possible example of stationary random sequence, consisting of mutually independent random variables each with mean zero and finite variance. Although other more advanced autoregressive models are available for modeling more complex covariance structures, the AR1 model suits *fMRI* error structures well because of high-pass filtering—a filtering method that leaves the data structure with only short-range dependencies in the correlations (e.g., only an autoregressive –1 process).

Time Series General Linear Model at the Voxel Level

The GLM provides a foundation for modeling time series data that can be extended to address time series analyses. Equation 9.10 provides the general linear equation specific to an individual voxel (Kiebel & Holmes, 2007, p. 122).

EQUATION 9.10. LINEAR MODEL AT THE LEVEL OF ONE VOXEL WITH MODIFIED ERROR TERM

$$Y^k = X\beta^k + \epsilon^k$$

- Y^k an Nx1 time series vector at voxel k.
- X an NxL design matrix.
- β^k the population parameter vector.
- ϵ^k the population error at voxel k modified to include the correlation matrix.

The error term in equation 9.10 is assumed to be approximately normally distributed and differs from the traditional linear model by incorporating the correlation matrix at the level of an individual voxel. In *fMRI* analyses, the voxel-specific correlation is assumed equal across all voxels, but the error variance component is allowed to vary across voxels. Given the assumption of the global equality of correlations (i.e., over the total number of voxels), an averaging scheme can be employed as illustrated in Equation 9.10 (Kiebel & Holmes, 2007, p. 122).

EQUATION 9.11. POOLED CORRELATION AS A MIXTURE OF VARIANCE COMPONENTS

$$V_Y = \sum_k X\beta^k \beta^{k^T} X^T + \epsilon^k \epsilon^{k^T}$$

and

$$Cov(\epsilon^k) = \sigma^{k^2} v$$

- V_Y the mixture of two variance components.
- X an NxL design matrix.
- β^k the parameter vector.
- ϵ^k the error at voxel k modified to include the correlation matrix.

Equation 9.11 for the voxel-level AR1 plus white noise and the error covariance component in Equation 9.12 are provided below and are credited to Kiebel and Holmes (2007, p. 124).

EQUATION 9.12. VOXEL-LEVEL AUTOREGRESSIVE-1 PLUS WHITE NOISE EQUATION

$$\epsilon(s) = z(s) + \delta_\varepsilon(s)$$
$$z(s) = az(s-1) + \delta_Z(s)$$

- $\delta_\varepsilon(s) \approx N(0, \sigma_\varepsilon^2)$ the error component at time-point s at voxel k.
- $\delta_Z(s) \approx N(0, \sigma_Z^2)$, incorporating the autoregressive component plus white noise.
- α is the autoregressive-1 component.

The error covariance matrix is given in Equation 9.13.

EQUATION 9.13. VOXEL-LEVEL ERROR COVARIANCE MATRIX

$$E(\varepsilon\varepsilon^T) = \sigma_Z^2 (I_N - A)^{-1}(I_N - A)^{-T} + \sigma_\varepsilon^2$$

Multilevel Models—the Hierarchical Linear Model

Multilevel modeling is used in a wide variety of disciplines for building complex models based on nested data structures. Multilevel models are descriptive of a general framework for fitting and analyzing data that naturally occur in some nested or hierarchical structure. A key component of multilevel models is specifying a series of hierarchically nested, less complex conditional distributions (Gelman & Hill, 2007; Raudenbush & Bryk, 2002; Bentler & Liang, 2003; Muthen, 1994) at specific levels of analysis. Hierarchical linear models (HLM) are considered special classes of multilevel models because the assumptions of HLMs are more restrictive regarding the error structure and covariance components. Such requirements include the linear nature of the data and the type of covariance structures allowed. Of particular importance in *fMRI* analyses is the estimation of covariance components. Covariance components play a central role in *fMRI* analyses caused by different types of variability occurring at different levels of analysis. Estimation procedures for covariance components are described in the next section.

Expectation Maximization

The expectation maximization (EM) algorithm is a procedure introduced by Hartley (1958) and generalized by Dempster et al. (1977). The EM method is an iterative method to obtain maximum likelihood estimators in incomplete or missing data. Briefly, the EM procedure works by (1) an E-step that finds the conditional expectation of the parameters, holding any prior information (i.e., hyperparameters) fixed, and (2) an M-step that updates the maximum likelihood estimates of the hyperparameters, while keeping the parameters fixed. The EM algorithm is also highly effective for estimating covariance components by providing a mechanism by which a fully Bayesian (described in the next section), MLEB, or ML estimation can proceed. In the absence of prior information or a hierarchical data structure, the EM algorithm provides the ML estimates of the error covariance for the Gauss-Markov model. The ML-based Gauss-Markov estimates are the optimal weighted least squares estimates (i.e., they exhibit minimum variance of all unbiased estimators).

In imaging analysis, hierarchical models (i.e., defined as hierarchical linear models with Gaussian error covariance components) are particularly useful for modeling the spatial and temporal covariance components in *fMRI* experiments (Friston & Penny, 2007, p. 275). Importantly, the HLM strategy can be expanded to the more general multilevel analytic approach, thereby providing a powerful way to analyze a variety of error covariance structures (e.g., heterogeneous or homogeneous temporal and/or spatial errors or autocorrected error structures over time). For example, linear and nonlinear covariance structure models are used to model complex time series covariance structures. Finally, conducting multilevel or hierarchical modeling within the Bayesian probabilistic framework provides a powerful framework for analyzing random and fixed effects in the analysis of imaging data. An introduction to Bayesian inference is provided in the next section.

Bayesian Methods of Analysis
Bayesian Probability and Inference

The history and development of Bayesian statistical methods are substantial and are closely related to frequentist statistical methods (Hald, 1998; Bayes, 1763). In fact, Gill (2002) has noted that the fundamentals of Bayesian statistics are older than the classical or frequentist paradigm. In some ways, Bayesian statistical thinking can be viewed as an extension of the traditional (i.e., frequentist) approach, in that it formalizes aspects of the statistical analysis that are left to uninformed judgment by researchers in classical statistical analyses (Press, 2003). The formal relationship between Bayesian (subjective) and Classical (direct) Probability Theory is provided in Equation 9.14

EQUATION 9.14. RELATIONSHIP BETWEEN BAYESIAN AND DIRECT PROBABILITY

$$p(\theta|x) \propto p(x|\theta) \propto L_x(\theta)$$

- $\propto$ = "proportional to"; meaning that the object to the left of the symbol differs only by a multiplicative constant in relation to the object to the right.
- p = probability.
- θ = the random variable theta.
- L_x = the likelihood of observed data x.
- x = observed data x.
- $p(\theta|x)$ = the probability of the parameter (a random variable) given the observed data (not random, but fixed).
- $p(x|\theta)$ = the probability of the observed (fixed) data given the parameter (a random variable—the sample data).
- $L_x(\theta)$ = the likelihood of the observed data times the parameter (random variable).

To illustrate Bayes' Theorem graphically, suppose that a researcher is interested in the proportion of people in a population who have been diagnosed with bipolar disorder. The researcher denotes this proportion as θ and it can take on any value between 0 and 1. Next, using information from a national database, 30 of 100 people are identified as having bipolar disorder. Next, two pieces of information are required—a range for the prior distribution and the likelihood, which is derived from the actual frequency distribution of the observed data. Bayes' Theorem multiplies the prior density and the maximum likelihood estimate to obtain the posterior distribution.

EQUATION 9.15 *bayes' theorem*

$$Posterior \propto Likelihood \times Prior$$

- $\propto$ = "proportional to"; meaning that the object to the left of the symbol differs only by a multiplicative constant in relation to the object to the right.
- Proportionality is required to ensure that the posterior density has its integral (i.e., that the area under the curve equals to a value of 1).
- Simply multiplying the likelihood and the prior does not ensure that the result will integrate to a value of 1.
- Therefore, to obtain the posterior density, the right-hand side must be scaled by multiplying it by

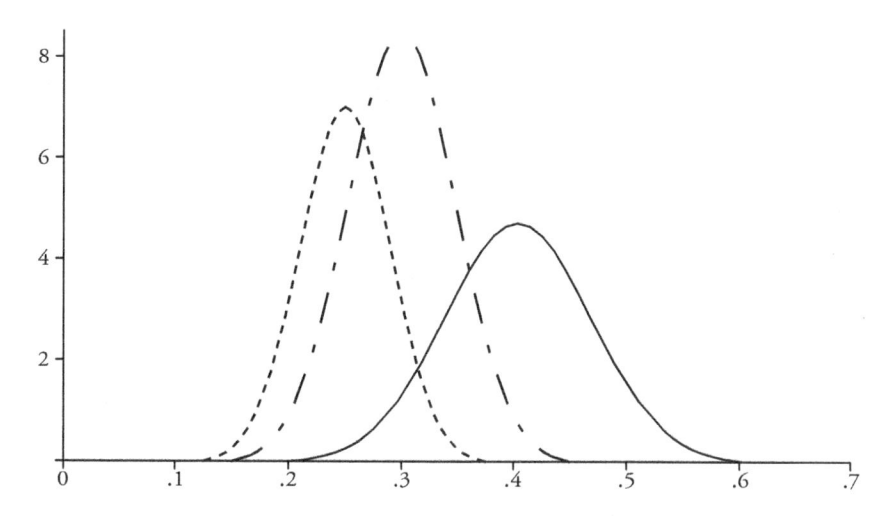

Figure 9.5 Bayesian example of bipolar incidence.

a suitable constant to ensure integration to a value of 1.

The process of Bayesian statistical estimation approximates the posterior density or distribution of say, y, $p(\theta|y) \propto p(\theta) L(\theta|y)$, where $p(\theta)$ is the prior distribution of θ, and $p(\theta|y)$ is the posterior density of θ given y. Continuing with the bipolar example, the prior density or belief (i.e., the solid curve) is for θ to lie between 0.35 and 0.45 and is unlikely to lie outside the range of 0.3 to 0.5 (Fig. 9.5).

The dashed line represents the likelihood, with θ being at its maximum at approximately 0.3 given the observed frequency distribution of the data. Now, Bayes' Theorem multiplies the prior density times the likelihood. If either of these two values are near zero, then the resulting posterior density will also be near negligible (i.e., near zero—for example, for $\theta < 0.2$ or $\theta > 0.6$). Finally, the posterior density (i.e., the dotted-dashed line) covers a much narrower range and is therefore more informative than either the prior or the likelihood alone.

Limitations of Classic Frequentist Probability in Imaging Analytics

Statistical parametric mapping introduced earlier in this chapter has proven effective for modeling activation and testing the hypothesis of no effect in fixed and random effects analyses. However, SPM is based on Frequentist or Classical Probability Theory. Limitations of the Classical Probability Theory approach are that the classic approach centers on *the likelihood of observing the data given no effect* (i.e., the null hypothesis). Conversely, the Bayesian analytic approach centers on the probability of *the effect given the data* (Friston & Penny, 2007, p. 276). In imaging analysis, Bayesian probability models provide an effective framework for generative models where neural activation propagates from one level to another.

Bayesian statistical inference is now the fundamental analytic approach in *fMRI* modeling because unknown population parameters are able to be modeled as random and then assigned a joint probability distribution. In Maximum Likelihood Empirical Bayes (MLEB), sample-based estimates are able to be incorporated into forward (i.e., generative) models moving from the voxel-level up to the regional activation level. The Bayesian approach allows for updated knowledge acquired using empirical Bayes (i.e., combining prior knowledge with the data at hand) or a fully Bayesian approach where priors are assigned before actual analyses are conducted. The posterior distribution or distributions of a parameter is the product of the initial likelihood function (accumulated over all possible values of θ) and the prior density of θ (Lee, 2007). The hierarchical Bayesian approach to *fMRI* analyses usually proceeds by using MLEB estimates as prior estimates for neural activation parameters (Friston et al., 2002a). In the MLEB case, Bayesian analysis proceeds by using noninformative diffuse prior distributions for activation parameters, which operationally involves allowing the actual data to inform the posterior parameter distributions and associated credible intervals (Lee, 2007). This approach works effectively with the Gaussian distributions associated with *fMRI* data, although a variety of prior distributions are able to be assigned if a researcher desires to do so. When researchers are interested in exploratory models at the level of regional effects (i.e., effective connectivity), Bayesian methods again provide powerful options. For example, using Bayes' factors, the Occam's Window algorithm can be applied to determine the optimum number and location of paths in a regional network model (Madigan & Raftery, 1994; Price 2012; Price et al., 2009; Price et al., 2008).

The Bayesian Hierarchical Model

The interrelated ensemble of brain architecture provides a natural structure for a Bayesian hierarchical or multilevel analytic approach. Figure 9.6 illustrates a two-level hierarchical model for imaging data that originates from the level of an individual voxel or voxels. The model in Figure 9.6 (adapted from Penny & Henson, 2007, p. 455) is formally defined as a two-level model because inferences are made about μ (second-level parameter) from y (voxel-level observations) and θ (first level parameter). The top or second level, μ, represents the mean random global activity effect for a single subject or subjects. At the top level (i.e., the population), the null hypothesis tested relates to the variation of effect size over voxels around the whole brain mean effect size of $\mu - 0$. Statistically, for a particular cognitive task, the activity response for a voxel randomly selected is zero (Friston et al., 2002b). Applying Bayes' Theorem, the posterior distribution based on Figure 9.6 is provided in Equation 9.16.

EQUATION 9.16. BAYES' THEOREM

$$p(\theta|y) \propto p(y|\theta)p(\theta)$$

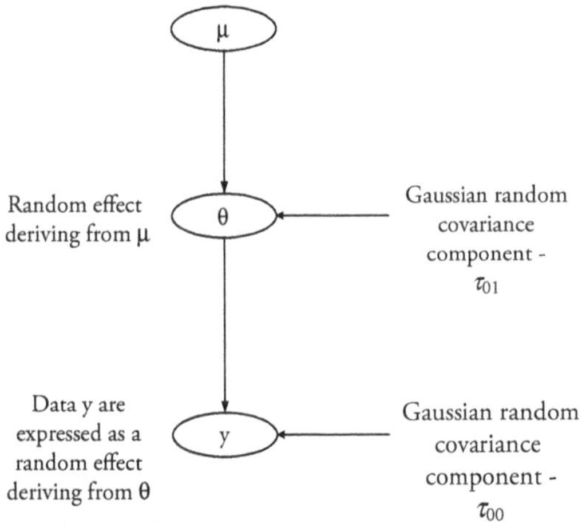

Figure 9.6 Hierarchical model for imaging analyses.

- $\propto$ = "proportional to"; meaning that the object to the left of the symbol differs only by a multiplicative constant in relation to the object to the right.
- $p(\theta|y)$ = posterior distribution of θ given the data at level one or y.
- $p(y|\theta)$ = posterior distribution of y given the data at level two or θ.
- $p(\theta)$ = the likelihood of θ.

The two-level hierarchical linear model corresponding to Figure 9.6 is expressed in equation form in Equation 9.17 (Penny & Henson, 2007, p. 149).

EQUATION 9.17. TWO-LEVEL HIERARCHAL LINEAR MODEL WITH KNOWN COVARIANCE COMPONENTS

$$y = X\theta + e$$
$$\theta = M\mu + z$$

and

$$COV[e] = \tau_{00}$$
$$COV[z] = \tau_{01}$$

- X design matrix composed of regression or β weights at level one.
- M design matrix composed of regression or β weights at level two.
- μ global or mean effect.
- θ random effect deriving from μ.
- y voxel-level data vector.
- $COV[e] = \tau_{00}$ is the covariance component at level one.
- $COV[z] = \tau_{01}$ is the covariance component at level two.

The posterior distribution using Bayes' rule is provided in Equation 9.18.

EQUATION 9.18. EQUATION FOR POSTERIOR PARAMETERS USING BAYES' THEOREM

$$p(\mu|y) = \frac{p(y|\mu)p(\mu)}{p(y)}$$

When no value for a prior is assigned, the level-two prior becomes equivalent to the likelihood (i.e., an uninformative prior in Bayesian inference). Finally, in the case where there is no prior assigned, the level-one and -two equations can be rearranged as illustrated in Equation 9.19.

EQUATION 9.19. TWO-LEVEL HIERARCHAL LINEAR MODEL

$$y = XM\mu + Xz + e$$

- X = design matrix composed of regression or β weights at level one.
- M = design matrix composed of regression or β weights at level two.
- μ = global or mean effect.
- z = error component from level two.
- y = voxel-level data vector.
- e = error component from level one.

An extended approach for fitting hierarchical models based on MLEB iterative estimation is now provided. In the MLEB approach, model specification is data-driven in that empirical priors serve as formal constraints for the generation of observed data. Specifically, predictions stemming from neural activity propagates upward from level one (voxel) through larger voxel-based cluster nodes in the hierarchy to the highest level (e.g., whole brain). The neural activity then propagates back down to level one, retracing the original path. In the upward and downward passes, the Bayesian approach provides a mechanism for updating the estimates at each level by deriving the joint distributions and by marginalizing over subsets of distributions. Hierarchical models in imaging neuroscience range from simple linear ones to spatiotemporal time series models. Penny and Henson (2007) provide a comprehensive overview of hierarchical models used in imaging analyses.

In Figure 9.7, level one in the model illustrates submodels expressed as an n_i element vector y_i, providing information about θ_i based on a design matrix X. Neuronal activity is derived using δ or boxcar functions that are convolved (i.e., mathematically combined) with hemodynamic response functions (HRFs). The resulting convolved information captured within *fMRI* propagates upward from level one. The level-one and -two design matrices are of block diagonal form. The covariance matrix at level one is diagonal and is composed of a column vector of 1s with n entries. Finally, using MLEB, Figure 9.8 (Penny, Mattout, & Trujillo-Barreto, 2007, p. 455) depicts how using Bayesian inference, information moves upward through a neural network to the highest level and then propagates back down.

Posterior means are the sum of the data and the prior means weighted by their respective precisions. The posterior distributions of the first- and second-level parameters are expressed in terms of the observed data, design, and error covariance matrices.

The MLEB approach incorporates traditional likelihood and Bayesian inference and proceeds in two steps. First, the priors (i.e., hyperparameters) of the parameter distributions are estimated from the marginal distribution of all the data, given the priors only. Specifically, the parameters for the population parameters are marginalized, leaving only the priors, which are estimated using maximum likelihood. In the second step, the prior (i.e., hyperparameter) estimates are inserted into the prior distribution of the parameters, and the posterior distribution of each parameter of interest is found by using Bayes' Theorem with that empirically found prior.

Spatial and Temporal Generative Bayesian Models for Functional Magnetic Resonance Imaging

Random effects generative models of neural activation using BOLD measures in *fMRI* are based on posterior probability maps (PPMs; Friston & Penny, 2007) evolving from the voxel level. Spatiotemporal generative models consist of T time points at N voxels yielding a $T \times N$ matrix Y. According to Friston, et al. (1995a), these data are described by a $T \times K$ design matrix X, containing values of K regression parameters at T time-points, and a $K \times N$ matrix of regression coefficients W, containing K regression coefficients at each of N voxels. The GLM equation from Friston (1995) for the model is given in Equation 9.20 (Penny, Flandin, & Trujillo-Barreto, 2007, p. 313).

EQUATION 9.20. GENERAL LINEAR EQUATION FOR GENERATIVE SPATIOTEMPORAL MODEL

$$Y = XW + E$$

- Y = a matrix composed of T time-points across N voxels.
- X = a design matrix composed of T time-points and K regression or β weights.
- W = $K \times N$ matrix of regression weights.
- E = $aT \times N$ error covariance matrix.

Time series data captured with *fMRI* posses serial correlations and sources of error that differs from other types of longitudinal models. For example, the nature of *fMRI* data acquisition produces low-frequency noise attributable to hardware, cardiac pulse noise, respiratory function noise, and residual motion artifacts. Typically, error attributable to low-frequency drift is removed by mathematical

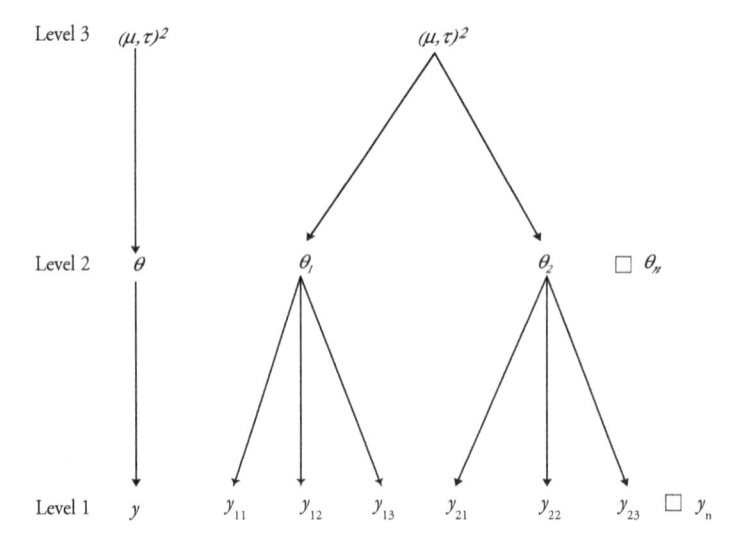

Figure 9.7 Representation of condensed and expanded hierarchical model

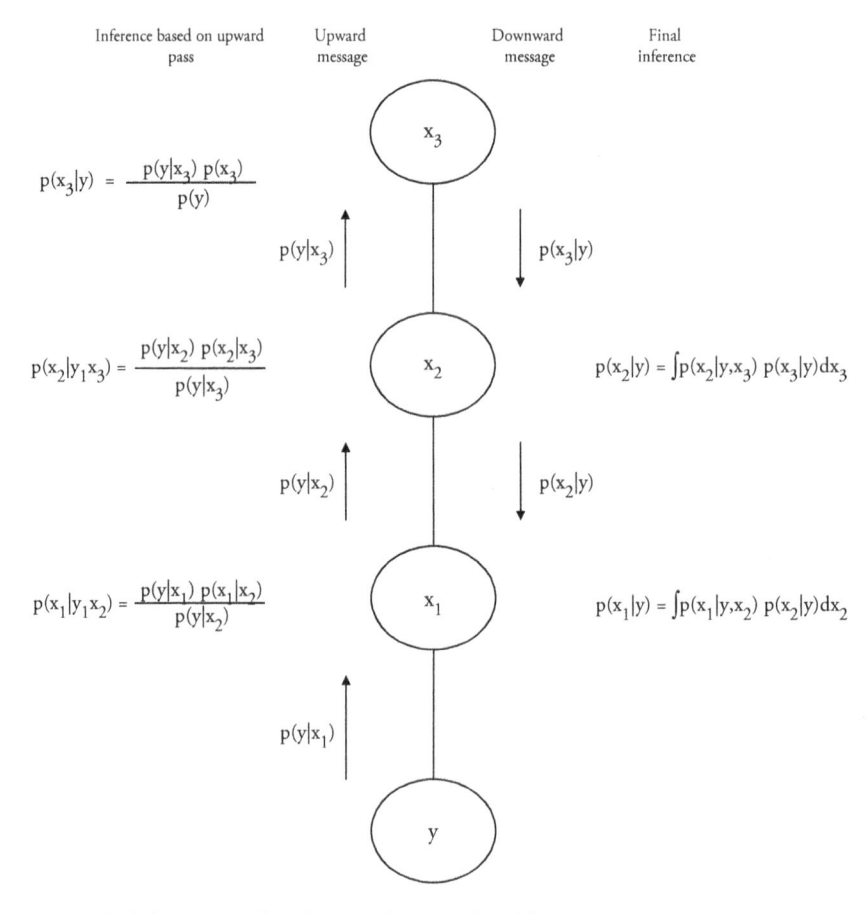

Figure 9.8 Bidirectional belief propagation for inference in hierarchical models. From Penny, Mattout, & Trujillo-Barreto, 2007; and Penny & Henson (2007).

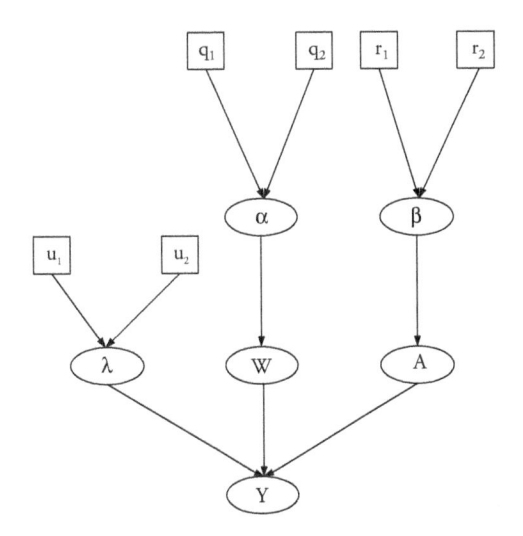

Figure 9.9 Generative model for fMRI data.
From Penny, Flandin, & Trujillo-Barreto, 2007, p. 314

transformation. After such transformation, the time series is accurately modeled using an autoregressive-1 approach. The generative model originating from the voxel level is illustrated in Figure 9.9 (Penny, Flandin, & Trujillo-Barreto, 2007, p. 314).

In Figure 9.9, the squares represent manifest variables (e.g., imposed constants), and the ovals represent random variables within the Bayesian inferential framework. The spatial coefficients are represented by α provide constraints on the regression coefficients W. The random variables or parameters γ and A define the autoregressive error properties of the measurements (e.g., Price, 2012). The spatial coefficients β constrain the autoregressive coefficients A. The joint probability of parameters and data are provided in Equation 9.21 (Penny, Flandin, & Trujillo-Barreto, 2007, p. 314).

EQUATION 9.21. JOINT PROBABILITY FOR GENERATIVE SPATIOTEMPORAL MODEL

$$p(Y, W, \lambda, \alpha, \beta) = p(Y|W, A, \lambda)p(W|\alpha)$$
$$p(A|\beta)p(\lambda|u_1, u_2)$$
$$p(\alpha|q_1, q_2)$$

Analytic Methods for Functional and Effective Connectivity
Functional and Effective Connectivity of Brain Regions

Imaging studies on functional connectivity focus on measuring and analyzing the associations between or among a voxel or clusters of voxels. Studies of functional connectivity incorporate multivariate statistical methods to jointly model the interactions (i.e., magnitude of association and direction) among clusters of voxels representing specific brain regions. Functional neuroimaging analyses seek answer to the question of whether the magnitude of physiological changes elicited by sensorimotor or cognitive challenges are explained by functional segregation or by integrated and distributed changes mediated by neuronal connections (Friston, 2007). Combining functional and effective connectivity analyses provide a mechanism by which to address this question.

Functional Connectivity Methods

Functional connectivity provides a framework for examining the magnitude and direction of correlations from the level of an individual voxel to associations among regional clusters of voxels in the brain. Functional connectivity does not address specific questions of mediation or causation among brain regions. Conversely, effective connectivity is defined as the influence one neural system exerts over another either at the synaptic or cortical level (Friston & Buchel, 2007, p. 492).

Functional connectivity specifically measures the statistical dependencies among a voxel or voxels comprising certain areas of the brain based on neurophysiological measurements (i.e., electrical spike trains in EEG and hemodynamic response functions in fMRI). The analytic approaches used in functional connectivity are primarily descriptive in that one only describes the direction of association and magnitude of neural activity as opposed to modeling generative or causal activation processes. Analytic methods specific to functional connectivity include (1) eigenimage analysis (i.e., mapping activation function into anatomic space); (2) multidimensional scaling (i.e., mapping anatomy into functional space); and (3) partial least squares (i.e., quantifying connectivity but not causation between nodes or systems) (Friston & Buchel, 2007, pp. 492–507).

In eigenimage analysis, the goal is to model the amount and pattern of activity in various connected areas of the brain. Identical to principle components analysis (PCA) with a time series component, the magnitude (amount) and pattern of variance is assessed in the acquired imaging data by the variance–covariance matrix (or correlation matrix in the standardized case). An additional step prior to conducting eigenimage analysis involves deriving normative vector information (i.e., vector length) that is able to be used to model the connectivity among a large number of voxels rather than only a few. To this end, neuroscientists have developed a normative process for identifying the degree to which a pattern of activity contributes to a covariance structure. The goal of modeling the magnitude and pattern of neural activity reduces to identifying the patterns that account for the most variation and covariation.

Mutlidimensional scaling (MDS) is a descriptive statistical tool used for mapping the pairwise structure (i.e., similarity defined by proximity and distance) of point in perceptual spaces. In imaging analysis, measures from a number of voxels can be plotted in multidimensional space. The nearer points are in space, the stronger the magnitude of relationship. The goal of MDS is to describe the maximum amount of variance through geometric rotational techniques. Conceptually, rotating the principle axes obtained in MDS provides vectors that describe the maximum volumetric space in the brain. Finally, partial least squares (PLS) is an extension of the previous two descriptive analytic methods and focuses on the functional connectivity among brain systems rather than voxels. Partial least squares has been useful for identifying intra-hemispheric systems that exhibit the greatest inter-hemispheric connectivity using covariance structure analysis (McIntosh et al., 1996).

Effective Connectivity

Functional processes within the brain are highly interrelated and involve a complex hierarchy of increasingly specialized and abstract processing. Given that regions within the brain influence one another regarding neural processing of information, studies of effective connectivity provide unique answers to questions related to perception, growth and development, adaptation to stress, and rehabilitation to injury.

Studying effective connectivity in imaging analysis is made possible by creating a mathematical model that approximates a physical or biological system. The driving factor regarding how the functions within the model work is based on the response to a direct experimental or indirect observational input. Inputs may be based on the invocation of hidden states (i.e., hidden Markov models) or ones that are based on the relation between inputs and outputs (e.g., modeled in MAR models) (Harrison, Stephan, & Friston, 2007, p. 508; Price, 2012). Identification of a model (describing a system) derives from using observed data to estimate model parameters. Models of effective connectivity can be linear or nonlinear, with measurements being discrete or continuous in time (Harrison et al., 2007).

The nonlinear nature of biological systems poses a substantial challenge in imaging analysis. For example, in biological systems analyses, there is a dynamic component such that the state of affairs in the system evolves in continuous time. Similarly, nonlinear reactions in biological systems are more common than linear ones. Unfortunately, nonlinear dynamic models are frequently untenable due to mathematical convergence problems. Therefore, a linear approximation to nonlinear systems is the most frequent comprised used in imaging analyses.

Dynamic Causal Models

Effective connectivity is defined as the influence that one neural system exerts over another (Friston, 2007). Dynamic causal models (DCM; Friston, 2007p. 541) represent an approach to modeling neuronal responses whereby responses are caused by directed or controlled changes to inputs. Dynamic causal models are nonlinear models where the system is subject to an input (i.e., a stimulus of some type), and based on this input a corresponding output is produced. The goal of DCM is to estimate parameters and make inferences regarding the associations among interdependent brain regions. To this end, effective connectivity within the DCM framework is composed of statistical parameters represented in terms of unobserved activity states in regions of the brain. The goal of DCM is to model output response measurements based on designed perturbations of the neural system within and experimental treatment or condition. DCM begins with a posited model of a neuronal response or responses to an experimental condition (e.g., time-dependent, cognitively-driven, or both). Such models are then posited as generative with the goal of capturing an accurate or valid representation of neuronal activity. Finally, DCM differs from MAR models introduced in the next section and SEMs in that in DCM the brain is treated as a deterministic (i.e., inputs are fixed) system, whereas in MAR and SEM the inputs are modeled as stochastic and lack a fixed point of origin.

Multivariate Autoregressive Models

The goal of MAR modeling is to provide a unified framework for modeling anatomical organization, functional integration, and effective connectivity

(Price, 2012). Researchers using MAR models seek to address the question of examining the large-scale network behavior among specialized regions by modeling random innovations within the network. Univariate and multivariate autoregressive models have a substantial history in the field of econometrics and provide a powerful framework for modeling multivariate time series in both linear and nonlinear systems. An additional strength of MAR models is the fact that contemporaneous (i.e., cross-sectional between regions) and temporal (i.e., over time) components can be integrated into a single analytic model. To optimize the statistical efficiency and power of MAR models, contemporaneous and temporal components can be estimated using linear or nonlinear SEM (Price, 2009; 2012). Finally, Bayesian MAR models can be used to aid in refining various components of the model such as the number of regions (e.g., using latent or manifest variable approaches), number of regression paths, and bidirectionality of relationships (i.e., non-recursive SEMs) between activation sites or regions. Figure 9.10 illustrates a MAR model with a lag-1 time series component (Price, 2012). Regions of interest and direction and inclusion of regression paths were selected based on activation likelihood meta-analysis (Turkeltaub et al., 2002; Brown, Ingham, Ingham, Laird, & Fox, 2005).

Modeling of Effective and Functional Connectivity With Structural Equation Modeling

Although establishing function–location relationships and uncovering areas of functional dissociation within the cortex is often a primary focus of imaging research, more investigators are progressing from simple identification of network nodes toward studying the interactions between brain regions. The aim is to understand how sets and subsets of networks function as a whole toward the intent of accomplishing specific cognitive goals. Previous studies have analyzed both correlational and covariance structures between brain regions. Techniques for applying SEM to neuroimaging data as a method to investigate connections between brain regions have been under development since 1991 (McIntosh & Gonzalez-Lima, 1991; McIntosh & Gonzalez-Lima, 1994a; McIntosh et al., 1994b; Price et al., 2009; Price 2012).

A common aim of functional brain mapping is to determine where and how various cognitive and perceptual processes are controlled in the normal and abnormal (diseased) human brain. In discussing the need for a comprehensive cognitive ontology, Price and Friston (2005) detailed a clear argument for the need for sophisticated network analysis tools. Because there are an immeasurably large number of thought processes that control cognition, perception, action, and interoception as well as a finite number of brain regions involved in carrying out these processes, it remains that these regions must interact in a highly complex and organized fashion. Determining and characterizing these interactions is a natural and obvious application of SEM.

Initial application of SEM techniques to functional neuroimaging data was limited to a handful of researchers with advanced statistical backgrounds. In recent years, interest in SEM has increased because of improvements and accessibility in commercial software and an unavoidable pressing need for the development of methods to test network models and investigate effective connectivity between neuroanatomical regions. Previous studies have applied SEM methods to PET and fMRI data as a means to investigate simple sensory and action processing, such as vision (McIntosh et al., 1994b), audition (Goncalves et al., 2001), and motor execution (Zhuang et al., 2005), as well as higher-order cognitive processing, such as working memory (Glabus et al., 2003; Honey et al., 2002), language (Bullmore et al., 2000), attention (Knodo et al., 2004), and multiple sclerosis (Au Duong et al., 2005).

The analytic strategies that researchers conducting these studies have used either posited starting path or structural equation latent variable models *a priori* based on a single theory alone and then proceeded in a confirmatory manner or an exclusively Bayesian approach to generate optimally weighted network models using little or no prior information. Two shortcomings of these previous studies is that the analytic strategies lacked the ability to distinguish from multiple other equally plausible network models, and they did not consider the impact of sample size and its effect on statistical power and parameter estimation bias. To address such issues, Price et al. (2009) presented a two-step approach incorporating quantitative activation likelihood (ALE) meta-analysis (Turkeltaub et al., 2002; Laird, et al., 2005a, 2005b; Brown, Ingham, Ingham, Laird, & Fox, 2005) for identification of ROIs specific to their research problem in combination with Bayesian SEM to generate a highly informed network model. Additionally, Price

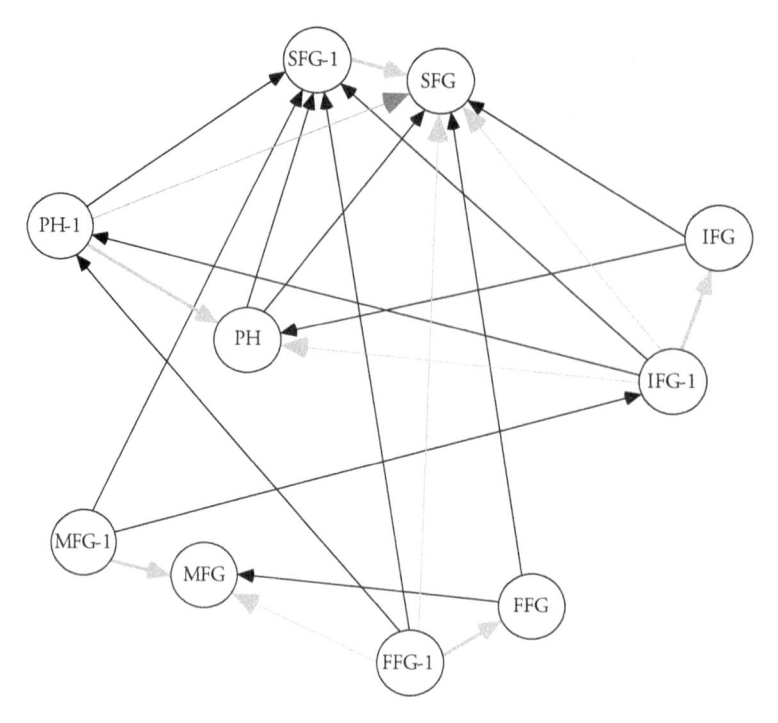

Figure 9.10 Multivariate autoregressive model with AR1 component. Dark nodes = regions of interest composed of clusters of voxels. Light nodes = regions of interest at measured at time t – 1. Black paths = contemporaneous regression paths. Light gray = autoregression of time (t) on t-1. Dark gray = cross-covariances. From: L. R. Price (2012)

et al. (2009b; 2012) evaluated issues such as sample size, statistical power, and parameter estimation bias, topics that previous SEM-based neuroimaging studies have failed to address.

Activation likelihood meta-analysis is performed by modeling each reported focus of activation from previous studies as the center of a three-dimensional Gaussian probability distribution. The three-dimensional Gaussian distributions are summed to create a whole-brain statistical map (Laird, et al., 2005c). The idea behind ALE is to take the data provided by the individual studies (which have been condensed from three-dimensional images to tabular format) and re-inflate the data back to three-dimensional space by modeling each cluster as a Gaussian distribution. From there, the process involves simply pooling all the clusters together to look for regions of overlap.

Relating to ALE meta-analysis is BrainMap (Laird et al., 2005c), a database of functional neuroimaging studies. Although databases of imaging data exist, such as fMRIDC and fBIRN, these include only raw data. However, BrainMap is different, because only coordinate data are archived. One of the standards in reporting is to present tables of stereotactic coordinates in Talairach or Montreal Neurologic Institute space (a three-dimensional proportional grid system that can be used to identify and measure brains from any number of patients despite the variability of brain sizes and proportions). Activation maps of voxels can be condensed to tabular form. To accomplish this, one takes each cluster in the activation map and reports the x, y, z coordinates of its center-of-mass. Basically, a three-dimensional image is condensed to a tabular format consisting of only coordinates—not the raw image data or the activation maps.

Consider a study where a researcher is interested in what data was acquired and what tasks the subjects did in the scanner. BrainMap is similar to Medline; for example, say the researcher is interested in the anterior cingulate area of the brain. BrainMap can be used to search for all papers that showed activation in the anterior cingulate. Because each coordinate entered gets processed through the Talairach Daemon, an anatomical label is provided. Conversely, say a researcher is interested in a particular region of cortex but is not sure of the specific name. The researcher performs an ROI search in BrainMap to find all papers that return activation results within a three-dimensional rectangular box. Both of these types of locations searches aid researchers in detecting common themes regarding the types of paradigms used to activate these regions, what subject groups, and what behavioral domains.

Conclusion

This chapter provided a brief history of methods of imaging research followed by a progression of analytic approaches used in imaging research. The modeling approaches have evolved by an increased understanding of how imaging signals are created. Developing highly informed models requires incorporating principles of biophysics and neuronal activity. Additionally, the research design component plays an integral role in deterministic and random component model analyses. The use of SEM in imaging research should increase given the flexibility of the approach to address certain types of questions that neuroscientists and clinical researchers pose. Bayesian SEM is an important advance for imaging research given the complex contemporaneous and temporal models that are estimated using small sample sizes. Bayesian model selection and averaging provides a mechanism for locating optimal models within dynamic neural systems. Finally, the use of DCM (or variants thereof) is likely to increase because of the fact that it is a deterministic approach that treats system perturbations as known rather than random and because of the integration of biophysical and neuronal mechanisms. In short, DCM treats the brain as a system that is dynamic and provides a framework for nonlinear time series models with feedback loops.

Future Directions

Imaging research is a very young endeavor with a myriad of research opportunities. For example, the following questions are at the precipice of the future of imaging research.

1. How might hierarchical, nonlinear time-series SEM be used to study problem in imaging research?

2. How might hierarchical, nonlinear time-series SEM with feedback loops be developed and used to study problems in imaging research?

3. How can the principles of causality established in the field of artificial intelligence be incorporated in DCMs?

4. What role can specification search algorithms play is developing and validating ROI network models?

5. How might Bayesian SEM be integrated with DCM to model the complex contemporaneous and temporal using small sample sizes?

6. What role can Bayesian model selection and averaging have in identifying dynamic neural activity in systems at the voxel and regional level?

7. What evidence exists that imaging analytic methods using classical or frequentist probability exhibit adequate statistical power?

Author Note

Larry R. Price, Ph.D., Director - Center for Interdisciplinary Research Design & Analysis, Professor Psychometrics & Statistics, Texas State University. National Science Foundation CAREER Award (2013–2018): Secure and Trustworthy Biometrics.

References

Alder, R. J, & Taylor, J. E. (2007). *Random fields and geometry*. New York, NY: Springer.

Ashburner, J., & Friston, K. J. (2007). *Computational Anatomy*. In *Statistical parametric mapping* (pp. 49–100). K. Friston, J. Ashburner, S. Kiebel, T. Nichols, & W. Penny (Eds.), San Diego, CA: Elsevier.

Au Duong, M. V., Boulanouar, K., Audoin, B., Treseras, S., Ibarrola, D., & Malikova, I. (2005). Modulation of effective connectivity inside the working memory network in patients at the earliest stage of multiple sclerosis. *Neuroimage, 24*, 533–538.

Bayes, T. (1763). An essay towards solving a problem in the doctrine of chances. *Philos. Trans. Royal Soc. London, 53*, 370–418.

Bentler, P. M., & Liang, J. (2003). *Two-level mean and covariance structures: Maximum likelihood via an EM algorithm*. In Multilevel modeling: Methodological advances, issues, and applications (pp. 53–70). Steven Reise & Naihua Duan (eds.). Mahwah, NJ: Erlbaum.

Brown, S., Ingham, R. J., Ingham, J. C., Laird, A. R., & Fox, P. T. (2005). Stuttered and fluent speech production: An ALE meta-analysis of functional neuroimaging studies. *Human Brain Mapping, 25*, 105–117.

Bullmore, E., Horwitz, B., Honey, G., Brammer, M., Williams, S., & Sharma, T. (2000). How good is good enough in path analysis? *Neuroimage, 11*, 289–301.

Dempster, A. P., Laird, N. M., & Rubin, D. B. (1977). Maximum likelihood from incomplete data via the EM algorithm. *Journal of the Royal Statistical Society Series B, 45*, 311–354.

Duffy, F. H., Bartes, P. H., Burchfiel, J. L. (1981). Significance probability mapping: an aid in the topographic analysis of brain electrical activity. *Electroencephalographic Clinical Neurophysiology, 51*, 455–462.

Fox, P. T., Mintun, M. A., & Raichle, M. E. (1986). Mapping the human visual cortex with positron emission tomography. *Nature, 323*, 806–809.

Fox, P. T., Mintun, M. A., Reiman, E. M., & Raichle, M. E. (1988). Enhanced detection of focal brain responses using intersubject averaging and change-distribution analysis of subtracted PET images. *Journal of Cerebral Blood Flow Metabolism, 8,* 642–653.

Fox, P. T., Laird, A. R., & Lancaster, J. L. (2005). Coordinate-based voxel-wise meta-analysis: Dividends of spatial normalization. *Human Brain Mapping, 25,* 1–5.

Friston, K. (2007). *Dynamic causal modeling.* In Statistical parametric mapping (pp. 541 – 589). K. Friston, J. Ashburner, S. Kiebel, T. Nichols, & W. Penny (Eds.), San Diego, CA: Elsevier.

Friston, K. J., Firth, C. D., & Liddle, P. F. (1991). Comparing functional PET images: the assessement of significant change. *Journal of Cerebral Blood Flow Metabolism, 11,* 690–699.

Friston, K., & Penny W. (2007). *Empirical Bayes and Hierarchical Models.* In Statistical parametric mapping (pp. 275–294). K. Friston, J. Ashburner, S. Kiebel, T. Nichols, & W. Penny (Eds.), San Diego, CA: Elsevier.

Friston, K., & Büchel, C. (2007). *Functional connectivity: eigenimages and multivariate analyses.* In Statistical parametric mapping (pp. 492–507). K. Friston, J. Ashburner, S. Kiebel, T. Nichols, & W. Penny (Eds.), San Diego, CA: Elsevier.

Friston, K. (2007). *Dynamic causal models for fMRI.* In Statistical parametric mapping (pp. 541–560). K. Friston, J. Ashburner, S. Kiebel, T. Nichols, & W. Penny (Eds.), San Diego, CA: Elsevier.

Fristion, K. J., Holmes, A. P., Worsely, K. J. (1995a). Statistical parametric maps in functional imaging: a general linear approach. *Human Brain Mapping, 2,* 189–210.

Friston, K. J., Glaser, D. E., & Henson, R. N. A. (2002b). Classical and Bayesian inference in neuroimaging: Applications. *Neuroimage, 16,* 484–512.

Friston, K. J., Penny, W. D., & Phillips, C. (2002a). Classical and Bayesian inference in neuroimaging: Theory. *Neuroimage, 16,* 465–483.

Gelman, A., & Hill, J. (2007). *Data analysis using regression and multilevel/hierarchical models.* New York: Columbia University Press.

Gentle, J. E. (2007). *Matrix algebra: Theory, computations, and applications in statistics.* New York: Springer.

Gill, J. (2002). *Bayesian methods: A social and behavioral sciences approach.* Boca Raton, FL: Chapman-Hall CRC.

Glabus, M. F., Horwitz, B., Holt, J. L. Kohn, P. D., Gerton, B. K., & Callicott, J. H. (2003). Interindividual differences in functional interactions among prefrontal, parietal and parahippocampal regions during working memory. *Cerebral Cortex, 13,* 1352–1361.

Gonclaves, M. S., Hall, D. A., Johnsrude, I. S., & Haggard, M. P. (2001). Can meaningful effective connectivities be obtained between auditory cortical regions? *Neuroimage, 14,* 1353–1360.

Greenhouse, S. W., & Geisser, S. (1959). On methods of the analysis of profile data. *Psychometrika, 24,* 95–112.

Hald, A. (1998). *A history of mathematical statistics from 1750 to 1930.* New York, NY: Wiley.

Harrison, L., Stephan, K., & Friston, K. (2007). *Effective connectivity.* In Statistical parametric mapping (pp. 508–521). K. Friston, J. Ashburner, S. Kiebel, T. Nichols, & W. Penny (Eds.), San Diego, CA: Elsevier.

Hartley, H. (1958). Maximum likelihood estimation from incomplete data. *Biometrics, 14,* 174–194.

Herscovitch, P., Markham, J., & Raichle, M. E. (1983). Brain blood flow measured with intravenous $H_2(15)O$. I. Theory and error analysis. Journal of Nuclear Medicine, *24,* 782–789.

Honey, G. D., Fu, C. H. Y., Kim, J., Brammer, M. J., Croudace, T. J., & Sucking, J. (2002). Effects of verbal working memory load on corticortical connectivity modeled by path analysis of functional magnets resonance imaging data. *Neuroimage, 17,* 573–582.

Kiebel, S.J., & Holmes, A. P. (2007). *The general linear model.* In Statistical parametric mapping (pp. 101-125). K. Friston, J. Ashburner, S. Kiebel, T. Nichols, & W. Penny (Eds.), San Diego, CA: Elsiver.

Kondo, H., Osaka, N., & Osaka, M. (2004). Cooperation of the anterior cingulate cortex and dorsolateral prefrontal cortex for attention shifting. *Neuroimage,* 23, 670–679.

Laird, A. R., Fox, P. M., Price, C. J., Glahn, D. C., Uecker, A. M., Lancaster, J. L., Turkeltaub, P. E., et al. (2005a). ALE meta-analysis: controlling the false discovery rate and performing statistical contrasts. *Human Brain Mapping, 25,* 155–164.

Laird, A. R., Lancaster, J. L., & Fox, P. T. (2005c). Brainmap: The social evolution of a human mapping database. *Neuroinformatics,* 3(1), 65–78.

Laird, A. R., McMillian, K. M., Lancaster, J. L., Kochunov, P., Turkeltaub, P. E., Pardo, J. V., P., & Fox, P. T. (2005b). A comparison of label-based review and ALE meta-analysis in the stroop task. *Human Brain Mapping, 25,* 6–21.

Lauter, J. L., Herscovitch, P., & Formby, C. (1985). Tonotopic organization in human auditory cortex revealed by positron emission tomography. *Hearing Research, 20,* 199–205.

Lee S.Y. (2007). *Structural Equation Modeling: A Bayesian Approach.* New York: Wiley.

Lutkepohl, H. (2006). *A new introduction to multiple time series analysis.* New York: Springer.

Madigan, E.J. & Raftery, A.E. (1994). Model selection and accounting for model uncertainty in graphical models using Occam's window. *Journal of the American Statistical Association, 89,* 1535–1546.

McIntosh A.R., Bookstein, F. L., & Haxby, J. B. (1996). Spatial pattern analysis of functional brain images using partial least squares. *Neuroimage, 3,* 143–157.

McIntosh A.R., & Gonzalez-Lima F. (1991). Structural modeling of functional neutral pathways mapped with 2-deoxyglucose: Effects of acoustic startle habituation on the auditory system. *Brain Res, 547,* 295–302.

McIntosh A.R., Gonzalez-Lima F. (1994a). Structural equation modeling and its application to network analysis in functional brain imaging. *Human Brain Mapping, 2,* 2–22.

McIntosh, A. R., Grady, C. L., Ungerleider, L. G., Haxby, J. V., Rapoport, S. I., & Horwitz, B. (1994b). Network analysis of corticial visual pathways mapped with PET. *Journal of Neuroscience, 14,* 655–666.

Muthen, B. O. (1994). *Multilevel covariance structure analysis.* Sociological methods & research, *22,* 376–98.

Neter, J., Kutner, M. H., Nachtsheim, & Wassmerman, W. (1996). *Applied linear statistical models.* Boston, MA: McGraw-Hill.

Penny, W. (2003). *Short course on Statistical Parametric Mapping.* Retrieved from: http://www.fil.ion.ucl.ac.uk/spm/course. London, England.

Penny, W., & Henson, R. (2007). *Hierarchical models.* In Statistical parametric mapping (pp. 148–155). K. Friston, J. Ashburner, S. Kiebel, T. Nichols, & W. Penny (Eds.), San Diego, CA: Elsevier.

Penny, W. D., Mattout, J., & Trujillo-Barreto, N. (2007). *Bayesian model selection and averaging*. In Statistical parametric mapping (pp. 454–470). K. Friston, J. Ashburner, S. Kiebel, T. Nichols, & W. Penny (Eds.), San Diego, CA: Elsevier.

Penny, W. D., Flandin, G., & Trujillo-Barreto, N. (2007). *Spatio-temporal models for fMRI*. In Statistical parametric mapping (pp. 313–322). K. Friston, J. Ashburner, S. Kiebel, T. Nichols, & W. Penny (Eds.), San Diego, CA: Elsevier.

Penny, W. D., Trujillo-Barreto, N., & Friston, K. J., (2005). Bayesian fMRI time series analysis with spatial priors. *Neuroimage, 24*, 350–362.

Press, J. S. (2003). *Subjective and objective Bayesian statistics: Principles, models, and applications, 2nd ed*. New York: Wiley Series in Probability & Statistics.

Price, L. R. (2009a). *A Bayesian autoregessive model for multivariate time series*. Paper presentation at the annual meeting of the American Educational Research Association, Structural Equation Modeling Special Interest Group, April 15, 2009, San Diego, CA.

Price, L. R. (2009b). Modeling dynamic functional neuroimaging data using structural equation modeling. *Structural equation modeling: A multidisciplinary journal, 16*(1), 147–162.

Price, L. R. (2010). *Small Sample Properties of Bayesian Multivariate Autoregressive Models*. Paper presentation at the annual meeting of the International Meeting of the Psychometric Society, University of Georgia, Athens, Georgia, July 7, 2010.

Price, L.R., Laird, A.R., Fox, P.T. (2008). Neuroimaging network analysis using Bayesian model averaging. Presentation at The International Meeting of the Psychometric Society, Durham, New Hampshire.

Price, L. R. (2012). Small sample properties of Bayesian multivariate autoregressive time series models. *Structural Equation Modeling, 19*(1), 51–64.

Price, C. J., & Friston, K. J. (2005). Functional ontologies for cognition: The systematic definition of structure and function. *Cognitive Neuropsychology, 22*, 262–275.

Raudenbusch, S., & Bryk, A, (2002). *Hierarchical linear models, 2nd ed*. Thousand Oaks, CA: Sage.

Statistical Parametric Mapping (SPM,2011) [Software]. *http://www.fil.ion.ucl.ac.uk/spm*.

Turkeltaub P.E., Guinevere, F.E., Jones, K.M., & Zeffiro T.A. (2002). Meta-analysis of the functional neuroanatomy of single-word reading: Method and validation. *Neuroimage, 16*, 765–780.

Talairach, P., & Tournoux, J. (1988). *A stereotactic coplanar atlas of the human brain*. Thieme, Stuttgart.

Worsley, K. (2007). *Random field theory*. In Statistical parametric mapping (pp. 232 – 236). K. Friston, J. Ashburner, S. Kiebel, T. Nichols, & W. Penny (Eds.), San Diego, CA: Elsevier.

Zhuang, J., LaConte, S., Peltier, S., Zhang, K. and Hu, X. (2005). Connectivity exploration with structural equation modeling: An fMRI study of bimanual motor coordination. *Neuroimage, 25*, 462–470.

CHAPTER 10

Twin Studies and Behavior Genetics

Gabriëlla A. M. Blokland, Miriam A. Mosing, Karin J. H. Verweij, *and* Sarah E. Medland

Abstract

Twin studies and behavior genetics address the questions raised by the nature versus nurture debate. Their aim is to estimate the extent to which individual differences in complex traits or phenotypes result from genetic and environmental influences. The vast majority of human behaviors and characteristics are complex traits and are influenced by both genetic and environmental influences, as well as the interplay between these two. Based on the differing genetic relatedness of monozygotic co-twins and dizygotic co-twins, the classical twin model allows for an estimation of the relative importance of these etiological factors. The classical twin model can be extended in multiple ways, depending on the phenotype, research question, and research design. In addition to the classical twin methodology, several such extensions are described in this chapter.

Key Words: Twin modeling; classical twin model; behavior genetics; individual differences; genes; environment; nature-nurture debate; monozygotic twins; dizygotic twins; path diagram; structural equation modeling

Introduction

In this chapter we will discuss some of the methodologies used in the genetic analysis of quantitative traits. The aim of this chapter is to provide an introduction to basic genetics and to the twin design as a method to study the etiology of individual differences in complex traits.

The phenotypic variation among species is extensive. In humans, this variation is observed across physical (e.g., height or weight), physiological (e.g., blood pressure or brain volume), cognitive (e.g., intelligence), and psychological (e.g., personality or depression) domains. The question of whether these individual differences in complex behavioral traits are caused by genetic (heritable) or environmental influences, or a combination of the two, is referred to as the *nature versus nurture debate* (Fig. 10.1), and dates back to ancient Greece (Loehlin, 2009).

Comparing individual variation at the population level to the variation within a family shows that there is less variation within families than between families, with the least variation observed between individuals sharing their entire genome (i.e., identical twins). In the late 1800s, Francis Galton developed a number of statistical techniques including the correlation coefficient and regression, in order to study the way in which family resemblance for many traits increased with family relatedness (Galton, 1889). These statistics underlie much of the behavioral and quantitative genetic techniques used today (Plomin, DeFries, McClearn, & McGuffin, 2001).

The broad aim of quantitative genetic analyses is to estimate the extent to which differences observed among individuals result from genetic and environmental influences, and can thus directly address the questions raised by the nature-nurture debate. As

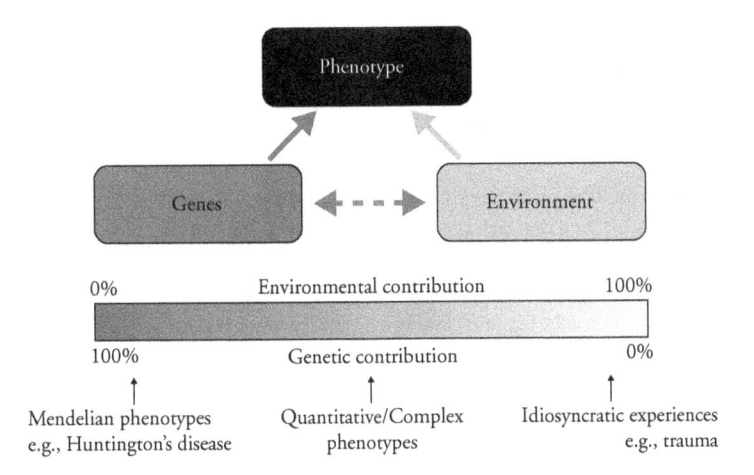

Figure 10.1 Nature versus Nurture.
Notes: Individual differences on traits result from genetic and/or environmental influences, or a combination of both. Mendelian traits, such as Huntington's disease, are (almost) entirely inherited, while traumatic brain injury can be caused by environmental exposures, such as a car accident. Quantitative traits are generally influenced by a combination of genetic and environmental influences.

shown in Figure 10.1, within the scientific community it is generally accepted that the vast majority of human behaviors and characteristics are complex traits and are influenced by both genetic and environmental influences, as well as the interplay between these two.

Although the degree of sharing of environmental factors among related (as well as unrelated) individuals is hard to measure, the sharing of genetic factors between individuals is easy to quantify, because inheritance of most genetic material follows very simple rules. These rules were first postulated by Gregor Mendel in 1866 and have come to be referred to as the *basic laws of heredity* (Plomin, DeFries, McClearn, & McGuffin, 2001). In his experimentation with pea plants, Mendel found that when crossing plants with different colored flowers (white and purple) the flowers of the resulting plant would still be purple (rather than lavender). These results led him to develop the idea of *genetic loci* (which he termed "heredity units"), which could either be additive or dominant. He concluded that each individual has two *alleles*, or versions of the genetic locus, one from each parent (note that didactic examples such as this one, are usually illustrated using the example of a bi-allelic locus with two variants, *A* and *a*; however, some types of loci have many more than two possible variants).

Within somatic cells, the DNA is arranged in two paired strands. Mendel established that, following the binomial distribution, within each individual the alleles at each locus can be paired as *aa*, *Aa*, or *AA*, with each pairing being referred to as a *genotype*. Cases where the genotype is composed of two copies of the same allele (i.e., *AA* or *aa*), are denoted *homozygotes*, while those with differing alleles (i.e., *Aa*), are referred to as *heterozygotes*. The frequency of each genotype reflects the frequency of each allele in the population. For example, if *a* has an allele frequency of *p*, and *A* has a frequency of *q* in the population, the frequencies of the three genotypes, *aa*, *Aa*, or *AA*, are p^2, $2pq$ and q^2. In didactic examples, $q = 1 - p$, however, this is not always true. Note also, that the frequency of the heterozygote is twice pq as this genotype can arise in two ways, *Aa* and *aA*, where the *A* allele can be inherited from either the mother or the father.

Mendel's findings are summarized in two laws: (1) the law of segregation; and (2) the law of independent assortment (Plomin, DeFries, McClearn, & McGuffin, 2001). The process of segregation occurs during *gametogenesis*, when the *gametes* or sex cells (egg and sperm) are formed. During this process the genotype separates; for example, a male with a heterozygous *Aa* genotype will usually develop approximately equal numbers of sperm carrying the *A* allele and the *a* allele. Thus, each of the parental alleles has an equal chance of being transmitted, regardless of the frequency of each allele within the population. Assortment refers to the process of segregation among many loci. This principle states that the inheritance of these loci is independent such that the process of segregation is random at each locus. An important caveat is that this principle does not hold if the loci are closely located on the same chromosome. This is because at the physical level stretches of DNA are co-inherited. This fact forms the basis of linkage analysis, which will be discussed in Chapter 11.

A genetic effect is described as dominant if the heterozygous individuals show the same behavior or phenotype as one of the homozygotes. By convention, a capital letter (e.g., *A*), is used to represent the dominant allele, while a lower case letter (e.g., *a*), is used to describe the recessive allele. However, if the gene effects are additive (i.e., the trait value increases with each additional *increasing* allele, denoted *A*), the observed trait or *phenotype* in the heterozygote will lie midway between the two homozygotes. While Mendelian laws were initially thought to apply only to traits influenced by single genes, it was subsequently shown by R.A. Fisher (1918) that they also apply to many complex and quantitative traits, where the phenotype results in part from the combined influence of multiple genes (Fig. 10.2).

At a genome-wide level the average amount of genetic sharing between two relatives can be calculated based on biometric genetic theory. A child shares 50% of their *autosomal* (i.e., non-sex chromosome) DNA with each of his parents. Similarly, siblings share on average 50% of their genetic material, and grandparents share on average 25% of their genetic material with their grandchildren (the same applies for half siblings and avuncular relationships). Analysis of data from related individuals, making use of the differences in genetic sharing between relatives, provides one way of estimating the relative magnitude of genetic (or *heritable*) and environmental influences on trait variation.

Heritability can be defined as the proportion of the phenotypic variance in a trait that is attributable to the effects of genetic variation (Neale & Maes, 2004). Generally, the more diverse the relatedness of the participants included (i.e., parents, siblings, and cousins), the greater the power to disentangle genetic and environmental influences on trait variation (Medland & Hatemi, 2009). A particularly attractive design to investigate genetic and environmental influences on trait variation is the adoption study. By comparing the resemblance between the adoptee and the adoptive family (environmental influence) versus the resemblance between the adoptee and the

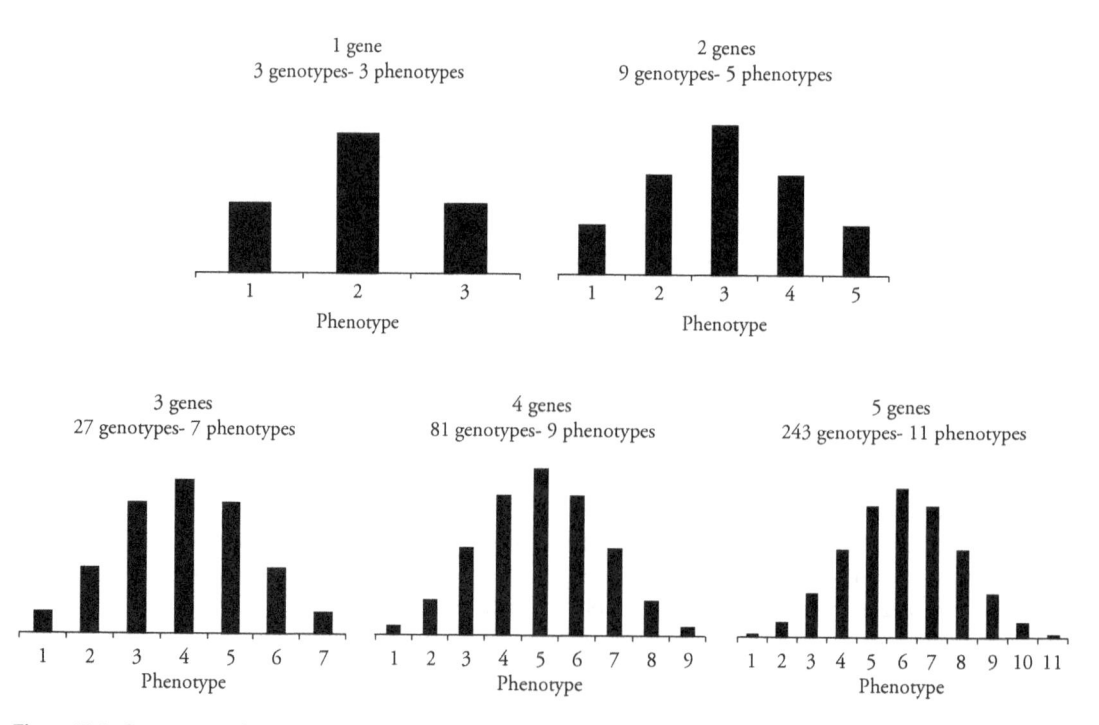

Figure 10.2 Genotypes to phenotypes: From single gene action to complex polygenic traits.
Notes: Given that each gene has 3 possible combinations of alleles (*aa*, *Aa*, and *AA*), under the assumption of additive genetic effects the homozygotes would be on the lower (*aa*) and the upper (*AA*) end of the phenotypic distribution, while the heterozygote is in the middle. If we extend this to include multiple genes, as would be the case for complex polygenic traits, with the inclusion of each new gene the distribution of phenotypic values in the sample increasingly resembles a normal distribution.

biological family (genetic influence) for a given trait, the relative contribution of genes and environment to variance in this trait can be estimated. However, this design is complicated by the difficulties associated with collecting data from the biological family, the nonrandom placement of adoptees and the effects of pre-adoptive experiences.

Arguably, the classical twin study represents the most practical and powerful family design available to researchers. This method compares the within-pair similarity of identical (*monozygotic*; MZ) and non-identical (*dizygotic*; DZ) twins. Monozygotic twins develop when the developing *zygote* (fertilized egg) divides, usually within 2 weeks of fertilization, and the two parts continue to develop independently (Fig. 10.3). In this case, both twins originate from the same sperm and egg, which makes them genetically identical and, therefore, they are always of the same sex. The later the twinning event occurs, the more likely the twins are to share chorion (which is comprised of the placenta and related membranes) and amniotic sacs (Derom et al., 2001; Baergen, 2011). In contrast, DZ twinning occurs when more than one egg is released by the ovaries at the same time and, subsequently, each of the eggs is fertilized by a separate sperm cell. As a result, DZ twins do not differ from normal siblings genetically, sharing on average 50% of their genetic loci. However, they do have shared prenatal environments, as they were conceived at the same time and shared the womb. Dizygotic twins, like normal siblings, can either be of the same or of the opposite sex (i.e., a male and a female).

In order to facilitate the use of twin designs many countries have set up twin registries, collecting information on twins and their families. The oldest national twin register is the Danish Twin Registry, initiated in 1954, currently listing more than 75,000 twin pairs (Skythe et al., 2006). Subsequently, many more countries have followed the Danish example by setting up large nationwide twin registries (e.g., Sweden, Australia, and the Netherlands). One of the biggest challenges for twin registries is the correct ascertainment of the zygosity of twins (MZ versus DZ). Until recently, zygosity was mainly determined by means of a questionnaire assessing twin similarity between same-sex twins. This method has proven to be efficient in 95% of

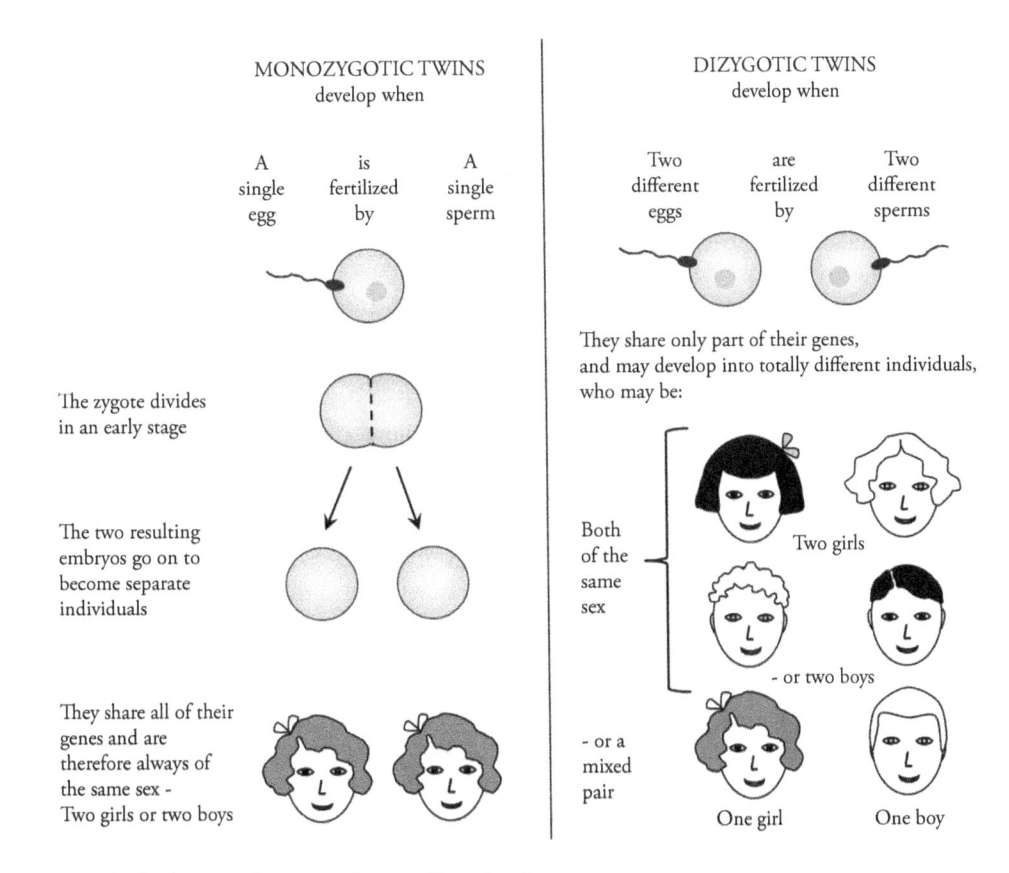

Figure 10.3 The development of monozygotic versus dizygotic twins.

cases (Kasriel & Eaves, 1976). Over the past thirty years, however, gene-finding methods became available, enabling the precise determination of zygosity status; these have largely been used to confirm and replace zygosity determination based on questionnaires (Plomin, DeFries, McClearn, & McGuffin, 2001). To date numerous twin studies on a very large variety of traits have been conducted. Although originally the focus was on "simple" (physical) traits such as height, soon twin studies were used to explore the variation in increasingly complex traits, such as intelligence, personality, psychiatric disorders, etc.

As mentioned above, the phenotypes and genotypes of related individuals are not independent, nor are they identically distributed; therefore, many standard statistical tests cannot and/or should not be applied in the analyses of relatives. Most analyses based on related individuals use statistical approaches based on likelihood, as this very general statistical framework has high modeling flexibility (e.g., Maes et al., 2009; Neale & Maes, 2004). These statistical approaches will be explained in this chapter.

The Classical Twin Model

As mentioned above, the classical twin design draws its explanatory power from the differences in genetic sharing of MZ and DZ twins. Using simultaneous equations, this knowledge can be used to partition the variance in a phenotype into that which results from additive genetic (A), dominant genetic (D), common or shared environmental (C) and unique or unshared environmental (E) influences. Additive and dominant genetic influences refer to the cumulative effect of genes acting in an additive or dominant manner. Common environmental influences refer to experiences shared by co-twins, including the intrauterine environment, and the social and cultural rearing environment (i.e., same socio-economic status, parents, diet, etc.) Unique environmental factors comprise all aspects of the physical and social environment experienced differentially by individuals in a family, such as illness, physical and psychological trauma, peers, teachers, etc. This component also includes measurement error and gene–environment interactions when not accounted for in the modeling (Eaves, Last, Martin, & Jinks, 1977; Jinks & Fulker, 1970).

The classical twin model assumes that phenotypic variation results from the sum of these sources, such that the total variance can be written as: A + C + D + E. Monozygotic twins share approximately 100% of their genetic information (A and D), as well as 100% of their common or shared environment (C). Thus, the MZ covariance (i.e., the covariance between twin 1 and 2 of an MZ pair) can be written as: A + C + D. Conversely, DZ twins are assumed to share, on average, 50% of their segregating genes, and 25% of the time they share the same paternal and maternal alleles (which are required to share dominant effects). In addition, they are assumed to share 100% of the common environment. Thus, the DZ covariance can be written as: 0.5A + C + 0.25D.

As will be obvious from these three equations, there is insufficient information within the classical twin model to simultaneously estimate the magnitude of all four sources of variance. As such, twin studies tend to estimate either C or D. This is because these measures are negatively confounded; that is, dominance effects tend to reduce the DZ correlation relative to the MZ correlation (i.e., make MZ twins more similar), whereas the common environment tends to increase the DZ correlation relative to the MZ correlation (i.e., makes DZ twins more similar). One or the other source can be assumed absent depending on whether the DZ twin correlation is greater or less than half the MZ correlation. In general an ACE model would be estimated if the DZ correlation is greater than half of the MZ correlation, and an ADE model if the DZ correlation is less than half of the MZ correlation.

In either case, the extent to which MZ twin pairs resemble each other more for a trait (i.e., show higher twin correlations) than DZ twin pairs gives information on the relative influence of genetic versus environmental factors on a trait. Under the ACE model, the proportion of variance resulting from additive effects (A) or the heritability (a^2), can be calculated as twice the difference between the MZ and DZ correlations (Holzinger, 1929): $a^2 = 2(r_{MZ} - r_{DZ})$. An estimate of shared environment (C or c^2) can be calculated via twice the DZ correlation minus the MZ correlation: $c^2 = 2r_{DZ} - r_{MZ}$. Because MZ twins do not share the non-shared environmental variance (E or e^2), 1 minus the MZ correlation gives the contribution of the non-shared environment: $e^2 = 1 - r_{MZ}$. Because correlations are standardized (with unit variance), the total phenotypic variance (A + C + E) is also standardized. Therefore, each variance component represents the relative contribution to a trait.

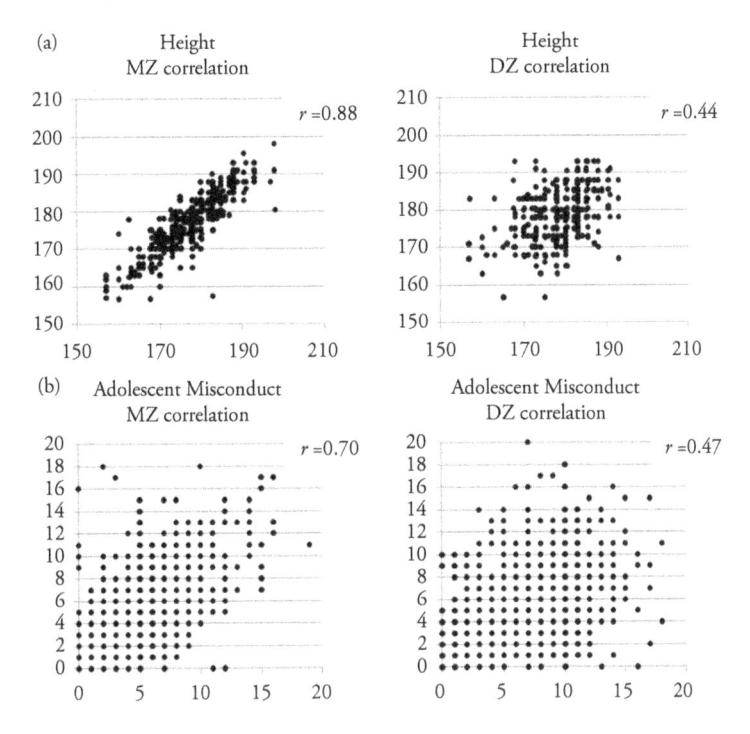

Figure 10.4 Twin correlations.

Notes: Scatter plots showing MZ and DZ twin pair correlations for (a) height in cm (males only) and (b) adolescent misconduct based on questionnaire data. Twin correlations for height indicate a high heritability for this trait, whereas twin correlations for adolescent misconduct point to moderate heritability. Data were provided by the Genetic Epidemiology Laboratory, Queensland Institute of Medical Research.

If we apply these formulas to the example data for height in Figure 10.4a, where the MZ twin correlation is 0.88 and the DZ correlation is 0.44, the heritability would be $a^2 = 2*(0.88 - 0.44) = 0.88$, and the common environmental influence would be $c^2 = (2*0.44) - 0.88 = 0$. A heritability of 0.88 should be interpreted to mean that 88% of the population variance in a trait can be attributed to variation at the genetic level. Importantly, this cannot be interpreted as height being genetically controlled for 88% of individuals. The estimate of the proportion of variance accounted for by E for this trait is 12%; notably, variance resulting from measurement error is also included in this estimate. For adolescent misconduct (Fig. 10.4b), where the MZ twin correlation is 0.70 and the DZ correlation is 0.47, the heritability would be $a^2 = 2*(0.70-0.47) = 0.46$ and the common environmental influence would be $c^2 = (2*0.47)-0.70 = 0.24$.

Figure 10.4b also illustrates how the range of values for the trait under investigation can affect the data distribution. In twin modeling it is important that the trait of interest shows a normal distribution in the entire sample, as well as in the MZ and DZ subsamples. If this is not the case, transformation of the data may be necessary. Otherwise, alternative models are available for data that violate this assumption (*see* section on the liability threshold model).

Structural Equation Modeling

The formulas developed by Holzinger (1929) are limited in their application to continuous phenotypes and univariate contexts. As much of the focus of modern quantitative genetics is on estimating the contribution of genetic effects to the covariation between phenotypes, the Holzinger method is seldom used in contemporary studies. The majority of current studies now use more sophisticated structural equation models to estimate these influences (Eaves, 1969; Eaves, Last, Martin, & Jinks, 1977; Martin & Eaves, 1977). These new methodologies allowed the development of models that more accurately reflect the complexities of human behavior and development (Mehta & Neale, 2005). *Structural equation modeling* (SEM) is used to test complex relationships between observed (measured) and unobserved (latent) variables and also relationships between two or more latent variables (Wright, 1921). For a more detailed explanation of structural equation modeling methodology, please refer to Chapter 15. The parameters of the structural equation model for the pattern of MZ and DZ variances and covariances can be estimated by several approaches, including *maximum likelihood* and *weighted least squares*. In this chapter we will assume that maximum likelihood methods are used.

Path diagrams (Fig. 10.5) provide a graphical representation of models. Path diagrams can be mapped directly to mathematical equations and are sometimes easier to understand. Structural equation modeling allows us to obtain maximum likelihood estimates of phenotypic means and genetic and environmental variance components, while also allowing for the explicit modeling of effects of covariates (e.g., sex, age, IQ) and interaction effects. The aim of maximum likelihood estimation is to find the parameter values that explain the observed data best. Likelihood ratio tests, which are asymptotically distributed as chi-square (χ^2), are used to compare the goodness of fit of reduced submodels (i.e., AE, CE, and E models) with that of the full ACE model. Model fit is evaluated according to the *principle of parsimony*, in which models with fewer parameters are considered preferable if they show no significant worsening of fit ($p > 0.05$) when compared to a full ACE model. A larger χ^2 (corresponding to a low probability) indicates a poor fit of the submodel; a smaller χ^2 (accompanied by a non-significant p value) indicates that the data are consistent with the fitted model.

For example, if dropping the A parameter from the ACE model (i.e., by equating the additive genetic path coefficient to zero) results in a significant worsening of model fit ($p < 0.05$), this signifies that the simpler CE model is not an accurate description of the observed data, and thereby indicates the significance of the genetic influences. Components of variance (A, C, or E) are calculated by dividing the squared value of the corresponding path coefficient by the total variance (i.e., the summed squared values of all path coefficients).

From Figure 10.5, the following algebraic statements can be derived for the variance/covariance matrices of MZ and DZ twins (Matrix 10.1), where the variance for each twin is located on the diagonal (shaded dark gray) with the covariance between twins on the off-diagonal (shaded light grey).

As mentioned previously, when estimating an ACE model it is assumed that there is no variance resulting from non-additive genetic influences (D).

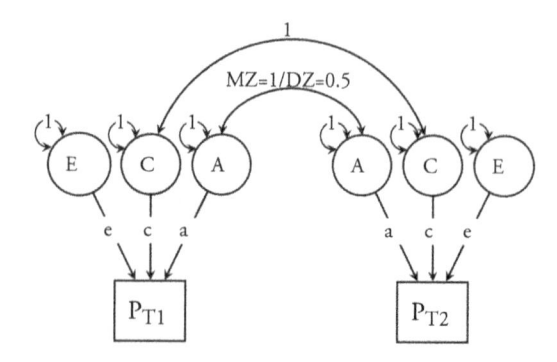

Figure 10.5 Path diagram depicting the classical twin model. Notes: P = phenotype; T1 = twin 1 of a pair; T2 = twin 2 of a pair; MZ = monozygotic; DZ = dizygotic; A = additive genetic influences; C = common environmental influences; E = unique environmental influences; a = additive genetic path coefficient; c = common environmental path coefficient; e = unique environmental path coefficient. Circles represent latent, unobserved variables; squares represent observed phenotypes; single-headed arrows represent influences of latent variables on observed variables; double-headed arrows represent (co)variances. Correlations between additive genetic factors (A) are fixed at 1 for MZ pairs and 0.5 for DZ pairs, because MZ twins share 100% of their segregating genes and DZ twins on average 50%. Correlations between common environmental factors (C) are fixed at 1 for both MZ and DZ twins, because both types of twins share 100% of their familial environment. By definition, E factors are left uncorrelated in both MZ and DZ twins because they are unique for each individual.

Matrix 10.1. ACE variance/covariance matrix.
Note: Occurrences of (0.5/1) refer to the alternate genetic correlations for DZ and MZ co-twins, respectively.

	Twin 1	Twin 2
Twin 1	$a^2 + c^2 + e^2$	$(0.5/1)a^2 + c^2$
Twin 2	$(0.5/1)a^2 + c^2$	$a^2 + c^2 + e^2$

Variance resulting from non-additive genetic influences (D) may also be estimated, where correlations between MZ twins are fixed at 1 and correlations between DZ twins are fixed at 0.25. The covariance structure of an ADE model is summarized in Figure 10.6 and in the matrix below (Matrix 10.2), where the variance for each twin is located on the diagonal (shaded dark gray) with the covariance between twins on the off-diagonal (shaded light grey).

The most commonly used software package for twin modeling is the flexible matrix algebra program, Mx (Neale, Boker, Xie, & Maes, 2002); Mx can be downloaded from: http://www.vcu.edu/mx/. The Mx website also

Matrix 10.2. ADE variance/covariance matrix.
Note: Occurrences of (0.5/1) and (0.25/1) refer to the alternate genetic correlations for DZ and MZ co-twins, respectively.

	Twin 1	Twin 2
Twin 1	$a^2 + d^2 + e^2$	$(0.5/1)a^2 + (0.25/1)d^2$
Twin 2	$(0.5/1)a^2 + (0.25/1)d^2$	$a^2 + d^2 + e^2$

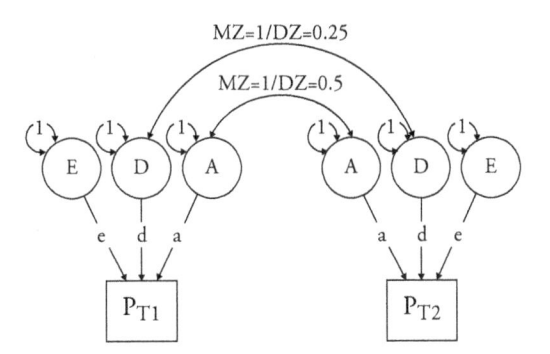

Figure 10.6 Path diagram depicting the ADE model. Notes: P = phenotype; T1 = twin 1 of a pair; T2 = twin 2 of a pair; MZ = monozygotic; DZ = dizygotic; A = additive genetic influences; D = dominance genetic influences; E = unique environmental influences; a = additive genetic path coefficient; d = dominance genetic path coefficient; e = unique environmental path coefficient. Circles represent latent, unobserved variables; squares represent observed phenotypes; single-headed arrows represent influences of latent variables on observed variables; double-headed arrows represent (co)variances.

contains (links to) example code for various models. Recently, Mx has been implemented within the R programming environment under the new name OpenMx (Boker et al., 2011); OpenMx and R can be downloaded from the following pages: http://openmx.psyc.virginia.edu/installing-openmx and http://www.r-project.org/, respectively. The OpenMx website also contains example code as well as a forum where OpenMx-related topics can be discussed. Another program suitable for twin modeling is Mplus (Muthén & Muthén, 1998–2010); the Mplus homepage can be found at: http://www.statmodel.com/. For family studies, when not utilizing twin data, SOLAR (Sequential Oligogenic Linkage Analysis Routines) can be used; the software can be downloaded from: http://solar.sfbrgenetics.org/download.html.

Assumptions of the Classical Twin Model

Several assumptions underlie the classical twin design, including generalizability, random mating, equal environments, and absence of genotype–environment interaction or genotype–environment correlation. These assumptions will be explained below.

GENERALIZABILITY

A frequently asked question regarding twin studies is whether their results can be generalized to the general population (i.e., singletons). The experience of being a twin, including the sharing of limited space and resources during gestation, and the differences in the birth process, may cause twins to be different from singletons. Generalizability can be assessed by comparing means and variances for a trait between twins and members of the general population, which are matched for age and sex. However, the best method of assessing generalizability is by extending the twin design to include the twins' own siblings within the analysis. Comparing the DZ co-twin correlation with twin–sibling correlations allows an examination of the role of pre- or perinatal factors on the trait of interest (correcting for age). One of the advantages of comparing twins with their own non-twin siblings is that by using siblings as the control group we can, at least partly, control for variance in maternal size (i.e., intrauterine size and body shape, which may influence the length of gestation and ease of delivery) and the effects of genetic transmission (as both DZ twins and their full siblings share, on average, 50% of their genetic material). Although twins do differ from singletons for some traits, especially those related to prenatal growth, most studies generally do not find differences in personality and social traits (Evans, Gillespie, & Martin, 2002). If this assumption is violated, additional twin-specific effects will need to be incorporated in the model.

RANDOM MATING

The assumption that DZ twins share on average 50% of their genes no longer holds true in the case of *assortative mating*. Visscher et al. (2006) used molecular data to get exact measures of average genetic sharing of sibling pairs, which in a sample of 4,401 sibling pairs ranged from 37% to 61%. Assortative mating may be based on phenotypic similarity (positive assortment) or dissimilarity (negative assortment). Positive assortative mating refers to the situation where prospective mating partners are more likely to select each other when they possess similar traits. As these traits will probably be at least partly caused by similar gene variants, their children are likely to share more than 50% of their genetic information, for genetic loci influencing the trait of interest. To illustrate, Maes et al. (1998) investigated assortative mating in the context of major depression, generalized anxiety disorder, panic disorder, and phobias, and found considerable associations between partners for most psychiatric diagnoses. Assortment was observed both within and between classes of psychiatric disorders. Variables correlated with the psychiatric diagnoses, such as age, religious attendance, and education, did explain part, but not all, of the assortment between partners.

Because assortative mating increases the correlations between mates, estimates of the relative genetic and environmental influences based on a twin design will be biased if assortative mating is present and is not appropriately accounted for. When parents are more genetically alike than expected by chance, the DZ twins' genetic resemblance will on average be more than 50% because of the transmission of the correlated parental genes. As a result, the resemblance of DZ twin pairs will increase relative to MZ twin pairs. Unmodeled assortative mating will therefore result in artificially inflated estimates of the shared environmental component and an underestimation of heritability. The presence of assortative mating can be studied by calculation of the phenotypic correlation between the parents of twins, or the phenotypic correlation between twins and their spouses, assuming that the extent of assortative mating does not change across generations.

THE DEGREE OF GENETIC SIMILARITY BETWEEN MZ TWINS

Although MZ twins are assumed to be genetically identical, a study of 19 MZ twin pairs detected subtle differences in copy number variations of the DNA (Bruder et al., 2008). These differences occur when a set of coding nucleotide bases in DNA are missing or when extra copies appear. It is currently theorized that at the time of conception MZ twins are genetically identical; however, during subsequent DNA replications and cell division, a small number of mutations may occur. The same phenomenon would also decrease the "known" degree of relatedness between DZ twins (50%), parents and children (50%), half siblings (25%), etc. This would also mean that age differences would influence the degree of relatedness in family studies (i.e., newborns would have fewer mutations than their older family members simply because they are younger).

EQUAL ENVIRONMENTS

The twin method partitions the environment into that which is shared between co-twins and that which is unshared. Generally the shared environment is assumed to include prenatal effects and the effects of growing up in the same household. This interpretation relies on the assumption that MZ and DZ twins experience shared environments to the same extent (i.e., that trait-relevant environmental influences contribute equally to the resemblance of MZ and DZ twin pairs). This assumption has received much attention. It has been found that MZ twins are treated more similarly than DZ twins in certain aspects; as young children they share a bedroom and are dressed alike more often, and they are more likely to share the same friends and stay in closer contact once they leave home (Cohen, Dibble, Grawe, & Pollin, 1973; Kendler, Heath, Martin, & Eaves, 1987; Loehlin & Nichols, 1976). However, it is not clear whether greater environmental similarity results in greater phenotypic similarity.

Furthermore, as highlighted by Heath et al. (1989), environmental inequality would only result in bias if the trait of interest happened to be affected by those environmental factors that differ between twins. Salient environmental influences that are more similar for MZ compared to DZ twins would increase twin correlations in MZ twins, inappropriately inflating estimates of trait heritability. Several methods have been used to test the equal environments assumption, including correlating perceived zygosity with the trait while controlling for actual zygosity (Kendler et al., 1993; Matheny, Wilson, & Dolan, 1976; Plomin, Willerman, & Loehlin, 1976; Scarr, 1982; Scarr & Carter-Saltzman, 1979), direct observation of family members and others to examine their self-initiated and twin-initiated behaviors toward the different twin types (Lytton, Martin, & Eaves, 1977), and correlating the similarity of the twin environments with the trait while controlling for actual zygosity (Borkenau, Riemann, Angleitner, & Spinath, 2002; Heath, Jardine, & Martin, 1989; Kendler et al., 1987; Martin et al., 1986).

A modeling-based approach is the extension of the classical ACE model by partitioning the common environment into the usual common environment, $C_{residual}$, which is completely correlated for all twin pairs, and that which is influenced by the perceived zygosity, $C_{specific}$, which is parameterized to be completely correlated if both twins perceive themselves to be MZ, completely uncorrelated if both twins perceive themselves to be DZ, and correlated at 0.5 if the twins disagree about their perceived zygosity (Hettema, Neale, & Kendler, 1995; Kendler et al., 1993; Scarr & Carter-Saltzman, 1979; Xian et al., 2000).

Furthermore, when data have been collected from non-twin siblings, checking for differences between the DZ covariance and the twin–sibling and sibling–sibling covariances can provide an additional test of the equal environments assumption. Arguably, if the more similar treatment of MZ twins were affecting their trait values, one might also expect more similar treatment of DZ twins as compared to regular siblings. When using ordinal data, equality of the thresholds of MZ and DZ twins indicates there are no differences in variances between MZ and DZ twin pairs, excluding the possibility of an extra environmental influence specific to MZ twins. The most recent method to remove equal environment biases allows heritability to be estimated from non-twin siblings (Visscher et al., 2006).

Although MZ and DZ mean differences have been found for traits such as birth weight (Koziel, 1998) and similar dress (Matheny, Wilson, & Dolan, 1976), rigorous and frequent testing of characteristics such as physical twin similarity (Hettema, Neale, & Kendler, 1995), self-perceived zygosity (Xian et al., 2000), perceived zygosity and associated parental approach to rearing their twins (Cronk et al., 2002; Kendler & Gardner, 1998; Kendler et al., 1993; Kendler et al., 1994), self-reported similarity of childhood experiences (Borkenau, Riemann, Angleitner, & Spinath, 2002), and physical and emotional closeness between the twins (Cronk et al., 2002; Kendler & Gardner, 1998; LaBuda, Svikis, & Pickens, 1997), has shown that these traits are uncorrelated with zygosity differences in intelligence, personality, and psychiatric disorders such as alcohol and illicit drug dependence, major depression, anxiety, and externalizing disorders, thereby supporting the validity of the equal environmental assumption in twin studies assessing these phenotypes.

GENOTYPE–ENVIRONMENT INTERACTION

The classical twin model does not take the possible presence of genotype–environment (GxE) interaction into account. *Gene–environment interaction* occurs when environments have differential effects on different genotypes. For example, Boomsma and colleagues (1999) found that a religious upbringing reduces the influence of genetic factors on disinhibition. A recent study of borderline personality disorder by Distel et al. (2011) also found evidence for GxE interaction. For individuals who had experienced a divorce/break-up, violent assault, sexual assault, or job loss, environmental variance for borderline personality disorder features was higher, leading to a lower heritability in exposed individuals. Jinks and Fulker (1970) suggested a screening test for GxE interaction using data from MZ twin pairs, whereby the intrapair differences are plotted against the sum of the co-twins' phenotypic values. A significant correlation between these two indicates the presence of GxE interaction. However, to avoid spurious results, this test requires data from MZ twins reared apart, and it is unsuitable for binary data. Purcell (2002) proposed another approach to the detection of GxE interaction, which allows the explicit modeling of the interaction through extension of the classical twin design. In order to model the interaction, the environmental covariate(s) must be entered into the analysis as an observed variable, thus limiting the application of this approach to the study of already known or suspected environmental covariates.

GENOTYPE–ENVIRONMENT CORRELATION

Gene–environment correlation (r_{GE}) occurs when individuals actively or passively expose themselves to different environments depending on their genotype, or when individuals' genotypes affect their social interactions or influence the responses they elicit from other individuals (Falconer & Mackay, 1996; Plomin, DeFries, & Loehlin, 1977). If r_{GE} is positive it could result in an increase in the total phenotypic variance of the trait. Alternatively, in the case of a negative r_{GE}, the total phenotypic variance would be decreased. Distel et al. (2011) also found evidence for gene–environment correlation. The genetic effects that influence borderline personality disorder features also increased the likelihood of being exposed to certain life events. Three types of r_{GE} have been described by Plomin et al. (1977), namely *cultural transmission, autocorrelation, and sibling effects.*

Cultural transmission refers to the environmental effect of the parental phenotype on the offspring's phenotype (Neale & Maes, 2004; i.e., resemblance between parents and offspring that results from a home environment created by the parents). To use a simplistic example, imagine two children taking part in a study of reading ability. Both children come from the same socio-economic strata and have very similar backgrounds. The parents of child A enjoy reading and have many books in their home, thus child A is read to as young child, observes his/her parents reading, and grows up in an environment where books are accessible. The parents of child B do not enjoy reading; they do not own many books and do not use the local library. Child B thus grows up in an environment where books are less accessible, and despite being read to as young child because the parents feel this is important, child B does not often observe his/her parents reading. As it is likely that the environmental differences between the two children are related to the genetic variants influencing reading ability, the environmental and genetic effects become correlated. Failure to model this correlation can inflate the heritability of reading ability in the children. The effects of cultural transmission may be examined by extending the twin design to include parental data. Such a design also allows for a test of the assumption of random or non-assortative mating (Neale & Maes, 2004).

Gene–environment autocorrelation occurs when environments are not randomly assigned to each individual but are, in part, individually selected on the basis of genetically influenced preferences. For example, when gifted individuals create or evoke situations that further enhance their intellectual ability, or when genetically introverted individuals choose to avoid situations where they may be the focus of attention.

Sibling interactions may be either cooperative, increasing the trait value of the co-twin (imitation effect), or competitive, decreasing the trait value in the co-twin (contrast effect; Carey, 1986). Cooperation effects increase the variance and decrease the covariance of MZ twins relative to DZ twins, while competition produces the opposite effects.

Correlated effects of genotypes and environments are difficult to detect. If not explicitly modeled, r_{GE} between the latent A and E variables behave like additive effects, whereas r_{GE} between the latent A and C variables acts like C.

Extensions to the Classical Twin Model

The classical twin model is the most basic twin model one can employ. There are many extensions available, the most basic of which is the incorporation of covariates to improve the estimation of phenotypic means. This allows for correction for effects such as age and gender, but also for effects of other variables that may confound the estimation of heritability. For example, if our trait of interest is cerebro-vascular disease in addition to age and gender, we may want to include smoking behavior as a covariate; if our trait of interest is education, we may want to include socio-economic status as a covariate.

SEX LIMITATION

Sex differences may obscure the data in different ways. Opposite-sex DZ twins can reduce the overall DZ twin covariance significantly if males and females differ greatly in their phenotypic values. Sex limitation refers to sex differences in the magnitude and/or proportion of the variance accounted for by genetic and environmental effects (Neale & Maes, 2004). If twin pair correlations differ between the sexes within zygosity, it is better to estimate A, C, and E separately for males and females. Three types of sex limitation have been described: quantitative, qualitative, and scalar.

In the *quantitative sex limitation model* the genetic and environmental sources of variance and covariance in males and females are assumed to be the same (i.e., sex-specific pathways are fixed to zero) but the magnitudes of these effects are allowed to differ and the correlations for additive genetic and common environmental influences in the opposite-sex DZ pairs are assumed to be 0.5 and 1, respectively. If data from opposite-sex DZ twins have been collected, the difference in fit (χ^2) between this model and the qualitative sex limitation model can be used to examine whether the same genetic or environmental factors are influencing males and females (Neale & Maes, 2004). Silventoinen et al. (2001) did this for height in two cohorts of twins (born in 1938–1949 and in 1975–1979) and found that the heritability estimates were higher among men ($h^2 = 0.87$ in the older cohort and $h^2 = 0.82$ in the younger cohort) than women ($h^2 = 0.78$ and $h^2 = 0.67$, respectively). Sex-specific genetic factors were not statistically significant in either cohort, suggesting that the same genes contribute to variation in body height for both men and women.

The hypothesis underlying *qualitative sex limitation models* is that different genetic or environmental factors influence trait variation in males and females. This model includes an extra genetic or environmental component (m^2) that contributes to either males or females. Differences in both genetic and environmental effects cannot be tested simultaneously when working with twin and sibling data. Therefore, one would usually run this model twice; once specifying m^2 as an additive genetic parameter ($r = 0.5$ for DZ twins) and once specifying m^2 as a common environment parameter ($r = 1$ for DZ twins). Derks and colleagues (2007) found this to be the case for attention deficit-hyperactivity disorder (ADHD) and oppositional defiant disorder (ODD). The heritabilities for both ADHD and ODD were high and of a similar magnitude for boys and girls. However, the source of this genetic variation differed between boys and girls, indicating that some genetic loci may be having sex-specific influences on these traits.

The *scalar sex limitation* is the simplest and most restrictive of the three models. Here the absolute magnitude of the total variance, and thus the unstandardized variance components, differ between males and females while the proportion of variance accounted for by genetic and environmental effects, that is, the standardized variance components, are equal across sexes. In the scalar model not only are the sex-specific effects removed, but the variance components for females are all constrained to be equal to a scalar multiple (k) of the male variance components, such that $a_f^2 = ka_m^2$, and $e_f^2 = ke_m^2$ (Neale & Maes, 2004). This model is a submodel of both the quantitative and qualitative sex limitation models, and can only be tested using continuous data, as variances are fixed to unity when working with ordinal data.

Normally you would test for the presence of sex limitation as part of testing a series of assumptions prior to fitting the ACE or ADE model. These assumptions include the equality of means and variances across zygosity and birth order, the equality of means and variances between twins and siblings, and the equality of means, variances, and covariances across the two sexes.

LIABILITY THRESHOLD MODEL

The classical twin design assumes that the trait of interest is a continuous variable, with a normal distribution. However, many traits that may be of interest are ordinal or dichotomous variables, such as medical or psychiatric diagnoses. For such variables, a liability threshold model can be used to estimate twin correlations and heritability. Threshold models assume that there is an underlying continuum of liability (e.g., to depression or ADHD) that is normally distributed in the population, and that our measurement categories (e.g., depressed/not depressed) result from one or more artificial divisions (thresholds) overlaying this normal distribution. Analyses are effectively performed on the underlying liability

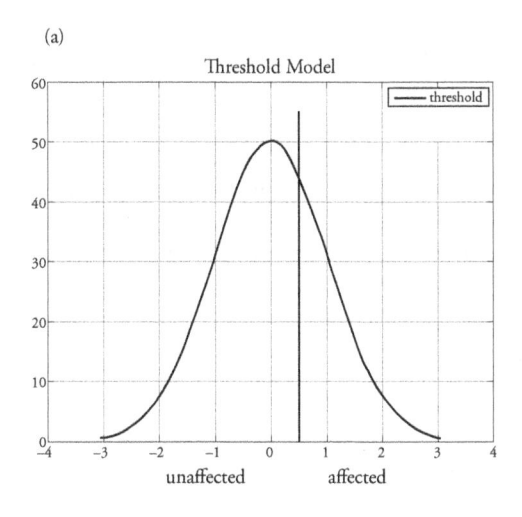

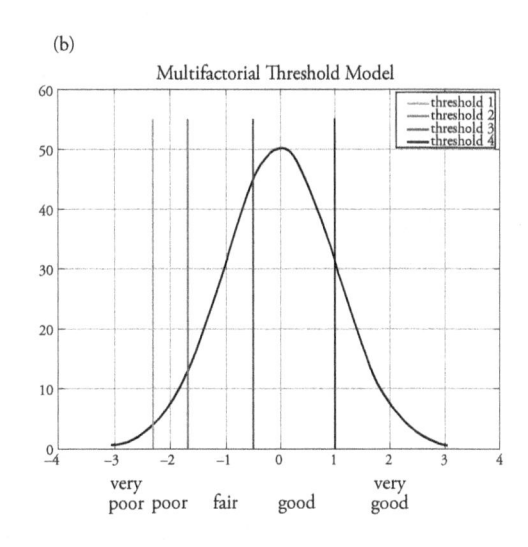

Figure 10.7 The threshold model.
Notes: (a) Univariate normal distribution for dichotomous phenotype. One threshold is shown (at z-value +0.5) corresponding to 2 categories with the frequencies 69% and 31%. (b) Univariate normal distribution with thresholds distinguishing ordered response categories. Four thresholds are shown (at z-values −2.30, −1.70, −0.5, and +1) corresponding to 5 categories with the frequencies, 1%, 3%, 27%, 53%, and 16%.

to the trait, resulting in estimates of the heritability of the liability. Figure 10.7 illustrates the threshold model. Panel A shows a model with a single threshold, separating persons into two classes, unaffected or affected, such as children with ADHD and controls. Panel B shows a liability threshold model with four thresholds (i.e., five categories), which could apply to a study of self-rated health, where the response categories were "very good," "good," "fair," "poor", and "very poor" (e.g., Mosing et al., 2009). Liability to psychiatric disorders such as ADHD, depression, anxiety, and schizophrenia has been found to be influenced by genetic factors (Hettema, Neale, & Kendler, 2001; Jepsen & Michel, 2006; Kendler, Gatz, Gardner, & Pedersen, 2006a, 2006b; Sullivan, Kendler, & Neale, 2003; Sullivan, Neale, & Kendler, 2000), with heritability estimates of >70%.

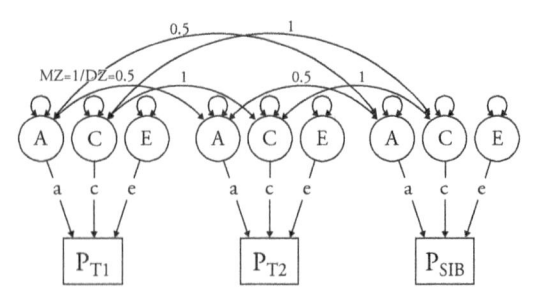

Figure 10.8 Path diagram depicting the extended twin model. Notes: P = phenotype; T1 = twin 1 of a pair; T2 = twin 2 of a pair; SIB = singleton sibling; MZ = monozygotic; DZ = dizygotic; A = additive genetic influences; C = common environmental influences; E = unique environmental influences; a = additive genetic path coefficient; c = common environmental path coefficient; e = unique environmental path coefficient. Circles represent latent, unobserved variables; squares represent observed phenotypes; single-headed arrows represent influences of latent variables on observed variables; double-headed arrows represent (co)variances.

INCLUDING DATA FROM ADDITIONAL FAMILY MEMBERS

As briefly mentioned above, the classical twin design can be extended by including singleton (non-twin) siblings, parents, children, and spouses. Including additional family members substantially enhances the statistical power to detect non-additive genetic and common environmental influences resulting from a greater number of observed covariance statistics (Posthuma et al., 2003). The power to detect common environmental influences is maximized when there are four times as many DZ pairs as MZ pairs (Nance & Neale, 1989). As siblings have the same amount of genetic material in common as DZ twins (on average 50%), including data from extra siblings in the model effectively increases the DZ to MZ ratio. As discussed above, adding data from non-twin siblings makes it possible to test for twin-specific environmental influences. The variance and covariance of additional siblings are modeled in the same way as for a DZ twin (Fig. 10.8). If we were to include the data of one extra sibling the typical variance-covariance matrix would be extended as shown in Matrix 10.3. Additional siblings can be added in the same way. Variances are on the diagonal highlighted in the darkest shade of gray, the intrapair covariances are a shade lighter on the off-diagonal, and the twin–sibling covariances are highlighted in the lightest shade of grey on the outermost row and column of the matrix.

The extended twin family model or the nuclear family model also allows for the estimation of more parameters and relaxed assumptions regarding mating and cultural transmission. For example, adding parental data to the model makes it possible to estimate effects from assortative mating, familial transmission, sibling environment, and the correlation between additive genetic effects and family environment (Keller et al., 2009), as well as allowing for the simultaneous estimation of C and D influences.

Another method allowing for the estimation of A, C, D and E in the same model is the twin adoption

Matrix 10.3. Extended variance/covariance matrix.
Note: Occurrences of (0.5/1) refer to the alternate genetic correlations for DZ and MZ co-twins, respectively.

	Twin 1	Twin 2	Sibling
Twin 1	$a^2 + c^2 + e^2$	$(0.5/1)a^2 + c^2$	$0.5a^2 + c^2$
Twin 2	$(0.5/1)a^2 + c^2$	$a^2 + c^2 + e^2$	$0.5a^2 + c^2$
Sibling	$0.5a^2 + c^2$	$0.5a^2 + c^2$	$a^2 + c^2 + e^2$

design. Here, twins raised apart (with no shared environmental influences) are compared to twins raised together. This design has a great explanatory power to facilitate separation of biological from environmental influences (Medland & Hatemi, 2009). However, because of ethical and legal hurdles, twin adoption studies are increasingly difficult to conduct. Also, modern adoption policies facilitate twins being adopted together, rapidly decreasing the number of twins reared apart. Finally, there are other methodological factors that have to be taken into account, such as contact with the biological family, age of adoption, time spent in state care or protective custody, and selective placement (i.e., matching of the infants' biological and adoptive environments), each of which may bias the sample. As a result of these caveats, which are hard to overcome, the twin adoption design is used only rarely and will not be explained here in further detail.

Multivariate Modeling

The twin model can also be extended to include multiple phenotypes. In the case of a multivariate design the aim is to decompose the covariance between traits into that caused by A, C, and E in the same way as one would with the phenotypic variance of a single trait. A multivariate design allows us to investigate the extent to which common sets of genes (genetic correlation, r_g), shared environmental factors (common environmental correlation, r_c) or unshared environmental factors (unique environmental correlation, r_e) underlie correlations between phenotypes. Matrix 10.4 shows a schematic representation of the variance/covariance matrix for a bivariate model. The corresponding path diagram is shown in Figure 10.9.

The model in Figure 10.9 employs Cholesky decomposition (named after its developer André-Louis Cholesky) and can be extended in a similar way to include many more phenotypes. In linear algebra, the Cholesky decomposition or Cholesky triangle is a decomposition of a symmetric, positive-definite matrix into the product of a lower triangular matrix and its conjugate transpose. Cholesky decomposition or triangular decomposition, illustrated in Figure 10.9 for two variables, can represent a multivariate analysis of simultaneously measured variables considered in some rationally defined order of priority (Loehlin, 1996; Neale & Maes, 2004). The first latent additive genetic variable (A1) explains the genetic influences on the first phenotype (P1) and the correlated genetic influences on the second phenotype (P2). The second latent additive genetic variable (A2) is uncorrelated with A1 and explains the remaining heritability of P2. Similar latent structures are estimated for E and C or D. From this basic model, parameters can be dropped or equated to test specific hypotheses regarding those parameters. The goal is to explain the data with as few underlying factors as possible, by testing which paths are significant (i.e., by setting the path coefficients to zero and noting whether this results in a significant decrease in model fit). For a review on how to use SEM programs to perform Cholesky decomposition please see, for example, Raykov, Marcoulides, and Boyd (2003).

Multivariate modeling can accommodate numerous variables, and can be used for both exploratory and confirmatory factor analysis, as well as longitudinal and causal analyses. It should be emphasized that the final results depend on the ordering—if we had considered the latent variables in the reverse order, A2 would be a factor with paths to both variables, and A1 a residual. Only in the case of uncorrelated variables is the order of selection irrelevant (Loehlin, 1996), but in that case multivariate modeling should not be used anyway.

One example application of multivariate twin modeling is the use of this method to examine genetic contributions to the comorbidity between psychiatric disorders. More than a dozen studies have revealed a shared genetic vulnerability between anxiety and depression, particularly between major depressive disorder and generalized anxiety disorder (*see* Cerda, Sagdeo, Johnson, & Galea, 2010, for a review).

COMMON PATHWAY MODEL

The common and independent pathway models can be considered submodels of the standard Cholesky decomposition. The *common pathway model* hypothesizes that the covariation between variables results from a single underlying "phenotypic" latent variable. A frequent application of this model is the examination of symptom dimensions in complex, heterogeneous diseases. For example, van Grootheest et al. (2008) applied this model to obsessive-compulsive behavior and found that the three symptom dimensions—Rumination, Contamination, and Checking—share variation with a latent common factor, denoted obsessive-compulsive behavior. Variation in this common factor was explained by both genes (36%) and environmental factors (64%). Only the Contamination dimension was influenced by specific genes and seemed to be a relatively

Matrix 10.4. Schematic presentation of the bivariate variance/covariance matrix.

Notes: Variances are on the diagonal (darkest shade of gray), the within-individual-cross-trait covariances are in the upper-left and lower-right quadrants on the off-diagonal, the within-trait-cross-twin covariances are in the upper-right and lower-left quadrants on the diagonal, and the cross-trait-cross-twin covariances are on the counter-diagonal (lightest shade of grey). Occurrences of (0.5/1) refer to the alternate genetic correlations for DZ and MZ co-twins, respectively. Abbreviations: P1 = phenotype 1; P2 = phenotype 2.

		Twin 1		Twin 2	
		P1	P2	P1	P2
Twin 1	P1	$a_{P1}^2 + c_{P1}^2 + e_{P1}^2$	$r_A a_{P1} a_{P2} + r_C c_{P1} c_{P2} + r_E e_{P1} e_{P2}$	$(0.5/1)a_{P1}^2 + c_{P1}^2$	$(0.5/1)r_A a_{P1} a_{P2} + r_C c_{P1} c_{P2}$
	P2	$r_A a_{P1} a_{P2} + r_C c_{P1} c_{P2} + r_E e_{P1} e_{P2}$	$a_{P2}^2 + c_{P2}^2 + e_{P2}^2$	$(0.5/1)r_A a_{P1} a_{P2} + r_C c_{P1} c_{P2}$	$(0.5/1)a_{P2}^2 + c_{P2}^2$
Twin 2	P1	$(0.5/1)a_{P1}^2 + c_{P1}^2$	$(0.5/1)r_A a_{P1} a_{P2} + r_C c_{P1} c_{P2}$	$a_{P1}^2 + c_{P1}^2 + e_{P1}^2$	$r_A a_{P1} a_{P2} + r_C c_{P1} c_{P2} + r_E e_{P1} e_{P2}$
	P2	$(0.5/1)r_A a_{P1} a_{P2} + r_C c_{P1} c_{P2}$	$(0.5/1)a_{P2}^2 + c_{P2}^2$	$r_A a_{P1} a_{P2} + r_C c_{P1} c_{P2} + r_E e_{P1} e_{P2}$	$a_{P2}^2 + c_{P2}^2 + e_{P2}^2$

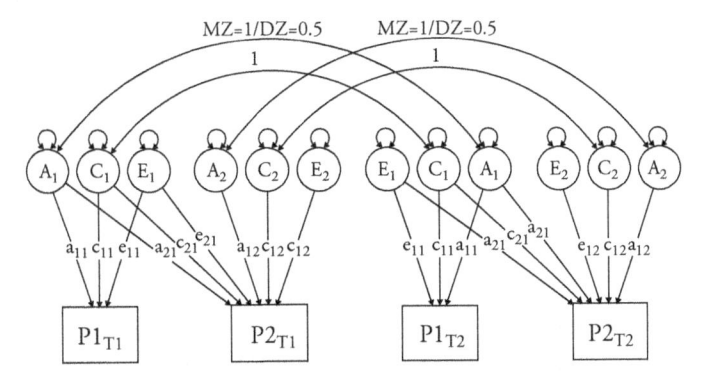

Figure 10.9 Path diagram depicting the bivariate twin model.
Notes: P1 = phenotype 1; P2 = phenotype 2; T1 = twin 1 of a pair; T2 = twin 2 of a pair; MZ = monozygotic; DZ = dizygotic; A1 = additive genetic influence 1; C1 = common environmental influence 1; E1 = unique environmental influence 1; A2 = additive genetic influence 2; C2 = common environmental influence 2; E2 = unique environmental influence 2; a = additive genetic path coefficient; c = common environmental path coefficient; e = unique environmental path coefficient. Circles represent latent, unobserved variables; squares represent observed phenotypes; single-headed arrows represent influences of latent variables on observed variables; double-headed arrows represent (co)variances.

independent dimension. The results suggest that a broad obsessive-compulsive behavioral phenotype exists, influenced by both genes and unshared environment. However, the common pathway model, although it is conceptually attractive, often does not fit the observed data well because the amount of genetic and environmental variation transmitted from the latent factor is defined by the phenotypic correlation between the measured and latent variables (Medland & Hatemi, 2009).

INDEPENDENT PATHWAY MODEL

On the other hand, the *independent pathway model* hypothesizes that the variance and covariance between the variables is expected to result from one (or sometimes two) common factor(s) with the residual variance reflecting variable-specific genetic and environmental effects. This is the case, for example, with cognitive domains and latency of event-related potentials (Hansell et al., 2005; Luciano et al., 2004). Both the common and independent pathway models are nested within the previously described Cholesky decomposition. The fit of these models may therefore be compared to the "saturated model" using a likelihood ratio test, which is asymptotically distributed as χ^2 with the degrees of freedom equal to the difference in the number of estimated parameters between the nested and saturated models.

CROSS-SECTIONAL COHORT AND LONGITUDINAL DESIGNS

Once the role of genetic factors in the variance of a particular trait has been established, an additional question that can be addressed is whether the magnitude of these genetic influences is stable over time. Instead of a costly and time-consuming longitudinal study (which is another possibility; see below), this can be investigated with a *cohort design*, in which genetic and environmental estimates are obtained from different cohorts. In such a design, subjects from different age cohorts are assessed on one or more phenotypes. For example, Lyons et al. (1998) used a cohort design to examine the diagnosis of early- and late-onset major depression in men. Early-onset (before 30 years of age) and late-onset (after 30 years of age) major depression were both significantly influenced by genetic factors (early-onset: $h^2 = 0.47$; late-onset: $h^2 = 0.10$) and unique environmental factors (early-onset: $e^2 = 0.53$; late-onset: $e^2 = 0.90$), but early-onset major depression (95% CI: 0.32, 0.61) was significantly more heritable than late-onset major depression (95% CI: 0.01, 0.29). However, determining whether the same genes are involved at different stages of life is not possible with a cohort design. In addition, phenotypic differences resulting from age are confounded with any other differences between the cohorts.

With *longitudinal twin data* it is possible to estimate to what extent the relative contributions of genetic and environmental factors to the observed phenotypic variance are stable over time, and to what extent these genetic and environmental contributions are specific to a certain time of life. One use of the Cholesky decomposition is in temporal contexts (Loehlin, 1996). For example, phenotypes P1 to P3 might represent measurements of a trait at three successive times. In this case, A1 would represent genetic influences present at time 1, affecting the observed trait at time 1 and on subsequent occasions; A2 would represent additional genetic influences that have arisen by time 2 and whose effects are added to those of A1; and, finally, A3 represents additional genetic influences, affecting only the third measurement (P3). To illustrate, studies on the heritability of cognitive abilities have repeatedly shown an increase in genetic influences and a decrease in common environmental influences over the life span (Ando, Ono, & Wright, 2001; Bartels, Rietveld, van Baal, & Boomsma, 2002; Boomsma & van Baal, 1998; Luciano et al., 2001; Petrill et al., 2004; Plomin, 1999; Posthuma, de Geus, & Boomsma, 2001).

Increasing heritability over the life span could result from genes that are activated or become more active later in life, or may result from a decrease in the influence of environmental factors, as a result of which the relative contribution of genetic influences increases. Although it is possible to use a standard Cholesky decomposition for the purposes of a longitudinal study (as mentioned above), various longitudinal models have been described, including the genetic simplex model (Boomsma & Molenaar, 1987; Eaves, Long, & Heath, 1986) and latent growth curve models (Baker, Reynolds, & Phelps, 1992; McArdle, 1986; Neale & McArdle, 2000).

The *genetic simplex model* is based on the frequent observation that correlations are highest among adjoining occasions and that they fall away systematically as the distance between time points increases. Such a pattern is called a *simplex structure* after Guttman (1955). The genetic simplex design allows for modeling of changes in latent true scores over time by fitting autoregressive or Markovian chains. In *autoregression* each latent true score is predicted to be causally related to the immediately preceding latent true score in a linear fashion (linear regression of latent factor on the previous latent factor), while allowing for genetic/environmental change or innovation that is uncorrelated with the previous latent factor at each consecutive time point. Using this design Gillespie et al. (2004) were able to show that although female neuroticism shows a degree of genetic continuity, there are also age-specific genetic effects (genetic innovation), which could be related to developmental or hormonal changes during puberty and psychosexual development.

Growth curve models can be applied to assess the heritability of rate of change (increase or decrease) in a trait (e.g., cognitive abilities, brain volumes) throughout development. Reynolds et al. (2005) applied the growth curve model to a measure of cognitive abilities in adulthood. They examined sources of variability for ability level (intercept) and rate of change (linear and quadratic effects) for verbal, fluid, memory, and perceptual speed abilities. With the exception of one verbal and two memory measures, estimated variance components indicated decreasing genetic and increasing non-shared environmental variation over age, providing support for theories of the increasing influence of the environment on cognitive abilities with age.

CAUSAL MODELS

When two correlated traits have rather different modes of inheritance (e.g., family resemblance is determined largely by family background, C, for one trait and by genetic factors, A or D, for the other trait), cross-sectional family data will allow for testing of unidirectional causal hypotheses ("A and B are correlated because A causes B" versus "because B causes A"), through the pattern of cross-twin cross-trait correlations (Gillespie & Martin, 2005; Heath et al., 1993). This model makes it possible to model specific environmental risk factors. For example, proposing a twin-family model that incorporates childhood parental loss as a specific environmental risk factor, Kendler et al. (1996) examined how much of the association between childhood parental loss (through separation) and alcoholism was causal (i.e., mediated by environmental factors) versus non-causal (mediated by genetic factors, with parental loss serving as an index of parental genetic susceptibility to alcoholism). Both the causal-environmental pathway and non-causal genetic paths were significant for alcoholism. However, the causal-environmental pathway consistently accounted for most of the association, suggesting childhood parental loss is a direct and significant environmental risk factor for the development of alcoholism in women. De Moor et al. (2008) tested the hypothesis that exercise reduces symptoms of anxiety and depression, and found that although regular exercise is associated with reduced anxious and depressive symptoms in the population, the association is not because of causal effects of exercise.

LATENT CLASS ANALYSIS

Latent class analysis can be used to investigate whether distinct classes of disease subtypes can be identified, which can be used to refine genetic analyses. Using this approach, Althoff et al. (2006) were able to identify inattentive, hyperactive, or combined subtypes for ADHD based on the Child Behavior Check List. Latent class analysis allows for modeling of etiological heterogeneity in disease subtypes; for example, it compares a model that allows for genetic heterogeneity that is expressed only in individuals exposed to a high-risk "predisposing" environment (i.e., differential sensitivity of latent classes to measured covariates) with a model that allows the environment to differentiate two forms of the disorder in individuals of high genetic risk (i.e., GxE interaction; Eaves et al., 1993).

The genetic models described above and the related matrix algebra have been explained in more detail elsewhere, such as in Neale and Maes' *Methodology for Genetic Studies of Twins and Families* (2004). This book is downloadable free of charge at http://ibgwww.colorado.edu/workshop2006/cdrom/HTML/BOOK.HTM.

Twin Studies and Beyond

Twin studies have shown that almost every trait is heritable to some extent. Although the behavior genetics approach allows for the determination of the ratio of genetic and environmental influences, neither the number of genetic loci influencing a trait, nor the direction of these genetic effects, nor the location, nor identity of the loci can be determined with this approach. Thus, the next interesting step in genetic research is to identify specific genetic variants underlying the trait. Identification of specific genetic variants influencing complex traits provides knowledge about underlying biological mechanisms and identified genetic variants could potentially be used as biomarkers for screening, prevention, and medical treatment.

Linkage and candidate gene association studies were the first to search for underlying genetic variants. Linkage studies test for coinheritance of genetic markers and traits within families and are used to localize regions of the genome where a locus is harbored that regulates the trait. Candidate gene association studies test for a correlation between a specific genetic marker and the trait of interest in population samples. The markers tested generally have a known function that is hypothesized to influence the trait. Linkage and candidate gene studies have identified numerous potential regions and genes underlying complex traits, but they have not always been consistently replicated (Bosker et al., 2011; Verweij et al., 2012).

Recent technological advances have enabled genome-wide association studies (GWAS), where single-nucleotide polymorphisms (SNPs) across the entire genome are systematically tested for association with the trait of interest. Genome-wide association studies do not take prior knowledge of gene function into account, so the approach is hypothesis-free. For complex traits, the results of GWAS are mixed. Genome-wide association studies have been successful in identifying genetic variants of large effect for a number of relatively rare disease traits (Burton et al., 2007; Visscher & Montgomery, 2009). There have also been some successes in identifying many genetic variants of small effect underlying complex traits (i.e., schizophrenia, autism, and smoking; Liu et al., 2010; The International Schizophrenia Consortium, 2009; Wang et al., 2009).

Other technological advances, such as next-generation sequencing, assessment of copy number variation (CNV) and methylation rates will provide new opportunities. These approaches are promising, but only the future can tell us whether these methods will enable us to better unravel the genetic etiology of complex traits. A more in-depth description of linkage and association studies and their methodological background can be found in Chapter 11.

Summary

Twin studies have contributed greatly to our knowledge about biological pathways. Although application of the twin model has revealed that almost every conceivable trait is partly genetically influenced, understanding the source of variance does not offer any indication of the number or location of genes influencing the trait. Twin studies provide one method of investigating the ongoing nature-nurture debate and are a very important and necessary first step in genetic analyses. In addition, multivariate twin analyses remain an important way to examine the nature and magnitude of covariation between traits and across time. Technological advances in both computational and laboratory techniques have led to the integration of variance component analyses with genetic information derived from DNA. The finding that a significant proportion of the variance in the trait of interest can be explained by genetic effects allows researchers to justify requesting funds to attempt to locate the genetic loci influencing the trait, as will be discussed in Chapter 11.

Author Note

Gabriëlla A. M. Blokland, Miriam A. Mosing, Karin J. H. Verweij, Sarah E. Medland-Genetic

Epidemiology Laboratory, Queensland Institute of Medical Research, Brisbane, Australia.gabriella.blokland@qimr.edu.au

References

Althoff, R. R., Copeland, W. E., Stanger, C., Derks, E. M., Todd, R. D., Neuman, R. J., et al. (2006). The latent class structure of ADHD is stable across informants. *Twin Res Hum Genet, 9*(4), 507–522.

Ando, J., Ono, Y., & Wright, M. J. (2001). Genetic structure of spatial and verbal working memory. *Behav Genet, 31*(6), 615–624.

Baergen, R. N. (2011). Chapter 9 Multiple gestation. In R. N. Baergen (Ed.), *Manual of Pathology of the Human Placenta* (2nd ed., pp. 124–125). New York, NY: Springer Science+Business Media.

Baker, L. A., Reynolds, C., & Phelps, E. (1992). Biometrical analysis of individual growth curves. *Behav Genet, 22*(2), 253–264.

Bartels, M., Rietveld, M. J., van Baal, G. C., & Boomsma, D. I. (2002). Genetic and environmental influences on the development of intelligence. *Behav Genet, 32*(4), 237–249.

Boker, S., Neale, M., Maes, H., Wilde, M., Spiegel, M., Brick, T., et al. (2011). OpenMx: An open source extended structural equation modeling framework. *Psychometrika, 76*(2), 306–317.

Boomsma, D. I., de Geus, E. J. C., van Baal, G. C. M., & Koopmans, J. R. (1999). A religious upbringing reduces the influence of genetic factors on disinhibition: Evidence for interaction between genotype and environment on personality. *Twin Res, 2*(2), 115–125.

Boomsma, D. I., & Molenaar, P. C. (1987). The genetic analysis of repeated measures. I. Simplex models. *Behav Genet, 17*(2), 111–123.

Boomsma, D. I., & van Baal, G. C. M. (1998). Genetic influences on childhood IQ in 5- and 7-year-old Dutch twins. *Dev Neuropsychol, 14*, 115–126.

Borkenau, P., Riemann, R., Angleitner, A., & Spinath, F. M. (2002). Similarity of childhood experiences and personality resemblance in monozygotic and dizygotic twins: A test of the equal environments assumption. *Pers Individ Dif, 33*(2), 261–269.

Bosker, F. J., Hartman, C. A., Nolte, I. M., Prins, B. P., Terpstra, P., Posthuma, D., et al. (2011). Poor replication of candidate genes for major depressive disorder using genome-wide association data. *Mol Psychiatry, 16*(5), 516–532.

Bruder, C. E., Piotrowski, A., Gijsbers, A. A., Andersson, R., Erickson, S., Diaz de Stahl, T., et al. (2008). Phenotypically concordant and discordant monozygotic twins display different DNA copy-number-variation profiles. *Am J Hum Genet, 82*(3), 763–771.

Burton, P. R., Clayton, D. G., Cardon, L. R., Craddock, N., Deloukas, P., Duncanson, A., et al. (2007). Genome-wide association study of 14,000 cases of seven common diseases and 3,000 shared controls. *Nature, 447*(7145), 661–678.

Carey, G. (1986). Sibling imitation and contrast effects. *Behav Genet, 16*(3), 319–341.

Cerda, M., Sagdeo, A., Johnson, J., & Galea, S. (2010). Genetic and environmental influences on psychiatric comorbidity: A systematic review. *J Affect Disord, 126*(1–2), 14–38.

Cohen, D. J., Dibble, E., Grawe, J. M., & Pollin, W. (1973). Separating identical from fraternal twins. *Arch Gen Psychiatry, 29*(4), 465–469.

Cronk, N. J., Slutske, W. S., Madden, P. A., Bucholz, K. K., Reich, W., & Heath, A. C. (2002). Emotional and behavioral problems among female twins: An evaluation of the equal environments assumption. *J Am Acad Child Adolesc Psychiatry, 41*(7), 829–837.

de Moor, M. H., Boomsma, D. I., Stubbe, J. H., Willemsen, G., & de Geus, E. J. C. (2008). Testing causality in the association between regular exercise and symptoms of anxiety and depression. *Arch Gen Psychiatry, 65*(8), 897–905.

Derks, E. M., Dolan, C. V., Hudziak, J. J., Neale, M. C., & Boomsma, D. I. (2007). Assessment and etiology of attention deficit hyperactivity disorder and oppositional defiant disorder in boys and girls. *Behav Genet, 37*(4), 559–566.

Derom, R., Bryan, E., Derom, C., Keith, L., & Vlietinck, R. (2001). Twins, chorionicity and zygosity. *Twin Res, 4*(3), 134–136.

Distel, M. A., Middeldorp, C. M., Trull, T. J., Derom, C. A., Willemsen, G., & Boomsma, D. I. (2011). Life events and borderline personality features: The influence of gene-environment interaction and gene-environment correlation. *Psychol Med, 41*(4), 849–860.

Eaves, L. J. (1969). Genetic analysis of continuous variation—a comparison of experimental designs applicable to human data. *Br J Math Stat Psychol, 22*, 131–147.

Eaves, L. J., Last, K., Martin, N. G., & Jinks, J. L. (1977). Progressive approach to non-additivity and genotype-environmental covariance in analysis of human differences. *Br J Math Stat Psychol, 30*, 1–42.

Eaves, L. J., Long, J., & Heath, A. C. (1986). A theory of developmental change in quantitative phenotypes applied to cognitive development. *Behav Genet, 16*(1), 143–162.

Eaves, L. J., Silberg, J. L., Hewitt, J. K., Rutter, M., Meyer, J. M., Neale, M. C., et al. (1993). Analyzing twin resemblance in multisymptom data: Genetic applications of a latent class model for symptoms of conduct disorder in juvenile boys. *Behav Genet, 23*(1), 5–19.

Evans, D. M., Gillespie, N. A., & Martin, N. G. (2002). Biometrical genetics. *Biol Psychol, 61*(1–2), 33–51.

Falconer, D. S., & Mackay, T. F. C. (1996). *Introduction to quantitative genetics* (4th ed.). Harlow, Essex, UK: Longmans Green.

Fisher, R. A. (1918). The correlation between relatives on the supposition of Mendelian inheritance. *Philos Trans R Soc Edinburgh, 52*, 399–433.

Galton, F. (1889). *Natural inheritance*. London: Macmillan (http://galton.org/books/natural-inheritance/pdf/galton-nat-inh-1up-clean.pdf; Retrieved 5 June, 2012).

Gillespie, N. A., Evans, D. E., Wright, M. M., & Martin, N. G. (2004). Genetic simplex modeling of Eysenck's dimensions of personality in a sample of young Australian twins. *Twin Res, 7*(6), 637–648.

Gillespie, N. A., & Martin, N. G. (2005). Direction of causation models. In B. S. Everitt & D. C. Howell (Eds.), *Encyclopedia of statistics in behavioral science* (Vol. 1, pp. 496–499). Chichester, UK: John Wiley & Sons, Ltd.

Guttman, L. A. (1955). A generalized simplex for factor analysis. *Psychometrica, 20*(3), 173–192.

Hansell, N. K., Wright, M. J., Luciano, M., Geffen, G. M., Geffen, L. B., & Martin, N. G. (2005). Genetic covariation between event-related potential (ERP) and behavioral non-ERP measures of working-memory, processing speed, and IQ. *Behav Genet, 35*(6), 695–706.

Heath, A. C., Jardine, R., & Martin, N. G. (1989). Interactive effects of genotype and social environment on alcohol consumption in female twins. *J Stud Alcohol, 50*(1), 38–48.

Heath, A. C., Kessler, R. C., Neale, M. C., Hewitt, J. K., Eaves, L. J., & Kendler, K. S. (1993). Testing hypotheses about direction of causation using cross-sectional family data. *Behav Genet, 23*(1), 29–50.

Hettema, J. M., Neale, M. C., & Kendler, K. S. (1995). Physical similarity and the equal-environment assumption in twin studies of psychiatric disorders. *Behav Genet, 25*(4), 327–335.

Hettema, J. M., Neale, M. C., & Kendler, K. S. (2001). A review and meta-analysis of the genetic epidemiology of anxiety disorders. *Am J Psychiatry, 158*(10), 1568–1578.

Holzinger, K. (1929). The relative effect of nature and nurture influences on twin differences. *J Educ Psych, 20*, 241–248.

Jepsen, J. L., & Michel, M. (2006). ADHD and the symptom dimensions inattention, impulsivity, and hyperactivity—A review of aetiological twin studies from 1996 to 2004. *Nord Psychol, 58*, 108–135.

Jinks, J. L., & Fulker, D. W. (1970). A comparison of the biometrical-genetical, MAVA and classical approaches to the analysis of human behavior. *Psychol Bull, 73*, 311–349.

Kasriel, J., & Eaves, L. J. (1976). Zygosity of twins—Further evidence on agreement between diagnosis by blood-groups and written questionnaires. *J Biosoc Sci, 8*(3), 263–266.

Keller, M. C., Medland, S. E., Duncan, L. E., Hatemi, P. K., Neale, M. C., Maes, H. H., et al. (2009). Modeling extended twin family data I: description of the Cascade model. *Twin Res Hum Genet, 12*(1), 8–18.

Kendler, K. S., & Gardner, C. O., Jr. (1998). Twin studies of adult psychiatric and substance dependence disorders: Are they biased by differences in the environmental experiences of monozygotic and dizygotic twins in childhood and adolescence? *Psychol Med, 28*(3), 625–633.

Kendler, K. S., Gatz, M., Gardner, C. O., & Pedersen, N. L. (2006a). Personality and major depression: A Swedish longitudinal, population-based twin study. *Arch Gen Psychiatry, 63*(10), 1113–1120.

Kendler, K. S., Gatz, M., Gardner, C. O., & Pedersen, N. L. (2006b). A Swedish national twin study of lifetime major depression. *Am J Psychiatry, 163*(1), 109–114.

Kendler, K. S., Heath, A. C., Martin, N. G., & Eaves, L. J. (1987). Symptoms of anxiety and symptoms of depression. Same genes, different environments? *Arch Gen Psychiatry, 44*(5), 451–457.

Kendler, K. S., Neale, M. C., Kessler, R. C., Heath, A. C., & Eaves, L. J. (1993). A test of the equal-environment assumption in twin studies of psychiatric illness. *Behav Genet, 23*(1), 21–27.

Kendler, K. S., Neale, M. C., Kessler, R. C., Heath, A. C., & Eaves, L. J. (1994). Parental treatment and the equal environment assumption in twin studies of psychiatric illness. *Psychol Med, 24*(3), 579–590.

Kendler, K. S., Neale, M. C., Prescott, C. A., Kessler, R. C., Heath, A. C., Corey, L. A., et al. (1996). Childhood parental loss and alcoholism in women: A causal analysis using a twin-family design. *Psychol Med, 26*(1), 79–95.

Koziel, S. M. (1998). Effect of disparities in birth weight on differences in postnatal growth of monozygotic and dizygotic twins. *Ann Hum Biol, 25*(2), 159–168.

LaBuda, M. C., Svikis, D. S., & Pickens, R. W. (1997). Twin closeness and co-twin risk for substance use disorders: Assessing the impact of the equal environment assumption. *Psychiatry Res, 70*(3), 155–164.

Liu, J. Z., Tozzi, F., Waterworth, D. M., Pillai, S. G., Muglia, P., Middleton, L., et al. (2010). Meta-analysis and imputation refines the association of 15q25 with smoking quantity. *Nat Genet, 42*(5), 366–368.

Loehlin, J. C. (1996). The Cholesky approach: A cautionary note. *Behavior Genetics, 26*(1), 65–69.

Loehlin, J. C. (2009). History of behavior genetics. In Y. K. Kim (Ed.), *Handbook of behavior genetics* (pp. 3–11). New York, NY: Springer.

Loehlin, J. C., & Nichols, R. C. (1976). *Heredity, environment, and personality: A study of 850 sets of twins*. Austin, TX: University of Texas Press.

Luciano, M., Wright, M. J., Geffen, G. M., Geffen, L. B., Smith, G. A., & Martin, N. G. (2004). A genetic investigation of the covariation among inspection time, choice reaction time, and IQ subtest scores. *Behav Genet, 34*(1), 41–50.

Luciano, M., Wright, M. J., Smith, G. A., Geffen, G. M., Geffen, L. B., & Martin, N. G. (2001). Genetic covariance among measures of information processing speed, working memory, and IQ. *Behav Genet, 31*(6), 581–592.

Lyons, M. J., Eisen, S. A., Goldberg, J., True, W., Lin, N., Meyer, J. M., et al. (1998). A registry-based twin study of depression in men. *Arch Gen Psychiatry, 55*(5), 468–472.

Lytton, H., Martin, N. G., & Eaves, L. J. (1977). Environmental and genetical causes of variation in ethological aspects of behavior in two-year-old boys. *Soc Biol, 24*(3), 200–211.

Maes, H. H., Neale, M. C., Kendler, K. S., Hewitt, J. K., Silberg, J. L., Foley, D. L., et al. (1998). Assortative mating for major psychiatric diagnoses in two population-based samples. *Psychol Med, 28*(6), 1389–1401.

Maes, H. H., Neale, M. C., Medland, S. E., Keller, M. C., Martin, N. G., Heath, A. C., et al. (2009). Flexible Mx specification of various extended twin kinship designs. *Twin Res Hum Genet, 12*(1), 26–34.

Martin, N. G., & Eaves, L. J. (1977). The genetical analysis of covariance structure. *Heredity, 38*(1), 79–95.

Martin, N. G., Eaves, L. J., Heath, A. C., Jardine, R., Feingold, L. M., & Eysenck, H. J. (1986). Transmission of social attitudes. *Proc Natl Acad Sci U S A, 83*(12), 4364–4368.

Matheny, A. P., Jr., Wilson, R. S., & Dolan, A. B. (1976). Relations between twins' similarity of appearance and behavioral similarity: Testing an assumption. *Behav Genet, 6*(3), 343–351.

McArdle, J. J. (1986). Latent variable growth within behavior genetic models. *Behav Genet, 16*(1), 163–200.

Medland, S. E., & Hatemi, P. K. (2009). Political science, biometric theory, and twin studies: A methodological introduction. *Polit Anal, 17*(2), 191–214.

Mehta, P. D., & Neale, M. C. (2005). People are variables too: Multilevel structural equations modeling. *Psychol Meth, 10*(3), 259–284.

Mosing, M. A., Zietsch, B. P., Shekar, S. N., Wright, M. J., & Martin, N. G. (2009). Genetic and environmental influences on optimism and its relationship to mental and self-rated health: A study of aging twins. *Behav Genet, 39*(6), 597–604.

Muthén, L. K., & Muthén, B. O. (1998–2010). *Mplus User's Guide* (6th ed.). Los Angeles, CA: Muthén & Muthén.

Nance, W. E., & Neale, M. C. (1989). Partitioned twin analysis: A power study. *Behav Genet, 19*(1), 143–150.

Neale, M. C., Boker, S. M., Xie, G., & Maes, H. H. (2002). *Mx: Statistical modeling* (6th ed.). Richmond, VA 23298: Department of Psychiatry, University of Virginia, VCU Box 900126.

Neale, M. C., & Maes, H. H. M. (2004). *Methodology for genetic studies of twins and families*. Dordrecht, The Netherlands: Kluwer Academic Publishers B.V.

Neale, M. C., & McArdle, J. J. (2000). Structured latent growth curves for twin data. *Twin Res, 3*(3), 165–177.

Petrill, S. A., Lipton, P. A., Hewitt, J. K., Plomin, R., Cherny, S. S., Corley, R., et al. (2004). Genetic and environmental contributions to general cognitive ability through the first 16 years of life. *Dev Psychol, 40*(5), 805–812.

Plomin, R. (1999). Genetics and general cognitive ability. *Nature, 402*(6761 Suppl), C25–C29.

Plomin, R., DeFries, J. C., & Loehlin, J. C. (1977). Genotype-environment interaction and correlation in the analysis of human behavior. *Psychol Bull, 84*(2), 309–322.

Plomin, R., DeFries, J. C., McClearn, G. E., & McGuffin, P. (2001). *Behavioral genetics* (4th ed.). New York, NY: Worth Publishers.

Plomin, R., Willerman, L., & Loehlin, J. C. (1976). Resemblance in appearance and the equal environments assumption in twin studies of personality traits. *Behav Genet, 6*(1), 43–52.

Posthuma, D., Beem, A. L., de Geus, E. J. C., van Baal, G. C., von Hjelmborg, J. B., Iachine, I., et al. (2003). Theory and practice in quantitative genetics. *Twin Res, 6*(5), 361–376.

Posthuma, D., de Geus, E. J. C., & Boomsma, D. I. (2001). Perceptual speed and IQ are associated through common genetic factors. *Behav Genet, 31*(6), 593–602.

Purcell, S. (2002). Variance components models for gene-environment interaction in twin analysis. *Twin Res, 5*(6), 554–571.

Raykov, T., Marcoulides, G. A., & Boyd, J. (2003). Using structural equation modeling programs to perform matrix manipulations and data simulation. *Struct Equ Modeling, 10*(2), 312–322.

Reynolds, C. A., Finkel, D., McArdle, J. J., Gatz, M., Berg, S., & Pedersen, N. L. (2005). Quantitative genetic analysis of latent growth curve models of cognitive abilities in adulthood. *Dev Psychol, 41*(1), 3–16.

Scarr, S. (1982). Environmental bias in twin studies. *Biodemography Soc Biol, 29*(3), 221–229.

Scarr, S., & Carter-Saltzman, L. (1979). Twin method: Defense of a critical assumption. *Behav Genet, 9*(6), 527–542.

Silventoinen, K., Kaprio, J., Lahelma, E., Viken, R. J., & Rose, R. J. (2001). Sex differences in genetic and environmental factors contributing to body-height. *Twin Res, 4*(1), 25–29.

Skytthe, A., Kyvik, K., Bathum, L., Holm, N., Vaupel, J. W., & Christensen, K. (2006). The Danish Twin Registry in the new millennium. *Twin Res Hum Genet, 9*(6), 763–771.

Sullivan, P. F., Kendler, K. S., & Neale, M. C. (2003). Schizophrenia as a complex trait: Evidence from a meta-analysis of twin studies. *Arch Gen Psychiatry, 60*(12), 1187–1192.

Sullivan, P. F., Neale, M. C., & Kendler, K. S. (2000). Genetic epidemiology of major depression: Review and meta-analysis. *Am J Psychiatry, 157*(10), 1552–1562.

The International Schizophrenia Consortium (2009). Common polygenic variation contributes to risk of schizophrenia and bipolar disorder. *Nature, 460*(7256), 748–752.

van Grootheest, D. S., Boomsma, D. I., Hettema, J. M., & Kendler, K. S. (2008). Heritability of obsessive-compulsive symptom dimensions. *Am J Med Genet B Neuropsychiatr Genet, 147B*(4), 473–478.

Verweij, K. J. H., Zietsch, B. P., Liu, J. Z., Medland, S. E., Lynskey, M. T., Madden, P. A. F., et al. (2012). No replication of candidate genes for cannabis use using a large sample of Australian twin families. *Addict Biol, 17*(3), 687-690.

Visscher, P. M., Medland, S. E., Ferreira, M. A., Morley, K. I., Zhu, G., Cornes, B. K., et al. (2006). Assumption-free estimation of heritability from genome-wide identity-by-descent sharing between full siblings. *PLoS Genet, 2*(3), e41.

Visscher, P. M., & Montgomery, G. W. (2009). Genome-wide association studies and human disease: From trickle to flood. *JAMA, 302*(18), 2028–2029.

Wang, K., Zhang, H. T., Ma, D. Q., Bucan, M., Glessner, J. T., Abrahams, B. S., et al. (2009). Common genetic variants on 5p14.1 associate with autism spectrum disorders. *Nature, 459*(7246), 528–533.

Wright, S. (1921). Correlation and causation. *J Agric Res, 20*, 557–585.

Xian, H., Scherrer, J. F., Eisen, S. A., True, W. R., Heath, A. C., Goldberg, J., et al. (2000). Self-reported zygosity and the equal-environments assumption for psychiatric disorders in the Vietnam Era Twin Registry. *Behav Genet, 30*(4), 303–310.

CHAPTER
11
Quantitative Analysis of Genes

Sarah E. Medland

> **Abstract**
>
> This chapter focuses on the complementary analytical techniques of *linkage* and *association*, which have traditionally been used to locate and identify genes influencing traits of interest. These techniques typically require a direct assay of genotypic variation. As such, the chapter will begin by providing a background to the concepts of DNA and genotyping. Following this, the most common methods used for linkage and association will be reviewed.
>
> **Key Words:** Linkage, association, genome-wide association study, single-nucleotide polymorphisms, case–control, family-based, identity by decent

Introduction

As explained in the previous chapter, *Twin Studies and Behavior Genetics*, at the population level, variation in behavioral, physical, and psychological traits results from genetic and environmental influences and the interaction of these influences. Genetic epidemiological techniques were developed in an attempt to understand individual differences—that is, to explain why individuals in a population differ from one another (Neale & Cardon 1992). The primary objective of behavioral genetics is to examine the extent to which genetic and environmental factors influence variation around a population mean rather than to what extent the mean is influenced by a specific predictor (or group of predictors). The finding that genetic influences effect a trait does not provide information regarding the number of genes influencing the trait, the direction of these genetic effects (i.e., whether these effects increase or decrease the mean), or the identity of the genes exerting this influence. These questions have traditionally been examined using the complementary analytical techniques of *linkage* and *association*, which are the focus of the current chapter.

The goals of linkage and association analysis and gene mapping in general, are to *localize* and *identify* genetic variants that regulate a trait of interest. Traditionally the initial localization of genetic variants was achieved through linkage analyses, whereas identification required association or functional analyses. However, technological developments have lead to a dramatic reduction in the number of linkage studies, and association has become the preferred technique used for both localization and identification of genetic variants. Although this chapter will provide a conceptual overview of both linkage and association analyses, it will begin by introducing some general concepts relating to the nature of genotypic data.

A Brief Overview of Genetic Data

The concepts of *genes* and *DNA* (deoxyribonucleic acid) have become ubiquitous through increased exposure to forensic science via the news and entertainment media. Colloquially, the term *DNA* is used to refer to the complete genetic information of an individual, whereas *gene* is generally understood to mean a section of DNA that shows variation within a population, such that different individuals may have different copies of the gene. Genes are commonly conceptualized as a set of blueprints or instructions that tell the organisms how cells should be organized physically and how processes should take place.

Within the scientific literature, these terms take on more precise meanings. The word *genome* is used to refer to the complete genetic information of each individual organism, both human and non-human. In general, this genetic information is encoded in DNA (although some organisms such as viruses encode this information in other ways). DNA is comprised of a series of *nucleotides,* which are comprised of one of four nitrogenous bases (adenine [A], cytosine [C], guanine [G] and thymine [T]) attached to a five-carbon sugar, and one to three phosphate groups. The covalent bonds between the sugar of one nucleotide and the phosphate group of the neighboring nucleotide result in the long strings of nucleotides that make up a DNA sequence. DNA is organized into two strands that are held together by weak hydrogen bonds to form a DNA duplex, or double helix. The bases in these strands are paired according to Watson-Crick rules so that adenine (A) specifically binds to thymine (T) with two hydrogen bonds and cytosine (C) specifically binds to guanine (G) with three hydrogen bonds. The genome is thus, encoded by the linear sequence of *base-pairs* (BPs) in the DNA strands (e.g., ACAGTGGGCAG) and is organized in discontinuous sections, called *chromosomes.*

The nucleuses of most human cells contain 22 pairs of autosomes (non-sex chromosomes) and 1 pair of sex chromosomes. Gametes (reproductive cells) have only one copy of each chromosome and so are called haploid cells; in the case of the sex chromosome, a female gamete will always have an X-chromosome, whereas a male gamete will either have an X or Y. Diploid cells result from the fusion of the parental gametes and so they have two copies of each chromosome, one from each parent. The two copies are called homologous chromosomes.

A gene corresponds to a specific DNA sequence that produces one or more proteins through the mechanisms of transcription and translation. At present, the human genome is estimated to have a total length of ~3.27 × 10^9 bases that code for ~20 000 genes. However, the genome is not neatly divided into genes. Genes vary markedly in length from histone cluster 4 (HIST4H4) at 412 BPs to dystrophin (DMD) at 2,220,382 BPs (http://www.ncbi.nlm.nih.gov/gene/121504; http://www.ncbi.nlm.nih.gov/gene/1756), with an average length of around 3,000 bases. Genes are separated by stretches of DNA sequence; although these intergenic regions are often described as *junk-DNA,* a great deal of variation is present in these regions and there is growing evidence that many of these variants are important. Within the genome there are regions that are gene-rich and also those that are gene-poor (often described as gene-deserts).

How Is Genotypic Data Obtained?

For linkage or association analysis to be conducted, a direct assay of genotypic variation is typically required. With the exception of the haploid sex cells, all nucleated cells within the body have a full complement of chromosomes and DNA. Thus, biological samples can come in many forms, such as blood, hair, skin, or saliva. For the purposes of obtaining DNA for use in linkage or association studies, the origin of the biological sample is not important. However, the quantity and quality of the DNA are of the upmost importance. Typically, hair does not provide enough DNA to run much more than a few basic forensic experiments. Blood provides the most DNA from current extraction methods (specifically from white blood cells), with saliva and cheek cells providing modest amounts of lower quality. Ten milliliters of blood typically yields more than 1 milligrams of DNA, or more than half a billion full copies of DNA, whereas saliva and cheek (buccal) cells normally yield 300 micrograms (which is more than sufficient for genotyping).

In addition to the DNA, biological samples contain additional material, including enzymes that will start degrading and digesting the DNA as soon as it is extracted from the body. Thus, the purification and extraction of DNA is undertaken as soon as possible once the sample has been collected. Genetic variants are typically assayed using site-specific primers, each of which is designed to attach to a unique section of DNA. Through a lengthy amplification process, these primers effectively enable us to measure the length of a section of DNA or molecular weight of a DNA fragment.

Types of DNA Variation Used in Linkage and Association Analysis

Although many types of genetic variation exist in the human genome, the most commonly assayed for association analyses are single-nucleotide polymorphisms (SNPs). Single-nucleotide polymorphisms are variations in the DNA sequence where a single nucleotide differs between individuals in a population (e.g., TTGT*A*ATGC vs. TTGT*G*ATGC), resulting in two possible forms or *alleles* for each

SNP. As humans are diploid (i.e., their chromosomes are organized in pairs, having inherited one of each pair from their mother and the other from their father), every individual has two copies of each SNP, which in tandem are known as a *genotype*. For example, given an A/G SNP, the three possible genotypes are AA, AG, and GG. Single-nucleotide polymorphisms are typically referred to by the Ref-SNP accession ID or rs number (e.g., rs61740690). When describing the location of a SNP, one usually provides the chromosome and BP location of the variant.

Single-nucleotide polymorphism data is generally stored in alphabetic (A/C/G/T) form. The frequencies of SNPs within populations are discussed with reference to the less common allele, known as the *minor allele frequency*. Single-nucleotide polymorphisms that result in a change of the amino acid sequence of the protein that is produced may have functional consequences and are known as *nonsynonymous* SNPs. Conversely, those that do not result in a change in the protein are *synonymous*.

Historically, association studies considered a relatively small number of genetic variants (<100) within a small region of DNA. With the advent of genome-wide SNP typing, it is now customary to type a much larger number of SNPs (500,000–1,000,000) distributed approximately every 1,500–2,00 bases across the genome.

Whereas the genetic variants used in association analysis often have functional consequences, the panels of *microsatellite markers* (also known as *variable* or *short-tandem repeats*) used in linkage analysis are typically neutral in nature. A typical linkage panel includes ~400 such variants typed across the genome. Although a SNP has only two possible variants, microsatellites are highly polymorphic with many variants. Microsatellites are repeating sequences, consisting of two, three, or four nucleotides (di-, tri-, and tetranucleotide repeats, respectively), repeated up to 100 times (e.g., TTGG*CACACACACA*GTGA). Raw microsatellite data is in the form of allele lengths measured in BPs; these data are typically binned prior to analysis. Generally, this is done by ranking the alleles observed in the genotyping sample and assigning the allele number 1 to the smallest allele. Ideally, a histogram of the allele lengths would show clear discontinuities, making binning a simple procedure. For example, if we had genotyped a CAG trinucleotide repeat, then we might expect to observe allele lengths of 3, 6, 9, 12, and 15, which we would recode as alleles 1 through 5. In reality, depending on the quality of the DNA and technology, the data often contain a small number of allele lengths that clearly do not fit the general pattern (i.e., an allele length of 7 in the above example). This was a common problem in early genome scans, especially with di- and tri-nucleotide repeats. This issue led to the development of algorithms that binned the data probabilistically.

Microsatellite markers are usually named using a convention that contains information about the chromosomal location of the variant—for example, D13S364 refers to the 364th marker registered on chromosome 13. However, many of these marker names were registered prior to the mapping of the human genome. One consequence of this is that there are a number of markers, such as *D18S543*, which were initially mapped to one chromosome (in this case chromosome 18), which were subsequently found to be located elsewhere (in this case on the psuedo-autosomal region of the X and Y chromosomes—a region of homologous sequence on the sex chromosomes that behave like autosomal, or non-sex, chromosomes).

Linkage Analysis

Linkage analysis aims to localize genetic variants that regulate a trait of interest by testing the extent to which a panel of known genetic variants are co-inherited, or *linked*, with a latent causal variant. Linkage was initially developed to identify genomic regions influencing diseases where the phenotype can be conceptualized as a binary variable—affected or unaffected, such as schizophrenia and obesity. Although the methods were broadened to allow for the analysis of phenotypes collected using continuous scales such as personality and body mass index, it is easier to explain the underlying concepts using a qualitative example.

Background

Consider a trio of relatives made up of two parents and an affected offspring. Let M represent a genotyped marker and D represent a locus or genetic variant that influences the disease affecting the child. The sperm and the egg cells that eventually combine to produce the offspring are formed during a process called *meiosis*. During this process, the maternal and paternal homologs of each chromosome pair together. (Note this process takes place prior to fertilization, so it is the grandparental chromosomes that are being paired. For example, in the formation of a sperm cell, it is the father's copy of the chromosome he received from this mother that pairs with the copy he received from this father that is paired.) While two homologous chromosomes remain paired, they can exchange segments in a random way through a process known as *recombination* or *crossover*. Typically only a fairly small number of recombination events occur at each meiosis; however, each pair of chromosomes will usually recombine at least once. This process of recombination, in conjunction with random mutation, across many hundreds of generations has led to the uniqueness of the DNA sequence at an individual level. The probability that a recombination event will occur between two points on a chromosome is related to the distance between them, with more crossovers expected between points that are further away. The probability that a recombinant is formed is referred to as the recombination fraction θ.

If the disease locus D and the marker locus M are unlinked (i.e., on the same chromosome but sufficiently far apart or on different chromosomes), then the two loci will not be inherited together. In this situation, $\theta = 0.5$, meaning we expect to observe as many recombinants (50%) as non-recombinants (50%). Therefore, D and M will be transmitted independently from parents to affected offspring. On the other hand, if two loci are located on the same chromosome and very close together (i.e., linked), $\theta < 0.5$, and therefore, we expect to observe fewer recombinants. In this situation, the segregation of alleles from both loci during meiosis is not independent: A certain D allele will tend to segregate jointly with a certain M allele within the family. It is this cosegregation of trait and marker alleles from parents to affected offspring that we aim to detect with a linkage test statistic. Linkage analysis exploits this logic to test genotyped markers across the genome to identify regions harboring genetic variants that may influence the trait.

In describing the location of a microsatellite marker, we use the unit of the centimorgan (cM). Although the BP units used to describe the location of SNPs are physical in nature, the centimorgan unit is based on the probability of recombination occurring within a stretch of sequence, such that there is a 1% probability of a recombination event between two markers that are located 1 centimorgan apart. As the probability of recombination varies across the genome, the relationship between centimorgan and BP is nonlinear. However, on average, 1 centimorgan equates to around 1,000,000 BP.

Types of Linkage Analysis

Linkage analyses are commonly divided into "model-based" (or "parametric") and "model-free" (or "non-parametric") methods. The distinction between the two styles of analysis is largely based on whether the researcher is required to specify the mode of inheritance (additive/recessive/dominant) and the *penetrance* (risk of being affected given the putative loci). Methods requiring researchers to specify these parameters *a priori* are denoted model-based, those that do not are termed model free. Model-based linkage tests for cosegregation between a given disease or a trait and marker by reconceptualizing the trait phenotype as an unobserved genotype and testing whether the recombination fraction observed between the unobserved genotype and the trait differs from 0.5. Conversely, model-free approaches focus on correlating allele-sharing among relatives with similarity in trait values.

MODEL-BASED LINKAGE

To test for linkage, we compare the likelihood, L_{H0}, of the null hypothesis of no linkage ($\theta = \frac{1}{2}$ between D and M) to likelihood, L_{H1}, of the alternative hypothesis of linkage ($0 \leq \theta < \frac{1}{2}$ between D and M). The outcome statistic for model-based linkage is, by convention, the logarithm of odds or LOD score, $\log_{10}(\frac{L_{H1}}{L_{H0}})$ (Morton, 1955).

Figure 11.1 shows a pedigree diagram or family tree, which illustrates the relationships across three generations of a single family. Males are represented by squares, whereas circles represent females. A closed or shaded symbol implies that an individual is affected with the disease of interest, whereas an open unshaded symbol indicates that the individual is either unaffected or, in the case of adult onset traits, may not have passed through the risk period. Mating resulting in offspring is represented by a horizontal line joining the two parents, with a vertical line to the offspring. A diagonal line through a symbol indicates the individual is deceased. The pedigree in Figure 11.1 shows segregation of a rare, dominant trait locus (*A/a*, where *A* is causal so genotypes *AA* and *Aa* are affected) and a fully informative marker (1/2). The father of the seven children in the pedigree carries A/2 and a/1 haplotypes. Of the seven children, five are non-recombinants and two are recombinants with respect to the paternal haplotype. Cases such as this where it is possible to determine the ancestral origin of each allele and thus to reconstruct the haplotype of an individual are described as phase known.

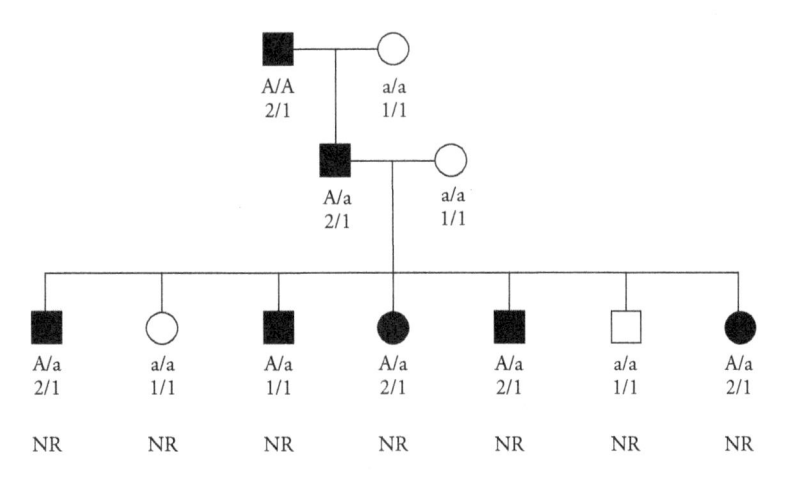

Figure 11.1 Pedigree segregating a rare completely dominant trait and a phase known marker. Recombinants (R) and non-recombinants (NR) between the trait locus and marker locus are indicated for the single possible (*known*) phase.

Under the null model for Figure 11.1, the likelihood, L_{H0}, of no linkage ($\theta = 0.5$) is $(0.5)^7$. Under the alternative model, the likelihood, L_{H1}, for the five non-recombinants is $(1 - \theta)^5$ and the likelihood for the two recombinants is $(\theta)^2$. To estimate θ, we maximize the likelihood function with respect to θ by calculating the likelihood for a range of values of θ. For the example in Figure 11.1, the LOD score is calculated as $z_i(\theta) = \log_{10}\left(\frac{L_{H1}}{L_{H0}}\right) = \log_{10}\left(\frac{((1-\theta)^5\theta^2)}{(0.5)^7}\right)$. At $\theta = 0.01$, 0.05, 0.1, 0.2, 0.3, and 0.4, one obtains the respective LOD scores of $-1.92, -0.61, -0.12, 0.23, 0.29,$ and 0.20.

Where phase is unknown and multiple recombinant and non-recombinant arrangements are possible and equally likely, we average the LOD for the family over these possibilities. For example, if no genotypes were available for the grandparents in Figure 11.1, there would be two possible phases: *Phase 1*, where five of the seven siblings are non-recombinant and two of the seven siblings are recombinant, and *Phase 2*, where five of the seven siblings are recombinant and two of the seven siblings are non-recombinant. Under *Phase 1*, the likelihood for the five non-recombinants is $(1-\theta)^5$ and the likelihood for the two recombinants is $(\theta)^2$. Under *Phase 2*, the likelihood for the two non-recombinants is $(1-\theta)^2$ and the likelihood for the five recombinants is $(\theta)^5$. Therefore, the LOD (θ) for this pedigree is $z_i(\theta) = \log_{10}\left(\frac{L_{H1}}{L_{H0}}\right) = \log_{10}\left(\frac{0.5((1-\theta)^5\theta^2)+0.5((1-\theta)^2\theta^5)}{(0.5)^7}\right)$. At $\theta = 0.01$, 0.05, 0.1, 0.2, 0.3, and 0.4, one obtains the respective LOD scores of $-2.21, -0.87, -0.35, 0.11, 0.29,$ and 0.38.

In the case of real data, the genotype at the trait locus is generally unknown, and the parameterization of the likelihood for model-based linkage can be generalized for any pedigree. The location of the trait locus is mapped by calculating the LOD score, for different values of θ to determine the maximum LOD score (*MLS*). The MLS for a set of independent pedigrees is equal to the sum of the LOD score for each pedigree.

The approach described here in which the data from each genotyped locus is considered sequentially is known as *singlepoint*. The alternative is to employ a *multipoint* approach that considers the information from two or more polymorphic markers concurrently, thus improving the ability to determine phase. Although more powerful, a multipoint approach is also more sensitive to genotyping, map order (Goring & Terwilliger, 2000), and pedigree errors.

MODEL-FREE LINKAGE

The two main statistical methods employed in model-free or *non-parametric* linkage are regression and variance component decomposition via structural equation modeling. The premise underlying both approaches is that in regions of the genome harboring loci that influence a trait, there will be increased covariance between genetic and phenotypic sharing. That is, relatives who are more similar phenotypically are expected to be more similar genetically.

Estimating Genotypic Similarity

Genotypic similarity can be assessed through a direct comparison of the relatives' alleles. A pair of relatives may share 0, 1, or 2 alleles at each locus. The presence of the same allele in a pair of individuals, termed *identity by state* (IBS), provides information regarding the genotypic covariation of the two individuals specific to the locus. Given that the aim of linkage analysis is to locate or map loci influencing the trait, a measure of genetic covariation at a given locus that provides information regarding the surrounding loci yields more information. This information is provided by assessing whether the alleles were inherited from a common ancestor—that is, whether the alleles at the locus are *identical by decent* (IBD). As the probability of a recombination event occurring within a small genetic distance is low, IBD provides information about both the directly genotyped marker and the ungenotyped markers nearby. Thus, given reasonably dense genotypic information (i.e., a 5cM genome scan if no parents are genotyped, or a 10cM scan if parental information is available), and a polymorphic marker set, IBD can be estimated across the genome with acceptable accuracy.

A number of methods have been developed to estimate IBD (Amos, Dawson, & Elston, 1990), the most general of these are based on the Elston-Stewart (Elston & Stewart, 1971) and Lander-Green (Lander & Green, 1987) algorithms. These algorithms can estimate IBD at either the singlepoint or multipoint levels. The Lander-Green algorithm is particularly suited to multipoint calculations involving multiple markers and small pedigrees and the computation time scales linearly with number of markers, but exponentially with the number of non-founders in the pedigree (Lander & Green, 1987).

To summarize, assuming perfectly informative marker loci, in a sample comprised of families with multiple offspring, for each sibship, there are 2^{2n} equally likely allele transmissions at each locus (where n is the number of non-founders—i.e., offspring—in the sibship). Each transmission may be specified by a unique inheritance vector that describes the outcome of paternal and maternal meioses that produced each non-founder: $v(x) = (p_1 m_1, p_2 m_2 \ldots p_n m_n)$. The resultant vector that summarizes gene flow through the pedigree is binary in nature, specifying whether the grand-maternal ($p_1 = 1$) or grand-paternal ($p_1 = 0$) allele is carried forward. As the inheritance vector cannot always be determined unequivocally (because of missing or uninformative markers) the information can be represented as a probability distribution over the possible inheritance vectors. The likelihood of a pedigree can be calculated as the sum of the probabilities of the 2^{2n} inheritance vectors. Thus, if V denotes all possible 2^{2n} inheritance vectors, then for any given locus:

$$P(IBD = k) = \sum_{w \in V} P\left[IBD = k | v(x) = w\right] \cdot P\left[v(x) = w\right],$$

where $P\left[IBD = k | v(x) = w\right]$ equals 1 or 0 depending on whether the vector w is compatible with IBD $= k$ and $P\left[v(x) = w\right]$ is the posterior probability of vector w.

For multipoint IBD estimation, the likelihood of the inheritance pattern at marker m can be informed by the inheritance patterns at the locus to either side of m, $m - 1$ and $m + 1$. The likelihood of an inheritance vector at a given marker m conditional on the observed genotypes can be characterized as a hidden Markov chain:

$$P(x_1, x_2, \ldots x_m) = 1^T \cdot Q_1 \cdot T_{\theta 1} \cdot Q_2 \cdot T_{\theta 2} \ldots \cdot T_{\theta m-1} \cdot Q_m \cdot 1,$$

where Q is a $2^{2n} \times 2^{2n}$ diagonal matrix containing the probabilities of the inheritance vectors at each marker, and T_θ are transition matrices describing the conditional probabilities between inheritance vectors for pairs of consecutive markers (reflecting the intermarker recombination rates). This allows the calculation of the probabilities of each inheritance vector given the genotypic data observed at the previous markers (Abecasis, Cherny, Cookson, & Cardon, 2002).

Thus, the probability of a given sibpair ij being IBD 0, 1, or 2 may be estimated at each marker or at a fixed interval across the genome. The proportion of alleles sibpair ij shares IBD, or *pihat* ($\hat{\pi}$), may be estimated as: $\hat{\pi}_{ij} = \frac{1}{2} P\left[IBD_{ij} = 1\right] + P\left[IBD_{ij} = 2\right]$.

Regression- Based Approaches

The regression based linkage methods derive from the pioneering work of Haseman and Elston (1972). Designed predominantly for use with sibpairs, in the original Haseman-Elston analysis, the squared difference of the trait values of the sibpair ij (Y_{ij}) are regressed on $\hat{\pi}$ at marker m. Thus, $E(Y_{ij} | \pi_{ijm}) = \alpha + \beta \pi_{ijm}$, where α is a constant ($2\sigma_g^2 + \sigma_e^2$) containing the genetic variance ($2\sigma_g^2$) (including that due to the qualitative trait loci [QTL]) and environmental (σ_e^2) variances, and $\beta = -2(1 - 2\theta)^2 \sigma_g^2$, where $(1 - 2\theta)^2$ is the correlation between the proportion of alleles shared IBD at the marker and trait loci under the assumption of linkage equilibrium. Evidence for linkage is assessed using a one-tailed t-test of the null hypothesis: $\beta = 0$ (Haseman & Elston, 1972). Numerous extensions of this method have been suggested, including modeling both the squared differences and cross-products of the phenotypes (Forrest, 2001; Visscher & Hopper, 2001; Wright, 1997).

Sample selection (which is generally based on trait values) can lead to violations of the expectation of bivariate normality between the phenotypic and genotypic similarity yielding biased estimates. The Reverse Haseman-Elston approach (Dudoit & Speed, 2000; Sham, Purcell, Cherny, & Abecasis, 2002) takes the opposite approach, modeling IBD conditional on trait values, thus correcting for this bias (as individuals are seldom directly selected for their IBD status). In this approach, $\hat{\pi}$ at marker m is simultaneously regressed on the squared differences and squared sums of the phenotypes. Sham et al.'s (2002) parameterization of this approach (implemented in MERLIN-REGRESS) can be applied to general pedigrees, providing the specification of the population mean, variance, and heritability. In nonselected samples, the power of this approach is similar to that observed with variance components analyses.

In Sham et al.'s (2002) parameterization, the independent variables (the squared sums and squared differences) are stacked in a mean-centered vector, $Y = [S, d]'$. The dependent variable ($\hat{\pi}_{ij}$) is placed in a mean-centered vector $\hat{\Pi}$. The multiple regression of $\hat{\Pi}$ on Y is given by: $\hat{\Pi} = \Sigma'_{Y\hat{\Pi}} \Sigma_Y^{-1} Y + e$, where $\Sigma'_{Y\hat{\Pi}}$ is the covariance matrix between Y and $\hat{\Pi}$, and Σ_Y^{-1} is the covariance matrix of Y and e is a vector of residuals. The matrix $\Sigma'_{Y\hat{\Pi}}$ is factorized into $Q\Sigma_{\hat{\Pi}}H$ (where Q is a diagonal matrix for the variance due to the QTL, and H is composed of two horizontally stacked diagonal matrices containing 2 and −2, respectively). Rewriting $H\Sigma_Y^{-1}Y$ as B, an optimally weighted estimate of Q is given by: $\hat{Q} = \frac{\Sigma(B'\hat{\Pi})}{\Sigma(B'\Sigma_{\hat{\Pi}}B)}$, yielding a test statistic: $T = \hat{Q}\Sigma(B'\hat{\Pi}) = \hat{Q}^2 \Sigma(B'\Sigma_{\hat{\Pi}}B)$ asymptotically distributed as χ_1^2.

Although this method depends on specification of the population mean, variance, and heritability (this is especially true in the case of the mean), it does not require the assumption of trait normality implicit within approaches that model trait similarity conditioning on IBD similarity. In addition, this approach as implemented in MERLIN-REGRESS is extremely fast (allowing the completion of a whole genome scan within minutes rather than hours). This recommends it to the empirical calculation of p-values, in which genotypic information is simulated under the null hypothesis for 1,000 to 5,000 replicates, preserving the informativeness of the data. Linkage is then conducted on each replicate, allowing the accurate probability of any given linkage result to be calculated. In addition, as there is no boundary constraint on the values of T, this method can provide evidence against linkage through negative LOD scores. Such scores indicate less than expected allele sharing among individuals with similar phenotypes (although an excess of negative LODs suggests that the data contain genotyping errors and/or misspecified relationships).

Variance Components Approaches

Within the context of a twin or family study, the parameterization of variance components QTL analysis represents a simple extension of the structural equation models described in the previous chapter *Twin Studies and Behavior Genetics*. Basically the model is reparameterized, repartitioning the genetic variation into that due to a specific locus and that due to the combined additive effects of genes at other loci (Almasy & Blangero, 1998; Amos, 1994; D. W. Fulker & Cherny, 1996; Goldgar, 1990; Nance & Neale, 1989; Schork, 1993). A QTL-linked variance component is added to the model, with the covariation between siblings defined by a measure of the similarity of the siblings' genotypes; the proportion of alleles shared IBD at a given loci or *pihat* ($\hat{\pi}$).

Thus, a QTL-linked variance component may be added to the classical twin design using $\hat{\pi}$ as the coefficient of covariation for the given locus m, yielding the following:

$$[\Sigma_N]_{ij} = \begin{cases} \sigma_A^2 + \sigma_C^2 + \sigma_Q^2 + \sigma_E^2 & \text{if } i = j \\ 1/2\sigma_A^2 + \sigma_C^2 + \hat{\pi}_{ijm}\sigma_Q^2 & \text{if } i \neq j \text{ and } i \text{ and } j \text{ are full siblings} \\ \sigma_A^2 + \sigma_C^2 + \sigma_Q^2 & \text{if } i \neq j \text{ and } i \text{ and } j \text{ are MZ twins} \end{cases}$$

where the subscripts A, C, Q, and E denote the variance due to additive genetic, common environmental, QTL, and unique environmental effects. In a sample comprised of full-sibling pairs, this can be reparameterized as follows:

$$[\Sigma_N]_{ij} = \begin{cases} \sigma_F^2 + \sigma_Q^2 + \sigma_E^2 & \text{if } i = j \\ \sigma_F^2 + \hat{\pi}_{ijm}\sigma_Q^2 & \text{if } i \neq j \text{ and } i \text{ and } j \text{ are full siblings} \end{cases}$$

This parameterization may also be described visually through the use of a path diagram as shown in Figure 11.2.

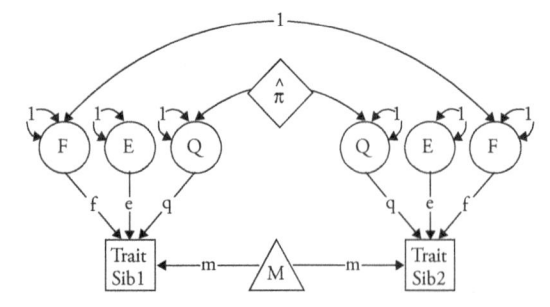

Figure 11.2 A path diagram summarizing a variance components style linkage analysis in a sample of (full) sibling pairs. The squares indicate the measured phenotypes for the two siblings. The circles indicate latent, unmeasured variables that are hypothesized to influence the trait. In this case, the latent variable F represents the familial sources of variation that are completely correlated between the two siblings. E represents the unique or unshared environmental sources of variation (which include measurement error). Q represents the quantitative trait locus (i.e., the linkage effect), which is correlated at $\hat{\pi}$ between the two siblings. The estimate of $\hat{\pi}$ is shown within a diamond to indicate that it changes dynamical between sib-pairs and across the genome. The mean is indicated by the triangle denoted M. Within these diagrams, single-headed arrows indicate paths, whereas double-headed arrows indicate covariance terms.

The likelihood of the observed data under this model ($-2\ln[L(x_i|\hat{\pi})] = -n\ln(2\pi) + \ln|\Sigma_i| + (x_i - \mu)' \cdot \Sigma_i^{-1}(x_i - \mu)$) is compared to a null model in which the QTL-linked variance component has been dropped from the model using the likelihood ratio chi-square test. As this test by definition does not allow negative variance components, the distribution of the test statistic is subject to a boundary constraint and results in a mixture distribution. Thus, twice the difference in natural log likelihoods between these models is asymptotically distributed as a ½:½ mixture of χ_1^2 and a point mass at zero and is consequently designated $\chi_{0,1}^2$ (Self & Liang, 1987). The likelihood ratio test statistic is usually expressed as a LOD score (the difference between the two likelihoods is divided by 2ln10; i.e., 4.6), comparable to the classical LOD score of parametric linkage analysis ($LOD = \log_{10} \frac{L(X|\theta=\hat{\theta})}{L(X|\theta=0.5)}$; (Williams & Blangero, 1999).

Assessing the Significance of Linkage

By definition, genome-wide linkage scans involve assessing evidence for linkage, either at genotyped markers or at fixed intervals across the genome. These procedures result in a large number of statistical tests: approximately 400 tests if the marker strategy is adopted (for a 10cM genome scan) or between 700 and 2000 for interval tests (depending on the genetic map used). Clearly then, the ability to correct for multiple testing when assessing linkage results is essential. In an attempt to standardize the multiple testing corrections within the emergent literature, Krugylak and Lander (1995) produced a seminal paper that provided guidelines for the thresholds that should be used to determine significant and suggestive linkage. They recommended a genome wise probability value of 0.05. That is, a LOD score that might be expected by chance in 1 of 20 genome scans should be adopted as a threshold for significance. The threshold recommended for suggestive linkage was a LOD score that might be observed by chance once in each genome scan. For allele-sharing methods in sib-pairs, Lander and Krugylak recommended that these thresholds be set at 3.6 and 2.2, respectively. The threshold recommended for replication of a significant peak was a *pointwise p*-value of 0.01 (i.e., a 1% probability that the linkage signal observed at the specific locus if a false–positive calculated without correcting for multiple testing).

Although these asymptotic thresholds may be adopted *a priori*, for any given study it is possible that these thresholds will be too conservative or too liberal, as the empirical distribution of the probability values is influenced by the informativeness of the families and markers and by the patterns of missingness within both phenotypic and genotypic data. Thus, simulation of empirical *p*-values for each study is preferred.

The most common approach to the simulation of empirical *p*-values involves simulating genome scan replicates that are unlinked to the trait under analysis but preserve the allele frequency, information content, and missingness of the true genotypic data. Linkage is assessed using the replicate null genome scan, yielding a set of completely spurious results and saving the highest LOD score from each chromosome. This process is repeated 1000 to 5000 times. The saved LOD scores are then sorted, and the significant and suggestive thresholds for the trait under analysis can be determined by finding the highest LOD score that might be expected by chance in 1 of 20 genome scans ($p = 0.05$) and once per genome scan, respectively. Although conceptually straightforward and easy to implement, this method can be time-consuming and is impractical for linkage analyses that take a long time to run or involve substantial data manipulation. In addition, although correcting for multiple testing when analyzing a single trait, it cannot correct for the multiple testing issues that arise by testing multiple traits.

SUMMARY

Although linkage methods were very successful in identifying regions harboring variants that influenced Mendelian-type diseases, the method was not particularly successful in identifying loci influencing complex traits. Moreover, when loci were identified, there was a notable lack of replication. Although contemporary theory supported the idea that most complex traits were highly polygenic, the type of loci identified through linkage analyses typically explained ~5% to 11% of the variance in a trait. Thus, it was generally expected that effects of this magnitude should show more replication than was generally reported. In addition, the apparent identification of loci for traits such as height on every chromosome led to queries regarding the veracity and generalizability of linkage results. In hind-sight, with the benefit of large genome-wide association meta-analyses, some of these findings have been born out and there are now more than 180 genetic variants scattered across the genome, which have been found to influence height (Lango Allen et al., 2010). However, at the time these findings lead to the adoption of association analysis as the primary method for locating quantitative trait loci.

Association Analysis

The aim of association analysis is to determine whether a *trait* or *disease* of interest correlates with *genetic variation* in the population. Such a correlation indicates that the surveyed genetic variation either predisposes to disease or acts as a proxy for the causal variant. As with linkage analysis, association analysis was initially developed for the analysis of binary disease states. The two primary association approaches for mapping disease loci are case–control and family-based studies. Methods for analyzing quantitative traits have been developed for analyzing both unrelated and family-based data.

Quality Control and Data Cleaning Prior to Analysis

Traditionally association studies tended to operate at a candidate gene/region level, with researchers usually selecting less than 100 variants to be genotyped. Around 2006, a series of technologies were developed that lead to the production of genome-wide SNP chips. These chips contain numerous probes, allowing researchers to genotype hundreds of thousands of SNPs in a single assay. As of 2012, chips containing 5 million SNPs are available. However, most researchers working with Caucasian samples are use chips that type 500K to 700K SNPs. Given the volume of data involved, it is important to undertake a series of preliminary quality control analyses prior to analysis. Data are typically screened for *call-rate* (the proportion of samples where the assay returns a genotype and no technical failure is observed), *minor-allele frequency* (MAF), *Hardy-Weinberg Equilibrium* (HWE; described below), and the relationship between these three metrics.

Considering a SNP marker with two alleles (theoretically denoted A_1/A_2; however, in practice this may be a A/G, A/T,C/G, or C/T SNP), there are three possible genotypes (AA, AG, and GG). Genotypes with two copies of the same allele (i.e., AA and GG) are termed *homozygotes*, and genotypes with a copy of each allele are termed the *heterozygote* (AG). Given a sample of genotypes from a population of interest, it is possible to estimate the proportions of the alleles A and G (which are typically labeled p and q, respectively, where $q = 1 - p$), as well as the proportions of the genotypes AA, AG, and GG. The expected frequencies for the genotype categories may be derived by assuming HWE, which occurs when mating in the population is random and the genotypes are equally viable (Hardy, 1908; Weinberg, 1908). These expected frequencies are p^2, $2pq$, and q^2 for AA, AG, and GG, respectively. Testing for a deviation of the observed genotype frequencies from HWE provides a good check for the quality of the genotype information, evidence of confounding, or assortative (non-random) mating. However, HWE tests are usually restricted to controls, because deviation from HWE is conflated with true association signal in cases (Cardon & Palmer, 2003).

Case–Control Association Tests

Given a sample comprised of unrelated individuals, where the participants can be classified into those who have the disease of interest (the *cases*) and those who are free of disease (the *controls*), where a given genotype has been assayed for the entire sample, there are a range of association tests that may be conducted. Much like any comparison between cases and controls, for a discrete predictor, a one degree of freedom Pearson's χ^2 test on allele counts may be calculated from the data organized as shown in Table 11.1.

The χ^2 is then defined as:

$$\chi^2 = \sum_{i=1}^{2}\sum_{j=1}^{2} \frac{(N_{ij} - M_{ij})^2}{M_{ij}},$$

Table 11.1. Notation for Counts of Alleles A_1 and A_2 in Cases (d_1 and d_2, respectively) and in Controls (u_1 and u_2, respectively)

	Allele counts		
	A_1	A_2	Total
Case	d_1	d_2	N_{case}
Control	u_1	u_2	$N_{control}$
Total	N_{A1}	N_{A2}	N_{total}

Table 11.2. Notation for Counts of Genotypes A_1A_1, A_1A_2 and A_2A_2

	Genotype counts			
	A_1A_1	A_1A_2	A_2A_2	Total
Case	d_{11}	d_{12}	d_{22}	N_{case}
Control	u_{11}	u_{12}	u_{22}	$N_{control}$
Total	N_{11}	N_{12}	N_{22}	N_{total}

d_{11}, d_{12}, and d_{22} are the respective genotype counts for cases, and u_{11}, u_{12}, and u_{22} are the corresponding genotype counts for controls.

where N_{ij} = number of j alleles observed in the i population ($i = 1$ represents cases; $i = 2$ represents controls); $N*j = N_{1j} + N_{2j}$; $Ni* = N_{i1} + N_{i2}$; and $M_{ij} = N_{i*} * N_{*j}/N_{total}$.

It is also possible to calculate a two degree of freedom Pearson's χ^2 from a table of genotype counts rather than allele counts, following the notation in Table 11.2.

The allelic test effectively employs an additive model, in which the genotypic mean of the heterozygote is estimated to be midway between that of the two homozygotes. Whereas the genotype test is effectively model-free, because the three genotype categories are specified separately. It is also possible to use the information in Table 11.2 to estimate the odds ratio or increase in disease risk conferred by the risk allele in cases as compared to controls:

$$OR = [(d_{12} + d_{22}) * u_{11}]/[d_{11} * (u_{12} + u_{22})]$$

An alternative to these Pearson χ^2 tests is to specify a logistic regression model for association analysis. For this regression model, the alleles for each individual are coded as an indicator variable, so the model is:

$$\log it(y_i) = \alpha + \beta x_i,$$

where y_i is the case or control status, α is the intercept, β is the regression coefficient for the locus, and x_i is an indicator variable for the number of copies of A_2. Note that only one of the two alleles is coded, because the second is linearly dependent on it (i.e., it is collinear). Essentially, this formulation specifies a multiplicative risk model for the effect of the allele in the population (i.e., the relative risk for genotype $A_1A_1 = R*A_1A_2 = R^2*A_2A_2$).

An alternative approach is to parameterize the model so that the risk for each genotype is estimated directly:

$$\log it(y_i) = \alpha + \beta_1 x_i + \beta_2 w_i,$$

where y_i is the case or control status; α is the intercept; β_1 is the regression coefficient for A_1A_1 homozygote; x_i is an indicator variable coded 0/1 for the presence or absence of genotype A_1A_1; β_2 is the regression coefficient for A_2A_2 homozygote; and w_i is an indicator variable coded 0/1 for the presence or absence of genotype A_2A_2.

As noted, the first regression model follows a multiplicative genetic model, in that it is based on the number of alleles and does not consider interaction between the alleles at the locus in question. However, it is possible to specify a model where the allelic effects operate according to a simple dominant or recessive mode of gene action. An allele is said to be dominant when only one copy of it is required for it to affect the phenotype; it is said to be recessive when two copies are required. Table 11.3 shows how models for dominant and recessive gene action may be parameterized.

The regression approaches are generally preferred as they are: (1) computationally efficient; (2) straightforward to incorporate other loci or covariates; and (3) possible to test for interactions between the alleles at a locus, between different loci, or between covariates (such as environmental exposure) and alleles. The regression models are also readily extended to the analysis of continuous data.

Table 11.3. Genotype Frequency and Penetrance Patterns Under Different Modes of Gene Action

	A_1A_1	A_1A_2	A_2A_2
Genotype frequency	p^2	$2pq$	q^2
Penetrance:	f_2	f_1	f_0
assuming recessive gene action	0	0	1
assuming dominant gene action	1	1	0
assuming multiplicative gene action	x^2	x	0

EXTENSION OF REGRESSION MODELS TO ASSOCIATION TESTS FOR CONTINUOUS PHENOTYPES IN UNRELATED SAMPLES

Given a locus L with alleles i and j (with forms A_1 and A_2), the phenotypic score of an individual y can be predicted using the following linear regression model:

$$y_{ij} = \beta_0 + \beta_1 X_{ij} + \varepsilon,$$

where β_0 is the intercept, β_1 is the regression coefficient for the additive effects at locus L, and ε is the residual. X_{ij} is the genotypic score, which is coded -1 for the A_2A_2 homozygotes, 0 for the A_1A_2 heterozygotes, and $+1$ for the A_1A_1 homozygotes. A second regression term can be included to allow for dominance; in this case, the genotypic score Z_{ij} equals X_{ij}^2, and thus takes on value 0 for the heterozygotes, and value 1 for the homozygotes (e.g., Allison, 1997).

Population Stratification

One potential pitfall of the analysis of unrelated samples is population stratification or substructure. Between populations, allele frequencies tend to differ at a range of loci through the processes of selection and *genetic drift*. This can lead to very diverse allelic frequencies, as illustrated in Figure 11.3 below. When such variation between populations is coupled with differences in the prevalence of a disease, or the mean or variance of a trait, spurious association may result. Hamer and Sirota (2000) have provided a useful didactic discussion of how such effects may arise. Although much attention is focused on population stratification as a source of false–positives, it is also possible that stratification might eliminate a genuine allelic effect and cause a false–negative finding.

Two main methods have been proposed to control for the problems arising from population stratification. The first of these uses genotypic data to estimate the ethnicity of participants. Based on their genetic ethnicity, any participants whose ancestry is divergent from the rest of the sample can be identified and excluded. Initially, this approach was considered quite costly, as it required researchers to genotype a panel of ancestry-informative markers in addition to their set of candidate SNPs. However, with the introduction of genome-wide association, genotyping this type of ancestry screening can be conducted without the need to undertake further genotyping. Using principal components or multidimensional scaling analyses, the data of a given sample may be compared to that available within large public reference samples (such as the HapMap project) to examine the ethnicities of individuals within a sample (as shown in Fig. 11.4).

The second main approach to dealing with the problem of population stratification is to use family-based association designs.

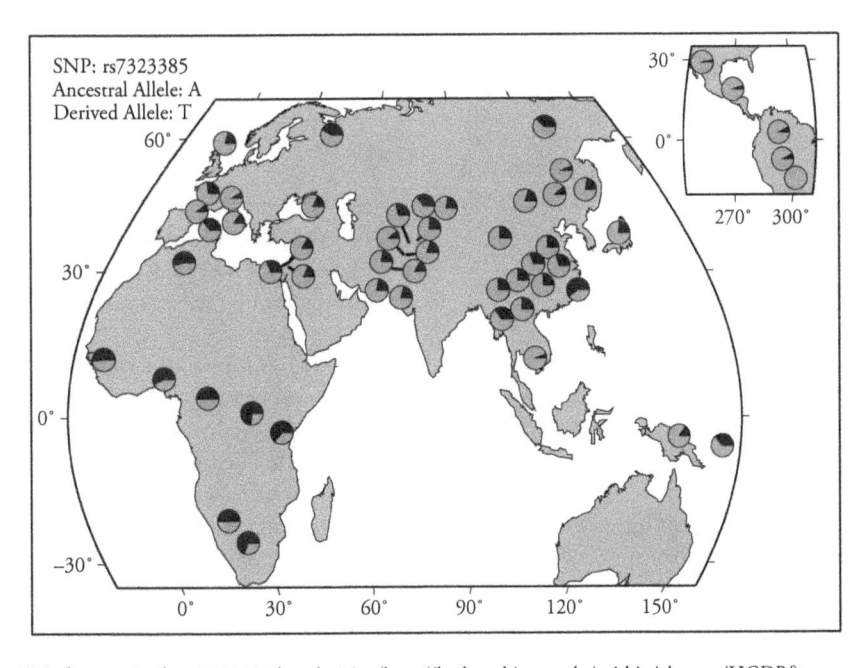

Figure 11.3 Allele frequencies for rs7323385 by ethnicity (http://hgdp.uchicago.edu/cgi-bin/gbrowse/HGDP/).

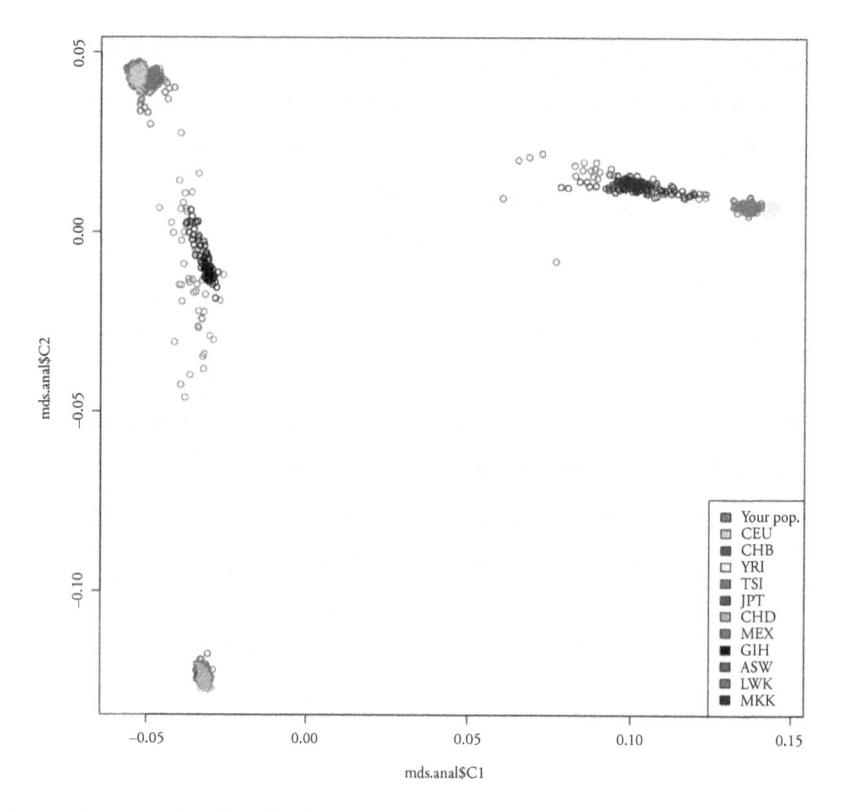

Figure 11.4 An example of an MDS plot of the first two MDS scores. In this case the sample indicated in red (labeled "your pop") is a sample of Australian adolescents recruited in Brisbane. The different reference populations are drawn from the HapMap 3 project (http://hapmap.ncbi.nlm.nih.gov/): ASW, African ancestry in Southwest USA; CEU, Utah residents with Northern and Western European ancestry from the CEPH collection; CHB, Han Chinese in Beijing, China; CHD, Chinese in Metropolitan Denver, Colorado; GIH, Gujarati Indians in Houston, Texas; JPT, Japanese in Tokyo, Japan; LWK, Luhya in Webuye, Kenya; MEX, Mexican ancestry in Los Angeles, California; MKK, Maasai in Kinyawa, Kenya; TSI, Toscans in Italy; YRI, Yoruba in Ibadan, Nigeria. As shown within the plot, the Australian data cluster tightly with the two European reference populations (CEU and TSI) reflecting the migration history of Australia.

Family-Based Association Tests

Unlike case–control designs for the identification of risk variants, family-based designs employ auto-control mechanisms, based on the hypothesis that parents share their genetic background with their offspring.

TRANSMISSION-BASED APPROACHES

The first family-based design proposed was the transmission disequilibrium test (TDT), which utilizes Mendel's Law of Segregation. The key principle is that the transmission of either allele from a heterozygous parent (i.e., genotype A_1A_2) is equally likely. However, affected offspring should be more likely to receive risk alleles than non-risk. Thus, it is possible to test for overtransmission of risk variants using the McNemar χ^2 as the transmission, or non-transmission, from heterozygous parents is a paired observation. The test is computed using the formula:

$$\chi^2 = \frac{(nt_1 - t_1)^2}{nt_1 + t_1} = \frac{(nt_2 - t_2)^2}{nt_2 + t_2}$$

Where nt_1 is the frequency of non-transmission of A_1, t_1 is the frequency of transmission of A_1, nt_2 is the frequency of non-transmission of A_2, and t_2 is the frequency of transmission of A_2 (note: $t_1 = nt_2$ and that $t_2 = nt_1$).

The TDT is robust to population stratification, because it only considers parents of a single genotype (i.e., heterozygotes). Although designed for situations in which parental genotypes are available, it is possible to use the same principle in study of sibling pairs (Horvath & Laird, 1998; Spielman & Ewens, 1998). Conceptually, if two siblings are discordant for the phenotype, then the affected sibling ought to harbor more risk variants than the unaffected sibling. As full siblings are *de facto* from the same stratum of the population, this design is not subject to population stratification artifacts. The basic test for the sib-TDT employs permutation. The genotypes of a pair of sibships are randomly reassigned and the difference in marker allele frequencies between case and control siblings is tested. This procedure is repeated a large number of times to determine the empirical distribution of the test. Finally, the true sample difference test statistic (i.e., when no randomization has been performed) is then compared to the empirical distribution to determine its significance. The sib-TDT and the TDT information have been combined together to form the family-based association test (Laird & Lange, 2006; Lange, DeMeo, Silverman, Weiss, & Laird, 2004; Lange, DeMeo, & Laird, 2002) and the pedigree disequilibrium test (Martin, Monks, Warren, & Kaplan, 2000).

STRUCTURAL EQUATION MODELING APPROACHES

An alternative approach to family-based association is to extend the modeling of familial resemblance using structural equations, as described in Chapter 9 (*Twin Studies and Behavior Genetics*). Within the combined maximum likelihood-based approach, we model the full covariance structure by maximizing the natural log of the likelihood of the data with respect to Σ_i (the expected covariance matrix among the variables for family i) and μ_i (the vector of expected means for family i). The structure of Σ_i, may be specified by the user. For example, if the sample were comprised of families that included mono- (identical) and dizygotic (non-identical) twins, then the trait variance could be decomposed into additive genetic (A), common environmental (C) and residual, or non-shared environmental (E) effects. Whereas given a sample of full siblings, the variance may be decomposed into familial (F) and residual (E) effects as described in the linkage section above.

Against this background covariance model, we can estimate the effect of the association within the model of the means. It is possible to incorporate the association model described above ($y_{ij} = \beta_0 + \beta_1 X_{ij} + \varepsilon$) within this structural equation model framework and assess evidence for association by comparing the fit of this model to one in which β_1 is fixed to 0, using a likelihood-ratio test. However, this *total* test of association is not robust to population stratification effects.

The association test can be reparameterized by taking advantage of the family-based strata correction by partitioning the allelic effects into *between* (β_b) and *within* (β_w) family effects (D. Fulker, Cherny, Sham, & Hewitt, 1999). In which case, these three models may be parameterized as follows, for the *j*th sib from the *i*th family:

$$y_{ij} = \beta_0 + \beta_b X_{bi} + \beta_w X_{wij} + \varepsilon,$$

where X_{bi} is the derived coefficient for the between-families additive genetic effect for the *i*th family, and X_{wij} is the coefficient for the within-families additive genetic effect for the *j*th sib from the *i*th family, as summarized in Table 11.4. Comparing the fit of a model in which both β_w and β_b are estimated to one in which β_w is fixed to 0 produces a

Table 11.4. Example Scoring of X_{bi} and X_{wij} in a Sibling Pair

Genotype		Genotypic effect		X_{bi}	X_{wij}	
Sib1	Sib2	Sib1	Sib2	Family j	Sib1	Sib2
A_1A_1	A_1A_1	1	1	1	0	0
A_1A_1	A_1A_2	1	0	½	½	−½
A_1A_1	A_2A_2	1	−1	0	1	−1
A_1A_2	A_1A_1	0	1	½	−½	½
A_1A_2	A_1A_2	0	0	0	0	0
A_1A_2	A_2A_2	0	−1	−½	½	−½
A_2A_2	A_1A_1	−1	1	0	−1	1
A_2A_2	A_1A_2	−1	0	−½	−½	½
A_2A_2	A_2A_2	−1	−1	−1	0	0

Following Fulker et al., 1999

test of association robust to population stratification known as the within-family test. In the absence of population stratification, the between-family effect β_b can be equated to the within-family effect β_w, without a significant loss of fit. In this case, the more powerful total test of association can be adopted.

Genome-Wide Association Studies

Genome-wide level data has a number of advantages over the candidate level study. First, the method is effectively hypothesis-free with respect to the variants being typed. As these chips are designed to tag the vast majority of common SNPs (MAF >5%), using this methodology reduces the time spent by researchers selecting the variants to be tested and designing and optimizing the primers to assay the SNPs. Second, as the variants included on the chips are effectively agnostic with respect to any given disease or trait, these genotypes can be used to test for association for any available phenotypes (conditional on any selection biases within the sample).

One of the best examples of the increased explanatory power of GWAS is the association of a risk variant (rs9930506) in the FTO gene with body mass index (BMI). This effect was initially found in a GWAS of type 2 diabetes that discovered a significant hit in a region on chromosome 16 (Frayling, 2007; Scott et al., 2007). In the process of attempting to replicate this finding, it was subsequently discovered to be associated with obesity and BMI rather than diabetes *per se*. The effect of this variant is large, with adults who are homozygous for the risk allele weighing about 3 kilograms more than those are homozygous for the non-risk alleles. In addition, across samples, obese individuals are 1.5 times more likely to have inherited risk genotypes than lean controls. Notably, the FTO gene had previously been characterized within the mouse. However, knocking-out this gene within the mouse lead to a deformation of mouse paws; based on this phenotype, the FTO gene had been registered in the databases as "Fatso"—a gene that led to a fused toes mutation in mice (Peters, Ausmeier, & Ruther, 1999). As there was no previous biological evidence to suggest FTO would be a useful candidate gene for BMI, this region had not previously been studied with reference to this trait. Amusingly, soon after the publication of the FTO–BMI associations, the gene was renamed within the databases and is now listed as "Fat mass and obesity associated" (http://www.ncbi.nlm.nih.gov/gene/79068).

The most common concern raised by researchers new to the approach is the sheer number of variants tested and the corresponding correction required to account for this multiple testing. Following from the design of genome-wide SNP chips that attempted to tag all common variants within the genome, the field has adopted a significance threshold that accounts for the number of independent regions within the genome, rather than adopting a Bonferoni correction for the actual number of SNPs directly tested. As such, a genome-wide significance threshold of 5×10^{-8} is generally used, which corrects for ~1 million independent common variants in the genome. In addition to reaching this threshold, replication in an independent sample is required to declare significance. Following the location of a significant effect, follow-up biochemistry studies are generally required to determine whether the loci identified has a causal effect or whether (as is more commonly the case) the SNP is acting as a proxy for the functional variant, which has been co-inherited with the loci under analysis.

Obviously, when analyzing genome-wide level genetic data, the efficiency and automation of data analysis is of the upmost importance. To this end, a number of software packages have been developed; the best known of these is PLINK (http://pngu.mgh.harvard.edu/~purcell/plink/). Researchers new to the field are strongly advised to use one of these existing packages to analyze their data rather than implementing their own analyses.

The results of GWAS analyses are typically presented visually in two formats. First, the data is presented as a QQ plot (Fig. 11.5). The QQ plot summarizes the number and magnitude of observed associations compared with the expectations under no association. Ideally the points should hug the identity line before rising above the identity line, indicating that the results are enriched for effects that approach significance. The nature of deviations from the identity line provide clues as to whether the observed associations are true associations or may result from population stratification or cryptic relatedness or technical problems.

The second method for summarizing genome-wide association results is the Manhattan plot (Fig. 11.6), which summarizes the significance of effects by location across the genome. Ideally any hit approaching significance will appear as a column of results indicating support from the surrounding SNPs.

One important factor to keep in mind when reading association studies is that results should not be considered deterministic. Genetic effects on complex traits are typically small, explaining less than

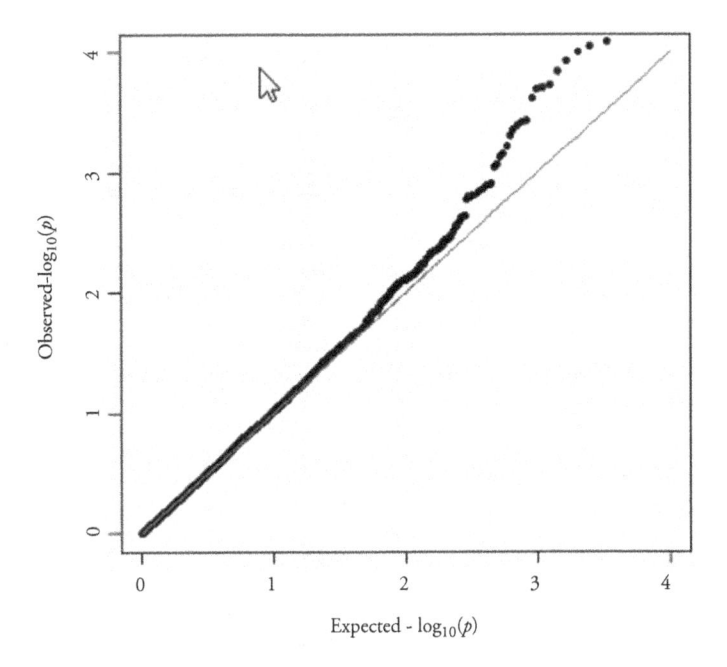

Figure 11.5 An example QQplot based on simulated data.

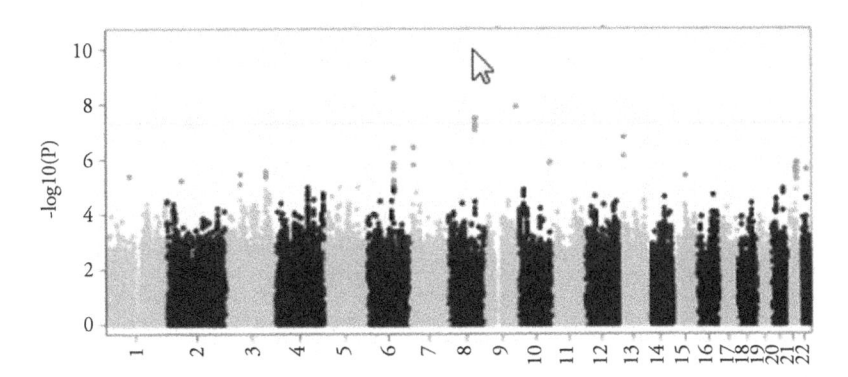

Figure 11.6 An example Manhattan plot based on simulated data.

1% of the variance. The language used in discussing results is very important—there are many variants within each gene; traits are influenced by many variants, and any given variant can influence many traits.

Summary

Association and GWAS in particular have been very successful in identifying genetic variants influencing diseases and behaviors. Moreover, GWAS has changed the way in which we think about genetic variation and the meaning of polygenicity. Whereas during the linkage era it was hypothesized that risk variants might explain up to 5% of the variance in a trait, many of the variants identified by GWAS explain less than 1% of the variation. This has led a reconceptualization of the nature of genetic effects within the genetics fields. Notably, these findings also contradict the single gene and hormonal hypotheses that are commonly proposed to explain behaviors within the biopsychology literature. To date, numerous GWAS have been conducted on traits of interest to psychology, including variation in personality and IQ within the normal range as well clinical disorders (using both DSM and ICD diagnostic criterion). As GWAS studies become more integrated within the psychological literature, we hope that these findings will inform theoretical and clinical practice.

Author Note

Sarah E. Medland, Genetic Epidemiology Laboratory, Queensland Institute of Medical Research, Brisbane, Australia, sarah.medland@qimr.edu.au

References

Abecasis, G. R., Cherny, S. S., Cookson, W. O., & Cardon, L. R. (2002). Merlin—rapid analysis of dense genetic maps using sparse gene flow trees. *Nat Genet, 30*(1), 97–101.

Allison, D. B. (1997). Transmission-disequilibrium tests for quantitative traits. *Am J Hum Genet, 60*, 676–690.

Almasy, L., & Blangero, J. (1998). Multipoint quantitative-trait linkage analysis in general pedigrees. *Am J Hum Genet, 62*(5), 1198–1211.

Amos, C. I. (1994). Robust variance-components approach for assessing genetic linkage in pedigrees. *Am J Hum Genet, 54*(3), 535–543.

Amos, C. I., Dawson, D. V., & Elston, R. C. (1990). The probabilistic determination of identity-by-descent sharing for pairs of relatives from pedigrees. *Am J Hum Genet, 47*(5), 842–853.

Cardon, L. R., & Palmer, L. J. (2003). Population stratification and spurious allelic association. *The Lancet, 361*, 598–604.

Dudoit, S., & Speed, T. P. (2000). A score test for the linkage analysis of qualitative and quantitative traits based on identity by descent data from sib-pairs. *Biostatistics, 1*(1), 1–26.

Elston, R. C., & Stewart, J. (1971). A general model for the genetic analysis of pedigree data. *Human Heredity, 21*, 523–542.

Forrest, W. F. (2001). Weighting improves the "new Haseman-Elston" method. *Hum Hered, 52*(1), 47–54.

Frayling, T. M. (2007). Genome-wide association studies provide new insights into type 2 diabetes aetiology. *Nat Rev Genet, 8*(9), 657–662.

Fulker, D., Cherny, S., Sham, P., & Hewitt, J. (1999). Combined linkage and association sib-pair analysis for quantitative traits. *American Journal of Human Genetics, 64*, 259–267.

Fulker, D. W., & Cherny, S. S. (1996). An improved multipoint sib-pair analysis of quantitative traits. *Behav Genet, 26*(5), 527–532.

Goldgar, D. E. (1990). Multipoint analysis of human quantitative genetic variation. *Am J Hum Genet, 47*(6), 957–967.

Goring, H. H., & Terwilliger, J. D. (2000). Linkage analysis in the presence of errors II: marker-locus genotyping errors modeled with hypercomplex recombination fractions. *Am J Hum Genet, 66*(3), 1107–1118.

Hamer, D., & Sirota, L. (2000). Beware the chopsticks gene. *Mol Psychiatry, 5*(1), 11–13.

Hardy, G. (1908). Mendelian proportions in mixed populations. *Science, 28*, 49–50.

Haseman, J. K., & Elston, R. C. (1972). The investigation of linkage between a quantitative trait and a marker locus. *Behav Genet, 2*(1), 3–19.

Horvath, S., & Laird, N. M. (1998). A discordant-sibship test for disequilibrium and linkage: no need for parental data. *American Journal of Human Genetics, 63*(6), 1886–1897.

Kruglyak, L., & Lander, E. S. (1995). Complete multipoint sib-pair analysis of qualitative and quantitative traits. *Am J Hum Genet, 57*(2), 439–454.

Laird, N., & Lange, C. (2006). Family-based designs in the age of large-scale gene-association studies. *Nature Reviews Genetics, 7*, 385–394.

Lander, E. S., & Green, P. (1987). Construction of multilocus genetic linkage maps in humans. *Proc Natl Acad Sci U S A, 84*(8), 2363–2367.

Lange, C., DeMeo, D., Silverman, E. K., Weiss, S. T., & Laird, N. M. (2004). PBAT: tools for family-based association studies. *American Journal of Human Genetics, 74*(2), 367–369.

Lange, C., DeMeo, D. L., & Laird, N. M. (2002). Power and design considerations for a general class of family-based association tests: quantitative traits. *American Journal of Human Genetics, 71*(6), 1330–1341.

Lango Allen, H. et al. (2010). Hundreds of variants clustered in genomic loci and biological pathways affect human height. *Nature, 467*, 832–838.

Martin, E., Monks, S., Warren, L., & Kaplan, N. (2000). A test for linkage and association in general pedigrees: the Pedigree Disequilibrium Test. *American Journal of Human Genetics, 67*, 146–154.

Morton, N. E. (1955). Sequential tests for the detection of linkage. *Am J Hum Genet, 7*, 227–318.

Nance, W. E., & Neale, M. C. (1989). Partitioned twin analysis: a power study. *Behav Genet, 19*(1), 143–150.

Neale, M. C., & Cardon, L. R. (1992). *Methodology for genetic studies of twins and families*, Dordrecht, the Netherlands: Kluwer Academic Publishers.

Peters, T., Ausmeier, K., & Ruther, U. (1999). Cloning of Fatso (Fto), a novel gene deleted by the Fused toes (Ft) mouse mutation. *Mamm Genome, 10*(10), 983–986.

Schork, N. J. (1993). Extended multipoint identity-by-descent analysis of human quantitative traits: efficiency, power, and modeling considerations. *Am J Hum Genet, 53*(6), 1306–1319.

Scott, L. J., Mohlke, K. L., Bonnycastle, L. L., Willer, C. J., Li, Y., Duren, W. L., et al. (2007). A genome-wide association study of type 2 diabetes in Finns detects multiple susceptibility variants. *Science, 316*(5829), 1341–1345.

Self, S., & Liang, K. (1987). Large sample properties of the maximum likelihood estimator and the likelihood ratio test on the boundary of the parameter space. *Journal of the American Statistical Association, 82*, 605–611.

Sham, P. C., Purcell, S., Cherny, S. S., & Abecasis, G. R. (2002). Powerful regression-based quantitative-trait linkage analysis of general pedigrees. *Am J Hum Genet, 71*(2), 238–253.

Spielman, R. S., & Ewens, W. J. (1998). A sibship test for linkage in the presence of association: The Sib Transmission/Disequilibrium Test. *American Journal of Human Genetics, 62*, 450–458.

Visscher, P. M., & Hopper, J. L. (2001). Power of regression and maximum likelihood methods to map QTL from sib-pair and DZ twin data. *Ann Hum Genet, 65*(Pt 6), 583–601.

Weinberg, W. (1908). Über den Nachweis der Vererbung beim Menschen. *Jahresh Ver Vaterl Naturk Württemb, 64*, 369–382.

Williams, J. T., & Blangero, J. (1999). Comparison of variance components and sibpair-based approaches to quantitative trait linkage analysis in unselected samples. *Genet Epidemiol, 16*, 113–134.

Wright, F. A. (1997). The phenotypic difference discards sib-pair QTL linkage information. *Am J Hum Genet, 60*(3), 740–742.

CHAPTER
12

Multidimensional Scaling

Cody S. Ding

Abstract

This chapter introduces multidimensional scaling (MDS) as a psychological and educational research tool. Using examples that are more familiar to psychological and educational researchers, I describe the major types of MDS models and their applications. Because the focus of the chapter is applied orientation, the presentation of materials is less technical. The chapter covers four types of MDS models: metric, nonmetric, individual differences, and preference. For individual differences models and preference models, there are both metric and nonmetric models. An example for each type of model is presented so that the reader may get a flavor of what research questions can be addressed. In addition, some main differences between MDS analysis, factor analysis, and cluster analysis are discussed. The chapter ends with some issues that need to be addressed in the future.

Key Words: multidimensional scaling, latent group configuration, individual differences and preferences

Introduction

In much of the quantitative and statistical literature, multidimensional scaling (MDS) is often referred to as a technique that represents the empirical relationships of data as a set of points in a space, typically in two or higher dimensional spaces. Traditionally, multidimensional scaling represents a family of statistical methods or models that portray the structure of the data in a spatial fashion so that we could easily see and understand what the data indicate. This may be the reason that MDS tends to be viewed as a data-visual technique. The unifying theme of different MDS models is the spatial representation of the data structure. However, MDS models do not have to be used only for the purpose of visual representation of the data. Rather, we could employ MDS models to investigate a wide range of issues in education and psychology such as perception of school climate by various age groups of students, changes in achievement, sensitivity of psychological measures, or individual differences in mental health. Moreover, it can also be used for the purpose of hypothesis testing, like that in structural equation modeling. Although MDS is a powerful tool, it appears to be underused in the current educational and psychological research.

In the literature, MDS has been defined in slightly different ways. For example, Davison (1983) defined MDS as a method for studying the structure of stimuli or individuals. Borg and Groenen (2005) defined MDS as a technique of representing distances between objects in a multidimensional space. In a nutshell, MDS can be defined as a family of analytical methods that use the geometric model (typically in the form of a distance equation) for analysis of inter-relationships among a set of variables or people. A distance equation could be the Euclidean distance, the city-block distance, or the Minkowski distance. Table 12.1 shows the definition of these distances, along with other terminologies and symbols used in this chapter. Thus, an MDS analysis involves employment of a specific

Table 12.1. Definition and Description of Terminology and Symbols Used in the Chapter

Terminology	Definition or description
Euclidean distance	The Euclidean distance between variable i and j in an m-dimensional configuration X is defined as: $$d_{ij} = \sqrt{\sum_{k=0}^{m} \left(x_{ik} - x_{jk}\right)^2}$$
City-block distance	The city-block distance between variable i and j in an m-dimensional configuration X is defined as: $$d_{ij} = \sum_{k=0}^{m} \left|x_{ik} - x_{jk}\right|$$
Minkowski distance	The Minkowski distance between variable i and j in an m-dimensional configuration X is defined as: $$d_{ij_{ij}}^{p} = \left(\sum_{k=0}^{m} \left|x_{ik} - x_{jk}\right|^p\right)^{\frac{1}{p}},$$ $p \geq 1$
d_{ij}	The MDS model-estimated distance between any two points or variables in an m-dimensional configuration X.
$\bar{d}$	The mean of model-estimated distances.
x_{ik}, x_{jk}	The coordinate of point or variable i and j along dimension k.
x_{iks}, x_{jks}	The coordinate of individual person s for variable i and j along dimension k.
x_{sk}	The individual s ideal point along dimension k. It designates the level along dimension k that the individual considers ideal.
δ_{ij}	The observed distance between any two points or variables i and j in an m-dimensional configuration X.
$\hat{\delta}_{ij}$	The disparity, the distance calculated so that: (1) it is monotonically related to the observed distance; and (2) it is as closely fit to the estimated distance d_{ij} as possible.
δ_{ijs}	The distance of individual s about the variable pair i, j.
w_{ks}	The dimension salience weight for individual s along dimension k.
δ_{is}	The distance between individual s and variable i. It represents the strength of the individual's preference for variable i.
b_{ks}	The linear regression weight for individual s along dimension k.
c_s	An additive constant unique to individual s.
w_s	The weight for individual s when the dimension salience is the same across dimensions.
$r'_{kk}s$	The correlation between dimensions k and k'.
A degenerate solution	An MDS solution where the points of variables in an m-dimensional configuration collapsed together rather than being distinctly separated.
An ideal point	A coordinate of individual s in an m-dimensional configuration that is considered ideal for that individual.
A monotonic transformation	The rank order of transformed data is the same as the original data.
Weights	The values that indicate the dimensional importance or salience given by individuals.

model of study, for example, how people view things in different ways.

The sample size required for an MDS analysis does not need to be large: it can range from a few people to a few hundred people or more. Because the MDS analysis is more descriptive (except for probabilistic MDS) and does not involve significance testing, the interpretation and accuracy of the analysis results are not tied to the sample size. Thus, the MDS analysis can be used for studies based on the single-case design to investigate how a small group of individuals responds to a treatment, for example. However, if one wants to make a generalization based on the people in the study, a representative sample is required. In addition, MDS models (except for probabilistic MDS) do not have distributional requirements such as normality of the coordinates. But the probabilistic MDS with maximum likelihood estimation assumes that the coordinates are normally and independently distributed and each object can have the same variance or different variances.

In this chapter, I will discuss MDS from several viewpoints. First, historical review of the MDS and its applications will be presented. Second, I will briefly discuss how MDS differs from similar statistical methods such as factor analysis. This comparison is necessary because I often encounter the questions regarding the uniqueness of MDS. Third, different MDS models and their primary applications will be discussed. In these sections, I will discuss each MDS model, its fundamental concepts, and how it can be applied. This part of the chapter occupies the majority of the space. Fourth, some new applications of MDS models will be presented. Finally, future directions will be discussed. The purpose of this chapter is to provide readers with a fundamental view of MDS so that they can better understand MDS and increase the likelihood that MDS models are employed in their research. In the discussion, I will keep the presentation of technical materials to a minimum and focus on essential concepts.

Historical Review

Up until the late 1980s, articles and books on MDS appeared at an ever-increasing rate, and MDS applications grew in a great number of disciplines, with the historical root in psychology. Because of such a large bibliography, it is hard to be exhaustive in tracking all technical materials on MDS as well as its applications. In the following sections, I present an overview of development of multidimensional scaling up to the late 1980s, because most of the MDS developments occurred before this time period. Beginning in 1990, MDS may have lost favor with the advent and popularity of structural equation modeling.

There are quite a few writings on the history of MDS developments (e.g., Shepard, Romney, & Nerlove, 1972; Young, 1987). The following review is based primarily on Young (1987).

Four Stages of MDS Development
THE FIRST STAGE: METRIC MDS MODEL

According to Young (1987), development of MDS models went through four stages. The first stage, started in the 1950s, is characterized by Torgerson's MDS model or algorithm (Torgerson, 1952). The algorithm determines or constructs the multidimensional map of points by: (1) obtaining a scale of comparative distances among these points; (2) converting the comparative distances into ratio distances; and (3) determining the dimensionality that underlies these ratio distances. In 1956, Messick and Abelson (1956) provided a better algorithm to Torgerson's original model to accomplish the same goal. The enhancement was made by improving the estimation of the additive constant, as in Torgerson's second step, that converts comparative distances to ratio distances based on firm mathematical grounds. These approaches to MDS have become known as *metric MDS* in the literature because the observed distances are assumed to be equal or proportional to model-derived distance in a multidimensional space in Torgerson's algorithm.

THE SECOND STAGE: NONMETRIC MDS MODEL

The assumptions of Torgerson's metric model are very restrictive (discussed in a later section), and thus his algorithm is rarely used in its original form. This limitation leads to the second stage of MDS developments in the 1960s. Thus, this second stage is characterized by development of what is now known as *nonmetric MDS* started by Shepard (1962) and followed by Kruskal (1964). Nonmetric MDS requires less restrictive assumptions than a metric MDS model by Torgerson (1952). The chief difference between nonmetric and metric MDS is that nonmetric MDS requires only that the rank order of observed distances be the same as (i.e., monotonically related to) the distance estimates derived from the prespecified MDS model.

Kruskal's contribution

It is worthy to note Kruskal's contribution to the development of nonmetric MDS at this stage, which will have implications for our interpretations of the findings. First, he introduced a least square fit function that objectively defined the goal of the MDS analysis by minimizing normalized residuals between a monotonic (i.e., rank order) transformation of the data and the model-derived distance based on multidimensional space. Second, he defined two optimization procedures that handled data that have equal distance between any two pairs of objects (called tied data): primary procedure (i.e., untie tied data) and secondary procedure (i.e., tied data remain tied). Third, his algorithm could analyze incomplete data matrices and is able to obtain MDS solutions in non-Euclidean distance space, such as the city-block distance space used by Attneave (1950).

Coombs' contribution

Another noteworthy contribution to nonmetric MDS development is by Coombs' data theory, which states that relationships among data can be represented in a space (Coombs, 1964). Although not directly related to MDS algorithm, Coombs' data theory is of central interest to MDS. Specifically, he suggested four types of data: (1) preferential choice data, when a person indicates he/she prefers a particular object or behavior (e.g., an adolescent girl prefers talking to her mother with respect to sexual behaviors); (2) liking data, when a person indicates whether he/she likes or dislike certain behaviors (e.g., a female may indicate she likes children while a male may indicate he likes playing computer games); (3) comparison data, when a person indicates which of the two objects is more of some attributes (e.g., a student may indicate that teachers are more helpful than students in school); and (4) similarity data, when a person indicates how similar the two objects are (e.g., an adolescent may indicate that smoking and drinking are the same with respect to deviant behaviors). All of these four types of data can be represented in multidimensional space. As we will see later in the chapter, different MDS analyses can be performed using these four types of data. For example, the MDS preference models can employ one of these types of data to study individual differences in behavioral preferences.

THE THIRD STAGE: INDIVIDUAL DIFFERENCES MODELS.

The third stage of MDS developments involves individual differences MDS models. The basic idea of *individual differences MDS* models is that when we analyze data from individuals, we have two choices: (1) analyze a single matrix of data, averaging across all individuals or (2) analyze each data matrix if we believe that the manipulation of independent variables has had an effect on individuals. Individual differences models, so named, have been used mainly to investigate variations of data structure across individuals, such as to describe variation in person's perceptions across time, settings, or treatment conditions. Thus, individual differences MDS models are able to simultaneously analyze a number of individual data matrices, producing indices of individual differences with respect to certain behavioral traits, with individual differences being represented by dimensional importance indices (called weights) in a Euclidean distance space.

INDSCAL

There are several individual differences MDS models. The most well-known model is the Weighted Euclidean Model, also called INDSCAL (for Individual Differences Scaling), developed by Carroll and Chang (1970). Several other researchers also contributed to this line of work such as Horan (1969), Bloxom (1968), McGee (1968), Tucker (1972), and Tucker and Messick (1963). However, the model developed by Carroll and Chang is most used because they developed the computer algorithm (also called INDSCAL) to implement the model, which turns out to be successful in many applications. Based on these developments, Takane, Young, and de Leeuw (1977) developed a computer algorithm called ALSCAL (alternating least squares scaling), which has been incorporated into statistical analysis programs such as SAS and SPSS, making MDS more accessible to a wider audience than before.

ALSCAL

In a sense, the ALSCAL program can be viewed as a consolidation of all previous developments during the first three stages. It includes metric MDS model (Torgerson, 1952), non-metric MDS models (Kruskal, 1964; Shepard, 1962), individual differences models (Carroll & Chang, 1970; McGee, 1968), and multidimensional unfolding (preference) models (Carroll, 1972; Coombs, 1964).

THE FOURTH STAGE: MAXIMUM LIKELIHOOD MDS.

The fourth stage of MDS development involves maximum likelihood multidimensional scaling, which makes it possible for MDS models to be an inferential tool rather than a descriptive tool. This inferential nature of MDS analysis is based on the idea that maximum likelihood MDS allows significance tests to determine dimensionality, the appropriate models, the appropriate error models, or confidence regions for stimuli and individuals.

The most well-known maximum likelihood MDS algorithm is *MULTISCAL* developed by Ramsay (Ramsay, 1991) and *PROSCAL* developed by MacKay and Zinnes (2005). In addition, there are many articles on maximum likelihood MDS and its applications such as those by Ramsay (1977), Takane (1978a, 1978b), Takane and Carroll (1981), DeSarbo, Howard, and Jedidi (1991), and more recently Treat, McFall, et al. (2002), MacKay (2007), and Vera, Macias, and Heiser (2009).

This brief historical review of the MDS developments provides a fundamental picture of where we are with MDS as a psychological and educational analytical tool. In here I did not discuss a great number of literature that dealt with various technical issues around the MDS, nor did I discuss the different applications using the MDS models. However, one can explore those issues and applications using the four themes of MDS developments as a roadmap. Moreover, one should realize that given about 40 years of development, MDS has reached to its young adulthood, as Schiffman, Reynolds, and Young (1981) suggested. In other words, MDS has become quite a sophisticated analytical tool that has yet to be taken full advantage of, especially when we have access to computing power unavailable for MDS analysis 20 years ago.

Differences and Similarities Between MDS, Factor Analysis, and Cluster Analysis

Before I present MDS models, it is imperative to discuss differences and similarities between MDS, factor analysis, and cluster analysis. Without a clear conceptual understanding of what MDS models are all about, one may have difficulty in utilizing MDS for their work, thus impeding further developments of MDS models in psychological and educational research. Consistent with my applied orientation, the discussion is focused more on conceptual grounds rather than mathematical aspects.

MULTIDIMENSIONAL SCALING AND FACTOR ANALYSIS

Conceptually, *factor analysis* is a technique that discovers latent relationships among a set of variables. The objective is to explain *a number of* observed variables (m), by a set of latent variables or factors (f), where (f) is much smaller in number than (m). The hypothesis is that only a few latent factors suffice to explain most of the variance of the data. In other words, the relationships among the observed variables exist because of the underlying latent variables. Likewise, the objective of MDS is to reveal geometrically the structure of data in fewer dimensions. Like MDS, factor analysis yields a quantitative dimensional representation of the data structure. Both have been used to study dimensionality among variables. It is often the case that the term *factor* and *dimension* are used interchangeably in factor analysis literature. Because of this similarity, it is not surprising that factor analysis and MDS are viewed as very similar if not the same.

Studies have been done to compare the two techniques (e.g., Davison, 1981; Hanson, Prediger, & Schussel, 1977; Schlessinger & Guttman, 1969). Based on the literature, the differences between the two may be summarized as follows: (1) factor analysis yields more dimensions than does MDS; (2) factor analysis typically represents linear relationships among variables, whereas MDS can represent both linear and nonlinear relationships; (3) MDS is traditionally more used as a data visualization tool than factor analysis, which is typically a measurement technique; and (4) MDS can employ a variety of kinds of data such as preference ratio data, whose values are coded between 0.0 and 1.0, indicating the degree to which a variable in a variable pair is preferred. However, factor analysis usually analyzes the correlation matrix, whose values indicate similarities between variables. Therefore, the applications of MDS can be more diverse than that of factor analysis. For example, MDS preference analysis can be used to study individuals' preferences to a set of coping behaviors (e.g., prefer shouting to talking with friends), whereas factor analysis usually is used in studying how a set of coping behaviors measures a particular coping construct (e.g., withdrawal coping).

MULTIDIMENSIONAL SCALING AND CLUSTER ANALYSIS

Another closely related method to MDS is *cluster analysis* (Kruskal, 1977). Traditional cluster analysis, such as hierarchical cluster analysis, is employed to identify individuals who share similar attributes (e.g., high-risk adolescents). **MDS** can be used in the same way. Davison (1983) pointed out three differences between MDS and cluster analysis. First, relationships between observed distance matrix and model-derived distance matrix in cluster analysis cannot be expressed in linear or even monotone fashion as in MDS. Second, dimensions in cluster analysis are typically represented in a tree diagram of many simple two-valued dimensions to represent data. As such, the number of dichotomous dimensions that needs to represent data structure becomes large in practice. Third, MDS defines clusters of individuals in terms of continuous dimensions rather than in either-or fashion. Thus, we can describe a group of individuals who possess more of one attribute (e.g., depression) than the other (e.g., anxiety) rather than having that attribute (e.g., depression) or not. In addition to these three differences, MDS is a model-based approach, while traditional cluster analysis is not. Recently, some researchers developed model-based cluster analysis (Fraley & Raftery, 2007). However, a key difference between model-based cluster analysis and MDS is still that MDS represents clusters in terms of dimension rather than dichotomous fashion.

In this section, I summarized some fundamental differences between MDS, factor analysis, and cluster analysis. One take-home message is that MDS is not simply a data-reduction method. Multidimensional scaling can be used for many other purposes in education and psychological applications such as longitudinal study of achievement, treatment preferences, or hypothesis testing of behavioral likings.

The MDS Models: Basics and Their Applications

Multidimensional scaling is a family of analytical techniques, consisting of many different models, each of which has its own uniqueness but also overlaps to some degree with other models in terms of what each model can accomplish. In order to enable readers to easily see the potential applications in their own research, I have organized this section in the following way. First, data characteristics that are unique to MDS models will be discussed. Then I will present MDS models based on the category to which they belong. Third, I will discuss the issues related to a particular model such as model fit, rotation, or interpretation. Fourth, a real dataset will be used to illustrate the application of the models discussed.

Data: More Than Just Numbers

Multidimensional scaling can be used for various analyses, and therefore different types of data can be involved. Young (1987) provided a thorough discussion of data for MDS models, as did some other authors (e.g., Borg & Groenen, 2005; Davison, 1983). I will discuss those aspects of data that are most relevant to MDS in the current research context.

Traditionally, data used in MDS analysis are typically called proximity measures. The term, *proximity*, is fairly vague, however, because it can indicate similarity data as well as dissimilarity data. For this reason, in this chapter I will use a specific term for a particular kind of data. For example, if distance matrix is to be used, I will refer to such data as distance data (c.f., dissimilarity or proximities).

Data source. The data in MDS usually come from direct judgment of certain stimuli with respect to some attribute. For example, participants are asked to judge which car's color is brighter or to judge which two schools are similar. Such judgment data are generated via four types of judgment tasks: magnitude estimation, category rating, graphic rating, or category sorting. Currently, the judgment data in education or psychology (except for some experimental studies) are not so common because of practical problems (e.g., time constraints) and participants' ability and willingness to perform the various tasks.

A type of data commonly used in today's research is Likert-type data generated by questionnaires or surveys. This type of data is typically not discussed in MDS literature; however, Likert-type data can be converted into either a distance data matrix by averaging across all participants or individual distance matrices, one for each participant. Such data are called indirect proximity measures in the literature. A distance matrix based on data generated from a survey can be used in research setting. Thus, the input data for MDS are more likely to be indirect data rather than direct judgment data. Jacoby (1993) has developed a SAS macro for calculating dissimilarity from survey research based on the approached by Rabinowitz (1976), which is suitable for non-metric MDS analysis.

Data design. One distinct feature of data used in MDS comes from data theories stipulated by Coombs (1964) and Young (1987). This feature involves the shape of the data (i.e., number of ways and number of modes) and measurement conditionality. Number of ways indicates the number of factors involved in collecting data (i.e., data design). This idea of number of ways is somewhat different from the idea of number of factors in analysis of variance (ANOVA). In MDS, number of ways implies the factors that produce variations. For example, if one participant is asked to rate differences among five coping behaviors, then this is a two-way data design because one participant does not produce variation but five coping behaviors are a source of variation in rating. On the other hand, if three participants are asked to judge the differences among five coping behaviors, this is a three-way data design because now different participants produce variations along with five coping behaviors. In ANOVA, this would be a one-way analysis because we only have one factor (i.e., coping behavior) with five levels.

The number of modes indicates the layout of the data in terms of data being either square or rectangular. A typical data layout of one mode is a square and symmetric data matrix such as correlation matrix or distance matrix, while a rectangular data layout is a person (row) by variable (column) data matrix. Thus, the data can be described with respect to number of ways and modes. A correlation or distance matrix averaged over a group of individuals is two-way one-mode data; but if we have several correlation or distance data matrices, one for each individual, the data will be three-way one-mode data. The commonly seen data layout from questionnaires or survey instruments is a two-way two-mode data layout, with two-way being participants and variables and two-mode being rectangular.

Data conditionality. Measurement conditionality refers to measurement characteristics of data (Young, 1987). There are four types of measurement conditionality: unconditional, matrix-conditional, row-conditional, and general-conditional. Multidimensional scaling models explicitly take into consideration data having different measurement characteristics by fitting the data in a least-square sense and maintaining the measurement characteristics of the data via optimal scaling of the observed data. Thus, richness of the data can be captured and maintained by employing an appropriate MDS model based on measurement characteristics. Specifically, *matrix-conditional data* occurs when having a group of participants respond to an item with a scale of, say, 1 to 10 in a questionnaire. It is likely that one participant's response of "6" may not be considered to be the same as another participant's response of "6." In fact, it is quite likely that they do not use the scale in the same way, as we may observe. Thus, the measurement characteristics are conditional on participants, with each participant having his/her own matrix and serving as a partition of the data. One possibly interesting application is to use such data measurement characteristics to study different response styles like acquiescent response style. So far, however, MDS has not been used to study such an issue.

On the other hand, *row-conditional data* refers to a data layout in which each row of data cannot be compared with one other. For example, a "4" in a first row of data has no bearing on a "4" in a second row (or any other rows). A response of a "4" in the first row merely indicates that a participant provides a rating of "4" on a particular item. Two "4" ratings in the different rows do not indicate the same degree of similarity or dissimilarity. Thus, each row of each individual's data serves as a partition of data.

Both matrix-conditional and row-conditional data are traditionally discussed in the context of similarity judgment by participants using a particular judgment tool, such as magnitude estimation, to rank the similarity among a set of stimuli or objects. Data obtained through such type of collection techniques are not commonly seen in most current research settings. However, a new habit of thinking can be developed with respect to how we conceptualize our data. For example, the data we commonly encounter today are person-by-variable multivariate data matrix, called column-conditional data. In column-conditional multivariate data, each column represents a variable and rows represent people. Thus, measurement characteristics are within columns of the data matrix, the first column representing gender, the second column representing achievement status, the third representing income, and so forth, with each variable having its own measurement level. But one can also view such multivariate data matrices as matrix- or row-conditional. Consider an example in which a group of five participants responds to 10 anxiety items on a scale of 1 to 6. If we are willing to make an assumption that each participant has his/her own internal standard with respect to anxiety level, and one participant's response of "3" on a particular anxiety item may indicate a different level of anxiety from another participant's response of "3" on the same item, then we can say that the meaning of measurements is conditional on each participant's response matrix. Thus, we can analyze the data as matrix-conditional data and preserve the original characteristics of measurement. On the other hand, we can also think of this 5 by 10 data matrix as row-conditional data if we are willing to assume that the response of one participant has no relationship with any other participants, and we cannot compare between participants, then we could analyze the data as row-conditional data. Historically, few multivariate data have been thought of in such ways and analyzed accordingly using the appropriate MDS model.

The third measurement conditionality is called *unconditional data*. Unconditional data occur when we think the response to a particular item is comparable across participants, which leads to one partition of the data. Accordingly, we can analyze one data matrix averaged across all participants. For example, a correlation matrix or distance matrix obtained from a group of participants is a typical unconditional data.

The fourth measurement conditionality is *general-conditional data*. Perhaps a better term should be situation-conditional data. General-conditional data occur when the same data are collected under different situations. As an example, a psychologist is interested in a client's perception of different treatments over a period of time. A different treatment will be used each day and data for each day are generated. Because the treatment that generates the data each day is different, she could view the data as being partitioned into subsets, with one partition for each day. Such data can be analyzed as general-conditional data. To the best of my knowledge, no studies have been conducted in such a fashion.

Some implications. Thinking about these different kinds of data structures opens up many possibilities for data analysis. A special strength of MDS is its ability to handle all these different kinds of data structures. In contrast, the commonly used analytical techniques such as hierarchical linear modeling or structural equation modeling typically use column-conditional data and do not take into consideration the other measurement characteristics. Theoretically, the strength of considering the measurement characteristics in our analysis is that it will force us to think more carefully about the different aspects of the data, which will have implications for our interpretations of the findings. These aspects may include, for example, what data say and what assumptions about the data we are willing to make. Of course, we need to further investigate the potential utility of MDS analysis when we make different assumptions about the multivariate data. For example, we do not typically have data generated from direct judgment or rating tasks such as having students rate similarity among a group of teachers with respect to helpfulness. Rather, we could have data generated from a Likert-type scale in assessing student perception of their teachers' helpfulness. Then it is possible that the data possess certain measurement characteristics so that the appropriate MDS model can be used to provide a better predictive or explanatory power for the study under inquiry. Certainly, more research is needed in this regard.

Conversely, another line of research could be conducted using MDS models with respect to measurement characteristics. For example, in column-conditional multivariate data, we take it for granted that one individual's response of "3," on a scale of 1 to 6 for an item is the same as another individual's response of "3" for the same item. Multidimensional scaling analysis could help to investigate whether such measurement characteristics are present in the data. If not, it may not be appropriate to analyze data by aggregating over individuals because such an indirect measurement does not keep individual data intact and may fail to detect systematic individual differences in the data. Thus, MDS models may be used as a measurement tool for identifying if we have different response styles represented in our sample.

In the following part, I will discuss each type of MDS model as used in many multidimensional scaling analyses, including model fitting and other related issues. Each section will end with an application of MDS analysis using model discussed under that section. Multidimensional scaling analysis is to apply an MDS model to certain data for purposes of description, prediction, or explanation.

Metric Model

Distance equations. An *MDS model* is an equation that represents distances between objects or variables in k dimensional space. Such an equation is applied to the data in an MDS analysis to turn the information into certain geometric representations so we may understand the underlying structure of the data for a better description, prediction, or explanation.

A very general MDS model is represented by the Minkowski distance equation, which is:

$$d_{ij}^p = \left(\sum_{k=0}^{m} |x_{ik} - x_{jk}|^p \right)^{\frac{1}{p}} \qquad (1)$$

where d_{ij}^p is distance between points i and j, m is number of dimensions, x_{ik} and x_{jk} are the coordinate of points i and j on dimension k, and p is the Minkowski exponent, which may take any value not less than one. In words, Equation 1 indicates that the distance between a pair of points or variables in m-dimensional configuration X is equal to the sum of the difference between two coordinates raised to a specific power, p.

One special case of Equation 1 is Euclidean distance, which is defined as:

$$d_{ij} = \sqrt{\sum_{k=0}^{m}(x_{ik} - x_{jk})^2} \qquad (2)$$

This equation defines the distance d_{ij} as the square root of the sum of squared differences between coordinates in k dimensional space. In this chapter, the distance implies Euclidean distance unless specified otherwise because Euclidean distance is more commonly encountered in psychology or education.

Torgerson's metric model. One of the first metric MDS models is Torgerson's metric model (Torgerson, 1952). In Torgerson's metric model, observed distance δ_{ij}, which is computed directly from the data, is assumed equal to distances d_{ij} in Euclidean space, that is:

$$\delta_{ij} = d_{ij} = \sqrt{\sum_{k=0}^{m}(x_{ik} - x_{jk})^2} \qquad (3)$$

Figure 12.1 illustrates the Euclidean distance in a two-dimensional configuration X.

Torgerson showed that when the observed distance δ_{ij} is double-centered (i.e., distance with both row and column means removed, also called row-standardized and column-standardized), this double-centered distance matrix δ_{ij}^* is the product of coordinates in k dimensional space as follows:

$$\delta_{ij}^* = \sum x_{ik} x_{jk} \qquad (4)$$

This δ_{ij}^* is called disparity or scalar product matrix because it is the sum of products between two coordinate values. The value of double-centered distance can be from $-\infty$ to ∞, although the original value of distance ranges from 0 to ∞. This is the case even if the raw data are standardized. Torgerson's model is called a metric MDS model because it requires that the observed distance data be proportional to or linearly related to model-derived distances in a Euclidean space.

Transformation of coordinates. In MDS models, Euclidean distances between two points are invariant with respect to transformation of distance points so that dimensionality does not change. The transformation includes rotation, translation, reflection, and dilation. Specifically, a rotation can be thought of as a rotation of the dimensions about their origin, and such a rotation may be needed to aid interpretation of the dimensions. On the other hand, translation involves adding a constant to all of the coordinates on each dimension; dilation involves multiplying the coordinates by a constant; reflection involves reversing the sign of each coordinate of dimensions. The implication of these concepts is that seemingly different dimensional configurations may be identical to each other because of the possibility of rotation, translation, dilation, or reflection of dimensions. Thus, interpretation of dimensions can be aided by taking these transformations into consideration.

Model fit. Like many other model-based analytical techniques, MDS also adopts the habit of using fit measures, which are typically called badness-of-fit measures because the higher the badness-of-fit measures, the worse the fit. Torgerson's algorithm minimizes the fit discrepancy between the model-derived distances and the observed distances (details of fit index will be discussed later).

Nonmetric Model

Nonmetric vs. metric model. The chief difference between metric and nonmetric MDS models is how the observed distances are assumed to be related to the model-derived distances. In metric MDS models, the observed distances are assumed to be linearly or proportionally related to model-derived distances. This assumption tends to be restrictive. Nonmetric models, proposed by Shepard (1962), assume that the observed distances are monotonically related to the model-derived distances; that is, the model-derived distances only need to reflect the rank order of the observed distances. Coxon (1982) called this *ordinal rescaling of the data* because the data are rescaled or transformed to be close to the model. However, it should be noted that in practice, the differences between metric and nonmetric MDS

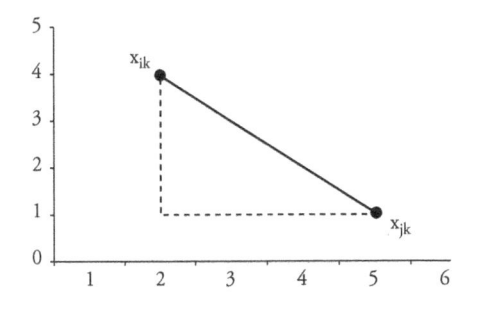

Figure 12.1 Euclidean distance (solid line) between two points in a two-dimensional configuration X.

are not that important (Borg & Groenen, 2005), and the results from both types of analyses tend to be similar rather than different, with nonmetric MDS models providing a better fit to the data.

Nonmetric model parameters. Nonmetric models have the following form:

$$\delta_{ij} = f(d_{ij}) \quad (5)$$

where f is a monotone function, including linear, power, exponential, and logarithmic functions. δ_{ij} is observed distance; d_{ij} is model estimated distance. Nonmetric MDS algorithm computes estimated d_{ij} based on model coordinate estimates x_{ik} and x_{jk} such that the rank order of estimated d_{ij} is as close as possible to the rank order of the rescaled distance, δ_{ij}.

Three sets of parameters are estimated by Equation 5. The first is coordinate estimates x_{ik} and x_{jk}, which represents the configuration of variables in the geometric space. The second is estimated distance d_{ij}, which is computed from coordinate estimates. The third set of parameters is called the *rank images* of data, *disparities, pseudo-distances, fitted distances,* or *transformed proximities.* These five terms may be used interchangeably and that may cause some confusion. In this chapter, I use the term *disparities* and designate it as $\hat{\delta}_{ij}$. Why do we need this third set of parameters? It turns out that disparity ($\hat{\delta}_{ij}$) is calculated in such a way that: (1) it is monotonically related to the observed distance; and (2) it is as closely fit to the estimated distance d_{ij} as possible. Thus, it is this $\hat{\delta}_{ij}$ that is used in measure of model fit.

Model fit index. Some common badness-of-fit measures used in MDS models include the following:

Kruskal's STRESS formula one (S_1) and STRESS formula two (S_2):

$$S_1 = \sqrt{\frac{\sum \left(\hat{\delta}_{ij} - d_{ij}\right)}{\sum d_{ij}}} \quad (6)$$

$$S_2 = \sqrt{\frac{\sum \left(\hat{\delta}_{ij} - d_{ij}\right)}{\sum \left(d_{ij} - \bar{d}\right)^2}} \quad (7)$$

Young's S-STRESS formula one (SS_1) and two (SS_2):

$$SS_1 = \sqrt{\frac{\sum \left(\hat{\delta}_{ij}^2 - d_{ij}^2\right)}{\sum d_{ij}^2}} \quad (8)$$

$$SS_2 = \sqrt{\frac{\sum \left(\hat{\delta}_{ij}^2 - d_{ij}^2\right)}{\sum \left(\delta_{ij}^2 - \bar{d}^2\right)^2}} \quad (9)$$

Normalized STRESS:

$$S_1^2 = \frac{\sum \hat{\delta}_{ij}}{\sum d_{ij}} \quad (10)$$

Coefficient of monotonicity:

$$u = \frac{\sum \hat{\delta}_{ij} d_{ij}}{\sqrt{\left(\sum \hat{\delta}_{ij}^2\right)\left(\sum d_{ij}^2\right)}} \quad (11)$$

Coefficient of alienation:

$$k = \sqrt{1 - u^2} \quad (12)$$

where $\hat{\delta}_{ij}$ is disparities, d_{ij} is model-estimated distance, and $\bar{d}$ is mean of model-estimated distances. The numerator of Equations 6 to 9 indicates the sum of differences between the observed distance and model-derived distance. S_1 and S_2 differ in the normalizing constant used in the denominator. It has been suggested that when the data are preferences, S_2 is a better choice for the fit measure (Takane et al., 1977). It should also be noted that the numerator of Equations 6 and 7 is a measure of *Raw Stress*, which is the sum of squares of differences between the model distances and disparities. On the other hand, $1 - S_1^2$ is equal to dispersion accounted for (DAF); that is, the proportion of residual variance from monotone regression.

An example. In this example, I used test data of a group of 1,169 kindergarteners. During the kindergarten school year, these children were tested three times (beginning, middle, and end of the school year) using subscales of Dynamic Indicators of Basic Early Literacy Skills (DIBELS) (Good & Kaminski, 2002). The DIBELS was designed to assess three key early word literacy areas: phonological awareness, alphabetic principles, and fluency with connected text. The measures included for this example were (the more detailed description of these measures can be found at DIBELS official website).[1]

Initial sounds fluency (ISF). This is a measure of phonological awareness that assesses a child's ability to recognize and produce the initial sound in an orally presented word. For example, the examiner says, "This is sink, cat, gloves, and hat. Which picture begins with /s/?" and the child points to the correct picture.

Letter naming fluency (LNF). This is a standardized, individually administered test that provides a measure of risk of early literacy. Students are presented with a page of upper- and lowercase letters arranged in a random order and are asked to name as many letters as they can in 1 minute.

Phoneme segmentation fluency (PSF). It is a measure that assesses a student's ability to segment three- and four-phoneme words into their individual phonemes fluently. The examiner orally presents words of three to four phonemes. It requires the student to produce verbally the individual phonemes for each word. For example, the examiner says "sat," and the student says "/s/ /a/ /t/" to receive three possible points for the word.

Nonsense word fluency (NWF). This is a measure of the alphabetic principle—including letter-sound correspondence in which letters represent their most common sounds and of the ability to blend letters into words in which letters represent their most common sounds. For example, if the stimulus word is "vaj," the student could say /v/ /a/ /j/ or say the word /vaj/ to obtain a total of three letter-sounds correct. The child is allowed 1 minute to produce as many letter-sounds as he/she can.

Word use fluency (WUF). It is a test of vocabulary and oral language to assess if children may be at-risk for poor language and reading outcomes.

Depending on the time of assessment during the kindergarten year, different subscales were used to assess word literacy progress. For example, at the beginning of the kindergarten year, ISF, LNF, and WUF were assessed; at the middle of the year, ISF, LNF, PSF, NWF, and WUF were assessed; at the end of the kindergarten year, LNF, PSF, NWF, and WUF were assessed. Although some of the same measures (e.g., LNF) were administered at different times, the same measure seemed to assess different aspects or difficulty levels of the word literacy. Some interesting questions are: What did these subscales have in common? How were they related to each other? Could we consider the same measure administered at a different time point to be the same measure? These questions can help us to clarify how the subscales of DIBELS could be used in the analysis to study children's word literacy development.

The nonmetric MDS model was applied to the data, with 12 measures used as input. These 12 measures came from three measures at the beginning of the kindergarten year, five at the middle of the kindergarten year, and four measures at the end of the kindergarten year. The analysis was performed using proximity scaling (*PROXSCAL*) procedure (Data Theory Scaling System Group) in *SPSS* version 17. In the analysis, I used simplex start as the initial MDS configuration, and the number of dimensions was specified to be 1 to 3. The results of fit measures from the analyses indicated that $S_1 = .09$ and Dispersion Accounted For (DAF) was .99 for the one-dimensional solution. The two- or three-dimensional solutions had smaller S_1 values, but Dispersion Accounted For (DAF) was essentially the same. Thus, it seemed that the one-dimensional solution could represent the structure underlying the data. Figure 12.2 shows the one-dimensional structure of the data. Inspection of the configuration indicated that the points along the dimension were distinct without any points collapsed together.

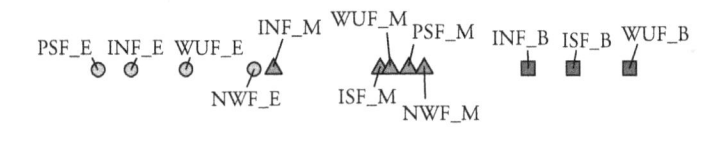

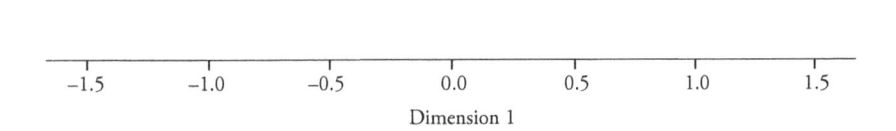

Figure 12.2 One dimension structure of subscales of DIBELS during kindergarten. ISF = *Initial sounds fluency*; LNF = *Letter naming fluency*; PSF = *Phoneme segmentation fluency*; NWF = *Nonsense word fluency*; WUF = *Word use fluency*. _E is end-of-year measurement, as indicated by circles; _M is middle-of-year measurement, as indicated by triangles; _B is beginning-of-year measurement, as indicated by squares.

Thus, the solution was not likely to be a degenerate solution.

The interesting information obtained from Figure 12.2 was that there was a time dimension underlying subscales of DIBELS. That is, the subscales administered at each time formed a distinct cluster on the basis of when the subscales were administered regardless of the content they assessed. Thus, it seemed reasonable that we could compute an average score of the subscales at each time point as an approximation of the word literacy progress at that time. For example, an average score at different time points can then be used for growth trajectory analysis of children's word literacy development.

The interpretation of the results from the MDS analysis can typically be based on patterns of configuration and the meaning attached to such patterns, such as what we know about the variables and what connotations they may have. Therefore, it is sometimes not possible to interpret the whole of a configuration but rather to focus on part of it. Moreover, the issues of similarity transformations such as rotation, reflection, dilation, and translation can directly affect the interpretations of the configuration. Coxon (1982) discusses in great detail about the interpretation of the configuration. Because of these issues, the interpretation of the results from MDS analysis is not as straightforward as that in other methods such as factor analysis or cluster analysis and requires more knowledge about the data.

Individual Differences Models

Weighted Euclidean model. In the literature of MDS analysis, two types of individual differences models are discussed. One is called the weighted Euclidean model or INDSCAL (Carroll & Chang, 1970), and the other one is called generalized weighted Euclidean model or the three-mode model (Tucker, 1972). Weighted Euclidean model can be considered as a special case of generalized weighted Euclidean model and it is more used in practice. Thus, I focus on weighted Euclidean model in this chapter.

In metric or nonmetric MDS models, the configuration estimated from the observed distances represents average configuration across all individuals, this is called group configuration. However, we also want to know how individuals differ with respect to the group configuration; that is, we not only want to know about nomothetic information, we also want to know about idiographic information. Each participant has his or her own configuration, x_{iks}, in relation to the group configuration, x_{ik}. Such an idiosyncratic configuration x_{iks} is related to the group configuration x_{ik} in the form:

$$x_{iks} = x_{ik} w_{ks} \quad (13)$$

where w_{ks} is the value that indicates the variation in the dimensional configuration across individuals. In other words, it is the weight for participant s along dimension k, indicating dimensional importance or salience given by an individual. The idiosyncratic configuration for participants can be expressed as:

$$\delta_{ijs} = \sqrt{\sum \left(x_{iks} - x_{jks}\right)^2} = \sqrt{\sum w_{ks}^2 \left(x_{ik} - x_{jk}\right)^2} \quad (14)$$

As in metric or nonmetric MDS models, in addition to parameter estimates of coordinate x_{ik} and x_{jk}, distance d_{ij}, and the *disparities* $\hat{\delta}_{ik}$, two more sets of parameters are estimated: (1) weight w_{ks}, which quantifies the differences among participants' rating along the k dimensions; and (2) participants' coordinate estimates x_{iks} and x_{jks}.

The interpretation of the results from the weighted Euclidean model follows the same principles as discussed previously with one exception: rotation. That is, the solution cannot be rotated because the group configuration is tied into the participants' configuration and the solution is unique to these individuals. Thus, the rotation problem disappears in the weighted Euclidean model.

An example. In this example, we use the same data as in the previous example, but the questions can be conceptualized differently. The previous research question concerns how the subscales of DIBELS are structured within a grade level. It is found that these measures are organized according to the time of measurement rather than the content they assess. In this example, I am interested in the question of how each child scored differently on a set of word literacy measures at a particular time point. That is, do children reach the same proficiency level on all the subscales at a given time?

For the purpose of illustration, I used the four subscales that were administered in the middle of the kindergarten year: ISF, LNF, PSF, and NWF. In order to simplify the analysis for didactic purposes, I randomly selected four children and examined their differences with respect to their standing on each of these four subscales. A high scale value between two subscales indicated children scored them differently. Thus, a distance matrix for each child could be considered as a measure of discrepancy between subscales.

differently on NWF. Children 2 and 4 scored more like the group configuration.

These individual configurations may have implications for education intervention. For example, we could examine the cognitive functions that underlie the differences in how children learn the materials as assessed by the DIBELS. By looking into what these differences are, we could also examine children's personal characteristics that may be related to word literacy progress. In addition, the weighted Euclidean model could serve as an analytical technique for single- or multiple-case(s) study in which the purpose is to analyze how people frame and solve problems. The results could produce empirical generalizations regarding intervention rationality, treatment, or normative reasoning.

The preference models. The preference models are often called unfolding models. The idea of MDS preference models is very appealing for studying individual differences, particularly in the case of single- or multiple-subject(s) design in which we would like to see how an individual responds to a particular treatment or a learning method as measured by a set of measurement items. The basic concept of MDS preference models is that the distance model can be used to represent both the items (called real objects) and the participants as points (called ideal points) in a geometric space. Thus, the MDS solution will consist of a configuration of i items or variable points and a configuration of s participant points in the same space. The closer a participant's point (i.e., ideal point) to the item's point (i.e., real object) in the space, the more ideal or preferred the item is by the participant. The large distance, therefore, indicates the less preference to an item or a variable. To put it another way, a large distance between a real object and an ideal point indicates that the real object has a high disutility.

In the basic metric model, the preferences are represented as:

$$\delta_{is} = d_{is} = \sqrt{\sum (x_{ik} - x_{sk})^2} \qquad (15)$$

where δ_{is} is estimated distance quantifying the degree of participant s preference for item i, that is, dislike for item i. x_{ik} is the location of item i along dimension k. x_{sk} is the participant's ideal or preference location along dimension k. The model implies that the participant's preference is manifested by comparing item location to his or her ideal location in the same geometric space. The

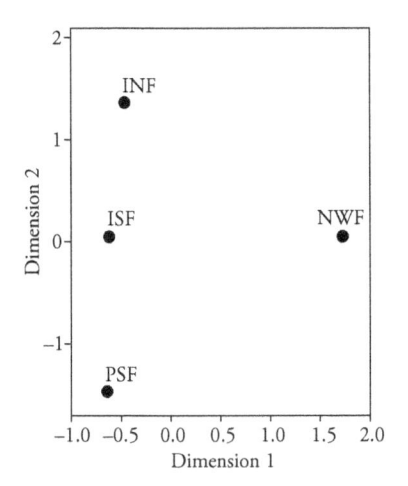

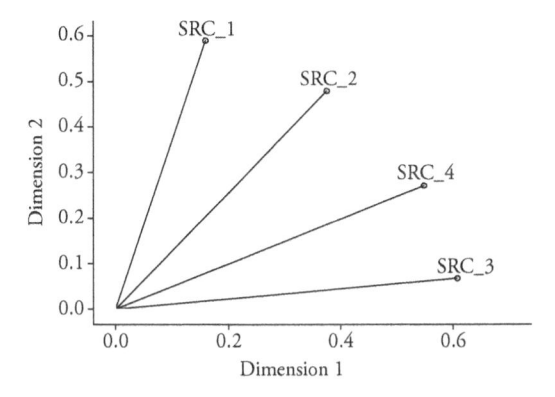

Figure 12.3 Latent-group configuration of subscales of DIBELS for the assessment at the middle of the kindergarten year and their weight space. LNF = *Letter naming fluency*; PSF = *Phoneme segmentation fluency*; NWF = *Nonsense word fluency*; SRC = *Child*; WUF = *Word use fluency*.

The weighted Euclidean model was conducted on the data from these four children. A two-dimensional solution was estimated, with fit measures indicating a good model fit. Figure 12.3 shows the group configuration (top portion) and individual dimensional weight (bottom portion). Dimension 1 seemed to indicate that, on average, children scored NWF differently from the other three subscales. Dimension 2 seemed to indicate that LNF and PSF scored differently from ISF and NWF. Individual weight plot indicated how these children scored differently on the four subscales, and these individual configurations were shown in Figure 12.4. As can be seen in Figure 12.4, Child 1's scores on these four subscales were more like that in Dimension 2, scoring similar on ISF and NWF but differently on LNF and PSF. On the other hand, Child 3 scored similar on LNF, ISF, and PSF but

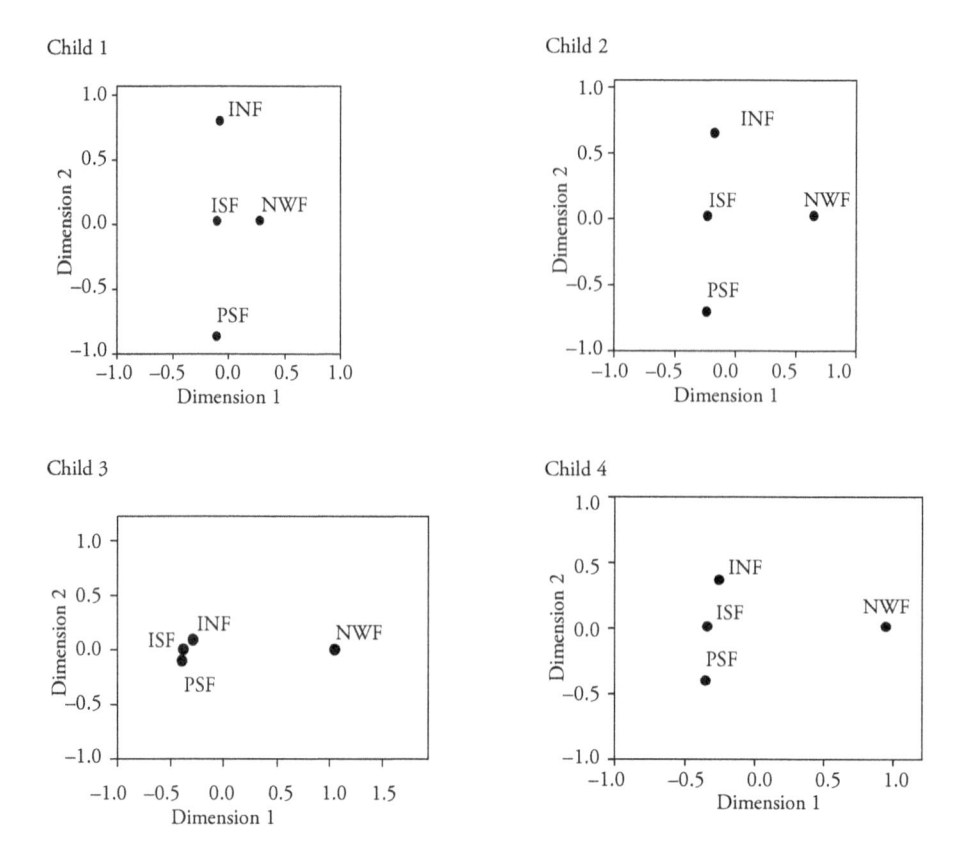

Figure 12.4 Each of four children's configurations with respect to subscales of DIBELS administered at the middle of the kindergarten year. LNF = Letter naming fluency; PSF = Phoneme segmentation fluency; NWF = Nonsense word fluency; WUF = Word use fluency.

preference model differs from individual differences model (i.e., weighted Euclidean model) because in preference model, participant space and item space are in the same space, whereas in weighted Euclidean model there are two separate dimensional configurations, one for participants and another for stimuli or variables.

There are two types of preference models, internal and external (Carroll, 1972), and both have metric and nonmetric forms. For internal preference model, the model provides parameter estimates of item coordinates, participant ideal points, and a fit measure. For external preference model, the item coordinates are assumed to be known from either theory or previous analysis. The model provides parameter estimates of participant ideal points and a fit measure for each participant. Because external preference model involves known item coordinates, it sometimes can be used to test a particular hypothesis about preference.

According to Davison (1983), external preference models include four preference models: the vector model, the simple Euclidean model, the weighted Euclidean model, and the general Euclidean model. The vector model is a linear model, while the other three models are distance models (therefore nonlinear models). These models can be estimated using standard multiple-regression methods. The estimates of various participant ideal points are regression coefficients or variants of regression coefficients. The input data for external preference analysis are prespecified item coordinates that are based on either theory or previous analyses and observed data (such as liking ratings) indicating participant preference.

The vector model is a linear model. That is, participant's ideal point is linearly or monotonically related to item scale value along the dimension k. It can be expressed as:

$$\delta_{is} = \sum b_{ks} x_{ik} + c_s \qquad (16)$$

where b_{ks} is linear regression weight or coefficient (i.e., ideal point), indicating participant's preference; c_s is a constant for each participant. In words, Equation 16 indicates an individual's preference, as measured by distance between an item and individual, δ_{is}, is equal to an individual's ideal point, b_{ks}, times item's location, x_{ik}, plus a constant.

The simple Euclidean model suggests that the more an item resembles a participant's ideal point along each dimension, the more the participant likes it. All dimensions are assumed to be equally salient to the participants. The model is:

$$\delta_{is} = \sum w_s^2 (x_{ik} - x_{sk})^2 + c_s$$
$$= w_s^2 \sum x_{ik}^2 + \sum b_{ks} x_{ik} + c_s \quad (17)$$

This model provides the participant's ideal point coordinate estimate, x_{sk}, the participant's dimension weight, w_s^2, and a fit measure. This model indicates that the participant's ideal point is curvilinearly (i.e., single-peaked) related to item scale value. In words, Equation 17 says that an individual's preference, as measured by distance between an item and individual, δ_{is}, is measured by three quantities: (1) item's location, x_{ik}, times the participant's dimensional weight, w_s, which is equal across all dimensions; (2) the individual's ideal point, b_{ks}, times item's location, x_{ik}; and (3) a constant, c_s.

The weighted Euclidean model differs from the simple Euclidean model only in that the dimensional salience varies across participants rather than assumed to be the same across the participants. Thus the model is:

$$\delta_{is} = \sum x_{ks}^2 (x_{ik} - x_{sk}) + c_s$$
$$= \sum w_{ks}^2 x_{ik}^2 + \sum b_{ks} x_{ik} + c_s \quad (18)$$

The model provides parameter estimates of the participant's ideal point, b_{ks}, the participant's dimension salience weights, w_{ks}^2, and a fit measure. In words, Equation 18 says that an individual's preference, as measured by distance between an item and the individual, δ_{is}, is measured by three quantities: (1) the item's location, x_{ik}, times the participant's dimensional weight, w_{ks}, that is different across all dimensions; (2) the individual's ideal point, b_{ks}, times the item's location, x_{ik}; and (3) a constant.

The fourth external preference model is the general Euclidean model, also called three-mode model (Tucker, 1972). This model is the most general model of all MDS preference models, as can be seen in Equation 19:

$$\delta_{is} = \sum w_{ks}^2 (x_{ik} - x_{sk})^2 + \sum_{k,k'} w_{ks} w_{k'}' s r_{kk}'$$
$$\times s(x_{ik} - x_{sk})(x_{ik}' - x_{sk}') + cs$$
$$= \sum w_{ks}^2 x_{ik}^2 + \sum b_{ks} x_{ik} + \sum_{k,k'} b_{kk'}' s x_{ik} x_{ik}' + cs$$
$$(19)$$

where $r_{kk'}'s$ indicates the correlation between dimensions. This model allows the interaction between dimensions and provides parameter estimates of the participant's ideal point location, x_{sk}, the participant's dimension salience weight, w_{ks}, and the participant dimensional interaction, $r_{kk'}'s$. If $r_{kk'}'s = 0$, then we have a weighted Euclidean model. That is, the difference between Equations 18 and 19 is that Equation 19 quantifies the interaction between dimensions, as measured by the correlation between dimensions in the participant's weight, $b_{kk'}'s$, and the items' coordinates, $x_{ik} x_{ik}'$.

An example. In this example, I used a small dataset ($n = 15$) to demonstrate the analysis using internal preference modeling. The data were a subsample of 486 Chinese students in Grade 7. A battery of various measures that assessed psychosocial adjustments was administered to the participants in the regular classroom setting. For the purpose of this example, I used a 12-item instrument of the Life Orientation Test (LOT; Scheier, Carver, & Bridges, 1994) that was developed to assess generalized optimism versus pessimism. The responses were coded along a 5-point Likert-type scale, ranging from "strongly disagree" to "strongly agree." The items were scored so that high values indicate optimism (i.e., a large distance from pessimism). Examples of items include: "In uncertain times, I usually expect the best;" and "If something can go wrong for me, it will;" or "I'm always optimistic about my future." In a sense, these items assessed adolescents' attitudinal preference toward life.

One of the questions I am interested in asking is: What kinds of life orientation preferences do these 15 adolescents in Grade 7 show as measured by these 12 items? The question can also be framed from a measurement perspective; we could ask: Do these items assess the same aspect of life orientation preferences? Given this question, I need to decide the MDS model that can be used. Because the question is related to preferences, an MDS preference model is a better choice. In addition, I assume that a rating of "2" on a 5-point Likert-type scale by one individual may not be compared with the same rating by another individual because they may have a different reference point. Thus, the "2" ratings as given by different individuals only indicate that a participant provides a rating of "2" on a particular item, and the same "2" ratings do not indicate the same degree of similarity or dissimilarity. Based on these two considerations, I selected the MDS preference model with the row-conditional data type as my analytical technique.

A two-dimensional MDS model was specified. The results of the MDS preference analysis using *SPSS* version 17 are shown in Figure 12.5, and the preference scaling (*PREFSCAL*) procedure yielded the following fit indices.

First, the algorithm converges to a solution after 130 iterations, with a penalized stress (marked final function value) of 0.72. The variation proximities are close to coefficient of variation for the transformed proximities, indicating the solution provides discrimination between 12 optimism items. The sum-of-squares of DeSarbo's intermixedness index (DeSarbo, Young, & Rangaswamy, 1997) is a measure of how well the points of the different set are intermixed. The closer to 0, the more intermixed the solution. In this example, the intermixedness is .059, indicating that the solution is well intermixed. Shepard's rough nondegeneracy index (Shepard, 1974), which assesses the percentage of distinct distances, is .729, indicating 73% of distinct distances. Taken together, the results indicate the solution was not degenerate; that is, the points along the dimensions were distinctly separated.

Second, for the goodness-of-fit indices (how well the model-based distance fit the observed distances), it is advisable to consider several measures together. Kruskal's Stress-II is scale-independent; variance accounted for (VAF) is equal to the square of correlation coefficient and is calculated over all values regardless of the conditionality of the analysis; in this example, Kruskal's Stress-II and VAF, and recovered preference orders (RPO) are acceptable.

Third, some relationships among indices with different names should be noted. Dispersion accounted for (DAF) is also referred to as the sum-of-squares accounted for (SSAF), which is equal to Tucker's congruence coefficient. The square of Kruskal's Stress-I is equal to normalized raw Stress. As Busing, Groenen, and Heiser (2005) indicated, the function values of normalized raw Stress, SSAF or DAF, and Kruskal's Stress-I are insensitive to differences in scale and sample size, and these values are suitable for comparing models with different dimensional solutions.

Based on joint plot in Figure 12.5, the following conclusion could be drawn. First, five optimism items (2, 7, 6, 8, and 10) seemed to be separate from other items in the same quadrant; these items seemed to focus more on physical aspects of optimism rather than attitudinal aspects. For example, item 2, *easy to relax*, item 6, *enjoy friends*, item 7, *keep busy*, and item 10, *do not easily get upset*, were about physical behaviors, particularly item 7, which was

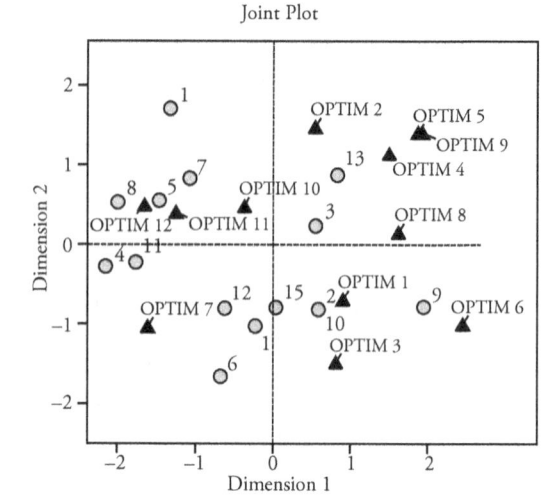

Figure 12.5 Fifteen children's ideal points with respect to their optimism as assessed by Life Orientation Test. OPTIM = optimism item. Circle indicates individual's ideal point and triangle indicates optimism item.

away from all other items. Second, nine participants' attitudinal preferences did not seem to match those assessed by the items. Participants 5, 7, and 8 preferred items 11 (*every cloud has a silver lining*) and 12 (*count on good things happening to me*); participants 2 and 10 preferred items 1 (*usually expect the best*) and 3 (*something will not go wrong for me*); participant 9 preferred item 6 (*enjoy friends*). Third, if we were to make inferences about the instrument based on these 15 people, the data might suggest that the instrument was not very sensitive to Chinese adolescents' attitudinal preferences because 9 out of 15 (60%) adolescents were not responsive to the items. On the other hand, if we were to make inferences about what these adolescents' attitudinal preferences were, five of them (33%) seemed to have attitudes of adolescent fable—invulnerability, and the rest of these seventh-graders did not seem to show any optimistic attitudes. Such results might be indicative of less cognitive development for this group of 15 Chinese students. Of course, we would not make such inferences for the adolescent population with a sample of 15 students. It was done here for didactic purposes.

The MDS Model Using Maximum Likelihood Estimation

The MDS models discussed so far are the least squares MDS models; that is, the model parameter estimation procedures are based on the least squares principle, with model-data fit measures being minimization between model-estimated distances and observed (or transformed) distances. The least squares MDS models are more commonly used in current practices in education or psychology. Such a usage is encouraged by readily available analytical procedures such as *PROXSCAL*, *PREFSCAL*, and *ALSCAL* in *SPSS* (SPSS Inc., 2007) or Proc MDS in *SAS* (*SAS/STAT 9.2 User's Guide: The MDS Procedure*, 2008).

However, the MDS models can also be estimated using maximum likelihood method. The primary research work was done by Ramsay (1977), Takane (1978b) and his associates (Takane & Carroll, 1981), and Zinnes & MacKay (1983). As of this writing, two software programs can provide maximum likelihood MDS analysis. One is Ramsay's *MULTISCAL* (Ramsay, 1977) and the other one is called *PROSCAL* (MacKay & Zinnes, 2005). The maximum likelihood MDS models are basically metric and are concerned with statistical inference. It is assumed that the distance data are erroneous rather than error-free so that confidence regions for items or participants (for weighted models) are provided in the estimation procedures. Thus, statistical tests between pairs of models can be conducted based on estimated standard errors. Such an approach changes multidimensional scaling from a descriptive method into an inferential one so that we can specifically test the appropriate dimensionality, the proper MDS model, and the error structure. That is, a chosen MDS model assumes a specific nature of error model that influences the data. If the nature of error model reflects the actual error processes in reality, the significance test of the MDS model is meaningful. Therefore, the choice of error models becomes crucial in conducting maximum likelihood MDS analysis. In Ramsay's work, error in distance can be assumed to be normally distributed (additive model) or lognormally distributed (multiplicative model). In MacKay and Zinnes' work, error in stimuli or items rather than distances is normally distributed.

Because both maximum likelihood MDS programs have extensive manuals, those who are interested in specific aspects of maximum likelihood MDS can consult the manual for how the different maximum likelihood MDS models with error terms are defined and specified. I do not provide detailed descriptions here given the limited space. It suffices to know that maximum likelihood MDS can provide a useful way to conduct psychological analyses. For example, we could test hypothesis of instrument sensitivity with respect to different symptoms or different populations. We also could test the dimensionality, single-ideal vs. multiple-ideal points model, or equal vs. unequal variance models.

An example. In this example, I used the data of the same 15 adolescents as in the internal preference modeling via *PREFSCAL* shown previously. Based on Figure 12.5, it seemed that there were two groups of adolescents with different life orientation preference. In other words, a model of two-ideal points seemed to underlie the data. However, it is also possible that a single-ideal point may be adequate to account for the differences in these adolescents' preference. Thus, I used maximum likelihood MDS to test a single-ideal point vs. a two-ideal point preference model. Of course, there were other possible models such as a two-dimensional vs. a one-dimensional model or a different combination of dimensionality and ideal points can also be tested.

The single-ideal vs. the two-ideal two-dimensional solutions estimated by *PROSCAL* are shown in Figure 12.6. The hypotheses were tested using information criterion statistics, such as Consistent Akaike Information Criterion (CAIC) (Bozdogan, 1987) or Bayesian Information Criterion (BIC) (Schwarz, 1978). The CAIC value for the single-ideal solution was 1882.67, whereas the two-ideal solution was 1880.66. The CAIC difference between the two models was less than 10, indicating that the single-ideal model was adequate to account for individual differences in life orientation preference (Burnham & Anderson, 2002). This finding was consistent with what I found in traditional nonmetric preference modeling conducted in *PREFSCAL*, in which a group of nine adolescents was not responsive to the items, and six adolescents indicated a life orientation preference.

Computer Programs for MDS Analysis

As mentioned previously, the most commonly used MDS analysis software programs can be found in either *SPSS* or *SAS*. However, there are many other stand-alone programs that can perform particular types of MDS analysis. For example, *MULTISCAL* or *PROSCAL* can be used for maximum likelihood MDS analysis. The many other programs are quite scattered in various places. A piece of good news is Coxon and his associates (Coxon, Brier, & Hawkins, 2005) developed a computer program called New MDS(X), which put together many different MDS analysis programs into one place. The MDS(X) program, thus, greatly

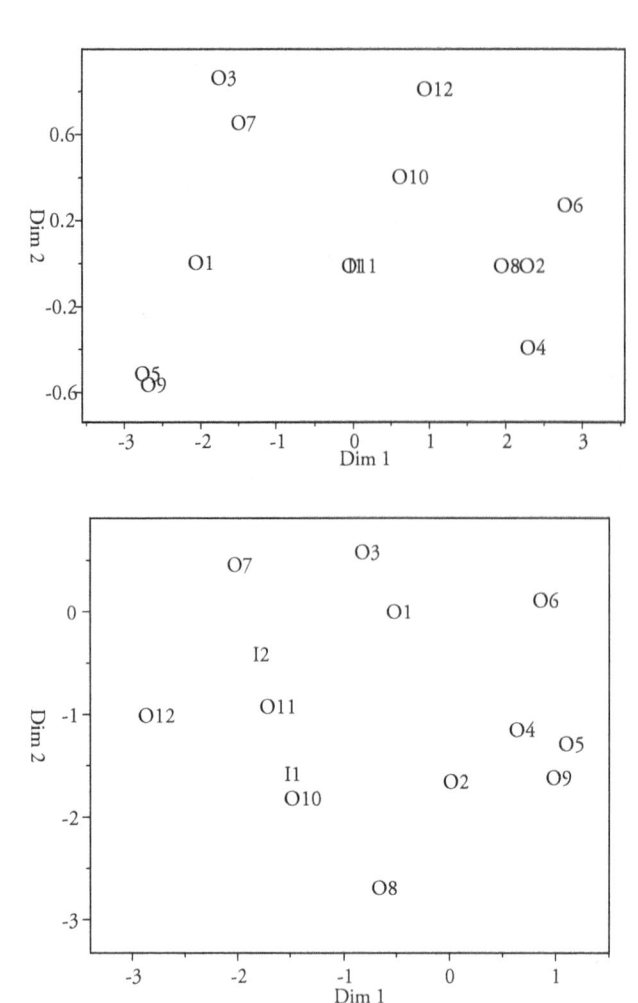

Figure 12.6 The top figure shows a two-ideal solution, as indicated by I1 and I2. The bottom figure shows a single-ideal solution, as indicated by I1. Circle indicates optimism item.

increases the accessibility of different MDS analysis programs and facilitates the applications of MDS models in educational and psychological research. In Table 12.2, I briefly describe some of the available programs in MDS(X) to provide one with a flavor of what can be done by these programs. The detailed description of all programs can be found in the New MDS(X) manual (Coxon et al., 2005).

New Applications of the MDS Models

Currently, continued efforts have been devoted to improving the estimation algorithms of MDS analysis (Busing et al., 2005; Busing, Heiser, & Cleaver, 2010; Busing & Rooij, 2009). On the other hand, the new applications of MDS models have been focused on latent profile analysis for both cross-sectional data (Davison, Gasser, & Ding, 1996) and longitudinal data (Ding, 2001; Ding, Davison, & Petersen, 2005). Latent-growth analysis via MDS models has been shown to be a viable alternative to explore developmental trajectories. At its core, MDS latent-growth analysis applies the distance model to a set of time-related variables and examines their configuration. Conceptually, the MDS latent-growth model has similar analytic goals as growth mixture models (GMM) (Muthen, 2001) and the group-based approach (GBA) (Nagin, 1999)—to determine the optimal number of latent-growth groups and the shape of the trajectory for each group that best fits the data. Then, outcome measures and covariates can be incorporated into the analysis with respect to the different latent-growth groups.

In the MDS model, a latent-growth class is called a "latent-growth profile," and it is represented by a single dimension. The dimension is estimated from a distance model and consists of a set of scale values that indicate the shape of the growth trajectory. For example, if a potential cubic trend exists in the data, the set of scale values estimated by the model would potentially recover that pattern. In a way, the set of scale values functions like a set of

Table 12.2. A Brief Description of Some Programs in the MDS(X)

Program name	Brief description
MINIRSA	It performs multidimensional unfolding analysis using internal mapping via the distance model. The analysis provides rectangle space analysis or internal analysis of two-way data in a row-conditional format of distance data.
MINISSA	It performs the basic nonmetric MDS analysis of two-way symmetric matrix of distances, with matrix conditional.
MRSCAL	It stands for metric scaling, which performs internal analysis of two-way data of a lower triangle distance measure by a Minkowski distance function. It can perform an MDS analysis by group (e.g., by male and female) and the configuration for each group can be compared by *PINDIS* analysis (see below).
PARAMAP	It stands for parametric mapping, which provides internal analysis of either a rectangle (row-conditional) or square symmetric two-way distance data by a distance model.
PREFMAP	It stands for preference mapping. It performs external analysis of two-way, row-conditional data.
PROFIT	It stands for property fitting, which performs external analysis of a configuration by mapping each participant into the configuration as a vector.
MDPREF	It stands for multidimensional preference scaling. It provides internal analysis of two-way preference for either row-conditional data or a set of paired comparisons matrices.
INDSCAL	It provides individual differences analysis, as that can be done by *PROXSCAL* or *ALSCAL* in *SPSS* or Proc MDS in *SAS*.
PINDIS	It stands for procrustean individual differences scaling. It can be used to compare configurations from different groups or compare models with different numbers of dimensions. It can be used for hypothesis testing in a sense.
TRISOCAL	It stands for triadic similarities ordinal scaling, which performs internal analysis of triadic distances by a Minkowski distance model. The basic idea is that the participants are asked to make judgments of similarities of objects or items by considering a group of three objects or items at a time.

The description of the measures in the present study is based on those from official website of DIBEL measures. DIBELS official website is: https://dibels.uoregon.edu/measures.php.

polynomial contrasts. Depending on the number of dimensions, one set of scale values for a given dimension reflects a particular shape of the trajectory for a given latent group. The number of dimensions can be determined by Akaike Information Criterion (AIC) (Akaike, 1973) in addition to traditional *Stress* values (Ding & Davison, 2010). Each participant can be assigned to a latent-growth profile group based on probability of profile membership (Ding, 2007). Moreover, MDS growth modeling can be used to explore the latent-growth trend by using deterministic MDS analysis as well as to conduct hypothesis testing regarding developmental trajectories by using maximum likelihood MDS analysis.

In summary, the key issues discussed are that the MDS latent-growth model can be used to identify distinct forms of growth/decline profiles in the data, which may reflect the source of heterogeneity. The distance-based MDS growth model is flexible because it does not restrict the functional form of trajectories across different latent groups, and no distributional assumptions are required. This approach provides the opportunity to analyze potential latent profiles via continuous or discrete observed variables, and to include covariates in the subsequent analyses.

Conclusion

In this chapter, I have covered some of the major topics on MDS models and analysis. As I mentioned at the beginning of the chapter, the literature on MDS is extensive and it is not possible to cover every line of work on MDS. As a conclusion, I mention strengths and limitations of MDS analysis with respect to its use in psychological and educational research.

Strengths. A main strength of MDS models is they can be used for analyzing various types of data such as row-conditional data, matrix-conditional data, and other types of preference data. These types of data contain rich information about individual differences and MDS models provide various ways to capture the information. In its application of longitudinal data analysis, it provides an alternative and complementary method to study growth heterogeneity in the population.

Second, because MDS models can accommodate more data types, it encourages researchers to think critically about the assumptions about the data. For example, in commonly encountered data of a person-by-variable matrix, does each individual use the scale (e.g., Likert-type response scale) in the same way? The other questions may be: How will a change in the wording of an item change participants' perception and liking of that item? Do male students and female students perceive mathematics concepts in the same way? How many different latent or subgroups are there in the data and how big are they? Which attribute of a construct should be emphasized in the assessment of that construct?

Third, the maximum likelihood MDS models can be used to test various hypotheses with regard to instruments as well as people. The application in this area is under-developed and has much potential in psychological research.

Limitations. One main limitation is that interpretation of configuration of MDS analysis is impacted by similarity transformation of the configuration. Thus a seemingly different but essentially the same configuration may be interpreted differently. For example, if we change the sign of the scale values along the dimensions, the configuration may appear different from the original one, which may lead to a different interpretation of the configuration.

Second, MDS has traditionally been viewed as a data visualizing method. However, data are not always visualized in two dimensions. Higher dimensionality, on the other hand, makes a dimensional solution difficult to be visualized, which defeats its original purpose.

Future Directions

Multidimensional scaling has not developed into a mature analysis technique, as predicted by some researchers (e.g., Young, 1987). The issues that need to be addressed include, but are not limited to, the following:

1. Covariates need to be incorporated into MDS models so that underlying structure of data can be better modeled.

2. Procedures for assessing equivalency in configurations are needed. Given that the interpretation of a configuration is influenced by similarity transformation, procedures need to be developed to present several equivalent configurations to be considered for interpretation.

3. Statistical procedures for assessing participants' ideal points with respect to latent-group configuration needs to be developed. Rather than relying on visual inspection of participants' ideal points, some statistical criteria need to be used to objectively examine the degree to which an individual prefers a particular behavior.

4. The analytical method of assessing participants' preference is typically standard multiple-regression analysis. It may be useful to incorporate logistic or multinomial regression to examine the probability of preference with respect to a set of behaviors.

5. In MDS latent-growth analysis, the person-model fit index is based on the R^2 statistic. But a better set of person-model fit indices needs to be developed so that we can perform statistical testing.

However, MDS models, particularly preference modeling, can provide a unique method for studying individual differences that cannot be revealed by a structural equation modeling analysis. For example, in research of moral reasoning, MDS preference modeling may be employed to investigate, using the concept of differential preferences, age differences or developmental trajectory that represents an emerging desire to imagine one's good behaviors as internally motivated, but one's bad behaviors are externally provoked. In addition, confirmatory MDS using maximum likelihood method can be used to test specific hypotheses regarding latent profiles of individuals, as that can be done in structural equation modeling analysis. These analytical possibilities, along with many others, for example, studying participants' multiple ideal points, can further advance MDS models as a psychological and educational research tool.

Author Note

Cody S. Ding, Educational Psychology, Research & Evaluation University of Missouri-St. Louis St. Louis, MO 63376.

References

Akaike, H. (1973). Information theory as an extension of the maximum likelihood principle. In B. N. Petrov, & F. Csaki (Eds.), *Second international symposium on information theory* (pp. 267–281). Budapest: Akademiai Kiado.

Attneave, F. (1950). Dimensions of similarity. *American Journal of Psychology, 63*, 516–536.

Bloxom, B. (1968). Individual differences in multidimensional scaling models. *Research Bulletin 68–45*. Princeton, NJ: Educational Testing Service.

Borg, I., & Groenen, P. J. F. (2005). *Modern multidimensional scaling: Theory and applications* (2nd ed.). New York, NY: Springer.

Bozdogan, H. (1987). Model selection and Akaike's information criterion (AIC): The general theory and its analytical extensions. *Psychometrika, 52*(3), 345–370.

Burnham, K. P., & Anderson, D., R. (2002). *Model selection and multimodel inference: A practical information-theoretic approach* (2nd ed.). New York, NY: Springer.

Busing, F. M. T. A., Groenen, P. J. K., & Heiser, W. J. (2005). Avoiding degeneracy in multidimensional unfolding by penalizing on the coefficient of variation. *Psychometrika, 70*(1), 71–98.

Busing, F. M. T. A., Heiser, W. J., & Cleaver, G. (2010). Restricted unfolding: Preference analysis with optimal transformations of preferences and attributes. *Food Quality and Preference, 21*(1), 82–92.

Busing, F. M. T. A., & de Rooij, M. (2009). Unfolding incomplete data: Guidelines for unfolding row-conditional rank order data with random missings. *Journal of Classification, 26*, 329–360.

Carroll, J. D. (1972). Individual differences and multidimensional scaling. In R. N. Shepard, A. K. Romney & S. Nerlove (Eds.), *Multidimensional Scaling: Theory and Applications in the Behavioral Sciences (Volume 1): Theory* (pp. 105–155). New York, NY: Seminar Press.

Carroll, J. D., & Chang, J. J. (1970). Analysis of individual differences in multidimensional scaling via an N-way generalization of "Eckart-Young" decomposition. *Psychometrika, 35*, 238–319.

Coombs, C. H. (1964). *A theory of data*. New York, NY: Wiley.

Coxon, A. P. M. (1982). *The user's guide to multidimensional scaling*. London: Heinemann Educational Books.

Coxon, A. P. M., Brier, A. P., & Hawkins, P. K. (2005). *The New MDSX program series, version 5*. Edinburgh: UK: New MDSX Project.

Data Theory Scaling System Group. *PROXSCAL (Version 1.0)*. Leiden University, Netherlands: Faculty of Social and Behavioral Sciences.

Davison, M. L. (1981, August 26). *Multidimensional scaling versus factor analysis of tests and items: Address to the American Psychological Association*. Los Angeles, CA.

Davison, M. L. (1983). *Multidimensional scaling*. New York, NY: Wiley.

Davison, M. L., Gasser, M., & Ding, S. (1996). Identifying major profile patterns in a population: An exploratory study of WAIS and GATB patterns. *Psychological Assessment, 8*, 26–31.

DeSarbo, W. S., Howard, D., & Jedidi, K. (1991). Multiclus: A new method for simultaneously performing multidimensional scaling and cluster analysis. *Psychometrika, 56*, 121–136.

DeSarbo, W. S., Young, M. R., & Rangaswamy, A. (1997). A parametric multidimensional unfolding procedure for incomplete nonmetric preference/choice set data. *Marketing Research. 34*, 499–516.

Ding, C. S. (2001). Profile analysis: Multidimensional scaling approach. *Practical Assessment, Research, and Evaluation, 7*(16). Available from http://PAREonline.net/getvn.asp?v=7&n=16

Ding, C. S. (2007). Studying growth heterogeneity with multidimensional scaling profile analysis. *International Journal of Behavioral Development, 31*(4), 347–356.

Ding, C. S., & Davison, M. L. (2010). Multidimensional scaling analysis using Akaike's information criterion. *Educational and Psychological Measurement, 70*(2), 199–214.

Ding, C. S., Davison, M. L., & Petersen, A. C. (2005). Multidimensional scaling analysis of growth and change. *Journal of Educational Measurement, 42*, 171–191.

Fraley, R. C., & Raftery, A. (2007). Model-based methods of classification: Using the mclust software in chemometrics. *Journal of Statistical Software, 18*(6), 1–13

Good, R. H., & Kaminski, R. A. (Eds.). (2002). *Dynamic indicators of basic early literacy skills* (6th ed.). Eugene, OR: Institute for the Development of Educational Achievement.

Hanson, G. R., Prediger, D. J., & Schussel, R. H. (1977). *Development and validation of sex-balanced interest inventory scales*. Iowa City, IA: The American College of Testing Program.

Horan, C. B. (1969). Multidimensional scaling: Combining observations when individuals have different perceptual structure. *Psychometrika, 34*, 139–165.

Jacoby, W. (1993). A SAS macro for calculating the line-of sight measure of interobject dissimilarity. *Psychometrika, 58*, 511–512.

Kruskal, J. B. (1964). Nonmetric scaling: A numerical method. *Psychometrika, 29*, 28–42.

Kruskal, J. B. (1977). The relationship between multidimensional scaling and clustering. In J. V. Ryzin (Ed.), *Classification and clustering* (pp. 17–44). New York, NY: Academic.

MacKay, D. B. (2007). Internal multidimensional unfolding about a single ideal: A probabilistic solution. *Journal of Mathematical Psychology, 51*, 305–318.

MacKay, D. B., & Zinnes, J. (2005). *PROSCAL professional: A program for probabilistic scaling*. Retrieved from www.proscal.com on May 16, 2011.

McGee, V. C. (1968). Multidimensional scaling of n sets of similarity measures: A nonmetric scaling. *Multivariate Behavioral Research, 3*, 233–248.

Messick, S. J., & Abelson, R. P. (1956). The additive constant problem in multidimensional scaling. *Psychometrika, 21*, 1–15.

Muthen, B. (2001). Second-generation structural equation modeling with a combination of categorical and continuous latent variables: New opportunities for latent class/latent growth modeling. In L. M. Collins & A. Sayer (Eds.), *New methods for the analysis of change* (pp. 291–322). Washington, DC: American Psychological Association.

Nagin, D. (1999). Analyzing developmental trajectories: A semiparametric, group-based approach. *Psychological Methods, 4*, 139–177.

Rabinowitz, G. B. (1976). A Procedure for ordering object pairs consistent with the multidimensional unfolding model. *Psychometrika, 41*, 349–373.

Ramsay, J. O. (1977). Maximum likelihood estimation in multidimensional scaling. *Psychometrika, 42*, 241–266.

Ramsay, J. O. (1991). *MULTISCALE Manual (Extended Version)*. Montreal, Canada: McGill University.

SAS, (2008). *SAS/STAT 9.2 User's Guide: The MDS Procedure*. Cary, NC: SAS Institute Inc.

Scheier, M. F., Carver, C. S., & Bridges, M. W. (1994). Distinguishing optimism from neuroticism (and trait anxiety, self-mastery, and self-esteem): A re-evaluation of the Life Orientation Test. *Journal of Personality and Social Psychology, 67*, 1063–1078.

Schiffman, S. S., Reynolds, M. L., & Young, F. W. (1981). *Introduction to multidimensional scaling: Theory, methods and applications*. New York, NY: Academic Press.

Schlessinger, I. M., & Guttman, L. (1969). Smaller space analysis of intelligence and achievement tests. *Psychological Bulletin, 71*, 95–100.

Schwarz, G. (1978). Estimating the dimension of a model. *Annals of Statistics, 6* (2), 461–464.

Shepard, L. (1962). The analysis of proximities: Multidimensional scaling with an unknown distance (I and II). *Psychometrika, 27*, 323–355.

Shepard, R. N. (1974). Representation of structure in similarity data: Problems and prospects. *Psychometrika, 39*, 373–421.

Shepard, R. N., Romney, A. K., & Nerlove, S. B. (Eds.). (1972). *Multidimensional scaling: Theory* (Vol. 1). New York, NY: Seminar Press.

SPSS Inc. (2007). *SPSS Statistics 17.0: Command syntax reference*. Chicago, IL: SPSS Inc.

Takane, Y. (1978a). A maximum likelihood method for nonmetric multidimensional scaling: I. The case in which all empirical pairwise orderings are independent-evaluation. *Japanese Psychological Research, 20*, 105–114.

Takane, Y. (1978b). A maximum likelihood method for nonmetric multidimensional scaling: I. The case in which all empirical pairwise orderings are independent-theory. *Japanese Psychological Research, 20*, 7–17.

Takane, Y., & Carroll, J. D. (1981). Nonmetric maximum likelihood multidimensional scaling from directional rankings of similarities. *Psychometrika, 46*, 389–405.

Takane, Y., Young, F. W., & De Leeuw, J. (1977). Nonmetric individual differences multidimensional scaling: An alternating least squares method with optimal scaling features. *Psychometrika, 42*, 7–67.

Torgerson, W. S. (1952). Multidimensional scaling: I. Theory and method. *Psychometrika, 17*, 401–419.

Treat, T. A., McFall, R. M., Viken, R. J., Nosofsky, R. M., MacKay, D. B., & Kruschke, J. K. (2002). Assessing clinically relevant perceptual organization with multidimensional scaling techniques. *Psychological Assessment, 14*, 239–252.

Tucker, L. R. (1972). Relations between multidimensional scaling and three-mode factor analysis. *Psychometrika, 37*, 3–27.

Tucker, L. R., & Messick, S. J. (1963). An individual differences model for multidimensional scaling. *Psychometrika, 28*, 333–367.

Vera, J., Macias, R., & Heiser, W. J. (2009). A latent class multidimensional scaling model for two-way one-mode continuous rating dissimilarity data. *Psychometrika, 2009*, 297–315.

Young, F. W. (1987). Multidimensional scaling: History, theory, and applications, ed. R. M. Hamer, Hillsdale, NJ: Lawrence Erlbaum Associates.

Zinnes, J. L., & MacKay, D. B. (1983). Probabilistic multidimensional scaling: Complete and incomplete data. *Psychometrika, 48*, 24–48.

CHAPTER
13 Latent Variable Measurement Models

Timothy A. Brown

Abstract

The focus of this chapter is on the principles and methods of latent variable measurement models in applied research. After a review of the common factor model, examples of exploratory factor analysis and confirmatory factor analysis are provided along with a recently developed hybrid of these two approaches (exploratory structural equation modeling). In addition, more advanced applications are illustrated, including multiple-group models, to evaluate measurement invariance and population heterogeneity, and various types of higher-order factor models (e.g., second-order factor analysis, bifactor models). Future directions are discussed, including more recent advances in these methodologies (e.g., factor mixture models, multilevel factor models, nonlinear factor models).

Key Words: common factor model, latent variable, exploratory factor analysis, confirmatory factor analysis, exploratory structural equation modeling, measurement invariance, multiple-group solutions, higher-order factor analysis, bifactor model

Introduction

The intent of latent variable measurement models (i.e., factor analysis) is to establish the number and nature of latent variables or *factors* that account for the variation and covariation among a set of observed measures, commonly referred to as *indicators*. Specifically, a factor is an unobservable variable that influences more than one observed measure and which accounts for the correlations among these observed measures. In other words, the observed measures are intercorrelated because they share a common cause (i.e., they are influenced by the same underlying construct); if the latent construct was partitioned out, the intercorrelations among the observed measures would be zero. Thus, factor analysis attempts a more parsimonious understanding of the covariation among a set of indicators because the number of factors is less than the measured variables.

These concepts emanate from the *common factor model* (Thurstone, 1947), which states that each indicator in a set of observed measures is a linear function of one or more common factors and one unique factor. Factor analysis partitions the variance of each indicator (derived from the sample correlation or covariance matrix) into two parts: (1) *common variance*, or the variance accounted for by the latent variable(s), which is estimated on the basis of variance shared with other indicators in the analysis; and (2) *unique variance*, which is a combination of reliable variance specific to the indicator (i.e., systematic latent factors that influence only one indicator) and random error variance (i.e., measurement error or unreliability in the indicator). There are two main types of analyses based on the common factor model: *exploratory factor analysis* (EFA) and *confirmatory factor analysis* (CFA; Jöreskog, 1969, 1971). Both EFA and CFA aim to reproduce the observed relationships among a group of indicators with a smaller set of latent variables. However, EFA and CFA differ fundamentally by the number and nature of *a priori* specifications and restrictions made on the latentvariable measurement model. Exploratory factor analysis is a data-driven approach such that no specifications are made in regard to the number of common factors (initially) or the pattern of relationships between the common factors and the indicators (i.e., the *factor loadings*). Rather, the researcher employs EFA as an exploratory or descriptive data technique to determine the appropriate number of common factors, and to ascertain which measured variables are reasonable indicators of the various latent dimensions (e.g., by the size and differential magnitude of factor loadings). In CFA, the researcher specifies the number of factors and the pattern of indicator-factor loadings in advance. In addition, other parameters of the factor model are prespecified such as those bearing on the independence or covariance of the factors and indicator unique variances (e.g., whether or not the indicators are presumed to be correlated for reasons other than the latent variables). The prespecified factor solution is evaluated in terms of how well it reproduces the sample covariance matrix of the measured variables. Unlike EFA, CFA requires a strong empirical or conceptual foundation to guide the specification and evaluation of the factor model. Accordingly, EFA is typically used earlier in the process of scale development and construct validation, whereas CFA is used in later phases when the underlying structure has been established on prior empirical and theoretical grounds. Other key differences between EFA and CFA are discussed later in this chapter.

Exploratory Factor Analysis

A data-based example is now introduced to illustrate some of the fundamental concepts of the common factor model and EFA, and to provide relevant background material for other latent variable measurement models discussed later in this chapter. Although it is beyond the scope of this chapter to present a comprehensive description of the best-practice procedures for EFA, Fabrigar, Wegener, MacCallum, and Strahan (1999) and Brown (2006) provide detailed guidelines for conducting EFA in applied data sets.

In this example, eight dimensional symptom ratings have been collected on 400 outpatients with emotional disorders. The ratings are depressed mood (D1), hopelessness (D2), feelings of worthlessness/guilt (D3), anhedonia (D4), shortness of breath (A1), feeling panicky (A2), dry mouth (A3), and trembling/shakiness (A4). The sample correlations of these ratings are presented in Table 13.1. A two-factor model is anticipated; that is, D1 through D4 are conceptualized as manifest indicators of the latent construct of Depression, and A1 through A4 are conjectured to be observed symptoms of the underlying dimension of Anxiety.

Using the correlations in Table 13.1 as input, a two-factor EFA solution was pursued.[1] Table 13.2 presents selected output for this analysis. The factor loadings for the eight ratings are completely standardized estimates of the regression slopes for predicting the indicators from the latent variables, and thus are interpreted along the lines of standardized regression coefficients in multiple regression. For example, the factor loading estimate for D1 (depressed mood) is .859, which would be interpreted as indicating that, holding the second factor constant (Anxiety), a standardized unit increase in the first factor (Depression) is associated with a .859 standardized score increase in depressed mood. The column of the output labeled "Residual Variances" provides the proportion of the variance in each indicator that is estimated to be unique variance (e.g., 25.9% of the total variance in D1 is not accounted for by the two latent variables). Although not specifically provided in Table 13.2, the proportion of variance in the indicators explained by the common factors (referred to as a *communality*) can be easily calculated by subtracting the proportion of unique variance from 1 (e.g., for D1: 1 − .259 = .741, indicating that 74.1% of the variance in D1 is accounted for by the two common factors).

A noteworthy aspect of the EFA results presented in Table 13.2 is that the promax rotated factor loading matrix is *saturated*, meaning all possible direct effects between the factors and indicators are estimated. Once the factor solution has been estimated, EFA generates a (unrotated) factor loading matrix that is a matrix of correlations between the factors and indicators (not shown in Table 13.2). However, additional transformations are made to the factor loading matrix because is it usually not easy to interpret this matrix in its initial form. Specifically, when two or more factors are involved, *rotation* is conducted to foster the interpretability of the factor solution (rotation does not apply to one-factor solutions). The term *simple structure* was coined by Thurstone (1947) to refer to the most readily interpretable solutions in which: (1) each factor is defined by a subset of indicators that load highly on the factor; and (2) each indicator (ideally) has a high loading on one factor (often referred to as a

Table 13.1. Sample Correlations, Standard Deviations (SD) and Means (M) for Depression and Anxiety Ratings (N = 400 Outpatients)

	D1	D2	D3	D4	A1	A2	A3	A4
D1	1.000							
D2	.683	1.000						
D3	.718	.690	1.000					
D4	.693	.636	.633	1.000				
A1	.206	.204	.229	.154	1.000			
A2	.360	.324	.389	.307	.522	1.000		
A3	.230	.195	.256	.214	.606	.506	1.000	
A4	.336	.346	.375	.276	.356	.621	.400	1.000
SD:	1.065	0.982	1.012	0.955	1.011	0.973	0.847	1.076
M:	1.025	1.253	0.938	0.678	0.903	0.963	0.585	1.205

Note: D1 = depressed mood, D2 = hopelessness, D3 = feelings of worthlessness/guilt, D4 = anhedonia, A1 = shortness of breath, A2 = feeling panicky, A3 = dry mouth, A4 = trembling/shakiness.

Table 13.2. Selected Output for Exploratory Factor Analysis (Two-Factor Solution)

	Factor loadings 1	Factor loadings 2	Residual variance
D1	0.859	0.004	0.259
D2	0.808	0.002	0.346
D3	0.804	0.069	0.301
D4	0.798	−0.030	0.384
A1	−0.097	0.757	0.481
A2	0.102	0.733	0.388
A3	−0.061	0.743	0.483
A4	0.161	0.569	0.572

Factor Correlations

	1	2
1	1.000	
2	0.429	1.000

Note: Promax-rotated factor loadings are shown; D1 = depressed mood, D2 = hopelessness, D3 = feelings of worthlessness/guilt, D4 = anhedonia, A1 = shortness of breath, A2 = feeling panicky, A3 = dry mouth, A4 = trembling/shakiness.

primary loading) and has a trivial or close to zero loading on the remaining factors (referred to as a *cross-loading* or *secondary loading*). Thus, for models with two or more factors, rotation is conducted to produce a solution with the best simple structure. It is important to emphasize that rotation does not alter the fit of the solution (e.g., the communalities for the indicators are the same before and after factor rotation). Because the factor matrix is saturated, the EFA solution is *indeterminate*, meaning that for any given multiple-factor model, there are an infinite number of equally good-fitting solutions (each represented by a different factor loading matrix). Rather, factor rotation is a mathematical transformation (i.e., rotation in multidimensional space) that is undertaken to foster interpretability by maximizing (primary) factor loadings close to 1.0 and minimizing (secondary) factor loadings close to 0.0.

There are two major types of rotation: *orthogonal* and *oblique*. In orthogonal rotation, the factors are constrained to be uncorrelated, whereas in oblique rotation, the factors are allowed to intercorrelate. There are many different types of orthogonal and oblique rotation. In applied research, orthogonal rotation is used most often, perhaps because it is the default in major statistical programs such as SPSS (specifically, varimax rotation). Moreover, orthogonal solutions are often perceived (incorrectly) to be easier to interpret than oblique solutions. For example, because the factors are constrained to be uncorrelated, squaring the factor loading provides the proportion of variance in the indicator that the factor explains (and summing these squared factor loadings provides the indicator's communality). Although communalities can be readily obtained from statistical software programs, hand calculation of these estimates is not as straightforward in oblique solutions because the factors are intercorrelated. The factor loadings in oblique solutions are partial regression coefficients (not simple correlations as in orthogonal solutions) and an indicator communality reflects the sum of the unique direct effects of the latent variables on the indicator as well as the variance in the indicator that the latent variables jointly explain.

Nonetheless, oblique rotation is generally recommended because it provides a more realistic representation of how factors are interrelated (cf. Brown, 2006; Fabrigar et al., 1999). If the factors are in fact uncorrelated, oblique rotation will produce a solution that is virtually the same as the one produced by orthogonal rotation. On the other hand, if the factors are interrelated, oblique rotation will yield a more accurate representation of the magnitude of these relationships. The estimation of factor correlations provides important information such as whether the direction and extent of the interrelationships among factors is in accord with substantive reasoning, the existence of redundant factors (i.e., latent dimensions with poor discriminant validity), or potentially viable higher-order factor solutions (based on the patterning of the factor correlations, see "Higher-Order Models" section of this chapter). Also, when EFA is used as a precursor to CFA, oblique solutions are more likely to generalize to CFA than orthogonal solutions (i.e., constraining factors to be uncorrelated in CFA will usually result in poor model fit).

Returning to the results in Table 13.2, it can be seen that oblique (promax) rotation was successful in attaining an interpretable simple structure. The D1 through D4 indicators evidenced strong primary loadings on the first factor, which could be labeled Depression, but had cross-loadings that were close to zero on the second factor (Anxiety). A similar pattern of primary and secondary loadings was obtained for the indicators of the Anxiety latent variable (A1 through A4). The estimated correlation between the latent dimensions of Depression and Anxiety was .429, indicating that these constructs were relatively distinct (i.e., possessed adequate discriminant validity).

Confirmatory Factor Analysis

Overview. As noted earlier, both CFA and EFA are based on the common factor model and thus many concepts apply to both approaches (e.g., simple structure, factor loadings, unique variances, communalities, residuals). In addition, although there are number of ways of statistically estimating latent variable measurement models, some of the same estimation methods are available to both CFA and EFA. For example, maximum likelihood (ML) can be used to estimate CFA and EFA (in fact, ML is the most commonly used CFA estimation method in applied research). If ML is used, the results arising from EFA and CFA can be evaluated in terms of how well the solution reproduces the observed relationships (e.g., correlations or covariances) among the input indicators (i.e., goodness-of-fit evaluation).

The key difference between CFA and EFA is that, as the name implies, all aspects of the CFA model must be prespecified (e.g., number of factors, pattern of indicator-factor loadings). In addition to this overarching distinction, CFA and EFA differ in many other ways. One aspect pertains to simple structure. Because the factor loading matrix is saturated in EFA, simple structure is obtained through the use of a rotational method (e.g., promax rotation as in the applied example summarized in Table 13.2). Rotation does not apply to CFA because most or all indicator cross-loadings are usually fixed to zero. Thus, simple structure is obtained in CFA by specifying indicators to load on only one factor. Consequently, CFA models are typically more parsimonious than EFA solutions because while primary loadings and factor correlations are freely estimated, no other relationships are specified between the indicators and factors.

Unlike EFA, the nature of relationships among the indicator unique variances can be modeled in CFA. Because of identification restrictions in EFA (in part because of its estimation of a saturated factor loading matrix), factor models must be specified under the assumption that measurement error is random. In contrast, correlated measurement error can be modeled in a CFA solution provided that this specification is substantively justified and that other identification requirements are met. When measurement error is specified to be random (i.e., the indicator unique variances are uncorrelated), the assumption is that the observed relationship between any two indicators loading on the same factor results entirely from the shared influence of the latent variable (i.e., if the factor was partitioned out, the correlation of the indicators would be zero).

The specification of correlated indicator uniqueness assumes that, whereas indicators are related in part because of the shared influence of the latent variable, some of their covariation results from sources other than the common factor. In latent variable measurement models, the specification of correlated errors may be justified on the basis of source or method effects that reflect additional indicator covariation that resulted from common assessment methods (e.g., observer ratings, questionnaires), reversed or similarly worded test items, or differential susceptibility to other influences such as response set, demand characteristics, acquiescence, reading difficulty, or social desirability. The inability to specify correlated errors is a significant limitation of EFA because this source of covariation among indicators that does not result from the substantive latent variables may be manifested in the EFA solution as additional factors (e.g., "methods" factors stemming from the assessment of a unidimensional trait with a questionnaire comprised of both positively and negatively worded items; cf. Brown, 2003; Marsh, 1996).

Other differences between CFA and EFA are the types of solutions they generate. Traditional EFA entails a *completely standardized* analysis. Specifically, a correlation matrix is used as input in EFA and the latent variables and indicators are completely standardized (i.e., factor variances equal one, factor loadings are interpreted as correlations or standardized regression coefficients). Although completely standardized results can be generated in CFA output, much of the analysis is focused on unstandardized values. In basic applications (e.g., situations where missing or nonnormal data are not an issue), CFA analyzes a variance-covariance matrix. Thus, the CFA input matrix is comprised of indicator variances on the diagonal (a variance equals the indicator's standard deviation, SD, squared; i.e., $VAR = SD^2$), and indicator covariances in the off-diagonal (a covariance can be computed by multiplying the correlation of two indicators by their SDs; i.e., $COV_{xy} = r_{xy} SD_x SD_y$). In addition to a completely standardized solution, the results of CFA include an *unstandardized solution* (parameter estimates expressed in the original metrics of the variables), and possibly a *partially standardized solution* (relationships where either the indicators or latent variable is standardized and the other is unstandardized). Also in contrast to EFA, if desired, CFA can entail the analysis of mean structure as part of the unstandardized solution (because EFA is completely standardized, all means are zero). When indicator means are included as part of the input in CFA, both the means of the latent variables and the intercepts of the indicators can be estimated (akin to multiple regression, an indicator intercept is interpreted as the predicted observed value of the indicator when the factor is zero). As discussed later in this chapter, the analysis of mean structures is relevant to multiple-group and longitudinal CFA models when the researcher is interested in comparing groups on the latent variable means or determining the equivalence of a test instrument's measurement properties across groups or across time.

Confirmatory factor analysis model identification. To estimate a CFA solution, the measurement model must be *identified*. A model is identified if, on the basis of known information (i.e., the variances and covariances in the sample input matrix), a unique set of estimates for each parameter in the model can be obtained (e.g., factor loadings, factor correlations, etc.). The two primary aspects of CFA model identification are scaling the latent variables and statistical identification.

Latent variables have no inherent metrics and thus their units of measurement must be set by the researcher. In CFA, this is accomplished in one of three ways. The most widely used method is the *marker indicator* approach whereby the unstandardized factor loading of one observed measure per factor is fixed to a value of 1.0. As will be illustrated shortly, this specification serves the function of passing the metric of the marker indicator along to the latent variable. In the second method, the variance of the latent variable is fixed to a value of 1.0. Although most CFA results are identical to the marker indicator approach when the factor variance is fixed to 1.0 (e.g., goodness-of-fit of the solutions are identical), only completely and partially standardized solutions are produced. Although perhaps useful in some circumstances (e.g., as a parallel to the traditional EFA model), the absence of an unstandardized solution often contraindicates the use of this approach (e.g., in scenarios where there is interest in comparing subgroups of the sample on the various measurement parameters). Recently, Little and colleagues (Little, Slegers, & Card, 2006) introduced a third method of scaling latent variables that is akin to effects coding in analysis of variance. In this approach, *a priori* constraints are placed on the solution such that the set of factor loadings for a given construct average to 1.0 and the corresponding indicator intercepts sum to zero. Consequently, the variance of the latent variables reflects the average of the indicators' variances explained by the construct, and the mean of the latent variable is the optimally weighted average of the means for the indicators of that construct. Thus, unlike the marker indicator approach where the variances and means of the latent variables will vary depending on which indicator is selected as the marker indicator, the method introduced by Little et al. (2006) has been termed "nonarbitrary" because the latent variable will have the same metric as the average of all its manifest indicators.

Statistical identification refers to the concept that a CFA solution can be estimated only if the number of freely estimated parameters (e.g., factor loadings, uniquenesses, factor correlations) does not exceed the number of pieces of information in the input matrix (e.g., number of sample variances and covariances). A model is *overidentified* when the number of knowns (i.e., individual elements of the input matrix) exceeds the number of unknowns (i.e., the freely estimated parameters of the CFA solution). The difference in the number of knowns and the number of unknowns constitutes the model's *degrees of freedom* (*df*). Overidentified solutions have positive *df*. For overidentified models, goodness-of-fit evaluation can be implemented to determine how well the CFA solution was able to reproduce the relationships among indicators observed in the sample data. If the number of knowns equals the number of unknowns, the model has zero *df* and is said to be *just-identified*. Although just-identified models can be estimated, goodness-of-fit evaluation does not apply because these solutions perfectly reproduce the input variance-covariance matrix. When the number of freely estimated parameters exceeds the number of pieces of information in the input matrix (e.g., when too many factors are specified for the number of indicators in the sample data), *df* are negative and the model is *underidentified*. Underidentified models cannot be estimated because the solution cannot arrive at a unique set of parameter estimates.

However, it is important to note that model identification is not determined solely by scaling the latent variables and ensuring that the model *df* equal or exceed zero. In some cases, the researcher may encounter an *empirically underidentified* solution. These are solutions in which the measurement model is statistically over- or just-identified, but there are aspects of the input matrix or the model specification that prevent the analysis from arriving at a unique and valid set of parameter estimates (i.e., the estimation will not reach a final solution, or the

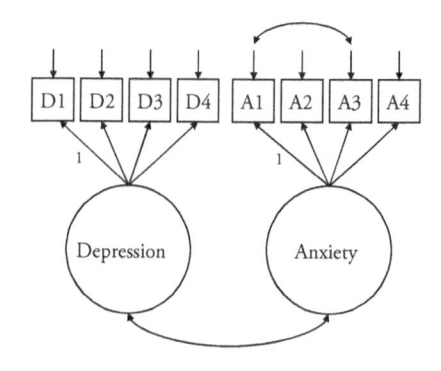

Figure 13.1 Two-Factor Measurement Model of Depression and Anxiety.

final solution will include one or more parameter estimates that have out-of-range values such as a negative indicator uniqueness). Although an exhaustive discussion of the various causes and remedies for empirically underidentified solutions is beyond the scope of this chapter (*see* Brown, 2006, and Wothke, 1993, for further discussion), a basic example would be the situation where the observed measure selected to be the marker indicator is in fact uncorrelated with all other indicators of the latent variable (thus, the metric of the latent variable would be unidentified). This issue is also discussed in the section of this chapter on second-order factor analysis.

Example. Using the information in Table 13.1 as input, a two-factor CFA model was fit to the data (*see* Fig. 13.1). Selected output of this analysis is presented in Table 13.3. As shown in Table 13.3, the unstandardized factor loadings of the D1 and A1 indicators were fixed to 1.0 to define the metrics of the Depression and Anxiety latent variables, respectively; all remaining factor loadings were freely estimated. Moreover, all error variances (uniquenesses), factor variances, and the factor covariance were freely estimated. All error covariances and indicator cross-loadings were fixed to zero, with one exception. Specifically, an error covariance for the A1 and A3 indicators was freely estimated based on the expectation that the symptoms of shortness of breath and dry mouth are more strongly intercorrelated relative to other indicators in the solution (because they are highly overlapping features of anxiety). Thus, this statement overrides the Mplus default of fixing error covariances to zero.

There are three major aspects of the results that should be examined to evaluate the acceptability of the CFA model. They are: (1) overall goodness-of-fit; (2) the presence or absence of localized areas of strain in the solution (i.e., specific points of

Table 13.3. Selected Output for Confirmatory Factor Analysis (Two-Factor Model of Anxiety and Depression)

	Measurement model parameter estimates				
	Unstandardized solution		Completely standardized solution		
	Loading	Residual	Loading	Residual	Communality
		Factor: Depression			
D1	1.0	0.293 (0.031)	0.861 (0.018)	0.259 (0.030)	0.741 (0.030)
D2	0.865 (0.045)	0.334 (0.030)	0.808 (0.021)	0.347 (0.034)	0.653 (0.034)
D3	0.925 (0.046)	0.305 (0.030)	0.838 (0.019)	0.299 (0.032)	0.701 (0.032)
D4	0.814 (0.045)	0.354 (0.031)	0.782 (0.023)	0.389 (0.036)	0.611 (0.036)
		Factor: Anxiety			
A1	1.0	0.692 (0.055)	0.567 (0.040)	0.679 (0.045)	0.321 (0.045)
A2	1.507 (0.146)	0.200 (0.047)	0.888 (0.029)	0.212 (0.052)	0.788 (0.052)
A3	0.841 (0.072)	0.484 (0.038)	0.569 (0.040)	0.676 (0.045)	0.324 (0.045)
A4	1.318 (0.130)	0.585 (0.055)	0.702 (0.034)	0.507 (0.047)	0.493 (0.047)

Latent-variable parameter estimates (unstandardized solution)			
Factor variances		Factor covariance	
Depression	0.838 (0.081)	Depression	
Anxiety	0.328 (0.058)	with Anxiety[a]	0.258 (0.040)

Note: Standard errors are provided in parentheses.
[a]The completely standardized estimate (factor correlation) is .492.

ill-fit); and (3) the interpretability, size, and statistical significance of the model's parameter estimates. Goodness-of-fit pertains to how well the parameter estimates of the CFA solution (i.e., factor loadings, factor correlations, error covariances) are able to reproduce the relationships that were observed in the sample data. For example, as seen in Table 13.3, the completely standardized factor loadings for D1 and D2 are .861 and .808, respectively. Using a basic tracing rule (further illustrated in the "Second-Order Factor Analysis" section of this chapter), the model-implied correlation of these indicators is the product of their factor loading estimates (i.e., .861[.808] = .696). Goodness-of-fit addresses the extent to which these model-implied relationships replicate the relationships seen in the sample data (e.g., as shown in Table 13.1, the sample correlation of D1 and D2 was .683).

There are a variety of goodness-of-fit statistics that provide a global descriptive summary of the ability of the model to reproduce the input covariance matrix. The classic goodness-of-fit index is χ^2. In the current example, the model $\chi^2 = 23.72$, $df = 18$, $p = .16$. The model df indicates that there were 18 more elements in the input matrix than there were freely estimated parameters in the two-factor CFA model (i.e., the solution was overidentified). Specifically, there are 36 variances and covariances in the input matrix (cf. Table 13.1) and 18 freely estimated parameters in the CFA model (i.e., six factor loadings [the factor loadings of D1 and A1 are not included because they were fixed to 1.0 to serve as marker indicators], two factor variances, one factor covariance, eight error variances, and one error covariance; *see* Fig. 13.1). Because the model $df = 18$, the critical value of the χ^2 distribution ($\alpha = .05$) is 28.87. Because the model χ^2 (23.72) does not exceed this critical value (computer programs provide the exact probability value, e.g., $p = .16$) the null hypothesis that the sample and model-implied variance-covariance matrices do not differ is retained. On the other hand, a statistically significant χ^2 would lead to rejection of the null hypothesis, meaning that the model estimates do not sufficiently reproduce the sample variances and covariances (i.e., the model does not fit the data well).

Although χ^2 is steeped in the traditions of maximum likelihood (ML) and structural equation modeling (SEM) (e.g., it was the first fit index to be developed), it is rarely used in applied research as a sole index of model fit. There are number of salient drawbacks of this statistic (e.g., *see* Brown, 2006, for review) including the fact that it is highly sensitive to sample size (i.e., solutions involving large samples would be routinely rejected on the basis of χ^2 even when differences between the sample and model-implied matrices are negligible). Nevertheless, χ^2 is used for other purposes such as nested model comparisons (discussed later in this chapter) and the calculation of other goodness-of-fit indices. Although χ^2 is routinely reported in CFA research, other fit indices are usually relied on more heavily in the evaluation of model fit.

Indeed, in addition to χ^2, the most widely accepted global goodness-of-fit indices are the standardized root mean square residual (SRMR), root mean square error of approximation (RMSEA), Tucker-Lewis index (TLI), and the comparative fit index (CFI). In practice, it is suggested that each of these fit indices be reported and considered because they provide different information about model fit (i.e., absolute fit, fit adjusting for model parsimony, fit relative to a null model; *see* Brown, 2006, for further details). Considered together, these indices provide a more conservative and reliable evaluation of the fit of the model. In one of the more comprehensive and widely cited evaluations of cutoff criteria, the findings of simulation studies conducted by Hu and Bentler (1999) suggest the following guidelines for acceptable model fit: (1) SRMR values are close to .08 or below; (2) RMSEA values are close to .06 or below; and (3) CFI and TLI values are close to .95 or greater. In the current two-factor model, each of these guidelines was consistent with acceptable overall fit; SRMR = .03, RMSEA = 0.03, TLI = 0.99, CFI = 1.00 (provided by Mplus but not shown in Table 13.3). However, it should be noted that this topic continues to be strongly debated by methodologists. For example, some researchers assert that these guidelines are far too conservative for many types of models (e.g., measurement models comprised of many indicators and several factors where the majority of cross-loadings and error covariances are fixed to zero; cf. Marsh, Hau, & Wen, 2004). Moreover, because the performance of fit statistics and their associated cut-offs have been shown to vary as a function of various aspects of the model (e.g., degree of misspecification, size of factor loadings, number of factors; e.g., Beauducel & Wittman, 2005), the fit statistic thresholds suggested by simulation studies may have limited generalizability to many types of measurement models in applied research.

The second aspect of model evaluation is to identify whether there are specific areas of ill-fit in the solution. A limitation of goodness-of-fit statistics (e.g., SRMR, RMSEA, CFI) is that they provide a *global*, descriptive indication of the ability of the model to reproduce the observed relationships among the indicators in the input matrix. However, in some instances, overall goodness-of-fit indices suggest acceptable fit despite the fact that some relationships among indicators in the sample data have not been reproduced adequately (or alternatively, some model-implied relationships may markedly exceed the associations seen in the data). This outcome is more apt to occur in complex models (e.g., models that entail an input matrix consisting of a large set of indicators) where the sample matrix is reproduced reasonably well on the whole, and the presence of a few poorly reproduced relationships have less impact on the global summary of model fit. On the other hand, overall goodness-of-fit indices may indicate a model poorly reproduced the sample matrix. However, these indices do not provide information on the reasons why the model fit the data poorly (e.g., misspecification of indicator-factor relationships, failure to model salient error covariances).

Two statistics that are frequently used to identify specific areas of misfit in a CFA solution are *standardized residuals* and *modification indices*. A residual reflects the difference between the observed sample value and model-implied estimate for each indicator variance and covariance (e.g., the deviation between the sample covariance of indicators D1 and D2 and the model-implied covariance). When these residuals are standardized, they are analogous to standard scores in a sampling distribution and can be interpreted like *z* scores. Stated another way, these values can be conceptually considered as the number of standard deviations that the residuals differ from the zero-value residuals that would be associated with a perfectly fitting model. For example, a standardized residual at a value of 1.96 or higher would indicate that there exists significant additional covariance between a pair of indicators that was not reproduced by the model's parameter estimates. Modification indices can be computed for each fixed parameter (e.g., parameters that are fixed to zero such as indicator cross-loadings and error covariances) and each constrained parameter in the model (e.g., parameter estimates that are constrained to be same the value). The modification index reflects an approximation of how much the overall model χ^2 will decrease if the fixed or constrained parameter is freely estimated. Because the modification index can be conceptualized as a χ^2 statistic with 1 df, indices of 3.84 or greater (i.e., the critical value of χ^2 at $p < .05$, 1 df) suggest that the overall fit of the model could be significantly improved if the fixed or constrained parameter was freely estimated. For example, when the two-factor model is specified without the A1 and A3 error covariance, the model $\chi^2(19) = 85.45$, $p < .001$, and the modification index for this parameter is 67.24. This suggests that the model χ^2 is expected to decrease by roughly 67.24 units if the error covariance of these two indicators is freely estimated. As can be seen, this is an approximation because the model χ^2 actually decreased 61.73 units (85.45 − 23.72) when this error covariance is included. Because modification indices are also sensitive to sample size, software programs provide expected parameter change (EPC) values for each modification index. As the name implies, EPC values are an estimate of how much the parameter is expected to change in a positive or negative direction if it were freely estimated in a subsequent analysis. In the current example, the unstandardized EPC for the A1 through A3 correlated error was .261. Like the modification index, this is an approximation (although not presented in Table 13.3, the estimate for the error covariance of A1 and A3 was .242). Although standardized residuals and modification indices provide specific information for how the fit of the model can be improved, such revisions should only be pursued if they can be justified on empirical or conceptual grounds (e.g., MacCallum, Roznowski, & Necowitz, 1992). Atheoretical specification searches (i.e., revising the model solely on the basis of large standardized residuals or modification indices) will often result in further model misspecification and overfitting (e.g., inclusion of unnecessary parameter estimates resulting from chance associations in the sample data).

The final major aspect of CFA model evaluation pertains to the interpretability, strength, and statistical significance of the parameter estimates. The parameter estimates (e.g., factor loadings and factor correlations) should only be interpreted in the context of a good-fitting solution. If the model did not provide a good fit to the data, the parameter estimates are likely biased (incorrect). For example, without the error covariance in the model, the factor loading estimates for A1 and A3 are considerably larger than the factor loadings shown in Table 13.3 because the solution must strive to reproduce the observed relationship between these indicators solely through the factor loadings; using the completely standardized solution in Table 13.3, the model-implied correlation of A1 and A3 is the product of their factor loadings plus their correlated error (i.e., .567[.569] + .283 = .61.)^2

In context of a good-fitting model, the parameter estimates should first be evaluated to ensure they make statistical and substantive sense. The parameter estimates should not take on out-of-range values (often referred to as *Heywood cases*) such as a negative indicator error variance. These results may be indicative of model-specification error or problems with the sample or model-implied matrices (e.g., a nonpositive definite matrix, small N). Thus, the model and sample data must be viewed with caution to rule out more serious causes of these outcomes (again, *see* Wothke, 1993, and Brown, 2006, for further discussion). From a substantive standpoint, the parameters should be of a magnitude and direction that is in accord with conceptual or empirical reasoning (e.g., each indicator should be strongly and significantly related to its respective factor, the size and direction of the factor correlations should be consistent with expectation). Small or statistically nonsignificant estimates may be indicative of unnecessary parameters (e.g., a nonsalient error covariance or indicator cross-loading). In addition, such estimates may highlight indicators that are not good measures of the factors (i.e., a small and nonsignificant primary loading may suggest that the indicator should be removed from the measurement model). On the other hand, extremely large parameter estimates may be substantively problematic. For example, if in a multifactorial solution the factor correlations approach 1.0, there is strong evidence to question whether the latent variables represent distinct constructs (i.e., they have poor discriminant validity). If two factors are highly overlapping, the model could be respecified by collapsing the dimensions into a single factor. If the fit of the respecified model is acceptable, it is usually favored because of its superior parsimony.

The first portion of the results shown in Table 13.3 is the measurement model parameter estimates (i.e., factor loadings, residual variances, communalities). In addition to point estimates of each freely estimated parameter, standard errors of the estimate are provided in parentheses. A test statistic can be computed by dividing the point estimate by its standard error (e.g., D2 factor loading = 0.865/0.045 = 19.22). These test ratios can be interpreted as a z statistic (i.e., values greater than 1.96 are significant at $\alpha = .05$, two-tailed). As seen in Table 13.3, standard errors and significance tests for the unstandardized factor loadings for D1 and A1 are unavailable because these variables were used as marker indicators (i.e., their unstandardized loadings were fixed to 1.0). The variances for the Depression and Anxiety latent variables are 0.84 and 0.33, respectively. These estimates were derived from the sample variances of the marker indicators multiplied by their respective communalities (shown in the last column of Table 13.3). For example, the communality estimate for D1 was .741 indicating that 74.1% of the variance in this indicator was explained by the Depression factor. Thus, 74.1% of the sample variance of D1 ($SD^2 = 1.065^2 = 1.134$; cf. Table 13.1) is passed along to become the variance of the Depression latent variable; 1.134(.741) = 0.84. As in EFA, the factor loadings are regression coefficients expressing the direct effects of the latent variables on the indicators, but in the unstandardized metric (e.g., a unit increase in Depression is associated with a .858 increase in D2). Table 13.3 indicates that the estimated covariance of the Depression and Anxiety factors is 0.258. The residual variances are the indicator uniquenesses or errors (i.e., variance in the indicators that was not explained by the Anxiety and Depression latent variables).

In addition, Table 13.3 provides the completely standardized measurement model parameter estimates (the partially standardized solutions are omitted from Table 13.3). Because each indicator loads on only one factor (i.e., all possible cross-loadings were fixed to zero), these factor loadings can be interpreted as the correlation between the indicator and the factor. Accordingly, squaring these loadings provides the indicator's communality (e.g., for D1, $.861^2 = .741$ which is the same as the values provided under the "Communality" column in Table 13.3). In some software programs (e.g., recent versions of Mplus), standard errors and test statistics are also provided for completely (and partially) standardized estimates. In the completely standardized solution, the residual variances reflect the proportion of indicators' sample variance that was not explained by the latent variables (e.g., 25.9% of the sample variance of D1 was not accounted for by Depression, also computed as 1 minus the communality). The completely standardized results also provide the correlations among the latent variables (as indicated in Table 13.3, the factor correlation for Depression and Anxiety is .492).

It is noteworthy that the CFA factor correlation estimate (.492) is somewhat larger than the estimate produced in EFA (.429). This is a common outcome that stems from the differences in how the factor loading matrix is parameterized in these analytic frameworks. Unlike EFA whereby the factor loading matrix is saturated, in CFA most if not all cross-loadings are fixed to zero (for purposes of model overidentification and simple structure). Thus, the model-implied correlation of indicators loading on separate factors in CFA is estimated solely by the primary loadings and the factor correlation; for example, using a basic tracing rule, the model-implied correlation of D2 and A2 is .808(.888)(.492) = .35 (product of their factor loadings multiplied by the factor correlation). For example, compared to oblique EFA (where the model-implied correlation of indicators with primary loadings on separate factors can be estimated in part by the indicator cross-loadings), in CFA there is more burden on the factor correlation to reproduce the correlation between D2 and A2 because there are no cross-loadings to assist in this model-implied estimate (i.e., in the ML iterative process to arrive at CFA parameter estimates that best reproduce the sample matrix, the magnitude of the factor correlation estimate may be increased somewhat to better account for the relationships of indicators that load on separate factors).

Hybrid Latent Variable Measurement Models

A common sequence in scale development and construct validation is to conduct CFA as the next step after latent structure has been explored using EFA. However, the researcher frequently encounters a poor-fitting CFA solution because of the potential sources of misfit that are not present in EFA. For example, unlike EFA, indicator cross-loadings and residual covariances are usually fixed to zero in initial CFA models. This convention of CFA model specification thus prompts the researcher to pursue a more parsimonious model than is appropriate for the data (e.g., in reality, some cross-loadings are significantly different than zero). When a poor-fitting solution arises, the researcher is then faced with potentially extensive post hoc model testing subject to the criticisms of specification searches in a single data set (MacCallum, 1986). Moreover, the misspecification of zero loadings may result in distorted factors. As noted above, when nonzero loadings are fixed at zero, the observed correlation among indicators on different factors must be reproduced through their factors, which can result in overestimated factor correlations.

There are two factor-analytic procedures available to researchers that are alternatives to the traditional EFA and CFA. The first approach, called "exploratory factor analysis within the CFA framework" (E/CFA; Jöreskog, 1969; Jöreskog & Sörbom, 1979) can be performed in any latent variable software program. The E/CFA procedure is a useful precursor to CFA that allows the researcher to explore measurement structures more fully before moving into a confirmatory framework. The E/CFA approach represents an intermediate step between EFA and CFA that provides substantial information important in the development of realistic confirmatory solutions. In this strategy, the CFA applies the same number of identifying restrictions used in EFA (m^2) by fixing factor variances to unity, freely estimating the factor covariances, and by selecting an anchor item for each factor whose cross-loadings are fixed to zero (the loadings of nonanchor items are freely estimated on each factor). Whereas this specification produces the same model fit as ML EFA, the CFA estimation provides considerably more information including the statistical significance of primary and secondary loadings and the potential presence of salient error covariances (e.g., modification indices). Thus, the researcher can develop a realistic measurement structure prior to moving into the more restrictive CFA framework. In addition, E/CFA can be used to bring other variables (i.e., predictors or distal outcomes of the factors) into an EFA-type solution, eliminating the need for factor scores. A detailed presentation of the procedures (and example syntax) of E/CFA can be found in Brown (2006); for illustrations of this approach in applied data sets, see Brown, White, and Barlow (2005), Brown, White, Forsyth, and Barlow (2004), and Campbell-Sills, Liverant, and Brown (2004).

The second method, called "exploratory structural equation modeling" (ESEM; Asparouhov & Muthén, 2009) is a new approach that is only available in the Mplus software program (beginning with version 5.21). The ESEM approach allows for the integration of EFA and CFA measurement models within the same solution. That is, within a given measurement model, some factors can be specified per the conventions of CFA (i.e., zero cross-loadings) whereas other factors can be specified as an EFA (i.e., rotation of a full factor loading matrix). Unlike traditional EFA, the EFA measurement model in ESEM provides the same information as ML CFA such as multiple indices of goodness-of-fit, standard errors for all rotated parameters, and modification indices (i.e., highlighting possible correlated residuals among indicators). Moreover, most of the modeling possibilities of CFA are available in ESEM including correlated residuals, regression of factors on covariates, regression among factors (among different EFA factor blocks or between EFA and CFA factors), multiple-group solutions, mean structure analysis, and measurement invariance examination across groups or across time. At this writing, ESEM possesses some relatively minor practical and analytic limitations including the inability to read in summary data (i.e., raw data must be used as input), and certain restrictions in the specification of structural parameters (e.g., exploratory factors from the same block cannot be regressed on each other and cannot be used as lower-order factors in a hierarchical factor model; if a structural path linking an exploratory factor to another variable must be specified for all factors within the same exploratory block). Moreover, given the recent advent of ESEM, best-practice guidelines for this procedure await future research and application. A technical description of ESEM can be found in Asparouhov and Muthén (2009); see Marsh et al. (2009, in press) and Rosellini and Brown (2011) for initial applied studies.

Table 13.4 presents Mplus syntax (version 6.0, Muthén & Muthén, 1998–2010) and selected output for the two-factor model of Depression and Anxiety in ESEM. Note that a raw data file has been read as input per Mplus requirements (see DATA command). In the MODEL command, the BY statement specifies that the factors DEP (Depression) and ANX (Anxiety) are measured by the indicators D1 through A4. The label (*1) after the BY statement is used to indicate that DEP and ANX are a block of EFA factors. Because a rotation option has not been specified, the Mplus default of oblique geomin rotation is used. As seen in Table 13.4, by Mplus default the variances of the factors are fixed to one; in addition, the intercepts and residual variances of the indicators are freely estimated and the residuals are not correlated as the default. However, the correlated residual default

Table 13.4. Mplus Syntax and Selected Output for Exploratory Structural Equation Modeling

```
TITLE: DEPRESSION AND ANXIETY ESEM
  DATA:
    FILE IS DEPANX.DAT;
    FORMAT IS F6,F2/F6,f2,7F1;
  VARIABLE:
    NAMES ARE SUBJID SEX SB2 D1 D2 D3 D4 A1 A2 A3 A4;
    USEVAR = D1 D2 D3 D4 A1 A2 A3 A4;
  MODEL:
    DEP ANX BY D1-A4 (*1);
    A1 WITH A3;
  OUTPUT: MODINDICES(4);
```

MODEL RESULTS

	Estimate	S.E.	Est./S.E.	Two-tailed P-value
DEP BY				
D1	0.915	0.046	19.695	0.000
D2	0.796	0.045	17.892	0.000
D3	0.813	0.047	17.255	0.000
D4	0.764	0.047	16.255	0.000
A1	−0.025	0.057	−0.435	0.663
A2	−0.003	0.003	−1.092	0.275
A3	0.017	0.049	0.341	0.733
A4	0.126	0.059	2.135	0.033
ANX BY				
D1	0.005	0.025	0.200	0.841
D2	−0.005	0.026	−0.178	0.858
D3	0.067	0.042	1.589	0.112
D4	−0.029	0.042	−0.685	0.493
A1	0.582	0.062	9.387	0.000
A2	0.893	0.052	17.115	0.000
A3	0.464	0.054	8.623	0.000
A4	0.673	0.065	10.287	0.000
ANX WITH				
DEP	0.452	0.053	8.595	0.000
A1 WITH				
A3	0.250	0.039	6.472	0.000

Table 13.4. (Continued)

		Intercepts		
D1	1.025	0.053	19.248	0.000
D2	1.253	0.049	25.517	0.000
D3	0.938	0.051	18.533	0.000
D4	0.678	0.048	14.177	0.000
A1	0.902	0.051	17.846	0.000
A2	0.962	0.049	19.791	0.000
A3	0.585	0.042	13.810	0.000
A4	1.205	0.054	22.396	0.000
		Variances		
DEP	1.000	0.000	999.000	999.000
ANX	1.000	0.000	999.000	999.000
		Residual variances		
D1	0.293	0.032	9.122	0.000
D2	0.333	0.031	10.750	0.000
D3	0.309	0.030	10.385	0.000
D4	0.349	0.031	11.244	0.000
A1	0.696	0.056	12.382	0.000
A2	0.152	0.066	2.314	0.021
A3	0.495	0.040	12.229	0.000
A4	0.613	0.057	10.778	0.000

MODEL MODIFICATION INDICES

Minimum M.I. value for printing the modification index 4.000

M.I.   E.P.C.   Std E.P.C.   Std YX E.P.C.

No modification indices above the minimum value.

has been overridden for A1 and A3 by the same programming used in CFA (*see* Table 13.3). Inspection of the geomin-rotated factor matrix shows that all primary loadings are statistically significant and all but one cross-loading (A4) is nonsignificant. The factor correlation between DEP and ANX is statistically significant but of somewhat smaller magnitude (.452) to the estimate obtained in CFA when all cross-loadings were fixed to zero. This is for the same reasons previously discussed in the comparison of traditional EFA and CFA results (i.e., in CFA, there is more burden on the factor correlation to reproduce the correlations of indicators loading on different factors because there are no cross-loadings to assist in this model-implied estimate).

Extensions of CFA

Multiple-group solutions. An advantage of CFA over traditional EFA is that the researcher is able to place a variety of substantively meaningful restrictions on the measurement model solution. In the examples discussed thus far, the parameters of the CFA model have been either freely estimated or fixed. A *free parameter* is unknown, and the researcher allows the analysis to find its optimal value that, in tandem with other model estimates, minimizes the differences between the observed and predicted variance-covariance matrices. A *fixed parameter* is prespecified by the researcher to be a specific value, most commonly either 1.0 (e.g., in the case of marker indicators or factor variances to define the metric of a latent variable) or 0 (e.g., the absence of cross-loadings or error covariances). A third type of estimate is a *constrained parameter*. As with a free parameter, a constrained parameter is also unknown. However, the parameter is not free to be any value, but rather the specification places restrictions on the values it may assume. The most common form of constrained parameter are *equality constraints*, in which unstandardized parameters are restricted to be equal in value.

Although equality constraints can be usefully applied to single-group CFA solutions (*see* Brown, 2006, for examples), they are most often used to examine the equivalence of the measurement and structural parameters of a factor model across multiple groups. The measurement portion of a CFA model, which deals with the measurement characteristics of the indicators, consists of the factor loadings, intercepts, and residual variances (uniquenesses). Thus, the evaluation of across-group equivalence of these parameters reflects tests of *measurement invariance*. The structural parameters of the CFA model relate to the latent variables themselves, and thus consist of the factor variances, covariances, and latent means. These parameters describe characteristics of the population from which the sample was drawn. Therefore, the examination of the across-group equivalence of structural parameters are often referred to as tests of *population heterogeneity*.

Multiple-group CFA solutions have many potential practical applications. For example, measurement invariance evaluation is a key aspect of the psychometric development of psychological tests. Do the items of a questionnaire measure the same constructs (same factor structure) and evidence equivalent relationships to these constructs (equal factor loadings) in all subgroups of the population for whom the measure will be used? Or, are there sex, ethnic/racial, age, or other subgroup differences that preclude responding to the questionnaire in comparable ways? Does the questionnaire contain items that are biased against a particular subgroup (i.e., yield substantially higher or lower observed scores in a group at equivalent levels of the latent or "true" score)? The evaluation of measurement invariance is also important in determining the generalizability of constructs across groups (e.g., does the construct underlying the formal definition of a given psychiatric diagnosis operate equivalently across cultures, sexes, and age groups?). Tests of structural parameters reveal potential group differences, adjusting for measurement error and an error theory. For example, tests of equality of factor covariances can be construed as the CFA counterpart to inferential evaluation of the differential magnitude of independent correlations (i.e., are two constructs more strongly correlated in one group than another?). Tests of the equality of latent means are analogous to the comparison of observed group means via ordinary least squares (OLS) statistics (e.g., t-test, ANOVA). However, a key advantage of the CFA approach is that such comparisons are made in the context of a latent variable measurement model which adjusts for measurement error, correlated residuals, and so forth.

For the reasons discussed below, the recommended sequence of multiple-group CFA invariance evaluation is as follows: (1) test the CFA model separately in each group; (2) conduct the simultaneous test of equal form (identical factor structure); (3) test the equality of factor loadings; (4) test the equality of indicator intercepts; (5) test the equality of indicator residual variances (optional); and, if substantively meaningful, (6) test the equality of factor variances; (7) test the equality of factor covariances (if applicable, i.e., > one latent variable); and (8) test the equality of latent means. Steps 1 to 5 are tests of measurement invariance; steps 6 to 8 are tests of population heterogeneity.

This sequence is now illustrated by examining the measurement invariance and population heterogeneity of the two-factor model of Depression and Anxiety in female ($n = 240$) and male ($n = 160$) outpatients.[3] Prior to conducting the multiple-group CFAs, it is important to ensure that the posited two-factor model is acceptable in both groups. If markedly disparate measurement models are obtained in each group, this would contraindicate further invariance evaluation. Although the full results are not provided here (except for goodness-of-fit statistics, *see* Table 13.5), the two-factor models (including the error covariance of A1 and A3) conducted separately for females and males were acceptable in regard to the three key aspects of model evaluation (i.e., overall goodness-of-fit, absence of specific areas of strain in the solutions, strength/significance of parameter estimates).

Table 13.5. Tests of Measurement Invariance and Population Heterogeneity of Two-Factor Model of Depression and Anxiety in Men and Women (N = 400)

	χ^2	df	$\Delta\chi^2$	Δ df	RMSEA	SRMR	CFI	TLI
Single-group solutions								
Women (n = 240)	22.35	18			.032	.032	.995	0.993
Men (n = 160)	37.44**	18			.062	.046	.969	0.952
Measurement invariance								
Equal form	59.79**	36			.057	.038	.985	0.976
Equal factor loadings	67.20**	42	7.41	6	.055	.041	.984	0.979
Equal indicator intercepts	77.57**	48	10.37	6	.055	.044	.981	0.978
Population heterogeneity								
Equal factor variances	79.37**	50	1.80	2	.054	.047	.981	0.979
Equal factor covariance	82.37**	51	3.00	1	.055	.047	.980	0.978
Equal latent means	84.57**	53	2.20	2	.055	.051	.980	0.979

Note: $\Delta\chi^2$ = change in χ^2; Δdf = change in degrees of freedom; RMSEA = root mean square error of approximation; SRMR = standardized root mean square residual; CFI = comparative fit index; TLI = Tucker-Lewis Index. **$p < .01$.

Next, the analysis of equal form was conducted. This analysis entails the simultaneous estimation of separate two-factor models for males and females. Accordingly, the equal form analysis uses separate input data for each group (depending on the software program used, either separate input data files for each group must be created and read into the analysis, or the input data file must contain a variable that denotes group membership). The specification of the measurement model for males and females is identical. For example, in this example D1 and A1 continue to be used as the marker indicators for the Depression and Anxiety latent variables in both groups; the remaining factor loadings, the indicator error variances, the error covariance of the A1 and A3 indicators, and the factor variances and covariance are freely estimated in both groups.

As shown in Table 13.5, the equal form solution provides an acceptable fit to the data. This solution will serve as the baseline model for subsequent tests of measurement invariance and population heterogeneity. Note that the *df* and model χ^2 of the equal form solution equal the sum of the *df*s and model χ^2s of the CFAs run separately for men and women (e.g., $\chi^2 = 59.79 = 22.35 + 37.44$).[4]

The next analysis evaluates whether the unstandardized factor loadings of the Depression and Anxiety indicators were equivalent in men and women. The test of equal factor loadings is a critical test in multiple-group CFA. In tandem with other aspects of measurement invariance evaluation, this test determines whether the indicators have the same meaning for different groups of respondents. Specifically, the test of equal factor loadings evaluates whether a unit increase in the factor is associated with the same amount of change in the observed measure for each group. This test also determines the suitability of subsequent group comparisons that may be of substantive interest (e.g., group equality of factor variances and factor means).

As shown in Table 13.5, the equal factor loadings model fit the data well. However, the test of equal loadings can be more directly evaluated by statistically comparing whether the fit of this more restricted solution is worse than a comparable solution without these constraints. Direct statistical comparison of alternative solutions is possible when the models are nested. A *nested model* contains a subset of the free parameters of another model (which is often referred to as the *parent model*). This is the case in the current example because the equal loadings model (nested model) contains a subset of the free parameters of the equal form model (parent model). When models are nested, the χ^2 statistic can be used to statistically compare the fit of the solutions. Used in this fashion, χ^2 is often referred to as the χ^2 difference test ($\Delta\chi^2$) or the nested χ^2 test. If a model is nested under a parent model, the simple difference in the model χ^2s is distributed as χ^2 under typical ML estimation (i.e., adjustments to the $\Delta\chi^2$ test must be made when using other estimators, such as those that accommodate nonnormal or categorical data; *see* Brown, 2006). Thus, the $\Delta\chi^2$ is 7.41 (67.20 − 59.79; *see* Table 13.5). In this example, $\Delta\chi^2$ has six *df*s, which reflects the difference in the number of freely estimated parameters in the equal form and equal loadings models. Specifically, the difference in degrees of freedom (*df* = 6) corresponds to the six factor loadings (D2 to D4, A2 to A4) that were freely estimated in both groups in the previous analysis. Because D1 and A1 were fixed to 1.0 in both groups to serve as marker indicators, they had already been constrained to equality between groups in the equal form model (and thus do not contribute to the *df* change in the equal loadings model). The critical value of the χ^2 distribution (α = .05, two-tailed) at $df = 6$ is 12.59. Because the $\Delta\chi^2$ (7.41) does not exceed this critical value, it can be concluded that the constraint of equal loadings did not significantly degrade fit of the model relative to the equal form solution (i.e., the factor loadings are equivalent for males and females).

The analysis proceeds to the evaluation of the equality of the indicator intercepts. The analysis of mean structures (e.g., indicator intercepts) poses additional identification issues. In addition to the sample variances and covariances, the sample means of the indicators must also be input as units of analysis. In this two-group analysis, there are 16 indicator means (eight per group) but potentially 20 free parameters of the mean structure solution (16 intercepts, four latent means). Moreover, latent variables must be assigned an origin in addition to a metric. Thus, the mean structure component of the multiple-group solution is underidentified in the absence of additional restrictions. In addition to holding the indicator intercepts to equality across groups in the measurement invariance solution, identification can be accomplished by fixing the origin (mean) of the latent variable(s) in one group to zero. The group whose latent mean(s) has been fixed to zero becomes the reference group (in this example, females). The latent means in the remaining groups are freely estimated, but these parameter estimates represent deviations from the reference group's latent means.

The equal indicator intercepts model is found to be good-fitting, and does not result in a significant degradation of fit relative to the equal factor loadings solution, $\Delta\chi^2(6) = 10.37$, *ns* (*see* Table 13.5). The gain of six degrees of freedom reflects the difference between the 16 observed indicator means (eight per group) minus eight indicator intercept estimates (the intercepts are held to equality in both groups) minus two freely estimated factor means (for men; the factor means for women are fixed to zero). Because the factor loadings and indicator intercepts are invariant in men and women, it can be concluded that for any given level of the latent variable (Depression or Anxiety), men and women will obtain the same observed score on the indicators of Depression and Anxiety (e.g., a given observed score on A2 reflects the same degree of the trait of Anxiety in both groups).

The remaining analyses are group comparisons on the structural parameters of the CFA model (i.e., tests of population heterogeneity).[5] The viability of these comparisons rests on the evaluation of measurement invariance. In other words, it is not useful to compare groups on aspects of the latent variables (factor variances, factor covariances, latent means) without first ascertaining that the factors represent the same constructs in the same fashion in each group. Specifically, group comparisons on factor variances are meaningful only if the factor loadings are invariant. Comparisons of the factor covariances are meaningful if both the factor loadings and factor variances are invariant. Finally, evaluation of group equality of latent means rests on the condition of invariant factor loadings and indicator intercepts.

Evaluation of the equality of a factor variance examines whether the amount of within-group variability (dispersion) of the construct differs across groups. Although crucial to all aspects of invariance evaluation, the test for equal factor variances best exemplifies why comparisons made by multiple-group CFA rely on the unstandardized solution. The test of invariant factor variances would be meaningless if the metric of the factor was defined by fixing its variance to 1.0. The question addressed by the test of factor variance equality often does not have clear substantive implications in applied research, although such evaluation is needed to establish the suitability of the potentially more interesting test of the invariance of factor covariances. In the current example, the factor variances of Depression and Anxiety were equivalent in men and women, $\Delta\chi^2(2) = 1.80$, *ns* (*see* Table 13.5; the increase of 2 *df* stems from the estimation of two factor variances instead of four in the preceding models).

Next, the equality of the factor covariance of Depression and Anxiety was examined. The equality constraint on the factor covariance did not result in a significant increase in the model χ^2; $\Delta\chi^2(1) = 3.00$, *ns*. Thus, it can be concluded that the strength of the relationship between the latent variables of Depression and Anxiety does not significantly differ for males and females. As in the previous analysis of the equality of indicator intercepts, the factor means in this model are fixed to zero for females and freely estimated for males. The estimated latent means (and standard errors) for males are as follows: Depression = 0.129 (0.099), Anxiety = −0.005 (0.064). As noted earlier, these estimates reflect deviations of the latent means from females (the reference group whose factor means were fixed to zero for identification purposes). For example, the latent mean estimate for Depression = 0.129, which indicates that, on average, males score 0.129 units higher than females on this dimension (based on the metric of the marker indicator, D1). The associated test statistic ($z = 0.129/0.099 = 1.30$) indicates this difference is nonsignificant ($p = .192$). However, because these test statistics can be biased (cf. Gonzalez & Griffin, 2001), group differences in latent means are more precisely evaluated by nested χ^2 testing. This was done in the final model, whereby the latent means for males were also fixed to zero. Because the $\Delta\chi^2$ test was nonsignificant (*see* Table 13.5), it can be concluded that the deviations of the latent means do not reliably differ from zero (i.e., males and females evidence equivalent levels of the underlying traits of depression and anxiety).

Higher-Order Models

Second-order factor analysis. Often, there is a substantive reason to examine the higher-order structure of a latent variable measurement model. Hierarchical factor analysis is often used for theory testing. For example, this analytic procedure is popular in intelligence research where it is believed that more specialized facets of ability (e.g., verbal comprehension, perceptual organization, memory) are influenced by a broader dimension of general intelligence (*g*). The examples discussed in this chapter thus far are *first-order* measurement models. In these multiple-factor models (e.g., Depression and Anxiety), the factors were specified to be intercorrelated (oblique); in other words, the factors are presumed to be interrelated, but the nature of these relationships is unanalyzed (i.e., the researcher makes no claims about the directions or patterns of factor interrelationships). In second-order factor analysis, the focus is on the intercorrelations among the factors. In essence, the factor correlations represent the input matrix for the second-order factor analysis. A goal of second-order factor analysis is to provide a more parsimonious account for the correlations among first-order factors. Second-order factors account for the correlations among first-order factors, and the number of second-order factors and second-order factor loadings is less than the number of factor correlations. Accordingly, the rules of identification used in first-order CFA apply to the higher-order component of a second-order solution. For example, the number of second-order factors that can be specified is dictated by the number of first-order factors (discussed below). Unlike first-order CFA, second-order CFA tests a theory-based account for the patterns of relationships among the first-order factors. These specifications assert that second-order factors have direct effects on first-order factors; these direct effects (and the correlations among second-order factors) are responsible for the covariation of the first-order factors.

An example of a second-order CFA model is presented in Figure 13.2. In this example, the researcher wishes to examine the latent structure of common mental disorders in a sample of 500 patients. It is predicted that a five-factor model will account for the covariance of 15 continuous measures of mental disorder features. The five factors are: Substance Use (e.g., drug/alcohol abuse and dependence), Conduct (e.g., antisocial personality), Anxiety (e.g., phobias, panic disorder), Mood (e.g., major depression), and Somatoform (e.g., hypochondriasis). In addition, a hierarchical structure is specified in which the relationships among the five mental disorder factors are explained by the second-order constructs of Externalizing (onto which Substance Use and Conduct load) and Internalizing (Anxiety, Mood, and Somatoform load).

The general sequence of second-order factor analysis is: (1) develop a well-behaved (e.g., good-fitting, conceptually valid) first-order solution; (2) examine the magnitude and pattern of correlations among factors in the first-order solution; and (3) fit the second-order factor model, as justified on conceptual and empirical grounds. Thus, using the data set presented in Figure 13.2, the first step is to fit a five-factor CFA model, allowing the correlations among the factors to be freely estimated. The five-factor solution provides a good fit to the data,

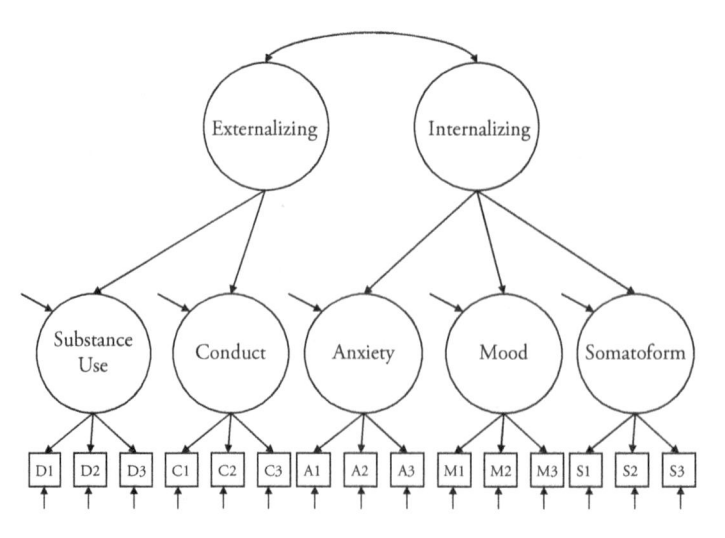

Figure 13.2 Example of a Second-Order Factor Model of Common Mental Disorders

Table 13.6. Intercorrelations Among Factors in the First-Order Model of Common Mental Disorders

	SUB	CON	ANX	MOOD	SOM
SUB	1.000				
CON	0.580	1.000			
ANX	0.323	0.308	1.000		
MOOD	0.347	0.318	0.637	1.000	
SOM	0.341	0.302	0.610	0.619	1.000

Note: SUB = Substance Use, CON = Conduct, ANX = Anxiety, MOOD = Mood, SOM = Somatoform.

$\chi^2(80) = 20.77, p = 1.0, \text{SRMR} = .012, \text{RMSEA} = 0.00, \text{TLI} = 1.02, \text{CFI} = 1.00$ (based on Mplus 6.0).

As seen in Table 13.6, the pattern of correlations speaks to the viability of the posited second-order model. This model asserts that Substance Use and Conduct are specific subdomains of Externalizing, while Anxiety, Mood, and Somatoform are subdomains of Internalizing. If this is true in the data, the magnitude of factor correlations should show a clear pattern (e.g., Substance Use and Conduct will be more strongly correlated with each other than with Anxiety, Mood, and Somatoform). The factor correlations in Table 13.6 follow this pattern. For example, the magnitude of the correlation between Substance Use and Conduct is considerably higher (.58) than the correlations between these constructs and the constructs that are construed to be subdomains of Internalizing (range of $rs = .30$ to .35).

A different pattern of factor correlations would contradict the posited second-order model. For example, if all factor correlations were roughly the same magnitude, this would favor a single second-order factor (which should be pursued only if justified by theory). Moreover, the higher-order portion of the model must be statistically identified. The rules of identification discussed earlier apply to second-order solutions. For example, the metric of the second-order factors must be identified either by specifying a first-order factor as a "marker indicator" for the second-order factor, or by standardizing the second-order portion of the solution (i.e., fixing the variance of the second-order factors to 1.0). In addition, the number of freely estimated parameters in the second-order portion of the model must not exceed the total number of factor variances and covariances in the first-order solution. For example, a single second-order factor cannot be specified to account for the factor correlation from a first-order CFA model with two factors (e.g., the Depression and Anxiety model discussed in previous sections of this chapter) because it would be underidentified unless other (potentially unreasonable) constraints are placed on the solution (e.g., constraining the second-order factor loadings to equality would just-identify the solution). If the first-order model has three factors, a solution with a single second-order factor would be just-identified (i.e., the second-order solution would produce the same goodness-of-fit as the first-order model in which the three factors are allowed to freely

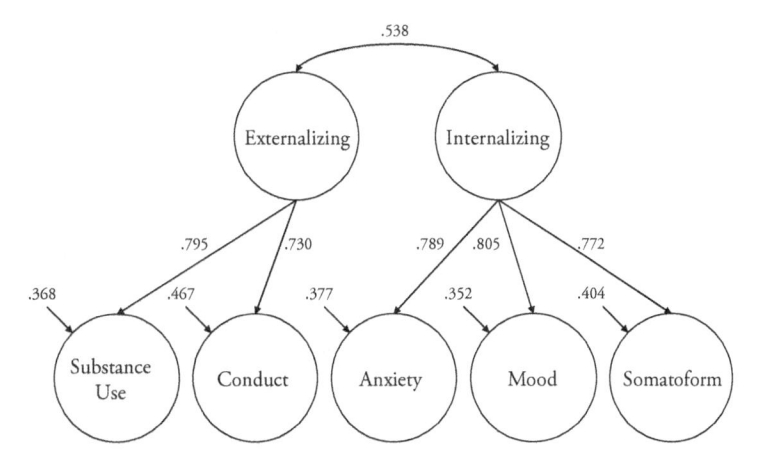

Figure 13.3 Second-Order Factor Model of Common Mental Disorders: Completely Standardized Estimates

covary). Even when the second-order portion of the solution is overidentified, it is possible that the researcher may encounter the problem of empirical underidentification. For example, empirical underidentification would occur in the Figure 13.2 model if the Substance Use and Conduct factors were not correlated (i.e., rs close to zero) with the remaining three first-order factors. In this case, the correlation between the second-order factors of Externalizing and Internalizing would be zero, and there would be infinite pairs of second-order factor loadings that would reproduce the correlation between Substance Use and Conduct, if these parameters were freely estimated.

This model also provided a good fit to the data (e.g., χ^2 [84] = 21.15, p = 1.0). Note that, compared to the first-order model, the model df increased by four, which reflects the fact that the second-order portion of the model is overidentified with four degrees of freedom. Specifically, the second-order solution is attempting to account for the 10 correlations among the first-order factors with six freely estimated parameters (i.e., the five second-order factor loadings and the correlation between the two second-order factors). Thus, the second-order solution cannot improve goodness-of-fit relative to the first-order solution because it is attempting to reproduce factor correlations with a smaller number of parameter estimates. When the second-order model is overidentified, the χ^2 difference test can be used to evaluate whether the specification produces a significant degradation in fit relative to the first-order solution. In this example, the second-order solution is equally good-fitting, $\Delta\chi^2(4) = 0.38$, ns (i.e., 21.15 – 20.77, df = 84 – 80), indicating that the imposed second-order structure was able to accurately reproduce the correlations among the first-order factors.

The acceptability of the second-order model should also be evaluated with regard to the magnitude of the second-order parameters (i.e., size of second-order factor loadings and second-order factor correlations). Figure 13.3 presents the completely standardized parameter estimates for the second-order portion of this solution. As seen in Figure 13.3, each of the first-order factors loads strongly onto the second-order factors (range of completely standardized loadings = .730 to .805). Squaring these loadings yields the proportion of variance in the first-order factors that is explained by the second-order factors; For example, Externalizing accounts for 53.3% of the variance in Conduct ($.73^2 = .533$). The correlation between the second-order factors is estimated to be .538. The remaining five values presented in Figure 13.3 are residual variances of the first-order factors (often referred to as *disturbances*). As completely standardized estimates, these values reflect the proportion of variance in the first-order factors that is not explained by the second-order factors; For example, 46.7% of the variance in Conduct is not accounted for by Externalizing (this value can also be calculated by 1 minus the squared second-order factor loading; e.g., $1 - .73^2 = .467$).

Because the second-order solution did not result in a significant decrease in model fit, it can be concluded that the model provided a good account for the correlations among the first-order factors. This can be demonstrated using the tracing rules presented earlier. For example, in the first-order CFA model, the correlation between Substance Use and Conduct was .58 (*see* Table 13.6). Multiplying

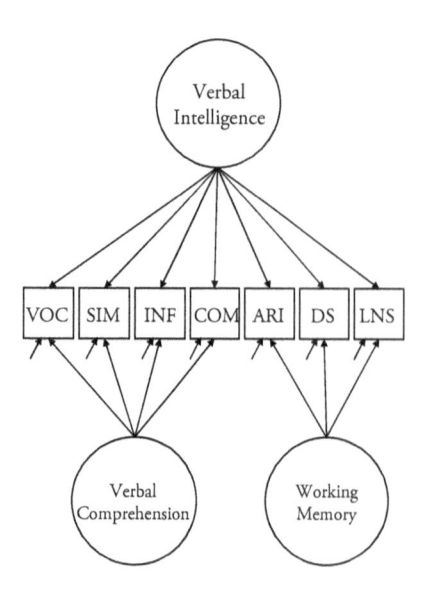

Figure 13.4 Example of a Bifactor Hierarchical Model of Verbal Intelligence. Note: VOC = Vocabulary, SIM = Similarities, INF = Information, COM = Comprehension, ARI = Arithmetic, DS = Digit Span, LNS = Letter-Number Sequencing.

the second-order factor loadings of Externalizing → Substance Use and Externalizing → Conduct reproduces this correlation (i.e., .795[.73] = .58). Similarly, in the initial CFA solution, the estimated correlation between Substance Use and Somatoform was .341. This relationship is accounted for multiplying the following three parameters: Externalizing → Substance Use (.795), Internalizing → Somatoform (.772), correlation between Externalizing and Internalizing (.538) (i.e., .795[.772][.538] = .330).

Bifactor models. Another less commonly used approach to higher-order factor analysis is the bifactor model (Harman, 1976; Holzinger & Swineford, 1937). A path diagram for a bifactor model specification is provided in Figure 13.4. In bifactor models, there exists a general factor that accounts for significance covariance in all the observed measures. In addition, there are multiple domain-specific factors that account for unique variance in the indicators of a specific domain over and beyond the general factor. In the model illustrated in Figure 13.4, there is a general Verbal Intelligence factor that underlies each of the specific verbal intelligence tests. Thus, unlike second-order models, the bifactor model specifies a direct effect of the higher-order dimension on the indicators.[6] In addition, there are two domain-specific factors (Verbal Comprehension, Working Memory) that each account for unique variance within the specific subdomain. Consistent with the typical parameterization of the bifactor model, the general and domain-specific factors are specified to be uncorrelated (i.e., the contribution of the domain-specific factors to explaining variability in the indicators is independent of the variance accounted for by the general factor).

Chen, West, and Sousa (2006) outlined several potential advantages of the bifactor model. Because the second-order model is nested within the bifactor model (Yung et al., 1999), the bifactor model can be used as a baseline model to which a second-order can be compared (via χ^2 difference evaluation). Moreover, the bifactor model can be used to evaluate the importance of domain-specific factors. For example, it is possible that a domain-specific factor will not be relevant to the prediction of the observed measures when the general factor is included in the model (i.e., once the general factor is partitioned out, the domain-specific factor does not account for unique variance in the indicators). If this is the case, estimation problems will be encountered because either the factor loadings of the irrelevant domain-specific factor will be small (e.g., close to zero) or the variance of the domain-specific factor will not significantly differ from zero. In addition, the bifactor model can be used in instances where the researcher is interested in examining whether the domain-specific factors predict external variables (i.e., outcome variables not part of the measurement model) when holding the general factor constant. This cannot be done in the typical second-order model because the domain-specific factors are represented by residual variances (disturbances) of the first-order factors (i.e., because the second-order factors have direct effects on the first-order factors, the "variance" of the first-order factors does not reflect the total variance of these dimensions but rather variability that is unexplained by the second-order factors). For similar reasons, measurement invariance evaluation cannot be conducted on the first-order factors in second-order models, whereas all aspects of the bifactor model can be tested for equivalence across multiple groups (including structural parameters such as differences in the latent means).

Although second-order models are more common in the applied research literature, see the following papers for recent applications of the bifactor model: Brouwer, Meijer, Weekers, and Baneke (2008), Osman et al. (2010), and Patrick, Hicks, Nichol, and Krueger (2007).

Conclusion

Hopefully, the examples in this chapter will demonstrate to the reader that latent variable measurement models are indispensible in addressing the types of empirical questions often asked by applied researchers (e.g., psychometric development of test instruments, construct validation, measurement invariance evaluation, data reduction, sources of bias in measurement). Although some of the most common applications were discussed in detail (e.g., multiple-group solutions, higher-order factor analysis), there are many other types of analyses that can be conducted within the latent variable measurement model framework. For example, given the ability to specify a measurement error theory, the CFA framework is an ideal approach for evaluating construct validity using multitrait-multimethod matrices (*see* Brown, 2006) and to estimate the scale reliability of test instruments (Raykov, 2001a, 2001b). As noted earlier in this chapter, a useful feature of CFA is the ability to bring external variables into the latent variable measurement model. Thus, empirical validation can be addressed using the latent variables themselves rather than factor scores. For example, CFA with covariates can be conducted to evaluate selected aspects of measurement invariance and population heterogeneity when multiple-group solutions are not feasible (Jöreskog & Goldberger, 1975; Muthén, 1989). Specifically, the CFA model can be specified such that the factors and indicators are regressed onto dummy codes reflecting group membership (e.g., Sex: 0 = male, 1 = female). The path from the Sex dummy code to the factor reflects sex differences in the underlying construct (population heterogeneity) and the path from the dummy code to the indicator represents group differences on its intercept (i.e., holding the factor constant, do the sexes differ on the observed level of the indicator—a test of measurement invariance). A detailed illustration of this approach can be found in Brown (2006). Finally, it is important to note that structural equation modeling (*see* next chapter in this volume) always involves a latent variable measurement model and thus a successful structural equation model depends on a high-quality CFA (e.g., poor-fitting structural equation models often result from problems with the latent variable measurement model). Thus, even when the development of a viable latent variable measurement model is not the ultimate purpose of the investigation, in many situations these analyses are crucial precursors to the ensuing analyses.

Future Directions

The concluding section of this chapter will highlight an issue associated with one of the types of latent variable measurement models discussed earlier in this chapter (multiple-group solutions), as well as discuss some relatively new modeling possibilities and their uses and areas in need of future research.

Reliance on χ^2 in multiple-group solutions. As shown in the illustration of multiple-group CFA, invariance evaluation relies strongly on the χ^2 statistic. For example, the omnibus test of equality of indicator intercepts across groups is conducted by determining whether the constrained solution (in which the intercepts are held equal across groups) produces a significant increase in χ^2 relative to a less constrained model (e.g., an equal factor loadings solution). When a significant degradation in model fit is encountered, procedures to identify noninvariant parameters also rely on χ^2-type statistics (i.e., modification indices). However, both model χ^2 and modification indices are sensitive to sample size. Researchers have noted that a double standard exists in the SEM literature (e.g., Cheung & Rensvold, 2002; Vandenberg & Lance, 2000). Given the limitations of χ^2, investigators are encouraged to use a variety of fit indices to evaluate the overall fit of a CFA solution (e.g., RMSEA, TLI, CFI, SRMR). However, in invariance evaluation, the χ^2 statistic is used exclusively to detect differences in more vs. less constrained solutions. This is because the distributional properties of χ^2 are known and thus critical values can be determined at various degrees of freedom. This cannot be done for other fit indices (e.g., a more constrained solution may produce an increase in the SRMR, but there is no way of determining at what magnitude this increase is statistically meaningful). Researchers have begun to recognize and address this issue (e.g., Cheung & Rensvold, 2002; Fan & Sivo, 2009; Meade, Johnson, & Braddy, 2008). Specifically, Monte Carlo simulation studies have been undertaken to determine whether critical values of alternative goodness-of-fit statistics (e.g., the CFI) could be identified to reflect the presence/absence of measurement invariance in multiple-group solutions (e.g., what point reduction in the CFI will reliably reject the null hypothesis that the measurement parameters are the same across groups?). Although these investigators have forwarded critical values for various fit statistics, the validity of these proposals awaits additional research.[7]

New modeling possibilities with latent variable measurement models. As discussed earlier in this chapter, ESEM is a new latent variable measurement modeling approach that represents a hybrid of EFA and CFA. Given the recent advent of ESEM, the field is in need of research to determine the best-practice guidelines for this methodology in applied data sets (e.g., issue with model identification, overfitting/specification searching, and model misspecification). This is also the case for two other recently developed latent variable measurement model methodologies, *factor mixture modeling* and *multilevel factor modeling*.

Factor mixture models are a combination of latent class models (cf. Lazarsfeld & Henry, 1968) and common factor models. Latent class models are used to explore unobserved population heterogeneity. Unobserved heterogeneity exists when it is not possible to identify the sources of heterogeneity beforehand (i.e., the sample may be heterogeneous because it is comprised of cases that belong to different subpopulations but it is not possible to identify these subgroups *a priori*). Factor mixture models identify *latent classes* (i.e., homogeneous clusters with a heterogeneous sample). Unlike the other examples discussed in this chapter, the latent variable in the latent class model is categorical, and the number of categories (i.e., latent classes) reflects the number of classes in the sample. These classes may differ qualitatively or quantitatively. For example, using the Figure 13.1 model, a factor mixture model might identify three classes: an "unaffected" class (i.e., cases with no depression and anxiety), a so-called "anxious" class (i.e., cases with no depression but with elevated anxiety), and a "comorbid distress" class (i.e., cases with elevated depression and anxiety). Various aspects of the model results (e.g., goodness-of-fit statistics such as the Bayesian information criterion, BIC, and interpretability/quality of classification and posterior probabilities) are used to evaluate the factor mixture model. After an appropriate number of classes is identified, the estimates (posterior class probabilities) of the factor mixture model can be used to divide the sample into subpopulations. Covariates and distal outcomes can be brought into the analysis to validate the factor mixture model. For example, an observed background variable (e.g., a genetic polymorphism linked to Depression) might be predictive of class membership. Such models may be more informative and interpretable than a single-group model that simply regresses the latent factors on a background variable (e.g., the background variable may be differentially predictive of classes). However, further study is needed on how and when covariates should be incorporated into the factor mixture model (i.e., at what stage of the analysis and by what method), as well as on the performance of statistical tests for identifying the correct combination of latent classes and factors. For further information on this methodology, the reader is referred to Lubke and Muthén (2005, 2007).

Another relatively new methodology is the multilevel factor model. Although multilevel models have been around for years (cf. hierarchical linear models; Raudenbush & Bryk, 2002), only recently has this methodology merged with CFA factor models in a manner readily accessible to applied researchers. Multilevel modeling is employed to avoid biases in parameter estimates, standard errors, and tests of model fit when data have been obtained by cluster or unequal probability sampling (e.g., data collected from students nested within classrooms, or children nested within families). In other words, if the hierarchical structure is ignored, so is the nonindependence of observations. Consequently, for example, the standard errors of parameter estimates are underestimated resulting in positively biased statistical significance testing. Moreover, the multilevel model can be estimated to learn more about within- and between-cluster relationships ("cluster" meaning of the data are hierarchically structured, e.g., families, classrooms). Multilevel models are also referred to as *random coefficient models*. Random coefficients are parameters in a model that may vary across clusters. Covariates can be included in the multilevel model to account for variability across and within clusters.

In addition to incorporating the proper corrections for the nonindependence in the data (e.g., correct standard errors for factor loadings), multilevel models can analyze within- and between-cluster factors in a latent variable measurement model. In fact, the number of factors can differ at the within- and between-cluster levels. Indeed, evidence in applied data sets suggests fewer factors are obtained at the between-cluster level because of a lack of variability across clusters. Covariates can be brought into the multilevel factor model to explain variability within and between clusters. Any parameter of the measurement model solution (e.g., a factor loading) can be treated as a random coefficient, if justified on substantive and empirical grounds (e.g., does the strength of the indicator-factor relationship significantly differ as a function of a characteristic of the cluster?). Most latent variable software programs (e.g., Mplus, EQS, LISREL) now have multilevel factor modeling capabilities. Recent applied illustrations of this methodology can be found in Dedrick and Greenbaum (in press), and Dyer, Hanges, and Hall (2005).

Author Note

Correspondence concerning this chapter should be addressed to: Timothy A. Brown, Center for Anxiety & Related Disorders, Department of Psychology, Boston University, 648 Beacon Street, 6th floor, Boston, MA 02215–2013.

Notes

1. Computer syntax, input data, and output files for this and other examples in this chapter can be found at the following website: <http://people.bu.edu/tabrown/index.html>.

2. The value of .283 is the completely standardized error covariance of the A1 and A3 indicators. The following formula converts a covariance into a correlation: $CORR_{1,2} = COV_{1,2}/SQRT(VAR_1 * VAR_2)$. To compute the model-implied correlated error of A1 and A3, divide the unstandardized error covariance (.242) by the product of the sample standard deviations of these indicators (from Table 13.1; i.e., .242 / [1.011 * 0.847] = .283).

3. Although this example is conducted as an extension of the single-group CFA presented earlier in this chapter, simulation research (e.g., Meade & Bauer, 2007) has indicated that sample sizes in multiple-group CFA should be larger than those in the current illustration to ensure sufficient power to detect group differences in measurement parameters (e.g., differential magnitude of factor loadings).

4. Although multiple-group solutions can be evaluated when the size of the groups vary (as in the current example), if the group sizes differ markedly, interpretation of the analysis may be more complex. This is because many aspects of the CFA are influenced by (sensitive to) sample size. For example, model χ^2 is computed by multiplying a fit function value (F_{ML}, which summarizes the discrepancies between the observed and predicted covariance matrices) by either sample size (N) or $N - 1$ (depending on the software program). Thus, the situation may arise in which F_{ML} is roughly the same across groups (e.g., males, and females), but each group's contribution to the equal form model χ^2 is substantially different because of the unbalanced group sizes. All other aspects of the CFA model that are based on χ^2 (e.g., overall fit statistics such as the CFI; modification indices) or are influenced by sample size (e.g., standard errors, standardized residuals) will be differentially impacted by the unbalanced group sizes. Thus, when the group ns differ considerably, the researcher must be mindful of this issue when interpreting the results.

5. Although the equality of error variances represents another potential test of measurement invariance, this evaluation is rarely conducted in applied research. Generally speaking, this test is regarded as being overly restrictive (e.g., rarely upheld in real data sets) and is usually not very germane to the endeavor of measurement invariance evaluation (e.g., Bentler, 1995).

6. However, a Schmid-Leiman transformation (Schmid & Leiman, 1957) can be applied to the second-order factor solution to elucidate the strength of the effects of the first- and second-order factors on the observed measures. In fact, the bifactor model and second-order model are statistically equivalent when the Schmid-Leiman transformation is applied to the latter (Yung, Thissen, & McLeod, 1999). For a more details and an applied illustration of the Schmid-Leiman transformation, see Brown (2006).

7. Another complication that may arise in measurement invariance evaluation is the situation where the true factor-to-indicator relationship is nonlinear (e.g., quadratic) when the solution is in fact invariant across groups. If a linear model is pursued, the factor loadings and indicator intercepts will increasingly differ across groups as the factor mean difference increases. Diagnostic procedures to identify nonlinear factor-indicator and factor-factor relationships have been developed (Bauer, 2005; Pek, Sterba, Kok, & Bauer, in press) as well as methods for fitting nonlinear factor models (Wall & Amemiya, 2007).

References

Aspharouhov, T., & Muthén, B. (2009). Exploratory structural equation modeling. *Structural Equation Modeling, 16,* 397–438.

Bauer, D.J. (2005). The role of nonlinear factor-to-indicator relationships in tests of measurement equivalence. *Psychological Methods, 10,* 305–316.

Beauducel, A., & Wittman, W.W. (2005). Simulation study on fit indices in CFA based on data with slightly distorted simple structure. *Structural Equation Modeling, 12,* 41–75.

Bentler, P.M. (1995). *EQS structural equations program manual.* Encino, CA: Multivariate Software, Inc.

Brouwer, D., Meijer, R.R., Weekers, A.M., & Baneke, J.J. (2008). On the dimensionality of the Dispositional Hope Scale. *Psychological Assessment, 20,* 310–315.

Brown, T.A. (2003). Confirmatory factor analysis of the Penn State Worry Questionnaire: Multiple factors or method effects? *Behaviour Research and Therapy, 41,* 1411–1426.

Brown, T.A. (2006). *Confirmatory factor analysis for applied research.* New York: Guilford Press.

Brown, T.A., White, K.S., & Barlow, D.H. (2005). A psychometric reanalysis of the Albany Panic and Phobia Questionnaire. *Behaviour Research and Therapy, 43,* 337–355.

Brown, T.A., White, K.S., Forsyth, J.P., & Barlow, D.H. (2004). The structure of perceived emotional control: Psychometric properties of a revised Anxiety Control Questionnaire. *Behavior Therapy, 35,* 75–99.

Campbell-Sills, L.A., Liverant, G., & Brown, T.A. (2004). Psychometric evaluation of the Behavioral Inhibition/Behavioral Activation Scales (BIS/BAS) in large clinical samples. *Psychological Assessment, 16,* 244–254.

Chen, F.F., West, S.G., & Sousa, K.H. (2006). A comparison of bifactor and second-order models of quality of life. *Multivariate Behavioral Research, 41,* 189–225.

Cheung, G.W., & Rensvold, R.B. (2002). Evaluating goodness-of-fit indices for testing measurement invariance. *Structural Equation Modeling, 9,* 233–255.

Dedrick, R., & Greenbaum, P. (in press). Multilevel confirmatory factor analysis of a scale measuring interagency collaboration of children's mental health agencies. *Journal of Emotional and Behavioral Disorders.*

Dyer, N.G., Hanges, P.J., & Hall, R.J. (2005). Applying multilevel confirmatory factor analysis techniques to the study of leadership. *The Leadership Quarterly, 16,* 149–167.

Fabrigar, L.R., Wegener, D.T., MacCallum, R.C., & Strahan, E.J. (1999). Evaluating the use of exploratory factor analysis in psychological research. *Psychological Methods, 4,* 272–299.

Fan, X., & Sivo, S.A. (2009). Using Δgoodness-of-fit indexes in assessing mean structure invariance. *Structural Equation Modeling, 16,* 54–69.

Gonzalez, R., & Griffin, D. (2001). Testing parameters in structural equation modeling: Every "one" matters. *Psychological Methods, 6,* 258–269.

Harman, H.H. (1976). *Modern factor analysis* (3rd ed.). Chicago: University of Chicago Press.

Holzinger, K.J., & Swineford, F. (1937). The bifactor method. *Psychometrika, 2,* 41–54.

Hu, L., & Bentler, P.M. (1999). Cutoff criteria for fit indexes in covariance structure analysis: Conventional criteria versus new alternatives. *Structural Equation Modeling, 6,* 1–55.

Jöreskog, K.G. (1969). A general approach to confirmatory maximum likelihood factor analysis. *Psychometrika, 34,* 183–202.

Jöreskog, K.G. (1971). Statistical analysis of sets of congeneric tests. *Psychometrika, 36,* 109–133.

Jöreskog, K.G., & Goldberger, A.S. (1975). Estimation of a model with multiple indicators and multiple causes of a single latent variable. *Journal of the American Statistical Association, 70,* 631–639.

Jöreskog, K.G., & Sörbom, D. (1979). *Advances in factor analysis and structural equation models* (J. Magidson, Ed.). Cambridge, MA: Abt Books.

Lazarsfeld, P.F., & Henry, N.W. (1968). *Latent structure analysis.* Boston: Houghton Mifflin.

Little, T.D., Slegers, D.W., & Card, N.A. (2006). A nonarbitrary method of identifying and scaling latent variables in SEM and MACS models. *Structural Equation Modeling, 13,* 59–72.

Lubke, G.H., & Muthén, B.O. (2005). Investigating population heterogeneity with factor mixture models. *Psychological Methods, 10,* 21–39.

Lubke, G.H., & Muthén, B.O. (2007). Performance of factor mixture models as a function of model size, covariate effects, and class-specific parameters. *Structural Equation Modeling, 14,* 26–47.

MacCallum, R.C. (1986). Specification searches in covariance structure modeling. *Psychological Bulletin, 100,* 107–120.

MacCallum, R.C., Roznowski, M., & Necowitz, L.B. (1992). Model modifications in covariance structure analysis: The problem of capitalization on chance. *Psychological Bulletin, 111,* 490–504.

Marsh, H.W. (1996). Positive and negative global self-esteem: A substantively meaningful distinction or artifactors? *Journal of Personality and Social Psychology, 70,* 810–819.

Marsh, H.W., Hau, K.T., & Wen, Z. (2004). In search of golden rules: Comment on hypothesis testing approaches to setting cutoff values for fit indexes and dangers in overgeneralizing Hu and Bentler's (1999) findings. *Structural Equation Modeling, 11,* 320–341.

Marsh, H.W., Lüdtke, O., Muthén, B., Asparouhov, T., Morin, A. J. S., Trautwein, U., & Nagengast, B. (in press). A new look at the big-five factor structure through exploratory structural equation modeling. *Psychological Assessment.*

Marsh, H.W., Muthén, B., Asparouhov, A., Lüdtke, O., Robitzsch, A., Morin, A.J.S., & Trautwein, U. (2009). Exploratory structural equation modeling, integrating CFA and EFA: Application to students' evaluations of university teaching. *Structural Equation Modeling, 16,* 439–476.

Meade, A.W., & Bauer, D.J. (2007). Power and precision in confirmatory factor analytic tests of measurement invariance. *Structural Equation Modeling, 14,* 611–635.

Meade, A.W., Johnson, E.C., & Braddy, P.W. (2008). Power and sensitivity of alternative fit indices in tests of measurement invariance. *Journal of Applied Psychology, 93,* 568–592.

Muthén, B. (1989). Latent variable modeling in heterogeneous populations. *Psychometrika, 54,* 557–585.

Muthén, L.K., & Muthén, B.O. (1998–2010). *Mplus user's guide* (6th ed). Los Angeles: Author.

Osman, A., Gutierrez, P.M., Smith, K., Fang, Q., Lozano, G., & Devine, A. (2010). The Anxiety Sensitivity Index-3: Analyses of dimensions, reliability estimates, and correlates in nonclinical samples. *Journal of Personality Assessment, 92,* 45–52.

Patrick, C.J., Hicks, B.M., Nichol, P.E., & Krueger, R.F. (2007). A bifactor approach to modeling the structure of the Psychopathy Checklist-Revised. *Journal of Personality Disorders, 21,* 118–141.

Pek, J., Sterba, S., Kok, B.E., & Bauer, D.J. (in press). Estimating and visualizing nonlinear relations among latent variables: A semi-parametric approach. *Multivariate Behavioral Research.*

Raudenbush, S.W., & Bryk, A.S. (2002). *Hierarchical linear models: Applications and data analysis methods* (2nd ed.). Newbury Park, CA: Sage.

Raykov, T. (2001a). Estimation of congeneric scale reliability using covariance structure analysis with nonlinear constraints. *British Journal of Mathematical and Statistical Psychology, 54,* 315–323.

Raykov, T. (2001b). Bias of Cronbach's alpha for fixed congeneric measures with correlated errors. *Applied Psychological Measurement, 25,* 69–76.

Rosellini, A.J., & Brown, T.A. (2011). The NEO Five-Factor Inventory: Latent structure and relationships with dimensions of anxiety and depressive disorders in a large clinical sample. *Assessment, 18,* 27–38.

Schmid, J., & Leiman, J.M. (1957). The development of hierarchical factor solutions. *Psychometrika, 22,* 53–61.

Thurstone, L.L. (1947). *Multiple-factor analysis.* Chicago: University of Chicago Press.

Vandenberg, R.J., & Lance, C.E. (2000). A review and synthesis of the measurement invariance literature: Suggestions, practices, and recommendations for organizational research. *Organizational Research Methods, 3,* 4–69.

Wall, M.M., & Amemiya, Y. (2007). A review of nonlinear factor analysis and nonlinear structural equation modeling. In R. Cudeck & R.C. MacCallum (Eds.), *Factor analysis at 100: Historical developments and future directions* (pp. 337–361). Mahwah, NJ: Erlbaum.

Wothke, W.A. (1993). Nonpositive definite matrices in structural modeling. In K.A. Bollen & J.S. Long (Eds.), *Testing structural equation models* (pp. 256–293). Newbury Park, CA: Sage.

Yung, Y.F., Thissen, D., & McLeod, L.D. (1999). On the relationship between the higher-order factor model and the hierarchical factor model. *Psychometrika, 64,* 113–128.

CHAPTER
14
Multilevel Regression and Multilevel Structural Equation Modeling

Joop J. Hox

Abstract

Multilevel modeling in general concerns models for relationships between variables defined at different levels of a hierarchical data set, which is often viewed as a multistage sample from a hierarchically structured population. Common applications are individuals within groups, repeated measures within individuals, longitudinal modeling, and cluster randomized trials. This chapter treats the multilevel regression model, which is a direct extension of single-level multiple regression, and multilevel structural equation models, which includes multilevel path and factor analysis. Multilevel analysis was originally intended for continuous normally distributed data. This chapter refers to recent extensions to non-normal data but does not treat these in detail. The end of the chapter presents some statistical issues such as assumptions, sample sizes, and applications to data that are not completely nested.

Key Words: Multilevel model, mixed model, random coefficient, cluster sampling, hierarchical data

Introduction

Social and behavioral research often concerns research problems that investigate the relationships between individuals and the larger context in which they live, such as families, schools, or neighborhoods. Similarly, longitudinal data are becoming more common, where individuals are followed for a period of time to observe and model their development. Multilevel models and software have been introduced to combine in a statistically sound way variables defined at the individual and the group level. These models were discussed in the educational and sociological research literature in the 1980s and described in monographs in the early 90s by, for example, Bryk and Raudenbush (1992) and Goldstein (1987). For an exhaustive review of the older multilevel literature, see Hüttner and Van den Eeden (1995). The monographs by Bryk and Raudenbush and by Goldstein are mathematically oriented; more introductory level handbooks appeared later—for example, Bickel (2007), Hox (2002), and Snijders and Bosker (1999).

Although multilevel modeling was initially discussed mostly in the context of individuals within groups, the model was rapidly extended to longitudinal and repeated measures data. The translation is simple—one just needs to replace individuals within groups with measurement occasions within individuals, and restructure the data from the conventional multivariate ("wide") structure to a stacked ("long") multilevel structure. This application was already described by Goldstein (1987). As it turns out, multilevel modeling of longitudinal data is a very powerful approach, because it enables a very flexible treatment of the metric of time, and it deals naturally with incomplete data resulting from incidental dropout and panel attrition. Just as multilevel analysis of individuals within groups does not assume that the group sizes are equal, multilevel analysis of repeated measures within individuals does not assume that all individuals have the same number of measures.

A more recent development is the introduction of multilevel structural equation modeling (SEM). Structural equation models are more flexible than (multilevel) regression models. Regression models assume predictor variables that are perfectly reliable, which is unrealistic. Structural equation models do not make that assumption, because they can include a measurement model for the predictor or outcome variables. In addition, they can model more complicated structures, such as indirect effects in a mediation analysis.

This chapter treats the multilevel regression model as applied to individuals within groups and as applied to measurement occasions within individuals. It follows with a description of (multilevel) SEM for measurement occasions within individual and for mediation analysis. Next, some issues are discussed concerning assumptions and sample sizes. The chapter ends with a brief discussion.

Multilevel Regression Modeling: Introduction and Typical Applications
Individuals Within Groups

The multilevel regression model for individuals within groups is often represented as a series of regression equations. For example, assume that we have data from pupils in classes. On the pupil level, we have an outcome variable, "pupil popularity." We have two explanatory variables on the pupil level, pupil gender (0 = boy, 1 = girl) and pupil extraversion, and one class level explanatory variable teacher experience (in years). There are data on 2,000 pupils in 100 classes, so the average class size is 20 pupils. The data are described and analyzed in more detail in Hox (2010) and available on the web (www.joophox.net).

The lowest level regression equation predicts the outcome variable as follows:

$$popularity_{ij} = \beta_{0j} + \beta_{1j} gender_{ij} + \beta_{2j} extraversion_{ij} + e_{ij}. \quad (1)$$

In this regression equation, β_{0j} is the intercept, β_{1j} is the regression slope for the dichotomous explanatory variable gender, β_{2j} is the regression slope for the continuous explanatory variable extraversion, and e_{ij} is the usual residual error term. The subscript j is for the classes ($j = 1...J$) and the subscript i is for individual pupils ($i = 1...n_j$). The major difference with the usual regression model is that we assume that each class has a different intercept β_{0j}, and different slopes β_{1j} and β_{2j}. This is indicated in the equation by attaching a subscript j to the regression coefficients. The residual errors e_{ij} are assumed to have a normal distribution with a mean of zero and some variance that is estimated. This chapter uses σ_e^2 to denote the variance of the lowest level residual errors.

Because the regression coefficients of the individual-level variables vary across classes, the next step is to explain this variation using explanatory variables at the second or class level:

$$\beta_{0j} = \gamma_{00} + \gamma_{01} Teacher\ Exp_j + u_{0j}, \quad (2)$$

and

$$\beta_{1j} = \gamma_{10} + \gamma_{11} Teacher\ Exp_j + u_{1j}$$
$$\beta_{2j} = \gamma_{20} + \gamma_{21} Teacher\ Exp_j + u_{1j}. \quad (3)$$

Equation 2 predicts the average popularity in a class (the intercept β_{0j}) by the teacher's experience. The equations under Equation 3 state that the *relationship* (as expressed by the slope coefficients β_j) between the popularity and the gender and extraversion of the pupil depends on the amount of experience of the teacher. The amount of experience of the teacher acts as a *moderator variable* for the relationship between popularity and gender or extraversion; this relationship varies according to the value of the moderator variable.

The u-terms u_{0j}, u_{1j}, and u_{2j} are residual error terms at the class level. These are assumed to have means of 0 and to be independent from the residual errors e_{ij} at the individual (pupil) level. The variance of the residual errors u_{0j} is specified as $\sigma_{u_0}^2$, and the variances of the residual errors u_{1j} and u_{2j} are specified as $\sigma_{u_1}^2$ and $\sigma_{u_2}^2$. The *covariances* between the residual error terms are denoted by σ_{u01}, σ_{u02}, and σ_{u12} and are generally *not* assumed to be 0.

Using standard multilevel regression software, we can estimate a series of models. Table 14.1 presents three models of increasing complexity. The first model is the intercept-only model, which allows us to calculate the intraclass correlation ρ as $\rho = \frac{\sigma_{u_0}^2}{\sigma_{u_0}^2 + \sigma_e^2}$. For the popularity data, the intraclass correlation is 0.36, which is relatively large. Model 2 adds the predictor variables, with a random slope for pupil extraversion (the variance of the slope for pupil gender is 0 and therefore omitted from the model). The last model adds the cross-level interaction to explain the variation of the extraversion

Table 14.1. Models for the Pupil Popularity Data

Model:	Intercept-only	Main effects	With interaction
Fixed part	Coefficient (SE)	Coefficient (SE)	Coefficient (SE)
Intercept	5.08(0.09)	0.74(0.20)	−1.21(0.27)
Pupil gender		1.25(0.04)	1.24(0.04)
Pupil extraversion		0.45(0.02)	0.80(0.04)
Teacher experience		0.09(0.01)	0.23(0.02)
Extra*T.exp			−0.03(0.003)
Random part			
σ_e^2	1.22(0.04)	0.55(0.02)	0.55(0.02)
σ_{u0}^2	0.69(0.11)	1.28(0.28)	0.45(0.16)
σ_{u2}^2		0.03(0.008)	0.005(0.004)
σ_{u02}		−0.18(0.05)	−0.03(0.02)
Deviance	6327.5	4812.8	4747.6

slope; after this interaction is included, the variance of this slope is no longer significant, as determined by a likelihood ratio test.

The interpretation of the main effects model (second model) in Table 14.1 is that girls and more extraverted pupils tend to be more popular. The significant variance for the slope of extraversion (σ_{u2}^2 in the random part) indicates that the effect of extraversion varies across classes. The interaction model (model 3) models this variance with an interaction between extraversion and teacher experience. The negative sign of the regression coefficient for this interaction indicates that the effect of extraversion on popularity is smaller with more experienced teachers. The interpretation of direct effects in the presence of a significant interaction is delicate; in general, it is recommended to support such interactions by drawing a graph using the observed range of the interacting variables (Aiken & West, 1991; Hox, 2010).

When predictor variables are added to the model, the resulting decrease in the residual error variance is often interpreted as explained variance. This interpretation is not quite correct, as Snijders and Bosker (1999) have shown. Table 14.1 illustrates this: when the predictors are added, the unexplained variance at the second level actually appears to increase. In this specific instance, this is the result of the changes in the random part, where a slope variance is added. This completely changes the model. When the random part is left unaltered, adding predictors generally results in decreasing residual error variances, and these are often interpreted as explained variance (Raudenbush & Bryk, 2002). Nevertheless, negative explained variances can and do occur, and interpreting decrease in variance as explained variance is at best an approximation (Hox, 2010).

Measurement Occasions Within Individuals

Longitudinal data, or repeated measures data, can be viewed as multilevel data with repeated measurements nested within individuals. Multilevel analysis of repeated measures is often applied to data from large-scale panel surveys. In addition, it can also be a valuable analysis tool in a variety of experimental designs—for example, intervention studies with an immediate and a later final follow-up measurement, where incomplete data resulting from attrition are common.

The example is a data file compiled by Curran (1997) from a large longitudinal data set. The data are a sample of 405 children who were within the first 2 years of entry to elementary school. The data consist of four repeated measures of both the child's antisocial behavior and the child's reading recognition skills. In addition, at the first measurement occasion, measures were collected of emotional support and cognitive stimulation provided by the mother. Other variables are the child's gender and age and the mother's age at the first measurement occasion. There was an appreciable amount of panel dropout: all 405 children and mothers were interviewed at measurement occasion 1, but on the three subsequent occasions the sample sizes were 374, 297, and 294. Only 221 cases were interviewed at all four occasions. These data have been analyzed extensively in Hox (2010) and can also be obtained from the web (www.joophox.net).

The multilevel regression model for longitudinal data is a straightforward application of the multilevel regression model described earlier. It is also written as a sequence of models for each level. At the lowest, the repeated measures level, we have:

$$Y_{ti} = \pi_{0i} + \pi_{1i}T_{ti} + \pi_{2i}X_{ti} + e_{ti}, \quad (4)$$

where Y_{ti} is the outcome variable for subject i at measurement occasion t, T_{ti} is a time indicator for the measurement occasion, and X_{ti} is some other time-varying predictor variable. The regression intercept and slopes are commonly denoted by π_j, so at the individual level we can again use β for the regression coefficients. In our example, the outcome variable could be reading skill, the time indicator could be 0, . . ., 3 for the four measurement occasions, and the time-varying predictor could be antisocial behavior. The intercept and slopes in Equation 4 are assumed to vary across individuals. Just as in two-level models for individuals within groups, this variation can be explained by adding individual level predictors and cross-level interaction effects:

$$\pi_{0i} = \beta_{00} + \beta_{01}Z_i + u_{0i}$$
$$\pi_{1i} = \beta_{10} + \beta_{11}Z_i + u_{1i} \quad (5)$$
$$\pi_{2i} = \beta_{20} + \beta_{21}Z_i + u_{2i}$$

By substitution, we get the single equation model:

$$Y_{ti} = \beta_{00} + \beta_{10}T_{ti} + \beta_{20}X_{ti} + \beta_{01}Z_i$$
$$+ \beta_{11}T_{ti}Z_i + \beta_{21}X_{ti}Z_i$$
$$+ u_{1i}T_{ti} + u_{2i}X_{ti} + u_{0i} + e_{ti} \quad (6)$$

Table 14.2 presents a sequence of models for these data, predicting reading skill from the available predictor variables, omitting non-significant effects.

The interpretation of Table 14.2 is that there is an increase in reading skill over time. Relatively older children and children that are cognitively stimulated have better reading skill. Children vary in the speed at which reading skill increases, which is partially explained by interactions with their age and cognitive stimulation. Relatively older children increase their reading skill less fast, and children who are cognitively stimulated increase faster.

A comparison of the intercept-only model with the model that includes measurement occasion shows the anomaly mentioned earlier; adding occasion results in an increase of the second level variance, hence in negative explained variance. The reason was also mentioned earlier, interpreting changes in the variance terms as explained variance is questionable. The variance decomposition in the intercept-only model depends on the assumption of random sampling at all available levels. In longitudinal panel designs, the sampling at the lowest level follows a very specific scheme, and as a result the occasion level variance is overestimated and the individual level variance is underestimated (for details, see Hox, 2010). The pragmatic approach is to use as a null-model a model with measurement occasion properly specified, which in Table 14.2 is the model that includes occasion with a random slope.

Two important advantages of multilevel modeling of longitudinal data should be mentioned. As is clear from the reading skill example, incomplete data resulting from missed measurement occasions are no special problem. In the stacked ("long") data file, the rows corresponding to missed occasions are simply left out, and the analysis proceeds as usual. Given the large fraction of missing data in these data, this is a major advantage. An even more important advantage is that an analysis using repeated measures MANOVA, with listwise deletion of incomplete cases, assumes that missing data are missing completely at random (MCAR), an unlikely assumption. Multilevel analysis assumes missing at random (MAR), which is a much weaker assumption (see chapter 27, this volume).

The second advantage of multilevel modeling for longitudinal data is the flexible treatment of time. Because time is included in the model as a time-varying predictor, we can attempt to specify the metric of time in ways that are more accurate than counting the measurement occasion. In our example, it appears theoretically sounder to use the actual age of the child at each measurement occasion as the time variable. It is more accurate, because it reflects real observed age differences rather than just measurement occasions, and in contrast to measurement occasion, it does have a theoretical interpretation. Table 14.3 highlights the differences between these two metrics of time.

When we use the real age rather than the measurement occasions, which are spaced 2 years apart, we halve the scale of the time variable. Thus, for the age slope, we obtain values that are precisely half the

Table 14.2. Multilevel Models for Longitudinal Data Reading Skill

Model	Intercept-only	Add occasion	Occasion varying	
Fixed part				
Predictor	Coefficient (SE)	Coefficient (SE)	Coefficient (SE)	Coefficient (SE)
Intercept	4.11(0.05)	2.70(0.05)	2.70(0.05)	−3.28(0.42)
Occasion		1.10(0.02)	1.12(0.02)	2.23(0.24)
Child age				0.80(0.06)
Cogn. Stim.				0.05(0.01)
Occasion*Child age				−0.19(0.03)
Occasion*Cogn. Stim.				0.02(0.01)
Random part				
σ_e^2	2.39(0.11)	0.46(0.02)	0.35(0.02)	0.35(0.02)
σ_{u0}^2	0.30(0.08)	0.78(0.07)	0.57(0.06)	0.30(0.04)
σ_{u1}^2			0.07(0.01)	0.06(0.01)
σ_{u01}			0.06(0.02)	0.11(0.02)
r_{u01}			0.29(0.13)	0.86(0.18)
Deviance	5051.8	3477.1	3371.8	3127.9

Table 14.3. Comparing Occasion and Child's Age for Longitudinal Data Reading Skill

Model				
Fixed part	Occasion	Occasion varying	Child age	Child age varying
Predictor	Coefficient (SE)	Coefficient (SE)	Coefficient (SE)	Coefficient (SE)
Intercept	2.70(0.05)	2.70(0.05)	2.19(0.05)	2.16(0.04)
Occasion	1.10(0.02)	1.12(0.02)	—	—
Child age	—	—	0.55(0.01)	0.56(0.01)
Cogn. Stim.				
Occasion*Child age				
Occasion*Cogn. Stim.				
Random part				
σ_e^2	0.46(0.02)	0.35(0.02)	0.45(0.02)	0.36(0.02)
σ_{u0}^2	0.78(0.07)	0.57(0.06)	0.65(0.06)	0.17(0.05)
σ_{u1}^2		0.07(0.01)		0.02(0.003)
σ_{u01}		0.06(0.02)		0.05(0.001)
r_{u01}		0.29(0.13)		0.88(0.30)
Deviance	3477.1	3371.8	3413.9	3226.8
AIC	3485.1	3383.8	3421.9	3238.8

values of the occasion slope. But the child level variances are quite different. When models are nested, meaning that we can proceed from one model to the next by adding (or deleting) terms, the model change can be tested using a test on the deviances of the models. However, replacing the predictor variable measurement occasion by actual age does not lead to nested models. Provided the dependent variable and the number of cases remain the same (which implies no additional missing values induced by using age), we can compare such models using the Akaike Information Criterion (AIC). The AIC (Akaike, 1987) is calculated as the deviance minus twice the number of estimated parameters; models with a lower AIC are considered to be better. Thus, the values of the AIC in Table 14.3 suggest that using the actual age results in better models. For a general discussion of these issues, *see* Willett and Singer (2003). A more detailed analysis of the reading skill data using child age as the metric of time can be found in Hox (2010), which also discusses the AIC and related indices in more detail.

Multilevel Structural Equation Modeling: Introduction and Typical Applications

Structural equation models are a very flexible family of models that allow estimation of relationships between observed and latent variables, direct and indirect effects, and assessment of the fit of the overall model. Conventional SEM software can be tricked to estimate two-level models by viewing the two levels as two groups and using the multigroup option of conventional software (Muthén, 1994). The approach outlined by Muthén is a limited information method. Mehta and Neale (2005) have described how general multilevel models can be incorporated in SEM, and how these models can be estimated by conventional SEM software. Using conventional SEM software requires incredibly complicated set-ups, but recent versions of most SEM software incorporates these complications internally and have special multilevel features in their command language, which make it easier to specify multilevel models.

Latent Curve Modeling

An interesting structural equation model for panel data is the latent curve model (LCM), sometimes referred to as the latent growth model (LGM). In the LCM, the measurement occasions are defined by the factor loadings in the measurement model of the latent intercept and slope factors. Figure 14.1 shows the path diagram of a simple LCM for the reading skill data. The loadings of the intercept factor are all constrained to 1, and the loadings of the slope factor are constrained to 0, 1, 2, and 3, successively. Thus, the loadings of the slope factor specify the four measurement occasions. The means of the intercept and slope factors are equal to the estimates of the intercept and slope in the corresponding multilevel model, and the variances are equal to the variances of the intercept and slope in multilevel regression.

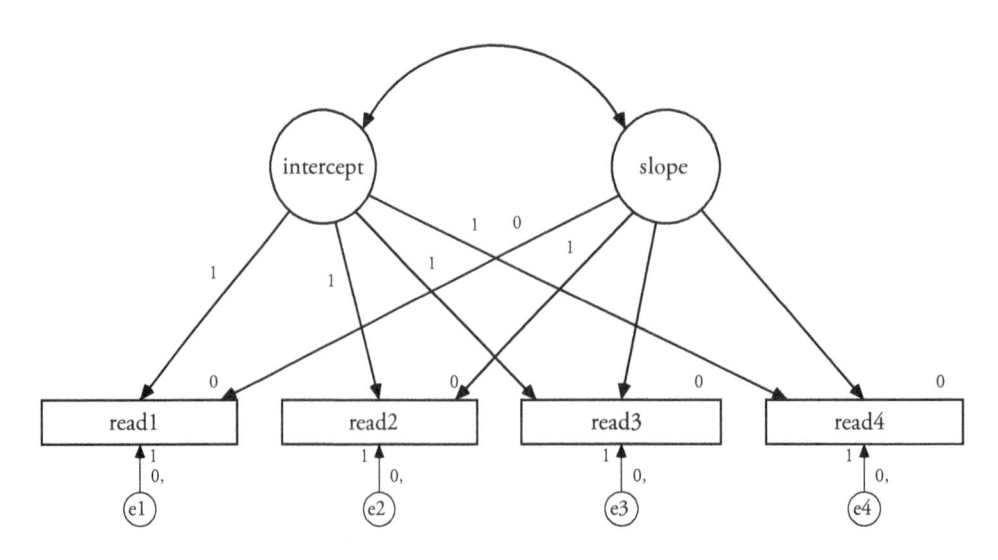

Figure 14.1 Path diagram for the intercept + slope model for reading skill.

It can be shown that the LCM and the multilevel regression model for longitudinal data are identical. That does not mean that there are no differences between the two approaches. For example, in SEM, it is trivial to use the intercept and slope factors in a GCM as predictors of some distant outcome. This is very difficult in a multilevel regression model. On the other hand, in multilevel regression software, it is trivial to extend the model with additional levels, whereas most current multilevel SEM software can deal with only two levels. In addition, in multilevel regression, the time variable is a predictor variable, which makes it easy to use the actual child ages rather than the measurement occasions (recent versions of SEM software like Mplus and Mx allow varying time-points as well but still have issues with widely varying numbers of measurement occasions). However, as MacCallum et al. have phrased it: "A wide range of models have equivalent representations in either framework" (MacCallum, Kim, Malarkey, & Kiecolt-Glaser, 1997, p. 246). The most important conclusion to draw from the comparison of GCM using a multilevel versus a structural equation approach is that these models are fundamentally the same but generally have a different representation in dedicated multilevel or SEM software. Hence, differences between these two approaches are more apparent than real (Bollen & Curran, 2006).

When the model presented in Figure 14.1 is estimated using conventional SEM software, the output highlights one important difference between the multilevel regression and the SEM approach. The SEM analysis produces the same estimates as the multilevel regression, but it also produces a global model test and several goodness-of-fit indices. The global chi-square test rejects the model ($\chi^2(5) = 174.6, p < 0.001$), and the fit indices indicate a very bad fit; Comparative Fit Index (CFI) = 0.78, Root Mean Square Error of Approximation (RMSEA) = 0.29 [95% CI 0.25–0.33]). This is important information that the multilevel regression approach does not provide. Further exploration of the model shows that the latent curve is decidedly nonlinear. If the slope loadings for readings 3 and 4 are estimated freely, then they are estimated as 1.6 and 2.1, respectively, which is quite different from the linear constraints of 2.0 and 3.0. The resulting model shows an excellent fit; ($\chi^2(3) = 4.3, p = 0.23$, CFI = 1.00, RMSEA = 0.03 [95% CI 0.00–0.11]). A more detailed multilevel regression analysis of these data in Hox (2010), using the actual child ages, also finds a strongly nonlinear curve.

Multilevel Structural Equation Modeling

The LCM is a real multilevel model, where the latent factors represent the random regression coefficients of the multilevel regression model, but it can be specified as a conventional single level structural model. Multilevel structural equation models in general need the aforementioned extensions in the SEM software to be estimated easily. Multilevel structural equation modeling assumes sampling at the individual and the group level, with both within-group (individual level) and between-group (group level) variation and covariation. In multilevel regression modeling, there is one dependent variable and several independent variables, with independent variables at both the individual and group level. At the group level, the multilevel regression model includes random regression coefficients and error terms. In the multilevel SEM, the random intercepts are second-level latent variables, capturing the variation in the means of the observed individual level variables. Some of the group level variables may be random slopes, drawn from the first level model, but other group level variables may be variables defined only at the group level, such as group size.

Mehta and Neale (2005) explain how multilevel SEM can be incorporated into conventional SEM. By viewing groups as observations, and individuals within groups as variables, they show that models for multilevel data can be specified in the full-information SEM framework. Unbalanced data—that is, unequal numbers of individuals within groups—are handled the same way as incomplete data in modern SEM estimation methods. So, in theory, multilevel SEM can be specified in any SEM package that supports FIML estimation for incomplete data. In practice, specialized software routines are used that take advantage of specific structures of multilevel data to achieve efficient computations and good convergence of the estimates. Extensions of this approach include extensions for categorical and ordinal data, incomplete data, and adding more levels. These are described in detail by Skrondal and Rabe-Hesketh (2004).

In two-level data, the observed individual level variables are modeled by:

$$y_W = \Lambda_W \eta_W + \varepsilon_W$$
$$\mu_B = \mu + \Lambda_B \eta_B + \varepsilon_B, \qquad (7)$$

where μ_B are the random intercepts for the variables y_W that vary across groups. The first equation models the within-groups variation, and the second equation models the between-groups variation and the group level means. By combining the within and between equations, we obtain

$$Y_{ij} = \mu + \Lambda_W \eta_W + \Lambda_B \eta_B + \varepsilon_B + \varepsilon_W. \quad (8)$$

In Equation 8, μ is the vector of group level means, Λ_W is the factor matrix at the within level, Λ_B is the factor matrix at the between level, and ε_W and ε_B are the residual errors at the within and the between level. With the exception of the notation, the structure of Equation 8 follows that of a random intercept regression model, with fixed regression coefficients (loadings) in the factor matrices Λ and a level-one and level-two error term. By allowing group level variation in the factor loadings, we can generalize this to a random coefficient model. The model in Equation 8 is a two-level factor model, by adding structural relationships between the latent factors at either level, we obtain a two-level SEM.

Multilevel SEMs are often estimated in separate steps. First, the intraclass correlations of the variables are inspected. If they are all small—for example, smaller than 0.05—the between-group variance is small and there may be no need for a complex group level model. The dependency in the data can be dealt with using standard analysis methods for cluster samples. If the between-group variances are considerable, then an investigation of the between structure is warranted. In general, because the sample size at the individual level is generally much larger than the sample size at the group level, the analysis is started with an analysis of the within structure. Standard analysis methods for clustered samples can be used here, such as the complex sample analysis methods used in survey research (cf. de Leeuw, Hox, & Dillman, 2008), which are implemented in, for example, Mplus. Next, the between structure is investigated in a two-level model with the within-structure fully specified.

Figure 14.2 depicts a two-level model that contains both observed and latent variables at both levels. It represents a model based on the theory of reasoned action (Ajzen & Fishbein, 1980) that predicts behavior from intention toward that behavior, and intention is in turn predicted from attitudes and social norms concerning that behavior. The attitudes and norms are latent factors, each indicated by three observed variables. In general, unless the intraclass correlation is 0, all observed variables exist at both the individual and the group level. Note that the variables that are observed variables at the individual level are latent variables at the group level; these

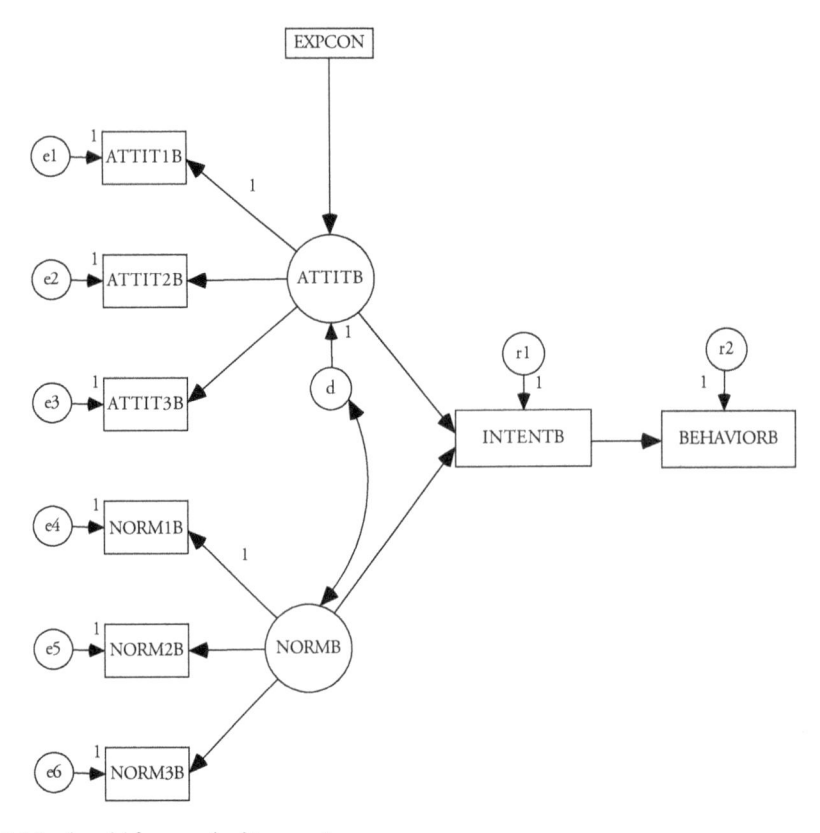

Figure 14.2 Multilevel model for group level intervention.

latent variables represent the group-level variation of the intercepts. There is one variable that exists only at the group level. The variable *expcon* represents some experimental intervention at the group level, aimed at changing the attitude toward the behavior. If the groups are assigned at random to the intervention or the control condition, then this example represents a group randomized trial.

Example data were generated directly from the model, for 100 groups of 10 subjects each and intraclass correlations of around 0.10, which is relatively high but not unusual. All variables are continuous; to simplify the modeling the intervention variable is ordered categorical with five categories.

The model depicted in Figure 14.2 is estimated using Mplus (Muthén & Muthén, 1998–2010). The program reports the intraclass correlations for all observed variables; these range from 0.15 to 0.22. Thus, multilevel modeling of these data is justified. The fit of the model is excellent ($\chi^2(44) = 26.7$, $p = 0.98$, CFI = 1.00, RMSEA = 0.00), which is unsurprising because the example data were generated from this model.

The model illustrates some issues that occur more generally in two-level SEM. First, we have a measurement model that specifies how attitude and norms are measured by the observed variables. Because the measurement model is the same at both levels, the question arises if we can impose equality constraints on the factor loadings across the two levels. If we impose these four constraints, the chi-square increases by 3.748, which with four degrees of freedom is not significant ($p = 0.44$). Table 14.4 presents the unstandardized factor loadings after imposing the equality constraints. Because we have established that there is measurement equivalence

Table 14.4. Unstandardized Factor Loadings (Standard Errors) for Attitude and Norms

Attit1	1.00*	–
Attit1	1.00(0.06)	–
Attit1	0.98(0.05)	–
Norm1	–	1.00*
Norm2	–	0.98(0.05)
Norm3	–	0.98(0.05)

Note: * indicates constrained for identification. Correlation between factors estimated as 0.50 (within) and 0.69 (between).

Table 14.5. Direct and Indirect Paths from Intervention to Behavior, Group Level

Dependent	Independent (mediating) variables path coefficient (standard error)		
	Intervention	Attitude	Intention
Attitude	0.52 (0.12)	–	–
Intention	0.34 (0.08)	0.64 (0.09)	–
Behavior	0.25 (0.07)	0.49 (0.08)	0.75 (0.06)

across the two levels, we can proceed to calculate the intraclass correlations for the two latent factors. If we specify a model without the intervention variable, then the intraclass correlation for attitude is 0.20 and for norms 0.16. The intraclass correlation for attitude is inflated because part of the variance in attitude is caused by the group-level intervention. If we analyze the model including the intervention variable, then the intraclass correlation for attitude is estimated as 0.17; this could be interpreted as a partial intraclass correlation, disregarding the variance in attitude caused by the intervention.

In addition to the inclusion of latent variables, SEM allows estimating and testing indirect effects. In our example, the effect of the intervention on the behavior is mediated at the group level by attitude and intention. Table 14.5 shows the standardized direct and indirect effects of the paths leading from the intervention to behavior, at the group (between) level.

The group-level explained variances are 0.27 for attitude, 0.74 for intention, and 0.57 for behavior. Predictably, the effect of the intervention becomes smaller when the chain of mediating variables becomes longer. The explained variance of the intervention on the attitude is 0.27, which translates to a correlation of 0.52—in Cohen's (1988) terms, a large effect size. In this example, the mediation is entirely at the group level. It is possible to model mediation chains where the group-level intervention affects individual-level variables (latent or observed) that in turn affect group or individual level outcomes. Especially when random slopes are involved, multilevel mediation is a complex phenomenon, and I refer to MacKinnon (2008) for a thorough discussion of the details.

Methodological and Statistical Issues
Assumptions

Multilevel regression and SEM make the same assumptions as their single-level counterparts. So, multilevel regression analysis assumes perfectly measured predictor variables, linearity of relationships, normal residual errors, homoscedasticity, and independence conditional on the grouping variables in the model. In addition, it assumes that the residual errors at the separate levels are independent. Structural equation modeling can incorporate a measurement model; thus, there is no assumption that variables are measured without measurement error, but otherwise the assumptions are much the same.

Investigating potential violations of assumptions is more complicated in multilevel models than in their single-level counterparts. For example, if there are random slopes in the model, then at the group level there is a set of residuals that are generally assumed to have a multivariate normal distribution. Investigating the normality assumption here implies investigating all residuals. In addition, the model itself is more complex. For example, Bauer and Cai (2009) have shown that if a nonlinear effect is not modeled as such, then this misspecification may show up as an entirely spurious variance parameter for a slope or a spurious cross-level interaction effect. Wright (1997) has shown that in multilevel logistic regression, sparse data resulting from skewed distributions or small samples may result in spurious overdispersion (a variance larger than implied by the underlying binomial distribution). So, investigating assumptions is both more difficult and more important in multilevel models. Specialized multilevel software such as HLM and MLwiN incorporate many procedures for investigating assumptions that are specific to multilevel regression models, but more general software like SAS, SPSS, or Mplus for multilevel SEM do not incorporate such features and rely completely on the ingenuity of the researcher to devise diagnostic checks.

Sample Size

In multilevel modeling, the most important limitation on sample size is generally the second or higher level, because the higher level sample sizes are usually smaller than the lower level sample sizes. Eliason (1993) recommends a minimum sample size of 60 when maximum likelihood estimation is used. In multilevel modeling, this would apply to the highest level. Maas and Hox (2005) have found that in multilevel regression modeling, a highest level sample size as low as 20 may be sufficient for accurate estimation, provided that the interest is in the regression coefficients and their standard errors. If the interest is in the variance estimates, then the higher level sample sizes must be much larger, and Maas and Hox have recommended at least 100 groups (although 50 groups may suffice for small models). Multilevel SEM are fundamentally based on the within-group and between-group covariance matrices, and hence it is not surprising that the recommendation for the accurate estimation of higher level variances in multilevel regression carries over to SEM: at least 100 groups are recommended, but in small models 50 groups may suffice (Hox, Maas, & Brinkhuis, 2010).

Unequal sample sizes at any of the levels are not a problem, as the model does not assume equal sample sizes at all. Missing values resulting from missing occasions or panel dropout can be dealt with easily in longitudinal models. However, incomplete data at the higher level are more difficult to handle. Structural equation software is sometimes able to analyze incomplete data directly using full information maximum likelihood procedures, but most multilevel software does not have such provisions. Multiple imputation is an option, but the problem is that the imputation model must also be a multilevel model. Van Buuren (2011) has discussed incomplete multilevel data in detail.

Small sample sizes at the lowest level do not pose a problem by themselves. For example, multilevel models have proven valuable in analysis of dyadic data, such as couples or twins (Atkins, 2005). Even groups of size 1 are fine, provided other groups are larger. However, small groups present some limitations, especially to the complexity of the within-groups (individual level) model. A model with a random intercept and one random slope is just identified, and more complex models cannot be estimated (Newsom, 2002). For a recent review of multilevel models for dyadic data, *see* Kenny and Kashy (2011).

Further Important Issues

In multilevel modeling, predictor variables are sometimes centered on some value. Centering on a single value, usually the grand mean of the predictor variable, poses no special problems. It facilitates estimation—especially when multicollinearity is present—and makes the interpretation of interactions easier. Centering predictor variables on their respective group means is different. Group mean centering totally changes the meaning of the model and should be used with caution. In particular, group mean centering removes all information about the group means from the model. Adding the group means as predictor variables to the model solves that issue, but the resulting model is still fundamentally different from a model that incorporates the original uncentered predictor variables. Enders and Tofighi (2006) have discussed these issues in detail and have provided some guidelines for when group mean centering is appropriate.

Effect sizes are somewhat problematic in multilevel models. In general, calculating explained variance is not different from calculating explained variance in similar single-level models. However, in multilevel modeling, one would want to be able to establish how much variance is explained at each of the available levels. This turns out to be problematic. Simply using the reduction in residual variance when predictor variables are added as suggested in Raudenbush and Bryk (2002) does not work, as this procedure can result in impossible values such as negative explained variances (Hox, 2010; Snijders & Bosker, 1994). There have been several proposals to cope with this problem (Roberts, Monaco, Stovall, & Foster, 2011; Snijders & Bosker, 1999), but these tend to be complicated and to have their own problems. In the end, Hox (2010) has recommended using the simple method (Raudenbush & Bryk, 2002), in combination with grand mean-centered predictors, and interpreting the resulting values as indicative, rather than mathematical truth.

In regression and SEM, the interest is often mostly on the fixed coefficients—that is, the regression coefficients, factor loadings, and path coefficients. Their significance can be tested using their standard errors. In latent growth models and in multilevel SEM, there is often considerable substantive interest in the variance components as well—for example, in testing whether the higher level variances are significant. Testing variances using the standard error is generally not a very accurate approach, because variances do not have a normal distribution. For significance testing, the recommended method is comparing a model that includes the variance component with a model that does not include it, using a likelihood ratio test or the equivalent deviance difference test (cf. Berkhof & Snijders, 2001). Establishing correct confidence intervals for variance components is possible using multilevel bootstrap methods (Goldstein, 2011) or Bayesian approaches (Hamaker & Klugkist, 2011).

The multilevel regression and the multilevel SEM were originally developed for continuous and (multivariate) normal variables. Both have been extended to include non-normal variables, such as dichotomous, ordered categorical, or count variables. With such variables, estimation problems tend to occur.

For multilevel logistic regression, estimation procedures have been developed based on Taylor series linearization of the nonlinear likelihood. These methods are approximate, and in some circumstances (such as the combination of small groups and high intraclass correlations) the approximation is not very good. Numerical methods that maximize the correct likelihood are superior (Agresti, Booth, Hobart, & Caffo, 2000), but they can be computationally intensive, especially in models that contain a large number of random effects. For such models, Bayesian estimation procedures are attractive. Some general software for multilevel modeling, such as MLwiN and Mplus, include Bayesian estimation options. General Bayesian modeling software such as (Win)BUGS can be used for multilevel modeling, but these require more complicated set-ups. For an introduction to Bayesian multilevel modeling, I refer the reader to Hamaker and Klugkist (2011), and a detailed discussion including set-ups in BUGS is given by Gelman and Hill (2007).

Conclusion

Multilevel models are increasingly used in a variety of fields. Initially these models were viewed as a means to properly analyze hierarchical data, with individual cases or measures nested within larger units such as groups. Although such applications still abound, applications have come to include models for cross-classified hierarchical data, dyadic data, network analysis, meta-analysis, and spatial modeling. The common characteristic of these models is that they contain complex relationships involving random effects. Multilevel analysis is a tool that allows great flexibility in the actual modeling, which is why it is an attractive option in analyzing these complex models.

Future Directions

As has been noted, multilevel models can be specified as simple SEM that can be analyzed using standard structural equation software. In practice, this leads to model set-ups that are unwieldy, and recent SEM software has incorporated special features to accommodate multilevel models. At the time of writing, multilevel structural equation software has practical limitations, such as a limited number of levels, convergence problems, or long execution times. As software development continues, structural equation software will outgrow these limitations.

Glossary of Key terms

Between groups	Model for the structure at the group level. Usual term in two-level SEM to refer to the group (second) level. As three- and more-level SEM develops, this term is becoming unclear, and better replaced with a reference to the level of interest (e.g., class or school level).
Cross-level interaction	Higher level variables may have a direct effect on the outcome in a multilevel model, or they may affect the effects of lower level variables on the outcome. This is generally modeled by an interaction between a higher level and a lower level predictor variable.
Fixed effect, fixed coefficient	Regression coefficients (including factor loadings and path coefficients) that do not vary across higher level units.
Intraclass correlation	The estimate of the similarity in the population between individuals belonging to the same group. Also defined as the proportion of variance (in the population) at the group level.
Mixed model	A model that contains both fixed effects and random effects.
Multilevel model	A model that contains variables defined at different levels of a hierarchically structured population. Other terms used are hierarchical linear model, mixed model and random coefficient model. Although these models are not identical, in practice these terms are often used interchangeably.
Random effect, random coefficient	Regression coefficients (including factor loadings and path coefficients) that are assumed to vary across higher level units. They are generally assumed to have a normal distribution with a mean of zero and some variance that is estimated.
Variance component	Generally used to refer to the higher level variances and covariances of the varying coefficients. In multilevel analysis of longitudinal data specific structures are sometimes assumed for the variances and covariances over time.
Within groups	Model for the structure at the lowest level. Usual term in two-level SEM to refer to the individual (first) level. As three- and more-level SEM develops, this term is becoming unclear and better replaced with a reference to the level of interest (e.g., individual or measurement-occasion level).

An extended glossary to key terms used in multilevel regression modeling is presented by Diez Roux (2002).

Symbols used

β_{pj}	Regression coefficient for variable p varying at the level indicated by j
γ_p	Fixed regression coefficient for variable p
π	Regression coefficient for time or measurement occasion indictor
u_{pj}	Residual error term for variable p varying at the level indicated by j
σ_u^2	Variance of residual error u
σ_e^2	Variance of lowest level residual error e
Λ	Factor matrix, subscript B or W indicates Between/Within level
η	Factor score, subscript B or W indicates Between/Within level

A difficult problem in actual research is often obtaining a large enough sample on the higher levels; the maximum likelihood estimation method requires a reasonable sample size to be accurate. Bayesian methods are promising in this respect—they tend to be more stable with smaller sample sizes and will always generate parameter values that are within their proper boundaries. However, Bayesian methods are still undergoing rapid development, and standard software lags behind in their implementation. As standard software (as opposed to specialized Bayesian software such as WINBUGS) develops to incorporate Bayesian methods (at the time of writing already available in the software MLwiN and Mplus), it is expected that their use will increase.

A problem that still awaits a good solution is incomplete multilevel data, including missing data at the higher levels. In SEM, estimation methods have been developed that provide parameter estimates based on the incomplete data themselves; no listwise or pairwise deletion or imputation of missing values is involved. Estimation methods for multilevel models generally lack this flexibility. In addition, multilevel multiple imputation must be considered to be in its infancy. Given the requirement that the imputation model must be at least as complex as the analysis model, developing proper procedures for multilevel multiple imputation is a daunting task.

Author Note

Joop Hox, Department of Methodology and Statistics, Faculty of Social Sciences, Utrecht University, the Netherlands, j.hox@uu.nl, www.joophox.net.

References

Agresti, A., Booth, J.G., Hobart, J.P., & Caffo, B. (2000). Random effects modeling of categorical response data, *Sociological Methodology, 2000, 30*, 27–80.

Aiken, L.S., & West, S.G. (1991). *Multiple regression: Testing and interpreting interaction*. Newbury Park, CA: Sage.

Ajzen, I., & Fishbein, M. (1980). *Understanding attitudes and predicting social behavior*. Englewood Cliffs, NJ: Prentice-Hall.

Akaike, H. (1987). Factor analysis and the AIC. *Psychometrika, 52*, 317–332.

Atkins, D.C. (2005). Using multilevel models to analyze couple and family treatment data: Basic and advanced issues. *Journal of Family Psychology, 19*, 98–110.

Bauer, D.J., & Cai, L. (2009). Consequences of unmodeled nonlinear effects in multilevel models. *Journal of Educational and Behavioral Statistics, 34*, 97–114.

Berkhof, J. & Snijders, T.A.B. (2001). Variance component testing in multilevel models. *Journal of Educational end Behavioral Statistics, 26*, 133–152.

Bickel, R. (2007). *Multilevel analysis for applied research: It's just regression!* New York: Guilford Press.

Bollen, K.A. & Curran, P.J. (2006). *Latent curve models*. New York: Wiley.

Bryk, A.S., & Raudenbush, S.W. (1992). *Hierarchical linear models*. Newbury Park, CA: Sage.

van Buuren, S. (2011). Multiple imputation of multilevel data. In J.J. Hox & J.K. Roberts (Eds). *Handbook of Advanced Multilevel Analysis* (pp. 173–196). New York: Routledge.

Cohen, J. (1988). *Statistical power analysis for the behavioral sciences*. Mahwah, NJ: Lawrence Erlbaum Associates.

Curran, P.J. (1997). *Supporting Documentation for Comparing Three Modern Approaches to Longitudinal Data Analysis: An Examination of a Single Developmental Sample*. Retrieved, May 2012 from http://www.unc.edu/ ~curran/srcd.html.

Diez Roux, A.V. (2002). A glossary for multilevel analysis. *Journal of Epidemiology and Community Health, 56*, 588–594.

Eliason, S.R. (1993). *Maximum Likelihood estimation*. Newbury Park, CA: Sage.

Enders, C.K., & Tofighi, D. (2006). Centering predictor variables in cross-sectional multilevel models: a new look at an old issue. *Psychological Methods, 12*, 121–138.

Gelman, A., & Hill, J. (2007). *Data analysis using regression and multilevel/hierarchical models*. New York: Cambridge University Press.

Goldstein, H. (1987). *Multilevel models in educational and social research*. London: Griffin/New York: Oxford University Press.

Goldstein, H. (2011). Bootstrapping in multilevel models. In J.J. Hox & J.K. Roberts (Eds). *Handbook of advanced multilevel analysis.* (pp. 163–172). New York: Routledge.

Hamaker, E.L., & Klugkist, I. (2011). Bayesian estimation of multilevel models. In J.J. Hox & J.K. Roberts (Eds.). *Handbook of advanced multilevel analysis.* (pp. 137–162). New York: Routledge.

Hox, J.J. (2002). *Multilevel analysis: Techniques and applications*. Mahwah, NJ: Erlbaum.

Hox, J.J. (2010). *Multilevel analysis: Techniques and applications. Second edition*. New York: Routledge.

Hox, J.J., Maas, C.J.M., & Brinkhuis, M.J.S. (2010). The effect of estimation method and sample size in multilevel structural equation modeling. *Statistica Neerlandica, 64*, 157–170.

Hüttner, H.J.M., & Van den Eeden, P. (1995). The multilevel design. London: Greenwood Press.

Kenny, D.A., & Kashy, D.A. (2011). Dyadic data analysis using multilevel modeling. In J.J. Hox & J.K. Roberts (Eds.). *Handbook of advanced multilevel analysis.* (pp. 335–370). New York: Routledge.

de Leeuw, E.D., Hox, J.J. & Dillman, D.A. (Eds.) (2008). *The International Handbook of Survey Methodology*. New York: Taylor & Francis.

Maas, C. J. M., & Hox, J. J. (2005). Sufficient Sample Sizes for Multilevel Modeling. *Methodology: European Journal of Research Methods for the Behavioral and Social Sciences, 1*, 85–91.

MacCallum, R.C., Kim, C., Malarkey, W.B., & Kiecolt-Glaser, J.C. (1997). Studying multivariate change using multilevel models and latent curve models. *Multivariate Behavioral Research, 32*, 215–253.

Mackinnon, D.P. (2008). Introduction to statistical mediation analysis. New York: Taylor & Francis.

Mehta, P.D., & Neale, M.C. (2005), People are variables too: multilevel structural equations modeling. *Psychological Methods*, *10*, 259–284.

Muthén, B.O. (1994). Multilevel covariance structure analysis. *Sociological Methods and Research*, *22*, 376–398.

Muthén, L.K. and Muthén, B.O. (1998–2010). Mplus User's Guide. Sixth Edition. Los Angeles, CA: Muthén & Muthén.

Newsom, J.T. (2002). A multilevel structural equation model for dyadic data. *Structural Equation Modeling*, *9*, 431–447.

Raudenbush, S.W., & Bryk, A.S. (2002). *Hierarchical linear models*. Second Edition. Thousand Oaks, CA: Sage.

Roberts, J.K., Monaco, J.P., Stovall, H., & Foster, V. (2011). Explained variance in multilevel models. In J.J. Hox & J.K. Roberts (Eds.). *Handbook of advanced multilevel analysis*. (pp. 219–230). New York: Routledge.

Singer, J.D., & Willett, J.B. (2003). *Applied Longitudinal Data Analysis: Modeling Change and Event Occurrence*. Oxford, United Kingdom: Oxford University Press.

Skrondal, A., & Rabe-Hesketh, S. (2004). *Generalized Latent Variable Modeling: Multilevel, Longitudinal and Structural Equation Models*. Boca Raton, FL: Chapman & Hall/CRC.

Snijders, T.A.B., & Bosker, R. (1994). Modeled variance in two-level models. *Sociological Methods & Research*, *22*, 342–363.

Snijders, T.A.B., & Bosker, R. (1999). *Multilevel analysis. An introduction to basic and advanced multilevel modeling*. Thousand Oaks, CA: Sage.

Wright, D.B. (1997). Extra-binomial variation in multilevel logistic models with sparse structures. *British Journal of Mathematical and Statistical Psychology*, *50*, 21–29.

CHAPTER
15 Structural Equation Models

John J. McArdle *and* Kelly M. Kadlec

Abstract

The purpose of this chapter is to present an accessible overview of recent research on what are termed *structural equation models* (SEM). This presentation is intended for graduate level students in the behavioral sciences, possibly taking a SEM class, but formal algebra or calculus is not required. First, SEM is broadly defined, and the increasing use of this approach to data analysis is described. In general, SEM techniques are increasingly used in the behavioral and social sciences. Second, some technical features of SEM are presented to illustrate key benefits of SEM. Some classical issues are described that highlight issues SEM researchers usually find to be important, and the big appeal of SEM comes when if offers some hope to deal with these issues. Third, we consider the inclusion of common factors as latent variables in path models that can be incorporated into SEM. We claim that the inclusion of common factors is what really makes SEM different than other statistical approaches. Fourth, we describe how SEM calculation works, and this gives rise to various indices of goodness-of-fit. Many researchers herald these techniques, although this seems to be a leftover from prior statistical training. Fifth, we provide an illustration of contemporary data generation and computer programming (using CALIS, Mplus, and OpenMx). In the final section, we illustrate some options from our previous SEM work, answer specific questions about SEM practices, and include a discussion of issues for future SEM uses.

Key Words: Structural equation models, LISREL, RAM, confirmatory factor analysis, latent variable path analysis, factorial invariance over time, latent curve analysis, cross-lagged panel analysis, time series analysis, dynamic factor analysis

Introduction

"The effect of a concept-driven revolution is to explain old things in new ways. The effect of a tool-driven revolution is to discover new things that have to be explained." (originally from Sir Frank Dyson, 1891; see Freeman Dyson, 1997, Imagined Worlds, pp. 50–51).

We think it is fair to say that recent research involving *structural equation models* (SEM) constitutes *both* a concept-driven revolution and a tool-driven revolution. That is, principles of SEMs can be used both for developing concepts and these same principles can also be used as data analyses tools. What makes SEM unique is the emphasis on using unobserved or *latent variables* (LVs). This chapter will define these two separate SEM functions, the concepts and the tools, and then try to bring them back together with some examples.

Structural Equation Models Defined

The popular term *structural equation models* (SEM) can be used to represent many different kinds of multivariable ideas. Statistical analyses as seemingly diverse as analysis of variance (ANOVA), multiple regression, factor analysis, path analysis, multidimensional scaling, time series analysis, and so on, can be organized under the same SEM heading. This generalization is correct because in all such cases, we consider SEM a reflection of three key ideas in modern statistical data analysis: (1) The term "model" is used to represent a "theory" in terms of propositions about the relationships between variables. (2) The term "equation" means that the relationships between variables are expressed in a formal fashion using the strict rules of algebra. (3) The term "structural" is used to suggest that these algebraic equations form a specific restrictive pattern about real data that is consistent with the model, and hence the theory.

Any SEM representation of the model scores is used to create expectations about the basic summary statistics—means and covariances—of the observed data. This is important because these expectations can be compared to the data observations to form a test of goodness-of-fit—that is, expected means (μ) compared to observed means (**m**), and expected covariances (Σ) compared to observed covariances (**S**). This also highlights one of the big limitations of SEM—we only compare means and covariances, so any other potential model versus data differences (i.e., skewness) are assumed not to be critical. Of course, this is also true of many other data analysis techniques, such as multiple regression and ANOVA, principal components and factor analysis, and canonical correlation and regression, so SEM is a natural generalization of this classic work.

Given these statistical limits, many scientific theories can be represented as testable models. Most importantly, SEM gives researchers a way to represent theories as models using LVs that are not directly measured. This is easy to do and is a major benefit of SEM because many key constructs in the behavioral sciences simply cannot be directly observed and measured. Of course, hypothesis testing is not always possible because our theories can quickly require more elaborations than we can do with the available data. We are consoled only because we will know that our model, and hence our theory, is far beyond any evaluation by our available data.

If we create a SEM on an *a priori* basis, we can then determine how well the expected model fits the observed data by calculating a variety of *a priori* defined "goodness-of-fit" indices. Unfortunately, any truly confirmatory analysis requires a great deal of prior information. For example, to really test any model, we would probably need to have point hypotheses about all the group (i.e., fixed) parameters (i.e., the one-headed arrows). This is not the typical case, and we often settle for testing the pattern or structural hypotheses of the parameters—that is,

is a specific correlation equal to the product of two parameters? Under these less rigid conditions, and if we assume all residuals are normally distributed, we can compare the model-based "likelihood-ratio" to a "chi-square" distribution and determine the probability of observing such an event—this model for these data—at random. This approach, of course, is virtually identical to calculating a *p*-value in an ANOVA or Regression model context (although a typical SEM often has more parameters), so all the assumptions and inference problems are similar as well. Although many people find SEM to have alleviated most statistical problems, it has not. Poor quality data will not miraculously provide robust results, just as cause-and-effect relationships cannot easily be formed from observational data. What SEM has done, and in a classical way, is allowed the representation of complex theories as complex models, and the basic expressions of models in terms of equations, so they can easily be used to examine ideas about the structure of a data set. Incidentally, we recognize that not all SEMs are based on *a priori* theory, and basically all we now ask is that SEM researchers try to tell us what they actually did (*see* McArdle, 2010).

When we consider SEM in this fashion, we find SEM is all around us, and it has been here for a very long time. The broad ideas of SEM, as both concept and tool, probably started with the "common factor analysis" model of Spearman (1904; *see* Horn & McArdle, 1980, 1992, 2007), and this led to extensions such as the "path analysis" concepts of Wright (1918, 1934) and the "variance components" ideas of Fisher (1918, 1924; *see* Li, 1975). These SEM ideas seemed to be dormant in academic research for about 50 years and only recently revived by a combination of the efforts of quantitatively minded sociologists (*see* Duncan, 1975; Goldberger & Duncan, 1973; Hauser & Goldberger, 1971) and psychologists (e.g., Werts & Linn, 1970). The early SEM seemed to be largely based on its conceptual and theoretical advantages rather than on the creation of analytic tools. But it also seems fair to say that these SEM concepts have enjoyed a revival in the last few decades, partially based on the generation of new SEM tools.

Confirmatory Factor Analysis and the Popular LISREL Movement

The current forms of SEM really took on a life of their own when they were placed into the context of what was termed a "confirmatory factor analysis" with "LVs (see Joreskog, 1973; McDonald, 1985). This approach was probably best represented in the general framework termed the *Linear Structural Equations Model* (LISREL; Joreskog, 1973; Wiley, 1973; Joreskog & Sorbom, 1979). In the LISREL approach, the researchers were interested in creating a general approach to data analysis, but one that was far more general than the ANOVA-based *general linear model* (see Bock, 1975; Muller & Stewart, 2006). LISREL advocates seemed to suggest that we should always consider an analytic framework that included hypotheses about "unobserved" variables based on both means and covariances.

In simplest terms, the LISREL concept suggested that the econometric concept of multivariable regression could be merged with the psychometric concepts of common factors (for example, see Wiley, 1973). That is, in the LISREL approach we may have many X-variables (i.e., independent, inputs, predictors, exogenous, or right-hand side) and many Y-variables (i.e., dependent, outputs, endogenous, or left-hand side), and as usual, the X-variables can affect the Y-variables with specific coefficients. However, rather than simply calculating multiple regression coefficients for entire sets of predictors and outcomes, the LISREL model allowed researchers to pose hypotheses about the relationships between unobserved common factors with common factor scores; specifically, unobserved common factors of X-side (or left hand side) variables could be thought of as based on common factor scores (termed η, although not estimated), and Y-side (or left hand side) variables could also have common factor scores (termed ξ, although not estimated). The Y-side factors could then be regressed on the X-side factors, possibly with additional constraints such as some regression coefficients being zero. These equations for the scores could be represented in X-side matrices of factor loadings (Λ_x), unique covariances (Θ_δ), and common factor covariances (Φ), whereas the common factors of the Y-side variables could be represented with factor loadings (Λ_y), unique covariances (Θ_ε) regressions between the Y-side common factors and the X-side common factors (Γ), regressions within the Y-side common factors (B), and all with common factor residual covariances (Ψ^2).

This fairly complex LISREL concept allowed researchers to place their theories in terms of unobserved constructs and still provide tests of goodness-of-fit using observables. It seems to us that LISREL would not have gained such momentum if it were not associated with a working computer program—the SEM concept was matched with a SEM tool! In fact, the flexible computer programming of the first versions of LISREL (see Joreskog & Sorbom, 1979; McDonald, 1985) allowed the unknown elements in these eight matrices of parameters to be (1) fixed at known values, (2) free to be estimated, or (3) estimated but equal to a different parameter. This new computer programming tool was a true innovation and came directly from the work of Joreskog (1969; see Lawley & Maxwell, 1971), where many new ideas for data analysis were emerging (e.g., Nesselroade & Baltes, 1984).

The SEM-LISREL approach allowed researchers both to think more clearly about what they were saying and, at the same time, fit models to data in ways that could not be done previously. This is viewed as a combination of concepts and tools. SEM-LISREL could be considered useful for its conceptual advances or because it added important tools (computer calculations) for behavioral scientists. For these kinds of reasons, it has been difficult to summarize all the advantages of SEM in one way (e.g., see Stapleton & Leite, 2005).

One thing that is clear is that the notion of confirmatory or *a priori* hypothesis-driven modeling represented powerful conceptual thinking. At the time LISREL was initiated, there was much work on the generic testing of hypotheses about specific multivariate patterns of group means, including repeated measures (see Bock, 1975; O'Brien & Kaiser, 1985). However, these statistical tests of mean differences were carried out within a severely limited framework for hypotheses about covariances (see Rao, 1965; Joreskog, 1973). Thus, the SEM-LISREL program was a tool that permitted analyses well beyond the standard framework of estimation and tests of mean differences in the ANOVA-based general linear model."

Because of the broad generality of the SEM-LISREL idea, and despite all the unfamiliar and occasionally odd choices of Greek terminology (i.e., Was there any real benefit in adding Greek letters for the unobserved and unestimated factors?), the SEM-LISREL concept and the related computer program became very popular because SEM-LISREL allowed seemingly unlimited ways to estimate and test hypotheses about both means and covariances. For these reasons, SEM-LISREL was studied and used in great depth (see Joreskog & Sorbom, 1979; see Horn & McArdle, 1980; Meredith, 1993; Meredith & Horn, 2001) and is still popular today.

The Current Status of Structural Equation Model Research

The early SEM research seems to have been focused on the concepts, whereas more recent SEM research seems to be focused on the tools. But it is a bit difficult to know exactly who is using SEM for what purpose. One recent article by Stapleton and Leite (2005) attempted to summarize all current SEM syllabi in classroom usage, but the classic conceptual treatments were necessarily overlooked. There are also online blogs (SEM-NET) and Internet websites devoted to the SEM enterprise, but the same could be said about almost any faddish idea.

To consider this question of current SEM usage more seriously now, we conducted a Google Scholar search for scholarly articles containing the phrase "Structural Equation Model," "Structural Equation Models," or "Structural Equation Modeling" in their title (and done about 08/2010). We excluded (1) articles that had only been cited, rather than found online; (2) patents; and (3) legal opinions and journals. Separate searches were conducted for seven disciplines identified by Google Scholar: (1) Biology, Life Sciences, and Environmental Science; (2) Business, Administration, Finance, and Economics; (3) Chemistry and Materials Science; (4) Engineering, Computer Science, and Mathematics; (5) Medicine, Pharmacology, and Veterinary Science; (6) Physics, Astronomy, and Planetary Science; and (7) Social Sciences, Arts, and Humanities. Within each discipline, we searched by date starting with articles published between 1900 and 1999, followed by yearly searches between 2000 and 2010.

Our search produced a total of $N = 1,810$ articles. Across disciplines, 22% of the articles on SEM were published during the twentieth century, whereas 78% were published during the first decade of the twenty-first century. A preponderance of the articles ($n = 856$; 47%) were published in the social sciences/arts/humanities, followed by engineering/computer science/mathematics ($n = 483$; 27%), and then business/administration/finance/economics ($n = 378$; 21%). In Figure 15.1 we have plotted the frequency of the term SEM in these articles over the past decade, and we can easily see that these three disciplines have also showed a steady increase of articles on SEM between 2000 and 2009. We did not distinguish the repeated authors, although we are certain there are many, and we did not take into account the likely increase in the number of overall publications. However, it is clear that almost half of scholarly articles on SEM are being produced by social scientists, and most all of them seem to be using SEM mainly as a new tool. But it seems that the SEM tools are now largely used in an appropriate fashion—to examine the utility of theoretical ideas about the effects of unobservable variables in terms of observable relationships.

Structural Equation Modeling As a Concept

A simple regression analysis (Fig. 15.2) does not really stimulate us to use SEM in any way, but some aspects of the formal basis of structural regression provide the needed motivation. In this case, the classic treatment of SEM by Goldberger (1973; in Goldberger & Duncan, 1973) is worth reconsidering. Goldberger initially suggested that the reason we do not use regression on all of our data

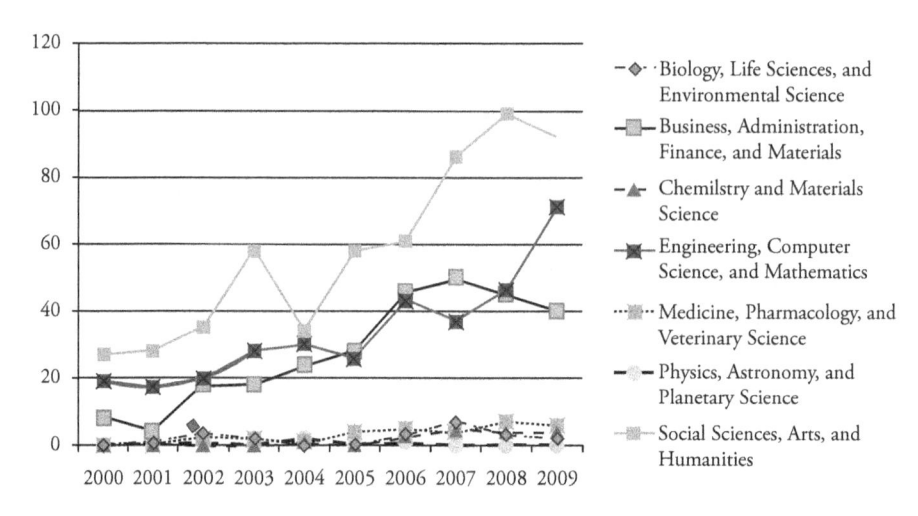

Figure 15.1 A Chart of recent SEM publications.

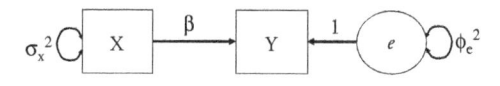

$\sigma_x^2 \bigcirc X \xrightarrow{\beta} Y \xleftarrow{1} e \bigcirc \phi_e^2$

Note: Estimates are typically calculated as
$\beta = \sigma_{yx} \sigma_{xx}^{-1}$
$\sigma_e^2 = \sigma_y^2 - (\beta \sigma_{xx} \beta')$

Figure 15.2 A simple linear regression model with no intercept.

analysis problems is that the simple linear model of regression is often incorrect and our results are biased. To be sure, it was well known that non-linear relations may exist and additional predictor variables may be needed, but this was a larger problem. Indeed, this may surprise some readers who do not think of regression analysis as a concept, Goldberger starts with the idea that regression analysis is used to make a "statement about causes" (*see also* Pearl, 2000). Goldberger seems to make the case that our standard data analyses should not be a search for the "highest" explained variance (i.e., maximum predictability) but the "correct" explained variance (i.e., maximum replicability). Of course, we can only begin to think this is true when our regression parameters remain the same from one analysis to another—Goldberger terms this principle "invariance" (p. 2). The search for invariance of parameters has now become a very basic principle in SEM.

In general, this means any regression analysis can be incorrect for a number of reasons, leading to "biased" coefficients. Goldberger shows how SEM concepts and algebra can be used to consider the resulting biases, and his basic concepts will be demonstrated here using both algebra and path diagrams.

Using Path Analyses Diagrams

We often presume that one of the observed variables (X) is an input to the other (Y). For simplicity, it is typical to eliminate the intercept (β_0) and calculate a single linear regression coefficient (β) to describe an X → Y relationship. We write the linear regression expression

$$Y_n = \beta_0 + \beta_1 X_n + e_n, \quad (1a)$$

where the Greek letters are used to represent population parameters to be estimated, the intercept (β_0), and slope (β_1), and the residual scores (*e*) are not directly observed. We also assume

$$E\{XX'\} = \sigma_x^2, E\{ee'\} = \phi_e^2, \text{ and}$$
$$E\{Xe'\} = 0, \quad (1b)$$

where the *E* is a symbol used for the expected values (rather than the usual summation symbol). This combined expression is considered the "structural equation model for the observed scores."

One other useful feature—the path diagram—was originally a conceptual device. The relation of the algebraic equations and the path diagram is important, useful, and may explain some of the popularity of SEM among novices. In any path diagram used here, observed variables are drawn as squares, unobserved variables are drawn as circles, and a constant (needed when means or intercepts are used) is included as a triangle. Using this notation, a path diagram of the traditional model of simple linear regression is depicted in Figure 15.2. This model has three variables: (1) an observed outcome (Y); (2) an observed predictor (X); and (3) an unobserved residual (*e*). The model also has three basic parameters: (1) a slope (β), (2) the variance of the predictor (σ_x^2), and (3) the variance of the residual (ϕ_e^2).

Perhaps it is obvious that this path diagram is not a plot of the raw data but, rather, a topographical representation of some of the assumptions in the model of analysis—that is, the residual has no mean, no correlation with the predictor, and so on. The path diagram does not say anything about the distribution requirements for the predictor X (this can be most anything) or the residuals—that is, the unobserved residual scores (*e*) need to be "normally distributed" for the statistical tests to be exact. One might reasonably ask, "Do we need to know all this just to define a simple linear regression?" The answer to this question depends on what we are going to do next.

These path diagrams can be conceptually useful devices for understanding basic concepts or tools. These diagrams are conceptually useful because they require a potentially complex theory to be portrayed in a single display. These diagrams are also practically useful as a tool because they can be used to represent the input and output of any of the SEM computer programs. But one note of caution is important: The SEM path diagrams do not fully substitute for the SEM algebraic interpretations, so the SEM diagrams can often be misleading. A few examples are described later.

By assuming that the residuals are independent ($E[X,e] = 0$) of the predictors, we know (from calculus) that the best estimate of this coefficient can be found by multiplying the observed covariance of Y and X (σ_{yx}) by the inverse of the variance of X (σ_{xx}^{-1}). That is, if we write

$$Y_n = \beta X_n \quad (2a)$$

or $(Y_n X_n') = \beta(X_n X_n')$,

then $(Y_n X_n')[(X_n X_n')]^{-1} = \beta$

or $\beta = E[YX']E[XX']^{-1}$

or $\beta = \sigma_{yx}\sigma_{xx}^{-1}$.

Rather, we could simply write the key structural expectation of the XY covariance as

$$\sigma_{yx} = \beta_{yx}\sigma_{xx}, \quad (2b)$$

so, in simple regression, we can see exactly why the slope formula in Equation 2a works—the structural form expressed in Equation 2b when divided by the value of σ_{xx} leaves us with β_{yx}. Of course, this simple regression is one of the simplest models we will discuss, and not all SEM calculations are so easy.

Missing Predictor Biases in Regression

As a first alternative, let us consider the biases resulting from a missing predictor in a SEM. Let us assume the correct structural model is drawn here as Figure 15.3. That is, the correct model is

$$Y_n = \beta_{yx} X_n + \beta_{yz} \cdot z_n + e_n. \quad (3a)$$

This is very similar to a linear regression for the observed data (Y and X are measured), with the exception that we have included an unobserved variable (z, drawn as a circle) that has an effect on the outcome (Y, with β_{yz}) and is allowed to be correlated with the other predictor (X, with σ_{yx}). This has a structure of observed covariances that is different than the standard linear regression model 2.

This implies that when we calculate the linear regression based on the expectation of the observables only (i.e., as $\beta = \sigma_{yx}\,\sigma_{xx}^{-1}$), we will calculate the incorrect value because

$$\sigma_{yx} = \beta_{yx}.\sigma_{xx} + \beta_{yz}.\sigma_{zx} \quad (3b)$$

so $\beta = (\beta_{yx}.\sigma_{xx} + \beta_{yz}.\sigma_{zx})\sigma_{xx}^{-1}$

or $\beta = (\beta_{yx}.\sigma_{xx}\sigma_{xx}^{-1}) + (\beta_{yz}.\sigma_{zx}\sigma_{xx}^{-1})$

or $\beta = (\beta_{yx}) + [\beta_{yz}.(\sigma_{zx}/\sigma_x^2)]$.

That is, the typical regression estimate (β) will lead to an incorrect or biased estimate of the true regression coefficient (β_{yx}) to the exact degree there is any non-zero effect of z on Y (β_{yz}) together with any non-zero correlation of z and Y (σ_{zx}). The missing z-variable can be any other variable, so this kind of bias is likely to occur with real data.

This kind of "missing predictor variable" bias can create changes of sign and is not strictly bounded. It is clear that one solution to this dilemma is to measure z and include it in the model together with X in a multiple regression. This is the reason why regression coefficients are altered when additional variables are included in the overall prediction model. This also means that when we find the parameter remains the same no matter what other variable is included, we assert parameter invariance and think we have found the structural parameter. The suggested solution, as usual, is to fit the correct model (Figure 15.3) directly to the observed data. Of course, this solution requires both the available data (measurements on X, Y, and Z) in addition to the regression tools.

Bias Resulting From Unreliability of Predictors

As a second alternative, let us consider the biases caused by the unreliability of a predictor in a SEM. Let us assume the correct model is one where the input variable that we measure (X) is decomposable into a true score (x^*) that produces the outcome (Y) and also an unreliable part (u) that does not. This is drawn in Figure 15.4, and can be expressed as a structural model

$$Y_n = \beta_{y*}.x_n^* + e_n \quad \text{and} \quad X_n = x_n^* + u_n. \quad (4a)$$

If this is assumed to be the correct model, but we calculate the value using standard regression formulas (i.e., $\beta = \sigma_{yx}\sigma_{xx}^{-1}$), then we would be incorrect. That is, using standard regression we find

$$\sigma_{yx} = \beta_{y*}.\sigma_*^2 \quad \text{and} \quad \sigma_{xx} = \phi_*^2 + \psi_u^2 \quad (4b)$$

so $\beta = (\beta_{y*}\phi^2)/(\phi_*^2 + \psi_u^2)$

or $\beta = \beta_{y*}.[\phi_*^2/(\phi_*^2 + \psi_u^2)]$

or $\beta = \beta_{y*}[\phi_*^2/\sigma_x^2]$.

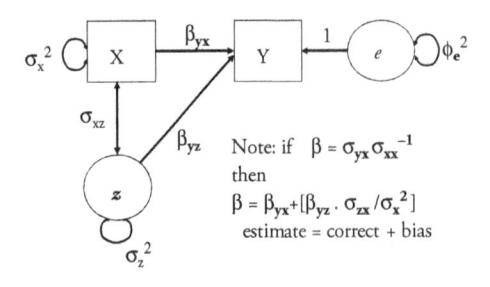

Figure 15.3 The population model is a regression, but with a latent predictor.

300 | STRUCTURAL EQUATION MODELS

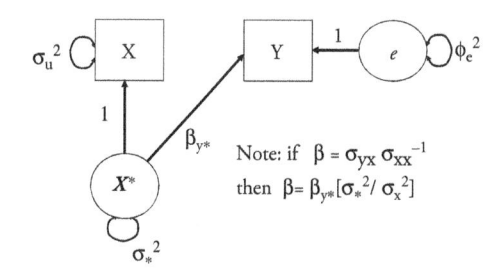

Figure 15.4 The correct model is a regression with an unreliable predictor.

This means the effect of having unreliable predictors pushes the true value of the regression coefficient downward by the size of the unreliability $(1 - [\phi_*^2/\sigma_x^2])$. It is useful to know that the estimated coefficient will always be smaller than the true coefficient, and this bias will not alter the sign of the coefficient, but this is actually not a desirable result. The suggested solution is to fit the correct model (Fig. 15.4) to the data, although this requires more data and more advanced programming (to be discussed).

Bias Resulting From Unreliability of Outcomes

As another case, let us consider the biases resulting from the unreliability of an outcome in a SEM. Let us assume the correct model is one where the outcome variable that we measure (Y) is decomposable into a true score (y*) that is produced by X and an unreliable part (u) that is not. This is drawn in Figure 15.5 and written as

$$y_n^* = \beta_{*x}X_n + e_n^* \quad \text{and} \quad Y_n = y_n^* + u_n, \quad (5a)$$

where there are two residual terms representing the true noise terms (e*) and the unreliability of the measurement (u). Indeed, unreliability of measures is clearly one of the big issues in SEM. If this is assumed to be the correct model, but we calculate

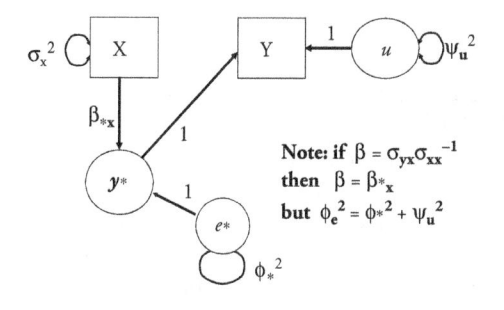

Figure 15.5 The correct model is a regression with an unreliable outcome.

the value using standard regression formulas (i.e., $\beta = \sigma_{yx}\sigma_{xx}^{-1}$), then we find

$$\sigma_{yx} = \beta_{*y}\sigma_x^2 \quad (5b)$$

so $\beta = \beta_{*y}$.

It follows that data with unreliable outcomes does not alter the true value of the regression coefficient. But the size of the unreliability will affect the error variance (which will increase by the size of the unreliability $\phi_e^2 + \psi_u^2$). Thus, the standardized coefficient and the explained variance will be lowered, and this is never a desirable result. The suggested solution is to fit the correct model (Fig. 15.5) directly to the data, again requiring more data and more programming.

Bias Resulting From Unreliability in Both Predictors and Outcomes

The biases resulting from the unreliability of both predictors and outcomes are an important part of SEM, so let us consider something not fully explored by Goldberger (1973). Let us assume the correct model is one in which the regression is a correct statement, but both measured outcome variables (Y) and measured predictor variables (X) have additional unobserved errors (u and v). This is drawn in Figure 15.6 as

$$y_n^* = \beta_{**}x_n^* + d_n, \quad (6a)$$

where $Y_n = y_n^* + u_n$ and $x_n^* = X_n + v_n$.

If this is assumed to be the correct model, but we calculate the value using standard regression formulas (i.e., $\beta = \sigma_{yx}\sigma_{xx}^{-1}$), then we find

$$\sigma_{yx} = \beta_{**}\phi_*^2 \quad \text{and} \quad \sigma_{xx} = \phi_*^2 + \sigma_v^2, \quad (6b)$$

so $\beta = \beta_{**}[\phi_*^2/\sigma_x^2]$ and $\phi_e^2 = \phi_*^2 + \sigma_v^2$.

Thus, if Model 6 is assumed to be the correct model, but we calculate the standard regression formulas, then we find the effect of having unreliable predictors and outcomes means both the true value of the regression coefficient will be biased downward by the size of the unreliability $(1-[\phi_*^2/\sigma_x^2])$, and the standardized coefficient and explained variance will be lowered. The suggested solution is to fit the correct model (Fig. 15.6) directly to the data, but this is not always possible. That is, to create a unique solution, we can use multiple indicators of the true variables (y*, x*).

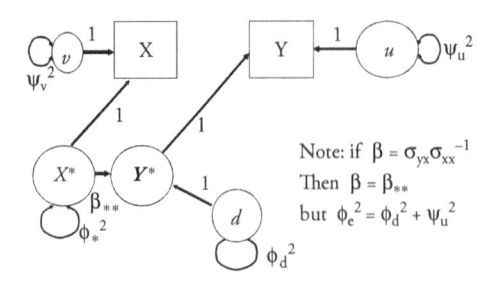

Figure 15.6 Assume the correct model is a regression but both are unreliable.

Bias Resulting From True Feedback Loops

The final case considered by Goldberger was the most complex, and here he considered the biases resulting from the possible feedback of effects in a SEM. Here, he assumes the correct model can be represented by a set of recursive linear equations where the variables that we measure (X and Y) both presumably have an effect on one another. This is drawn in Figure 15.7 and written as

$$Y_n = \beta_y X_n + u_n \quad \text{and} \quad X_n = \beta_x Y_n + v_n, \quad (7a)$$

with two residual terms. If this is assumed to be the correct model, but we calculate the value using standard regression formulas (i.e., $\beta = \sigma_{yx}\sigma_{xx}^{-1}$), then we find

$$\sigma_{yx} = (\beta_x \phi_v^2 + \beta_y \phi_u^2)\delta^2 \quad \text{and}$$
$$\sigma_{xx} = (\phi_v^2 + \beta_y^2 \phi_u^2)\delta^2, \quad (7b)$$

where $\delta = 1/(1 - (\beta_x\beta_y)) = 1 + \beta_x\beta_y$
$+ (\beta_x\beta_y)^2 + (\beta_x\beta_y)^3 + \ldots (\beta_x\beta_y)^r$,

so $\beta = \beta_x \cdot [\kappa + (1/\beta_y)(1 - \kappa)]$ with

$$\kappa = \phi_v^2/(\phi_v^2 + \beta_y^2 \phi_u^2).$$

If this feedback (Fig. 15.7) is assumed to be the correct model, but we calculate the value using standard regression formulas, then we find the effect of

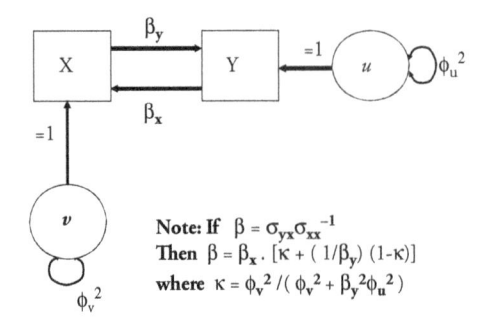

Figure 15.7 Assume the correct model is a feedback of "non-recursive" equations.

having a true feedback loop among the predictors means the true value of the regression coefficient will be biased in complex ways (i.e., the δ and κ). Thus, this general problem is not actually solved when we do a regression analysis and assume we calculate the true effect. The suggested solution is to fit the correct model (Fig. 15.7) directly to the data, but we now know this feedback model does not have any unique solution with just two or more measured variables (*see* Hauser, Tsai, & Sewell, 1983).

Additional Issues When Considering Both Means and Covariances

Although we have not highlighted this issue here, the same general approach can be used to examine the intercept term (β_0) in regression, and this can be illustrated in the path diagram of Figure 15.8. Once we estimate the slope, this leads to the estimates of other unknown parameters

$$\phi_e^2 = \sigma_y^2 - (\beta_1 \sigma_{xx} \beta_1') \quad \text{and}$$
$$\beta_0 = \mu_y - \beta_1 \mu_x. \quad (8)$$

To estimate the intercept parameter at the same time as the regression coefficient, we can include a constant term in the model (as a measured predictor, labeled 1, drawn here as a constant triangle). It follows that we need to include this constant into the model of expectations, but this is easily done by augmenting the covariance matrix with a mean vector or by estimating the model from the average cross-products matrices (*after* Rao, 1965). This approach will be described in more detail in the Technical Appendix. Most importantly, this general approach, using means and covariances together, forms the basis of many complex models being used today (*see* McArdle, 1994, 2007, 2009). While the simple inclusion of means does not alter the prior biases, it does help us understand them better. That is, in all cases above, the intercept is biased as well as the slope. One solution to these problems is to represent the model in terms of the true parameters, often requiring more measurements to be included.

Including Common Factors/Latent Variables in Models

We think it is fair to say that a key reason researchers have moved toward SEM is because of the *a priori* inclusion of LVs representing common factors (*see* Lawley & Maxwell, 1971; McDonald, 1985). That is, we include LVs because we are trying to estimate the unbiased parameters of the models just discussed (Figures 15.2–15.8) from the data. In

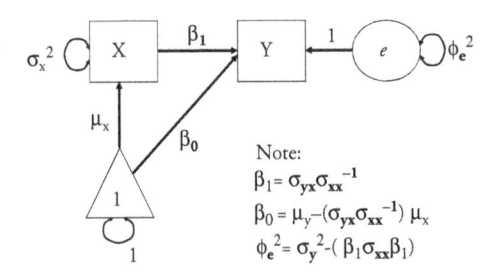

Figure 15.8 A simple regression model with an intercept.

Note:
$\beta_1 = \sigma_{yx}\sigma_{xx}^{-1}$
$\beta_0 = \mu_y - (\sigma_{yx}\sigma_{xx}^{-1})\mu_x$
$\phi_e^2 = \sigma_y^2 - (\beta_1\sigma_{xx}\beta_1)$

this section, we will explore a few selected particular uses of SEM with LVs in path models. We try to point out how this can create an advantage for SEM over other forms of data analysis.

The Structure of Common Factor Models

Figure 15.9 is a SEM path diagram representing a single common factor as a new LV. The common factor score (the circle termed F) is not directly measured. But it is thought to have its own variability ($\phi_?^2$) and to produce the variation in each of the six observed variables ($Y(m)$) through the common factor loadings ($\lambda(m)$). Each of the measured variables also has a unique variance ($\psi(m)^2$) that is assumed to be composed of variance that is both specific to that variable and variance that is based on errors of measurement. Using these terms, the model for the observed variables is thought to be

$$Y(m)_n = \lambda(m)F_n + u(m)_n \text{ for } m = 1 \text{ to } M. \quad (9a)$$

So, although we have many measured variables ($Y(m)$), we only have one unobserved common factor (F). This set of assumptions implies that the expectation we have for the covariance terms among measures includes only common factor variance, whereas the expected variance terms includes both common and specific variance. That is, if this model

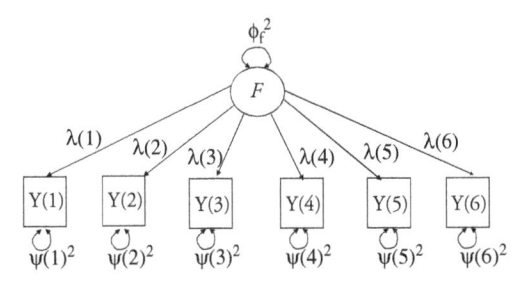

Note: The expected variance of $Y(k) = \sigma(k)^2 = \lambda(k)\phi_f^2\lambda(k) + \psi(k)^2$ and the expected covariance of $Y(k)$ and $Y(j) = \sigma(k,j) = \lambda(k)\phi_f^2\lambda(j)$

Figure 15.9 A one-common factor "population" model.

is true, then each variance and covariance has a very simple structure describable as

$$\sigma(m)^2 = \lambda(m)\phi_?^2\lambda(m)' + \psi(m)^2 \text{ and}$$
$$\sigma(j,k) = \lambda(j)\phi_?^2\lambda(k)'. \quad (9b)$$

The collective parameters of this model all include the factor variance term ($\phi_?^2$), so an additional restriction will be needed to make the parameters "uniquely identified." This is typically done by either restricting the unknown factor variance ($\phi_?^2 = 1$) or by restricting one of the factor loadings ($\lambda(1) = 1$). The specific choice of the identification "constraint" (also referred to as "setting the metric") should not alter the estimation, fit, or interpretation of the result, but this is only guaranteed if the model is largely correct. If so, the unique property of the model is the ratio of the pairs of factor loadings (i.e., $\lambda(j)/\lambda(k)$). That is, after the identification constraint ($\phi_?^2 = 1$), the new covariance expectations are now more restricted and can be written in the seemingly much simpler form of

$$\sigma(m)^2 = \lambda(m)\lambda(m)' + \psi(m)^2 \text{ and}$$
$$\sigma(j,k) = \lambda(j)\lambda(k)'. \quad (9c)$$

As it turns out, this provides enough information for us to estimate the loadings and tell which measured variables are most closely aligned with the unobserved common factor and which are not—that is, the ratio of the loadings are used to provide a label for the unobserved common factor.

We can now examine whether the one-factor model fits the data by comparing the observed variances and covariance (**S**) to the model expected variances and covariance (Σ, from [9b]). If the model seems to fit, then there are many ways to restrict this model even further. For example, we could say that all the factor loadings are equal (as done in a Rasch-type model; see McDonald, 1999; McArdle, Grimm, Bowles, Hamagami, & Meredith, 2009). As a very general alternative, we could simply say there is no common factor at all (and all correlations are collectively zero), and this is a typical "baseline" model that we really must be able to say does not fit our data (i.e., if this model fits we are effectively finished). These are both testable alternatives to the one common factor model.

Alternatively, if this simple one common factor model does not seem to provide a good fit, then we can go the other way, and relax some of the model constraints. For example, we can posit the existence of a second common factor (F_2), and one simple version of this model is drawn as Figure 15.10. In

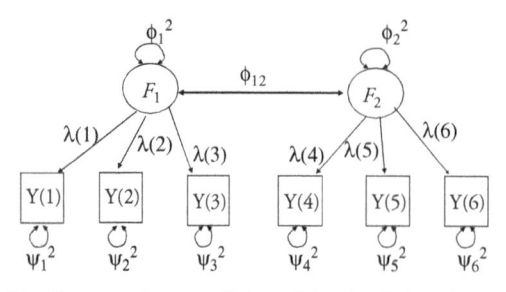

Note: The expected variance of Y(k) = σ(k)² = λ(k) φ_f² λ(k) + ψ(k)²
and the expected covariance of Y(1) and Y(6) = σ(1,6) = λ(1) φ₁₂ λ(6)

Figure 15.10 A simple two-common factor "population" model.

this simple model, we posit that each common factor is related to a specific set of observed variables. In this case, each factor is indicated by three measured variables. Of course, because each common factor is unobserved, we need to identify the model by either fixing the common factor variances (e.g., $\phi_1^2 = 1$ and $\phi_2^2 = 1$) or by restricting a factor loading on each (e.g., $\lambda(1) = 1$ and $\lambda(6) = 1$). The only difference between this two-factor model and the one-factor model is the covariance among the common factors (ϕ_{12}). That is, if this value turns out to be the same as the variance terms (or the factor intercorrelation $\rho_{12} = 1$), then this model reduces to become the previous one-factor model. This subtle difference could be important in the model fit, where there is now one degree of freedom difference between these models, testing the covariance hypothesis, and we can evaluate the gain in fit.

Unfortunately, these simple kinds of SEM are not the only ones that can be fitted. For example, we can start with this simple two-factor model and add two additional factor loadings, where factor 1 is indicated by variables 4 and 5, and two additional factor loadings, where factor 2 is indicated by variables 2 and 3. These additional parameters reduce the number of parameters we need to estimate, but the overall two-factor model is still identified, and unique estimates can be found for all parameters. It quickly becomes evident that these are not the only restrictions that can be allowed in the context of factor analysis. In this specific model with 6 variables and 2 common factors, at least 10 factor loadings can be placed in different locations. Because the overall two-factor model can be represented with different diagrams (i.e., "rotated" into a different position) without any change in fit, this means that we have possibly different parameter values and factorial interpretations.

In general, it is known that an alternative factor model cannot be judged by fit alone (*see* McArdle & Cattell, 1994). Perhaps more importantly, this also illustrates that the highly restricted two-factor model (of Fig. 15.10) is a specific factorial hypothesis that can have a "unique solution" and "cannot be rotated" any further. This is the essential benefit of what is usually termed *confirmatory factor analysis* (*see* Joreskog, 1970; Lawley & Maxwell, 1971; McDonald, 1985). Just as a clarifying note, in our view, if the factor loading values were all specified in advance, then this would really be considered a "confirmatory" approach to model evaluation. But to be sure, this somewhat rigid form of confirmatory analysis is hardly ever used.

The range of possibilities for factorial structure is so vast that it is rare to consider all possible alternatives. Instead we consider the goodness of fit of the models to be an indicator of whether a specific model does not fit the data, and we never explicitly know whether any specific model is the best one to fit. That is, using the classical arguments of Popper (1970), "we can reject models with data, but we can never know we have the best model for any set of data." Another way to say this is that we can use the data to tell us which models are "false," but we cannot use the data to tell us which models are "true."

The careful reader will notice that we have also not mentioned the very big problem of the calculation of the unobserved common factor scores—this is because factor scores for individuals can be calculated in many alternative ways, so they are usually "indeterminant" (for elaboration, *see* McDonald, 1985). One simple way to understand this problem is to consider that a Pearson correlation coefficient (r_{yx}) can be uniquely calculated from observed data on two variables (Y and X), but if we simply know the size of the correlation (e.g., $r_{yx} = 0.6$), then we cannot recreate the distribution of the observed data (on Y and X) that produced this correlation—there are an unlimited set of scores that could lead to this specific correlation. This is a considerable problem, because in SEM we do not usually obtain a plot of the unobserved common factor scores. It is typical for some to say the SEM evaluation "does not require factor score estimates" rather than they "cannot uniquely estimate factor scores." This allows SEM users to appear to be correct, but also means that all the information about the factor scores must come from the model assumptions (i.e., normality of unique factors) rather than the empirical evidence from the score distribution.

The Structure of Common Factors Within Latent Path Regression

We can now consider the addition of other variables into the LV model. If we include two measured input variables (X_1 and X_2) and consider the common factor score (F) to be the critical feature of all other outcomes (Y), then we can create a LV regression model with parameters ($\beta(1)$ and $\beta(2)$) where the outcome has no error that could be attributed to its measurement. That is, the common factor model is used to separate the common variance from the unique variance, and the latter includes all errors of measurement. This scenario of a restricted LV path analysis is depicted in Figure 15.11. This kind of model can be represented by two structural equations of the form

$$Y(m)_n = \lambda(m)F_n + u(m)_n \quad \text{and}$$
$$F_n = \beta(1)X(1)_n + \beta(2)X(2)_n + d_n, \quad (10a)$$

so the impacts of measured Xs on Ys are mediated through the common factor (F), and their impacts (β) are also estimated a function of the same factor loadings ($\lambda(m)$). Incidentally, because the factor scores, by definition, do not contain measurement error, the residuals (d) in the prediction of the factor scores do not contain measurement error and are often termed *disturbances* (see Hsiao, 2003) to represent the effect of other unmeasured, but potentially reliable, sources of variation in the factor scores.

If the model of Equation 10a is true, then some key structural expectations of the variances and covariance are required to follow the specific pattern defined by

$$\sigma(m)^2 = \lambda(m)\lambda(m) + \psi(m)^2 \quad \text{and} \quad (10b)$$
$$\sigma(m, 1) = \lambda(m)\{\beta(1)\sigma(1)^2 + \beta(2)\sigma(1, 2)\},$$

among many other covariance restrictions (see Fig. 15.11). Thus, we hope to tell if this model is grossly incorrect for our data. If this latent path model seems reasonable it can be used to test the accuracy of this pattern in real data here (see Structural Equation Modeling As a Tool section), and it can also be used as a reasonable test of the available SEM computer software (see the Computer Appendix section).

The Structure of Invariant Common Factors Over Time

One of the best features of SEM is that the basic ideas are broad and general and can be used to consider many different problems. For example, an alternative type of SEM naturally arises when we have common factors at both occasions, and this has some interesting additions. This is depicted in the path diagram of Figure 15.12, and this is a model that can be used with multivariate longitudinal data (see McArdle & Nesselroade, 1994; McArdle, 2005; McArdle, 2010). In these cases, we assume some of the same variables have been measured on both occasions. We term these M measured variables as $Y(m)[1]$ and $Y(m)[2]$. Using a basic array of two-occasion data, we can consider two key SEM issues: (1) the "Invariance of the Common Factors" over occasions, and (2) the "Cross-Lagged Analysis" of the common factor scores.

The first consideration is fairly unique to SEM, but it is very useful. Because we have measured the same observed variables over time we might just assume we have measured the same unobserved factors over time. In principle, this should be an easy concept, especially because we have asserted we have measured the same persons on the same observed variables over two times. Indeed, this is one basic form of factorial equivalence, and it is almost always assumed using standard procedures such as MANOVA or Canonical Regression (see Tabachinik & Fidell, 2007), and this would allow us to go directly to the Cross-Lagged Regression analysis, perhaps with some aggregated scores. But when we think about it a bit more, we come to realize that many things could change over time, including the people's responses to the same stimuli. Thus, if we make the mistake of mislabeling the key factors at this initial level, then our mistakes are likely to become compounded in any subsequent analysis (see McArdle, 2007). So SEM is useful because it can help us avoid a big mistake at this initial level. That is, SEM allows us to examine this interesting concept of *Multiple Factors Invariance Over Time* (MFIT) as a testable hypothesis. In fact, this a very basic test, because if the same people are not responding from

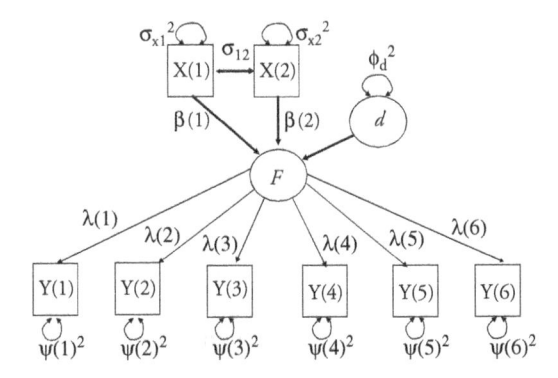

Figure 15.11 A "population" latent path model.

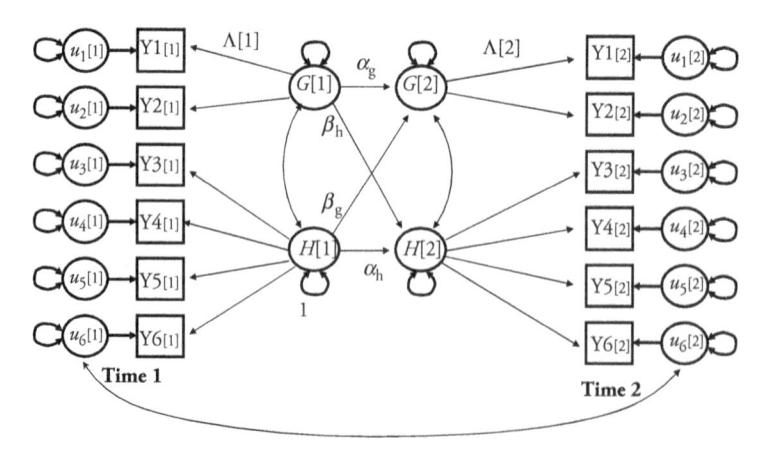

Figure 15.12 A theoretical model of cross-lagged regression applied to longitudinal common factor scores (from McArdle, 2010).

the same latent sources at both occasions, this model should not fit very well. We do want to achieve this goal, so possibly we may need more than one common factor (as in Fig. 15.12) with a more complex pattern of loadings to achieve MFIT.

In SEM we first hypothesize a structural equation that could be applied at both occasions. Within this set of restrictions is the basic requirement of MFIT. That is, we can state

$$Y(m)[1]_n = \lambda(m)F[1]_n + u(m)[1]_n, \quad (11a)$$

$$Y(m)[2]_n = \lambda(m)F[2]_n + u(m)[2]_n, \quad \text{and}$$

$$F[2]_n = \alpha_f F[1]_n + d[2]_n,$$

so the common factor ($F[t]$) is assumed to have the same set of factor loadings within each time ($\lambda(m)$). Although the measured variable ($Y(m)[t]$) indicates the common factor score ($F[t]$) in the same way at any time, the factor score itself can be changing. Here we only use a simple regression function of the prior $t = 1$ factor score. If this MFIT concept is true, then some key structural expectations might be

$$\sigma(m)[1]^2 = \lambda(m)^2 + \psi(m)[1]^2, \quad (11b)$$

$$\sigma(m)[2]^2 = \lambda(m)\phi[2]^2\lambda(m) + \psi(m)[2]^2,$$

$$\text{and} \quad \phi[2]^2 = \alpha_f^2 + \phi_d^2,$$

among many other covariance restrictions (see Fig. 15.12). This latent path model is interesting because it is not necessarily true, and it can be tested using all observed variable expectations between time 1 and time 2. These expectations require the pattern of the correlations to be exactly proportional (via $\phi[2]^2$); thus, all correlations can get higher or lower together, and because the loadings are required to be the same within each time,

the relative ratios ($\lambda(j)/\lambda(k)$) and factorial interpretation must remain as well. This MFIT may not be easy to find on an empirical basis, but it is a desirable property to have because it implies we have found a set of common factors that provide a useful template for other changes. Of course, we may find more than one common factor (as in Fig. 15.12), possibly with some unusually complex combination of loadings (see McArdle, 2007; McArdle & Cattell, 1994).

Once we assume the MFIT expressions, we can concentrate on the sequential changes in the factor scores. Assuming we have two factor scores ($G[t]$ and $H[t]$) within each time (as in Fig. 15.12), we can next consider a score model that comes from cross-lagged panel analysis (see Joreskog & Sorbom, 1979; Hsiao, 2003) written here as

$$G[2]_n = \alpha_g G[1]_n + \beta_g H[1]_n + d_{gn} \quad \text{and} \quad (12a)$$

$$H[2]_n = \alpha_h H[1]_n + \beta_h G[1]_n + d_{hn},$$

where we broadly assert that the "past leads to the future," (i.e., scores at time 1 affect scores at time 2). Most importantly here, we suggest that the each common factor at time 1 has both a "lagged" effect (α_g and α_h) on the same factor and a "crossed" effect (β_g and β_h) on the other factor. Regressions are typically used in these SEM for simplicity, and there are two separate but possibly correlated disturbance terms (d_g and d_h). Besides working with factor scores that have no measurement error, we are also trying to understand their independent stability over time ($1 - \alpha$) and their independent impact on the other (β_g and β_h). This leads to some key structural expectations for the over-time variances and covariances, such as

$$\phi_g[2]^2 = \alpha_g^2 + \beta_g^2 + 2\alpha_g\beta_g\rho_{gh} + \phi_{dg}^2 \quad (12b)$$

$$\phi_g[1,2] = \alpha_g + \beta_g\rho_{gh}, \quad \text{and}$$

$$\phi_h[1,2] = \alpha_h + \beta_h\rho_{gh},$$

among many other covariance restrictions. As it turns out, this initial model will fit just as well as the overall factor model, because all we have done is turn the covariances into regressions.

We can simply look at the values (and possibly the standard errors and significance) of the crossed coefficients to get some idea of the sequential impacts (i.e., does $G \to H$ or does $H \to G$) in light of the lagged features. But because crossed coefficients often represent critical issues of inference, we can use this general SEM approach in a more sophisticated fashion. To further specify and fit an alternative model where $G[1]$ does not impact $H[2]$ (i.e., $\beta_h = 0$), we simply alter the expectations of Equation 12b. If this model still fits the data as well as the previous and less restricted model, then we conclude we have no evidence for an effect of $G \to H$. To deal with the bigger questions, we can also fit alternative models where $H[1]$ does not impact $G[2]$ (i.e., $\beta_g = 0$), or where neither factor affects the other (i.e., $\beta_g = 0$, $\beta_h = 0$), and possibly other models too.

This basic use of cross-lagged logic is one classical way to examine "causality in observational data" (*see* Cochran & Cox, 1950; Duncan, 1975; Sobel, 1995; Pearl, 2000; Shrout, 2010), and although there are clear limits to our modeling (i.e., perhaps some other unobserved variables $Z[t]$ cause both), at least we can test these basic ideas with variables that are assumed to have no measurement error. These kinds of SEMs are hopefully useful to create a basic understanding of the sequential inferences. Recent work on randomized experiments (see McArdle & Prindle, 2008; Prindle & McArdle, 2012) and other froms of *mediation modeling* is often being done in the absence of common factors, and this can be quite misleading (for good examples, *see* Cole & Maxwell, 2003).

The Structure of Common Factors for Multiple Repeated Measures

An important first set of models for repeated measures data have emerged from the "time-series" perspective (*see* Anderson, 1957; Browne & Nesselroade, 2005). These models essentially suggest, once again, that the "future is predicable from the past,"

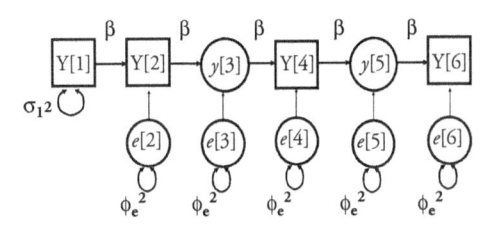

Figure 15.13 An equal-time Markov model of longitudinal data used so the parameters are equal over unequal intervals of time.

and we should use this as a main feature of our analysis. The path diagram of Figure 15.13 describes some options for these kinds of time-series analyses. In this diagram everything in the past is used to produce (or predict) the future behaviors. This kind of model is termed *fully recursive* because it requires as many parameters to be calculated as there are observed correlations in the data so it is really not testing any major substantive idea. To be clear, in this popular formulation, we are not really able to test whether the past predicts the future, or even vice versa, but we can use this approach to calculate the predicted values.

The model in Figure 15.13 can be modified by adding some important constraints. For example, we can say that the only predictors needed for future scores are the ones in the immediate past. That is, the first affects the second, the second affects the third, and the third affects the fourth, and that is all that is needed to predict the future values. In general, we can eliminate three parameters from Figure 15.2, and we can test this comparison of parameters as a formal hypothesis with three *df*. We emphasize that we are actually testing the importance of parameters that are not present rather than the ones that are present. By fitting this alternative model, we can examine whether these restrictions seem reasonable for our data.

This model is written where the future deviation at any time-point ($[t]$) was predicted from the deviation at the prior time-point ($[t-1]$) using a linear regression model with "fixed" group parameters ($\alpha[t]$) and independent disturbances ($d[t]$). One version of this model can be written as

$$Y[t]_n = \alpha[t-1]Y[t-1] + e[t-1]_n, \quad (13a)$$

so some of the expected variances and covariances are

$$\sigma[t]^2 = \alpha[t-1]\sigma[t]^2\alpha[t-1]$$
$$+ \phi(e[t-1])^2 \quad \text{and} \quad (13b)$$

$$\sigma[t, t-1] = \alpha[t-1]\sigma[t-1]^2.$$

The utility of time-series regression obviously comes when we add more variables and examine cross-lagged models, but this basic time-series structure resonates with some researchers more than others (McArdle & Epstein, 1987; Walls & Schaffer, 2006).

We can add another important component to this basic model—a LV—typically drawn as a circle with an arrow pointing directly to the square. This kind of LV is introduced to indicate that the time-series process does not apply to the observed or "manifest variable" (MV) but, rather, to one key source of the variation in the MV—namely, the LV over time. Here we assume there is one LV at each time, that the part of the MV that is not attributable to the LV is "unique" (e.g., it may be partly "error of measurement"), and it has the same variation at all times. This is exactly like a common factor model, but here the common factor has only one indicator, so it is not broad in any sense, nor is it testable in a rigorous way. However, we should not underestimate the importance of this LV idea. One benefit of using LVs here is that it enables the estimation of the process in the presence of random error (see Heise, 1975; Joreskog & Sorbom, 1979). In this formulation, the time series for the LV is "error-free," so we expect it to have predictions that are absent of error, and thus higher in accuracy. The model may fit the data better using this LV approach, but we do not have, nor can we obtain, estimated scores for the LVs. What we can examine is the effect of measurement error on our understanding of the process.

There are some important conditions for this model to be useful. In interpretation of these time-series models, we typically assume the time points are equally spaced, so any α coefficient could be substituted for another with the same specific time-interval. We may need to use unobserved variables representing the time-points without data to deal with the "unbalanced" data over time (see McArdle & Aber, 1990). But these are not typical constraints in this model. Another more typical restriction on time-series models is an assumption of "stationarity"—that the variances (and covariances) remain the same over all times because the system has reached a "steady state of equilibrium" (see Walls & Schaffer, 2006). Equilibrium does not seem to be a reasonable assumption for many data sets, so this particular model is probably not a good idea. Finally, the means of the scores at each time are not considered so they do not count against us here. This may sound foolish at first, but there are many examples where these group level statistics are not needed. This problem does not create more misfit, but it can certainly be a problem when the change for the whole group is a key part of the substantive questions.

To ameliorate some of these problems, a seemingly completely different set of models was also used, and this is presented in Figure 15.14. These are broadly termed *latent curve models* (LCMs), and they can be fitted by either approximate ANOVA methods or exact SEM methods (from Meredith & Tisak, 1990; *see* McArdle, 1986, 1988; McArdle & Epstein, 1987). This LCM approach typically starts by assuming we have a *trajectory* equation for each occasion for each person formed as the sum of (1) unobserved or *latent scores* representing the individual's initial level ($G\{0\}$); (2) unobserved or latent scores representing the individual *change over time* or *slope* ($G\{1\}$); and (3) unobserved and independent unique features of measurements ($u[t]$). In this model, the arrows from the latent slopes to observed variables are a set of group coefficients or *basis weights* that define the timing or *shape of the trajectory over time* (e.g., $\alpha[t] = t - 1$). Note how this carefully selected set of basis weights (as $\alpha[t] = [0, 1, 3, 5]$) easily takes care of the unbalanced time delay between occasions.

In the LCM of Figure 15.14, the initial level and slopes are often assumed to be random variables with "fixed" means ($\mu\{0\}, \mu\{1\}$) but "random" variances ($\phi\{0\}^2, \phi\{1\}^2$) and correlations ($\rho\{0, 1\}$). The standard deviations ($\phi\{j\}$) are drawn here to permit the direct representation of the correlations (*see* McArdle & Hamagami, 1991). This LCM path diagram can also be interpreted as a two common factor model with means. The first latent factor score is an intercept or level score (labeled $G\{0\}$), and the second latent factor score is a slope or change score (labeled $G\{1\}$). The relationships between the latent levels $G\{0\}$ and all observed scores Y[t] are fixed at a value of 1. In contrast, the relationships between the latent slopes $G\{1\}$ and all observed scores Y[t] are assigned a value based on the time parameter $\alpha[t]$, which, depending on the application, may be fixed or estimated. For simplicity, the unique components ($u[t]$) are defined as having constant unique deviations (ψ) and are presumably uncorrelated with other components. This seems like a typical setup for such models.

In this longitudinal model, the change score ($G\{1\}$) is assumed to be constant *within* an individual but it is not assumed to be the same *between* individuals. The LVs are written in italics ($G\{0\}$, $G\{1\}$) because they are similar to the predicted scores

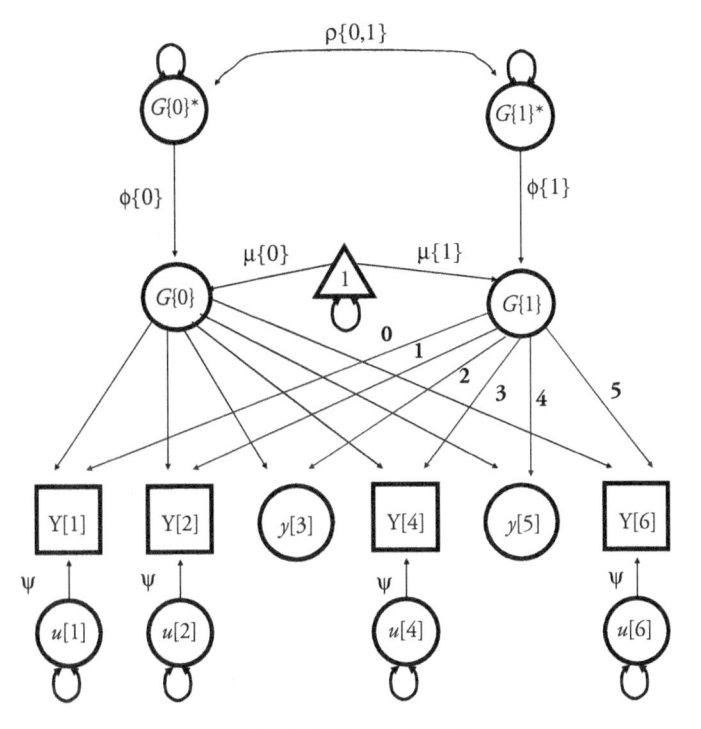

Figure 15.14 A path diagram for the latent curve model (LCM) with a linear "basis."

in a standard regression equation. (That is, we do not use Greek notation because these scores do not need to be estimated). One new feature here is the use of a triangle to represent a measured variable that has no variation—that is, the unit constant. The key reason this new option is added to the path diagram is to allow us to make hypotheses about the group means. In LCM we want to evaluate hypotheses about the group means and covariances that require the same parameters of proportionality (i.e., the basis $\alpha[t]$) because this is an indirect way to evaluate the patterns of the score trajectories.

Perhaps it is obvious, but this LCM is not the same as the prior time-series model of Equation 13. This LCM structural equation model can be written as

$$Y[t]_n = G\{0\}_n + \alpha[t]G\{1\}_n + u[t]_n, \quad (14a)$$

so some of the expected means, variances, and covariances are

$$\mu[t] = \mu\{0\} + \alpha[t]\mu\{1\}, \quad (14b)$$

$$\sigma[t]^2 = \phi\{0\}^2 + \alpha[t]\phi\{1\}^2\alpha[t] + \psi^2, \text{ and}$$

$$\sigma[t, t-1] = \phi\{0\}^2 + \alpha[t]\phi\{1\}^2\alpha[t-1],$$

and the careful reader will see that this is a model for means as well as covariances, and these covariance assumptions are not identical to those of the time-series model in Equation 13.

Although a linear scaling of the basis is very popular (*see* Singer & Willett, 2003), it is only one of many that could be used. For example, it is possible to add a lot of nonlinear complexity based on age or time to the simple growth curve models for the study of within-person changes. Wishart (1938) introduced a fundamental way to examine a nonlinear shape—the use of power polynomials to better fit the curvature apparent in growth data. The individual growth curve (consisting of $t = 1$, T occasions) is summarized with a small set of linear orthogonal polynomial coefficients based on a fixed power-series of time ($\alpha[t]$, ½$\alpha[t]^2$, 1/3 $\alpha[t]^3$, ... 1/p $\alpha[t]^p$) describing the general nonlinear shape of the growth curve. A second-order (quadratic) polynomial growth model implies that the loadings of the second component are fixed to be a function of the first components (i.e., the derivative is linear with time).

The quadratic form of this basic model can be depicted as a path diagram as well (not included here). This can appear to be a bit complicated because it requires a third latent component with a basis that is related to the first one (i.e., ½$\alpha[t]^2$), but all of this is done so the implied change is linear with time (i.e., we add acceleration). Additional variance and covariance terms can be used to account for individual differences in these new LVs. Typically we find that introducing some curvature allows the model to approximate the data points more closely. Of course, a model of growth data might require this form of a second-order (quadratic), third-order (cubic), or even higher-order polynomial model fitted to the data. The polynomial family kind of nonlinear models is very popular (e.g., Bryk & Raudenbush, 1992).

One reason researchers like the LCM logic is that it permits a rich variety of alternative extensions. For example, a different alternative to the linear growth model was brought to light by Meredith and Tisak (1990)—the model proposed by Rao (1958) and Tucker (1958) in the form of summations of "latent curves." These innovative techniques were important because they added the benefits of the SEM techniques – SEM made it possible to represent a wide range of alternative growth and change models (McArdle, 1986, 2009; McArdle & Epstein, 1987; McArdle & Anderson, 1990; McArdle & Hamagami, 1991). Our use of this latent curve concept can be accomplished with only a minor adjustment to the LCM of Figure 15.3a. We allow the curve basis to take on a form dictated by the empirical data. In this example we simply write a model for the same person at multiple occasions where the last two basis coefficients $\alpha[3]$ and $\alpha[4]$ are *free to be estimated* (the first two are still fixed at $\alpha[1] = 0$ and $\alpha[2] = 1$). The actual time of the measurement is known, but the basis parameters are allowed to be freely estimated so we can end up with different distances between time-points, an optimal shape for the whole curve. The estimated basis has been termed a "meta-meter" or "latent time" scale that can be plotted against the actual age curve for clearer interpretation (Rao, 1958; Tucker, 1958; McArdle & Epstein, 1987). There are many ways to estimate these model parameters in a LCM framework, and all such options are not considered here.

The time series and LCMs are only two approaches to the analysis of within-person changes that, although representing major modeling approaches, barely scratch the surface of all the possibilities (e.g., *see* Walls & Schaffer, 2006; McArdle, 2009). These illustrations mainly show that any SEM, based on AR-type models or LCM-type models, is used to make a prediction about longitudinal trajectory. Thus, both kinds of models have their place in the array of possible analytic frameworks, and choices between models are not often so easy. Some of these choices are simply defined by the data.

For example, we might have a data set where the individuals are measured repeatedly at many more time-points (i.e., T = 100). In this sense, a collection of complete cases at a few time-points (T = 4) within a panel study design is fairly easy to consider, even the timing is unbalanced, and this has allowed us to go a bit further.

This LCM has become a very popular model, and it clearly highlights the differences between SEM and ANOVA. In SEM, the entire model is used to pattern the means and covariances (*see* McArdle, 1988; McArdle & Epstein, 1987), whereas in ANOVA the means are fully patterned, and the covariances are either highly restricted (i.e., in repeated measures ANOVA we assume Compound Symmetry; *see* Muller & Stewart, 2006), or the covariances are allowed to be completely free (i.e., repeated measures MANOVA). If the univariate ANOVA assumptions are correct, then the tests of mean differences over time is the most powerful. But if these assumptions are not met, then the same questions about means differences are biased (*see* Bock, 1975). The multivariate repeated measures model is always correct, but in general it will not be as powerful as the LCM. Thus, there are a lot of basic statistical reasons to use LCM rather than MANOVA.

The introduction of measured predictors of the LVs is a natural aspect of LV path models, and it is no different here. In fact, this reflects the best thinking in "multilevel" modeling (Bryk & Raudenbush, 1992). Here, a set of the first level variables ($Y[t]$) are used to form the latent level and slopes ($G\{0\}$ and $G\{1\}$), and the second level variables (X) are used as predictors of the levels and slopes. There should be no doubt that multilevel thinking has allowed much progress in the simplicity of the required calculations, but there is also no doubt that this "new" approach does not automatically produce novel results (*see* McArdle & Hamagami, 1996; Ferrer, Hamagami, & McArdle, 2004).

In this specific case, path diagrams of longitudinal data were originally used with autoregression models, and these models seemed to reflect actions or predictions moving forward in time (e.g., *see* Figure 15.13). However, it was very unclear whether any movement was actually taking place or if anyone was actually doing any traveling at all (not really). Subsequent work showed how these diagrams can be used in the context of growth and change with LVs (e.g., Fig. 15.14; McArdle, 1986, 2009; McArdle & Epstein, 1987; McArdle & Anderson, 1990; McArdle & Woodcock, 1997).

Indeed, the usefulness of path diagrams as tools emerge as we move to the more complex examples.

Structural Equation Modeling As a Tool

When we want to calculate values for the parameters of a model, we may need specialized SEM software. There are many elegant treatments of SEM in the current literature (e.g., Loehlin, 2004; Kline, 2011), but a simple treatment is a worthwhile start. A sample of the current SEM programs are listed in Table 15.1. As can be seen here, there are many other computer programs that carry out SEM, and many more are not listed or are under current development. But those listed will serve our purposes here. These are all computer programs that largely focus on SEM analyses, and it is useful to know what they are actually doing. The SEM programs listed here differ in several key options, including data entry, model construction, iterative schemas and options, model output, and general ease of use, so different but knowledgeable researchers will advocate one program over another (i.e., Mplus instead of CALIS).

Structural Equation Modeling As a General Data Analysis Technique

There is no doubt that these SEM computer programs listed above can be used to calculate a wide variety of regression-based parametric models, and some of these might be incorrect (as just seen). In fact, the SEM computer program can calculate almost any model, including square roots and exponents (*see* McArdle & Boker, 1990). But these kinds of calculations do not represent the true benefits of SEM, or the real reason why so many researchers now use SEM programs.

In our own uses of SEM, we initially demonstrated that all available software for fitting a specific model with a specific data set (i.e., longitudinal growth models of the WISC) could be programmed to produce the same results (e.g., Ferrer, Hamagami, & McArdle, 2004). This led us to recognize an important general principle for SEM—*All SEM computer programs produce the same result for the same model*. To the degree this is true, it really should not matter which program is used as long as a correct expression of the model is our goal. Having said that, it is important to make sure that you have specified exactly the same model in each program—relying on computer program defaults may lead to different results for seemingly identical models. It is confusing why more researchers do not understand this basic

Table 15.1. Currently Available SEM Programs

1. LISREL (by Joreskog & Sorbom, 1979, 2010)—this program was the first of its kind and probably has been the most widely used and cited, and it is based on the classical structural equation modeling concepts.
2. Mplus (by Muthen & Muthen, 2009)—this is the newest general program, and it makes complex analyses very easy to input. It has a flavor of combining different forms of analyses, but it is relatively expensive.
3. OpenMx (by Neale, Boker, Xie & Maes, 2010)—this is one of the newest general programs in R. It is based on the well-tested Mx program, and it is free.
4. Other free R code packages—lavaan (by Rosell, 2012; *see* Ghisletta & McArdle, 2011) and sem (by Fox, 2006).
5. SPSS - AMOS (Wotke, 2001)—this package works off path diagrams.
6. SAS - PROC CALIS and PROC NLMIXED (Littell, et al., SAS Institute, 1996)—these are not often thought of as SEM, but they do work.
7. STATA - GLAMM (Rabe-Hesketh & Skrondal, 2010).
8. SYSTAT - RAMONA (Browne, 2000)—an interesting approach is used here.
9. WINBUGS (Lee, 2007; Ntzoufras, 2009)—This program offers a different type of calculation, and it should be more popular (see McArdle et al., 2009), especially when researchers have a formal basis for "informative priors."

SEM principle, but it certainly seems they do not. Perhaps this is because the calculation of parameter estimates using SEM can be overly complicated. We will briefly describe some key SEM ideas here, and we will use a variety of SEM programs, such as SAS PROC Calis, Mplus, and OpenMx (*see* the Technical Appendix). Some researchers have been surprised how many innovations have emerged first in SEM—dealing with multiple populations, incomplete data, and longitudinal data—and this made the original LISREL matrix concepts far less important than once thought (*see* McArdle, 2005; Muthen & Muthen, 2002; for further reasons, *see* Kline, 2011).

As will be illustrated in the next section, any SEM program requires a tradeoff of SEM concepts for SEM tools, but the Mplus program offers a good example of easy input, correct calculations, and the need to work hard to carry out a real SEM analysis. Other programs we will use (CALIS and OpenMx) can produce the same estimates but are not as easy to use.

Creating Structural Equation Modeling Expectations

The way we create model expectations is not exactly clear to many researchers, but it is an essential technique. What we generally do is place values (or symbols) inside model matrices and then use matrix algebra to generate the expected values. This is required and automatically done by all of the computer programs, but not enough emphasis is placed on this calculation. Let us revisit an earlier thought—an SEM representation of the scores is used to create model expectations about the means (μ, for means $\mathbf{m}$) and covariances (Σ, for covariances $\mathbf{S}$) of the observed data. This is most important because it is these expectations that can be compared to the data observations to form a test of fit. The formal basis of LISREL notation was designed to produce a set of expected values (symbolized as E) from the eight-matrix notation.

It is well-known now that a specific matrix algebra formulation such as SEM-LISREL is not the only way to create model expectations. Without any loss of enthusiasm for the basic premises of SEM, it is fair to say that there were other knowledgeable researchers who suggested that the LISREL concept and computer program was not actually the best way to deal with such problems, and McDonald (1980) was among the most vocal (see McDonald, 1985; Loehlin, 2004). In McDonald's alternative approach, the newly available computer programming he created allowed an unrestricted level of higher-order common factors, which he termed *covariance structure analysis* (COSAN). The resulting concept and computer program produced exactly the same values as LISREL, but it was not nearly as popular as LISREL, which was unfortunate because COSAN was free software.

Our own interest in path diagrams also led to another innovation in the calculation schemes. Our own use of COSAN proved instrumental in asserting that the eight-matrix notation, and the entire LISREL concept, was not the only correct way to carry out SEM (see Horn & McArdle, 1980). In fact, a practical comparison of COSAN and LISREL applications led directly to RAM theory (McArdle & McDonald, 1984; McArdle, 2005) where only three model matrices were necessary to consider any model: (1) a filter matrix (**F**) of completely fixed ones and zeros designed to distinguish the manifest variables from the LVs in a model; (2) an arrow matrix (**A**) of potential one-headed arrows (regression coefficients and means) based on directional hypotheses; and (3) a sling matrix (Ω) of potential two-headed arrows based on nondirectional hypotheses.

Of course, the main point of RAM notation is that these three matrices also were based on a one-to-one identity with the path analysis graphics (for details, see McArdle, 2005; McArdle & Boker, 1990). In various demonstrations we showed how this three-matrix approach produced exactly the same values as the eight (or more)-matrix approach (e.g., McArdle & McDonald, 1984; McArdle, 2005). We also suggested that the existing SEM computer programs could be quite useful (e.g., LISREL, COSAN), but all available matrices in these programs were not needed because only these three parameter matrices were needed to produce all the correct model expectations (Σ). This simplified programming made exceedingly complex models relatively easy to consider (e.g., McArdle & Hamagami, 2003; Grimm & McArdle, 2005). Nevertheless, any SEM only consists of variables that are either measured (squares) or not (circles) and relationships that are either directed (arrows) or not (slings). All other statements about the reasons why a specific approach should be used (i.e., combining econometrics with psychometrics) could still be useful, but they are certainly not essential. As with the earlier COSAN concept, it was no surprise that the RAM concept was not uniformly recognized by the community of scholars who had put so much time and energy into LISREL concepts, notation, and programming.

Statistical Indicators in Structural Equation Modeling

There are many statistical features that have been considered in SEM. A typical SEM has fewer parameters than observed covariances, so the model can be said to have *degrees-of-freedom* (df). Each df represents one way the model can be incorrect about the expectations. That is, the df represent ways the model does not need to look like the observed data, and the more of these df, the stronger the *a priori* nature of the model. Of course, not all dfs represent the same parameter restrictions or model information, so we need to deal with this with one model at a time.

Any overall goodness-of-fit index typically requires some idea of the desired relation of the data observations (**m**, **S**) and the model expectations (**μ**, **Σ**). Some function of the distance between observations and expectations is chosen, and we can calculate individual "misfits." If we want the model to reflect a good fit to the data, then we want the expectations to be close to the observations and, hence, small misfits. Of course, the term "close" can mean many things, so we need to define this in further detail. In simple regression, we often attempt to minimize the squared distance between the observations and the expectations—the least squares function (i.e., $\Sigma[O - E)^2]$). But there are other reasonable alternatives to consider. For example, we may wish to find the value that minimizes the squared distance of the observations and the expectations divided by the squared observations (i.e., $\Sigma[O - E)^2/O^2]$). This is one expression of the principle of "generalized least squares" (GLS). Alternatively, we may wish to find the values that minimize the squared distance of the observations and the expectations divided by the squared expectations (i.e., $\Sigma[O - E)^2/E^2]$). This is one simple expression of *maximum likelihood estimation* (MLE).

When we define a model on an *a priori* basis, the "probability of perfect fit" can be obtained by assuming the misfits are normally distributed, searching for GLS or MLE, and comparing the difference between the likelihood to a chi-square distribution (or random misfits). If the obtained misfits do not behave like random misfits, and the chi-square is relatively high for the associated *df*, then we conclude the model does not fit the data. If we are concerned that this index is asking for too much, which it usually is, then we may choose to estimate the "probability of close fit" using the root mean square error of approximation (e.g., ε_a or *RMSEA*; Browne & Cudeck, 1993). Often we do not define the model on an *a priori* basis, but we have used some key aspect of the data to help us choose a model, so we probably need to be careful to report this approach and we should not try to generate a probability statement at all (see McArdle, 2010).

The estimate of any model parameter has some important features that follow the functional form. For example, if we estimate some models using the ordinary least squares (OLS), now termed *unweighted least squares* (ULS) function, we can say we have *best linear unbiased estimates* (BLUE; see Fox, 1997). If we estimate with a more complex function, such as GLS or MLE, then we can say we have GLS or MLE. In any case, the standard error of the parameter can also be calculated and used to create a confidence boundary for the parameter ($t = est/se(est)$), and this ratio is thought to be useful in model interpretation. In many cases, researchers ignore parameters that are not more than two standard errors away from zero, but they often do not say why they do this. It seems this is a rather crude evaluation of the individual virtue of a parameter in a model by assuming it is uncorrelated with other parameters, and this strategy that is probably based on the use of an arbitrary $\alpha < 0.05$ criterion (i.e., because $t > 1.96$ and this is fairly close to $t > 2$).

Nevertheless, this overall principle was used in the simplification of otherwise complex models by Hauser, Tsai, and Sewell (1983) who unfortunately termed it "model trimming" and made it seem statistically defensible. Their tests actually represented *a priori* hypotheses so their particular application is not suspect. However, because key SEM parameters may be correlated with other parameters in the model, this "trimming" approach is in fact highly suspect. The only procedure that can be justified on a statistical basis is to set the key parameter to zero, allowing the other parameters to take the place of the key one, and see if the model fit is significantly altered (using χ^2 comparison logic). If there is a great loss of fit, then the key parameter is important. Although this approach can be much more tedious, there does not seem to be a simpler way to carry out this evaluation in a statistically meaningful fashion.

Structural Equation Modeling Estimation of Linear Multiple Regression

To illustrate these points in more detail, let us assume we have measured several persons (*N*) on two variables (Y and X) and we want to describe their functional relationship as X → Y. This expression is considered the "structural equation model for the observed scores." For simplicity, we can eliminate the intercept (β_0) and calculate a single linear regression coefficient (β) to describe this X → Y relationship. By assuming that the residuals are independent of the predictors, we know (from calculus) that the best estimate of this coefficient has a specific numerical value ($\beta = \sigma_{yx}\sigma_{xx}^{-1}$) that is considered as the BLUE. So we use this prior and well-known result to calculate the regression coefficient, and we use this to define the other statistical features of the model (see Fox, 1997).

Now that we have set up the structural model, we can examine several other ways to obtain reasonable values for the parameters of a SEM. In general, what we are trying to do is to find a set of parameters for the estimated relationships hypothesized that come as close to our observed relationships as possible. That is, we want to find those values that minimize some prespecified function of the observables, and we know this function could take on many different forms. So this definition of our goal can be accomplished in many ways, including by the direct result of the calculus (as above).

Now that we have created a functional goal, let us consider an iterative approach to model estimation. We can start by doing the following:

1. *Create a Set of Starting Values*—Make an educated guess for every parameter value. These can all be unities (ones) or they can be created in different ways based on previous findings from the substantive area of interest.

2. *Calculate the Function at this Iteration*—Take the values for every unknown model parameter and put these values into the positions of the matrix (in Table 15.A1). We can see we will create some differences between these guesses and the observations, and we can create a total function value for the overall model at this point.

3. *Use Some Technique to Find Better Values*—Here, there are several options to obtain an improved guess at the parameter values. If we are relying on standard SEM, then we would calculate the next best values by fundamental calculus—we estimate the first and second order derivatives of the parameters with respect to this function (and this can be complicated), and we then use the ratio of first and second derivatives as the most desired change in each parameter. Of course, if we use a Bayesian-type estimator (i.e., WINBUGS; *see* Lee, 2007; Ntzoufras, 2009) we might instead just simulate new scores for every LV and see how well these new values fit the data.

Table 15.A1 SAS Output of Generated Data for SEM-LVP

Variable	N	Mean	Std Dev	Sum	Minimum	Maximum
ID	1001	501.00000	289.10811	501501	1.00000	1001
y1	1001	-0.02178	1.25483	-21.80388	-4.39351	4.10147
y3	1001	0.03489	1.25608	34.92494	-4.09204	3.32691
y4	1001	-0.00118	1.14394	-1.17674	-2.89942	4.17124
y6	1001	0.02969	1.15476	29.71830	-3.18675	3.69231
x1_score	1001	-0.02167	1.03793	-21.69399	-3.39152	3.28872
x2_score	1001	-0.04871	1.01137	-48.75798	-3.23752	2.81972
Y_aver	1001	0.01791	0.76292	17.92970	-2.65687	2.46838
F_score	1001	-0.00378	1.27766	-3.78554	-3.79686	3.73907

Pearson Correlation Coefficients, N = 1001

	ID	y1	y3	y4	y6
ID	1.00000	0.04878	0.03562	0.04754	0.03824
y1	0.04878	1.00000	0.36498	0.33079	0.30962
y3	0.03562	0.36498	1.00000	0.24903	0.25623
y4	0.04754	0.33079	0.24903	1.00000	0.21166
y6	0.03824	0.30962	0.25623	0.21166	1.00000
x1_score	-0.01630	0.01179	-0.00830	-0.00691	0.00188
x2_score	0.03805	0.39046	0.34012	0.27284	0.32810
Y_aver	0.05712	0.69072	0.68227	0.58463	0.59170
F_score	0.04988	0.60799	0.59738	0.46149	0.5017

	x1_score	x2_score	Y_aver	F_score
ID	-0.01630	0.03805	0.05712	0.04988
y1	0.01179	0.39046	0.69072	0.60799
y3	-0.00830	0.34012	0.68227	0.59738
y4	-0.00691	0.27284	0.58463	0.46149
y6	0.00188	0.32810	0.59170	0.50176

4. *Put the New Values into the Calculation*—After we obtain a new set of changes in the parameters, we can create new parameter values. We then plug these back into the matrix expressions, and we do the basic calculations (expression 2 and 3) all over again.

5. *Terminate When We Cannot Do Better*—We terminate the iterative sequence when we do not get a big enough change in the parameters from one iteration to the next. We term this as "convergence."

There are a series of important proofs that show how this iterative approach can be used to estimate the best possible values for all model parameters (see Joreskog & Sorbom, 1979). This is true of multiple regression models for sure. Of most importance now is that this iterative approach can also be used when we do not know what values are optimal by straightforward algebra or calculus (*see* Technical Appendix). This is often the case when we have more complicated SEMs, involving LVs, recursive relationships, or both. We will deal with some of these more complex models in a later section.

Considering Common Factors/Latent Variables in Models

As stated earlier, the merger of SEM concepts using the SEM tools is the basis of many real SEM applications. The SEM literature is filled with interesting forms of analysis, from the "Experimental" work of Blalock (1985a, 1985b) to the "Observational" examples in Rabe-Hesketh & Skrondal (2006; *see* Cochran & Cox, 1950). However, all such interesting applications include the concepts of LVs in path models, so we extend this merger by highlighting features of a few real data applications of our own.

Considering Benefits and Limitations of Including Common Factors

There are many ways we can use LVs or common factors in SEMs. But we must ask "Are we just fooling ourselves when we add unobservables to a model?" Some people seem to think so (*see* McArdle, 1994), so it is important to reconsider what we are doing here. Let us list reasons why it is useful to consider LVs:

1. *Unbiased*—If LVs are used and not needed, then no bias should result. In this sense, LVs models are not dangerous.

2. *Missing*—If LVs are not used, but the data were actually created by a correlated predictor, then substantial bias can result.

3. *Unreliable Inputs*—If LVs are not used for input variables X, but are needed, then downward bias will result.

4. *Unreliable Outcomes*—If LVs are not used for output variables Y, but are needed, then there will be bias in standardized estimates.

5. *Unreliable Inputs and Outcomes*—If LVs are not used for X and Y, but are needed, then severe biases can result.

a. Because these cases are very likely in real data, it is wise to consider SEMs with LVs. At the same time, of course, there are also several problems that can emerge when using LVs:

6. *Indeterminancy*—In many models, there is no direct way to estimate a value for the LVs of an individual. This means the LVs cannot be plotted or explored in the usual way (i.e., for outliers, etc.), and new analyses need to be created.

7. *Manifest Explanations*—In many cases, there are alternative explanations for the data that are based only on MVs and are just as good (in terms of fit) as the first model with LVs.

8. *Latent Explanations*—In many cases, there are alternative explanations for the data that are based on other forms of LVs and are just as good (in terms of fit) as the first model of LVs. It is possible that researchers can fool themselves with LVs!

9. *Communication*—In many cases, the LV models are harder to explain in terms of basic theory and outcomes. Although these LV models may be correct, other may not understand.

10. *Naming Fallacy*—The wrong name may be attached an LV, partly because of low loadings or missing indicators, and this may persist and create more problems (*see* Cliff, 1983).

Common Factors With Cross-Sectional Observations

Some research demonstrates the sequential nature of building a LV path model from cross-sectional data gathered at a single occasion. In one of our analyses, McArdle and Prescott (1992) used data on N > 1,600 adults from the national sample of data on the *Wechsler Adult Intelligence Scale-Revised* (WAIS-R; *see* Wechsler, 1981). Although there was much discussion of the merits of different models, the final model depicted in this article includes two common factors (termed Gf and Gc) and two key predictors (age and high school graduation status). Attempts were made here to consider many different kinds of models, including polynomial forms of age and nonlinear interactions with high school graduation. In this research, successive models with a sequence of restrictions suggested that that nonlinearity and interactions were not needed when the outcomes were the two most reliable common factors.

A related question is whether something can be gained by splitting persons into subgroups. Splitting data into groups is some evaluation of the evidence for the equality of the meaning of the LVs over groups. This introduction of multiple-group analysis, initially promoted by Lawley and Maxwell (1971) and Sörbom (1979), turns out to be a remarkable advance over classical ANOVA thinking. That is, nothing needs to be lost here, because there can be one overarching model for the whole data set, and parameters can be invariant over groups. This was demonstrated by Horn and McArdle (1992) using the same WAIS-R data to express these basic ideas. The data were split into four separate age groups, and a multiple-group analysis was conducted without path diagrams. What they tried to examine was the rationale for the equality or inequality of the basic factor structure over age groups.

Multiple-group concepts were put into path diagram form in McArdle et al. (2001), where data from the Hawaii High School study was used to examine multiple-group hypotheses using the CESD. In the models from the HHS study, persons who were ethnically different (Hawaiian vs. non-Hawaiian) were split into separate groups to see whether the factor patterns were the same across groups. They seemed to be, but others can check this out.

The multiple-group models were used in the theoretical analyses of McArdle and Cattell (1994) but go one step further. A multiple-group SEM was used to assert that if the model of factorial invariance did not hold over groups, we needed to relax some of the major simple structure restrictions on the factor pattern but not the invariance constraints. This was largely the opposite of the tradition at the time, where invariance constraints were added to simple structures. That is, when doing comparative factor analyses of real data, we may need many common factors (K) before we achieve factorial invariance, and we should not expect the resulting invariant factor pattern to also be simple. This research also showed how rotation of the final multifactor invariant pattern may be needed for substantive understanding.

This use of multiple-group factor invariance model leads to an interesting observation. If we can assume metric factorial invariance, then we do not need to measure every person on every variable to estimate SEMs. In this example, a one- versus two-factor model for the WAIS was considered the key issue, and a "fractional factorial design of measures" was chosen as a quick way to test the specific hypothesis. In this data collection design, presented in this paper, a first group of persons was chosen at random, and only four WAIS-R scales (of eight) were administered. Such a data collection, if it were actually undertaken, should take only about half of the usual testing time. A second randomly selected group was then administered another set of four WAIS-R scales. This process was repeated until eight groups with a different pattern of four measures each were obtained. The result from an eight-group SEM with factorial invariance constraints was compared for one versus two common factors, and the misfit suggested two factors were needed.

The power of the statistical tests for one versus two common factors was compared when there were between $M = 1$ and $M = 8$ variables measured in each required subgroup. The resulting power calculations, based on the Satorra and Saris (1985) method, were plotted for different sample sizes, and the results are surprising. For example, if we used the fractional factorial blocks design based on $M = 4$ variables in each group, and we wanted to achieve a power of 0.95, then we would only need about $n = 80$ persons in each of the eight subgroups. Of course, as the power requirements grow larger, so do the required samples sizes, and as the number of variables measured goes down, so does the resulting power. But, in general, to retain relatively high power for the test of one versus two common factors, it seems relatively few individuals are actually needed in each subgroup.

Common Factors With Longitudinal Observations

The case of repeated measures is an important one in modern data analysis, especially because of the importance placed on repeated measures in ANOVA (see Bock, 1975). Our simplest model was presented here as Figure 15.12, and this was used in McArdle and Nesselroade (1994). In that paper, we assumed the measurement of four different variables (W, X, Y, and Z) were repeated at two occasions. The data we used were four WISC Verbal subscales measured in the first grade and then again in the sixth grade on the same set of children ($N = 204$).

Again the topic of metric factor invariance is raised, but now it can be applied to the same observations over time. The most obvious question, of course, is "Do the means change over time?" This informative question can be answered using a number of different ANOVA techniques (see O'Brien & Kaiser, 1985). But the first SEM question raised is slightly different—"Is exactly the same common factor measured at each occasion?" The techniques of ANOVA typically assume the answer is yes, and we used these procedures here. However, this was not a testable assumption and it is not usually asked because, after all, we have measured the same people using the same instruments. So, although this may seem like an easy question to answer in the affirmative, it is actually not. That is, just because we can measure the same variables at each time does not mean the persons respond to the same features on the tests at both times. There are many real-life situations where we might think the people have changed in a qualitative way, and the factors have changed, so the comparison of means, even for the same observed variables, is really comparing latent apples to latent oranges.

This SEM question was initially answered by fitting a model to the invariance of the factor pattern over time in the WISC verbal scores. Once the best number of factors was determined within each timepoint, a model of metrically invariant loadings (same exact values) was fitted over time, and the loss of fit was examined. Now there is no doubt that we wanted to find invariant factors, so some loss of fit was deemed acceptable. Once the common factors were considered invariant, we could examine the mean changes in the common factor scores, and this became the focus of our analyses. We determined that this gave a different result than either the ANOVA or MANOVA, which created components that appeared to have maximum differences over time. In addition, we added several different features, including the possibility of specific factor covariances over time (see Meredith & Horn, 2001). The correlation of the specific factors over time was also added to this analysis, but this set of parameters proved far less important.

As a byproduct of this two-time invariance analysis, we were also able to show that the factors of the sums over time was the same as the common factors of the changes over time. This was used to show several variations on the way means and covariances could be used, including the creation of a *latent change score* (LCS). In addition, this approach led to a more general expression and a test of the general assumption of metric factorial invariance in multilevel data (see McArdle, 2007; McArdle, Fisher, & Kadlec, 2007).

In the next case of Figure 15.12, we assumed that two factors were apparent at each of the two occasions (see McArdle, 2010), and now we were interested in testing hypotheses about their dynamic nature over time using longitudinal panel data (Blalock, 1985b; Hsiao, 2003). That is, once the same factors are measured at both times, it is reasonable to consider their scores in a cross-lagged analysis. It is also reasonable to define latent factors that have particular patterns of change over time (i.e., G_1 produces H_2, but not the other way around; see McArdle, 2007).

Common Factors With Multiple Longitudinal Observations

Next we assume we have a longitudinal sequence of repeated observations ($Y[t]$, where $t > 2$). In the past, these kinds of data would also typically be analyzed using the ANOVA models for repeated measures, perhaps adding polynomials (see O'Brien & Kaiser, 1985). But the main SEM point here is that these GLM tests are mainly about the group differences in mean changes over repetitions and do not deal with hypotheses about covariances.

In the path diagram of Figure 15.14, we considered an LCM (, after Meredith & Tisak, 1990; see McArdle, 1986). In all cases, more than 200 children were measured at specific occasions (i.e., grades 1, 2, 4, and 6), and we used a LV approach to space the latent measurements out in an equal time lag. That is, when there was no observed data, we simply used a LV as a placeholder. That is, we assumed they had the scores but we never asked for them because of budgetary constraints (i.e., no funding for grades 3 and 5). This basic use of an LV as a placeholder turns out to be a very useful idea in SEMs.

The introduction of measured predictors of the LVs is a natural aspect of LV path models, and this reflects the best thinking in what is now termed *hierarchical* or *multilevel modeling* (Bryk & Raudenbush, 1992). In one case (McArdle, 2005), we fitted some cognitive data over many ages using a LCM, and we estimated the effect of educational attainment of the person, mother, and father on these latent scores. We found that the person's education is mainly influenced by their mother, and this in turn influences the person's slope in cognition over age. There are very few influences on the initial level, or from the father. Now, there should be no doubt that multilevel thinking has allowed much progress in the simplicity of the required calculations, but there is also no doubt that this "new" approach does not automatically produce novel results (*see* McArdle & Hamagami, 1996; Ferrer et al., 2004; Ferrer & McArdle, 2010).

The final LCM is based on work done by McArdle and Woodcock (1997). Here we wanted to estimate a full LCM over many occasions, but a premium was placed on people's time (largely because we wanted to administer up to 17 tests). So we used the basic logic of LVs as incomplete data to design a data collection plan. We measured each individual at a first occasion, and then at a second occasion that was spaced out in time by our data collection design. The basis of the LCM we fitted is drawn as a path diagram ($t = 0$) or was not measured "circle in the square," indicating the person may or may not have been measured, and we did this for up to four follow-up times ($t = 1$ to 4). We applied this principle of a random "time-lag" to estimate and test developmental functions where the person was measured only twice but where we could estimate a multi-occasion LCM. We also found we could apply a second slope component that connected the two points in time, and this led to our independent estimate of a nontrivial *practice function* (with μ_p and σ_p^2). The same approach was applied to multiple indicators of multiple constructs where, by assuming factorial invariance, we could separate the true score changes from state dependent changes, and from test-specific practice effects (*see* McArdle & Woodcock, 1997).

Much of the prior LV thinking was expressed in the recent overviews of McArdle (2009) and Ferrer and McArdle (2010). In one analysis of real data by McArdle and Hamagami (2006), the task was to examine longitudinal changes in both verbal skills and memory skills over age. The basic dynamic hypothesis (from the theory of J.L. Horn) was that memory losses would lead to verbal losses, but not

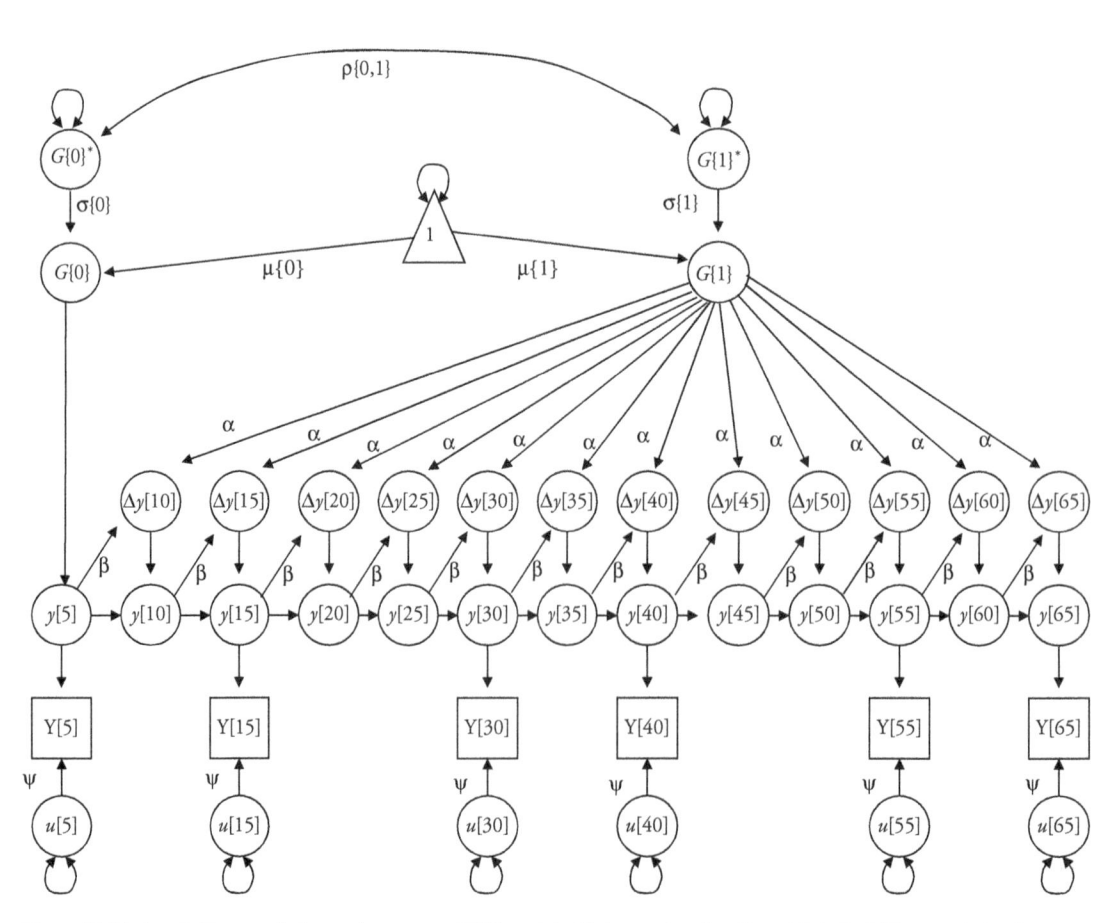

Figure 15.15 A path diagram of a latent change score (LCS) model with incomplete data (from McArdle & Hamagami, 2006).

the other way around. Figure 15.15 is a diagram of a univariate sequence of latent scores ($y[t]$) where only six occasions of measurement ($Y[t]$) have been spread out over a 60-year period (from ages 5 to 65 years). One obvious complexity to this LCM was that the six occasions of measurement were spread out unequally over age, and one non-obvious complexity is that not everyone was measured at each of the six occasions. In addition, the full sample was relatively small ($N = 111$), so only a minimal set of parameters could be accurately estimated. In this first model we proposed that there was a level of latent change scores (symbolized as $\Delta y[t]$ here) that occurred with regularity ($\Delta t = 5$ years here) and were separated from the measurement uniquenesss ($u[t]$). We then suggested that the source of the latent changes were two-part: (α) some of the variation in latent changes came from a constant latent slope ($G\{1\}$), and (β) some of the variation in latent changes came from the immediately prior latent score ($y[t-1]$). Very few parameters were considered here, resulting in an exponential shape for each function, but this LCS-LGM fit each univariate score at least as well as our previous latent basis LCMs.

This result gave us some courage to fit a bivariate dynamic model where there are two sequences of latent changes, as depicted in Figure 15.16. There is no doubt that this bivariate model requires more explanation and elaboration (*see* McArdle, 2001, 2009; Ferrer & McArdle, 2010), but it can be seen now as a model for the observed scores in terms of a combination of latent sources. The latent change in any variable is a three-part function: (α_y) some of the variation in latent changes came from a constant latent slope $G\{1\}$, (β_y) some of the variation in latent changes came from the immediately prior latent score ($y[t-1]$), and (γ_{yx}) some of the variation in latent change came from the other variables prior latent score ($x[t-1]$). We concluded that this effect was indeed in the predicted direction (M → V) and not the other way around.

The Future of Structural Equation Modeling

Up to this point, we have tried to set the stage in the need for SEM analysis, but we have been careful not to actually fit any SEMs to real data nor have we tried to explain why we need to make specific

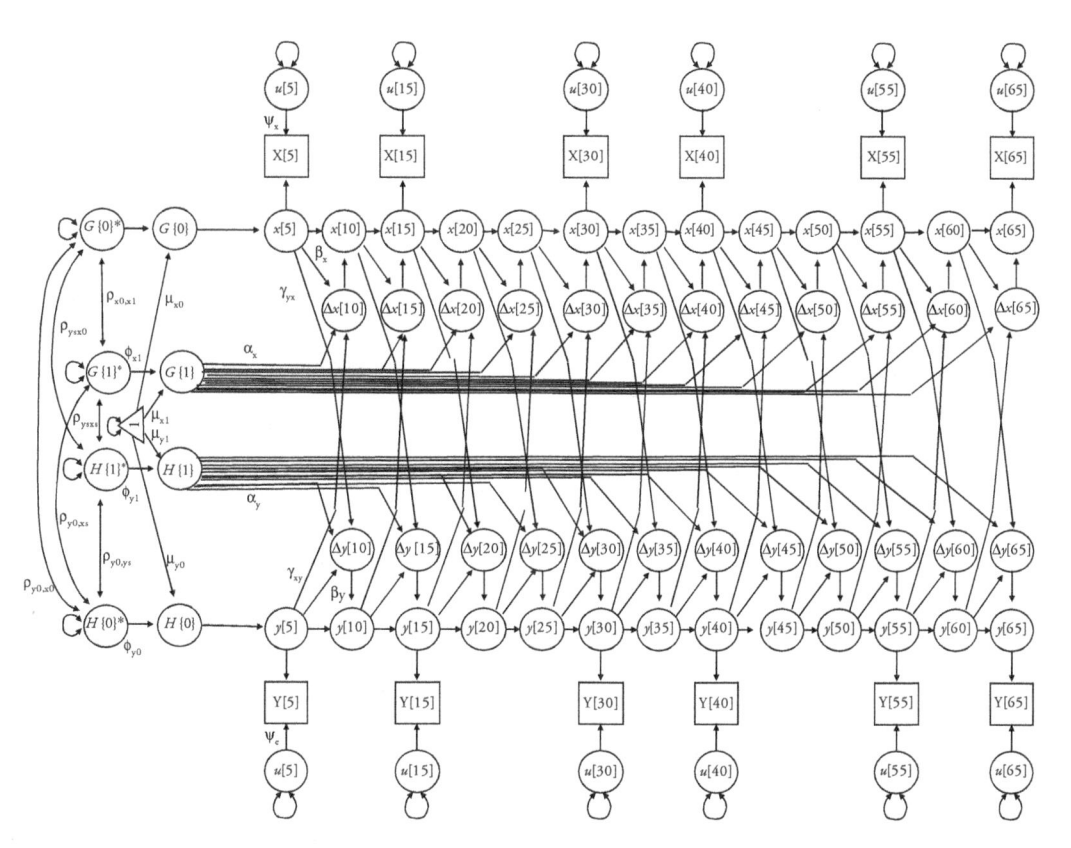

Figure 15.16 A bivariate LCS model (from McArdle & Hamagami, 2006)

analytic choices. For interested readers, there are many good examples of SEM in the growing literature (e.g., Ferrer-Caja, Crawford, & Bryan, 2002; Widaman, 1985; King, King, & Foy, 1996; Kline, 2011). We can also say that a few novel SEM ideas were published in the context of a real problem in "Latent Variable Analysis of Age Trends in Tests of Cognitive Ability in the Health and Retirement Survey, 1992–2004" by McArdle, Fisher, & Kadlec (2007). As we quickly found, aspects of the available theory and available data led us to use very different SEMs than those that seem prominent in this literature.

There are so many contemporary statistical models that can be said to have a SEM form and can be fitted using SEM software, it is often best to say that *SEM is an idea rather than a technique*. In the terms used here, SEM is a concept rather than a tool. We know that one first necessary feature of SEM is of the requirement for clear model specification. When we write out a SEM—any SEM—we really need to know what we are thinking. If we do not have any thoughts, then we do not have any SEM either. This exercise is very useful when creating simulations for demonstrations (as done here), for evaluation of software, or even for Monte Carlo simulation of complex mathematical-statistical issues. The SEM approach offers a level of precision not readily available to other approaches, and this is one reason it is so widely heralded. However, when it comes to actual data analysis, as shown here, the use of SEM does not always improve our understanding beyond that found by simpler and more standard methods (*see* McArdle, 1994). *So perhaps SEM is best thought of as a theoretical tool rather than a practical tool.*

On the other hand, the SEM tools have become rather elegant. Perhaps it is now obvious that either CALIS or Mplus or OpenMx or any of the other programs in Table 15.1 can be used for SEM analyses, and it will not really matter which program we choose. As we have tried to show, the philosophy of CALIS and OpenMx, as with LISREL and others, is that the analyst must ask directly for the parameters of a specific SEM. This was a simple approach adopted by the original programmers of LISREL, and some of this rigidity is now changing. For example, in contrast to CALIS/LISREL and other programs, the working philosophy of Mplus/AMOS and other programs seems to be that the complexity of SEM should be simplified to the point where we do not have to know exactly what we are doing to make this SEM work. If we wanted to base all our analysis strictly around path diagrams, and avoid most algebra, then AMOS (Wothke, 2000) can be a most useful tool. In some cases, we may worry that these elegant SEM tools are falling into the hands of people who do not know what they are doing—*But then we should ask ourselves, who should be the judge here?* The verdict is not yet out on many important issues about who will carry out the best data analysis and who will find the most repeatable result. These are intriguing questions.

So why do we use SEM at all? Well, it is not true that we use SEM because of the path diagrams—many traditional models can be represented using path diagrams, and we really do not need to use SEM tools to use SEM concepts. Also, some of the standard multivariate tools are now very easy to use. But there are three very good reasons why we use SEM for data analysis:

1. We use SEM because we have *a priori* ideas that we want to examine in real data, and some of these ideas are well beyond ANOVA and the so-called GLM framework. We would certainly like to know if we are wrong about these ideas, so we can appreciate much of the ongoing work on SEM estimators, statistical indices, and overall goodness-of-fit indices.

2. We use SEM because we want to consider the inclusion of unobserved variables in our models—that is, *LVs*. We often think about LVs in our theories, variables that are not directly measured or measurable, and we want to represent them in our models of these theories. In this sense, the inclusion of LV is for clarity, not for obscurity. It is also clear that the accurate representation of observed variable distributions may require more complex measurement models than the typical normality assumptions.

3. We use SEM because we would like to select the "true" or "correct" model, or at least an "adequate" model, for a set of data. We believe we can tell we have found an adequate model when we estimate parameters that do not differ with different samplings of person or variables or occasions—that is, the parameters are *invariant*. In the terms of linear regression, we do not always want the model with the highest explained variance for the current set of data, but we do want the model that is most likely to replicate over and over again.

Researchers who are interested in more details on SEM can consider the Technical Appendix that follows. Because these three goals listed above seem reasonable and continue to be part of most behavioral science research, SEM combined as both a concept and a tool is now very popular, and multivariate data analysis is likely to remain this way for a long time to come.

Technical Appendix: Algebraic Notes and Computer Programs for the SEMs Presented
1. Reconsidering Simple Linear Regression

We often presume that one of the variables (X) is an input to the other (Y) and we repeat the common linear regression expression

$$Y_n = \beta_0 + \beta_1 X_n + e_n \text{ with} \quad (1a)$$

$$E\{XX'\} = \sigma_x^2, E\{ee'\} = \phi_e^2, \text{ and}$$

$$E\{Xe'\} = 0. \quad (1b)$$

Here, E is the symbol used for the expected values (rather than the usual greek summation symbol). This combined expression is considered the "structural equation model for the observed scores," and a diagram of this simple model was presented earlier as Figure 15.8.

The same general approach can be used to examine the intercept term (β_0). To estimate the intercept parameter at the same time as the regression coefficient, we need to include a constant term in the model (as a measured predictor, 1, drawn here as a constant triangle). It follows that we need to include this constant into the model of expectations, but this is easily done by augmenting the covariance matrix with a mean vector (μ) or by estimating the model from the average cross-products matrices (Σ; see Table 15.8; Rao, 1958). This approach using means and covariances together forms the basis of many complex models being used today (see McArdle, 1994, 2007, 2009).

A simple way to create the required expected covariance matrix is to write out the SEM in terms of three RAM matrices. That is: (1) the unit elements of the **F** matrix means that the row variable (in the data) and column variable (of the model) should be assigned the same label; (2) the non-zero elements of the **A** matrix represents one-headed arrows where the row variable is input to the column variable; and (3) the non-zero elements of the Ω matrix represents two-headed arrows where the row variable is connected to the column variable. These relations are used to form all model expectations (μ and Σ).

In using RAM notation, we first write the score vectors for all observed and unobserved variables using these definitions, which in this particular model can be listed as

$$\mathbf{m}(3 \times 1) = [X \ Y \ 1], \text{ and}$$

$$\mathbf{v}(4 \times 1) = [X \ Y \ e \ 1]. \quad (1c)$$

Then we can write the three matrices of relationships among these variables as

$$\mathbf{F}(3 \times 4) = \begin{bmatrix} 1 & 0 & 0 & 0 \\ 0 & 1 & 0 & 0 \\ 0 & 0 & 1 & 0 \end{bmatrix}$$

$$\mathbf{A}(4 \times 4) = \begin{bmatrix} 0 & 0 & 0 & 0 \\ 0 & \beta_1 & 1 & \beta_0 \\ 0 & 0 & 0 & 0 \\ 0 & 0 & 0 & 0 \end{bmatrix} \text{ and} \quad (1d)$$

$$\Omega(4 \times 4) = \begin{bmatrix} \sigma_x^2 & 0 & 0 & \mu_x \\ 0 & 0 & 0 & 0 \\ 0 & 0 & \phi_e^2 & 0 \\ 0 & 0 & 0 & 1 \end{bmatrix}$$

This was not presented earlier, but this kind of specification in matrix form leads to the basic calculation of the resulting expected value matrix Σ??g???g measured ???????? g

$$\Sigma(3 \times 3) = \mathbf{F}(\mathbf{I} - \mathbf{A})^{-1} \Omega (\mathbf{I} - \mathbf{A})^{-1'} \mathbf{F}', \quad (1e)$$

?????g????????g????g????? and covariances (see McArdle, 2005). This is not always easy to understand from a matrix point of view, but it does allow us to use the path diagrams more effectively. From the resulting expressions we find that the model expected value of the covariance of Y and X is where Y and X intersect in this matrix (at column 1, row 2), and from our model we know this observed value (σ_{yx}) is supposedly composed of the regression weight (β) multiplied by the variance of X (σ_x^2). Perhaps it is also easy to see that these matrices are simply descriptions of the path graphic display. All other models described below follow the same RAM matrix logic so they will not be presented in detail.

Of course, for simplicity, we can eliminate the intercept (β_0) and the constant (1) and just calculate a single linear regression coefficient (β_1) to describe this X → Y relationship. By assuming that the residuals are independent ($E[X,e] = 0$) of the predictors, we know (from calculus) that the best estimate of this coefficient can be found by multiplying the observed covariance of Y and X (σ_{yx}) by the inverse of the variance of X (σ_{xx}^{-1}), which in algebraic terms is the same as equations 2a and 2b. In simple regression, we can see exactly why this works by writing the structural expectations of the model in the matrix equation for the Σ. This matrix expression is considered the "structural equation model of the observed covariances."

Furthermore, from this expression we can see that the model expected value of the covariance of Y and X, where Y and X intersect in this matrix (at column 1, row 2), and from our model we know this observed value (σ_{yx}) is supposedly composed of the regression weight (β) multiplied by the variance of X (σ_x^2). Thus, if we simply divide by the variance of Y by the variance of X we will have the desired regression coefficient. If we assume the correct model is one of the ones presented in Figures 15.3–15.7 but we fit a standard regression model like Figure 15.2 we obtain the biases previously described.

2. An Example of Structural Equation Model Fitting

One good way to check the SEM computer programming is to create a fictitious data set and then have the SEM program estimate the population values. This is accomplished here using a simple latent path model to illustrate the use of three different kinds of computer programs: (1) SEM in SAS-CALIS (SAS Institute, 2006); (2) SEM in Mplus (Muthen & Muthen, 2002); and (3) SEM in OpenMx (Boker, 2011).

The three SEM programs were chosen for illustration because they are now widely used but seem to represent extremes of the philosophy of SEM techniques. That is, CALIS is one of the programs (like the early versions of LISREL and the current OpenMX) that requires the user to specify all model parameters to be fitted, so very few defaults are invoked, and there is extensive documentation of the techniques. The second program, Mplus (like AMOS or the current version of LISREL), requires the minimal amount of information about the model parameters, many defaults are invoked (including identification), and very little documentation of the techniques is available. The third program, OpenMx, is much like the first program in input style, but this program is completely free. The choice of which program to choose depends on the prior SEM experience of the user. Of course, any other SEM programs (see Table 15.1) could be used instead. In addition to generating the data, each program allows a first set of analyses to be designed to see if we can recover SEM values using any statistical technique.

Let us assume a LV path model can be written for a set of six observed variables (Y(m), $m = 1$ to 6) with two potentially correlated predictors (X(1) and X(2)). Here we assume a latent variable path model can be written for observed variables (Y) with two observed predictors (X). The general model might be written as

$$Y(m)_n = \lambda(m)F_n + u(m)_n \quad \text{for}$$
$$m = 1 \text{ to } M \tag{2a}$$
$$\text{and } F_n = \beta(1)X(1)_n + \beta(2)X(2)_n + d_n.$$

If we further assume the values of M = 6, $\lambda(1, 2, 3) = 0.6$, $\lambda(4, 5, 6) = 0.4$, and $\beta(1) = 0.0$, $\beta(2) = 0.2$ then we have a model that can be rewritten as

$$Y(m)_n = 0.6F_n + u(m)_n \quad \text{for}$$
$$m = 1 \text{ to } 3, \tag{2b}$$
$$Y(m)_n = 0.4F_n + u(m)_n \quad \text{for} \quad m = 4 \text{ to } 6,$$
$$\text{and } F_n = 0.0X(1)_n + 0.2X(1)_n + d_n,$$

and this model appears back in Figure 15.10.

This model can be placed in RAM notation by writing the score vectors for all observed and unobserved variables as

$$\mathbf{m}(8 \times 1) = [Y(1)Y(2)Y(3)Y(4)$$
$$Y(5)Y(6)X(1)X(2)], \text{ and} \tag{2c}$$
$$\mathbf{v}(9 \times 1) = [Y(1)Y(2)Y(3)Y(4)$$
$$Y(5)Y(6)X(1)X(2)F].$$

Then we can write the matrices of relationships as

$$F(8 \times 9) = \begin{bmatrix} 1 & 0 & 0 & 0 & 0 & 0 & 0 & 0 & 0 \\ 0 & 1 & 0 & 0 & 0 & 0 & 0 & 0 & 0 \\ 0 & 0 & 1 & 0 & 0 & 0 & 0 & 0 & 0 \\ 0 & 0 & 0 & 1 & 0 & 0 & 0 & 0 & 0 \\ 0 & 0 & 0 & 0 & 1 & 0 & 0 & 0 & 0 \\ 0 & 0 & 0 & 0 & 0 & 1 & 0 & 0 & 0 \\ 0 & 0 & 0 & 0 & 0 & 0 & 1 & 0 & 0 \\ 0 & 0 & 0 & 0 & 0 & 0 & 0 & 1 & 0 \end{bmatrix}$$

$$A(9 \times 9) = \begin{bmatrix} 0 & 0 & 0 & 0 & 0 & 0 & 0 & 0 & \lambda(1) \\ 0 & 0 & 0 & 0 & 0 & 0 & 0 & 0 & \lambda(2) \\ 0 & 0 & 0 & 0 & 0 & 0 & 0 & 0 & \lambda(3) \\ 0 & 0 & 0 & 0 & 0 & 0 & 0 & 0 & \lambda(4) \\ 0 & 0 & 0 & 0 & 0 & 0 & 0 & 0 & \lambda(5) \\ 0 & 0 & 0 & 0 & 0 & 0 & 0 & 0 & \lambda(6) \\ 0 & 0 & 0 & 0 & 0 & 0 & 0 & 0 & 0 \\ 0 & 0 & 0 & 0 & 0 & 0 & 0 & 0 & 0 \\ 0 & 0 & 0 & 0 & 0 & 0 & \beta(1) & \beta(2) & 0 \end{bmatrix} \text{ and} \tag{2d}$$

$$\Omega(9 \times 9; \text{symmetric}) =$$

$$\begin{bmatrix} \psi(1)^2 & & & & & & & & \\ 0 & \psi(2)^2 & & & & & & & \\ 0 & 0 & \psi(3)^2 & & & & & & \\ 0 & 0 & 0 & \psi(4)^2 & & & & & \\ 0 & 0 & 0 & 0 & \psi(5)^2 & & & & \\ 0 & 0 & 0 & 0 & 0 & \psi(6)^2 & & & \\ 0 & 0 & 0 & 0 & 0 & 0 & \sigma_{x1}^2 & & \\ 0 & 0 & 0 & 0 & 0 & 0 & 0 & \sigma_{12} & \sigma_{x2}^2 \\ 0 & 0 & 0 & 0 & 0 & 0 & 0 & 0 & \phi_d^2 \end{bmatrix}$$

Whereby using formula 1e above leads to the direct calculation of the structural model of covariances (later listed in Table 15.A1).

Let us next assume the values of $\lambda(1, 2, 3) = 0.6$, $\lambda(4, 5, 6) = 0.4$, and $\beta(1)g = 0.0$ and $\beta(2) = 0.8$. In this model we have one common factor with six indicators, one measured variable (X(1)) that is unrelated to the common factor and one measured variable that does produce it (X(2)). The values chosen are relatively small ($\lambda(1) = 0.6$, $\lambda(4) = 0.4$, $\beta(1) = 0.0$, and $\beta(2) = 0.8$) and the additional variance terms, created so all residual variables in the population have zero means and unit variances, make the net effects even smaller. This places numerical values on the parameters of Figure 15.10, and this is drawn in Figure 15.A1, and it often called a *multiple indicator multiple causes* (MIMIC) model (Hauser & Goldberger, 1971).

Details of the required computer program are presented in the Technical Appendix, and just a few details are presented here. Random score vectors that are consistent with this specific model may be created using many different computer programs (e.g., we present code for the SAS DATA step here using RANNOR functions in Table 15.A2). The output is generated by specific line of code, and it is a summary description of the simulated data in terms of means, standard deviations, and correlations, created from each program for $N = 1,001$ entities

Figure 15.A1 A "population" latent path model useful for CALIS programming.

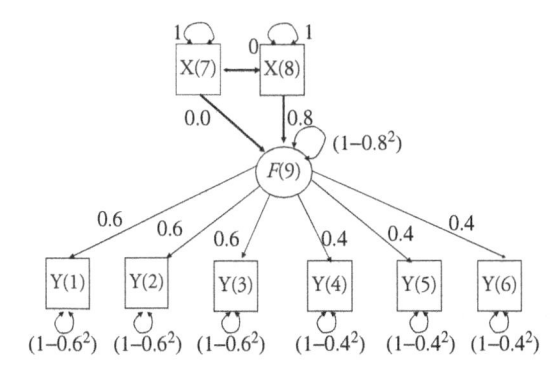

(another program option). Here, we have included the actual factor score created (F_score) as well as one of the many empirical estimates of this factor score (the F_aver).

Fitting the Simulated MIMIC Data With Standard Modeling Software

The three program outputs (Table 15.A3–15.A5) also show the results of scripts for running a few conventional analyses on these simulated data. For example, we might run a simple factor analysis of the six observed outcomes (Y; e.g., using SAS-FACTOR). The output of this analysis is presented in Table 15.A3. Using the traditional Scree Plot and the Scree logic (Cattell, 1978), we clearly find one dominant factor. Using the Maximum-Likelihood Factor extraction technique (*see* Lawley & Maxwell, 1971), we obtain a test statistic that shows the zero-common factor model is a poor fit to the data ($\chi^2 = 860$ on $df = 15$, p(perfect fit) < 0.0001), but the one-factor model is much better ($\chi^2 = 21$ on $df = 9$, p(perfect fit) > 0.01), and the resulting difference in fit resulting from inclusion of 6 loadings was worthwhile ($d\chi^2 = 839$ on $df = 6$, p(no difference) < 0.0001). The ML estimated factor loadings $\Lambda = [0.61, 0.60, 0.60, 0.46, 0.49, 0.47]$ are very close to the true values $\Lambda = [0.6, 0.6, 0.6, 0.4, 0.4, 0.4]$, and we would probably not be misled in any way. Of course, this is the correct model for the data so this seems appropriate. Obviously this standard approach to factor analysis seems very reasonable for these simple latent path scores, using either the Scree or ML approach.

After this, we might run a linear regression where one of the most reliable outcomes, the average of the Y(m), is regressed on the two input Xs. This results (*see* Output Tables 15.A4–15.A5) in a significant overall F ($p < 0.0001$), $\beta(0) = 0.04$ (ns), $\beta(1) = 0.04$ (ns), and $\beta(2) = 0.39$ ($p < 0.0001$), with an $R^2 = 0.26$. This was obviously considered significant (i.e., accurately different than zero) because of the large sample size (N = 1001). In this case, the regression model is largely correct, but we know the true regression values should be $\beta(0) = 0.0$, $\beta(1) = 0.0$, and $\beta(2) = \lambda(1)^*\beta(2) = 0.6^*0.8 = 0.46$, and the explained variance of the true factor scores is only $R^2 = 0.8^2/(0.8^2 + 1) = 0.19$. Thus, the linear regression has done what it can to get the correct answer using the approximate solution because the average is presumed to account for all the unreliability – and it does not.

Table 15.A2 SAS Input Script to Generate Data for SEM-LVP

```
TITLE2 'Generating Simulation Data using random normal theory';
TITLE3 'Where Correct Model is one factor y(m) = L f + u(m) and f=B0+B1*X+e';
DATA sim_lvp1;
* setting mathematical parameters;
  mu_F = 0; sigma_F = 1; mu_u = 0; sigma_u = 1;
  mu_d = 0; sigma_d = 1; mu_x = 0; sigma_x = 1;
  Lf1 = .6; Lf2 = .4;  Bf1 = .0; Bf2 = .8;
* setting statistical parameters;
  N = 1001;   seed = 20110325;
* setup arrays for vector variables;
ARRAY u_score{6} u1-u6; ARRAY y_score{6} y1-y6;
* generating raw data;
  DO _N_ = 1 TO N; ID=_N_;
* first the true structural regression model;
     x1_score = mu_x + sigma_x * RANNOR(seed); x2_score = mu_x + sigma_x * RANNOR(seed);
     d_score  = mu_d + sigma_d * RANNOR(seed);
     f_score = Bf1 * x1_score + Bf2 * x2_score + d_score;
* now the measurement model ;
        DO m = 1 TO 3;
           u_score{m} = mu_u + sigma_u * RANNOR(seed); y_score{m} = Lf1 * F_score + u_score{m};
        END;
        DO m = 4 TO 6;
           u_score{m} = mu_u + sigma_u * RANNOR(seed); y_score{m} = Lf2 * F_score + u_score{m};
        END;
* finally save some data ;
     Y_aver = (y1 + y2 + y3 + y4 + y5 + y6)/6;
     KEEP ID y1--y6 x1_score x2_score F_score Y_aver;
     OUTPUT;
  END;
RUN;
```

Table 15.A3 SAS Input for Analysis of Generated Data

```
*************************************************************;
TITLE2 'Analysis 1: Correct Factor Analyses on the Generated
Data';
*************************************************************;
PROC FACTOR SCREE ROUND; VAR y1--y6;  RUN;
PROC FACTOR SCREE ROUND METHOD=ML NFACT=1; VAR y1--y6; RUN;
PROC FACTOR SCREE ROUND METHOD=ML NFACT=2 ROTATE=PROMAX;
VAR y1--y6;  RUN;


*************************************************************;
TITLE2 'Analysis 2: Correct Regression Analyses on Various
Sets of Data';
*************************************************************;
PROC REG; MODEL y1 = x1_score x2_score / STB; RUN;
PROC REG; MODEL y1--y6 = x1_score X2_score / STB; RUN;
PROC REG; MODEL y_aver = x1_score x2_score / STB; RUN;
PROC CANCORR ALL; VAR y1--y6;  WITH x1_score x2_score;  RUN;
```

Table 15.A4 SAS Output of ML Factor Analysis

```
Convergence criterion satisfied.
              Significance Tests Based on 1001 Observations
                                                                Pr >
        Significance Tests Based on 1001 Observations

                                                                Pr >
              Test                      DF      Chi-Square     ChiSq

        H0: No common factors            15      860.1274     <.0001
        HA: At least one common factor
        H0: 1 Factor is sufficient        9       21.2389     0.0116
        HA: More factors are needed
        H0: 2 Factors are sufficient      4        4.7959     0.3089
        HA: More factors are needed

The FACTOR Procedure
              Initial Factor Method: Maximum Likelihood

                       Factor Pattern

                          Factor1

                   y1      61 *
                   y2      60 *
                   y3      60 *
                   y4      46
                   y5      49
                   y6      47
```

The next likely analysis is a canonical regression of the relationships between all Y(m) variables and the two X input variables. The output (Table 15.A5) shows a significant canonical $F = 29$ on $df_b = 12$ and $df_w = 1996$, so $p < 0.0001$, and the canonical $R^2 = 0.27$, so this is close to the true $R_f^2 = 0.19$, but it is somewhat inflated. However, the second canonical component is not significant ($p > 0.40$) so only the first component would be considered in actual research. The canonical correlations between the six Y variables and the two X variable estimates the canonical weights as $\beta = [-0.005, -1.000]$, correctly pointing to the second X variable as the source of this component. The canonical loadings on the Y side are estimated as $\Lambda = [0.74, 0.71, 0.65, 0.52, 0.49, 0.63]$, rather than the true values of $\Lambda = [0.6, 0.6, 0.6, 0.4, 0.4, 0.4]$, so these estimates are also slightly inflated. However, an this is impotant, the general canonical regression conclusion seems correct—there is at least one small but significant relationship between the X(2) and the Y(6) variables, and the first three outcomes (especially Y(1)) are more related to the relationship than the last three outcomes (the least of which is Y(5)).

Fitting the Simulated MIMIC Data With SEM-CALIS

These simulated data in SAS can be directly compared with the model expectations. Input (Table 15.A6) includes two SAS-CALIS script for a first SEM analyses we might carry out on the observed data. In the first script, LVP#0, we only consider the data from the now observed variables (Y(1)–Y(6) and X(1) and X(2)) and we use the RAM notation option of SAS-CALIS. In this option, the variables are assumed to be numbered by their entry in the observed data, so observed variables (1–8) are augmented with any LVs (numbers > 8). In this case, we have only described one new variable (number 9) and this is the common factor (F). Although

Table 15.A5 SAS Output Multiple Regression on the Average Outcome

```
The REG Procedure
                        Model: MODEL1
                   Dependent Variable: y_aver

          Number of Observations Read        1001
          Number of Observations Used        1001
```

Analysis of Variance

Source	DF	Sum of Squares	Mean Square	F Value	Pr > F
Model	2	153.72423	76.86212	179.09	<.0001
Error	998	428.32225	0.42918		
Corrected Total	1000	582.04648			

Root MSE	0.65512	R-Square	0.2641
Dependent Mean	0.01791	Adj R-Sq	0.2626
Coeff Var	3657.47239		

Parameter Estimates

Variable	DF	Parameter Estimate	Standard Error	t Value	Pr > |t|	Standardized Estimate
Intercept	1	0.03686	0.02073	1.78	0.0758	0
x1_score	1	0.00294	0.01996	0.15	0.8828	0.00400
x2_score	1	0.38760	0.02049	18.92	<.0001	0.51383

it is possible to enter another LV for the disturbance term (d, termed 10), for simplicity we do not need to do so here.

After doing this, each non-zero entry in the matrix is listed in terms of: (1) Matrix Number (or number of arrowheads), (2) Row Number (output variable), (3) Column Number (input variable), (4) Start Value (best guess), and (5) an optional label for the "free" parameters. This is done in order here for the first elements, which can be understood as "Matrix = 1, Row = 1, Column = 9, value = 0.6, fixed (resulting from no label)," indicating that LV 9 is input to manifest variable 1. The next five entries are similar, giving the specific fixed values of the factor loadings, and the seventh entry is understood as "Matrix = 1, Row = 9, Column = 7, Value = 0.0," indicating that manifest variable 7 is input to LV 9 with a starting value = 0.0. The two-headed arrows of the model (see Figure 15.10) are first entered as elements that can be understood as "Matrix = 2, Row = 1, Column = 1, value = 1, termed U12," This is done to indicate that manifest variable 1 is connected to manifest variable 1 with a two-headed arrow termed "U12" that can be estimated from the data. The next five entries are similar, giving the starting values of the unique variances ($\psi(m)^2$) at unity, but the seventh entry is understood as "Matrix = 2, Row = 9, Column = 9, Value = 1, Label = "Vd," indicating that latent variable 9 has a variance term, and the last entry indicates LV 9 has a variance term. Figure 15.A1 can be termed a "compact diagram" because the unique factors have not been displayed. Any LVs that have fixed loadings of 1 and only produce one other outcome need not be put in the path diagram (e.g., McArdle, 2005), or in the program, so we only include their parameters. The ";" followed by the "RUN;" command is used to initiate the calculation.

The first output of the SAS-CALIS program gives a thorough description of the input model, input data, and iterative steps, but all this output is not included here. Instead, we simply jump to the results of goodness-of-fit listed in another section of the output (see Table 15.A7). It seems SAS-CALIS

Table 15.A6 SAS Output of Canonical Regression Analysis

```
Canonical Correlation Analysis
                            Adjusted      Approximate        Squared
              Canonical     Canonical       Standard        Canonical
             Correlation   Correlation       Error         Correlation
        1     0.521979      0.517968       0.023007         0.272462
        2     0.071472      0.043861       0.031461         0.005108
                         Eigenvalues of Inv(E)*H
                          = CanRsq/(1-CanRsq)
              Eigenvalue    Difference    Proportion       Cumulative
        1       0.3745        0.3694        0.9865           0.9865
        2       0.0051                      0.0135           1.0000
Test of H0: The canonical correlations in the current row and all that follow are zero
              Likelihood    Approximate
                Ratio         F Value     Num DF    Den DF     Pr > F
        1     0.72382144      29.03         12       1986      <.0001
        2     0.99489179       1.02          5        994      0.4040

Standardized Canonical Coefficients for the WITH Variables
                               W1               W2
              x1_score       -0.0050          1.0002
              x2_score        1.0001         -0.0137
Canonical Structure Correlations Between the VAR Variables and Their Canonical Variable
                               V1               V2
                 y1           0.7480           0.0901
                 y2           0.7128          -0.1069
                 y3           0.6517          -0.1814
                 y4           0.5228          -0.1490
                 y5           0.4897           0.8075
                 y6           0.6286          -0.0366
```

calculates and lists almost every statistical index ever invented (with the exception of some in Horn & McArdle, 1992). Without being hypercritical, we need to pick the indices of importance to our own work. In our SEM experience, the only indices that matter are: (1) the $\chi^2 = 38$. (as usual, no decimal places are needed); (2) the dfs = 26; (3) the p(perfect) > 0.063; (4) the $\varepsilon_a = 0.021$; and (5) the p(close fit) = 0.999, so this model fits the data very well. Incidentally, from the first two indices (and the N), we can derive all other indices on the output.

The estimates from the model are presented in Table 15.A8. Some of the other estimates are the unique variance terms $\Psi^2 = [0.67, 0.64, 0.60, 0.86, 0.94, 0.90]$, and these are very close to the true values of $\Psi^2 = [0.64, 0.64, 0.64, 0.84, 0.84, 0.84]$. The other terms are related to the Xs, and the program seems to eliminate the X(1) score (it does not) because we have set $\beta(1) = 0$, while it keeps X(2) because it is related at $\beta(2) = 0.8$. The other two terms are the variance of the predictor (estimated $\sigma_x^2 = 1.02$ vs. true $\sigma_x^2 = 1.00$) and variance of the disturbance (estimated $\phi_d^2 = 0.89$ vs. true $\phi_d^2 = 0.96$). The standardized estimates (the estimates as if all variables have unit variance) are also listed, but these are less relevant here.

We can see that this Confirmatory LVP or MIMIC model fits these data very well indeed. This, of course, should be no surprise, because we generated the data in exactly this way. This result merely shows the SAS programming worked correctly. This confirmatory latent path model assumes we have the correct pattern hypothesis, as well as all one-headed arrows. That is, we are not willing to let the algorithm optimize all parameter estimates. Incidentally, the reason we fixed the one-headed arrows in LVP #0 was that under some specific forms of sampling of persons, these parameters should be invariant (see Meredith, 1964, 1993; Meredith & Horn, 2001). On the other hand, the two-headed arrows would typically depend on the sample selection mechanism. In essence, the LVP #0 is exactly the kind of *a priori* model we hope to achieve,

Table 15.A7 SAS Scripts for Confirmatory LVP #0 and LVP#1

```
*************************************************************;
TITLE2 'Analysis LVP#0: Confirmatory LVP Analysis on Full Manifest Data';
*************************************************************;
PROC CALIS COV DATA=sim_lvp1;
      VAR y1--y6 x1_score x2_score;
    * so first common factor is number 9;
      RAM
      1 1 9 0.6,   1 2 9 0.6,   1 3 9 0.6,    1 4 9 0.4,   1 5 9 0.4,   1 6 9 0.4,
      1 9 7 0.0,   1 9 8 0.8,
      2 1 1   1 U12,  2 2 2   1 U22,  2 3 3   1 U32, 2 4 4   1 U42,  2 5 5   1 U52,  2 6 6   1 U62,
      2 7 7   1 Vx1,  2 8 8   1 Vx2,  2 9 9   1 Vd,
      2 8 7   0 C12;
      RUN;


*************************************************************;
TITLE2 'Analysis LVP#1: Correct LVP Analysis on Full Manifest Data';
*************************************************************;
PROC CALIS
      COV
      DATA=sim_lvp1;
      VAR y1--y6 x1_score x2_score; ! so first common factor is 9
      RAM
      1 1 9 .1 L1,   1 2 9 .1 L2,   1 3 9 .1 L3,
      1 4 9 .1 L4,   1 5 9 .1 L5,   1 6 9 .1 L6,
      1 9 7 .1 Bf1,  1 9 8 .1 Bf2,

      2 1 1   1 U12, 2 2 2   1 U22, 2 3 3   1 U32,
      2 4 4   1 U42, 2 5 5   1 U52, 2 6 6   1 U62,
      2 7 7   1 Vx1, 2 8 8   1 Vx2, 2 9 9   1 Vd,
      2 7 8 0.1 C12;

      RUN;
```

although this is certainly rare (i.e., more typically, only the structural pattern would count). The fact that the program recovered the correct answer for LVP #0 shows that the SAS-CALIS program actually works!

Next we try to fit this model to these data using other optional forms. In the other input of Table 15.A8 we use the same correct structural pattern, but now we try to estimate all but one of the true factor loadings (i.e., fixing $\lambda(1) = 1$) and the factor regression (done by supplying labels for all one-headed arrows). The output of this LVP #1 is the typical way models are fit to data. The output shows the fit is excellent (i.e., $\chi^2 = 18.$, df s = 20, p(perfect) > 0.59, the $\varepsilon_a = 0.000$, and p(close fit) = 1.000.) The estimated values in this output show how the ratio of the loadings is largely preserved by the estimates ($\lambda_1/\lambda_2 = 1/0.97$ instead of 0.6/0.6, $\lambda_1/\lambda_4 = 1/0.69$ instead of 0.6/0.4, and $\lambda_4/\lambda_5 = 0.69/0.67$ instead of 0.4/0.4). This means SAS-CALIS worked again, even when we did not use a complete *a priori* specification of the loadings and regression in advance.

The next line of input scripts (LVP#2 and LVP#3 of Table 15.A9) are a bit different, because here we explicitly restrict the $\beta(1) = 0$ (see line 8). This, of course, is the way we generated the data so this model should fit without failure, and it fits about the same as the prior model ($\chi^2 = 57.$ df s = 19, p(perfect) < 0.01, the $\varepsilon_a = 0.08$, and p(close fit) = 0.36). In the next script we explicitly restrict the $\beta(2) = 0$ (see line 8). This of course, is not the way we generated the data so this model should not fit so well anymore. The shows a $\chi^2 = 157.$, df s = 19, p(perfect) < 0.0001, the $\varepsilon_a = 0.18$, and p(close fit) = 0.001. The same output also shows the other model parameters are affected but not by very much. As we know from many studies of statistical power (e.g., Satorra & Saris, 1985), the inclusion of small sized effects can only be found in large-scale data sets.

There are many other models that could be fit to these data, and we encourage the reader to try some

Table 15.A8 SAS Goodness-of-Fit Output for Confirmatory LVP #0

```
Fit Function                                              0.0378
       Goodness of Fit Index (GFI)                        0.9906
       GFI Adjusted for Degrees of Freedom (AGFI)         0.9869
       Root Mean Square Residual (RMR)                    0.0357
       Standardized Root Mean Square Residual (SRMR)      0.0266
       Parsimonious GFI (Mulaik, 1989)                    0.9198
       Chi-Square                                        37.8469
       Chi-Square DF                                          26
       Pr > Chi-Square                                    0.0626
       Independence Model Chi-Square                      1186.1
       Independence Model Chi-Square DF                       28
       RMSEA Estimate                                     0.0213
       RMSEA 90% Lower Confidence Limit                        .
       RMSEA 90% Upper Confidence Limit                   0.0353
       ECVI Estimate                                      0.0580
       ECVI 90% Lower Confidence Limit                         .
       ECVI 90% Upper Confidence Limit                    0.0786
       Probability of Close Fit                           0.9999

       Normal Theory Reweighted LS Chi-Square            38.1079
       Akaike's Information Criterion                   -14.1531
       Bozdogan's (1987) CAIC                          -167.7807
       Schwarz's Bayesian Criterion                    -141.7807
       McDonald's (1989) Centrality                       0.9941
       Bentler & Bonett's (1980) Non-normed Index         0.9890
       Bentler & Bonett's (1980) NFI                      0.9681
       James, Mulaik, & Brett (1982) Parsimonious NFI     0.8989
       Z-Test of Wilson & Hilferty (1931)                 1.5345
       Bollen (1986) Normed Index Rho1                    0.9656
       Bollen (1988) Non-normed Index Delta2              0.9898
       Hoelter's (1983) Critical N                          1029
```

of these. Another set of input scripts can be made which differ from the other SEMs in one important respect—here we include only variables Y(1), Y(2), Y(3), and X(2). That is, four potentially measured variables Y(4), Y(5), Y(6) and X(1) can been eliminated from the SAS-CALIS input. The question we can try to answer here is will the correct values emerge from the analysis even though all the variables are not used? The answer should be yes, because we have left just enough variables in the data to identify the model, but we are not sure how SAS-CALIS will like this selection of variables. As we find looking at the output (this can be tried by the reader), SAS-CALIS finds this to be a very reasonable model for the data ($\chi^2 = 1.0$, dfs = 2, p(perfect) > 0.7, $\varepsilon_a = 0.02$, and p(close fit) = 0.96). In addition, this shows the values for the parameters estimated are reasonable ($\lambda_1/\lambda_4 = 1.0/0.7$ vs. $0.6/0.4$) with the key $\beta = 0.15$ ($t > 5$). These are not completely incorrect, but we must recognize that the LVP model has lost a lot of dfs, because of seemingly missing observed scores, and the precision is lowered. This illustrates an important SEM message—if you want to pick up small effects and patterns in data, then you need large samples of variables and persons.

Fitting the Simulated MIMIC Data With SEM-Mplus

The same points made above will be illustrated using the Mplus computer program (Muthen & Muthen, 2002). One way to write an Mplus script for the LVP model appears (Table 15.A10). The TITLE line and the DATA line have several options, and the previous data could been output from SAS simulation (of Input 1) to a text file ("sim_lvp1.dat") with space delimiters and read back into Mplus. However, here we do not illustrate an option in the

Table 15.A9 SAS-MLE Output for Confirmatory LVP #0

The CALIS Procedure

```
                  Covariance Structure Analysis: Maximum Likelihood Estimation
                                        RAM Estimates

                                                                         Standard
Term    Matrix    -----Row------    ----Column----    Parameter    Estimate       Error      t Value

  1        2      y1         1      F1          9         .         0.60000
  1        2      y2         2      F1          9         .         0.60000
  1        2      y3         3      F1          9         .         0.60000
  1        2      y4         4      F1          9         .         0.40000
  1        2      y5         5      F1          9         .         0.40000
  1        2      y6         6      F1          9         .         0.40000
  1        2      F1         9      x2_score    8         .         0.80000
  1        3      E1         1      E1          1        U12        0.97655      0.05142     18.99
  1        3      E2         2      E2          2        U22        0.98872      0.05195     19.03
  1        3      E3         3      E3          3        U32        1.01454      0.05306     19.12
  1        3      E4         4      E4          4        U42        1.03530      0.04935     20.98
  1        3      E5         5      E5          5        U52        0.92325      0.04437     20.81
  1        3      E6         6      E6          6        U62        1.03782      0.04947     20.98
  1        3      E7         7      E7          7        Vx1        1.07729      0.04818     22.36
  1        3      E8         8      E7          7        C12        0.01963      0.03320      0.59
  1        3      E8         8      E8          8        Vx2        1.02287      0.04574     22.36
  1        3      D1         9      D1          9        Vd         1.04110      0.07637     13.63


                              Standardized Estimates (NOT CRITICAL!)

              ------Row------       ----Column-----     Parameter      Estimate

                  y1         1      F1          9           .          0.62021
                  y2         2      F1          9           .          0.61785
                  y3         3      F1          9           .          0.61292
                  y4         4      F1          9           .          0.45569
                  y5         5      F1          9           .          0.47658
                  y6         6      F1          9           .          0.45525
                  F1         9      x2_score    8           .          0.62133
```

Mplus program that allows us to generate the data using statistical simulation—MONTECARLO. We could only ask for one replication (REP = 1) but we could ask for many more (i.e., REP = 101). In essence, the Mplus program allows the user to create repetitions of data based on one model and then fit the same or a different model to these data. The VARIABLE line allows names for all the variables in the file (and USEVAR is used to select the ones to consider in the model). Of course, we are not using many other useful features of Mplus (e.g., CATEGORICAL, MISSING). The ANALYSIS line is used to describe the kind of analysis required (TYPE = MEANSTRUCTURE). Once again, we are not using many other analytic features of Mplus (MISSING, CLUSTER, MIXTURE, etc.). The "MODEL POPULATION:" command allows us to create any population model we would like to examine. This allows us to add a LV to the model simply by creating a new name (F_score) that is not among the VARIABLES, and the BY statement (f_score BY Y1–Y3 0.6 Y4–Y6 * 0.6;) indicates that this is a common factor formed from the three Y(m) variables but with different loadings. The second line asks for the addition of a regression of the "f_score ON X1*0.0 X2*0.8;" so this is the designation of the βs in the MIMIC model. The "MODEL:" command is a request to fit a specific model to the simulated data, and here we fit essentially the population model without fixed values (i.e., MODEL: f_score ON Y1–Y3; f_score ON X1 X2;), but this is not necessary. Any alternative could be attempted at this point. The OUPUT line allows many other options.

Table 15.A10 SAS-CALIS Input for LVP #2 and LVP #3

```
*************************************************************;
TITLE2 'Analysis LVP#2: Correctly Restricted LVP Analysis';
*************************************************************;
PROC CALIS COV DATA=sim_lvp1; VAR y1--y6 x1_score x2_score;
    * so first common factor is number 9;
    RAM
    1 1 9 1.0  ,  1 2 9 .1 L2,  1 3 9 .1 L3,
    1 4 9 .1 L4,  1 5 9 .1 L5,  1 6 9 .1 L6,
    1 9 7 0   ,  1 9 8 .1 Bf2,
    2 1 1  1 U12,  2 2 2  1 U22,  2 3 3  1 U32,
    2 4 4  1 U42,  2 5 5  1 U52,  2 6 6  1 U62,
    2 7 7  1 Vx1,  2 8 8  1 Vx2,  2 9 9  1 Vd,
    2 8 7  .0 C12;
    RUN;
*************************************************************;
TITLE2 'Analysis LVP#3: InCorrectly Restricted LVP Analysis ';
*************************************************************;
PROC CALIS COV DATA=sim_lvp1; VAR y1--y6 x1_score x2_score;
RAM
    1 1 8 1.0,   1 2 8 .1 L2,  1 3 8 .1 L3,
    1 4 8 .1 L4, 1 5 8 .1 L5,  1 6 8 .1 L6,
    1 9 7 0,     1 9 8 0,
    2 1 1  1 U12,  2 2 2  1 U22,  2 3 3  1 U32,
    2 4 4  1 U42,  2 5 5  1 U52,  2 6 6  1 U62,
    2 7 7  1 Vx1,  2 8 8  1 Vx2,  2 9 9  1 Vd,
    2 8 7  .1 C12;

    RUN;


*************************************************************;
TITLE2 'Analysis 3.4: Correctly Identified LVP Analysis on Less Manifest Data';
*************************************************************;
PROC CALIS
    COV
    DATA=sim_lvp1;
    VAR y1--y3 x2_score;
    RAM
    1 1 5 1.0,   1 2 5 .1 L2,  1 3 5 .1 L3,
    1 5 4 .1 Bf2,
    2 1 1  1 U12,  2 2 2  1 U22,  2 3 3  1 U32,
    2 4 4  1 Vx,   2 5 5  1 Vd;
    RUN;
```

The first result from Mplus is simply a description of our data and main analysis problem. This output starts with a listing of the summary statistics calculated by Mplus from the raw data, and these are equivalent to the SAS results (in Table 15.A11). This result also gives an indication that the iterations have converged (so the model is identified), and the results are nearly equivalent to SAS-CALIS ($\chi^2 = 19$, dfs $= 19$, p(perfect) > 0.8, the $\varepsilon_a = 0.000$, and p(close fit) $= 1.000$). The estimated values in Table 15.A9 show how the ratio of the loadings is again largely preserved by the estimates

Table 15.A11 **Mplus Input Script for LVP #3**

```
TITLE: First Latent Variable Path model;
DATA: FILE = 'sim_lvp1.dat';

VARIABLE: NAMES = ID y1-y6 x1_score x2_score
   y_aver F_score;
   USEVAR = y1-y3 x1_score x2_score;

ANALYSIS: TYPE = MEANSTRUCTURE;

MODEL: f_score BY y1-y3;
       f_score ON X2_score;

OUTPUT: SAMPSTAT STANDARDIZED RESIDUAL;
```

($\lambda_1/\lambda_2 = 1/.97$ instead of 0.6/0.6), and here the Mplus program automatically created the required identification constraint ($\lambda_1 = 1$) and freely estimated the other parameters. The MLE, its standard error (S.E.), their ratio (z-value), and a two-tailed p(non-zero) are all listed for every parameter. To get at some population values, Table 15.A9 may be useful, and here we see the standardized effect of the observed X on the unobserved F is $\beta = 0.26$ with $R^2 = (1 - 0.932) = 0.068$. Of course, this means Mplus worked even when we did not use an *a priori* specification of the loadings and regression in advance, and when we did not have to include all the indicators of the common factor.

Without any doubt, the Mplus program is easy to use, and many researchers find this to be the most critical feature (*see* Maydeau-Olivares, 2000). In addition, Mplus now allows users to easily: (1) access advanced measurement techniques, such as dealing with measurement models such as ordinal, nominal, censored, and Poisson-based responses; (2) access advanced statistical techniques, such as sampling weights, multiple-group SEM, two-level SEM with a cluster structure, latent mixture SEMs of a general variety; (3) the direct inclusion of survival analyses with base-hazards and time-censoring; (4) the estimation of missing data using either maximum likelihood or multiple imputation; and (5) the use of Monte Carlo generation of simulated data uses the same input language. Among the most common complaints about Mplus are: (6) the default options do not always make the best sense (i.e., why correlate all LVs?); (7) there are few options for data input—that is, we can only use short names (up to 8 characters), we cannot read input data directly from standard statistical software, and we cannot read past a pre-specified number of columns; (8) user input errors are often hard to track down (i.e., it does not point to a line number in a script); and (9) as with many other SEM programs, Mplus does not allow Path Diagrams for input and/or output. All these problems can be overcome and they probably will be altered in future versions.

Fitting the Simulated MIMIC Data With R Code – OpenMx, lavaan, sem

The OpenMx program (*see* Boker, 2011) is relatively new and seems largely untried, but it is also the only general SEM program that is entirely free to use (*see* Table 15.1). This program has many different options, including the flexible use of matrix algebra and fitting functions. The example given here (*see* Appendix Table 15.A12) is identical in every respect to the MIMIC model presented above, so it is not surprising that the SEM results are equivalent as well.

The first thing we will do is generate the data using the built in R "rnorm(1)" functions. Each line in the code generates a vector of scores, and these are placed together into a matrix of data (termed "MIMICData"). These data were defined to have the same features as the simulation previously described and we expect to find no differences – and we do not!

The second phase of the analysis is to try to fit a SEM to their data using the new "OpenMx" commands, and to do this we need to load the OpenMx library onto our machine (using "require(OpenMx)"). The "mxModel" command is used to accumulate the model components, and here we use another option

Table 15.A12 **Mplus Output for LVP #3**

MODEL RESULTS				Two-Tailed
	Estimate	S.E.	Est./S.E.	P-Value
F_SCORE BY				
Y1	1.000	0.000	999.000	999.000
Y2	0.967	0.082	11.721	0.000
Y3	0.917	0.078	11.744	0.000
X2_SCORE ON				
F_SCORE	0.441	0.068	6.453	0.000
Variances				
F_SCORE	0.355	0.043	8.199	0.000
Residual Variances				
X2_SCORE	0.949	0.044	21.629	0.000
Y1	0.660	0.039	16.719	0.000
Y2	0.654	0.038	17.017	0.000
Y3	0.616	0.036	17.303	0.000

Table 15.A13 **R Input for LVP**

```
# MIMIC1.R
# Author: Jack McArdle
require(psych) # this is only needed in order to output summary stats
library(lattice)
setwd("your_choice")
options(width=100) # make the printout wide enough for the summary stats
options(digits=4)
# could read in the data and print summary statistics
# ReadData <- read.csv("read.csv"
# SET Constants
set.seed(20110416)
N=101; L1=0.6; L2=0.4; B1=0.0; B2=0.8
#Generate Simulated Data
X1 <- numeric(N); X2 <- numeric(N); F_Score <- numeric(N); id <- numeric(N)
Y1 <- numeric(N); Y2 <- numeric(N); Y3 <- numeric(N);
Y4 <- numeric(N); Y5 <- numeric(N); Y6 <- numeric(N);
for (i in 1:N){ id[i]=i; X1[i]=rnorm(1); X2[i]=rnorm(1)
#model creation
F_Score[i]=B1*X1[i]+B2*X2[i]+rnorm(1)
Y1[i]=L1*F_Score[i]+rnorm(1);Y2[i]=L1*F_Score[i]+rnorm(1);Y3[i]=L1*F_Score[i]+rnorm(1
Y4[i]=L2*F_Score[i]+rnorm(1);Y5[i]=L2*F_Score[i]+rnorm(1);Y6[i]=L2*F_Score[i]+rnorm(1
MIMICData <- (c( "Y1", "Y2","Y3", "y4", "Y5", "Y6", "X1", "X2" ))
print(MIMICData); pcorr <- cor(MIMICData); describe(MIMICData)
```

(type = "RAM") to invoke the use of RAM notation. From this point, we can then define each path coefficient in a SEM using the "mxPath" command/Each mxPath command line requires a simple statement of: (1) a "from" and "to" variable number or label; (2) the type of "arrowhead" proposed (1 or 2 headed); (3) whether the parameter is free of fixed (free = false); (4) the numerical value (a starting value or a fixed non-zero value); and (5) and optional label (useful if the parameter is equivalent to another). This "list of parameters" approach is the same as what has been used in PROC CALIS and is based on the list notation of McArdle (1988, 2005; McArdle & Boker, 1990).

Table 15.A14 **R Input for** OpenMx

```
#Part II: Fit a model to the available data - from comments of S. Boker (03/2012)
require(OpenMx)
# select which variables from the data to use in the model
indicators <- c("Y1", "Y2", "Y3", "Y4", "Y5", "Y6"); predictors <- c("X1", "X2")
# name the latent variable
latents <- c("F_Score")
# create the unconditional MIMIC model
MIMICModel <- mxModel("Correct MIMIC Model", type="RAM",
    manifestVars=c(indicators), latentVars=latents,
    mxPath(from=F_Score, to=Y1, arrows=1, free=FALSE, values=1),
    mxPath(from=F_Score, to=Y2-Y6, arrows=1, free=True, values=1),
    mxPath(from=indicators, arrows=2, free=TRUE, values=1, labels="VarU"),
    mxPath(from=F_Score, arrows=2, free=TRUE, values=1, labels=c("VarF"),
    mxPath(from=predictors, to=F_Score, all=TRUE, arrows=1, free=TRUE, values=.1),
    mxPath(from=predictors, arrows=2, free=TRUE, values=1, labels=c("Var1", "Var2")),
    mxPath(from="X1", to="X2", arrows=2, free=TRUE, values=.1, labels=c("Cov12")),
    mxPath(from="one", to=indicators, arrows=1, free=FALSE, values=0),
    mxPath(from="one", to=predictors, arrows=1, free=TRUE, values=0,
labels=c("MeanX1", "MeanX2")),
    mxPath(from="one", to=latents, arrows=1, free=TRUE, values=0, labels=c("MeanF")),
    mxData(observed=MIMICData, type="raw")
    )
# run the model
MIMICModelOut <- mxRun(MIMICModel)
```

As stated before, this OpenMx program offers many other options, and some of the best have not been used here. But the fact that it can incorporate the RAM list means it will also work for SEMs of any complexity (*see* McArdle, 2005). For this and other reasons, this program is worthwhile investigating further. The exact same sentiment applies to at least two other R code programs for SEM — the lavaan package (Rosell, 2012) and the sem package (Fox, 2006). Both programs are free and easy to use, and these are worthy of further consideration.

Author Note

1. John J. McArdle, PhD, Senior Professor, Department of Psychology, University of Southern California.

2. Please send any written correspondence to SGM 711, 3620 S. McClintock Ave., University of Southern California, Los Angeles, CA 90089.

3. Funding for this chapter was provided by the National Institute on Aging (Grant # AG–07137–22).

References

Anderson, T.W. (1957). *An Introduction to Multivariate Statistical Analysis*. New York: Wiley.

Blalock, H.M. (Ed., 1985a). *Causal Models in the Social Sciences*, 2nd Ed. New York: Aldine.

Blalock, H.M. (Ed., 1985a). *Causal Models in Panel and Experimental Designs*. New York: Aldine.

Bock, R. D. (1975). *Multivariate statistical methods in behavioral research*. New York: McGraw-Hill.

Boker, S.M. (2011). The OpenMx Project. See http://openmx.psyc.virginia.edu/about-openmx-project (as of November 2012).

Browne, M. W. & Cudeck, R. (1993). Alternative ways of assessing model fit. In: Bollen, K. A. & Long, J. S. (Eds.) *Testing Structural Equation Models*. (pp. 136–162). Beverly Hills, CA: Sage.

Browne, M. W. & Nesselroade, J. R. (2005). Representing psychological processes with dynamic factor models: Some promising uses and extensions of ARMA time series models. In A. Maydeau-Olivares & J. J. McArdle (Eds.), *Advances in psychometrics: A festschrift to Roderick P. McDonald* (pp. 415–451). Mahwah, NJ: Erlbaum.

Bryk, A. S., & Raudenbush, S. W. (1992). *Hierarchical linear models: Applications and data analysis methods*. Newbury Park, CA: Sage.

Cattell, R.B. (1978). *The Scientific Use of Factor Analysis in Behavioral and Life Sciences*. New York: Plenum.

Cochran, W.G. & Cox, G.M. (1950). *Experimental Design* (2nd Ed.). New York: Wiley

Cole, D. A., & Maxwell, S. E. (2003). Testing mediational models with longitudinal data: Questions and tips in the use of structural equation modeling. *Journal of Abnormal Psychology*, 112, 558–577.

Duncan, O.D. (1975). *Introduction to Structural Equation Models*. New York: Academic Press.

Dyson, F. (1997). *Imagined Worlds*. Cambridge, MA: Harvard University Press.
Ferrer, E., Hamagami, F., & McArdle, J.J. (2004). Modeling latent growth curves with incomplete data using different types of structural equation modeling and multilevel software. *Structural Equation Modeling, 11* (3), 452–483.
Ferrer, E. & McArdle, J.J. (2010). Longitudinal Modeling of Developmental Changes in Psychological Research. *Current Directions in Psychological Science, 19* (3), 149–154.
Ferrer-Caja, E., Crawford, J.R., & Bryan, J. (2002). A structural modeling examination of the executive decline hypothesis of cognitive aging through reanalysis. *Aging, Neuropsychology, and Cognition, 9*, 231–249.
Fisher, R.A. (1918). The correlation between relatives on the supposition of Mendelian inheritance. *Transactions of the Royal Society of Edinburgh, 52*, 399–433.
Fisher, R.A. (1924). The Conditions Under Which χ^2 Measures the Discrepancy Between Observation and Hypothesis. *Journal of the Royal Statistical Society, 87*, 442–450.
Fox, J. (1997). *Applied Regression Analysis, Linear Models, and Related Methods*. Thousand Oaks, CA: Sage.
Fox, J. (2006). Structural equation modeling with the sem package in R. *Structural Equation Modeling, 13* (3), 465–486.
Ghisletta, P. & McArdle, J.J. (2012). Latent Curve Models and Latent Change Score Models Estimated in R. *Structural Equation Modeling, 19*, 651–682.
Goldberger, A.S. (1973). Structural Equation Models: An Overview. In A.S. Goldberger & O.D. Duncan, (Eds.) *Structural Equation Models in the Social Sciences*. (pp. 1–18) New York: Seminar Press.
Goldberger, A.S. & Duncan, O.D. (1973). *Structural Equation Models in the Social Sciences*. New York: Seminar Press.
Grimm, K.J. & McArdle, J.J. (2005). A Note on the Computer Generation of Mean and Covariance Expectations in Latent Growth Curve Analysis. In F. Danserau & F.J. Yammarino (Ed.), *Multi-level issues in strategy and Methods*. (pp. 335–364). New York: Elsiver.
Hauser, R.M. & Goldberger, A.S. (1971). The treatment of unobservables in path analysis. In H.L. Costner (Ed.). *Sociological Methodology*. (pp. 81–117). San Francisco, CA: Jossey-Bass.
Hauser, R.M., Tsai, S-L., & Sewell, W.H. (1983). A model of stratification with response error in social and psychological variables. *Sociology of Education, 56*, 20–46.
Heise, D.R. (1975). *Causal Analysis*. New York: Wiley.
Horn, J.L. & McArdle, J.J. (1980). Perspectives on Mathematical and Statistical Model Building (MASMOB) in Research on Aging. In L. Poon (Ed.), *Aging in the 1980's: Psychological Issues*. Washington, D. C.: American Psychological Association, 503 541.
Horn, J.L. & McArdle, J.J. (1992). A practical guide to measurement invariance in aging research. *Experimental Aging Research, 18* (3), 117–144.
Horn, J. L. & McArdle, J.J. (2007). Understanding human intelligence since Spearman. In R. Cudeck & R. MacCallum, (Eds.). *Factor Analysis at 100 years* (pp. 205–247). Mahwah, NJ: Lawrence Erlbaum Associates.
Hsiao (2003). *Analysis of panel data. Second edition*. Cambridge, UK: Cambridge University Press.
Joreskog, K. & Sorbom, D. (1979). *Advances in Factor Analysis and Structural Equation Models*. Cambridge, MA; Abt Books.
Joreskog, K.G. (1969). A general approach to confirmatory maximum likelihood factor analysis. *Psychometrika, 34*, 183–202.
Joreskog, K.G. (1973). A general method for estimating a linear structural equation system. In A.S. Goldberger & O.D. Duncan, (Eds.) *Structural Equation Models in the Social Sciences*. (pp. 85–112). New York: Seminar Press.
King, D.W., King, L.A., Foy, D.W. (1996). Prewar factors in combat-related posttraumatic stress disorder: Structural equation modeling with a national sample of female and male Vietnam veterans. J. *Consulting and Clinical Psychology, 64* (3), 520–531.
Kline, R.B. (2011). *Principles and Practice of Structural Equation Modeling* (3rd Ed). New York: Guilford Press.
Lawley, D.N. & Maxwell, A.E. (1971). *Factor Analysis as a Statistical Method* (2nd Ed.). London: Butterworths.
Lee, S-Y. (2007). *Structural Equation Modeling: A Bayesian Approach*. New York: Wiley.
Li, C.C. (1975). *Path Analysis: A Primer*. Pacific Grove, CA: Boxwood Press.
Loehlin, John C. (2004). *Latent Variable Models: An Introduction to Factor, Path, and Structural Analysis* (4th Ed.) Mahwah, NJ: Lawrence Erlbaum Associates.
Maydeau-Olivares, A. (2000). Review of Mplus. *Multivariate Behavioral Research, 35* (4), 501–515.
McArdle, J.J. (1986). Latent variable growth within behavior genetic models. *Behavior Genetics, 16* (1), 163–200.
McArdle, J.J. (1988). Dynamic but structural equation modeling of repeated measures data. In J.R. Nesselroade & R.B. Cattell (Eds.), *The Handbook of Multivariate Experimental Psychology, Volume 2*. New York, Plenum Press, 561–614.
McArdle, J.J. (1994). Structural factor analysis experiments with incomplete data. *Multivariate Behavioral Research, 29* (4), 409–454.
McArdle, J.J. (2001). A latent difference score approach to longitudinal dynamic structural analysis. In R. Cudeck, S. du Toit, & D. Sorbom (Eds.). *Structural Equation Modeling: Present and future*. (pp. 342–80). Lincolnwood, IL: Scientific Software International.
McArdle, J.J. (2005). The development of RAM rules for latent variable structural equation modeling. In A. Maydeau & J.J. McArdle, (Eds.). *Contemporary Advances in Psychometrics*. (pp. 225–273). Mahwah, NJ: Lawrence Erlbaum Associates.
McArdle, J.J. (2007). Five Steps in the Structural Factor Analysis of Longitudinal Data. In R. Cudeck & R. MacCallum, (Eds.). *Factor Analysis at 100 years*. (pp. 99–130). Mahwah, NJ: Lawrence Erlbaum Associates.
McArdle, J.J. (2009). Latent variable modeling of longitudinal data. *Annual Review of Psychology, 60*, 577–605.
McArdle, J.J. (2010). Some Ethical Issues in Factor Analysis. In A. Panter & S. Sterber (Eds.) *Quantitative Methodology Viewed through an Ethical Lens*. (pp. 313–339).Washington, DC: American Psychological Association Press.
McArdle, J.J. & Aber, M.S. (1990). Patterns of change within latent variable structural equation modeling. In A. von Eye (Eds.). *New Statistical Methods in Developmental Research* (pp. 151–224). New York: Academic Press.
McArdle, J.J. & Anderson, E. (1990). Latent variable growth models for research on aging. In J.E. Birren & K.W. Schaie (Eds.), *The Handbook of the Psychology of Aging*. (pp. 21–43). New York: Plenum Press.

McArdle, J.J. & Boker, S. M. (1990). *RAMpath: A Computer Program for Automatic Path Diagrams*. Hillsdale, NJ: Lawrence Erlbaum Publishers.

McArdle, J.J. & Cattell, R.B. (1994). Structural equation models of factorial invariance in parallel proportional profiles and oblique confactor problems. *Multivariate Behavioral Research, 29* (1), 63–113.

McArdle, J.J. & Epstein, D.B. (1987). Latent growth curves within developmental structural equation models. *Child Development, 58*(1), 110–133.

McArdle, J.J., Fisher, G.G. & Kadlec, K.M. (2007). Latent Variable Analysis of Age Trends in Tests of Cognitive Ability in the Health and Retirement Survey, 1992-2004. *Psychology and Aging, 22*(3), 525–545.

McArdle, J.J., Grimm, K., Hamagami, F., Bowles, R., & Meredith, W. (2009). Modeling Life-Span Growth Curves of Cognition Using Longitudinal Data With Multiple Samples and Changing Scales of Measurement. *Psychological Methods, 14*(2), 126–149.

McArdle, J.J. & Hamagami, F. (1991). Modeling incomplete longitudinal and cross-sectional data using latent growth structural models. In L. Collins & J.L. Horn (Eds.), *Best Methods for the Analysis of Change* (pp. 276304). Washington, D.C.: APA Press.

McArdle, J.J. & Hamagami, F. (1996). Multilevel models from a multiple group structural equation perspective. In G. Marcoulides & R. Schumacker (Eds.), *Advanced Structural Equation Modeling Techniques.* (pp. 89–124). Hillsdale, NJ: Erlbaum.

McArdle, J.J. & Hamagami, F. (2003). Structural equation models for evaluating dynamic concepts within longitudinal twin analyses. *Behavior Genetics, 33*(2), 137–159.

McArdle, J.J. & Hamagami, F. (2006). Longitudinal tests of dynamic hypotheses on intellectual abilities measured over sixty years. In C. Bergeman & S.M. Boker (Eds.), *Methodological Issues in Aging Research.* (pp. 43–98). Mahwah: Erlbaum.

McArdle, J.J., Johnson, R.C., Hishinuma, E.S., Myamoto, R.H., & Andrade, N. (2001). Structural equation modeling of group differences in CES-D ratings of native Hawaiian and non-native Hawaiian high school students. *Journal of Adolescent Research 16* (2), 108–149.

McArdle, J.J. & McDonald, R.P. (1984). Some algebraic properties of the Reticular Action Model for moment structures. *British Journal of Mathematical and Statistical Psychology, 37,* 234–251.

McArdle, J.J. & Nesselroade, J.R. (1994). Using multivariate data to structure developmental change. In S.H. Cohen & H.W. Reese (Eds.), *Life Span Developmental Psychology: Methodological Innovations.* (pp. 223–267). Hillsdale, NJ: Erlbaum.

McArdle, J.J. & Prescott, C.A. (1992). Age based construct validation using structural equation models. *Experimental Aging Research, 18*(3), 87–115.

McArdle, J.J. & Prindle, J.J. (2008). A latent change score analysis of a randomized clinical trial in reasoning training. *Psychology and Aging, 23* (4), 702–719.

McArdle, J.J. & Woodcock, J.R. (1997). Expanding test rest designs to include developmental time lag components. *Psychological Methods, 2* (4), 403–435.

McDonald, R.P. (1980). A simple comprehensive model for the analysis of covariance structures. *British Journal of Mathematical and Statistical Psychology, 31,* 161–183.

McDonald, R.P. (1985). *Factor Analysis and Related Methods.* Hillsdale, NJ: Erlbaum.

McDonald, R.P. (1999). *Test Theory: A Unified Treatment.* Mahwah, NJ: Erlbaum.

Meredith, W. (1964). Notes on factorial invariance. *Psychometrika, 29,* 177–185.

Meredith, W. (1993). Measurement invariance, factor analysis and factorial invariance. *Psychometrika, 58,* 525–543.

Meredith, W., & Horn, J. (2001). The role of factorial invariance in modeling growth and change. In A. Sayer & L. Collins (Eds.), *New methods for the analysis of change* (pp. 203–240). Washington, DC: American Psychological Association.

Meredith, W., & Tisak, J. (1990). Latent curve analysis. *Psychometrika, 55,* 107–22.

Muller, K.E. & Stewart, P.W. (2006). *Linear Model Theory: Univariate, Multivariate, and Mixed Models.* New York: Wiley.

Muthén, L.K. & Muthén, B.O. (2002). *Mplus, the comprehensive modeling program for applied researchers user's guide.* Los Angeles, CA: Muthén & Muthén.

Nesselroade, J.R. & Baltes, P.B. (1984). From traditional factor analysis to structural-causal modeling in developmental research. In. V. Sarris & A. Parducci (Eds.). *Perspectives in Psychological experimentation.* (pp. 267–287). Hillsdale, NJ: Erlbaum

Ntzoufras, I. (2009). *Bayesian Modeling Using WinBUGS.* New York: Wiley.

O'Brien, R. G. & Kaiser, M.K. (1985). MANOVA Method for Analyzing Repeated Measures Designs: An Extensive Primer. *Psychological Bulletin, 97*(2), 316–333.

Pearl, J. (2000). *Causality: models, reasoning, and inference.* Cambridge University Press.

Popper, K. (1970). Normal Science and its Dangers, In Lakatos, I. & Musgrave, A. (Eds.) *Criticism and the Growth of Knowledge* (pp. 51–58). Cambridge: Cambridge University Press.

Prindle, J. J. & McArdle, J.J. (2012). An Examination of Statistical Power in Multigroup Dynamic Structural Equation Models. *Structural Equation Modeling, 19* (3) 351–372.

Rabe-Hesketh, S. & Skrondal, A. (2006). *Multilevel and longitudinal modeling using Stata,* 2nd Ed. College Station, Texas: Stats Press.

Rao, C. R. (1958). Some statistical methods for the comparison of growth curves. *Biometrics, 14,* 1–17.

Rao, C.R. (1965). Linear statistical inferences and its applications. New York: Wiley.

Roseell, Y. (2012). *lavaan: an R package for structural equation modelling and more.* Unpublished Manuscript, Department of Data analysis, Ghent University, Belgium.

SAS Institute (2006). PROC CALIS ->http://support.sas.com/documentation/cdl/en/statug/63347/HTML/default/viewer.htm#statug_calis_sect021.htm (as of November 2012).

Satorra, A., & Saris, W. E. (1985). Power of the likelihood ratio test in covariance structure analysis. *Psychometrika, 50,* 83–90.

Shrout, P. (2010). Integrating causal analysis into psychopathology research. In Shrout, P.E. Keyes, K.M. & Ornstein, K. (Eds.). *Causality and Psychopathology: Finding the Determinants of Disorders and Their Cures.* (pp. 3–24). New York: Oxford University Press.

Singer, J.D. & Willett, J. B. (2003). *Applied Longitudinal Data Analysis: Modeling Change and Event Occurrence.* New York: Oxford University Press.

Sobel, M. (1995). Causal inference in the behavioral sciences. In Arminger, G., Clogg, C.C. & Sobel, M.E. (Eds.). *Handbook of Statistical Modeling for the Social and Behavioral Sciences.* (pp. 1–38). New York: Plenum Press.

Spearman, C. (1904). "General intelligence" objectively determined and measured. *American Journal of Psychology, 15*, 201–293.

Stapleton, L.M. & Leite, W.L. (2005). Teacher's Corner: A Review of Syllabi for a Sample of Structural Equation Modeling Courses. *Structural Equation Modeling: A Multidisciplinary Journal, 12* (4), 642–664.

Sörbom, D. (1979). An alternative to the methodology for analysis of covariance. *Psychometrika, 43,* 381–396.

Tabachnick, B. G., & Fidell, L. S. (2007). *Using Multivariate Statistics,* 5th ed. Boston: Allyn and Bacon.

Tucker, L.R (1958). Determination of parameters of a functional relation by factor analysis. *Psychometrika, 23*, 19–23.

Walls, T.A. & Schaffer, J.L. (Eds., 2006). *Models for intensive longitudinal data.* New York: Oxford University Press.

Werts, C.E. & Linn, R.L. (1970). Path analysis: Psychological examples. *Psychological Bulletin, 74*, 193–212.

Wechsler, D. (1981). *WAIS-R: Wechsler Adult Intelligence Scale Revised.* New York: Harcourt, Brace & Jovanovich.

Widaman, K. F. (1985). Hierarchically nested covariance structure models for multitrait- multimethod data. *Applied Psychological Measurement, 9*, 1–26.

Wiley, D. (1973). The identification problem for structural equation models with unmeasured variables. In A.S. Goldberger & O.D. Duncan, (Eds.) *Structural Equation Models in the Social Sciences.* (pp. 69–84). New York: Seminar Press.

Wishart, J. (1938). Growth rate determination in nutrition studies with the bacon pig, and their analyses. *Biometrika, 30,* 16–28.

Wright, S. (1918).On the Nature of Size Factors. *Genetics 3,* 367–374.

Wright, S. (1934). The Method of Path Coefficients. *Annals of Mathematical Statistics 5,* 161–215.

Wothke, W. (2000) Longitudinal and multi-group modeling with missing data. In T.D. Little, K.U. Schnabel, & J. Baumert (Eds.) *Modeling longitudinal and multiple group data: Practical issues, applied approaches and specific examples.* Mahwah, NJ: Lawrence Erlbaum Associates.

CHAPTER
16 Developments in Mediation Analysis

David P. MacKinnon, Yasemin Kisbu-Sakarya, *and* Amanda C. Gottschall

Abstract

Theories in many substantive disciplines specify the mediating mechanisms by which an antecedent variable is related to an outcome variable. In both intervention and observational research, mediation analyses are central to testing these theories because they describe how or why an effect occurs. Over the last 30 years, methods to investigate mediating processes have become more refined. The purpose of this chapter is to outline these new developments in four major areas: (1) significance testing and confidence interval estimation of the mediated effect, (2) mediation analysis in groups, (3) assumptions of and approaches to causal inference for assessing mediation, and (4) longitudinal mediation models. The best methods to test mediation relations are described, along with methods to assess mediation relations when they may differ across groups. Methods for addressing causal inference and models for assessing temporal precedence in mediation models are used to illustrate some remaining unresolved issues in mediation analysis, and several promising approaches to solving these problems are presented.

Key Words: Mediation, moderation, indirect effects, causal inference, longitudinal models, significance testing, confidence intervals

Introduction

A mediator (M) is a variable that transmits the effect of an antecedent variable (X) to an outcome variable (Y) in a causal sequence such that X causes M and M causes Y. Theories across many substantive disciplines focus on mediating processes as explanations for how and why an antecedent variable is related to an outcome variable. Intervention programs are designed to change mediating variables theorized to be causally related to the outcome variable. If an intervention program substantially changes a mediating variable that is causally related to an outcome, then a change in the mediator will produce a change in the outcome. The effect of the antecedent variable on the mediator variable is called the action theory because a manipulation is introduced to change the mediator. The effect of the mediator variable on the outcome variable is called the conceptual theory because the mediator is not directly manipulated but is theorized to affect the outcome. Mediating variables can be psychological (e.g., knowledge, beliefs, and attitudes), behavioral (e.g., interpersonal skills), or biological (e.g., serum cholesterol level). The purpose of this chapter is to review current methods used to investigate mediating variables. As comprehensive descriptions of mediation analysis are available in the literature (MacKinnon, 2008; MacKinnon, Fairchild, & Fritz, 2007), only an overview of mediation analysis is presented here. The purpose of this chapter is to supplement these resources with a description of recent advances in four major areas: (1) significance testing and confidence interval estimation of the mediated effect, (2) mediation analysis in groups,

(3) assumptions of and approaches to improving causal inference for mediation, and (4) longitudinal mediation models.

History

Mediation analysis was introduced as a way to explain observed relations among variables. Modern methods for quantifying mediation models started with Wright's path analysis methods (1920, 1921). Path analysis provides a framework for the causal relations among variables and estimation of the size of those relations. About 30 years later, the elaboration method was described by Lazarsfeld and colleagues (Kendall & Lazarsfeld, 1950; Lazarsfeld, 1955) to demonstrate how an original relation between two variables would change when other variables were added into the statistical analysis. The elaboration method provided a set of analyses to investigate mediation and other third-variable effects (Hyman, 1955). Also during this time, Rozeboom (1956) described mediation as a set of functional relations where the mediator is a function of the independent variable and the dependent variable is a function of the mediator. During the '60s and '70s, models for sets of causal relations were described (Blalock, 1971; Duncan, 1966, 1975; Rosenberg, 1968), including covariance structure modeling, which combined path analysis and measurement traditions (Jöreskog, 1970; Keesling, 1972; Wiley, 1973).

Since the 1970s, many advances in methodological, statistical, and substantive aspects of mediation analysis have been made. Sobel (1982, 1986) derived the standard error for any indirect effect. Inspired by earlier work on the elaboration method (Hyman, 1955; Kenny, 2008; Mathiew, DeShon, & Bergh, 2008), Kenny and colleagues (Baron & Kenny, 1986; Judd & Kenny, 1981) described the regression equations and outlined the tests necessary for a causal steps method to assess mediation. MacKinnon and Dwyer (1993) specified the mediation regression equations, proposed different approaches to estimate the mediated effect, and provided several formulas for the standard error of the mediated effect. Applications of mediation analysis to answer substantive questions were given in social psychology (Baron & Kenny, 1986), applied psychology (James & Brett, 1984), prevention programs (MacKinnon & Dwyer, 1993), and epidemiology (Robins & Greenland, 1992). Bootstrap methods for mediation analysis were outlined (Bollen & Stine, 1993; Lockwood & MacKinnon, 1998), as were conceptualizations of longitudinal mediation (Gollob & Reichardt, 1991). A causal inference perspective on mediation was outlined by Holland (1988) for the social sciences and by Robins and Greenland (1992) for epidemiology. Recently, the similarity of mediation methods across fields such as epidemiology, medicine, psychology, and sociology have been recognized and led to several advances (MacKinnon, 2008). Since 2000, advances in mediation analysis have occurred for significance testing and confidence interval estimation (MacKinnon, Lockwood, Hoffman, West, & Sheets, 2002; MacKinnon, Lockwood, & Williams, 2004), mediation in grouped data (Krull & MacKinnon, 2001; Preacher, Zyphur, & Zhang, 2010), causal inference (Imai et al., 2010; Jo, 2008; Pearl, 2009; Sobel 2007; VanderWeele, 2008) and longitudinal data (Cheong, MacKinnon, & Khoo, 2003; Cole & Maxwell, 2003; von Eye, Mun, & Mair, 2009).

Modern Appeal

At least part of the recent interest in mediation models stems from its application to the design of interventions. The intervention is designed to change mediating variables that are hypothesized to be causally related to an outcome variable. Many drug prevention programs, for example, are designed to increase resistance skills, educate people about the risks associated with drug use, and change social norms, all of which are expected to reduce drug use. Researchers from many substantive areas have stressed the importance of assessing mediation in the evaluation of prevention and treatment studies (Baranowski, Anderson, & Carmack, 1998; Begg & Leung, 2000; Donaldson, 2001; Judd & Kenny, 1981; MacKinnon, 1994; Sandler, Wolchik, MacKinnon, Ayers, & Roosa, 1997; Weiss, 1997). The broad appeal of mediation analysis for intervention studies is evident by recommendations for its use across many fields, including nursing (Bennett, 2000, p. 419), nutrition (Kristal, Glanz, Tilley, & Li, 2000, p. 123), medicine (Begg & Leung, 2000, p. 27), and randomized clinical trials (Kraemer, Wilson, Fairburn, & Agras, 2002, p. 877).

Mediation analysis informs both action theory (the theory relating the intervention program components to the targeted mediators) and conceptual theory (the theory relating the mediating variables to the outcome variable) (Chen, 1990; Lipsey, 1993; MacKinnon, Taborga, & Morgan-Lopez, 2002), making its application to intervention studies a popular area of substantive and statistical interest

(MacKinnon, 1994). First, mediation analysis provides a way to evaluate if the intervention program has affected the mediators it was designed to change (i.e., tests of the action theory). For example, if a program is designed to change social norms, then program effects on normative measures should be statistically significant. Failure of the program to affect the mediating variables may occur because the program was ineffective or because measures of the mediating construct were inadequate. Second, mediation analysis provides a check on the conceptual theory of the program. If there is a not a significant relation of the mediating variable to the outcome, then this may indicate a failure of conceptual theory, that effects may emerge later, or that the mediator, the outcome, or both were not measured accurately. Third, an overall understanding of how the prevention program achieved, or failed to achieve, effects on the outcome can be obtained. For each mediator, tests of both action and conceptual theory provide a way to examine whether the lack of an intervention effect may result from the failure of the program to change the mediator, the failure of the mediator to change the outcome, or both. Overall, mediation analysis is useful for identifying the most effective components of a prevention program so that they can be retained or enhanced in future interventions.

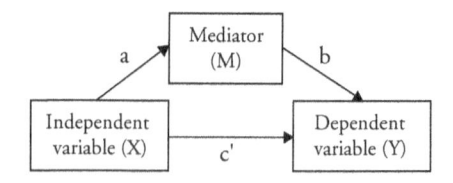

Figure 16.1 The single mediator model.

Estimating the Mediated Effect

Several methods have been used to investigate mediating processes. An ideal way to study mediation is to manipulate mediators directly by randomly assigning subjects to different mediators or to investigate mediators in separate randomized studies (MacKinnon, 2008; MacKinnon, Taborga, et al., 2002; Spencer, Zanna, & Fong, 2005; West & Aiken, 1997). These designs will be discussed later in this chapter. However, these studies are impractical in many fields because manipulations often contain related components and it is inefficient to separate them, especially in the early stages of research. Even when subjects are randomly assigned to levels of a mediator, estimation of mediated effects is important, as it provides a test of whether the manipulation process worked as planned.

One widely used method to assess mediation is to measure mediating variables and outcome variables and conduct a series of statistical tests (Baron & Kenny, 1986; Kenny, Kashy, & Bolger, 1998). The first test assesses the extent to which the antecedent variable affects the outcome variable. Second, antecedent effects on the hypothesized intervening or mediating variables are evaluated. Third, if effects on the outcome and the hypothesized mediating variables are substantial, then the process by which effects on the mediating variable affect changes in the outcome is assessed. More recent mediation methods have been shown to be more accurate than this causal steps method. These newer methods directly estimate the mediated effect and its standard error using the regression equations described in the next section (MacKinnon, Lockwood, et al., 2002).

Point Estimation

Difference in Coefficients Approach. In Figure 16.1 and the regression equations below, X is the antecedent variable, M is the mediator, and Y is the outcome variable. In the single mediator model (*see* Fig. 16.1), the mediated effect can be calculated in two ways (MacKinnon & Dwyer, 1993). One method, commonly used in the medical sciences, estimates the two regression equations shown below:

$$Y = i_1 + cX + e_1 \qquad (1)$$
$$Y = i_2 + c'X + bM + e_2, \qquad (2)$$

where i_1 and i_2 are intercepts, c is the coefficient relating the antecedent to the outcome, c' is the coefficient relating the antecedent to the outcome adjusting for the effects of the mediator, b is the coefficient relating the mediator to the dependent variable adjusting for antecedent variable, and e_1 and e_2 are unexplained variability (i.e., error). In Equation 1, the outcome variable is regressed on the antecedent variable. In Equation 2, the mediating variable is included as an additional predictor of the outcome. Using the difference in coefficients approach $(c - c')$, the mediated (i.e., indirect) effect equals the difference between c, the effect of X on Y, and c', the effect of X on Y adjusting for M. This can also be thought of as the reduction in the antecedent variable effect on the outcome variable when the mediator is included in the model. If the direct program effect coefficient c does not differ from zero when the mediator is included in the model, then the antecedent variable effect is entirely transmitted through the mediating variable.

Product of Coefficients Approach. A second method to assess the mediated effect also involves estimation of two regression equations (Alwin & Hauser, 1975): Equation 2, presented earlier, and an additional equation shown below,

$$M = i_3 + aX + e_3, \qquad (3)$$

where i_3 is an intercept, and e_3 is the unexplained variability. First, the a coefficient in Equation 3 relates the antecedent variable to the mediating variable. Second, the b coefficient in Equation 2 relates the mediator to the outcome adjusting for the antecedent variable. The product of these two coefficients (ab) is the mediated or indirect effect. The c' coefficient in Equation 2, which relates the antecedent variable to the outcome adjusting for the mediator, is the nonmediated or direct effect. The rationale behind the product of coefficients approach is that mediation depends on the extent to which the antecedent variable changes the mediator (a) and the extent to which the mediator affects the outcome variable (b). The path from the antecedent variable to the mediator to the outcome is the mediation process. The ab and $c - c'$ estimates of mediation are algebraically equivalent for ordinary least squares regression (MacKinnon, Warsi, & Dwyer, 1995). Because the ab method is easily generalized to more complicated mediation models, the product of coefficients method is recommended over the difference in coefficients method for mediation analysis.

Assumptions. For the ab estimator of the mediated effect, the model assumes that e_2 and e_3 are independent and that M and e_2 are independent (McDonald, 1997; Merrill, 1994). Other assumptions are that Equations 2 and 3 represent causal relations that are linear, additive, and recursive (James & Brett, 1984; James, Mulaik, & Brett, 2006; McDonald, 1997). Violations of this assumption can sometimes be addressed. For example, the additivity assumption implies that there is no interaction between X and M (Collins, Graham, & Flaherty, 1998; Judd & Kenny, 1981), but this interaction can be included in the model, which would allow the effect of the mediator on the outcome to differ across groups. Mediation analysis for nonrecursive models (McDonald, 1997; Sobel, 1986) and for nonlinear mediation effects (Stolzenberg, 1979) have been described in the literature.

Other important assumptions include correct causal order (e.g., X → M → Y), correct causal direction (e.g., no reciprocal causation between the mediator and the dependent variable), no misspecification due to omitted variables, and minimal measurement error (Baron & Kenny, 1986; Holland, 1988; James & Brett, 1984; MacKinnon, 2008; McDonald, 1997; Pearl, 2009). Tests of sensitivity to violation of the model assumptions are the most challenging aspects of mediation analysis. As a result, the investigation of mediation processes requires a cumulative program of research using evidence from a variety of sources, including clinical observation, qualitative studies, and replication (MacKinnon, 2008).

Adding Covariates. Equations 1, 2, and 3 can be expanded to include covariates as shown below by the inclusion of variable C in Equations 4, 5, and 6. The inclusion of covariates may increase power to detect effects and may provide helpful information when investigating the sensitivity of results to different alternative explanations based on causal inference.

$$Y = i_1 + cX + dC + e_1 \qquad (4)$$
$$Y = i_2 + c'X + bM + d'C + e_2 \qquad (5)$$
$$M = i_3 + aX + fC + e_3 \qquad (6)$$

Adding the covariate C yields a d coefficient in Equation 4 and a d' coefficient in Equation 5, corresponding to the relation of the covariate to the outcome variable controlling for the other independent variables. Similarly, the f coefficient in Equation 6 captures the relation between the covariate and M, controlling for X. For simplicity, one covariate is described here, but in practice there may be several covariates. By including one or more covariates, the values of a, b, c, and c' will likely differ from the values obtained using Equations 1, 2, and 3, where the covariate(s) are excluded from the model. Selection of covariates for a mediation model can be complicated and should typically not include posttreatment variables or colliders (*see* Pearl, 2009).

Multiple Mediators. Equations 1, 2, and 3 are easily expanded to include additional mediating variables (MacKinnon, 2000, 2008). There are separate equations for the effect of X on each mediator (Equation 3). In Equation 2, all mediators are included as predictors of Y. Multiple mediator models are postulated in several fields of research. In school-based drug prevention programs, for example, mediators such as resistance skills, social norms, attitudes about drugs, and communication skills are often targeted. The multiple mediator model more accurately reflects the multiple causes of effects on the outcome. Formulas for testing the equality of multiple mediated effects were given in MacKinnon (2000). Designs for assessing multiple mediator models in tobacco prevention research were also outlined in MacKinnon, Taborga, et al. (2002) and West and Aiken (1997). The multiple mediator model allows for positive and negative mediated effects, called inconsistent models (Blalock, 1969; Davis, 1985). These inconsistent models and their relation to suppression and confounding effects are described in MacKinnon, Krull, and Lockwood (2000). An inconsistent mediation model can occur when an intervention component does not work as planned, leading to a change in a mediator that actually increases problem behavior, whereas other components of the program reduce the problem behavior. In a study of the mediating mechanisms in a program to prevent anabolic steroid use among high school football players, the program increased knowledge of the reasons to use anabolic steroids, which actually increased intentions to use steroids in the future (MacKinnon, Goldberg, et al., 2001). Fortunately, there were other mediational processes that led to an overall beneficial effect of the intervention program (i.e., reduced intentions to use steroids in the future). These types of counterproductive mediators can be identified with multiple mediator models, which improves future programs by avoiding these iatrogenic effects.

Another type of multiple mediator model has several mediators in a sequence. In a three-path mediation model, an independent variable is hypothesized to affect one mediator, which affects a second mediator, which, in turn, affects an outcome (i.e., program → mediator1 → mediator2 → outcome). Taylor, MacKinnon, and Tein (2008) evaluated several tests of mediation for the three-path mediation model and found that a joint significance test of each of the three paths, as well as resampling methods, were the best tests of this more complicated mediation relation.

Models with multiple antecedent variables, mediators, and outcomes require structural equation modeling to more accurately estimate the relevant parameters. Matrix equations are used to organize the many parameters for these models and estimate the many mediated effects. Mediated (i.e., indirect) effects are commonly included in comprehensive structural equation models (Bollen, 1987; MacKinnon, 2008; Sobel, 1982).

Standard Error

Confidence intervals and significance tests require a measure of the estimate's variability. The standard error of the product of two random variables, a and b, is $\sigma_{ab} = (\sigma_a^2 b^2 + \sigma_b^2 a^2 + \sigma_a^2 \sigma_b^2)^{1/2}$ (Goodman, 1960, 1962). Alternatively, the multivariate delta standard error (Sobel, 1982) does not include the $\sigma_a^2 \sigma_b^2$ term (Baron & Kenny, 1986; MacKinnon & Dwyer, 1993). The standard error of the ab mediated effect obtained using either method has low relative bias in sample sizes of at least 50 for the single mediator model when the data are normally distributed (MacKinnon et al., 1995; MacKinnon, Lockwood, et al., 2002). As summarized by MacKinnon, Lockwood, et al. (2002), there are also formulas for the standard error of $c-c'$, such as $(\sigma_c^2 + \sigma_{c'}^2 - 2r\sigma_c\sigma_{c'})^{1/2}$, where $r\sigma_c\sigma_{c'}$ is the covariance between c and c' (McGuigan & Langholtz, 1988; Clogg, Petkova, & Shihadeh, 1992; Freedman & Schatzkin, 1992). The standard error can be used to compute confidence limits for the mediated effect for $c-c'$. Confidence intervals have been widely recommended for reporting research results because they enable researchers to consider the size of an effect as well as its statistical significance (Harlow, Mulaik, & Steiger, 1997; Krantz, 1999).

Significance Testing and Confidence Interval Estimation of the Mediated Effect

There have been extensive statistical and methodological developments in significance testing and confidence interval estimation of mediated effects during the last 25 years. Significance tests are typically based on normal theory. The product of two normally distributed random variables, such as the ab product estimator of the mediated effect, is not normally distributed (Craig, 1936; Springer & Thompson, 1970). Rather, the distribution of the product of two normally distributed random variables is a complicated function (Springer, 1979) that is normal only in special cases. Consider two standard normal random variables with a mean of 0—their product will have a kurtosis of six (Meeker, Cornwell, & Aroian, 1981). As a result, significance tests based on normal theory are not appropriate for testing an estimate of the mediated effect. Simulation studies have demonstrated that the statistical power and Type I error rates are too low for most tests of significance based on normal theory (i.e., using the ratio of the mediated effect to its standard error) (MacKinnon, Lockwood, et al., 2002). In one study examining the necessary sample size to detect a mediated effect, Fritz and MacKinnon (2007) showed that tests for mediation based on normal theory or causal steps (Baron & Kenny, 1986) have larger sample size requirements than either bootstrapping methods or tests based on the distribution of the product because the latter methods account for the non-normal distribution of the product.

Because the *ab*-mediated effect is not normally distributed, confidence limits based on normal theory are imbalanced (Fritz & MacKinnon, 2007; MacKinnon, Lockwood, et al., 2004; MacKinnon et al., 1995). MacKinnon and colleagues (MacKinnon, Fritz, Williams, & Lockwood, 2007) have described a computer program that computes critical values for confidence limits based on the distribution of the product. Resampling methods such as bootstrapping also provide more accurate confidence limits for the mediated effect because they accommodate the non-normal distribution of the product (Arbuckle, 1997; Bentler, 1995; Hall, 1992; Jöreskog & Sorbom, 2001). MacKinnon, Lockwood, et al. (2004) and Williams and MacKinnon (2008) compared single-sample methods (including the distribution of the product) to several computer-intensive methods and found that the distribution of the product and bootstrap sampling methods led to the most accurate confidence limits. Although the bias-corrected bootstrap appeared to have the most accurate confidence limits, there was some evidence that for small sample sizes and small mediated effects there were excess Type I error rates (e.g., 0.07 instead of 0.05). These inflated Type I error rates do not appear to occur for the distribution of the product and are reduced in larger sample sizes (Fritz, Taylor, & Mackinnon, 2010).

Bayesian Methods

One promising new approach to mediation analyses is based on Bayesian mediation methods (Yuan & MacKinnon, 2009), which can complement the frequentist approaches to mediation analysis described in this chapter by providing an alternative framework to investigate mediation. Bayesian methods allow for the incorporation of prior information about mediation relations such as the size of the relation or the distribution of relevant variables. Bayesian methods may be especially useful for studies with small sample sizes in research areas where there is considerable prior information from other studies that can be incorporated into the statistical analysis. Although Bayesian methods may require changes in the approach to data analysis, they allow for straightforward applications to both complex and simple mediation models. Bayesian approaches may also provide a natural way to investigate complicated assumptions regarding causal mediation (Elliott, Raghunathan, & Li, 2010). The application of Bayesian versus frequentist statistical approaches has generated some controversy (Little, 2006) but there is plenty of room for Bayesian and frequentist methods to provide complementary approaches to the scientific investigation of mediation.

Effect Size Measures

In addition to the statistical significance of a mediated effect, recent research has addressed the need for mediation effect size measures that provide a practical and intuitive understanding of the effect. For individual paths in the mediation model, standardized regression coefficients are useful measures of effect size because they are partial correlations (MacKinnon, 2008). For example, a researcher could state that 10% of the variance in the mediator is explained by the antecedent variable. For the mediated effect, the proportion of the total effect that results from the indirect effect, also called the proportion mediated $(1 - (c'/c) = ab/(ab + c'))$, and the ratio of the indirect effect to the direct effect (ab/c') are measures of effect size. For example, a researcher could state that 30% of the antecedent effect on the outcome variable was associated with the mediating variable. Simulation studies have found that the proportion mediated requires a sample size of at least 500 to stabilize unless the effects are large, particularly the direct effect c' (Freedman, 2001; MacKinnon et al., 1995). For the ratio of the indirect effect to the direct effect, larger sample sizes of close to 1000 are required. It is important to emphasize that the accuracy of these methods is also a function of population effect size. Finally, the R^2 effect size measure focuses on the amount of variance in Y explained by both X and M, and this method works well for many different mediation models (Fairchild, MacKinnon, Taborga, & Taylor, 2009). One promising effect size measure is the mediated effect divided by the standard deviation of the outcome variable; this scales the mediated effect in standard deviation units of the outcome variable.

Categorical and Count Outcomes

In many studies, the dependent variable is categorical (e.g., whether a person used drugs or not) or a count (e.g., the number of times an event occurred). In the binary categorical case, Equations 1 and 2 are estimated with logistic or probit regression. Logistic and probit regression coefficients can be distorted because not only are the coefficients a function of the true relations between variables, but they are also a function of a fixed error term in each regression equation. The $c-c'$ method of estimating mediation can be distorted in these models because the parameter estimate of c' depends on both the indirect effect and the scaling of Y in Equation 2 (MacKinnon & Dwyer, 1993). Because the $c-c'$ estimate can be incorrect when the outcome is categorical, it is no longer equivalent to the ab estimate. One method to put the $c-c'$ estimate in the same metric as the ab estimate is to standardize the regression coefficients prior to estimating the mediated effect (Winship & Mare, 1983). With standardization of the coefficients, $c-c'$ is close to ab (MacKinnon & Dwyer, 1993; MacKinnon, Taylor, Yoon, & Lockwood, 2009). However, it is usually best to use the product of coefficients approach, ab, in logistic and probit regression mediation analysis because it is more general and does not require standardization. To construct confidence intervals, the distribution of the product and resampling methods are best for mediation estimation with categorical data.

An extension of the mediation model to the generalized linear model framework, which accommodates both logistic and probit regression as well as other methods such as survival analysis, has been outlined (MacKinnon, Lockwood, Brown, Wang, & Hoffman, 2007). In a preliminary study of mediation analysis of count outcomes using Poisson regression models, it was found that ab and $c-c'$ were usually comparable (Coxe & MacKinnon, 2010). Like the logistic and probit regression models, ab does not equal $c-c'$ when the outcome is time to an event (e.g., death) and survival analysis is used (Tein & MacKinnon, 2003). Tein and MacKinnon (2003) investigated the proportional hazards regression procedure, which allows for covariates to be incorporated into the survival model. The study found that the differences between ab and $c-c'$ decreased as the sample size increased; however, the standard errors of ab and $c-c'$ were nearly identical in sample sizes of at least 100. Recently, Pearl (2010b) has proposed a *Mediation Formula*, which presents a general approach to estimating mediation for both parametric and nonparametric relations among categorical variables. An interesting aspect of this method is that the difference score (i.e., $c-c'$) and the product of coefficients (i.e., ab) methods represent two unique ways to approach mediation, and each approach may be appropriate in different contexts.

Non-Normality

Research on non-normality and mediation analysis (Bollen & Stine, 1993, Finch, West, & MacKinnon, 1997; Lockwood, 2000) suggests the use of resampling approaches to mediation analysis, as these methods make fewer assumptions about the underlying distribution of the indirect effect (Bollen & Stine, 1990; Manly, 1997; Noreen, 1989). Computer programs have been written to conduct bootstrap estimation of the mediated effect (Lockwood & MacKinnon, 1998; Preacher & Hayes, 2004) and extended to include more computer-intensive tests (MacKinnon et al., 2004; Williams & MacKinnon, 2002). Resampling methods are a method of choice to investigate models with non-normal distributions (Williams & MacKinnon, 2008; Cumming & Finch, 2001). Recent approaches relax assumptions about the distribution of the variables involved in mediation analysis, including variables that may be affected by outliers (Zu & Yuan, 2010); when data are not normally distributed, nonparametric methods tend to outperform parametric methods.

Small Samples

When one of the two paths in the mediated effect is small, tests of the mediated effect have low power, and the confidence interval tends to be too wide to detect the mediated effect for sample sizes less than 400 (Fritz & MacKinnon, 2007). Many important studies have sample sizes ranging from 30 to 200, such as studies examining a specific population (e.g., autistic children, high risk groups, burn victims, persons at a drug treatment clinic), using very expensive measurement (e.g., magnetic resonance imaging, positron emission tomography), or collecting very intensive repeated measurements (e.g., daily assessments). Several methods have been proposed for increasing power in research studies with limited sample sizes (Hoyle, 1999) by improving the research design, measurement, or analysis.

Design. Power to detect the mediated effect can be increased through the design of a study by using extreme groups or planned missing data. Extreme group analyses are conducted to enlarge the effect size of an intervention in situations where it is possible to select groups at extreme levels of the mediator or outcome. Because extreme groups are selected, the corresponding effect size will theoretically be larger. Given a fixed sample size, researchers select participants based on scores on the mediator or the outcome variable to maximize statistical power (Alf & Abrahams, 1975). One example is the case of selecting persons for a research study that are the lowest on a mediator targeted by the intervention (Pillow, Sandler, Braver, Wolchik, & Gersten, 1991; West, Sandler, Baca, Pillow, & Gersten, 1991). In this approach, the size of the *a* path relating the intervention to the mediator is maximized. Similarly, participants could be selected based on their level of the dependent variable at baseline. An alternative is to oversample extreme cases based on principles of optimal design to detect effects (McClelland & Judd, 1993) and to obtain one or more pretest measures to assess regression to the mean (Pitts, 1997). Although the extreme group method for increasing power to detect a mediation effect shows promise, there are limitations (Preacher, Rucker, MacCallum, & Nicewander, 2005). One limitation to the extreme group method is the phenomenon of regression to the mean, whereby extremes at one time will tend to score closer to the mean at a later time.

When high-quality but expensive (or time-consuming, difficult, or labor-intensive) measurements are required, power can be improved by using a planned missing data design (Graham, Hofer, & MacKinnon, 1996; Graham, Hofer, & Piccinin, 1994; Graham, Taylor, & Cumsille, 2001) where the expensive measurement is obtained for only a subsample of participants. Here the subsample of participants who were only administered the inexpensive measure(s) can provide some additional power when incorporated into an analysis that uses the expensive measurement (Enders, 2010; Schafer, 1997). The power to detect mediation with small sample sizes is likely influenced by the amount of missing data and the number of measured variables and is an important area of investigation (Graham, Hofer, Donaldson, MacKinnon, & Schafer, 1997).

Measurement. Collecting baseline measures of variables in the mediation model can reduce unexplained variability, thereby increasing the ability to detect effects. To the extent that the baseline measures are strongly related to the other measures, there will be an increase in statistical power. Another way to increase power is with improved measurement of the constructs, which can reduce measurement error and increase statistical power. Even when the reliability of variables in a mediation model is close to 1, it may be possible to increase power to detect mediation relations by purifying measures so that they have greater validity. To illustrate, assume that norms are an important mediator of an intervention effect on an outcome variable. It may be possible to increase power to detect a mediated effect in this intervention study by measuring the most potent part of norms that leads to the mediation relation. For example, norms among friends may be a more valid mediator of the intervention effect and the use of this mediator, rather than the general norm mediator, will increase power to detect mediated effects. As described elsewhere (MacKinnon, 2008), one way to view mediation analysis is as a measurement task, where understanding and evidence of a true mediator accumulates as the measure of the mediator is improved.

Analysis. Bayesian methods (Yuan & MacKinnon, 2009) can be applied to mediation analysis when prior information on the parameter values is available. Prior information is incorporated into the parameter estimates, and this is especially useful when the sample size is small and effects are underpowered. Permutation tests may also be ideal for small sample sizes because they use the available data to construct all possible data sets that could have been observed. Permutation tests for mediation have been outlined (MacKinnon, 2008) but not yet thoroughly investigated in small sample sizes (MacKinnon & Lockwood, 2001; Taylor & MacKinnon, 2012). Early work on the permutation test suggests an elevated Type I error rate when one of the two paths in the mediation relation is zero and the other path is non-zero.

Mediation Analysis in Groups

Models with moderation and mediation are important because they provide information about how X affects Y and for which groups of participants X affects Y. Models with moderation and mediation can be used to investigate the extent to which individual paths differ across subgroups, whether a mediated effect differs across subgroups, and whether a moderator effect is explained by a mediator. In moderation of a mediated effect, the mediated effect differs for subgroups of participants (James & Brett, 1984; Judd, Kenny, & McClelland, 2001). For example, mediated effects may differ across cohorts (MacKinnon, Cheong, Goldberg, Williams, & Moe, 2002), age groups, gender, or ethnic groups. A statistical test for the equivalence of the mediated effect and tests of the equality of a, b, and c' also provide information about whether the action theory (i.e., how the program will change mediators) holds across subgroups (i.e., is invariant) and whether the conceptual theory (i.e., how mediators are related to the outcome) holds across subgroups (MacKinnon, 2008). Moderation of a mediated effect is more complex when the moderator variable is continuous, and researchers often categorize the continuous variable but categorization may lead to loss of information (MacCallum, Zhang, Preacher, & Rucker, 2002).

In mediation of a moderator effect, the mediator is intermediate in the causal sequence from an interaction effect to a dependent variable. The purpose of mediation of a moderator effect is to determine whether a mediating variable explains the interaction effect because the mediator transmits the effect of the interaction to the outcome variable. For example, assume there is an interaction effect between program exposure and self-esteem such that program effects on drug use differ as a function of self-esteem. The program effect that changes as a function of self-esteem leads to changes in the resistance skills mediator, which then leads to reduced drug use. Morgan-Lopez and MacKinnon (2001) and MacKinnon (2008) have described an estimator of the mediated moderator effect, but this proposed estimator requires further development and evaluation.

In treatment and prevention studies, the examination of mediation in program effects addresses *how* the program achieves its effects (Donaldson, 2001; MacKinnon, 2001; MacKinnon & Dwyer, 1993; MacKinnon, Weber, & Pentz, 1989; MTA Cooperative Group, 1999; Sandler et al., 1997). Moderator variables address *for whom* the intervention is effective (Aiken & West, 1991; Baron & Kenny, 1986). Models with both mediators and moderators allow for the simultaneous assessment of how a program works (mediation) and whether the program works differentially for groups of participants (moderation). These models represent an attempt to incorporate multiple elements of the program design into a single analysis for program evaluation (Lipsey, 1993; Sidani & Sechrest, 1999; West & Aiken, 1997).

A General Model of Moderation and Mediation

Early strategies to test models that combine moderator effects (i.e., interactions) and mediator effects tended to focus on estimating the two effects in separate situations (Baron & Kenny, 1986; James & Brett, 1984; Merrill, 1994; Merrill, MacKinnon, & Mayer, 2006; Morgan-Lopez, 2002; Morgan-Lopez, Castro, Chassin, & MacKinnon, 2003; Morgan-Lopez & MacKinnon, 2001). Recently, comprehensive models with both moderation and mediation have been described (Edwards & Lambert, 2007; Fairchild & MacKinnon, 2009; Hoyle & Robinson, 2004; MacKinnon, 2008; Preacher, Rucker, & Hayes, 2007) but require more evaluation. The equations below describe a combined moderator and mediator model for a single mediator and a single moderator (Fairchild & MacKinnon, 2009; MacKinnon, 2008). The model includes moderation of a mediated effect, mediation of a moderator effect, and other types of moderator and mediator effects as special cases of the model. The single mediator model is extended in several ways. First, the moderator variable, Z, is added along with its interaction with X, represented by XZ. Second, the interaction of the moderator with M is represented by MZ. In this model, a test of homogeneous action theory is included in the test of the a_3 coefficient; this tests whether the *a* parameter differs across the Z groups. A test of homogeneous conceptual theory is included in the test of the b_2 coefficient; this tests whether the *b* parameter differs across the Z groups. The test of whether the c' parameter is different across the Z groups is obtained by testing the c'_3 coefficient. The results from these tests are algebraically equivalent to the model where effects are estimated separately in each group when there are no higher-order interactions, heterogeneous variability, and functional form across two groups (MacKinnon, 2008).

$$Y = i_1 + c_1 X + c_2 Z + c_3 XZ + e_1 \qquad (7)$$

$$Y = i_2 + c'_1 X + c'_2 Z + c'_3 XZ + b_1 M + b_2 MZ + e_2 \qquad (8)$$

$$M = i_3 + a_1 X + a_2 Z + a_3 XZ + e_3 \qquad (9)$$

Moderation of a mediated effect is tested by taking the difference between the mediated effects from each group and dividing this difference by its standard error (MacKinnon, 2008). If there are more than two groups, then contrasts between mediated effects for pairs of groups can be tested if the number of groups is low. If the moderator is continuous, a statistical test of the moderation of a mediated effect is more complex.

The above model can be made even more general by adding two more interaction terms, thereby allowing for testing of more complicated forms of moderation and mediation. The XM and XMZ interactions can be added to Equation 8 to form a more general model (MacKinnon, 2008). These interactions test whether the relation of M to Y differs across levels of X and Z. Often these relations are assumed to not exist and the terms are omitted from the model. In general, these models test mediation effects conditional on one or more moderator variables.

Point estimates and standard errors for mediation of a moderator effect in the single mediator model are accurate at sample sizes as small as 100 (Merrill et al., 2006). However, the standard errors can be too small with non-zero direct effects (Morgan-Lopez & MacKinnon, 2001, 2006). A non-zero direct effect implies that after including the mediator in the model, there is a residual relation between the independent variable and the outcome. It is common in social science research to have mediators that do not fully explain the relation between the independent variable and the outcome; this is called partial mediation. Morgan-Lopez (2003) also explored Type I error rates and empirical power of four different methods to detect simple mediation effects in a mediated moderation model. This work showed that the method using asymmetric confidence intervals had Type I error rates closest to the nominal Type I error rate of 0.05. The bias-corrected bootstrap method was the most powerful method overall, although the differences between the bias-corrected bootstrap and the asymmetric confidence interval methods were minimal. Because the bias-corrected bootstrap had elevated Type I error rates in some circumstances, the overall recommendation is to use the asymmetric confidence interval method or the percentile bootstrap. Fairchild (2008) examined the performance of several tests for moderation of a mediated effect using interaction effect sizes typically found in the literature (i.e., explaining 1%–3% of the total variance). When the interaction effect explained 1% of the overall variance, none of the tests had 0.8 power to detect effects for sample sizes less than 1000. When the interaction effect explained 3% of the overall variance, tests had at least 0.8 power to detect effects for sample sizes of at least 300. The distribution of the product test had greater power to detect interaction effects than either the multivariate δ test or the test of joint significance.

Multilevel Mediation

Multilevel mediation models also include grouping of participants, but the grouping is determined by sampling characteristics such as one's school, clinic, or family. Individual observations are not independent of the other observations within the same group (i.e., cluster). Thus, if clustered data is evaluated at the individual level, ignoring the multilevel data structure, then the assumption of independent observations is violated. This violation may lead to underestimated standard errors of estimates, which result in an inflated Type I error rate (Krull & Mackinnon, 1999, 2001). Violating the assumption of independent observations can be resolved by incorporating multilevel analysis into mediation analysis. In addition, conducting mediation analysis in the multilevel framework allows researchers to investigate mediation effects at different levels and reach more detailed conclusions about mediating mechanisms (Hofmann & Gavin, 1998). For example, when evaluating the mediating mechanisms of a prevention program delivered at the school level, investigators may find that the mediating mechanisms working at the school level are different from the mechanisms working at the individual level. At the school level, overall drug norms may mediate the program effect on the individual student's drug use, whereas an individual's resistance skills may work as a mediator at the individual level. Mediation methods for multilevel data (e.g., data from schools, clinics, families) have been described (Krull & MacKinnon, 1999, 2001; MacKinnon, 2008; Raudenbush & Sampson, 1999) and evaluation of these models has been conducted in simulation studies (Krull & MacKinnon, 1999, 2001; Pituch, Stapleton, & Kang, 2006).

There are several options for specifying mediation effects in multilevel modeling, depending on whether the independent variable, mediator, and/or the dependent variables are at the individual or group (cluster) level (Krull & MacKinnon, 2001). In some situations, the independent variable represents group-level characteristics, whereas the mediator and the dependent variable represent individual level characteristics. For example, one might hypothesize that style of the team leader (X at the team level) may affect individual employee's job satisfaction (Y at the employee level) indirectly by affecting the employee's perceived autonomy (M at the employee level). In other situations, the independent and mediating variables are group-level variables, whereas the dependent variables are individual-level variables, such as the relation between the class size and individual student's achievement mediated by teacher's level of fatigue. Equations 7, 8, and 9 can be written at the individual and group level depending on the levels of the independent, mediating, and dependent variables (*see*

Krull & MacKinnon, 1999; MacKinnon, 2008). Consequently, the path coefficients *a* and *b* are estimated at the individual or group level.

Another flexibility of multilevel mediation is that one or both of the *a* and *b* path coefficients can be modeled as fixed or random effects. In other words, the effect of the independent variable on the mediator and/or the effect of the mediator on the dependent variable can be treated as constant (i.e., fixed) or varying (i.e., random) across clusters. For example, in a study of group therapy treatments (e.g., behavior focused vs. cognition focused) on patient's social anxiety, researchers may be interested in the mediating mechanism of social interaction skills. Patients are clustered into therapy groups, and the treatment is administered at the cluster level (not at the individual level). In such cases, the path coefficient *b* may vary across therapy groups (i.e., clusters), and, therefore, no single values of *b* can be applied to all therapy groups. In other cases, both the *a* and *b* path coefficients vary significantly across groups, which can result in a non-zero covariance between the *a* and *b* paths ($\sigma_{ab} \neq 0$). Thus, the covariance of *a* and *b*, σ_{ab}, is taken into account to estimate standard errors and point estimates of the mediated effects (Kenny et al., 1998). There are several ways to estimate the covariance between the random coefficients *a* and *b*. Kenny et al. (1998) used resampling methods to estimate the covariance between *a* and *b*. Bauer, Preacher, and Gil (2006) have demonstrated that this covariance can be calculated by combining Equations 2 and 3 into the same analysis and directly estimating the covariance among the random effects, as is possible in SEM software programs such as Mplus (Muthén & Muthén, 2001). More recent developments provide multilevel approaches (Zhang, Zyphur, & Preacher, 2009) and a comprehensive structural equation model that incorporates the multilevel structure of the data (Preacher, Zyphur, et al., 2010). Mediation models for data collected from dyads (i.e., clusters with only two members, such as husband–wife and mother–child pairs) have also been outlined (Dagne, Brown, & Howe, 2007; Ledermann & Macho, 2009).

Causal Inference in Mediation

Recently, promising approaches to improve causal inference in mediation analysis have been proposed (Frangakis & Rubin, 2002; Holland, 1988; Jo, 2008; Kaufman, MacLehose, & Kaufman, 2004, Murphy, Van der Laan, Robins, & Conduct Problems Prevention Research Group, 2001; Pearl, 2009, 2010a; Robins & Greenland, 1992; Robins, Mark, & Newey, 1992; Rubin, 2004; Shipley, 2000; Sobel, 1998a, 1998b, 2007; Winship & Morgan, 1999) but have not been systematically evaluated in simulation studies and applied settings. These new models primarily address the effects of omitted variables on a mediation analysis (MacKinnon, 2008). In the single-mediator model, bias introduced by omitted variables occurs for the X to M and M to Y relations. Randomization of X balances the omitted variables to experimental conditions and reduces bias in the X to M relation. Holland (1988), who first noted the potential bias in the relation of M to Y, applied Rubin's (1974) causal model to mediation and showed that under some assumptions (especially random assignment), the typical regression coefficient for the effect of randomized X on Y, *c*, and the randomized effect of X on M, *a*, are valid estimators of the true causal effect (*see also* Sobel, 2007, for a recent extension of this approach). The regression coefficient of M on Y, *b*, is not an accurate estimator of the causal effect because this relation is correlational. So even when X is randomized, alternative explanations exist for mediation because M is not randomly assigned but, rather, is self-selected by participants. The estimator, *c′*, is also not an accurate causal estimator of the direct effect controlling for M. The limitations of interpreting the *b* coefficient have been described in different substantive areas (Robins & Greenland, 1992; Winship & Morgan, 1999).

Sequential Ignorability Assumption

The problems raised by Holland (1988) in the causal interpretation of the single-mediator model are more clearly specified in the sequential ignorability assumption (Imai, 2010; Lynch, Cary, Gallop, & ten Have, 2008; ten Have et al., 2007). There are two parts of the sequential ignorability assumption. Sequential Ignorability A assumes that the relation of X to M is not affected by other variables. Randomization of participants to levels of X ensures that this assumption is satisfied asymptotically. The many possible omitted variables from the X to M relation are ignorable because randomization of X makes all other variables equivalent between the levels of X. Sequential Ignorability B requires that M is ignorable in its relation to Y. It is assumed that M is randomly assigned to participants at each level of X. That is, at all levels of M the values of Y are unrelated to other variables because of the assumed random assignment of persons to the levels of M. In reality, M is not randomly assigned as the participant usually self-selects their value of M. Using a treatment versus control design, Sequential Ignorability B, assumes that both X and M are randomly assigned. However, the values of M are not randomly assigned, and there are likely differences in the M to Y relation for the same participant if in the control condition versus in the treatment condition. It is even possible that the same participant in the control condition would have an M–Y relation that is opposite to the M–Y relation had they been in the treatment condition. Sequential Ignorability B is a difficult assumption to satisfy, but there are several methods to address this issue.

The extent to which sequential ignorability is a valid assumption may differ depending on the type of mediating variable. In intervention research, the mediators are selected because theory and prior empirical research suggest that they are causally related to the outcome variable. As a result, the *b* effect is often considered to be known and merely requires that the levels of M be changed. In this case, the manipulation that changes the X–M relation will have the same expected change in the M–Y relation. However, it may be possible that the relation of M to Y is not completely causal. Researchers can address the sequential ignorability assumption with theoretical consideration of the mediators measured in the study and the extent to which both X and M can be considered randomized across participants by the treatment assignment. For example, if dose is the mediator and administration of pills is the intervention, then it is likely that there is a monotonic relation between M and Y, and therefore Sequential Ignorability B may be a valid assumption. If the intervention is encouragement to take pills, then the M–Y relation may be more complicated because of the participant's choice in their exposure to M, and Sequential Ignorability B may be less likely to hold.

Sensitivity Analysis. Sensitivity analysis is a way to assess the influence of omitted variables on the observed mediation relations, including the relation of M to Y. The goal of these methods is to assess how large a confounder effect (i.e., Sequential Ignorability B) on the M–Y relation must be to invalidate conclusions about mediation (Frank, 2000; Li, Bienias, & Bennett, 2007; Lin, Psaty, & Kronmal, 1998; Rosenbaum, 2002). One way to conduct sensitivity analyses for mediation would be to systematically increase the correlation between the errors in Equations 2 and 3 and evaluate how much the coefficients change. The covariance between the errors in Equations 2 and 3 reflects the contribution of omitted variables to the observed relation of M on Y. When one or both assumptions of Sequential Ignorabilty have been violated, VanderWeele (2008, 2010) has formalized several useful methods to probe bias in mediation relations based on the marginal structural model.

Instrumental Variable Methods. Instrumental variable methods provide another way to address the influence of omitted variables. Instrumental variable methodology is a general approach to improve the causal interpretation of coefficients in a statistical model (Angrist & Krueger, 2001; Angrist, Imbens, & Rubin, 1996; Bound, Jaeger, & Baker, 1995; Hanushek & Jackson, 1977, p. 234–9; Shadish, Cook, & Campbell, 2002; Stolzenberg & Relles, 1990). In mediation, an estimate of the causal relation between M and Y is obtained by using X as an instrumental variable. An instrumental variable makes a relationship more like an experimental relationship, and ideally it is equivalent to a randomized experiment. For the mediation model, the idea is to use an instrument X for the prediction of M and then use the predicted values of M to predict Y. The statistical significance of the coefficient relating predicted value of M to Y is the causal test of the *b* path for the mediated effect. There are several assumptions required for the *b* path to have a causal interpretation, two of which are described here (see MacKinnon, 2008; Shadish, Cook, & Campbell, 2002). First, it is assumed that the randomizing qualities of the instrumental variable X lead to randomization of the mediator M. The stronger the relation of X to M, the better the instrument, with the ideal instrument having a correlation of 1 for X with M. When the correlation is 1, X and M can be considered the same variable and so the randomization of X allows M to reflect randomization. Because M can be considered randomized, the influence of any omitted variable on the relation of M to Y is removed. Another assumption is that M completely mediates the effect of X on Y. In the instrumental variables literature, this assumption is called the exclusion restriction and it means that there is complete mediation. However, complete mediation is rare and may be unrealistic in many research contexts. If complete mediation is not plausible for the entire sample, then it may be possible to design a research study to identify subgroups where the assumption of complete mediation is reasonable. The applicability of the instrumental variable methods is likely limited because of the requirement of a strong relation between the instrument and M as well as the need for complete mediation. More applications of instrumental variable mediation methods are needed to assess the benefits of this approach.

Principal Stratification

Several promising methods to strengthen causal inference in mediation analysis are based on the classification of different possible response patterns for how X affects M and M affects Y. This approach specifies subsets of persons based on how the relation between M and Y could change in response to treatment X. For example, in a treatment/control study there are four different types of hypothetical responses (Jo, 2008): (1) never-improvers, whose mediator would not improve if they were in either treatment group; (2) forward-improvers, whose mediator would improve only if they received the treatment; (3) backward-improvers, whose mediator would improve only if they were in the control group; and (4) always-improvers, whose mediator would improve if they were in either treatment group. These four types of persons are determined outside the experiment so their classification is independent of their experimental assignment. Typically, it is assumed that there are no backward-improvers because it is often difficult to conceive of situations where the mediator would improve for participants in the control condition. Once the classifications are made, the mediated effect is estimated within and between these stratifications (Angrist, Imbens, & Rubin, 1996; Frangakis & Rubin, 2002; Jo, 2008). In these models, covariates are often used to provide information about the stratifications to identify parameters in the model (Jo, Stuart, MacKinnon, & Vinokur, 2010; Stuart, Perry, Le, & Ialongo, 2008). Related approaches use the actual and counterfactual data for each participant and estimate model parameters in the context of the additional counterfactual condition in which the participants actually did not partake (Robins, 1989; Robins & Greenland, 1992; Witteman et al., 1998). In other words, these counterfactual models consider how control participants would behave if, in fact, they were in the treatment condition and how treatment participants would behave if, in fact, they were in the control condition. Like other causal inference methods, the application of these methods to many real data sets is critical to assess their usefulness for uncovering mediation.

Experimental Designs

Experimental studies can be used to bolster evidence for a mediation relation. A cumulative experimental approach is the most widely used method to identify and validate mediating variables in psychology and other substantive areas. As recognized by researchers, one or a few experiments are not enough to convincingly demonstrate a true mediation relation. The literature suggests research designs to directly test the mediation relation (MacKinnon, 2008; Mark, 1986; West, Aiken, & Todd, 1993; West & Aiken, 1997). The typical research design to assess mediation has a randomized intervention, and the mediator and outcome are measured in each group. An assumption of this design is that the relation of M to Y represents a real causal relation so that directly changing M will lead to a change in Y.

There are other possible experimental designs to assess mediation (MacKinnon, 2008). One such research design is called the blockage design, where a manipulation is used to block the mediation process (Robins & Greenland, 1992). If the intervention to block the mediation process does remove the mediation relation, then this provides additional evidence for the mediation process. As a hypothetical example of the blockage design, consider a study to investigate whether an intervention reduces drug use by changing social norms among friends. Intervention participants may be randomly assigned to a treatment condition where contact among friends was eliminated or to a control condition that allowed regular contact among friends. If social norms among friends is a mediator of the drug prevention program, then reduced drug use should be observed in the control group but not in the treatment group, where norm change was not possible because of the lack of contact among friends.

An enhancement design is similar to a blockage design, with the exception that mediation effects are enhanced, rather than eliminated, in the treatment group (for examples, *see* Maxwell, Bashook, & Sandlow, 1986, and Klesges, Vasey, & Glasgow, 1986). For example, in the drug use intervention study described above, social contact among friends would be enhanced in the treatment group. If social norms among friends are a mediator of the drug use intervention, then the treatment group should show a greater reduction in drug use than the control group. Another type of experimental design called double randomization uses one randomized study to evaluate the X–M relation and a second randomized study to evaluate the M–Y relation adjusting for X (MacKinnon, 2008; MacKinnon & Pirlott, 2010; Spencer et al., 2005). Other experimental designs focus on testing the consistency and specificity of mediation relations across different contexts, subgroups, and measures of the mediating and outcome variables (MacKinnon & Pirlott, 2010).

Longitudinal Mediation

The mediation model is a longitudinal model where X precedes M and M precedes Y. Previous research has demonstrated the limitations of using cross-sectional data to investigate longitudinal mediation processes (Cole & Maxwell, 2003; Maxwell & Cole, 2007). Repeated measures are a feature of well-designed studies because they enhance power to detect program effects and allow for the measure of change in response to a treatment (Cohen, 1988; Singer & Willett, 2003). The importance of temporal precedence in the investigation of mediation has been emphasized (Gollob & Reichardt, 1991; Judd & Kenny, 1981; Kraemer et al., 2002; MacKinnon, 1994) and methods for assessing longitudinal mediation have been described (Cheong et al., 2003; Cole & Maxwell, 2003; MacKinnon, 2008; Maxwell & Cole, 2007). As a result, the evaluation of longitudinal mediation models is an important step in advancing mediation methods. Several choices for longitudinal mediation models have been described, including autoregressive, latent growth curve, and latent change score models. Latent growth curve models are a common choice for analyzing repeated measures data and have been applied to longitudinal mediation models (Cheong, 2002; Cheong et al., 2003). Although autoregressive mediation models (e.g., Cole & Maxwell, 2003) and latent change score mediation models (MacKinnon, 2008) have been outlined, much work remains to be done to evaluate how these models perform in the analysis of real data. It is likely that these different modeling approaches are suited to different research situations.

Two Wave Models

The simplest type of longitudinal study has two waves of data, such as measurement at baseline and follow-up. These two-wave models differ in several ways from the single-wave X, M, and Y models that have been the most thoroughly studied to date. The most common two-wave methods are: (1) analysis of covariance (ANCOVA), (2) difference score analysis, and (3) residualized change score analysis (Bonate, 2000; Tornqvist, Vartia, & Vartia, 1985; Willett & Sayer, 1994). Analysis of covariance includes baseline measures of the variables as predictors of follow-up measures in each mediation equation to adjust for baseline differences.

Difference scores and residualized change scores are options for single-mediator models because the two waves of measurement can be reduced to a single change score. In a difference score model, X is the change in X from baseline to follow-up, M is the change in M from baseline to follow-up, and Y is the change in Y from baseline to follow-up. Using the difference score as a dependent variable has been controversial because measurement error may be too high (Burr & Nesselroade, 1990; Cronbach & Furby, 1970; Rogosa, 1988). The residualized change score is often used as an alternative to the difference score and ANCOVA methods, at least in part because it adjusts for baseline differences and avoids some of the problems with the unreliability of difference scores (Lord, 1963). Often the conclusions based on the residualized change score are indistinguishable from the conclusions based on ANCOVA because both approaches adjust for baseline measurement.

Three (or More)-Wave Models

One limitation of the analysis of two waves of data is that the relation of the mediator to the dependent variable is still a cross-sectional relation. If three waves of data are collected, then the longitudinal relation of X and M and the longitudinal relation of M to Y can be examined. With many repeated measures, more accurate modeling of growth over time can be assessed prior to and after the intervention. If more than two waves of data collection are available, there are several longitudinal mediation models that can be applied, including the autoregressive model (Cole & Maxwell, 2003; Maxwell & Cole, 2007), the latent growth curve model (Cheong, MacKinnon, & Khoo, 2001, 2003), and the latent change score model (McArdle, 2001; see MacKinnon, 2008). There are additional complexities for three and more wave models, including assumptions regarding the stability of scores over time, stationarity (the same relations among variables across time), equilibrium (the relations among variables are stable enough to be estimated), and timing (the timing of how variables change across time is correct and measured at the right time to detect effects). Space limitations preclude further discussion of these topics, but interested readers can consult MacKinnon (2008). Although longitudinal mediation models are complex, they provide potentially more accurate information regarding the relations among variables (Cohen, 2008; Cole & Maxwell, 2003; MacKinnon, 1994, 2008; Jöreskog, 1979).

Autoregressive Models. The autoregressive mediation model is an extension of the model described in Gollob and Reichardt (1991) and elaborated on by Cole and Maxwell (2003). It specifies the dependency between adjacent longitudinal relations, in addition to the relations consistent with longitudinal mediation. There are several important aspects of this model. First, relations one lag (i.e., one measurement wave) apart are specified. With three waves of data, it is possible to consider effects that are two waves apart as lag-two effects, but these effects are usually not included in the mediation model. Second, examining the relations within a variable over time assesses the stability of that measure. Third, only longitudinal relations consistent with longitudinal mediation are specified among the variables (i.e., X1 is related to M2, and M2 is related to Y3). Fourth, the covariances among variables at the first wave are included (e.g., the covariance between X1 and Y1), as are the covariances among the residuals of X, M, and Y at each later wave (e.g., the covariance between the X2 residuals and the Y2 residuals). This reflects the unknown causal order of these measures within the same wave.

Other forms of the autoregressive model include contemporaneous mediation relations among X, M, and Y (e.g., X1–M1 and M1–Y1), as well as the longitudinal mediation effects described above. Another option for an autoregressive longitudinal mediation model allows for cross-lagged relations among variables (e.g., X1–M2 and M1–X2) so that the direction of relations among X, M, and Y are all free to vary. This model violates the assumed temporal precedence of X to M to Y, as specified by the mediation model, because paths in the opposite direction are also estimated (i.e., M–X and Y–M). However, this model could be used to assess the possibility of cross-lagged relations among variables.

Latent Growth Curve Models. The latent growth curve approach models longitudinal data in a different manner than the autoregressive approach (Duncan, Duncan, Strycker, Li, & Alpert, 2006). In a simple growth model, there are two growth parameters: (1) the random intercept factor, representing the initial status of the growth trajectory at Time 1, and (2) the random slope factor, representing the linear growth rate per time unit. The mediation process includes the relations between the slope factor of the independent variable, the slope factor of the mediating variable, and the slope factor of the outcome variable (Cheong, MacKinnon, & Pentz, 2002; MacKinnon, 2008; Hertzog, Lindenberger, Ghisletta, & Oertzen, 2006). Linear, quadratic, cubic, and higher order trends can be estimated to reflect the growth over time. A two-stage piecewise parallel process latent growth model provides a way to evaluate the effect of earlier change in the growth of the mediator on later change in the growth of the outcome variable.

The latent growth curve framework (Cheong, MacKinnon, & Khoo, 2001, 2003) models the growth curves of the mediator and the outcome as distinct parallel processes influenced by a program. This method has been applied to the evaluation of several prevention studies (e.g., Cheong, MacKinnon, & Khoo, 2001, 2003; Cheong, MacKinnon, & Pentz, 2002; Cheong & MacKinnon, 2008). Cheong (2011) found that testing mediation in the latent growth curve framework requires large sample sizes to obtain accurate estimates and adequate statistical power. For example, a sample size of 500 is needed when the size of the true mediated effect is moderate (i.e., proportion mediated of 0.30). The accuracy of estimates and the statistical power for testing mediation in the latent growth curve framework were also influenced by the fit of the hypothesized trajectory shape to the data; better fit in the growth trajectory portion of the model led to improved estimates and statistical power. More work is needed on the performance of different latent growth curve approaches to assess mediation.

Latent Change Score Models. The latent change score model is related to the latent growth model. A latent change score model allows a researcher to examine the change in a variable between pairs of measurement waves (Ferrer & McArdle, 2003, 2010; McArdle, 2001; McArdle & Hamagami, 2001; McArdle & Nesselroade, 2003). In this model, fixed parameters and modeled latent variables are used to specify latent change scores. By specifying latent change, the model represents dynamic change in a variable (i.e., the acceleration or deceleration of the change in that variable between measurement waves). This model may be especially useful in situations where it is expected that the predictors of change differ based on the wave of measurement. One common example of these effects may occur in experimental research where the manipulation affects change early in the process, but these effects may not be present later in the process (i.e., at later waves). That is, the intervention affects change in a dependent variable between wave 1 and wave 2, but the intervention does not affect change in the dependent variable between later waves (e.g., between waves 3 and 4). The original latent change score model is constrained to represent change between two waves but it is possible to specify models that represent the acceleration/deceleration of the change between waves (i.e., second derivatives; Malone, Lansford, Castellino, Berlin, & Dodge, 2004) and models that represent moving averages. Another version of the latent change score model includes paths relating the latent differences in one variable to the latent differences in another variable. There are many potential mediation effects in this type of model corresponding to mediation effects for concurrent change and mediation effects for longitudinal change, including correlated change between waves and relations among longitudinal change in X, M, and Y.

Person-Centered Approaches

Person-oriented approaches, such as trajectory classes (Muthén & Muthén, 2001), staged response across trials (Collins et al., 1998) and configural frequency analysis (von Eye et al., 2009) represent new ways to understand mediation processes consistent with the goal of examining both individual-level processes and group-level processes. Rather than examining whether relations between variables (e.g., X–M and M–Y adjusted for X) are consistent with mediation, this approach considers whether patterns of data for individual persons are consistent with mediation. A significance test for the person-centered approach has recently been proposed (Fairchild & MacKinnon, 2005; MacKinnon, 2008). These person-centered methods are a welcome addition to traditional variable-centered mediation analysis (von Eye, Mun, & Mair, 2009).

Summary and Future Directions

Many substantive theories specify mediating mechanisms by which an antecedent variable is related to an outcome variable. Although these processes are important for observational studies, it is their application in intervention research, which has led to the recent growth in statistical and methodological research on mediation methods. Action theory, the relation of intervention exposure to the mediator, and conceptual theory, the relation of the mediator to the outcome, are two important theoretical components of the mediation approach in intervention design and evaluation. Tests of action and conceptual theory reveal if and how an intervention program works to change outcomes. Over the last 30 years, new approaches to statistical mediation analysis have been developed. The purpose of this chapter was to describe developments in four major areas: (1) significance testing and confidence interval estimation of the mediated effect, (2) mediation analysis in groups, (3) assumptions of and approaches to causal inference for mediation, and (4) longitudinal mediation models.

The mediated effect is estimated using the difference in coefficients, $c-c'$, method or the product of coefficients, ab, method. The single mediator model can easily be expanded to include covariates or additional mediators. Significant tests and confidence intervals based on normal theory result in reduced statistical power and inflated Type I error rates, primarily because the distribution of the mediated effect is not normal. More accurate statistical tests and confidence intervals can be obtained with methods that are based on the distribution of the product or that incorporate the non-normal distribution of the mediated effect (e.g., bootstrapping methods). Bayesian methods also incorporate the non-normal distribution of the mediated effect and incorporate prior information, which may be particularly useful when estimating mediation models in small samples. For these and other reasons, Bayesian methods may be especially useful for mediation analysis and merit further research attention. Effect sizes measures in mediation analysis gage the practical meaning of effects in complement to significance testing. Correlation measures of effect size are useful for individual paths in the mediation model. The proportion mediated, ratio of the indirect effect to the direct effect (ab/c'), and mediated effect divided by the standard deviation of Y are promising effect size measures for the entire mediated effect. Methods for mediation analysis of count and categorical outcomes are available, along with methods for non-normal variables in the mediation model. One issue in testing mediation effects is that relatively large sample sizes are needed. Power can be improved through study design, measurement, and statistical analysis.

Mediation effects may differ across groups such as age or gender (i.e., moderator variables). Mediation describes how an antecedent variable changes an outcome, and moderation describes for whom the antecedent variable changes an outcome. The general moderation and mediation model allows for tests of moderation of a mediated effect (i.e., the mediated effects differs across subgroups of participants) and mediation of a moderated effect (i.e., the mediator is intermediate in the causal sequence from an interaction effect to the outcome). When there are more than a few subgroups in the sample (e.g., schools), using a categorical moderator is not ideal. Rather, the multilevel modeling framework can be applied to mediation models. These multilevel mediation models are interesting because the independent variable, the mediator, and the outcome can be specified at the individual level or the group (i.e., cluster) level, or at both levels. The development of models that combine mediation and subgroup analyses is ongoing.

Causal inference is probably the most rapidly growing area in mediation methodology. When X is a randomly assigned variable, the relations of X to M and X to Y can be interpreted as causal effects. The M–Y relation, however, is not directly randomized so causal interpretation is suspect. The threat of omitted variables to the M–Y relation is a violation of the Sequential Ignorability B assumption, but sensitivity analysis and instrumental variable analysis can address this violation. Applying a principal stratification approach to the mediation model is another way to strengthen causal inference in mediation. Cumulative experimental studies can validate mediating variables. The rapid developments in causal inference for mediation models will likely continue. Ideally, a clear set of conceptual and statistical approaches for causal inference in mediation will emerge.

The mediation model is a longitudinal model where X precedes M and M precedes Y. Temporal precedence is central to a mediation model. Although cross-sectional data have been used to investigate mediation processes, the utility of these models is limited. When there are only two waves of data, the most common methods used to examine mediation effects are ANCOVA, difference score, and residualized change score. For three or more waves of data, several types of longitudinal mediation models have recently been developed, including autoregressive, latent growth curve, and latent change score models. Person-centered approaches to mediation have also begun to emerge in the literature. The next step in research will be to evaluate the performance of these proposed models with real data. It is likely that different modeling approaches are suited to different research situations.

Mediation analyses have the potential to test the theoretical questions commonly posed in many fields. In treatment and prevention research, mediation analysis can identify critical intervention components, thereby reducing intervention costs and increasing scientific understanding of behavior. Mediation analysis addresses the fundamental nature of theories that explain processes by which one variable affects another variable. This chapter demonstrates the rapid growth in methods to identify mediating variables. There is no reason to believe that the demand for accurate mediation analysis or the development of these methods will decline.

Acknowledgments

This article was supported in part by National Institute on Drug Abuse grant DA09757. We thank several members of the Research in Prevention Laboratory for comments on the manuscript.

Author Note

1. David P. MacKinnon, Ph.D., Professor Department of Psychology, Arizona State University, 950 S. McAllister, Room 237, Tempe, AZ 85287–1104, E-mail: David.MacKinnon@asu.edu

2. Yasemin Kisbu-Sakarya, M. A., Graduate Research Assistant, Department of Psychology, Arizona State University, 950 S. McAllister, Room 237, Tempe, AZ 85287–1104, E-mail: ykisbu@asu.edu

3. Amanda Gottschall, M.A., Statistical Analyst, Parenting & Family Research Center, University of South Carolina, 1233 Washington St., 2nd Floor Columbia, SC 29208, Office: 803–978–7412, Fax: 803–978–7410, E-mail: Amanda.Gottschall@sc.edu. The chapter was supported in part by National Institute on Drug Abuse grant DA009757.

References

Aiken, L. S., & West, S. G. (1991). *Multiple Regression: Testing and interpreting interactions.* Newbury Park, CA: SAGE.

Alf, E. F., & Abrahams, N. M. (1975). Use of extreme groups in assessing relationships. *Psychometrika, 40,* 563–572.

Alwin, D. F., & Hauser, R. M. (1975). The decomposition of effects in path analysis. *American Sociological Review, 40,* 37–47.

Angrist, J. D., Imbens, G. W., & Rubin, D. B. (1996). Identification of causal effects using instrumental variables (with discussion). *Journal of the American Statistical Association, 91,* 444–472.

Angrist, J. D., & Krueger, A. B. (2001). Instrumental variables and the search for identification: From supply and demand to natural experiments. *Journal of Economic Perspectives, 15*(4), 69–85.

Arbuckle, J. L. (1997). *AMOS user's guide version 3.6.* Chicago, IL: SmallWaters Corp.

Baranowski, T., Anderson, C., & Carmack, C. (1998). Mediating variable framework in physical activity interventions. How are we doing? How might we do better? *American Journal of Preventive Medicine 15,* 266–297.

Baron, R. M., & Kenny, D. A. (1986). The moderator-mediator variable distinction in social psychological research: Conceptual, strategic, and statistical considerations. *Journal of Personality and Social Psychology, 51,* 1173–1182.

Bauer, D. J., Preacher, K. J., & Gil, K. M. (2006). Conceptualizing and testing random indirect effects and moderated mediation in multilevel models: New procedures and recommendations. *Psychological Methods, 11,* 142–163.

Begg, C. B., & Leung, D. H. Y. (2000). On the use of surrogate end points in randomized trials. *Journal of the Royal Statistical Society, 163,* 15–28.

Bennett, J. A. (2000). Mediator and moderator variables in nursing research: Conceptual and statistical differences. *Research in Nursing & Health, 23,* 415–420.

Bentler, P. M. (1995). *Theory and implementation of EQS: A structural relations program.* Los Angeles, CA: BMDP Statistical Software.

Blalock, H. M. (1969). *Theory construction: From verbal to mathematical formulations.* Englewood Cliffs, NJ: Prentice Hall.

Blalock, H.M. (Ed.) (1971). *Causal models in the social sciences.* Chicago, IL: Aldine-Atherton.

Bollen, K.A. (1987). Total, direct, and indirect effects in structural equation models. In Clifford Clogg (Ed.), *Sociological Methodology* (pp. 37–69). Washington, DC: American Sociological Association.

Bollen, K. A., & Stine, R. (1990). Direct and indirect effects: Classical and bootstrap estimates of variability. *Sociological Methodology, 20,* 115–140.

Bollen, K. A., & Stine, R.A. (1993). Bootstrapping goodness-of-fit measures in structural equation models. In K.A. Bollen & J.S. Long (Eds.), *Testing structural equation models* (pp. 111–135). Newbury Park, CA: Sage.

Bonate, P. L. (2000). *Analysis of pretest-posttest designs.* Boca Raton, FL: Chapman & Hall.

Bound, J., Jaeger, D. A., & Baker, R. M. (1995). Problems with instrumental variables estimation when the correlation between the instruments and the endogenous explanatory variable is weak. *Journal of the American Statistical Association, 90,* 443–450.

Burr, J. A., & Nesselroade, J. R. (1990). Change measurement. In A. von Eye (Ed.), *Statistical methods in longitudinal research, vol. 1* (pp. 3–34). New York: Academic Press.

Chen, H. -T. (1990). *Theory-driven evaluations.* Newbury Park, CA: Sage.

Cheong, J. (August, 2002). *Investigation of a method to evaluate mediating mechanisms to reduce adolescent DUI in a school-based prevention program.* Unpublished doctoral dissertation, Arizona State University.

Cheong, J. (2010). Accuracy of estimates and statistical power for testing mediation in latent growth modeling. *Structural Equation Modeling, 18,* 195–211.

Cheong, J. & MacKinnon, D. P. (May, 2008). Accuracy of estimates and statistical power for testing mediation in latent growth modeling. Paper presented at the annual convention of the Association for Psychological Science, Chicago, IL.

Cheong, J., MacKinnon, D. P., & Khoo, S.-T. (2001). A latent growth modeling approach to mediation analysis [Abstract]. In L. M. Collins & A. Sayer (Eds.), *New methods for the analysis of change* (pp. 390–392). Washington, DC: American Psychological Association.

Cheong, J., MacKinnon, D.P., & Khoo, S.-T. (2003). Investigation of mediational processes using parallel process latent growth curve modeling. *Structural Equation Modeling, 10,* 238–262.

Cheong, J., MacKinnon, D. P., & Pentz, M. A. (June, 2002). *Evaluation of the mediating mechanisms of a drug prevention program to reduce adolescent DUI.* Poster presented at the annual meeting of the Research Society on Alcoholism, San Francisco, CA.

Clogg, C. C., Petkova, E., & Shihadeh, E. S. (1992). Statistical methods for analyzing collapsibility in regression models. *Journal of Educational Statistics, 17,* 51–74.

Cohen, J. (1988). *Statistical power analysis for the behavioral sciences.* Hillsdale, NJ: Erlbaum.

Cohen, P. (2008). Applied data analytic techniques for turning points research. New York: Taylor & Francis.

Cole, D. A., & Maxwell, S. E. (2003). Testing mediational models with longitudinal data: Questions and tips in the use of structural equation modeling. *Journal of Abnormal Psychology, 112,* 558–577.

Collins, L. M., Graham, J. W., & Flaherty, B. P. (1998). An alternative framework for defining mediation. *Multivariate Behavioral Research, 33,* 295–312.

Coxe, S., & MacKinnon, D. P. (2010). Mediation Analysis of Poisson distributed count outcomes. *Multivariate Behavioral Research, 45,* 1022.

Craig, C. (1936). On the frequency function of xy. *Annals of Mathematical Statistics, 7,* 1–15.

Cronbach, L. J., & Furby, L. (1970). How should we measure "change" or should we? *Psychological Bulletin, 74,* 68–80.

Cumming, G., & Finch, S. (2001). A primer on the understanding, use, and calculation of confidence intervals that are based on central and noncentral distributions. *Educational and Psychological Measurement, 61,* 532–574.

Dagne, G. A., Brown, C. H., & Howe, G. W. (2007). Hierarchical modeling of sequential behavioral data: Examining complex association patterns in mediation models. *Psychological Methods, 12,* 298–316.

Davis, J. A. (1985). *The logic of causal order.* In: Sage university paper series on quantitative applications in the social sciences. Beverly Hills, CA: Sage Publications.

Donaldson, S. I. (2001). Mediator and moderator analysis in program development. In S. Sussman (Ed.), *Handbook of program development for health behavior research and practice* (pp. 470–496). Thousand Oaks, CA: Sage.

Duncan, O.D. (1966). Path analysis: Sociological examples. *American Journal of Sociology, 72,* 1–16.

Duncan, O.D. (1975). *Introduction to structural equation models.* New York: Academic Press.

Duncan, T. E., Duncan, S. C., Strycker, L. A., Li, F., & Alpert, A. (2006). *An introduction to latent variable growth curve modeling: Concepts, issues, and applications.* Mahwah, NJ: Erlbaum.

Edwards, J. R., & Lambert, L. S. (2007). Methods for integrating moderation and mediation: A general analytical framework using moderated path analysis. *Psychological Methods, 12,* 1–22.

Elliott, M. R., Raghunathan,T. E., & Li, Y. (2010). Bayesian inference for causal mediation effects using principal stratification with dichotomous mediators and outcomes. *Biostatistics, 11,* 353–372.

Enders, C. (2010). *Applied missing data analysis.* Guilford: New York.

Fairchild, A.J. (2008). A comparison of frameworks for the joint analysis of mediation and moderation effects. Unpublished dissertation.

Fairchild, A. J., & MacKinnon, D. P. (2005). Developing significance tests for a person-centered approach to mediation. Poster presented at the 113th annual convention of the American Psychological Association, Washington, D.C.

Fairchild, A. J., & MacKinnon, D. P. (2009). A General Model for Testing Mediation and Moderation Effects. *Prevention Science, 10,* 87–99.

Fairchild, A. J., MacKinnon, D. P., Taborga, M., & Taylor, A. B. (2009). R^2 Effect-size Measures for Mediation Analysis. *Behavioral Research Methods. 41,* 486–498.

Ferrer, E. & McArdle, J. J. (2003). Alternative structural models for multivariate longitudinal data analysis. *Structural Equation Modeling, 10,* 493–524.

Ferrer, E. & McArdle, J. J. (2010). Longitudinal modeling of developmental changes in psychological research. *Current Directions in Psychological Science, 19,* 149–154.

Finch, J. F., West, S. G., & MacKinnon, D. P. (1997). Effects of sample size and nonnormality on the estimation of mediated effects in latent variable models. *Structural Equation Modeling, 4,* 87–107.

Frangakis, C. E., & Rubin, D. B. (2002). Principal stratification in causal inference. *Biometrics, 58,* 21–29.

Frank, K. A. (2000). Impact of a confounding variable on a regression coefficient. *Sociological Methods and Research, 29,* 147–194.

Freedman, L. S. (2001). Confidence intervals and statistical power of the 'validation' ratio for surrogate or intermediate endpoints. *Journal of Statistical Planning and Inference, 96,* 143–153.

Freedman, L. S., & Schatzkin, A. (1992). Sample size for studying intermediate end-points within intervention trials or observational studies. *American Journal of Epidemiology, 136,* 1148–1159.

Fritz, M. S., & MacKinnon, D. P. (2007). Required sample size to detect the mediated effect. *Psychological Science, 18*(3), 233–239.

Fritz, M. S., Taylor, A., & MacKinnon, D. P. (2010). *When does the bias-corrected bootstrap test of mediation produce elevated Type I error rates and why?* Poster presented at the annual meeting of the Society for Prevention Research, Denver, CO.

Gollob, H. F., & Reichardt, C. S. (1991). Interpreting and estimating indirect effects assuming time lags really matter. In L. M. Collins & J. L. Horn (Eds.), *Best methods for the analysis of change: Recent advances, unanswered questions, future directions* (pp. 243–259). Washington DC: American Psychological Association.

Goodman, L. A. (1960). On the exact variance of products. *Journal of the American Statistical Association, 55,* 708–713.

Goodman, L. A. (1962). The variance of the product of K-random variables. *Journal of the American Statistical Association, 57,* 54–60.

Graham, J. W., Hofer, S. M., Donaldson, S. I., MacKinnon, D. P., & Schafer, J. L. (1997). Analysis with missing data in prevention research. In K. Bryant, M. Windle, & S. G. West (Eds.), *The science of prevention: Methodological advances from alcohol and substance abuse research* (pp. 325–365). Washington, DC: American Psychological Association.

Graham, J. W., Hofer, S. M., & MacKinnon, D. P. (1996). Maximizing the usefulness of data obtained with planned missing value patterns: an application of maximum likelihood procedures. *Multivariate Behavioral Research, 31*(2), 197–218.

Graham, J. W., Hofer, S. M., & Piccinin, A. M. (1994). Analysis with missing data in drug prevention research. In Collins, L. & Seitz, L. (Eds.), *National Institute on Drug Abuse Research Monograph Series,* Vol. 142 (pp. 13–62). Washington, DC: National Institute on Drug Abuse.

Graham, J. W., Taylor, B. J., & Cumsille, P. E. (2001). Planned missing data designs in the analysis of change. In L.M. Collins & A.G. Sayer (Eds.), *New Methods for the Analysis of Change* (pp. 335–353). Washington, DC: American Psychological Association.

Hall, P. (1992). On the removal of skewness by transformation. *Journal of the Royal Statistical Society, Series B, 54,* 221–228.

Hanushek, E. A., & Jackson, J. E. (1977). *Statistical methods for social scientists.* New York: Academic Press.

Harlow, L. L., Mulaik, S. A., & Steiger, J. H. (Eds.). (1997). *What if there were no significance tests?* Mahwah, NJ: Erlbaum.

Hertzog, C., Lindenberger, U., Ghisletta, P., & Oertzen, T. (2006). On the power of multivariate latent growth curve models to detect correlated change. *Psychological Methods, 11*(3), 244–252.

Hofmann, D. A., & Gavin, M. B. (1998). Centering decisions in hierarchical linear models: Implications for research in organizations. *Journal of Management, 24,* 623–641.

Holland, P. W. (1988). Causal inference, path analysis, and recursive structural equation models. *Sociological Methodology, 18,* 449–484.

Hoyle, R. H. (1999). *Statistical strategies for small sample research.* Thousand Oaks: Sage.

Hoyle, R. H., & Robinson, J. C. (2004). Mediated and moderated effects in social psychological research: Measurement, design, and analysis issues. In C. Sansone, C. C. Morf & A. T. Panter (Eds.), *The sage handbook of methods in social psychology* (pp. 213–233). Thousand Oaks, CA: Sage.

Hyman, H. H. (1955). *Survey design and analysis: Principles, cases, and procedures.* Glencoe, IL: Free Press.

Imai, K., Keele, L., & Tingley, D. (2010). A general approach to causal mediation analysis. *Psychological Methods, 15,* 309–334.

Imai, K., Keele, L., & Yamamoto, T. (2010). Identification, inference, and sensitivity analysis for causal mediation effects. *Statistical Science, 25,* 51–71.

James, L. R., & Brett, J. M. (1984). Mediators, moderators, and tests for mediation. *Journal of Applied Psychology, 69,* 307–321.

James, L. R., Mulaik, S. A., & Brett, J. M. (2006). A tale of two methods. *Organizational Research Methods,* 9, 233–244.

Jo, B. (2008). Causal inference in randomized experiments with mediational processes. *Psychological Methods, 13,* 314–336.

Jo, B., Stuart, E. A., MacKinnon, D. P., & Vinokur, A. D. (2010). The use of propensity scores in mediation. *Multivariate Behavioral Research, 46,* 425–452.

Jöreskog, K.G. (1970). A general method for analysis of covariance structures. *Biometrika, 57,* 239–251.

Jöreskog, K. G. (1979). Statistical estimation of structural models in longitudinal-developmental investigations. In J. R. Nesselroade & P. B. Baltes (Eds.), *Longitudinal research in the study of behavior and development* (pp. 303–352), New York: Academic.

Jöreskog, K. G., & Sorbom, D. (2001). *LISREL 8: User's reference guide.* Lincolnwood, IL: Scientific Software.

Judd, C. M., & Kenny, D. A. (1981). *Estimating the effects of social interventions.* New York: Cambridge University Press.

Judd, C. M., Kenny, D. A., & McClelland, G. H. (2001). Estimating and testing mediation and moderation in within-subject designs. *Psychological Methods, 6,* 115–134.

Kaufman, J. S., MacLehose, R. F., & Kaufman, S. (2004). A further critique of the analytic strategy of adjusting for covariates to identify biologic mediation. *Epidemiologic Perspectives & Innovations, 1*(4), 1–13.

Keesling, J.W. (June, 1972). *Maximum Likelihood approached to causal analysis.* Unpublished doctoral dissertation, University of Chicago.

Kendall, P.L., & Lazarsfeld, P.F. (1950). Problems of survey analysis. In R.K. Merton & P.F. Lazarsfeld (Eds.), *Continuities in social research: Studies in the scope and method of "The American Soldier"* (pp. 133–196). Glencoe, IL: Free Press.

Kenny, D. A. (2008). Reflections on mediation. *Organizational Research methods, 11,* 353–358.

Kenny, D. A., Kashy, D. A., & Bolger, N. (1998). Data analysis in social psychology. In D. Gilbert, S. T. Fiske, & G. Lindzey (Eds.), *Handbook of social psychology, Volume 1* (pp. 233–265). New York: McGraw-Hill.

Klesges, R. C., Vasey, M. M., & Glasgow, R. E. (1986). A worksite smoking modification competition: Potential for public health impact. *American Journal of Public Health, 76,* 198–200.

Kraemer, H. C., Wilson, T., Fairburn, C. G., & Agras, S. (2002). Mediators and moderators of treatment effects in randomized clinical trials. *Archives of General Psychiatry, 59,* 877–883.

Krantz, D. H. (1999). The null hypothesis testing controversy in psychology. *Journal of the American Statistical Association, 44,* 1372–1381.

Kristal, A. R., Glanz, K. Tilley, B. C., & Li, S. H. (2000). Mediating factors in dietary change: Understanding the impact of a worksite nutrition intervention. *Health Education and Behavior, 27,* 112–125.

Krull, J. L., & MacKinnon, D. P. (1999). Multilevel mediation modeling in group-based intervention studies. *Evaluation Review, 23,* 418–444.

Krull, J. L., & MacKinnon, D. P. (2001). Multilevel modeling of individual and group level mediated effects. *Multivariate Behavioral Research, 36,* 249–277.

Lazarsfeld, P.F. (1955). Interpretation of statistical relations as a research operation. In P.F. Lazarsfeld & M. Rosenberg (Eds.), *The language of social research: A reader in the methodology of social research* (pp. 115–125). Glencoe, IL: Free Press.

Ledermann, T. & Macho, S. (2009). Mediation in dyadic data at the level of the dyads: A structural equation modeling approach. *Journal of Family Psychology, 23,* 661–670.

Li, Y., Bienias, J., & Bennett, D. (2007). Confounding in the estimation of mediation effects. *Computational Statistics & Data Analysis, 51,* 3173–3186.

Lin, D. Y., Psaty, B. M., & Kronmal, R. A. (1998). Assessing the sensitivity of regression results to unmeasured confounders in observational studies. *Biometrics, 54,* 948–963.

Lipsey, M. W. (1993). Theory as method: Small theories of treatments. In L. B. Sechrest & H. G. Scott (Eds.), *Understanding causes and generalizing about them* (pp. 5–38). San Francisco, CA: Jossey-Bass.

Little, R. (2006). Calibrated Bayes: A Bayes/frequentist roadmap. *The American Statistician, 60,* 213–223.

Lockwood, C. M. (2000). *Effects of nonnormality on tests of mediation.* Unpublished master's thesis, Arizona State University.

Lockwood, C. M., & MacKinnon, D. P. (1998). Bootstrapping the standard error of the mediated effect. *Proceedings of the 23rd Annual Meeting of SAS Users Group International* (pp. 997–1002). Cary, NC: SAS Institute.

Lord, F. M. (1963). Elementary models for measuring change. In C. W. Harris (Ed.) *Problems in measuring change* (pp. 21–38). Madison, WI: University of Wisconsin Press.

Lynch, K. G., Cary, M., Gallop, R., & ten Have, T. R. (2008). Causal mediation analyses for randomized trials. *Health Services and Outcome Methodology, 8,* 57–76.

MacCallum, R. C., Zhang, S., Preacher, K. J., & Rucker, D. D. (2002). On the practice of dichotomization of quantitative variables. *Psychological Methods, 7,* 19–40.

MacKinnon, D. P. (1994). Analysis of mediating variables in prevention intervention studies. In A. Cazares & L. A. Beatty (Eds.), *Scientific methods for prevention intervention research. NIDA research monograph 139* (DHHS Pub. No. 94-3631, pp. 127–53). Washington, DC: Supt. of Docs., U. S. Government Printing Office.

MacKinnon, D. P. (2000). Contrasts in multiple mediator models. In J. Rose, L. Chassin, C. C. Presson, & S. J. Sherman (Eds.), *Multivariate applications in substance use research: New methods for new questions* (pp.141–160). Mahwah, NJ: Lawrence Erlbaum.

MacKinnon, D. P. (2001). Commentary on Donaldson: Mediator and moderator analysis in program development. In S. Sussman (Ed.), *Handbook of program development for health behavior research and practice* (pp. 497–500). Thousand Oaks, CA: Sage.

MacKinnon, D. P. (2008). *Introduction to statistical mediation analysis.* Mahwah, NJ: Erlbaum.

MacKinnon, D. P., Cheong, J., Goldberg, L., Williams, J., & Moe, E. (May, 2002). *Mediating mechanisms in the second cohort of a program to prevent anabolic steroid use.* Paper presented at the annual meeting of the Society for Prevention Research, Seattle, WA.

MacKinnon, D. P., & Dwyer, J. H. (1993). Estimating mediated effects in prevention studies. *Evaluation Review, 17,* 144–158.

MacKinnon, D. P., Fairchild, A. J., & Fritz, M. S. (2007). Mediation analysis. *Annual Review of Psychology, 58,* 593–614.

MacKinnon, D. P., Fritz, M. S., Williams, J., & Lockwood, C. M. (2007). Distribution of the product confidence limits for the indirect effect: Program PRODCLIN. *Behavior Research Methods, 39,* 384–389.

MacKinnon, D. P., Goldberg, L., Clarke, G. N., Elliot, D. L., Cheong, J., Lapin, A., Moe, E. L., et al. (2001). Mediating mechanisms in a program to reduce intentions to use anabolic steroids and improve exercise self-efficacy and dietary behavior. *Prevention Science, 2,* 15–28.

MacKinnon, D. P., Krull, J. L., & Lockwood, C. M. (2000). Equivalence of the mediation, confounding, and suppression effect. *Prevention Science, 1,* 173–181.

MacKinnon, D. P., & Lockwood, C. M. (May, 2001). *An approximate randomization test for the mediated effect.* Paper presented at the annual meeting of the Western Psychological Association Convention, Maui, Hawaii.

MacKinnon, D. P., Lockwood, C. M., Brown, C. H., Wang, W. & Hoffman, J. M. (2007). The intermediate endpoint effect in logistic and probit regression. *Clinical Trials, 5,* 499–513.

MacKinnon, D. P., Lockwood, C. M., Hoffman, J. M., West, S. G., & Sheets, V. (2002). Comparison of methods to test mediation and other intervening variable effects. *Psychological Methods, 7,* 83–104.

MacKinnon, D. P., Lockwood, C. M., & Williams, J. (2004). Confidence limits for the indirect effect: Distribution of the product and resampling methods. *Multivariate Behavioral Research, 39,* 99–128.

MacKinnon, D. P., & Pirlott, A. (2010). The unbearable lightness of b. Paper presented at the Annual Meeting of the Society for Personality and Social Psychology.

MacKinnon, D. P., Taborga, M. P., & Morgan-Lopez, A. A. (2002). Mediation designs for tobacco prevention research. *Drug and Alcohol Dependence, 68,* S69–S83.

MacKinnon, D. P., Taylor, A. B, Yoon, M., & Lockwood, C. M. (2009). A comparison of methods to test mediation and other intervening variable effects in logistic regression. Unpublished Manuscript.

MacKinnon, D. P., Warsi, G., & Dwyer, J. H. (1995). A simulation study of mediated effect measures. *Multivariate Behavior Research, 30,* 41–62.

MacKinnon, D. P., Weber, M. D., & Pentz, M. A. (1989). How do school-based drug prevention programs work and for whom? *Drugs and Society, 3,* 125–143.

Malone, P. S., Lansford, J. E., Castellino, D. R., Berlin, L. J., & Dodge, K. A. (2004). Divorce and child behavior problems: Applying latent change score models to life event data. *Structural Equation Modeling, 11,* 401–423.

Manly, B. F. J. (1997). *Randomization, bootstrap, and Monte Carlo methods in biology.* London: Chapman & Hall.

Mark, M. M. (1986). Validity typologies and the logic and practice of quasi-experimentation. In W. M. K. Trochim, (Ed.), *Advances in quasi-experimental design and analysis* (pp. 47–66). San Francisco: Jossey-Bass.

Mathieu, J. E., DeShon, R. P., & Bergh, D. D. (2008). Mediational inferences in organizational research. *Organizational Research Methods, 11,* 203–223.

Maxwell, J. A., Bashook, P. G., & Sandlow, L. J. (1986). Combining ethnographic and experimental methods in educational evaluation: A case study. In D. M. Fetterman & M. A. Pittman (Eds.), *Educational evaluation: Ethnography in theory, practice, and politics,* (pp. 121–143). Newbury Park, CA: Sage.

Maxwell, S. E., & Cole, D. A. (2007). Bias in cross-sectional analyses of longitudinal mediation. *Psychological Methods, 12,* 23–44.

McArdle, J. J. (2001). A latent difference score approach to longitudinal dynamic structural analysis. In R. Cudeck, S. du Toit, & D. Sörbom (Eds.) *Structural equation modeling: Present and future. A festschrift in honor of Karl Jöreskog* (pp. 341–380). Lincolnwood, IL: Scientific Software International.

McArdle, J. J., & Hamagami, F. (2001). Latent difference score structural models for linear dynamic analyses with incomplete longitudinal data. In L. M. Collins & A. G. Sayer (Eds.) *New methods for the analysis of change* (pp. 139–175). Washington, DC: APA.

McArdle, J. J., & Nesselroade, J. R. (2003). Growth curve analysis in contemporary psychological research. In J. Schinka & W. Velicer (Eds.), *Comprehensive handbook of psychology, Vol. II: Research methods in psychology* (pp. 447–480). New York: Pergamon Press.

McClelland, G.H., & Judd, C.M. (1993). Statistical difficulties of detecting interactions and moderator effects. *Psychological Bulletin, 114,* 376–390.

McDonald, R. P. (1997). Haldane's lungs: A case study in path analysis. *Multivariate Behavioral Research, 32,* 1–38.

McGuigan, K., & Langholtz, B. (1988). *A note on testing mediation paths using ordinary least-squares regression.* Unpublished note.

Meeker, W. Q., Cornwell, L. W., & Aroian, L. A. (1981). *Selected tables in mathematical statistics, Vol. 7.* Providence, RI: Institute of Mathematical Statistics.

Merrill, R. (1994). *Treatment effect evaluation in nonadditive mediation models.* Arizona State University Dissertation.

Merrill, R., MacKinnon, D. P., & Mayer, L. (2006). *Estimating mediated moderator effects in treatment studies.* Manuscript in preparation.

Morgan-Lopez, A. A. (2002). *Bias-corrected bootstrap estimation of mediated baseline by treatment interaction effects in intervention trials.* Invited colloquium presented at Quantitative Methodology in Prevention Seminar Series, The Methodology Center, The Pennsylvania State University, University Park, PA, November 8, 2002.

Morgan-Lopez, A. A. (2003). A simulation study of the mediated baseline by treatment interaction effect in preventive intervention trials (Doctoral dissertation, Arizona State University, 2003). *Dissertation Abstracts International, 64,* 4673.

Morgan-Lopez, A. A., Castro, F. G., Chassin, L., & MacKinnon, D. P. (2003). A mediated moderation model of cigarette use among Mexican-American youth. *Addictive Behaviors, 28,* 583–589.

Morgan-Lopez, A. A., & MacKinnon, D. P. (May-June, 2001). *A mediated moderation model simulation: Mediational processes that vary as a function of second predictors.* Paper submitted for presentation at the 9th Annual Meeting of the Society for Prevention Research, Washington, DC.

Morgan-Lopez, A. A., & MacKinnon, D. P. (2006). Demonstration and evaluation of a method for assessing mediated moderation. *Behavior Research Methods, 38,* 77–87.

MTA Cooperative Group. (1999). Moderators and mediators of treatment response for children with attention-deficit/Hyperactivity disorder. *Archives of General Psychiatry, 56,* 1088–1096.

Murphy, S. A., Van der Laan, M. J., Robins, J. M. & Conduct Problems Prevention Research Group. (2001). Marginal mean models for dynamic regimes. *Journal of the American Statistical Association, 96,* 1410–1423.

Muthén, L. K., & Muthén, B. O. (2001). *Mplus: The comprehensive modeling program for applied researchers.* Los Angeles, CA: Muthén & Muthén.

Noreen, E. W. (1989). *Computer-intensive methods for testing hypothesis: An introduction.* New York: Wiley & Sons.

Pearl, J. (2009). *Causality: Models, reasoning, and inference.* Cambridge, England: Cambridge University Press.

Pearl, J. (2010a). The foundations of causal inference. *Sociological Methodology, 40,* 75–149.

Pearl, J. (2010b). *The mediation formula: A guide to the assessment of causal pathways in non-linear models.* (Tech. Rep.) Los Angeles, CA: University of California, Los Angeles.

Pillow, D. R., Sandler, I. N., Braver, S. L., Wolchik, S. A., & Gersten, J. C. (1991). Theory-based screening for prevention:

Focusing on mediating processes in children of divorce. *American Journal of Community Psychology, 19,* 809–836.

Pitts, S. (1997). *The utility of extreme groups analysis to detect interactions in the presence of correlated predictor variables.* Masters document. Arizona State University.

Pituch, K., Stapleton, L. M., & Kang, J. Y. (2006). A comparison of single sample and bootstrap methods to assess mediation in cluster randomized trials. *Multivariate Behavioral Research, 41,* 367–400.

Preacher, K. J., & Hayes, A. F. (2004). SPSS and SAS procedures for estimating indirect effects in simple mediation models. *Behavior Research Methods, Instruments, & Computers, 36,* 717–731.

Preacher, K. J., Rucker, D. D., & Hayes, A. F. (2007). Addressing moderated mediation hypotheses: Theory, Methods, and Prescriptions. *Multivariate Behavioral Research, 42,* 185–227.

Preacher, K. J., Rucker, D. D., MacCallum, R. C., & Nicewander, W. A. (2005). Use of the extreme groups approach: a critical reexamination and new recommendations. *Psychological Methods, 10,* 178–192.

Preacher, K. J., Zyphur, M. J., & Zhang, Z. (2010). A general multilevel SEM framework for assessing multilevel mediation. *Psychological Methods, 15,* 209–233.

Raudenbush, S. W., & Sampson, R. (1999). Assessing direct and indirect effects in multilevel designs with latent variables. *Sociological Methods and Research. 28,* 123–153.

Robins, J.M. (1989). The control of confounding by intermediate variables. *Statistics in Medicine, 8,* 679–701.

Robins, J. M., & Greenland, S. (1992). Identifiability and exchangeability for direct and indirect effects. *Epidemiology, 3,* 143–155.

Robins, J. M., Mark, S. D., & Newey, W. K. (1992). Estimating exposure effects by modeling the expectation of exposure conditional on confounders. *Biometrics, 48,* 479–495.

Rogosa, D. R. (1988). Myths about longitudinal research. In K. W. Schaie, R. T. Campbell & W. M. Meredith & S. C. Rawlings (Eds.), *Methodological issues in aging research.* (pp. 171–209). New York: Springer.

Rosenbaum, P. R. (2002). *Observational studies.* New York : Springer.

Rosenberg, M. (1968). *The logic of survey analysis.* New York : Basic Books.

Rozeboom, W.W. (1956). Mediation variables in scientific theory. *Psychological Review, 63,* 249–264.

Rubin, D. B. (1974). Estimating causal effects of treatments in randomized and nonrandomized studies. *Journal of Educational Psychology, 66,* 688–701.

Rubin, D.B. (2004). Direct and indirect causal effects via potential outcomes. *Scandinavian Journal of Statistics, 31,* 161–170.

Sandler, I. N., Wolchik, S. A., MacKinnon, D. P., Ayers, T. S., & Roosa, M. W. (1997). Developing linkages between theory and intervention in stress and coping processes. In S. A. Wolchik & I. N. Sandler (Eds.), *Handbook of children's coping: Linking theory and intervention.* (pp. 3–40) New York: Plenum Press.

Schafer, J. L. (1997). *Analysis of incomplete multivariate data.* London: Chapman & Hall.

Shadish, W. R., Cook, T. D., & Campbell, D. T. (2002). *Experimental and quasi-experimental designs for generalized causal inference.* Boston: Houghton Mifflin Company.

Shipley, B. (2000). *Cause and correlation in biology.* Cambridge, England: Cambridge University Press.

Sidani, S., & Sechrest, L. (1999). Putting program theory into operation. *American Journal of Evaluation, 20,* 227–238.

Singer, J. D., & Willett, J. B. (2003). *Applied longitudinal data analysis: Modeling change and event occurrence.* London: Oxford University Press.

Sobel, M. E. (1982). Asymptotic confidence intervals for indirect effects in structural equation models. In S. Leinhardt (Ed.), *Sociological Methodology* (pp. 290–312). Washington, DC: American Sociological Association.

Sobel, M. E. (1986). Some new results on indirect effects and their standard errors in covariance structure models. In N. Tuma (Ed.), *Sociological Methodology* (pp. 159–186). Washington, DC: American Sociological Association.

Sobel, M. E. (1998a). Causal inference in statistical models of the process of socioeconomic achievement: A case study. *Sociological Methods & Research, 27,* 318–348.

Sobel, M. E. (March, 1998b). *Causality: New ideas on mediated effects.* Paper presented at Arizona State University's Conference on Mediation Models in Prevention Research, Tempe, AZ.

Sobel, M.E. (2007). Identification of causal parameters in randomized studies with mediating variables. *Journal of Educational and Behavioral Statistics, 33,* 230–251.

Spencer, S.J., Zanna, M.P., & Fong, G.T. (2005). Establishing a causal chain: Why experiments are often more effective than meditational analyses in examining psychological processes. *Journal of Personality and Social Psychology, 89,* 845–851.

Springer, M. D. (1979). *The algebra of random variables.* New York: Wiley.

Springer, M. D., & Thompson, W. E. (1970). The distribution of products of Beta, Gamma, and Gaussian variables. *Journal of SIAM Applied Mathematics, 18,* 721–737.

Stolzenberg, R. M. (1979). The measurement and decomposition of causal effects in nonlinear and non additive models. In K. F. Schuessler (Ed.), *Sociological Methodology* (pp. 459–488). San Francisco, CA: Jossey-Bass.

Stolzenberg, R. M., & Relles, D. A. (1990). Theory testing in a world of constrained research design. *Sociological Methods & Research, 18*(4), 395–415.

Stuart, E. A., Perry, D. F., Le, H., & Ialongo, N. S. (2008). Estimating intervention effects of prevention programs: Accounting for noncompliance. *Prevention Science, 9,* 288–298.

Taylor, A. B., & MacKinnon, D. P. (2012). Four applications of permutation methods to testing a single-mediator model. *Behavior Research Methods,* xxx–xxx.

Taylor, A. B., MacKinnon, D., & Tein, J.-Y. (2008). Test of the three-path mediated effect. *Organization Research Methods.* 11, 241–269.

Tein, J.-Y., & MacKinnon, D. P. (2003). Estimating mediated effects with survival data. H. Yanai, A. O. Rikkyo, K. Shigemasu, Y. Kano, J. J. Meulman (Eds.) *New Developments on Psychometrics* (pp. 405–412). Tokyo, Japan: Springer-Verlag Tokyo.

ten Have, T. R., Joffe, M. M., Lynch, K. G., Brown, G. K., Maisto, S. A., & Beck, A. T. (2007). Causal mediation analysis with rank preserving models. *Biometrics, 63,* 926–934.

Tornqvist, L., Vartia, P., & Vartia, Y. O. (1985). How should relative changes be measured? *American Statistician, 39,* 43–46.

VanderWeele, T. J. (2008). Simple relations between principal stratification and direct and indirect effects. *Statistics and Probability Letters, 78,* 2957–2962.

VanderWeele, T. J. (2010). Bias formulas for sensitivity analysis for direct and indirect effects. *Epidemiology, 21,* 540–51.

von Eye, A., Mun, E. Y., & Mair, P. (2009). What carries a mediation process? Configuralanalysis of mediation. *Integration of Psychology and Behavior, 43,* 228–247.

Weiss, C. H. (1997). How can theory-based evaluation make greater headway? *Evaluation Review, 21,* 501–524.

West, S. G., & Aiken, L. S. (1997). Toward understanding individual effects in multiple component prevention programs: Design and analysis strategies. In K. Bryant, M. Windle, & S. G. West (Eds.), *The science of prevention: Methodological advances from alcohol and substance abuse research* (pp. 167–209). Washington, DC: American Psychological Association.

West, S. G., Aiken, L. S., & Todd, M. (1993). Probing the effects of individual components in multiple component prevention programs. *American Journal of Community Psychology, 21,* 571–605.

West, S. G., Sandler, I., Baca, L., Pillow, D., & Gersten, J. C. (1991). The use of structural equation modeling in generative research: Toward the design of a preventive intervention for a bereaved children. *American Journal of Community Psychology, 19,* 459–480.

Wiley, D.E. (1973). The identification problem for structural equation models with unmeasured variables. In A.S. Goldberger & O.D. Duncan (Eds.), *Structural equation models in the social sciences* (pp. 69–83). New York: Seminar Press.

Willett, J. B., & Sayer, A. G. (1994). Using covariance structure analysis to detect correlates and predictors of individual change over time. *Psychological Bulletin, 116,* 363–381.

Williams, J., & MacKinnon, D.P. (2002). *Selection bias and the estimation of the mediated effect.* Poster presented at the Western Psychological Association conference, Irvine, CA.

Williams, J., & MacKinnon, D. P. (2008). Resampling and distribution of the product methods for testing indirect effects in complex models. *Structural Equation Modeling, 15,* 23–51.

Winship, C., & Mare, R. D. (1983). Structural equations and path analysis for discrete data. *American Journal of Sociology, 89,* 54–110.

Winship, C., & Morgan, S. L. (1999). The estimation of causal effects from observational data. *Annual Review of Sociology, 25,* 659–707.

Witteman, J. C. M., D'Agostino, R. B., Stijnen, T., Kannel, W. B., Cobb, J. C., de Ridder, M. A. J., Hofman, A., & Robins, J. M. (1998). G-estimation of causal effects: Isolated systolic hypertension and cardiovascular death in the Framingham Heart Study. *Journal of Epidemiology, 148,* 390–401.

Wright, S. (1920). The relative importance of heredity and environment in determining the piebald pattern of guinea-pigs. *Proceedings of the National Academy of Sciences, 6,* 320–332.

Wright, S. (1921). Correlation and causation. *Journal of Agricultural Research, 20,* 557–585.

Yuan, Y., & Mackinnon, D. P. (2009). Bayesian Mediation Analysis. *Psychological Methods, 14,* 301–322.

Zhang, Z., Zyphur, M. J., & Preacher, K. J. (2009). Testing multilevel mediation using hierarchical linear models. *Organizational Research Methods, 12,* 695–719.

Zu, J., & Yuan, K. (2010). Local influence and robufst procedures for mediation analysis. *Multivariate Behavioral Research, 45,* 1–44.

CHAPTER 17

Moderation

Herbert W. Marsh, Kit-Tai Hau, Zhonglin Wen, Benjamin Nagengast, *and* Alexandre J.S. Morin

---

Abstract

Moderation (or interaction) occurs when the strength or direction of the effect of a predictor variable on an outcome variable varies as a function of the values of another variable, called a moderator. Moderation effects address critical questions, such as under what circumstances, or for what sort of individuals, does an intervention have a stronger or weaker effect? Moderation can have important theoretical, substantive, and policy implications. Especially in psychology with its emphasis on individual differences, many theoretical models explicitly posit interaction effects. Nevertheless, particularly in applied research, even interactions hypothesized on the basis of strong theory and good intuition are typically small, nonsignificant, or not easily replicated. Part of the problem is that applied researchers often do not know how to test interaction effects, as statistical best practice is still evolving and often not followed. Also, tests of interactions frequently lack power so that meaningfully large interaction effects are not statistically significant. In this chapter we provide an intuitive overview to the issues involved, recent developments in how best to test for interactions, and some directions that further research is likely to take.

Key Words: Interaction effect; moderator, moderated multiple regression; mediation; latent interaction; product indicator; structural equation model

---

Introduction

Moderation and interactions between variables are important concerns in psychology and the social sciences more generally (here we use moderation and interaction interchangeably). In educational psychology, for example, it is often hypothesized that the effect of an instructional technique will interact with characteristics of individual students, an aptitude-treatment interaction (Cronbach & Snow, 1979). For example, a special remediation program developed for slow learners may not be an effective instructional strategy for bright students (i.e., the effect of the special remediation "treatment" is moderated by the ability "aptitude" of the student). Developmental psychologists are frequently interested in how the effects of a given variable are moderated by age in longitudinal or cross-sectional studies (i.e., effects interact with age or developmental status). Developmental psychopathologists may also be interested to know whether a predictor variables is, in fact, a risk factor, predicting the emergence of new symptoms and useful in preventive efforts, or an aggravation factor, mostly useful in curative efforts (i.e. effects interact with the baseline level on the outcome in longitudinal studies; Morin, Janoz, & Larivée, 2009). Social psychologists and sociologists are concerned with how the effects of individual characteristics are moderated by groups in which people interact with others. Organizational psychologists study how the effects of individual employee characteristics interact with workplace characteristics. Personnel psychologists want to know whether a selection test is equally valid at predicting work performance for different demographic groups. Fundamental to the rationale of differential psychology is the assumption that people differ in the way that they respond to all sorts of external stimuli.

Many psychological theories explicitly hypothesize interaction effects. Thus, for example, some forms of expectancy-value theory hypothesize that resultant motivation is based on the interaction between expectancy of success and the value placed on success by the individual (e.g., motivation is high only if both probability of success and the value placed on the outcome are high). In self-concept research, the relation between an individual component of self-concept (e.g., academic, social, physical) and global self-esteem is sometimes hypothesized to interact with the importance placed on a specific component of self-concept (e.g., if a person places no importance on physical accomplishments, then these physical accomplishments—substantial or minimal—are not expected to be substantially correlated with self-esteem). More generally, a variety of weighted-average models posit—at least implicitly—that the effects of each of a given set of variables will depend on the weight assigned to each variable in the set (i.e., the weight assigned to a given variable interacts with the variable to determine the contribution of that variable to the total effect).

Interaction or moderation can be seen as the opposite of generalizabilty. For example, if the effect of an intervention is the same for males and females, it is said to generalize across gender. However, if the effect of the intervention differs for men and women, then it is said to interact with gender.

Classic Definition of Moderation

In their classic presentation of moderation, Baron and Kenny (1986, p. 1174) defined a moderator variable to be a "variable that affects the direction and/or strength of the relationship between an independent or predictor variable and a dependent or criterion variable." An interaction occurs when the effect of at least one predictor variable and an outcome variable is moderated (i.e., depends on or varies as a function of) by at least one other predictor. Moderation studies address issues like "when (under what conditions/situations)" or "for whom" X has a stronger/weaker (positive/negative) relation with or effect on Y.

Consider the effect of a variable X_1 on an outcome Y: If the effect of X_1 on Y is affected by another variable X_2, then we say X_2 is a moderator; the relation between X_1 and Y is moderated by X_2. Under this circumstance, the size or direction of the effect of X_1 on Y varies with the value of the moderator X_2. As used here, X_1 and X_2 are symmetrical and can be interchanged, such that either of them can moderate the effect of the other. However, depending on the design of the study, the goals of the research, or the specific research questions, it might be reasonable to designate one of the predictor variables to be a moderator variable. Implicit in the discussion of interaction effects is the assumption that the outcome variable is determined, at least in part, by a combination of the main effects of the two predictor variables and their interaction.

Moderators can be categorical variables (e.g., gender, ethnicty, school type) or continuous variables (e.g., age, years of education, self-concept, test scores, reaction time). They can be a manifest observed variable (e.g., gender, race) or a latent variable measured with multiple indicators (e.g., self-concept, test scores). Different analytic methods of testing interactions are associated with the different types of moderators. In tests of interaction effects, the interaction term is typically the product of two variables and treated as a separate variable (e.g., the $X_1 X_2$ interaction is often denoted as X_1-by-X_2 or $X_1 \times X_2$). A significant interaction effect indicates that the simple slopes of the predictor vary when the moderator takes on different values. We begin by discussing methods for analyzing interactions between observed variables and then discuss alternative approaches to probing the meaning of these interactions. We then give a brief account of the development of more sophisticated but statistically (and theoretically) stronger models in the estimation of latent interactions.

Particularly for categorical independent variables, manifest variables as outcome, and experimental designs with random assignment to groups, ANOVA is commonly used to evaluate interactions. The initial tests of these interactions are performed almost completely automatically by statistical packages with little intervention by the researcher. Even here, however, probing the appropriate interpretation and meaning of statistically significant interactions requires careful consideration. In contrast to ANOVAs, interaction terms in regression analyses are usually based on *a priori* theoretical predictions. Although statistically all ANOVA models can be respecified as multiple regression models (e.g., by using dummy variables), ANOVA is appropriate when all the independent variables are categorical with a relatively small number of levels. In the present chapter, we concentrate on the detection and estimation of interactions in regression analyses with the understanding that with appropriate coding of the different design factors, these analytical techniques can be applied equally effectively to experimental designs.

Graphs of Interaction Effects

Whatever the statistical approach used to test interaction effects, it is always helpful to graph statistically significant interaction effects. For example, suppose you want to test the prediction that there is no relation between X_1 and Y for boys but that X_1 and Y are positively related for girls. The finding that gender interacts significantly with X_1 only says that the relation between X_1 and the outcome Y is different for boys and girls but not whether the nature of this interaction is consistent with a specific *a priori* prediction. The starting point for probing the nature of this interaction is typically to graph the results.

Although we discuss more statistically sophisticated ways to probe significant interaction effects, a graph is always helpful in understanding the nature of the interaction effect. In Figure 17.1 we illustrate a number of different graphs of paradigmatic interaction effects, which are sometimes given specific labels in the literature. For purposes of the example, we can consider these as interactions in which one of the predictor variables is dichotomous (e.g., male/female; experimental/control), whereas the other predictor and the outcome variable are continuous. However, later we will describe how such graphs can be constructed when all variables are continuous.

Even with relatively simple models, interaction effects can be very diverse (Fig. 17.1). In Figure 17.1 we have plotted different forms of interactions in which X_1 is a continuous predictor variable and X_2 (the other predictor, the moderating variable) is a dichotomous grouping variable (here labelled as boys and girls). The key distinguishing feature is that the lines (regression plots) for boys and girls are parallel in the first graph (indicating no interaction), whereas they are significantly non-parallel for all the other graphs.

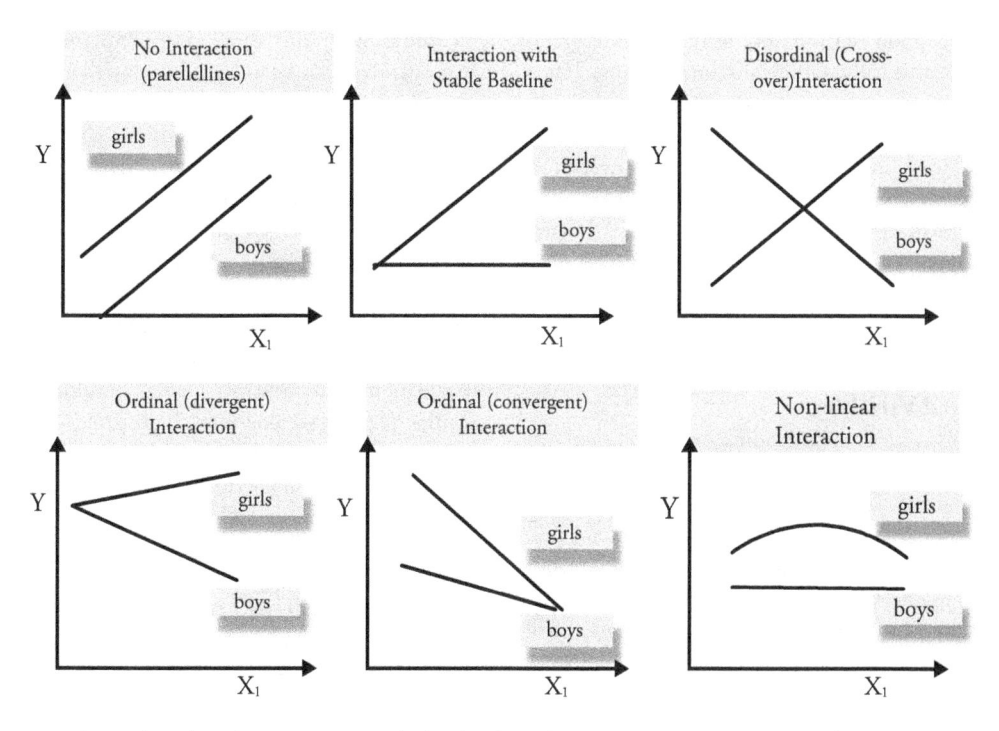

Figure 17.1 Diverse hypothetical outcomes testing whether the relation between a continuous predictor variable (X_1) and a continuous outcome variable (Y) varies as a function of the dichotomous grouping variable, gender (X_2, the moderating variable). The distinguishing feature is that the line (regression plots) for boys and girls are parallel in the first graph (indicating no interaction), whereas they are not parallel for any of the other graphs. Regression plots that contain only linear terms necessarily result in graphs that are strictly linear. However, the final graph illustrates an interaction that is nonlinear in relation to X_1 (i.e., the differences between the two lines is small when X_1 is large or small, but larger when X_1 is intermediate).

Specific forms of interactions are sometimes referred to by different names. In particular, it is typical to distinguish between disordinal graphs, where the lines cross, and ordinal graphs, where the lines do not cross, for the range of possible or plausible values that the predictor variables can take on. It is important to note that these graphs represent the predicted values from the regression model used to test the interaction effect (and should be limited to a range of values for X_1 and X_2 that are plausible and actually considered in the analyses). Thus, for example, all but the last graph are strictly linear in that only the linear effects of X_1 were included in the model (because X_2 is dichotomous, it can only have a linear effect). However, the final model includes a nonlinear (quadratic) component of X_1; the difference between the two lines is small when X_1 is small, large when X_1 is intermediate, and small when X_1 is large. Because of the nature of this interaction in this last model, it is likely that there would have been no statistically significant interaction if only the linear effects of X_1 were considered. It would also be possible to control for one or more covariates in any of these models, and this typically would change the form of the interaction.

Plotting regression equations like those in Figure 17.1 is a good starting point in the interpretation of statistically significant interactions, but a casual visual inspection of the graphs is not sufficient. Particularly for studies based on modest sample sizes, researchers are likely to overinterpret the results, leading to false–positive errors. We now turn to appropriate strategies to test the statistical significance of interactions and probe their meaning.

Traditional (Non-Latent) Approaches for Observed Variables

In this section, we introduce analytical methods for interaction models, depending on the nature of the variables. The critical feature common to all these approaches is that all the constructs are presented by a single indicator. Hence, these are not latent variable models in which the constructs are represented by multiple indicators (which we will discuss latter).

Interactions between Categorical Variables: Analysis of Variance

When the independent variables X_1 and X_2 are both categorical variables that can take on a relatively small number of levels and the dependent variable is a continuous variable, interaction effects can be easily estimated with traditional analysis of variance (ANOVA) procedures (for more general discussions of ANOVA, *see* classic textbooks such as Kirk, 1982; *see also* Jaccard, 1998). In the simplest factorial design, both X_1 and X_2 have two levels (i.e., a 2 × 2 design). In addition to the main effects of X_1 and X_2, this factorial ANOVA provides a test of the statistical significance of the interaction between X_1 and X_2.

The null hypothesis for the interaction effect is that the effect of neither predictor variable (X_1 or X_2) depends on the value of the other. More complex factorial designs can have more than two levels of each variable and more than two predictor variables. There can also be higher-order interactions involving more than two variables (e.g., the nature of the $X_1 X_2$ interaction depends on a third variable, X_3).

Although ANOVAs are typically used in experimental studies in which participants are randomly assigned to different levels of a grouping variable (e.g., experimental and control), this design can also be evaluated with more general regression approaches, representing the factors with dummy or indicator variables. Likewise, nonexperimental studies with only categorical predictor variables (e.g., gender) can be analyzed with either ANOVA or regression approaches.

The deceptive ease with which ANOVAs can be conducted has tempted researchers to transform reasonably continuous variables into a few discrete categories so that they can be evaluated with traditional ANOVA approaches. For example, with independent variables that are originally reasonably continuous, it might be possible to divide one or both of the variables into two (e.g., using a mean or median split) or a small number of categories (e.g., low, medium, high groups) so that they can be evaluated with ANOVAs. There are, however, potentially serious problems that dictate against this strategy, including (1) a reduction in reliability of the original variables, resulting in a loss of power in detecting main and particularly the interaction effects; (2) a reduction in variance explained by the original variables and particularly the interaction terms; (3) absence of a commonly used summary estimate of the strength of the interaction effect (using categories, we have t-values in different groups only; Jaccard, Turrisi, & Wan, 1990); and (4) difficulty in determining the nature of potential nonlinear relations (particularly when a continuous variable is represented by only two categories). A possible exception is that if the categorization is a natural cut-off of particular interest (e.g., minimum test scores to qualify for acceptance into a program or classification schemes). For example, Baron and Kenny (1986) discuss a threshold form of moderation such that a predictor variable has no effect when the moderator value is low, but has a positive effect when the moderator takes on a value above a certain threshold. In this case, if the threshold value is know *a priori*, it might be reasonable to dichotomize the moderator at the level of the threshold. Even here, however, there are typically stronger models that test, for example, whether the effects of the predictor variable are unaffected by variation in the moderator below the threshold or variation above the threshold. Nevertheless, the general strategy forming a small number of categories from a reasonably continuous variable should usually be avoided (for further discussion, *see* MacCallum, Zhang, Preacher, & Rucker, 2002). Although researchers have been warned of the inappropriateness of this practice for more than a quarter of a century (e.g., Cohen, 1978), it still persists. In summary, researchers should (almost) never transform continuous variables into discrete categories.

Interactions With One Categorical Variable: Separate Group Multiple Regression

When one independent variable is a categorical variable (e.g., X_2)—particularly with only a few naturally occurring levels (e.g., gender as in Fig. 17.1, or ethnic groups)—and the other one is a continuous variable (e.g., X_1), a possible approach is to conduct a separate regression for each group (*see also* subsequent discussion about multiple-group tests in the section on latent variable interactions). The interaction effect is represented by the differences between unstandardized regression coefficients obtained with the separate groups (Aiken & West, 1991; Cohen & Cohen, 1983; Cohen, Cohen, Aiken, & West, 2003). Assume we draw these regression equation lines: If these lines from different groups are parallel, then we conclude that there is no interaction (*see* the first graph in Fig. 17.1).

If one of the predictor variables (X_2) is dichotomous, then it is possible to test for the statistical significance of the difference between to regression coefficients relating X_1 and Y (Cohen & Cohen, 1983, p. 56). If the hypothesis is rejected, then the interaction is significant. This approach is particularly useful if there are differences in the error variances at different levels of the moderator (*see also* subsequent discussion of latent variable tests of invariance across multiple groups). Although useful in some special cases, this multiple-group approach is typically more limited in terms of facilitating the interpretation of interaction effects, reducing power because of lower sample size in each group considered separately, and, of course, because it requires at least one of the predictor variables to be a true categorical variable. Therefore, we now present a more general approach that is appropriate when predictor variables are categorical, continuous, or a mixture of the two.

Interactions With Continuous Variables: Moderated Multiple Regression Approaches

Now we move from analyses of moderation involving categorical observed independent variables to those using continuous observed independent variables. Consider the familiar regression equation involving two predictors, X_1 and X_2:

$$Y = \beta_0 + \beta_1 X_1 + \beta_2 X_2 + e,$$

which assumes no interaction; the effects of X_1 and X_2 are additive (Judd, McClelland, & Ryan, 2009; Klein, Schermelleh-Engel, Moosbrugger, & Kelava, 2009). That means the effect of a predictor (e.g., X_1) does not depend the value of the other (i.e., X_2) and the effects of the two predictors on Y can simply be added. The first graph in Figure 17.1 (with parallel lines) was based on a model of this form.

However, this assumption of strictly additive effects might be false. Irrespective of whether X_1 or X_2 has a main effect on Y, an interaction effect might exist in that the effect of X_1 on Y depends on the value of X_2. The mathematical equation representing this can be expressed as:

$$Y = \beta_0 + \beta_1 X_1 + \beta_2 X_2 + \beta_3 X_1 X_2 + e, \quad (1)$$

where β_1 and β_2 represent the main effects of with X_1 and X_2, β_3 represents the interaction effect, $X_1 X_2$ is the product of X_1 and X_2 (the interaction term), and e is a random disturbance term with zero mean that is uncorrelated with X_1 and X_2.

Suppose that

$$Y = b_0 + b_1 X_1 + b_2 X_2 + b_3 X_1 X_2$$

represents the estimated values of Equation 1. When X_1 is treated as the moderator, it can also be expressed as:

$$Y = (b_0 + b_1 X_1) + (b_2 + b_3 X_1) X_2,$$

where the intercept ($b_0 + b_1X_1$) as well as the slope ($b_2 + b_3X_1$) of X_2 are a linear functions of X_1. Similarly, the equation can be represented as:

$$Y = (b_0 + b_2X_2) + (b_1 + b_3X_2)X_1,$$

with the intercept and effect (slope) of X_1 on Y being moderated by X_2. With simple derivations using either X_1 or X_2 as the moderator, it can be shown that the interactive effect can be operationalized by adding a product term X_1X_2 into the regression equation (for details, see, for example, Jaccard et al., 1990; Judd, McClelland, & Ryan, 2009). This shows that the moderating relation is symmetric in that if the effect of X_1 on Y depends on the value of X_2, then the effect of X_2 on Y also depends on the value of X_1. Although this equation only represents the linear effects of X_1, X_2, and X_1X_2, it could easily be expanded to include nonlinear components of X_1 and X_2 as well as additional covariates. Although this means that statistically either one of the variables forming the interaction effect can be treated as the moderator, this choice should be guided by the design of the study or substantive theory.

The variables in Equation 1 can also be centered ($M = 0$, as the variable mean is subtracted from each value; see Equation 2):

$$Y_C = \beta_{C0} + \beta_{C1}X_{1C} + \beta_{C2}X_{2C} + \beta_{C3}X_{1C}X_{2C} + e_C \quad (2)$$

Standardized estimates are the parameter estimates that are obtained when all independent and dependent variables in the regression model are standardized (i.e., z-scores; subtracting the variables with their respective means and then divided by their respective standard deviations):

$$Z_Y = \beta_{Z0} + \beta_{Z1}Z_{X1} + \beta_{Z2}Z_{X2} + \beta_{Z3}Z_{X1}Z_{X2} + e_Z \quad (3)$$

The centered and standardized form of the regression equation that are based on centered and standardized variables, respectively, are given by where the subscripts Z and C on the regression weights are used to indicate that these parameter estimates based on centered scores (Equation 2) and standardized scores (Equation 3) are not the same as the corresponding parameter estimates based on raw scores (Equation 1).

For the raw score regression (Equation 1), β_0 is the *intercept* or the predicted value of Y when X_1 and X_2 equal 0. The intercept (β_0) might be meaningless if X_1 and X_2 never take on a value of 0. However, when the predictor variables are centered or standardized (Equation 2 or Equation 3), the intercept (β_{C0} or β_{Z0}) is the value of Y at the mean of X_1 and X_2, which is typically meaningful.

β_1 is the estimated change in Y associated with 1 unit of change in X_1 when $X_2 = 0$ (i.e., the slope of the relation between X_1 and Y when $X_2 = 0$). Again this may be meaningless in the raw score equation. However, with centered or standardized predictors, it is the association between X_1 and Y at the mean of X_2. With centered predictors, β_{C1} represents the change in the outcome if X_1 changes one unit in the raw metric. If the predictors are standardized, then β_{Z1} represents the change in Y in standard deviation (SD) units if X_1 changes one SD. Although main effects should always be interpreted cautiously when there is an interaction, this is typically a meaningful result in the standardized equation. Because the interaction is symmetric in relation to X_1 and X_2, β_2 is merely the change in Y associated with a 1-unit change in X_2 when $X_1 = 0$. For Equations 1 and 2, the 1-unit change is in the original (raw score) metric, whereas in Equation 3 it is in standard deviation units. If the units of the predictor variables are in a meaningful metric, it might be useful to use the centered predictor variables, as changes are then in the same metric as the original variables. However, particularly when the metric is arbitrary, it often is more meaningful to standardize the variables so that changes are in terms of standard deviation units. However, when one of the predictor variables is a categorical variable, it is traditional to use values of 0 and 1 (or appropriate dummy variables if there are more than two categories).

β_3 represents the interaction effect, the amount by which the effect of X_1 on Y changes with a 1-unit increase in X_2. Equivalently, because of the symmetry of the interaction effect, it is the amount by which the effect of X_2 on Y changes with a 1-unit increase in X_1. In the raw and centered form, this value may or may not be interpretable, depending on the nature of the metric of X_1 and X_2. In the standardized form, the interpretation of β_{Z3} is the same, with the exception that all changes are in terms of SD units.

It is important to understand the relation between the regression equation and graphs like those presented in Figure 17.1. Regression plots are constructed by substituting values for the X_1 and X_2 predictor variables into the regression equation. In this regard, the regression plots represent the *predicted* values based on the model that is being tested, not the raw data. Thus, for example, even if there is nonlinearity in the raw data, this will not be reflected in regression plots based on a model with no nonlinear terms. To address this issue, researchers sometimes include a scatterplot of the individual cases (or the raw mean values for categorical variables) as well as the regression plot.

The regression plot can be based on raw scores, centered scores, or standardized scores. In terms of plotting, it is, of course, critical that values plotted are the same as those used to estimate the regression parameters. Hence, if predictor variables are standardized in the regression, then the standardized values should be used to construct the plot. However, it is reasonable to construct different plots in relation to raw, centered, or standardized scores—whichever is most appropriate—as the shape of the plot will be similar except for the metric of the axes of the graph.

When there are more than two groups, typical practice is to use dummy coding (in which one group is "left out" and serves as a baseline of comparison for other groups). However, the whole range of orthogonal and nonorthogonal coding schemes (e.g., effect coding, polynomial coding, difference coding, as well as coding specific to the nature of the study; e.g., Cohen et al., 2003; Marsh & Grayson, 1994) are available to the researcher and may have strategic advantages depending on the nature of the study design, the goals of the researcher, the meaning of the variables, and so forth. Whatever coding scheme is used, it is useful that all of the predictor variables have a meaningful zero point to facilitate the interpretation of the regression equations.

When both the predictors (X_1 and X_2) are continuous variables, it is traditional to plot regression lines for at least two strategically chosen values and typically three or more values (although complicated interactions involving nonlinear components might require more than three values). The representative values are typically selected to be the mean, 1 or 2 SDs above the mean, and 1 or 2 SD below the mean. In each case, the graphs can be constructed by simply substituting these representative values into the regression equation.

In Figure 17.2 we represent some of the correspondences between the regression equation and the graphs. We have graphed only two regression lines, as would be appropriate if one of the predictor variables was dichotomous (it is also appropriate in a model with only linear effects of X_1 and X_2 but more conventional to include three lines). To facilitate interpretation, these are presented in standard deviation units (i.e., all variables are standardized before conducting the multiple regression). The regression equation is plotted for $X_1 = 0$ (the mean of X_1

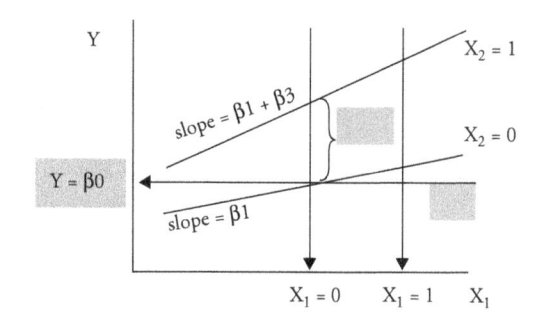

Figure 17.2 Graphical representation of the regression equation. X_1 and X_2 are predictor variables and Y is the outcome variable (to facilitate interpretation, these are presented in standard deviation units). The regression equation is plotted for $X_1 = 0$ (the mean of X_1) and $X_1 = 1$ (1 SD above the mean of 1). β_0 (the intercept) is the value that Y takes on when both $X_1 = 0$ and $X_2 = 0$. β_1 (the regression weight for X_1) is the change in Y associated with a 1-unit change in X_1 when $X_2 = 0$. β_2 (the regression weight for X_2) is the change in Y associated with a 1-unit change in X_2 when $X_1 = 0$. This form of the interaction term (the product of X_1 and X_2) is typical in social science research, but other forms of interaction could be considered.

when it is standardized) and $X_1 = 1$ (1 SD above the mean of X_1 when it is standardized). β_0 (the intercept) is the value that Y takes on when both $X_1 = 0$ and $X_2 = 0$. β_1 (the regression weight for X_1) is the change in Y associated with a 1-unit change in X_1 when $X_2 = 0$. β_2 (the regression weight for X_2) is the change in Y associated with a 1-unit change in X_2 when $X_1 = 0$. The relation between Y and X_2 when $X_1 = 1$ is given by the sum of β_2 and β_3.

There are, however, important caveats in the interpretation of the results that are highlighted by this graph. In particular, the effects of X_1 and X_2 on Y are conditional upon the value that the other variable takes on. The regression parameters β_1 and β_2 cannot be unconditionally interpreted as main effects of X_1 and X_2, respectively. This would only be possible if there were no interaction effect—that is, if $\beta_3 = 0$. The values of these regression weights represent the effect of their predictor at the point where the other predictor takes on a value of 0. In most cases in social science research, neither X_1 nor X_2 actually take on values of 0, or the value of 0 is arbitrary (i.e., ratio scales with an absolute 0 are rare). In these circumstances, it makes no sense to base substantive interpretations on the values of the regression weights unless the variables are centered or standardized. In this case, the zero point has a meaningful interpretation as the mean of the variable considered.

Some authors (e.g., Carte & Russell, 2003) are so adamant about this point that they have argued that regression coefficients should never be interpreted unless continuous X_1 and X_2 predictors are measured on a ratio scale that has an absolute 0. However, we emphasize that regression weights can be meaningfully interpreted when predictor variables are centered or when all variables in the regression equation are standardized or, perhaps, when zero is meaningful. Thus, for example, β_2 (the regression weight for X_2) is the change in Y associated with a 1-unit change in X_2 when $X_1 = 0$. When values are standardized, this means the change in Y (in SD units) associated with a change of 1 SD in X_2 at the mean of X_1. Hence, in relation to standardized or centered values, this is an interpretable result. It is, of course, important to emphasize that the change in Y will differ when X_1 takes on different values. Similarly, for standardized values it is interpretable to report β_2, the marginal change in Y associated with a 1 SD change in X_2 at the mean of X_1. It is important that the values of the predictor variables are scaled so that 0 is a meaningful value—whether a 0 and 1 coding of experimental groups, a zero-centered coding of continuous predictor variables, or appropriately standardized values so that all predictor variables have $M = 0$ and SD $= 1$. However, although we argue that it is meaningful to evaluate interaction effects in relation to scores transformed to have a meaningful zero value, it is important to evaluate simple effects of the predictor variable at different levels of the moderator variable.

Standardized Solutions for Models With Interactions Terms

Standardized estimates (*see* Equation 3) are useful for comparing results based on different variables in a standardized metric, even when the original variables are based on different, possibly arbitrary metrics. Standardizing a variable can be treated as two steps: centering (subtracting the variable with its mean) and rescaling (multiplying by a constant, e.g., meter is replaced by centimeter). Although the main effects of predictors on outcome variables are unaffected by centering in analyses for models without an interaction term, they may be affected substantially in models with interaction terms (Cohen, 1978; Cohen et al., 2003). However, centering does not affect the coefficient for the interaction term (*see* Cohen et al., 2003) or the nature (e.g., ordinal vs. disordinal) of the interaction. We also note that when predictors are not centered, product or nonlinear (e.g., X^2) terms will typically be highly correlated with the original variables, leading to multicollinearity problems such as large standard errors for the regression coefficients (Aiken & West, 1991; Cohen et al., 2003).

The computation of the appropriate standardized effects involving interaction terms in regression analyses is not straightforward with most commercial statistical packages (*see* Aiken & West, 1991; Cohen et al., 2003). In particular, the standardized regression coefficients are typically *not* correct for the interaction term. To obtain correct standardized regression coefficients (Friedrich, 1982):

1. standardize (*z*-score) all variables to become Z_Y, Z_{X1}, Z_{X2};
2. form the interaction term by multiplying the two standardized variables $Z_{X1}Z_{X2}$ (but do not re-standardize the product term);
3. use Z_{X1}, Z_{X2}, and $Z_{X1}Z_{X2}$ in a regression analysis to predict Z_Y, determine the statistical significance of all predictors using their respective *t*-values, and report the *unstandardized* regression coefficients as the appropriate standardized coefficients. That is, the coefficients of the Equation 2. (Note: The intercept term β_0 is necessary and generally not equal to 0 because the product term $Z_{X1}Z_{X2}$ typically does not have a mean of 0).

Tests of Statistical Significance of Interaction Effects.

In the application of a multiple regression model, it is straightforward to test the statistical significance of main effects and interactions by using the so-called hierarchical regression approach. This can be done in relation to raw, centered, or standardized variables:

1. For the additive model (with no interaction terms) predict Y with X_1 and X_2 and obtain the squared multiple correlation (percentage of variance explained) R_1^2;
2. For the interaction model, predict Y with X_1, X_2 and X_1X_2 using Equation 1, obtain the squared multiple correlation R_2^2 and compute the change in the squared multiple correlation, $R_2^2 - R_1^2$.

Based on Equation 1, to test whether the interaction effect is statistically significant, the hypothesis $H_0 : \beta_3 = 0$ the test statistic is

$$t = \frac{\hat{\beta}_3}{\text{SE}(\hat{\beta}_3)},$$

where $\text{SE}(\hat{\beta}_3)$ is the standard error of estimated β_3. More generally, when there is only one interaction term in the regression model, an equivalent test is whether R_2^2 is significantly higher than R_1^2 with the following F-test,

$$F = [(R_2^2 - R_1^2)/(k_2 - k_1)]/[(1 - R_2^2)/(N - k_2 - 1)],$$

where R_2^2 is from the equation involving the interaction term of k_2 predictors, R_1^2 is from the original equation with k_1 predictors, and N is the sample size. This is evident in that the squared t-statistic is equal to the F-statistic with $df = 1$ in the numerator. This value will be the same regardless of whether X_1 and X_2 have been centered or standardized.

The greater the partial regression coefficient β_3, and the change in R^2 (i.e., $R_2^2 - R_1^2$) resulting from the introduction of the interaction terms, the greater the moderating effect of X_1 on the relation of X_2 on Y (or symmetrically X_2 on the relationship of X_1 on Y). As pointed out by various researchers (e.g., Aiken & West, 1991; McClelland & Judd, 1993), it is important that the hierarchical regression be conducted with a model in which the interaction term is tested after controlling for both X_1 and X_2. That is, regression models testing the interaction term (X_1X_2) must also contain the corresponding predictor variables (X_1 and X_2). Otherwise the effect of the interaction is confounded with the main effects of X_1 and X_2. For models involving categorical variables in which more than one dummy variable is needed to represent one of the predictor variables (i.e., there are more than two categories), then all the related product terms must be entered simultaneously in the same regression step. Whether analyses are done in one step (including all predictor and interaction variables) or two steps (testing additive effects first and then including interaction terms), it is critical that interaction terms are evaluated in a model that contains all the additive terms for all variables in the interaction.

If additional covariates are included as control variables, they should be entered as the very first set of variables in the hierarchical regressions, followed by those involved in the interaction terms (Frazier, Tix, & Barron., 2004). However, this recommendation is based on the assumption that covariates come before the predictor and outcome variables in relation to their causal ordering. For some covariates, this is reasonable (e.g., gender, ethnicity, pretest variables), but in others it might not (*see* further discussion of mediated effects below). It is also relevant to evaluate whether the covariates really have similar effects on the outcome variable at different values of the other predictor variables by testing interactions between covariates and other variables (Cohen et al., 2003; Frazier et al., 2004).

Post hoc *Examination of the Interactions With Continuous Observed Variables.* Even when there is a statistically significant interaction effect, the interpretation of the values of the regression weights is hazardous, particularly when based on raw scores in the original metric. Hence, we recommend that researchers should always graph the regression equation at representative values of the predictor variables. Although this can be done in relation to the original (raw score) metric, there are sometimes interpretational advantages in constructing these graphs based on centered or standardized values. Logical questions might include (1) what is the pattern of changes in the slope (e.g., does the slope increase or decrease with increasing values of X_2)? and (2) is the regression of Y on X_1 significant at a particular value of X_2 or for a range of X_2 values?

Graphically this simple approach can be depicted by plots like those in Figure 17.2. When one of the predictor variables is a dichotomous grouping variable and the other is a continuous variable, the group-by-linear interaction can be depicted by two straight lines. Simple slopes refer to the fact that for each value of one predictor variable, it is possible to plot the relation of the other predictor variable to the outcome. This approach can still be used even when the effect of the continuous variable is nonlinear. Even when both of the variables are continuous, such plots of the effects of predictor variable at representative values of the other predictor variable provide a heuristic pictorial representation of an interaction. We generally recommend that all interactions should be represented graphically to better understand and communicate the nature of the interaction.

More formally, to explore the pattern of changing slopes in the regression of Y on X_1 at different values of X_2, it is customary to plot at least two or more of these lines (Y against X_1—i.e., simple slopes) at specific values of X_2 (e.g., the mean of X_2 and $X_2 = +1SD$ and $-1SD$; Aiken & West, 1991; Cohen et al., 2003). Mathematically, we can substitute X_2 (or symmetrically X_1) with values at $-1SD$, 0, $+1SD$ from its mean into the regression equation and manually calculate the appropriate t-values for the respective regression weights for X_1 (*see* Aiken & West, 1991, for an illustrated example). It is also possible to plot simple slopes either in terms of the original regression equation or the completely standardized regression equation, whichever is easier and most interpretable. Based on values provided from most computer packages, it is also possible to compute standard errors and appropriate t-values to test the statistical significance of slopes for a predictor at a given value of the moderator or to test the difference in slopes at two different values of the moderator variable (for further discussion, *see* Aiken & West, 1991; Darlington, 1990; Jaccard et al., 1990). However, a possibly more expedient approach is to center the value of the moderator at the desired value and re-run the regression model with the new terms (i.e., the newly centered moderator variable and corresponding new cross-product terms based on the newly centered moderator variable). As is always the case, the effect of X_1 can be interpreted as its effect when $X_2 = 0$. Hence, if X_2 is centered on a particular value of interest, the test of statistical significance of X_1 provides a test of the simple slope of X_1 at that value of X_2. A similar logic can be used with categorical variables by choosing different categories as the reference (or "left-out") category that is assigned a value of zero. Thus, for example, when X_2 is gender, with boys = 0 and girls = 1, the test of statistical significance of X_1 provides a test of the simple slope of X_1 for boys. However, redoing the analysis with boys = 1 and girls = 0 provides a test of the simple slope for girls. (For further discussion, *see* Cohen et al., 2003).

The Johnson-Neyman approach is a more general alternative to the simple slopes approach that is particularly relevant when both predictor variables are continuous (Johnson & Neyman, 1936; Potthoff, 1964). This approach is used to define *regions of significance* to represent the range (or ranges) of values of one predictor variable for which the slope of the other predictor variable is significantly different than zero. Thus, a *region of significance* is the range of X_2 (moderator) values for which the relation between X_1 (predictor) and Y are statistically significant. For each region of significance, there is at most one upper and one lower bound, although one or the other of these values might be outside of the range of possible values of the moderator (or even take on the value of infinity) so that there is effectively only one bound. Alternatively, regions of nonsignificance are the ranges of values of one predictor variable for which the slope relating the other predictor variable is not significantly different from 0. As noted by Preacher, Curran, and Bauer (2006; *see also* Dearing & Hamilton, 2006), the logic of regions of significance is the converse of that used to interpret simple slopes. Simple slopes identify a slope coefficient (and its standard error, confidence interval, and statistical significance) at chosen values of the moderator. In contrast, regions of significance provide the range of values of the moderator for which the simple slopes are significant.

The manual calculation and plotting involved in probing significant interactions (e.g., simple slopes and regions of significance) is tedious and prone to error. Fortunately, Preacher et al. (2006) have provided a useful online program that helps the examination of two- and three-way interactions in multiple regression, multilevel modeling, and latent curve analysis (*see* Appendix of this chapter for more detail). Users just input regression coefficients, the variances/covariances of these coefficients, degrees of freedom, and α levels. Simple slopes and intercepts for conditional values of the moderator at predetermined points of interest, their standard errors, critical ratios, *p*-values, as well as confidence bands around them are either provided or can be easily generated (*see* Appendix for an example of this presented in detail).

Based on the tools introduced by Preacher et al. (2006; *see also* Appendix of this chapter for more detail) we constructed a graph of simple slopes (Fig. 17.3A) and regions of significance (Fig. 17.3B). The graph of relations between X_1 (a predictor variable) and Y (the outcome variable) at different values of X_2 (the moderator variable) shows that this is a disordinal interaction (Fig. 17.3A) in that the three regression plots cross (at the "point of intersection") within the range of X_1 and X_2 values that were considered. The effect of X_1 on Y is very positive for X_2 = −1, less positive for $X_2 = 0$ (the mean of the moderator variable X_2), and close to 0 for $X_2 = +1$. Figure 17.3B represents the relation between the moderator (X_2) and the simple main slope of the relation of X_1 on Y—the regression plot that is a solid dark-gray line. The relation between the simple slope and the moderator is negative; the simple slope is positive for sufficiently low values of X_2, 0 for some intermediate value of X_2, and negative for sufficiently high values of X_2. The curved lines on either side of the regression line are the 95% confidence bands for the simple slope at each value of X_2. The solid dark line for the simple slope of 0 represents the values of X_2 for which X_1 is not related to Y; this occurs at a value of $X_2 = 0.87$. The 95% confidence interval around the value of X_2 where the simple slope is 0 is the "region of nonsignificance" (represented by the two horizontal dashed lines—that is, the values for X_2 for which the simple slope of X_1 on Y is not significantly different from 0; $X_2 = +0.55$ to $X_2 = +1.40$ in our example). There are two regions of significance; the effect of X_1 on Y is positive for

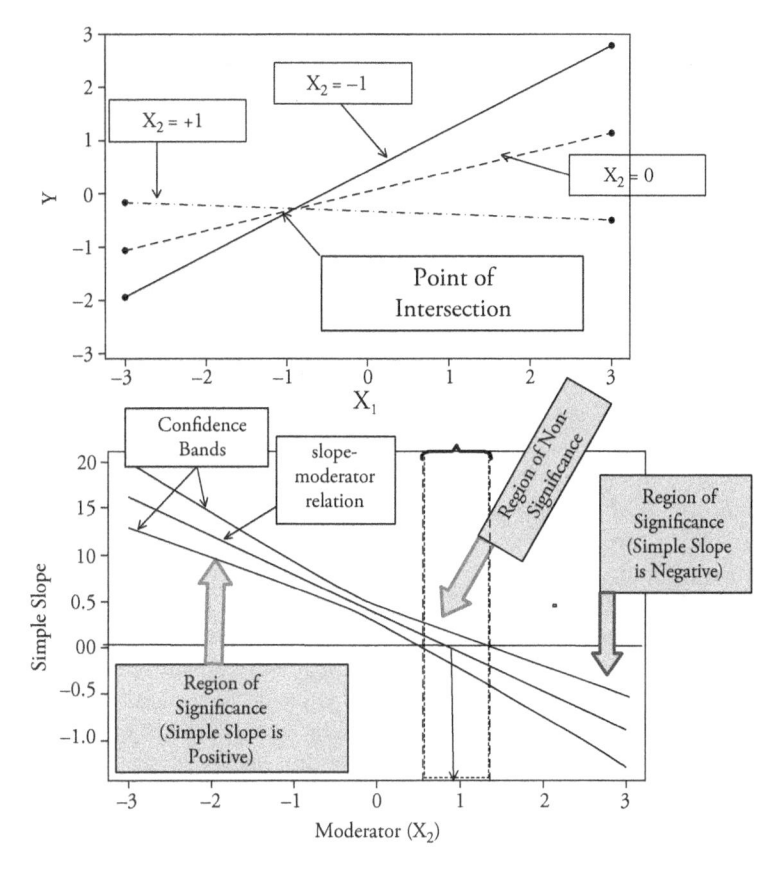

Figure 17.3 Plot of a Two-way interaction (**A**) and regions of significance and nonsignificance (**B**). Y = outcome variable, X_1 = predictor variable, X_2 = moderator. In (**A**), simple slopes are represented as regression plots of the relation between X_1 and Y at different values of X_2. (**B**) shows the relation between the simple slope (relating X_1 to Y) and the moderator X_2. Regions of significance show the ranges of values of X_2 for which the simple slope is statistically significant (i.e., X_1 is significantly related to Y), whereas regions of nonsignificance show the range for the values of X_2 for which the simple slope is not statistically significant.

values of X_2 less than +0.55 but negative for values of X_2 greater than 1.40.

Point of Intersection for Disordinal Interactions. For a regression equation with a significant interaction, the simple slopes may cross within or outside the possible (or plausible) range of the predicting variables (e.g., the disordinal interaction in Fig. 17.1). In an ordinal interaction the set of lines merely fan out or fan in with the nominal crossover point outside of the range of plausible values of X_1 (see ordinal interaction in Fig. 17.1). Thus, for example, for the disordinal interaction in Figure 17.1, the point of intersection represents the value for X_1 at which gender (X_2) has no effect on the outcome variable (i.e., where the lines cross so that scores for boys and girls are the same). In this graph, for all values of X_1 to the right of the intersection (i.e., more positive values of X_1), girls score higher than boys. Depending on the size of the confidence intervals, for some value of X_1 sufficiently above the intersection, girls

have outcomes significantly higher than boys. Likewise, for values X_1 below the intersection, boys have higher values than girls, and this difference is statistically significant for values of X_1 less than the lower bound of the region of nonsignificance.

For disordinal interactions where all the effects are linear, there can be only one region of nonsignificance and at most two regions of significance. For ordinal interactions based on linear effects, it is possible to have no regions of nonsignificance and no more than one region of significance. However, for nonlinear effects, it is possible to have disordinal interactions with more than one point of intersection and multiple regions of significance and nonsignificance.

For a disordinal interaction based on linear effects, we can determine mathematically the intersection or crossing point. With some simple algebra based on the appropriate regression equation (Aiken & West, 1991), it can be shown that when X_1 is the moderator, $X_2 = -b_1/b_3$ is the intersection and that when X_2 is the moderator, $X_1 = -b_2/b_3$ is the intersection. For example, in Figure 17.3A, $b_2 = -0.355$ and $b_3 = -0.397$ so that the point of interaction is .89 $(-b_2/b_3 = -(-0.355/-0.397) = -0.89$

Power in Detecting Interactions. Using standard multiple regression procedures, it is not difficult to test the statistical significance of interaction effects. Nevertheless, McClelland and Judd (1993) emphasized that researchers have had great difficulty in identifying substantively meaningful, statistically significant interactions that are replicable—particularly in nonexperimental research. Reasons for this situation include (1) overall model error is generally smaller in controlled experiments than nonexperimental studies; (2) measurement errors are exacerbated when X_1 and X_2 are multiplied to form the product term X_1X_2 (*see also* Frazier et al., 2004) and are likely to be larger in nonexperiments than in experimental studies when values are manipulated to take on a few fixed values at predetermined levels; (3) the magnitude of interactions is typically constrained in field studies in which researchers cannot assign participants to optional levels of the predictor variables; and (4) power to detect interactions is compromised because of nonlinearities of the effects of X_1 and X_2 and their interaction (e.g., products of higher order terms), which is more problematic for field studies with more levels of measurements. Finally, the values that factors in experimental studies are assigned are often selected to maximize the sizes of effects (e.g., extreme values) and to be optimal in relation to research predictions—even if not representative of values typically observed, whereas the values in nonexperimental studies are more likely to be representative of the population from which the sample was drawn.

Particularly relevant to this chapter, McClelland and Judd (1993) demonstrated that because of the reduced residual variance of the product X_1X_2 after controlling for X_1 and X_2 in typical field studies, the efficiency of the interaction coefficient estimates and its associated power are much lower. This is likely to dramatically reduce the power to detect interactions in field studies as compared to more optimal design in true experiments. Thus, for example, Aguinis (2004; McClelland & Judd, 1993) has shown that the power of the test of an interaction effect is typically less than 50% so that large sample sizes might be needed to evaluate interaction effects. The situation becomes worse when the variances of X_1 and X_2 are limited, truncated, or reduced in a particular study. For these reasons, it is reasonable to conduct a preliminary power analysis before collecting data to determine how large an N is needed to have a reasonably high probability of finding a moderately sized interaction to be statistically significant (for further discussion, *see* Cohen et al., 2003).

Before conducting research, Frazier et al. (2004) suggested that researchers ensure that they have sufficient power to detect hypothesized interactions. In particular, sample size should be sufficiently large, especially when interaction effects are likely to be small, as is typically the case. For categorical variables, it is best to have approximately similar sample sizes across subgroups. Further, if error variances within subgroups are not similar, then alternative tests of significance are needed (e.g., a multiple-group approach with heterogeneous error terms; *see* subsequent discussion). For continuous predictor and outcome measures, reliabilities should be high and samples leading to restriction of the range should be avoided. Several researchers (e.g., Frazier et al., 2004; Marsh, Wen, & Hau, 2004) have also suggested the use of latent factors in structural equation modeling (SEM) to control for measurement errors (*see* subsequent discussion of latent-variable approaches to interaction models).

Multicollinearity Involved With Product Terms. Multicollinearity results when multiple predictor variables are correlated with each other such that the values of one variable systematically vary with the other variable (Marsh, Dowson, Pietsch & Walker, 2004). Hence, multicollinearity is a function of relations among predictor variables and their relation to the outcome variable. There are three quite different meanings of multicollinearity that are often confused. The first, and the focus of this section, is when the two or more predictor variables are correlated, thus complicating the interpretation of each considered separately. This form of multicollinearity occurs in almost all studies in which the predictor variables are not experimentally manipulated so as to be orthogonal. The second meaning of multicollinearity is when the predictor variables are so highly correlated that the typical tests of statistical significance are distorted or cannot be done (e.g., matrices become nonpositive definite so they cannot be inverted). This almost never happens and so is not a major concern. [Actually this sometimes happens when researchers inadvertently use different variables that are a linear combination of each other but this should be easy to recognize.] The third meaning, perhaps, is when multicollinearity is sufficiently large that SEs of coefficients are so large that meaningful interpretations of the parameter estimates cannot be made. This is not a statistical problem *per se* but, rather, the inability to disentangle the effects of each separate variable when they are highly correlated. Although there are numerous guidelines as to how large multicollinearity has to be before it is a serious problem, these are rough rules of thumb typically based on arbitrary cut-off values (*see* discussion by Cohen et al., 2003) and not "golden rules" (Marsh, Hau, & Wen, 2004) to be followed blindly in all instances. Importantly, any non-zero correlation between predictor variables results in multicollinearity. Nevertheless, reducing multicollinearity can substantially enhance the interpretability of regression weights and, in extreme cases, affect statistical tests of these effects.

Whenever product terms are computed to represent interaction effects (e.g., X_1X_2)—and particularly nonlinear effects (e.g., X^2 to represent a quadratic effect)—there is likely to be substantial amounts of multicollinearity. That is, the product terms are likely to be substantially correlated with the variables used to construct the product terms. Cohen et al. (2003; *see also* Marquardt, 1980) have distinguished between what they refer to as essential and nonessential multicollinearity. Nonessential multicollinearity can be seen as artificial effects resulting from the scaling of predictor variables in relation to the means of the predictor variables, whereas essential multicollinearity is a function of the correlation between the predictor variables (and would be 0 if X_1 and X_2 are uncorrelated). Cohen et al. have noted that nonessential multicollinearity can be reduced substantially by centering the predictor variables (or by standardizing them).

Even when there is substantial levels of "essential" multicollinearity resulting in substantial SEs that undermine interpretability, alternative models can be specified to circumvent these problems. Thus, for example, Marsh, Downson, Pietch, and Walker (2004) reanalyzed data apparently showing that paths leading from self-efficacy to achievement (0.55, $p < 0.05$) were apparently much larger than those from self-concept (–0.05, *ns*). However, the interpretation was problematic because the correlation between self-concept and self-efficacy (0.93) was so high, resulting in very large SEs for both paths. In an alternative model, the two paths were constrained to be equal. This constraint did not result in a statistically significant decline in fit, provided a better more parsimonious fit to the data, and also substantially reduced the sizes of SEs (from 0.50 to 0.03).

Multicollinearity can be reduced even more by applying the more general, hierarchical (sequential) approach analogous to residualizing procedure like that proposed by Landram and Alidaee (1997; Lance, 1988; Little, Bovaird, & Widaman, 2006; but *see also* Lin, Wen, Marsh, & Lin, 2010; Marsh, Wen, Hau, Little, Bovaird, & Widaman, 2007) for polynomial components. With this approach, variance attributable to the predictor (X_1 and X_2) variables is partialed out of the X_1X_2 interaction (product) term, main effect and first-order interactions are partialed out of second-order interactions, and so forth. This strategy is consistent with the hierarchical approach used to test interactions (based on the change in R^2) but has the advantage of substantially reducing levels of multicollinearity. However, it also introduces interpretational problems because the coefficients of the interaction terms are no longer in the same metric as the predictor variables and so it is not so easy to graph the interaction effect (*see* King, 1986, on problems with analyses of residuals). Hence, we recommend that this approach should only be used with appropriate caution and this it is generally better to use centering and standardizing strategies). Importantly, multicollinearity may sometimes indicate that the model has been in some ways misspecified (e.g., when the predictor and the moderator should, in fact, be considered as indicators of the same construct) and should not be simply partialled out of the model.

Summary of Traditional (Non-Latent) Approaches to Interaction Effects

In this section, we briefly reviewed approaches to testing interaction effects based on observed (non-latent) variables. We began with a brief discussion of ANOVA when all predictor variables are categorical, noting in particular the dangers in transforming continuous predictors into categorical variables that are appropriate for ANOVA. We then moved to the more general moderated multiple regression approach that can be applied to continuous or categorical predictors (and thus include ANOVA models as a special case). We emphasized that graphs of interactions are typically a useful starting place in the interpretation of results, but these should always be supplemented with tests of statistical significance of interaction effects overall and supplemental analyses such as tests of simple slopes and regions of significance. We recommended consideration of, and discussed issues related to, a number of transformations of the original data (centering predictor variables or standardizing all variables). We concluded with a discussion of the related issues of power and multicollinearity (and the little-used residualizing procedure). A critical limitation in most psychological research is that when tests of interactions are appropriately constructed, *a priori* interaction effects that are intuitive and based on a strong theoretical rationale are typically small, non-significant, or not replicable. The implication is that most research lacks the statistical power to detect interaction effects—particularly in non-experimental studies where interaction effects are typically small. A critical issue related to power is the substantial measurement error associated particularly in interaction terms. Latent variable models of interaction effects that control for measurement error might substantially reduce measurement error as well as having more general strategic advantages. Hence, we now turn to an overview of these approaches.

Latent Variable Approaches to Tests of Interaction Effects

The critical feature common to each of the above non-latent approaches is that all of the dependent and independent variables are *observed* variables inferred on the basis of a single indicator rather than latent variables inferred by multiple indicators. Particularly when there are multiple indicators of these variables (e.g., multiple items in rating scales or achievement tests), latent variable approaches provide a much stronger basis for evaluating the underlying factor structure relating multiple indicators to their factors, controlling for measurement error, increasing power, testing the implicit factor structure used to create scale scores, and, ultimately, providing more defensible interpretations of the interaction effects.

Despite the ongoing emphasis on interaction effects, empirical support for predicted interactions has been disappointingly limited. One reason might be that the independent variables are contaminated by measurement error and do not provide accurate estimates of true interaction effects (Moulder & Algina, 2002). Indeed, because the measurement error of each of the main effect variables combines multiplicatively in the formation of the interaction term, measurement error in the interaction is likely to be substantially larger than in either of the main effects variables (*see* earlier discussion). When each of the independent variables is a latent variable inferred from multiple indicators, SEM provides many advantages over the use of analyses based on observed variables.

Nevertheless, despite the widespread use of SEMs for the purposes of estimating relations among latent variables and the importance of interaction effects, there have been very few substantive applications of SEMs to estimating interactions between two latent variables. Obviously, the paucity of such interaction applications does not result from a lack of relevant substantive applications that require interaction terms. Rather, as noted by Rigdon, Schumacker, and Wothke (1998), inherent problems in the specification of SEMs with interactions between latent variables have led researchers to pursue other approaches. Similarly, Jöreskog (1998) warned that latent variable approaches require the researcher to understand how to specify complicated nonlinear constraints. Although a variety of different approaches to estimating latent interactions were described in the book edited by Schumacker and Marcoulides (1998), and some new approaches have been developed by Algina and Moulder (2001), Wall and Amemiya (2001), and Klein and Moosbrugger (2000), there has been no consensus that any one of these approaches was optimal. Further, most of these approaches are not practically useful for the applied researcher because of the difficulties in specifying the nonlinear constraints. Another possible reason for the infrequent use of the latent approach is the difficulty in deciding how to construct or select the multiple indicators to form the latent factors, as typically required by all traditional latent approaches.

Latent interactions fall into two broad categories. In the first and generally simpler situation, at least one of the variables involved in the interaction is a categorical variable with only a few categories (e.g., gender: male and female). In this situation, a multiple-group SEM is appropriate in which the different categories are treated as separate groups within the same model. Even when both variables involved in the interaction are categorical, they can be used to form groups reflecting the main and interaction effects (e.g., two dichotomous variables can be used to form four groups reflecting the two main effects and one interaction effect; which is like an ANOVA within a SEM framework but providing control for measurement error). Although it might be argued that the interaction in this case is not really latent, it is still a latent variable model as long as the dependent (or other predictor) variables are inferred on the basis of multiple indicators.

In the second situation, both independent variables involved in the interaction are latent and continuous. Here there are various approaches to estimating their interaction effects, and "best practice" is still evolving. Marsh, Wen, and Hau 2004; (see also Marsh, Wen & Hau, 2006) reviewed various alternative approaches for estimating these latent interaction effects, including the unconstrained (Marsh et al., 2004), constrained (Algina & Moulder, 2001), generalized appended product indicator (GAPI; Wall & Amemiya, 2001), and the distribution-analytic (Klein & Moosbrugger, 2000; Klein & Muthén, 2007; see also Moosbrugger, Schermelleh-Engel, Kelava, & Klein, 2009) approaches[1].

In the remainder, we will first discuss multiple-group SEMs that are appropriate to analyze interactions when one of the predictors is categorical. We will then turn to the discussion of approaches to study interaction between latent continuous variables.

Multiple Group Structural Equation Modeling Approach to Interaction

Consider an interaction between a latent variable (ξ_1) and an observed variable (X_2) on a latent variable (η), and assume that X_2 is a categorical variable with a few naturally existing categories. We can use a multiple-group SEM approach (e.g., Bagozzi & Yi, 1989; Byrne, 1998; Rigdon, Schumacker, & Wothke, 1998; Vandenberg & Lance, 2000) with the categorical variable (X_2) as the grouping variable. Once the sample is divided into a small number of groups according to the values of X_2, we conduct multiple-group SEM for the latent variable ξ_1 and compare the model with and without restraining the effect of ξ_1 on the dependent variable η to be equal across the groups. Let χ_1^2 (with df_1) and χ_2^2 (with df_2) be the chi-square test statistics, respectively, with and without restraining the effect of ξ_1 on η to be equal in all the groups. If there is substantial decline in the goodness of fit with the invariance constraint (i.e., $\chi_1^2 - \chi_2^2$ with $df_1 - df_2$ is significant and there is a substantial deterioration in selected goodness of fit indexes), then the effects in the different groups are not identical and there is an interaction between the categorical predictor X_2 and the latent variable ξ_1. Of course, the invariance of the corresponding loadings and factor variances (i.e., constraining them to be the same in the different groups) must have been examined earlier (for details, see, e.g., Marsh, Muthén et al., 2009; Marsh, Lüdtke et al., 2010; Vandenberg & Lance, 2000; see also subsequent discussion and further discussion in Chapter 15, this volume).

Historically this approach has been used often and has some advantages—particularly in terms of ease of implementation. If one of the independent variables is an observed variable that can be used to divide the sample naturally into a small number of groups, then multiple-group SEM is a simple, direct, yet effective approach (Bagozzi & Yi, 1989; Rigdon, Schumacker, & Wothke, 1998), which can be easily implemented in most common commercial SEM softwares. However, as emphasized earlier, this approach is generally not appropriate when two or a small number of groups are formed from a reasonably continuous predictor variable in that it ignores measurement error in the variable used to divide the sample into multiple groups and actually increases the unreliability in the grouped variable relative to the original continuous variable. Strategically there are limitations in that it is not easy to estimate the size of the interaction effect and some of the groups can become unacceptably small. In general we recommend not using this approach unless one of the interacting variables is a true categorical variable with a small number of categories and at least moderate sample sizes.

Structural Equation Models with Product Indicators

Kenny and Judd (1984) first used a SEM model with an interaction term to estimate latent interaction effects. In their approach, the dependent variable y is an observed variable, whereas the independent variables ξ_1, ξ_2 each has two observed indicators x_1, x_2 and x_3, x_4, respectively, with all variables being centered (mean = 0). If the latent variables are identified by fixing the loading of the first indicator to 1, then the measurement equations of the model are:

$$x_1 = \xi_1 + \delta_1, x_2 = \lambda_2 \xi_1 + \delta_2;$$
$$x_3 = \xi_2 + \delta_3, x_4 = \lambda_4 \xi_2 + \delta_4.$$

The structural equation is:

$$y = \gamma_1 \xi_1 + \gamma_2 \xi_2 + \gamma_3 \xi_1 \xi_2 + \zeta, \quad (4)$$

where $\xi_1 \xi_2$ is the interaction term of ξ_1 and ξ_2 on y. In the model, it is assumed that latent variables and the error terms are all normally distributed and there is no correlation between the latent variables and the error terms or between any two error terms.

Equation 4 is not linear with respect to ξ_1 and ξ_2 and is different from the SEM equations generally used. If we consider $\xi_1\xi_2$ as a separate third latent variable, then having no indicators for this variable remains a problem. To solve this, Kenny and Judd used the products of all possible pairs of the centered indicators x_1x_3, x_1x_4, x_2x_3, x_2x_4 as the indicators for $\xi_1\xi_2$ with a lot of constraints added for identification.

Kenny and Judd's (1984) ingenious work was heuristic, stimulating many published studies that present alternative approaches to the use of products of indicators to estimate latent interactions (e.g., Algina & Moulder, 2001; Coenders, Batista-Foguet & Saris, 2008; Hayduk, 1987; Jaccard & Wan, 1995; Jöreskog & Yang, 1996; Marsh et al., 2004; Ping, 1996; Wall & Amemiya, 2001). However, their original approach was unduly cumbersome and overly restrictive in terms of the assumptions on which it was based (see Marsh et al., 2004), leading to the development of new approaches.

Unconstrained Approach for Latent Interaction. Compared to the traditional constrained approach (e.g., Algina & Moulder, 2001; Marsh et al., 2004) and the partially constrained approach (Wall & Amemiya, 2001; Marsh et al., 2004), the unconstrained approach is fundamentally different and impressively simple to implement in that many of the complicated constraints in the original Kenny and Judd (1984) approach are no longer necessary. Marsh et al. (2004) showed that the unconstrained approach performed nearly as well as the constrained approach when all assumptions of the constrained approach were met and substantially better under more realistic conditions.

For the sake of simplicity, suppose that the endogenous latent variable has three indicators: y_1, y_2, y_3; the exogenous latent variables ξ_1 and ξ_2 also have three indicators, respectively: x_1, x_2, x_3 and x_4, x_5, x_6. Lin et al. (2010) proposed a double-mean-centering strategy for the unconstrained model that does not require a mean structure. First they centered all indicators to their mean, then formed a more parsimonious set of product indicators, and finally centered the product again (double-mean-centering). When SEM software (such as LISREL) is employed in practice, however, the product indicators do not really need to be re-centered again. Because when the model does not consist of a mean structure, the estimation results are identical with and without re-centering the product indicators. In other words, SEM software routinely treats the data being mean-centered if there is no mean structure in the model. Noting this point, Wu, Wen, and Lin (2009) suggested that researchers can directly use single-mean-centered data to analyze a latent interaction model without a mean structure. We note, however, that some statistical packages (e.g., Mplus) include a mean structure as the default so that this potential advantage of being able to ignore the mean structure might not be so important. Thus, the steps for analyzing the latent interaction are as below:

1. center all indicators to their mean, still denoted as y_1, y_2, y_3; x_1, x_2, x_3; x_4, x_5, x_6;
2. form the product indicators x_1x_4, x_2x_5, x_3x_6;
3. use y_1, y_2, y_3 as the indicators of η, x_1, x_2, x_3 as the indicators of ξ, x_4, x_5, x_6 as the indicators of ξ_2, x_1x_4, x_2x_5, x_3x_6 as the indicators of ξ_3 (ξ_3 is the centered interaction term $\xi_1\xi_2 - E(\xi_1\xi_2)$, see Lin et al., 2010; Wu et al, 2009). The structural equation has three exogenous latent variables:

$$\eta = \gamma_1\xi_1 + \gamma_2\xi_2 + \gamma_3\xi_3 + \zeta. \qquad (5)$$

ξ_1, ξ_2, and ξ_3 are allowed to be correlated with each other, but each is uncorrelated with measurement errors and the residual term ζ.

In Equation 4 γ_1 and γ_2 represent the conditional main effects, γ_3 represents the interaction effect (for the path diagram, see Fig. 17.4). A simple LISREL syntax is given in Appendix 3). Readers who are familiar with the usual LISREL syntax may easily revise it for their researches involved in latent interactions).

Construction of Product Indicators of the Latent Interaction. A potential problem with the indicator approach is how to form the product indicators. In contrast to earlier, *ad hoc* approaches to create produce indicators, Marsh, Hau, and Wen (2004, 2006) proposed the guiding principles: (1) use all the multiple indicators from both interacting variables in the formation of the indicators of the latent interaction factor, and (2) do not re-use the same indicator in forming the indicators for the latent interaction factor. Thus, each indicator in ξ_1 *and* ξ_2 should be used once and only once in forming the indicators for the latent interaction factor.

In some situations there is a natural matching that should be used to form product indicators (e.g., the items used to infer ξ_1 and ξ_2 have parallel wording). More generally, when the two first-order effect factors ξ_1 and ξ_2 have the same number of indicators, Marsh et al. (2004; see also Saris, Batista-Foguet, & Coenders, 2007) suggested that it would be better to match indicators in terms of the reliabilities of the indicators (i.e., the best item from the first factor with the best item from the second factor, etc.).

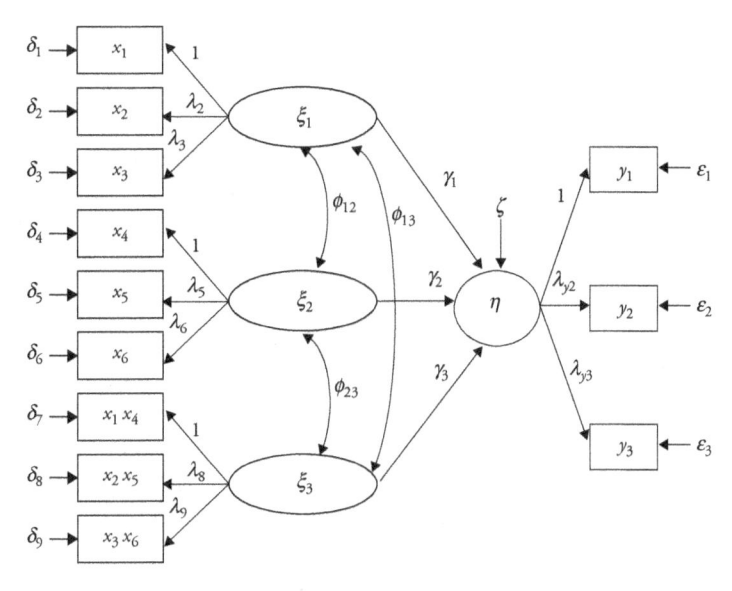

Figure 17.4 The notional path diagram of the latent interaction model. ξ_3 is the centered interaction term $\xi_1\xi_2 - E(\xi_1\xi_2)$.

However, if the number of indicators differs for the two first-order effect factors, then a simple matching strategy does not work. Assume, for example, that there were 5 indicators for the first factor and 10 for the second. One approach would be to use the 10 items from the second factor to form five (item pair) parcels by taking the average of the first 2 items to form the first item parcel, the average of the second 2 items to form the second parcel, and so forth. In this way, the first factor would be defined in terms of 5 (single-indicator) indicators, the second factor would be defined by 10 (single-indicator) indicators, and the latent interaction factor would be defined in terms of 5 matched-product indicators (cross-product terms based on 5 single-indicators for the first factor and 5 item-pair parcels for the second factor).

Appropriate Standardized Solution for Latent Interactions Standardized parameter estimates are important because they facilitate the comparison of the effects of different predictor variables in the equation. Analogous to the corresponding problem in multiple regression with the manifest interaction described earlier, the usual standardized coefficients of SEMs with latent interaction are not appropriate. Wen, Marsh, and Hau 2010; (*see also* Wen, Hau & Marsh, 2008) derived an appropriate standardized solution for latent interaction. They proved that these appropriate standardized estimates of the main and interaction effects as well as their standard errors and *t*-value are all scale-free (for further discussion, *see* Wen et al., 2010). Although specifically designed for the latent interaction model, this one-step approach might also be appropriate to manifest models based on single indicators of predictor variables.

Distribution-Analytic Approaches

In contrast to the product-indicator approaches that model the latent interaction by specifying a separate latent interaction variable, the distribution-analytic approaches (Klein & Moosbrugger, 2000; Klein & Muthén, 2007; Moosbrugger, Schermelleh-Engel, Kelava, & Klein, 2009) explicitly model the distribution of the latent outcome variables and their manifest indicators in the presence of latent nonlinear effects and provide a promising alternative for the estimation of nonlinear SEM. Two methods are currently available: the Latent Moderated Structural Equations (LMS) approach (Klein & Moosbrugger, 2000) that is implemented in Mplus (Muthén & Muthén, 1997–2008) and the Quasi-Maximum Likelihood (QML) approach (Klein & Muthén, 2007) that has not yet been implemented in a readily available software package (but is available from its author Andreas Klein).

Both QML and LMS directly estimate the parameters of the latent interaction model given in Equation 4 (and are flexible enough to handle quadratic effects of latent variables as well) without having to resort to the use of product-indicators. They differ in the distributional assumptions made about the latent dependent variable η and its indicators and in the estimation method used to obtain the parameter estimates (for more technical description, *see* Klein & Moosbrugger, 2000; Klein & Muthén, 2007).

In contrast to product-indicator approaches following from Kenny and Judd's (1984) research, it is not necessary to have indicators of the latent interaction variable in the distribution-analytic approaches. The product-indicator approaches assume normality of indicators and latent constructs to estimate parameter and standard errors. In general, both assumptions are violated in models with latent interactions, although results seem to be robust in relation to these violations. In addition, alternative approaches such as bootstrapping (*see* Wen et al., 2010) can be used. Bootstrapping is becoming more readily available in standard statistical packages and provides a more accurate estimate of SEs—particularly when N is small. The distribution-analytic approaches, on the other hand, maximize special fitting functions that take the non-normality of the indicators of the dependent latent variable explicitly into account (but still rely on normality assumptions about the indicators of the latent predictor variables). However, these advantages are offset by the need to use specialized software to estimate these models (Mplus and the QML-program) and the high computational demands of the LMS approach that limit its applicability.

Simulation studies that compared distribution-analytic approaches (Klein & Muthén, 2007; Marsh et al., 2004) to the unconstrained approach showed that QML appears to be sufficiently robust in relation to non-normal data. LMS, on the other hand, can yield biased standard errors when distributional assumptions about the indicators of the predictor variables are violated. The QML program provides a fully standardized solution that assumes that all manifest and latent variables are standardized but no standard errors for the standardized effects. These estimates are equal to the parameters of the appropriately standardized solution. Standardized effects for LMS are harder to obtain, as the current implementation does neither provide a standardized solution nor an estimator for the variance of the latent product variable $\xi_1\xi_2$ to calculate the standardized solution.

Comparisons of LMS and QML (Klein & Muthén, 2007) indicate that LMS is slightly more efficient when its distributional assumptions are fulfilled, but QML is comparatively more robust to violations of normality. It appears that the QML approach will be more useful for applied researchers, but there have been too few studies with real data to fully evaluate its potential in actual practice. Indeed, this concern can be applied to all of the various approaches to latent interaction.

Summary of Latent-Variable Approaches to Interaction Effects

Non-latent variable tests of interaction effects traditionally lack power because of the substantial amount of measurement error, particularly in the interaction component. In this section we briefly described new and evolving approaches to testing latent interaction effects. When one of the predictor variables is a manifest grouping variable with a small number of categories (e.g., male/female) the traditional approach to multigroup SEM can be applied. This approach is well established, easily implemented, and facilitates a detailed evaluation of invariance assumptions (e.g., invariance of factor loadings over groups) that are largely ignored in other approaches. However, the multigroup approach is generally not recommended when all the predictor variables are continuous or based on multiple indicators. Historically, the product indicator approaches have dominated latent interaction research. Although these approaches are still evolving, there is good evidence in support of the unconstrained approach in terms of robustness and ease of implementation in terms of all commercial SEM packages. More recently, distribution-analytic approaches (LMS and QML) hold considerable promise and apparently have strategic advantages over the product-indicator approach. Although LMS is available in Mplus, the QML approach is not available in any major statistical package (but is available from its author Andreas Klein upon request). Despite a long history dating back to 1984, latent interaction effects are rarely used in applied research. Furthermore, even the limited numbers of demonstration and simulation articles have focused on statistical issues involved in estimating the models and have not adequately dealt with many of the issues faced by applied researchers (including some of those discussed here in relation to the moderated multiple regression approach).

Summary

Tests of interaction effects are central to psychology. The implications of being able to test and interpret interaction effects are critical for theory, substantive understanding, and applied practice. Yet, typical practice in the evaluation of interaction effect is surprisingly weak. In our chapter we have provided an overview of the topic of moderation based on both manifest and latent variable models. In doing so, we have attempted to summarize current best practice. The good news is that there has been important progress in both best practice and typical practice. Applied researchers are apparently becoming more aware of the basic issues in the testing and interpretation of interaction effects. The bad news is that many well-established methodological requirements continue to be ignored in applied research. Although there are some stunning new developments in the application of latent models to testing interaction effects, these new approaches have not yet had much impact on applied research. Further, these new developments have focused primarily on the substantial statistical issues involved in fitting data to the latent variable models and have not made much progress in resolving many of the complications that have been the focus of manifest applications. Hence, it is perhaps unsurprising that evolving latent variable approaches to moderation effects have had limited effect on typical practice in applied research.

In this chapter, we have tried to promote a substantive-methodological synergy (Marsh & Hau, 2007), bringing to bear new, strong, and evolving methodology to tackle complex substantive issues with important implications for theory and practice. Here, as in other areas of applied psychological research, theory, good measurement, research, and practice are inexorably related such that the neglect of one will undermine pursuit of the others. Marsh and Hau (2007) claimed: (1) some of the best methodological research is based on the development of creative methodological solutions to problems that stem from substantive research; (2) new methodologies provide important new approaches to current substantive issues; and (3) methodological-substantive synergies are particularly important in applied research. In the study of moderation, this synergy is particularly important.

Limitations and Directions for Further Research

We now turn to a set of issues that are beyond the scope of the present chapter. In some cases these are ongoing or evolving issues that have not been resolved in the literature and reflect our thoughts about directions for further research.

Quadratic Effects: Confounding Nonlinear and Interaction Effects

Examples with quadratic effect are common. For example, nonlinear effects may be hypothesized between strength of interventions (or dosage level) and outcome variables such that benefits increase up to an optimal level, and then level off or even decrease beyond this optimal point. At low levels of anxiety, increases in anxiety may facilitate performance but at higher levels of anxiety, further increases in anxiety may undermine performance. Self-concept may decrease with age for young children, level out in middle adolescence, and then increase with age into early adulthood. The level of workload demanded by teachers may be positively related to student evaluations of teaching effectiveness for low to moderate levels of workload but may have diminishing positive effects or even negative effects for possibly excessive levels of workload. Quadratic effects can be seen as a special case of non-linearity effect that can be very complicated but are not discussed here in detail.

The existence of quadratic effects can complicate the analysis and interpretation of interaction effects. A strong quadratic effect may give the appearance of a spurious significant interaction effect, and it is sometimes difficult to distinguish them (Klein et al., 2009; Lubinski & Humphreys, 1990; MacCallum & Mar,1995). Thus, without the proper analysis of the potential quadratic effects, the investigator might easily misinterpret, overlook, or mistake a quadratic effect as an interaction effect. Particularly when both X_1 (the predictor) and the moderator are positively correlated, it is likely that the product (quadratic and interaction) terms are also correlated. That is, the quadratic function of X_1 (i.e., $X_1 \times X_1 = X_1^2$) is likely to be correlated with the interaction $(X_1 \times X_2)$. Unless there is a well-established causal ordering of X_1 and X_2, then there is no easy solution as to how to disentangle the potential confounding between the quadratic and moderation terms. In most cases, the variance that can uniquely be explained by the interaction effect will be diminished by controlling for quadratic effects. However, this is the same sort of confounding that is typical in multiple regression analyses even when product terms are not considered; some variance can be uniquely attributed to one predictor, some to the other predictor, and some can be explained by either predictor. Hence, it is reasonable to include both the nonlinear and the interaction effects in the same model to more fully specify that pattern of relations among the variables.

When all variables are manifest, the inclusion of quadratic effects is a relatively straightforward extension of approaches outlined here. Indeed, the construction of the statistical model is likely to be much easier than the interpretation of the results. However, for latent variable models when all predictor variables are based on multiple indicators, the simultaneous inclusion of latent interaction and latent quadratic terms is likely to prove more complicated. Nevertheless, there has been some recent work on this issue involving both the multiple-indicator and distributional approaches to latent variable modeling (*see* Klein et al., 2009; Marsh et al., 2006; Kelava & Brandt, 2009). Furthermore, as is the case with interaction effects more generally, the focus of latent variable models has been more on the statistical issues involved in fitting the model than the interpretational concerns that have been the focus of studies based on manifest variables (and our chapter).

We also note that in applied research it is sometimes suggested that nonlinear relations should be specified *a priori* on the basis of theory or previous research. However, the linearity of the observed relationships is an implicit assumption of any form of model that does not include nonlinear terms. Hence, it is always reasonable to test the appropriateness of the linearity assumption through the inclusion of nonlinear terms.

Moderation versus Mediation and the Role of Causal Ordering

The concept of moderation (or interaction) is often confused with that of mediation (*see* Holmbeck, 1997; Baron & Kenny, 1986; also see Chapter 16 of this Handbook). As noted by Frazier et al.(2004, p. 116): "Whereas moderators address 'when' or 'for whom' a predictor is more strongly related to an outcome, mediators establish 'how' or 'why' one variable predicts or causes an outcome variable." Mediation refers to the mechanism that explains the relation between X_1 and Y.

Mediation occurs (*see* Fig. 17.5) when some of the effects of an independent variable (X) on the dependent variable (Y) can be explained in terms of another mediating variable (MED) that falls between X_1 and Y in terms of the causal ordering: $X_1 \rightarrow$ MED $\rightarrow Y$. A mediator is an intervening variable that accounts for—at least in part—the relation between a predictor and an outcome such that the predictor influences an outcome indirectly through the mediator. Thus, for example, the effects of mathematical ability prior to the start of high school (X) on mathematics achievement test scores at the end of high school (Y) are likely to be mediated in part by mathematics coursework completed during high school (MED). In Figure 17.5A the model assumes

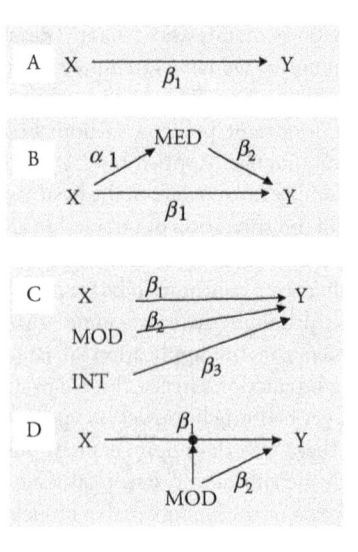

Figure 17.5 The distinction between mediation (MED) and moderation (MOD). X = predictor variable. Y = outcome variable. INT = interaction. In (**A**), X effects Y with no mediation or moderation. In (**B**), the effect of X on Y is mediated in part by MED. There is total mediation if the direct effect of X on Y is 0 ($\beta_1 = 0$) or partial medication if $\beta_1 \neq 0$. The indirect effect of X on Y thru that is mediated by MED is the product of α_1 and β_2. (**C**) and (**D**) offer two representations of the interaction effect. In (**C**), the interaction is depicted as a separate construct (typically defined as the product of X and MOD, but sometimes after both have been centered or standardized). (**D**) offers demonstrates more explicitly that MOD moderates the relation between X and Y.

that the effect of X_1 on Y is unmediated ($X_1 \rightarrow Y$). In Figure 17.5B the model assumes that part of the effect of X_1 on Y is direct ($X_1 \rightarrow Y$, the path that goes directly from X_1 to Y) and that some of the effect is mediated ($X_1 \rightarrow$ MED $\rightarrow Y$) by the indirect path that goes from X_1 to MED and then from MED to Y). If both the direct ($X_1 \rightarrow Y$) and indirect ($X_1 \rightarrow$ MED $\rightarrow Y$) effects are non-zero, then the X–Y relation is said to be partially mediated, whereas in Figure 17.5B, the X_1–Y relation is said to be completely mediated by MED if the $X_1 \rightarrow Y$ effect is 0.

In contrast, and as discussed extensively above, moderation is said to have taken place when the size or direction of the effect of X_1 on Y varies with the value of a moderating variable (MOD). Thus, for example, the effect of a remedial course in mathematics rather than regular mathematics coursework (X) on subsequent mathematics achievement (Y) may vary systematically depending on the student's initial level of mathematics ability (MOD); the effect of the remedial course may be very positive for initially less able students, negligible for average-ability students, and even detrimental for high-ability students who would probably gain more from regular or advanced mathematics coursework. Figure 17.5C shows the interaction as a separate construct (INT) and the effect of the interaction on the outcome (INT → Y) as a separate regression coefficient (β_3). Alternatively the representation of the interaction effect in Figure 17.5D shows more clearly that the moderator influences the relation between two variables.

Although a full discussion of mediation is beyond the scope of this chapter, a critical requirement of mediation is that there is a clear causal ordering from X → MED → Y. Particularly as mediation analyses are typically applied in nonexperimental studies, this is an important consideration. Frazier et al. (2004) have proposed that the most defensible strategy is a longitudinal study in which all three variables are tested on at least three occasions (e.g., Marsh, Trautwein, Lüdtke, Köller, & Baumert, 2005; Marsh & O'Mara, 2008). Without clear support for the causal ordering of the X_1 and MED variables, traditional tests of mediation make no sense. Unless there is a clear causal ordering, it is not possible to rule out (empirically, theoretically, or commonsensically) the possibility that X_1 and MED are reciprocally related (i.e., both X_1 → MED, and MED → X_1; see Marsh & Craven, 2006, for further discussion of reciprocal effects). This point is at the heart of the Judd and Kenny (2010) critical re-evaluation of the Baron and Kenny (1986; Judd & Kenny, 1981) assumptions of what are necessary and sufficient conditions to demonstrate mediation. The issue of causality in mediation requires strong theory, a good design, appropriate statistical analyses, and probably an ongoing research programme that addresses the same issues from multiple perspectives. It is our contention that the vast majority of studies purporting to test mediation—particularly when based on a single wave of data—are either wrong or cannot be defended in relation to the typically implicit, untested assumption of causal ordering. Without strong assumptions of causality, tests of mediation are typically uninterpretable.

For purposes of this chapter, we argue that there needs to be no causal ordering established between X_1 and MOD to test interaction effects. The statistical tests cannot distinguish between interpretations that X_1 moderates MOD and MOD moderates X_1; the two perspectives are equivalent in terms of statistical significance, variance explained, and so forth. Our recommendation is that unless there is a clearly established causal ordering, then both possibilities should be considered, although one might be more substantively or theoretically useful (Brambor, Clark, & Golder, 2006). However, if a strong basis of causal ordering can be established on the basis of theory or the design of the study (e.g., with longitudinal data), then the interpretability of the results is greatly enhanced. In the evaluation of interaction effects, there is, of course, the assumption that both X_1 and MOD precede Y in the causal ordering and tests of interactions typically are not symmetric in relation to X_1 and Y (or for MOD and Y). Thus, for example, if there is not a theoretical or substantive rationale for assuming X_1 → Y rather than Y → X_1 (e.g., X_1 is an intervention based on random assignment) Traci and Russell (2003) have suggested that researchers should consider different models in which X_1 is considered the outcome rather than the predictor variable.

Although we have emphasized the distinction between mediation and moderation, they are obviously not mutually exclusive. It is quite conceivable to have moderated mediation or mediated moderation. Here the issues of direction of causality become even more important (for further discussion, see Judd & Kenny, 2010; Muller, Judd, & Yzerbyt, 2005).

Interactions with More Than Two Continuous Variables

The moderated regression approach described above can be extended to include more than two independent variables with multiple two-way or other higher-order interactions involving more than two variables. Should we include all possible interactions in the regression equation? In general, the inclusion of interaction terms should be theory driven. It is also tempting to exclude non-significant effects to simplify the regression equation, increase the degrees of freedom, and increase the power of the remaining statistical tests. Nevertheless, Jaccard et al. (1990) and many others have recommended that interaction terms supported by strong theory—as well as the predictor variables used to construct the interaction terms—should always be included irrespective of whether they are significant. In particular, failure to include main effects (or lower-order interaction) will typically bias coefficient estimates for the higher-order interactions (see earlier discussion). Also, for hypothesized interaction effects that are based on theory, the values of even non-significant effects can be important, for example, for meta-analyses that seek to combine the effects from many different studies.

When multiple interaction effects are examined in the same regression equation, one approach to safeguard against an inflated Type I error is to use an omnibus F-test to compare squared multiple correlations with and without the entire set of interactions terms. Interactions are individually inspected only when this ombibus F-test is significant (Aiken & West, 1981; Frazier et al., 2004). Analogous to analyses of higher-order interactions in ANOVA, the interpretation of the three-way (or other higher order) interaction in regression may not be straightforward and easily interpretable. When a certain three-way interaction is significant, for example, we can construct simple slopes similar to those for the two-way interactions. Operationally, to find the slope of X_1 at certain values of X_2 and X_3 (or symmetrically, slope of X_2 at certain values of X_1 and X_3), substitute these values of X_2 and X_3 into the full regression equations with known coefficients and the coefficient of X_1 will be the required slope. Corresponding t-tests on these coefficients can also be computed with the appropriate standard errors of the coefficients (*see* Jaccard et al., 1990) as in the case with two-way interactions.

Measurement error is likely to be an even larger problem for the evaluation of higher-order interactions. As noted earlier with two-way interactions, measurement errors associated with each of the separate predictor variables combines multiplicatively so that measurement error is typically much larger for the interaction terms. This issue is likely to be exacerbated even more for higher-order interactions. Hence, there is the need for latent variable models that control for unreliability. However, latent variable models of interaction have primarily focused on models of two-way interactions, and there has been little progress on extending these models to include higher-order interaction.

Tests of Measurement Invariance

Of particular substantive importance for applied psychological research are mean-level differences across multiple groups (e.g., male vs. female; age groups; single-sex vs. co-educational schools) or over time (i.e., observing the same group of participants at multiple occasions, perhaps before and after an intervention) as well as interactions between these variables. What have typically been ignored in such studies are tests of whether the variables have the same meaning in the different groups or for multiple occasions. When there are multiple indicators of the constructs, typical approach is to test the invariance over groups or time of the factor structure and the item intercepts. An important assumption underlying tests of mean differences is that group differences in the latent mean are reflected in each of the multiple indicators of the latent construct. For example, if the underlying factor structure for the outcome variable Y differs for boys and girls, or over time, then interpretations of mean level differences are problematic. Also, if mean level differences are not consistent across items used to infer the outcome, given comparable levels on the estimated outcome (i.e., there is differential item functioning), then the observed differences might be idiosyncratic to the particular items used. Obviously these issues are critical in the interpretation of interaction effects. If the meaning of a predictor variable is qualitatively different for boys and girls, then it makes no sense to test the effect of the interaction between the predictor variable and gender

The evaluation of model invariance over different groups (e.g., gender) or over time for the same group is widely applied in SEM studies (Jöreskog & Sörbom, 1988; Meredith & Teresi, 2006; Vandenberg & Lance, 2000). Indeed, such tests of invariance might be seen as a fundamental advantage of CFA over traditional approaches to EFA (but *see also* recent applications of exploratory structural equation modeling that integrate EFA and CFA approaches in the evaluation of measurement invariance; *see* Marsh, Muthén et al., 2009, Marsh, Lüdtke, et al., 2010). Tests of measurement invariance begin with a model with no invariance of any parameters (*configural invariance*) followed by tests of whether factor loadings are invariant over groups (*weak invariance*). *Strong measurement invariance* requires that the indicator intercepts and factor loadings are invariant over groups or time and is an assumption for comparison of latent means. *Strict measurement invariance* requires invariance of item uniquenesses (i.e., each item's residual variance) in addition to invariant factor loadings and intercepts and is an assumption for the comparison of manifest means over groups or time. Unless there is support for at least strong measurement invariance, then the comparison of latent means is not justified (because of the problem of differential item functioning). The comparison of manifest means requires the much stronger assumption of strict measurement invariance (as a necessary, but not a sufficient condition).

The multiple-group approach to measurement invariance is easily formulated and tested when in relation to a predictor that is a true grouping variable with a relatively small number of discrete categories. However, for continuous variables, the multiple-group approach would require researchers to transform continuous variables into a relatively small number of categories that constitute the multiple groups—a practice we have criticized earlier. Marsh, Tracey, and Craven (2006; *see also* Marsh, Lüdtke et al., 2010) have proposed a hybrid approach involving an integration of interpretations based on both multiple-indicator-multiple-cause (MIMIC) and multiple group approaches. In the MIMIC approach, the predictor variables (X_1 and X_2) and their interaction are included in the model based on the total sample; they can be categorical or continuous, latent or manifest. In this respect, the distinction between the MIMIC and multiple-group approaches is analogous to the multiple-group and single (total) group distinction already discussed in relation to the moderated regression approach. The main difference is that in the MIMIC and multiple-group approach as used here, some of the variables are latent variables based on multiple indicators.

Moderated multiple regression models like those considered in the first half of this chapter are based on manifest variables that might not have multiple indicators. Although some constructs might be appropriately measured with a single indicator that has no measurement error (e.g., gender), most cannot. However, tests of single-indicator (manifest) variables make the same assumptions of measurement invariance, as do latent variables. Indeed, the assumptions are even more stringent (strict measurement invariance is needed rather than strong measurement invariance). The problem is that typical approaches to measurement invariance cannot be used to test the appropriateness of these assumptions for single-indicator manifest constructs. Although issues of measurement invariance have been largely ignored in tests of interactions, this situation is likely to change with the increased focus on latent variable models in general and latent interactions in particular.

Multilevel Designs and Clustered Samples

There is a special type of interaction in that data points are related as clusters and are not collected totally independently (e.g., students' questionnaire responses from 100 schools, with data from the same school sharing some commonalities). The effects of the independent variables on dependent variables (or their relations) may change according to their subgroup units (e.g., school) or their characteristics. For example, parental influence on students' achievement depends on the characteristics of the schools (e.g., whether the student is studying in a school with low or high average socioeconomic status). Indeed, a key question in many multilevel studies is how the effect of an individual variable varies from group-to-group, and whether there are group-level variables that can explain the group-level variation. Although the groups are typically considered as a random effect, rather than a fixed effect, the issue is still an interaction question—is the effect of one variable moderated by another variable (e.g., the particular school that a student attends).

Historically, multilevel researchers have tended to work with manifest variables that ignore measurement error, whereas SEM researchers have tended to work with latent variable models that ignore multilevel structures in their data. However, these two dominant analytic approaches are increasingly being integrated within more comprehensive multilevel SEMs (e.g., Lüdtke, Marsh et al., 2008; Marsh, Lüdtke et al., 2009). Inevitably, this integration will lead to increased sophistication in the study of latent interactions, a better understanding of the cross-level interactions between individual-level and group-level variables, and a clearer distinction between fixed-effects that have been emphasized in our chapter and random effects that are emphasized in multilevel analyses. Although clearly beyond the scope of our chapter (*but see* chapter "Multilevel regression and Multilevel SEM" in this monograph), this is an important emerging area in quantitative analysis.

Author Note

The authors would like to thank the following colleagues for input in relation to earlier drafts of this chapter: Eric Dearing, Kathleen McCartney; David Kenny, Matthew R Golder; and Thomas Brambor.

Note

1. As in many other statistical models, there are Bayesian approaches and non-Bayesian approaches in estimating latent interaction models. Although well developed (see, e.g., Arminger & Muthén, 1998; Lee, Song & Poon, 2004), Bayesian approaches and their calculation algorithms are relatively difficult for general applied researchers and thus although available in the special WinBUGS software, these approaches have not been adopted for the most popular commercial SEM software (but also see the Bayesian approach recently introduced in Mplus).

References

Aguinis, H. (2004). *Moderated regression.* New York: Guilford.

Aiken, L. S., & West, S. G. (1991). *Multiple regression: Testing and interpreting interactions.* Newbury Park, CA: Sage.

Algina, J., & Moulder, B. C. (2001). A note on estimating the Jöreskog-Yang model for latent variable interaction using LISREL 8.3. *Structural Equation Modeling: A Multidisciplinary Journal, 8*, 40–52.

Arminger, G., & Muthén, B. (1998). A Bayesian approach to nonlinear latent variable models using the Gibbs sampler and the Metropolis-Hastings algorithm. *Psychometrika, 63*, 271–300.

Bagozzi, R. P., & Yi, Y. (1989). On the use of structural equation models in experimental designs. *Journal of Marketing Research, 26*, 271–284.

Baron, R. M., & Kenny, D. A. (1986). The moderator-mediator variable distinction in social psychological research: Conceptual, strategic, and statistical considerations. *Journal of Personality and Social Psychology, 51*, 1173–1182.

Brambor, T., Clark, W. R., & Golder, M. (2006). Understanding interaction models: Improving empirical analyses. *Political Analysis, 14*, 63–82.

Byrne, B. M. (1998). *Structural equation modeling with LISREL, PRELIS, and SIMPLIS: Basic concepts, applications and programming.* Mahwah, NJ: Erlbaum.

Carte, T. A. & Russell, C. J. (2003). In Pursuit of Moderation: Nine Common Errors and Their Solutions. *Management Information Systems Quarterly, 27*, 479–501.

Coenders, G., Batista-Foguet, J.M. & Saris. W. E. (2008). Simple, efficient and distribution-free approach to interaction effects in complex structural equation models. *Quality & Quantity, 42*, 369–396.

Cohen, J. (1968). Multiple regression as a general data analytic system. *Psychological Bulletin 70*(6), 426–443.

Cohen, J. (1978). Partialed products are interactions; partialed powers are curve components. *Psychological Bulletin, 85*, 858–866.

Cohen, J., & Cohen, P. (1983). *Applied multiple regression/correlation analysis for the behavioral sciences.* Hillsdale, NJ: Lawrence Erlbaum.

Cohen, J., Cohen, P., Aiken, L. S., & West, S. G. (2003). *Applied multiple regression/correlation analysis for the social sciences* (3rd ed.). Mahwah, NJ: Lawrence Erlbaum.

Cronbach, L. J., & Snow, R. E. (1977). *Aptitudes and instructional methods: A handbook for research on interactions.* Oxford, England: Irvington.

Darlington, R. B. (1990). *Regression and linear models.* New York: McGraw-Hill.

Dearing, E., & Hamilton, L. C. (2006). Contemporary approaches and classic advice for analyzing mediating and moderating variables. *Monographs of the Society for Research in Child Development, 71* (Serial No. 285).

Frazier, P. A., Tix, A. P., & Barron, K. E. (2004). Testing moderator and mediator effects in counseling psychology. *Journal of Counseling Psychology, 51*, 115–334.

Friedrich, R. J. (1982). In defense of multiplicative terms in multiple regression equations. *American Journal of Political Science, 26*, 797–833.

Hayduk, L. A. (1987). *Structural equation modeling with LISREL: Essentials and advances.* Baltimore: Johns Hopkins University.

Holmbeck, G. N. (1997). Toward terminological, conceptual, and statistical clarity in the study of mediators and moderators: Examples from the child-clinical and pediatric psychology literatures. *Journal of Consulting and Clinical Psychology, 65*, 599–610.

Jaccard, J. (1998). *Interaction effects in factorial analysis of variance.* Thousand Oaks, CA, US, Sage Publications.

Jaccard, J., Turrisi, R., & Wan, C. K. (1990). *Interaction effects in multiple regression.* Newbury Park, CA: Sage.

Jaccard, J., & Wan, C. K. (1995). Measurement error in the analysis of interaction effects between continuous predictors using multiple regression: multiple indicator and structural equation approaches. *Psychological Bulletin, 117*, 348–357.

Johnson, P. O., & Neyman, J. (1936). Tests of certain linear hypotheses and their application to some educational problems. *Statistical Research Memoirs, 1*, 57–93.

Jöreskog, K. G. (1998). Interaction and nonlinear modeling: issue and approaches. In R.E. Schumacker, G.A. Marcoulides, (Eds.), *Interaction and nonlinear effects in structural equation modelling* (pp. 239–250). Mahwah, NJ: Erlbaum.

Jöreskog, K. G., & Sörbom, D. (1988). *LISREL 7—A guide to the program and applications* (2nd ed.). Chicago, IL: SPSS.

Jöreskog, K. G., & Yang, F. (1996). Nonlinear structural equation models: The Kenny-Judd model with interaction effects. In. G. A. Marcoulides & R. E. Schumacker, (Eds.), *Advanced structural equation modeling: Issued and techniques* (pp. 57–88). Mahwah, NJ: Erlbaum.

Judd, C. M., & Kenny, D. A. (1981). Process analysis: Estimating mediation in treatment evaluations. *Evaluation Review, 5*, 602–619.

Judd, C. M., & Kenny, D. A. (2010). Data analysis in Social Psychology: Recent and recurring issues (pp. 115–139). In S. T. Fiske, D. T. Gilbert & G. Lindzey. *Handbook of Social Psychology* (5th ed). Hoboken NJ: Wiley.

Judd, C. M., McClelland, G. H., & Ryan, C. S. (2009). *Data analysis: A model comparison approach* (2nd ed.). New York: Routledge.

Kelava, A., & Brandt, H. (2009). Estimation of Nonlinear Latent Structural Equation Models using the Extended Unconstrained Approach. *Review of Psychology, 16*, 123–131.

Kenny, D. A., & Judd, C. M. (1984). Estimating the nonlinear and interactive effects of latent variables. *Psychological Bulletin, 9*, 201–210.

King, G. (1986) How not to lie with statistics: Avoiding common mistakes in political science. *American Journal of Political Science, 30*, 666–687.

Kirk, R. (1982). *Experimental Design: Procedures for the Behavioral Sciences.* Belmont CA: Brooks/Cole.

Klein, A. G., & Moosbrugger, H. (2000). Maximum likelihood estimation of latent interaction effects with the LMS method. *Psychometrika, 65*, 457–474.

Klein, A. G., & Muthén, B. (2007). Quasi-maximum likelihood estimation of structural equation models with multiple interaction and quadratic effects. *Multivariate Behavioral Research, 42*, 647–674.

Klein, A. G., Schermelleh-Engel, K., Moosbrugger, H., & Kelava, A. (2009). Assessing spurious interaction effects. In T. Teo & M. S. Khine (Eds.), *Structural equation modeling in educational research: Concepts and applications* (pp. 13–28). Rotterdam, The Netherlands: Sense Publishers.

Lance, Charles E. (1988). Residual centering, exploratory and confirmatory moderator analysis, and decomposition of effects in path models containing interactions.

Lance, C. E. (1988). Residual centering, exploratory and confirmatory moderator analysis, and decomposition of effects in path models containing interactions. *Applied Psychological Measurement, 12*, 163–175.

Landram, F. G. & Alidaee, B. (1997). Computing orthogonal polynomials. *Computers Operations Research, 24*, 473–476.

Lee, S. Y., Song, X. Y., & Poon, W. Y. (2004). Comparison of approaches in estimating interaction and quadratic effects of latent variables. *Multivariate Behavioral Research, 29*, 37–67.

Lin, G-C., Wen, Z. L., Marsh, H. W. & Lin, H-S. (2010). Structural equation models of latent interactions: clarification of orthogonalizing and double-mean-centering strategies. *Structural Equation Modeling, 17*(3), 374–391.

Little, Todd D.; Bovaird, James A.; Widaman, Keith F. (2006). On the merits of orthogonalizing powered and product terms: Implications for modeling interactions among latent variables.

Little, T. D., Bovaird, J. A., & Widaman, K. F. (2006). On the merits of orthogonalizing powered and product terms: Implications for modeling interactions among latent variables. *Structural Equation Modeling, 13*, 497–519.

Lubinski, D., & Humphreys, L. G. (1990). Assessing spurious "moderator effects": Illustrated substantively with the hypothesized ("synergistic") relation between spatial and mathematical ability. *Psychological Bulletin, 107*, 385–393.

Lüdtke, O., Marsh, H. W., Robitzsch, A., Trautwein, U., Asparouhov, T., & Muthén, B. (2008). The multilevel latent covariate model: A new, more reliable approach to group-level effects in contextual studies. *Psychological Methods, 13*, 203–229.

MacCallum, R. C., & Mar, C. M. (1995). Distinguishing between moderator and quadratic effects in multiple regression. *Psychological Bulletin, 118*, 405–421.

MacCallum, R. C., Zhang, S., Preacher, K. J., & Rucker, D. D. (2002). On the practice of dichotomization of quantitative variables. *Psychological Methods, 7*, 19–40.

Marquardt, D. W. (1980). You should standardize the predictor variables in your regression models. *Journal of the American Statistical Association, 75*, 87–91.

Marsh, H. W. & Craven, R. G. (2006). Reciprocal effects of self-concept and performance from a multidimensional perspective: Beyond seductive pleasure and unidimensional perspectives. *Perspectives on Psychological Science, 1*, 133–163.

Marsh, H. W., Dowson, M., Pietsch, J., & Walker, R. (2004). Why multicollinearity matters: A re-examination of relations between self-efficacy, self-concept and achievement. *Journal of Educational Psychology, 96*, 518–522.

Marsh, H. W., & Grayson, D. (1994). Longitudinal stability of latent means and individual differences: A unified approach. *Structural Equation Modeling, 1*, 317–359.

Marsh, H. W., & Hau, K-T. (2007). Applications of latent-variable models in educational psychology: The need for methodological-substantive synergies. *Contemporary Educational Psychology, 32*, 151–171.

Marsh, H. W., Hau, K.T. & Wen, Z., (2004). In search of golden rules: Comment on hypothesis testing approaches to setting cutoff values for fit indexes and dangers in overgeneralising Hu & Bentler's (1999) findings. *Structural Equation Modelling, 11*, 320–341.

Marsh, H. W., Lüdtke, O., Muthén, B., Asparouhov, T., Morin, A. J. S., Trautwein, U. & Nagengast, B. (2010). A new look at the big-five factor structure through exploratory structural equation modeling. *Psychological Assessment, 22*, 471–491.

Marsh, H. W., Muthén, B., Asparouhov, T., Lüdtke, O., Robitzsch, A., Morin, A. J. S., & Trautwein, U. (2009). Exploratory Structural equation modeling, integrating CFA and EFA: Application to students' evaluations of university teaching. *Structural Equation Modeling,16*, 439–476.

Marsh, H. W., & O'Mara, A. (2008). Reciprocal effects between academic self-concept, self-esteem, achievement, and attainment over seven adolescent years: Unidimensional and multidimensional perspectives of self-concept. *Personality and Social Psychology Bulletin, 34*, 542–552.

Marsh, H. W., Tracey, D. K., & Craven, R. G. (2006). Multidimensional self-concept structure for preadolescents with mild intellectual disabilities: A hybrid multigroup-mimic approach to factorial invariance and latent mean differences. *Educational and Psychological Measurement, 66*, 795–818.

Marsh, H. W., Trautwein, U., Lüdtke, O., Köller, O. & Baumert, J. (2005) Academic self-concept, interest, grades and standardized test scores: Reciprocal effects models of causal ordering. *Child Development, 76*, 297–416.

Marsh, H. W., Wen, Z., & Hau, K.T. (2004). Structural equation models of latent interactions: Evaluation of alternative estimation strategies and indicator construction. *Psychological Methods, 9*, 275–300.

Marsh, H. W., Wen, Z., & Hau, K. T. (2006). Structural equation models of latent interaction and quadratic effects. In G. Hancock & Mueller (Eds). *Structural equation modeling: A second course* (pp. 225–265). Greenwich, CT: Information Age Publishing.

Marsh, H. W., Wen, Z. L., Hau, K. T, Little, T. D. Bovaird, J. A. & Widaman, K. F. (2007). Unconstrained structural equation models of latent interactions: Contrasting residual- and mean-centered approaches. *Structural Equation Modelling, 14*, 570–580.

McClelland, G. H., & Judd, C. M. (1993). Statistical difficulties of detecting interactions and moderator effects. *Psychological Bulletin, 114*, 376–390.

Meredith, W., & Teresi, J. A. (2006). n Essay on Measurement and Factorial Invariance. *edical Care, 44*, S69–S77.

Moosbrugger, H., Schermelleh-Engel, K., Kelava, A., & Klein, A. G. (2009). Testing multiple nonlinear effects in structural equation modeling: A comparison of alternative estimation approaches. In T. Teo & M. S. Khine (Eds.), *Structural equation modeling in educational research: Concepts and applications* (pp.103–136). Rotterdam, The Netherlands: Sense Publishers.

Morin, A. J. S., Janoz, M. & Larivée, S. (2009). The Montreal adolescent depression development project (MADDP): School life and depression following high school transition. *Psychiatry Research Journal, 1*(3), 1–50.

Moulder, B. C., & Algina, J. (2002). Comparison of methods for estimating and testing latent variable interactions. *Structural Equation Modeling, 9*, 1–19.

Muller, D., Judd, C. M., & Yzerbyt, V. Y. (2005). When moderation is mediated and mediation is moderated. *Journal of Personality and Social Psychology, 89*, 852–863.

Muthén, L. K., & Muthén, B. O. (1997–2008). *Mplus user's guide*. Los Angeles, CA: Muthén & Muthén.

Ping, R. A., Jr. (1996). Latent variable interaction and quadratic effect estimation: A two-step technique using structural equation analysis. *Psychological Bulletin, 119*, 166–175.

Potthoff, R. F. (1964). On the Johnson-Neyman technique and some extensions thereof. *Psychometrika, 29*, 241–256.

Preacher, K. J., Curran, P. J., & Bauer, D. (2006). Computational tools for probing interactions in multiple linear regression, multilevel modeling, and latent curve analysis. *Journal of Educational and Behavioral Statistics, 31*, 437–448.

Rigdon, E. E., Schumacker, R. E. & Wothke, W. (1998). A comparative review of interaction and nonlinear modeling. In R. E. Schumacker & G. A. Marcoulides (Eds.), *Interaction and nonlinear effects in structural equation modeling* (pp. 1–16). Mahwah, NJ: Lawrence Erlbaum Associates.

Saris. W. E., Batista-Foguet, J.M. & Coenders, G. (2007). Selection of indicators for the interaction term in structural equation models with interaction. *Quality & Quantity, 41*, 55–72.

Schumacker, R. E., & Marcoulides, G. A. (Eds.) (1998). *Interaction and nonlinear effects in structural equation modeling*. Mahwah, NJ: Erlbaum.

Traci, A. C., & Russell, C. J. (2003). *In pursuit of moderation: Nine common errors and their solutions*. MIS Quaterly, 27, 479–501.

Vandenberg, R. J., & Lance, C. E. (2000). A review and synthesis of the measurement invariance literature: Suggestions, practices, and recommendations for organizational research. *Organizational Research Methods, 3*, 4–69.

Wall, M. M., & Amemiya, Y. (2001). Generalized appended product indicator procedure for nonlinear structural equation analysis. *Journal of Educational and Behavioral Statistics, 26*, 1–29.

Wen, Z., Hau, K. T., & Marsh, H. W. (2008). Appropriate standardized estimates for moderating effects in structural equation models. *Acta Psychologica Sinica, 40*(6), 729–736.

Wen, Z., Marsh, H. W., & Hau, K. T. (2010). Structural equation models of latent interactions: An appropriate standardized solution and its scale-free properties. *Structural Equation Modeling, 17*, 1–22.

Wu, Y., Wen, Z., & Lin, G. C. (2009). Structural equation modeling of latent interactions without using the mean structure. *Acta Psychologica Sinica, 41*(12), 1252–1259.

CHAPTER
18 Longitudinal Data Analysis

Wei Wu, James P. Selig, *and* Todd D. Little

Abstract

Longitudinal data analysis is an increasingly popular approach because evaluating change is of central interest in many areas of research. Using advanced statistical techniques such as multilevel modeling (MLM) and structural equation modeling (SEM), longitudinal data analysis allows for the simultaneous evaluation of intra-individual change and interindividual differences in intra-individual change. This chapter presents an overview of both MLM and SEM approaches to evaluating change with different functional forms for continuous panel data, including linear, curvilinear, nonlinear, and spline curve models. This chapter also covers a variety of longitudinal models that take advantage of the flexibility of SEM over MLM, including autoregressive cross-lagged, latent difference, fully latent, parallel process, and second-order curve models. The chapter closes with a discussion of the advantages and disadvantages of MLM and SEM in modeling change, along with a brief review of advances in longitudinal data analysis.

Key Words: Longitudinal data analysis, multilevel modeling, structural equation modeling, repeated measures, latent curve model, change trajectory, parallel process curve model

Introduction
The Importance of Longitudinal Data Analysis

Longitudinal data refer to repeated observations or measures over time (Singer & Willett, 2003) and are widely present in educational, social, and behavioral science studies. Longitudinal research designs are often classified according to the frequency of repeated observations. If individuals are repeatedly measured for a limited number of time-points, each separated by several months or more (e.g., five yearly measures of school achievement), then the study follows a longitudinal panel design (Collins, 2006). In contrast, if individuals are repeatedly measured for a large number of time-points with relatively brief intervals between occasions (e.g., daily measure on depression levels for 30 days), the design is referred to as an intensive longitudinal design (Collins, 2006). Different techniques are needed to analyze the two types of data. The current chapter focuses on longitudinal data analysis for panel designs. The techniques for analyzing intensive longitudinal data are discussed in Walls (Chapter 18, this volume).

Longitudinal data can also be described as balanced or unbalanced. When all individuals share the same measurement occasions, data are considered balanced on time (e.g., all individuals are measured at ages 12, 13, and 14 years). When individuals are measured on different occasions, the data are unbalanced on time (e.g., individual 1 is measured at ages 12, 13, and 14 years, but individual 2 is measured at ages 15, 16, and 17 years). The methods introduced in this chapter can be applied to both balanced and unbalanced data. In addition, the response variable measured at each occasion can be either continuous or discrete. This chapter is only focused on continuous outcomes. Those who are interested in longitudinal data analysis for discrete outcomes can refer to Fitzmaurice, Laird, and Ware (2004).

A variety of research questions related to change can be answered in longitudinal data analysis. Typical research questions include (1) How does a population mean change over time? (e.g., What is the change trend for average academic achievement as grade in school increases? Is it a linear or nonlinear function of grade?); (2) How do individual responses change over time? (e.g., What is the change in achievement for each student?); (3) Is there interindividual variability in intra-individual change? (e.g., Do the students differ in their rates of change or their trajectories of change in school achievement?); (4) Can individual differences in change be explained by covariates? (e.g., Are individual differences in change in school achievement explained by gender?); and (5) Is there a relationship between changes in different outcomes (e.g., Is change in school engagement related to change in academic achievement?)?

Although some of the basic ideas of longitudinal data analysis can be traced back to the nineteenth century (e.g., Gompertz, 1825; Quetelet, 1835; *see* Bollen & Curran, 2006, for a further review), modern longitudinal data analysis has only been developed in the past 30 years. One major challenge researchers have faced in analyzing longitudinal data is that the individual deviations from the mean responses over time (i.e., residuals) are not independent, which violates the independence assumption made by traditional techniques such as regression and analysis of variance (ANOVA). As a result, the traditional techniques yield biased estimates of standard errors and misleading statistical inferences when used to analyze longitudinal data.

Two approaches have been proposed to address the associations among residuals: (1) directly specifying the covariance matrix of the residuals allowing the residuals from the means to covary with one another over time and (2) introducing random effects into the model by allowing the time effect to vary across individuals. In the first approach, one needs to specify the form of change for mean responses over time and the covariance structure of residuals from the means. In statistics, this type of model is often referred to as a marginal or repeated measures regression model. Although the second approach is less straightforward than the marginal approach, introducing random effects induces covariances among residuals (we will illustrate this point later in the chapter). In this random effects approach, the form of change for individual responses needs to be specified. Random effects models are often referred to as conditional, random coefficient regression (Laird & Ware, 1982), multilevel modeling (MLM), or mixed models (Goldstein, 1987; Bryk & Raudenbush, 1992). These name differences largely result from the fact that these models were developed in different research areas. For example, the random coefficient regression model is most often used in biostatistics and the multilevel model is most often used in education. In the following, we will use the term MLM longitudinal models to represent these types of models.

Both the marginal and MLM approaches have their own target use. The marginal model is useful for inference about change in population mean responses. Multilevel modeling is useful for inference about individual-specific changes, thus it can be used to answer research questions focusing on, for example, individual differences in growth trajectories. In fact, if the functional form of a change trajectory is linear or curvilinear (*see* definition later), then aggregating (e.g., averaging) the individual change trajectories will reproduce the change trajectory of population mean responses. Thus MLM longitudinal models can also be used to answer research questions centering on the change in population mean responses. For this reason, MLM longitudinal models are often favored by researchers. However, if the functional form of change is nonlinear or the outcome variable is discrete, aggregating (e.g., averaging) the individual change trajectory cannot reproduce the trajectory for the population mean response. In those cases, researchers prefer marginal models for research questions on the trajectory of population mean responses.

Researchers have shown that both approaches can be implemented within the framework of latent variable analysis or structural equation modeling (SEM) by treating the random effects as latent variables (Meredith & Tisak, 1990; Willett & Sayer, 1994). Researchers have also shown that SEM offers tremendous flexibility in modeling relationships among variables (e.g., Chou, Bentler & Pentz, 1998; Curran & Peterman, 2005; Mehta & West, 2000) and this flexibility allows for the specification of a wider variety of models to answer research questions related to change (*see* more detailed discussion later in the chapter).

Goal of this Chapter

This chapter is not intended as an exhaustive review of the techniques for longitudinal data analysis. Rather, we will focus on *MLM* and *SEM* approaches to modeling change in *continuous panel data*. The longitudinal models for panel data come in two classes: the traditional autoregressive cross-lagged (ARCL) and the growth curve model (GCM). The ARCL models tend to fit the correlational or predictive relationship between pairs of repeated measures. In contrast, the GCMs aim to address change trajectory across time. Growth curve models can be specified as multilevel models (MLM GCMs) or as structural equation models (SEM GCMs). In contrast, the ARCL models can only be estimated as SEM models. Methods have also been developed to incorporate the two perspectives in one model. The current chapter covers both classes of longitudinal models.

We organized the chapter in the following way: We start with the MLM approach to fitting GCMs with different functional forms of change trajectories. The functional forms include linear, curvilinear, nonlinear, and piecewise trajectories (Singer & Willett, 2003; Cudeck & du Toit, 2003; Cudeck & Klebe, 2002). We then map those models onto structural equation models. After that, we present a variety of SEM longitudinal models that cannot, or cannot be easily, estimated using MLM, including the ARCL model, the latent difference score model, the fully latent model with freely estimated time basis coefficients (level and shape model), the parallel process GCM, and the second-order GCM. We conclude the chapter by presenting some advances in longitudinal data analysis such as growth mixture modeling, three-level and cross-classified MLM longitudinal models, and integrative data analysis.

Multilevel Modeling Approach to Longitudinal Data Analysis

Multilevel modeling is an advanced data analytical technique for clustered or nested data (Bryk & Raudenbush, 1992; Cohen, Cohen, West, & Aiken, 2003). In the special case of longitudinal data, measurement occasions are nested within individuals. The basic idea of MLM is to include random effects of time in regression models to take into account the effect of repeated observations and the resulting correlations among residuals over time (MacCallum, Kim, Malarkey, & Kiecolt-Glaser, 1997).

Specifying an appropriate functional form for a pattern of change is the first step in applying GCMs. This specification is not a simple task given the diversity of growth patterns in the real world. Figure 18.1 displays several functional forms for change over time that will be described in the chapter. Because the individual change pattern do not always agree with the pattern of mean change, one should specify a functional form that is suitable not only to the mean pattern of change but also to the individual change patterns (Singer & Willett, 2003; Wu, West, & Taylor, 2009). A so-called spaghetti plot can help in selecting an appropriate functional form. A spaghetti plot is a plot of the observed individual trajectories for a subset of individuals (usually 20–30) that are randomly drawn from the full sample. To inspect and identify an appropriate functional form, the repeated observations are plotted and connected with straight lines (splines). One might also impose a systematic change trajectory or a smoothing line. Figure 18.2 shows a spaghetti plot for change in math achievement over a 4-year period for 25 elementary school students. As can be seen in Figure 18.2, a linear trajectory seems to provide a close approximation to most of the individual trends, although there is evidence of curvature in a few of the individual trajectories. Evaluation of these differences can be further determined in model fitting and testing.

In this section, we will illustrate MLM GCMs with a variety of functional forms, focusing on model specifications and interpretation of parameters in the models. Despite the different functional forms, MLM GCMs share some common features or general specifications. For example, a two-level MLM model is needed to represent a basic GCM. The first level is used to specify the functional form of the change trajectory for each individual, which is also called repeated measures or within-individual level. The second level is used to capture the individual difference in their change trajectories, often called the between-individual level. In the following, we use the linear trajectory, the simplest change trend, to illustrate the general specifications. We then show the functional forms for more complicated curvilinear and nonlinear GCMs. We also discuss how to include covariates to predict interindividual differences in intra-individual change trajectories and how covariates can be used to explain the variability in an outcome variable that cannot be accounted for by a specific change trajectory.

Linear Growth Curve Model

Perhaps because of its simplicity and the fact that it requires fewer time-points than more complex trajectories, the linear GCM is the most widely used

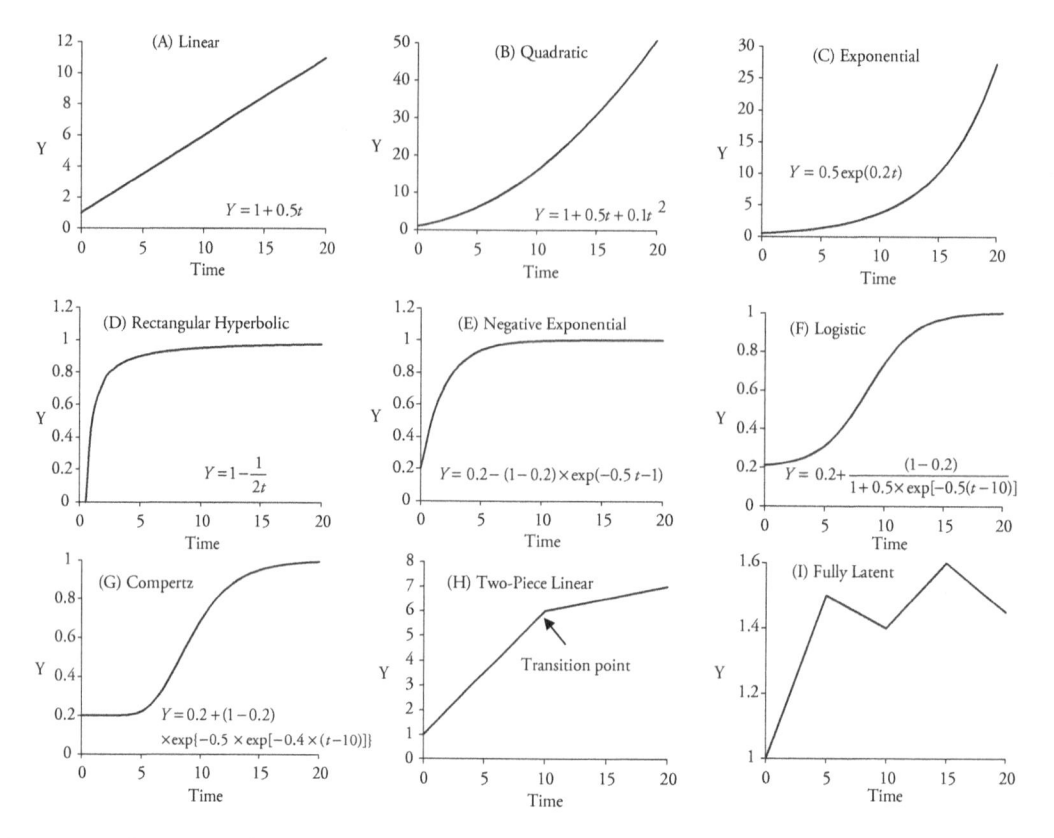

Figure 18.1 Different shapes of change trajectories.

GCM. A linear change follows a straight line, which means that the amount of expected change is constant given the same amount of increment in time. The shape of a linear change trajectory is defined by two parameters: (1) an intercept and (2) a slope (or rate of change). See Figure 18.1(A) for an example of linear trajectory.

Model Specification. As mentioned above, a GCM can be represented as a MLM with two levels. For a linear GCM, the first level (level-1) expresses individual outcome as a linear function of time. Equation 1 shows a linear GCM for longitudinal data with five waves of measures.

$$Level - 1 : y_{ij} = \beta_{0i} + \beta_{1i} t_{ij} + e_{ij}, e_{ij} \sim N(0, \sigma^2), \quad (1)$$

where i indicates individual and j indicates measurement occasion or time-point ($j = 1, 2, 3, 4,$ or 5 in our example), y_{ij} is the individual i's response at time j, and t_{ij} is the time when individual i was measured at the jth measurement occasion.

If one ignores the subscripts in the equation, Equation 1 is very much like a linear regression equation, which expresses the predictive relationship between the response variable and predictor *time*.

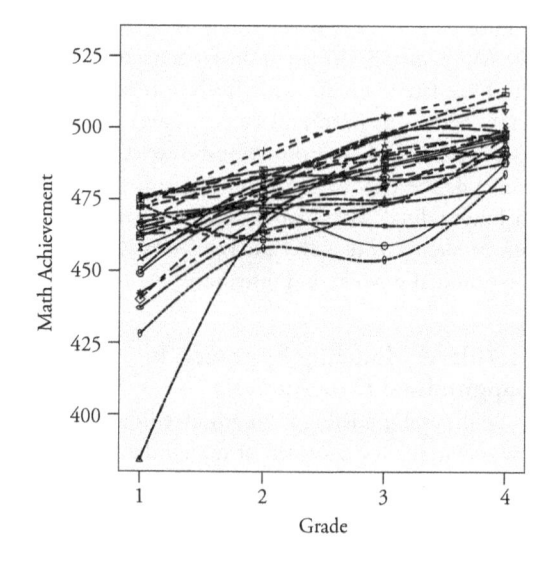

Figure 18.2 An example of spaghetti plot.

β_{0i} is the intercept that represents initial status of the outcome variable when $t_{ij} = 0$. Note that one can *center* time at different occasions (e.g., mean time) to change the interpretation of β_{0i}. β_{1i} is the slope of predicting y_{ij} from t_{ij}, which describes the expected

390 | LONGITUDINAL DATA ANALYSIS

change in y_{ij} for a 1-unit change in t_{ij}. Because β_{0i} and β_{1i} determine the shape of the individual change trajectories, they are often called *growth parameters*. The level 1 model also includes residuals (e_{ij}) that represent deviations of the observed data from the predicted individual curves. e_{ij} is often assumed to follow a normal distribution with mean of 0 and a constant variance (σ^2) over time. The covariance matrix for the level 1 residuals is called the **R** or *within-individual covariance* matrix. With five waves of measurement,

$$R_i = \begin{bmatrix} \sigma^2 & 0 & 0 & 0 & 0 \\ 0 & \sigma^2 & 0 & 0 & 0 \\ 0 & 0 & \sigma^2 & 0 & 0 \\ 0 & 0 & 0 & \sigma^2 & 0 \\ 0 & 0 & 0 & 0 & \sigma^2 \end{bmatrix}.$$

The difference between the level 1 equation and an ordinary linear regression equation is that there is a subscript i associated with the intercept and slope in Equation 1. This implies that the intercept and slope are unique to each individual. In other words, although the change in *an outcome variable* follows a straight line for all of the individuals, the intercept and slope of the straight line can vary across individuals. The variability of the individual-specific intercept and slope is modeled by the second level model, as shown in Equation 2.

$$\text{Level} - 2 : \beta_{01} = \gamma_{00} + u_{0i}$$
$$\beta_{1i} = \gamma_{10} + u_{1i}$$
$$\begin{bmatrix} u_{0i} \\ u_{1i} \end{bmatrix} \sim MVN \left(\begin{bmatrix} 0 \\ 0 \end{bmatrix}, \right.$$
$$\left. G = \begin{bmatrix} \tau_{00} & \\ \tau_{10} & \tau_{11} \end{bmatrix} \right), \quad (2)$$

where MVN stands for multivariate normally distributed. At level 2, the individual growth parameters (β_{0i} and β_{1i}) conceptually become outcome variables where predictors that might account for their variation across individuals can be specified. When no predictor is specified, β_{0i} and β_{1i} are represented by their population means (γ_{00} and γ_{10}) and deviations of individual growth parameters from the population means (u_{0i}, u_{1i}) γ_{00} and γ_{10} are constant across individuals and thus are termed *fixed effects*. u_{0i} and u_{1i} vary across individuals and thus are termed *random effects*.

For random effects, researchers usually do not care about the individual deviation values but their variances and covariances. Their variances and covariance are elements in the covariance matrix of u_{0i} and u_{1i}, which is called the **G**-matrix or between-individual covariance matrix. If the variances of u_{0i} and u_{1i} (τ_{00} and τ_{11}) are significantly different from 0, then there is significant individual variability in the intercept and slope. If the covariance between u_{0i} and u_{1i} (τ_{10}) is significant, then the intercept and slope are related to each other. For example, a negative covariance between intercept and slope for math achievement indicate that lower initial math achievement is often accompanied by a faster increase in math achievement in the future.

Using the average growth parameters (γ_{00} & γ_{10}), one can calculate predicted mean response at a certain time-point, as shown in Equation 3. Using the level 1 residual variance and the elements in the **G** matrix, one can calculate the model implied covariance matrix of repeated measures, as shown in Equation 4.

$$E(y_{ij}) = \gamma_{00} + \gamma_{10} t_{ij}; \quad (3)$$

$$\hat{\Sigma}_i = COV(Y_i);$$

$$= \begin{pmatrix} Var(y_{i1}) & Cov(y_{i1},y_{i2}) & Cov(y_{i1},y_{i3}) & Cov(y_{i1},y_{i4}) & Cov(y_{i1},y_{i5}) \\ Cov(y_{i2},y_{i1}) & Var(y_{i2}) & Cov(y_{i2},y_{i3}) & Cov(y_{i2},y_{i4}) & Cov(y_{i2},y_{i5}) \\ Cov(y_{i3},y_{i1}) & Cov(y_{i3},y_{i2}) & Var(y_{i3}) & Cov(y_{i3},y_{i4}) & Cov(y_{i3},y_{i5}) \\ Cov(y_{i4},y_{i1}) & Cov(y_{i4},y_{i2}) & Cov(y_{i4},y_{i3}) & Var(y_{i4}) & Cov(y_{i4},y_{i5}) \\ Cov(y_{i5},y_{i1}) & Cov(y_{i5},y_{i2}) & Cov(y_{i5},y_{i3}) & Cov(y_{i5},y_{i4}) & Var(y_{i5}) \end{pmatrix}$$
$$(4)$$

where $VAR(y_{i1}) = \tau_{00} + 2t_{i1}\tau_{01} + t_{i1}^2 \tau_{11} + \sigma$,

$COV(y_{i1}, y_{i2}) = \tau_{00} + (t_{i1} + t_{i2})\tau_{01} + t_{i1}t_{i2}\tau_{11}$,

Here, $E(y_{ij})$ is the model implied mean at time j. $\hat{\Sigma}_i$ is the model implied covariance matrix for individual i. As we can see in Equations 3 and 4, each individual can have different measurement occasions, as well as different means and covariance matrices. Thus, this approach can easily accommodate unbalanced data.

In addition, Equation 4 reveals why the associations among repeated measures can be accounted for by introducing random effects into the model. As one can see, the covariances among repeated measures are solely functions of the components in the between-individual covariance matrix (τ_{00}, τ_{11}, & τ_{10}). In other words, if there is no individual variability in the growth parameters or no random effects (i.e., τ_{00}, τ_{11}, and τ_{10} are all 0), the covariances among repeated measures will be 0. On the other hand, if any of the parameters is significant, then the repeated measures are correlated with one another in the model.

The model implied means and covariance matrix can be compared to the observed means and covariance matrix to evaluate the extent to which the model fits the data. The closer the model implied means and covariance matrix are to the observed means and covariance matrix, the better the model fits the data. Many model fit indices—for example, the likelihood ratio test statistic (chi-square), root mean square error of approximation (RMSEA), and standard root mean square residuals (SRMR)—have been developed based on this principal to inform the researchers the goodness of fit of the model (Wu, West, & Taylor, 2009). In practice, if no theory can specify the form of change, then it might be a good idea to audit different functional forms to see which fits the population best or which is more generalizable to the samples drawn from the same population. Generalizability is often captured by model selection indices or information indices such as Akaike Information Criterion (AIC) and Bayesian Information Criterion (BIC). One needs to refer to those indices to select among competing longitudinal models. Model fit and model selection are discussed in Brown (Chapter 13, this volume) and Jaccard (Chapter 5, Volume 1).

Curvilinear Growth Curve Model

Although the linear GCM is easy to specify and interpret, in practice, growth rarely follows a purely linear trend but, rather, often follows a more complex nonlinear trend if a construct is followed for a sufficiently long period of time (Vandergrift, 2004; Boker & Graham, 1998). Generally, nonlinear trajectories feature a nonconstant change rate (slope) across time. Two types of nonlinearity are differentiated: (1) nonlinearity in the covariate(s) or predictor(s) (e.g., time) and (2) nonlinearity in the regression coefficients (e.g., growth parameters).

For the first type of nonlinearity, a curve is nonlinear in covariate(s) but linear in the coefficients. Equation 5 shows an example of nonlinearity in only covariates. Although the covariate(s) are nonlinear functions of time, the outcome variable can be expressed as a linearly weighted sum of the *coefficients*. This type of model is often called a curvilinear model (Cohen et al., 2003). Curvilinear GCMs can be estimated as linear models by simply creating new covariates that are nonlinear functions of time (e.g., t_{ij}^2 or $\exp(t_{ij})$). The most commonly used curvilinear GCM is the polynomial GCM, where the covariates are power functions of time.

$$y_{ij} = \beta_{0i} + \beta_{1i} t_{ij}^2 + \beta_{2i} \exp(t_{ij}) + e_{ij} \quad (5)$$

The second type of nonlinearity is nonlinear in the coefficients. For this type of nonlinearity, the outcome variable can no longer be expressed as a weighted sum of the coefficients. For example, as shown in Equation 6, the coefficient β_{2i} is in the exponent. There is no way to express the outcome as a weighted sum of β_{2i} unless a transformation is used. This type of model is sometimes called a truly nonlinear GCM (Singer & Willett, 2003; Vandergrift, 2004). Modeling a truly nonlinear GCM comes with many challenges. First, it often requires computationally intensive estimation methods. Second, it requires more waves of repeated measures than linear or curvilinear models given the number of parameters being equivalent. Finally, the interpretation of parameters in a truly nonlinear GCM is usually less straightforward than those in a linear or curvilinear model.

$$y_{ij} = \beta_{1i} \exp(\beta_{2i} t_{ij}) + e_{ij} \quad (6)$$

Next we present polynomial GCMs as an example of curvilinear GCMs and then a few truly nonlinear functions that have been utilized in the social and behavioral sciences.

Polynomial Growth Curve Model. As mentioned before, polynomial GCMs are special cases of curvilinear GCMs. The general form that can be employed to represent a polynomial GCMs of any order is presented in Equation 7 (Raudenbush & Bryk, 2002; Rogosa, Brandt, & Zimowski, 1982):

$$y_{ij} = \beta_{0i} t_{ij}^0 + \beta_{1i} t_{ij}^1 + \beta_{2i} t_{ij}^2 + \cdots + \beta_{pi} t_{ij}^p + e_{ij} \quad (7)$$

In Equation 7, p is the order of the polynomial model. For a pth order polynomial model, there are $p - 1$ bends in the trajectory. When p is equal to 1, this model is a linear growth model, thus the linear model is a special case of the general polynomial model. When p is equal to 2, we get a quadratic growth model, in which there is one bend in the trajectory (*see* Fig. 18.1(B) for an example of a quadratic trajectory). A quadratic model is shown in Equations 8 and 9. Again it is a two-level model, with the first level specifying the quadratic functional form for the individual change trajectory and the second level capturing the individual variability in the growth parameters.

$$\text{Level 1:} \quad y_{ij} = \beta_{0i} t_{ij}^0 + \beta_{1i} t_{ij}^1 + \beta_{2i} t_{ij}^2 + e_{ij} \quad (8)$$

$$\text{Level 2:} \quad \beta_{0i} = \gamma_{00} + u_{0i},$$
$$\beta_{1i} = \gamma_{10} + u_{1i},$$
$$\beta_{2i} = \gamma_{20} + u_{2i}.$$

$$\begin{bmatrix} u_{0i} \\ u_{1i} \\ u_{2i} \end{bmatrix} \sim MVN \left(\begin{bmatrix} 0 \\ 0 \\ 0 \end{bmatrix}, \mathbf{G} = \begin{bmatrix} \tau_{00} & & \\ \tau_{10} & \tau_{11} & \\ \tau_{20} & \tau_{21} & \tau_{22} \end{bmatrix} \right). \quad (9)$$

In the level 1 equation, there is one more growth parameter β_{2i} in the quadratic model than in the linear model, which represents the rate of change in the instantaneous slope over time. Remember that in the linear model, the instantaneous slope is constant over time. Quadratic models allow the instantaneous slope to vary across time introducing curvature in the change trajectory. As the higher order term, β_{2i} (the regression coefficient associated with predictors with higher power) is introduced, the interpretation of the lower order term (β_{1i}) becomes conditional on the origin of time (i.e., when time = 0). Rather than describing linear change over all values of time, β_{1i} becomes the instantaneous linear slope at time = 0. The same regularity also holds for higher order polynomial growth models such that the highest order coefficient is not conditional on the origin of time, but the lower order coefficients are conditional on the origin of time. Similarly to the linear model, the growth parameters are allowed to vary across individuals. The individual variability is captured in the level 2 model. u_{0i}, u_{1i}, and u_{2i} in the level 2 equations represent the deviations of the intercept, linear slope, and quadratic slope for the individual i's change trajectory from the average intercept, linear slope, and quadratic rate (γ_{00}, γ_{10}, & γ_{20}).

Theoretically, one can construct a polynomial model with any order as long as there are a sufficient number of time-points. If one has j time-points, then she can construct a polynomial model with an order up to $j - 2$. However, as higher order terms are introduced into a model, the model becomes more complex and difficult to interpret. It is also important to remember that j time-points in the sample is the absolute minimum required to estimate a model of order $j - 2$, but more time-points may be required to optimally estimate a model of this order (Hertzog, Lindenberger, Ghisletta, & von Oertzen, 2006; MacCallum et al., 1997). Note that this argument is also applied to the case where individuals are measured at a different set of time-points (random time). One still needs at least j measures *in the sample* to estimate a trajectory with $j - 2$ orders, although each individual does not have to be measured for j time-points. For example, one still need at least four measures to estimate a quadratic trajectory. However, some participants may only have data for the first three time-points and some might only have data for the last three time-points.

Moreover, adding higher order terms may not improve the model fit substantially. Thus, choosing a suitable order of polynomial growth is not simply a matter of how high an order can be estimated given the number of occasions. Singer and Willett (2003) provided some useful practical suggestions on this issue.

Nonlinear Growth Curve Models

Let's now turn to nonlinear GCMs. A general form for nonlinear GCMs can be found in Equation 10 (Neter, Kutner, Nachtsheim, & Wasserman, 1996). To save space, we will only present the level-1 (within-individual) equation for the GCMs described below. Similar to the level-2 models for the linear and quadratic GCMs, the level-2 models for the other GCMs contain equations for each of the random parameters (parameters varying across individuals) in the level-1 models.

$$y_{ij} = f(t_{ij}, \boldsymbol{\alpha}, \boldsymbol{\beta}_i) + e_{ij}, \quad (10)$$

where $\boldsymbol{\beta}_i$ represents the growth parameter(s) for individual i (e.g., the intercept and change rate), and $\boldsymbol{\alpha}_i$ represents the asymptote(s) for individual i. The reason an asymptote term is included in the general form is that empirically most forms of nonlinear growth have at least one asymptote (lower, upper, or both). For example, a learning trajectory is always increasing but approaches a plateau or asymptote. Assuming sufficient data, the asymptote(s) can be also treated as random and allowed to vary across individuals, which is why there is an associated subscript *i associated with the asymptote(s)*. That is, each individual can have his/her own plateau.

There are a wide variety of nonlinear functional forms (Cudeck & du Toit, 2003; Davidian & Giltinan, 1995; Pinheiro & Bates, 2000; Singer & Willett, 2003). Based on the shape of the trajectories and whether there is an asymptote, we next describe some typical nonlinear functional forms in three categories: monotonically changing without asymptote, monotonically changing with asymptote(s), and S-shaped with asymptotes. Here monotonically changing has nothing to do with the outcome variable but instantaneous linear slope (first derivative). Monotonically increasing or decreasing means that the instantaneous linear slope always increases or decreases over time.

Monotonically Changing without Asymptote. A common functional form used to capture a monotonically changing trajectory without an asymptote is the exponential growth model (*see* Equation 11). For this model, the increase in y_{ij} at any point depends on the current size of y_{ij} at that point. Otherwise stated, the larger the value of y_{ij}, the greater the increase in y_{ij} (instantaneous growth rate) at that point (Seber & Wild, 2003; Singer & Willett, 2003).

$$y_{ij} = \beta_{0i} \exp(\beta_{1i} t_{ij}) \qquad (11)$$

where β_{0i} and β_{1i} are growth parameters that determine the shape of the curve. β_{0i} denotes the initial status of the response variable for individual i when time is 0, thus it serves as an intercept parameter. β_{1i} is the change rate in the curve and thus serves as a slope parameter. As time increases 1 unit, y_{ij} changes exponentially with an exponent of β_{1i}. In other words, y_{ij} would be multiplied by $\exp(\beta_{1i})$. There is no asymptote in this model, thus the model represents unlimited increasing growth. Figure 18.1(C) displays an exponential curve with $\beta_{0i} = 0.5$ and $\beta_{1i} = 0.2$.

Monotonically Changing with Asymptote. Two nonlinear functions are introduced in this category: Rectangular hyperbolic (Equation 12) and negative exponential GCMs (Equation 13). In the hyperbolic growth model, the change in y_{ij} at any point is inversely related to the distance of y_{ij} from the upper asymptote α_{1i} (Cohen et al., 2003). Note that time cannot be 0 in Equation 12. As time approaches 0, y_{ij} would approach negative or positive infinity depending on the sign of β_{1i}. β_{1i} determines how fast the trajectory approaches the asymptote (α_{1i}). The growth trajectory approaches the asymptote faster as β_{1i} is smaller. See Figures 18.1(D) for an example of rectangular hyperbolic growth trajectory.

$$y_{ij} = \alpha_{1i} - 1/(\beta_{1i} t_{ij}) + e_{ij} \qquad (12)$$

The negative exponential growth model (*see* Equation 13) has a lower (α_{1i}) and an upper asymptote (α_{2i}). Similarly, β_{1i} determines how fast the trajectory approaches the upper asymptote (α_{2i}). As β_{1i} increases, y_{ij} approaches the upper asymptote more quickly. See Figure 18.1(E) for an example of a negative exponential growth trajectory.

$$y_{ij} = \alpha_{1i} - (\alpha_{2i} - \alpha_{1i})[\exp(-\beta_{1i} t_{ij}) - 1] + e \qquad (13)$$

S-Shaped (Sigmoid) Growth Model. In the previous nonlinear model, the instantaneous change rate increased or decreased monotonically (i.e., change consistently and systematically). S-shaped growth does not have this property. The instantaneous growth rate increases first and then decreases. Thus, there is a point of inflection (surge point) in the growth curve at which the growth rate is at its maximum (Choi, Harring, & Hancock, 2009; Serroyen, Molenberghs, Verbeke, & Davidian, 2009). Here, we introduced two S-shaped GCMs with lower and upper asymptotes: the logistic and Gompertz growth models (Cudeck & du Toit, 2003; Grimm & Ram, 2009; Seber & Wild, 2003; Singer & Willett, 2003). The functional forms for the two change trajectories are shown in Equations 14 and 15, respectively. *See also* Figures 18.1(F) and 18.1(G) for examples of logistic and Gompertz trajectories. The difference between the two trajectories is that the logistic is a symmetric curve but the Gompertz is not.

$$y_{ij} = \alpha_{1i} + \frac{(\alpha_{2i} - \alpha_{1i})}{1 + \beta_{0i} \exp(-\beta_{1i} t_{ij})} + e_{ij} \qquad (14)$$

$$y_{ij} = \alpha_{1i} + (\alpha_{2i} - \alpha_{1i}) \exp(-\beta_{0i} \\ \times \exp(-\beta_{1i} t_{ij})) + e_{ij} \qquad (15)$$

Four parameters are to be estimated in both functional forms: the intercept (β_{0i}), a slope term (β_{1i}), as well as the lower (α_{1i}) and upper asymptotes (α_{2i}). The intercept term determines the initial status of the outcome variable. The slope term determines how fast an individual will grow from the lower to the upper asymptote. One can use the estimated β_{0i} and the asymptotes to calculate the point of inflection. In the logistic curve, y_{ij} is equal to a value halfway between the lower and upper asymptote, $(\alpha_{2i} + \alpha_{1i})/2$, at the inflection point of time, at which the maximum growth rate is $\beta_{1i} \alpha_{2i}/4$. In comparison, in the Gompertz growth model, y_{ij} is equal to $[\alpha_{2i} + (e - 1)\alpha_{1i}]/e$ at the inflection point, at which the maximum growth rate is $\beta_{1i} \alpha_{2i}/e$.

One can reparameterize the function so that the maximum growth rate at the point of inflection can be captured by a parameter in the function. For example, one can rewrite the logistic function as Equation 16 and the Gompertz function as Equation 17 (*see* Grimm & Ram, 2009). In the reparameterized equation, there are still four parameters to be estimated. However, rather than estimating the intercept term, the maximum change rate at the point of inflection is estimated and is represented by λ_{1i}. One benefit of doing this is that one can directly test for the significance of λ_{1i}. In addition, reparameterization is also a way to improve convergence during model estimation.

$$y_{ij} = \alpha_{1i} + \frac{\alpha_{2i} - \alpha_{1i}}{1 - \exp(-\beta_{1i}(t_{it} - \lambda_{1i}))} + e_{ij} \quad (16)$$

$$y_{ij} = \alpha_{1i} + (\alpha_{2i} - \alpha_{1i})\exp(-\exp(-\beta_{1i}(t_{it} - \lambda_{1i}))) + e_{ij} \quad (17)$$

Spline Curve Models

All the GCMs described above assume that the change trend during the duration of a study follows one systematic form. If there are qualitatively distinct periods of growth—for example, before and after an intervention or during different Piagetian developmental stages—it can be optimal to divide the growth curve into several pieces representing each of the distinct periods (Li, Duncan, Duncan, & Hops, 2001; Singer & Willett, 2003). Different growth curves can be fit to each of these pieces simultaneously. This type of model is often called a spline or piecewise model. Equation 18 shows the simplest spline model: a two-piece linear curve model which contains two segments with linear change in each segment; *see* Figure 18.1(H) for an example of two-piece linear spline model.

$$y_{ij} = \beta_{0i} + \beta_{1i}t_{1ij} + \beta_{2i}t_{2ij} + e_{ij} \quad (18)$$

where t_{1ij} represents the time-related variable coded for the first piece. t_{2ij} represents the time-related variable coded for the second piece. There are different coding schemes for the time-related variables. These coding schemes do not change the estimated curve but do change the interpretation of particular growth parameters in the model. Table 18.1 shows two coding schemes for a two-piece linear GCM with the transition point at the third measurement occasion. Each coding scheme is designed for different research questions and hypothesis tests.

The first coding scheme allows us to test the difference in slopes between the two pieces. With the first coding scheme, β_{0i} represents the initial status of the outcome variable at the first measurement occasion, β_{1i} represents the slope for the first piece, and β_{2i} represents the change in slope from piece 1 to piece 2. The second coding scheme allows us to test the slopes at each of the two pieces. The second coding scheme differs from the first coding scheme in only the coding of t_{1ij}. The interpretation of β_{0i} and β_{1i} remain the same. However, β_{2i} now represents the exact slope for piece 2 rather than the difference in slopes between the two pieces. Note that the zero-point in t_{1ij} always indicates the point where time is centered, and the last zero-point in

Table 18.1. Two Coding Schemes for a Two-Piece Linear Model with Five Time-Points

Time	1	2	3	4	5
Coding Scheme 1					
t_{1ij}	0	0	1	2	3
t_{2ij}	0	0	0	1	2
Coding Scheme 2					
t_{1ij}	0	1	2	2	2
t_{2ij}	0	0	0	1	2

t_{1ij} indicates the point of transition. In our example above, time is centered at occasion 1.

In fact, more complex form of growth can be fit to each piece as long as there are sufficient time-points. In addition, the two-piece model can be readily extended to more pieces (Flora, 2008). As an example, to fit a quadratic growth curve to the second piece, one needs only to add a quadratic term of time (t_{2ij}) to the previous model, as shown in Equation 19 (Flora, 2008).

$$y_{ij} = \beta_{0i} + \beta_{1i}t_{1ij} + \beta_{2i}t_{2ij} + \beta_{3i}t_{2ij}^2 + e_{ij} \quad (19)$$

where β_{0i} and β_{1i} retain the same meaning as those of the previous two-piece linear model; however, the interpretation of β_{2i} changes. For coding scheme 1, β_{2i} represents the difference in instantaneous growth rate at the transition point between two pieces. For the coding scheme 2, β_{2i} would represent the *instantaneous* growth rate at the transition point for piece 2. For both coding schemes, β_{3i} represents the quadratic growth rate or rate of change in *instantaneous* growth rate for piece 2.

Applications of the spline curve model can be found in many literatures (Chassin, Presson, Rose, & Sherman, 2001; Chou, Yang, Pentz, & Hser, 2004; Cudeck & Klebe, 2002; Fergus, Zimmerman, & Caldwell, 2007; Wu, West, & Hughes, 2008. Chassin and her colleagues (2001) examined age-related changes in health-relevant beliefs from the middle school years through age 37 years in a large, Midwestern, community sample. They split the age range into five age periods and found that beliefs about the personalized risks of smoking declined and then increased. Beliefs about generalized health risks increased beginning in the middle school years, and the value placed on health as an outcome decreased in the high school years and then increased.

Error Structures

The models presented above assume constant within-individual residual variances over time (the diagonal elements in the **R**-matrix are the same). In addition, there is no correlation among the residuals (the off-diagonal elements are all 0s). In real-world data, the error structure is rarely this simple. For example, some leftover correlations among the residuals that are not accounted for by the fitted growth trajectories often occur. Also the error variances may vary across time. For this reason, researchers have proposed many alternative error structures. Here we present some of them including the compound symmetry (CS), first-order autoregressive structure (AR1), the first-order moving average structure (MA1), the autoregressive moving average structure (ARMA(1,1)), and the Toeplitz autocorrelation structure. Those error structures are briefly described below.

In the CS structure, both the covariances and variances are constant across repeated measures. In the AR1 structure, the variance of the errors is constant across time and the correlations are the same with the same time lag. In the MA1 structure, the error at a time-point is equal to the disturbances at that time-point plus a correlated part of the disturbance. ARMA(1,1) is a combination of AR1 and MA1 structures, in which the errors are a function of the errors of the just-previous time and the disturbances of the previous time. The Toeplitz error structure assumes that any pairs of errors that are equally separated in time have the same correlation. In some cases, the correlation between pairs of errors might decay to 0 beyond certain intervals. This kind of pattern is called a banded pattern. The interval beyond which the correlations are banded shows the band size. For example, TOEP(2) below is a banded Toeplitz structure with correlation between pairs of errors beyond two intervals fixed at 0. The number given in the parenthesis is the band size.

$$CS = \sigma^2 \begin{bmatrix} 1 & \rho & \rho & \rho \\ \rho & 1 & \rho & \rho \\ \rho & \rho & 1 & \rho \\ \rho & \rho & \rho & 1 \end{bmatrix}$$

where ρ is the constant correlation and σ^2 is the constant variance across repeated measures.

$$AR(1) = \sigma^2 \begin{bmatrix} 1 & \rho & \rho^2 & \rho^3 \\ \rho & 1 & \rho & \rho^2 \\ \rho^2 & \rho & 1 & \rho \\ \rho^3 & \rho^2 & \rho & 1 \end{bmatrix},$$

$$ARMA(1,1) = \sigma^2 \begin{bmatrix} 1 & \gamma & \gamma\rho & \gamma\rho^2 \\ \gamma & 1 & \gamma & \gamma\rho \\ \gamma\rho & \gamma & 1 & \gamma \\ \gamma\rho^2 & \gamma\rho & \gamma & 1 \end{bmatrix}$$

where γ is the moving average coefficient. ρ is the autoregressive coefficient.

$$TOEP = \sigma^2 \begin{bmatrix} 1 & \rho_1 & \rho_2 & \rho_3 \\ \rho_1 & 1 & \rho_1 & \rho_2 \\ \rho_2 & \rho_1 & 1 & \rho_1 \\ \rho_3 & \rho_2 & \rho_1 & 1 \end{bmatrix}$$

$$TOEP(2) = \sigma^2 \begin{bmatrix} 1 & \rho_1 & 0 & 0 \\ \rho_1 & 1 & \rho_1 & 0 \\ 0 & \rho_1 & 1 & \rho_1 \\ 0 & 0 & \rho_1 & 1 \end{bmatrix}$$

where ρ_1, ρ_2, and ρ_3 are the correlations between errors with 1, 2, and 3 intervals (lags), respectively.

Selection of an appropriate error structure is important for accurate statistical inference (Grimm & Widaman, 2010; Kwok, West, & Green, 2007; Sivo, Fan, & Witta, 2005). Kwok et al. (2007) found that over-misspecification (freeing too many elements in the matrix) of the error structure leads to underestimated standard errors, and thus inflated type I error. In contrast, under-misspecification (constraining too many elements in the matrix) of the error structure leads to overestimated standard errors and thus reduced statistic power. Kwok et al. (2007) recommended using both substantive and statistical theory to specify the optimal error structure.

Time-Constant and Time-Varying Covariates

Time-Constant Covariates. As described above, longitudinal data analysis allows the examination of individual differences in the trajectory of an outcome variable, which is captured by the variances in the growth parameters that determine the shape of a change trajectory (e.g., variance in intercept and slope). If there is substantial individual variability, the next issue to address is whether some covariates can explain such individual differences. Time-constant covariates vary across individuals but are constant across time (e.g., gender or treatment). A time-constant covariate is added in the between-individual level (level 2) to predict individual growth parameters. Equation 20 shows how to incorporate a time-constant covariate Z in a linear curve model.

Level 1: $y_{ij} = \beta_{0i} + \beta_{1i}t_{ij}, \varepsilon_{ij} \sim N(0, \sigma^2)$,

Level 2: $\beta_{0i} = \gamma_{00} + \gamma_{01}z_i + u_{0i}$

$\beta_{1i} = \gamma_{10} + \gamma_{11}z_i + u_{1i}$

$$\begin{bmatrix} u_{oi} \\ u_{1i} \end{bmatrix} \sim MVN\left(\begin{bmatrix} 0 \\ 0 \end{bmatrix}, G = \begin{bmatrix} \tau_{00} & \\ \tau_{10} & \tau_{11} \end{bmatrix}\right) \quad (20)$$

where γ_{01} and γ_{11} represent the effect of the time-constant covariate Z on the individual-specific intercept and slope. γ_{00} and γ_{10} now represent the population average intercept and slope at $Z = 0$. Note that one can *center* Z to change the interpretation of γ_{00} and γ_{10}. As the covariate Z is introduced into the level 2 equations, u_{0i} and u_{1i} now represent the residuals in intercept and slope that cannot be accounted for by Z.

Time-Varying Covariates. In addition to time-constant covariates, there are covariates that are changing across time. Those covariates are called time-varying covariates which might also predict change in an outcome variable in addition to the index of time and any time-invariant variable. A time-varying covariate is added in the within-individual level (level 1) to predict change in individual responses (*see* Equation 21). For example, Grimm (2007) examined depression as a time-varying covariate for change in achievement over years. Including time-varying covariates allows researchers to ask a variety of questions, such as (1) how is a time-varying covariate X related to an outcome Y while controlling for individual change in Y (e.g., what is the effect of depression on achievement when the individual change in achievement is controlled?)?; and (2) how does Y change over time controlling for the time-varying covariate (e.g., what is the change in achievement controlling for depression level at each time point?)? Equation 21 shows how to add a time-varying covariate (X) in a linear GCM.

Level 1: $y_{ij} = \beta_{0i} + \beta_{1i}t_{ij} + \beta_2 x_{ij} + e_{ij}, \varepsilon_{ij}$

$\sim N(0, \sigma^2)$,

Level 2: $\beta_{0i} = \gamma_{00} + u_{0i}$

$\beta_{1i} = \gamma_{10} + u_{1i}$

$$\begin{bmatrix} u_{oi} \\ u_{1i} \end{bmatrix} \sim MVN\left(\begin{bmatrix} 0 \\ 0 \end{bmatrix}, G = \begin{bmatrix} \tau_{00} & \\ \tau_{10} & \tau_{11} \end{bmatrix}\right) \quad (21)$$

The subscript *ij* associated with X indicates that X varies across time and individuals. β_{0i} now represents the expected outcome for individual i at both $t_{ij} = 0$ and $X = 0$. Note that *centering time and X* can change the interpretation of β_{0i}. β_{1i} represents the time effect (slope) for individual i with X partialled out. β_2 represents the effect of the time-varying covariate X with the time effect partialled out. Note that there is no i subscript with β_2 because the effect of the time-varying covariate (X) is assumed to be constant (fixed) across individuals. This assumption may be relaxed by adding a random effect associated with the effect of the time-varying covariate. In addition, the effect of the time-varying covariate is often assumed constant over time, which can be easily relaxed in the SEM but not in the MLM framework. e_{ij} now represents the residuals in the outcome variable that cannot be accounted for by either time or X.

Structural Equation Modeling Approaches to Longitudinal Data Analysis

Structural equation modeling is a comprehensive statistical technique used to test hypotheses about relations among observed and latent variables (Bollen, 1989; Hoyle, 1995). Structural equation modeling is an extension of the general and generalized linear model. One well-known advantage of SEM is its ability to model *latent* structure: Measurement errors associated with manifest variables can be removed permitting the relations between latent variables to be accurately estimated. Meredith and Tisak (1990) showed that SEM can be used for growth curve modeling if we treat the growth parameters as latent variables and repeated measures as multiple indicators of the latent variables. These types of SEMs has been called latent curve models (LCMs). At its core, a LCM is a MLM for change. Mapping of the MLM for change onto the general mean and covariance structure model provides an alternative approach to model specification and estimation. Moreover, the flexibility of SEM can dramatically extend the analytic possibilities (*see* a later discussion of the advantages and disadvantages of MLM and SEM in modeling change). As a result, a wider variety of longitudinal models can be estimated as SEMs.

Linear Latent Curve Model

A linear GCM can be readily mapped onto a SEM. Figure 18.3 shows a linear LCM, which is identical to the linear model shown in Equation 1. As shown in Figure 18.3, the random intercept and slope are treated as latent variables which are indicated by the repeated measures. The means of the latent variables represent the population mean

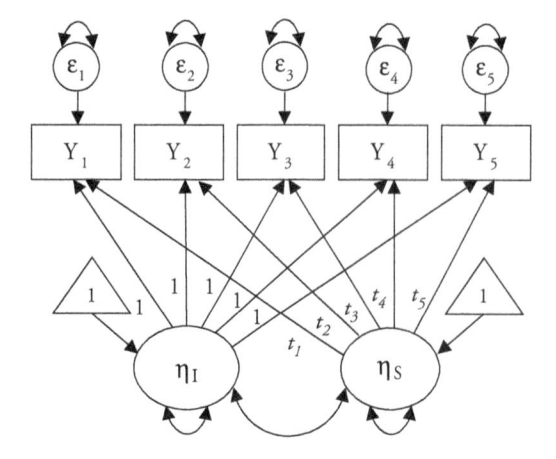

Figure 18.3 Linear LCM
Note: Y_1–Y_5 are repeated measures of the outcome variable. t_1–t_5 are times at each of the measurement occasions. e_1–e_5 are within-individual residuals at each of the measurement occasions that cannot be explained by time or the linear trajectory. η_I and η_S are latent intercept and slope, respectively. The triangles with arrows pointing to the latent intercept and slope indicate that means of the two latent variables are also estimated in the model. A double-headed arrow shows that the variance of a latent variable is estimated.

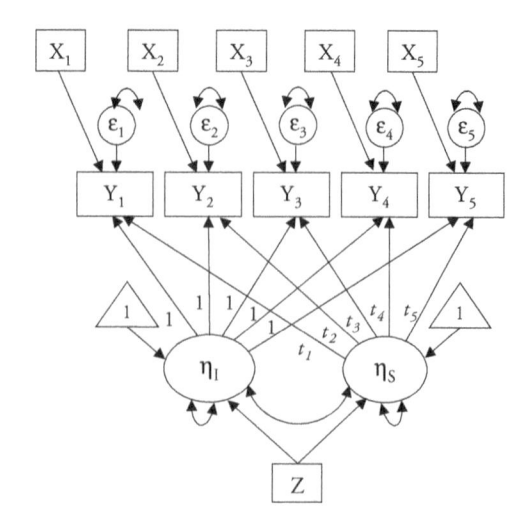

Figure 18.4 Linear latent curve model with time-varying and time-constant covariates.
Note: Z is a time-constant covariate. X_1–X_5 are repeated measures of a time-varying covariate. e_1–e_5 are within-individual residuals at each of the measurement occasions. η_I and η_S are latent intercept and slope, respectively. The triangles with arrows pointing to the latent intercept and slop indicate that intercepts of the intercept and slope on Z are estimated in the model. The double-headed arrows associated with η_I and η_S represent that the residual variances of η_I and η_S that cannot be explained by Z.

intercept and slope, and the variances of the latent variables quantify the interindividual differences in the intercept and slope. The loadings associated with the intercept are all fixed at 1, and the loadings associated with the slope are fixed at the time of each measurement occasion ($t_1, t_2, t_3, t_4,$ and t_5 in Fig. 18.3).

Model Implied Mean and Covariance Matrix. The mathematical expression of the linear LCM is shown below. Note that standard SEM notation is followed in the forthcoming equations.

$$\begin{bmatrix} Y_1 \\ Y_2 \\ \vdots \\ Y_t \end{bmatrix} = \begin{bmatrix} 1 & t_1 \\ 1 & t_2 \\ 1 & \vdots \\ 1 & t_t \end{bmatrix}$$

$$\times \begin{bmatrix} \eta_{\text{intercept}} \\ \eta_{\text{slope}} \end{bmatrix} + \begin{bmatrix} \varepsilon_1 \\ \varepsilon_2 \\ \vdots \\ \varepsilon_t \end{bmatrix}$$

$$y = \Lambda_y \times \eta + \varepsilon,$$

$$E(\eta) = \alpha, \quad E(\varepsilon) = 0, \quad \text{COV}(\eta, \eta') = \Phi,$$

$$\text{COV}(\varepsilon, \varepsilon') = \Theta_\varepsilon \text{ and COV}(\eta, \varepsilon) = 0. \quad (22)$$

Here y is a vector of t waves of repeated measures, Λ is a $t \times 2$ factor loading matrix, η is a vector of latent variables (growth parameters), and ε is a vector of unique factors (corresponding to level-residuals in MLM). Latent variable means are contained in the vector α, Φ is a 2×2 matrix of covariances among latent variables, and Θ_ε is a $t \times t$ matrix of residual covariances. These matrices combine to obtain the model implied mean and covariance matrix:

$$E(Y) = \Lambda\alpha,$$
$$\text{COV}(Y, Y') = \Lambda\Phi\Lambda' + \Theta_\varepsilon. \quad (23)$$

It is also easy to incorporate time-constant and time-varying covariates in the SEM framework. Figure 18.4 displays a linear LCM with both a time-varying covariate (X) and a time-constant covariate (Z). In Figure 18.4, the latent intercept and slope are predicted by Z. $X_1 - X_5$ are repeated measures of the time-varying covariate at each of the five time-points. The arrows pointing from $X_1 - X_5$ to $Y_1 - Y_5$ suggest that the individual differences in Y are not only affected by time but also by X at each time-point. The effect of X on Y can be either constant or different across time. To allow the effect of X on Y to vary across time, one just needs to freely estimate the path coefficients from X to Y.

Curvilinear Latent Curve Model

Similarly, the curvilinear GCM can be easily estimated as a SEM by treating the random intercept,

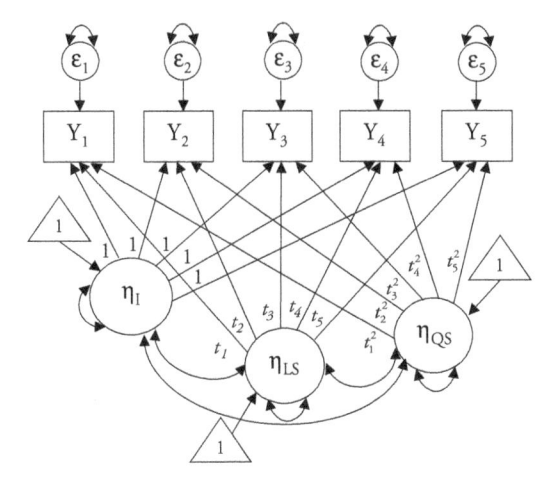

Figure 18.5 Quadratic LCM.
Note: I = intercept; LS = linear slope; QS = quadratic rate.

linear rate of change, and quadratic rate of change as latent variables (*see* Equation 24 for the matrix expression and Fig. 18.5 for the path diagram for a quadratic LCM with five time-points). The loadings associated with the latent intercept and linear rate of change are the same as those in the linear model. The loadings associated with the quadratic rate are fixed at the square of time for each measurement occasion ($t_1^2, t_2^2, t_3^2, t_4^2,$ and t_5^2 in Fig. 18.5), but other fixed codings can be used (e.g., orthogonal contrast codes).

$$\begin{bmatrix} Y_1 \\ Y_2 \\ Y_3 \\ Y_4 \\ Y_5 \end{bmatrix} = \begin{bmatrix} 1 & t_1 & t_1^2 \\ 1 & t_2 & t_2^2 \\ 1 & t_3 & t_3^2 \\ 1 & t_4 & t_4^2 \\ 1 & t_5 & t_5^2 \end{bmatrix} \times \begin{bmatrix} \eta_{\text{intercept}} \\ \eta_{\text{linear}} \\ \eta_{\text{quad}} \end{bmatrix} + \begin{bmatrix} \varepsilon_1 \\ \varepsilon_2 \\ \varepsilon_3 \\ \varepsilon_4 \\ \varepsilon_5 \end{bmatrix}$$
(24)

Nonlinear Latent Curve Model

Although linear and curvilinear GCMs can be easily translated to SEMs, mapping nonlinear GCMs onto SEMs is not a simple task. The reason is that SEM is intrinsically a framework for estimating linear equations. When the nonlinear function cannot be transformed to a linear combination of variables, it creates challenges for SEM to accommodate those nonlinear functions. Three approaches have been developed to estimate nonlinear trajectories in SEM: (1) the structured LCM (Browne, 1993); (2) the hybrid LCM (Cudeck, 1996; du Toit & Cudeck, 2001); and (3) the level and shape model (or fully latent model; Meredith & Tisak, 1990).

Structured Latent Curve Model. Structured latent curve models (SLCMs) use a first-order Taylor series to approximate a nonlinear trajectory as a polynomial function that can be easily handled by SEM (*see* Equation 25; Browne, 1993). The SEM estimates the approximate nonlinear trajectory by placing nonlinear constraints on the factor loadings. Different from the linear or curvilinear GCMs in which factor loadings are fixed at time or a function of time, SLCMs specify the factor loadings as first derivatives of a nonlinear function with respect to the parameters in the function. Those first derivatives are often referred to as basis functions. SLCMs allow both the fixed and random effects of the parameters in the function to be estimated.

$$Y = f(\theta, t) + \eta_1 f_1'(\theta, t) + \eta_2 f_2'(\theta, t) + \cdots + \eta_j f_j'(\theta, t),$$

$$f_j'(\theta, t) = \frac{\delta f(\theta, T)}{\delta \theta_j},$$
(25)

where $f(\theta, t)$ is a nonlinear function of time (t) with θ as growth parameters to be estimated. $f_j'(\theta, t)$ is the first derivative of the nonlinear function with respect to the jth parameter (θ_j). For example, $f_1'(\theta, t)$ is the first derivative of the nonlinear function with respect to the first parameter (θ'_1).

Let's use the exponential function in Equation 11 as an illustration. To follow the SEM notation tradition, we replaced β in Equation 11 by η ($y_{ij} = \eta_{0i} \exp(\eta_{1i} t_{ij}) + e_{ij}$). The function contains two parameters: intercept and slope (η_0 and η_1). To fit the model as a SLCM, the factor loadings associated with η_0 are fixed as the first derivative with respect to η ($\frac{\partial y_{ij}}{\partial \eta_{0i}} = \exp(\mu_{\eta_1} t_{ij})$; here, μ_{η_1} is the estimated mean of η_1). The factor loadings associated with the second parameter (η_1) are fixed as the first derivative of the nonlinear function with respect to η ($\frac{\partial y_{ij}}{\partial \eta_{1i}} = \mu_{\eta_0 i} \exp(\mu_{\eta_1 i} t_{ij}) t_{ij}$, where μ_{η_0} is the estimated mean of η_0). Equation 26 shows the matrix equation for the SLCM for the exponential curve model.

$$\begin{bmatrix} Y_1 \\ Y_2 \\ Y_3 \\ Y_4 \\ Y_5 \end{bmatrix} = \begin{bmatrix} \exp(\mu_{\eta_1} t_1) & \mu_{\eta_0} \exp(\mu_{\eta_1} t_1) t_1 \\ \exp(\mu_{\eta_1} t_2) & \mu_{\eta_0} \exp(\mu_{\eta_1} t_2) t_2 \\ \exp(\mu_{\eta_1} t_3) & \mu_{\eta_0} \exp(\mu_{\eta_1} t_3) t_3 \\ \exp(\mu_{\eta_1} t_4) & \mu_{\eta_0} \exp(\mu_{\eta_1} t_4) t_4 \\ \exp(\mu_{\eta_1} t_5) & \mu_{\eta_0} \exp(\mu_{\eta_1} t_5) t_5 \end{bmatrix}$$

$$\times \begin{bmatrix} \eta_0 \\ \eta_1 \end{bmatrix} + \begin{bmatrix} \varepsilon_1 \\ \varepsilon_2 \\ \varepsilon_3 \\ \varepsilon_4 \\ \varepsilon_5 \end{bmatrix} \qquad (26)$$

Note that the fixed effect (mean) of η_1 is to be estimated through the factor loadings. As a result, one needs to fix the mean of the latent variable η_1 to be 0 to avoid redundancy of the parameter estimates (fixing the mean of η_1 also ensures that the model implied mean function is the mean of the trajectory; see Grimm, Ram, & Hamagami, 2011). The random effect (variance) of η_1 is estimated through the latent variable. One can also allow the covariance between the two growth parameters to be estimated. The specification of the model can also be seen in the path diagram in Figure 18.6(A).

Hybrid Latent Curve Model. Similarly to SLCMs, hybrid latent curve models (HLCMs) also use the first derivatives to specify the factor loadings. However, the hybrid model does not estimate the random effects for all of the growth parameters in a nonlinear function; rather, it only allows the parameters that enter the function linearly to vary across individuals. For example, in the exponential equation, η_0 enters the model linearly but η_1 enters the model nonlinearly (in the exponent); thus the hybrid model only allows η_0 but NOT η_1 to vary across individuals (see Equation 27 and Fig. 18.6(B)). To accomplish this, the HLCM only has η_0 as the latent variable for which the mean and variance are estimated. One can still estimate the fixed effect for η_1 through the factor loadings in the hybrid model.

$$\begin{bmatrix} Y_1 \\ Y_2 \\ Y_3 \\ Y_4 \\ Y_5 \end{bmatrix} = \begin{bmatrix} \exp(\mu_{\eta_1} t_1) \\ \exp(\mu_{\eta_1} t_2) \\ \exp(\mu_{\eta_1} t_3) \\ \exp(\mu_{\eta_1} t_4) \\ \exp(\mu_{\eta_1} t_5) \end{bmatrix} \times [\eta_0] + \begin{bmatrix} \varepsilon_1 \\ \varepsilon_2 \\ \varepsilon_3 \\ \varepsilon_4 \\ \varepsilon_5 \end{bmatrix}. \qquad (27)$$

Fully Latent Curve Model. Fully latent curve models (FLCMs) are often used to explore the shape of growth when a trajectory cannot be approximated using a well-defined function of time. The path diagram for a FLCM looks similar to a linear LCM. There are also two growth parameters (latent variables) in a FLCM that capture the level and shape of the curve, respectively. For this reason, a FLCM is also called a level and shape model (Meredith & Tisak, 1990). However, unlike linear LCMs in

(A) Structured exponential latent curve model

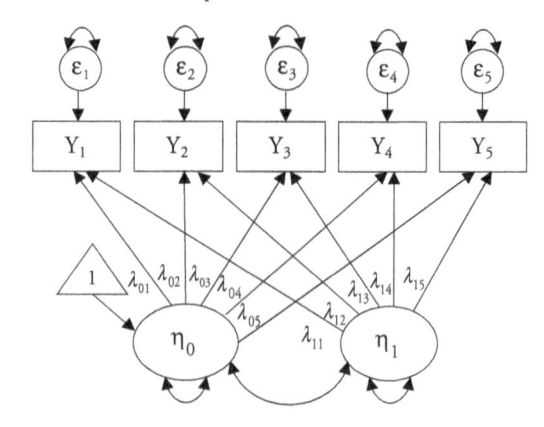

$$\Lambda = \begin{bmatrix} \lambda_{01} & \lambda_{11} \\ \lambda_{02} & \lambda_{12} \\ \lambda_{03} & \lambda_{13} \\ \lambda_{04} & \lambda_{14} \\ \lambda_{05} & \lambda_{15} \end{bmatrix} = \begin{bmatrix} \exp(\mu_{\eta_1} t_1) & \mu_{\eta_0} \exp(\mu_{\eta_1} t_1) t_1 \\ \exp(\mu_{\eta_1} t_2) & \mu_{\eta_0} \exp(\mu_{\eta_1} t_2) t_2 \\ \exp(\mu_{\eta_1} t_3) & \mu_{\eta_0} \exp(\mu_{\eta_1} t_3) t_3 \\ \exp(\mu_{\eta_1} t_4) & \mu_{\eta_0} \exp(\mu_{\eta_1} t_4) t_4 \\ \exp(\mu_{\eta_1} t_5) & \mu_{\eta_0} \exp(\mu_{\eta_1} t_5) t_5 \end{bmatrix}$$

(B) Hybrid exponential latent curve model

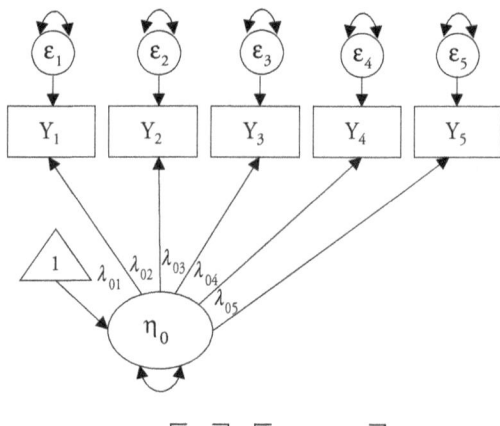

$$\Lambda = \begin{bmatrix} \lambda_{01} \\ \lambda_{02} \\ \lambda_{03} \\ \lambda_{04} \\ \lambda_{05} \end{bmatrix} = \begin{bmatrix} \exp(\mu_{\eta_1} t_1) \\ \exp(\mu_{\eta_1} t_2) \\ \exp(\mu_{\eta_1} t_3) \\ \exp(\mu_{\eta_1} t_4) \\ \exp(\mu_{\eta_1} t_5) \end{bmatrix}$$

Note. the λ_s are defined in the Λ matrix. μ_{η_0} = estimated mean η_0; μ_{η_1} = estimated

Figure 18.6 Exponential LCM.
(A) Structured exponential LCM (B) Hybrid exponential LCM
Note: the λ_s are defined in the Λ matrix. $\mu_{\eta 0}$ = estimated mean η_0; $\mu_{\eta 1}$ = estimated mean $\eta 1$

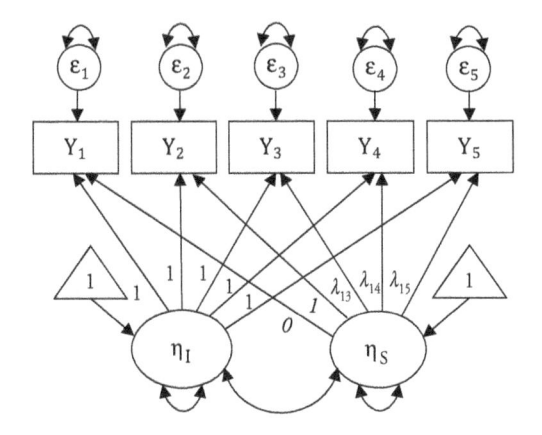

Figure 18.7 Fully LCM (level and shape model). *Note*: λ_{13}, λ_{14}, and λ_{15} are freely estimated.

which the factor loadings are defined as a specific function of time, FLCMs freely estimate those loadings. For the purpose of model identification and interpretation, the factor loading at the baseline is usually set at 0—that is, where the start of growth is assumed—and the factor loading at first follow-up is set at 1 as a reference for the scale of the slope factor (other scales are possible). The estimates of loadings of each follow-up, therefore, indicate the relative growth of each follow-up compared with that at the first follow-up (Chou, Bentler, & Pentz, 1998; Meredith & Tisak, 1990; Vandergrift, 2004).

Figure 18.7 displays a FLCM with five repeated measures. The first two factor loadings associated with the slope factor are fixed at 0 and 1, respectively. Thus, the latent slope captures the reference growth, which is the change from time 1 to time 2. The latent intercept still represents the initial status of the outcome at time 1. As can be seen in Figure 18.7, the loadings associated with the last three time-points are freely estimated. Suppose the estimates for the last three factor loadings are 0.8, 1.2, and 2, respectively. One would then conclude that the change from time 1 to time 3 is 80% of the amount of change from time 1 to time 2, the change from time 1 to time 4 is 1.2 times this amount, and the change from time 1 to time 5 is two times this amount. Although the latent slope only captures the change in a certain period, the changes in any other periods are all proportional to it. For this reason, the latent slope is also termed *generalized slope* in the FLCM. Note that one can assign 0 and 1 to any pair of factor loadings to change the reference for the scale change at a different period. For example, one might assign 0 and 1 to the loadings at time 1 and time 5. In this way, the latent slope would represent the total change between time 1 to time 5 and the estimated loadings would be estimated as a proportion of the total change.

Vandergrift (2004) compared structural latent, hybrid, and fully latent approaches to modeling a monomolecular nonlinear change curve (*see* Equation 28). He found that the fully latent model performed similarly to the hybrid latent model because of the fact that they both estimate the random effects of only two parameters (β_{0i} and β_{1i}). The SLCM outperformed the fully latent model and the hybrid latent model in terms of overall model fit to the data. All of the models fit the marginal means well; however, the FLCM better recovered the covariance matrix.

$$y_{ij} = \beta_{0i} - \beta_{1i}(\exp(-\beta_{2i}t_{ij}) - 1) + e_{ij} \qquad (28)$$

The models described thus far can be estimated in both the MLM and SEM frameworks. As mentioned above, the flexibility of SEM opens up more modeling possibilities. In the following, we will show a few longitudinal models that can be easily estimated in SEM but not in MLM, including autoregressive cross-lagged models (ARCL), latent difference models, parallel process LCMs, and second-order LCMs.

Autoregressive Cross-Lagged Models

The ARCL (Bollen & Curran, 2006; Jöreskog, 1970) model is alternatively referred to as a cross-lagged panel model or linear panel analysis model (Kessler & Greenberg, 1981). Use of this model has a long history tracing back many decades to the early applications of SEM (Heise, 1970; Duncan, 1969). In fact, because of its history, the ARCL can be considered the traditional longitudinal model. The equations for a two-variable (X and Y), two-occasion (T_1 and T_2) ARCL model can be written as follows. See Figure 18.8 for a path diagram of the

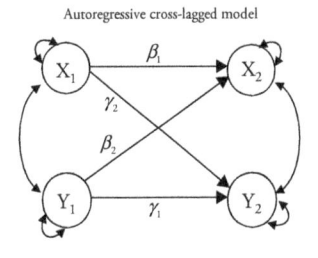

Figure 18.8 Autoregressive cross-lagged model.

ARCL model.

$$X_2 = \beta_0 + \beta_1 X_1 + \beta_2 Y_1 + \zeta,$$
$$Y_2 = \gamma_0 + \gamma_1 X_1 + \gamma_2 Y_1 + \zeta_Y, \qquad (29)$$

Here, β_0 and γ_0 are intercepts, or the expected value of X_2 and Y_2, respectively, when both X_1 and Y_1 are equal to 0. The coefficients β_1 and γ_1 represent autoregressive effects, or the effect of the variable at T_1 on the same variable at T_2. These coefficients are also referred to as stability coefficients in that the magnitude of the coefficient reflects stability in individual differences across time controlling for the influence of the other variable(s) in the model. The coefficients β_2 and γ_2 represent cross-lagged effects, or the effect of one variable at T_1 on another variable at T_2. These effects are often of interest when researchers examine the lagged effects of one variable on another or the reciprocal lagged effects for a pair of variables. After controlling for the level of the variable at the earlier occasion, the residual variance in Y_2 is the variance that cannot be accounted for by Y_1. Thus the cross-lagged effects predict residual change in relative standing on Y from T_1 to T_2. This is the reason that ARCL models are sometimes referred to as *residual change* models. ζ_X and ζ_Y represent residuals, or that part of X_2 and Y_2 that cannot be accounted for by the T_1 predictors. In typical applications, X_1 and Y_1 are correlated at T_1 and the residuals ζ_X and ζ_Y are correlated. The equations above describe a structural model. Measurement error can be addressed by using multiple indicators for both X and Y and modeling these as latent variables. Here, we emphasize the ARCL structural model because it is the same whether X and Y are measured or latent variables.

Different from the other models described in this chapter, ARCL models emphasize variability and change based on interindividual differences rather than aspects of intra-individual change trajectories. For example, a small stability coefficient, or AR effect, means that individuals' rank order on Y is changing from T_1 to T_2. A large cross-lagged (CL) effect means that individual standing on X_1 at Time 1 is related to individual standing on Y_2 at Time 2 (controlling for standing on Y_1 at Time 1). Autoregressive cross-lagged models do not incorporate time directly as many of the other models described in the chapter. Rather, effects are interpreted as occurring after a certain lag. Although it is not often considered, the use of an ARCL model assumes that a proper time lag has been chosen such that sufficient time has passed for a lagged predictor to have its effect on the outcome. The CL and AR effects from an ARCL model are specific to a particular time lag, and the use of a different time lag for the same analysis could substantially change the magnitude of the effects. Selig, Preacher, and Little (2009; in press) have provided an approach that incorporates time into the estimation of ARCL effects by treating time lags as moderator variables.

Autoregressive cross-lagged models may be attractive because they map well onto tests of specific theories. Stability coefficients can shed light on whether a variable appears to change over time and CL effects provide information about lagged predictive effects. Autoregressive cross-lagged models are also frequently used for tests of statistical mediation. Mediation is said to occur when a relationship between two variables can be explained by some intermediate variable. Three-variable longitudinal panel data can be used to test hypotheses about longitudinal mediation. Cole and Maxwell (2003) have provided a comprehensive review of the use of ARCL models for testing longitudinal mediation (*see also* Little, Card, Bovaird, Preacher, & Crandall, 2007).

Hawkley, Preacher, and Cacioppo (2010) used an ARCL model to examine the effects of loneliness and depressive symptoms on sleep duration and daytime dysfunction. The flexibility of the ARCL model is highlighted by this study because the lags between occasions were 1 day. The three occasions of the study were 3 consecutive days that participants completed a daily diary. Use of the ARCL model allowed Hawkley et al. (2010) to test time-specific hypotheses about whether feeling lonely or depressed one day predicted poor sleep the following day. In another ARCL application, Cillessen and Mayeux (2004) examined the "causal architecture" (p. 156) of social preference, popularity, and aggression. The authors used data from five occasions to model AR and CL effects among these variables to examine the casual effects of these variables on one another over time.

These types of question cannot be addressed with the various growth models we have described. The different models ask and answer different questions about change. For the most part, ARCL models address relative change and predictors of individual differences in those changes, whereas GCM models address questions about absolute changes (or absolute change functions) and predictors of the individual differences in these functions. Both types of model are useful and important to understand change processes inherent in a longitudinal study.

Latent Difference Score Models

The latent difference score (LDS) model is another testimony to the flexibility of SEM in modeling change (McArdle, 2009; McArdle & Hamagami, 2001). LDS can capture any nonlinear trajectories assuming that the change between two consecutive time-points ($Y_t - Y_{t-1}$) is a linear function of the previous state (Y_{t-1}) and given that the intervals between any pairs of adjoining points are equal and well established. Latent difference scores offer more flexibility and complexity in modeling dynamic change, such as additive change, proportional change, or both. It is also easy to add covariates in the LDS model or generalize the LDS model to more than one outcome variable (McArdle, 2001). Applications of the LDS model can be found in many areas of psychology (Finkel, Reynolds, McArdle, Hamagami, & Pedersen, 2009; Gerstorf, Hoppmann, Anstey, & Luszcz, 2009).

The use of difference scores has a long history. For longitudinal data, the difference score is found by computing, for each person, the difference between a variable at one occasion and the same variable at the previous occasion (thereby calculating the absolute difference for each person). These difference scores can then be used as a dependent measure to determine the predictors of individual change. Kessler and Greenberg (1981) and Stoolmiller and Bank (1995) have examined models for panel data in which the difference score (i.e., $Y_2 - Y_1$, or ΔY) is predicted by lagged covariates. The use of difference scores has been severely criticized (Cronbach & Furby, 1970; Lord, 1956) principally because difference scores can exhibit low levels of reliability; however, Rogosa (1995) has demonstrated that when there are sufficient individual differences in change over time, difference scores can show reasonable levels of reliability.

More recent uses of the difference score have employed LDS models (McArdle & Nesselroade, 1994; McArdle, 2001). LDS models do not directly compute difference scores prior to analysis but, rather, use a structural model with strategically fixed parameters to model the difference score as a latent variable. Figure 18.9 shows a diagram of a simple two-occasion difference score model. Y_1 and Y_2 are assumed to be latent variables with an underlying measurement model. This model has three estimated parameters: ψ_1 is the variance of Y at T_1; ψ_Δ represents variability in difference scores across individuals; and $\psi_{\Delta,1}$ is covariance between the initial level of Y and change in Y. In some models, this covariance is estimated as a regression path that

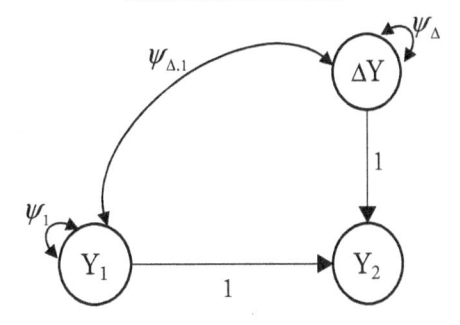

Figure 18.9 Latent difference score model.

serves to control for the aspect of change in Y that is related to initial levels of Y.

One advantage of the LDS model is that it focuses on within-person change similarly to the GCM. In fact, the LDS can be construed as a two-occasion linear curve model. In addition, the LDS is very flexible and can be used for multi-occasion data to model complex nonlinear trajectories. It does so in a fashion similar to the previously described piecewise model in which the various linear segments together depict a nonlinear trajectory. Finally, similarly to the ARCL model, a multivariate LDS model can be used to investigate lagged predictors of change. For example, Ferrer, McArdle, Shaywitz, Holahan, Marchione, and Shaywitz (2007) used a bivariate LDS model to examine the lagged relationships between reading and cognition. The same analysis also examined nonlinear trajectories for both of these constructs. Another similarity the LDS model shares with the ARCL model is the capacity to model mediation effects. In a LDS mediation model, it is possible to use individual level change in any or all of the three roles the variables play in a mediation model (MacKinnon, 2008; Selig & Preacher, 2009).

Parallel Process Latent Curve Model

Parallel process LCMs are used to model the relationship between changes in two or more outcome. The model that involves changes of two outcome variables is specifically called a bivariate LCM (McArdle, 1988; Grimm, 2007). Many questions can be answered using a bivariate LCM. For example, if two outcomes (X and Y) increased linearly across time, then there is an intercept and slope for each of the outcomes. One can ask: Does initial status (intercept) of X predict individual differences in the rate (slope) of change in Y? Is there a relationship between change in X and change in Y? In other words, is a faster increase in X associated with

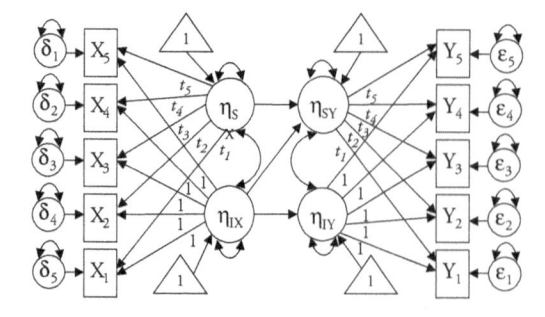

Figure 18.10 Parallel process LCM.
Note: η_{IX} and η_{SX} are latent intercept and slope for X; η_{IY} and η_{SY} are latent intercept and slope for Y. e_1–e_5 are within-individual residuals for X. d_1–d_5 are within-individual residuals for Y.

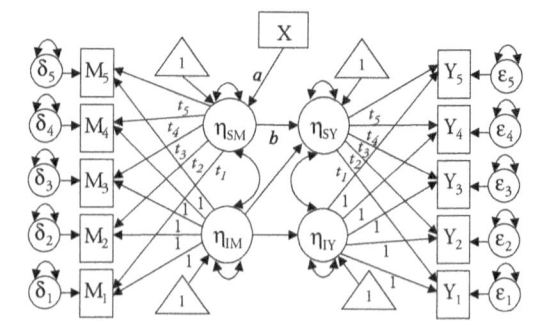

Figure 18.11 Parallel process LCM with mediation effect ($X \rightarrow$ Slope of $M \rightarrow$ Slope of Y).
Note: η_{IM} and η_{SM} are latent intercept and slope for the mediator; X is the predictor. η_{IY} and η_{SY} are latent intercept and slope for the outcome variable. a = the strength of the effect of X on the slope of M. b = the strength of the effect of M on the slope of Y.

a faster increase in Y or slower increase in Y? To answer these questions, simultaneous estimation of the longitudinal models for the outcome variables is required. Figure 18.10 displays a parallel process model for changes in X and Y where the intercept and slope of X predict the slope of Y. Applications of parallel process models can be found in many literatures. Curran, Stice, and Chassin (1997) examined the relationship between parallel trajectories of adolescent and peer alcohol use over 3 years. They found that both adolescent and peer alcohol use increased over time. There was a positive correlation between the slopes of the two outcomes. In other words, a faster increase in adolescent alcohol use was accompanied by a faster increase in peer alcohol use.

Parallel LCMs can be also used in examining longitudinal mediation effects (Cheong, MacKinnon, & Khoo, 2003; MacKinnon, 2008). Different than the ARCL mediation models which use a variable at a certain time-point as a mediator, a parallel LCM allows examination of how the effect of X on the change rate of Y is mediated by the initial status, or change rate of a mediator M, or both. Figure 18.11 shows a parallel model in which the slope of M mediates the effect of X on the change rate of Y. Cheong and colleagues (2003) used parallel LCM to evaluate the longitudinal effect of a prevention program developed to improve the nutrition behavior of high school football players. They found that the perceived importance of the team leader as an information source mediated the effect of the prevention program. The prevention program increased the rate of change for the mediator and consequently increased the rate of change for nutrition behavior across six waves (2 years) of measurements.

Second-Order Latent Curve Model

The models described above are all first-order LCMs in the sense that change was examined at the observed or manifest variable level. A major limitation of this type of model is that the measurement errors embedded in the observed variable can obscure the true change trajectory and the factorial invariance of the constructs is assumed rather than tested. A solution to the problem is to measure the construct at each wave using more than one variable (item) or from different perspectives (e.g., youths' antisocial behavior reported by youth, their parents, and their teachers; Patterson, 1993) and treat the construct as a latent variable and the items as indicators of the latent variable. Using the SEM framework, one can address measurement error by partitioning the observed variance into the variance shared by the items and that which is unique to each item (*see* Little, Preacher, Selig, & Card, 2007). The change trajectory of the latent variables is evaluated. Because the latent variable is not subject to measurement error, the change evaluated at the level of the latent variable reflects true change in the construct. Second-order LCMs usually contain two parts: a measurement model for the latent construct at each measurement occasion (first order) and the change model of the latent variables across the measurement occasions (second order) (Hancock, Kuo, & Lawrence, 2001; Leite, 2007; Meredith & Tisak, 1990). Figure 18.12 displays a second-order LCM with linear change on the latent variables.

The factorial invariance of the latent constructs has to be established before change in the construct can be modeled (Chan, 1998; Khoo, West, Wu, &

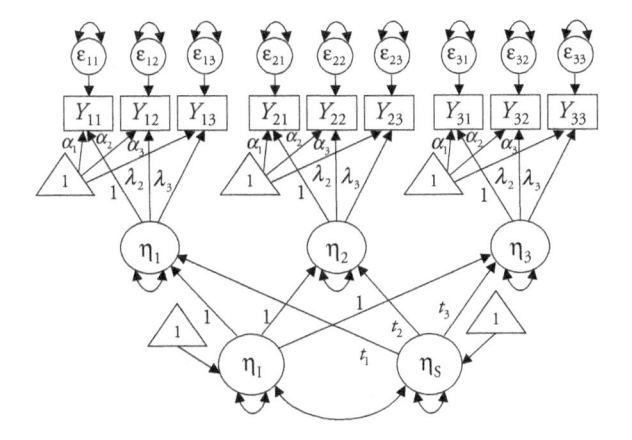

Figure 18.12 Second-order linear LCM.

Note: $\eta_1 - \eta_3$ are repeated (first-order) latent variables at each of the three measurement occasions. Each first-order latent variable is indicated by three observed variables (e.g., η_1 is indicated by $Y_{11} - Y_{13}$). η_I and η_S are latent intercept and slope for the change of the first-order latent variables across three time-points. This model presents a case where strong factorial invariance is satisfied: (1) the loadings of Y on η (1, λ_2, and λ_3) are equal across time, and (2) the intercepts on the observed variables (α_1, α_2, and α_3) are equal across time.

Kwok, 2005; Little, in press; Little, Card, Slegers, & Ledford, 2007). To make inferences that the same construct was measured at each time-point, at least strong factorial invariance (both the factor loadings and intercepts are constant across time) needs to be satisfied (Ferrer, Balluerka, & Widaman, 2008; Meredith, 1993; Meredith & Horn, 2001). Strong invariance ensures that the construct was measured in the same metric at each occasion, and the relationship among the latent variables are constant regardless of which observed variable was selected as the reference indicator of the latent structure. The steps to evaluate factorial invariance of latent structure can be found in Widaman, Ferrer, and Conger (2010).

Because second-order LCMs are often more complex than the first-order LCMs, larger sample sizes (usually > 200) are typically required to obtain stable parameter estimates of second-order LCMs. Also, it can be difficult to achieve adequate model fit given the complexity of the model (Leite, 2007).

An application of a second-order LCM can be found in Sayer and Cumsille (2001). The authors examined change in latent positive alcohol expectancy across five grades (5, 6, 7, 9, and 10). Latent positive alcohol expectancy was indicated by three items at each grade. Sayer and Cumsille (2001) fit a two-piece linear second-order growth model because they expected that change occurred in two discontinuous periods, with grade 7 as the transition point. On average positive expectancy increased from grade 5 to grade 10. However, the rate of change after grade 7 was faster than that before grade 7.

General Assumptions

In this chapter, we introduced both growth curve models and autoregressive models for continuous panel data. The basic assumptions for these models can be divided into two categories: distributional assumptions and independence assumptions.

Distributional Assumptions. Longitudinal models for continuous outcomes usually assume that the responses have an approximate multivariate normal distribution. However, departures from this assumption, unless they are very extreme (e.g., highly skewed response data), are not so critical for estimation when the data are complete or are missing at random. In addition, in GCMs, within-individual residuals and random effects are often assumed to be normally distributed. Both assumptions can be relaxed with more robust estimation methods (Verbeke & Molenberghs, 2000; Verbeke & Lesaffre, 1997).

Independence Assumptions. In all of the longitudinal models illustrated in the chapter, it is assumed that the observations are independent across individuals. That is, the repeated measures from one individual should provide no information on the repeated measures from another individual in the sample. If the independence assumption is violated, then the dependency needs to be taken into account in the estimation procedure. In the section of recent advances, we discussed available strategies to handle this kind of dependency. In addition, in GCMs, it is assumed that the level 2 random effects are uncorrelated with level 1 residuals. According to Satorra (1992), the independence assumption is more fundamental than the distributional assumption. Even when the distributional assumption is violated, if the independence assumption is met, then the test statistics will still have asymptotic robustness.

Conclusion and Discussion

The current chapter presents an overview of the MLM and SEM approaches to modeling change over time for continuous panel data. We have demonstrated how models with linear, curvilinear, nonlinear, and spline functional forms can be estimated in both frameworks. As Raudenbush (2001) described, the two frameworks reflect different aspects of the longitudinal model: "The model is multilevel because it describes data that vary at two levels: within individuals and between individuals. It is a latent curve model because the trajectory or curve is unobservable, depending on latent growth parameters" (p. 39). Thus, although the MLM and SEM approaches represent the growth model in different ways, they share the same basic rationale when modeling growth and yield similar results across a wide range of models, including linear and curvilinear models as well as some nonlinear models (Curran, 2003; Chou, Bentler, & Pentz, 1998; Maccallum, Kim, Malarkey, & Kiecolt-Glaser, 1997; Mehta & West, 2000; Muthen & Curran, 1997).

The two approaches have also unique advantages and limitations. SEM has a major advantage over MLM in modeling flexibility. As introduced in the chapter, SEM can estimate a GCM where loadings are estimated rather than fixed to a specified value (e.g., FLCM). SEM can also handle multiple indicators at each time-point so that the effect of measurement error can be eliminated (second-order LCM, MacCallum, et al., 1997; Meredith & Tisak, 1990; Muthen & Curran, 1997). Structural equation modeling can also model the relationships between growth parameters and other variables that can serve as either correlates, predictors, or consequences of those parameters. In contrast, MLM is very limited in representing such relationships: The covariates can be only included as predictors of growth parameters in MLM (MacCallum et al., 1997). In addition, SEM can easily parallel two or more trajectories in one model. Finally, SEM can provide tests of overall model fit including likelihood ratio test statistics, SRMR, and RMSEA, although the performance of those fit indices for longitudinal models awaits thorough study (Wu, West, & Taylor, 2009).

On the other hand, MLM allows for simpler model specification and is more efficient computationally in yielding results. This advantage may be important when there are unequal intervals between observations across individuals, distinct populations with different growth curves, or time-varying predictors with random effects (see Mehta & West, 2000). In addition, although both MLM and SEM can be used for nonlinear models, SEM is limited in modeling random effects of a parameter if the parameter is captured by a latent factor. Multilevel modeling is also better at incorporating additional levels of clustering (e.g., repeated measures on individuals clustered within groups; Muthen & Curran, 1997).

Some Advances

To date, there have been many advances in modeling change beyond the models illustrated in the chapter. The use of growth mixture modeling (GMM) is one such advance. For many of the phenomena examined with longitudinal models, it is clear that a single average trajectory is a limited means of describing the nuanced patterns of change over time. Growth mixture modeling addresses this issue and extends the random coefficients approach by assuming there may be subpopulations each with its own particular pattern of change over time (i.e., some of the participants might be more similar to each other than the others in their change over time). The goal of the GMM is to simultaneously determine the number of subpopulations and the form of growth within each group (Muthén, 2001; Muthén et al., 2002). Such information can be very useful. For example, people with different risks of substance use tend to have different patterns of change. Identifying the subgroups may help identify high risk groups and facilitate the application of targeted prevention programs (Muthén & Muthén, 2000). Growth mixture modeling can also allow researchers to examine the variables that predict group membership. The known characteristics of an individual may provide information about the probability of group membership. Given these capabilities, GMM has become an appealing method in the past decades with applications in many research areas. It should be noted, however, that the use of the GMM can be controversial in that it is possible—especially when models assumptions are violated—to find evidence for subpopulations when none exist (Bauer & Curran, 2003, 2004). Detailed discussion on GMM can be found in Masyn and Nylund-Gibson (Chapter 25, this volume) and Rupp (Chapter 24, this volume).

The aforementioned models apply to data with only two levels: repeated measures (within-individual) and individual (between-individual). In practice, there might be situations where more than two levels exist. For example, in educational settings, it is common to have students nested within classroom. If students are repeatedly measured over time, then three levels are to be addressed: repeated measures (within-student), student, and classroom. In this case, it is necessary to take into account the within-classroom correlation in the estimation procedure to obtain correct standard error estimates. This type of model with a higher level unit can be handled using a three-level multilevel model or a two-level structural equation model (Bovaird, 2007). Those models will partition the total covariance matrix of the repeated measures to those resulting from the multiple levels to take into account the clustering effect of the multiple levels on the standard error estimates.

Sometimes, a data set has a more complicated nested structure. For example, the lower level units (e.g., students) might be nested to more than one higher-level unit or share multiple memberships (e.g., classroom and neighborhood). In this case, the influence of both units needs to be addressed. Furthermore, higher level units might change over time (e.g., students are nested within different teachers over time). Cross-classified multilevel models or cross-random effects models need to be used to address those more complicated nesting structures (Goldstein, 1994; Hox & Kreft, 1994; Raudenbush, 1993).

Another advance we would like to draw attention to is integrative data analysis (IDA: Curran & Hussong, 2009; Hofer & Picinnin, 2009), which is not tied directly to a particular model for longitudinal data analysis but, rather, is a collection of techniques for analyzing data pooled from different studies. Pooling data from different studies offers the ability to address research questions involving periods that extend longer than a single study, with a much larger sample size than any one study, and incorporating the measures of more constructs than may be easily measured in a single study. Although there are several issues that must be addressed before the goals of IDA are achieved, especially those having to do with insuring measurement invariance across studies and establishing that samples from distinct studies can be considered as samples from the same target population, there is much to be gained from this approach. Using an IDA framework, Curran and Hussong (2009) have proposed an approach in which several studies could use a common set of items to make it possible to integrate data into a very large comprehensive body of information that would far exceed the information that could be collected in a single study.

Author Note

Partial support for this project was provided by grant NSF 1053160 (Wei Wu & Todd D. Little, co-PIs) and by the Center for Research Methods and Data Analysis at the University of Kansas (Todd D. Little, director). Correspondence: Wei Wu, University of Kansas (wwu@ku.edu); James P. Selig, University of New Mexico (selig@umn.edu); and Todd D. Little, University of Kansas (yhat@ku.edu). Web support: crmda.ku.edu.

References

Bauer, D. J., & Curran, P. J. (2003). Distributional assumptions of growth mixture models: Implications for overextraction of latent trajectory classes, *Psychological Methods, 8,* 338–363.

Bauer, D. J. & Curran, P. J. (2004). The integration of continuous and discrete latent variable models: Potential problems and promising opportunities. *Psychological Methods, 9,* 3–29.

Boker, S. M., & Graham, J. W. (1998). A dynamical systems analysis of adolescent substance use. *Multivariate Behavioral Research, 33,* 479–507.

Bollen, K. A. (1989). *Structural Equations with Latent Variables.* New York. Wiley.

Bollen, K. A. & Curran, P. J. (2006). *Latent curve models: A structural equation approach.* Hoboken, NJ: Wiley.

Bovaird, J. A. (2007). Multilevel structural equation models for contextual factors. In T. D. Little, J. A. Bovaird, & N. A. Card. *Modeling contextual effects in longitudinal studies* (pp. 149–182). Mahwah, NJ: Erlbaum.

Browne, M. W. (1993). Structured latent curve models. In C. M. Cuadras & C. R. Rao (Eds.), *Multivariate analysis: Future directions 2* (pp. 171–197). Amsterdam: Elsevier Science.

Bryk, A. S., & Raudenbush, S. W. (1992). *Hierarchical linear models: Applications and data analysis methods.* Newbury Park, CA: Sage Publications.

Chan, D. (1998). The conceptualization and analysis of change over time: An integrative approach incorporating longitudinal mean and covariance structures analysis (LMACS) and multiple indicator latent growth modeling (MLGM). *Organizational Research Methods, 1,* 421–483.

Chassin, L., Presson, C. C., Rose, J., & Sherman, S. J. (2001). From adolescence to adulthood: Age-related changes in beliefs about cigarette smoking in a midwestern community sample, *Health Psychology, 20,* 377–386.

Cheong, J., MacKinnon, D. P., & Khoo, S-T. (2003). Investigation of mediational processes using latent growth curve modeling. *Structural Equation Modeling, 10,* 238–262.

Choi, J., Harring, J. R., & Hancock, G. R. (2009). Latent growth modeling for logistic response functions. *Multivariate Behavioral Research, 44,* 620–645.

Chou, C-P., Bentler P. M., & Pentz M. A. (1998). Comparison of two statistical approaches to study growth curves:

The multilevel model and latent curve analysis. *Structural Equation Modeling, 5,* 247–266.

Chou, C-P., Yang, D-Y., Pentz, M. A., & Hser, Y-L. (2004). Piecewise growth curve modeling approach for longitudinal prevention study, *Computational Statistics and Data Analysis, 46,* 213–225.

Cillessen, A. H. N., & Mayeux, L. (2004). From censure to reinforcement: Developmental changes in the association between aggression and social status. *Child Development, 75,* 147–163.

Cohen, J., Cohen, P., West, S. G., & Aiken, L. S. (2003). *Applied multiple regression/correlation analysis for the behavioral sciences.* (3rd ed.). Mahwah, NJ: Lawrence Erlbaum Associates.

Cole, D. A., & Maxwell, S. E. (2003). Testing mediational models with longitudinal data: Questions and tips in the use of structural equation modeling. *Journal of Abnormal Psychology, 112,* 558–577.

Collins, L. M., (2006). Analysis of longitudinal data: The integration of theoretical model, temporal design, and statistical model. *Annual Review of Psychology, 57,* 505–528.

Cronbach, L. J., Furby, L. (1970). How should we measure "change"—or should we? *Psychological Bulletin, 74,* 68–80.

Cudeck, R. (1996). Mixed-effects models in the study of individual differences with repeated measures data. *Multivariate Behavioral Research, 31,* 371–403.

Cudeck, R. & du Toit, S. H. C. (2003). Nonlinear multilevel models for repeated measures data. In N. Duan & S. P. Reise (Eds.), *Multilevel modeling: Methodological advances, issues and applications* (pp. 1–24). Mahwah, NJ: Erlbaum.

Cudeck, R., & Klebe, K. J. (2002). Multiphase mixed-effects model for repeated measures data. *Psychological Methods, 7,* 41–63.

Curran, P. J. (2003). Have multilevel models been structural equation models all along? *Multivariate Behavioral Research, 38,* 529–569.

Curran, P. J., & Hussong, A. M. (2009). Integrative data analysis: The simultaneous analysis of multiple data sets. *Psychological Methods, 14,* 81–100.

Curran, P. J., & Peterman, M. (October, 2005). *A curious discrepancy between multilevel and structural equation growth curve models with time-varying covariates.* Paper presented at the 2005 meeting of the Society of Multivariate Experimental Psychology, Lake Tahoe, NV.

Curran, P. J., Stice, E., & Chassin, L. (1997). The relation between adolescent alcohol use and peer alcohol use: a longitudinal random coefficients model. *Journal of Consulting and Clinical Psychology, 65,* 130–140.

Davidian, W., & Giltinan, D. M. (1995). *Nonlinear models for repeated measurement data.* London: Chapman & Hall.

Duncan, O. D. (1969). Some linear models for two-wave, two-variable panel analysis. *Psychological Bulletin, 72,* 177–182.

du Toit, S. H. C. & Cudeck, R. (2001). The analysis of nonlinear random coefficient regression models with LISREL using constraints. In R. Cudeck, S. H. C. du Toit, & D. Sörbom (Eds). *Structural Equation Modeling: Present and Future* (pp. 259–278). Lincolnwood, IL: Scientific Software International.

Fergus, S., Zimmerman, M. A., & Caldwell, C. H. (2007). Growth trajectories of sexual risk behavior in adolescence and young adulthood. *American Journal of Public Health, 97,* 1096–1101.

Ferrer, E., Balluerka, N., & Widaman, K. F. (2008). Factorial invariance and the specification of second-order latent growth models. *Methodology, 4,* 22–36.

Ferrer, E., McArdle, J. J., Shaywitz, B. A., Holahan, J.M., Marchione, K., & Shaywitz, S.E. (2007). Longitudinal models of developmental dynamics between reading and cognition from childhood to adolescence. *Developmental Psychology, 43,* 1460–1473.

Finkel, D., Reynolds, C. A., McArdle, J. J., Hamagami, F., & Pedersen, N. L. (2009). Genetic Variance in Processing Speed Drives Variation in Aging of Spatial and Memory Abilities. *Developmental Psychology, 45,* 820–834.

Fitzmaurice, G. M., Laird, N. M., & Ware, J. H. (2004). *Applied longitudinal analysis.* New Jersey: Wiley.

Flora, D. B. (2008). Specifying Piecewise Latent Trajectory Models for Longitudinal Data *Structural Equation Modeling, 15,* 513–533.

Gerstorf, D., Hoppmann, C. A., Anstey, K. J., & Luszcz, M. A. (2009). Dynamic links of cognitive functioning among married couples: Longitudinal evidence from the Australian longitudinal study of ageing, *Psychology and Aging, 24,* 296–309.

Goldstein, H. (1987). *Multilevel models in educational and social research.* London, United Kingdom: Oxford University Press.

Goldstein, H. (1994) Multilevel cross-classification models, *Sociological Methods and Research, 22,* 364–375.

Gompertz, B. (1825). On the nature of the function expressive of the law of human mortality. *Philosophical Transactions of the Royal Society, 115,* 513–585.

Grimm, K. J. (2007). Multivariate longitudinal methods for studying developmental relationships between depression and academic achievement. *International Journal of Behavioral Development, 31,* 328–339.

Grimm, K. J., & Ram, N. (2009). Nonlinear growth models in M*plus* and SAS. *Structural Equation Modeling, 16,* 676–701.

Grimm, K. J., Ram, N., & Hamagami, F. (2011). Nonlinear growth curves in developmental research. *Child Development., 82,* 1357–1371.

Grimm, K. J., & Widaman, K. F. (2010). Residual structures in latent growth curve modeling. *Structural Equation Modeling, 17,* 424–442.

Hancock, G. R., Kuo, W-L., & Lawrence, F. R. (2001). An illustration of second-order latent growth models. *Structural Equation Modeling, 8,* 470–489.

Hawkley, L. C., Preacher, K. J., & Cacioppo, J. T. (2010). Loneliness impairs daytime functioning but not sleep duration. *Health Psychology, 29,* 124–129.

Heise, D. R. (1970). Causal inference from panel data. *Sociological Methodology, 2,* 3–27.

Hertzog, C., Lindenberger, U., Ghisletta, P., & von Oertzen, T. (2006). On the power of latent growth curve models to detect correlated change. *Psychological Methods, 11,* 244–252.

Hofer, S. M., & Picinnin, A. M. (2009). Integrative data analysis through coordination of measurement and analysis protocol across independent longitudinal studies. *Psychological Methods, 14,* 150–164.

Hox, J. J. & Kreft, I. G. (1994). Multilevel analysis methods. *Sociological Methods and Research, 22,* 283–299.

Hoyle, R.H. (1995). *Structural equation modeling.* Thousand Oaks, CA: Sage.

Jöreskog, K. G. (1970). Estimation and testing of simplex models. *British Journal of Mathematical and Statistical Psychology, 23*, 121–146.

Kessler, R. C. & Greenberg, D. F. (1981). *Linear panel analysis: Models of quantitative change.* New York: Academic Press.

Khoo, S-T., West, S. G., Wu, W., & Kwok, O-M. (2005). Longitudinal methods. In M. Eid & E. Diener (Eds.), *Handbook of multimethod measurement in psychology* (pp. 301–317), Washington, DC: American Psychological Association.

Kwok, O., West, S. G., & Green, S. B. (2007) The impact of misspecifying the within-subject covariance structure in multiwave longitudinal multilevel models: A Monte Carlo study. *Multivariate Behavioral Research, 42*, 557–592.

Laird, N. M., & Ware, J. H. (1982). Random-effects models for longitudinal data. *Biometrics, 38*, 963–974.

Leite, W. L. (2007). A comparison of latent growth models for constructs measured by multiple items. *Structural Equation Modeling, 14*, 581–610.

Li, F., Duncan, T. E., Duncan, S. C., & Hops, H. (2001). Piecewise growth mixture modeling of adolescent alcohol use data. *Structural Equation Modeling, 8*, 175–204.

Little, T. D. (in press). Longitudinal structural equation modeling: Individual difference panel models. New York: Guilford Press.

Little, T. D., Card, N. A., Bovaird, J. A., Preacher, K. J., & Crandall, C. S. (2007). Structural equation modeling of mediation and moderation with contextual factors. In T. D. Little, J. A., Bovaird, & N. A. Card (Eds.), *Modeling contextual effects in longitudinal studies* (pp. 207–230). Mahwah, NJ: Lawrence Erlbaum.

Little, T. D., Card, N. A., Slegers, D. W. & Ledford, E. C. (2007). Representing contextual effects in multiple-group MACS models. In T. D. Little, J. A., Bovaird, & N. A. Card (Eds.), Modeling contextual effects in longitudinal studies (pp. 121–147). Mahwah, NJ: Lawrence Erlbaum.

Little, T. D., Preacher, K. J., Selig, J. P., & Card, N. A. (2007). New developments in SEM panel analyses of longitudinal data. *International Journal of Behavioral Development, 31*, 357–365.

Lord, F. M. (1956). The measurement of growth. *Educational and Psychological Measurement, 16*, 421–437.

MacCallum, R. C., Kim, C., Malarkey, W. B., & Kiecolt-Glaser, J. K. (1997). Studying multivariate change using multilevel models and latent curve models. *Multivariate Behavioral Research, 32*, 215–253.

MacKinnon, D.P. (2008). *Introduction to statistical mediation analysis.* New York: Lawrence Erlbaum.

Maxwell, S. E., & Cole, D. A. (2007). Bias in cross-sectional analyses of longitudinal mediation. *Psychological Methods, 12*, 23–44.

McArdle, J. J. (1988). Dynamic but structural equation modeling of repeated measures data. In J.R. Nesselroade & R.B. Cattell (Eds.), *Handbook of multivariate experimental psychology* (Vol. 2, pp. 561–614). New York: Plenum Press.

McArdle, J. J. (2001). A latent difference score approach to longitudinal dynamic structural analysis. In R. Cudeck, S. du Toit, & D. Sorbom (Eds.). *Structural equation modeling: Present and future.* (pp. 342–380). Lincolnwood, IL: Scientific Software International.

McArdle, J. J. (2009). Latent variable modeling of differences and changes with longitudinal data. *Annual Review of Psychology, 60*, 577–605.

McArdle, J. J. & Hamagami, F. (2001). Linear dynamic analyses of incomplete longitudinal data. In L. Collins & A. Sayer (Eds.). *Methods for the analysis of change.* (pp. 137–176) Washington, DC: American Psychological Association.

McArdle, J. J., & Nesselroade, J. R. (1994). Using multivariate data to structure developmental change. In S. H. Cohen & H. W. Reese (Eds.), *Life-span developmental psychology: Methodological contributions* (pp. 223–267). Hillsdale, NJ: Lawrence Erlbaum.

Mehta, P. D., & West, S. G. (2000). Putting the individual back in individual growth curves. *Psychological Methods, 5*, 23–43.

Meredith, W. (1993). Measurement invariance, factor analysis and factorial invariance. *Psychometrika, 58*, 525–543.

Meredith, W., & Horn, J. L. (2001). The role of factorial invariance in modeling growth and change. In L. M. Collins & A. G. Sayer (Eds.), *New methods for the analysis of change* (pp. 203–240). Washington, DC: American Psychological Association.

Meredith, W., & Tisak, J. (1990). Latent curve analysis. *Psychometrika, 55*, 107–122.

Muthén, B. (2001). Latent variable mixture modeling. In G. A. Marcoulides & R. E. Schumacker (Eds.), *New Developments and Techniques in Structural Equation Modeling* (pp. 1–22). Lawrence Erlbaum.

Muthén, B., Brown, C. H., Masyn, K., Jo, B., Khoo, S-T., Yang, C-C., et al. (2002). General growth mixture modeling for randomized preventive interventions. *Biostatistics, 3*, 459–475.

Muthén, B., & Muthén, L. (2000). Integrating person-centered and variable-centered analysis: growth mixture modeling with latent trajectory classes. *Alcoholism: Clinical and Experimental Research, 24*, 882–891.

Muthen, B. O., & Curran, P. (1997). General longitudinal modeling of individual differences in experimental design: A latent variable framework for analysis and power estimation. *Psychological Methods, 2*, 371–402.

Neter, J., Kutner, M. H., Nachtsheim, C. J., & Wasserman, W. (1996). *Applied linear regression models.* (3rd ed.). Chicago, IL: Irwin.

Patterson, G. R. (1993). Orderly change in a stage world. The antisocial trait as a chimera. *Journal of Consulting and Clinical Psychology, 61*, 911–919.

Pinheiro, J. C., & Bates, D. M. (2000). *Mixed-effects models in S and S-PLUS.* New York: Springer.

Quetelet, L. A. J. (1835). Sur l'homme et le dévelopment de ses facultés ou essai de physique sociale. In E. Boyd, B. S. Savara, & J. F. Schilke (Eds.) (1980), *Origins of the study of human growth* (pp. 317–332). Portland, OR: University of Oregon Health Sciences Center Foundation.

Raudenbush, S. W., & Bryk, A. S. (2002). *Hierarchical linear models: Applications and data analysis methods* (2nd ed.). Thousand Oaks, CA: Sage Publications.

Raudenbush, S. W. (1993). A crossed random effects model for unbalanced data with applications in cross-sectional and longitudinal research. *Journal of Educational Statistics, 18*, 321–349.

Raudenbush, S. W. (2001). Toward a coherent framework for comparing trajectories of individual change. In L. Collins, & A. Sayer (Eds.), *New methods for the analysis of change* (pp. 33–64). Washington DC: American Psychological Association.

Rogosa, D., Brandt, D., & Zimowski, M. (1982). A growth curve approach to the measurement of change. *Psychological Bulletin, 92*, 726–748.

Rogosa, D. R. (1995). Myths and methods: "Myths about longitudinal research," plus supplemental questions. In J. M. Gottman (Ed.), *The analysis of change* (pp. 3–65). Hillsdale, NJ: Lawrence Erlbaum.

Satorra, A. (1992). Asymptotic robust inferences in the analysis of mean and covariance structures. *Sociological Methodology, 22*, 249–278.

Sayer, A. G., & Cumsille, P. E. (2001). Second-order latent growth models. In L. M. Collins & A. G. Sayer (Eds.), *New methods for the analysis of change* (pp. 179–200). Washington, DC: American Psychological Association.

Seber, G. A. F., & Wild, C. J. (2003). *Nonlinear regression*. New York: John Wiley.

Selig, J. P., & Preacher, K. J. (2009). Mediation models for longitudinal data in developmental research. *Research in Human Development, 6*, 144–164.

Selig, J. P., Preacher, K. J., & Little, T. D. (2009). Abstract: Lag as moderator models for longitudinal data. *Multivariate Behavioral Research, 44*, 853.

Selig, J. P., Preacher, K. J., & Little, T. D. (in press). Modeling time-dependent association in longitudinal data: A lag as moderator approach. *Multivariate Behavioral Research*.

Serroyen, J., Molenberghs, G., Verbeke, G., & Davidian, M. (2009). Nonlinear models for longitudinal data. *The American Statistician, 63*, 378–388.

Singer, J. D. & Willett, J. B. (2003). *Applied longitudinal data analysis: Modeling change and event occurrence*. New York: Oxford University Press.

Sivo, S. A., Fan, X., & Witta, E. L. (2005). The biasing effects of unmodeled ARMA time series processes on latent growth curve model estimates. *Structural Equation Modeling, 12*, 215–231.

Stoolmiller, M., & Bank, L. (1995). Autoregressive effects in structural equation models: We see some problems. In J. M. Gottman & G. Sackett (Eds.), *The analysis of change* (pp. 263–276). Hillsdale, NJ: Erlbaum.

Vandergrift, N. A. (2004). *Latent curve models for nonlinear target functions: a review and simulation*. Doctoral dissertation, University of North Carolina, Chapel Hill.

Verbeke, G., & Lesaffre, E. (1997). The effect of misspecifying the random-effects distribution in linear mixed models for longitudinal data. *Computational Statistics & Data Analysis, 23*, 541–556.

Verbeke, G., & Molenberghs, G. (2000). *Linear mixed models for longitudinal data*. New York: Springer.

Widaman, K. F., Ferrer, E., & Conger, R. D. (2010). Factorial invariance within longitudinal structural equation models: Measuring the same construct across time. *Child Development Perspectives, 4*, 10–18.

Willett, J., & Sayer, A. (1994). Using covariance structure analysis to detect correlates and predictors of individual change over time. *Psychological Bulletin, 116*, 363–380.

Wu, W., West, S. G., & Hughes, J. N. (2008). Effect of retention in first grade on children's achievement trajectories over four years: A piecewise growth analysis using propensity score matching. *Journal of Educational Psychology, 100*, 727–740.

Wu, W., West, S., & Taylor, A. (2009). Evaluating model fit for growth curve models: Integration of fit indices from SEM and MLM frameworks. *Psychological methods, 14*, 183–201.

CHAPTER
19 Dynamical Systems and Models of Continuous Time

Pascal R. Deboeck

Abstract

Historically it has been easier to focus on measuring and describing differences between groups of people rather than try to describe the dynamic ways that individuals change. Dynamical systems are mathematical models that aim to describe how constructs change over time. Frequently these models are continuous time models; models that try to capture the function that underlies a set of observations. This chapter introduces the concept of a dynamical system and of continuous time models. Two methods are introduced for the fitting of continuous time models to observed data: one using the approximate discrete model for a first-order autoregressive model and the second using a method of estimating latent derivatives for a second-order autoregressive model.

Key Words: Dynamical System(s), Dynamic System(s), Continuous Time, Discrete Time, Differential Equation Model(s)(ing), Derivative Estimation, Approximate Discrete Model

Introduction

Short time-scale, intra-individual variability is often hard to model in the social sciences. It is of little surprise that researchers chose to begin by modeling more macroscopic, interindividual features first (e.g., mean differences among groups). Increasingly, perhaps because of an interest in causal relationships, the questions being asked by some researchers have moved from questions about group differences to questions of change. In answering how constructs change, emphasis has been placed on more macroscopic features first (e.g., long-term linear or quadratic change). But these long-term changes are not the essence of living—they are the product of countless minutes, hours, and days of incremental changes. The analysis of individuals on shorter time-scales is still frequently ignored because the data often appear so complex that they could be confused with random variation.

But to understand the essence of how individuals grow and adapt in response to their environment, the analysis of very short time-scales is necessary. Sitting at a wedding, one might ask oneself: "Will this couple be happy 10 years from now?" One could look for macroscopic predictors of success—perhaps similarities in political disposition—but this would only begin to unravel the picture. John Gottman's "5 to 1 ratio" of positive to negative interactions, however, suggests that the key to positive marriages may be built in daily events and moment-to-moment interactions. Many useful predictors that don't change over the course of many days have been identified. The usefulness of these predictors, however, may be due to their ability to reflect what is occurring at much shorter time scales. For example, people of similar political dispositions would seem likely to have a few less topics on which they could have negative interactions, which in turn might lead couples with similar dispositions to be closer on average to the 5 to 1 ratio than couples with differing political dispositions. If long-term outcomes are the product of many smaller events and decisions, studies that examine long-term development may average over rich, informative variability, just as averaging over a group can average over the rich differences between individuals. But even if the analysis of individuals at short time-scales is essential to understanding how people develop, how could one go about conceptualizing and modeling such change?

This chapter introduces tools for the conceptualizing and modeling of nonlinear change through the concepts of dynamical systems and continuous time models. There are many excellent introductions to dynamical systems (e.g., Smith & Thelen, 2003; Thelen & Smith, 2006); the present chapter blends some introductory concepts with two tools that have been developed for empirical research on relatively short time series (< 100 observations). This chapter begins by discussing concepts related to dynamical systems and continuous time modeling. Two methods for analysis of time series are then presented: the approximate discrete model (Bergstrom, 1988; Oud, 2007) and a method that estimates latent derivatives (Boker & Nesselroade, 2002). Sample code for each of the methods is provided in the appendices and on the website of the author.

Dynamical Systems: The Concept

Many statistics are based on the analysis of the consistent parts of a system: the steady-states of constructs, trait-like constructs, constructs that have high test–retest reliability. To speak of dynamical systems, on the other hand, is to convey an interest in that which changes, and that which is not constant, that which is inherently unstable. The first concept to address is that of a *system*. A system is all of the interrelated elements in the domain being studied. Systems could consist of one person or several people, a single construct or several constructs. A *dynamic system* is a system where the elements change over time. This differs from a *dynamical system*, which is a mathematical model of a dynamic system. The translation of dynamic systems—systems that change—into the language of mathematics is the goal of dynamical systems.

Dynamical systems are broadly categorized into one of two classes: linear dynamical systems and nonlinear dynamical systems. The distinguishing feature of these classes is how the predictors are combined. If the predictors in all equations are multiplied only by constants and added up, as is typically how predictors are entered into regression equations, then the dynamical system is linear. If the predictors are multiplied with each other, or there are terms such as the exponent of a predictor, then the dynamical system is nonlinear. The classification of dynamical systems is by the linearity or nonlinearity of the *equations*—not of the resulting trajectory. Many seemingly complex, nonlinear trajectories can be described using linear equations—that is, linear dynamical systems.

In linear dynamical systems, changes in the predictors result in proportional changes in the dependent variables. Systems where there are non-proportional changes—for example, sudden transitions between states are indicative of a nonlinear dynamical system. One example is axon firing. The firing of an axon is often described as an all-or-none event, where a very small change in input could result in no change to the axon or alternatively could tip an axon into firing. Such threshold effects are one example of a feature that may convey the need for a nonlinear dynamical system. The present chapter focuses on introducing linear dynamical systems, but there are many resources for readers interested in nonlinear dynamical systems (e.g., Kaplan & Glass, 1995; Strogatz, 1994; Thompson & Stewart, 1986).

One remarkable thing about dynamical systems is that even linear systems can produce intricate change over time. The time series in Figure 19.1 are examples of the complexity that can be observed with a linear system; note that there is no error in these time series, they are the result of linear, regression-like equations. The possibility of describing change—particularly complex changes in observed variables—stirs the excitement of many fields, and so literature on dynamical systems can be found in a variety of natural and social sciences (e.g., physics, chemistry, biology, medicine, physiology, psychology, economics, etc.). The study of dynamical systems tends to leave many researchers with an indelible excitement because it presents fascinating and seemingly counter intuitive ideas, for example: the idea that extremely complex changes over time do not have to be the result of complex processes or models. In trying to explain the daily fluctuations of a complex system—perhaps the construct of stress—one could seek a model that tries to include predictors to explain every hill and valley that occurs—a complex model (many parameters) to explain seemingly complex process; no doubt the reader can think of a dozen factors or more that

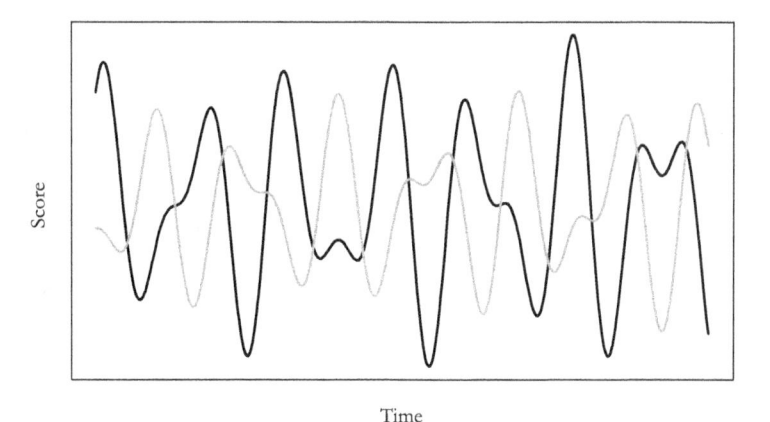

Figure 19.1 Example of two time series produced by a linear dynamical system.

contribute to stress, all of which might need to be included to model stress. From a dynamical systems perspective, however, many of the observed changes may be attributable to the dynamics of stress itself—perhaps the self-regulation of stress or the simple interactions of stress with another part of the system (e.g., negative affect; Montpetit, Bergeman, Deboeck, Tiberio, & Boker, 2010). Even if stress and negative affect tended to fluctuate with a weekly schedule and there were absolutely no external influences (a simple model), one could see complex trajectories such as those in Figure 19.1 if they affect each other; complex trajectories can arise even without a complicated set of external influences. Fundamentally these mathematical models are intricately bound to a quest for simplicity and functionality that conveys an elegance that elicits the emotions typically reserved for things of overwhelming beauty. People got so lost in the beauty of dynamical systems that in the 1980s and 90s that much of dynamical systems theory was co-opted by *Chaos Theory*; Chaos Theory was introduced by many writers as a new way of thinking, the herald of a true scientific revolution. Chaos Theory and dynamical systems are, however, older than many writers convey and can be traced at least as far back as the work of mathematician Henri Poincaré (1854–1912).

The Language of Dynamical Systems

The essence of dynamical systems are models of systems that change. The mathematical models used therefore must be able to describe how a construct is changing with respect to time. In mathematics, describing the change in one variable with respect to another variable is usually accomplished using derivatives. Introduction to derivatives occurs early in many education systems when students first learn about the slope of the line—that is, "rise over run" or the change in y divided by the change in x. Although the name may not have been used, the linear slope is also called the *first derivative* of y with respect to x. Although the word derivative seems to be fear-provoking for many people, the first derivative sneaks into our daily lives in many ways. Innocuous letters go by like "mph" without announcing that miles per hours is just shorthand for the first derivative of position—that is, a change in position (measured in miles) with respect to a change in time (hours).

The *second derivative* builds on the first by expressing the change in the first derivative with respect to time. In our cars, the second derivative expresses the change in mph per unit time—that is, it expresses how quickly one is changing the *speed* (first derivative) of the car whether through *acceleration* or *deceleration* (e.g, braking). One other derivative that is commonly used is the *zeroth derivative*. This derivative expresses the position of the car at some time. The terms *zeroth*, *first*, and *second* refer to the *order* of the derivative. Derivatives are by no means limited to the second order (acceleration) and one can think about higher order derivatives—the third order, for example, would convey information about how quickly acceleration is changing with time.

In the social sciences there is frequent talk about the zeroth derivative—the level of a person's construct at some time. Many constructs change with time, however, and we could then used two pieces of information to described a person—the level of a person's construct at some time, and the speed at which the construct is changing (imagine the slope of a line). Many forms of change are not well described with lines. Rather than continuing up or down at some constant speed, frequently there will be one or more changes in speed, such that the line curves in some manner. This curve represents a change in speed with respect to time and indicates a non–zero second derivative. We could then imagine that at any given time, a person has a particular score on some construct, but that construct is changing with some speed (linear slope), and simultaneously the speed that the person is changing may be increasing or decreasing (accelerating or decelerating). Equivalently, we could describe the construct of a person at any given time and how that construct is changing using the zeroth, first, and second derivatives.

For people interested in change, the question then becomes: At any given time, what predicts whether a person's scores are increasing or decreasing (positive or negative first derivative)? accelerating or decelerating (positive or negative second derivative)? One can imagine trying to find predictors of the first and/or second derivative(s) to address what might relate to how a person's scores change. Any model with a derivative, on either side of the equation, is called a *differential equation model*. Differential equation models can be used to express changes in a system of constructs; they can be used to describe the relationships between the current state of a construct and how that construct is changing, how a construct changes in response to the level of a another construct, or how a construct changes is response to changes in other constructs.

Attractors and Self-Regulation

The idea of relationships between the state of a construct and how it changes brings up one dynamical systems concept that may be particularly relevant to the social sciences; that concept is *self-regulation*. In the process of trying to describe all the small changes in a construct we could think about using a large number of predictors to try to explain every small change observed. Alternatively, we might find that we can model constructs in terms of a relationship between current states and change, such that people perturbed from their typical state might have a tendency to change so as to return to their typical state or *equilibrium*—they might self-regulate. The concept of self-regulation is a natural one for social scientists, as many constructs seem to exhibit homeostasis. In dynamical systems, one will often read of the concept of an *attractor*. An attractor is a state or set of states around which a dynamical system will fluctuate or converge. Many people will imagine the idea of a marble moving in a bowl, with the bottom of the bowl being an attractor; one can also imagine weaker and stronger attractors, much like a bowl with shallower or steeper sides. The idea of an attractor seems to map well onto the ideas of homeostasis, equilibrium, one's "typical" state, or one's trait.

Systems are not limited to one attractor but can have many attractors. Waddington's epigenetic landscape (Fig. 19.2) is a famous visualization of a dynamical system with a changing number of attractors (Waddington, 1957). Waddington's figure involves imagining a marble rolling toward the viewer as time progresses. Initially the ball can easily waver to the right and left in a single attractor. As the ball rolls forward, it may find itself in either one of two attractor states. The ball can still vary to the right and left, and with enough of a push could even surmount the hilly obstacle in the center and vary around the alternative attractor. As time goes on, the number of attractor states changes and the various attractors differ in their depth. Some attractors will consist of deep wells, allowing relatively little variation in the ball's movements and few possibilities to change attractors; other attractors will be more shallow, allowing for more variation and more possibility of switching attractors.

Waddington's interests were in the process of tissue differentiation. A chicken begins as a set of undifferentiated cells that over time becomes increasingly differentiated so as to produce organs, muscles, bones, and so forth. Early in the process, if one removes several of the undifferentiated cells, then the chicken will still develop normally—one does not expected that by removing a few undifferentiated cells that one can produce a boneless chicken. Early on the cells are gathered around a single, shallow attractor that allows for change to occur easily. Over time the attractor wells deepen, such that late in the process, cells have a much harder (if not close to impossible) time surmounting the attractor walls so to become another type of tissue; muscle and bone will not change to replace a missing kidney.

For psychological constructs, we might imagine a slightly different landscape. We might imagine that early in life, people are predisposed to certain traits but that those traits are not specifically defined. Through interactions with their environment, the landscape changes. Perhaps the valley of the attractor becomes deeper than people were initially predisposed, leading people to vary less in a construct and suggesting that there are periods that traits would be

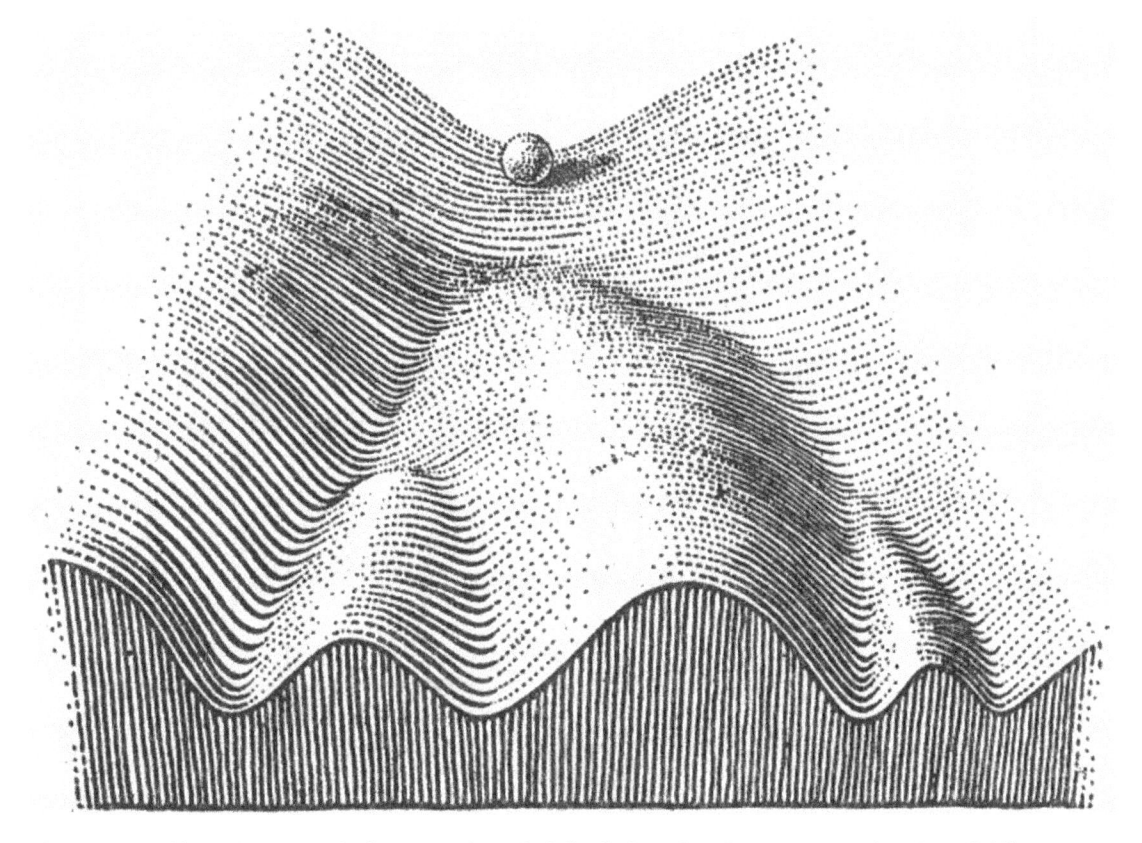

Figure 19.2 Waddington's epigenetic landscape (1957). As the ball rolls down the valley (progression of time), small differences in initial conditions lead the ball to different paths (attractors). The application of the correct force, however, could push the ball from one attractor to another. One can also imagine the ball varying within an attractor basin.

more precisely measured. However, it is well known that even mighty rivers, over time, can begin to carve a new path. Perhaps similarly, these constructs might be altered over time such that the position of the valley switches. Figure 19.3 is one way to imagine the effects of events "pulling" on the landscape (perspective from under the landscape), changing its shape. The conceptualization gets more complex, as one can imagine events (such as a traumatic life event) either changing the shape of the landscape or moving people from one attractor to another. Furthermore, people could differ in the depth of their attractor(s); with some people being easily perturbed within or between shallow valleys and some people varying only within very deep valleys.

The attractors described so far have primarily been *point attractors* or combinations of a few point attractors. There are several types of attractors, of which the point attractor is just one. For example, one could think about a *point repeller*. As its name implies, this is a state from which a system diverges rather than converges. It is a point of instability from which a system will depart, given a small amount of energy. Rather than imagining a ball in a bowl (attractor) or a valley, imagine balancing a marble on top of a larger ball. With a bowl, the marble is attracted to the lowest part of a basin. On the other hand, if one balances a marble on top of another ball, then it is unlikely to remain there for very long because a small amount of energy will knock the marble from its current state. Like the valley example, repellers can have very steep or very shallow walls—they can differ in their strength. Imagine balancing a marble on something with very steep sides (perhaps the head of a pin) versus something with less steep sides (perhaps a basketball). There are also many different shapes of attractors; frequently they are divided into categories that define the attractors as either a point attractor, a periodic attractor, or a chaotic attractor. Attractors become increasingly complex beyond a point attractor, but all are based on the fundamental idea of the state or states to which a system converges (or for repellers—diverges).

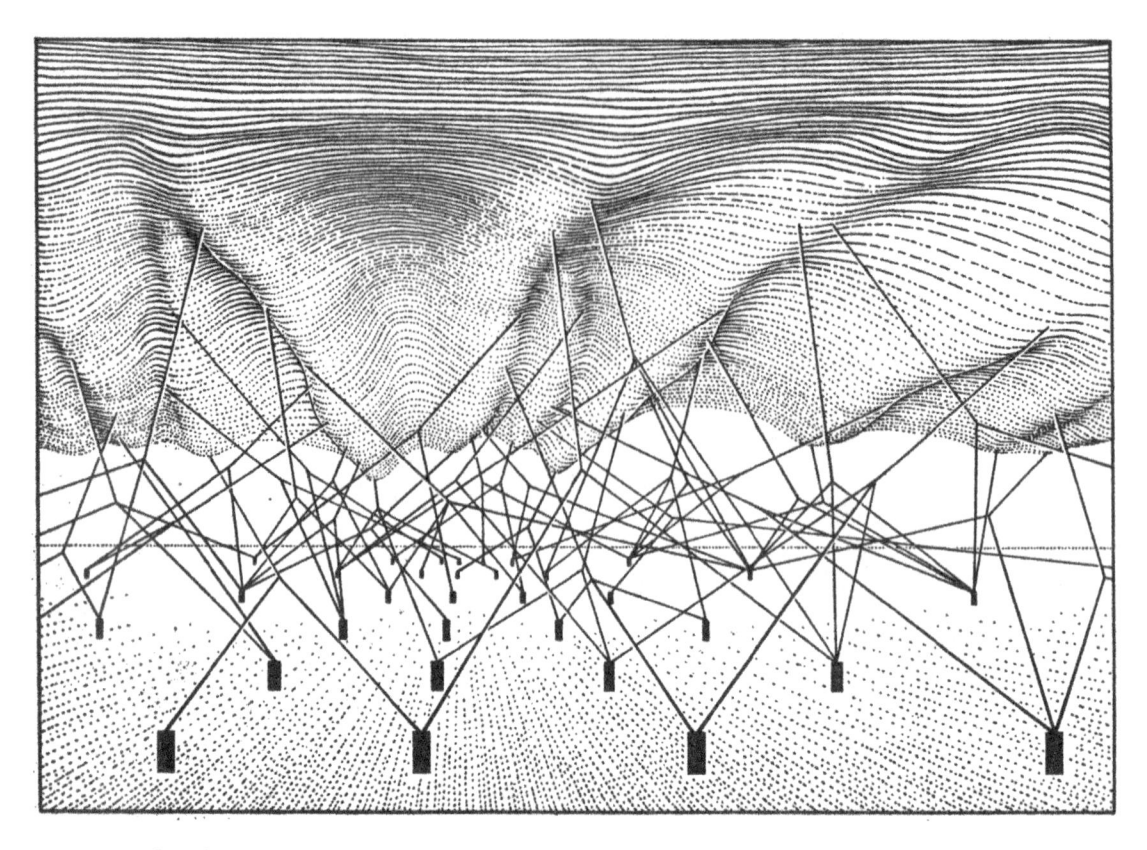

Figure 19.3 A figure from Waddington (1957) depicting the effect of various influences on an attractor landscape. Waddington thought about this from the perspective of genes (black pegs) effecting chemical tendencies (strings), which affects the epigenetic landscape.

Discrete and Continuous Time

This chapter began by introducing the ideas of systems of dynamic variables, models of change, derivatives, and differential equation models to introduce the mathematical tools and language of dynamical systems. The ideas of attractors and self-regulation gave a sampling of the concepts and metaphors often used by people working with dynamical systems. This section begins to move the reader toward the application of a dynamical system to data. When considering a changing construct, it seems almost natural to consider change with respect to time—that is, time is often selected as the baseline variable with respect to which other variables change. Although time is often not the variable of central focus, differing modeling techniques treat time very differently. One primary way that models can differ is the treatment of time as either discrete or continuous.

The expression of changes in variables using derivatives and differential equation models was coming into its full swing by the time Newton and Leibniz were telling the world about calculus, but it was not until almost 100 to 150 years later (late 1700s to mid-1800s) that differential equation models started to be approximated using *difference equations* (Lakshmikantham & Trigiante, 2002). Difference equations are expressions of the relationships between consecutively observed values—for example, that the observation at some time is equal to the previous observation times a constant plus some error ($x_t = Ax_{t-1} + \epsilon$) with no attempt to model the system at times between $t-1$ and t. These difference equations, which treat time as if it is discrete, are much easier to work with than differential equations, which treat time as if it is continuous.

For the physical sciences, where measurements could be rapidly and frequently made (relative to the social sciences) with relatively little error and with little change occurring between subsequent measurements, difference equations produced very reasonable approximations. This was particularly convenient, as it would not be until the early and mid–twentieth century before tools were becoming available for the fitting of stochastic differential equation models (essentially differential equation models with random errors). In the mean time, however, the use of difference equations spread to many other fields, including the social sciences. By the mid–twentieth century there was trouble on the horizon. As Bergstrom described the history of econometric analysis: "At the time when Bartlett's paper [1946] was published, econometricians were becoming increasingly aware of the problems created by interaction between variables within the unit observation period." (Bergstrom, 1988)

What econometricians like Bergstrom realized was described by Bartlett (1946)

> "The discrete time nature of our observations in many economic and other time series does not reflect any lack of continuity in the underlying series. Thus theoretically it should often prove more fundamental to eliminate this imposed artificiality. An unemployment index does not cease to exist between readings, nor does Yule's pendulum cease to swing."

Barlett's concern was the way that discrete time models treated the data. Difference equations treat subsequent observations as if they were caused by previous observations, ignoring the interaction of constructs between observations, as in Figure 19.4a. If we imagine this figure to represent two psychological variables (perhaps the monthly interactions between mother and child), then discrete time approaches can yield models that are strange from a theoretical perspective. For example, Figure 19.4a suggests that a child's current score is related to his/her score a month prior and the mother's score a month prior, but that the mother and child have not continued to affect each other daily over the course of the month. Discrete time models treat the mother–child interaction as if it ceases to exist between measurements, that they interact at a few, discrete moments rather than continuously. But mothers and children do "not cease to exist between readings...."

The primary consequence of the seemingly innocent choice to use a discrete time model is that all of the results depend on the specific rate data were sampled; this issue has been addressed in the psychological literature in the context of longitudinal mediation (Gollob & Reichardt, 1987, 1991). There are several problems that follow. Three have the potential to lead to serious conflicts in the literature. First, the selection of the best model will depend on the observation interval. For example, if one collects monthly data conforming to a process that depends on the previous two observations ($x_t = A_1 x_{t-1} + A_2 x_{t-2} + \epsilon$), then by collecting quarterly data, one will find that these data will satisfy a completely different model (a moving average model; Bergstrom, 1988). Second, the relationships between variables will change depending on the frequency of observation. It has been shown that the effect of one variable on another can change from being positive, to non existent, to negative depending on the frequency that one makes observations (Oud, 2007). Finally, the magnitude of effects can also vary with sampling rate. Asking whether construct A has more of an effect on construct B, or vice versa, is a question whose answer will depend on the sampling rate—for some sample rates, A may have more effect on B (than vice versa), and for other sampling rates, B may have more of an effect on A (Oud, 2010).

These consequences have the potential to create important conflicts in the literature, merely due to researchers using different sampling rates and the use of discrete time methods (e.g., cross–lagged panel models). One way to think about these conflicts is to think about discrete time methods as a microscope focused on only a single sampling interval; analyzing monthly data with a discrete time model, we only get answers regarding a monthly interval but we can't be sure that results extrapolate to other sampling intervals (e.g., bimonthly measurements or biweekly measurements). Aside from these conflicts, discrete time models often can have problems handling unequally spaced observations or missing data; in these cases, one must either start estimating differing parameters for the two differing time intervals (two different parameters in Fig. 19.5b) or find ways to create equal intervals such as the use of latent variables (e.g., Fig. 19.5c)[1]

The mismatch with theory, the overwhelming dependance of results on the sampling rate, the limited interpretation of results, and the problems with unequal intervals (or missing data) would seem to be serious deterrents to the use of discrete time methods. Yet, despite the work of many economists, much of economic research is still based on discrete time methods, as is the case in much of the other social sciences. No doubt, in part, the reason is that it is easy to specify discrete time models—models where one observation is regressed on the previous observation are abundant in psychology. It may also be that researchers are not widely familiar with the weaknesses of discrete time models. Although more challenging to implement, continuous time models can be used with exactly the same data as discrete time models and surmount the weaknesses discussed.

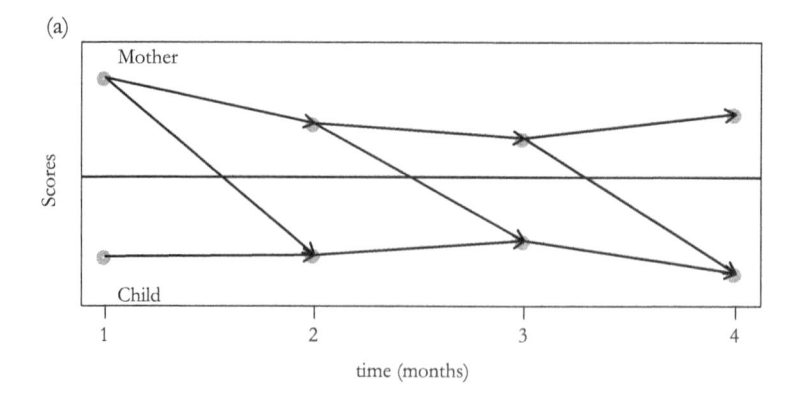

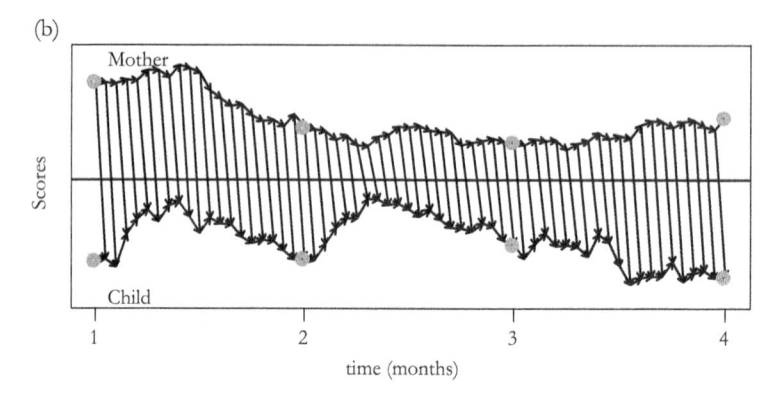

Figure 19.4 Of the many possible times that observations can be made, only a few observations are made on any one subject (gray circles). Discrete time models treat observations as if observation is caused by the previous observations (a). Continuous time models (b) take into account the continual affects of constructs on themselves and on other constructs, even when not observed (e.g., the effect of mother on child).

One can think of continuous time models as trying to understand the functions that underlie the data, like the lines shown in Figure 19.6. Rather than saying one observation was caused by another, each observation is just a sample of many possible observations from an ongoing process. As studies sample individual subjects from some larger population, for a continuous time model the observations are a sample of individual observations (dark circles) from some larger population of possible observations (gray circles). With two constructs, there are two such functions. When one starts to think about how these functions affect each other, one can imagine changes in one construct at any moment being related to small, ongoing changes in the other construct—that is, changes in one construct continuously affect the other, like the many arrows in Fig. 19.4b, rather than just at specific discrete times. In addition, thinking about the observations as samples from a larger whole means missing observations and unequally spaced intervals are frequently less of an issue for these methods, much like how we are not usually concerned about people that aren't sampled, unless there is something systematic about the people that weren't sampled.

The following sections move from theory to application by demonstrating two methods for applying two different continuous time models. The first model is a first-order differential equation model, for which an autoregressive process is a solution in discrete time; an example of a discrete time version of such a model is shown in Figure 19.5a. This continuous time model will be fit using the *Approximate Discrete Model* (Bergstrom, 1988; Oud, 2007, 2010). The second continuous time model will be a second-order differential equation model—that of a damped linear oscillator or pendulum. This model can be fit using a second-order autoregressive model in discrete time, such as in Figure 19.5d. This continuous time model will be fit using *Latent Differential Equations* (Boker, Neale, & Rausch, 2004). It should be noted that

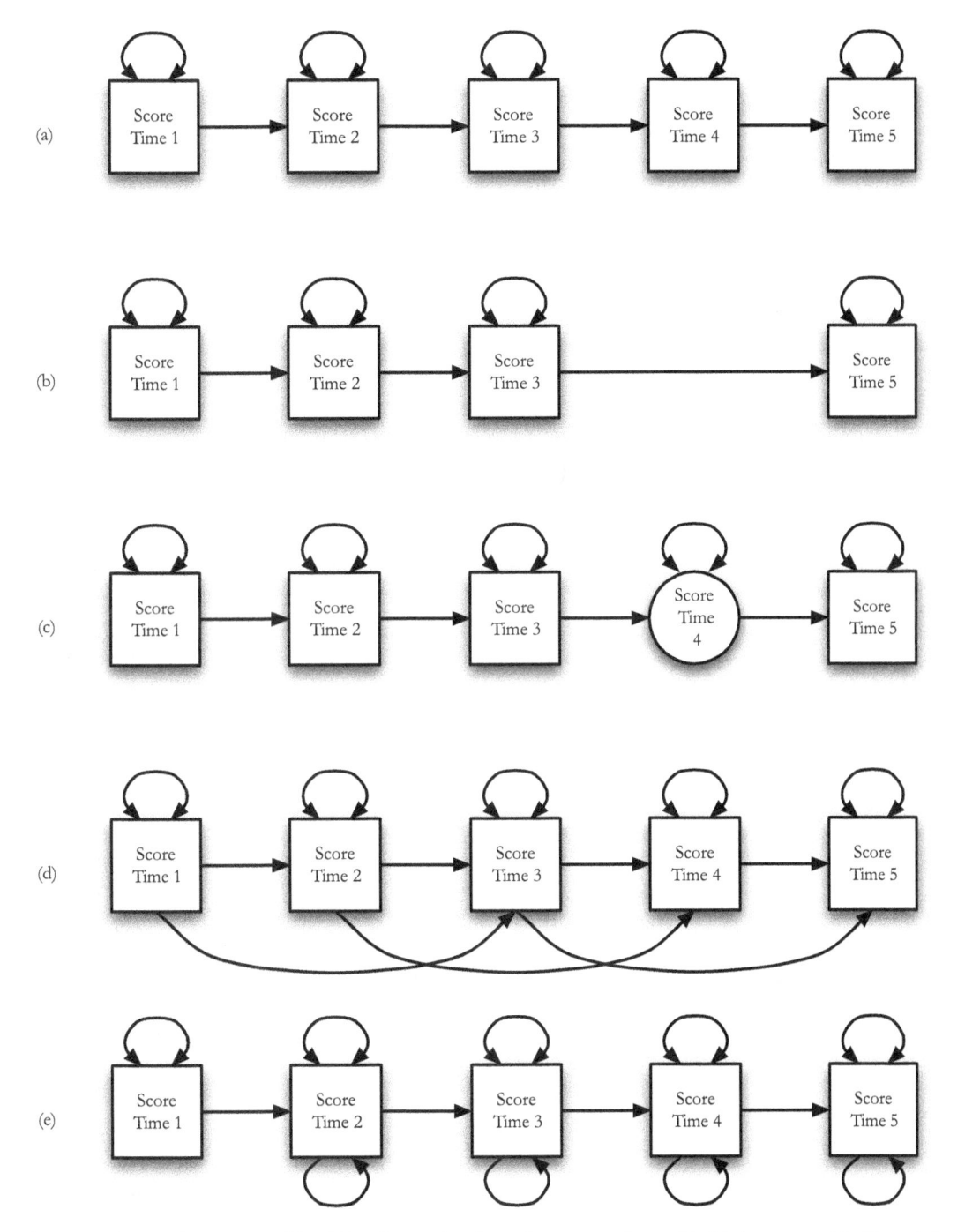

Figure 19.5 Structural equation models of (a) a discrete time first-order autoregressive model, (b) the same model with a missing observation, (c) the same model with a way to estimate the autoregressive parameter, (d) a discrete time second-order autoregressive model, and (e) a way to think about the approximate discrete model, including instantaneous recursive paths (constraints not represented).

either method can be used to fit either model, with differing advantages and disadvantages; the two methods are demonstrated with differing models so as to expose the reader to more options both for models and for methods. Moderate familiarity with structural equation modeling (SEM) is assumed for the sections that follow; readers unfamiliar with SEM might consider first reading Chapter 15 (this volume) or perusing an introductory book (e.g., Kline, 2004).

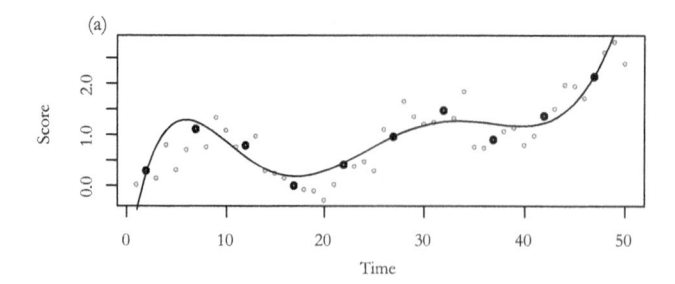

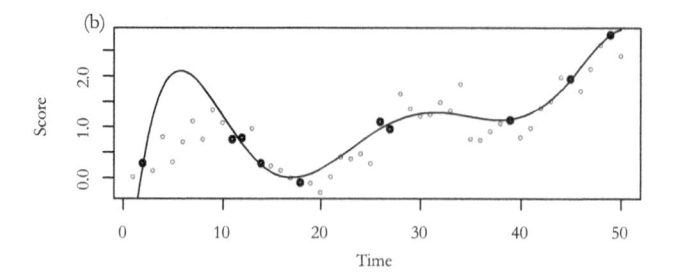

Figure 19.6 Continuous time models aim to understand the continuous function underlying a set of observations (continuous line). As one is trying to understand the underlying function, these models are applicable with both equally (a) and unequally (b) spaced observations (black circles). The gray circles represent a larger population of possible observations.

First-Order Differential Equation Model

Recall that discrete time models were used as an alternative to continuous time models as a method to simplify estimation. One very common discrete time model is the first-order autoregressive model,

$$x_t = A_\Delta x_{t-\Delta} + w_t, \qquad (1)$$

where x_t is the observed value at some time t, $x_{t-\Delta}$ is the observed value at some prior time $t - \Delta$, Δ is the time between subsequent observations, and w is an error (sometimes called innovation) that is often assumed to be normally distributed with mean of zero and with values that are independent. The relationship between x_t and $x_{t-\Delta}$ is captured in the parameter A_Δ; the Δ subscript is used here to indicate that this value of A will depend on the sampling rate—that is, the time between subsequent observations. This equation can be shown to be a solution for the continuous time equation

$$\frac{dx_t}{dt} = Ax_t + G\frac{dW_t}{dt}, \qquad (2)$$

which states that the first derivative of a variable at some time $\left(\frac{dx_t}{dt}\right)$ is equal to the zeroth derivative at some time (x_t) multiplied by a constant (A), plus error $\left(G\frac{dW_t}{dt}\right)$. The second part of the error term, $\frac{dW_t}{dt}$, is a continuous time equivalent of w_t called the Wiener process. Like w_t, when integrated over some period of time this process produces independent, normally distributed values, with a mean of zero. The first part of the error term, G, is included because the Wiener process has a fixed variance; by multiplying a distribution with a fixed variance by a constant, one can allow the errors to have any variance.

The key difference in Equations 1 and 2 is the estimation of the autoregressive relationships A_Δ and A, which are conceptually related but not equivalent. The parameter A_Δ tells a researcher about the autoregressive relationship for one sampling rate (e.g., "this is the autoregressive relationship for daily measurements"). The parameter A, being a continuous time value, describes the expected relationships for all possible lagged relationships (within the limits of the smallest and largest intervals covered by the data). These parameters are related through the equation

$$A_\Delta = e^{A\Delta}, \qquad (3)$$

where e is the symbol for exponent. In many applications A_Δ is expected to range between 0 and 1, the equivalent for A is to range from $-\infty$ to 0; so a discrete time autoregressive relationship near 1 will be equal to a continuous time autoregressive relationship that is a negative number approaching zero[2].

As an example, let's say that A_Δ is equal to 0.9 and that measurements on our construct have been made every half-hour, then rewriting Equation 3 to solve for A

$$A = ln(A_\Delta)/\Delta = ln(0.9)/0.5 = -0.211. \qquad (4)$$

Note that ln is the symbol for natural log (log base e). One way to interpret A is to solve for the discrete time effect (A_Δ) for many possible sampling intervals (Δs), as in Figure 19.7a. In this figure, the line consists of the discrete time autoregressive values (y-axis) for a range of sampling intervals (x-axis). That is, this continuous time parameter can be interpreted as giving information as to what the discrete time parameter would have been had we measured every 15 minutes, every 101 minutes, or any other possible sampling interval. The circle, on the other hand, is the information conveyed by A_Δ, the discrete time parameter. It is not that the discrete and continuous time approaches are different models, but rather, they convey the information in one's data in very different ways, with the information offered by the discrete time approach being more limited. Unfortunately, it has been shown that fitting the discrete model and converting to the continuous time model parameter(s) (called the "indirect method"), as was done in this example, can lead to serious problems in parameter estimation that can result in misleading inferences (Hamerle, Nagl, & Singer, 1991). This means that to get the continuous time parameter, one needs to fit the continuous time model directly to data.

The application of Equation 2 to data can be accomplished in structural equation modeling software (Oud, 2007; Oud & Jansen, 2000). The exact fitting of this equation, unfortunately, requires a program that is adept with nonlinear constraints and can take the exponential of a matrix (e.g., Mx or OpenMx; Neale, Boker, Xie, & Maes, 2003; Boker et al., 2011). The *Approximate Discrete Model* is an approximation of Equation 2 that has been shown to provide reasonable approximations for the continuous time parameter A—much better than fitting the discrete time model and calculating A from A_Δ (Bergstrom, 1988; Oud, 2010)[3]. The approximate discrete model fits a model that is partially described in the SEM in Figure 19.5e. On first inspection this figure would seem to be impossible to fit with SEM software. The single-headed arrow of an observed variable to itself is not an error variance but, rather, an instantaneous path from the observed variable to itself (recursive path). This oddity is possible through a set of linear constraints, constraints that define what the paths between observations and recursive paths should be equal to, given a value of A. In setting the linear constraints properly, one can achieve an estimate of A (continuous time) rather than A_Δ (discrete time).

Appendix A provides code for the software program R (using the package OpenMx; R, 2012; Boker et al., 2011)[4]. Examining this code, the reader will see that it sets up an SEM, as in Figure 19.5e. More importantly are the list of constraints; these constraints relate the paths in the figure back to the parameter A. Constraints on the instantaneous paths (recursive paths) and lagged paths (paths between different time) are:

$$A_{instantaneous} = \frac{1}{2} A_{approx} \Delta \qquad (5)$$

$$A_{lagged} = 1 + \frac{1}{2} A_{approx} \Delta, \qquad (6)$$

where A_{approx} is a reasonable approximation to the continuous time parameter A. As all of the paths have constrained relationships with the parameter A_{approx}, in a case such as the one being illustrated the continuous time structural equation model (Fig. 19.5e) will be based on the same number of parameters as the discrete time model (Fig. 19.5a)—that is, the degrees of freedom will be equivalent for the two models. Additional discussion of these constraints, as well as the constraints placed on the parameter G, is available in Oud (2007, 2010).

It should be noted that the model presented in this section is the simplest of the possible models. This model can be made substantially more realistic through the inclusion of a measurement equation (relating latent variables rather than observed variables), inclusion of mean structure related to time (e.g., a developmental trajectory), inclusion of changes in relation to other time-varying variables, autocorrelation matrices A that vary with time (a changing dependence on previous observations), and random effects for different individuals. The equations and presentation also focused on the examination of only a single variable; however, Equation 2 is easily altered to accommodate multiple variables and the relationships among those variables (discussed in discrete time as cross–lags), by changing the parameters and variables to matrices and changing the "1" in Equation 6 to an identity matrix. Example of these additions are discussed in several articles (e.g., Delsing, Oud, & De Bruyn, 2005; Delsing & Oud, 2008; Toharudin, Oud, & Billiet, 2008).

What is perhaps most interesting about the continuous time models is the additional understanding it can convey regarding one's data. Figure 19.7b and 19.7c show some examples of discrete time parameter estimates (A_Δ, y-axis) for a particular sampling interval (x-axis) based on three coupled constructs. The lines in Figure 19.7b represent the effects of constructs on themselves (two variables shown of three); the lines Figure 19.7c represent the

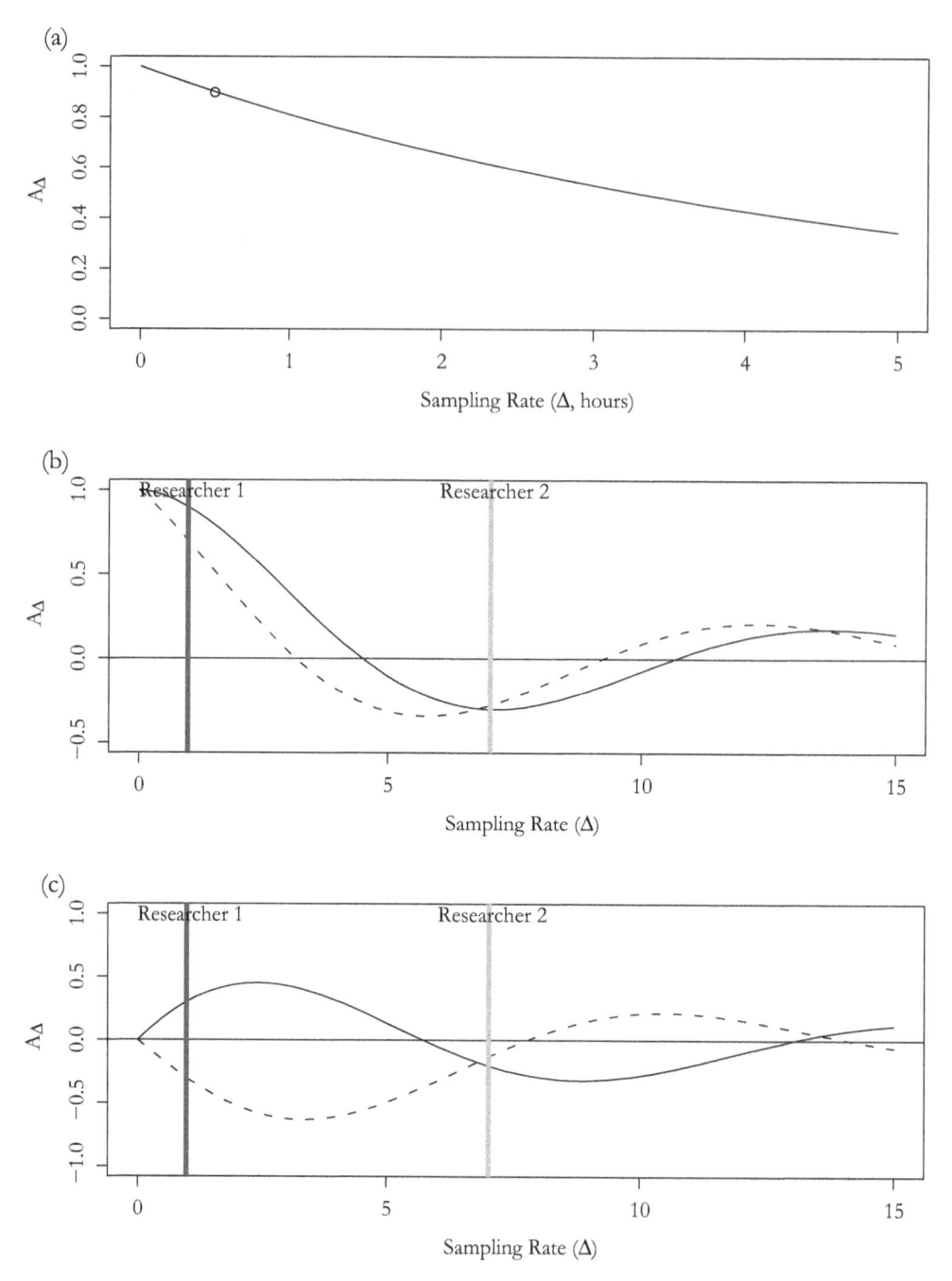

Figure 19.7 Plots of the discrete time autoregressive parameters (A_Δ) calculated for a range of sampling intervals (e.g., daily, every 2 days, every 3 days...). Figures b and c correspond to a system with three coupled variables. The values of b correspond to the effects of a construct on itself. The values of c correspond to two of the relationships between constructs. The horizontal lines correspond to the results seen by researchers using a discrete time model and either daily measurements (#1) or weekly measurements (#2).

effects of constructs on each other (two relationships shown of six). Using a discrete time analysis, one would only examine a singular value on the x-axis. Consequently two researchers collecting daily and weekly measurements (vertical lines) would find the effects of constructs on themselves (Figure 19.7b) to be positive and negative, respectively. In addition, the first researcher would say that there is a positive relationship between constructs, whereas the second would insist there is a negative relationship (solid line, 19.7c). Both would report their results, and the literature would be divided: Is the effect of A on B positive or negative? To add to the confusion, there would be similarities in their results (dashed line, 19.7c). These misunderstandings could be reconciled using a continuous time model, which could be used to produce figures such as Figure 19.7b and 19.7c and, therefore, give an impression as to the effect of one variable on the other for many possible sampling intervals.

Second-Order Differential Equation Model

Another continuous time model that one could consider would be a second-order differential equation model; this chapter specifically examines the second-order model that corresponds to a damped linear oscillator—that of a pendulum. This model is interesting from several perspectives. First, it has been shown that this model can be described using a second-order autoregressive model in discrete time (e.g., Figure 19.5d; Yule, 1927); some applications of second-order autoregressive models may be cases where the damped linear oscillator is appropriate. Second, this model is interesting from a theory perspective, as it offers one way to model and conceptualize self-regulation.

Many simple pendulums vary around a point called the *equilibrium*; this is the point where a pendulum would come to rest given friction. The equation for this second-order differential equation is

$$\frac{d^2x}{dt^2} = \eta x + \zeta \frac{dx}{dt}, \qquad (7)$$

where $\frac{d^2x}{dt^2}$, $\frac{dx}{dt}$, and x are the second, first, and zeroth derivatives (acceleration, speed, and observed score) of the construct, η is related to the frequency of oscillation, and ζ is related to the amount damping. In this equation, it is assumed that the equilibrium is constant, and has been set to zero. The parameter η is negative for a system that oscillates, such that when the construct score is high, there is a large negative acceleration; that is, if a person's construct were to get far from their equilibrium there is an acceleration that will change their speed so that they start moving back toward equilibrium. If η is small then this restorative acceleration will be small and it will take a long time for the person to return to their equilibrium (low frequency), whereas a large negative number would provide a large restorative acceleration (high frequency). Over time—the addition of external forces on the pendulum can lead the pendulum to increase or decrease how far it swings (its amplitude). Changes in amplitude, regardless of whether they increase or decrease the amplitude, are called *damping*. Increases or decreases in the amplitude of the pendulum are conveyed in the ζ parameter, with positive values corresponding to an increase in amplitude and negative values corresponding to a decrease in amplitude.

Most constructs are unlikely to change with the perfect oscillations expected of a pendulum. This, however, is not a requirement of the damped linear oscillator model if it is fit as a differential equation rather than using nonlinear estimation of a function such as sine. The differential equation only expresses a relationship between derivatives, stating that the distance a construct is from the equilibrium is related to the amount and direction of its acceleration. So, although this model matches the movements of a pendulum, it does not require the trajectories produced over time to conform to perfect oscillations. It is the ideas of equilibrium and restorative forces that make this model an interesting way that self-regulation could be conceptualized and modeled. The second-order differential equation with negative damping also conforms to the idea of a point attractor[5]. Figure 19.8 shows two time series: one that corresponds to a pendulum–like oscillation and one that does not have perfect oscillation (left and right columns, respectively). The rows show the construct with respect to time (top) and plots of the relationships between derivatives (middle and bottom). Even when there are large departures from a pendulum-like oscillation, the relationships among derivatives remain similar to those of a pendulum.

Rather than solve the second-order differential equation in the manner done with the first-order differential equation, this section considers another option using SEM. In this approach, latent estimates of derivatives are estimated from observed data as described by Boker et al. (Latent Differential Equation Modeling; 2004). The second-order differential equation model is then fit by examining the paths between latent derivatives. The specification of this model does not require series of constraints, as is the case with the approximate discrete model. However, this model does require the time series data to be formatted in a specific way.

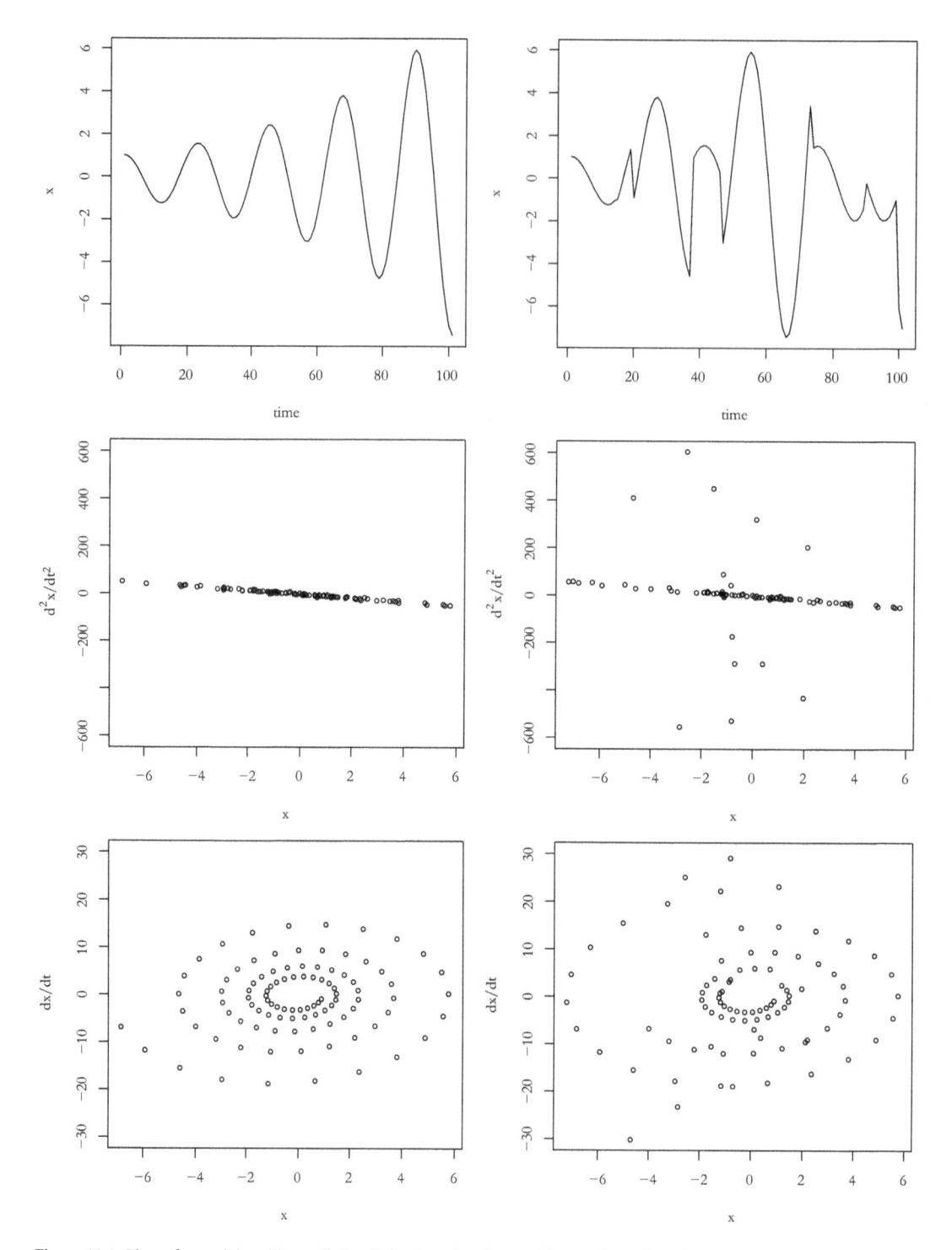

Figure 19.8 Plots of a pendulum-like oscillation (left column) and an oscillator with random disturbances (right column). The top row shows the plot of the construct over time, the subsequent rows show the relationships between estimates of the zeroth and first derivative with estimates of the second derivative.

The data format that is necessary is called and *embedded matrix*—a concept from the state space literature. For out current purposes, we are interested in reconstructing a specific system (the damped linear oscillator model), so this treatment of embedded matrices can be relatively short. The key element to an embedded matrix is the number of *embedding dimensions*—the number of dimensions used to reconstruct a system (Takens, 1981). One way to think about the embedding dimension is that it will determine the number of observations used to estimate the moment-to-moment derivatives of a time series. As we are interested in a second-order model (i.e., a model with acceleration), we need to be able to estimate not just a straight line from data but also the curvature; we know that to estimate a curved line a minimum of three observations is required (four, if one wants to allow for error).

For the second-order model, this requirement of three or four observations to estimate the second derivative sets the lower bound for the embedding dimension—the minimum embedding that will faithfully reconstruct the dynamics of this system. However, how high the number of dimensions should be above the minimum is selected by the researcher and is motivated by two diametrically opposing goals. If one thinks about the embedding dimension as the number of observations that will be used to estimate any one derivative, then one can imagine using a lesser or greater number of observations. If using a lesser number of observations, then estimates will be more influenced by errors in the data and will be further (on average) from their true values than if one were to estimate the derivatives using a larger number of observations (i.e., higher variance in estimation). On the other hand, using a large number of observations, one will begin to average over true change of interest—that is, the true change variance will be reduced. The selection of the embedding dimension in other literatures is primarily motivated by the reconstruction of the system. In psychology and other social sciences, the selection of embedding dimensions must be considered in terms of how quickly the true system of interest is changing and selecting a dimension that strikes a balance between the amount of error reduction that occurs (by using a large embedding dimension) and maximizing the amount of true variance examined (by using a smaller embedding dimension).

Once the embedding dimension is selected, the physical creation of an embedded matrix is straightforward. To create an embedded matrix from a time series x, where x has values $x_1, x_2, ..., x_t$, one must rearrange multiple copies of the series into a matrix where adjacent columns are offset in time. For example, for an embedded matrix with embedding dimension four, we would produce a four column matrix

$$\mathbf{X} = \begin{bmatrix} x_1 & x_2 & x_3 & x_4 \\ x_2 & x_3 & x_4 & x_5 \\ \vdots & \vdots & \vdots & \vdots \\ x_{t-3} & x_{t-2} & x_{t-1} & x_t \end{bmatrix}. \quad (8)$$

This matrix will be entered into SEM software as if it consists of four observed variables, or however many columns one has selected as the embedding dimension. Interested readers can read more introduction to the selection of embedding dimensions and creation of an embedded matrix in Boker et al. (2004) and Deboeck (2011).

Figure 19.9 shows the SEM that will fit the model in Equation 7 to the embedded matrix. Each of the columns of the embedded matrix correspond to one of the observed variables. The paths from the latent variables to the observed variables, like in latent growth curve modeling, are all fixed so that the meaning of the latent variables is defined. The key difference here, in comparison to latent growth curve modeling, is the embedded matrix that treats the data as if we wish to specify lots of little growth curves along the entire length of the time series. The specification of the paths is not quite the same as in latent growth curve modeling—particularly for the second derivative and higher order derivatives—but still bears a resemblance in its estimation of the score of a construct at some time (intercept/zeroth derivative), estimation of how that construct is changing (slope/first derivative), and estimation of how the speed of the scores is accelerating or decelerating (curvature/second derivative). The syntax provided in Appendix B gives the path values for an embedding dimension four and can be altered for any embedding dimension (*see*, Boker et al., 2004)[6].

As with the first-order differential equation model, this section has primarily focused on the simplest of cases: fitting a second-order differential equation model to a single time series. Not discussed here are topics such as how to set the equilibrium to zero, how to include multiple measures of the same construct, or how to analyze the data from multiple individuals. Many of these topics are discussed in the Boker et al. (2004) article and another chapter by Deboeck (2011), as well as examples that have been published using Latent Differential Equation Modeling (Bisconti, Bergeman, & Boker, 2004, 2006; Boker & Laurenceau, 2006; Boker, Leibenluft, Deboeck, Virk, & Postolache, 2008). There are also methods available for producing observed derivative estimates using equally spaced observations (Local Linear Approximation; Boker & Nesselroade,

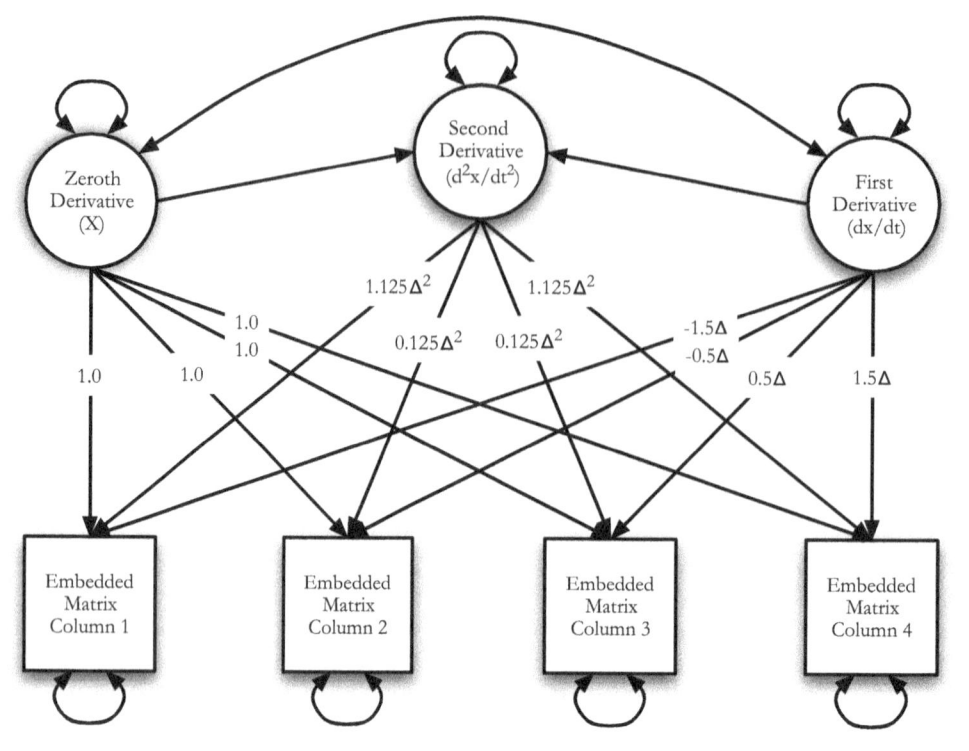

Figure 19.9 Structural equation model using latent differential equation modeling to fit a damped linear oscillator model to an embedded matrix of observed values.

2002; Boker & Graham, 1998), and unequally spaced observations (Generalized Orthogonal Local Derivative Estimates; Deboeck, 2010). Like the first-order differential equation model, we can also think about the coupling of multiple oscillators. Boker and Lauranceau (2006) have worked on several examples of coupled oscillators, examining the intimacy and disclosure patterns of husbands and wives; two coupled pendulums can produce remarkably complex change over time (e.g., Figure 19.1). The work by Boker and Lauranceau also has demonstrated some of the more nuanced questions that can be asked about coupling through this model, such as: Is it the husband's *level* of intimacy that affects his wife, or is it the *change in level* of his intimacy that affects his wife?

Conclusions & Future Directions

This chapter has given a brief introduction to dynamical systems, continuous time models, and methods for applying these ideas to data. The methods for the first-and second-order differential equation models, in particular, demonstrate some relatively new ways to address questions about change in data sets consisting of time series with significant proportions of measurement error. These models are the work of fusing dynamical systems with statistics, taking into account the data constraints often experienced in the social sciences. These tools continue to expand, and the next decade is likely to continue to see the emergence of better methods as well as new ideas for other differential equation models that may be widely applicable to the social sciences.

This chapter did not go into great detail on many topics but has aimed to introduce key terms and ideas to give direction for further reading. Although two methods were mentioned in this article, there are a variety of other methods being used to fit dynamical systems to data. For example there are methods that directly apply equations to observed data such as in Dynamical Causal Modeling (Friston, Harrison, & Penny, 2003), direct comparison of observed and expected matrices (Deboeck & Boker, 2010), and methods that through iterative prediction try to obtain better estimates of observed values and parameter estimates such as Kalman filtering (Chow, Ferrer, & Nesselroade, 2007). The two methods introduced in this chapter were selected because they have been implemented in SEM software, making them (at present) a bit more accessible than other methods. No doubt this will change as more researchers ask questions about the relationships between the current state of constructs and how they are changing.

Dynamical Systems Theory, however, does come at a cost of re-evaluating some of the ways that data are routinely collected and analyzed. Related to dynamical systems is an area called *Ergodic Theory*. The mathematics in this area have highlighted that unless that all people have the same dynamical relationships—that is, all people change according to the same rules—inferences made using interindividual analyses are unlikely to be informative about any particular individual (Molenaar, 2004). This suggests that if one wishes to discuss the individual, which seems pertinent to much of psychology, models will have to be applied within individual before looking at interindivudal differences. Intraindividual models will require many intraindividual measurements.

Despite the problems of data collection and the difficulty of fitting novel models, dynamical systems have become a point attractor. Researchers caught in this attractor are addressing new questions about how people change, sometimes analyzing old data with new methods and coming to a new understanding of those data. And although in the past dynamical systems seemed to require an impossibly large number of observations (many articles would discuss the need for thousands of observations), the combination of new methods for ambulatory assessments and statistical methods developed for shorter time series will no doubt continue to improve our ability to glean information from the seemingly random, complex variation of individuals.

Appendix A: Approximate Discrete Model

The following syntax applies the approximate discrete model to a matrix named "data" with N rows (one row per subject) and 5 columns. The syntax is written for the statistical program R (2012). Users will need to install the R package OpenMx (Boker et al., 2011) prior to running this syntax. This syntax is also available on the website of the author.

Mant comments have been placed in the code, following the # character. The observations in this example were spaced to occur at times 0, 1, 3, 6 and 10; that is, there are different lags between each pair of observations. These lags can be changed by altering the "Delta" matrices in the code below. The model summary provides an estimate of "Aapprox" which is the approximation of the continuous time parameter A. This code uses a raw data matrix and Full Information Maximum Likelihood estimation.

```
rm(list=ls()) # clear workspace
library(OpenMx) #load OpenMx package
colnames(data) <- paste("x",c(1:5),sep="") #assign names to data matrix columns
manifestvariables <- colnames(data)

# begin model, provide raw data matrix
ADMModel5 <- mxModel("ADM5",mxData(data,type="raw"),
    # set up matrices with lag information
    mxMatrix(type="Full",nrow=1,ncol=1,free=FALSE,values=1,name="Delta1"),
    mxMatrix(type="Full",nrow=1,ncol=1,free=FALSE,values=2,name="Delta2"),
    mxMatrix(type="Full",nrow=1,ncol=1,free=FALSE,values=3,name="Delta3"),
    mxMatrix(type="Full",nrow=1,ncol=1,free=FALSE,values=4,name="Delta4"),

    #Create Asymmetric matrix
    mxMatrix(type="Full",nrow=5,ncol=5,byrow=TRUE, name="Asymmetric",
        # tell OpenMx with values will be estimated
        free=c(    FALSE,FALSE,FALSE,FALSE,FALSE,
                   TRUE,TRUE,FALSE,FALSE,FALSE,
                   FALSE,TRUE,TRUE,FALSE,FALSE,
                   FALSE,FALSE,TRUE,TRUE,FALSE,
                   FALSE,FALSE,FALSE,TRUE,TRUE),
        # give estimate values unique names
        labels=c(     NA,NA,NA,NA,NA,
```

```
                "Alag1","Ainst2",NA,NA,NA,
                NA,"Alag2","Ainst3",NA,NA,
                NA,NA,"Alag3","Ainst4",NA,
                NA,NA,NA,"Alag4","Ainst5")),
    # create matrix for Aapprox, relate to Asymmetric values
    mxMatrix(type="Full",nrow=1,ncol=1,free=c(TRUE),values=c(-.5),
                labels=c("Aapprox"), name="Amatrix"),
    mxConstraint(.5*Delta1*Aapprox=="Ainst2"),
    mxConstraint(.5*Delta2*Aapprox=="Ainst3"),
    mxConstraint(.5*Delta3*Aapprox=="Ainst4"),
    mxConstraint(.5*Delta4*Aapprox=="Ainst5"),
    mxConstraint(1+.5*Delta1*Aapprox=="Alag1"),
    mxConstraint(1+.5*Delta2*Aapprox=="Alag2"),
    mxConstraint(1+.5*Delta3*Aapprox=="Alag3"),
    mxConstraint(1+.5*Delta4*Aapprox=="Alag4"),

    # create Symmetric matrix
    mxMatrix(type="Full",nrow=5,ncol=5,byrow=TRUE, name="Symmetric",
        free=c(   TRUE,FALSE,FALSE,FALSE,FALSE,
                  FALSE,TRUE,FALSE,FALSE,FALSE,
                  FALSE,FALSE,TRUE,FALSE,FALSE,
                  FALSE,FALSE,FALSE,TRUE,FALSE,
                  FALSE,FALSE,FALSE,FALSE,TRUE),
        labels=c(     "var1",NA,NA,NA,NA,
                      NA,"var2",NA,NA,NA,
                      NA,NA,"var3",NA,NA,
                      NA,NA,NA,"var4",NA,
                      NA,NA,NA,NA,"var5")),
    # create matrix for G, relate to Symmetric values
    mxMatrix(type="Full",nrow=1,ncol=1,free=TRUE,labels=c("G"), name="Gmatrix"),
    mxConstraint(Delta1*G%*%G=="var2"),
    mxConstraint(Delta2*G%*%G=="var3"),
    mxConstraint(Delta3*G%*%G=="var4"),
    mxConstraint(Delta4*G%*%G=="var5"),

    # create other matrices needed to calculate covariance
    mxMatrix(type="Iden",nrow=5,free=FALSE,name="I"),
    # calculate expected covariance
    mxAlgebra(solve(I-Asymmetric)%*%Symmetric%*%t(solve(I-Asymmetric)),
        name="ExpCov"),
    # create matrix of means
    mxMatrix(type="Full",nrow=1,ncol=5,free=TRUE,labels=paste("M",c(1:5)),
        name="Means",values=apply(data,2,mean)),
    # identify optimization objective
    mxFIMLObjective("ExpCov","Means",dimnames=manifestvariables)
) # finished writing model

model <- mxRun(ADMModel5) # run model, save output as "model"
summary(model) # get summary of output
```

Appendix B: Latent Differential Equation Modeling

The following syntax used latent differential equation modeling to apply the damped linear oscillator model to a single time series named "timeseries." The syntax is written for the statistical program R (2012). Users will need to install the R package OpenMx (Boker et al., 2011) prior to running this syntax. This syntax is also available on the website of the author. Many comments have been placed in the code, following the # character. The model summary provides estimates of the frequency (η) and damping (ζ) parameters. This code uses Full Information Maximum Likelihood estimation. A function "Embed" is provided to embed the time series.

```
rm(list=ls()) #clear workspace
library(OpenMx) #load OpenMx package

# create function to embed data
# x=time series, E=embedding dimension
Embed <- function(x,E) {
    len <- length(x)
    out <- x[1:(len-E+1)]
    for(i in 2:E) { out <- cbind(out,x[(1+i-1):(len-E+i)])}
    return(out)
    }

data <- Embed(timeseries,4) # embed timeseries
colnames(data) <- paste("x",c(1:4),sep="") # add names to embedded matrix

lag <- 1 #time between equally space observations
# manifest and latent variable names
ObsVar <- paste("x",c(1:4),sep="")
MatNames <- c(ObsVar,c("zeroth","first","second"))

# create Asymmetric matrix
A <- mxMatrix(type="Full",nrow=length(MatNames),ncol=length(MatNames),
    free=FALSE,name="A")
A@values[1:4,5] <- c(1,1,1,1)
A@values[1:4,6] <- c(-1.5,-0.5,0.5,1.5)*lag
A@values[1:4,7] <- c(1.125,0.125,0.125,1.125)*(lag^2)
A@labels[7,5] <- "Eta"
A@free[7,5] <- TRUE
A@labels[7,6] <- "Zeta"
A@free[7,6] <- TRUE

# create symmetric matrix
S <- mxMatrix(type="Symm",nrow=length(MatNames),ncol=length(MatNames),
    free=FALSE,name="S")
diag(S@labels) <- c(paste("eObs",c(1:length(ObsVar)),sep=""),
    "eZeroth","eFirst","eSecond")
diag(S@lbound[5:7,5:7]) <- 0
diag(S@free) <- TRUE
S@free[5,6] <- TRUE
S@free[6,5] <- TRUE
S@labels[5,6] <- "CovFirstZeroth"
S@labels[6,5] <- "CovFirstZeroth"

# other matrices needed for covariance algebra, mean estimation
I <- mxMatrix(type="Iden",nrow=length(MatNames),name="I")
F <- mxMatrix(type="Full",nrow=length(ObsVar),ncol=length(MatNames),
    free=FALSE,name="F")
diag(F@values[,1:4]) <- 1
M <- mxMatrix("Full",ncol=1,nrow=length(MatNames),name="M",
    labels=c("M1","M2","M3","M4",rep(NA,3)),
    free=c(rep(TRUE,4),rep(FALSE,3)))
```

```
# create DLO model
DLOmodel <- mxModel("Model",A, S, I, F, M, # include matrices
    # covariance algebra
    mxAlgebra(F%*%solve(I-A)%*%S%*%t(solve(I-A))%*%t(F),
        name="ECov1",dimnames=list(ObsVar,ObsVar)),
    # mean algebra
    mxAlgebra(t(F%*%solve(I-A)%*%M),name="ExpM",dimnames=list(NA,ObsVar)),
    # provide data
    mxData(data,type="raw"),
    # provide optimization objective
    mxFIMLObjective("ECov1","ExpM")
) # finished writing model

DLOout <- mxRun(DLOmodel) # run model, save output as "DLOout"
summary(DLOout) # get summary of output
```

Author Note

Correspondence concerning this chapter can be addressed to Pascal R. Deboeck, Ph.D., University of Kansas, Department of Psychology, 1415 Jayhawk Blvd., Lawrence, Kansas 66045. http://people.ku.edu/~pascal/.

Notes

1. Clearly, this only works if all of the differing intervals have a common multiple.
2. The relationship between Equation 1 and Equation 2—that is, how to solve for Equation 3—is addressed in many introductory resources on stochastic differential equations(e.g., Björk, 2009; Phillies, 2000; van Kampen, 2007). In the statistical physics literature the Wiener process is also called Brownian motion. Langevin's Equation, for example, describes the motion of a Brownian particle and is very similar to the equations presented with velocity v replaced by position x (Langevin, 1908). This same first-order system has also been solved assuming that A is an $n \times n$ matrix rather than a constant, where n represents the number of variables being analyzed (Bergstrom, 1990).
3. Essentially, the approximate discrete model is the result of using a trapezoidal rule, rather than truly integrating the model.
4. There is code published for the approximate discrete model for LISREL in Oud (2007).
5. With positive damping (increasing amplitude), it conforms to the idea of a point repeller, and with no damping it conforms to the idea of a cyclic attractor.
6. Appendix B also provides a function to embed a time series. Mplus code is provided on the website of the author to fit the SEM.

References

Bartlett, M. (1946). On the theoretical specification and sampling properties of autocorrelated time-series. *Journal of the Royal Statistical Society Supplement*, 8, 27–41.

Bergstrom, A. R. (1988). The history of continuous–time econometric models. *Econometric Theory*, 4(3), 365–383.

Bergstrom, A. R. (1990). *Continuous time econometric modelling*. New York, NY: Oxford University Press.

Bisconti, T. L., Bergeman, C. S., & Boker, S. M. (2004). Emotional well-being in recently bereaved widows: A dynamical systems approach. *Journal of Gerontology*, 59B(4), 158–167.

Bisconti, T. L., Bergeman, C. S., & Boker, S. M. (2006). Social support as a predictor of variability: An examination of the adjustment trajectories of recent widows. *Psychology and Aging*, 21(3), 590–599.

Björk, T. (2009). *Arbitrage theory in continuous time, third edition*. New York, NY: Oxford University Press.

Boker, S. M., & Graham, J. (1998). A dynamical systems analysis of adolescent substance abuse. *Multivariate Behavioral Research*, 33(4), 479-507.

Boker, S. M., & Laurenceau, J. P. (2006). Dynamical systems modeling: An application to the regulation of intimacy and disclosure in marriage. In T. A. Walls & J. L. Schafer (Eds.), *Models for intensive longitudinal data* (pp. 195–218). Oxford: Oxford University Press.

Boker, S. M., Leibenluft, E., Deboeck, P. R., Virk, G., & Postolache, T. T. (2008). Mood oscillations and coupling between mood and weather in patients with rapid cycling bipolar disorder. *International Journal of Child Health and Human Development*, 1(2), 181–202.

Boker S, Neale M, Maes H, Wilde M, Spiegel M, Brick T et al. (2011) OpenMx: an open source extended structural equation modeling framework. *Psychometrika*, 76(2), 306–317.

Boker, S. M., Neale, M. C., & Rausch, J. R. (2004). Latent differential equation modeling with multivariate multi-occasion indicators. In K. V. Montfort, J. Oud, & A. Satorra (Eds.), *Recent developments on structural equation models: Theory and applications* (pp. 151–174). Amsterdam, Kluwer: Kluwer Academic Publishers.

Boker, S. M., & Nesselroade, J. R. (2002). A method for modeling the intrinsic dynamics of intraindividual variability: Recovering the parameters of simulated oscillators in multi-wave panel data. *Multivariate Behavioral Research*, 37(1), 127–160.

Chow, S., Ferrer, E., & Nesselroade, J. R. (2007). An unscented kalman filter approach to the estimation of nonlinear dynamical systems models. *Multivariate Behavioral Research*, 42(2), 283–321.

Deboeck, P. R. (2010). Estimating dynamical systems, derivative estimation hints from sir ronald a. fisher. *Multivariate Behavioral Research*, 43, 725–745.

Deboeck, P. R. (2011). Modeling non-linear dynamics. In M. R. Mehl & T. S. Conner (Eds.), *The handbook of research methods for studying daily life*. Guilford.

Deboeck, P. R., & Boker, A. M. (2010). Modeling noisy data with differential equations using observed and expected matrices. *Psychometrika*, 75(3), 420–437.

Delsing, M. J., & Oud, J. H. (2008). Analyzing reciprocal relationships by means of the continuous-time autoregressive latent trajectory model. *Statistica Neerlandica*, 62, 58–82.

Delsing, M. J., Oud, J. H., & De Bruyn, E. E. (2005). Assessment of bidirectional influences between family relationships and adolescent problem behavior: Discrete vs. continuous time analysis. *European Journal of Psychological Assessment*, 21, 226–231.

Friston, K. J., Harrison, L., & Penny, W. (2003). Dynamic causal modelling. *NeuroImage*, 19, 1273–1302.

Gollob, H. F., & Reichardt, C. S. (1987). Taking account of time lags in causal models. *Child Development*, 58, 80–92.

Gollob, H. F., & Reichardt, C. S. (1991). Interpreting and estimating indirect effects assuming time lags really matter. In L. M. Collins & J. L. Horn (Eds.) Best methods for the analysis of change: Recent advances, unanswered questions, future directions (pp. 243–259). Washington, DC: American Psychological Association.

Hamerle, A., Nagl, W., & Singer, H. (1991). Problems with the estimation of stochastic differential-equations using structural equations models. *The Journal of mathematical sociology*, 16(3), 201–220.

Kaplan, D., & Glass, L. (1995). *Understanding nonlinear dynamics*. New York: Springer.

Kline, R. B. (2004). *Principles and practice of structural equation modeling*. New York: The Guilford Press.

Lakshmikantham, V., & Trigiante, D. (2002). *Theory of difference equations: numerical methods and applications*, 2nd ed. New York: Marcel Dekker, Inc.

Langevin, P. (1908). Sur la théorie du mouvement brownien. *Comptes-rendus de l'Académie des Sciences*, 146, 530–532.

McArdle, J. J. & Kadlec, K. M. (2012). Structural equation models. In T. D. Little (Ed.), *The Oxford Handbook of Quantitative Methods, Vol. 2* (Chapter 15). New York: Oxford University Press.

Molenaar, P. C. (2004). A manifesto on psychology as idiographic science: Bringing the person back into scientific psychology, this time forever. *Measurement*, 2(4), 201–218.

Montpetit, M. A., Bergeman, C. S., Deboeck, P. R., Tiberio, S. S., & Boker, S. M. (2010). Resilience–as–process: Negative affect, stress, and coupled dynamical systems. *Psychology and Aging*, 25(3), 631–640.

Oud, J. H. L. (2007). Continuous time modeling of reciprocal relationships in the cross-lagged panel design. In S. Boker & M. Wenger (Eds.), *Data analytic techniques for dynamical systems in the social and behavioral sciences* (pp. 87–129). Mahwah, NJ: Lawrence Erlbaum Associates.

Oud, J. H. L. (2010). Continuous time modeling of panel data by means of sem. In K. van Montfort, J. Oud, & A. Satorra (Eds.), *Longitudinal research with latent variables* (pp. 201–244). New York: Springer.

Oud, J. H. L., & Jansen, R. A. R. G. (2000). Continuous time state space modeling of panel data by means of sem. *Psychometrika*, 65, 199–215.

Phillies, G. D. J. (2000). *Elementary lectures in statistical mechanics*. New York, NY: Springer–Verlag.

R Development Core Team. (2012). R: *A Language and Environment for Statistical Computing*. Vienna, Austria: R Foundation for Statistical Computing. http://www.R-project.org/

Smith, L. B., & Thelen, E. (2003). Development as a dynamic system. *Trends in Cognitive Science*, 7(8), 343–348.

Strogatz, S. H. (1994). *Nonlinear dynamics and chaos: with applications to physics, biology, chemistry, and engineering*. Cambridge, MA: Westview Press.

Takens, F. (1981). Detecting strange attractors in turbulence. In D. A. Rand & L. S. Young (Eds.), *Dynamical systems and turbulence, lecture notes in mathematics, vol. 898*. Berlin: Springer–Verlag.

Thelen, E., & Smith, L. B. (2006). Dynamic systems theories. In R. M. Lerner (Ed.), *Handbook of child psychology, 6th edition, volume 1, theoretical models of human development* (pp. 258–312). Hoboken, New Jersey: John Wiley & Sons, Inc.

Thompson, J. M., & Stewart, H. B. (1986). *Nonlinear dynamics and chaos: Geometrical methods for engineers and scientists*. New York, NY: John Wiley & Sons.

Toharudin, T., Oud, J. H., & Billiet, J. B. (2008). Assessing the relationships between nationalism, ethnocentrism, and individualism in flanders using bergstrom's approximate discrete model. *Statistica Neerlandica*, 62, 83–109.

van Kampen, N. G. (2007). *Stochastic processes in physics and chemistry, third edition*. Amsterdam, Netherlands: Elsevier.

Waddington, C. H. (1957). *The strategy of the genes: A discussion of some aspects of theoretical biology*. New York, NY: The Macmillan Company.

Yule, G. U. (1927). On a method of investigating periodicities in disturbed series, with special reference to wolfer's sunspot numbers. *Philosophical Transactions of the Royal Society of London. Series A*, 226, 267–298.

CHAPTER 20

Intensive Longitudinal Data

Theodore A. Walls

Abstract

This chapter summarizes briefly recent developments in the area of intensive longitudinal data analysis. These data arise frequently in technology-enabled research studies. Attention is given to the important theoretical distinction of idiographic versus nomothetic inference, in part because the longer and rich series frequently available when devices are used for measurement supports new and profitable inferential opportunities in the idiographic arena of modeling. Additionally, the advent of technology-based measurement and associated opportunities in study deployment and modeling are discussed. Some concerns about the role of reactivity in current and emerging studies are outlined.

Key Words: Intensive longitudinal data, idiographic-nomothetic distinction, microsensors, technology-enabled research studies

With few exceptions, longitudinal studies of human behavior traditionally have involved a handful of occasions of measurement over a study term. However, in the 1980s, following increased use of diary approaches and technology-supported measurement protocols, studies began regularly to attain 30, 50, over even more occasions of measurement in studies generally targeted at describing or explaining behavior. Most of these studies were focused on naturalistic measurement of health behavior and/or psychosocial parameters tracked *in vivo* and over *contexts*. Examples include stressful triggers, motivational states, marital relations, substance use, and criminal behavior, to name a few. Walls and Schafer (2006) suggested that data from these studies conform to a new class of data and referred to it as *intensive longitudinal data* (ILD) in a volume of case studies of statistical models in application mainly to health data. At the same time, a companion volume edited by Stone et al. (2007), also published by Oxford, described the science of collecting self-reports on subjects over time, frequently with the aid of technology. Both volumes covered the range of theoretical, instrumentation-focused, methodological, and substantive health behavioral topics. Similar practitioner-oriented titles have emerged on experience sampling techniques (Hektner, Csikszentmihalyi, & Schmidt, 2007) and on a diversity of measurement approaches for studying daily life (Mehl & Connor, 2012).

In this chapter, I review the state-of-the-art in methodological approaches to the analysis of intensive longitudinal data. First, I review important themes encountered in the collection and analysis of ILD data; some of these were described in Walls and Schafer (2006). Second, I review an important theoretical scientific topic, the idiographic-nomothetic distinction, and outline why this topic bears heavily on design of study and data analytic decisions in ILD investigations. Third, I present, in short form, some statistical models identified by Walls and Schafer (2006) and further chronicle models emerging since 2006 with relevance to analysis of

ILD. In light of the foregoing, I conclude with consideration of some challenges and opportunities faced by the community in ensuring that this class of studies will advance science and maintain an important position in funded scholarship. In particular, I review the concept of reactivity and describe some ways in which emerging device-oriented studies may present new manifestations of participant reactance.

Review of Intensive Longitudinal Data

Intensive longitudinal data arise in any situation where quantitative or qualitative characteristics of multiple individuals or study units are recorded at more than a handful of time-points. The number of occasions may be in the tens, hundreds, or thousands. The frequency or spacing of measurements in time may be regular or irregular, fixed or random, and the variables measured at each occasion may be few or many. Intensive longitudinal data may also arise in situations involving continuous-time measurement of recurrent events, provided that the period of measurement is long enough for a large number of these events to be potentially observed for each subject.

Although a larger number of occasions gave rise to the concept of ILD, and the number of dimensions under consideration at once is central to the analytical challenge researchers face; the features that make ILD unique and worthy of special consideration pertain to the scientific motivations for collecting them, the unusual nature of the hypotheses they are intended to address, and the complex features of the data that need to be revealed and parameterized by statistical models.

Sources of Data

Some of the oldest ILD from human participants came from diary studies. Individuals were asked to complete by paper and pencil, usually at the end of the day, a log of their experiences or actions (Walls, Jung, & Schwartz, 2006). For analytic purposes, diary data were often aggregated into means, totals, or other coarse summaries. In many cases, the high frequency of measurement was not central to the scientific questions being addressed; the primary reason for obtaining daily reports was to reduce bias and variance in the measurement process by having participants respond while the experiences were still relatively fresh in their minds. Recent technological developments have made the collection of diary data more convenient for respondents and researchers alike. Subjects are now given small electronic devices (e.g., palmtop computers) that prompt them at various times throughout the day to ask questions and record responses. Among psychologists, the frequent recording of thoughts, feelings, or actions by electronic means has been referred to as the experience-sampling method (ESM; Csikszentmihalyi & Larson, 1987) and ecological momentary assessment (EMA; Stone & Shiffman, 2002). Other techniques, as covered by Nusser (2006), involve automatic sensing of physical behaviors (e.g., number of steps taken) or bodily states (e.g., blood pressure or glucose levels) by using ambulatory devices that unobtrusively monitor participants in their natural environments outside of a laboratory (Mehl & Conner, 2012). A vast array of other microsensors have been emerging rapidly in the past few years, ranging from electrodermal sensors to movement sensors to rapid assay devices (Poh, Swenson, & Picard, 2011; Sadana, 2003; Varkey, Pompili, & Walls, 2011). Frequently, ambulatory behavioral monitoring measurement devices and technology-enabled questionnaires have been employed in these studies. Of course, devices measuring actions and states may also be used in laboratories and clinics. Audio or video recordings of individuals as they interact with their physical environment or with one another, which are subsequently reviewed and coded by researchers, can also generate high volumes of ILD. Although most of the data examples used in this chapter involve human participants, ILD are also compiled from administrative records regarding institutions, organizational units, localities, retail outlets, and so on.

Recurring Themes in Intensive Longitudinal Data Modeling

There are several distinguishing features of ILD and concomitant modeling efforts to date. The first feature is *the complexity and variety of individual trajectories and the need to move beyond simple time-graded effects*. With shorter series, patterns of average growth or change over time may be reasonably described by incorporating the effects of time through a linear or quadratic trend. Individual variation in trends, if necessary, can be accommodated by allowing intercepts, slopes, and so on, to randomly vary from one subject to another. With ILD, however, describing temporal change by conventional polynomials is rarely appropriate. Many waves of measurement produce complicated trajectories that are difficult to describe by simple parametric curves. Moreover, we often find that the empirically derived shapes of these trajectories, even after smoothing over time, may vary wildly from one subject to another. With such strong variation, the relevance of a population-average time trend becomes questionable, because in comparison to the individual curves, the average may be highly atypical. If the period of data collection represents a very narrow slice of the participants' lifespan, then a pattern of average growth may be irrelevant or undetectable; long-term trends may be swamped by short-term variation. Sometimes it is reasonable to completely remove any absolute measure of time from the mean structure and view each subject's data as a realization of an autocorrelated process that is stable or stationary. Another common theme, which is closely related to the previous one, is *the need to rethink the role of time as a covariate.* With ILD, there may be no obvious way to align the trajectories so that the time variable has an equivalent meaning across subjects; this problem is called curve registration (Ramsay & Li, 1998). If the study involves an intervention, then the start of the intervention may provide a natural anchor point; in some cases, it could be the time of a major life event (e.g., a change in marital status). In other situations, no natural origin exists, and time may need to be characterized in some other way.

With high intensities of measurement, however, we may need to recognize that time is heterogeneous. Morning is different from evening; Wednesday is different from Sunday; this Tuesday may be very different from next Tuesday. Effects may be cyclic, periodic, or vary randomly over the discrete units of time by which biological and social processes are organized. With ILD, descriptors of time, such as time of day or day of week, are often more influential than time itself, and the data analyst may need to introduce these features in new and creative ways. The need to decide whether an assumed temporal pattern holds for any one, any subset of, or all subjects also arises. A third theme of ILD analyses is that *effects of interest are often found in the covariance structure.* Most books and articles on longitudinal data assume that the parameters of greatest concern are the effects of covariates on the mean of a response variable, either in a population-average or subject-specific sense. Longitudinal analysis is usually presented as an extension of classical regression, and inferences about regression coefficients are seen as the primary goal. Although these coefficients are important, the most interesting features of ILD may lie elsewhere. With many waves of measurement, we may find that subjects vary not only in their means but also in their variances and covariances. Some individuals are stable, whereas others are erratic. Some may show strong positive relationships among measured variables, whereas others may show weak or negative relationships. If we seek to understand and explain this variation in the covariance structure, then we can no longer treat that structure as a nuisance but must model it carefully and systematically. A fourth emergent theme is *a focus on relationships that change over time.* In traditional longitudinal analyses, the effects of time-varying covariates are often taken to be fixed. That is, with a small number of occasions, one would typically estimate a single coefficient that reflects an average association between the time-varying covariate and the response. With a moderate number of occasions, we may discern that this association actually varies from one subject to another and include variance components to account for that variation. With intensive longitudinal measurement, however, we may have the opportunity to discover that the association not only varies among individuals but also within individuals over time. Trends in association parameters are often complex, not easily described by simple time-by-covariate interactions, and we may need to consider models with nonparametrically time-varying coefficients. A fifth feature is *an interest in autodependence and regulatory mechanisms.* Traditional longitudinal models focus on how a response varies over time, on the relationship between a time-varying response and covariate, or on a hazard rate that varies in relation to covariates. Many analyses of ILD, however, involve issues of an autodependent or self-regulatory nature. How does a high level of a response at one occasion, or a change in response from one occasion to the next, influence the distribution of the response at later occasions? Does the occurrence of an event temporarily elevate or depress the probability of additional arrivals later in time? Does self-regulation lead to oscillatory behavior? Questions like these move the toolbox for ILD away from basic regression into the realm of multiple-subject time series, dynamical systems, point process models, and control processes.

The Idiographic-Nomothetic Continuum

One of the themes mentioned in an earlier section involves effects of interest possibly residing in the covariance structure. Some models already published by Rovine and Walls (2006) and several papers in the domains of state space modeling and dynamic factor analysis explicitly cover models that attend to the covariance structure well (Chow et al., 2009;

Wood and Brown, 1994.), both for the within-subject case and multiple-subject case. However, this theme can be viewed as part of a larger theoretical scientific trend toward the allocation of models on a continuum between idiographic and nomothetic models. This distinction stemmed from Munsterberg (1899) who suggested that in the idiographic conception, particular descriptions are too unique to gain accurate information through generalities, so they cannot be defined by a general nomothetic description. This distinction was refined by Allport (1957) in the context of personality research and involves a pair of distinctions, whereas an idiographic view on personality holds that each person's life history is unique and operates on its own properties, and whereas, by contrast, a nomothetic view requires that all persons share features that are species-wide and each person is a person replicate of those properties to varying extents. This distinction may have several implications for modeling of intensive longitudinal data and warrants some more attention for this reason. If the idiographic–nomothetic distinction is held as a dichotomous split, that is, to adopt one distinction means that one does not adhere to theories of science attendant to the other, this may have a rather immobilizing impact on attempts at developing understanding of a phenomenon. For example, work by Molenaar (2004) has been consistent with the view that the idiographic position must be primary for study of humans psychological processes. He argues that processes under study in psychology are ergodic, and hence intra-individual variation is not equal to interindividual variation. In fact, under Allport's description, in the idiographic approach, every case is unique and so should be considered on an individual basis (Allport, 1962). This position contrasts sharply with traditional approaches in statistics and epidemiology and, of course, with attendant mainstream analytical strategies in psychology.

An alternative is to view the distinction as a continuum of conceptions in which the analysis vantage points implied by either end of the continuum need to be entertained simultaneously and mutually respected. As a continuum of nomothetic to idiographic conceptions, the dialogue moves to the level of the observation; a maxim could be that any data point could be considered in idiographic (unique) or nomothetic (general) terms. That is, no given observation, whether from a study or an analysis that is nominally more or less idiographic, need be framed as inherently one or the other. Accordingly, Silverstein (1981) suggested that events can be abstracted into universal or particular descriptions to regard specific (idiographic) or general (nomothetic) processes. Windelband (1921) argued that the particular is subordinate to the general and the general must ever accommodate the particular. In general, one can conclude that the vantage points implied by either end of the continuum of conceptions along the idiographic to nomothetic continuum need to be entertained simultaneously and mutually respected. This is the case for two reasons. First, the description of all individual (idiographic) processes comprise the general (nomothetic) definition of the processes. Inversely stated, nomothetic descriptions include all cases of the particulars they describe, and are a general description of what is always common to all (Lamiell, 1998). The general law covers any instance of that phenomenon (Lamiell, 1998). This is in line with the original Windelband definition of nomothetic, which holds that statements that are true in general include all instances of the particular they cover (Windelband, 1921). An alternative perspective on this note suggests that purposive, individual-specific life histories consist of the species-level tract of possible human functioning. In this view, the term nomothetic refers to the utilization of comprehensive models to test and explain process, assuming each individual's uniqueness within the generality (Silverstein, 1988, p. 425). That individuals can develop individualized life histories is evidence of the principle of the thing (human) unfolding from its purposes (Silverstein, 1988, p. 427). Individuals house functional (purpose-driven) processes that consist of requisite cases for functioning at the higher levels of complexity. Extending this idea, Molenaar (2004) has suggested that the complete set of life histories of a population of human participants can be represented as a collection of trajectories in the same behavior space.

A second unifying concept suggests that individual cases arise from an underlying universal process of the species. In this view, the nomothetic conception is concerned with the laws under which each fact stands, such as in psychology (Munsterberg, 1899). The species is then defined by the presence of given universal processes manifested by individuals as instantiations (Silverstein, 1988).

These considerations are both intellectually intriguing and also somewhat polarizing with respect to inference. It may be worth considering that nomothetic and idiographic conceptions should correspond to each other in some way. For example, error deviations from centroid estimates reflecting individual scores versus individual specific trend estimates need not be viewed as right or wrong. Rather, it is important to simply recognize what the two might mean and how they might inform each other. Similarly, a robust description of individual processes could also be upwardly aggregated, as in k-means clustering. Such vantage points are crucial to the future of modeling for ILD, because with the large amount of data, many more possible inferences can be pursued. Analysts must navigate serious theoretical scientific issues such as the ones outlined here before embarking on modeling.

Reactivity

A second scientific issue of great importance to modeling ILD involves the issue of reactivity. Introducing monitoring devices and surveillance systems into research with human subjects immediately raises the specter of reactivity. *Reactivity*, also called reactive arrangements, means that individuals may change their behavior simply because they know they are being watched. More generally, it refers to any issue of external invalidity arising from novelty and surveillance effects in experiments and observational studies (Campbell & Stanley, 1963). Reactivity comes into play whenever a testing situation is not simply a passive recording of behavior but itself becomes a stimulus to change (Campbell & Stanley, 1963, p. 9). One of the earliest and most famous examples of reactivity is the Hawthorne effect, in which the productivity of factory workers was seen to improve regardless of the experimental condition applied (Franke & Kaul, 1978). Diaries and electronic devices that collect ILD can produce new forms of reactivity. We might observe a priming effect, an initial rise or fall in the mean response, as participants gain familiarity with a device and gradually settle into a routine. Some researchers have noted decreasing variation and increasing rates of nonresponse over time. Subjects may tire when repeatedly prompted for what they perceive to be the same information and may respond inertly, settle on a favored score, or fail to respond altogether. Time and place also matter. When subjects are asked to respond in different contexts—homes, offices, play places, cars, and so on—and at different times of day, the nature of the measurement process could drastically change. Quite naturally, one might question the validity and reliability of self-report data in the initial stages of a study as participants grow accustomed to the device. Moreover, as the study progresses, one could imagine that individuals' responses may no longer be highly correlated with their instantaneous true scores; after subjects have adjusted to the protocol, their answers may become essentially random or hover within a relatively limited range. In many cases, not much can be done to measure reactivity or adjust for its effects within a single study. However, an awareness of these issues may help—knowing, for example, that diminished within-person variation over time could be an artifact of measurement—influence the way we interpret the results of our analyses or design future studies. Empirical evidence in experiments and observational studies indicate that reactivity tends to diminish as devices become easier to use (Hufford & Shields, 2002).

In addition, with the development of the next wave of devices and device configurations (which include nanoscale biological sensors and signaling devices, devices tied to social networks, geographic indicators such as GPS or cell phone networks, interfaces among sensors and electronic data storage repositories, and computers algorithms that can compute and provide summarized information back into these multiple nodes of these systems), the role of reactivity may rise to previously unknown levels. Or, as the case may be, certain users of devices may be so comfortable with a life context that includes multiple electronic that the impact of device use may be overstated. Further, the forms of the devices and their functionality may give rise to other reactions in participants that could bias study results or, worse, cause human subjects participation issues such as injury, loss of privacy, legal consequences, or lesser levels of discomfort. These issues are particularly prominent in four areas: biological health, socio-emotional functioning, attention and cognition, and societal risk. These areas roughly match those covered in standard human subjects protections, but their manifestations in ILD studies warrants some careful consideration (National Institute of Justice, 2011). In the area of *biological health*, for example, use of adherable or injectable devices may carry the risk of infection, impairment of physical movement, or immunological response. Multiple electronic devices may also generate electrical patterns or radiation effects that could induce unknown impacts on the body or possibly aggravate functions of sweat glands, skin functions, or other biological processes. Whereas traditional studies in psychology typically involve only passing exposure to technology in a lab, ILD studies frequently involve integration of devices into the normal lifestyle for extended periods. In the areas of *attention and cognition*, although some devices may be unobtrusive and require no conscious engagement from the user other than awareness that the device is there, others may require attention to a degree that some may find detracts from volitional personal experience. For example, a device that is used to track heart rate may be mostly unobtrusive, but constant attention to deviations such as in apparent but subclinical tachycardia may detract from normal experience unnecessarily. In addition, a device that requires two-way interaction, such as in the case of a device-enabled intervention, may detract from natural experience in ways that prevent the true course of events. For example, recognition on the part of a drinker that he is providing data to a device about his drinking behavior, location, and company may alter the experience of processing thoughts about the behavior. In the area of *socio-emotional functioning*, it is easy to imagine that the sensation of "being tracked" may present a threat to emotional or social well-being of subjects, especially if the behaviors under study are illicit, such as illegal drug use, or involve subjects with criminal histories or restrictions. Less dramatically, but of equal or greater concern, a perception that parents may be able to obtain behavior about children would certainly impact compliance in protocols for adolescents, and researchers work very hard to assure these kinds of participants are aware of their rights and of how data are used. Several of the same examples outlined in the case of socio-emotional functioning also may translate into actual *societal risks* if data are lost or if laws and policies enable the use of information collected in ways that could harm participants. For example, if an insurance company offers web-based or other tracking of health behaviors to help covered members attain health improvements, then it is possible that data could be used to change rates or reduce claim payments if behaviors were the basis of rates. With increasing pressure on health costs and insurers to maintain costs, this risk seems quite real at present. Of even greater concern, if data from the study could in some way be used against people in their jobs or private lives, then resistance to electronically enabled tracking could meet with wide societal resistance. Although these risks exist in traditional studies not facilitated by technology, the instantaneous and continuous monitoring and upload of data about behavior producing a rather "Orwellian" condition is threatening even to many technologists (Orwell, 1949). Moreover, features of data storage and computer processing equipment may enable a host of other behaviors in the context of a study that simply would not be possible in a paper-and-pencil survey or lab experience. Whereas these studies typically involve the observation of behaviors by scientists, subjects can conceivably control the instruments themselves by reprogramming or feeding misinformation to it. This is possible because increasingly devices not only send information to researchers, but they could be manipulated to send it to others or whole networks of others (such as online social networking sites), and they also receive information. As in the case of drinking behavior noted above, device use may deter drinkers from seeing a participant as a desirable partner in the joint behavior. It is not difficult to imagine that technology savvy and electronic context-oriented communities may interact about an entire protocol, comment on the functionality of devices, and provide assistance to one another to manipulate signals for well-intentioned, harmless, or less well-intentioned and harmful acts. Hence, the use of technological monitoring is inextricably linked to societal experience with communication technology and its rapid and frequently changing functionality. These are concerns and challenges that exciting field must face thoughtfully.

Statistical Models

The models covered in Walls and Schafer (2006) fall in three categories. First, they covered extensions of the general linear mixed model to include robust or diverse parameterizations of the response and explain the heterogeneity of variance across cluster units (frequently data series of human subjects) through the use of theoretically important covariates. Second, they introduced several approaches that capture the dynamics of human behavior based on multivariate time series—for example, through extensions of time series analysis, state-space modeling, control modeling, and dynamical models. Third, they considered the possibility of point process and other event history models being relevant in cases where series and the processes they describe likely conform to these kinds of models. It is fair to say that this volume provided a valuable resource for consolidating diverse analytical frameworks that bore relevance to the analysis of ILD, and many of these approaches have been employed. Reviewers of the volume have pointed out some areas for additional consideration. These include greater attention to models for single-subject analyses, models for recurrent events and multiple spells, and issues in variable reduction (Cook, 2007; Land, 2007; van Montfort, 2007). Since the publication of the volume, several new and exciting modeling developments have occurred, and researchers have realized more about the possibilities, collecting these data in ways that will make modeling more profitable. I review a few of these here, however, a complete review is beyond the scope of this chapter.

First, regime-switching state-space model as proposed by Kim and Nelson (1999) is used for a system that switches back and forth between two or more regimes. This is important for many ILD studies because basic models for shapes will poorly represent series with dramatic changes in amplitude or covariance. Another modeling framework that certainly bears relevance and that has progressed recently in application to ILD is the hidden Markov model for individual time series in the case of discrete data. Visser and Speekenbrink (2010) have developed an R package for deploying these models and a chapter in Visser and colleagues (2009) in which clear examples describe how individual time series can be modeled with this approach. Through somewhat related approaches, Chow and colleagues (2009) have explored several other ways to model the dynamics in ILD with attention to the influence of mutual states in dyads. In fact, the area of dyadic relations has been particularly leveraged by model development for ILD (Boker & Laurenceau, 2006; Ferrer et al., 2010; Hsieh et al., 2010).

Second, by contrast, when the interest is in the effect of an intervention and an interest is in whether a switch in the process took place, the approach would be to see whether something actually changed then by comparing the parameters before and after. For this need, traditional time series interruption models can be used or change-point or structural-break models can be employed (Cohen, 2008). Consistently, Walls and colleagues (2012) have described a set of design considerations that may be used to craft studies when the interruption is based on multiple time-scales. Extensions of change-point and structural-break models for these designs should be straightforward in some cases, although in others, ways to deal with the clustered nature of data within time-scale blocks will be necessary.

Third, some extensions to new data forms have been explored. Von Eye and Bogat (2009) have handled categorical intensive longitudinal data in a modification of configural frequency analysis. In addition, work by several authors have explored ways to handle categorical data with respect to modeling of clustered data (see work by Verbeke & Molenberghs, 2005, and subsequent extensions in application of adaptive quadrature), causal inference in the case of binary data (Albert, 2008), as well as diverse, expansive, and widely available new work on the application of mixture models to serial data. Several authors, notably, Chow (2010), have also begun to capitalize on model advancement opportunities in cases with ILD arise from research on dyads measured in daily life or in experimental settings.

Challenges and Opportunities

Intensive longitudinal data are generated by diary studies, electronic tracking devices, and research protocols that generate multivariable measures on many occasions. This chapter has retraced the approaches covered in Walls and Schafer (2006) and considered some important themes that have become prominent in the consideration of ILD over the short 5 years since its publication. Methods for consideration of these data include many applied statistical techniques extended for use with these data and increasingly involve strategies intended to reflect important phenomenological dynamics and qualitative shifts. Further, innovations in design, further fieldwide experience with devices and their related reactivity, and further elaboration of modeling approaches for specific analytical needs, data forms, and in light of other modeling technology have become commonplace.

A few other issues come to mind. One involves the extent to which so-called ILD are actually rich or sparse. Although the emergence of these data in psychology contrasted starkly with traditional longitudinal studies (several cross-sections over time), it may be the case that the dynamics of interest to many psychologists are still not measured at the time-scale at which they actually reside or, therein, with the frequency of measurement needed to employ models used in other disciplines (such as physics or engineering) needed to describe dynamics parsimoniously. The complexity of whether idiographic or nomothetic type inference should prevail also generates an overlay that further constrains model selection for various databases.

Another issue involves the fact that the technological state-of-the-art for collecting ILD, the design of study and measurement considerations, and the statistical models are still evolving and driving each other's development. For example, in years to come we can expect that public policy will respond to research participants' needs for privacy in device use. Studies may be proscribed to be deployed within the boundaries of tighter regulation than currently exists.

In general, we can be certain that the diversity of model development activity around ILD is still in its early infancy, with myriad opportunities for innovation in design and statistical development apparent. In fact, this chapter only incompletely documents many quantitative developments and applications in diverse areas that emerge almost daily with the burgeoning of electronic measurement at the international societal level as electronic devices with tracking and intervention capability pervade our existence.

References

Albert, J.M. (2008). Mediation analysis via potential outcomes models. *Statistics in Medicine. 27,* 1282–1304.

Allport, G. W. (1957). European and American theories of personality. In H. David and H. von Bracken (Eds) *Perspectives in personality theory*. Oxford: Basic Books.

Allport, G. W. (1962). The general and the unique in psychological science. *Journal of Personality, 30* (3), 405–422.

Boker, S. M., & Laurenceau, J-P. (2006). Dynamical systems modeling: An application to the regulation of the intimacy and disclosure in marriage. In T. A. Walls & J. L. Schafer (Eds.), *Models for intensive longitudinal data* (pp. 195–218). New York: Oxford University Press.

Campbell D. T., & Stanley, J. C. (1963). Experimental and quasi-experimental designs for research on teaching. In N. L. Gage (Ed.), *Handbook of research on teaching* (pp. 171–246). Chicago, IL: Rand McNally.

Chow, S.-M., Hamaker, E. L., Fujita, F. & Boker, S. M. (2009). Cyclic state-space models as a representation of change. *British Journal of Mathematical and Statistical Psychology, 62,* 683–716.

Cook, R.J. (2007). Models for intensive longitudinal data. International Statistical Review, *75(2),* 274–275.

Csikszentmihalyi, M. & Larson, R. (1987). Validity and reliability of the experience sampling method. *Journal of Nervous and Mental Disease, 175,* 526–536.

Ferrer, E., Chen, S., Chow, S.M., & Hsieh, F. (2010). Exploring intra-individual, inter-individual and inter-variable dynamics in dyadic interactions. In S.M. Chow, E. Ferrer, & F. Hsieh (Eds.), *Statistical methods for modeling human dynamics: An interdisciplinary dialogue* (pp. 381–411). New York: Taylor and Francis.

Franke, R.H. & Kaul, J.D. (1978). The Hawthorne Experiments: First statistical interpretation. *American Sociological Review, 43,* 623–643.

Hektner, J. M., Schmidt, J. A., & Csikszentmihalyi, M. (2007). *Experience sampling method: Measuring the quality of everyday life*. Thousand Oaks, CA: Sage.

Hsieh, F., Ferrer, E., Chen, S., & Chow, S-M. (2010). Exploring nonstationary dynamics in dyadic interactions via hierarchical segmentation. *Psychometrika 75(2),* 351–372.

Hufford, M. & Shields, A. (2002). Electronic diaries applications and what works in the field. *Applied Clinical Trials* (online) 46–59.

Kim, C.-J., & Nelson, C. R. (1999). *State-space models with regime switching: Classical and Gibbs-sampling approaches with applications*. Cambridge, MA: The MIT Press.

Lamiell, J. T. (1998). "Nomothetic" and "idiographic": Contrasting windelband's understanding with contemporary usage. *Theory and Psychology, 8*(1), 23–38.

Land, K.C. (2007). Models for intensive longitudinal data. *American Journal of Sociology, 113* (September), 596–598.

Mehl, M. R. & Conner, T. S. (Eds.) (2012). *Handbook of research methods for studying daily life*. New York: Guilford Press

Molenaar, P. C. M. (2004). A manifesto on psychology as idiographic science: Bringing the person back into scientific psychology, this time forever. *Measurement: Interdisciplinary Research and Perspectives, 2*(4), 201–218.

Munsterberg, H. (1899). Psychology and history. *Psychological review, 6* (1), 1–31.

National Institute of Justice (2011). Human Subjects and Privacy Protection. Retrieved from http://www.ojp.usdoj.gov/nij/funding/humansubjects/welcome.htm. Last accessed September 11, 2012.

Nusser, S., Intille, S. S., & Maitra, R. (2006). Emerging technologies and nextgeneration intensive longitudinal data collection. In Walls, T. A. and Schafer, J. S. (Eds.). *Models for intensive longitudinal data*. New York: Oxford University Press.

Orwell, G. (1949). *Nineteen Eighty-Four*. New York: Harcourt, Brace and Jovanovitch.

Poh, M.Z., Swenson, N.C., & Picard, R.W. (2010). A Wearable Sensor for Unobtrusive, Long-term Assessment of Electrodermal Activity. *IEEE Transactions on Biomedical Engineering, 57*(5), 1243–1252.

Ramsay, J. O. & Li, X. (1998) Curve registration. *Journal of the Royal Statistical Society, Series B, 60,* 351–363.

Rovine, M. R. & Walls, T. A. (2006). Multilevel autoregressive modeling of interindividual differences in the stability of a process. In Walls, T. A. and Schafer, J. S. (Eds.). *Models for intensive longitudinal data*. New York: Oxford University Press.

Sadana, A. (2003). *Biosensors: Kinetics of binding and dissociative fractals*. Oxford, UK: Elsevier.

Silverstein, A. (1988). An Aristotelian resolution of the idiographic versus nomothetic tension. *American Psychologist, 43*(6), 425–430.

Stone, A.A. & Shiffman, S. (2002). Capturing momentary, self-report data: A proposal for reporting guidelines. *Annals of Behavioral Medicine, 24,* 236–243.

Stone, A., Shiffman, S., Atienza, A. & Nebelling, L. (2007). *The science of real-time data.* capture. New York: Oxford.

Van Montfort, K. (2007). Review of Models for Intensive Longitudinal Data. *Psychometrika, 72*(3), 451–454.

Varkey, J-P., Pompili, D., & Walls, T. A. (2011). Human motion recognition using a wireless sensor-based wearable system. *Personal and Ubiquitous Computing* [On-line first].

Verbeke, G. & Molenberghs, G. (2005). *Models for discrete longitudinal data*. New York: Springer.

Visser, I. Maartje, E. J., Raijmakers & van der Maas, H.L.J. (2009). Hidden Markov Models for Individual Time Series. In J. Valsiner, P.C.M. Molenaar, M.C.D.P. Lyra, N. Chaudhary(Eds.). *Dynamic Process Methodology in the Social and Developmental Sciences* (pp. 269–289), New York: Springer.

Visser, I. & Speekenbrink, M. (2010). depmixS4: An R Package for Hidden Markov Models. *Journal of Statistical Software, 36*(7), 1–21.

von Eye, A., & Bogat, G.A. (2009). Analysis of intensive categorical longitudinal data. In J. Valsiner, P.C.M. Molenaar, M.C.D.P Lyra, & N. Chaudhary (Eds.), *Dynamic Process*

Walls, T.A., Barta, W.D. Stawski, R.S., Collyer, C. & Hofer, S.M. (2012). Time-scale Dependent Longitudinal Designs. In B. Laursen, T.D. Little, & N. Card. (Eds.). *Handbook of Developmental Research Methods*. New York: Guilford Press.

Walls, T. A., Jung, H., & Schwartz, J. (2006). *Multilevel models and intensive longitudinal data*. In Walls, T. A. and Schafer, J. S. (Eds.). *Models for intensive longitudinal data*. New York: Oxford University Press.

Walls, T.A. & Schafer, J.S. (2006). *Models for Intensive Longitudinal Data*. New York: Oxford University Press.

Windelband, W. (1921). *An introduction to philosophy.* London: Unwin.

Wood, P. and Brown, D. (1994). The study of intraindividual differences by means of dynamic factor models: Rationale, implementation, and interpretation. *Psychological Bulletin, 116*(1), 166–186.

Yu, Q., Scribner, R., Carlin, B., Theall, K., Simonsen, N., Ghosh-Dastidar, B., Cohen, D., & Mason, K. 2008, Multilevel spatiotemporal dual changepoint models for relating alcohol outlet destruction and changes in neighborhood rates of assaultive violence, *Geospatial Health, 2*(2), 161–172.

CHAPTER
21 Dynamic Factor Analysis: Modeling Person-Specific Process

Nilam Ram, Annette Brose, *and* Peter C. M. Molenaar

Abstract

Modern data collection technologies are providing large data sets, with many repeated observations of many individuals on many variables—and new opportunities for application of analytical techniques that consider individuals as unique, complex, multivariate, dynamic entities. In this chapter we review the conceptual and technical background for dynamic factor analysis and provide a primer for application to multivariate time series data. Step-by-step procedures are illustrated using daily diary data obtained from three women over 100+ days. Specifically, we provide background on and demonstrate (1) formulation of DFA research questions; (2) study design and data collection; (3) variable selection and data pre-processing procedures; (4) the fitting and evaluation of person-specific DFA models; and (5) examination of between-person differences/similarities. We conclude by pointing to some extensions that might be elaborated and used to articulate additional complexities of within-person process.

Key Words: longitudinal, P-technique, dynamic systems, idiographic, ecological momentary assessment

A number of "dynamic" longitudinal models are being adapted and used to more clearly understand biological, psychological, and behavioral processes. Generally, the aim of these models is to articulate and test hypotheses about how an established series of events or actions transform an entity from one state to another. Specifically, the objective is to model how an individual's state at one point in time is influenced by his or her past states and/or influences his or her future states.

Recent advances in mobile and computing technology have opened new possibilities to obtain biobehavioral data, model it in real-time, and remotely deploy interventions at population scale. The electronic devices many of us now carry with us as we go about our daily lives provide a wide array of opportunities to collect more and more data from more and more participants and to deliver time- and context-specific guidance to them. Such data streams have tremendous implications for how biobehavioral phenomena can be approached, both in principle and in practice. As new study designs bring moment-to-moment data "online" it shall be possible to track, model, and guide the progression of behavioral transformations—in real-life and in real-time, as individuals go about their daily lives. In this chapter, we provide an overview of one approach for modeling within-person processes—dynamic factor analysis (Molenaar, 1985)—that holds substantial utility for application to these emerging data streams.

The speed and capacity of modern computers brings with it new possibilities for computation. As has been shown with the advent of Internet search engine data mining, we can now estimate the parameters and fit of thousands of models to a given set of data in less than 1 second. This means that it is now feasible to implement person-specific approaches to data analysis. Rather than presupposing, "top-down," that all individuals fall into a single population described by an "average" process, we can instead take a "bottom-up" approach and model *individual* biobehavioral functioning, one person at a time (Cattell, 1966; Lamiell, 1981; Molenaar, 2004; Nesselroade, 2007; Ram & Gerstorf, 2009; Stern, 1911; Valsiner, 1986). This provides an opportunity to test basic assumptions of homogeneity and equivalence of within- and between-person structures that are known to be problematic (i.e., ergodicity of dynamic processes; Molenaar, 2004), eliminates the need to interpret sample-level findings as though they apply to within-person processes (i.e., commit an ecological fallacy; Estes, 1956; Robinson, 1950) and sets the stage for *personalized* intervention at population scale.

In the following sections, we review the conceptual and technical background for person-specific dynamic models and provide a primer for application of dynamic factor analysis to multivariate time series data. Step-by-step procedures are illustrated using "classic" daily diary data obtained from a small number of women over 100-plus days (The Lebo Data; Lebo & Nesselroade, 1978). Finally, we point to some extensions of the dynamic factor model that may be used to articulate even more complex aspects of within-person change.

Background

Factor analysis is a method for investigating the structure of a set of variables. The basic principle is to represent the covariation among many observed variables in terms of linear relations among a *smaller number* of abstract or latent variables. The underlying idea is that if two or more characteristics covary in a systematic manner, they may reflect a shared underlying construct. In practice, the patterns of covariation reveal the *latent* dimensions that lie beneath the *measured qualities* (Gorsuch, 1983; Tabachnick & Fidell, 2007).

P-technique. P-technique factor analysis is the application of factor analysis to P-data—a multi-occasions × multi-variables (× single person) matrix of scores (Cattell, Cattell, & Rhymer, 1947). Applied to this multivariate time series data, the *P-technique* factor model provides a parsimonious description of intra-individual variation and covariation. As such, the P-technique model provides a framework for examining the latent dimensions that lie beneath repeated measures for an individual. The modeling approach has been used in numerous areas to describe individual-level structures of affect, personality, psychophysiology, and other domains (*see* Jones & Nesselroade, 1990; Luborsky & Mintz, 1972; and Russell, Jones, & Miller, 2007, for reviews). For example, portending our forthcoming illustrations, consider the daily reports of six affective states obtained from one study participant over 100-plus days that are plotted in the upper panel of Figure 21.1. The objective of the P-technique analysis is to parsimoniously describe relations among this woman's daily self-reports of *cheerful, happy, contented, sluggish, tired,* and *weary* feelings. The objective of the analysis is to test the hypothesis that the day-to-day variation in the six observed variables can be adequately described as a manifestation of two latent, unobserved factors, positive *well-being* and *fatigue*. As will be described in detail below, the common factor model is applied to time-series data to obtain a more parsimonious description of the processes that contribute to an individual's day-to-day experiences. This latent process representation is plotted in the lower panel of Figure 21.1.

Time series. P-data, like those shown in the upper panel of Figure 21.1, consist of observations obtained from the same entity on multiple occasions. Given that organisms maintain some sort of continuity over time, repeated measurements obtained from the same person are likely to be related. Thus, time series data likely violate a key assumption required by many statistical analyses (including factor analysis)—that observations are independent and identically distributed. Even early critiques of P-technique factor analysis pointed out that the model ignored the time dependencies in the data (e.g., Anderson, 1963; Cattell, 1963). In the decades that followed, time series analysis emerged as a way to explicitly model and accommodate the dependencies in such data (e.g., Box & Jenkins, 1976; Jenkins & Watts, 1968). A plethora of techniques are now available for dealing with and making use of the time ordering, sequences, and dependencies inherent in time series data (Shumway & Stoffer, 2006). Of particular importance for our purposes here was the advent of autoregression (and moving average) models, wherein relations among successive occasions are modeled as autoregression and cross-regression.

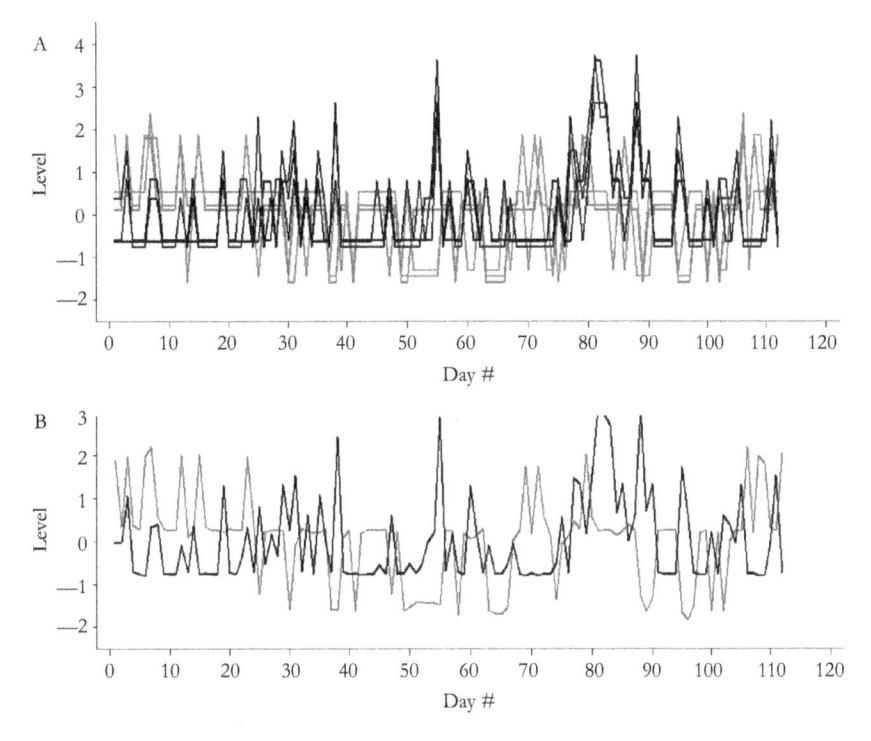

Figure 21.1 Panel A: Observed six-variate time series for Individual 1. Panel B: Model derived two-variate latent time series for Individual 1.

Dynamic factor analysis. Molenaar (1985) introduced dynamic factor analysis (DFA) as a combination of P-technique factor analysis and time series analysis. The objective was to both deal with the independence violations and provide a framework for modeling the dynamic nature of ongoing processes. In brief, the underlying notion of the DFA model is that the (multivariate) state of the individual at any given time is a function of both concurrent influences and past states. Following our example, an individual's present level of fatigue may, in part, be influenced by what happened yesterday. That is, fatigue may linger or *carryover* from one day to the next. Similarly, regulatory processes may promote the *maintenance* of well-being from one day to the next. Events that influence well-being may contribute not only to current levels but also carry forward for some limited amount of time. The DFA framework provides an opportunity to explicitly model such processes.

Often articulated as *state-space models*, many fields make use of DFA-type frameworks (Durbin & Koopman, 2001). In fact, much of the machinery that takes us from place to place (e.g., planes, trains, automobiles) depends on such frameworks to model, forecast, and help guide movements in real-time. Substantive applications in psychology include modeling of affective and psychophysiological changes (Chow et al., 2004; Ferrer & Nesselroade, 2003; Gates et al., 2010; Wood & Brown, 1994), where ongoing processes (e.g., adaptation, regulation, homeostasis) can be extracted from time series data collected on relatively short time-scales.

Person-specific approach. Person-specific approaches seek to articulate the dynamics of the adaptive, regulatory, and other processes that proceed at the individual level (Nesselroade, 2001; Ram & Gerstorf, 2009). The objective is to extract a viable representation of an ongoing process from the covariation that manifests in multiple observations of a person across time (Nesselroade, 1991). The focus is on describing, explaining, predicting, and potentially modifying *individual* behavior, *not* sample- or population-level behavior. Knowledge about how variables relate across individuals at a single time-point (between-person covariation) cannot be used to make inferences about any individuals' actual behavior (Estes, 1956; Robinson, 1950; *see also* recent discussions in Sterba & Bauer, 2010, and associated commentaries). Recently, Molenaar (2004) underscored this point using mathematical proofs. Outlining the relevance of ergodicity theorems, he demonstrated that within- and between-person structures are equivalent (i.e., ergodic) only under very strict (and likely rare) conditions—namely, (1) stationarity of variables' attributes and (2) equivalence of the relations among variables for *all* individuals. Following this logic, it is simply not possible to theorize about between-person differences (the hallmark of most of our inquiries) and meet the methodological requirement that the patterns of variability across time are *identical* for all individuals. In sum, when using between-person analytic techniques to examine psychological phenomena, we are very likely forced to commit egregious ecological fallacies that are, by definition, at odds with the very phenomenon (i.e., processes) we want to examine. As such, it seems imperative that researchers make use of person-specific analysis frameworks in the formulation and testing of psychological theory (Hamaker, Dolan, & Molenaar, 2005). Interindividual differences in the individual-level processes can be studied in a subsequent step. After providing some additional mathematical background, we shall, in the sections that follow, work through a step-by-step illustration of how dynamic factor models can be implemented with sufficiently long data streams.

Technical Background

P-technique factor analysis is procedurally similar to the familiar between-person (R-technique) factor analysis to which most researchers are exposed as part of their graduate research methods training. What differs are the data to which the models are applied. In the usual R-technique factor analysis, the common factor model is applied to multivariate observations obtained from multiple subjects at a single measurement occasion (a persons x variables matrix of scores). In contrast, in P-technique factor analysis, the common factor model is applied to multivariate single subject time series data (an occasions x variables matrix of scores). The model can be written as

$$y(t) = \Lambda \eta(t) + \varepsilon(t), \tag{1}$$

where, $y(t)$ is a p-variate time series of observations indexed by time ($t = 1, 2, \ldots, T$), Λ is a p × q factor loading matrix, $\eta(t)$ is a q-variate time series of latent factor scores, and $\varepsilon(t)$ is a p-variate residual (specific error + measurement error) time series. An example model is depicted graphically in Figure 21.2a. The path model depicts how a six-variate $y(t)$ time series (squares labeled y1 to y6) is "driven" by two common factor score series (circles labeled η1 and η2) that are appropriately weighted by the factor loadings λ1 to λ6, and six residual series (circles labeled ε1 to ε6). From the model, and a set of identification constraints (e.g., factor loading or variance = 1), a set of covariance expectations can be developed and tested against the data to assess the viability of the model.

In P-technique factor analysis, the common factor model, $y(t) = \Lambda \eta(t) + \varepsilon(t)$, is used to model data obtained from one individual over many occasions, t = 1 to T, under the assumption that the observations are *independent*. Depicted graphically in Figure 21.2a, there are no sequential dependencies (arrows) between the variables (latent and manifest) at occasion t − 1 and those at t. The labels for the two occasions could be swapped, t and t − 1, without effect on the model fit or model parameters. Given organismic continuity, this is an unlikely circumstance. Rarely would we find that repeated measures obtained from the same organism are truly independent observations in the sense that there is no relation between the states on different occasions (*see* Fiske & Rice, 1955, and Ram & Gerstorf, 2009, for discussions of net intra-individual variability).

Dynamic factor analysis (Molenaar, 1985) relaxes the assumption that all observations are independent observations of an individual's states. The occasion-to-occasion dependencies of a time series with *equally spaced* observations are modeled explicitly (addressing some of the early critiques of P-technique; e.g., Anderson, 1963) and allowing for *carryover*, *spillover*, or *system memory* from one occasion to the next. A few configurations of the model have been presented and used (*see*, e.g., Nesselroade, McArdle, Aggen, & Meyers, 2002). In a simplistic form, a dynamic factor model can be written as

$$y(t) = \Lambda \eta(t) + \varepsilon(t), \tag{2}$$

$$\eta(t) = B_1 \eta(t-1) + B_2 \eta(t-2)$$
$$+ \cdots + B_s \eta(t-s) + \zeta(t), \tag{3}$$

where the q-variate latent state series $\eta(t)$ is now modeled as a function of $k = 1, 2, \ldots, s$ prior latent states, $\eta(t-1)$ to $\eta(t-s)$, that are weighted by B_1 to B_s. Present time "disturbances" are then introduced as a q-variate set of latent "innovations," $\zeta(t)$, and residual (measurement + specific) errors, $\varepsilon(t)$, the latter of which may be correlated across occasions. Figure 21.2b graphically depicts an example model. In contrast to the P-technique model, time dependencies are now explicitly incorporated at the latent factor level through a set of autoregression and cross-regression (and may also be incorporated at the measurement error level through

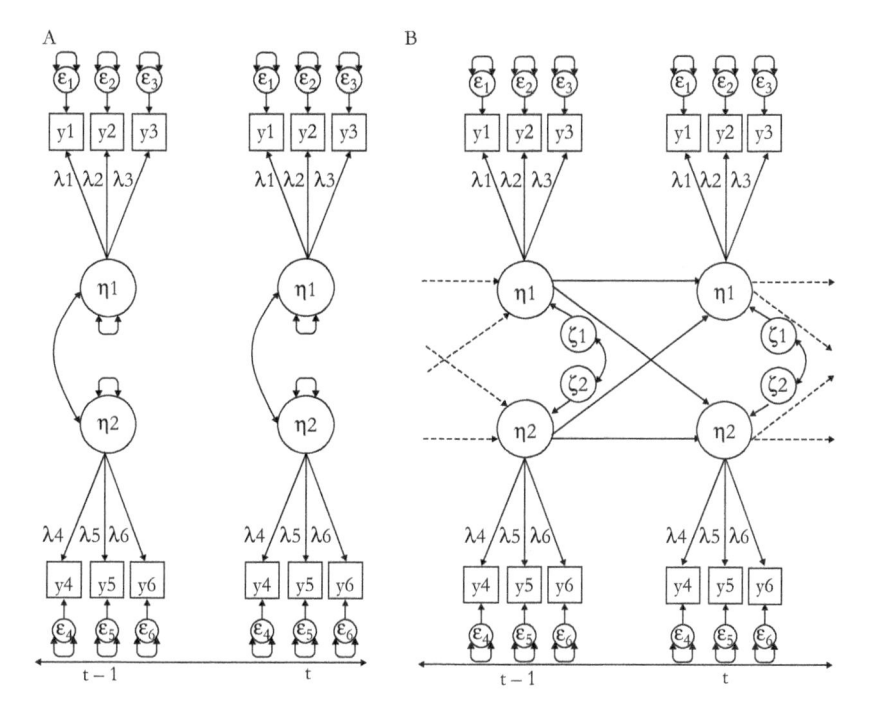

Figure 21.2 Panel A: P-technique factor model. Panel B: Dynamic factor model.

between-occasion correlations, not shown in figure). Substituting Equation 3 into Equation 2 and with a tad of rearranging, we obtain

$$y(t) = \Lambda[\zeta(t) + B_1\eta(t-1) + B_2\eta(t-2) + \cdots + B_s\eta(t-s)] + \varepsilon(t). \quad (4)$$

In general form, the DFA model can be written as

$$y(t) = \Lambda_0\eta(t) + \Lambda_1\eta(t-1) + \Lambda_2\eta(t-2) + \cdots + \Lambda_s\eta(t-s) + \varepsilon(t), \quad (5)$$

where the time dependencies are now modeled through a set of lagged factor loadings, Λ_k, $k = 0, 1, 2, \ldots, s$. We note that there are a number of nuanced differences between DFAs with different configurations and the nature of the processes captured or implied by each model (see, e.g., Browne & Nesselroade, 2005; Browne & Zhang, 2007; Nesselroade et al., 2002). In particular, Equation 4 is a special case of, and can be rotated to, Equation 5 (Molenaar & Nesselroade, 2001). Selection of one configuration over another should be necessarily informed by substantive considerations—how the specific parameters of the model can be mapped to the particular process of interest. In our forthcoming example and discussion, we use the (state-space) representation given in Equation 4 (with an additional practical, but unnecessary, constraint that the measurement errors are uncorrelated over time).

Investigations of individual-level *processes* require consideration of the time-structured variability (Ram & Gerstorf, 2009). The theories presume transactions or activities that connect an individual's prior state to his or her present and future states— behavioral transformations that are contiguous. The data in which those processes manifest are, by definition, not independent and require explicit rendering of the sequential dependencies. Dynamic factor analysis offers a robust framework for modeling process-oriented theory in time series data (Molenaar, 2010). In recent years, the methodological literature surrounding DFA and availability of software programs for model estimation has expanded (*see* Webpages for C. Dolan, L. L. Lo, G. Zhang, and Z. Zhang, among others). The literature illustrates use of maximum likelihood, ordinary least squares, Kalman filter, and Bayesian approaches (Zhang, Hamaker, & Nesselroade, 2008), use of the model for estimations of reliability of change (Lane & Shrout, 2010), and implementations as structural equation models or as state-space models (Chow et al., 2010). In sum, the availability of software tools and computational power now afford the possibility to conduct person-specific DFA with relative ease and speed.

Five Steps for Conducting Dynamic Factor Analysis

The following sections describe a five-step heuristic for conducting DFA. We illustrate implementation using data obtained from a small sample of pregnant women who provided ratings of their daily mood on 100-plus consecutive days (Lebo & Nesselroade, 1978; *see also* Brose & Ram, 2012 Molenaar & Nesselroade, 2001; Nesselroade & Molenaar, 1999; Nesselroade et al., 2007; Nesselroade, McArdle, Aggen, & Meyers, 2002; Zhang & Browne, 2010). We purposively note that there is some irony in our use of this "classic" data, given that we believe that the applications of DFA will expand as modern technologies provide for more and more intensive data collection. However, there is an interesting contrast between the explosion of experience sampling/ecological momentary assessment studies and the still low availability of relatively long psychologically oriented time series data suitable for DFA—particularly data with equal spacing between assessments.

Step 1: Research Questions

As noted earlier, DFA models allow for articulation and testing of process-oriented questions. Process involves patterns of changes that are organized over time (Ram & Gerstorf, 2009). The objective is to provide a set of variables and parameters that can be used to capture some of the forces that produce these patterns of change—at the level of the individual. Models of process include variables that represent the forces that cause change and the behaviors in which the changes manifest as well as parameters that capture the temporal flow in the relationships between the forces of change and the observed behavioral outcomes (*see* Browne & Nesselroade, 2005).

Specific to the parameterizations given above, research questions center on the autoregressive and cross-regressive parameters that capture how innovations (e.g., external events) and prior states influence or carryover from occasion to occasion. The stationarity assumptions, in essence, keep bounds on the extent of possible changes. By definition, the individual cannot "explode" by continued travel very far away from equilibrium. As such, dynamic factor models are useful for articulating a class of stability maintenance processes (Ram & Nesselroade, 2007). Model parameters then can be interpreted as quantifications of the "competing" forces that both move the individual away from and back toward his or her equilibrium. Useful characterizations of the processes captured by DFA models include *carryover, spillover, maintenance, contagion, buffering,* and *decay*. As with other forms of factor analysis, DFA models and their representations of the data can be used in exploratory or confirmatory ways. In our forthcoming illustration, multiple models, each articulating a particular configuration of the process of interest, are compared and evaluated so as to obtain the most useful and parsimonious representation.

Step 1: Empirical Illustration

As we all know from personal experience and observations of others (as well as a plethora of empirical research), individuals' affective states fluctuate from day to day in response to endogenous and exogenous events. There is also evidence of regulatory processes that manage those responses. Our specific interest here was in articulating two processes: a *stability maintenance* process that promotes persistence of an individual's positive well-being from one day to the next and a *buffering* process wherein increases in well-being contribute to decreases in feelings of fatigue the following day. To operationalize these questions in available data, we made use of a measurement model wherein day-to-day changes in well-being and fatigue would manifest in daily reports of affective feeling states and a dynamic model capturing dependencies between consecutive day's well-being and fatigue. Specifically, we sought to confirm that for each individual in the study, there was systematic day-to-day spillover and buffering. Further, we were interested in between-person differences in these stability maintenance and buffering processes. Considering that the endogenous and exogenous variables driving the structure and dynamics of affective experiences differ from one individual to the next (e.g., people live in different contexts), we expected substantial between-person differences in how these processes would manifest in different women. We explored whether individuals in the study would be characterized by similar or different processes.

Step 2: Study Design and Data Collection

The data requirements for dynamic factor analysis are that each individual must be measured on multiple variables repeatedly on many occasions. The resulting time series (P-data) must be (1) of considerable length, (2) collected on a time-scale that matches the phenomena of interest, and (3) sampled at equally spaced intervals. Although there are no clear rules, it has been recommended that factor analytic studies use not less than 100 observations in any analysis (Gorsuch, 1983, p. 332), and that there be at least five observations for each parameter being estimated in the model (Loehlin, 1998). Time series of length 100 observations per individual can be considered as a kind of minimum starting point for person-specific dynamic analysis (cf. Wood & Brown, 1994, recommendations for 300+). Further, it is essential that the study design capture variability—the core of any statistical analysis—at the individual level. Key concerns are the time-scale on which the observations were obtained and that the interval between successive occasions is long enough that change can occur but not so long an interval that the progression of the process is entirely missed (Boker, Molenaar, & Nesselroade, 2009; Collins, 2006; Shiyko & Ram, 2011).

Similarly, measurement instruments should be sensitive enough to capture the variation produced by the processes of interest. Subtle occasion-to-occasion changes may be lost in the granularity of the response scale. For example, when occasion-to-occasion changes are not so large as to prompt individuals to move their response to the next higher or lower category, the granularity of the response scale may be inadvertently imposing a limit on what constitutes "meaningful" change. This is not to say that one should always strive to use interval scales. Dynamic factor analysis models can be implemented with interval, ordinal, and categorical variables (G. Zhang & Browne, 2010; Z. Zhang & Nesselroade, 2007). The point is that care should be taken that the measurement instruments are well suited to capture the particular process of interest.

Step 2: Empirical Illustration

Lebo collected the data we use for our illustration as part of his investigation of mothers' affective experiences leading up to and surrounding the birth of their first child. Data were obtained from five pregnant women who rated their mood on 100-plus successive days using 75 adjectives (0–4 response scale) covering a wide swath of constructs prevalent in the literature of the time. The resulting time series (1) span more than 100 occasions; (2) were collected once per day, a time-scale that allows for modeling day-to-day continuity of affective experiences; and (3) were obtained at equally spaced intervals, once each evening. We note that although the response scale was quite granular (5-point scale), we have treated it as an interval scale.

Step 3: Variable Selection and Data Preprocessing

Variable Selection. Once individuals' time series of observations have been collected, it is important to determine whether the data are, in actuality, suitable for application of DFA. Most importantly, there must be reliably measured variation in scores on the specific variables to be analyzed (Comrey & Lee, 1992, p. 238). Variables with no within-person variance across time cannot, by definition, be subjected to analysis of variation and covariation. Various rules of thumb have been used to identify and remove variables that do not have "sufficient" variance for analysis. These include removing variables with (intra-individual) standard deviations below 0.10, or variables with more than 80% of scores being identical (*see*, e.g., Lebo & Nesselroade, 1978; Zevon & Tellegen, 1982). The issue becomes complicated when individuals exhibit insufficient variance on different items. Three routes can be taken. (1) Specific items can be excluded from each individual-level analysis, potentially resulting in a different set of variables being analyzed for each individual in the sample. The advantages of this route are that as much information as possible is maintained in the analyses, and idiosyncratic manifestations of the same phenomena can be acknowledged and modeled (Nesselroade et al., 2007). (2) Alternatively, individuals who have insufficient variability on one or more items are excluded from the analyses. The advantage of this approach is that between-person comparisons among the remaining sample are easy. (3) Strike a balance between finding a common set of items and a "common" set of persons by placing equal weight on the selective sampling of persons and selective sampling of items. The idea is to hone in on the subsample of individuals for whom a particular set of items is relevant. This acknowledges the possibility of qualitatively different measurement models (i.e., idiosyncratic interpretation of items), while preserving the benefits of across-person measurement invariance within each subsample of individuals.

Data Preprocessing. Before the main analysis, the data should be examined for suitability for application of the dynamic factor model. In principle, the main objective of the preprocessing is to obtain time series that are *weakly stationary*. As usual, there are no clear guidelines on what preprocessing steps are most appropriate. Depending on the specifics of the research question, and how much "nonstationarity" was collected along with the phenomena of interest, researchers may choose among many possibilities to identify and remove trends (or cycles) and other anomalous features. This can be accomplished using linear, quadratic, or other polynomial regressions (e.g., detrending), frequency analysis (i.e., spectral analysis), or through application of various differencing techniques, filters, or smoothers (see, e.g., Shumway & Stoffer, 2006, for concise review). The choice of preparations can consider both statistical criteria for testing whether the resulting time-series are stationary and theoretical evaluation of what processes should be identified and removed from (and/or modeled in) the data.

Statistical methods for identifying nonstationarity include use of evolutionary spectra (Priestley, 1981), the Augmented Dickey-Fuller Test (Dickey & Fuller, 1979), and fitting of multiple models to the data. However, there is not always an obvious way to use these tests or explore possible models for nonstationarity (see Chatfield, 2004, 13.2–13.4). Theoretical considerations revolve around the idea that each trend, cycle, or other "noise" component that is present in the data is driven by one or more processes (e.g., learning, circadian rhythms, measurement error). Modeling and removing these elements is, in essence, a procedural setting aside of particular processes to concentrate on underlying structures that are independent of those processes.

Step 3: Empirical Illustration

Variable Selection. Following Lebo and Nesselroade's (1978) original procedures, we removed, for each woman, items where more than 80% of responses were identical. Taking the third of the three alternatives listed above, we selected a subset of items that fit with our theoretical notions of a positively valenced *well-being* factor and a negatively valenced *fatigue* factor, and a subset of persons for whom those items were available for analysis. To keep our example parsimonious, we honed in on a set of six items (cheerful, happy, contented, sluggish, tired, weary) that exhibited sufficient variance for three of the five women. This subset of items and persons becomes the focus of further analysis, with the added benefit that subsequent examination of between-person differences/similarities would be relatively straightforward.

We note that, as is often the case when working with real data, there has been some "offline" iteration between the development of the research questions and the selection of variables and persons for analysis. Sometimes these iterations occur before the data are collected but in our case have proceeded some 40 years after data collection was completed.

Data Preprocessing. Our next goal was to prepare the selected data from these three individuals so that they met stationarity requirements. To this end, we took the following steps. First, we standardized each variable for each individual ($M = 0$, $SD = 1$) to remove potential differences in overall variance and use of the response scale. Second, each individual's time series was plotted and inspected visually. The prepared six-variate time-series for Participant 1 are the data we used for Figure 21.1. By observation, the item-level trajectories did not show trends across time, nor did we have reason to presume the presence of systematic trends. Thus, we treated the data as though they were weakly stationary and conducted *post hoc* tests to check the viability of the final models for different portions of the data (e.g, first half vs. second half) as an approximate indicator of adherence to stationarity assumptions.

Step 4: Fitting and Evaluating Person-Specific Dynamic Factor Models

Dynamic factor analysis can be implemented in a variety of ways. Methodologists, in recent years, have demonstrated and evaluated the possibilities for using structural equation modeling-based maximum likelihood approaches (e.g., LISREL, Mplus, OpenMx, SAS PROC CALIS, etc.), Kalman filter approaches (mkfm6), Bayesian approaches (Winbugs), and ordinary least squares (OLS) approaches (Dyfa) and have provided many resources regarding the specifics of implementation (Browne & Zhang, 2007; Chow, Ho, Hamaker, & Dolan 2010; Molenaar & Nesselroade, 1998; Nesselroade et al., 2002; Wood & Brown, 1994; Zhang & Browne, 2010; Zhang, Hamaker, & Nesselroade, 2008). The model is specified in accordance with theoretical expectations (e.g., a specific hypothesis about structure and time dependencies, including the number of lags) and then fitted to the data using Kalman filter, maximum likelihood, OLS, Bayesian, or other procedures. Models are fit to each individual's data separately; fit statistics (e.g., χ^2, −2LL) and parameter estimates are obtained and interpreted in relation to theory and other empirical evidence. In the context of a person-specific analysis approach, the fit criteria and solutions can be used to determine which of the hypothesized structures provide an adequate and/or better description of that individual's data. Between-person comparisons are done in a subsequent step.

Step 4: Empirical illustration

To examine the dynamic structure of well-being and fatigue for each of the three women, we fit confirmatory P-technique and DFA models separately to each of the three women's data using *mkfm6* (contact C. V. Dolan). For each analysis, the P-data being analyzed consisted of a 100-plus occasions (days) × six variables matrix of scores. The measurement portion of the model (Equation 2) was specified with two factors: a *well-being* factor (η_1) indicated by the items cheerful, happy, and contented ($y_1 - y_3$), and a *fatigue* factor (η_2) indicated by the items sluggish, tired, and weary ($y_4 - y_6$). As in Figure 21.2, the two factors had simple structure (no cross-loadings) and were allowed to correlate. The dynamics portion of the model (Equation 3) was specified in two ways. Specifically, the elements of B were either (1) constrained to equal zero as in a typical P-technique factor model assuming independence of observations, or (2) freely estimated as a one-lag DFA model. The models were identified by fixing the variance of the innovations equal to one. Individual level results are provided in Table 21.1.

The evaluation and interpretation of the other person-specific solutions proceeded one individual at a time. With the P-technique model being nested under the DFA model, we were able to test, using likelihood ratio tests, whether the DFA model provided a better statistical fit to the data than the more parsimonious P-technique model. This test was done separately for each individual. For Individual 1, the DFA model provided a better fit to the data than the more constrained P-technique model ($\Delta - 2LL = 26.64, df = 4, p < 0.05$), meaning that there were indeed time-related processes to be extracted. Auto-regression parameters for both the well-being ($\beta = 0.42$) and the fatigue ($\beta = 0.28$) factors were significant, indicating carryover in feelings from one day to the next. The non-significant cross-regression parameters provide no evidence of buffering. For Individual 2, the DFA model also fit better than the P-technique model ($\Delta - 2LL = 17.24, df = 4, p < 0.05$). There was evidence of carryover in fatigue ($\beta = 0.32$) but not in well-being. However, there was a significant cross-regression, with higher well-being leading to higher fatigue the following day ($\beta = 0.33$), the opposite of the expected buffering process. Perhaps this results from increased activity engagement on the previous day, resulting in some exhaustion on the present day. For Individual 3, the DFA model again fit the data better than the P-technique model ($\Delta - 2LL = 19.16, df = 4, p < 0.05$). However, the only significant lagged effect was an autoregression for fatigue ($\beta = 0.43$), suggesting carryover in fatigue from one day to the next, but with no evidence of other spillover or buffering processes.

Step 5: Between-Person Differences

The person-specific approach used here maintains that the analyses first examine the phenomena of interest at the individual level. Models are fit to individual-level P-data and the solutions and fits of those models evaluated one individual at a time. Nevertheless, proponents of person-specific approaches also emphasize that the individual solutions must at some point be integrated for purposes of generalization (Nesselroade, 2007; Nesselroade & Molenaar, 1999). For example, working in the clinical context with subjects suffering from borderline personality disorder, one may seek to classify individuals into phenotypes, with some individuals' day-to-day changes in negative emotions and self-destructive behaviors being well characterized by persistence dynamics and other individuals being characterized by more random changes. It may also be of interest to understand how differences in individuals' dynamic processes are related to other individual differences. For example, theories of cognitive development suggest that the abilities differentiate and dedifferentiate over the lifespan. Interindividual differences in age would be related to interindividual differences in the number of factors needed to describe fluctuations in performance on cognitive tasks.

The step-by-step procedures for conducting dynamic factor analysis are purposively ordered to maintain the integrity of the *individual* as the proper unit of analysis when investigating psychological processes. Between-person comparisons are made only after the person-specific solutions have been obtained. Several approaches have been used to identify the similarities and differences among the individual-level models. Solutions from multiple individuals can be examined with respect to specific characteristics of the model and its parameters, including, for example, the number of factors, the pattern of factor loadings, and the autoregression and cross-regression (e.g., Hamaker, Nesselroade, & Molenaar, 2007). Given the generally small sample sizes used in DFA studies, identification of similarities and differences in structure can usually be summarized through qualitative descriptions of

Table 21.1. Parameter Estimates and Fit Statistics From Person-Specific P-Technique Factor Analyses and Dynamic Factor Analyses

	Individual 1				Individual 2				Individual 3			
	P-Technique		DFA		P-Technique		DFA		P-Technique		DFA	
Std. loadings, Λ	WB	F	WB	F	WB	F	WB	F	WB	F	WB	F
Cheerful	0.92	—	0.85	—	0.87	—	0.85	—	0.71	—	0.71	—
Happy	0.77	—	0.67	—	0.80	—	0.80	—	0.84	—	0.79	—
Contented	0.63	—	0.54	—	0.71	—	0.70	—	0.77	—	0.74	—
Sluggish	—	0.86	—	0.83	—	0.94	—	0.87	—	0.89	—	0.83
Tired	—	0.94	—	0.89	—	0.93	—	0.84	—	0.88	—	0.78
Weary	—	0.76	—	0.74	—	0.79	—	0.72	—	0.76	—	0.66
	Factor correlations, Ψ											
Fatigue	1.0	—	—	—	1.0	—	—	—	1.0	—	—	—
Well-being	−0.14	1.0	—	—	−0.25*	1.0	—	—	−0.52*	1.0	—	—
	Correlation of innovations, ζ											
	—	—	1.0	—	—	—	1.0	—	—	—	1.0	—
	—	—	−0.22*	1.0	—	—	−0.34*	1.0	—	—	−0.59*	1.0
	Latent regression coefficients, β											
Well-being	—	—	0.42*	—	—	—	0.10	—	—	—	0.23	—
Fatigue	—	—	0.28*	—	—	—	0.32*	—	—	—	0.43*	—
Well-being–Fatigue	—	—	0.04	—	—	—	0.33*	—	—	—	0.04	—
Fatigue–Well-being	—	—	0.12	—	—	—	0.14	—	—	—	0.04	—
	Model fit											
−2LL	529.84		503.19		421.00		403.76		546.73		527.57	
	Model comparison[a]											
Δ −2LL	26.64*				17.24*				19.16*			

Note: DFA = dynamic factor analysis; F = fatigue; WB = well-being; *$p < 0.05$. [a]Critical value for Likelihood ratio test with 4 degrees of freedom = 9.49.

individual-level results. As the sample size increases, these descriptions can be quantified as follows. Similarities and differences among patterns of factor loadings and/or regressions obtained from multiple samples (i.e., individuals) can be quantified using congruence coefficients or other measures of pattern similarity. Modern computing provides the possibility to assess the fit of several *a priori* models to many individuals' P-data quickly and efficiently. This allows that models from multiple individuals can be integrated and compared through formal statistical tests. In particular, making use of multiple-group equality constraints, it is possible to formally test whether two or more individuals' data can be described by the same factor model parameters. The logic of such pairwise tests exactly follows the logic underlying tests for measurement invariance across multiple groups or occasions (Meredith, 1993). Specifically, observations from each individual are conceptualized as separate groups, with confirmatory models being fit to the multigroup data with and without equality constraints. Nested model comparisons provide evidence that the individual models can be considered equivalent or different. Like individuals can be described by the same model and separated from unlike individuals. We underscore that, as per the bottom-up strategy, identification, description, and testing of between-person similarities and differences should be completed only after individual-level models have been obtained and examined.

Step 5: Empirical Illustration

Looking across participants at a global level, each of the three participants' day-to-day experiences were better represented by some type of dynamic process than as a collection of independent states. The factor loadings for the indicator items were generally high for all participants, and there was some type of carryover from one day to the next, most consistently in fatigue, which carried over from day-to-day for all three women. Similarities among the solutions were tested formally using multigroup models. Specifically, treating each individual as a separate group, we tested whether the parameters for each pair of individuals/groups were invariant (i.e., factor loadings and the autoregression and cross-regression coefficients were constrained equal across groups). Results are given in Table 21.2. None of the three pairwise tests were significant (all $\Delta - 2LL < 11$, critical value [df = 10] = 18.31), suggesting that the women were highly similar. A three-group (-person) invariance test was also non-significant ($\Delta - 2LL = 18.62$, critical value [df = 20] = 31.41), indicating that the dynamics within all three participants' data could be represented by the same model. The parameter estimates for this invariant model, shown in the first column of Table 21.2, suggest spillover-type processes that contribute to the ongoing maintenance of both well-being and fatigue, without evidence for buffering of one affective state on the other. In sum, the between-person similarities suggest some homogeneity of maintenance processes across this group of three women. However, before generalizing further, we should not forget that two other women were not included in the analysis because their daily reports on this particular item set did not show sufficient variance for meaningful analysis. Their affective experiences may be characterized by a different set of processes or by the same processes but different indicators (as will be discussed in the following section).

Future Directions

The first papers on DFA appeared in the psychological literature in the 1980s (e.g., Molenaar, 1985). However, despite the recent increase in methodologically oriented papers, the application of these models in substantively oriented studies remains rather limited (cf. Chow et al., 2004). This lack may be rooted in the fact that many areas of social and behavioral science have been focused on modeling of between-person differences (in presumed stable traits—e.g., personality). The time-series data needed for focused study of within-person processes have simply not been collected. In other fields, including engineering and economics, where time-series data are obtained as a matter of course, within-person or within-entity modeling traditions hold significant traction (*see* Chow et al., 2010). In those fields, dynamic models are part of the standard paradigm. As the social and behavioral sciences evolve from use of relatively "static" core representations of phenomena (e.g., traits) toward more "dynamic" representations, dynamic factor models and person-specific modeling approaches will become more pervasive. Already we see substantial movement toward collection of more intensive time series in the promotion and use of intensive longitudinal, diary, and ecological momentary assessment designs (e.g., Bolger et al., 2003; Shiffman et al., 2008; Walls & Schafer, 2006). As mobile technologies become more and more ubiquitous, the data constraints will fall away, and there will be tremendous opportunities for application of

Table 21.2. Results From the Multigroup DFA Model Invariance Tests

	Individual 1 = 2 = 3		Individual 1 = 2		Individual 1 = 3		Individual 2 = 3	
	WB	F	WB	F	WB	F	WB	F
Std. loadings, Λ								
Cheerful	0.83	–	0.87	–	0.81	–	0.80	–
Happy	0.76	–	0.74	–	0.73	–	0.80	–
Contented	0.67	–	0.63	–	0.64	–	0.72	–
Sluggish	–	0.85	–	0.86	–	0.83	–	0.86
Tired	–	0.86	–	0.88	–	0.84	–	0.83
Weary	–	0.72	–	0.74	–	0.71	–	0.70
Correlation of innovations, ζ								
Individual 1	−0.22*		−0.24*		−0.20		–	
Individual 2	−0.34*		−0.34*		−0.33*		–	
Individual 3	−0.66*		−0.65*		−0.65*		–	
Latent regression coefficients, β								
Well-being	0.26*		0.28*		0.35*		0.15	
Fatigue	0.35*		0.29*		0.36*		0.39*	
Well-being–Fatigue	0.12		0.15		0.03		0.20*	
Fatigue–Well-being	0.12		0.13		0.12		0.10	
Model fit								
−2LL	1453.15		916.98		1041.27		938.78	
Model comparison								
Δ−2LL	18.62[a]		10.02[b]		10.50[b]		7.45[b]	

Notes: Df = degrees of freedom; DFA = dynamic factor analysis F = fatigue; WB = well-being; *$p < 0.05$;
[a]Critical value for Likelihood ratio test with 20 degrees of freedom = 31.41; [b]Critical value for Likelihood ratio test with 10 degrees of freedom = 18.31.

dynamic factor analysis and other similar types of models. As the data evolve, we see three aspects of the basic person-specific DFA approach in need of further elaboration: non-stationarity, adaptive guidance, and idiographic filters.

Non-Stationarity

Within the developmental literature on change, a distinction emerged between intra-individual change—those within-person changes that proceed slowly and are relatively enduring, and intra-individual variability—those within-person changes that proceed more quickly and are relatively reversible (Nesselroade, 1991). The former are typically characterized as directional changes or "development" and modeled using growth-curve and other similar methods. The latter are typically characterized by fluctuations or cycles (modeled using time series methods) and used to describe individuals' dynamic characteristics and dynamic processes (Ram & Gerstorf, 2009). When exhibiting invariance in means and covariance functions over time, the intra-individual variability is considered (weakly) stationary (see Shumway & Stoffer, 2006). Lucky for our capacity to maintain life, but unlucky for the parsimony of our modeling, human systems are not stationary. The processes that keep us alive and moving change, adapt, and grow (intra-individual change). That is, stationary processes that manifest as fluctuations and cycles (intra-individual variability) change over time and context and are influenced by internal or external factors. This is the nature of development (see, e.g., Molenaar, 2004, and Nesselroade, 1991, for more in-depth discussion).

From a modeling perspective, this suggests that stationary models, like the DFAs outlined above, are limited. Non-stationary extensions are needed to adequately capture the changes that are proceeding simultaneously at multiple time-scales. Dynamic factor analysis models have been extended to accommodate and model non-stationary time series (Molenaar, 1994; Molenaar, De Gooijer, & Schmitz, 1992). In the P-technique and DFA models presented here, the parameters (e.g., Λ, B) were assumed to be constant over time—*time-invariant*. In the non-stationary extensions, the parameters become *time-varying*, so that transient or trend-type changes in the parameters accommodate and describe how the structure or process (e.g., factor loadings, autoregressions) changes or transforms over time. We point to some additional state-space models that may provide for useful extensions of the DFA approach.

Kim and Nelson (1999) outlined the use and estimation of multiregime state space models (*see also* Hamaker, Grasman, & Kamphuis, 2010). The core idea is that ongoing processes may switch among two or more regimes. For one period of time, the process may be well described by one set of parameters. However, after some event, change in context, or on particular occasions, the process is described by a different set of parameters. Consider the one-lag DFA (as a state-space model) given in Equations 2 and 3, with an additional subscript denoting a time-varying, categorical *switching* variable, $S(t)$

$$y(t) = \Lambda_{S(t)}\eta(t) + \varepsilon(t), \qquad (6)$$

$$\eta(t) = B_{1S(t)}\eta(t-1) + \zeta(t), \qquad (7)$$

where the elements of Λ and B_1 now differ depending on the value of $S(t)$. When $S(t) = 0$, the evolution of the process is governed by one set of parameters, Λ_0 and B_{10}, and when $S(t) = 1$ by a different set of parameters, Λ_1 and B_{11}. This family of models accommodates the types of non-stationarity that might accompany discrete changes in context (e.g., experimental conditions) or measured or latent Markov (i.e., sequentially dependent) switching.

For more continuous evolution, the multiregime model can be straightforwardly extended to a model with fully time-varying parameters. Here, all the parameters are time-varying,

$$y(t) = \Lambda(t)\eta(t) + \varepsilon(t), \qquad (8)$$

$$\eta(t) = B_1(t)\eta(t-1) + \zeta(t), \qquad (9)$$

with the constraint that the parameter matrices, $\Lambda(t)$ and $B_1(t)$, change in a smooth fashion and slowly relative to the states, $\eta(t)$. Building on applications from engineering, Molenaar and colleagues have recently described and fitted such models to psychological time series using extended Kalman filtering with iterated smoothing (Molenaar, Sinclair, Rovine, Ram, & Corneal, 2009; Molenaar & Ram, 2009). Initial results have demonstrated the viability and promise of such models. However, further work is needed to establish the limitations of the procedure and the types of processes and changes that can be captured by such models.

Given the preponderance of cyclic trends in bio-behavioral processes (e.g., diurnal and circadian activity), additional forms of change and non-stationarity that accommodate cyclic dynamics may also be useful (*see* Chow, Hamaker, Fujita, & Boker, 2009). State-space models that incorporate time-varying parameters that are tied to cyclic components (e.g., sine and cosine functions) of specific frequencies or even time-varying frequencies can be used to model complex nonlinear changes in how processes manifest over time (e.g., Harvey & Streibel, 1998; Young, Pedregal, & Tych, 1999). In principle, the elements of $\Lambda(t)$ and $B_1(t)$ are filled with sinusoidal elements. These models potentially provide a framework for mixing models from the time-domain and the frequency-domain, for modeling changes in amplitude and frequency of oscillatory processes, and discrete shifts in cyclicity or phase (when integrated with the regime shift model given above). Emerging from the econometrics literature, application to bio-behavioral processes is just beginnning. Further work is needed to establish the specific processes and data streams to which cyclic versions of the dynamic factor models are best suited. In sum, non-stationarity is a reality of human function to be dealt with. Models that can do so are available and are currently being adapted for use with human data. As that trend (mind the pun) continues, our ability to describe and predict the complex changes that characterize real life will expand.

Adaptive Guidance

Moving beyond description and prediction, our scientific goals include the explanation and potential modification of human behavior. Control theory developed in engineering and mathematics as a framework for guiding systems toward desired states or outputs (e.g., Kwon & Han, 2005). In brief, a controller manipulates time-varying inputs into a system to steer an ongoing process. An additional vector of input variables is introduced into the state space model

$$y(t) = \Lambda(t)\eta(t) + \varepsilon(t), \qquad (10)$$

$$\eta(t) = B_1(t)\eta(t-1) + \Gamma(t)u(t-1) + \zeta(t), \quad (11)$$

so that the current state, $\eta(t)$, is now a function of its past states, (random) innovations, and some (external) input. In cases where the input can be controlled, $u(t)$ can be manipulated in such a way that $\eta(t)$ can be steered toward a desired or optimal level (see Molenaar, 2010; Molenaar & Ram, 2010). For example, inputs of insulin can be used to control an individuals' blood glucose level (Molenaar, Ulbrecht, Gold, Rovine, Wang, & Zhou, in press). Ubiquitous in engineering applications (e.g., steering rockets, managing electric grids, optimizing chemical processes), sophisticated extensions of this simple model allow for analysis and guidance of systems with multiple inputs and outputs, nonlinearities, and complex evolutions over time. Theoretical descriptions of many psychological and behavioral processes make use of adaptive guidance and control-type language (e.g., Carver & Scheier, 1998). As interdisciplinary efforts foster the emergence of a combined engineering and social science, it is likley that the analytical technologies of control theory will be among the central foci of consideration. The match between theory and method is strong. For example, in medicine, psychotherapy, and even physical therapy, the main objective is to develop personalized programs that optimize and guide individuals towards healthy states. Models making use of control theory principles and estimation algorithms are at the forefront of the person-specific modeling enterprise.

Idiographic Filters

The move toward personalized medicine suggests that person-specific approaches consider further how and in what ways models both generalize across persons and can be tailored to specific persons. In our example, we highlighted the importance of first examining the phenomena of interest at the individual level and only later considering between-person similarities and differences. Among the procedures used were confirmatory tests of model invariance, which provide a statistically rigorous framework for testing similarity. Specifically we examined invariance in both the factor loadings and autoregression and cross-regression, $\Lambda_i = \Lambda$ and $B_{1i} = B_1$ for all (or each pair of) individuals. Traditionally, invariance tests have concentrated only on the factor loadings (Meredith, 1993). Extending how between-person differences in structure or dynamics are approached, Nesselroade and colleagues recently proposed that invariance tests should *instead* concentrate on similarity of factor correlations or autoregressions and cross-regressions (see Nesselroade, Gerstorf, Hardy, & Ram, 2007, and accompanying commentaries/critiques). The proposal is that the latent processes or structures may be highly similar or even equivalent across individuals, although the indicator variables may be different. Idiographic filters allow for person-level differences in the manifestation of the same processes. For example, consider the simple dynamic factor model

$$y(t) = F_i \odot \Lambda \eta(t) + \varepsilon(t), \quad (12)$$

$$\eta(t) = B_1 \eta(t-1) + \zeta(t), \quad (13)$$

where F is a matrix filled with 1s and 0s, and $\odot$ denotes the Hadamard product (i.e., entrywise product), $(A \odot B)_{p,q} = A_{p,q} \cdot B_{p,q}$. Through this algebraic mechanism the person specific F_i matrix serves as a filter that organizes the latent states into particular manifest states—in different ways for different people (see also Widaman & Grimm, 2007).

Pushing these ideas a bit further, person-specific models might allow for filtering or tailoring in many different places—in the state equations, in the measurement equations (as above), in the configurations of dynamic noise, or in the configurations of measurement noise. Although the implications for measurement theory, and whether a new conceptualization is truly needed, remain unclear, evidence is building that highly tailored models hold utility (note extensive use of tailoring in therapy and prevention efforts). Further work is needed to establish how additional algebraic tools, like the Hadamard product, can be used to expand the repertoire of processes and changes that can be captured by dynamic factor modeling frameworks.

Synopsis

The purpose of this chapter was to introduce dynamic factor analysis to researchers interested in modeling within-person processes. We reviewed a "bottom-up," person-specific approach to hypothesis testing and data analysis, wherein the relations among variables are first examined one individual at a time. Applied to within-person data, DFA can be used to identify and describe how a set of variables travel together across time and to reveal the parsimonious structures that may underlie occasion-to-occasion changes and/or "carryover" in an individual's behavior. Once the dynamic patterns are established at the individual level, they can be compared one person to the next, and the between-person differences and similarities described, quantified, and examined. It seems through recent extensions and developments, DFA is increasingly able to capture complex and dynamic aspects of human behavior. We hope through our step-by-step illustration we have provided a guide for when and how dynamic factor models may be incorporated into empirical research programs and take us further along the route toward describing, predicting, explaining, and potentially modifying individuals' behavior.

Glossary

Person-specific analyses: Analyses of single entities' time series (a single individual; $N = 1$)

Person-specific approach: Person-specific approaches seek to articulate the dynamics of the adaptive, regulatory, and other processes that proceed at the individual level

Time series: observations obtained from the same entity on multiple occasions/repeated measurements obtained from the same person

Sequential dependencies: Relationships across time between repeated measurements of the same variable (lagged effects)/between different variables measured on subsequent occasions (cross-lagged effects)

Dynamic factor analysis: A combination of P-technique factor analysis and time-series analysis. The multivariate state of the individual at a given time is a function of both concurrent influences and influences of past states.

References

Anderson, T. W. (1963). The use of factor analysis in the statistical analysis of multiple time series. *Psychometrika, 28*, 1–25.

Boker, S. M., Molenaar, P. C. M. & Nesselroade, J. R. (2009). Issues in intraindividual variability: Individual differences in equilibria and dynamics over multiple time scales. *Psychology and Aging, 24*, 858–862. Doi 10.1037/A0017912

Bolger, N., Davis, A. & Rafaeli, E. (2003). Diary methods: Capturing life as it is lived. *Annual Review of Psychology, 54*, 579–616.

Box, G. E. P. & Jenkins, G. M. (1976). *Time Series Analysis: Forecasting and Control* (revised ed.). San Francisco, CA: Holden Day.

Brose, A. & Ram, N. (2012). Within-person factor analysis: Modeling how the individual fluctuates and changes across time. In M. Mehl & T. Conner (Eds.) *Handbook of Research Methods for Studying Daily Life* (pp. 459–468). New York: Guilford.

Browne, M. W., & Nesselroade, J. R. (2005). Representing psychological processes with dynamic factor models: Some promising uses and extensions of ARMA time series models. In A. Maydeu-Olivares & J. J. McArdle (Eds.), *Psychometrics: A festschrift to Roderick P. McDonald* (pp. 415–452). Mahwah, NJ: Lawrence Erlbaum.

Browne, M. W., & Zhang, G. (2007). Developments in the factor analysis of individual time series. In R. Cudeck & R. C. MacCallum (Eds.), *Factor analysis at 100: historical developements and future directions* (pp. 265–291). Mahwah, NJ: Erlbaum.

Carver, C. S., & Scheier, M. F. (1998). *On the self-regulation of behavior*. New York: Cambridge University Press.

Cattell, R. B. (1963). The structuring of change by P-technique and incremental R-technique. In C. W. Harris (Ed.), *Problems in measuring change* (pp. 167–198). Madison, WI: University of Wisconsin Press.

Cattell, R. B. (1966). Guest editorial: Multivariate behavioral research and the integrative challenge. *Multivariate Behavioral Research, 1*, 4–23.

Cattell, R. B., Cattell, A. K. S., & Rhymer, R. M. (1947). P-technique demonstrated in determining psychophysiological source traits in a normal individual. *Psychometrika, 12*, 267–288.

Chatfield, C. (2004). *The analysis of time series: An introduction* (6th ed.). London: Chapman and Hall.

Chow, S-M., Hamaker, E. L., Fujita, F., & Boker, S. M. (2009). Representing time-varying cyclic dynamics using multiple-subject state-space models. *British Journal of Mathematical and Statistical Psychology, 62*, 683–716.

Chow, S-M., Ho, M. R., Hamaker, E. L., & Dolan, C. V. (2010). Equivalence and differences between structural equation modeling and state-space modeling techniques. *Structural Equation Modeling, 17*, 303–332.

Chow, S-M., Nesselroade, J. R., Shifren, K., & McArdle, J. J. (2004). Dynamic structure of emotions among individuals with Parkinson's disease. *Structural Equation Modeling, 11*, 560–582.

Collins, L. M. (2006). Analysis of longitudinal data: The integration of theoretical model, temporal design, and statistical model. *Annual Review of Psychology, 57*, 505–528.

Comrey, A. L., & Lee, H. B. (1992). *A first course in factor analysis* (2nd edition). Hillsdale, NJ: Erlbaum.

Dickey, D. & Fuller, W. (1979). Distribution of the estimators for autoregressive time series with a unit root. *Journal of the American Statistical Association, 74*, 427–431.

Durbin, J. & Koopman, S. J. (2001). *Time-series analysis by state-space methods*. New York: Oxford University Press.

Estes, W. (1956). The problem of inference from curves based on group data. *Psychological Bulletin, 53*, 134–140.

Ferrer, E. & Nesselroade, J. (2003). Modeling affective processes in dyadic relations via dynamic factor analysis. *Emotion, 3*, 344–360.

Fiske, D. W. & Rice, L. (1955). Intra-individual response variability. *Psychological Bulletin, 52*, 217–250.

Gates, K. M., Molenaar, P. C. M., Hillary, F., Ram, N., & Rovine, M. (2010). Automatic search in fMRI connectivity mapping: An alternative to Granger causality using formal equivalences between SEM path modeling, VAR, and unified SEM. *NeuroImage, 53*, 1118–1125.

Gorsuch, R. L. (1983). *Factor analysis* (2nd edition). Hillsdale, NJ: Erlbaum.

Hamaker, E. L., Dolan, C. V., & Molenaar, P. C. M. (2005). Statistical modeling of the individual: Rationale and application of multivariate stationary time series analysis. *Multivariate Behavioral Research, 40*, 207–233.

Hamaker, E. L., Grasman R. P. P. P., & Kamphuis, J. H. (2010). Regime-switching models to study psychological processes. In P. C. M. Molenaar & K. M. Newell (Eds). *Individual pathways of change: Statistical models for analyzing learning and development* (pp. 155–168). Washington, DC: APA.

Hamaker, E. L., Nesselroade, J. R., & Molenaar, P. C. M. (2007). The integrated trait-state model. *Journal of Research in Personality, 41*, 295–315.

Harvey, A. C. & Streibel, M. (1998). Tests for deterministic versus indeterministic cycles. *Journal of Time Series Analysis, 19*, 505–529.

Jenkins, G. M. & Watts, D. G. (1968). *Spectral Analysis and its Applications.* San Francisco, CA: Holden-Day.

Jones, C. J., & Nesselroade, J. R. (1990). Multivariate, replicated, single-subject designs and P-technique factor analysis: A selective review of the literature. *Experimental Aging Research, 16*, 171–183.

Kim, C.-J. & Nelson, C. R. (1999). *State-space models with regime switching: Classical and Gibbs-sampling approaches with applications.* Cambridge, MA: MIT Press.

Kwon, W.H., & Han, S. (2005). Receding horizon control: Model predictive control for state models. London: Springer.

Lamiell, J. T. (1981). Toward an idiothetic psychology of personality. *American Psychologist, 36*, 276–289.

Lane, S. P. & Shrout, P. E. (2010). Assessing the Reliability of Within-Person Change Over Time: A Dynamic Factor Analysis Approach. *Multivariate Behavioral Research, 45*, 1027. DOI: 10.1080/00273171.2010.534380

Lebo, M. A., & Nesselroade, J. R. (1978). Intraindividual differences dimensions of mood change during pregnancy identified in five P-technique factor analyses. *Journal of Research in Personality, 12*, 205–224.

Loehlin, J. C. (1998). *Latent variable models: An introduction to factor, path, and structural analysis.* Mahwah, NJ: Erlbaum.

Luborsky, L., & Mintz, J. (1972). The contribution of P-technique to personality, psychotherapy, and psychosomatic research. In R. M. Dreger (Ed.), *Multivariate personality research: Contributions to the understanding of personality in honor of Raymond B. Cattell* (pp. 387–410). Baton Rouge, LA: Claitor's Publishing Division.

Meredith, W. (1993). Measurement invariance, factor analysis and factorial invariance. *Psychometrika, 58*, 525–543.

Molenaar, P. C. M. (1985). A dynamic factor model for the analysis of multivariate time series. *Psychometrika, 50*, 181–202.

Molenaar, P.C.M. (1994). Dynamic latent variable models in developmental psychology. In A. von Eye & C.C. Clogg (Eds.), *Analysis of latent variables in developmental research* (pp.155–180). Newbury Park, CA: Sage.

Molenaar, P. C. M. (2004). A manifesto on psychology as idiographic science: Bringing the person back into scientific psychology, this time forever. *Measurement, 2*, 201–218.

Molenaar, P. C. M. (2010). Testing all six person-oriented principles in dynamic factor analysis. *Development and Psychopathology, 22*, 255–259.

Molenaar, P. C. M., De Gooijer, J. G., & Schmitz, B. (1992). Dynamic factor analysis of nonstationary multivariate time series. *Psychometrika, 57*, 333–349.

Molenaar, P. C. M., Nesselroade, J. R. (1998). A comparison of pseudo-maximum likelihood and asymptotically distribution-free dynamic factor analysis parameter estimation in fitting covariance-structure models to Block-Toeplitz matrices representing single-subject multivariate time-series. *Multivariate Behavioral Research, 33*, 313–342.

Molenaar, P. C. M. & Nesselroade, J. R. (2001). Rotation in the dynamic factor modeling of multivariate stationary time series. *Psychometrika, 66*, 99–107.

Molenaar, P. C. M., & Ram, N. (2009). Advances in dynamic factor analysis of psychological processes. In J. A. Valsiner, P. C. M. Molenaar, M. C. D. P. Lyra, & N. Chaudhary (Eds.) *Dynamic process methodology in the social and developmental sciences* (pp. 255–268). New York: Springer.

Molenaar, P. C. M., & Ram, N. (2010). Dynamic modeling and optimal control of intra-individual variation: A computational paradigm for non-ergodic psychological processes. In S. M. Chow, E. Ferrer, & F. Hsieh (Eds.), *Statistical methods for modeling human dynamics: Notre Dame Series on Quantitative Methods* (pp. 13–35). New York: Routledge.

Molenaar, P. C. M., Sinclair, K. O., Rovine, M. J., Ram, N., & Corneal, S. E. (2009). Analyzing Developmental Processes on an Individual Level Using Nonstationary Time Series Modeling. *Developmental Psychology, 45*(1), 260–271. doi: Doi 10.1037/A0014170

Molenaar, P. C. M., Ulbrecht, J., Gold, C., Rovine, M. J., Wang, Q., & Zhou, J. (in press). State-space modeling of continuously monitored blood glucose time series of Type I diabetic patients: A new inductive approach to prediction and dynamic regression on insulin dose and meal intake.

Nesselroade, J. R. (1991). The warp and the woof of the developmental fabric. In R. M. Downs, L. S. Liben & D. S. Palermo (Eds.), *Visions of aesthetics, the environment and development: The legacy of Joachim F. Wohlwill* (pp. 213–240). Hillsdale, NJ: Lawrence Erlbaum.

Nesselroade, J. R. (2001). Intraindividual variability in development within and between individuals. *European Psychologist, 6*, 187–193.

Nesselroade, J. R. (2007). Factoring at the individual level: Some matters for the second century of factor analysis. In R. Cudeck & R. MacCallum (Eds.), *100 years of factor analysis* (pp. 249–264). Mahwah, NJ: Erlbaum.

Nesselroade, J. R., Gerstorf, D., Hardy, S. A., & Ram, N. (2007). Idiographic filters for psychological constructs. *Measurement, 5*, 217–235.

Nesselroade, J. R., McArdle, J. J., Aggen, S. H., & Meyers, J. M. (2002). Dynamic factor analysis models for representing process in multivariate time-series. In D. S. Moskowitz & S. L. Hershberger (Eds.), *Modeling intraindividual variability with repeated measures data* (pp. 233–265). Mahwah, NJ: Erlbaum.

Nesselroade, J. R., & Molenaar, P. C. M. (1999). Pooling lagged covariance structures based on short, multivariate time series for dynamic factor analysis. In R. H. Hoyle (Ed.), *Statistical strategies for small sample research* (pp. 223–250). Thousand Oaks, CA: Sage Publications.

Priestley, M. B. (1981). *Spectral analysis and time series.* New York: Academic Press.

Ram, N., & Gerstorf, D. (2009). Time-structured and net intraindividual variability: Tools for examining the development of dynamic characteristics and processes. *Psychology and Aging, 24*(4), 778–791. doi: 10.1037/A0017915

Ram, N. & Nesselroade, J. R. (2007). Modeling intraindividual and intracontextual change: Rendering developmental contextualism operational. In T. D. Little, J. A. Bovaird & N. A.

Card (Eds.), *Modeling contextual effects in longitudinal studies* (pp. 325–342). Mahwah, NJ: Lawrence Erlbaum.

Robinson, W. S. (1950). Ecological correlations and the behavior of individuals. *American Sociological Review, 15*, 351–357.

Russell, R. L., Jones, M. E., & Miller, S. A. (2007). Core process components in psychotherapy: A synthetic review of P-technique studies. *Psychotherapy Research, 17*, 271–288.

Shiffman, S., Stone, A. A., & Hufford, M. R. (2008). Ecological momentary assessment. *Annual Review of Clinical Psychology, 4*, 1–32.

Shiyko, M., & Ram, N., (2011). Conceptualizing and estimating process speed in studies employing ecological momentary assessment designs: A multilevel variance decomposition approach. *Multivariate Behavioral Research, 46*, 875–899.

Shumway, R. H. & Stoffer, D. S. (2006). *Time Series Analysis and Its Applications.* New York: Springer.

Sterba, S. K., & Bauer, D. J. (2010). Matching method with theory in person-oriented developmental psychopathology research. *Development and Psychopathology, 22*, 239–254.

Stern, W. (1911). *Differentielle pschologie: Ihre methodischen grundlagen (Differntial psychology: Methodological foundations).* Leipzig, Barth Verlag.

Tabachnick, B. G. & Fidell, L. S. (2007). *Using multivariate statistics,* 5th edition. New York: Pearson.

Valsiner, J. (1986). Where is the individual subject in scientific psychology? In J. Valsiner (Ed.), *The individual subject and scientific psychology* (pp. 1–14). New York: Plenum Press.

Walls, T. A., & Schafer, J. L. (Eds.). (2006). *Models for intensive longitudinal data.* New York: Oxford University Press.

Widaman, K. F., & Grimm, K. G. (2009). Invariance, or noninvariance: That is the question. *Measurement, 7*, 8–12.

Wood, P. & Brown, D. (1994). The study of intraindividual differences by means of dynamic factor models: Rationale, implementation, and interpretation. *Psychological Bulletin, 116*, 166–186.

Young, P. C., Pedregal, D. J., & Tych, W. (1999). Dynamic harmonic regression. *Journal of Forecasting, 18*, 369–394.

Zevon, M. A., & Tellegen, A. (1982). The structure of mood change: An idiographic/nomothetic analysis. *Journal of Personality and Social Psychology, 43*, 111–122.

Zhang, G. & Browne, M. W. (2010). Bootstrap standard error estimates in dynamic factor analysis. *Multivariate Behavioral Research, 45*, 453–482.

Zhang, Z., Hamaker, E. L., & Nesselroade, J. R. (2008). Comparisons of four methods for estimating dynamic factor models. *Structural Equation Modeling, 15*, 377–402.

Zhang, Z., & Nesselroade J. R. (2007). Bayesian estimation of categorical dynamic factor models. *Multivariate Behavioral Research, 42*, 729–756.

CHAPTER 22

Time Series Analysis

William W.S. Wei

Abstract

This chapter deals with time domain statistical models and methods on analyzing time series and their use in applications. It covers fundamental concepts, stationary and nonstationary models, nonseasonal and seasonal models, intervention and outlier models, transfer function models, regression time series models, vector time series models, and their applications. We discuss the process of time series analysis including model identification, parameter estimation, diagnostic checks, forecasting, and inference. We also discuss autoregressive conditional heteroscedasticity model, generalized autoregressive conditional heteroscedasticity model, and unit roots and cointegration in vector time series processes.

Key Words: Autoregressive model, moving average model, autoregressive moving average model, autoregressive integrated moving average model, intervention, outlier, transfer function model, autoregressive conditional heteroscedasticity model, generalized autoregressive conditional heteroscedasticity model, vector autoregressive model, vector moving average model, vector autoregressive moving average model

---

Introduction

In studying a phenomenon, we often encounter a data set where the observations are taken according to the order of time. This time-ordered sequence of observations is called a *time series*. Examples of such data sets are numerous, such as daily closing stock prices, monthly unemployment figures, quarterly crime rates, and annual birth rates. The fundamental characteristic of a time series is that its observations are correlated. Most standard statistical methods based on random samples are not applicable, and different methods are needed. The body of statistical methods for analyzing time series is referred to as *time series analysis*. Some of these methods are descriptive, emphasizing mainly the description of a time series based on non-stochastic methods. The other approach—that is, the stochastic approach—is to treat a time series as a realization of a stochastic time series process or model, and the main purpose of analyzing time series in this approach is to construct a possible underlying process and use it for forecasting, inference, and control. It is on this approach that we will focus our attention in the following discussion.

Time series analysis includes time domain approach and frequency domain approach. In the time domain approach, we use time functions like the *autocorrelation function* (*ACF*) and the *partial autocorrelation function* (*PACF*) to describe the characteristics of a time series process whose evolution is represented through various time-lag relationships. In the frequency domain approach, we try to use a spectral function to study how the variation of a time series may be accounted for by the mixture of sines and cosines at various frequencies. Because of space restrictions, we will concentrate our discussion on the time domain approach. For the frequency domain approach, we refer readers to the introductory chapter, Spectral Analysis, given by Wei (2008).

After introducing some fundamental concepts, we will start with univariate time series and introduce some commonly used stationary and non-stationary time series models, including seasonal time series models. We will describe a systematic model-building process that has been found useful in constructing a time series model from a given time series data set. We then extend the method to study the relationship of several time series variables. Examples will be used throughout the discussion to illustrate the concepts and procedures.

Some Fundamental Concepts
Strictly and Weakly Stationary Processes

A time series is a realization of a *stochastic process*, which is a family of time-indexed random variables. Let us use Z_t to denote a time series process, where for convenience and with no loss of generality we assume that the time index set is the set of all integers. The process is characterized by the joint probability distribution of these variables. We call the process *strictly stationary* if its joint distribution is invariant with respect to a change of time origin. That is, for a strictly stationary process, we have

$$F_{Z_{t_1},\ldots,Z_{t_n}}(x_1,\ldots,x_n) = F_{Z_{t_1+k},\ldots,Z_{t_n+k}}(x_1,\ldots,x_n) \quad (1)$$

for any n-tuple $(t_1,\ldots,t_n)$ and any k of integers, where $F_{Z_{t_1},\ldots,Z_{t_n}}(x_1,\ldots,x_n)$ is the joint distribution function defined by $F_{Z_{t_1},\ldots,Z_{t_n}}(x_1,\ldots,x_n) = P\{Z_{t_1} \leq x_1,\ldots,Z_{t_n} \leq x_n\}$. The terms *strongly stationary* and *completely stationary* are also used to denote a strictly stationary process. Unfortunately this assumption is very difficult or impossible to check. For most practical purpose, to identify the underlying model, it is often sufficient to know the first few moments of the time series process. Thus, we will consider the concept of a weakly stationary process.

A process is said to be *second order* or *weakly stationary* if its first two moments are time invariant. That is, if the *mean function* of the process,

$$\mu_t = E(Z_t) = \mu, \quad (2)$$

and the *variance function* of the process,

$$\sigma_t^2 = Var(Z_t) = E(Z_t - \mu)^2 = \sigma^2, \quad (3)$$

are constant, and the *covariance function* between Z_s and Z_t,

$$\gamma(s,t) = Cov(Z_s, Z_t) = E(Z_s - \mu)(Z_t - \mu), \quad (4)$$

is only a function of the time difference, $(t-s)$. Thus, we can simply write the covariance function between Z_t and Z_{t+k} of a weakly stationary process as

$$\gamma(t, t+k) = E(Z_t - \mu)(Z_{t+k} - \mu) = \gamma_k. \quad (5)$$

Because, in practice, it is this class of second-order weakly stationary processes with which we often work, henceforth, when we say that the process is stationary it is understood that we are referring to a second-order weakly stationary process.

The Autocorrelation Function

In time series analysis, the covariance function at lag k is often called the *autocovariance function* at lag k because it represents the covariance between Z_t and Z_{t+k} from the same process, separated by k time lags. Hence, the ACF between Z_t and Z_{t+k} is simply the standardized autocovariance function,

$$\rho_k = \frac{\gamma_k}{\gamma_0} = \frac{Cov(Z_t, Z_{t+k})}{\sqrt{Var(Z_t)}\sqrt{Var(Z_{t+k})}}, \quad (6)$$

where we note that for a stationary process, $Var(Z_t) = Var(Z_{t+k}) = \gamma_0$. It is easy to see that for a stationary process, the ACF has the properties: (1) $\rho_0 = 1$; (2) $|\rho_k| \leq 1$; (3) $\rho_{-k} = \rho_k$, which follows from the fact that the time difference between Z_t and Z_{t+k} and between Z_t and Z_{t-k} are the same; and (4) ρ_k is positive semidefinite—that is, $\sum_{i=1}^{n}\sum_{j=1}^{n} \alpha_i \alpha_j \rho_{|t_i - t_j|} \geq 0$, for any set of time-points, $t_1, \ldots,$ and t_n and any real numbers $\alpha_1, \ldots,$ and α_n. Using property 3, we plot an ACF only for the non-negative lags, which is also called a *correlogram*.

The Partial Autocorrelation Function

Other than the autocorrelation between Z_t and Z_{t+k}, we may also want to study the correlation between Z_t and Z_{t+k} after their mutual linear dependency on the intervening variables $Z_{t+1}, \ldots,$ and Z_{t+k-1} has been removed. This conditional correlation,

$$\varphi_{kk} = Corr(Z_t, Z_{t+k} | Z_{t+1}, \ldots, Z_{t+k-1}), \quad (7)$$

is referred to as the *partial autocorrelation*, and it equals

$$\varphi_{kk} = \frac{\begin{vmatrix} 1 & \rho_1 & \cdots & \rho_{k-2} & \rho_1 \\ \rho_1 & 1 & \cdots & \rho_{k-3} & \rho_2 \\ \vdots & \vdots & \cdots & \vdots & \vdots \\ \rho_{k-1} & \rho_{k-2} & \cdots & \rho_1 & \rho_k \end{vmatrix}}{\begin{vmatrix} 1 & \rho_1 & \cdots & \rho_{k-2} & \rho_{k-1} \\ \rho_1 & 1 & \cdots & \rho_{k-3} & \rho_{k-2} \\ \vdots & \vdots & \cdots & \vdots & \vdots \\ \rho_{k-1} & \rho_{k-2} & \cdots & \rho_1 & 1 \end{vmatrix}}. \quad (8)$$

White Noise and Gaussian Processes

A process is called a *white noise process*, to be denoted by $\{a_t\}$, if it is a sequence of uncorrelated random variables from a fixed distribution with a constant mean, usually assumed to be 0, and constant variance. Thus it has the ACF

$$\rho_k = \begin{cases} 1, & k = 0, \\ 0, & k \neq 0, \end{cases} \quad (9)$$

and the PACF

$$\varphi_{kk} = \begin{cases} 1, & k = 0, \\ 0, & k \neq 0. \end{cases} \quad (10)$$

This process plays an important role as a basic building block in the construction of time series models.

A time series process is said to be a *Gaussian* or *normal process* if its joint distribution is normal. Like most other areas in statistics, most results in time series analysis are established for Gaussian processes. Because a normal distribution is uniquely characterized by its first two moments, strictly stationary and weakly stationary are equivalent for a Gaussian process. As a result, mean, variance, ACF, and PACF also become fundamental measures used in the identification of time series models.

Estimation of the Mean, the Variance, the Autocorrelation Function, and the Partial Autocorrelation Function

Given a time series, $Z_1, \ldots, Z_n$, of n observations from a stationary process, we will use the *sample mean*,

$$\overline{Z} = \frac{1}{n} \sum_{t=1}^{n} Z_t, \quad (11)$$

to estimate the mean, μ, the *sample variance*,

$$\hat{\gamma}_0 = \frac{1}{n} \sum_{t=1}^{n} (Z_t - \overline{Z})^2, \quad (12)$$

to estimate the variance, $\gamma_0 = \sigma_Z^2$, and the *sample autocovariance function*,

$$\hat{\gamma}_k = \frac{1}{n} \sum_{t=1}^{n-k} (Z_t - \overline{Z})(Z_{t+k} - \overline{Z}), \quad (13)$$

to estimate the autocovariance function, γ_k. Similarly, we will use the *sample ACF*,

$$\hat{\rho}_k = \frac{\hat{\gamma}_k}{\hat{\gamma}_0} = \frac{\sum_{t=1}^{n-k} (Z_t - \overline{Z})(Z_{t+k} - \overline{Z})}{\sum_{t=1}^{n} (Z_t - \overline{Z})^2}, \quad (14)$$

and the *sample PACF*,

$$\hat{\varphi}_{kk} = \frac{\begin{vmatrix} 1 & \hat{\rho}_1 & \cdots & \hat{\rho}_{k-2} & \hat{\rho}_1 \\ \hat{\rho}_1 & 1 & \cdots & \hat{\rho}_{k-3} & \hat{\rho}_2 \\ \vdots & \vdots & \cdots & \vdots & \vdots \\ \hat{\rho}_{k-1} & \hat{\rho}_{k-2} & \cdots & \hat{\rho}_1 & \hat{\rho}_k \end{vmatrix}}{\begin{vmatrix} 1 & \hat{\rho}_1 & \cdots & \hat{\rho}_{k-2} & \hat{\rho}_{k-1} \\ \hat{\rho}_1 & 1 & \cdots & \hat{\rho}_{k-3} & \hat{\rho}_{k-2} \\ \vdots & \vdots & \cdots & \vdots & \vdots \\ \hat{\rho}_{k-1} & \hat{\rho}_{k-2} & \cdots & \hat{\rho}_1 & 1 \end{vmatrix}}, \quad (15)$$

to estimate the ACF, ρ_k, and the PACF, φ_{kk}, respectively.

For a stationary Gaussian process that has the autocorrelations $\rho_k = 0$ for $k > m$, the large-lag standard error of $\hat{\rho}_k$ from Bartlett (1946) is

$$S_{\hat{\rho}_k} = \sqrt{\frac{1}{n}(1 + 2\hat{\rho}_1^2 + \cdots + 2\hat{\rho}_m^2)}. \quad (16)$$

Thus, to test a white noise process from a sample series of n observations, we use

$$S_{\hat{\rho}_k} = \sqrt{\frac{1}{n}}, \quad (17)$$

and

$$S_{\hat{\varphi}_{kk}} = \sqrt{\frac{1}{n}}. \quad (18)$$

Moving Average and Autoregressive Representations of Time Series Processes

In time series analysis, we often write a process Z_t as a linear combination of a sequence of white noise random variables, known as the *moving average (MA) representation*,

$$Z_t = \mu + \sum_{j=0}^{\infty} \psi_j a_{t-j}, \quad (19)$$

where $\psi_0 = 1$. Defining the backshift operator $B^j a_t = a_{t-j}$, we can write Equation 19 as

$$Z_t = \mu + \psi(B) a_t, \qquad (20)$$

where $\psi(B) = \sum_{j=0}^{\infty} \psi_j B^j$. For a stationary process, we require that the ψ_j is absolutely summable—that is, $\sum_{j=0}^{\infty} |\psi_j| < \infty$, and μ is the mean of the process.

Another useful form known as *autoregressive (AR) representation* is to regress the value of Z_t on its past values plus a random shock,

$$Z_t = \theta_0 + \sum_{j=0}^{\infty} \pi_j Z_{t-j} + a_t, \qquad (21)$$

or

$$\pi(B) Z_t = \theta_0 + a_t, \qquad (22)$$

where $\pi(B) = 1 - \sum_{j=1}^{\infty} \pi_j B^j$. We call the process Z_t invertible if it can be written in Equation 21 such that the π_j is absolutely summable—that is, $\sum_{j=1}^{\infty} |\pi_j| < \infty$.

Univariate Time Series Models

Although the AR and MA representations are useful, they are not the model forms that we will construct from a given time series of n observations because they contain an infinite number of parameters, which cannot be estimated from a finite number of available observations. We need to consider models with a finite number of parameters. For a given n observations, it is known that the more parameters in a model, the less efficient the estimation of the parameters will be. Thus, an important rule in model construction is the principle of parsimony, where all other things being equal, we will, in general, choose a simpler model.

Stationary Time Series Models

In the AR representation, if only a finite number of π_j weights are non-zero—that is, $\pi_1 = \varphi_1, \ldots, \pi_p = \varphi_p$, and $\pi_j = 0$, for $j > p$, the resulting model is said to be an *AR model (process) of order p*, to be denoted as $AR(p)$,

$$Z_t = \theta_0 + \varphi_1 Z_{t-1} + \cdots + \varphi_p Z_{t-p} + a_t, \qquad (23)$$

or

$$\varphi_p(B) Z_t = \theta_0 + a_t, \qquad (24)$$

where $\varphi_p(B) = (1 - \varphi_1 B - \cdots - \varphi_p B^p)$. Because $\sum_{j=1}^{\infty} |\pi_j| = \sum_{j=1}^{p} |\varphi_j| < \infty$, the process is always invertible. To be stationary, the roots of $\varphi_p(B) = 0$ must be outside of the unit circle so that its moving average representation in Equation 19 exists. The $\varphi_j, j = 1, \ldots, p$, are often referred to as the AR coefficients or parameters.

For $p = 1$, we have the first-order $AR(1)$ model,

$$Z_t = \theta_0 + \varphi_1 Z_{t-1} + a_t, \qquad (25)$$

or

$$(1 - \varphi_1 B) Z_t = \theta_0 + a_t. \qquad (26)$$

For a stationary $AR(1)$ process, the root of $(1 - \varphi_1 B) = 0$ must be outside of the unit circle and hence $|\varphi_1| < 1$. It can be easily seen that the mean μ of the process is related to the constant term θ_0 by $\theta_0 = (1 - \varphi_1)\mu$. Let $\dot{Z}_t = Z_t - \mu$. Equation 25 becomes $\dot{Z}_t = \varphi_1 \dot{Z}_{t-1} + a_t$, and we have

$$\gamma_k = E(\dot{Z}_{t-k} \dot{Z}_t) = \varphi_1 E(\dot{Z}_{t-k} \dot{Z}_{t-1}) + E(\dot{Z}_{t-k} a_t)$$
$$= \varphi_1 \gamma_{k-1}, \ k \geq 1,$$

and

$$\rho_k = \varphi_1 \rho_{k-1} = \varphi_1^k, \ k \geq 1, \qquad (27)$$

where we note that $\rho_0 = 1$. The PACF of the process from Equation 8 is

$$\varphi_{kk} = \begin{cases} \rho_1 = \varphi_1, & k = 1, \\ 0, & \text{for } k \geq 2. \end{cases} \qquad (28)$$

Thus, for a stationary $AR(1)$ model, its ACF decays exponentially and its PACF cuts off after lag 1. More generally, for a stationary $AR(p)$ model, its ACF decays exponentially and its PACF cuts off after lag p. The fundamental characteristic of a stationary $AR(p)$ is that its PACF cuts off after lag p.

In the MA representation, if only a finite number of ψ_j weights are non-zero (i.e., $\psi_1 = \theta_1, \ldots, \psi_q = \theta_q$, and $\psi_j = 0$, for $j > q$) then the resulting model is said to be a *moving average model (process) of order q*, to be denoted as $MA(q)$,

$$Z_t = \mu + a_t + \theta_1 a_{t-1} + \cdots + \theta_q a_{t-q}, \qquad (29)$$

or

$$\dot{Z}_t = \theta_q(B) a_t, \qquad (30)$$

where $\theta_q(B) = (1 - \theta_1 B - \cdots - \theta_q B^q)$. Because $\sum_{j=0}^{\infty} |\psi_j| = 1 + \sum_{j=1}^{q} |\theta_j| < \infty$, the process is always stationary. To be invertible, the roots of $\theta_q(B) = 0$ must be outside of the unit circle so that its AR representation in Equation 21 exists. The $\theta_j, j = 1, \ldots, q$, are often referred to as the MA coefficients or parameters.

For $q = 1$, we have the first-order moving average $MA(1)$ model,

$$Z_t = \mu + a_t - \theta_1 a_{t-1}, \qquad (31)$$

or
$$\dot{Z}_t = (1 - \theta_1 B)a_t. \qquad (32)$$

For a stationary $MA(1)$ process, the root of $(1 - \theta_1 B) = 0$ must be outside of the unit circle and hence $|\theta_1| < 1$. It can be easily seen that

$$\rho_k = \begin{cases} \dfrac{-\theta_1}{1 + \theta_1^2}, & k = 1, \\ 0, & k > 1. \end{cases} \qquad (33)$$

The PACF of the process from Equation 8 is

$$\varphi_{kk} = \dfrac{-\theta_1^k(1 - \theta_1^2)}{1 - \theta_1^{2(k+1)}}, \text{ for } k \geq 1. \qquad (34)$$

Thus, for a stationary $MA(1)$ model, its ACF cuts off after lag 1 and its PACF decays exponentially. More generally, for a stationary $MA(q)$ model, its ACF cuts off after lag q and its PACF decays exponentially. The fundamental characteristic of a stationary $MA(q)$ is that its ACF cuts off after lag q.

Naturally, a model may contain both AR and MA parameters, and we have the $ARMA(p, q)$ *models*,

$$\varphi_p(B)Z_t = \theta_0 + \theta_q(B)a_t, \qquad (35)$$

where

$$\varphi_p(B) = (1 - \varphi_1 B - \cdots - \varphi_p B^p),$$

and

$$\theta_q(B) = (1 - \theta_1 B - \cdots - \theta_q B^q).$$

For the process to be stationary, the roots of $\varphi_p(B) = 0$ must be outside of the unit circle. To be invertible, the roots of $\theta_q(B) = 0$ must be outside of the unit circle.

For $p = 1$ and $q = 1$, we have the $ARMA(1, 1)$ model,

$$Z_t = \theta_0 + \varphi_1 Z_{t-1} + a_t - \theta_1 a_{t-1}, \qquad (36)$$

or

$$(1 - \varphi_1 B)Z_t = \theta_0 + (1 - \theta_1 B)a_t. \qquad (37)$$

For stationarity, we require that $|\varphi_1| < 1$, and for invertibility, we require that $|\theta_1| < 1$. Note that the mean μ of Z_t and θ_0 are related by $\theta_0 = (1 - \varphi_1)\mu = (1 - \varphi_1 B)\mu$. The AR representation of the invertible $ARMA(1, 1)$ model is

$$\pi(B)\dot{Z}_t = a_t,$$

where

$$\pi(B) = (1 + \pi_1 B + \pi_2 B^2 + \cdots) = \dfrac{(1 - \varphi_1 B)}{(1 - \theta_1 B)},$$

and hence

$$\pi_j = \theta_1^{j-1}(\varphi_1 - \theta_1), \text{ for } j \geq 1. \qquad (38)$$

The MA representation of the stationary $ARMA(1, 1)$ model is

$$\dot{Z}_t = \psi(B)a_t,$$

where

$$\psi(B) = (1 + \psi_1 B + \psi_2 B^2 + \cdots) = \dfrac{(1 - \theta_1 B)}{(1 - \varphi_1 B)},$$

and

$$\psi_j = \varphi_1^{j-1}(\varphi_1 - \theta_1), \text{ for } j \geq 1. \qquad (39)$$

Because the $ARMA(p, q)$ process contains $AR(p)$ model and $MA(q)$ model as its special cases, both of its ACF and PACF decays exponentially.

Figure 22.1 illustrates the fundamental properties of some simple AR, MA, and ARMA models in terms of their ACF and PACF.

Nonstationary Time Series Models

In the Stationary Time Series Models section, we introduced stationary time series models. However, in practice, there are many time series that clearly show nonstationary phenomena such as a nonconstant mean and/or nonconstant variance as shown in Figure 22.2 for the yearly U.S. tobacco production between 1871 and 1984.

From earlier discussions, we see that a stationary process is very well characterized by its mean, variance, ACF, and PACF. Because we are using ACF and PACF as our identification tools, we need to use transformations to remove nonstationary phenomena before employing these tools to identify the underlying model. To remove a nonconstant mean, we often use a differencing operator,

$$W_t = (1 - B)^d Z_t, \qquad (40)$$

where d is a positive integer. The most commonly used d is 1. For example, Z_t is nonstationary but the series of its changes, $(1 - B)Z_t = Z_t - Z_{t-1}$, is often stationary. To remove a nonconstant variance, we can use various variance stabilizing transformations such as Box and Cox's (1964) power transformation,

$$T(Z_t) = \dfrac{Z_t^\lambda - 1}{\lambda}, \qquad (41)$$

which includes logarithmic and many other transformations as special cases. Because the power transformation is defined only for positive series, we may need to add a constant to a series before taking the transformation, which will not affect the correlation structure of the series. With this

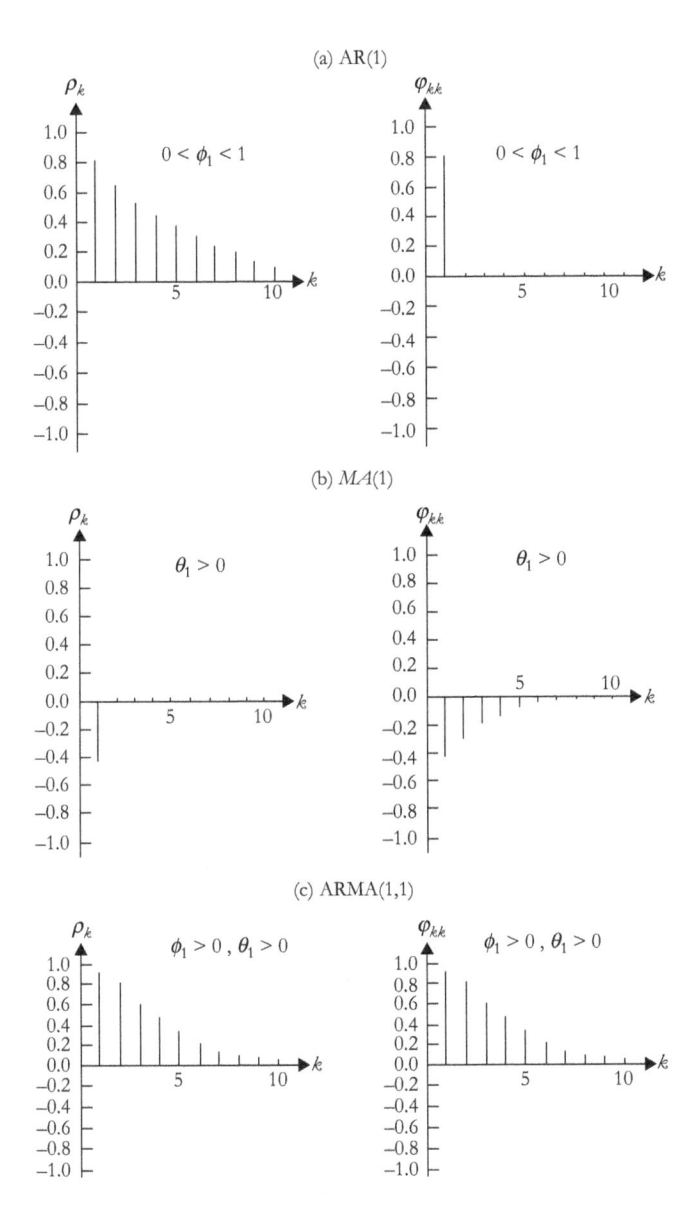

Figure 22.1 ACF and PACF for various time series models.

consideration, we should also apply the power transformation first before taking any differencing. Thus, for a given nonstationary time series, let Z_t be the resulting series from some proper variance stabilizing transformation if necessary. We will extend ARMA(p, q) models to the following *autoregressive integrated moving average* ARIMA(p, d, q) models,

$$\varphi_p(B)(1 - B)^d Z_t = \theta_0 + \theta_q(B) a_t, \quad (42)$$

where the stationary AR polynomial, $\varphi_p(B) = (1 - \varphi_1 B - \cdots - \varphi_p B^p)$, and the invertible MA polynomial, $\theta_q(B) = (1 - \theta_1 B - \cdots - \theta_q B^q)$, are assumed to have no common roots. It should be noted that the parameter θ_0 plays very different roles for $d = 0$ and $d > 0$. When $d = 0$, the process is stationary, and θ_0 is related to the mean of the process—that is, $\theta_0 = (1 - \varphi_1 - \cdots - \varphi_p)\mu$. When $d > 0$, θ_0 is actually equal to the coefficient α_d of t^d from applying the difference operator $(1 - B)^d$ on a deterministic trend $(\alpha_0 + \alpha_1 t + \cdots + \alpha_d t^d)$. For a process without a deterministic trend, the differenced series will have a zero mean. Hence, in general, when $d > 0$, we assume $\theta_0 = 0$ unless the series clearly contains a deterministic component.

Seasonal Time Series Models

Many time series contain a seasonal phenomenon that repeats itself after a regular period of time. The smallest time period for this repetitive phenomenon is called the *seasonal period*. For example, in the U.S.

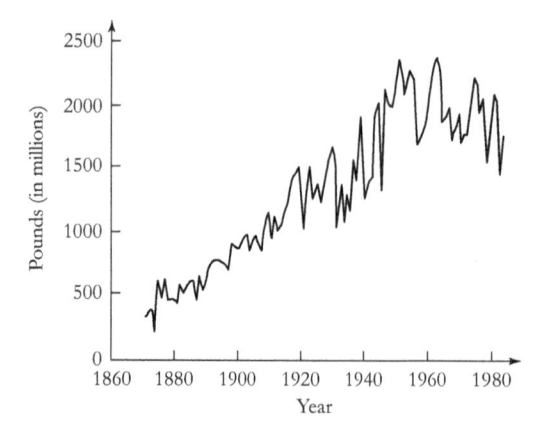

Figure 22.2 Example of a nonstationary time series.

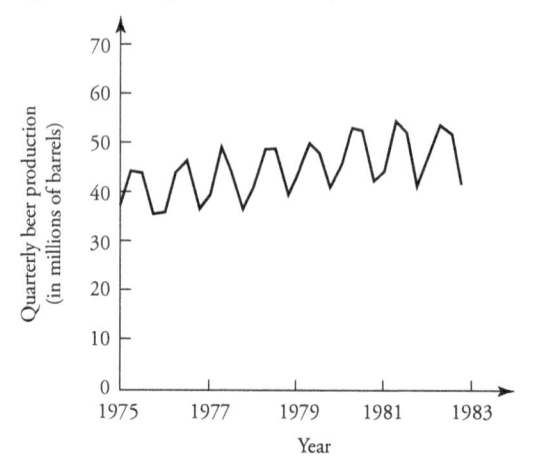

Figure 22.3 Example of a seasonal time series.

quarterly beer production, as shown in Figure 22.3, the beer production is higher during the summer, and the phenomenon repeats itself each year, giving a seasonal period of four.

Suppose we have a seasonal time series with a seasonal period s but fit it with a nonseasonal ARIMA model,

$$\varphi_p(B)(1-B)^d Z_t = \theta_q(B) b_t, \qquad (43)$$

where the series b_t will not be white noise because it contains unexplained seasonal correlations. Let

$$\rho_{j(s)} = \frac{E(b_{t-j(s)} - \mu_b)(b_t - \mu_b)}{\sigma_b^2}, \quad j = 1, 2, 3, \ldots$$

be the ACF representing the unexplained seasonal relationship. We can use the following ARIMA model to represent the relation

$$\Phi_P(B^s)(1-B^s)^D b_t = \Theta_Q(B^s) a_t, \qquad (44)$$

where $\Phi_P(B^s) = (1 - \Phi_1 B^s - \cdots - \Phi_P B^{Ps})$, $\Theta_Q(B^s) = (1 - \Theta_1 B^s - \cdots - \Theta_Q B^{Qs})$, and a_t is a white noises series with mean 0 and variance σ_a^2. Combining Equations 43 and 44, we obtain the following *seasonal ARIMA model*,

$$\begin{aligned}\Phi_P(B^s)\varphi_p(B)(1-B^s)^D(1-B)^d Z_t &= \theta_0 \\ &+ \Theta_Q(B^s)\theta_q(B) a_t,\end{aligned} \qquad (45)$$

which is often denoted as $ARIMA(p,d,q) \times (P,D,Q)_s$, where the index s refers to the seasonal period. For convenience, we often call $(1-B)^d$ and $(1-B^s)^D$ the regular and seasonal difference operators, $\varphi_p(B)$ and $\Phi_P(B^s)$ the regular and seasonal AR polynomials, and $\theta_q(B)$ and $\Theta_Q(B^s)$ the regular and seasonal MA polynomials, respectively.

Time Series Model Building
Model Identification

Given a time series, the first important task is to use the following steps to identify the possible underlying time series model.

Step 1. Plot the time series and if necessary, choose the proper transformation.

Through careful examination of the plot, we usually get a good idea about whether the underlying model is either stationary or nonstationary and seasonal or nonseasonal.

Step 2. Compute and examine the sample ACF and sample PACF of the original series to decide whether differencing is necessary.

Given a series of n observations, we normally compute $n/4$ sample ACF and PACF. If the sample ACF decays slowly and the sample PACF cuts off after lag 1, then it indicates that differencing is needed. The process can be repeated and used to find the order, d, of differencing. Sometimes a decision based on visual inspection may be difficult. More rigorously, we can develop a test statistic to determine whether a series is nonstationary and needs differencing. Let us consider the following process,

$$Z_t = \varphi Z_{t-1} + a_t, \qquad (46)$$

where a_t is Gaussian $N(0, \sigma_a^2)$ white noise. Given $Z_1, Z_2, \ldots,$ and Z_n, we know that the least square estimator given by,

$$\hat{\varphi} = \frac{\sum_{t=2}^n Z_{t-1} Z_t}{\sum_{t=2}^n Z_{t-1}^2}, \qquad (47)$$

is the best linear unbiased estimator and $\tau = (\hat{\varphi} - \varphi)/S_{\hat{\varphi}}$ follows a t–distribution when $|\varphi| < 1$. When $\varphi = 1$, the process becomes nonstationary. It is tempting to use the same test statistic, τ, and the standard t-distribution to test the hypothesis, $H_0 : \varphi = 1$. However, it has been shown by Dickey and Fuller (1979) and Chan and Wei (1988) that it is hardly a t-distribution. In fact,

$$\tau = \frac{\hat{\varphi} - 1}{S_{\hat{\varphi}}} \rightarrow \frac{\frac{1}{2}\{[W(1)]^2 - 1\}}{\left\{\int_0^1 [W(x)]^2\, dx\right\}^{1/2}}, \quad (48)$$

where $W(x)$ is a standard Brownian motion process. The percentiles of the distribution were computed by Dickey and Fuller and the critical values are much less than the values from the standard t-distributions. Therefore, the test rejects $H_0 : \varphi = 1$ when τ is "too negative." The use of a similar test statistic, $R = n(\hat{\varphi} - 1)$, was also studied by Dickey and Fuller (1979), who constructed tables of critical values for both τ and R. They extend the above result to the $AR(1)$ with non-zero mean, $Z_t = \alpha + \varphi Z_{t-1} + a_t$, and the $AR(1)$ with a linear time trend, $Z_t = \alpha + \delta t + \varphi Z_{t-1} + a_t$. They also generalized the result to a general $AR(p)$ process, where testing for a unit root is equivalent to testing $\varphi = 1$ in the following model

$$Z_t = \varphi Z_{t-1} + \sum_{j=1}^{p-1} \phi_j \Delta Z_{t-j} + a_t, \quad (49)$$

where $\Delta Z_{t-j} = (Z_{t-j} - Z_{t-j-1})$. The test is commonly known as the *unit root test*, *Dickey-Fuller test*, or *augmented Dickey-Fuller test*. The test can be repeatedly used on differenced series to determine the order of required differencing and is available in many statistical packages including R (2012), SAS (Statistical Analysis System) (2009), SCA (Scientific Computing Associates) (2008), and SPSS (Statistical Package for the Social Sciences) (2009).

Similarly, for a seasonal time series with the seasonal period s, if the sample ACF decays slowly at multiple lags of s and the sample PACF cuts off after lag s, then it indicates that a seasonal differencing, $(1 - B^s)^D$, is needed for some D. To help identification, we often print these sample ACF and PACF with s of them per line. The seasonal unit root test can also be used to determine the order of required seasonal differencing using the table developed by Dickey, Hasza, and Fuller (1984).

Step 3. Compute and examine the sample ACF and PACF of the properly transformed and differenced series to identify p and q for a regular $ARIMA(p, d, q)$ model or $p, q, P,$ and Q for a seasonal $ARIMA(p, d, q) \times (P, D, Q)_s$ model.

Table 22.1. Characteristics of Theoretical ACF and PACF for Stationary Processes

Process	ACF	PACF
$AR(p)$	Tails off as exponential decay or damped sine wave	Cuts off after lag p
$MA(q)$	Cuts off after lag q	Tails off as exponential decay or damped sine wave
$ARMA(p, q)$	Tails off	Tails off

Again, because variance-stabilizing transformations such as the power transformation are defined only for positive series, they should be performed before any other transformation such as differencing. If necessary, a constant can be added to produce a positive valued series without changing the pattern of the series.

The summary in Table 22.1 should be helpful.

The P and Q for seasonal processes with the seasonal period s are determined similarly based on the ACF and PACF patterns at the lags of multiple s. For example, when $s = 12$, the ACF decays exponentially at $s = 12, 24, 36, \ldots$, and the PACF cuts off after lag 12, implying a seasonal $AR(1)$ model, $(1 - \Phi_1 B^{12})Z_t = a_t$.

One useful procedure to identify the orders of a mixed ARMA model is the use of the *extended sample autocorrelation function* (ESACF) or the *smallest canonical correlation* (SCAN) introduced by Tsay and Tiao (1984, 1985). They showed that using indicator symbols, with X referring to values greater than or less than ± 2 standard deviations and 0 (zero) for values within ± 2 standard deviations, the orders of an $ARMA(p, q)$ model are determined by the vertex of the triangle formed by these zeros in the ESACF table or the upper-left vertex of the rectangle formed by these zeros in the SCAN table. For example, the ESACF and SCAN tables in Table 22.2 correspond to an $ARMA(1, 1)$ model.

Step 4. Test the deterministic trend term θ_0 when $d > 0$.

One can test for its inclusion by comparing the sample mean $\overline{W}$ of the differenced series $W_t = (1 - B)^d Z_t$, with its approximate standard error

$$S_{\overline{W}} = \left[\frac{\hat{\gamma}_0}{n}(1 + 2\hat{\rho}_1^2 + \cdots + 2\hat{\rho}_k^2)\right]^{1/2} \quad (50)$$

Table 22.2. ESACF and SCAN Tables for an $ARMA(1, 1)$ Model

ESCAF						
AR\MA	0	1	2	3	4	⋯
0	X	X	X	X	X	⋯
1	X	0	0	0	0	⋯
2	X	X	0	0	0	⋯
3	X	X	X	0	0	⋯
4	X	X	X	X	0	⋯
⋮	⋮	⋮	⋮	⋮	⋮	⋱

SCAN						
AR\MA	0	1	2	3	4	⋯
0	X	X	X	X	X	⋯
1	X	0	0	0	0	⋯
	X	0	0	0	0	⋯
3	X	0	0	0	0	⋯
4	X	0	0	0	0	⋯
⋮	⋮	⋮	⋮	⋮	⋮	⋱

Under the null hypothesis $\rho_k = 0$ for $k \geq 1$, it reduces to

$$S_{\overline{W}} = \sqrt{\hat{\gamma}_0/n}. \qquad (51)$$

Parameter Estimation

After identifying the orders of a tentative model in Equation 45, we will estimate the parameters in the model. The following are some of the most commonly used estimation methods adopted in various software such as R, SAS, SCA, and SPSS.

1. The method of moments: We express the parameters as functions of moments such as the mean, the variance, the autocovariances, or autocorrelations and then replace these moments by their sample estimates.

2. The maximum likelihood method: We assume a_t following a certain underlying distribution such as a normal distribution, express it as a function of parameters, and then maximize the resultant likelihood function. With a given fixed number of observations, because the expression of a_t involves some unavailable observations and depending on whether any assumption of these unavailable observations is used and how it is used, we have the conditional maximum likelihood estimation, unconditional maximum likelihood estimation, and the exact maximum likelihood estimation.

3. Nonlinear estimation method: Because the expression of a_t as a function of parameters is mostly nonlinear, we can use the nonlinear least squares procedure to find their nonlinear least squares estimates.

Diagnostic Checking

After parameter estimation, we can assess model adequacy by examining whether the model assumption about a_t being white noise is satisfied through various residual analyses such as examining the sample ACF and sample PACF of the residuals. One can also use the portmanteau lack of fit test to test the joint assumption, $H_0: \rho_1 = \cdots = \rho_K = 0$ with the test statistic

$$Q = n(n+2) \sum_{j=1}^{K} \hat{\rho}_j^2/(n-j), \qquad (52)$$

where $\hat{\rho}_j^2$ is the residual sample ACF. Under the null hypothesis of model adequacy, the Q statistic was shown by Ljung and Box (1978) to follow approximately a $\chi^2(K-m)$ distribution, where m is the number of AR and MA parameters in the model.

Once we have an adequate model, we can use the model for forecasting, inference, and control. It is important to note that model building is an iterative process as summarized in Figure 22.4.

Model Selection

In data analysis, several models may adequately represent a given data set of n observations. Thus, some criteria have been introduced to help with model selection.

AKAIKE'S *AIC*

Akaike (1974) introduced the following information criterion,

$$AIC(M) = \ln(\hat{\sigma}_a^2) + \frac{2M}{n}, \qquad (53)$$

where $\hat{\sigma}_a^2$ is the maximum likelihood estimate of σ_a^2, n is the number of observations, and M is the number of parameters in the model. The optimal order of the model is chosen by the value of M so that $AIC(M)$ is minimum.

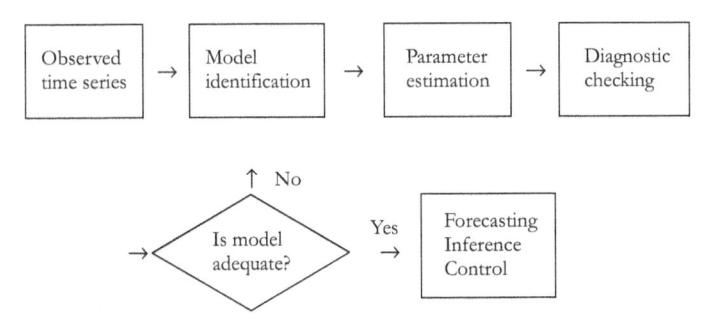

Figure 22.4 Iterative model-building process.

SCHWARTZ'S *SBC*

Schwartz (1978) suggested the following Bayesian criterion of model selection:

$$SBC(M) = \ln(\hat{\sigma}_a^2) + \frac{M\ln(n)}{n}. \quad (54)$$

Again, the model is chosen by the value of M so that $SBC(M)$ is minimum.

PARZEN'S *CAT*

Because a stationary process can always be approximated by an $AR(p)$ model, Parzen (1977) suggested using AR approximations and computed the following

$$CAT(p) = \begin{cases} -(1 + \frac{1}{n}), & p = 0, \\ \frac{1}{n}\sum_{j=1}^{p}\frac{1}{\hat{\sigma}_j^2} - \frac{1}{\hat{\sigma}_p^2}, & p = 1, 2, \ldots, \end{cases} \quad (55)$$

where $\hat{\sigma}_j^2$ is the unbiased estimate of σ_a^2 when an $AR(j)$ model is fitted to the series. The optimal order of p is chosen so that $CAT(p)$ is minimum.

As an aid to model selection—especially in selecting orders p and q in an ARMA(p,q) model—SAS has implemented these criteria through its procedure, MINIC. However, it should be noted that either MINIC or ESACF and SCAN methods that were introduced earlier are recommended for suggesting orders p and q of a regular ARMA but not for the orders P and Q of a seasonal ARMA model.

An Illustrative Example of Model Building

The crime index rates are vital statistics that concern many citizens and governments. Figure 22.5 shows a time series Z_t of 49 observations, which is the yearly aggravated assault rate per 100,000 inhabitants of Pennsylvania between 1960 and 2008 obtained from the U.S. FBI Uniform Crime Reports. The series is clearly nonstationary.

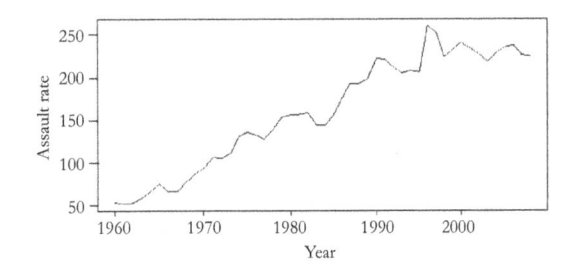

Figure 22.5 The yearly Pennsylvania aggravated assault rate between 1960 and 2008.

Table 22.3. Results of the Power Transformation on Aggravated Assault Rates

λ	Residual mean square error
1.0	309.133
0.5	312.584
0.0	333.326
−0.5	323.860
−1.0	329.683

We first apply Box-Cox power transformation analysis to the series with the result given in Table 22.3. The residual mean square error is lowest when $\lambda = 1$. Thus, no variance stabilizing transformation is needed.

Another nonstationary phenomenon of the series is its increasing trend. This nonstationarity is also shown by the slowly decaying ACF and a single large PACF at lag 1 in Table 22.4 and Figure 22.6. More rigorously, we can apply the Dickey-Fuller unit root tests to the series as shown in Table 22.5. The large p-values for both R and τ statistics for all possible cases clearly indicate that the underlying process for the series contains a unit root.

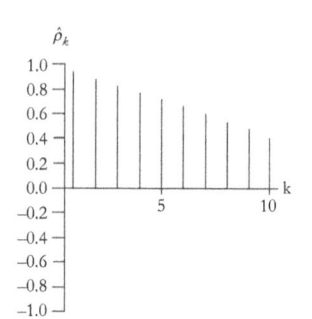

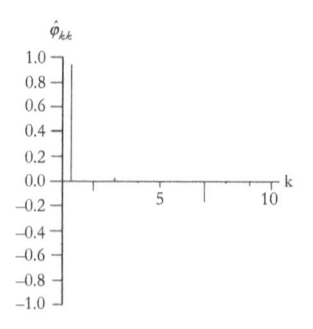

Figure 22.6 Sample ACF and sample PACF of the Pennsylvania aggravated assault rates between 1960 and 2008.

Table 22.4. Sample ACF and Sample PACF of the Pennsylvania Aggravated Assault Rates between 1960 and 2008

k	1	2	3	4	5	6	7	8	9	10
$\hat{\rho}_k$	0.94	0.88	0.82	0.77	0.72	0.67	0.60	0.54	0.48	0.41
St.E.	0.14	0.14	0.14	0.14	0.14	0.14	0.14	0.14	0.14	0.14
$\hat{\varphi}_{kk}$	0.94	−.08	0.03	−.01	−.02	−0.00	−0.17	−0.01	−0.03	−.07
St.E.	0.14	0.14	0.14	0.14	0.14	0.14	0.14	0.14	0.14	0.14

Table 22.5. Dickey-Fuller Unit Root Tests on the Aggravated Assault Rates

Type	Lags	R	Pr < R (p-value)	τ	Pr < τ (p-value)
Zero mean	0	0.6747	0.8423	1.33	0.9521
	1	0.6446	0.8352	1.14	0.9324
Single mean	0	−1.8037	0.7953	−1.37	0.5910
	1	−2.0912	0.7602	−1.49	0.5306
Trend	0	−9.8459	0.4039	−1.93	0.6264
	1	−15.4288	0.1260	−2.23	0.4606

Because theoretical ACF and PACF do not exist for a nonstationary series, we cannot use Table 22.4 and Figure 22.6 to identify its underlying model. Thus, we compute the sample ACF and PACF of its differenced series, $W_t = (1 − B)Z_t$, which are reported in Table 22.6 with their plots in Figure 22.7. Although the significant PACF cutting off after lag 2 suggests a possible $AR(2)$ model, the significant ACF cutting off after lag 2 suggests an alternative $MA(2)$ model. These selections also agree with the suggested models from ESACF on Table 22.7. The t-ratio, $\overline{W}/S_{\overline{W}} = 3.5667/.3123 = 11.42072$, suggests adding a deterministic trend term. Hence, the following $ARIMA(2, 1, 0)$ and $ARIMA(0, 1, 2)$ models will be entertained:

$$(1 − \varphi_1 B − \varphi_2 B)(1 − B)Z_t = \theta_0 + a_t, \quad (56)$$

and

$$(1 − B)Z_t = \theta_0 + (1 − \theta_1 B − \theta_2 B^2)a_t. \quad (57)$$

The estimation of $AR(2)$ model gives

$$(1 − 0.05B + 0.39\ B^2)(1 − B)Z_t = 5.008 + a_t,$$
$$\quad\ \ (0.137)\quad\ (0.139)\qquad\qquad\qquad (1.248)$$
$$(58)$$

with $\hat{\sigma}_a^2 = 132.7446$ and AIC = 374.094. The estimation of $MA(2)$ model gives

$$(1 − B)Z_t = 3.79 + (1 − 0.02B − 0.37\ B^2)a_t,$$
$$\qquad\qquad (1.051)\quad\ \ (0.141)\quad\ (0.146)$$
$$(59)$$

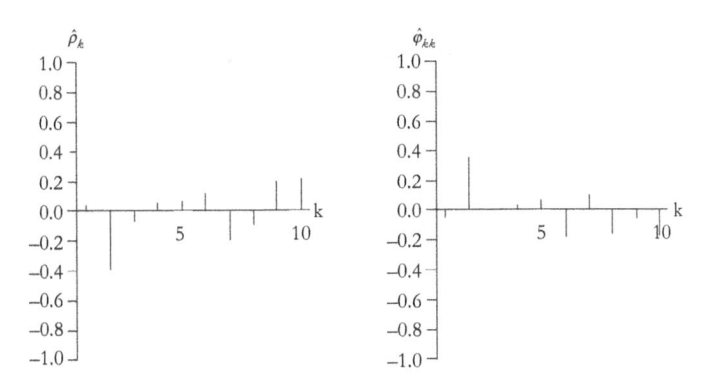

Figure 22.7 Sample ACF and sample PACF for $W_t = (1-B)Z_t$, where Z_t is the yearly Pennsylvania aggravated assault rate between 1960 and 2008.

Table 22.6. Sample ACF and Sample PACF for $W_t = (1-B)Z_t$ Where Z_t is the Yearly Pennsylvania Aggravated Assault Rate Between 1960 and 2008.
$\overline{W} = 3.5667$, $S_W = .3123$.

k	1	2	3	4	5	6	7	8	9	10
$\hat{\rho}_k$	0.04	−0.39	−0.07	0.06	0.07	0.12	−0.19	−0.09	0.20	0.22
St.E.	0.14	0.14	0.14	0.14	0.14	0.14	0.14	0.14	0.14	0.14
$\hat{\varphi}_{kk}$	−0.05	0.36	0.01	0.03	0.07	−0.18	0.10	−0.16	−0.05	−0.16
St.E.	0.14	0.14	0.14	0.14	0.14	0.14	0.14	0.14	0.14	0.14

Table 22.7. The ESACF for the Differenced Aggravated Assault Rates

AR\MA	0	1	2	3	4	5
0	0	X	0	0	0	0
1	0	X	0	0	0	0
2	0	0	0	0	0	0
3	X	0	0	0	0	0
4	0	X	0	0	0	0
5	0	0	0	0	0	0

with $\hat{\sigma}_a^2 = 134.0952$ and AIC $= 374.5403$. Both models are adequate and pass diagnostic checks. Based on model selection criteria discussed in the Model Selection section, because $\hat{\sigma}_a^2$ and AIC are smaller for the $AR(2)$ model, we will select the $AR(2)$ model as the possible underlying model for the series. However, before we use it for forecasting, inference, and control, we will drop the insignificant parameter φ_1 and re-estimate the model. The final result is

$$(1 + 0 \underset{(0.137)}{.39} B^2)(1-B)Z_t = \underset{(0.197)}{5.177} + a_t, \quad (60)$$

with $\hat{\sigma}_a^2 = 130.1907$ and AIC $= 372.2134$, which are smaller than those in the full model in Equation 58.

Time Series Forecasting

One of the most important objectives in the analysis of a time series is to forecast its future values. Let us consider the time series Z_t from the general $ARIMA(p,d,q)$ process

$$\varphi_p(B)(1-B)^d Z_t = \theta_0 + \theta_q(B)a_t, \quad (61)$$

where θ_0 is normally 0 if $d \neq 0$ and is related to the mean μ of the series when $d = 0$, $\varphi_p(B) = (1 - \varphi_1 B - \cdots - \varphi_p B^p)$, $\theta_q(B) = (1 - \theta_1 B - \cdots - \theta_q B^q)$, $\varphi_p(B) = 0$ and $\theta_q(B) = 0$ share no common roots that lie outside of the unit circle, and the series a_t is a Gaussian $N(0, \sigma_a^2)$ white noise process.

Minimum Mean Square Error Forecasts and Forecast Limits

The general ARIMA process in Equation 61 can be written as

$$(1 - \phi_1 B - \cdots - \phi_{p+d} B^{p+d}) Z_t = \theta_0$$
$$+ (1 - \theta_1 B - \cdots - \theta_q B^q) a_t, \quad (62)$$

where $(1 - \phi_1 B - \cdots - \phi_{p+d} B^{p+d}) = \varphi(B)(1 - B)^d$, or equivalently,

$$Z_t = \theta_0 + \phi_1 Z_{t-1} + \cdots + \phi_{p+d} Z_{t-p-d}$$
$$+ a_t - \theta_1 a_{t-1} - \cdots - \theta_q a_{t-q}. \quad (63)$$

Suppose that at time $t = n$ we want to forecast the value of $Z_{n+\ell}$. The minimum mean square error forecast $\hat{Z}_n(\ell)$ of $Z_{n+\ell}$ is given by the following conditional expectation

$$\hat{Z}_n(\ell) = E(Z_{n+\ell} | Z_t, t \leq n)$$
$$= \theta_0 + \phi_1 \hat{Z}_n(\ell - 1) + \cdots + \phi_{p+d}$$
$$\hat{Z}_n(l - p - d) + \hat{a}_n(\ell) - \theta_1 \hat{a}_n(\ell - 1)$$
$$- \cdots - \theta_q \hat{a}_n(\ell - q), \quad (64)$$

where

$$\hat{Z}_n(j) = E(\hat{Z}_{n+j} | Z_t, t \leq n), \quad j \geq 1,$$
$$\hat{Z}_n(j) = Z_{n+j}, \quad j \leq 0,$$
$$\hat{a}_n(j) = 0, \quad j \geq 1,$$

and

$$\hat{a}_n(j) = Z_{n+j} - \hat{Z}_{n+j-1}(1) = a_{n+j}, j \leq 0.$$

By rewriting Equation 62 as

$$Z_t = \alpha + \psi(B) a_t = \alpha + \sum_{j=0}^{\infty} \psi_j a_{t-j}, \quad (65)$$

where $(1 - \phi_1 B - \cdots - \phi_{p+d} B^{p+d})(1 + \psi_1 B + \psi_2 B^2 + \cdots) = (1 - \theta_1 B - \cdots - \theta_q B^q)$, α is normally 0 when $d \neq 0$, and $\alpha = \theta_0/(1 - \varphi_1 - \cdots - \varphi_p) = \mu$ when $d = 0$, we can see that the ℓ − step ahead forecast error is

$$e_n(\ell) = Z_{n+\ell} - \hat{Z}_n(\ell) = \sum_{j=0}^{\ell-1} \psi_j a_{n+\ell-j}, \quad (66)$$

where $\psi_0 = 1$. Because $E(e_n(\ell)) = 0$, the forecast is unbiased with the error variance

$$Var(e_n(\ell)) = \left(\sum_{j=0}^{\ell-1} \psi_j^2 \right) \sigma_a^2. \quad (67)$$

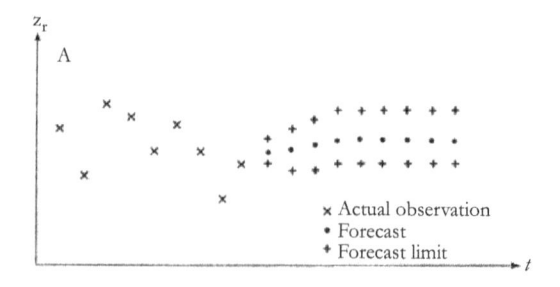

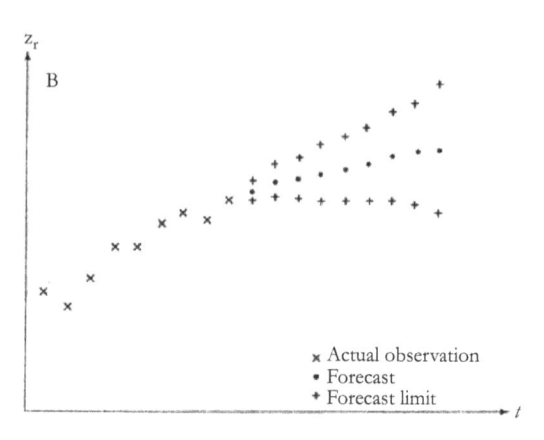

Figure 22.8 Forecasts for (a) stationary processes and (b) nonstationary processes.

For a normal process, the $(1 - \alpha)100\%$ forecast limits are

$$\hat{Z}_n(\ell) \pm N_{\alpha/2} \left[\sum_{j=0}^{\ell-1} \psi_j^2 \right]^{1/2} \sigma_a, \quad (68)$$

where $N_{\alpha/2}$ is the standard normal deviate such that $P(N > N_{\alpha/2}) = \alpha/2$.

As shown in Figure 22.8, for a stationary process, $\lim_{\ell \to \infty} \sum_{j=0}^{\ell-1} \psi_j^2$ exists and its eventual forecast limits approach to two horizontal lines. For a nonstationary process, because $\sum_{j=0}^{\ell-1} \psi_j^2$ increases as ℓ increases, the forecast limits become wider and wider. The result simply implies that in a nonstationary case, the forecaster becomes less certain about the result as the forecast lead time gets larger.

Updating Forecasts

Note that from Equation 66, we have

$$e_n(\ell + 1) = Z_{n+\ell+1} - \hat{Z}_n(\ell + 1)$$
$$= \sum_{j=0}^{\ell} \psi_j a_{n+\ell+1-j}$$
$$= e_{n+1}(\ell) + \psi_\ell a_{n+1}$$
$$= Z_{n+\ell+1} - \hat{Z}_{n+1}(\ell) + \psi_\ell a_{n+1}.$$

Table 22.8. Yearly Forecasts for the Aggravated Assault Rate per 100,000 Inhabitants in Pennsylvania

Year	Forecast	Std Error	95% Confidence Limits	
2009	234.345	11.4101	211.9579	256.6848
2010	240.146	16.1363	208.4921	271.7453
2011	241.601	17.5829	207.1401	276.0637
2012	244.516	18.9191	207.4489	281.6104

Hence, we obtain the following equation for updating forecasts,

$$\hat{Z}_{n+1}(\ell) = \hat{Z}_n(\ell+1) + \psi_\ell [Z_{n+1} - \hat{Z}_n(1)]. \quad (69)$$

Forecasting Example

From the example in the section An Illustrative Example of Model Building, we have the following model for the series of aggravated assault rate per 100,000 inhabitants in Pennsylvania

$$(1 + 0\underset{(0.137)}{.39} B^2)(1-B)Z_t = \underset{(0.197)}{5.177} + a_t, \quad (70)$$

where a_t is Gaussian white noise with mean 0 and variance 130.1907. Given the 49 values of the series from 1960 to 2008, for example, $Z_{47} = 237.6$ for 2006, $Z_{48} = 226.4$ for 2007, and $Z_{49} = 224.82$ for 2008, we can now use the model to forecast future values as follows:

$$\hat{Z}_{49}(1) = 5.177 + Z_{49} - 0.39 Z_{48} + 0.39 Z_{47}$$
$$= 5.177 + 224.8 - 0.39(226.4)$$
$$+ 0.39(237.6) = 234.345$$

$$\hat{Z}_{49}(2) = 5.177 + \hat{Z}_{49}(1) - 0.39 Z_{49} + 0.39 Z_{48}$$
$$= 5.177 + 234.345 - 0.39(224.8)$$
$$+ 0.39(226.4) = 240.146$$

$$\hat{Z}_{49}(3) = 5.177 + \hat{Z}_{49}(2) - 0.39\hat{Z}_{49}(1) + 0.39 Z_{49}$$
$$= 5.177 + 240.146 - 0.39(234.345)$$
$$+ 0.39(224.8) = 241.601,$$

and for $\ell \geq 4$, we simply use the following forecast equation from the model

$$\hat{Z}_{49}(\ell) = 5.177 + \hat{Z}_{49}(\ell-1) - 0.39\hat{Z}_{49}(\ell-2)$$
$$+ 0.39\hat{Z}_{49}(\ell-3).$$

Using Equation 68, we can also compute their 95% forecast limits together with the forecast values given in Table 22.8, which become wider and wider as the forecast lead time gets larger because the model is nonstationary.

Intervention and Outlier Analysis

Time series are often affected by external events such as new treatments, sales promotions, strikes, outbreaks of war, and policy changes. We call these external events interventions and the method of evaluating the effect of the dynamic change for these external events *intervention analysis*.

There are many types of intervention. Some interventions occur at time T and thereafter, which can be represented by

$$I_t = \begin{cases} 1, & t \geq T, \\ 0, & t < T. \end{cases} \quad (71)$$

Some interventions occur only at one time period T, as represented by

$$I_t = \begin{cases} 1, & t = T, \\ 0, & t \neq T. \end{cases} \quad (72)$$

Obviously, there are some interventions that occur at multiple time periods, such as applying a new treatment at time $T_1, T_2, \cdots,$ and T_k, and we can represent this type of intervention as

$$I_t = \begin{cases} 1, & t = T_1, T_2, \cdots, T_k, \\ 0, & t \neq = T_1, T_2, \cdots, T_k. \end{cases} \quad (73)$$

There are many possible responses to an intervention. It can be a fixed unknown response after b periods,

$$\omega B^b I_t, \quad (74)$$

a gradual response after b periods,

$$\frac{\omega B^b}{(1-\delta B)} I_t, \quad (75)$$

or more generally, a response that can be described by a rational function,

$$\frac{\omega(B) B^b}{\delta(B)} I_t, \quad (76)$$

where $\omega(B) = \omega_0 - \omega_1 B - \cdots - \omega_s B^s$ and $\delta(B) = 1 - \delta_1 B - \cdots - \delta_r B^r$ are polynomials in B, b represents the time delay for the intervention effect, and the weights ω_j's in the polynomial $\omega(B)$ often represent the expected initial effects of the intervention. The polynomial $\delta(B)$, on the other hand, measures the behavior of the permanent effect of the intervention. The roots of $\delta(B) = 0$ are assumed to be on or outside the unit circle. The unit root represents an impact that increases linearly, and the root outside the unit circle represents a phenomenon that has a gradual response.

Clearly, Equation 76 contains Equations 74 and 75 as special cases. Thus, in general with multiple interventions, we can represent the phenomenon with the following *intervention model*,

$$Z_t = \theta_0 + \sum_{j=1}^{K} \frac{\omega_j(B) B^{b_j}}{\delta_j(B)} I_{jt} + \frac{\theta(B)}{\phi(B)} a_t, \quad (77)$$

where $I_{jt}, j = 1, \cdots, K$ are intervention variables. The form $\omega_j(B) B^{b_j}/\delta_j(B)$ for the jth intervention is postulated based on the expected form of the response given knowledge of the intervention. Because the main purpose of intervention models is to measure the effect of interventions, Box and Tiao (1975), who introduced the intervention model, called the time series free of interventions, represented by $[\theta(B)/\phi(B)]a_t$, where $\phi(B) = \varphi_p(B)(1-B)^d$, as the noise model. The noise model is usually identified using the time series Z_t before the intervention date. For a nonstationary process, the model in Equation 77 normally does not contain a constant term θ_0.

Time series are sometimes affected by interruptive events. The consequences of these interruptions create spurious observations that are inconsistent with the rest of the series. Such observations are usually referred to as *outliers*. When the timing and causes of interruptions are known, their effects can be accounted for by using the intervention model. However, the timing and causes of interruptions are often unknown. Because outliers are known to wreak havoc in data analysis, making the resultant inference unreliable or invalid, it is important to have procedures that will detect and/or remove such outlier effects. There are many types of time series outliers including *additive outliers (AO)*, *innovational outliers (IO)*, *level shift (LS)*, and *transitory change (TC)*.

Let Z_t be the observed series and X_t be the outlier-free series. Assume that X_t follows a general ARMA(p,q) model, $\varphi_p(B) X_t = \theta_q(B) a_t$. An AO is the outlier that affects only the Tth observation, Z_T, and so

$$Z_t = \omega I_t^{(T)} + X_t = \omega I_t^{(T)} + \frac{\theta_q(B)}{\varphi_p(B)} a_t, \quad (78)$$

where

$$I_t^{(T)} = \begin{cases} 1, & t = T, \\ 0, & t \neq T, \end{cases}$$

is the indicator variable representing the presence or absence of an outlier at time T. An IO is the outlier that affects all observations beyond T through the memory of the system described by $\theta_q(B)/\varphi_p(B)$, and so

$$Z_t = \frac{\theta_q(B)}{\varphi_p(B)} \omega I_t^{(T)} + X_t = \frac{\theta_q(B)}{\varphi_p(B)} \left(\omega I_t^{(T)} + a_t \right). \quad (79)$$

A LS outlier is the outlier that corresponds to a shift of the level of the process starting from time T and continues afterward,

$$Z_t = \frac{1}{(1-B)} \omega I_t^{(T)} + X_t = \frac{1}{(1-B)} \omega I_t^{(T)} + \frac{\theta_q(B)}{\varphi_p(B)} a_t, \quad (80)$$

which is equivalent to a sequence of additive outliers of the same size occurring at time T and afterward. A TC outlier is a level shift that produces an initial impact but the impact decays exponentially as $1/(1 - \delta B)$, so

$$Z_t = \frac{1}{(1-\delta B)} \omega I_t^{(T)} + X_t = \frac{1}{(1-\delta B)} \omega I_t^{(T)} + \frac{\theta_q(B)}{\varphi_p(B)} a_t. \quad (81)$$

The detection of time series outliers was first introduced by Fox (1972). Other references include Chang, Tiao, and Chen (1988), Tsay (1988), Chen and Liu (1991), and Lee and Wei (1995). These procedures have been implemented in many time series software such as SAS, SCA, and SPSS.

In searching for the causes of an outlier, one may find the nature of the disturbance. Some outliers may turn out to be important intervention variables that the analyst overlooked during the preliminary stages of the analysis. We can obviously have a combined *intervention-outlier model*, as illustrated in the following example.

Example of Outlier and Intervention Analysis

As an example, let us consider the monthly airline passengers in the United States from January 1995 to March 2002 plotted in Figure 22.9.

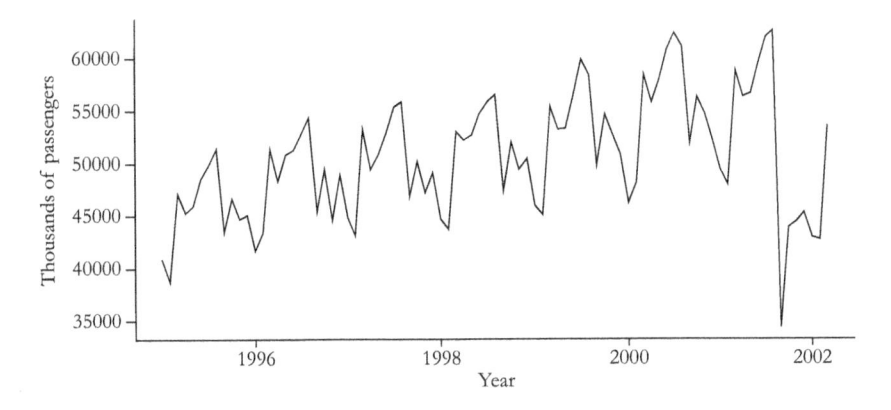

Figure 22.9 The monthly airline passengers in the United States from January 1995 to March 2002.

Without looking at the plot and blindly applying the outlier detection method introduced above with SCA, we obtain the following result:

Detected outliers	
Time	Type
81	TC
82	TC

Parameter	Estimate	St. Error
ω	$-18,973.5$	1299.3
δ	0.76	0.06
φ_1	0.62	0.1
φ_2	0.21	0.1

The impact of the September 11th tragedy on the airline industry is clearly devastating.

If we use a significance level less than 0.01, the only outlier found is the observation at time 81 that corresponds to September 2001, the month of the World Trade Center tragedy in New York City. The incident clearly is an intervention event. The outlier procedure not only detects the event but also suggests the form of the intervention.

The standard time series modeling on the subseries from January 1995 to August 2001 suggests the $ARIMA(2, 0, 0) \times (0, 1, 0)_{12}$ seasonal model:

$$(1 - \varphi_1 B - \varphi_2 B^2)(1 - B^{12})Z_t = a_t. \quad (82)$$

Thus, we will combine Model 82 and the information about the observation at time 81 in the following intervention model:

$$Z_t = \frac{\omega}{(1 - \delta B)} I_t + \frac{1}{(1 - \varphi_1 B - \varphi_2 B^2)(1 - B^{12})} a_t, \quad (83)$$

where

$$I_t = \begin{cases} 0, & t < 81 \,(\text{Sept., 2001}), \\ 1, & t \geq 81 \,(\text{Sept., 2001}). \end{cases}$$

The estimation results are:

Transfer Function and Time Series Regression Models

In earlier sections, we were concerned with univariate time series models. In this section, we will consider models where an output series is related to one or more input series.

Transfer Function Models

Assume that X_t and Y_t are properly transformed series so that they are both stationary. The *transfer function model* is the following model that relates input and output variables:

$$\begin{aligned} Y_t &= \upsilon_0 X_t + \upsilon_1 X_{t-1} + \upsilon_2 X_{t-2} + \cdots + N_t \\ &= \upsilon(B) X_t + N_t, \end{aligned} \quad (84)$$

where $\upsilon(B) = \sum_{j=0}^{\infty} \upsilon_j B^j$ is the transfer function for the system and the υ_j are known as impulse response weights. Figure 22.10 illustrated this dynamic system.

In practice, we often represent $\upsilon(B)$ with the following rational function,

$$\upsilon(B) = \frac{\omega_s(B)}{\delta_r(B)} B^b, \quad (85)$$

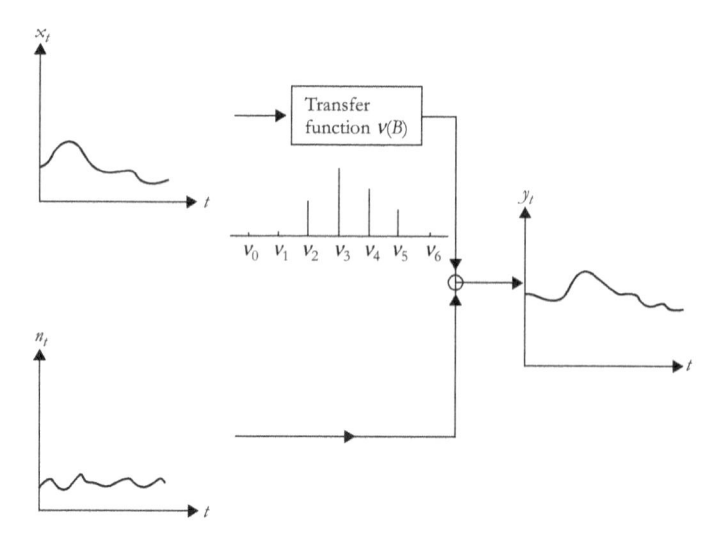

Figure 22.10 Dynamic transfer function system.

where $\omega_s(B) = \omega_0 - \omega_1 B - \cdots - \omega_s B^s$, $\delta_r(B) = 1 - \delta_1 B - \cdots - \delta_r B^r$, b is the delay parameter representing the time lag that elapses before the input variable produces an effect on the output variable, and N_t is the noise series of the system that is independent of the input series. For a stable system, we assume that the roots of $\delta_r(B) = 0$ are outside of the unit circle. When X_t and N_t are assumed to follow some ARMA processes, the system is also known as the *ARMAX model*.

A useful measure for studying the relationship between time series variables is the *cross-correlation function* (CCF),

$$\rho_{XY}(k) = \frac{\gamma_{XY}(k)}{\sigma_X \sigma_Y}, \qquad (86)$$

where $\gamma_{XY}(k) = E[(X_t - \mu_X)(Y_{t+k} - \mu_Y)]$ is the *cross-covariance function* between X_t and Y_t. The sample CCF is given by,

$$\hat{\rho}_{XY}(k) = \frac{\hat{\gamma}_{XY}(k)}{S_X S_Y}, \qquad (87)$$

where

$$\hat{\gamma}_{XY}(k) = \begin{cases} \dfrac{1}{n} \sum_{t=1}^{n-k} (X_t - \overline{X})(Y_{t+k} - \overline{Y}), & k \geq 0, \\ \dfrac{1}{n} \sum_{t=1-k}^{n} (X_t - \overline{X})(Y_{t+k} - \overline{Y}), & k < 0, \end{cases} \qquad (88)$$

$S_X = \sqrt{\hat{\gamma}_{XX}(0)}$, $S_Y = \sqrt{\hat{\gamma}_{YY}(0)}$,

and $\overline{X}$ and $\overline{Y}$ are the sample means of the X_t and Y_t series, respectively. Under the hypothesis that X_t and Y_t are uncorrelated and X_t is white noise, we have

$$\text{Var}[\hat{\rho}_{XY}(k)] \approx (n - k)^{-1}.$$

When the input series is white noise, it can be shown that

$$v_k = \frac{\sigma_Y}{\sigma_X} \rho_{XY}(k). \qquad (89)$$

This result leads to the following procedure of transfer function model identification:

1. Prewhiten the input series:

$$\varphi_X(B) X_t = \theta_X(B) \alpha_t.$$

So

$$\alpha_t = \frac{\varphi_X(B)}{\theta_X(B)} X_t, \qquad (90)$$

and α_t is a white noise series with mean 0 and variance σ_α^2.

2. Calculate the filtered output series:

$$\beta_t = \frac{\varphi_X(B)}{\theta_X(B)} Y_t. \qquad (91)$$

3. Calculate the sample CCF, $\hat{\rho}_{\alpha\beta}(k)$, between α_t and β_t to estimate v_k:

$$\hat{v}_k = \frac{\hat{\sigma}_\beta}{\hat{\sigma}_\alpha} \hat{\rho}_{\alpha\beta}(k). \qquad (92)$$

The significance of the CCF and its equivalent v_k can be tested by comparing it with its standard error $(n - k)^{-1/2}$.

4. Identify the delay parameter b, the order r in $\delta_r(B) = (1 - \delta_1 B - \cdots - \delta_r B^r)$, and the order s in $\omega_s(B) = (\omega_0 - \omega_1 B - \cdots - \omega_s B^s)$ using the pattern of $\hat{v}_k$. Table 22.9 illustrates some typical impulse weights and their corresponding transfer

Table 22.9. Some Typical Impulse Weights and Their Corresponding Transfer Functions

(b,r,s)	Transfer function	Typical impulse weights
(2, 0, 0)	$v(B)x_t = \omega_0 x_{t-2}$	
(2, 0, 1)	$v(B)x_t = (\omega_0 - \omega_1 B)x_{t-2}$	
(2, 0, 2)	$v(B)x_t = (\omega_0 - \omega_1 B - \omega_2 B^2)x_{t-2}$	
(2, 1, 0)	$v(B)x_t = \dfrac{\omega_0}{(1 - \delta_1 B)} x_{t-2}$	
(2, 1, 1)	$v(B)x_t = \dfrac{(\omega_0 - \omega_1 B)}{(1 - \delta_1 B)} x_{t-2}$	
(2, 1, 2)	$v(B)x_t = \dfrac{(\omega_0 - \omega_1 B - \omega_2 B^2)}{(1 - \delta_1 B)} x_{t-2}$	

functions with $b = 2$. Thus, we have our preliminary transfer function for the system:

$$v(B)X_t = \frac{\omega_s(B)}{\delta_r(B)} B^b X_t. \qquad (93)$$

5. Once we obtain the preliminary transfer function, we can calculate the estimated noise series,

$$\hat{N}_t = Y_t - \frac{\hat{\omega}_s(B)}{\hat{\delta}_r(B)} B^b X_t.$$

We then use identification statistics such as sample ACF and PACF to identify the noise model,

$$\varphi(B)N_t = \theta(B)a_t. \qquad (94)$$

Combining Equations 93 and 94, we have our entertained transfer function model:

$$Y_t = \frac{\omega_s(B)}{\delta_r(B)} X_{t-b} + \frac{\theta(B)}{\varphi(B)} a_t. \qquad (95)$$

Because Equations 95 can be rewritten in terms of a_t as a function of $Y'_t s, X'_t s$, and past values of a_t, the estimation methods discussed in the Parameter Estimation section can be used to estimate the parameters. Once the parameters are estimated, we will check the model adequacy by examining the CCF, $\hat{\rho}_{\alpha\hat{a}}(k)$, between α_t and $\hat{a}_t$, and ACF and PACF of $\hat{a}_t$ to make sure they are all insignificant and do not show any patterns as specified in the assumptions of our model. We can then use the adequate model for forecasting, inference, and control. We refer readers to Box, Jenkins, and Reinsel (2008, Chapters 11 and 12) for more details.

Regression Time Series Models

A regression model is used to study the relationship of a dependent variable with one or more independent variables. The standard regression model is represented by the following equation:

$$Y = \beta_0 + \beta_1 X_1 + \beta_2 X_2 + \ldots + \beta_k X_k + \varepsilon,$$

where Y is the dependent variable, $X_1, \cdots, X_k$ are the independent variables, $\beta_0, \beta_1, \cdots, \beta_k$ are the regression coefficients, and ε is the error term. When time series data are used in the model, it becomes *time series regression*, and the model is often written as

$$Y_t = \beta_0 + \beta_1 X_1 + \beta_2 X_2 + \ldots + \beta_k X_k + \varepsilon_t,$$

or equivalently,

$$Y_t = \mathbf{X}'_t \boldsymbol{\beta} + \varepsilon_t, \qquad (96)$$

where $\mathbf{X}'_t = [1, X_{1,t}, \cdots, X_{k,t}]$ and $\boldsymbol{\beta} = [\beta_0, \beta_1, \cdots, \beta_k]'$.

The standard regression assumptions for the error variable are that the ε_t are i.i.d. $N(0, \sigma_\varepsilon^2)$. Under these standard assumptions, it is well known that the *ordinary least squares (OLS) estimator* $\hat{\boldsymbol{\beta}}$ of $\boldsymbol{\beta}$ is a minimum variance unbiased estimator and distributed as multivariate normal, $N(\boldsymbol{\beta}, \sigma_\varepsilon^2 \mathbf{I})$. When $\mathbf{X}'_t$ is stochastic in Model 96 and conditional on $\mathbf{X}'_t$, the results about the OLS estimator $\hat{\boldsymbol{\beta}}$ of $\boldsymbol{\beta}$ also hold as long as ε_s and $\mathbf{X}'_t$ are independent for all s and t. However, the standard assumptions associated with these models are often violated when time series data are used.

REGRESSION WITH AUTOCORRELATED ERRORS

When $\mathbf{X}'_t$ is a vector of a constant 1 and k lagged values of Y_t—that is, $\mathbf{X}'_t = (1, Y_{t-1}, \cdots, Y_{t-k})$ and ε_t is white noise, the model in Equation 96 states that the variable Y_t is regressed on its own past k lagged values and hence is known as autoregressive model of order k—that is, $AR(k)$ model

$$Y_t = \beta_0 + \beta_1 Y_{t-1} + \ldots + \beta_k Y_{t-k} + \varepsilon_t. \quad (97)$$

The OLS estimator $\hat{\boldsymbol{\beta}}$ of $\boldsymbol{\beta}$ is still a minimum variance unbiased estimator. However, this result no longer holds when the ε_t are autocorrelated. In fact, when this is the case, the estimator is not consistent and the usual tests of significance are invalid. This is an important caveat.

When time series are used in a model, it is the norm rather than the exception that the error terms are autocorrelated. Even in univariate time series analysis when the underlying process is known to be an AR model as in Equation 97, the error terms ε_t could still be autocorrelated unless the correct order of k is chosen. Thus, a residual analysis is an important step in regression analysis when time series variables are involved in the study.

There are many methods that can be used to test for autocorrelation of the error term. For example, one can use the test based on the Durbin-Watson statistic. More generally, to study the autocorrelation structure of the error term, we can perform the residual analysis with time series model identification statistics like the sample ACF and sample PACF. Through these identification statistics, one can detect not only whether the residuals are autocorrelated but also identify its possible underlying model. A final analysis can then be performed on a model with autocorrelated errors as follows:

$$Y_t = \mathbf{X}'_t \boldsymbol{\beta} + \varepsilon_t \quad (98)$$

for $t = 1, 2, \ldots, n$, where

$$\varepsilon_t = \varphi_1 \varepsilon_{t-1} + \ldots + \varphi_p \varepsilon_{t-p} + a_t \quad (99)$$

and the a_t are i.i.d. $N(0, \sigma_a^2)$.

Let

$$\mathbf{Y} = \begin{bmatrix} Y_1 \\ \vdots \\ Y_n \end{bmatrix}, \mathbf{X} = \begin{bmatrix} \mathbf{X}'_1 \\ \vdots \\ \mathbf{X}'_n \end{bmatrix}, \text{ and } \boldsymbol{\xi} = \begin{bmatrix} \varepsilon'_1 \\ \vdots \\ \varepsilon'_n \end{bmatrix}.$$

The matrix form of the model in Equation 98 is

$$\mathbf{Y} = \mathbf{X}\boldsymbol{\beta} + \boldsymbol{\xi} \quad (100)$$

where $\boldsymbol{\xi}$ follows a multivariate normal distribution $N(\mathbf{0}, \boldsymbol{\Sigma})$. When $\varphi_1, \ldots, \varphi_p$, and σ^2 are known in Equation 99, $\boldsymbol{\Sigma}$ can be easily calculated. The diagonal element of $\boldsymbol{\Sigma}$ is the variance of ε_t, the jth off-diagonal element corresponds to the jth autocovariance of ε_t, and they can be easily computed from Equation 99. Given $\boldsymbol{\Sigma}$, the *generalized least squares (GLS) estimator*,

$$\hat{\boldsymbol{\beta}} = (\mathbf{X}'\boldsymbol{\Sigma}^{-1}\mathbf{X})^{-1}\mathbf{X}'\boldsymbol{\Sigma}^{-1}\mathbf{Y} \quad (101)$$

is known to be a minimum variance unbiased estimator.

Normally, we will not know the variance–covariance matrix $\boldsymbol{\Sigma}$ of $\boldsymbol{\xi}$ because even if ε_t follows an $AR(p)$ model given in Equation 99, the σ^2 and AR parameters φ_j are usually unknown. As a remedy, the following iterative GLS is often used:

1a. Calculate OLS residuals $\hat{\varepsilon}_t$ from OLS fitting of Model 98.

1b. Estimate φ_j and σ^2 for the $AR(p)$ model in Equation 99 based on the OLS residuals, $\hat{\varepsilon}_t$, using any time series estimation method. For example, a simple conditional OLS estimation can be used.

1c. Compute $\boldsymbol{\Sigma}$ from model in Equation 99 using the values of φ_j and σ^2 obtained in Step 1b.

1d. Compute GLS estimator, $\hat{\boldsymbol{\beta}} = (\mathbf{X}'\boldsymbol{\Sigma}^{-1}\mathbf{X})^{-1}\mathbf{X}'\boldsymbol{\Sigma}^{-1}\mathbf{Y}$, using the $\boldsymbol{\Sigma}$ obtained in Step 1c.

Compute the residuals $\hat{\varepsilon}_t$ from the GLS model fitting in Step 1d, and repeat the above Steps 1b through 1d until some convergence criterion (such as the maximum absolute value change in the estimates between iterations become less than some specified quantity) is reached.

More generally, the error structure can be modified to include an ARMA model. The above GLS iterative estimation can still be used with the exception that a nonlinear least squares estimation rather than OLS is needed to estimate the parameters in the error model. Alternatively, by substituting the error process in the regression model Equation 98, we can also use the nonlinear estimation or maximum likelihood estimation to jointly estimate the regression and error model parameters $\boldsymbol{\beta}$ and $\varphi'_j s$, which is available in many standard software.

It should be pointed out that although the error term, ε_t, can be autocorrelated in the regression model, it should be stationary. A nonstationary error structure could produce a spurious regression, where a significant regression can be achieved for totally unrelated series.

REGRESSION WITH HETEROSCEDASTICITY

One of the main assumptions of the standard regression model in Equation 96 or the regression model with autocorrelated errors in Equation 98 is that the variance, σ_ε^2, is constant. In many applications, this assumption may not be realistic. For example, in financial investments, it is generally agreed that the stock market's volatility is rarely constant.

A model with a non-constant error variance is called a *heteroscedasticity model*. There are many approaches that can be used to deal with heteroscedasticity. For example, the weighted regression is often used if the error variances at different times are known or if the variance of the error term varies proportionally to the value of an independent variable. In time series regression, we often have a situation where the variance of the error term is related to the magnitude of past errors. This phenomenon leads to the conditional heteroscedasticity model, introduced by Engle (1982), where in terms of Equation 96 we assume that

$$\varepsilon_t = \sigma_t e_t \quad (102)$$

where e_t is the series of i.i.d. random variables with mean 0 and variance 1, and

$$\sigma_t^2 = \theta_0 + \theta_1 \varepsilon_{t-1}^2 + \theta_2 \varepsilon_{t-2}^2 + \ldots + \theta_s \varepsilon_{t-s}^2. \quad (103)$$

Given all of the information up to time $(t-1)$, the conditional variance of the ε_t becomes

$$\begin{aligned} \text{Var}_{t-1}(\varepsilon_t) &= E_{t-1}(\varepsilon_t^2) \\ &= E(\varepsilon_t^2 | \varepsilon_{t-1}, \varepsilon_{t-2}, \ldots) = \sigma_t^2 \\ &= \theta_0 + \theta_1 \varepsilon_{t-1}^2 + \theta_2 \varepsilon_{t-2}^2 \\ &\quad + \ldots + \theta_s \varepsilon_{t-s}^2, \end{aligned} \quad (104)$$

which is related to the squares of past errors, and it changes over time. A large error through ε_{t-j}^2 gives rise to the variance, which tends to be followed by another large error. This is a common phenomenon of volatility clustering in many financial time series. From the forecasting results, we see that Equation 103 is simply the optimal forecast of ε_t^2 from the following $AR(s)$ model:

$$\varepsilon_t^2 = \theta_0 + \theta_1 \varepsilon_{t-1}^2 + \theta_2 \varepsilon_{t-2}^2 + \ldots + \theta_s \varepsilon_{t-s}^2 + a_t, \quad (105)$$

where the a_t is a $N(0, \sigma_a^2)$ white noise process. Thus, Engle (1982) called the model of the error term ε_t with the variance specification given in Equations 102 and 103 or equivalently in Equation 105 the *autoregressive conditional heteroscedasticity model of order s (ARCH(s))*.

Bollerslev (1986) extended the ARCH(s) model to the *GARCH(r, s) model (generalized autoregressive conditional heteroscedasticity model of order (r, s))* so that the conditional variance of the error process is related not only to the squares of past errors but also to the past conditional variances. Thus, we have the following more general case,

$$\varepsilon_t = \sigma_t e_t, \quad (106)$$

where e_t is the series of i.i.d. random variables with mean 0 and variance 1,

$$\begin{aligned} \sigma_t^2 &= \theta_0 + \phi_1 \sigma_{t-1}^2 + \ldots + \phi_r \sigma_{t-r}^2 \\ &\quad + \theta_1 \varepsilon_{t-1}^2 + \ldots + \theta_s \varepsilon_{t-s}^2, \end{aligned} \quad (107)$$

and the roots of $(1 - \phi_1 B - \ldots - \phi_r B^r) = 0$ are outside the unit circle. To guarantee $\sigma_t^2 > 0$, we assume that $\theta_0 > 0$, and ϕ_i and θ_j are non-negative.

More generally, the regression model with autocorrelated error can be combined with the conditional heteroscedasticity model—that is,

$$Y_t = \mathbf{X}'_t \beta + \varepsilon_t, \quad (108)$$

where

$$\varepsilon_t = \phi_1 \varepsilon_{t-1} + \cdots + \phi_p \varepsilon_{t-p} + a_t, \quad (109)$$

$$\varepsilon_t = \sigma_t e_t, \quad (110)$$

$$\begin{aligned} \sigma_t^2 &= \theta_0 + \phi_1 \sigma_{t-1}^2 + \cdots + \phi_r \sigma_{t-r}^2 \\ &\quad + \theta_1 a_{t-1}^2 + \cdots + \theta_s a_{t-s}^2, \end{aligned} \quad (111)$$

and the e_t are i.i.d. $N(0, 1)$. To test for the heteroscedasticity in this model, we perform the following steps:

1a. Calculate OLS residuals $\hat{\varepsilon}_t$ from the OLS fitting of Equation 108.

1b. Fit an $AR(p)$ Model 109 to the $\hat{\varepsilon}_t$.

1c. Obtain the residuals $\hat{a}_t$ from the AR fitting in Model 109.

1d. Form the series $\hat{a}_t^2$, compute its sample ACF and PACF, and check whether these ACF and PACF follow any pattern. A pattern of these ACF and PACF not only indicates ARCH or GARCH errors, it also forms a good basis for their order specification. Alternatively, we can also use the following portmanteau Q statistic to test for $\rho_i(a_t^2) = 0, i = 1, 2, \ldots, k$,

$$Q(k) = n(n+2) \sum_{i=1}^{k} \frac{\hat{\rho}_i^2(\hat{a}_t^2)}{(n-i)}, \quad (112)$$

which approximately follows a $\chi^2(k)$ distribution. The significance of the $Q(k)$ statistic occurring only for a small value of k indicates an ARCH model, and a persistent significance for a large value of k implies a GARCH model.

Vector Time Series Models

In transfer function and time series regression models, we study the relationship between an output or a dependent variable and a set of input or independent variables. In many applications, the relationship represented in these models may not be appropriate. In this section, we introduce the extension of the univariate time series models from the section on Univariate Time Series Models to vector time series models and use them to describe the relationships among several time series variables.

Just like univariate time series models are characterized by their moments such as means, variances, ACFs, and PACFs, vector time series models are also characterized by their moments such as mean vectors, variance–covariance matrices, correlation matrix functions, and partial correlation matrix functions.

Correlation and Partial Correlation Matrix Functions

Let $\mathbf{Z}_t = [Z_{1,t}, Z_{2,t}, \cdots, Z_{m,t}]'$, $t = 0, \pm 1, \pm 2, \ldots$, be a m-dimensional jointly stationary real-valued vector process so that $E(Z_{i,t}) = \mu_i$ is constant for each $i = 1, 2, \ldots, m$ and the cross-covariance between $Z_{i,t}$ and $Z_{j,s}$, for all $i = 1, 2, \ldots, m$ and $j = 1, 2, \ldots, m$, are functions only of the time difference $(s - t)$. Hence, we have the *mean vector*

$$E(\mathbf{Z}_t) = \boldsymbol{\mu} = \begin{bmatrix} \mu_1 \\ \mu_2 \\ \vdots \\ \mu_m \end{bmatrix}, \quad (113)$$

and the *lag-k covariance matrix*

$$\boldsymbol{\Gamma}(k) = Cov\{\mathbf{Z}_t, \mathbf{Z}_{t+k}\} = E[(\mathbf{Z}_t - \boldsymbol{\mu})(\mathbf{Z}_{t+k} - \boldsymbol{\mu})']$$

$$= E \begin{bmatrix} Z_{1,t} \\ Z_{2,t} \\ \vdots \\ Z_{m,t} \end{bmatrix} [Z_{1,t+k} - \mu_1, \quad Z_{2,t+k} - \mu_2, \\ \cdots, \quad Z_{m,t+k} - \mu_m]$$

$$= \begin{bmatrix} \gamma_{11}(k) & \gamma_{12}(k) & \cdots & \gamma_{1m}(k) \\ \gamma_{21}(k) & \gamma_{22}(k) & \cdots & \gamma_{2m}(k) \\ \vdots & \vdots & \vdots & \vdots \\ \gamma_{m1}(k) & \gamma_{m2}(k) & \cdots & \gamma_{mm}(k) \end{bmatrix}, \quad (114)$$

where

$$\gamma_{ij}(k) = E(Z_{i,t} - \mu_i)(Z_{j,t+k} - \mu_j)$$

for $k = 0, \pm 1, \pm 2, \ldots$, $i = 1, 2, \ldots, m$, and $j = 1, 2, \ldots, m$. As a function of k, $\boldsymbol{\Gamma}(k)$ is called the *covariance matrix function* for the vector process $\mathbf{Z}_t$. For $i = j$, $\gamma_{ii}(k)$ is the autocovariance function for the ith component process $Z_{i,t}$; and for $i \neq j$, $\gamma_{ij}(k)$ is the cross-covariance function between component series $Z_{i,t}$ and $Z_{j,t}$. The matrix $\boldsymbol{\Gamma}(0)$ is easily seen to be the contemporaneous variance–covariance matrix of the process.

The *correlation matrix function* for the vector process is defined by

$$\boldsymbol{\rho}(k) = \mathbf{D}^{-1/2} \boldsymbol{\Gamma}(k) \mathbf{D}^{-1/2} = [\rho_{ij}(k)] \quad (115)$$

for $i = 1, 2, \ldots, m$, and $j = 1, 2, \ldots, m$, where $\mathbf{D}$ is the diagonal matrix in which the ith diagonal element is the variance of the ith process; that is, $\mathbf{D} = diag[\gamma_{11}(0), \gamma_{22}(0), \ldots, \gamma_{mm}(0)]$. Thus, the ith diagonal element of $\boldsymbol{\rho}(k)$ is the ACF for the ith component series $Z_{i,t}$ whereas the (i,j)th off-diagonal element of $\boldsymbol{\rho}(k)$ is the cross-correlation function between component series $Z_{i,t}$ and $Z_{j,t}$.

Unlike the correlation matrix function that follows the standard definition given in Equation 115, the concept of a partial correlation matrix function has been introduced much later (the correlation matrix function was introduced before 1900 and the concept of a partial correlation matrix function was introduced only after 1980) and there are different versions.

Heyse and Wei (1985) extended the definition of univariate partial autocorrelation to vector time series and derived the correlation matrix between $\mathbf{Z}_t$ and $\mathbf{Z}_{t+s}$ after removing the linear dependence of each on the intervening vectors $\mathbf{Z}_{t+1}, \ldots, \mathbf{Z}_{t+s-1}$. This correlation matrix is defined as the correlation between the residual vectors

$$\mathbf{U}_{s-1,t+s} = \mathbf{Z}_{t+s} - \boldsymbol{\alpha}_{s-1,1}\mathbf{Z}_{t+s-1} - \cdots - \boldsymbol{\alpha}_{s-1,s-1}\mathbf{Z}_{t+1}$$

$$= \begin{cases} \mathbf{Z}_{t+s} - \sum_{j=1}^{s-1} \boldsymbol{\alpha}_{s-1,j}\mathbf{Z}_{t+s-j}, & s \geq 2, \\ \mathbf{Z}_{t+1}, & s = 1, \end{cases} \quad (116)$$

and

$$\mathbf{V}_{s-1,t} = \mathbf{Z}_t - \boldsymbol{\beta}_{s-1,1}\mathbf{Z}_{t+1} - \cdots - \boldsymbol{\beta}_{s-1,s-1}\mathbf{Z}_{t+s-1}$$

$$= \begin{cases} \mathbf{Z}_t - \sum_{j=1}^{s-1} \boldsymbol{\beta}_{s-1,j}\mathbf{Z}_{t+j}, & s \geq 2, \\ \mathbf{Z}_{t+1}, & s = 1. \end{cases} \quad (117)$$

Let $C_{VU}(s)$ be the covariance between $V_{s-1,t}$ and $U_{s-1,t+s}$—that is, $C_{VU}(s) = Cov(V_{s-1,t}, U_{s-1,t+s})$, Heyse and Wei (1985) showed that

$$C_{VU}(s) = \Gamma(s) - \begin{bmatrix} \Gamma(s-1) & \Gamma(s-2) & \cdots & \Gamma(1) \end{bmatrix}$$
$$\begin{bmatrix} \Gamma(0) & \Gamma'(1) & \cdots & \Gamma'(s-2) \\ \Gamma(1) & \Gamma(0) & \cdots & \Gamma'(s-3) \\ \vdots & \vdots & & \vdots \\ \Gamma(s-2) & \Gamma(s-3) & \cdots & \Gamma(0) \end{bmatrix}^{-1}$$
$$\begin{bmatrix} \Gamma(1) \\ \Gamma(2) \\ \vdots \\ \Gamma(s-1) \end{bmatrix}, \quad (118)$$

where $\Gamma(k) = Cov\{Z_t, Z_{t+k}\}$. Note that $Var(U_{s-1,t+s}) = C_{UU}(s)$ and $Var(V_{s-1,t}) = C_{VV}(s)$. Thus, the *partial lag autocorrelation matrix at lag s* is

$$P(s) = [D_V(s)]^{-1} C_{VU}(s) [D_U(s)]^{-1}, \quad (119)$$

where $D_V(s)$ is the diagonal matrix in which the *i*th diagonal element is the square root of the *i*th diagonal element of $C_{VV}(s)$ and $D_U(s)$ is similarly defined for $C_{UU}(s)$.

Tiao and Box (1981) defined the *partial autoregression matrix at lag s*, denoted by $\Phi_{s,s}$, to be the last matrix coefficient when the data is fitted to a vector AR process of order *s*. It can be shown that

$$\Phi_{s,s} = C'_{VU}(s) [D_V(s)]^{-1}. \quad (120)$$

Ansley and Newbold (1979) defined the *multivariate partial autocorrelation matrix at lag s* to be

$$Q(s) = [W_U(s)]^{-1} C'_{VU}(s) [W_V(s)]^{-1}, \quad (121)$$

where $W_U(s)$ and $W_V(s)$ are the symmetric square roots of $C_{UU}(s)$ and $C_{VV}(s)$, defined such that $|W_U(s)|^2 = C_{UU}(s)$ and $|W_V(s)|^2 = C_{VV}(s)$. However, it should be noted that although $P(s)$, $\Phi_{s,s}$ and $Q(s)$ all share the same cut-off property for vector $AR(s)$ models, the elements of $P(s)$ are proper correlation coefficients but those of $\Phi_{s,s}$ and $Q(s)$ are not correlation coefficients, with the exception of when $m = 1$—that is, except in the univariate case in which $P(s) = \Phi_{s,s} = Q(s)$.

Vector Autoregressive, Vector Moving Average, and Vector Autoregressive Moving Average Models

STATIONARY VECTOR TIME SERIES MODELS

A *m*-dimensional stationary vector time series process Z_t can always be written as a linear combination of a sequence of vector white noises—that is,

$$Z_t = \mu + a_t + \psi_1 a_{t-1} + \psi_2 a_{t-2} + \cdots$$
$$= \mu + \sum_{k=0}^{\infty} \psi_k a_{t-k}, \quad (122)$$

where the A_t is a sequence of *m*-dimensional white noise processes with mean **0** vector and covariance matrix function

$$E(a_t a'_{t+k}) = \begin{cases} \Sigma, & \text{if } k = 0, \\ 0, & \text{if } k \neq 0, \end{cases} \quad (123)$$

and Σ is a $m \times m$ symmetric positive definite matrix. $\psi_0 = I$ is the $m \times m$ identity matrix and the ψ_k is a sequence of absolutely summable $m \times m$ coefficient matrices in the sense that if we let $\psi_k = [\psi_{ij,k}]$, then each of the $m \times m$ sequences $\psi_{ij,k}$ is absolutely summable—that is, $\sum_{k=0}^{\infty} |\psi_{ij,k}| < \infty$ for $i = 1, \ldots, m$ and $j = 1, \ldots, m$. The Equation 122 is known as the *vector moving average* (VMA) representation. A vector time series process Z_t is said to be invertible if it can be written as a *vector autoregressive* (VAR) representation

$$\dot{Z}_t = \Pi_1 \dot{Z}_{t-1} + \Pi_2 \dot{Z}_{t-2} + \cdots + a_t$$
$$= \sum_{k=1}^{\infty} \Pi_k \dot{Z}_{t-k} + a_t, \quad (124)$$

so that the sequence of $m \times m$ AR coefficient matrices Π_k is absolutely summable where $\dot{Z}_t = Z_t - \mu$.

A useful class of parsimonious vector time series models is the *vector autoregressive moving average* (VARMA) *process*

$$\Phi_p(B) \dot{Z}_t = \Theta_q(B) a_t, \quad (125)$$

where $\Phi_p(B) = \Phi_0 - \Phi_1 B - \cdots - \Phi_p B^p$ and $\Theta_q(B) = \Theta_0 - \Theta_1 B - \cdots - \Theta_q B^q$ are AR and MA matrix polynomials of order *p* and *q*, respectively; Φ_0 and Θ_0 are nonsingular $m \times m$ matrices; and the A_t is a sequence of *m*-dimensional white noise processes with mean zero vector and positive definite variance–covariance matrix Σ. Because one can always invert Φ_0 and Θ_0 and combine them into Σ, with no loss of generality, we will assume in the following discussion that $\Phi_0 = \Theta_0 = I$, the $m \times m$ identity matrix.

Following the extension of the stationary univariate time series models of the Univariate Time Series Models section, we have the following stationary vector time series models.

1. *VAR(p) models*:

$$(I - \Phi_1 B - \cdots - \Phi_p B^p) \dot{Z}_t = a_t, \quad (126)$$

where the zeros of $|\mathbf{I} - \boldsymbol{\Phi}_1 B - \cdots - \boldsymbol{\Phi}_p B^p|$ lie outside of the unit circle or, equivalently, the roots of $|\lambda^p \mathbf{I} - \lambda^{p-1} \boldsymbol{\Phi}_1 - \cdots - \boldsymbol{\Phi}_p| = 0$ are all inside of the unit circle.

2. VMA(q) models:

$$\dot{Z}_t = (\mathbf{I} - \boldsymbol{\Theta}_1 B - \cdots - \boldsymbol{\Theta}_q B^q) \mathbf{a}_t. \quad (127)$$

3. VARMA(p, q) models:

$$(\mathbf{I} - \boldsymbol{\Phi}_1 B - \cdots - \boldsymbol{\Phi}_p B^p) \dot{Z}_t$$
$$= (\mathbf{I} - \boldsymbol{\Theta}_1 B - \cdots - \boldsymbol{\Theta}_p B^p) \mathbf{a}_t. \quad (128)$$

Consider the following VAR(1) model,

$$(\mathbf{I} - \boldsymbol{\Phi} B) \dot{Z}_t = \mathbf{a}_t, \quad (129)$$

or

$$\dot{Z}_t = \boldsymbol{\Phi} \dot{Z}_{t-1} = \mathbf{a}_t, \quad (130)$$

where the $\mathbf{A}_t$ is a m-dimensional white noise process with mean $\mathbf{0}$ and covariance matrix $\boldsymbol{\Sigma}$. For $m = 2$, we have

$$\begin{bmatrix} \dot{Z}_{1,t} \\ \dot{Z}_{2,t} \end{bmatrix} = \begin{bmatrix} \phi_{11} & \phi_{12} \\ \phi_{21} & \phi_{22} \end{bmatrix} \begin{bmatrix} \dot{Z}_{1,t-1} \\ \dot{Z}_{2,t-1} \end{bmatrix} + \begin{bmatrix} a_{1,t} \\ a_{2,t} \end{bmatrix},$$
(131)

or

$$\begin{aligned} \dot{Z}_{1,t} &= \phi_{11} \dot{Z}_{1,t-1} + \phi_{12} \dot{Z}_{2,t-1} + a_{1,t} \\ \dot{Z}_{2,t} &= \phi_{21} \dot{Z}_{1,t-1} + \phi_{22} \dot{Z}_{2,t-1} + a_{2,t}. \end{aligned} \quad (132)$$

Thus, apart from current shocks, each $\dot{Z}_{i,t}$ depends not only on its past values of $\dot{Z}_{i,t}$ but also the past values of other variables $\dot{Z}_{j,t}$. For the VAR(1) to be stationary, the zero of the determinant equation $|\mathbf{I} - \boldsymbol{\Phi} B|$ must be outside the unit circle or the eigenvalues of $|\lambda \mathbf{I} - \boldsymbol{\Phi}| = 0$ are inside the unit circle.

It is important that one should not conclude from Equation 132 that there is no contemporaneous relationship between $\dot{Z}_{1,t}$ and $\dot{Z}_{2,t}$. In the form of VARMA models, because of our choice of $\boldsymbol{\Phi}_0 = \boldsymbol{\Theta}_0 = \mathbf{I}$, the contemporaneous relationship between components of vector series is modeled through the off-diagonal elements of $\boldsymbol{\Sigma}$.

It is also interesting to note that when $\phi_{12} = 0$ in Equation 131, then we have

$$\begin{bmatrix} 1 - \phi_{11} B & 0 \\ -\phi_{21} B & 1 - \phi_{22} B \end{bmatrix} \begin{bmatrix} \dot{Z}_{1,t} \\ \dot{Z}_{2,t} \end{bmatrix} = \begin{bmatrix} a_{1,t} \\ a_{2,t} \end{bmatrix},$$
(133)

or

$$\begin{cases} \dot{Z}_{1,t} = \dfrac{1}{1 - \phi_{11} B} a_{1,t}, \\ \dot{Z}_{2,t} = \dfrac{\phi_{21} B}{1 - \phi_{22} B} \dot{Z}_{1,t} + \dfrac{1}{1 - \phi_{22} B} a_{2,t}. \end{cases}$$
(134)

Thus, the model can be reduced to a transfer function type of model. However, from Equation 134, we should not mistakenly think that $\dot{Z}_{2,t}$ is affected only by the past values of $\dot{Z}_{1,t}$. As pointed out earlier, the contemporaneous relationship between $\dot{Z}_{1,t}$ and $\dot{Z}_{2,t}$ is contained in the off-diagonal elements of $\boldsymbol{\Sigma}$. Unless $\boldsymbol{\Sigma}$ is a diagonal matrix, $\dot{Z}_{1,t}$ and $a_{2,t}$ are correlated, which clearly violates the fundamental assumption of the transfer function model. To make it a proper transfer function model, one needs to use some transformations so that the error term in the equation is independent of input variables. We refer readers to Wei (2006, chapter 16) for more details.

NONSTATIONARY VECTOR TIME SERIES MODELS AND COINTEGRATED PROCESSES

In univariate time series analysis, a nonstationary time series is reduced to a stationary time series by proper power transformations and differencing. They can still be used in vector time series analysis. However, it should be noted that these transformations should be applied to component series individually because not all component series can be reduced to stationary by exactly the same power transformation and the same number of differencing. To be more flexible, after applying proper power transformations to the component series, we will use the following presentation for a nonstationary vector time series model:

$$\boldsymbol{\Phi}_p(B) \mathbf{D}(B) \dot{Z}_t = \boldsymbol{\Theta}_q(B) \mathbf{A}_t, \quad (135)$$

where $D(B)$

$$= \begin{bmatrix} (1 - B)^{d_1} & 0 & \cdots & 0 & 0 \\ 0 & (1 - B)^{d_2} & \ddots & \cdots & 0 \\ \vdots & & \ddots & \ddots & \vdots \\ 0 & \cdots & & \ddots & 0 \\ 0 & \cdots & & 0 & (1 - B)^{d_m} \end{bmatrix}.$$
(136)

In many applications, the $d_i's$ in Equation 136 may be equal. In this case, one needs to be very careful in constructing a vector time series model because its component series could be cointegrated. A vector time series is said to be cointegrated if each component series is nonstationary but some linear combinations of them become stationary. For example, consider the following two-dimensional VAR(1) process

$$\begin{bmatrix} Z_{1,t} \\ Z_{2,t} \end{bmatrix} = \begin{bmatrix} 1 & 0 \\ -\phi & 0 \end{bmatrix} \begin{bmatrix} Z_{1,t-1} \\ Z_{2,t-1} \end{bmatrix} + \begin{bmatrix} a_{1,t} \\ a_{2,t} \end{bmatrix}.$$
(137)

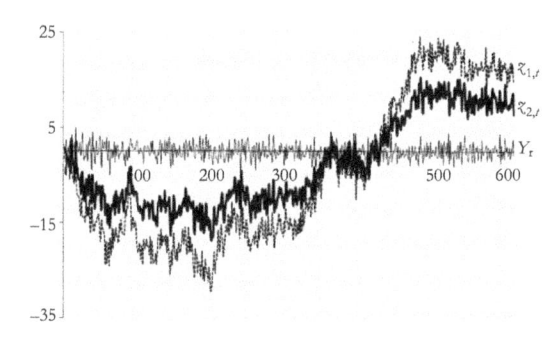

Figure 22.11 A cointegrated process where $Z_{1,t}$ and $Z_{2,t}$ are each nonstationary, but their linear combination $Y_t = 0.6Z_{1,t} + Z_{2,t}$ is stationary.

Clearly, the component $Z_{1,t} = Z_{1,t-1} + a_{1,t}$ is a random walk, which is nonstationary. For the component $Z_{2,t}$, we have $Z_{2,t} = -\phi Z_{1,t-1} + a_{2,t}$, which as the sum of a constant multiple of $Z_{1,t}$ and a white noise process is also nonstationary. However, the linear combination, $Y_t = \phi Z_{1,t} + Z_{2,t} = \phi Z_{1,t} - \phi Z_{1,t-1} + a_{2,t} = \phi a_{1,t} + a_{2,t}$, is stationary. Hence, $Z_{1,t}$ and $Z_{2,t}$ are cointegrated. Figure 22.11 illustrates the phenomenon.

For a cointegrated nonstationary vector process $\mathbf{Z}_t$, one cannot consider its differences, $\Delta \mathbf{Z}_t$ where $\Delta = (1 - B)$, and build a model only in terms of the differences. In other words, its AR representation in terms of only its differences, $(\mathbf{I} - \mathbf{\Phi}_1 B - \cdots - \mathbf{\Phi}_p B^p)\Delta \mathbf{Z}_t = \mathbf{a}_t$, does not exist for any p. The vector AR representation of a *cointegrated process* must be in terms of $\mathbf{Z}_t$ directly. If a presentation using its differences, $\Delta \mathbf{Z}_t$, and lagged values, $\Delta \mathbf{Z}_j$ for $j < t$, is preferable, one has to use the error-correction representation by including an error-correction term in the model. For more details, we refer interested readers to Granger (1986), Engle and Granger (1987), and Wei (2006, Chapters 16 and 17).

Vector Time Series Model Building
IDENTIFICATION OF VECTOR TIME SERIES MODELS

In constructing a vector time series model, just like in univariate time series model building, the first step is to plot the vector time series, as shown in Figure 22.12, for the vector series of sales and advertizing expenditures of a company. By plotting all of the component series in one graph, we obtain a good idea of the movements of different components and the general pattern of their relationships. In principle, vector time series model-building procedure is similar to the univariate time series model building procedure discussed in the Time Series Model Building section. We identify an underlying model from its correlation and partial correlation matrix functions. Table 22.10 gives a useful summary.

Given an observed vector time series $\mathbf{Z}_1, \ldots, \mathbf{Z}_n$, we compute its sample correlation and partial correlation matrices after proper transformations are applied to reduce a nonstationary series to a stationary series.

Sample Correlation Matrix Function

The *sample correlation matrix function* is computed as

$$\hat{\boldsymbol{\rho}}(k) = [\hat{\rho}_{ij}(k)], \qquad (138)$$

where the $\hat{\rho}_{ij}(k)$ is the sample cross-correlation function for the ith and jth component series,

$$\hat{\rho}_{ij}(k) = \frac{\sum_{t=1}^{n-k}(Z_{i,t} - \overline{Z}_i)(Z_{j,t+k} - \overline{Z}_j)}{[\sum_{t=1}^{n}(Z_{i,t} - \overline{Z}_i)^2 \sum_{t=1}^{n}(Z_{j,t} - \overline{Z}_j)^2]^{1/2}}, \qquad (139)$$

and $\overline{Z}_i$ and $\overline{Z}_j$ are the sample means of the corresponding component series. For a stationary vector process, Hannan (1970, p. 228) showed that $\hat{\boldsymbol{\rho}}(k)$ is a consistent estimator that is asymptotically normally distributed. When the vector process is white noise, we have

$$Cov[\hat{\rho}_{ij}(k), \hat{\rho}_{ij}(k+s)] \approx \frac{1}{(n-k)}, \qquad (140)$$

and

$$Var[\hat{\rho}_{ij}(k)] \approx \frac{1}{(n-k)}. \qquad (141)$$

For large samples, $(n - k)$ is often replaced by n in the above expressions.

Sample Partial Lag Correlation Matrix Function

The *sample partial lag correlation matrices*, denoted by $\hat{\mathbf{P}}(s)$, are obtained by using $\hat{\mathbf{\Gamma}}(j)$ in place of $\mathbf{\Gamma}(j)$ for $j = 0, 1, \ldots, (s-1)$ in $\mathbf{P}(s)$, as shown in Equations 118 and 119. Because $\hat{\mathbf{P}}(s)$ is a proper correlation matrix, the results of sample correlation matrices can be used for its inference. Specifically, the elements of $\hat{\mathbf{P}}(s)$, denoted by $\hat{p}_{ij}(s)$, are independent and asymptotically normally distributed with mean 0 and variance $1/n$. Thus,

$$X(s) = n \sum_{i=1}^{m} \sum_{j=1}^{m} [\hat{p}_{ij}(s)]^2 \qquad (142)$$

is asymptotically distributed as a χ^2 with m^2 degrees of freedom.

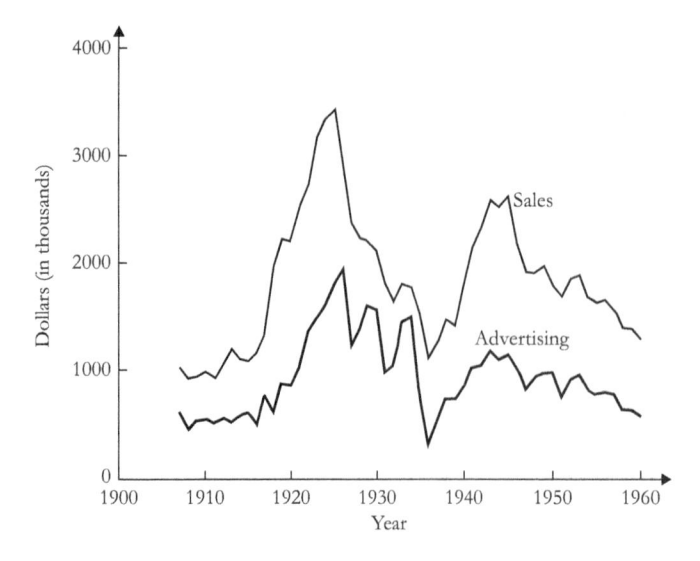

Figure 22.12 Example of a vector time series.

Table 22.10. Characteristics of Stationary Vector Time Series Models

Process	Correlation matrix function	Partial correlation matrix function
VAR(p)	Non-zero matrix with diminishing elements	Zero matrix after lag p
VMA(q)	Zero matrix after lag q	Non-zero matrix with diminishing elements
VARMA(p,q)	Non-zero matrix with diminishing elements	Non-zero matrix with diminishing elements

PARAMETER ESTIMATION, DIAGNOSTIC CHECKING, AND FORECASTING

Once a tentative model is identified, efficient estimates of the parameter matrices $\mathbf{\Phi}_i, \mathbf{\Theta}_j$, and $\mathbf{\Sigma}$ are obtained using a maximum likelihood method that is available in many statistical packages such as SAS, SCA, and SPSS. The adequacy of the fitted model can be checked through a careful analysis of the residuals

$$\hat{\mathbf{a}}_t = \dot{\mathbf{Z}}_t - \hat{\mathbf{\Phi}}_1\dot{\mathbf{Z}}_{t-1} - \cdots - \hat{\mathbf{\Phi}}_p\dot{\mathbf{Z}}_{t-p} + \hat{\mathbf{\Theta}}_1\hat{\mathbf{A}}_{t-1} + \cdots + \hat{\mathbf{\Theta}}_q\hat{\mathbf{a}}_{t-q}, \quad (143)$$

where $\dot{\mathbf{Z}}_t$ is now used to denote $\mathbf{Z}_t$ if $\mathbf{\mu} = 0$ and $(\mathbf{Z}_t - \hat{\mathbf{\mu}})$ otherwise. For an adequate model, the sequence of residual vectors should behave as a vector white noise process.

After residual analysis, if the model is adequate, then it can be used for forecasting future values. For the general model in Equation 128, the ℓ − step ahead forecast at time n is given by,

$$\hat{\dot{\mathbf{Z}}}_n(\ell) = \hat{\mathbf{\Phi}}_1\hat{\dot{\mathbf{Z}}}_n(\ell-1) + \cdots + \hat{\mathbf{\Phi}}_p\hat{\dot{\mathbf{Z}}}_n(\ell-p) \\ + \hat{\mathbf{a}}_n(\ell) - \hat{\mathbf{\Theta}}_1\hat{\mathbf{a}}_n(\ell-1) \\ - \cdots - \hat{\mathbf{\Theta}}_q\hat{\mathbf{a}}_n(\ell-q), \quad (144)$$

where $\hat{\dot{\mathbf{Z}}}_n(j) = \dot{\mathbf{Z}}_{n+j}$ for $j \leq 0, \hat{\mathbf{a}}_{n+j} = \mathbf{0}$ for $j > 0$, and $\hat{\mathbf{a}}_{n+j} = \mathbf{a}_{n+j}$ when $j \leq 0$. It can also be used for inference and control using the estimates of parameters and the relationship presented in the vector model.

Concluding Remarks and Future Directions

In this chapter, we have discussed many useful time domain methods and their applications in time series analysis. These include AR, MA, ARMA, and ARIMA models, intervention models, outlier detection, transfer function models, time series regression, GARCH model, vector time series models, cointegrated processes, and their iterative model-building processes and applications. Although most time series data used for our illustrations are from business and social sciences, these models and methods are general statistical methodology and can be used in any field where time series analysis is needed.

We do not cover state space models, fractional differencing, and nonlinear time series models, but with the background provided in this chapter, readers should be able to pick up these topics on their own without difficulty.

After making a conjecture or a proposition about the underlying phenomenon, a researcher often wants to test his or her proposition against observable data. In a time series study, this time series data set may be available in many forms. For example, one can choose a weekly data set, a monthly data set, or a quarterly data set. What time unit should we use in the analysis? Does the time unit chosen make a difference? It is important to point out that the same time unit should be used in both the underlying proposition and the data analysis. This normally would not be a problem in a setting where controlled experiments are possible. However, in many social science studies, a controlled experiment may not be possible, and data are often available only through aggregation or systematic sampling. In such a case, one must be very careful and aware of the consequences of aggregation and systematic sampling on model structure, parameter estimation, and forecasting discussed in Wei (2006, Chapter 20) and other references therein.

In some studies, there is a natural time unit to be used in the analysis. For example, regarding patient care at a hospital, a doctor using a certain medication will monitor a patient at certain time intervals (such as hourly) simply based on the instructions of the drug company. In some studies, there may be no apparent natural time unit, and data are available in different intervals. This is often true in many empirical studies. Natural issues to address in such cases are whether there is a best time unit to be used in the analysis and, if there is, how to determine what it is. These questions are challenging and their answers remain to be discovered.

Because of high-speed internet and the power and speed of the new generation of computers, a researcher is facing some very challenging phenomena. First, he/she has to deal with an ever increasing amount of data. To find useful information and hidden patterns underlying the data, a researcher may use various data-mining methods and techniques. Adding a time dimension to these large databases certainly introduces new aspects and challenges. In the process, one may also encounter cases where the underlying distribution is non normal, which was often assumed to be the underlying distribution for most traditional time series models.

Appendix
Summary Table of Some Commonly Used Terms, Notations, and Equations in Time Series Analysis

Terms	Notations	Equations
Mean function	μ_t	$\mu_t = E(Z_t) = \mu$ for a stationary process
Variance function	σ_t^2	$\sigma_t^2 = Var(Z_t) = E(Z_t - \mu)^2 = \sigma^2$ for a stationary process
Auto*correlation function*	ACF	$\rho_k = \dfrac{Cov(Z_t, Z_{t+k})}{\sqrt{Var(Z_t)}\sqrt{Var(Z_{t+k})}} = \dfrac{\gamma_k}{\gamma_0}$
Partial autocorrelation function	PACF	$\varphi_{kk} = Corr(Z_t, Z_{t+k} \mid Z_{t+1}, \ldots, Z_{t+k-1})$
White noise process	a_t	$Z_t = a_t$
Autoregressive model of order p	AR(p)	$Z_t = \theta_0 + \varphi_1 Z_{t-1} + \cdots + \varphi_p Z_{t-p} + a_t$ $\varphi_p(B) Z_t = \theta_0 + a_t$ $\varphi_p(B) = 1 - \varphi_1 B - \cdots - \varphi_p B^p$
Moving average model of q	MA(q)	$Z_t = \mu + a_t + \theta_1 a_{t-1} + \cdots + \theta_q a_{t-q}$ $Z_t = \mu + \theta_q(B) a_t$ $\theta_q(B) = 1 - \theta_1 B - \cdots - \theta_q B^q$
Autoregressive moving average model of order (p, q)	ARMA(p, q)	$\varphi_p(B) Z_t = \theta_0 + \theta_q(B) a_t$

Appendix (Continued)
Summary Table of Some Commonly Used Terms, Notations, and Equations in Time Series Analysis

Terms	Notations	Equations
Autoregressive integrated moving average model order (p, d, q)	$ARIMA(p, d, q)$	$\varphi_p(B)(1-B)^d Z_t = \theta_0 + \theta_q(B)a_t$
Cross-correlation function	CCF	$\rho_{XY}(k) = \dfrac{\gamma_{XY}(k)}{\sigma_X \sigma_Y}$ $\gamma_{XY}(k) = E[(X_t - \mu_X)(Y_{t+k} - \mu_Y)]$
Transfer function model	ARMAX	$Y_t = \dfrac{\omega_s(B)}{\delta_r(B)} X_{t-b} + \dfrac{\theta_q(B)}{\varphi_p(B)} a_t$ $\omega_s(B) = \omega_0 - \omega_1 B - \cdots - \omega_s B^s$ $\delta_r(B) = 1 - \delta_1 B - \cdots - \delta_r B^r$
Autoregressive conditional heteroscedasticity model of order s	$ARCH(s)$	$\varepsilon_t = \sigma_t e_t$ where $e_t \sim i.i.d.\ N(0,1)$ and $\sigma_t^2 = \theta_0 + \theta_1 \varepsilon_{t-1}^2 + \cdots + \theta_s \varepsilon_{t-s}^2$
Generalized autoregressive conditional heteroscedasticity model of order (r, s)	$GARCH(r, s)$	$\varepsilon_t = \sigma_t e_t$ where $e_t \sim i.i.d.\ N(0,1)$ and $\sigma_t^2 = \theta_0 + \phi_1 \sigma_{t-1}^2 + \cdots + \phi_r \sigma_{t-r}^2$ $+ \theta_1 \varepsilon_{t-1}^2 + \cdots + \theta_s \varepsilon_{t-s}^2$
Vector autoregressive model of order p	$VAR(p)$	$(\mathbf{I} - \mathbf{\Phi}_1 B - \cdots - \mathbf{\Phi}_p B^p)\dot{\mathbf{Z}}_t = \mathbf{A}_t$ $\dot{\mathbf{Z}}_t = \mathbf{Z}_t - \boldsymbol{\mu}$
Vector moving average model of order q	$VMA(q)$	$\dot{\mathbf{Z}}_t = (\mathbf{I} - \mathbf{\Theta}_1 B - \cdots - \mathbf{\Theta}_q B^q)\mathbf{A}_t$
Vector autoregressive moving average model of order (p, q)	$VARMA(p, q)$	$(\mathbf{I} - \mathbf{\Phi}_1 B - \cdots - \mathbf{\Phi}_p B^p)\dot{\mathbf{Z}}_t = (\mathbf{I} - \mathbf{\Theta}_1 B - \cdots - \mathbf{\Theta}_q B^q)\mathbf{A}_t$

In addition to the large amount of data, one is also encountering more and more high-dimensional data sets. Traditional time series methods are not designed to deal with these kinds of high-dimensional variables. Even with today's computer power and speed, there are many difficult problems that remain to be solved. As most statistical methods are developed for a random sample, the use of highly correlated time series data certainly introduces a new set of complications and challenges.

Acknowledgments

The authors thank the referees and the editor for their helpful comments and suggestions, which have improved the presentation of this paper.

Author Note

William W.S. Wei, Department of Statistics, Temple University, 1810 North 13th Street, Philadelphia, PA 19122, USA, Email: wwei@temple.edu.

References

Akaike, H. (1974). A new look at the statistical identification, *IEEE Transactions on Automatic Control*, AC-19, 716–723.

Ansley, C. F. & Newbold, P. (1979). Multivariate partial autocorrelations, *American Statistical Association Proceedings of Business and Economic Statistics Section*, 349–353.

Bartlett, M. S. (1946). On the theoretical specification of sampling properties of autocorrelated time series, *Journal of Royal Statistical Society*, B8, 27–41.

Box, G. E. P. & Cox, D. R. (1964). An analysis of transformations, *Journal of Royal Statistical Society*, B26, 211–252.

Box, G. E. P., Jenkins, G. M. & Reinsel, G. C. (2008). *Time Series Analysis: Forecasting and Control, 4th Ed.,* New York: Wiley.

Box, G. E. P. & Tiao, G.C. (1975). Intervention analysis with applications to economic and environmental problems, *Journal of American Statistical Association, 70,* 70–79.

Bollerslev, T. (1986). Generalized autoregressive conditional heteroskedasticity, *Journal of Econometrics, 31,* 307–327.

Chan, N. H. & Wei, C. Z. (1988). Limiting distribution of least squares estimates of unstable autoregressive processes, *Annals of Statistics, 16,* 367–401.

Chang, I., Tiao, G.C., & Chen C. (1988). Estimation of time series parameters in the presence of outliers, *Technometrics, 30* (2), 193–204.

Chen, C. & Liu, L. M. (1991). Forecasting time series with outliers, *Journal of Forecasting, 12,* 13–35.

Dickey, D. A. & Fuller, W. A. (1979). Distribution of the estimates for autoregressive time series with a unit root, *Journal of American Statistical Association, 74,* 427–431.

Dickey, D. A., Hasza, D. P., & Fuller, W. A. (1984). Testing for unit roots in seasonal time series, *Journal of American Statistical Association, 79,* 355–367.

Engle, R.F. (1982). Autoregressive conditional heteroscedasticity with estimates of the variance of United Kingdom inflation, *Econometrica, 50,* 987–1007.

Engle, R. F. & Granger, C. W. J. (1987). Co-intrgration and error correction: representation, estimation, and testing, *Econometrica, 55,* 251–276.

Fox, A.J. (1972). Outliers in time series, *Journal of Royal Statistical Society, B43,* 350–363.

Granger, C. W. J. (1986). Developments in the study of co-integrated economic variables, *Oxford Bulletin of Economics and Statistics, 48,* 213–228.

Hannan, E.J. (1970). *Multiple Time Series,* New York: Wiley.

Heyse, J. F. & Wei, W. W. S. (1985). Inverse and partial lag autocorrelation for vector time series, *American Statistical Association Proceedings of Business and Economic Statistics Section, 233*–237.

Lee, J.H. & Wei, W.W.S. (1995). A model-independent outlier detection procedure, *Journal of Applied Statistical Science, 2,* 345–359.

Ljung, G. M. & Box, G. E. P. (1978). On a measure of lack of fit in time series models, *Biometrika, 65,* 297–303.

Parzen, E. (1977). Multiple time series modeling: Determining the order of approximating autoregressive schemes. In P. Krishnaiah (Ed.). *Multivariate Analysis IV* (pp. 283–295). Amsterdam, The Netherlands: North-Holland.

R Foundation (2012). The R project for statistical computing, version 2.15.0, Vienna, Austria. URL http://www.r-project.org.

SAS Institute, Inc. (2009). SAS for Windows, 9.2, Cary, North Carolina.

SCA Corp. (2008). SCA WorkBench User's Guide, Release 5.4, Villa Park, Illinois.

Schwartz, G. (1978). Estimating the dimension of a model, *Annal of Statistics, 6,* 461–464.

SPSS, Inc. (2009). SPSS 15.0 for Windows, Chicago, Illinois.

Tiao, G. C. & Box, G. E. P. (1981). Modeling multiple time series with applications, *Journal of American Statistical Association, 76,* 802–816.

Tsay, R. S. & Tiao, G. C. (1984). Consistent estimates of autoregressive parameters and extended sample autocorrelation function for stationary and non-stationary ARIMA models, *Journal of American Statistical Association, 79,* 84–96.

Tsay, R. S. & Tiao, G. C. (1985). Use of canonical analysis in time series model identification, *Biometrika, 72*(2), 299–315.

Tsay, R. S. (1988). Outliers, level shifts, and variance changes in time series. *Journal of Forecasting, 7,* 1–22.

Wei, William W.S. (2006). *Time Series Analysis—Univariate and Multivariate Methods, 2nd Ed.,* Boston, MA: Pearson Addison-Wesley.

Wei, William W.S. (2008). Spectral analysis. In S. Menard (Ed.). *Hand Book of Longitudinal Research* (pp. 601–620). Burlington, MA: Academic Press..

CHAPTER 23

Analyzing Event History Data

Trond Petersen

Abstract

The chapter gives an instruction to event history analysis. The central goals are first to justify why what perhaps must be considered an unusual modeling approach is needed and next to explicate in some detail what the key ideas from probability theory are and how these ideas solve the problems that arise when using more standard techniques such as regression analysis for continuous dependent variables or logit analysis for binary dependent variables. Elaborations for how to take account of measured variables are given. It elaborates on what the dependent variable is in event history analysis, on the framework for repeated event processes, multi-state processes, and continuous-state space processes.

Key Words: Event history analysis, hazard-rate models, time-independent covariates, time-dependent covariates, repeated-event processes, multi-state processes, continuous state-space processes

Introduction

Event histories are generated by so-called failure-time processes and take this form. The dependent variable or, more correctly, an aspect of the dependent variable—for example, being unemployed—is discrete or continuous. Over time it evolves as follows. For finite periods of time (from one calendar date to another), it stays constant at a given value. At a later date, which is a random variable, the dependent variable changes (or jumps) to a new value. The process evolves in this manner from the calendar date (when one change occurs) to a later date (when another change occurs). Between the dates of the changes, the dependent variable stays constant.

Data on such processes typically contain information about the date a sample member entered a state (e.g., an employment state), the date the state was subsequently left or the date the person was last observed in the state, and if the state was left, the value of the next state entered, and so on.

In analyzing such data, the foci are on what determines (e.g., gender, race, education) the amount of time spent in each state and the value of the next state entered. A key feature of such processes is that it is unknown at the time a state is entered (say, being employed), how long the subject will remain in the state, and at each later point in time, while the subject still is in the state, it is uncertain how much longer the subject will remain it. In event history analysis, at each point in time a subject is observed as being present in a state, the method focuses on whether the state is left (and if so to where) in the next short time interval (say, next month), given that the state had not been left prior to entry into the interval. This is an approach to modeling that appears foreign compared to most cross-sectional analysis of data, and which to comprehend requires reflection and rethinking of traditional ways to approach data analysis. Therefore, rather than elaborating on extensions and hence achieving a more comprehensive treatment of the subject, I spend considerable space on fundamentals in the hope to elucidate the key ideas and the problems these are designed to solve.

The paper discusses three types of failure-time or jump processes.[1] The first and simplest type, called a single-state nonrepeatable event process, obtains when there is a single state that can be occupied only once. A person currently in the state may leave it or not. If it is left, one does not distinguish among different reasons for leaving or different destination states. The state, once left, cannot be reentered. An example is entry into first marriage, provided one makes no distinction between religious and secular marriages (Hernes, 1972). Another example is mortality (Vaupel, Manton, & Stallard 1979). Being alive is a state that cannot be reentered, and typically one does not distinguish between different destination states, heaven, purgatory, or hell.

The second type I consider is the repeatable event process. In this process a person can occupy a state several times. Job histories fall within this class of process (Tuma, 1976). The researcher focuses on the amount of time spent in each job. Each sample member may contribute more than one job. Typically, such processes also have multiple states: employed, unemployed, and out of the labor force (Flinn & Heckman, 1983).

The third type is the so-called multistate process. In such a process, the state currently occupied can be left for several distinct reasons. For example, in labor market research, an employee may leave a job for another job, for unemployment, for return to school, or for other reasons. Or in cancer research, a patient may die from the cancer, from the cancer treatment, or from other reasons. In most cases the number of states is finite—that is, the state space is discrete. In some instances, it is however continuous, as, for example, in the analysis of individual earnings histories.

In all three types of failure-time processes, the objective of the empirical analysis is, as stated above, to analyze the determinants of the amount of time that elapses between changes and the value of the destination state once a change occurs.[2]

It is important to understand that not all dependent variables with a measure of time spent in a state, or measures of time more generally, lend themselves to event history analysis. For example, in many democratic countries, a fixed number of years elapses between presidential or other general elections. There would be no point in analyzing the number of years that elapses between such elections, neither by event history analysis nor by other techniques, since the number of years is fixed by law. One may, of course, make comparisons between countries in the amount of time between elections but not by using event history analysis. Or, in prison sentencing, a judge may give the guilty party a specific number of months or years to serve in prison. The length of sentences may well be analyzed by linear regression analysis, and be regressed on characteristics of the judge, the defendant, and the crime. But the sentencing process is not a process to be analyzed using event history techniques, simply because although there is uncertainty about sentence length prior to any ruling, once the judge has ruled, there is no further uncertainty with respect to the length. There may, of course, be uncertainty with respect to how long the defendant actually will stay imprisoned, but that is a process that unfolds subsequent to sentencing. In processes suitable for event history analysis, in contrast, there is uncertainty at each point in time as the process unfolds with respect to how much longer the unit of analysis will stay in a state before leaving it.

The remainder of the paper is organized in nine sections. The Motivation section discusses why ordinary regression and logit models are not suited for analyzing event histories, identifying the challenges that event history analysis is designed to solve. The Hazard-Rate Framework: Discrete-Time Formulation section outlines the basic strategy for analyzing event histories by means of hazard-rate models in the discrete-time framework. The Hazard-Time Framework: Continuous-Time Formulation section extends the framework from discrete to continuous time. The Time-Independent Covariates section explains how time-independent explanatory variables can be introduced into the hazard rate. The Time-Dependent Covariates section explains how time-dependent explanatory variables can be introduced into the hazard rate. In the section Observability of the Dependent Variable comparisons to more familiar regression-type models are made. The Repeated Events section discusses repeatable event processes. The Multistate Processes: Discrete State Space section discusses multi-state processes with a discrete state space. The Multistate Processes: Continuous State Space section discusses multi-state processes with a continuous state space. The Conclusion concludes the paper.

Many of the sections include empirical examples, using real-life data.

Motivation

The purpose of this section is to clarify why (1) linear regression analysis and (2) logit or probit models are not appropriate tools for analyzing event histories, and thus identify the problems that the tools of event history analysis are designed to solve. To recall, one has information on the amount of time a subject has spent in a state and whether the state was left by the last time the subject was observed in it and if, left, which state was next entered. One might be tempted to use linear regression methods to analyze the amount of time (a continuous variable) in the state and logit or probit methods to analyze whether the state was left (a binary variable). As will be shown below, both methods will work satisfactorily or somewhat satisfactorily only in specific situations, but neither will work well in general.

Statement of the Problems: Censoring and Time-varying Covariates

Suppose the researcher has collected career histories on employees in a hierarchically organized company. The researcher might be interested in analyzing the determinants of promotion or the amount of time that elapses before a promotion occurs.

Let t_k be the amount of time that elapsed before an employee was promoted, or before he or she left the company without having been promoted, or before he or she was last observed in the company without having received a promotion. The use of the subscript k to t will be explained in the section on The Hazard-Rate Framework: Continuous-Time Formulation. Let x denote the vector of explanatory variables—for example, race, sex, and marital status.

One may formulate a linear regression model

$$t_k = \beta x + \epsilon, \quad (1)$$

where β the effect parameters pertaining to x, and ϵ a stochastic error term.

There are at least two problems with the approach in Equation 1.

First, it treats employees who were never promoted or who left the company without receiving a promotion in the same way as those who did experience a promotion. The former cases are referred to as right-censored. We know only that they had not experienced the event of interest when they were last observed in the company. A *second* problem with the formulation in Equation 1 arises when the covariates in x change over time. The number of patterns that x may take over time can be very large, and to account for all of these on the right-hand side of Equation 1 may be close to impossible, and it would be hard, if not impossible, to derive a general formulation.

One response to the censoring problem is to restrict analysis to those employees who were promoted. This solution, however, generates other problems. For one, there may be systematic differences between those who were promoted and those who were not. If the research interest is to assess the determinants of promotions, then the bias introduced by excluding those who were not promoted may be severe. We will only learn about the amount of time that elapsed before a promotion occurred among those who were promoted in the data set.

Another response to the problem of right-censoring would be to define a dummy variable C that is equal to one if a promotion occurred and zero otherwise and then estimate a logit (or probit) model predicting the probability of having been promoted, as follows (in the logit case)

$$P(C = 1 \mid x) = \exp(\alpha x)/[1 + \exp(\alpha x)]. \quad (2)$$

However, this procedure ignores the amount of time that elapsed before a promotion or censoring occurred. Being promoted after 6 months is a different career trajectory from being promoted after 6 years, but Equation 2 does not distinguish the two cases. Introducing t_k on the right-hand side would not help. It would be tantamount to treating a dependent as an independent variable, which would make matters worse. Also, Equation 2 cannot account for time-varying covariates, unless one defines the probability in Equation 2 separately for each observed time unit—say, each week or month (*see* Allison, 1982). In the latter case, one has defined a discrete-time model. It will be treated in more detail below.

Illustration of the Censoring Problem

It is instructive to elaborate on the problem of right-censored data using some stylized examples. In Table 23.1 I show two different data patterns for event histories. I list data for 6 men and 6 women, altogether 12 subjects, each of whom was observed for up to 10 months (time periods) in a state from the time it was entered (in month 1) until the subject either left it (whichever month that occurred) or was still in it (month 10). In the far left column, the months are listed from 1 to 10. For each man and each women (numbered $i = 1-12$), their

Table 23.1. Examples of Event Histories Creating Problems for Standard Techniques

Panel A: No Problem with Linear Regression Analysis, Logit Analysis Is Useless
No Right-Censored Observations
Differences in Time Before Event

	Men (i = 1–6)						Women (i = 7–12)					
Month (j)	1	2	3	4	5	6	7	8	9	10	11	12
1	0	0	0	0	0	0	0	0	0	0	0	0
2	0	0	0	0	0	0	0	0	0	0	0	0
3	0	0	0	0	0	0	0	0	0	0	0	0
4	0	0	0	0	0	0	0	0	0	0	0	0
5	1	1	1	1	1	1	0	0	0	0	0	0
6							0	0	0	0	0	0
7							0	0	0	0	0	0
8							0	0	0	0	0	0
9							0	0	0	0	0	0
10							1	1	1	1	1	1
T	5	5	5	5	5	5	10	10	10	10	10	10
C	1	1	1	1	1	1	1	1	1	1	1	1

Panel B: Problem with Linear Regression Analysis, Less Problem With Logit
Right-censoring for Men and Women, Differences in Proportions with Event

Month	Men						Women					
1	0	0	0	0	0	0	0	0	0	0	0	0
2	0	0	0	0	0	0	0	0	0	0	0	0
3	0	0	0	0	0	0	0	0	0	0	0	0
4	0	0	0	0	0	0	0	0	0	0	0	0
5	0	0	0	0	0	0	0	0	0	0	0	0
6	0	0	0	0	0	0	0	0	0	0	0	0
7	0	0	0	0	0	0	0	0	0	0	0	0
8	0	0	0	0	0	0	0	0	0	0	0	0
9	0	0	0	0	0	0	0	0	0	0	0	0
10	0	0	1	1	1	1	0	0	0	0	1	1
T	10	10	10	10	10	10	10	10	10	10	10	10
C	0	0	1	1	1	1	0	0	0	0	1	1

entire event history is listed for each month (numbered $j = 1-10$), with one column per subject. If no promotion occurred in a month, then the entry in the table is 0. If no promotion occurred at all in the 10 months, then each of the 10 months will have an entry of 0. If a promotion occurred in a given month, the entry in that month will be 1, and there will be no further entries in the table. The entry for each individual i ($i = 1-12$) in period j ($j = 1-10$) is denoted C_{ij}. It is equal to 0 if no promotion occurred for individual i in period j and equal to 1 if a promotion occurred. At the bottom of the table, I list the the number of months (t_i) for which the individual is observed either with or without a promotion and whether a promotion occurred (C_i). None of the individuals left the company either before getting promoted or before month 10.

For these data, I compute the estimates corresponding to three methods: linear regression analysis, linear probability (and logit) analysis, and event history analysis. As will be shown shortly, in the first data pattern (Panel A in Table 23.1), there is no problem for linear regression analysis, but logit analysis is useless. In the second data pattern (Panel B), linear regression analysis is useless, whereas linear probability (and logit) analysis is better, although not problem-free. For each of the two data patterns, event history analysis gives the correct answer.

Consider now two models:

$$t_i = \beta_0 + \beta_1 \text{Female}_i + \epsilon_i, \qquad (3)$$

$$C_i = \alpha_0 + \alpha_1 \text{Female}_i + \varepsilon_i, \qquad (4)$$

where we in Equation 3 regress the amount of time spent in a state (t_i) on a constant term and a dummy variable for being female, whereas in Equation 4 we regress whether a promotion occurred (C_i) on the same variables. Here, β_0, β_1, α_0, and α_1 are the coefficients to be estimated and ϵ_i and ε_i are error terms. To simplify computations and make results more transparent, I focus on the linear regression model without taking the logarithm of the dependent variable in Equation 3 and the linear probability model in Equation 4. For the latter, the logit model presented in Equation 2 would be preferable, but would require slightly more complex computations to find estimates, but with no gain in insight.

In Panel A, all the men and all the women received the promotion. A linear regression analysis would give a constant term for the men of 5.0, corresponding to the average number of months before men received a promotion, and a coefficient for being female of 5.0, showing that women on average spent an additional 5.0 months before experiencing a promotion, a total duration of 10 months. This would be a correct description of what goes on. A linear probability model with whether a promotion occurred (C_i) as the dependent variable would, in contrast, give a constant term for men of 1.0 and a coefficient for female of 0.0, as all the men and all the women were promoted (the constant term in the corresponding logit model would be plus infinity, estimated typically at 15, and a coefficient for female of 0.0). The linear probability (or logit) model would correctly conclude that everyone was promoted, and that there is no difference in this regard between men and women. But it would miss the crucial fact that women had to wait twice as long as the men before the promotion occurred.

An event history analysis of the data would look at the probability of promotion per month by sex, in contrast to the probability of promotion over the entire period. The 6 men were observed for an entire 30 months (6 × 5 months) and each of them received a promotion in month 5—that is, 6 promotions over 30 months. Hence, the average monthly probability of promotion is 0.20 (=6/30). The women were observed for an entire 60 months (6 × 10 months), and each of them received a promotion in month 10—that is, 6 promotions over 60 months. The average monthly probability of promotion is hence 0.10 (=6/60). The event history analysis reveals that the average monthly promotion probability is twice as high for men as for women. This, in turn, translates into women having to wait twice as long as men before getting promoted.

For this particular data pattern, we do not learn anything more from the event history analysis than from the linear regression analysis. But we see that the linear probability (or logit) model misses a key feature of what goes on, the large sex difference in monthly promotion probability and time before promotion.

In Panel B, we have a different data pattern. Here, each of the men and each of the women were observed for 10 months, and two-thirds of the men received a promotion in month 10, whereas one-third of the women received such a promotion. We could apply linear regression analysis here but would encounter problems. The estimate of the constant term for men would be 10, and the estimate for being female would be 0. The analysis would show no difference between men and women. That is clearly incorrect, as two-thirds of the men got promoted, whereas only one-third of the women did so. The regression model here furthermore does not distinguish employees according to their promotion status; getting promoted versus not getting promoted are clearly different outcomes. To address this problem, one might be tempted, therefore, to restrict the regression analysis to subjects that received the promotion. But in this case the linear regression would not solve the problem. It would give the same results, a constant term of 10 and a coefficient for being female of 0, incorrectly showing no differences between men and women. A linear probability model analysis would here work better, yielding a constant term of 0.666 and an effect of being female of –0.333 (with logit coefficients of 0.693 and –1.386). The linear probability (or logit) model will correctly describe that men are twice as likely to get promoted.

An event history analysis of the data would look at the average probability of promotion per month by sex. The men were observed for an entire 60 months (6 × 10 months), and 4 of 6 received a promotion in month 10—that is, with 4 promotions over 60 months. The average monthly probability of promotion is hence 0.0666 (=4/60). The women were also observed for an entire 60 months (6 × 10 months), and 2 of the 6 received a promotion in month 10—that is, with 2 promotions over 60 months. The average monthly probability of promotion is hence 0.0333 (=2/60). The event history analysis reveals that the monthly promotion probability is twice as high for men as for women or that two-thirds of the men get promoted and one-third of the women.

Note that although the linear probability (or logit) model for Panel B is correct in so far as it reports that the promotion probability for men is twice that of women, it says nothing about the average monthly promotion probability or the amount of time that elapses before the promotion. It would have given the exactly same estimates if all the promotions had occurred in month 5 rather than month 10. The event history analysis would then, in contrast, have reported monthly promotion probabilities twice as high as in the case where the promotions all occurred in month 10, and again with men having twice the promotion probability of women.

In summary, Panel A gives a data pattern where linear regression analysis yields a correct answer, but where the linear probability (or logit) model is useless. Panel B gives a data pattern where linear regression analysis is useless, but where the linear probability (or logit) model gives a better, although not satisfactory, answer. In both panels, event history analysis focusing on the average probability of a promotion (i.e., an event) per month gives the correct answer. Or if the men got promoted in month 5 and the women in month 10, the estimates from the linear probability (or logit) model would still be the same, whereas the event history analysis would have shown much higher promotion probabilities for men but with no change in monthly probabilities for women.

Real-life data will clearly combine features of the data patterns in both panels. Neither linear regression analysis of the time spent in state nor linear probability (or logit) model of whether an event occurred will then provide the correct answer. Event history analysis will handle both data patterns correctly.

Initial Statement of the Solution to the Problems

We can now, with few formalities, state what the event history method really does, through the following linear probability model

$$C_{ij} = \delta_0 + \delta_1 \text{Female}_i + e_{ij}. \quad (5)$$

In this model, for *each* individual, one specifies a linear probability (or logit) model for *each* time period the individual is observed. The dependent variable takes the value of 0 in each time period that does not end in the individual getting promoted, and then takes the value of 1 in the time period where the individual gets promoted. For each period one models the probability of getting promoted or not getting promoted. For a given individual, the number of probability models specified will equal the number of periods for which the individual is observed.

If one applies linear least squares to the model in Equation 5 one gets estimates of the constant term and the coefficient for being female of 0.20 and –0.10 in Panel A and of 0.0666 and –0.0333 in Panel B, with corresponding logit estimates of –1.386 and –0.811 in Panel A and –2.640 and –0.728 in Panel B. These estimates gives precisely the results for the average monthly probability of getting promoted for each gender.

This then in a nut-shell—in the formulation in Equation 5—is what event history analysis does: It estimates the average probability per month (or whatever time unit one measures time spent in a state) and how this probability varies with measured covariates such as sex, education, and more, as well as the number of months that has passed without having received a promotion.

From Equation 5, one can also see how we could account for time-varying covariates. Suppose that in addition to female we also have a covariate for marital status, a variable that can change value many times, from single to married to separated to divorced as well as to widowed. For the current purposes, we code marital status as unmarried (=0) versus married (=1) (denoted M_{ij}), giving the marital status for individual i at time j. In the framework in Equation 5, which specifies one regression equation per month the individual is observed, one could in each month enter the person's actual marital status, which, for example, could be single in months 1 through 3, and married in months 4 through 10. Time-varying covariates thus pose no particular problem. One could in Equation 5 also include, for each month, the amount of time that has already elapsed without a promotion having occurred. In month 1, the value of this variable would be 0, in month 2 it would be 1, and so on. The specification including marital status and time elapsed without a promotion would be:

$$C_{ij} = \delta_0 + \delta_1 \text{Female}_i + \delta_2 M_{ij} + \gamma(j-1) + e_{ij}, \quad (6)$$

where γ measures the impact of number of months that have elapsed without a promotion, and δ_2 is the impact of being married.

In the next three sections I discuss and give a justification for why this framework works. I will introduce the standard tool of the hazard-rate framework and how it can be used to solve the two identified problems of the regression framework—namely, censored durations and time-varying covariates.

The Hazard-Rate Framework: Discrete-time Formulation

Above we stated the key idea in the hazard-rate framework: For each time interval an individual (or other unit) is observed, to focus on whether an event occurs (least common) or not (most common) in the time interval. As shown, this idea works well and is intuitively appealing. It produces results that make sense and solves the problems of right censoring and time-dependent covariates. We shall now make this framework more explicit, dressing the intuition up in a formal apparatus by giving it a justification from probability theory.

Toward this end, it is instructive to develop the hazard-rate framework in a discrete-time setting first, which is the focus of this section. To do so, one needs a fundamental rule of probability theory—namely, the *chain-rule* for probabilities.

Suppose one wants to specify the probability of three things occurring—namely, C_1, C_2, and C_3, denoted $P(C_1, C_2, C_3)$. The chain-rule for probabilities now states:

$$P(C_1, C_2, C_3) = P(C_1) \times P(C_2 \mid C_1)$$
$$\times P(C_3 \mid C_1, C_2). \quad (7)$$

This states that the probability of C_1, C_2, and C_3 occurring equals the product of three probabilities: (1) the probability of C_1 occurring times (2) the probability of C_2 occurring, given (or conditional) that C_1 has occurred, times (3) the probability that C_3 occurs, given that both C_1 and C_2 have occurred. This is a way to rewrite the probability of three things occurring in terms of the probabilities of the first thing occurring, the probability of the second thing occurring, and the probability of the third thing occurring, in the latter two conditional on the first and then both the first and second thing having occurred.

To make this more concrete in the case of event history analysis, let $C_1 = 0$ denote that no event (or transition) happened in the first period someone was observed, $C_2 = 0$ that no event happened in the second period, $C_3 = 0$ that no event happened in the third period, and conversely where $C_j = 1$ will denote that an event happened in period j. The probability that no event happens in the first three periods then equals the probability of $C_1 = 0$, $C_2 = 0$, and $C_3 = 0$, which in turns equals the probability of no event in first period times the probability of no event in the second period, given no event in the first period, times the probability of no event in the third period, given no event in the first and second periods.

We can then write this as

$$P(C_1 = 0, C_2 = 0, C_3 = 0) =$$
$$P(C_1 = 0) \times P(C_2 = 0 \mid C_1 = 0)$$
$$\times P(C_3 = 0 \mid C_1 = 0, C_2 = 0). \quad (8)$$

If an event occurred in the third period, then the sequence for the three variables would be $C_1=0$, $C_2=0$, $C_3=1$, and by the chain rule we will get:

$$P(C_1 = 0, C_2 = 0, C_3 = 1) =$$
$$P(C_1 = 0) \times P(C_2 = 0 \mid C_1 = 0)$$
$$\times P(C_3 = 1 \mid C_1 = 0, C_2 = 0). \quad (9)$$

This specification of probabilities generalizes to any number of periods, where (as above) the subs inputs i and j index individuals and periods respectively. For each period where no event (or transition) occurs, one specifies the probability of $C_{ij} = 0$, and in a period where an even (or transition) occurs, one specifies the probability of $C_{ij} = 1$. Let $H_{i,j-1} = 0$ denote that $C_{i1} = \ldots = C_{i,j-1} = 0$—that is, that no event happened from period 1 through period $j - 1$. In the case of a logit specification for the probabilities, one could specify:

$$P(C_{ij} = 1 \mid H_{i,j-1} = 0) = \exp[\alpha + \gamma(j - 1)]/$$
$$\{1 + \exp[\alpha + \gamma(j - 1)]\} \quad (10)$$

and $P(C_{ij} = 0 \mid H_{i,j-1} = 0) =$
$$1 - P(C_{ij} = 1 \mid H_{i,j-1} = 0) = 1/$$
$$\{1 + \exp[\alpha + \gamma(j - 1)]\}. \quad (11)$$

For each time unit where no transition occurs, one specifies the probability of no transition occurring—namely, $1 - P(C_{ij} = 1 \mid H_{i,j-1} = 0)$. For the time unit where a transition occurs—one specifies the probability of a transition occurring—namely, $P(C_{ij} = 1 \mid H_{i,j-1} = 0)$. For a censored observation, where no transition occurs at all, each time unit would get specified by Equation 11—namely, $1 - P(C_{ij} = 1 \mid H_{i,j-1}) = 0$. For a non-censored observation, where a transition occurs in the last period, each time unit before the last gets specified by Equation 11 [$1 - P(C_{ij} = 1 \mid H_{i,j-1} = 0)$], whereas the last time unit gets specified by Equation 10 [$P(C_{ij} = 1 \mid H_{i,j-1} = 0)$]. There would be one logit equation (or some other probability model) specified per time unit that an individual was observed. Only in the last time unit may the variable C_{ij} be equal to 1, if a transition occurs in that time unit. Otherwise the individual is censored and C_{ij} is equal to 0 for all time units.

This is a very straightforward and intuitively appealing way to analyze event histories. It requires good knowledge of logit (or probit) models, which is widespread. It also requires an understanding of the chain-rule for probabilities, which, although less well known, easily can be taught. The chain rule justifies specifying one logit model per time unit an individual is observed in a state, and justifies that multiplying together these probabilities yields the probability for the entire sequence of no events ($C_{ij} = 0$) possibly ending in the last period with an event ($C_{ij} = 1$).

The discrete-time formulation as applied to continuous-time processes has two drawbacks. First, the estimated coefficients may depend on the length of the time interval for which one specifies the probability of no event occurring or an event occurring. That means that results may not be comparable across studies that vary in the lengths of the time intervals for which the probabilities are specified. Fortunately, in most models (e.g., the logit model), only the constant term will be severely affected by the length of the same unit, whereas the coefficients of explanantory variables tend to be less affected by the length of the time interval.

Second, in software packages—say, for logit or probit models—the discrete-time formulation requires the researcher to create one record of data per observed time unit on an individual, as illustrated for 12 individuals in Table 23.1, with one line per individual per period he or she was observed. All records that do not end in a transition are coded as censored, $C_{ij}=0$, whereas the last record on a case, if it ends in a transition, is coded as noncensored, $C_{ij}=1$. So there will be many more records of data than there are individuals. This imposes burdens on the researcher in terms of data management and increases computation time. Note, however, that multiple records per observation and different number of records across observations *do not deflate standard errors or induce other biases* (Petersen 1986, pp. 229–233). That is, observations do not become differentially weighted by this procedure. This is a feature that arises out of the hazard-rate framework.

The Hazard-Rate Framework: Continuous-time Formulation
Basic Concepts

In many applications, researchers use a continuous-time formulation for event history data. The central idea is identical to the discrete-time formulation. It is based on the chain-rule for probabilities. One specifies the probability of no event or of an event in each time unit an individual is observed, conditional on no event prior to entry into the time unit, possibly conditional on the amount time spent in the state, and possibly conditional on covariates and prior history of the process. But rather than the time unit being a day, week, month, or some other finite unit of measurement, one considers a time unit that is very small. This leads to some technical novelty, arising from how one deals with small quantities in probability theory, but it results in no conceptual novelty relative to the discrete-time formulation. To focus on core ideas, we here discuss the case without measured covariates. The extension to covariates raises no new conceptual issues.

To explicate the continuous-time framework, I drop the subscript i to individuals used in the section The Hazard-Rate Framework: Discrete-Time Formulation above. For each individual, one has a total duration for which he or she was observed,

t_k, where the role of the subscript k will become clear shortly. As in the discrete-time framework, rather than focusing on the entire duration t_k, one proceeds by dividing the duration t_k into several segments. Set $t_0=0$. Then divide t_k into k segments of time from duration 0 to duration t_k. The first segment covers the interval 0 to t_1, the second covers t_1 to t_2, and so on up until t_{k-1} to t_k, where $0=t_0 < t_1 < t_2 < \cdots < t_{k-1} < t_k$. Each segment has length Δt, defined as:

$$\Delta t = t_{j+1} - t_j. \quad (12)$$

Now let T be the random variable denoting the amount of time spent in a state before a transition or censoring occurs. The hazard-rate framework proceeds by specifying the probability that the state is left during the duration interval t_j to t_{j+1}, given that it was not left before t_j—namely:

$$P(t_j \leq T < t_j + \Delta t \mid T \geq t_j), \text{ where } t_j + \Delta t = t_{j+1}. \quad (13)$$

In a given time interval there are two outcomes: the state is left or is not left. The probability that the state is not left in the duration interval t_j to t_{j+1}, given that it was not left before t_j, is therefore just one minus the probability that it was left (given in Equation 13)—namely

$$P(T \geq t_{j+1} \mid T \geq t_j) =$$
$$1 - P(t_j \leq T < t_{j+1} \mid T \geq t_j),$$
$$\text{where } t_{j+1} = t_j + \Delta t. \quad (14)$$

By means of these two probabilities Equations 13 and 14—defined for each small segment of time t_j to t_{j+1}, one can derive the probability that the state was not left before duration t_k as follows

$$P(T \geq t_k) = \prod_{j=0}^{k-1} P(T \geq t_{j+1} \mid T \geq t_j),$$
$$\text{where } t_0=0 \text{ and } t_{j+1}=t_j + \Delta t, \quad (15)$$

which follows from rules for conditional probabilities and Π is the product sign, denoting a product with terms numbering from $j = 0$ to $j = k$.

The interpretation of Equation 15 is this: The probability of not having an event before duration t_k equals the probability of surviving beyond duration t_1, times the probability of surviving beyond duration t_2, given survival to t_1, and so on up until the probability of surviving beyond duration t_k, given survival to t_{k-1}. This corresponds to Equation 8 in the discrete-time formulation.

Similarly, the probability that the state was left between duration t_k and $t_k + \Delta t$ follows as

$$P(t_k \leq T < t_k + \Delta t) = P(T \geq t_k)$$
$$\times P(t_k \leq T < t_k + \Delta t \mid T \geq t_k)$$
$$= \prod_{j=0}^{k-1} P(T \geq t_{j+1} \mid T \geq t_j)$$
$$\times P[t_k \leq T < t_k + \Delta t \mid T \geq t_k], \quad (16)$$

which again follows from rules for conditional probabilities, as in Equation 9.

The interpretation of Equation 16 is this: The probability of leaving the state in the duration interval t_k to $t_k + \Delta t$ equals the probability of not leaving it before duration t_k—that is, Equation 15—times the probability of leaving the state between duration t_k and $t_k + \Delta t$, given that it was not left before duration t_k. This corresponds to Equation 9 in the discrete-time formulation, and as in that case, follows from the chain-rule for probabilities.

In conclusion, if one can specify the probability of a transition in a small time interval—that is, Equation 13—given no transition before entry into the interval, then one can derive each of the three probabilities in Equations 14, 15, and 16. One can specify the probability accounting for the entire duration in a state by means of the product of the probabilities for each time interval into which the duration is split. The chain-rule allows one to do this.

Continuous-time Formulations

Above, the formulation is still in discrete time, and the length of the time interval is Δt. The need to consider a continuous-time formulation (wherein the length of the time interval becomes infinitesimally small) arises in part for technical reasons (how one deals with continuous variables in probability theory), and in part because the length of the time interval (week, month, etc.) for which Equation 12 is specified, is arbitrary. One would like to obtain a formulation that yields consistency across studies as well as facility of notation; mathematics is often simpler for continuous than discrete variables. The convention, therefore, because time is continuous, is to let Δt approach 0—namely,

$$\lim_{\Delta t \downarrow 0} P(t_j \leq T < t_j + \Delta t \mid T \geq t_j),$$
$$\text{where } t_j + \Delta t = t_{j+1}, \quad (17)$$

where "lim" denotes taking the limit.

Because duration T is an absolutely continuous variable, the probability of any specific realization of T is 0 and Equation 17 is hence also equal to 0. A probability quantity that is 0 is useless; there is no variation to analyze. As with probabilities for other continuous variables, one therefore divides the probability in Equation 17 by Δt, which yields a probability per time unit divided by the length of the time unit itself. Then one takes the limit of this ratio as the time unit goes to 0. This operation yields the central concept in event-history analysis, the *hazard rate*

$$\lambda(t_j) \equiv \lim_{\Delta t \downarrow 0} P(t_j \leq T < t_j + \Delta t \mid T \geq t_j)/\Delta t. \quad (18)$$

This is a conditional density function: the probability density that the state is left at duration t_j, given that it was not left before duration t_j. This quantity is never negative and is typically larger than zero, provided that there is a positive probability that an event will occur. One here divides two quantities, which both are positive, hence yielding a positive ratio, and both quantities approach zero. Their ratio in this case is larger than zero because the denominator approaches zero faster than the numerator.

From Equation 18 we find that for small Δt a good approximation to the probability of a transition, initially specified in Equation 13, becomes

$$P(t_j \leq T < t_j + \Delta t \mid T \geq t_j)$$
$$\approx \lambda(t_j)\Delta t, \quad \text{when } \Delta t \text{ is small.} \quad (19)$$

Then, inserting Equation 19 into Equation 14,

$$P(T \geq t_{j+1} \mid T \geq t_j)$$
$$\approx 1 - \lambda(t_j)\Delta t, \quad \text{where } t_{j+1} = t_j + \Delta t. \quad (20)$$

Next, insert Equation 20 into Equation 15

$$P(T \geq t_k) \approx \prod_{j=0}^{k-1} [1 - \lambda(t_j)\Delta t]. \quad (21)$$

Inserting Equation 21 into Equation 19 into Equation 16 yields

$$P(t_k \leq T < t_k + \Delta t) \approx \prod_{j=0}^{k-1}[1-\lambda(t_j)\Delta t] \times \lambda(t_k)\Delta t. \quad (22)$$

Equations 21 and 22 have the same interpretations as Equations 15 and 16, but the right-hand sides are now expressed exclusively in terms of the hazard rate in Equation 18.

The approximations in Equations 19 through 22 can be made exact by replacing Δt on the right-hand sides with Δt^*, where $\Delta t^* < \Delta t$. This gives

$$P(t_j \leq T < t_j + \Delta t \mid T \geq t_j) = \lambda(t_j)\Delta t^*,$$
$$P(T \geq t_{j+1} \mid T \geq t_j) = 1 - \lambda(t_j)\Delta t^*,$$
$$P(T \geq t_k) = \prod_{j=0}^{k-1}[1 - \lambda(t_j)\Delta t^*],$$
$$P(t_k \leq T < t_k + \Delta t) = \prod_{j=0}^{k-1}[1 - \lambda(t_j)\Delta t^*]$$
$$\times \lambda(t_k)\Delta t^*.$$

When $\Delta t = 1$ in Equations 19 through 22 and $\lambda(t_j)$ stays constant from t_j to t_j+1, then the value of Δt^* needed to make the approximation exact depends only on the rate $\lambda(t_j)$. Set now $\Delta t = 1$—that is, $t_j + 1 = t_{j+1}$. Then, when the rate is 0.05, Δt^* is 0.975, while when the rate is 0.50, Δt^* is 0.787. The smaller the rate, the closer Δt^* is to 1.0.[3] As will be shown in the section Time-Independent Covariate the approximation in Equation 21 is very good for small rates even when we set $\Delta t^* = 1$.

Since duration is absolutely continuous, the expressions in Equations 21 and 22 must, as in Equation 18, be evaluated as Δt goes to 0. When Δt goes to 0, the number of segments k goes to infinity, since $k = t_k/\Delta t$. Computing the limit of Equation 21, as $\Delta t \downarrow 0$ and $k \to \infty$, yields the famous expression for the probability of surviving beyond duration t_k

$$P(T \geq t_k) = \lim_{\substack{\Delta t \downarrow 0 \\ k \to \infty}} \prod_{j=0}^{k-1}[1 - \lambda(t_j)\Delta t]$$
$$= \exp[-\int_0^{t_k} \lambda(s)ds], \quad (23)$$

known as the *survivor function*. In the last equality of Equation 23, s denotes duration in state.

Here, I consider a proof of Equation 23 in the special case when the hazard rate equals a constant θ for all t. The integral of $\lambda(t) = \theta$ from 0 to t_k then equals θt_k and the survivor function in Equation 23 is hence $\exp(-\theta t_k)$. To show this, using the limit operations on the right-hand side of the first equality in Equation 23, set first $\Delta t = t_k/k$. Then let $k \to \infty$

(i.e., $\Delta t \downarrow 0$), which, for a fixed t_k, yields

$$P(T \geq t_k) = \lim_{k \to \infty} \prod_{j=0}^{k-1} (1 - \theta t_k/k)$$
$$= \lim_{k \to \infty} (1 - \theta t_k/k)^k \qquad (24)$$
$$= \exp(-\theta t_k),$$

where the last equality follows from a well-known fact in calculus (see Apostol, 1967, eq. [10.13], p. 380).

Finally, consider the limit of Equation 22 as Δt goes to 0 and k goes to infinity, but now first dividing by Δt on both sides of Equation 22, for the same reason as in Equation 18. We obtain the *density function* for the duration t_k as

$$f(t_k) \equiv \lim_{\Delta t \downarrow 0} P(t_k \leq T < t_k + \Delta t)/\Delta t$$
$$= \lim_{\substack{\Delta t \downarrow 0 \\ k \to \infty}} \prod_{j=0}^{k-1} [1 - \lambda(t_j)\Delta t] \times \lambda(t_k)\Delta t/\Delta t$$
$$= \exp[-\int_0^{t_k} \lambda(s)ds] \times \lambda(t_k). \qquad (25)$$

The key point of all this is that by specifying the hazard rate, as in Equation 18, one can derive the survivor function and the density function for the duration t_k. The survivor function, Equation 23, accounts for right-censored observations, those that did not experience a transition. The density function, Equation 25, accounts for observations that did experience a transition. Once one has specified the hazard rate, the survivor and density functions follow directly from Equations 23 and 25. So the researcher needs first to choose a particular hazard rate that makes sense for describing the process. Thereafter, the rest follows.

Specifications and Estimation

It may be instructive to consider some specifications of the hazard rate. Perhaps the most famous specification of Equation 14 is the exponential model (now dropping subscripts to period j)

$$\lambda(t) = \exp(\alpha). \qquad (26)$$

Here, the rate at duration t is independent of t. Exponentiation of α is done to ensure non-negativity of the rate, an issue that is of importance when covariates are introduced, but that does not arise in the rate above.

A straightforward extension of the exponential rate, which allows the rate to depend on duration t, is the so-called piecewise constant rate,

$$\lambda(t) = \exp[\sum_{j=0}^{k} \alpha_j D_j(t)], \qquad (27)$$

where $D_j(t)=1$ when t lies in the interval t_j to t_{j+1} and 0 otherwise. The rate stays constant at $\exp(\alpha_j)$ within each period t_j to t_{j+1} but varies arbitrarily between periods. The length of each period is chosen by the researcher. When $\alpha_j = \alpha$ for all j the constant rate model in Equation 26 above follows as a special case.

Explicit expressions exist for the estimators of the rates in Equations 26 and 27. I consider the former. Let $C = 0$ if an observation is right-censored and 1 if not. The likelihood, log-likelihood, and gradient of an observation is then

$$\mathcal{L} = [\lambda(t)]^C \exp[-t \times \lambda(t)]$$
$$= [\exp(\alpha)]^C \exp[-t \times \exp(\alpha)] \qquad (28)$$
$$L = C \times \ln[\lambda(t)] - t \times \lambda(t)$$
$$= C \times \alpha - t \times \exp(\alpha) \qquad (29)$$

and $\partial L / \partial \alpha = C - t \times \exp(\alpha). \qquad (30)$

Let π denote the proportion of noncensored observations (i.e., observations that ended in a transition) in a sample, and let $\bar{t}$ denote the average duration of the observations in the sample, where the average is computed across censored and noncensored observations. The ML estimators of α and of the rate itself follow from Equation 30 above, as

$$\hat{\alpha} = \ln(\pi/\bar{t}), \qquad (31)$$

and

$$\widehat{\lambda(t)} = \pi/\bar{t}. \qquad (32)$$

As Equation 32 shows, for a fixed proportion of noncensored observations, the higher the average duration the lower the estimated rate. This makes sense, because the lower the rate the more time will, on average, be spent in the state. Conversely, for a fixed average duration $\bar{t}$, the higher the proportion of noncensored observations the higher the estimated rate. This also makes sense. For a fixed average duration in the sample, which often means a fixed observation period for the durations, the higher the rate, the higher the proportion of observations that experiences a transition.

Several other specifications allow the rate to depend on duration t. A simple but general specification would be

$$\lambda(t) = \exp(\alpha + \gamma_1 t + \gamma_2 \ln t), \qquad (33)$$

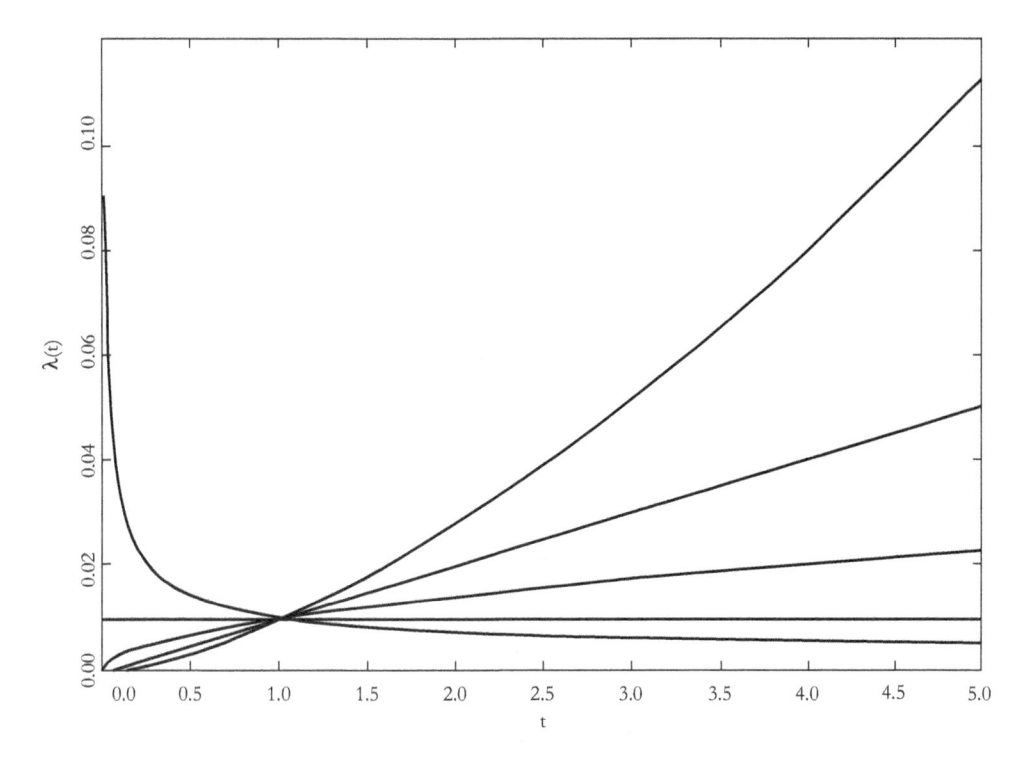

Figure 23.1 The Weibull rate for five values of γ_2 (γ_2=−0.5, 0.0, 0.5, 1.0, 1.5) and for α=−4.61 from equation (4.20) when γ_1=0. Starting from the right vertical axis of the figure, the curve at the bottom of the figure corresponds to γ_2=−0.50, whereas the curves above it correspond to increasing values of γ_2.

in which case the exponential model obtains as a special case when $\gamma_1 = \gamma_2 = 0$; the so-called Gompertz when $\gamma_2 = 0$; and the so-called Weibull when $\gamma_1 = 0$ and $\gamma_2 > -1$ (see, e.g., Box-Steffensmeier & Jones 2004, Chapter 3). Each specification allows for different shapes of the hazard rate over time. The Gompertz specification allows the rate to follow three functions of time (1) no change when $\gamma_1 = 0$; (2) decreasing when $\gamma_1 < 0$; and (3) increasing when $\gamma_1 > 0$.

In Figure 23.1 the Weibull specification is plotted for various parameter values.

In the Weibull model, the survivor function has the form

$$P(T \geq t_k) = \exp[-\frac{1}{\gamma_2 + 1} t_k^{\gamma_2+1} \exp(\alpha)]. \quad (34)$$

In the case of the Weibull model, no analytic solution exists for the estimates of α and γ_2. They must be obtained by means of iterative procedures.

Examples

I present an example of the rates in Equations 26 through 27 and 33 using data from the personnel records of a large U.S. insurance company. For each employee in the company, we know the date he or she entered the company and the dates of all movements within the company up until the end of the study or the date the person quit the company (end of study is December 1978). For further descriptions of the data, *see* Petersen and Spilerman (1990). In this section, I present estimates of the rates of departure from the company.

I restrict the analysis to lower-level clerical employees in the company, all of whom are employed in salary grade levels 1 to 6. I use data on a 50 % random sample of the employees, leaving data on 10,850 employees.

In this analysis, the duration t is the seniority of the employee in the company. It is measured in months. For the piecewise constant rate, I report estimates for 10 groups of seniority. For seniority of 9 years or less, there are nine groups captured by the coefficient α_j, one for each year of seniority less than or equal to nine. For seniority greater than 9 years, there is one group, 9-plus years of seniority, captured by the coefficient α_9.

The parameter estimates are given in Table 23.2. The constant rate model gives an estimate of β_0 of −3.747, which means that the estimated expected time before a departure is 42.3 [=1/ exp(−3.747)] months among lower-level clerical employees. From

Table 23.2. Estimates of the Rate of Departure from Company (Estimated Standard Errors in Parentheses)

	Constant rate Eq. 26	Piecewise constant rate[a] Eq. 27	Gompertz Eq. 27 $\gamma_2 = 0$	Weibull Eq. 27 $\gamma_1 = 0$
	−3.747 (0.011)		−3.215 (0.012)	−2.829 (0.023)
γ_1			−0.015 (0.000)	
γ_2				−0.330 (0.008)
α_0		−3.019 (0.014)		
α_1		−3.684 (0.026)		
α_2		−4.082 (0.038)		
α_3		−4.319 (0.048)		
α_4		−4.674 (0.065)		
α_5		−4.759 (0.078)		
α_6		−4.699 (0.087)		
α_7		−4.985 (0.115)		
α_8		−4.987 (0.131)		
α_9		−4.850 (0.056)		
L[b]	−37,695	−35,852	−36,511	−36,388
N	10,089	10,089	10,089	10,089
Number of events	7,947	7,947	7,947	7,947

Note: Data are taken from the personnel records of a large U.S. insurance company. The dependent duration variable is the number of months since entry into the company (i.e., seniority) before a departure or censoring (end of study) occurs. See section 3.3 for further description of the data. The estimation routine is described in Petersen (1986b). See Blossfeld, Hamerle, and Mayer (1989, Chapter 6) for an extensive discussion of the BMDP-implementation of the routine. All computations are done in BMDP (1985). All coefficients are significantly different from zero at the five-percentage level (two-tailed tests). A 50 % random sample of all individuals about which we have data are used in this analysis. For spells that were started prior to January 1, 1970 and that were still in progress at that date, the likelihood contribution is given by equation (14.12) in Section 14.1 in Petersen (1995a). Spells that started and ended prior to January 1, 1970 are not included in our sample.

[a] For the piecewise constant rate, the duration is divided into 10 groups of seniority. For seniority of less or equal to 9 years, there are nine groups, one for each year of seniority, where each group is captured by the coefficient α_j, where j refers to the number of years of seniority ($j=0,\ldots,8$) at the beginning of the period to which α_j pertains. For seniority greater than 9 years, there is one group, 9-plus years of seniority, captured by the coefficient α_9.

[b] This is the loglikelihood of the model.

the Gompertz and Weibull models we see that seniority has a significant negative effect on the rate of departure. The longer someone has been with the company the less likely he or she is to leave. The piecewise constant rate confirms the findings of the Gompertz and Weibull models. The rate declines with every year of seniority, until it reaches a low level after about 8 years.

Estimates of the rates for the piecewise constant and the Weibull model are plotted in Figure 23.2. We see that the Weibull model, relative to the piecewise constant rate, overestimates the departure rate somewhat for employees with 4 to 5 years or more seniority, but that the agreement between the models is quite close for seniority of less than 5 years (60 months).

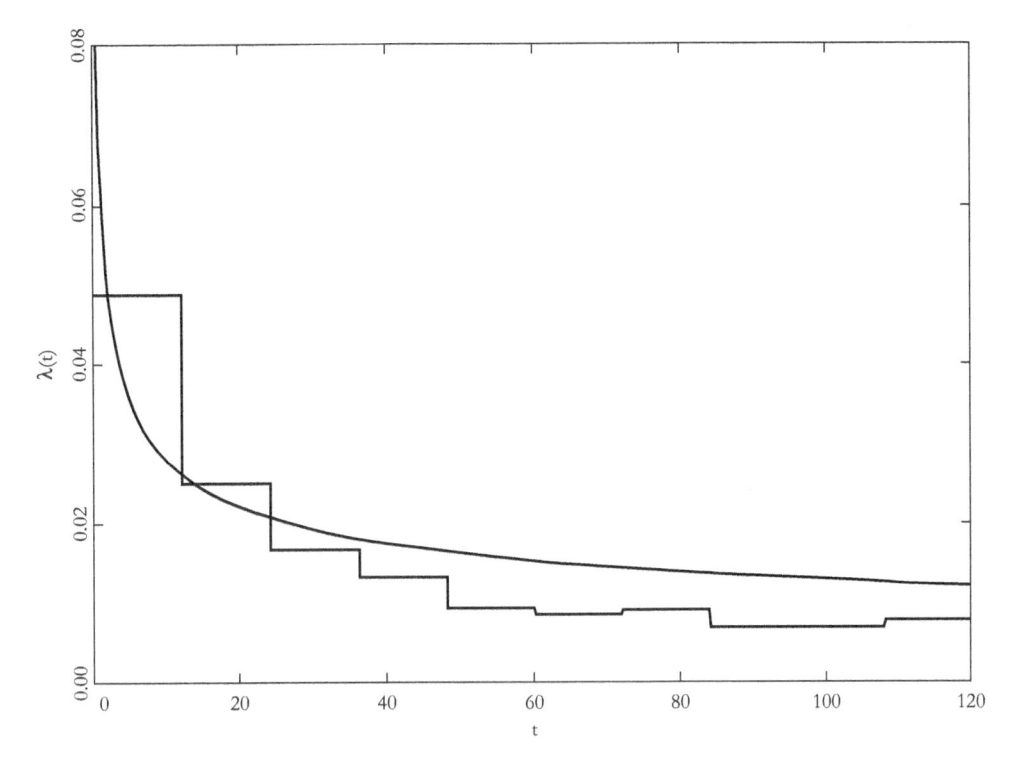

Figure 23.2 Plots of the rates estimated in columns 2 and 4 of Table 23.2. The trapeziodal curve is the piecewise constant rate in equation 27 and the smooth curve is the Weibull rate in equation 33, when $\gamma_1 = 0$. Duration (t) is measured in months.

Relationship Between the Rate and Probability of Event in a Period

It is useful to consider in more detail the accuracy of the approximation $\Delta t = 1$ in Equation 21 and hence how well the rate approximates the probability of an event in the next time interval. Assume that the rate is

$$\lambda(t) = \lambda_j \quad \text{if } t_j < t \leq t_j + 1. \quad (35)$$

The probability of no event between duration t_j and duration $t_j + 1$, given no event prior to t_j, is then given by

$$P(T > t_j+1 \mid T > t_j) = \exp(-\lambda_j), \quad (36)$$

and the probability of an event between duration t_j and duration $t_j + 1$, given no event prior to t_j, is

$$P(t_j < T \leq t_j+1 \mid T > t_j) = 1-\exp(-\lambda_j). \quad (37)$$

Note now that for a small λ_j,

$$\lambda_j \approx 1 - \exp(-\lambda_j). \quad (38)$$

For $\lambda_j = 0$, the approximation is exact. Note also that

$$\lambda_j > 1 - \exp(-\lambda_j) \quad \text{for all } \lambda_j > 0. \quad (39)$$

This means that the rate λ_j always is larger than the probability of an event in the relevant time interval, but that when small, the rate is close to the probability of an event in the next time interval.

Figure 23.3 plots the relationship between λ_j and the probability of an event between duration t_j and duration t_j+1, given no event prior to t_j, for values of λ_j in the interval 0 to 0.25. It shows that the discrepancy between λ_j and the probability of an event in the interval increases with λ_j and that the rate is larger than the true probability. For small rates—say, $\lambda_j \leq 0.10$—the two are very close. So, the approximation $\Delta t = 1$ is quite accurate when the rate is low. This is an important fact. It helps interpretation and presentation of results. When rates are small (e.g., 0.10 or lower), they can, for all practical purposes, be interpreted as the probability of an event (or transition) occurring in the next time interval of length one unit (e.g., week, month, year).

Time-independent Covariates

The hazard rate at duration t may depend not only on t, as in Equation 27 or 33 but also on explanatory variables. Explanatory variables can be grouped broadly into two types, which I treat separately: those that stay constant over time and those that change or may change over time. Examples of the former are sex, race, and birthplace. Examples of the latter are marital status, number of children,

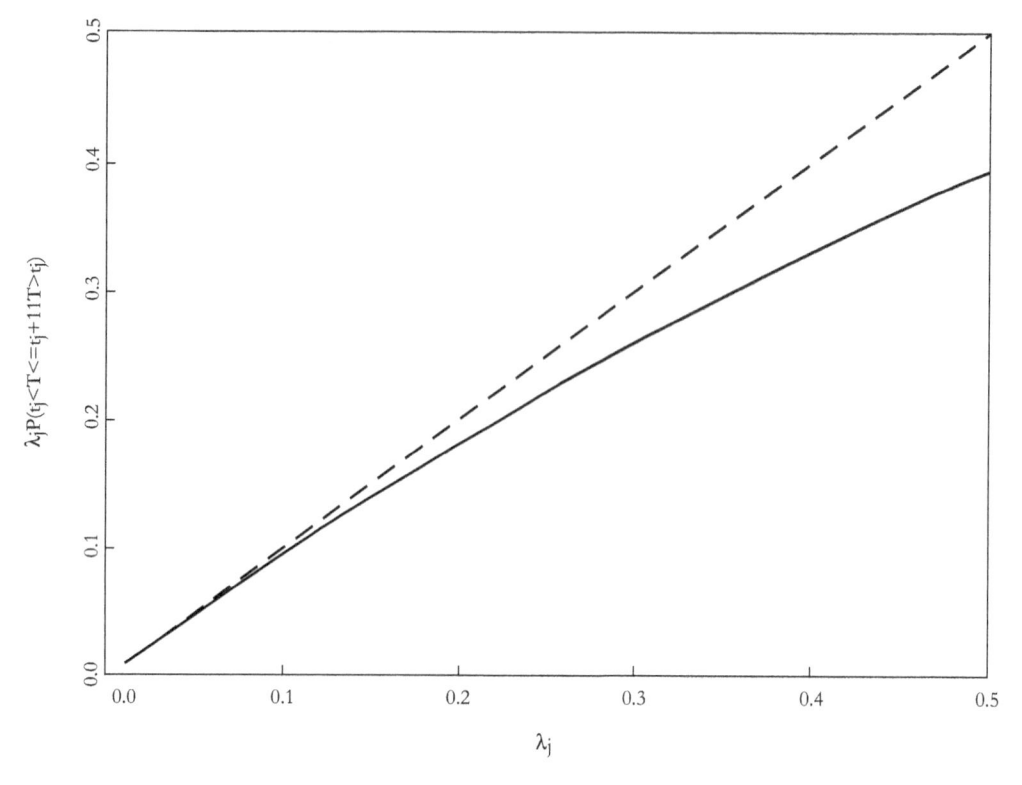

Figure 23.3 Plots of the relationship between the rate λ_j and the probability of an event between duration t_j and duration t_j+1, given no event prior to t_j, $P(t_j < T \leq t_j+1 \mid T > t_j)$, for values of λ_j in the interval 0 to 0.25, when the rate stays constant at λ_j in the interval t_j to t_{j+1}. The horizontal axis gives λ_j, whereas the vertical axis gives λ_j (the 45-degree dashed line) and $P(t_j < T \leq t_j+1 \mid T > t_j)$ (the full-drawn curve).

and socioeconomic status. This section describes the simpler case where the covariates stay constant over time; The Time-Dependent Covariates section discusses the more complicated case where they depend on time.

Let x denote the set of time-constant covariates. The hazard rate at duration t, given the covariates x, is now defined as

$$\lambda(t \mid x) \equiv \lim_{\Delta t \downarrow 0} P(t \leq T < t + \Delta t \mid T \geq t, x)/\Delta t, \quad (40)$$

giving the rate at which a transition occurs at duration t, given no transition before t, and given the covariates x. The hazard rate at each duration is allowed to vary not only by duration t, but also by measured covariates such as race and sex.

The survivor function, given the covariates x, is

$$P(T \geq t_k \mid x) = \exp[-\int_0^{t_k} \lambda(s \mid x)ds]. \quad (41)$$

It might be instructive to consider some specific examples of the hazard rate. This can easily be done within the framework of Equations 27 and 33 of the section on The Hazard-Rate Framework:

Continuous-Time Formulation. In the case of the exponential model, the approach is to say that the parameter α differs between groups in the sample, so that individual i has parameter, say, $\alpha_i = \beta x_i$, where x_i are the covariates for individual i, and β is a vector of effect parameters conforming to x_i, where x_i usually contains the constant 1, and the first element of β usually is the constant term. The rate in Equation 27 then becomes

$$\lambda(t \mid x_i) = \exp(\beta x_i). \quad (42)$$

The covariates shift the rate up and down. Therefore, differences may occur in the rates between individuals because of differences in the covariates. If $\beta_h > 0$, the corresponding covariate increases the rate; if $\beta_h = 0$, then has no effect on the rate; and if $\beta_h < 0$, then the covariate lowers the rate.

Specifications, Estimates, and Size of Coefficients

If x_i only contains a constant 1 and a single categorical covariate (e.g., race), that is, $x_i = (1, x_{1i})$—then the ML estimator of β in Equation 42 has an analytic expression. It is informative to consider this case. In the more general case where x_i contains either a continuous explanatory variable (e.g., years of education) or two or more explanatory variables (e.g., sex and race), no explicit expressions exist for the parameter estimates. They must be obtained by means of iterative procedures.

Suppose x_{1i} is a dummy variable equal to 0 or 1, in which case $\beta = (\beta_0, \beta_1)$, where, for example, 0 is equal to male and 1 to female. Let π_0 denote the proportion of noncensored observations for cases with $x_{1i} = 0$ and let π_1 denote the proportion of noncensored observations for cases with $x_{1i} = 1$. Further, let $\bar{t}_0$ denote the average duration for cases with $x_{1i} = 0$ and let $\bar{t}_1$ denote the average duration for cases with $x_{1i} = 1$. The ML estimators of β_0, $\beta_0 + \beta_1$, and β_1 are

$$\hat{\beta}_0 = \ln(\pi_0/\bar{t}_0), \qquad (43)$$

$$\widehat{\beta_0 + \beta_1} = \ln(\pi_1/\bar{t}_1), \qquad (44)$$

$$\hat{\beta}_1 = \ln[(\bar{t}_0/\bar{t}_1)(\pi_1/\pi_0)], \qquad (45)$$

and for the two rates

$$\hat{\lambda}(t \mid x_{1i} = 0) = \exp(\hat{\beta}_0) = \pi_0/\bar{t}_0, \qquad (46)$$

$$\hat{\lambda}(t \mid x_{1i} = 1)] = \exp(\hat{\beta}_0 + \hat{\beta}_1) = \pi_1/\bar{t}_1. \qquad (47)$$

As Equation 46 shows, the estimate of the rate for men equals the proportion of noncensored cases among men divided by the average duration for men, with the same relationship holding for the estimate of the rate for women. This is no different from the case without covariates in Equation 32.

We see from Equation 45 that the estimate of the effect β_1 of being female depends on two ratios: $\bar{t}_0$ to $\bar{t}_1$ and π_0 to π_1. Fixing $\pi_0 = \pi_1$ (the proportion of noncensored cases is equal for the two groups), the effect parameter β_1 for females is positive if the average duration for men $\bar{t}_0$ is larger than that for women, $\bar{t}_1$. This makes sense. The higher the rate, the lower the average duration. A positive value for β_1 indicates a higher rate for women. If, in contrast, the opposite holds (i.e., $\bar{t}_0$ is less than $\bar{t}_1$), then the estimate of β_1 will be negative. If $\bar{t}_0$ equals $\bar{t}_1$, then the estimate of β_1 will be zero: there are no differences in the rates between the two groups.

Conversely, fixing $\bar{t}_0 = \bar{t}_1$ (the average durations are equal for the two groups), then, if the proportion of noncensored cases is larger for men than for women, the estimate of β_1 is positive. Women have a higher rate. The opposite occurs when the proportion of noncensored cases is smaller for men than for women. When the two proportions are equal, the effect of being female is zero. This makes sense. Fixing the average durations to be equal, the group with the lower rate will experience a lower proportion of noncensored cases and vice versa.

In the case of the more general rate in Equation 33, the approach is the same. Typically, one assumes that γ_1 and γ_2 do not vary among groups in the sample (although one could allow this also to be the case), but that α does, yielding

$$\lambda(t \mid x_i) = \exp(\beta x_i + \gamma_1 t + \gamma_2 \ln t). \qquad (48)$$

Now, differences may occur in the rates between individuals at a given duration, because of differences in the covariates, and *intra*-individual differences may occur in the rate over time because of the effect of duration itself.

In the case of the Weibull model, where $\gamma_1 = 0$ in Equation 48, the survivor function becomes

$$P(T \geq t_k \mid x_i) = \exp[-\frac{1}{\gamma_2 + 1} t_k^{\gamma_2 + 1} \exp(\beta x_i)]. \qquad (49)$$

The size of the coefficients in Equations 42 and 48 will depend on (1) the units in which duration is measured, that is, days, weeks, and so on; (2) the units in which x is measured, as always; and (3) how often transitions occur, that is, the rate at which changes occur. Regarding (1), if duration is measured in months, the estimated monthly rates will be roughly four times bigger than the estimated weekly rates had durations been measured in weeks. Except for the constant term, the coefficients in β will not be affected by the units in which duration is measured. The reason for this is that a coefficient can be roughly interpreted as the percentage deviation in the rate from the baseline group captured by the constant term. This percentage deviation will be unaffected by the units in which duration is measured, in the same way as when the logarithm of a continuous dependent variable is regressed on covariates (only the constant term is affected by the scale of the dependent variable, i.e., whether it is measured in dollars or cents). These properties come well across in the ML estimators in Equations 43 and 45. For the constant term, the estimate from Equation 43 clearly depends on the units in which durations are measured. If duration is measured in years and fractions of years, then the denominator on the right of side of Equation 43 will be 12 times smaller than when durations are measured in months and fractions of months. This means that the constant term with durations measured in yearly units will be equal to $\ln 12 = 2.48$

plus the constant term when durations are measured in monthly units.[4] So the constant term merely gets adjusted the natural logarithm of 12. For the effect parameter β_1, we see that the estimate in fact is independent of the units in which durations are measured, because when one goes from monthly to yearly measurement, the monthly measurements in the first term on the right-hand side of Equation 45 are divided by 12 in both the numerator and denominator, thus cancelling each other. In the rate considered in Equation 43, the rate itself is twelve times larger for yearly than monthly measurements, so a monthly rate of .10 translates into an annual rate of 1.2, as can be seen from Equation 46. But in terms of the survivor function as well as all other relevant measures that can be derived from the rate, the meaning of the two numbers 0.10 and 1.2 are the same. For example, the probability of surviving the first year will be given by $\exp(-0.10 \times 12) = 0.30$ and $\exp(-1.2 \times 1) = 0.30$ in the case of monthly and annual measurements of durations, respectively.

Not much can be said about the number of observations needed to estimate the parameters of a rate. My experience is that hazard-rate models do not require more observation than binary logit and probit models do, nor are they harder to estimate. Parameter estimates are usually stable with respect to where one starts the iteration routine needed for estimating most hazard-rate models. For the model in Equation 42, final estimates are indeed independent of initial guesses, as the model contains no local maxima of the likelihood.

Illustration

An illustration of these procedures is found in Table 23.3, column 1. I use the same data as in Table 23.2 (*see* the section on The Hazard-Rate Framework: Continuous-Time Formulation) and estimate the same rate—the rate of departure—but add the covariates sex and race (White, Black, Hispanic, or Asian). The Weibull model is used—namely,

$$\lambda_d(t \mid x_i) = \exp(\beta_d x_i + \gamma_d \ln t), \quad (50)$$

where the subscript d denotes that this is the departure rate and that the coefficients β_d and γ_d pertain to that rate, so as to distinguish it from the promotion rate considered in the sections on Observability of the Dependent Variable and Repeated Events.

The seniority effect (i.e., γ_d) is similar to the one reported in Table 23.2. Men and Whites have higher departure rates than the other groups.

To illustrate the meaning of the size of the coefficients, it is useful to consider the constant rate model in equation Equation 42. That model allows one easily to calculate several measures. If we estimate this model using the same data and exclude duration from the variables listed in column 1 of Table 23.3, then we get the following estimates of the constant and the sex effect: -3.642 and -0.125. The estimated rate for White males is then $\hat{\lambda}(t \mid \text{Sex} = 0, \text{Race} = 0) = \exp(-3.642) = 0.026$ and for White women it is $\hat{\lambda}(t \mid \text{Sex} = 1, \text{Race} = 0) = \exp(-3.642 - 0.125) = 0.023$. Thus, the monthly probability of leaving the company is approximately 0.026 for White men and 0.023 for White women.

Because every employee sooner or later will leave the company, these rates can also be used straightforwardly to compute the expected time before a departure. For White men, the estimate is $\hat{E}(T \mid \text{Sex} = 0, \text{Race} = 0) = 1/0.026 = 38.4$ months, whereas for White women it is $\hat{E}(T \mid \text{Sex} = 1, \text{Race} = 0) = 1/.023 = 43.4$ months. Similarly, if we look at the survivor function, the probabilities of no departure occurring before 12 months are these. For White men it is 0.730, using the standard expression for the survivor function in Equation 23, or 0.727 using the approximation with $\Delta t = 1$ in Equation 21. For White women it is 0.757, using Equation 23, or 0.755, using the approximation with $\Delta t = 1$ in Equation 21. As we see, the approximation with $\Delta t = 1$ in Equation 21 is accurate.

Time-dependent Covariates
Basic Ideas

In this section, I treat the considerably more difficult case where the hazard rate depends on time-dependent covariates. These are covariates that may change over time. For example, in the analysis of departure rates, as in the previous two sections, some of the covariates on which the departure rate depends may change over time. This typically will be the case for salaries, for position within the company, and sometimes for work location. In the analysis of the rate, one would generally like to take account of these changes in the explanatory variables.

Time-dependent covariates are often grouped into three classes (Kalbfleisch & Prentice, 1980, pp. 122–127). First, there are the deterministic time-dependent covariates, such as calendar time or any function of time that is prespecified. Second, there are stochastic covariates that are generated by a stochastic mechanism external to the process being studied. An example may be fluctuations in interest

Table 23.3. Estimates of Effect Parameters on the Rates of Departure from and Promotion Within Company (Estimated Standard Errors in Parentheses)

	Departure		Promotion	
Constant	−2.7392 (0.0434)	−1.6095 (0.0730)	−0.0535*(0.0565)	1.4154 (0.1083)
Constant of hazard[a]			−6.1211 (0.0555)	−6.7603 (0.0619)
Duration[b]	−0.3345 (0.0083)	−0.2342 (0.0112)	1.0334 (0.0326)	0.9299 (0.0273)
Seniority[c]				−0.0024 (0.0003)
Time in grade[d]		−0.0025 (0.0010)		
Age[e]		−0.0134 (0.0012)		−0.0176 (0.0011)
Sex[f]	−0.0611*(0.0390)	−0.2288 (0.0398)	−0.2965 (0.0343)	−0.2448 (0.0353)
Race[g]				
Black	−0.0569*(0.0290)	−0.0543*(0.0295)	0.0164*(0.0265)	−0.1988 (0.0274)
Asian	−0.0226*(0.0962)	−0.0269*(0.0944)	0.0972*(0.0880)	0.0653*(0.0881)
Hispanic	−0.1817 (0.0481)	−0.1856 (0.0482)	0.1139 (0.0404)	−0.0846*(0.0409)
Education[h]		−0.4221 (0.0477)		0.2200 (0.0507)
Company Location[i]		−0.4797 (0.0283)		0.2387 (0.0236)
Salary grade level[j]				
2		−0.1478 (0.0336)		−0.2359 (0.0351)
3		−0.2580 (0.0349)		−0.3927 (0.0352)
4		−0.4610 (0.0400)		−0.5132 (0.0381)
5		−0.7344 (0.0516)		−0.5605 (0.0434)
6		−0.7111 (0.0845)		−0.8792 (0.0507)
L[k]	−36,368	−35,904	−39,949	−39,322
N	10,089	10,089	10,089	10,089
Number of events	7,947	7,947	32,815	32,815

*Not significantly different from zero at the five-percentage level (two-tailed tests).
Note: Data and estimation procedures are described in the note to Table 23.1 and in the Time-Independent Covariates section for the numbers in column 1, Time-Dependent Covariates for the numbers in column 2, and in the Repeated Events section for the numbers in columns 3 and 4. For the departure rate the Weibull model is used, see Equation 50 for the estimates in column 1 and Equation 56 for the estimates in column 2. For the promotion rate the proportional-hazards version of the log-logistic model is used; see Equation 69.
[a] This is the γ_0 parameter in the log-logistic model in Equation 69.
[b] For departures, duration is measured as months since employment in the company started (i.e., seniority). For promotions, duration is measured as months since the currently occupied salary grade level was entered.
[c] Seniority is measured as months of employment in the company. In the promotion rate its path is approximated by a step function, updated as a time-dependent covariate every 12 months.
[d] Time in grade is measured as months since the currently occupied salary grade level was entered. In the departure rate its path is approximated by a step function, updated as a time-dependent covariate every 12 months.
[e] This is the age of the employee measured in years. In both rates its path is approximated by a step function, updated as a time-dependent covariate every 12 months.
[f] Reference category: male.
[g] Reference category: White.
[h] High school education or more = 1; less than high school education = 0.
[i] Home office branch = 1; branch in another city = 0.
[j] Reference category: salary grade level 1.
[k] This is the log-likelihood of the model.

rates, which may influence the behavior of an individual but that themselves are not influenced by his or her behavior. But it could also be a covariate measured at the individual level, such as the age of one's children, presence of spouse, as long it is not influenced by the dependent failure-time process itself. Below, these types of covariates are referred to as exogenous. Third, there are stochastic covariates that are generated by a stochastic mechanism that is internal to the process being studied. An example might be how the number of children a couple has depends on whether they remain married. Now, whether the couple remains married or not may also depend on the number of children they acquire. Hence, marital status is a covariate that partly has been determined by the dependent fertility process. The latter types of covariates are referred to as endogenous to the dependent failure-time process.

The first type of covariates do not create any specific conceptual problems. The second and third do. The likelihood equations needed for estimation do not depend on whether covariates are deterministic or stochastic and, among the latter, on whether they are exogenous or endogenous. But the interpretation of the equations do. The part of the likelihood equation that has the mathematical form of survivor function, has the interpretation of a survivor function only when covariates are exogenous to the dependent failure-time process. The are many distinctions to be made here, the technicalities are at times involved. Below I just give some of the key points.

Let $x(t)$ be the vector of explanatory variables at duration t, where $x(t)$ may include lagged values of the explanatory variables. Let the entire history of the covariates all the way up to duration t be denoted $X(t)$, where the history could list the dates and values of variables such as marital status, children, earnings, and more. Finally let the value of the covariates and the history of the covariates at time t^-, which is immediately prior to time t, be denoted $x(t^-)$ and $X(t^-)$. In practice, the value of the covariates at time t^- would be the value in the prior week or month or some other time unit.

The hazard rate at duration t can now be defined as

$$\lambda[t \mid X(t^-)] \equiv \lim_{\Delta t \downarrow 0} P[t \leq T < t + \Delta t \mid T \geq t, X(t^-)]/\Delta t, \quad (51)$$

giving the rate at which a transition occurs at duration t, given no transition before t, and given the covariates up until but not including t. The reason that one conditions on the covariates up to but not including t is that the "cause" must preceed the effect in time.[5] Operationally, this means that in specifying the hazard rate at t, one uses lagged rather than contemporaneous values of the covariates. The length of the lag depends on the process and the frequency with which measures are available. If the process is measured down to monthly intervals, then one would, in specifying the hazard rate in month t, condition on the covariate process X up to and including month $t-1$ but not up to and including month t.

Exogeneity of Covariates

As mentioned above, covariates that change over time may either be endogenous or exogenous relative to the dependent failure-time process. The covariates are exogenous when they influence the probability of a failure but are themselves not influenced by the failure-time process. Otherwise they are endogenous. The relevant exogeneity condition, in the case when the covariates do not change at duration t, is [i.e., $x(t) = x(t^-)$]:

$$\lambda[t \mid X(t_k)] = \lambda[t \mid X(t^-)] \quad \text{for all } t_k > t, \quad (52)$$

which is an extension to continuous-time processes of Chamberlain's (1982) generalization of Sims' (1972) exogeneity condition for time-series data (see Petersen, 1995b). On the left-hand side of Equation 52 the conditioning at duration t on X is also on its future values all the way up to and including t_k.[6]

The exogeneity condition in Equation 52 says that when the covariates are exogenous to the dependent failure-time process, future values of the covariates are not informative with respect to the probability of a present failure. In contrast, when the covariates are endogenous to the dependent failure-time process, in which case they are outcomes of the failure-time process, their future values will add information about the probability of a current failure. The intuition is straightforward. If the covariates are influenced by the dependent failure-time process, then knowledge about their future values also adds knowledge about the current value of the failure-time process, because the latter also influenced the covariates.

The condition makes sense only when the covariates are stochastic. That is, covariates may exist whose future values will influence the likelihood of a present failure, but that are not endogenous, because they are nonstochastic. An example would be an inheritance determined at birth that is to be received at the age of 20 years. It may influence behavior before age 20 years, but is itself not influenced by that behavior.

One should also note that Equation 52 does not preclude expectations about the future influencing the probability of a transition at t, but expectations are assessments made in the present of what the future will be like and are to be distinguished from realizations of the future.

The Survivor Function

To obtain the survivor function, I consider the case where X and the dependent failure-time process can not change at the same time (see Petersen, 1995b). The survivor function, irrespective of whether the covariates are exogenous or endogenous, given the covariates from 0 to t_k, is then

$$P[T \geq t_k \mid X(t_k)] = \exp\{-\int_0^{t_k} \lambda[s \mid X(t_k)]ds\}. \quad (53)$$

As stated on the left-hand side of (6.3), one conditions at each $s < t_k$, not only on the covariates up to s but also on future values of the covariates (up until t_k).

Under the assumption of exogeneity of the covariates—that is, Equation 52—the survivor function, given the sequence of covariates from 0 to t_k, becomes:

$$P[T \geq t_k \mid X(t_k)] = \exp\{-\int_0^{t_k} \lambda[s \mid X(s^-)]ds\}. \quad (54)$$

In the integral on the right-hand side of Equation 54, one conditions at each $s < t_k$, on the history of the covariates up until and including s. This is justified by the exogeneity condition in Equation 52.

In most applications, the covariates in x change according to step-functions of time. That is, the covariates stay constant at, say, $x(t_j)$, from duration t_j to t_{j+1}, at which time they jump to $x(t_{j+1})$, and so on. In such cases, one needs to compute a conditional survivor function for each time period the covariates stayed constant. This yields:

$$P[T \geq t_{j+1} \mid T \geq t_j, X(t_{j+1})]$$
$$= \exp\{-\int_{t_j}^{t_{j+1}} \lambda[s \mid X(s^-) = X(t_j)]ds\}. \quad (55)$$

It gives the probability of surviving beyond duration t_{j+1}, given survival at t_j and given the covariates from 0 to t_{j+1}. The integral from t_j to t_{j+1} in Equation 55 is easy to evaluate. One just uses the covariates as evaluated at t_j, because X stays constant from t_j to t_{j+1}. For estimating the survivor function, this is tantamount to using X only up to t_j, because $x(t_{j+1}^-) = x(t_s) = x(t_j)$ for all s in the interval t_j to t_{j+1}^-. Note, however, that in the interpretation of the survivor function Equation 55, the conditioning is on X in the entire interval up to t_{j+1}.

The entire survivor function from duration 0 to duration t_k would consist of the product of the conditional survivor functions for each time period where the covariates stayed constant at $x(t_j)$ from t_j to t_{j+1}. There would be as many terms in this product as there are changes in the covariates. For example, if there is a single time-dependent covariate, such as the number of children a women has given birth to, then for a women with no births, there would be just one term in the survivor function, whereas for a women with two births, there would be three terms, one covering the first period from having no children to the first birth, a second covering the period from first to second birth, and the third the period from the second birth to the end of the observation period at t_k (when the women was last observed). The value of the covariate number of children would change from 0 to 1 to 2 between the three time periods.

With respect to estimation, much can be said, but the central results are these. If the covariates are exogenous, just use Equation 55 for each period within which the covariates X stayed constant, or more generally the expression in Equation 54 covering all periods. At the points in time when a failure occurs, the contribution is just the hazard rate. If the covariates are endogenous, then the same procedure can be used, as Kalbfleisch and Prentice (1980, pp. 121–127) have shown, but this is a topic that requires separate treatment. The central difference then is that when X is endogenous to the dependent failure-time process, the expressions on the right-hand side in Equations 54 and 55 no longer have interpretations as survivor functions.[7]

The construction of the likelihood equations used for estimation is independent of whether the covariates are exogenous or endogenous. When exogenous, the key part of the likelihood equation (on the right-hand side of Equations 54 and 55) have the interpretation of a survivor function. When endogenous, they no longer can be interpreted as such, and the relevant expression would be from the right-hand side of Equation 52, where we at each duration t take into account future in addition to past values of the covariates. This is not a quantity we would find interesting to estimate, nor a survivor function that we would like to compute. It is, however, an expression that could form the basis for testing whether the covariates are endogenous.

Data Management

Data management is cumbersome in the presence of time-dependent covariates. In most applications, the covariates change according to step-functions of time, and if they do not, their paths can be approximated by step-functions of time. The typical strategy is then to create a new record of data each time a change in one of the covariates occurs. There will be as many records of data as there are periods within which the covariates stayed constant. Each record will cover a period in which the covariates stayed constant. Each record then contains information about duration in the focal state (the dependent failure-time process) at the beginning of the period the record covers, duration at the end of the period the record covers, and whether a transition occurred at the end of the period the record covers, as well as the values of the covariates during the period the record covers (i.e., equal to their values at the beginning of the period). Justification for this procedure is found in the survivor function in Equation 55 above, where each piece of the survivor function pertains to a period in which the covariates stayed constant. This does not deflate standard errors or inflate statistical significance (*see* Petersen, 1986, pp. 229–233). Blossfeld, Hamerle, and Mayer (1989, pp. 199–205) have provided a detailed description of this procedure for data management in the presence of time-dependent covariates.

Illustration

An illustration of the use of time-dependent covariates is found in column 2 in Table 23.3. Added to the variables in column 1 are the following time-dependent covariates: the person's age (years), the time (months) spent in the currently occupied salary grade level, his or her education (high school vs. less), the salary grade level currently occupied, and the work location (home office versus branch in other city). The variables age of employee and time spent in the currently occupied salary grade level, change continuously with time. In this analysis, I approximate their continuous change by a step function. I let their values change every 12 months. The alternative solutions are either to let their values change every month or to let them change continuously. The first alternative is computer-intensive. The second requires numerical integration of the hazard rate and is, therefore, also computer-intensive. The rate is

$$\lambda_d[t \mid x_i(t^-)] = \exp[\beta_d x_i(t^-) + \gamma_d \ln t], \quad (56)$$

where the subscript d denotes departure rate and that the coefficients β_d and γ_d pertain to that rate—to distinguish it from the promotion rate considered in the sections Observability of the Dependent Variable and Repeated Events.

As in the results in Table 23.1 and in column one of Table 23.3, the departure rate declines with seniority. Time since last promotion has a negative effect on the rate of leaving the company. The longer one has waited without having received a promotion the less likely one is to leave. Age (years) has a negative effect, about half the effect of time in grade (months), when the latter is multiplied by 12. Employees with a high school degree have lower rates of departure than those without.[8] The rate of departure is lower in the home office than elsewhere. The rate of departure declines with the salary grade level among these lower-level clerical employees.

Observability of the Dependent Variable

Sometimes researchers write that the dependent variable in hazard-rate models is an unobservable quantity: the instantaneous rate or instantaneous probability of transition, the mathematical quantity the hazard rate. This is incorrect. It is worse than incorrect. It is obfuscation. We do not observe probabilities, and we do not observe any instantaneous probabilities. The dependent variable in hazard-rate models is not the hazard rate, but one of the two following, depending on one's point of view.

According to the first view, which I will call the event-history formulation, the dependent variable is whether an event takes place in a small time interval t to $t + \Delta t$ (now dropping the subscripts to periods of time used in The Hazard-Rate Framework: Continuous-Time Formulation section). That is, it is a zero-one variable that takes the value of 1 if an event takes place in the small time interval and 0 if not, given that no event had occurred prior to entry into the interval. We need as many such zero-one variables as there are observed time intervals for an individual.

According to the second view, which I will call the duration formulation, the dependent variable is the amount of time that elapses before an event or censoring occurs.

Both ways of viewing the dependent variable are equally valid, and they amount to the same specification, estimation, and interpretation of the models. Now I explore both viewpoints.

Let

$$D(t + \Delta t) = \begin{cases} 1 & \text{if a transition occurs in the time interval } t \text{ to } t + \Delta t, \\ 0 & \text{if no transition occurs in the time interval } t \text{ to } t + \Delta t. \end{cases} \quad (57)$$

From Equation 57,

$$P[D(t + \Delta t) = 1 \mid T \geq t, x] \approx \lambda(t \mid x)\Delta t, \quad \text{for small } \Delta t, \quad (58)$$

which can be made exact by replacing Δt on the right-hand side with Δt^*, where $\Delta t^* < \Delta t$, as in the section on The Hazard-Rate Framework: Continuous-Time Formulation.

If, at most, one change in D can occur between t and $t + \Delta t$, it follows that

$$D(t + \Delta t) = \lambda(t \mid x)\Delta t \\ + \epsilon(t), \quad \text{when } T \geq t \text{ and } \Delta t \text{ is small,} \quad (59)$$

where $\epsilon(t)$ is a stochastic error term with expectation 0, conditional on $T \geq t$, and x. This is a regression model with a binary dependent variable, whether an event takes place in a small time interval. Here, $D(t+\Delta t)$ is observable, $\lambda(t \mid x)\Delta t$ is the probability of $D(t+\Delta t)$ changing from 0 to 1 in the duration interval t to $t+\Delta t$, the quantity that we want to estimate, and $\epsilon(t)$ is the deviation between the observed dependent variable and what we want to estimate. This mirrors exactly any regression model with an observed dependent variable on the left-hand side of the equation, and its mean value and an error term on the right-hand side of the equation. Further, from Equation 59

$$E[D(t + \Delta t) \mid T \geq t, x] \\ \approx \lambda(t \mid x)\Delta t \quad \text{for small } \Delta t, \quad (60)$$

which also can be made exact by replacing Δt on the right-hand side with Δt^*, as above.

The point here is that in Equation 59, which captures the event-history formulation, the dependent variable is whether an event takes place between t and $t + \Delta t$, given no event before to t. This dependent variable takes the value of 0 in all time units in which no event takes place. Only in the last time unit may it take the value of 1, if the observation is noncensored. We use a model for this dependent variable where the focus is the hazard rate, the rate of transition at each point in time. Because Δt goes to 0, there will be infinitely many such zero-one variables that will account for the entire duration in a state. *We can conclude that the dependent variable in event-history analysis is observable.*

Once the hazard rate has been specified, the survivor function, $P(T \geq t \mid x)$, and the probability density function, $f(t \mid x)$, follow, by Equations 23 and 25. The mean value of the duration T can be derived from the probability density function, as

$$E(T \mid x) = \int_0^\infty s f(s \mid x) ds, \quad (61)$$

from which follows that

$$T = E(T \mid x) + \epsilon \\ = \int_0^\infty s f(s \mid x) ds + \epsilon, \quad (62)$$

where ϵ is a stochastic error term with mean 0, conditional on x.

For example, if the rate is

$$\lambda(t \mid x) = \exp(\beta x), \quad (63)$$

then

$$E(T \mid x) = \exp(-\beta x), \quad (64)$$

and hence

$$T = \exp(-\beta x) + \epsilon, \quad (65)$$

where we can estimate β by nonlinear least squares (henceforth NLLS). However, because we have specified a hazard rate, it is preferable to compute the ML rather than the NLLS estimates.[9]

Above, in Equation 65, we model the dependent variable—the amount of time that elapses before a transition occurs—as its mean value plus an error term, just as in standard regression analysis. The mean value is defined in terms of the parameters of the hazard rate. As in linear regression analysis for a continuous dependent variable, we model the mean of the dependent variable, conditional on covariates, as a linear or nonlinear function of the covariates. But, also as in standard regression analysis, it is not the mean of the dependent variable that is the dependent variable.

Again, *the central point is that the dependent variable is not some unobservable instantaneous rate*. In the representation in Equation 62, which corresponds to the duration formulation, the dependent variable is the amount of time that elapses before an event takes place. We focus on one aspect of this amount of time, the hazard rate, and we try to estimate the parameters of this rate.

Repeated Events

Sometimes a state once left can be re-entered. For example, once a tenant leaves a dwelling, a new tenancy in another dwelling can be entered, or once a job is left, a new job can immediately be re-entered or re-entered after unemployment, schooling or other events. Such processes are called *repeated event processes*.

I consider the case of job mobility. Each person in the sample has held at least one job and some have held two or more jobs. The focus of the analysis will still be on the determinants of the amount of time spent in each job. A straightforward extension of the framework developed in the earlier sections will accomplish this.

Consider a person who, when last observed, had held m jobs with durations $t_1, t_2, \ldots, t_m$, where the last duration may be censored. Note that t_j now refers to the amount of time spent in job j, not to the duration at which period j within a job was entered, as in the section on The Hazard-Rate Framework: Discrete-Time Formulation. Let $C_m = 0$ if the last job was censored and $C_m = 1$ if not.

Within the ML framework we need to derive the probability density of the entire job history of the person, which now is the unit of the analysis and which may consist of more than one job. Define

$$H_{j-1} \equiv \{t_g\}_{g=1}^{j-1} \quad \text{for } j \geq 2, \quad (66)$$

which gives the sequence of job durations for job 1 through job $j-1$.

The probability density of the entire job history can now be written

$$f(t_1, \ldots, t_m)$$
$$= f(t_1) \prod_{j=2}^{m-1} f(t_j \mid H_{j-1})$$
$$\times [\lambda(t_m \mid H_{m-1})]^{C_m} P(T_m \geq t_m \mid H_{m-1}), \quad (67)$$

where $f(t_j \mid H_{j-1})$ gives the density of the duration in job j, given the sequence of previous jobs 1 through $j-1$. The specification allows for full dependence of the duration in, say, job j on the previous job history. Covariates can be introduced in the manner discussed in the sections on Time-Independent Covariates and Time-Dependent Covariates.

Taking the logarithm of Equation 67 yields the log-likelihood of the job history of the individual as

$$L = \ln f(t_1) + \sum_{j=2}^{m-1} \ln f(t_j \mid H_{j-1})$$
$$+ C_m \ln \lambda(t_m \mid H_{m-1})$$
$$+ \ln P(T_m \geq t_m \mid H_{m-1}). \quad (68)$$

We see that the log-likelihood of the entire job history consists of the sum of the log-likelihoods of each job.

In specifying the hazard rate of leaving, say, job j, two procedures are common. In the first, one assumes that the shape of the rate and the parameters of the rate are the same for all jobs. Dependence on previous history may be captured through explanatory variables. In the second procedure, one assumes that the rate and its parameters differ from job to job, or at least between subsets of jobs (say, early and late jobs; see, e.g., Blossfeld & Hamerle 1989).[10]

When the form for the hazard rate and its parameters are common to all jobs, one just pools all the jobs on each individual, and estimates the parameters from the data on all the jobs. When the hazard rate and its parameters vary between jobs, depending on, say, the job number, one estimates the parameters separately for each job number. The parameters for job j are estimated from the durations in job j, and so on.

In both cases, one creates one record of data for each job a person held. Justification for this can be seen from Equation 68, where the log-likelihood of a person's job history is the sum of the log-likelihoods of each job. This sum can be computed from m different records of data on a person who held m jobs. It is important to note that this procedure for arranging the data makes no assumption about independence between the jobs on the same individual. The rate of transition in job j may, for example, depend on the amount of time spent in job $j-1$ or other aspects of the prior job history.

The procedure is valid if the rate in each job does not depend on unobserved variables that are common to or correlated across jobs within an individual's job history. Under this assumption each job can be treated as a separate observation, provided that we condition correctly on the past history of the process.

Note also that even if a possibly unobserved variable is neither common to nor correlated across jobs, ignoring it will still create biases. The bias created does not arise because each job is treated separately, but because the unobservable is not taken into account in deriving the likelihood, a problem that arises even if each sample member held only one job. Thus, restricting the analysis to only first jobs will still yield inconsistent estimates if there are unobservables and these are not taken into account in the likelihood.

Sometimes researchers also worry that individuals who held many jobs are given more weight in the analysis than individuals who held few jobs. This is a misunderstanding. Suppose we observed job histories for the first 10 years after graduation from college, for a total of 120 months. Some individuals may have held only one job, which then lasted 120 months, whereas other individuals may have held many more—for example, 10 jobs each lasting 1 year or 12 months. A researcher may be tempted to restrict the analysis only to the first job. For the first group of individuals, they would each contribute 120 months of data, whereas for the second group of individuals, each would contribute only 12 months of data. Focusing on the discrete-time formulation discussed earlier, which captures everything that is relevant for the event history formulation, the first group would contribute 120 probabilities to the likelihood equation, whereas the second group would only contribute 12 probabilities. The first group would be weighted 10 times more heavily. We thus would vastly oversample the job histories of individuals who stay with their employers for a long time. Had in contrast the interest been on the amount of time spent in the first job, as opposed to the amount of time spent in jobs, then analyzing only the first job would have yielded the correct results.

An analysis of repeated events is presented in columns 3 and 4 in Table 23.3, using the same data as in the section on The Hazard-Rate Framework: Discrete-Time Formulation through the section on Time-Independent Covariates. The focus is now on the promotion process, and estimates of the rate of promotion in the company are presented. The dependent duration variable is the number of months, measured as time spent in the currently occupied salary grade level that elapses before a promotion, departure, or censoring occurs. A person can be promoted several times. Hence, it is a repeatable-event process. The variables are the same as in columns 1 and 2, which were discussed in the sections The Hazard-Rate Framework: Continuous-Time Formulation and Time-Independent Covariates. The rate is specified as a proportional-hazards log-logistic model

$$\lambda_p(t \mid x(t^-)) = \frac{\exp(\gamma_0 + \gamma_p \ln t)}{[1 + \exp(\gamma_0 + (\gamma_p + 1)\ln t)]} \\ \times \exp[\beta_p x(t^-)], \quad (69)$$

where $\gamma_p > -1$ and β_p is a vector of parameters conforming to $x(t)$ (for a use of this model, see Petersen, Spilerman, & Dahl, 1989). When $\gamma_p < 0$, the rate declines monotonically with duration t. When $\gamma_p > 0$, the rate first increases with duration in grade, it then reaches a peak, whereafter it declines. That is, the rate is a bell-shaped function of time, which seems reasonable in the context of promotion processes (see, e.g., Petersen, Spilerman, & Dahl, 1989). In the specification, it is assumed that the shape of the hazard and its parameters are the same for all repetitions of the process.

Focusing on column 4, we see that the rate of promotion declines with the salary grade level. The higher up in the hierarchy a lower-level clerical employee is, the less likely he or she is to get promoted. The sex and race effects are as one would expect. Female and Black employees are less likely to be promoted. The effects of age and seniority on the promotion rate are negative. Employees in the home office have higher promotion rates than those employed elsewhere. Because $\gamma_p > 0$, the promotion rate is a bell-shaped function of time in grade, low during the initial months, then rising to a peak, whereafter it declines.

In Figure 23.4 the promotion rate, as a function of time in a grade level, is plotted for White men and White women. The plots are based on the estimates in column 3 of Table 23.3. The plots show that the promotion rate reaches its peak after about 20 months in a grade and that the rate for women is substantially lower than the rate for men.

Multistate Processes: Discrete State-Space

In most applications, when a failure or transition occurs, the person enters a new state or the transition occurs for a specific reason. Sometimes, the number of states that can be entered is finite. The state-space is then referred to as discrete, an example of which is labor force transitions between being employed and unemployed or out of the labor force, or in mortality research, a death can occur from illness, old age, murder, or suicide. There may also be a continuum of states, in which case the state space is referred to as continuous. Examples of the latter are individual-level socioeconomic status and earnings histories.

In this section, I discuss discrete state-space processes. In the next section, I discuss continuous state-space processes.

Let Z be a random variable denoting the state entered when a transition occurs, and let z denote a specific realization of Z, where Z is categorical—that is, it has a finite number of values. The *destination-specific* rate of transition, $\lambda_z(t \mid z_j)$, where z_j denotes the state occupied immediately prior to t, is defined as

$$\lambda_z(t \mid z_j) \equiv \lim_{\Delta t \downarrow 0} P(t \leq T < t \\ + \Delta t, Z = z \mid T \geq t, z_j)/\Delta t, \quad (70)$$

again dropping the subscripts to subperiods of time t_j. Equation 70 gives the rate at which a transition to state z occurs at duration t, given no transition prior to t and given that state z_j was occupied immediately prior to t. We specify the rate $\lambda_z(t \mid z_j)$ for all $z \neq z_j$. Covariates can be introduced in the same manner as in the sections on Time-Independent

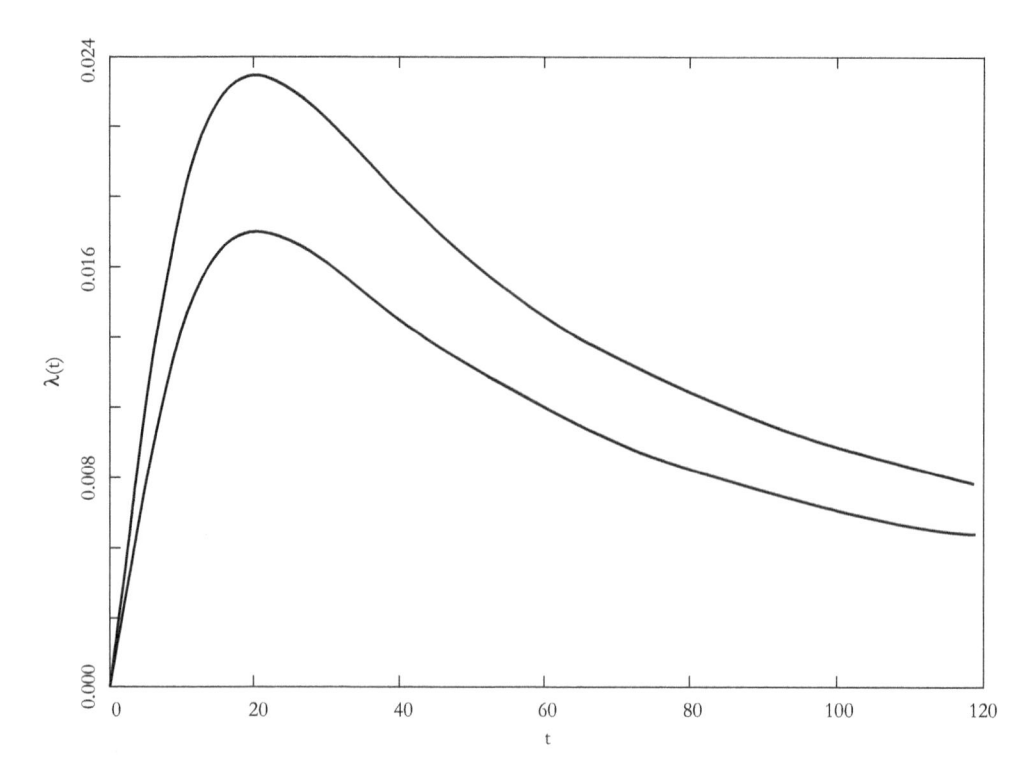

Figure 23.4 Plots of the estimated promotion rates in column 3 of Table 23.9, from the log-logistic model in Equation 63. Upper curve is the rate for White men and lower curve is the rate for White women. Duration (t) is measured in months.

Covariates and Time-Dependent Covariates and the rates may depend on the entire past history of the process, including the nature of previous transitions and durations.

Let z' denote the number of possible destination states. The overall rate of transition at duration t, irrespective of the destination state, follows by straightforward probability calculus as

$$\lambda(t \mid z_j) = \sum_{z=1}^{z'} \lambda_z(t \mid z_j), \quad (71)$$

because the z' states are mutually exclusive.

Let $P(Z = z \mid T = t, z_j)$ denote the probability that state z was entered, given that a transition occurred at t, and given that state z_j was occupied before the transition. It is defined as

$$P(Z = z \mid T = t, z_j)$$
$$= \lim_{\Delta t \downarrow 0} P(Z = z \mid t \leq T < t + \Delta t, z_j). \quad (72)$$

Because the states are mutually exclusive and exhaust the possible transitions, we get

$$\sum_{z \neq z_j} P(Z = z \mid T = t, z_j) = 1. \quad (73)$$

Using the chain-rule for probabilities, one can decompose the destination-specific rate of transition as follows

$$\lambda_z(t \mid z_j) = \lambda(t \mid z_j) \times P(Z = z \mid T = t, z_j), \quad (74)$$

that is, into the overall rate of transition times the probability of the destination state, given that a transition occurred.

The survivor function follows as

$$P[T \geq t \mid z_j] = \exp[-\int_0^t \sum_{z=1}^{z'} \lambda_z(s \mid z_j) ds], \quad (75)$$

which obtains by inserting the overall rate of transition in Equation 71 into the general expression for the survivor function in Equation 23 of the section The Hazard-Rate Framework: Continuous-Time Formulation.

In analyzing discrete state-space processes one can either specify the destination-specific rate of transition directly, as in Equation 70, or the overall rate of transition and the probability of the destination state, given a transition, as on the right-hand side of Equation 74. In the first case, one estimates the destination-specific rates directly. In the second case,

510 | ANALYZING EVENT HISTORY DATA

one estimates first the overall rate of transition, using a hazard rate routine, and then the probabilities of the destination states, given a transition, using—for example, a multinomial logit model.

Focusing on the destination-specific rate as in Equation 70, one can, for purposes of estimation, use a hazard-rate routine for estimating single-state space processes. Estimates of each of the destination-specific rates can be obtained by separate analyses. In estimating, say, $\lambda_1(t \mid z_j)$, each transition that occurred for reason 1 is treated as noncensored; all the other observations—that is, transitions to other states or censored observations, are treated as censored. To estimate all the z' different rates, just perform z' separate estimations, one for each destination state. This procedure is valid provided there are no restrictions on the parameters across the destination-specific rates and no unobserved variables common to, or correlated across, the rates. Each of the destination-specific rates may be given a separate functional form—Weibull, Gompertz, and so forth—and may depend on different explanatory variables.

An example of analysis of a multiple-state process is given in Table 23.4. Getting promoted and leaving the company are the two states. If a departure occurs, then a promotion cannot. However, if one is promoted, which is a repeatable-event process, one is still at risk for departing as well as at risk for further promotions.

In the departure analysis, the dependent duration variable is the number of months that elapses from the time a person enters the company until he or she leaves or until censoring (end of study) occurs. In the promotion analysis, the dependent duration variable is the number of months that elapses in a given salary grade before a promotion, departure, or censoring occurs.

Both sets of estimates were discussed in the sections on Time-Independent Covariates, Time-Dependent Covariates, and Observability of the Dependent Variable. I stress here what can be learned additionally from considering the two-state model.

First, we see that both the rates of departure and of promotion decline strongly with the salary grade level occupied. The higher up in the company, the less likely an employee is to leave and the longer it takes to get promoted. This probably means that the benefits accruing from being in the upper echelons of the salary grade levels for lower-level clerical employees must outweigh the drawback of the lower promotion rates once these grades have been reached. Otherwise, one would expect departure rates to increase with salary grade level.

Second, the rate of promotion is higher in the home office than elsewhere, whereas the rate of departure is lower. When opportunities for advancement are high, quit rates are lower, given the level of already obtained achievement—that is, the salary grade level. Thus, the two-state model gives insight into how employees respond in terms of departure rates to the opportunity structure of the company.

Multistate Processes: Continuous State-Space

For some processes the state-space is continuous. Examples arise in analysis of intragenerational mobility studies, where one focuses on changes in socioeconomic status, and in analysis of individual-level wage and earnings dynamics. If the state-space is continuous, then the framework of Equation 70 must be modified correspondingly (see Petersen, 1988, 1990b).

Let Y be the random and now continuous variable, and let y denote a specific realization of Y. In specifying the destination-specific rate of transition, focus on the probability density of y being entered in a small time interval, given what has happened up to the start of the interval (see Petersen, 1988, p. 144). The destination-specific rate of transition, $\lambda(t, y \mid y_j)$, where y_j is the state occupied immediately prior to, is defined as

$$\lambda(t, y \mid y_j) \equiv \lim_{\substack{\Delta t \downarrow 0 \\ \Delta y \downarrow 0}} P[t \leq T < t + \Delta t,$$
$$y \leq Y < y + \Delta y \mid T \geq t, y_j]/\Delta t \Delta y. \quad (76)$$

The definition of the rate in Equation 76 differs from the definition of the rate in the discrete state-space case in Equation 70 in that one divides by and takes the limit with respect to both Δy and Δt, whereas in Equation 70 one divides by and takes the limit only with respect to Δt. In Equation 76 one needs to take the limit also with respect to Δy because y is continuous and probability measures for continuous variables are defined in terms of the limits that give densities, as was already discussed in The Hazard-Rate Framework: Continuous-Time Formulation section.

Covariates can be introduced into the rate in Equation 76 in the same manner as in the sections on Time-Independent Covariates and Time-Dependent Covariates, and the rates may depend on the entire past history of the process,

Table 23.4. Estimates of the Effects on the Rate of Upward Shifts in Socioeconomic Status and of the Density of the New Socioeconomic Status Given that an Upward Shift Occured (Standard Errors in Parentheses)

Variables	Equation (82)[a]	Equation (83)[b]
Constant	−3.6420 (.0416)	10.7800 (.2052)
Duration (in months), γ	0.0005*(.0004)	
Labor force experience (in months), α	−0.0050 (.0004)	
Socioeconomic status before shift	−0.0780 (.0033)	0.6353 (.0181)
Education (1=high school or more)[c]	0.6630 (.0399)	5.0980 (.2272)
Sector (1=public, 0=private)	0.0960*(.0520)	−0.2470*(.2893)
Occupation[d]		
Manager	−0.7970 (.2564)	5.3560 (1.370)
Professional	−0.3608 (.1342)	−0.8122*(.7165)
Craftsman	−0.1081 (.0463)	1.1770 (.2630)
Log-likelihood[e]	−22727.4	
Number of events[f]	6523	3730

*Not significantly different from zero at the 0.05 level, two-tailed tests.
Source: Visher (1984, Table 5.2 and Table D). For exact definitions of the sample and variables, see Visher (1984, Chapter 5-6). The table was also published in Petersen (1988, Table 1, p. 160).
Note. The data were taken from the Norwegian Life History Study for Men (*see* Rogoff Ramsøy 1977, pp. 43-60; Visher 1981).
[a] These are ML estimates of the rate of upward shifts in socioeconomic status (from Visher 1984, Table 5.2, col. 1). For estimation procedures, *see* the note to Table 1.
[b] These are estimates of θ_1 and δ_1 in the density for the new value of socioeconomic status, given that an upward shift occured (from Visher 1984, Table D, panel B, col. 1). The estimates were obtained by least squares, which coincide with the ML estimates when the error term in Equation 83 is normally distributed.
[c] The reference category is educational attainment equal to junior high school, its equivalent (in years) or less.
[d] The reference category is manual workers.
[e] Using a likelihood ratio test, we can reject the constant rate model, $\lambda(t) = \lambda$, against the model in Equation 82 at any reasonable level of significance.
[f] In column 1, the number of observed spells is 6523, out of which 3730 are noncensored. In column 2, the number of observed upward shifts is 3730.

including the nature of previous transitions and durations (as discussed in Petersen, 1988).

The overall rate of transition follows, in a manner analogous to the discrete state-space framework in Equation 71, by integrating over all the destination-specific rates–namely,

$$\lambda(t \mid y_j) = \int_{D(y)} \lambda(t, y \mid y_j) dy, \quad (77)$$

where $D(y)$ denotes the domain of y.

Define, in a manner analogous to Equation 72, the density of the destination state, given a transition at duration t and given that state y_j was occupied prior to t, as

$$g(y \mid T = t, y_j) \equiv \lim_{\substack{\Delta t \downarrow 0 \\ \Delta y \downarrow 0}} P[y \leq Y < y + \Delta y \mid t \leq T < t + \Delta t, y_j]/\Delta y. \quad (78)$$

Because $g(y \mid T = t, y_j)$ is a density function for y, given that a change in y occurred at t, we find, analagously to Equation 73 in the discrete case, that

$$\int_{D(y)} g(y \mid T = t, y_j) dy = 1. \quad (79)$$

The destination-specific rate of transition can be decomposed into the overall rate of transition times the probability density of the destination state, analogously to Equation 74 in the discrete state-space framework–namely,

$$\lambda(t, y \mid y_j) = \lambda(t \mid y_j) \times g(y \mid T = t, y_j). \quad (80)$$

For estimation, one can either focus on the destination-specific rate directly (*see* Petersen 1990*b*), as in Equation 76, or on its decomposition into the overall rate of transition times the probability density of the destination state, given a transition (see Petersen 1988), as on the right-hand side of Equation 80.

The survivor function follows in complete analogy to Equation 75 in the discrete state-space case, as

$$P(T \geq t \mid y_j) = \exp[-\int_0^t \int_{d(y)} \lambda(s, y \mid y_j) dy ds], \quad (81)$$

which one may obtain either by specifying $\lambda(t, y \mid y_j)$ directly as in Equation 76 or by using the decomposition in Equation 80. In the latter case, one first integrates $g(y \mid T = t, y_j)$ over the domain of y, which yields 1. Thereafter, one integrates the overall rate of transition in Equation 77 from 0 to t.

I present an example of this framework using an empirical study by Visher (1984), as reported in Petersen (1988, pp. 157–161), using the two-step procedure where one specifies the overall rate of transition and the density of the destination state given that a transition occurred, as in Equation 78. The data were taken from the Norwegian Life History Study for Men, which was directed by Natalie Rogoff Ramsøy at the Institute of Applied Social Research in Oslo and is described in detail in Rogoff Ramsøy (1977, pp. 43–60). The Norwegian Central Bureau of Statistics collected and organized the data. A representative sample of 3,470 Norwegian men born in 1921, 1931, and 1941 were interviewed retrospectively on their life histories from age 14 years up to the date of interview in 1971. Detailed month-by-month employment histories as well as histories in other life spheres were collected.

The analysis focuses on the rate of upward shifts in socioeconomic status and on the value of socioeconomic status after an upward shift occurred. An upward shift is defined as a job change that results in an increase in socioeconomic status over the highest level previously attained. Almost all changes in socioeconomic status in this data set are upward. Job shifts leading to either no change or a downward change in socioeconomic status are treated as if no change occurred, as theories of intragenerational status attainment are primarily about gains in attainment and have little to say about downward and lateral changes in socioeconomic status (see Sørensen, 1984, pp. 91–93, 97). If a person holds more than one job before improving his attainment over the previous highest level, the duration before the upward shift is the sum of the durations in the jobs held since the previous highest level of attainment was reached. The measure of socioeconomic status (see Skrede, 1971) runs from a low of 3 to a high of 52 and can, for all practical purposes, be considered continuous.

The rate at which upward shifts occur depends on the sector in which the person works (private or public), on the highest level of socioeconomic status previously attained (i.e., y_j), educational attainment (junior high school or less, or high school or more), on occupational position (manager, professional, craftsman, or manual worker), on labor force experience, and on duration since the last upward shift. Other than y_j, all variables are treated as time-dependent, including labor force experience. The latter is allowed to vary continuously with time since the last upward shift (as detailed in Petersen, 1986, pp. 231–232). Visher (1984, p. 123) specifies the rate of upward shifts as (suppressing subscripts to individual observations)

$$\lambda_1[t \mid y_j, x^{(t-)}, L_j]$$
$$= \exp[\beta x^{(t-)} + \rho y_j + \alpha(L_j + t) + \gamma t], \quad (82)$$

where β is a vector of parameters giving the effects of the covariates in x, which includes a constant 1, education, sector, and occupation, measured as of the job held immediately prior to duration t; L_j is the employee's labor force experience (measured in months) at the date the last upward shift occurred; $L_j + t$ is the labor force experience at duration t after the last shift occurred, with effect α; y_j is the highest socioeconomic status previously reached and ρ its effect; and γ is the effect of duration since the last shift.

The specification for the new value of socioeconomic status, given that an upward shift occurred, is

$$y_{j+1} = \theta_1 x_j + \delta_1 y_j + \epsilon, \quad (83)$$

where θ_1 is a vector of parameters giving the effects of the covariates in x_j, which includes a constant 1, education, sector, and occupation; δ_1 gives the effect of the highest level of socioeconomic status previously attained, and ϵ is a stochastic error term (see Visher, 1984, p. 158). Sector and occupation are measured as of the job held immediately prior to the change in Y (if that job differs from the job held when status y_j was entered). It is assumed that the parameters pertaining to the new value of Y, given a shift in direction d, differ for upward and downward shifts. Hence, we can correctly estimate Equation 83 on the basis of upward shifts alone, with no correction for truncation, because there is no truncation problem, as discussed in Petersen (1988, eq. [19]).

In Visher's specification, therefore, the rate of an upward change in Y depends on its highest value previously reached, on the time since that value was obtained, and on the exogenous variables, as seen from Equation 82. The density of the new value of Y, given that an upward shift occurred, depends on the highest value of Y prior to the change and on the exogenous variables, but not on time since y_j was reached, as seen from Equation 83. There is, however, nothing in the general model specification that prevents one from entering the time elapsed since status y_j was achieved as a predictor in Equation 83.

Assuming that there is no autocorrelation in the ϵ's and that the expectation of ϵ, conditional on an upward shift and on the right-hand-side variables in Equation 83, is zero, the parameters of Equation 83 can be consistently estimated by linear least squares. No distribution needs to be imposed on the error term. If the latter is normal, then least squares and ML coincide, and if not, then least squares still yields consistent estimates, under the usual assumptions. The parameters of the hazard rate were estimated by ML (e.g., Tuma & Hannan, 1984, Chapter 5).

Table 23.4 gives the estimates of Equations 82 and 83 (taken from Visher 1984, Table 5.2, col. 1 and Table D, panel B, col. 1). I will not comment on every number in the table. Rather I will focus on the conclusions from this analysis that one could not obtain solely from analyses of the rate of upward shifts or of the size of shifts. In the first column we see that managers have a lower rate of upward shifts than the other occupational groups. That is, on the average they wait longer before experiencing an upward shift (net of the other variables).

From the analysis of upward shifts alone, as in Sørensen and Tuma (1981), one would conclude that managers are the most constrained in their opportunities for increasing rewards, a conclusion that seems plausible in light of their already high rewards and the ceiling effects that may set in. In the second column, we see that managers on the average make the largest jumps, given that an upward shift occurred. From the analysis of the size of the gain alone, as in Sørensen's (1974) difference equation model approach, one would conclude that managers are the least constrained in their opportunities to get ahead. Considering both Equations 82 and 83 yields a more nuanced picture. The process of intragenerational mobility appears to differ between managers and the reference group, manual workers,

in the following way. The former wait longer before they experience upward shifts, but once they shift, they also jump farther. Managers climb in few, but long, steps, whereas manual workers climb in many, but correspondingly shorter, steps. The approach taken here to the study of continuous state-space failure time processes, allows us to characterize the difference in the processes in this way.

Conclusion

I have given an introduction to event history analysis. The central goals, rather than giving a comprehensive, and thus—by necessity—cursory treatment, have been first to attempt to justify why what perhaps must be considered an unusual modeling approach is needed (in the second section above), and next to explicate in some detail what the key ideas from probability theory are and how these ideas solve the problems that arise when using more standard techniques such as regression analysis for continuous dependent variables or logit analysis for binary dependent variables. Elaborations for how to take account of measured variables were given in the sections on Time-Independent Covariates and Time-Dependent Covariates. After discussing at some length a topic that is not always obvious to researchers—namely, what the dependent variable is in event history analysis—elaborations of the framework to repeated event processes.

Much more could be written, including details on estimation, the consequences of unobserved variables, bias arising from measuring durations only in grouped intervals (e.g., Petersen, 1991b), the use of continuous versus discrete-time models, how to deal with grouped measurements of the duration in state, the role of sampling plans, and much more. Each of these topics raises interesting and important questions.

I thank the editor and an anonymous reviewer for comments. The paper draws on Petersen (1995a).

Notes

1. This paper expands on the materials in Petersen (1990a, 1991a, 1995a). There are several monograph-length treatments of event-history analysis, such as Tuma and Hannan (1984), Blossfeld, Hamerle, and Mayer (1989), Lancaster (1990), and Box-Steffensmeier and Jones (2004) in the social sciences, and Kalblfeisch and Prentice (1980), Fleming and Harrington (1991), and Laan and Robins (2003) in statistics.

2. An exception to this characterization is the counting-process framework (see Andersen & Borgan 1985), where the concept of a failure time plays only a marginal role.

3. The relationship between the rate $\lambda(t_j)$ and Δt^*, when $\lambda(t_j)$ stays constant in the interval t_j to t_j+1 (i.e., $\Delta t=1$), is $\Delta t^* = \{1 - \exp[-\lambda(t_j)]\}/\lambda(t_j)$.

4. This follows because $\hat{\beta}_0 = \ln(\pi_0/\bar{t}_0/12) = \ln(\pi_0/\bar{t}_0) + \ln 12$.

5. Andersen and Gill (1982) provide additional technical justifications for this type of specification.

6. Petersen (1995b) provides a more extensive treatment of exogeneity conditions in hazard-rate models. These issues are difficult and no comprehensive treatment exists in the literature. Lancaster (1990, especially Chapter 2) gives a partial treatment, drawing on an earlier (1986) version of Petersen (1995b).

7. Petersen (1995b) treats these issues in considerable detail and discusses alternative approaches.

8. In Petersen (1991a, Table 2) the education variable was incorrectly coded so that the reported estimate of having a high school degree was positive.

9. The hazard rate uniquely defines the survivor and density functions. NLLS relies on specification of the hazard rate and hence on the entire probability distribution of the duration. But then ML is more efficient, whereas NLLS has no gains in terms of being more robust.

10. Using the same data as in Tables 23.1 and 23.2 to analyze promotion processes, Petersen, Spilerman, and Dahl (1989) employ the first procedure, whereas a variant of the second is used in Petersen and Spilerman (1990).

References

Allison, P. D. (1982). Discrete-time methods for the analysis of event histories. In S. Leinhardt (ed.), *Sociological Methodology 1982* (pp. 61–98). San Francisco, CA: Jossey-Bass.

Andersen, P. K., & Borgan, Ø. (1985). Counting process models for life history data: A review (with discussion). *Scandinavian Journal of Statistics 12*, 97–158.

Andersen, P. K., & Gill, R. D. (1982). Cox regression model for counting processes: A large sample study. *Annals of Statistics 10*, 1100–1120.

Apostol, T. M. (1967). (2nd ed.) *Calculus. Volume 1*. New York: Wiley.

Blossfeld, H.-P., Hamerle, A. & Mayer, K. U. (1989). *Event History Analysis*. Hillsdale, NJ: Erlbaum.

Box-Steffensmeier, J. M., & Jones, B. S. (2004). *Event History Modeling. A Guide for Social Scientists*. New York: Cambridge University Press.

Chamberlain, G. (1982). The general equivalence of Granger & Sims causality. *Econometrica 50*, 569–581.

Fleming, T. R., & Harrington, D. P. (1991). *Counting Processes and Survival Analysis*. New York: John Wiley and Sons.

Flinn, C. J., & Heckman, J. J. (1983). Are unemployment and n out of the labor force behaviorally distinct labor force states. *Journal of Labor Economics 1*, 28–42.

Hernes, G. (1972). The process of entry into first marriage. *American Sociological Review 37*, 173–182.

Kalbfleisch, J. D., & Prentice, R. L. (1980). *The Statistical Analysis of Failure Time Data*. New York: Wiley.

Laan, M. J. van der, & J. M. Robins. (2003). *Unified Methods for Censored Longitudinal Data and Causality*. New York: Springer.

Lancaster, T. (1990). *The Econometric Analysis of Transition Data*. New York: Cambridge University Press.

Petersen, T. (1986). Estimating fully parametric hazard rate models with time- dependent covariates. Use of Maximum Likelihood. *Sociological Methods and Research 14*, 219–246.

Petersen, T. (1988). Analyzing change over time in a continuous dependent variable: Specification and estimation of continuous state space hazard rate models. In C. C. Clogg (Ed.), *Sociological Methodology 1988* (pp. 137–164). Washington, D.C.: American Sociological Association.

Petersen, T. (1990a). Analyzing event histories. In A. von Eye (Ed.), *New Statistical Methods in Longitudinal Research. Volume 2* (pp. 258–288). Orlando, FL: Academic Press.

Petersen, T. (1990b). Analyzing continuous state space failure time processes: Two further results. *Journal of Mathematical Sociology 10*, 247–256.

Petersen, T. (1991a). The Statistical Analysis of Event Histories. *Sociological Methods and Research 19*, 270–323.

Petersen, T. (1991b). Time-aggregation bias in continuous-time hazard-rate models. In P. V. Marsden (Ed.), *Sociological Methodology* 1991, Volume 21, (pp. 263–290). Cambridge, MA: Basil Blackwell.

Petersen, T. (1995a). Analysis of Event Histories. Chapter 9 In G. Arminger, C. C. Clogg, & M. E. Sobel (Eds.). *Handbook of Statistical Modeling for the Social and Behavioral Sciences*. (pp. 453–517) New York: Plenum Press.

Petersen, T. (1995b). Models for Interdependent Event History Data: Specification and Estimation. In P. V. Marsden (Ed.). *Sociological Methodology* 1995, Volume 25, (Pp. 317–375). Cambridge, MA: Basil Blackwell.

Petersen, T., & Spilerman, S. (1990). Job–quits from an internal labor market. In K. U. Mayer & N. B. Tuma (Eds.), *Applications of Event History Analysis in Life Course Research*. Madison, WI: University of Wisconsin Press.

Petersen, T., Spilerman, S. & Dahl, S.-Å. (1989). The structure of employment termination among clerical employees in a large bureaucracy. *Acta Sociologica 32*(4), 319–338.

Rogoff Ramsøy, N. (1977). *Sosial Mobilitet i Norge* (Social Mobility in Norway). Oslo: Tiden Norsk Forlag.

Sims, C. A. (1972). Money, income, and causality. *American Economic Review 62*, 540–552.

Skrede, K. (1971). *Sosioøkonomisk Klassifisering av Yrker i Norge, 1960* (Socioeconomic classification of Occupations in Norway, 1960). Report 71-1. Oslo: Institute of Applied Social Research.

Sørensen, A. B. (1974). A Model for Occupational Careers. *American Journal of Sociology 80*, 44–57.

Sørensen, A. B. (1984). Interpreting Time Dependency in Career Processes. In A. Diekman & P. Mitter (Eds.). *Stochastic Modelling of Social Processes*, (pp. 89–122). New York: Academic Press.

Sørensen, A. B., & Tuma, N. B. (1981). Labor Market Structure and Job Mobility. In D. Treiman & R. V. Robinson (Eds.).

Research in Social Stratification and Mobility, Vol. 1, ed. D. Treiman and R. V. Robinson. Greenwich, CT: JAI Press.

Tuma, N. B. (1976). Rewards, resources and the rate of mobility: a nonstationary multivariate stochastic model. *American Sociological Review 41*, 338–360.

Tuma, N. B., & Hannan, M. T. (1984). *Social Dynamics. Models and Methods*. Orlando, FL: Academic Press.

Vaupel, J. W., Manton, K. G. & Stallard, E. (1979). The impact of heterogeneity in individual frailty on the dynamics of mortality. *Demography 16*, 439–54.

Visher, M. G. (1984). The Workers of the State and the State of State Workers: A Comparison of Public and Private Employment in Norway. Ph.D. diss., Department of Sociology, University of Wisconsin, Madison.

CHAPTER
24 Clustering and Classification

André A. Rupp

Abstract

In this chapter I first describe core terminology, notation, and related readings for certain core clustering and classification techniques. I then discuss the theoretical underpinnings and practical applications of nonparametric techniques that do not require distributional assumptions on outcome variables followed by parametric/model-based techniques that do require such assumptions. In the former set, I specifically discuss hierarchical clustering techniques and K-means clustering techniques. In the latter set I specifically discuss univariate and multivariate finite mixture models, unrestricted latent class models, and restricted latent class models. I further show how so-called diagnostic classification models are a particularly useful class of restricted latent class models for calibration and scaling purposes in educational and psychological measurement.

Key Words: Clustering, classification, K-means cluster analysis, hierarchical cluster analysis, finite mixture models, unrestricted latent class models, restricted latent class models, diagnostic classification models

Introductory Remarks

In this chapter I describe core statistical techniques that are used across various fields and disciplines for the purposes of clustering and classification. Generally speaking, clustering techniques are designed to sort a set of observations into groups that are not directly observed, whereas classification techniques are designed to assign a set of observations into groups that are directly observed. This leads to a linguistic distinction between clustering techniques as techniques for *unsupervised learning* and classification techniques as techniques for *supervised learning* in the literature; some techniques even combine attributes of both types of technique and might be called techniques for *semi-supervised learning*.

Similarly, some authors suggest that clustering techniques are designed to perform sorting operations on a given data set to *explain* its underlying structure, whereas classification techniques are designed to *predict* the group membership of observations in future data sets. Viewed from this methodological angle, clustering techniques do not require an explicitly declared outcome variable, whereas classification techniques do require such a variable for prediction.

Although these distinctions have some intuitive appeal on a surface level, nuances in the techniques and their applications mask overlapping characteristics of both types of techniques, however. First, as with other statistical techniques, the stability of any solution and the defensibility of any resulting interpretations are at issue in applications of both clustering and classification techniques. Second, clustering cases is akin to creating unobserved subsets or groups in the data. Consequently, although the process is not one of statistical prediction, existing cases are "classified," in the everyday sense of the word, into one of these different groups. Third, certain types of restricted latent class models that I discuss at the end of this chapter can be used to describe a number of unobserved groups in the data, akin to clustering techniques, but also to probabilistically classify respondents into the resulting groups in a given and in future data sets, akin to classification techniques.

In short, rather than dogmatically and uncritically using either the term *clustering* or the term *classification*, I believe it is much more beneficial to carefully reflect on the objectives of any given technique, its implementation, and the evidentiary narratives its application can support. Consistent with this belief, I sometimes use one of the two terms in isolation and sometimes I use both terms in juxtaposition, depending on the particularities of the narrative at that point in the chapter.

Range of Applications

Clustering and classification techniques are often associated with the general umbrella term of *multivariate data analysis*, because multiple outcome variables are involved in the analyses. To truly appreciate the breadth of research and practice around various clustering and classification techniques across different disciplines and fields of study, however, it is necessary to go beyond this description. For example, consider that searches on clustering and classification techniques in professional data bases for peer-reviewed research such as *PsychInfo* yield thousands of results that include both real-life applications and new methodological studies.

Similarly, areas of application for clustering and classification techniques listed under various key words in Wikipedia include biology, medicine, market research, mathematical chemistry, petroleum geology, physical geography, crime analysis, sociology, software engineering, and data mining. Consequently, the interpretations and decisions that are made on the basis of the clustering and classification techniques range widely in terms of their purpose, their complexity, and their associated stakes for individuals and institutions (for a similar argument supported by 10 exemplar studies, *see* Kettenring, 2006).

Scope of Chapter

My introductory remarks underscore that it would be impossible for me to comprehensively cover the entirety of methodological and practical approaches that could be conceptually associated with clustering and classification techniques. Rather, my aim in this chapter is to give readers a sense of the core dimensions, boundaries, and complexities of the methodological space that serves to characterize clustering and classification techniques. It is my hope that upon reading this chapter, readers will feel empowered to dig deeper into particular methodological techniques that suit their particular application purposes best. I also hope that readers will be able to engage intelligently in debates with members of interdisciplinary teams regarding the nuances of different assumptions, choices, and interpretations that are made for evidentiary reasoning using clustering and classification techniques.

Chapter Organization

I have divided this chapter into two core sections that characterize a particular journey through the methodological space of clustering and classification techniques. In the first core section, I will mimic traditional discussions of clustering techniques in multivariate textbooks. Roughly speaking, I will discuss *nonparametric clustering techniques* that fall under the umbrella terms *hierarchical* and *partitioning* techniques. This requires me to discuss some of the key underpinnings of these techniques, such as interobject distances in multivariate space, measures of intercluster distances between clusters, and algorithms for combining objects into clusters.

I want to note that these are the two most commonly used umbrella terms for these methods, but researchers generally make further distinctions. For example, Gan, Ma, and Wu (2007) have distinguished between hierarchical clustering techniques, fuzzy clustering algorithms, center-based clustering algorithms, search-based clustering algorithms, graph-based clustering algorithms, grid-based clustering algorithms, density-based clustering algorithms, model-based clustering algorithms, subspace clustering, and miscellaneous algorithms that do not fit any of these categories well. Obviously, I cannot discuss all of these techniques in this chapter, but the two selected sets of techniques are representative of the basic ideas of many techniques in the literature.

In the second core section of this chapter, I will then transition to *parametric/model-based clustering and classification techniques* grounded in latent class analysis, which are quite commonly used in the social and behavioral sciences generally and educational and psychological measurement specifically. I will specifically discuss *univariate finite mixture models*, *multivariate finite mixture models*, *unrestricted latent class models*, and *restricted latent class models*. As part of the set of restricted latent class models, I will discuss a subset of models known as cognitive diagnosis models or *diagnostic classification models* (DCMs), which are the focus of my own research (e.g., Rupp & Templin, 2008; Rupp, Templin, & Henson, 2010). They are also, in some sense, the state of the art for creating multivariate profiles of respondents for diagnostic assessment contexts, which is one of the key areas of research and practical interest in modern educational and psychological measurement. Before concluding the chapter, I will also briefly discuss the assessment of model-data fit at different global and local levels.

As this description has suggested, the organization of this chapter is driven, in part, by the somewhat natural progression from nonparametric to parametric techniques resulting from theoretical connections that exist between them and, in part, by my own expertise in the area of restricted latent class models for educational and psychological measurement. Before I begin the two core sections in this book, however, I want to outline some key terminology, suggested references, and notation.

Terminological Foundations, Suggested Readings, and Chapter Notation
Terminological Foundations
OBSERVATIONS VERSUS VARIABLES

As has already been apparent, it can be challenging to describe clustering and classification techniques using a common vocabulary, especially if interdisciplinary applications are considered. To create a reasonable sense of coherence in this chapter, I will describe the resulting sets that define group membership as *clusters* or *groups* when nonparametric techniques are used and as *classes/latent classes* when parametric/model-based techniques are used. I will use the term *cases* when non-human entities such as computers, cars, or mice are being clustered/classified and the term *respondents* when human beings are being clustered/classified. Finally, I will use the term *outcome variables* when cases are clustered/classified and the term *response variables* when respondents are clustered/classified.

VARIABLE TYPES VERSUS MEASUREMENT SCALES

The most commonly used terminology for describing the structure of a data set to which a clustering or classification technique is applied is describing it as a *two-mode structure* (i.e., a two-dimensional tabular structure), where one mode represents the cases/respondents (i.e., the rows) and one mode represents the outcome/response variables (i.e., the columns). In many clustering and classification techniques, the raw data get transformed into matrices that represent *similarities/dissimilarities/distances* between cases/respondents in the multivariate space that is spanned by the multiple outcome/response variables.

Based on the seminal, yet not undisputed, work of Stevens (1946), most specialists distinguish between four *measurement scales* for a variable: nominal, ordinal, interval, and ratio. Put simply, for nominal scales an assignment of observations to unordered levels of a variable has to be well-defined, for ordinal scales a linear ordering of the observations across the levels of a variable has to be well-defined, for interval scales differences between numerical scores have to be well-defined, and for ratio scales ratios of numerical scores have to be well-defined. For example, a sex categorization (i.e., "male" vs. "female") results in a nominal variable, a graded Likert scale (e.g., "do not agree," "undecided," "strongly agree") results in an ordinal score variable, a proficiency score estimate in a large-scale assessment is an interval-scaled variable, and a measure such as response times is a ratio-scaled variable.

Alongside the measurement scale distinction, there are also distinctions among different *variable types*: researchers recognize *continuous variables* versus *discrete variables*, *quantitative variables* versus *qualitative variables*, and *categorical variables* versus *noncategorical variables*. Specifically, variables measured on nominal scales are discrete/categorical qualitative variables, whereas variables measured on ordinal scales are discrete/categorical quantitative variables. Variables measured on interval scales are continuous/noncategorical quantitative variables, whereas variables measured on ratio scales are continuous/noncategorical quantitative variables also.

Despite this seeming clarity, there are a few nuances to this organization. For example, count variables such as the number of attempts for performing a task within a given time interval are somewhat different because they require unique statistical distributions in parametric statistical models. They can be said to be quantitative discrete variables measured on ratio scales because ratios of counts are well defined, but most practitioners would probably first and foremost associate continuous variables with ratio scales. In addition, the literature on categorical data analysis (e.g., Agresti, 2007) is focused primarily on variables measured on nominal and ordinal scales but also includes count variables.

In the end, for the purpose of this chapter, it is less important to understand the nuances of theories about measurement scales. Rather, it is important to keep in mind that each variable has descriptive statistics that are appropriate for it and inferential statistics that depend on appropriate distributional assumptions tied to its measurement scale and the data collection design that gave rise to the data. Thus, if key assumptions of a clustering and classification technique are violated, then there may be (1) biases in the recovery of the true cluster structure for nonparametric techniques or (2) biases of point estimates of parameters or their associated standard errors for parametric/model-based techniques, unless a technique is reasonably robust to the particular violations that exist.

NON-PARAMETRIC VERSUS PARAMETRIC/MODEL-BASED TECHNIQUES

As has been implicitly clear, I will refer to any statistical approach for clustering and classification generically as a *technique* in this chapter and will reserve the term *method* for computational algorithms that are used for parameter estimation or for steps like variable standardizations. Similarly, I believe that a didactically useful distinction can be made between *nonparametric techniques* and *parametric/model-based techniques*, which is reflected in the two main sections of this chapter. Both of these sets of techniques minimize or maximize *objective functions* to obtain computational solutions, but they differ in whether they make *distributional assumptions* about the outcome variables to specify the objective functions.

Nonparametric techniques do not rely on distributional assumptions of the outcome/response variables unless secondary inferential statistical tests are invoked as part of the evidentiary reasoning process. They typically utilize second-order representations (e.g., covariance matrices/similarity matrices/distance matrices) of the data to perform the requisite computations. The techniques in the first core section of this chapter, hierarchical clustering techniques and K-means cluster analysis, can be subsumed under this general heading for didactic purposes.

Parametric/model-based techniques make specific distributional assumptions about the outcome/response variables (e.g., a multivariate normal distribution assumption for all outcome/response variables, an independent Bernoulli distribution assumption for each outcome/response variable). Consequently, they contain particular model parameters that need to be estimated along with their standard errors, which allows for inferential statistical tests to be applied.

Estimation proceeds via either *maximum likelihood estimation* within a *frequentist estimation framework* using numerical methods such as the *expectation-maximization algorithm* (e.g., Bock & Aitken, 1981, 1982; Dempster, Laird, & Rubin, 1977) as well as *empirical Bayes* or *fully Bayesian estimation* within a *Bayesian estimation framework* (e.g., Gelman, Carlin, Stern, & Rubin, 1995; Lynch, 2007; Rupp, Dey, & Zumbo, 2004). The models in the second core section of this chapter, univariate and multivariate finite mixture models as well as unrestricted and restricted latent class models, are estimated with either maximum likelihood or fully Bayesian approaches. .

Note that there are nonetheless technical similarities that can be conceptually placed between these two sets of techniques. For example, all of the approaches in this chapter are different from nonparametric latent-variable models, which avoid distributional assumptions within a model-based structure altogether; however, they can be computationally rather expensive to implement, and I will not discuss them further here (but see, e.g., Schmitt et al., 2006; Vermunt, 2001, 2004).

EXPLORATORY VERSUS CONFIRMATORY TECHNIQUES

The techniques in the first core section of this chapter are typically viewed as *exploratory techniques*, because no constrained statistical model is used for testing the absolute fit of the model to the data to confirm a particular research hypothesis. The same is often said about mixture models and unrestricted latent class models in the second core section of this chapter, which is why there is a natural link between these approaches. Diagnostic classification models, however, are restricted latent class models and, thus, *confirmatory statistical models*. Note that the distinction between exploratory and confirmatory techniques is based on whether models contain *parameter restrictions* vis-à-vis a more complex statistical model.

This is not the same as the distinction between *exploratory analyses* and *confirmatory analyses*. Generally speaking, most statistical analyses are driven by some hypothesis about a phenomenon of interest, because the plausibility of interpretations would be impossible to judge without such hypotheses. This is true even for applications in areas such as data mining, although the exploratory character of analyses is more in the foreground of the evidentiary narrative and resulting decisions. Yet, even if a particular confirmatory statistical model with parameter constraints is fit to a particular data set to investigate the tenability of a particular hypothesis, the model is typically refined if the fit is poor at a global or global level. This induces an exploratory character into the process of model-based reasoning although confirmatory statistical models are used.

Suggested Readings

In this section I want to briefly point out a few resources that may be of interest to readers for further in-depth study of particular techniques and their applications.

INTRODUCTORY BOOKS FOR MULTIVARIATE STATISTICS

To gain a basic understanding of clustering and classification techniques, any multivariate textbook arguably provides a good starting point for study. Some multivariate textbooks are more conceptual in nature (e.g., Hair, Black, Babin, & Anderson, 2009), some are more mathematical/statistical in nature (e.g., Johnson & Wichern, 2007), but most strike a reasonable balance between those two objectives (e.g., Lattin, Carroll, & Green, 2002).

SPECIALIZED BOOKS FOR PARTICULAR TECHNIQUES

There are a variety of specialized reference books on the market that are dedicated to particular clustering and classification techniques useful for the social and behavioral sciences generally; I cannot enumerate all of them comprehensively here but want to point out a few representative resources. A recent overview of cluster analytic techniques and their implementation in the software program MATLAB (e.g., Quarteroni & Saleri, 2006) is provided by Hubert, Köhn, and Steinley (2009). Similarly, the recent books by Gan, Ma, and Wu (2007), Jajuga, Sokolowski, and Bock (2002), Kaufman and Rousseeuw (2005), and Xu and Wunsch (2008) have provided broad—if not necessarily introductory—readings to this area. Care in dissemination is required, however, because not all of them provide recommendations that are fully up-to-date from a research perspective although their titles and publication dates might suggest otherwise (*see*, e.g., the review of Gan, Ma, & Wu, 2007, by Steinley, 2008a).

The book by Borg and Groenen (2009) has provided a comprehensive overview of techniques for multidimensional scaling, which can be integrated with algorithmic cluster analysis techniques (e.g., Heiser & Groenen, 1997; Kiers, Vicari, & Vichi, 2005). The books by Faraway (2004) and Kim and Timm (2006) have provided comprehensive overviews of general linear modeling techniques, whereas the books by Dobson and Barnett (2008), Faraway (2005), and McCullagh, Searle, and Neuhaus (2008) have provided comprehensive overviews of generalized general linear modeling techniques. These techniques can be integrated with nonparametric cluster analysis techniques (e.g., Kauermann, Ormerod, & Wand, 2010; Qian, Wu, & Shao, 2009) albeit not necessarily without problems (e.g., Brusco, Cradit, Steinley, & Fox, 2008).

There are also several books dedicated to specific sets of clustering and classification techniques such as ensemble approaches (e.g., Rokach, 2010), classification and regression trees (e.g., Breiman, Friedman, Stone, & Olshen, 1984; Rokach & Maimon, 2008), and discriminant function analysis (e.g., Huberty & Olejnik, 2006). In general, the field of data mining (e.g., Hastie, Tibshirani, & Friedman, 2009; Nisbet, Elder, & Miner, 2009) is concerned very heavily with clustering and classification in high-dimensional spaces.

In the area of educational and psychological measurement specifically, readers may want to consult general books on finite mixture models and latent class analysis (e.g., Collins & Lanza, 2009; Hagenaars & McCutcheon, 2009; McLachlan & Peel, 2000). For DCMs specifically, the book by Rupp, Templin, and Henson (2010) is dedicated to the theory, methods, and applications of diagnostic measurement using DCMs within a general unified estimation framework. Similarly, the book by Tatsuoka (2009) is dedicated to a particular semi-parametric technique called the *rule-space methodology* and the book by Almond, Williamson, Mislevy, and Yan (in press) is devoted to a parametric family of models called *Bayesian inference networks* or *Bayes nets*, for short.

PEER-REVIEWED PUBLICATIONS AND PROFESSIONAL ASSOCIATIONS

Several journals are dedicated to methodological advances for clustering and classification techniques in the social and behavioral sciences generally. Two of the most prominent journals are certainly the *Journal of Classification* and the journal *Advances in Data Analysis and Classification*. Other journals that may be of interest to readers include *Biometrika*, the *British Journal of Mathematical and Statistical Psychology*, the *Journal of Multivariate and Behavioral Research*, the *Journal of the American Statistical Association*, the *Journal of Mathematical Psychology*, and the journal series of the *Royal Statistical Society*.

Similarly, the conference proceedings from the *International Federation of Classification Societies* are a useful starting point into the technical literature. Readers interested in networking with colleagues may consider joining one of the 14 international member societies within this federation such as the *Classification Society* (formerly known as the *Classification Society of North America*), the *British Classification Society*, and the *Gesellschaft für Klassifikation*; more broadly, the *American Statistical Association* may also be of interest.

For more theoretical and technical advancements related to clustering and classification techniques in the field of educational and psychological measurement, readers may want to follow publications in key journals such as *Applied Psychological Measurement*, *Educational and Psychological Measurement*, *Methodology*, *Psychological Methods*, and *Psychometrika*. Readers interested in networking with colleagues may want to consider joining the *European Association of Methodology*, the *National Council of Measurement in Education*, the *Psychometric Society*, and Division D of the *American Educational Research Association*.

Chapter Notation

I will use the subscript $i = 1, \ldots, N$ to denote cases/respondents, $j = 1, \ldots, J$ to denote outcome/response variables, and $k = 1, \ldots, K$ to denote groups/clusters/latent classes. Further, I will use x_{ij} to denote the value of case/respondent i on outcome variable j, $\mathbf{X}$ to denote the matrix of raw observations on the outcome/response variables for the cases/respondents, $\mathbf{Z}^{(\cdot)}$ to denote the matrix of observations on the outcome/response variables for the cases/respondents when they have been standardized using a particular method, ^{T} to denote a transpose of a matrix, $^{-1}$ to denote the inverse of a matrix, $P(\cdot)$ to denote the probability of an event, $\Sigma(\cdot)$ to denote a sum of different terms, and $\Pi(\cdot)$ to denote a product of different factors.

Nonparametric Techniques
Hierarchical Techniques
BASIC CONCEPTS

Hierarchical clustering techniques are prototypically designed to sequentially partition a set of N cases into K mutually exclusive clusters based on the joint information contained in the J outcome variables. I should note that it is also possible to perform clustering on variables rather than cases or to perform a joint clustering on both cases and variables (e.g., Banerjee et al., 2007). Arguably, however, the clustering of variables is conceptually akin to a nonparametric item factor analysis for many practical applications (*see*, e.g., the HCA-CCPROX procedure for the nonparametric dimensionality assessment program DIMTEST investigated in Froelich & Habing, 2008). Because the literature of factor analysis and item response theory is so vast, however, I have decided not to include a separate section on the clustering of variables using nonparametric techniques in this chapter.

AGGLOMERATIVE VERSUS DIVISIVE APPROACHES

There are two distinct approaches for hierarchical clustering techniques. The first one, which is called an *agglomerative approach*, starts by treating each case as its own cluster and then sequentially merges (i.e., agglomerates) cases until all cases form a single cluster. The second approach, which is called a *divisive approach*, starts by placing all cases in one cluster and then sequentially partitions (i.e., divides) the cases into distinct clusters until each case represents its own cluster. Importantly, the segmentation of the cases in these two approaches is sequential and leads to nested clusters. That is, once a case is joined with other cases in an agglomerative approach, it can never again be separated from these cases. Similarly, once a case is separated from other cases in a divisive approach, it can never again be merged with the cases in the original cluster from which it was separated.

STOPPING RULES AND NUMERICAL REPRESENTATION OF CLUSTER MEMBERSHIP

These descriptions underscore that there are no "natural" stopping points for hierarchical algorithms. At any given point at which an algorithm is stopped, however, cases are deterministically classified as belonging into one particular cluster. Statistical software packages will generally save a single new variable that represents the cluster membership in the data file. This new variable can then be used to compute descriptive statistics on variables for each cluster, which may be the outcome variables for the cluster analysis itself or secondary explanatory variables that are collected to help guide interpretations of the cluster structure. Researchers typically inspect means and standard deviations of variables across clusters similar to a parametric one-way *analysis of variance* (ANOVA) but may also use medians and other percentiles similar to descriptive analyses for a nonparametric one-way ANOVA.

GRAPHICAL REPRESENTATION OF CLUSTER STRUCTURE AND MEMBERSHIP

Graphically, there are several different means to represent the resulting cluster structure. A very common two-dimensional display is a *dendrogram*, which complements numerical information about the emerging cluster structure for hierarchical techniques. It displays the iteration history of the cluster structure and show at what steps in an algorithm cases have been merged into common clusters or divided into separate clusters. For illustration purposes, Figure 24.1 shows a dendrogram from the software program SPSS 17.0 for a random sample of $N = 75$ cases from a population with $K = 3$ clusters and $J = 5$ variables.

As indicated by the labels at the bottom of Figure 24.1, the dendrogram visually supports the existences of two or three larger clusters in the data. Statistically, when Cluster 1 and Cluster 2 are merged, their macrocluster would be about 15 units away from Cluster 3; if they are kept separate, then Cluster 1 and Cluster 2 are about 10 units away from each other and various distances away from the remaining cases that eventually make up Cluster 3. Numerically, as noted above, the cluster membership for different solutions can be saved by a statistical program; for example, saving the cluster membership indicator for a three-cluster solution would create a single new nominal-scaled variable in the data set whose values for each case correspond to the visual organization in the dendrogram.

However, the dendrogram does not show whether the cluster structure and resulting cluster memberships correspond to the true cluster structure in the population and whether this structure can be meaningfully interpreted vis-à-vis domain-specific theories. In general, some degree of subjective judgment is always needed to determine an appropriate cluster structure based on visual information alone, which is why numerical means are used as well.

KEY PRE-PROCESSING CHOICES FOR HIERARCHICAL TECHNIQUES

Clustering techniques require analysts to make a few choices before computational algorithms are run to determine resulting cluster structures. Both hierarchical and partitioning techniques require choices that relate to (1) the *standardization/weighting* of the variables that is to be used to compute this metric and (2) the *selection and/or weighting* of those variables that contribute substantial statistical information to the definition of the cluster structure.

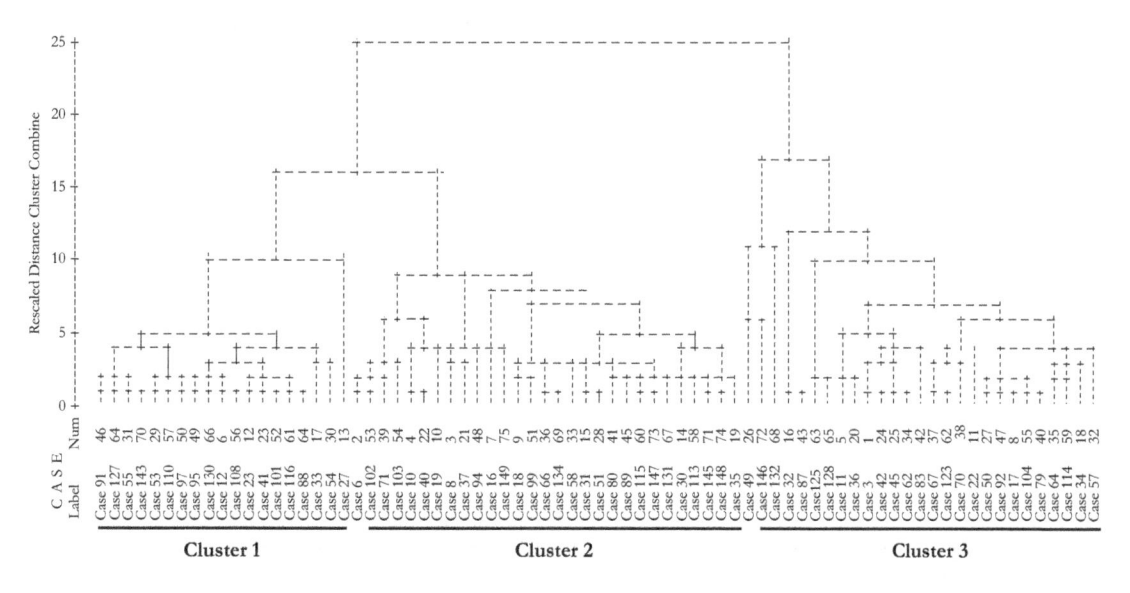

Figure 24.1 Dendrogram from an agglomerative hierarchical cluster analysis for a three-cluster population structure.

Hierarchical clustering techniques further require a choice regarding (3) the *distance or similarity/dissimilarity measure* of the multidimensional space within which the clustering is to be performed and (4) the measure of *intercluster distance* within the space that is used to define how far away clusters with multiple cases are from one another. In contrast, partitioning clustering techniques require choices regarding (5) the initial selection of cluster centers and the number of random initializations that are used.

Standardization Approaches for Variables

There are four standardization approaches that are most commonly used in the literature on cluster analysis, which are (1) no standardization (i.e., using the raw data) (**X**); (2) a standardization by means and standard deviations (i.e., using traditional z-scores) ($\mathbf{Z}^{(1)}$); (3) a standardization by the range ($\mathbf{Z}^{(2)}$); and (4) a combined standardization by mean, range, and variance ($\mathbf{Z}^{(3)}$). Table 24.1 shows the formulas for the three standardization methods.

Note that the $\mathbf{Z}^{(3)}$ standardization can be viewed as a multistep process that consists of (1) computing M_j for each variable and determining $\min(M_j)$ as well as $R(z_{\min(1)})$; (2) computing RC_j for each variable; and then (3) reweighting the $\mathbf{Z}^{(1)}$ values by the square root term. RC_j is called a measure of *relative clusterability* for each variable such that the least clusterable variable will have $RC_j = 1$ and all other variables will have values larger than 1. Thus, RC_j indicates how much more "clusterable" (i.e., influential in an intuitive sense) each variable is; this comparison of values for RC_j is valid within a data set but not across different data sets.

Although the formula for $\mathbf{Z}^{(3)}$ may look a bit complicated at first sight, it is easy to implement in statistical software packages. Recent research has demonstrated that this method outperforms other standardization measures for K-means clustering when a Euclidian metric is used (Steinley & Brusco, 2008a), which expanded earlier results on the utility of eight different standardization techniques (Milligan & Cooper, 1988; *see also* Steinley, 2004a).

Selection Procedures for Variables

The key issue to understand for variable selection procedures is that not all variables in a data set contribute statistical information for recovering the true cluster structure in the population, although all may be used to initialize a particular clustering algorithm. Variables that contribute exclusively, or at least mostly, *statistical noise* that can lead a particular clustering algorithm away from finding the true population cluster structure are known as *masking variables* (e.g., Brusco, 2004; Brusco & Cradit, 2001).

A common strategy for high-dimensional data structures with several potential masking variables is to apply dimensionality reduction techniques before applying clustering techniques to capture dominant dimensions of variation in the data. Techniques include *projection pursuit* (e.g., Bolton & Krzanowski, 2003), *independent components analysis* (e.g., Zeman, Till, Livingston, Tanaka, & Driessen, 2007), and *factor analysis* (e.g., Gershoff, Pedersen, & Aber, 2009), among others.

Recent research by Steinley and Brusco (2008a, 2008b) has suggested that a variable weighting and selection algorithm that capitalizes on the relative

Table 24.1. Standardization Formulas for Cluster Analysis

Standardization method	Components	Formula
$\mathbf{Z}^{(1)}$	Mean, Variance	$z_{ij}^{(1)} = \dfrac{x_{ij} - \bar{x}_j}{\sqrt{Var(x_j)}}$
$\mathbf{Z}^{(2)}$	Range	$z_{ij}^{(2)} = \dfrac{x_{ij}}{R(x_j)}$
$\mathbf{Z}^{(3)}$	Mean, Range, Variance	$z_{ij}^{(3)} = z_{ij}^{(1)} \sqrt{\dfrac{RC_j[R(z_{\min}^{(1)})]^2}{[R(z_j^{(1)})]^2}}$ where $RC_j = \dfrac{M_j}{\min(M_j)}$ and $M_j \dfrac{12 \times Var(x_j)}{[R(x_i)]^2}$

Note. $R(\cdot)$ denotes the range of a variable, "Var" denotes the variance of a variable, $\min(M_j)$ is computed across all j variables, and $R(z_{\min}^{(1)})$ is the range of the traditional z-score variable with the minimum M_j value.

clusterability of variables using standardization $\mathbf{Z}^{(3)}$ in the previous section outperforms other variable selection and weighting algorithms (*see* Steinley, 2006a, for an overview) in the presence of masking variables for K-means clustering. However, they point out that additional research is needed to obtain a more comprehensive understanding of which variable weighting and selection algorithm works best under which population cluster structures.

For example, it is as of yet unclear how to select the key clustering variables in the presence of masking variables when the masking variables themselves form a pertinent cluster structure that is not of interest to the researcher. Similarly, relative performance under different objective functions remains to be comprehensively investigated as well. Finally, it is also unclear how the variable standardization and selection algorithm performs for hierarchical clustering techniques.

Distance Measures for the Multivariate Space

Distance measures are statistical quantifications of how far away points are in multivariate space. There are three key properties that distance measures can possess; if a particular measure possesses all three then it is a statistical *metric* for the space:

$$d_{ii'} > 0 \quad \text{for all } i, i' \quad positivity \quad (1)$$

$$d_{ii'} = d_{i'i} \quad \text{for all } i, i' \quad symmetry \quad (2)$$

$$d_{(i'i'')}(< d_{(ii')}) + d_{(ii'')} \quad \text{for all } i, i', i'' \quad triangle\ equality, \quad (3)$$

where the indices i, i', and i'' indicate three different points in multivariate space. Simply put, any proper distance measure needs to provide a positive distance between two distinct points in multivariate space (*positivity*), needs to provide the same distance going from point A to point B as from point B to point A (*symmetry*), and needs to reflect that any three points form a triangle such that the sum of the lengths of any two sides is always larger than the length of the remaining side (*triangle inequality*).

One may wonder whether there are any distance measures that violate these three properties because they are so intuitive. As it turns out, however, if $0 < p < 1$ in the L^p-norm below, then the triangle inequality is violated so that norms with those ranges of values are not proper distance measures. Violations of the triangle inequality coupled with asymmetric proximity measures pose computational problems for exact clustering techniques such as the *p*-median technique that I will discuss in the Alternatives to K-means section (*see*, e.g., the discussion in Brusco & Köhn, 2009, and Köhn, Steinley, & Brusco, 2010).

It is helpful to understand that any two-dimensional representation of cases in multivariate statistics is a simplification of the problem in that it only represents the situation when two, rather than J, outcome variables are involved in a clustering and classification problem. For example, Figure 24.2 shows two points/cases/respondents in a two-dimensional space to illustrate the differences in different distance metrics for two quantitative variables; conceptually, a case with 10 variables would have to be represented with a 10-dimensional graph.

A very useful framework for distances for quantitative variables is the $L^p - norm$ framework represented by the *Minkowski distance*. The reason why this metric is so useful is that three of the most commonly used distances are special cases of it. The general formula for the Minkowski distance is as follows, with $p \geq 1$:

$$d_{ii'}(p) = \left[\sum_{j=1}^{J} |x_{ij} - x_{i'j}|^p \right]^{1/p}. \quad (4)$$

If $p = 1$, then one obtains the *city-block* or *Manhattan distance*; if $p = 2$, then one obtains the *Euclidian distance*; and if $p = q = \infty$, then one obtains the

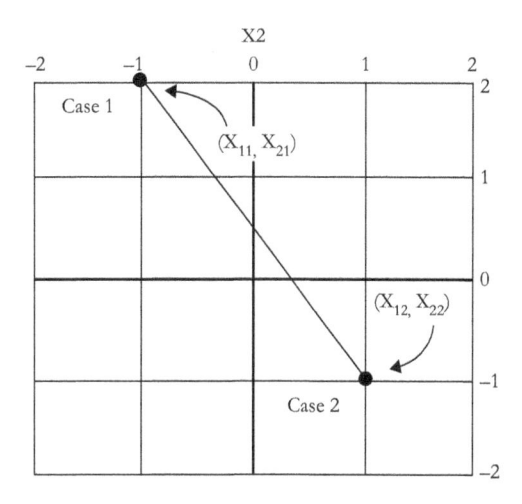

Figure 24.2 A two-dimensional graph for illustrating the computation of different distances.

maximum or *supremum distance*:

$$d_{ii'}(1) = \sum_{j=1}^{J} |x_{ij} - x_{i'j}| \quad (5)$$

$$d_{ii'}(2) = \sqrt{\sum_{j=1}^{J}(x_{ij} - x_{i'j})^2}$$

$$= \sqrt{(\mathbf{x}_i - \mathbf{x}_{i'})^T(\mathbf{x}_i - \mathbf{x}_{i'})}. \quad (6)$$

$$d_{ii'}(\infty) = \max(|x_{i1} - x_{i'1}|, |x_{i2} - x_{i'2}|, \ldots, |x_{iJ} - x_{i'J}|) \quad (7)$$

Furthermore, one can consider the *squared Euclidian distance*:

$$d_{ii'}^2(2) = \sum_{j=1}^{J}(x_{ij} - x_{i'j})^2$$

$$= (\mathbf{x}_i - \mathbf{x}_{i'})^T(\mathbf{x}_i - \mathbf{x}_{i'}) \quad (8)$$

which is a special case of a generalized L^p-norm formulation with powers p and q:

$$d_{ii'}(p, q) = \left[\sum_{j=1}^{J}|x_{ij} - x_{i'j}|^p\right]^{1/q}. \quad (9)$$

For example, for the two cases in Figure 24.2, the city-block distance between the two cases would be 5.00, the Euclidean distance would be 3.61, the squared Euclidean distance would be 13.00, and the maximum distance would be 3.00.

The squared Euclidean distance is useful because its matrix formulation can be easily extended to incorporate information about the covariance structure of the variables, which leads to the common *Mahalanobis distance*:

$$D_{ii'}^2(2) = (\mathbf{x}_i - \mathbf{x}_{i'})^T \mathbf{S}^{-1}(\mathbf{x}_i - \mathbf{x}_{i'}), \quad (10)$$

where $\mathbf{S}^{-1}$ is the inverse of the covariance matrix for all J outcome/response variables. The Mahalanobis distance can be viewed as a squared Euclidean distance where the distance is computed on the *principal components axes* in multivariate space.

Perhaps not surprisingly, additional distances for quantitative variables exist; for example, Legendre and Legendre (1983) proposed an *average Euclidian distance* as well as the *Geodesic distance*, which itself is based on a distance known as the *Chord distance* (see Gan, Ma, & Wu, 2007, for more details). Obviously, the key question for practitioners is not so much how many distance measures one could possible theoretically define but, rather, which distance measure may be most appropriate for any given data set. Typically, the measurement scales, distributions of the variables, or covariance structure of the outcome/response variables are used to choose a metric. It is probably fair to say that the Euclidian or squared Euclidian distance are very commonly used for continuous and even ordinal discrete variables followed by the city-block distance for binary discrete variables. In some cases, however, choices are much more driven by facilities of software programs or the interpretability of cluster solutions under different metrics.

In contrast, categorical data require a reformulation of the concept of association between variables vis-à-vis numerical data because cases are cross-classified on multiple categorical variables. Thus, most measures of association are designed to capture the distribution of cases in a J-way cross-classification table. The measures are referred to as *similarity* or *dissimilarity measures* in the literature, depending on their orientation and interpretation.

One of the simplest cases is when all outcome variables have only two levels resulting in binary data. For example, Gan, Ma, and Wu (2007, p. 78) have presented nine different basic measures for binary data expressed as both similarity and dissimilarities and discussed the distinction between symmetrical and asymmetrical measures, which differ in whether they include double zeros or not, respectively. The authors list nine different symmetrical measures and six different asymmetrical measures, which are typically defined on the intervals [0, 1], [0, ∞], or [−1, 1] with the exception of one measure that is defined on [0, 0.5].

In terms of relative performance of different distance measures, Takeuchi, Saito, and Yadohisa (2007) compared various agglomerative hierarchical clustering techniques for asymmetric measures within a unified framework. Similarly, Fan, Chiu, Köhn, and Douglas (2009) compared the relative performance of selected distance measures for categorical data in educational and psychological measurement.

Measures of Intercluster Distance

The choice of a distance or similarity/dissimilarity measure provides only a direct distance between all cases individually in multivariate space but does not prescribe how one quantifies the distance of clusters of cases relative to one another. For hierarchical clustering techniques, the choice of a measure of intercluster distance is critical, which is also known as the *linkage* because it connects (i.e., links) different clusters. Conceptually, there are three scenarios to distinguish, the computation of (1) distances between two clusters each with only one case in them (i.e., distances between two points), (2) distances between one cluster with multiple cases and another cluster with a single case, and (3) distances between two clusters with multiple cases in them.

For hierarchical clustering techniques, the three most commonly known intercluster distance measures are (1) *minimum/single linkage*, (2) *mean/average linkage*, and (3) *maximum/complete linkage*, which refer to taking (1) the shortest distance between any two points in two different clusters, (2) the arithmetic mean of all pairwise distances between points in two different clusters, and (3) the largest distance between any two points in two different clusters, respectively. Note that it is also possible to differentially weight distances between pairs of cases in different clusters when computing the mean intercluster distance, which is referred to as a *weighted mean/weighted average linkage*.

Another commonly used distance measure is the *centroid linkage*, which refers to defining the distance between any two clusters as the distance between the points corresponding to the arithmetic means of the two clusters. This point typically does not exist in the data set, which is one of the arguments why some researchers have investigated the viability of clustering techniques based on the *median linkage*. Statistically, however, one can view median linkage also as a *weighted centroid linkage*. Furthermore, as we shall see in the next section on partitioning clustering techniques, there is a closely related partitioning clustering linkage called p-median clustering that is recommended when cluster centers need to exist in the data and to improve the robustness of cluster solutions. Finally, as noted by Gan, Ma, and Wu (2007, pp. 96–97), most commonly used intercluster distance measures are special cases of a more general formula that was initially proposed by Lance and Williams (1967) and then extended by Jambu (1978).

In contrast to the previous criteria, *Ward's method* (Ward, 1963) assigns cases to clusters such that the within-cluster variance of cases is minimized. This reflects intuitively the basic idea of cluster analysis, which is to classify cases into maximally homogeneous groups who are maximally different from one another. It is also conceptually akin to what one tries to achieve in experimental designs when one tries to create interventions for groups of subjects whose distributions on outcome variables overlap the least and have the smallest amount of within-group variance possible. In other words, Ward's method is related to the idea of minimizing *within-group* or *error variance*. It leads very naturally to the most commonly discussed partitioning clustering technique in the literature, which is known as K-means.

Once key clustering variables have been selected, those variables have been properly standardized, a proper distance or similarity/dissimilarity measure has been defined, and a measure of inter-cluster distance has been chosen, then hierarchical clustering algorithms are deterministic. That is, cluster membership is iteratively assigned by joining the two clusters that are closest to one another in multivariate space.

Partitioning Clustering Methods

Perhaps not surprisingly, there is also a reasonably large number of partitioning clustering techniques available in the literature. To provide useful guidelines for practitioners, I have decided to focus specifically on the most commonly used method, which is K-means (*see* MacQueen, 1967, for the original presentation of the method). For readers interested in a careful overview of the K-means algorithm, I recommend the very comprehensive review by Steinley (2006a), and for readers interested in a historical review of the K-means algorithm, I recommend Bock (2007).

K-MEANS CLUSTERING

As I stated at the end of the previous section, this clustering technique is conceptually related to Ward's method. The key similarity between the two techniques is that both attempt to minimize the within-group variance of cases in their respective clusters in multivariate space. The key difference between the two techniques is that Ward's method is connected to a hierarchical clustering technique, which prevents separated cases from rejoining other cases, whereas K-means is a partitioning clustering technique, which does allow for a re-allocation of cases across clusters.

Mechanics of K-Means Clustering

As the name implies, the K-means algorithm assumes a fixed number of K clusters, which are characterized first and foremost by their means (i.e., multivariate centroids based on arithmetic averages). Because it is an algorithm that allows for the re-allocation of cases across clusters, it requires a stopping criterion that makes the algorithm stop when only very minor improvements in the within-cluster variance can be made by re-allocation. This characterizes K-means clustering as a numerical optimization problem where the within-cluster variance is the target or objective function that is to be minimized. Technically, however, a locally optimal minimum may, in certain cases, represent a superior solution to the cluster recovery problem than a globally optimal minimum (Steinley & Hubert, 2008).

Steinley and Brusco (2008a) have provided an elegant representation of the particular objective function in K-means, which is the within-cluster variance aggregated across all clusters. They have discussed three different representations of this formula, which are a *compact representation* (Equation 11), a *cluster decomposition* representation (Equation 12), and a *variable decomposition* representation (Equation 13):

$$SSE^{(C)} = \sum_{j=1}^{J}\sum_{k=1}^{K}\sum_{i \in C_k}(x_{ij}-\bar{x}_j^{(k)})^2 \quad (11)$$

$$SSE^{(K)} = \sum_{j=1}^{J}\sum_{i \in C_k}(x_{ij}-\bar{x}_j^{(1)})^2$$

$$+ \ldots + \sum_{j=1}^{J}\sum_{i \in C_K}(x_{ij}-\bar{x}_j^{(K)})^2 \quad (12)$$

$$SSE^{(J)} = \sum_{k=1}^{K}\sum_{i \in C_k}(x_{i1}-\bar{x}_1^{(k)})^2$$

$$+ \ldots + \sum_{k=1}^{K}\sum_{i \in C_k}(x_{iJ}-\bar{x}_J^{(k)}) \quad (13)$$

The cluster decomposition $SSE^{(K)}$ has as many double-sum terms as there are clusters (K), whereas the variable decomposition expression $SSE^{(J)}$ has as many double-sum terms as there are variables (J).

The compact representation should be familiar to readers from general linear modeling contexts such as factorial ANOVA. The cluster decomposition underscores that clusters with larger within-cluster variances have a greater effect on the overall SSE, whereas the variable composition underscores that variables with larger within-cluster variances have a greater effect on the overall SSE. Thus, minimizing the overall SSE in K-means, as in the compact representation, masks the differential influences of within-cluster variances for individual variables across clusters and within-cluster variance for individual clusters across variables. Cluster solutions obtained via the K-means algorithm should be driven by the former and not by the latter.

Initial Selection of Cluster Centers for K-Means

As I mentioned in the previous section, there are a variety of choices regarding variable selection and variable weighting that influence the performance of both hierarchical and partitioning clustering techniques. To appreciate the range of choices, consider that Steinley (2006a) discusses six variable standardization methods, seven variable selection methods, and five variable weighting methods for K-means cluster analysis. As I noted earlier, all clustering techniques may further utilize dimension reduction techniques before cluster analyses are performed.

Further, solutions obtained by commercial programs may be locally optimal, rather than globally optimal, because of the fact that a single set of cases/respondents is chosen as the initial cluster centers (Steinley, 2003, 2006b, 2008b). Ideally, the stability of cluster solutions across multiple initializations should be empirically investigated. Research has shown that thousands of initializations should be used to find a consensual globally optimal solution based on diverse locally optimal solutions (Steinley, 2008b). If this is computationally too expensive, then an initialization of K-means with the cluster solution found via a hierarchical technique using Ward's method is recommended next (Steinley & Brusco, 2007). Steinley (2003) has provided code for the program MATLAB (e.g., Quarteroni & Saleri, 2006) to perform K-means analyses with multiple random starts; *see also* Hubert, Köhn, and Steinley (2009) for a detailed description on how to perform cluster analyses within MATLAB.

Selected Technical Advances for K-Means Clustering

Recent research by de Craen, Commandeur, Frank, and Heiser (2006) has demonstrated how the accuracy of cluster structure recovery is driven predominantly by the shape of the cluster structures, which is determined by the variance–covariance structures of the clusters, as well as to a smaller extent by the relative size of the different clusters (*see also* related discussions in Steinley, 2006a). Steinley (2008b) has shown how the effectiveness of K-means clustering can be improved by utilizing statistical information from locally optimal solutions that arise from different random initializations. The resulting final solution created by this type of *stability analysis* is thus a statistical consensus of different locally optimal solutions and can provide nonparametric probabilistic cluster membership assignments (*see also* Steinley, 2006b).

Steinley and Hubert (2008) have further shown how an imposition of order constraints in K-means can lead to locally optimal cluster solutions that are superior to alternative solutions, underscoring how the objective function drives the interpretation of cluster solutions. Similarly, Steinley and Brusco (2008b) have demonstrated superior performance of a novel standardization and variable selection method for K-means.

Alternatives to K-Means Clustering

K-means is, of course, not the only partitioning technique for clustering, although it is the most commonly used one. Recent research has also reflected a renewed interest in the so-called p-median model, which is essentially a K-median clustering algorithm (*see* Steinley, 2006a). Brusco and Köhn (2009) have stated that this algorithm is (1) more robust than K-means or other K-centroid procedures; (2) has tremendous flexibility, as it does not require particular variable scales or distributional forms; and (3) can frequently produce globally optimal solutions (*see also* Avella, Sassano, & Vasil'ev, 2007; Hansen & Mladenović, 2008; Köhn, Steinley, & Brusco, 2010).

The optimization problem is much harder, however, which is why the algorithm's relative performance had not been thoroughly investigated until recently. Brusco and Köhn (2008) have proposed and investigated a three-stage optimization procedure to solve the p-median estimation problem. The procedure consists of what is known as a greedy heuristic coupled with a Langrangian relaxation coupled with a branch-and-bound algorithm; they have shown that the first two stages appear to be frequently sufficient to achieve adequate cluster recovery. The same authors have further proposed a simulated annealing heuristic, which outperforms previous implementations of this type of technique (Brusco & Köhn, 2009).

The bottom line of this research at present is that the p-median model has become is conceptually more desirable whenever cluster centers that actually exist as exemplars in the data are desired and has become computationally feasible due to recently developed robust estimation methods. However, the implementation of such routines is just beginning to become more user-friendly and still relies on routines written by researchers rather than GUI interfaces in commercial software packages. As I will discuss in the Finite Mixture and Latent Class Models section, K-means technique also have close relationships with parametric/model-based techniques, which can be used to uncover hierarchical cluster structures as well (e.g., Kurihara & Welling, 2009).

Software Packages for Nonparametric Techniques

Because clustering and classification techniques are a common set of multivariate analysis techniques, it probably comes as no surprise that essentially all popular software packages and programming environments have clustering and classification routines available. For example, the routine CLUSTER in SAS 8.0 (e.g., Delwiche & Slaughter, 2008) can be used for hierarchical clustering methods, the routine FASTCLUS in SAS and the routine "kmeans" in MATLAB (e.g., Quarteroni & Saleri, 2006) can be used for K-means clustering methods, and various routines in SPSS 17.0 (SPSS Inc., 2009) can be used for both hierarchical and partitioning clustering methods.

To illustrate the strengths and limitations of popular clustering and classification packages, I will use SPSS 17.0 as an example because it is a very popular general-purpose statistical estimation software program. This is not designed to either laud or criticize SPSS *per se* but, rather, to illustrate the kinds of considerations that practitioners could have in mind when selecting a particular software package for their particular purpose.

At the time of this writing, the base version of SPSS Version 17 contained menus for performing hierarchical and K-means clustering analyses as well as two-step and nearest neighbor clustering analyses along with discriminant function analysis. The hierarchical clustering menu contained six of the most common distance metrics (including the ability to separately specify the power coefficients and the root coefficients of the Minkowski metric up to the order four), seven of the most common intercluster distance measures, and seven different variable standardization methods. The program was able to provide dendrograms and icicle plots, which could be varied in orientation, and could save the cluster membership for specific solutions or a range of solutions. The K-means menu allowed the user to read in initial cluster centers and write out the final cluster centers for a particular solution and to select either the first K cases as cluster centers or use a sequential procedure based on a single pass through the data set that tried to maximize the initial distance of cluster centroids.

Although these choices certainly cover a wide range of options of interest, SPSS 17.0 lacked a few features that have been shown to be useful for cluster analysis. For example, for K-means analysis, the program did not allow the user to specify a certain number of random starts for the clustering procedure along with a process for aggregating the results across the multiple runs (e.g., Steinley & Brusco, 2007). It also did not contain the more recently proposed algorithms for variable standardization and selection proposed by Steinley and Brusco (2008a). Because proper variable standardization and selection as well as multiple runs are commonly suggested in the research literature, this limits the utility of SPSS to find the most stable and trustworthy solution. In other words, the SPSS graphical user interface is very user-friendly for determining clustering solutions for a few combinations of important input characteristics and methods, but chances are high that users will retain and use locally optimal clustering solutions unless specialized runs are programmed using the syntax language (*see* Steinley, 2003).

Finally, there are many additional clustering routines that have been written by researchers in the area of clustering and classifications, mostly as standalone codes; brief technical descriptions of specialized clustering algorithms can be found in, for example, Gan, Ma, and Wu (2007) as well as Kaufman and Rousseeuw (2005). As is the case for many fields, the highest level of cutting-edge innovation can be found in these author-written codes, but their appeal for general-purpose users is rather limited because of the limited accessibility and specialized programming languages or environments that are being used.

Additional Example

To illustrate the performance of cluster analysis techniques with an additional brief example, I will use a data set on body measurements published by Heinz, Peterson, Johnson, and Kerk (2003), which was used as one of several data sets in a validation study by Brusco and Köhn (2008). It contains data from $N = 507$ respondents, and I will use $J = 5$ variables, which are $X_1 =$ Height (in *cm*), $X_2 =$ Weight (in *kg*), $X_3 =$ Chest girth (in *cm*), $X_4 =$ Waist girth (in *cm*), and $X_5 =$ Hip girth (in *cm*); the known grouping variable that is used for comparison purposes with a derived cluster structure is $X_6 =$ Gender. I standardized the variables using the $Z^{(3)}$ standardization as described earlier and used two clustering techniques. These were (1) an agglomerative technique that uses the squared Euclidian distance and Ward's method and (2) a K-means clustering technique with $K = 2$ clusters; for simplicity I did not reinitialize the K-means procedure multiple times.

The dendrogram for the hierarchical technique supported, at best, a two-cluster solution, whereas the K-means solution was set by me *a priori* to $K = 2$ clusters. The results showed that Ward's method classified 434 / 507 = 85.60% of the respondents in alignment with the two gender groups, whereas the K-means technique classified 439 / 507 = 86.59% of the respondents in alignment with the two gender groups with an agreement of 434 / 507 = 85.60% across the two methods. Correcting these classification results for chance agreement using the adjusted Rand index (e.g., Hubert & Arabie, 1985; Warrens, 2008; Steinley, 2004b) as computed in the package "mclust" (Fraley & Raftery, 2003) in R (www.r-project.org) gives values of 0.51 and 0.53. This shows that the K-means technique performs slightly better than, but essentially identical to, the hierarchical technique with Ward's method in this case, which is to be expected because of the relative statistical similarity between the two techniques.

Finite Mixture and Latent Class Models

The previous section was concerned with hierarchical and partitioning clustering techniques. All of these techniques were nonparametric in nature, which is to say that they did not make any particular distributional assumptions regarding the distribution of the outcome variables. Technically, as I stated earlier, distributional assumptions may still be necessary for nonparametric techniques when particular inferential statistical tests are connected to them but these are not required to find the cluster structure and to assign cases to these clusters.

In this section, I will look at four different types of parametric/model-based techniques for clustering cases, which are particularly useful for the social and behavioral sciences. Thus, I will refer to the cases as respondents and to the outcome variables as response variables. The four types are all special case of so-called *latent class* models. Similarly to the clustering techniques in the previous section, a latent class model is concerned with assigning respondents to unobserved (i.e., latent) groups, which are called *classes* in this literature. Contrary to these clustering methods, however, latent class models assume specific distributions for the response variables.

Because the latent classes can be thought of as representing a sorting of respondents from heterogeneous populations, these models are also known as *finite mixture models* in the literature (e.g., Fraley & Raftery, 1998; McLachlan & Peel, 2000). Moreover, the assignment to the unobserved latent classes is done probabilistically, rather than deterministically. The probability of belonging to a particular latent class k is represented by the *latent class membership probability* or *mixing proportion* in the population. Note that a probabilistic group assignment via a latent class structure is conceptually similar to probabilistic computational clustering techniques like *fuzzy partitioning methods*, which I did not have space to discuss in detail in this chapter.

The four types of latent class models that I will discuss in the following subsections are (1) finite mixture models for single quantitative response variables; (2) finite mixture models for multiple quantitative response variables; (3) unconstrained latent class models for multiple categorical response variables; and (4) constrained latent class models for multiple categorical response variables.

Finite Mixture Models for Single Quantitative Response Variables

Typically, finite mixture models utilize distributions for continuous quantitative response variables on interval or ratio scales as well as counts while distributions for categorical qualitative variables on nominal and ordinal scales lead to unrestricted and restricted latent class models. As the name implies, univariate finite mixture models are designed to model the distribution of a single quantitative response variable that takes on different distributional shapes in different unobserved populations.

These models consist of two components, which are a set of *mixing proportions* (υ_k), and class-specific *probability density functions* $f(X|\omega)$, which are typically of the same distributional form but have different population parameters ω in each latent class. For example, in a situation with $K=3$ latent classes and a univariate normal distribution structure for $J=1$ response variable, the response data for each class would follow a univariate normal distribution with a class-specific mean and a class-specific standard deviation. This statistical model can be represented as:

$$f(X|\mu,\sigma,\upsilon) = \Sigma_{k=1}^{3}[\upsilon_k f(X|\omega)]$$
$$= \upsilon_1 N(X|\mu_1,\sigma_1)$$

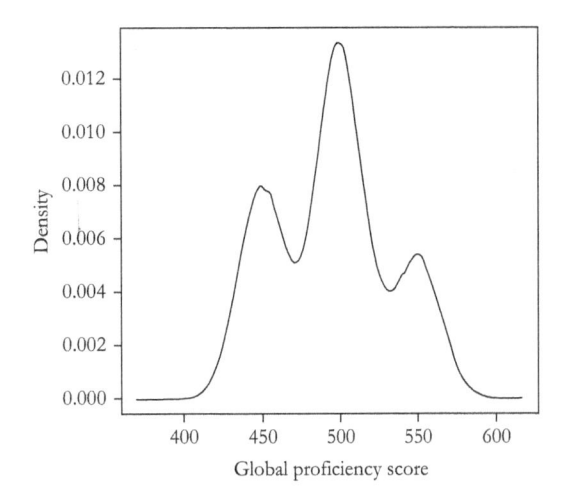

Figure 24.3 Kernel density plot for univariate normal mixture distribution of proficiency scores from $K=3$ groups.

$$+ \upsilon_2 N(X|\mu_2,\sigma_2)$$
$$+ \upsilon_3 N(X|\mu_3,\sigma_3) \quad (14)$$

where the mixing proportions υ_k are subject to the constraint $\upsilon_1 + \upsilon_2 + \upsilon_3 = 1$.

As an example, consider a scenario where there are three subpopulations of respondents, which correspond to low-, moderate-, and high-achieving students on a large-scale achievement test of mathematics such as the *Programme for International Student Achievement* (PISA) (www.pisa.oecd.org). Assume that the populations' mean scores are $\mu_1 = 450$, $\mu_2 = 500$, and $\mu_3 = 550$ points, the populations' standard deviations are $\sigma_1 = \sigma_2 = \sigma_3 = 25$ points, and the populations' mixing proportions are $\upsilon_1 = 30\%$, $\upsilon_2 = 50\%$, and $\upsilon_3 = 20\%$. For illustration purposes, Figure 24.3 shows a univariate kernel density plot based on 200,000 respondents simulated for this scenario.

The objective of a univariate mixture model estimation would be to take such data and estimate the mixing proportions and distribution parameters for each of the three populations; this would typically be done for different choices of numbers and types of mixtures until a best-fitting model has been found. Thus, for a mixture model with three groups that matched this data-generation scenario, one would have to estimate a total of eight parameters. These consist of three population means, three population standard deviations, and two mixing proportions; the last mixing proportion is determined by the sum-to-one constraint.

In general, other parametric distributions apart from the normal distribution may be chosen for the response variables. The distributions are typically members of the exponential family (see, e.g., Casella & Berger, 2001, Chapter 3) with popular choices including a Poisson distribution for unbounded counts, a binomial distribution for the proportion of events of interests out of a fixed number of events, and an exponential distribution for monotonic trends.

Finite Mixture Models for Multiple Quantitative Response Variables

As the name suggests, finite mixture models for multiple response variables extend the idea of the previous subsection to multivariate distributions for the response variables. Continuing with the previous example, we may consider a case where there are $K = 3$ latent classes and $J = 5$ outcome variables. In this case, the data within each latent class would follow a five-dimensional multivariate normal distribution with class-specific mean vector and class-specific variance–covariance matrix. The statistical model can be represented as:

$$f(\mathbf{X}|\mu, \Sigma, \upsilon) = \Sigma_{k=1}^{3} \upsilon_k f(X|\omega)$$
$$= \upsilon_1 MVN(X|\mu_1, \Sigma_1)$$
$$+ \upsilon_2 MVN(X|\mu_1, \Sigma_2)$$
$$+ \upsilon_3 MVN(X|\mu_1, \Sigma_3) \quad (15)$$

such that $\mathbf{X}_k \sim MVN(\mu_k, \Sigma_k)$ and the mixing proportions υ_k are subject to the constraint $\upsilon_1 + \upsilon_2 + \upsilon_3 = 1$.

As this representation underscores, a multivariate finite mixture model is a simple extension of a univariate finite mixture model. The most commonly used distribution is a multivariate normal distribution, as in the illustration above, but other multivariate distributions are certainly possible.

As an extension of the example for univariate mixture models above, consider a scenario where there are three populations of respondents, which correspond again to low-, moderate-, and high-achieving students on two subscales of mathematics for a large-scale achievement test such as PISA. Assume that the population mean vectors are $\mu_1 = [470, 530]$, $\mu_2 = [500, 500]$, and $\mu_3 = [530, 470]$ points. The identical population covariance matrix for the three groups is $\Sigma = \begin{bmatrix} 625 & 437.50 \\ 437.50 & 625 \end{bmatrix}$ to represent univariate standard deviations of 25 points and a bivariate score correlation of 0.70 within each group and the population mixing proportions are again $\upsilon_1 = 30\%$, $\upsilon_2 = 50\%$, and $\upsilon_3 = 20\%$. For

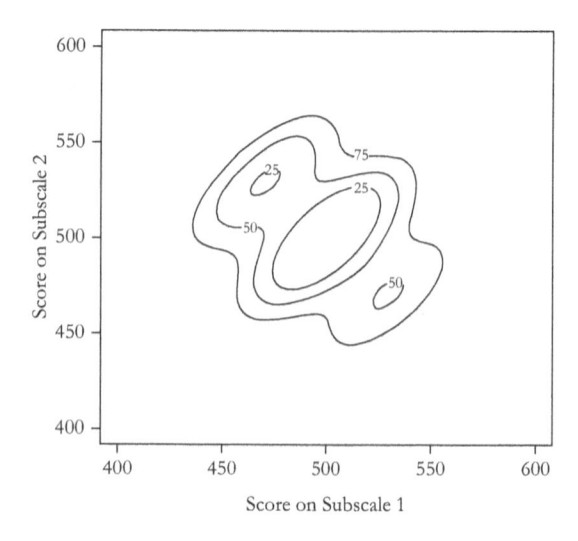

Figure 24.4 Contour plot for bivariate normal mixture distribution of two proficiency scores from $K = 3$ groups with unequal sizes.

illustration purposes, Figure 24.4 shows a bivariate contour plot with highlighted 25th, 50th, and 75th percentile contours for this scenario.

Again, the objective of a multivariate mixture model estimation would be to take such data and estimate the mixture proportions and population parameters for each of the three groups for different models until a best-fitting model has been found. Thus, for a multivariate mixture model with three groups that matched this data-generation scenario, one would have to estimate a total of 17 parameters. These consist of three population mean vectors with two score means each, three covariance matrices with two variances and one covariance each, and two mixing proportions; the last mixing proportion is determined by the sum-to-one constraint.

A finite multivariate mixture model is closely related to a K-means clustering method. Intuitively, both modeling approaches are concerned with grouping objects/respondents into unobserved clusters or classes using multiple outcome/response variables. These modeling techniques become identical in specification if a multivariate normal distribution for uncorrelated outcome/response variables is assumed within each cluster in K-means and if the class membership probabilities are set to 0 or 1 for each observation in a finite mixture model to make class assignment deterministic (Steinley, 2006a). In general, however, the key difference between the two modeling approaches is the prototypical nonparametric versus parametric nature of model specification and estimation for K-means and finite mixture models, respectively, along with the resulting implications for statistical inference.

Unconstrained Latent Class Models

Finite multivariate mixture models are primarily designed for quantitative discrete count variables or quantitative continuous variables measured on interval or ratio scales. In contrast, unconstrained latent class models are finite multivariate mixture models for discrete categorical variables measured on nominal or ordinal scales. They are, in many ways, the prototypical latent class models from both a historical and an application perspective.

However, the conceptualization of modeling unobserved population heterogeneity in data structures (i.e., mixtures) via latent classes is much more general. This has led to the specification and estimation of model families such as growth mixture models (e.g., Bauer, 2007), mixture structural equation models (e.g., Dolan, 2009), and mixture regression models (e.g., van Horn et al., 2009)—to name but a few. In this subsection of the chapter, I want to focus on the prototypical latent class model, however, and will refer readers interested in additional variants of latent class models to the more specialized resources cited at the beginning of this chapter.

INSTRUMENT CALIBRATION VERSUS RESPONDENT SCALING

The primary statistical objectives of these unconstrained latent class models, as well as the DCMs in the next subsection, are known as the *calibration of the measurement instrument* and the *scaling of the respondents*. Latent class models share these objectives with other latent variable techniques in the area of *confirmatory factor analysis* (e.g., Brown, 2006; McDonald, 1999), *structural equation modeling* (e.g., Hancock & Mueller, 2006; Kline, 2010), and *item response theory* (e.g., de Ayala, 2009; Yen & Fitzpatrick, 2006).

Calibrating a measurement instrument essentially means determining the *operating characteristics* of the questions/items/tasks on an instrument associated with the response variables. These include their relative difficulty, discriminatory power, and potential characteristics under guessing. The response variables are typically *dichotomous* (i.e., have two levels such as "incorrect"/"correct" or "endorsed"/"not endorsed") or *polytomous* (i.e., have more than two levels such as "incorrect"/"partially correct"/"completely correct" or "not endorsed"/"partially endorsed"/"fully endorsed"). Scaling the respondents essentially means determining their profiles on the latent (i.e., unobservable) characteristics that the measurement instrument is trying to tap. In the latent variable frameworks cited above, this is done with continuous latent variables, whereas latent class models contain discrete latent variables that are used to sort/group/classify respondents into homogeneous subsets.

CLASS-SPECIFIC ITEM RESPONSE PROBABILITIES

In an unconstrained latent class model for purely binary response variables, there is a class-specific probability of correct response for each item. Because these probabilities are allowed to differ across latent classes, these models are known specifically as *unconstrained* latent class models. Consider an example with $K = 3$ latent classes and $J = 5$ binary response variables, which could represent a short five-item screening instrument consisting of yes–no questions at a hospital. In this case, there would be five item response probabilities within each latent class corresponding to the five binary response variables as well as three mixing proportions for the latent classes.

LOCAL/CONDITIONAL INDEPENDENCE ASSUMPTION

An unconstrained latent class model assumes *local* or *conditional independence* among the item responses, which means that one can express the joint likelihood of the data within each class as a product of the class-specific item response probabilities (i.e., responses to items are independent for respondents within any given latent class). Mathematically, this is an instantiation of the Basic Probability Theorem that states that the joint probability for a set of independent outcomes is the product of the probabilities for the individual outcomes. As an aside, a latent class model with increasing or decreasing order restrictions on the response probabilities across latent classes, as discussed in the Constrained Latent Class Models section, is a discrete version of a unidimensional factor analysis or item response theory model. In those models, the item responses are also assumed to be conditionally independent, with the exception that interval-scaled quantitative latent variables are used to create the conditional independence.

STATISTICAL STRUCTURE OF UNRESTRICTED LATENT CLASS MODEL

Consider again the example with $K = 3$ latent classes and $M = 5$ binary response variables from above. The unconstrained latent class model can be statistically represented as follows:

$$X_k \sim \text{Bernoulli}(\pi_k)$$

$$f(\mathbf{X}|\pi, \upsilon) = \sum_{k=1}^{3} \upsilon_k \prod_{j=1}^{5} f(X|\pi_{jk})$$

$$= \sum_{k=1}^{3} \upsilon_k \prod_{j=1}^{5} (\pi_{jk})^x (1 - \pi_{jk})^{1-x} \quad (16)$$

$$= \upsilon_1 \prod_{j=1}^{5} (\pi_{j1})^x (1 - \pi_{j1})^{1-x}$$

$$+ \upsilon_2 \prod_{j=1}^{5} (\pi_{j2})^x (1 - \pi_{j2})^{1-x}$$

$$+ \upsilon_3 \prod_{j=1}^{5} (\pi_{j3})^x (1 - \pi_{j3})^{1-x}$$

subject to the constraint that $\upsilon_1 + \upsilon_2 + \upsilon_3 = 1$.

This model can also be represented in tabular form as shown in Table 24.2, which highlights its parameter structure.

As Table 24.2 shows, there are 17 parameters that need to be estimated for this model, which are 15 item response probabilities and two mixing proportions; the last mixing proportion is determined automatically because of the sum-to-one constraint. As a result of the estimation process, respondents are thus classified into these three latent classes. This is typically done using a *maximum a posteriori* estimation process within an empirical Bayes or fully Bayesian estimation framework, which means that respondents are assigned to the latent class for which the posterior probability of membership is highest (i.e., to the mode/maximum value of the posterior distribution).

For illustration purposes, consider the scenario where the five items correspond to five mathematical questions about linear algebra that are arranged in the table from easiest to most difficult. Further, imagine that the three latent classes correspond to groups of respondents with different ability levels (i.e., an ordered latent class structure) such that respondents in the first latent class are below a targeted minimum proficiency level, respondents in the second latent classes are at a targeted minimum proficiency level, and respondents in the third latent class are above a targeted minimum proficiency level. This mixture distribution is a continuation of the examples for univariate and multivariate mixture models from the previous two subsections.

Table 24.3 shows potential parameter values for such a scenario.

In this case, $\upsilon_1 = 20\%$ of the respondents are classified as "below proficient," $\upsilon_2 = 50\%$ of the respondents are classified as "proficient," and $\upsilon_3 = 30\%$ of the students are classified as "above proficient." Further, in accordance with the scenario, the response probabilities for the items decrease from Item 1 to Item 5 within each latent class but increase for each item across latent classes. If these order constraints were included in the model specification a priori then an order-restricted latent class model, as discussed in the next section, would result.

These parameter values have some grounding in realistic applications as follows. Latent class models can be used as alternative modeling approaches for the empirical determination of cut-scores along a single conceptual proficiency continuum within standard-setting approaches, which are used in large-scale standardized assessments of student achievement (e.g., Hambleton & Pitoniak, 2006; Zieky & Perie, 2006). These assessments are common at the district or state level, at national levels (e.g., NCES, 2007), or at international levels (e.g., NCES, 2006). In these scenarios, having three ordered classes of respondents for reporting

Table 24.3. Parameter Values for Sample Unconstrained Latent Class Model

Mixing proportion	Item 1	Item 2	Item 3	Item 4	Item 5
0.20	0.60	0.50	0.35	0.30	0.25
0.50	0.75	0.65	0.40	0.50	0.40
0.30	0.90	0.80	0.70	0.65	0.60

Table 24.2. Population Parameter Structure for Sample Unconstrained Latent Class Model

Mixing proportion	Item 1	Item 2	Item 3	Item 4	Item 5
υ_1	π_{11}	π_{12}	π_{13}	π_{14}	π_{15}
υ_2	π_{21}	π_{22}	π_{23}	π_{24}	π_{25}
υ_3	π_{31}	π_{32}	π_{33}	π_{34}	π_{35}

purposes as well as having about 70% of respondents classified as "proficient" or "above proficient" is quite desirable.

Constrained Latent Class Models/Diagnostic Classification Models

Constrained latent class models are confirmatory analogs to exploratory unconstrained latent class models, which contain equality or order constraints for the class-specific item response or class membership probabilities in the model. Such constraints can serve a variety of different purposes. For example, imposing equality constraints of item response probabilities for a single item across all latent classes can be used to test whether this item can be deleted from the model. The reasoning behind this is that latent class models are designed to carve out distributional differences in latent classes for response variables and if the distributions are identical across latent classes, then response variables do not contribute to defining the latent class structure.

Similarly, imposing order constraints can be used to represent specific hypotheses about the performance of respondents in different latent classes. For example, if the different respondent groups represent subpopulations with different mean proficiency levels as in the example above, then order constraints could be used during estimation to reflect the differential item response probabilities for these questions for the different groups. If such a hypothesis were appropriate, then a model that produces parameter estimates like those in Table 24.3 would likely show a good fit to the data.

LATENT CLASSES AS ATTRIBUTE PROFILES

The particular models that I want to discuss in this section are special types of constrained latent class models that blend ideas from multidimensional factor analysis and multidimensional item response theory and basic constrained latent class models. The core idea of these models is that a certain number of discrete latent variables are postulated at the outset of the problem, which reflect either dichotomous or polytomous mastery states on *latent attribute variables*.

I use the term "attribute" in a generic sense here to suggest that the attributes could reflect unobserved characteristics such as proficiencies, dispositions, or other constructs. The idea is that all possible combinations of mastery states on these variables represent distinct attribute profiles whose number is pre-determined by the levels of the latent variables and the number of latent variables.

Importantly, each attribute profile represents a distinct latent class so that the number of latent classes is predetermined.

DEFINITION OF DIAGNOSTIC CLASSIFICATION MODELS

Technically, according to Rupp, Templin, and Henson (2010, p. 83),

> DCMs are confirmatory multidimensional latent-variable methods. Their loading structure/Q-matrix can be complex to reflect within-item multidimensionality or simple to reflect between-item multidimensionality. DCMs are suitable for modeling observable response variables with various scale types and distributions and contain discrete latent predictor variables. The latent predictor variables are combined by a series of linear-modeling effects that can result in compulsory and/or noncompensatory ways for predicting observable item responses. DCMs thus provide multi-variate attribute profiles for respondents based on statistically derived classifications.

Historically, DCMs had been specified separately with different notation and different estimation algorithms. More recently, several authors have embedded the large majority of parametric DCMs within unified specification and estimation frameworks. The three most commonly cited frameworks are the *log-linear cognitive diagnosis model* framework (e.g., Henson, Templin, & Willse, 2009), the *general diagnostic model* framework (e.g., von Davier, 2010), and the *generalized DINA model* framework (e.g., de la Torre, 2008b, 2011).

For simplicity of illustration, I will consider only the case of dichotomous latent variables in this subsection, although polytomous extensions are nowadays relatively straightforward to conceive of and implement. Consider a case with $A = 4$ dichotomous latent attribute variables and $J = 5$ dichotomous item response variables. Thus, there are a total of $2^A = 2^4 = 16$ distinct attribute profiles or latent classes in this problem. Conceptually, each latent class could have a total of five distinct item response probabilities for the five dichotomous item response variables, as shown in Table 24.4.

PARAMETER CONSTRAINTS VIA THE Q-MATRIX

Because such a model specification would lead to a very large number of model parameters to be estimated (e.g., 80 item response probabilities across latent classes and 15 mixing proportions in this example), additional constraints are imposed on the

Table 24.4. Baseline Population Parameter Structure for Sample Constrained Latent Class Model

Class	α	Item 1	Item 2	Item 3	Item 4	Item 5
1	[0,0,0,0]	$\pi_{1,1}$	$\pi_{2,1}$	$\pi_{3,1}$	$\pi_{4,1}$	$\pi_{5,1}$
2	[0,0,0,1]	$\pi_{1,2}$	$\pi_{2,2}$	$\pi_{3,2}$	$\pi_{4,2}$	$\pi_{5,2}$
3	[0,0,1,0]	$\pi_{1,3}$	$\pi_{2,3}$	$\pi_{3,3}$	$\pi_{4,3}$	$\pi_{5,3}$
4	[0,0,1,1]	$\pi_{1,4}$	$\pi_{2,4}$	$\pi_{3,4}$	$\pi_{4,4}$	$\pi_{5,4}$
5	[0,1,0,0]	$\pi_{1,5}$	$\pi_{2,5}$	$\pi_{3,5}$	$\pi_{4,5}$	$\pi_{5,5}$
6	[0,1,0,1]	$\pi_{1,6}$	$\pi_{2,6}$	$\pi_{3,6}$	$\pi_{4,6}$	$\pi_{5,6}$
7	[0,1,1,0]	$\pi_{1,7}$	$\pi_{2,7}$	$\pi_{3,7}$	$\pi_{4,7}$	$\pi_{5,7}$
8	[0,1,1,1]	$\pi_{1,8}$	$\pi_{2,8}$	$\pi_{3,8}$	$\pi_{4,8}$	$\pi_{5,8}$
9	[1,0,0,0]	$\pi_{1,9}$	$\pi_{2,9}$	$\pi_{3,9}$	$\pi_{4,9}$	$\pi_{5,9}$
10	[1,0,0,1]	$\pi_{1,10}$	$\pi_{2,10}$	$\pi_{3,10}$	$\pi_{4,10}$	$\pi_{5,10}$
11	[1,0,1,0]	$\pi_{1,11}$	$\pi_{2,11}$	$\pi_{3,11}$	$\pi_{4,11}$	$\pi_{5,11}$
12	[1,0,1,1]	$\pi_{1,12}$	$\pi_{2,12}$	$\pi_{3,12}$	$\pi_{4,12}$	$\pi_{5,12}$
13	[1,1,0,0]	$\pi_{1,13}$	$\pi_{2,13}$	$\pi_{3,13}$	$\pi_{4,13}$	$\pi_{5,13}$
14	[1,1,0,1]	$\pi_{1,14}$	$\pi_{2,14}$	$\pi_{3,14}$	$\pi_{4,14}$	$\pi_{5,14}$
15	[1,1,1,0]	$\pi_{1,15}$	$\pi_{2,15}$	$\pi_{3,15}$	$\pi_{4,15}$	$\pi_{5,15}$
16	[1,1,1,1]	$\pi_{1,16}$	$\pi_{2,16}$	$\pi_{3,16}$	$\pi_{4,16}$	$\pi_{5,16}$

item response probabilities across the latent classes. This is done via two core modeling components. The first one is known as the *design matrix* or *Q-matrix* in educational and psychological assessment and represents the *loading structure* for the instrument. Using binary indicators, it specifies which items measure which attributes (i.e., which latent attribute variables are associated with which observed item response variables). This matrix is common to a wide range of confirmatory latent variable models, most prominently confirmatory factor analysis models Table 24.5 shows a possible Q-matrix for the example from above.

The second component is a *linear predictor* that specifies how the mastery of particular attributes relates to an increase in probability of responding to individual items. This specification effectively reduces the complexity of the model, because a smaller number of parameters can now be used to model, and subsequently constrain, the item response probabilities across latent classes. For each item, the number of possible main and interaction effects is driven by the number of attributes that are measured by each item. For example, Item 1 in this example measures both addition and multiplication. Hence, the maximum number of main effects is two: one for the discrete latent variable representing addition and one for the variable representing multiplication, as well as a two-way interaction effect between these two variables.

STATISTICAL STRUCTURE OF DIAGNOSTIC CLASSIFICATION MODELS

Specifically, let X_{jk} be the response to item j for a respondent in latent class k, π_{jk} be the predicted response/response probability for a respondent in latent class k to item j, and α_k be the attribute profile for respondents in latent class k. Equation 17 shows the general expression for the linear predictor with all main effect and all interaction effect terms up to the highest-order interaction effect term in compact notation using a so-called helper function vector **h**:

$$\pi_{jk} = P(X_{jk} = 1 | \boldsymbol{\alpha}_k)$$
$$= \frac{\exp(\lambda_{j,0} + \boldsymbol{\lambda}_j^T \mathbf{h}(\boldsymbol{\alpha}_k, \mathbf{q}_j))}{1 + \exp(\lambda_{j,0} + \boldsymbol{\lambda}_j^T \mathbf{h}(\boldsymbol{\alpha}_k, \mathbf{q}_j))} \quad (17)$$

In this equation, the expression within the parentheses is known as the *kernel* of this expression, which has the following form in the most general case:

$$\lambda_{j,0} + \boldsymbol{\lambda}_j^T \mathbf{h}(\boldsymbol{\alpha}_k, \mathbf{q}_j) = \lambda_{j,0} + \sum_a^A \lambda_{j,1,(a)} \alpha_{ka} q_{ja}$$
$$+ \sum_{a=1}^A \sum_{a'>a} \lambda_{j,2,(a,a')} \alpha_{ka} \alpha_{ka'} q_{ja} q_{ja'}$$
$$+ \ldots + \lambda_{j,A,(a,a',\ldots)} \prod_{a=1}^A \alpha_{ka} q_{ja}, \quad (18)$$

where q_{ja} is a binary indicator from the Q-matrix, indicating whether item j measures attribute a, α_{ka} is a binary indicator indicating whether attribute a is mastered by respondents in latent class k, $\lambda_{j,0}$ is the intercept parameter for item j, and the remaining λ parameters specify two-way and higher-order interaction effects.

Put simply, this expression is akin to a regression model expression with binary dummy variables that includes an intercept term, main effect terms, and higher-order interaction effect terms; the important difference between such an expression in general linear ANOVA models and DCMs is that the binary dummy variables are observed in the former models (i.e., they represent observed factor levels) but

Table 24.5. Q-Matrix for Sample Assessment

Item #	Item stem	Attribute 1 addition	Attribute 2 subtraction	Attribute 3 multiplication	Attribute 4 division
Item 1	$2 + 6 = ?$	1	0	0	0
Item 2	$15/5 - 3 = ?$	0	1	0	1
Item 3	$10 * 2 + 6/3 = ?$	1	0	1	1
Item 4	$3 * 4 = ?$	0	0	1	0
Item 5	$12 - 8 = ?$	0	1	0	0

are unobserved/latent in the latter models (i.e., they represent estimated attribute mastery states).

For simplicity of illustration, I will consider only models with main effects for this example because interaction effects can be difficult to estimate precisely in samples of even moderate size (e.g., Kunina-Habenicht, Rupp, & Wilhelm, 2010):

$$\lambda_{j,0} + \lambda_j^T \mathbf{h}(\boldsymbol{\alpha}_k, \mathbf{q}_j) = \lambda_{j,0} + \sum_{a=1}^{A} \lambda_{j,1,(a)} \alpha_{ka} q_{ja} \quad (19)$$

Thus, the kernel expression in Equation 18 above simplifies notably and leads to a model that is known as the *compensatory reparameterized unified model* in the literature (see Rupp, Templin, & Henson, 2010, Chapters 6 and 7). Table 24.6 shows the symbolic representation of the parameters for these items for respondents in all 16 latent classes.

For illustration purposes, I set $\lambda_{j,0} = -1.40$ for Item 1, Item 4, and Item 5, which involve one attribute, $\lambda_{j,0} = -1.73$ for Item 2, which involves two attributes, and $\lambda_{j,0} = -2.20$ for Item 3, which involves three attributes. These decreasing values imply a roughly 20% chance of a correct answer for respondents who have not mastered any relevant attribute(s) to any item requiring one attribute, a 15% chance for items requiring two attributes, and a 10% chance for items requiring three attributes. Thus, answers to items measuring more attributes are more difficult to guess correctly than answers to items measuring fewer attributes for respondents who have not mastered any attributes.

Further, I set $\lambda_{j,1,(1)} = \lambda_{j,1,(2)} = 3.30$ for mastery of either addition or subtraction and $\lambda_{j,1,(3)} = \lambda_{j,1,(4)} = 2.60$ for the mastery of either multiplication or division across items that measure these attributes. Thus, in this example, items involving multiplication and division are modeled as more difficult to solve than items involving addition and subtraction if only one of the required attributes is mastered. This is because the additional "credit" for the response probability on the logit scale for the former items is larger; Table 24.7 shows all resulting probabilities for respondents in the 16 latent classes. Note that all of the values above are created specifically for this example but reflect reasonable values of these parameters in real-life applications of DCMs.

As a result of the estimation process for this example, respondents are classified into the 16 latent classes postulated by the model. As with unrestricted latent class models, this is typically done using a maximum *a posteriori* estimation process within an empirical Bayes or fully Bayesian estimation framework (see, e.g., Huebner, 2010, for a discussion of the impact of different classification approaches within the DCM context).

Further typical estimation output for DCMs consists of (1) the distribution of respondents across the latent classes, (2) the marginal proportions of masters for each attribute across the latent classes, (3) the bivariate correlations between the discrete latent attribute variables, and (4) estimates of the reliability of classifications across the latent classes. On the item side, typical estimation output for DCMs consists of (1) the item parameter estimates (i.e., the λ estimates) with standard errors as well as estimates of the discriminatory ability of individual items for respondents with different mastery states of (2) single attributes and (3) multiple attributes.

NONPARAMETRIC ALTERNATIVES TO DIAGNOSTIC CLASSIFICATION MODELS

Diagnostic classification models, as parametric restricted latent class models, are not the only modeling approaches that have been used in the literature to calibrate items and / or classify respondents into a

Table 24.6. Parameter Values for Five Assessment Items Across All Latent Classes

Latent class	Attribute profile	Item 1	Item 2	Item 3	Item 4	Item 5
1	[0,0,0,0]	$\lambda_{1,0}$	$\lambda_{2,0}$	$\lambda_{3,0}$	$\lambda_{4,0}$	$\lambda_{5,0}$
2	[0,0,0,1]	$\lambda_{1,0}$	$\lambda_{2,0} + \lambda_{2,1,(4)}$	$\lambda_{3,0} + \lambda_{3,1,(4)}$	$\lambda_{4,0}$	$\lambda_{5,0}$
3	[0,0,1,0]	$\lambda_{1,0}$	$\lambda_{2,0}$	$\lambda_{3,0} + \lambda_{3,1,(3)}$	$\lambda_{4,0} + \lambda_{4,1,(3)}$	$\lambda_{5,0}$
4	[0,0,1,1]	$\lambda_{1,0}$	$\lambda_{2,0} + \lambda_{2,1,(4)}$	$\lambda_{3,0} + \lambda_{3,1,(3)} + \lambda_{3,1,(4)}$	$\lambda_{4,0} + \lambda_{4,1,(3)}$	$\lambda_{5,0}$
5	[0,1,0,0]	$\lambda_{1,0}$	$\lambda_{2,0} + \lambda_{2,1,(2)}$	$\lambda_{3,0}$	$\lambda_{4,0}$	$\lambda_{5,0} + \lambda_{5,1,(2)}$
6	[0,1,0,1]	$\lambda_{1,0}$	$\lambda_{2,0} + \lambda_{2,1,(2)} + \lambda_{2,1,(4)}$	$\lambda_{3,0} + \lambda_{3,1,(4)}$	$\lambda_{4,0}$	$\lambda_{5,0} + \lambda_{5,1,(2)}$
7	[0,1,1,0]	$\lambda_{1,0}$	$\lambda_{2,0} + \lambda_{2,1,(2)}$	$\lambda_{3,0} + \lambda_{3,1,(3)}$	$\lambda_{4,0} + \lambda_{4,1,(3)}$	$\lambda_{5,0} + \lambda_{5,1,(2)}$
8	[0,1,1,1]	$\lambda_{1,0}$	$\lambda_{2,0} + \lambda_{2,1,(2)} + \lambda_{2,1,(4)}$	$\lambda_{3,0} + \lambda_{3,1,(3)} + \lambda_{3,1,(4)}$	$\lambda_{4,0} + \lambda_{4,1,(3)}$	$\lambda_{5,0} + \lambda_{5,1,(2)}$
9	[1,0,0,0]	$\lambda_{1,0} + \lambda_{1,1,(1)}$	$\lambda_{2,0}$	$\lambda_{3,0} + \lambda_{3,1,(1)}$	$\lambda_{4,0}$	$\lambda_{5,0}$
10	[1,0,0,1]	$\lambda_{1,0} + \lambda_{1,1,(1)}$	$\lambda_{2,0} + \lambda_{2,1,(4)}$	$\lambda_{3,0} + \lambda_{3,1,(1)} + \lambda_{3,1,(4)}$	$\lambda_{4,0}$	$\lambda_{5,0}$
11	[1,0,1,0]	$\lambda_{1,0} + \lambda_{1,1,(1)}$	$\lambda_{2,0}$	$\lambda_{3,0} + \lambda_{3,1,(1)} + \lambda_{3,1,(3)}$	$\lambda_{4,0} + \lambda_{4,1,(3)}$	$\lambda_{5,0}$
12	[1,0,1,1]	$\lambda_{1,0} + \lambda_{1,1,(1)}$	$\lambda_{2,0} + \lambda_{2,1,(4)}$	$\lambda_{3,0} + \lambda_{3,1,(1)} + \lambda_{3,1,(3)} + \lambda_{3,1,(4)}$	$\lambda_{4,0} + \lambda_{4,1,(3)}$	$\lambda_{5,0}$
13	[1,1,0,0]	$\lambda_{1,0} + \lambda_{1,1,(1)}$	$\lambda_{2,0} + \lambda_{2,1,(2)}$	$\lambda_{3,0} + \lambda_{3,1,(1)}$	$\lambda_{4,0}$	$\lambda_{5,0} + \lambda_{5,1,(2)}$
14	[1,1,0,1]	$\lambda_{1,0} + \lambda_{1,1,(1)}$	$\lambda_{2,0} + \lambda_{2,1,(2)} + \lambda_{2,1,(4)}$	$\lambda_{3,0} + \lambda_{3,1,(1)} + \lambda_{3,1,(4)}$	$\lambda_{4,0}$	$\lambda_{5,0} + \lambda_{5,1,(2)}$
15	[1,1,1,0]	$\lambda_{1,0} + \lambda_{1,1,(1)}$	$\lambda_{2,0} + \lambda_{2,1,(2)}$	$\lambda_{3,0} + \lambda_{3,1,(1)} + \lambda_{3,1,(3)}$	$\lambda_{4,0} + \lambda_{4,1,(3)}$	$\lambda_{5,0} + \lambda_{5,1,(2)}$
16	[1,1,1,1]	$\lambda_{1,0} + \lambda_{1,1,(1)}$	$\lambda_{2,0} + \lambda_{2,1,(2)} + \lambda_{2,1,(4)}$	$\lambda_{3,0} + \lambda_{3,1,(1)} + \lambda_{3,1,(3)} + \lambda_{3,1,(4)}$	$\lambda_{4,0} + \lambda_{4,1,(3)}$	$\lambda_{5,0} + \lambda_{5,1,(2)}$

Table 24.7. Item Response Probabilities for Five Assessment Items Across All Latent Classes

Latent class	Attribute profile	Item 1	Item 2	Item 3	Item 4	Item 5
1	[0,0,0,0]	0.20	0.15	0.10	0.20	0.20
2	[0,0,0,1]	0.20	0.87	0.60	0.20	0.20
3	[0,0,1,0]	0.20	0.15	0.60	0.77	0.20
4	[0,0,1,1]	0.20	0.87	0.95	0.77	0.20
5	[0,1,0,0]	0.20	0.87	0.10	0.20	0.87
6	[0,1,0,1]	0.20	0.99	0.60	0.20	0.87
7	[0,1,1,0]	0.20	0.87	0.60	0.77	0.87
8	[0,1,1,1]	0.20	0.99	0.95	0.77	0.87
9	[1,0,0,0]	0.87	0.15	0.75	0.20	0.20
10	[1,0,0,1]	0.87	0.87	0.98	0.20	0.20
11	[1,0,1,0]	0.87	0.15	0.98	0.77	0.20
12	[1,0,1,1]	0.87	0.87	1.00	0.77	0.20
13	[1,1,0,0]	0.87	0.87	0.75	0.20	0.87
14	[1,1,0,1]	0.87	0.99	0.98	0.20	0.87
15	[1,1,1,0]	0.87	0.87	0.98	0.77	0.87
16	[1,1,1,1]	0.87	0.99	1.00	0.77	0.87

Note: These probabilities are based on the following values for the parameters in Table 6: $\lambda_{1,0} = \lambda_{4,0} = \lambda_{5,0} = -1.40, \lambda_{2,0} = -1.73$, and $\lambda_{3,0} = -2.20; \lambda_{j,1,(1)} = \lambda_{j,1,(2)} = 3.30$ and $\lambda_{j,1,(3)} = \lambda_{j,1,(4)} = 2.60$.

distinct set of groups/clusters/classes. For example, the rule-space methodology (e.g., Tatsuoka, 2009) combines a parametric unidimensional model from item response theory and a residual-based person fit index for the same purpose within a semi-parametric approach. Similarly, for the *attribute hierarchy method* (e.g., Gierl, Leighton, & Hunka, 2007), researchers have used maximum-likelihood and neural network classification techniques behind the scenes to derive respondent classifications. Both of these techniques are grounded in *Knowledge–Space Theory* (e.g., Ünlü, 2006; Schrepp, 2005), which is a classification approach driven by mathematical set theory.

On the parametric side, Bayes nets (e.g., Almond, Williamson, Mislevy, & Yan, in press) can be used to classify respondents and to capture directional relationships between the discrete attribute variables that create the attribute profiles, which is conceptually comparable to a structural equation modeling approach with discrete latent variables.

Importantly, the use of semi-parametric and non-parametric clustering and classification approaches for the calibration of assessment items and the creation of attribute profiles for respondents is driven, in part, by the fact that complex parametric models can be challenging to estimate. Specifically, they require large numbers of items per dimension for the reliable classification of respondents and large numbers of respondents per item for the reliable estimation of item operating characteristics such as item difficulty and item discrimination (e.g., Haberman & Sinharay, 2009; Puhan, Sinharay, Haberman, & Larkin, 2010; Rupp, in press). Nevertheless, it should be noted that DCMs require relatively less of such information compared to other parametric multidimensional models because the distinction of proficiency levels on each dimension is coarser (*see,* e.g., Templin & Henson, 2009).

Consequently, it is not surprising that adaptations of *K*-means clustering techniques have recently been developed as nonparametric alternatives to DCMs. The most comprehensive documentation of the current state of the art of these techniques for educational and psychological assessment is the dissertation by Chiu (2008), which combined analytical results, simulation study results, and real-data results to make the case that traditional clustering algorithms can perform reasonably well compared to DCMs under certain conditions (*see also* Chiu & Douglas, 2009).

In the area of educational data mining, Nugent, Dean, and Ayers (2010) have developed an algorithm for determining optimal starting centers for *K*-means clustering as an alternative to DCMs. The algorithm further allows certain clusters to be empty, which improves its computational performance and can be related to an exploratory approach for uncovering *attribute hierarchies* in DCMs. These hierarchies are a key component of the rule–space and attribute hierarchy methods because they reflect empirical hypotheses about conditional attribute dependencies that render certain attribute profiles logically impossible. Statistically, they represent a simplification of the estimation/computation problem as they reduce the number of possible latent classes/clusters.

DESIGNS FOR INVESTIGATING THE RELATIVE PERFORMANCE OF DIFFERENT TECHNIQUES

Methodologically, it is important to note that researchers who investigate the relative performance of nonparametric clustering techniques vis-à-vis DCMs use particular DCMs to generate data with certain latent class structures and then investigate how well techniques like modified *K*-means recover this structure.

Researchers who investigate the relative performance of different nonparametric techniques themselves use multivariate mixture distributions—typically multivariate normal distributions—with particular degrees of overlap, within-cluster covariance structure, and cluster sizes to generate data (*see,* e.g., de Craen et al., 2006; Chiang & Mirkin, 2010; Qiu & Joe, 2006a, 2006b; Steinley & Henson, 2005). For example, researchers now have access to data generation routine for cluster recovery studies such as "clustergeneration" in R (www.r-project.org). The use of such parametric distributions for data generation in a simulation set-up leads researchers to describe the distribution, volume, orientation, and shape of cluster structures as "spherical," "diagonal," "ellipsoidal," or "elongated," for example (*see* Fraley & Raftery, 2003, Table 24.1). Independently of the study set-up, however, the *adjusted Rand index* is generally recommended for capturing the degree to which particular techniques are able to recover the true underlying cluster/latent class structure and provide consistent results (e.g., Hubert & Arabie, 1985; Milligan & Cooper, 1986; Steinley, 2004b, 2006a).

Software Packages for Finite Mixture and Latent Class Models

Owing to the recent unification of many statistical models with latent variables within the family of *generalized linear and nonlinear latent mixed effects models* (e.g., Skrondal & Rabe-Hesketh, 2004), many latent mixture models, unrestricted latent class models, and DCMs can be estimated with general-purpose latent variable estimation programs such as Mplus 6.0 (Muthén & Muthén, 2010), SAS GLIMMIX (*see* Wedel, 2001), and GLLAMM (e.g., Rabe-Hesketh, Skrondal, & Pickles, 2002; www.gllamm.org). However, there exist also specialized programs for latent class and finite mixture analysis such as Latent Gold 4.5 (Vermunt & Magidson, 2005) that can be combined with classification/segmentation programs like SI-CHAID (Magidson, 2005), specialized programs for discrete mixture models with categorical variables including mixture item response theory models such as Winmira 2001 (von Davier, 2001), and specialized programs for DCMs such as MDLTM (von Davier, 2006) or the code for the G-DINA model by de la Torre (2011).

Assessing Model-Data Fit at Different Levels

The results of any statistical analysis are only useful if the fit of the model to the data is of an acceptable nature, which is equally true of the parametric latent class models that I have discussed in this section. The assessment of model-data fit can proceed at five levels—namely, at the level of (1) global relative fit between nested models, (2) global relative fit between non-nested models, (3) global absolute fit for a particular model, (4) local item fit, and (5) local person fit. I will briefly discuss some strategies for performing model-data fit assessment at these levels for latent class models in this subsection.

Relative Fit Assessment

In finite mixture models for single quantitative response variables, competing models are typically defined by the number of latent classes that are estimated; for example, one may want to compare the fit of one-, two-, and three-class models for a single normally distributed response variable. In finite mixture models for multiple quantitative variables, competing models are typically defined both by the number of latent classes that are estimated as well as by the structure of the variance–covariance matrix across latent classes. For example, one may want to compare the fit of one-, two-, and three-class models with identical variance–covariance matrices across latent classes or the fit of these models with different variance–covariance matrices across latent classes.

In unrestricted latent class models for multiple qualitative response variables, competing models are typically defined by the number of latent classes that are estimated similar to finite mixture models for single quantitative response variables. However, item parameter restrictions across latent classes can be imposed to impose equality or order constraints in alignment with a theory of responding, as stated earlier in this section. In restricted latent class models for multiple quantitative response variables, there are even more choices that are possible. For example, one could compare the relative fit of models with and without interaction effects for items that measure multiple attributes or one could compare the relative fit of models with different numbers of attributes, which leads to a different number of latent classes.

In general, one statistical model is considered *nested* within a competing statistical model if the simpler nested model can be obtained by placing constraints on certain parameters in the more complex model. In these cases, the statistical test of choice is a *likelihood-ratio* (LR) test, which follows well-known χ^2 sampling distributions. The exact degrees of freedom for any particular LR test are the difference in the number of parameters for both models, and because the number of parameters in these models depends on their complexity I cannot provide a single simple formula.

If it is not possible to obtain a simpler statistical model from a particular competing statistical model by placing constraints on parameters in the latter, then the two models are said to be *non-nested*. In this case, the method of choice is to use descriptive indices of relative model fit based on statistical information theory. Different *information criteria* (IC) have been proposed in the literature in both uncorrected and various corrected versions. The most common information indices are the uncorrected *Akaike's information criterion* (AIC) (e.g., Akaike, 1974), the consistent AIC (CAIC) (e.g., Bozdogan, 1987), and the *Bayesian information criterion* (BIC) (e.g., Schwarz, 1976) within a frequentist or empirical Bayes estimation framework as well as the *deviance information criterion* (DIC) and the *Bayes factor* within a fully Bayesian estimation framework (e.g., Spiegelhalter, Best, Carlin, & van der Linde, 2002).

Specifically, the general structure for key information criteria can be expressed as:

$$IC = -2lnL + \tau(penalty) \quad (20)$$

$$AIC = -2lnL + \tau 2 \quad (21)$$

$$BIC = -2lnL + \tau ln(N) \quad (22)$$

$$CAIC = -2lnL + \tau(ln(N) + 1), \quad (23)$$

where lnL represents the log-likelihood of the data, N represents the sample size, and τ represents the number of estimated model parameters for a given model. Yang (1998) showed how a variety of fit indices for frequentist or empirical Bayes estimation frameworks can be expressed as special cases of a general formula and have been extended to include additional adjustments based on sample size. Recent research by Yang and Yang (2007) has shown how sample-size-adjusted versions of these indices outperform other versions for various parametric latent class models.

All of these indices are functions of the likelihood of the model under question and penalty terms that statistically penalize overparameterizations of particular models, which is to say that they increase the baseline information value as a function of the number of parameters that are included in the model. This is done to prevent so-called *overfitting* of models, because it is a well-known fact that the fit of a model to data can generally be improved if more variables and associated parameters are included in it even if they do not improve the fit by much. Among the three indices shown above, the penalization is least strong in the AIC, stronger in the BIC, and strongest in the CAIC. The guideline for making decisions about relative global model fit is to choose the model that has the lowest value for a chosen information criterion. In practice, different information criteria may point to different models because they penalize differentially strong for model complexity.

Absolute Fit Assessment

One of the drawbacks of relative fit assessment is that it cannot determine whether any of the models actually fits the data well; put differently, the best-fitting model determined by a relative model-data fit assessment strategy may still be fitting the data poorly. Thus, an assessment of global absolute model fit is needed next, which I will do specifically in the context of unrestricted latent class models.

Determining the global fit for these types of latent class model is typically done using a LR statistic denoted L^2, which follows a χ^2 sampling distribution. It compares the observed and expected (i.e., model-predicted) frequencies across response categories across latent classes:

$$L^2 = 2 \sum_{i=1}^{n} \sum_{j=1}^{J} \sum_{k=1}^{K} \sum_{m=1}^{M_j} f_{ijkm} \ln\left[\frac{\widehat{f}_{ijkm}}{f_{ijkm}}\right], \quad (24)$$

where $i = 1, \ldots, n$ denotes respondents, $j = 1, \ldots, J$ denotes items, $m = 1, \ldots, M_j$ denotes the response categories for item j, $k = 1, \ldots, K$ denotes the latent classes, f_{ijkm} denotes the observed frequency of responses, and $\widehat{f}_{ijkm}$ denotes the expected frequency of responses. Intuitively, if the model fits the data well, then it would be able to reproduce the observed frequencies very well, in which case the L^2 statistic would be close to 0.

One caveat with this statistic is that its sampling distribution is not well approximated by a χ^2 distribution when many cells are sparse, which can be frequently the case when unrestricted latent class models and DCMs are applied to longer tests with many items. In this case, a *resampling* or *bootstrapping approach* for estimating an *empirical sampling distribution* for this statistic or a fully Bayesian estimation approach with suitable prior distributions is recommended.

Item-Fit Assessment

Depending on the stakes of the decisions that are attached to the parameter interpretations of a particular latent class model, it may be desirable to dig further into the fit of a model at local levels. Note that this is mostly of interest for unrestricted and restricted latent class models, rather than finite mixture models, because the former models are specifically concerned with modeling the structure of assessment instruments where such information is most critical for reporting and decision-making purposes.

A simple strategy for assessing the utility of including a particular item within unrestricted latent class models was already alluded to earlier. It is to constrain the response probabilities for this item to equality across latent classes and to perform a relative model-fit test for nested models to determine whether this restriction is tenable. If it is, then the item does not contribute to the differentiation of respondents into different latent classes and can be deleted; if it is not, then the item should be retained.

For DCMs, the use of χ^2 statistics for individual items is sometimes discussed. These statistics compare the observed and expected (i.e., model-predicted) frequencies across response categories for items for each latent class, summed and weighted across latent classes. If the expected frequencies are strikingly different from the observed frequencies, then the associated hypothesis test for the χ^2 statistics will be statistically significant, and the fit of a particular item is said to be poor. As with other applications of the χ^2 statistic, it is rather sensitive to even mild differences between expected and observed frequencies.

Recent research for DCMs by Kunina-Habenicht, Rupp, and Wilhelm (2012) has investigated the performance of four-item-level fit indices that differ in the way that they weight observed and expected response frequencies across the latent classes and in the way that they compute these differences. Specifically, two indices used the squared difference versus the absolute value difference between the observed and expected values, and two indices used an equal weighting versus a mixing proportion weighting for these differences. The four indices are referred to as two versions of a *mean absolute deviation* (MAD) index (i.e., equally weighted and differentially weighted) and two versions of a *root mean square error of approximation* (RMSEA) index (equally weighted and differentially weighted):

$$MAD_j^{(equal)} = \frac{\sum_{k=1}^{K} |\pi_{jk}^{obs} - \pi_{jk}^{pred}|}{2K} \quad (25)$$

$$MAD_j^{(different)} = \sum_{k=1}^{K} v_k |\pi_{jk}^{obs} - \pi_{jk}^{pred}| \quad (26)$$

$$RMSEA_j^{(equal)} = \sqrt{\frac{\sum_{k=1}^{K} \left(\pi_{jk}^{obs} - \pi_{jk}^{pred}\right)^2}{2K}} \quad (27)$$

$$RMSEA_j^{(different)} = \sqrt{\sum_{k=1}^{K} v_k \left(\pi_{jk}^{obs} - \pi_{jk}^{pred}\right)^2} \quad (28)$$

where $j = 1, \ldots, J$ denotes a particular item, $k = 1, \ldots, K$ denotes the latent classes, π_{jk}^{obs} denotes the observed proportion of correct responses to item j by respondents in latent class k, and π_{jk}^{pred} denotes the expected (i.e., model-predicted) proportion of correct responses to item j by respondents in latent class k.

Previous research on the RMSEA had suggested that values below 0.05 indicate an excellent fit, values between 0.05 and 0.10 indicate a moderate fit, and values above 0.10 indicate a poor fit at the item level, which roughly resemble guidelines similar to applications of an RMSEA index for global model-fit assessment confirmatory factor analysis. However, preliminary findings from the research on all four indices suggests that these values may have to be adjusted depending on factors such as the number of attributes that are measured by each item and the index chosen.

Similarly, Lee and de la Torre (2010) have shown how the Wald test is generally powerful for performing item-level fit assessment under local model misspecification. Taking a slightly different modeling approach, de la Torre (2008a) has proposed an item-fit index for certain DCM that he is currently extending to a broader family of DCMs; this index is based on an optimization process that seeks to determine places in the Q-matrix where potential misspecifications have occurred.

Person-Fit Assessment

Relatively little research is currently available at the level of individual respondents. Generally speaking, similarly to item-fit assessment, one could estimate a particular latent class model twice, once with a particular person removed and once with that person included, and then conduct a χ^2 test for nested models. However, because the number of respondents is generally relatively large, such an iterative approach is not practically feasible.

Rather, it is more feasible to use indices that can detect aberrant (i.e., unusual) response patterns for individual respondents similarly to such work in nonparametric item response theory (e.g., Emons, Sijtsma, & Meijer, 2005). In one recent paper, Liu, Douglas, and Henson (2009) have investigated the feasibility of using a likelihood-ratio test for assessing person fit. The test followed the theoretical sampling distribution in the tail and was useful for detecting the kind of aberrant respondent behavior that was more strongly different from what one would expect under the model; however, it was only mildly powerful for detecting mildly aberrant respondent behavior, as that is harder to detect.

The definition of the index was based on a general framework for modeling person misfit that could be adapted to broader classes of DCMs and more varied types of aberrant respondent behavior. Similarly, von Davier and Molenaar (2003) proposed a variant of the l_z statistic for latent class models that would seem to be a promising candidate. In short, the work on person fit for DCMs is in its infancy, relatively speaking, but more work is undoubtedly going to appear in the years to come, as it represents an important aspect of the overall assessment of the fit of the model to the data.

Concluding Remarks

In this chapter I have reviewed a variety of techniques for clustering and classifying cases/respondents into different clusters/latent classes on the basis of multiple-outcome/response variables. The techniques included nonparametric techniques from hierarchical and K-means cluster analysis and parametric/model-based techniques from finite mixture model and latent class analysis. As with any field whose boundaries are fuzzy, whose applications are interdisciplinary, and whose methodological toolbox is vast, I was only able to provide a brief snapshot of different approaches here.

As I have discussed in this chapter, many related applications that draw on the conceptual ideas of clustering and classification for the purposes of explanation and prediction exist. Nevertheless, the snapshot of some of the key ideas and core principles that underlie clustering and classification techniques that I have provided in this chapter should empower readers to read primary and secondary sources in their own fields to make even deeper and richer connections.

Importantly, research in these areas is constantly expanding. Driven by computational advances—especially multiprocessor machines and cloud computing—I expect the field of simulation studies for these techniques to explode even further in the following years. It is my hope that the journey through the methodological space that I presented in this chapter is robust enough that it will remain useful for readers for a few years to come.

Author Note

This work was made possible, in part, by two grants from the National Science Foundation awarded to the University of Wisconsin at Madison (DRL-0918409 and DRL-0946372). The opinions, findings, and conclusions or recommendations in this paper are those of the authors and do not necessarily reflect the views of the funding agencies, cooperating institutions, or other individuals.

Glossary of Selected Key Terms

Key term	Explanation
Attribute profile	A combination of latent variable indicator values that is used to characterize respondents in different latent classes based on a set of underlying unobserved latent characteristics/attributes
Bayesian estimation framework	A general set of estimation techniques that rely on prior and posterior distributions of parameters to obtain parameter estimates and associated standard error estimates
City-block distance	A commonly used distance measure based on absolute value differences of coordinate values of points in multivariate space
Classification techniques	Techniques that are used to predict group membership and thus classify cases/respondents into a number of known groups/classes
Clustering techniques	Techniques that are used to sort/group a number of cases/respondents into a number of unobserved groups/clusters based on a number of outcome/response variables
Dendrogram	A visual display of the sequential cluster structure for a hierarchical clustering technique
Diagnostic classification models	Confirmatory latent class models that predict the latent class membership using multiple unobserved latent attribute variables
Distance/Similarity/Dissimilarity measure	A statistical quantity that is used to quantify how far cases are away from each other in a multivariate space
Euclidian distance	A commonly used distance measure based on squared differences of coordinate values of points in multivariate space
Expected *a posteriori* estimate	A parameter estimate based on the mean of the posterior distribution within a Bayesian estimation framework
Factor analysis	A set of statistical techniques that are used to summarize the covariation among a set of typically continuous item responses via a smaller set of continuous unobserved latent variables
Fit assessment	A process for identifying whether a statistical model does an acceptable job of reproducing key characteristics of the observed data structure in a relative, absolute, item-level, or person-level sense
Frequentist estimation framework	A general set of estimation techniques that are used to obtain parameter estimates and estimates of their associated standard errors
Hierarchical clustering techniques	A set of techniques that leads to a series of nested groups/clusters based on sequential partitions (divisive techniques) or aggregations (agglomerative techniques) of cases
Information criterion	A statistical quantity that can be used to assess which of several non-nested model provides the best fit for a given data set

Glossary of Selected Key Terms (Continued)

Key term	Explanation
Item response theory	A set of statistical techniques that are used to summarize the covariation among a set of typically discrete item responses via a smaller set of continuous unobserved latent variables
K-means clustering	A particularly popular partitioning technique where the number of resulting groups/clusters is prespecified to be K; the cases in the resulting groups/clusters are maximally homogeneous while the groups/clusters are maximally heterogeneous
Latent class models	Parametric statistical models that model the joint distribution on outcome/response variables using a certain number of unobserved latent classes
Likelihood-ratio test	A statistical test whose formulation is based on the comparison of the empirical likelihood under a null and an alternative hypothesis
Linear predictor	A regression-type expression that combines intercept, main-effect, and interaction-effect terms in a linear manner to predict certain outcomes
Linkage	A measure of intercluster distance in hierarchical clustering methods based on the smallest (single linkage), largest (complete linkage), or average (mean linkage) distance between any two points in any two clusters
Local/conditional independence	An assumption made by latent variable models that specifies that the responses on a set of outcome/response variables are independent for respondents with identical values on the latent variables
Mahalanobis distance	A multivariate extension of the squared Euclidian distance that incorporates information about the covariance structure of the variables that are used to compute the distance
Masking variable	A variable that does not contribute much essential information about the true underlying cluster structure
Maximum a posteriori estimate	A parameter estimate based on the mode of the posterior distribution within a Bayesian estimation framework
Measurement scale	A description of the nature of an outcome/response variable that includes nominal, ordinal, interval, and ratio scales for discrete and continuous variables
Minkowski distance	A framework for computing a variety of distance measures, which can be obtained by setting a particular parameter p to certain values
Mixing proportion	The proportion of cases/respondents that are classified into each unobserved latent class in a latent class model
Multivariate data analysis	An umbrella term that subsumes a wide variety of statistical techniques for analyzing the joint variation and covariation among a set of outcome/response variables
Multivariate finite mixture models	A set of statistical models that postulate a particular response distribution for multiple outcome/response variables along with multiple unobserved latent groups/classes for which the parameters for this joint distribution can differ
Nested models	A term for two statistical models where one of the models can be obtained from the other model by placing certain parameter restrictions
Non-nested models	A term for two statistical models where one of the models cannot be obtained from the other model by placing certain parameter restrictions

Glossary of Selected Key Terms (Continued)

Key term	Explanation
Non-parametric techniques	Techniques that do not make distributional assumptions about the response variables.
Objective function	A statistical expression whose value is to be minimized or maximized, depending on the computational approach, to determine a solution for a clustering or classification technique
Parametric techniques	Techniques that make distributional assumptions about the response variables
Partitioning clustering techniques	A set of techniques that leads to a series of non-nested groups/clusters based on iterative case assignment and re-assignment
p-median clustering	A popular alternative method to K-means clustering based on objective functions that utilize differences around medians rather than means
Probability density function	A distribution function for a single or multiple outcome/response variable(s) such as a univariate or multivariate normal distribution
Q-matrix	A design table/loading matrix that indicates which items on an assessment measure which unobserved latent attributes
Relative clusterability	A quantity that is used in a particularly effective standardization for outcome/response variables that quantifies how much information a variable carries about the true underlying cluster structure
Restricted latent class models	A set of statistical models for categorical outcome variables, which include a certain number of unobserved latent classes with some restrictions on either the number of latent classes and/or parameters across latent classes
Structural equation modeling	An umbrella term for a wide range of statistical techniques that summarize the relationship between multiple outcome/response variables via multiple unobserved latent variables on different measurement scales
Supremum distance	A distance measure based on the largest difference of two coordinate values of points in multivariate space
Univariate finite mixture models	A set of statistical models that postulate a particular response distribution for a single outcome/response variables along with multiple unobserved latent groups/classes for which the distributional parameters for this variable can differ
Unrestricted latent class models	A set of statistical models for categorical outcome variables, which include a certain number of unobserved latent classes with no particular restrictions on the number of latent classes
Ward's linkage	A measure for obtaining a cluster structure in hierarchical clustering methods that minimizes the within-cluster variance similar to the objective function in K-means clustering

References

Agresti, A. (2007). *Categorical data analysis* (2nd ed.). Hoboken, NJ: Wiley.

Akaike, H. (1974). A new look at the statistical identification model. *IEEE Transactions on Automated Control, 19,* 716–723.

Almond, R. G., Williamson, D. M., Mislevy, R. J., & Yan, D. (in press). *Bayes nets in educational assessment.* New York: Springer.

Avella, P., Sassano, A., & Vasil'ev, I. (2007). Computational study of large-scale *p*-median problems. *Mathematical Programming A, 109,* 89–114.

Banerjee, A., Dhillon, I., Ghosh, J., Merugu, S., & Modha, D. S. (2007). A generalized maximum entropy approach to Bregman co-clustering and matrix approximation. *Journal of Machine Research Learning, 8,* 1919–1986.

Bauer, D. (2007). 2004 Cattel Award address: Observations on the use of growth mixture models in psychological research. *Multivariate Behavioral Research, 42,* 757–786.

Bock, H. H. (2007). Clustering methods: A history of K-means algorithms. In P. Brito, P. Bertrand, G. Cucumel, & F. De Carvalho (Eds.), *Selected contributions in data analysis and classification* (pp. 161–172). Berlin: Springer.

Bock, R., & Aitken, M. (1982). Errata: Marginal maximum likelihood estimation of item parameters: Application of an EM algorithm. *Psychometrika, 47,* 369.

Bock, R. D., & Aitken, M. (1981). Marginal maximum likelihood estimation of item parameters: Application of an EM algorithm. *Psychometrika, 46,* 443–459.

Bolton, R. J., & Krzanowski, W. J. (2003). Projection pursuit clustering for exploratory data analysis. *Journal of Computational and Graphical Statistics, 12,* 121–142.

Borg, I., & Groenen, P. J. F. (2009). *Modern multidimensional scaling: Theory and applications.* New York: Springer.

Bozdogan, H. (1987). Model selection and Akaike's Information Criterion (AIC): The general theory and its analytical extensions. *Psychometrika, 52,* 345–370.

Breiman, L., Friedman, J., Stone, C. J., & Olshen, R. A. (1984). *Classification and regression trees.* Boca Raton, FL: Chapman & Hall/CRC.

Brown, T. A. (2006). *Confirmatory factor analysis for applied research.* New York: Guilford Press.

Brusco, M. J. (2004). Clustering binary data in the presence of masking variables. *Psychological Methods, 9,* 510–523.

Brusco, M. J., & Cradit, J. D. (2001). A variable-selection heuristic for K-means clustering. *Psychometrika, 66,* 249–270.

Brusco, M. J., Cradit, J. D., Steinley, D., & Fox, G. J. (2008). Cautionary remarks on the use of clusterwise regression. *Multivariate Behavioral Research, 43,* 29–49.

Brusco, M. J., & Köhn, H.-F. (2008). Optimal partitioning of a data set based on the p-median model. *Psychometrika, 73,* 89–105.

Brusco, M. J., & Köhn, H.-F. (2009). Exemplar-based clustering via simulated annealing. *Psychometrika, 74,* 457–475.

Casella, G., & Berger, R. L. (2001). *Statistical inference* (2nd ed.). Belmont, CA: Duxbury Press.

Chiang, M. M.-T., & Mirkin, B. (2010). Intelligent choice of clusters in K-means clustering: An experimental study with different cluster spreads. *Journal of Classification, 27,* 3–40.

Chiu, C.-Y. (2008). *Cluster analysis for cognitive diagnosis: Theory and applications.* Unpublished doctoral dissertation, University of Illinois at Urbana-Champaign, Urbana-Champaign, IL.

Chiu, C.-Y., & Douglas, J. (2009). Cluster analysis for cognitive diagnosis: Theory and applications. *Psychometrika, 74,* 633–665.

Collins, L. M., & Lanza, S. T. (2009). *Latent class and latent transition analysis with applications in the social, behavioral, and health sciences.* New York: Wiley.

de Ayala, R. J. (2009). *The theory and practice of item response theory.* New York: Guilford Press.

de Craen, S., Commandeur, J. J. F., Frank, L. E., & Heiser, W. J. (2006). Effects of group size and lack of sphericity on the recovery of clusters in K-means cluster analysis. *Multivariate Behavioral Research, 41,* 127–145.

de la Torre, J. (2011). The generalized DINA model framework. *Psychometrika, 76,* 179–199.

de la Torre, J. (2008a). An empirically based method of Q-matrix validation for the DINA model: Development and applications. *Journal of Educational Measurement, 45,* 343–362.

de la Torre, J. (July, 2008b). *The generalized DINA model.* Paper presented at the annual International Meeting of the Psychometric Society (IMPS), Durham, NH.

Delwiche, L. D., & Slaughter, S. J. (2008). *The little SAS book.* SAS Institute.

Dempster, A. P., Laird, N. M., & Rubin, D. B. (1977). Maximum likelihood from incomplete data via the EM algorithm. *Journal of the Royal Statistical Society, Series B (Methodological), 39,* 1–38.

Dobson, A. J., & Barnett, A. (2008). *An introduction to generalized linear models* (3rd ed.). Boca Raton, FL: Chapman & Hall/CRC.

Dolan, C. V. (2009). Structural equation mixture modeling. In R. E. Milsap & A. Maydeu-Olivares (Eds.), *The SAGE handbook of quantitative methods in psychology* (pp. 568–591). Thousand Oaks, CA: Sage.

Emons, W. H. M., Sijtsma, K., & Meijer, R. R. (2005). Global, local, and graphical person-fit analysis using person-response functions. *Psychological Methods, 10,* 101–119.

Fan, Z., Chiu, C., Köhn, H.-F., & Douglas, J. (2009). *Performance of several distance measures for clustering data arising from some common models in educational testing.* Presented at the Joint Annual Meeting of the Interface and the Classification Society, St. Louis, MO.

Faraway, J. J. (2004). *Linear models with R.* Boca Raton, FL: Chapman & Hall/CRC.

Faraway, J. J. (2005). *Extending the linear model with R: Generalized linear, mixed effects, and nonparametric regression models.* Boca Raton, FL: Chapman & Hall/CRC.

Fraley, C., & Raftery, A.E. (1998). How many clusters? Which clustering method? Answers via model-based cluster analysis. *The Computer Journal, 41,* 578–588.

Fraley, C., & Raftery, A.E. (2003). Enhanced model-based clustering, density estimation, and discriminant analysis software: MCLUST. *Journal of Classification, 20,* 263–286.

Froelich, A. G., & Habing, B. (2008). Conditional covariance-based subtest selection for DIMTEST. *Applied Psychological Measurement, 32,* 138–155.

Gan, G., Ma, C., & Wu, J. (2007). *Data clustering: Theory, algorithms, and applications.* Alexandria, VA: American Statistical Association.

Gelman, A., Carlin, J. B., Stern, H. S., & Rubin, D. B. (2003). *Bayesian data analysis* (2nd ed.). Boca Raton, FL: Chapman & Hall/CRC.

Gershoff, E. T., Pedersen, S., & Aber, J. L. (2009). Creating neighborhood typologies of GIS-based data in the absence of neighborhood-based sampling: A factor and cluster analytic strategy. *Journal of Prevention & Intervention in the Community, 37,* 35–47.

Gierl, M. J., Leighton, J. P., & Hunka, S. M. (2007). Using the attribute hierarchy method to make diagnostic inferences about respondents' cognitive skills. In J. P. Leighton & M. J. Gierl (Eds.), *Cognitive diagnostic assessment for education: Theory and applications* (pp. 242–274). Cambridge, UK: Cambridge University Press.

Haberman, S., & Sinharay, S. (2009). Reporting of subscores using multidimensional item response theory. *Psychometrika, 75,* 209–227.

Hagenaars, J. A., & McCutcheon, A. L. (2009). *Applied latent class analysis.* New York: Cambridge University Press.

Hair, J. F., Black, W. C., Babin, B. J., & Anderson, R. E. (2009). *Multivariate data analysis* (7th ed.). New York: Prentice Hall.

Hambleton, R. K., & Pitoniak, M. J. (2006). Setting performance standards. In R. L. Brennan (Ed.), *Educational measurement* (4th ed.) (pp. 433–470). Washington, DC: American Council on Education.

Hancock, G. R., & Mueller, R. O. (2006). *Structural equation modeling: A second course*. Charlotte, NC: Information Age Publishing.

Hansen, P., & Mladenović, N. (2008). Complement to a comparative analysis of heuristics for the p-median problem. *Statistics and Computing, 18*, 41–46.

Hastie, T., Tibshirani, R., & Friedman, J. (2009). *The elements of statistical learning: Data mining, inference, and prediction* (2nd ed.). New York: Springer.

Heinz, G., Peterson, L. J., Johnson, R. W., & Kerk, C. J. (2003). Exploring relationships in body dimensions. *Journal of Statistics Education*, 11. Available at www.amstat.org/publications/jse/v11n2/datasets.heinz.html

Heiser, W. J., & Groenen, P. J. F. (1997). Cluster differences scaling with a within-cluster loss component and a fuzzy successive approximation strategy to avoid local minima. *Psychometrika, 62*, 63–83.

Henson, R., Templin, J., & Willse, J. (2009). Defining a family of cognitive diagnosis models. *Psychometrika, 74*, 191–210.

Hubert, L., & Arabie, P. (1985). Comparing partitions. *Journal of Classification, 2*, 193–218.

Hubert, L., Köhn, H.-F., & Steinley, D. (2009). Cluster analysis: A toolbox for MATLAB. In R. Millsap & A. Maydeu-Olivares (Eds.), The *SAGE handbook of quantitative methods in psychology* (pp. 444–512). Los Angeles, CA: Sage.

Huberty, C. J., & Olejnik, S. (2006). *Applied MANOVA and discriminant analysis*. New York: Wiley.

Huebner, A. (2010, May). *Comparing classification methods for cognitive diagnosis models*. Presented at the annual meeting of the American Educational Research Association (AERA), Denver, CO.

Jajuga, K., Sokolowski, A., & Bock, H.-H. (2002). *Classification, clustering, and data analysis: Recent advances and applications*. New York: Springer.

Jambu, M. (1978). *Classification automatique pour l'analyse de données* [Automatic classification for data analysis]. Paris: Dunod.

Johnson, R. A., & Wichern, D. W. (2007). *Applied multivariate statistical analysis* (6th ed.). New York: Prentice Hall.

Kauermann, G., Ormerod, J. T., & Wand, M. P. (2010). Parsimonious classification via generalized linear mixed models. *Journal of Classification, 27*, 89–110.

Kaufman, L., & Rousseeuw, P. J. (2005). *Finding groups in data: An introduction to cluster analysis*. New York: Wiley.

Kettenring, J. R. (2006). The practice of cluster analysis. *Journal of Classification, 23*, 3–30.

Kiers, H. A. L., Vicari, D., & Vichi, M. (2005). Simultaneous classification and multidimensional scaling with external information. *Psychometrika, 70*, 433–460.

Kim, K., & Timm, N. (2006). *Univariate and multivariate general linear models: Theory and applications with SAS*. Boca Raton, FL: Chapman & Hall/CRC.

Kline, R. B. (2010). *Principles and practice of structural equation modelling* (3rd ed.). New York: Guilford Press.

Köhn, H.-F., Steinley, D., & Brusco, M. J. (2010). The p-median model as a tool for clustering psychological data. *Psychological Methods, 15*, 87–95.

Kunina-Habenicht, O., Rupp, A. A., & Wilhelm, O. (2012). The impact of model misspecification on parameter estimation and item-fit assessment in log-linear diagnostic classification models. *Journal of Educational Measurement, 49*, 59–81.

Kurihara, K., & Welling, M. (2009). Bayesian k-means as a "maximization-expectation" algorithm. *Neural Computation, 21*, 1145–1172.

Lance, G., & Williams, W. (1967). A general theory of classificatory sorting strategies II: Clustering systems. *The Computer Journal, 10*, 271–277.

Lattin, J., Carroll, J. D., & Green, P. E. (2002). *Analyzing multivariate data*. Pacific Grove, CA: Brooks/Cole-Thomson Learning.

Lee, Y.-S., & de la Torre, J. (May, 2010). *Item-level comparisons of saturated and reduced cognitive diagnosis models*. Presented at the annual meeting of the National Council on Measurement in Education (NCME), Denver, CO.

Legendre, L., & Legendre, P. (1983). *Numerical ecology*. New York: Elsevier Scientific.

Liu, Y., Douglas, J. A., & Henson, R. A. (2009). Testing person fit in cognitive diagnosis. *Applied Psychological Measurement, 33*, 579–598.

Lynch, S. (2007). *Introduction to applied Bayesian statistics and estimation for social scientists*. New York: Springer.

MacQueen, J. (1967). Some methods of classification and analysis of multivariate observations. In L. M. Le Cam & J. Neyman (Eds.), *Proceedings of the fifth Berkeley symposium on mathematical statistics and probability* (Vol. 1, pp. 281–297). Berkeley, CA: University of California Press.

Magidson, J. (2005). *SI-CHAID 4.0 user's guide*. Belmont, MA: Statistical Innovations.

McCullagh, P., Searle, S. R., & Neuhaus, J. M. (2008). *Generalized, linear, and mixed models*. New York: Wiley.

McDonald, R. P. (1999). *Test theory: A unified treatment*. Mahwah, NJ: Erlbaum.

McLachlan, G. J., & Peel, D. (2000). *Finite mixture models*. New York: Wiley.

Milligan, G. W., & Cooper, M. C. (1986). A study of the comparability of external criteria for hierarchical cluster analysis. *Multivariate Behavioral Research, 21*, 441–458.

Milligan, G. W., & Cooper, M. C. (1988). A study of variable standardization. *Journal of Classification, 5*, 181–204.

Muthén, L. K., & Muthén, B. O. (2010). *Mplus Version 6.0* [Computer software]. Los Angeles, CA: Muthén & Muthén.

National Center for Education Statistics (2006). *Comparing mathematics content in the National Assessment of Educational Progress (NAEP), Trends in International Mathematics and Science Study (TIMSS), and Program for International Student Assessment (PISA) 2003 assessments* (Report # 1006-029). Washington, DC: NCES.

National Center for Education Statistics (2007). *Mapping 2005 state proficiency standards onto the NAEP scales* (Report # 2007-482). Washington, DC: NCES.

Nisbet, R., Elder, J., & Miner, G. (2009). *Handbook of statistical analysis and data mining applications*. Burlington, MA: Elsevier.

Nugent, R., Dean, N., & Ayers, E. (2010), Skill set profile clustering: The empty K-means algorithm with automatic specification of starting cluster centers. In R. S. J. D. Baker, A. Merceron, & P. I. Pavlik Jr. (Eds.), *Proceedings from Educational Data Mining 2010: 3rd International Conference* on *Educational Data Mining*, 151–160. Available online at http://www.stats.gla.ac.uk/~nd29c/publications.html

Puhan, G., Sinharay, S., Haberman, S., & Larkin, K. (2010). The utility of augmented subscores in licensure exams: An evaluation of methods using empirical data. *Applied Measurement in Education, 23*, 266–285.

Qian, G., Wu, Y., & Shao, Q. (2009). A procedure for estimating the number of clusters in logistic regression clustering. *Journal of Classification, 26*, 183–199.

Qiu, W.-L. & Joe, H. (2006a) Generation of random clusters with specified degree of separation. *Journal of Classification, 23*, 315–334.

Qiu, W.-L. & Joe, H. (2006b) Separation index and partial membership for clustering. *Computational Statistics and Data Analysis, 50*, 585–603.

Quarteroni, A., & Saleri, F. (2006). *Scientific computing with MATLAB and Octave*. New York: Springer.

Rabe-Hesketh, S., Skrondal, A. & Pickles, A. (2002). Reliable estimation of generalized linear mixed models using adaptive quadrature. *The Stata Journal, 2*, 1–21.

Rokach, L. (2010). *Pattern classification using ensemble methods*. Hackensack, NJ : World Scientific Publishing Company.

Rokach, L., & Maimon, O. (2008). *Data mining with decision trees : Theory and applications*. Hackensack, NJ : World Scientific Publishing Company.

Rupp, A. A. (in press). Psychological vs. psychometric dimensionality in diagnostic language assessments: Subscore issues in multidimensional measurement theory. In J. Sabatini & E. R. Albro (Eds.), *Assessing reading in the 21st century: Aligning and applying advances in the reading and measurement sciences*. New York: Rowan & Littlefield Education.

Rupp, A. A., Dey, D. K., & Zumbo, B. D. (2004). To Bayes or not to Bayes, from whether to when: Applications of Bayesian methodology to modelling. *Structural Equation Modeling, 11*, 424–421.

Rupp, A. A., & Templin, J. (2008). Unique characteristics of cognitive diagnosis models: A comprehensive review of the current state-of-the-art. *Measurement: Interdisciplinary Research & Perspectives, 6*, 219–262.

Rupp, A. A., Templin, J., & Henson, R. J. (2010). *Diagnostic measurement: Theory, methods, and applications*. New York: Guilford Press.

Schmitt, J. E., Mehta, P. D., Aggen, S. H., Kubarych, T. S., & Neale, M. C. (2006). Semi-nonparametric methods for detecting latent non-normality: A fusion of latent trait and ordered latent class modeling. *Multivariate Behavioral Research, 41*, 427–443.

Schrepp, M. (2005). About the connection between knowledge structures and latent class models. *Methodology, 1*(3), 93–103.

Schwarz, G. (1976). Estimating the dimension of a model. *Annals of Statistics, 6*, 461–464.

Skrondal, A., & Rabe-Hesketh, S. (2004). *Generalized latent variable modeling: Multilevel, longitudinal, and structural equation models*. Boca Raton, FL: Chapman & Hall/CRC.

Spiegelhalter, D. J., Best, N. G., Carlin, B. P., & van der Linde, A. (2002). Bayesian measures of model complexity and fit (with discussion). *Journal of the Royal Statistical Society, Series B (Statistical Methodology), 64*, 583–639.

SPSS Inc. (1998). *SPSS Base 17.0 for Windows user's guide*. Chicago, IL: SPSS.

Steinley, D. (2003). Local optima in K-means clustering: What you don't know may hurt you. *Psychological Methods, 8*, 294–304.

Steinley, D. (2004a). Standardizing variables in K-means clustering. In D. Banks, L. House, F. R. McMorris, P. Arabie, & W. Gaul (Eds.), *Classification, clustering, and data mining applications* (pp. 53–60). New York: Springer.

Steinley, D. (2004b). Properties of the Hubert–Arabie adjusted Rand index. *Psychological Methods, 9*, 386–396.

Steinley, D. (2006a). K-means clustering: A half-century synthesis. *British Journal of Mathematical and Statistical Psychology, 59*, 1–34.

Steinley, D. (2006b). Profiling local optima in K-means clustering: Developing a diagnostic technique. *Psychological Methods, 11*, 178–192.

Steinley, D. (2008a). Data clustering: Theory, algorithms, and applications. [Book review]. *Journal of the American Statistical Association, 103*, 1710–1711.

Steinley, D. (2008b). Stability analysis in K-means clustering. *British Journal of Mathematical and Statistical Psychology, 61*, 255–273.

Steinley, D., & Brusco, M. J. (2007). Initializing K-means batch clustering: A critical evaluation of several techniques. *Journal of Classification, 24*, 99–121.

Steinley, D., & Brusco, M. J. (2008a). A new variable weighting and selection procedure for K-means cluster analysis. *Multivariate Behavioral Research, 43*, 77–108.

Steinley, D., & Brusco, M. J. (2008b). Selection of variables in cluster analysis: An empirical comparison of eight procedures. *Psychometrika, 73*, 125–144.

Steinley, D., & Henson, R. (2005). OCLUS: An analytic method for generating clusters with known overlap. *Journal of Classification, 22*, 221–250.

Steinley, D., & Hubert, L. (2008). Order-constrained solutions in K-means clustering: Even better than being globally optimal. *Psychometrika, 73*, 647–664.

Stevens, S.S. (1946). On the theory of scales of measurement. *Science, 103*, 677–680.

Takeuchi, A., Saito, T., & Yadohisa, H. (2007). Asymmetric agglomerative hierarchical clustering algorithms and their evaluation. *Journal of Classification, 24*, 123–143.

Tatsuoka, K. K. (2009). *Cognitive assessment: An introduction to the rule-space method*. Florence, KY: Routledge.

Templin, J., & Henson, R. (April, 2009). *Practical issues in using diagnostic estimates: Measuring the reliability and validity of diagnostic estimates*. Presented at the annual meeting of the National Council of Measurement in Education, San Diego, CA.

Ünlü, A. (2006). Estimation of careless error and lucky guess probabilities for dichotomous test items: A psychometric application of a biometric latent class model with random effects. *Journal of Mathematical Psychology, 50*, 309–328.

Van Horn, M. L., Jaki, T., Masyn, K., Ramey, S. L., Smith, J. A., & Antaramian, S. (2009). Assessing differential effects: Applying regression mixture models to identify variations in the influence of family resources on academic achievement. *Developmental Psychology, 45*, 1298–1313.

Vermunt, J. K. (2001). The use of restricted latent class models for defining and testing nonparametric and parametric item response theory models. *Applied Psychological Measurement, 25*, 283–294.

Vermunt, J. K. (2004). An EM algorithm for the estimation of parametric and nonparametric hierarchical nonlinear models. *Statistica Neerlandica, 58*, 220–233.

Vermunt, J. K., & Magidson, J. (2005). *Latent GOLD 4.0 user's guide*. Belmont, MA: Statistical Innovations.

von Davier, M. (2001). *WINMIRA* [Computer program]. St. Paul, MN: Assessment Systems Corporation.

von Davier, M. (2006). Multidimensional latent trait modelling (MDLTM) [Software program]. Princeton, NJ: Educational Testing Service.

von Davier, M. (2010). Hierarchical mixtures of diagnostic models. *Psychological Test and Assessment Modeling*, 52, 8–28.

von Davier, M., & Molenaar, I. W. (2003). A person-fit index for polytomous Rasch models, latent class models, and their mixture generalizations. *Psychometrika, 68*, 213–228.

Ward, J. H. (1963). Hierarchical grouping to optimize an objective function. *Journal of the American Statistical Society, 58*, 236–244.

Warrens, M. J. (2008). On the equivalence of Cohen's Kappa and the Hubert-Arabie Adjusted Rand Index. *Journal of Classification, 25*, 177–183.

Wedel, M. (2001). GLIMMIX: Software for estimating mixtures and mixtures of generalized linear models [Software review]. *Journal of Classification, 18*, 129–135.

Yen, W., & Fitzpatrick, A. R. (2006). Item response theory. In R. L. Brennan (Ed.), *Educational measurement* (4th ed.) (pp. 111–153). Westport, CT: Praeger.

Xu, R., & Wunsch, D. (2008). *Clustering*. IEEE Press Series on Computational Intelligence. New York: Wiley-IEEE Press.

Yang, C.-C. (1998). *Finite mixture model selection with psychometric applications*. Unpublished doctoral dissertation. Los Angeles, CA: University of California.

Yang, C.-C., & Yang, C.-C. (2007). Separating latent classes by information criteria. *Journal of Classification, 24*, 183–203.

Zeman, P. M., Till, B. C., Livingston, N. J., Tanaka, J. W., & Driessen, P. F. (2007). Independent component analysis and clustering improve signal-to-noise ratio for statistical analysis of event-related potentials. *Clinical Neurophysiology, 118*, 2591–2604.

Zieky, M., & Perie, M. (2006). *A primer on setting cut scores on tests of educational achievement*. Princeton, NJ: Educational Testing Service.

CHAPTER 25

Latent Class Analysis and Finite Mixture Modeling

Katherine E. Masyn

Abstract

Finite mixture models, which are a type of latent variable model, express the overall distribution of one or more variables as a *mixture* of a *finite* number of component distributions. In direct applications, one assumes that the overall population heterogeneity with respect to a set of manifest variables results from the existence of two or more distinct homogeneous subgroups, or latent classes, of individuals. This chapter presents the prevailing "best practices" for direct applications of basic finite mixture modeling, specifically latent class analysis (LCA) and latent profile analysis (LPA), in terms of model assumptions, specification, estimation, evaluation, selection, and interpretation. In addition, a brief introduction to structural equation mixture modeling in the form of latent class regression is provided as well as a partial overview of the many more advanced mixture models currently in use. The chapter closes with a cautionary note about the limitations and common misuses of latent class models and a look toward promising future developments in mixture modeling.

Key Words: Finite mixture, latent class, latent profile, latent variable

Introduction

Like many modern statistical techniques, mixture modeling has a rich and varied history—it is known by different names in different fields; it has been implemented using different parameterizations and estimation algorithms in different software packages; and it has been applied and extended in various ways according to the substantive interests and empirical demands of different disciplines as well as the varying curiosities of quantitative methodologists, statisticians, biostatisticians, psychometricians, and econometricians. As such, the label *mixture model* is quite equivocal, subsuming a range of specific models, including, but not limited to: latent class analysis (LCA), latent profile analysis (LPA), latent class cluster analysis, discrete latent trait analysis, factor mixture models, growth mixture models, semi-parametric group-based models, semi-nonparametric group-mixed models, regression mixture models, latent state models, latent structure analysis, and hidden Markov models.

Despite the equivocal label, all of the different mixture models listed above have two common features. First, they are all *finite mixture* models in that they express the overall distribution of one or more variables as a *mixture of* or composite of a *finite* number of component distributions, usually simpler and more tractable in form than the overall distribution. As an example, consider the distribution of adult heights in the general population. Knowing that males are taller, on average, than females, one could choose to express the distribution of heights as a mixture of two component distributions for males and females, respectively. If $f(height)$ is the probability density function of the distribution of heights in the overall population, it could be expressed as:

$$f(height) = p_{male} \cdot f_{male}(height) \\ + p_{female} \cdot f_{female}(height), \quad (1)$$

where p_{male} and p_{female} are the proportions of males and females in the overall population, respectively, and $f_{male}(height)$ and $f_{female}(height)$ are the distributions of heights within the male and female subpopulations, respectively. p_{male} and p_{female} are referred to as the *mixing proportions* and $f_{male}(height)$ and $f_{female}(height)$ are the *component distribution* density functions.

The second common feature for all the different kinds of mixture models previously listed is that the components themselves are not directly observed—that is, mixture component membership is unobserved or *latent* for some or all individuals in the overall population. So, rather than expressing the overall population distribution as a mixture of *known* groups, as with the height example, mixture models express the overall population distribution as a finite mixture of some number, K, of unknown groups or components. For the distribution of height, this finite mixture would be expressed as:

$$f(height) = p_1 \cdot f_1(height) + p_2 \cdot f_2(height) \\ + \cdots + p_K \cdot f_K(height), \quad (2)$$

where the number of components, K, the mixing proportions, $p_1, \ldots, p_K$, and the component-specific height distributions, $f_1(height), \ldots, f_K(height)$, are all unknown but can be estimated, under certain identifying assumptions, using height data measured on a representative sample from the total population.

Finite Mixture Models As Latent Variable Models

It is the unknown nature of the mixing components—in number, proportion, and form—that situates finite mixture models in the broader category of latent variable models. The finite mixture distribution given in Equation 2 can be re-expressed in terms of a latent unordered categorical variable, usually referred to as a *latent class variable* and denoted by c, as follows:

$$f(height) = \Pr(c = 1) \cdot f(height|c = 1) \\ + \cdots + \Pr(c = K) \cdot f(height|c = K), \quad (3)$$

where the number of mixing components, K, is the number of categories or classes of c ($c = 1, \ldots, K$); the mixing proportions are the class proportions, $\Pr(c = 1), \ldots, \Pr(c = K)$; and the component distribution density functions are the distribution functions of the response variable, conditional on latent class membership, $f(height|c = 1), \ldots, f(height|c = K)$.

Recognizing mixture models as latent variable models allows use of the discourse language of the latent variable modeling world. There are two primary types of variables: (1) *latent* variables (e.g., the latent class variable, c) that are not directly observed or measured, and (2) *manifest* variables (e.g., the response variables) that are observable and are presumed to be influenced by or caused by the latent variable. The manifest variables are also referred to as *indicator* variables, as their observed values for a given individual are imagined to be imperfect indications of the individual's "true" underlying latent class membership. Framed as a latent variable model, there are two parts to any mixture model: (1) the *measurement model*, and (2) the *structural model*. The statistical measurement model specifies the relationship between the underlying latent variable and the corresponding manifest variables. In the case of mixture models, the measurement model encompasses the number of latent classes and the class-specific distributions of the indicator variables. The structural model specifies the distribution of the latent variable in the population and the relationships between latent variables and between latent variables and corresponding observed predictors and outcomes (i.e., latent variable antecedent and consequent variables). In the case of unconditional mixture models, the structural model encompasses just the latent class proportions.

Finite Mixture Modeling As a Person-Centered Approach

Mixture models are obviously distinct from the more familiar latent variable factor models in which the underlying latent structure is made up of one or more continuous latent variables. The designation for mixture modeling often used in applied literature to highlight this distinction from factor analytic models does not involve the overt *categorical* versus *continuous* latent variable scale comparison but instead references mixture modeling as a *person-centered* or *person-oriented* approach (in contrast to *variable-centered* or *variable-oriented*). Person-centered approaches describe similarities and differences *among individuals* with respect to how variables relate to each other and are predicated on the assumption that the population is heterogeneous with respect to the relationships between variables (Laursen & Hoff, 2006, p. 379). Statistical techniques oriented toward categorizing individuals by patterns of associations among variables, such as LCA and cluster analysis, are person-centered. Variable-centered approaches describe associations *among variables* and are predicated on the assumption that the population is homogeneous with respect to the relationships between variables (Laursen & Hoff, 2006, p. 379). In other words, each association between one variable and another in a variable-centered approach is assumed to hold for all individuals within the population. Statistical techniques oriented toward evaluating the relative importance of predictor variables, such as multivariate regression and structural equation modeling, are variable-centered.

Although "person-centered analysis" has become a popular and compelling catchphrase and methods-jingle for researchers to recite when providing the rationale for selecting a mixture modeling approach for their data analysis over a more traditional variable-centered approach, the elaborated justification, beyond the use of the catchphrase, is often flawed by placing person-centered and variable-centered approaches in juxtaposition as rival or oppositional approaches when, in fact, they are complementary. To understand this false dichotomy at the conceptual level, imagine that the data matrix, with rows of individuals and columns of variables, is a demarcated geographic region. You could explore this region from the ground (person-centered), allowing you to focus on unique, salient, or idiosyncratic features across the region, or you could explore this region from the air (variable-centered), allowing you to survey general and dominant features of the full expanse (e.g., the mean and covariance structure). Perhaps you might even elect to view the region both ways, recognizing that each provides a different perspective on the *same* region and that both advance your understanding of the region. That is, the region itself doesn't change but the information that can be gleaned about the region does change according to the type of search, and determining which search is more useful depends entirely on the objectives of the exploration.

The false dichotomy can also be explained in analytic terms, as Horn (2000) does so effectively in describing the linear decomposition of a n person × m variable data array:

"In person-centered compared with variable-centered analyses, the theorem of Eckart and Young [(1936)] indicates that the linear relationships among variables have a counterpart in relationships among people. Or, to put the matter the other way around, the relationships among people that indicate types have a counterpart in relationships among variables that indicate factors . . . Quite simply, there is no variance in person-centered types that cannot be accounted for in terms of variable-centered factors, and vice-versa" (Horn, 2000, p. 925).

Beyond the conceptual and analytic considerations, there is also a practical rejection of the dichotomy between person- and variable-centered approaches. Although a majority of applications of mixture models claim and motivate an exclusive person-centered approach, most utilize strategies that combine person-centered and variable-centered elements. For example, it is not uncommon for a study to use a person-centered analysis to identify latent classes or groups of individuals characterized by different response patterns on a subset of variables and then use a variable-centered analysis to examine predictors and outcomes (antecedent and consequent correlates) of class membership. There are also many examples of "hybrid" models, such as growth mixture models, that use both latent factors (variable-centered) and latent classes (person-centered) to describe interindividual differences in intra-individual change.

With the dichotomy between person-centered and variable-centered approaches dispelled, you may be left wondering how to determine which approach to take or whether, indeed, your choice matters at all. The fact that it is possible to represent person-centered findings in variable-centered terms does not obfuscate the choice of approach but does make the explicit consideration of the fundamental assumptions of each approach in the context of the actual research question and available data all the more important. Further, explicit consideration must also be given to the consequences of choosing to represent a construct as one or more latent factors versus latent classes for the subsequent specification and testing of relationships between the construct and its hypothesized correlates. If your planned study aims at a person-centered level, and you can reasonably assume that your target population is heterogeneous in that there are actual types or classes to be revealed by an empirical study, then you have sufficient rationale for utilizing a person-centered or combined person-/variable-centered approach, and the choice is clear. However, these rationales are not necessary for the purposed application of mixture models and I will touch on this topic again throughout the chapter, to recapitulate what constitutes principled use of mixture models.

Chapter Scope

This chapter is intended to provide the reader with a general overview of mixture modeling. I aim to summarize the current "best practices" for model specification, estimation, selection, evaluation, comparison, interpretation, and presentation for the two primary types of cross-sectional mixture analyses: latent class analysis (LCA), in which there are observed categorical indicators for a single latent class variable, and latent profile analysis (LPA), also known as latent class cluster analysis (LCCA), in which there are observed continuous indicators for a single latent class variable. As with other latent variable techniques, the procedures for model building and testing in these settings readily extend to more complex data settings—for example, longitudinal and multilevel variable systems. I begin by providing a brief historic overview of the two primary roots of modern-day mixture modeling in the social sciences and the foci of this chapter—*finite mixture modeling* and *LCA*—along with a summary of the purposed applications of the models. For each broad type of model, the general model formulation is presented, in both equations and path diagrams, followed by an in-depth discussion of model interpretation. Then a description of the model estimation including a presentation of current tools available for model evaluation and testing is provided, leading to a detailed illustration of a principled model building process with a full presentation and interpretation of results. Next, an extension of the unconditional mixture models already presented in the chapter is made to accommodate covariates using a latent class regression (LCR) formulation. I conclude the chapter with a brief cataloging of (some of) the many extensions of finite mixture modeling beyond the scope of this chapter, some cautionary notes about the misconceptions and misuses of mixture modeling, and a synopsis of prospective developments in the mixture modeling realm.

A Brief and Selective History of Mixture Modeling
Finite Mixture Modeling

Finite mixture modeling, in its most classic form, is a cross-sectional latent variable model in which the latent variable is nominal and the corresponding manifest variables are continuous. This form of finite mixture modeling is also known as LPA or LCCA. One of the first demonstrations of finite mixture modeling was done by a father of modern-day statistics, Karl Pearson, in 1894 when he fit a two-component (i.e., two-class) univariate normal mixture model to crab measurement data belonging to his colleague, Walter Weldon (1893), who had suspected that the skewness in the sample distribution of the crab measurements (the ratio of forehead to body length) might be an indication that this crab species from the Bay of Naples was evolving to two subspecies (McLachlan & Peel, 2000). Pearson used the method-of-moments to estimate his model and found evidence of the presence of two normally distributed mixing components that were subsequently identified as crab subspecies. There weren't many other mixture model applications that immediately followed suit because the daunting moments-based fitting was far too computationally intensive for mixtures. And it would take statisticians nearly 80 years to find more viable, as well as superior, alternative estimation procedures. Tan and Chang (1972) were among the researchers of their time that proved the maximum likelihood solution to be better for mixture models than the method-of-moments. Following on the heels of this insight was the release of the landmark article by Dempster, Laird, and Rubin (1977) that explicated, in general terms, an iterative estimation scheme—the expectation-maximization (EM) algorithm—for maximum-likelihood estimation from incomplete data. The recognition that finite mixture models could be easily reconceived as missing data problems (because latent class membership is missing for all individuals)—and thus estimated via the EM algorithm—represented a true turning point in the development of mixture modeling. Since that time, there has been rapid advancement in a variety of applications and extensions of mixture modeling, which are covered briefly in the section on "The More Recent Past" following the separate historical accounting of LCA.

Before moving on, there is another feature of the finite mixture history that is worth remarking on, as it relates to the earlier discussion of person-centered versus variable-centered approaches. Over the course of the twentieth century, there was a bifurcation in the development and application of finite mixture models in the statistical community following that early mixture modeling by Pearson, both before and after the advancement of the estimation algorithms. There was a distinction that

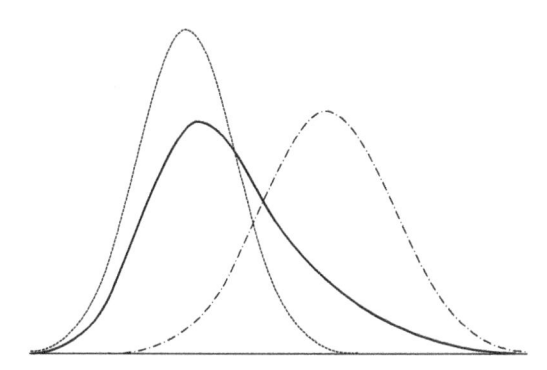

Figure 25.1 Hypothetical overall univariate non-normal population distribution (solid line) resulting from a mixing of two normally distributed subpopulations (dashed lines).

began to be made between *direct* and *indirect* applications (Titterington, Smith, & Makov, 1985) of finite mixture modeling. In direct applications, as in person-centered approaches, mixture models are used with the a priori assumption that the overall population is heterogeneous, and made up of a finite number of (latent and substantively meaningful) homogeneous groups or subpopulations, usually specified to have tractable distributions of indicators within groups, such as a multivariate normal distribution. In indirect applications, as in variable-centered approaches, it is assumed that the overall population is homogeneous and finite mixtures are simply used as more tractable, semi-parametric technique for modeling a population distribution of outcomes for which it may not be possible (practically or analytically speaking) to specify a parametric model. Mathematical work was done to prove that virtually any continuous distribution (even highly skewed, highly kurtotic, multimodal, or in other ways non-normal) could be approximated by the mixing of K normal distributions if K was permitted to be indiscriminately large and that a reasonably good approximation of most distributions could be obtained by the mixing of a relatively small number of normal distributions (Titterington, Smith, & Makov, 1985). Figure 25.1 provides an illustration of a univariate non-normal distribution that is the result of the mixing of two normally distributed components. The focus for indirect applications is then not on the resultant mixture components nor their interpretation but, rather, on the overall population distribution approximated by the mixing.

I find the *indirect* versus *direct* application distinction for mixture modeling less ambiguous than the *person-centered* versus *variable-centered* labels and, thus, will favor that language throughout the remainder of this chapter. Furthermore, the focus in this chapter is almost exclusively on direct applications of mixture models as I devote considerable time to the processes of class enumeration and interpretation and give weight to matters of classification quality, all of which are of little consequence for indirect applications.

Latent Class Analysis

Latent class models can be considered a special subset of finite mixture models formulated as a mixture of generalized linear models; that is, finite mixtures with discrete response variables with class-specific multinomial distributions. However, LCA has a rich history within the psychometric tradition, somewhat independent of the development of finite mixture models, that is worthy of remark, not unlike the way in which analysis of variance (ANOVA) and analysis of covariance (ANCOVA) models, although easily characterized as a special subset of multiple linear regression models, have their own historical timeline.

It didn't take long after Spearman's seminal work on factor analysis in 1904 for suggestions regarding categorical latent variables to appear in the literature. However, it wasn't until Lazarsfeld and Henry summarized their two decades of work on latent structure analysis (which included LCA as a subdomain of models) in 1968 that social scientists were presented with a comprehensive treatment of the theoretical and analytic features of LCA that had been in serious development since the 1950s.

Despite the expansive presentation and motivation for LCA provided by Lazarsfeld and Henry (1968), there were still two primary barriers to larger scale adoption of latent class models by applied researchers: (1) the categorical indicators could only be binary, and (2) there was no general, reliable, or widely implemented estimation method for obtaining parameter estimates (Goodman, 2002). Goodman (1974) resolved the first and part of the second problem with the development of a method for obtaining maximum likelihood estimates of latent class parameters for dichotomous and polytomous indicators. Once Goodman's estimation algorithm was implemented in readily available statistical software, first by Clogg in 1977, and Goodman's approach was shown to be closely related to the EM algorithm of Dempster, Laird, and Rubin (1977), currently the most widely utilized estimation algorithm for LCA software (Collins & Lanza, 2010), the remaining portion of the second barrier to the application of LCA was annulled. I will return to matters related to maximum likelihood estimation for LCA parameters later in this chapter.

As with the history of finite mixture modeling, there is some comment necessary on the features of LCA history related to person-centered versus variable-centered approaches. Latent class models, with categorical indicators of a categorical latent variable, have, at different times, been described in both person-centered and variable-centered terms. For example, one of the fundamental assumptions in classical LCA is that the relationship among the observed categorical variables is "explained" by an underlying categorical latent variable (latent class variable)—that is, the observed variables are conditionally (locally) independent given latent class membership. In this way, LCA was framed as the pure categorical variable-centered analog to continuous variable-centered factor analysis (in which the covariances among the observed continuous variables is explained by one or more underlying continuous factors). Alternatively, LCA can be framed as a multivariate data reduction technique for categorical response variables, similarly to how factor analysis may be framed as a dimension-reduction technique that enables a system of m variables to be reduced to a more parsimonious system of q factors with $q \ll m$. Consider a set of 10 binary indicator variables. There are $2^{10} = 1024$ possible observed response patterns, and one could exactly represent the $n \times 10$ observed data matrix as a frequency table with 1024 (or fewer) rows corresponding to the actual observed response patterns. Essentially, in the observed data there are a maximum of 1024 groupings of individuals based on their observed responses. Latent class analysis then enables the researcher to group or cluster these responses patterns (and, thus, the individuals with those response patterns) into a smaller number of K latent classes ($K \ll 1024$) such that the response patterns for individuals within each class are more similar than response patterns across classes. For example, response patterns (1 1 1 1 1 1 1 1 1 1) and (0 1 1 1 1 1 1 1 1 1) might be grouped in the same latent class, different from (0 0 0 0 0 0 0 0 0 0) and (0 0 0 0 0 0 0 1 0). The classes are then characterized not by exact response patterns but by response *profiles* or typologies described by the relative frequencies of item endorsements. Because grouping the observed response patterns is tantamount to grouping individuals, this framing of LCA is more person-oriented. Thus, in both the psychometric tradition in which LCA was developed and in the classical mathematical statistics tradition in which finite mixture modeling was developed, mixture models have been used as both a person-centered and variable-centered approach, leading to some of the confusion surrounding the misleading association of mixture models as implicitly person-centered models and the false dichotomy between person-centered and variable-centered approaches.

The More Recent Past

In both finite mixture modeling and LCA, the utilization of the EM algorithm for maximum likelihood estimation of the models, coupled with rapid and widespread advancements in statistical computing, resulted in a remarkable acceleration in the development, extension, application, and understanding of mixture modeling over the last three decades, as well as a general blurring of the line that delineated latent class models from more general finite mixture models. A few of the many notable developments include the placement of latent class models within the framework of log linear models (Formann, 1982, 1992; Vermunt, 1999); LCR and conditional finite mixture models, incorporating predictors of class membership (Bandeen-Roche, Miglioretti, Zeger, & Rathouz, 1997; Dayton & Macready, 1988); and the placement of finite mixture modeling within a general latent structure framework, enabling multiple and mixed measurement modalities (discrete and continuous) for both manifest and latent variables (Hancock & Samuelson, 2008; Muthén & Shedden, 1999; Skrondal & Rabe-Hesketh, 2004). For an overview of the most recent developments in finite mixture modeling, *see* McLachlan and Peel (2000) and Vermunt and McCutcheon (2012). For more recent developments specifically related to LCA, *see* Hagenaars and McCutcheon (2002) and Collins and Lanza (2010).

There has also been conspicuous growth in the number of statistical software packages that enable the application of a variety of mixture models in real data settings. The two most prominent self-contained modeling software packages are Mplus V6.11 (Muthén & Muthén, 1998–2011), which is the software used for all the empirical examples in this chapter, and Latent GOLD V4.5 (Statistical Innovations, Inc., 2005–2011), both capable of general and comprehensive latent variable modeling, including, but not limited to, finite mixture modeling. The two most popular modular packages that operate within existing software are PROC LCA and PROC LTA for SAS (Lanza, Dziak, Huang, Xu, &

Collins, 2011), which are limited to traditional categorical indicator latent class and latent transition analysis models, and GLLAMM for Stata (Rabe-Hesketh, Skrondal & Pickles, 2004), which is a comprehensive generalized linear latent and mixed model framework utilizing adaptive quadrature for maximum likelihood estimation.

Access to software and the advancements in high-speed computing have also led to a remarkable expansion in the number of disciplines that have made use of mixture models as an analytic tool. There has been particularly notable growth in the direct application of mixture models within the behavioral and educational sciences over the last decade. Mixture models have been used in the empirical investigations of such varied topics as typologies of adolescent smoking within and across schools (Henry & Muthén, 2010); marijuana use and attitudes among high school seniors (Chung, Flaherty, & Schafer, 2006); profiles of gambling and substance use (Bray, 2007); risk profiles for overweight in adolescent populations (BeLue, Francis, Rollins, & Colaco, 2009); patterns of peer victimization in middle school (Nylund-Gibson, Graham, & Juvonen, 2010); liability to externalizing disorders (Markon & Krueger, 2005); profiles of academic self-concept (Marsh, Lüdtke, Trautwein, & Morin, 2009); profiles of program evaluators' self-reported practices (Christie & Masyn, 2010); rater behavior in essay grading (DeCarlo, 2005); mathematical ability for special education students (Yang, Shaftel, Glasnapp, & Poggio, 2005); patterns of public assistance receipt among female high school dropouts (Hamil-Luker, 2005); marital expectations of adolescents (Crissey, 2005); and psychosocial needs of cancer patients (Soothill, Francis, Awwad, Morris, Thomas, & McIllmurray, 2004).

Latent Class Analysis

Although latent class models—mixture models with exclusively categorical indicator variables for the latent class variable—emerged more than a half-century after the inception of finite mixture models, I choose to use LCA for this initial foray into the details of mixture modeling because I believe it is the most accessible point of entry for applied readers.

Model Formulation

As with any latent variable model, there are two parts to a latent class model: (1) the measurement model, which relates the observed response variables (also called indicator or manifest variables) to the underlying latent variable(s); and (2) the structural model, which characterizes the distribution of the latent variable(s) and the relationships among latent variables and between latent variables and observed antecedent and consequent variables. In a traditional latent variable model-building process, the unconditional measurement model for each latent variable of interest is established prior to any structural model-based hypothesis testing. It is the results of the final measurement model that researchers use to assign meaning to the latent classes that are then used in the substantive interpretations of any structural relationships that emerge. Thus, the formal LCA model specification begins here with an unconditional model in which the only observed variables are the categorical manifest variables of the latent class variable.

Suppose there are M categorical (binary, ordinal, and/or multinomial) latent class indicators, $u_1, u_2, \ldots, u_M$ observed on n study participants where u_{mi} is the observed response to item m for participant i. It is assumed for the unconditional LCA that there is an underlying unordered categorical latent class variable, denoted by c, with K classes where $c_i = k$ if individual i belongs to Class k. The proportion of individuals in Class k, $\Pr(c = k)$, is denoted by π_k. The K classes are exhaustive and mutually exclusive such that each individual in the population has membership in exactly one of the K latent classes and $\Sigma \pi_k = 1$. The relationship between the observed responses on the M items and the latent class variable, c, is expressed as

$$\Pr(u_{1i}, u_{2i}, \ldots, u_{Mi}) = \sum_{k=1}^{K} \left[\pi_k \cdot \Pr(u_{1i}, u_{2i}, \ldots, u_{Mi} | c_i = k) \right]. \quad (4)$$

The above expression *is* the latent class measurement model. The measurement parameters are all those related to the class-specific response pattern probabilities, $\Pr(u_{1i}, u_{2i}, \ldots, u_{Mi} | c_i = k)$, and the structural parameters are those related to the distribution of the latent class variable, which for the unconditional model are simply the class proportions, π_k.

The model expressed in Equation 4 can be represented by a path diagram as shown in Figure 25.2. All the path diagrams in this chapter follow the diagramming conventions used in the Mplus V6.11 software manual (Muthén & Muthén, 1998–2011): boxes to enclose observed variables; circles to enclose latent variables; single-headed arrow paths

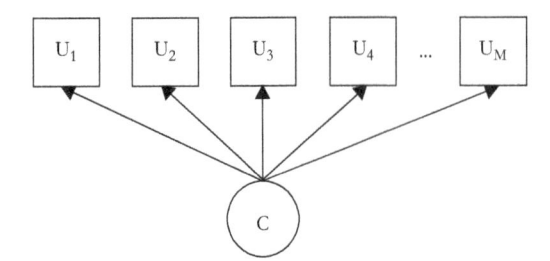

Figure 25.2 Generic path diagram for an unconditional latent class model.

to represent direct (causal) relationships; double-headed arrow paths to represent nondirection (correlational) relationships; "*u*" to denote observed categorical variables; "*y*" to denote observed continuous variables; "*c*" to denote latent categorical variables (finite mixtures or latent class variables); and "*η*" to denote latent continuous variables (factors).

Similarly to the typical default model specification in traditional factor analysis, *conditional* or *local independence* is assumed for the *M* items conditional on class membership. This assumption implies that latent class membership explains *all* of the associations among the observed items. Thus, the formation of the latent classes (in number and nature) based on sample data will be driven by the set of associations among the observed items in the overall sample. If all the items were independent from each other in the sample—that is, if all the items were uncorrelated in the overall sample—then it would not be possible to estimate a latent class model with more than $K = 1$ classes because there would be no observed associations to be explained by class membership. Under the local independence assumption, Equation 4 simplifies to

$$\Pr(u_{1i}, u_{2i}, \ldots, u_{Mi})$$
$$= \sum_{k=1}^{K} \left[\pi_k \cdot \left(\prod_{m=1}^{M} \Pr(u_{mi}|c_i = k) \right) \right]. \quad (5)$$

This assumption is represented in Figure 25.2 by the *absence* of any nondirectional (double-headed arrow) paths between the *u*s that would represent item correlations *within* or *conditional on* latent class membership. The tenability of the local independence assumption can be evaluated and may also be *partially* relaxed (*see*, e.g., Huang & Bandeen-Roche, 2004). However, some degree of local independence is necessary for latent class model identification. It is not possible to fully relax this assumption for models with $K > 1$ classes—that is, an unconditional latent class model with all the items allowed to co-vary with all other items within class is not identified for $K > 1$ classes unless other parameter restrictions are imposed. I will revisit this assumption in the context of finite mixture modeling with continuous indicators. In that setting, models with $K > 1$ classes are identified even with all items co-varying within latent classes under certain other assumptions—for example, the distributional assumption of multivariate normality of the indicators within class.

Model Interpretation

As I mentioned earlier, it is the results of the final unconditional LCA, the measurement model, that are used to assign meaning to the latent classes, which augments the substantive interpretations of any structural relationships that emerge. Unless you are using mixture models in an indirect application as a semi-parametric approximation for an overall homogeneous population such that your attention will only be on parameter estimates for the overall (re)mixed population, you will focus your interpretation on the separate mixing components, interpreting each latent class based on the relationships between the classes and their indicators just as you use factor loadings and item communalities to interpret factors in a factor analysis. And just as with factor analysis, to reasonably interpret the latent class variable, you must have "good" measures of each of the classes.

A good item is one that measures the latent class variable well (i.e., reliably). A good latent class indicator is one for which there is a strong relationship between the item and the latent class variable. Strong item–class relationships must have both of the following features: (1) a particular item response—for example, item endorsement in the case of binary items, epitomizes members in at least one of the K latent classes in the model; and (2) the item can be used to distinguish between members across at least one pair of classes among the K latent classes in the model. The first quality is referred to as latent class *homogeneity* and the second quality is referred to as latent class *separation* (Collins & Lanza, 2010).

To better understand the concepts of latent class homogeneity and latent class separation, and how these concepts both relate to the parameters of the unconditional measurement model and ultimately qualify the interpretation of the resultant latent classes, consider a hypothetical example with five binary response variables ($M = 5$) measuring a three-class categorical latent variable ($K = 3$). The unconditional model is given by

$$\Pr(u_{1i}, u_{2i}, u_{4i}, u_{4i}, u_{5i}) = \sum_{k=1}^{3} \left[\pi_k \cdot \left(\prod_{m=1}^{5} \omega_{m|k} \right) \right], \quad (6)$$

where $\omega_{m|k}$ is the probability that an individual belonging to Class k would endorse item m—that is, $\Pr(u_{mi} = 1 | c_i = k) = \omega_{m|k}$.

Class Homogeneity. To interpret each of the K classes, you first need to identify items that epitomize each class. If a class has a high degree of homogeneity with respect to a particular item then there is a particular response category on that item that can be considered a response that typifies that class. In the case of binary items, strong associations with a particular class or high class homogeneity is indicated by high or low model-estimated probabilities of endorsement—that is, $\hat{\omega}_{m|k}$ or $1 - \hat{\omega}_{m|k}$ close 1, with "close" defined by $\hat{\omega}_{m|k} > .7$ or $\hat{\omega}_{m|k} < .3$. For example, consider a class with an estimated class-specific item probability of 0.90. This means that in that class, an estimated 90% of individuals will endorse that particular item whereas only 10% will not. You could then consider this item endorsement as "typical" or "characteristic of" that class and could say that class has high homogeneity with respect to that item. Now consider a class with an estimated class-specific item probability of 0.55. This means that in that class, only an estimated 55% of individuals will endorse that particular item whereas 45% will not. Item endorsement is neither typical nor characteristic of that class, nor is lack of item endorsement, for that matter, and you could say that class has low homogeneity with respect to that item and would not consider that item a good indicator of membership for that particular class.

Class Separation. To interpret each of the K classes, you must not only have class homogeneity with respect to the items such that the classes are each well characterized by the item set, you also need to be able to distinguish *between* the classes—this quality is referred to as the degree of class separation. It is possible to have high class homogeneity and still have low class separation. For example, consider two classes, one of which has an estimated class-specific item probability of 0.90 and another class with an estimated class-specific item probability of 0.95. In this case, since item endorsement is "typical" for both of these classes and the two classes can be characterized by a high rate of endorsement for that item, they are not distinct from each other with respect to that item. Now consider two classes, one of which has an estimated class-specific item probability of 0.90 and another with an estimated class-specific item probability of 0.05. In this case, each class has good homogeneity with respect to the item and they also have a high degree of separation because the first class may be characterized by a high rate of item endorsement whereas the other class may be characterized by a high rate of item non-endorsement. To quantify class separation between Class j and Class k with respect to a particular item, m, compute the estimated item endorsement odds ratio as given by:

$$\hat{OR}_{m|jk} = \frac{\left(\hat{\omega}_{m|j} / 1 - \hat{\omega}_{m|j} \right)}{\left(\hat{\omega}_{m|k} / 1 - \hat{\omega}_{m|k} \right)}. \quad (7)$$

Thus, $\hat{OR}_{m|jk}$ is the ratio of the odds of endorsement of item m in Class j to the odds of endorsement of item m in Class k. A large $\hat{OR}_{m|jk} > 5$ (corresponding to approximately $\hat{\omega}_{m|j} > .7$ and $\hat{\omega}_{m|k} < .3$) or small $\hat{OR}_{m|jk} < .2$ (corresponding to approximately $\hat{\omega}_{m|j} < .3$ and $\hat{\omega}_{m|k} > .7$) indicates a high degree of separation between Classes j and k with respect to item m. Thus, high class homogeneity with respect to an item is a necessary but not sufficient condition for a high degree of class separation with respect to an item.

I should note here that although simply taking the ratio of the class-specific item response probabilities may seem more intuitive, the use of the odds ratio of item response rather than the response probability ratio is preferred because the odds ratio doesn't depend on whether you emphasize item endorsement or item non-endorsement separation or whether you are assessing the item-endorsement separation for classes with relatively high endorsement rates overall or low endorsement rates overall for the item in question. For example, an $\hat{OR}_{m|jk}$ of 0.44 corresponding to $\hat{\omega}_{m|j} = .80$ versus $\hat{\omega}_{m|k} = .90$ is the same as the $\hat{OR}_{m|jk}$ corresponding to $\hat{\omega}_{m|j} = .10$ versus $\hat{\omega}_{m|k} = .20$, whereas class-specific item probability ratios would be $.80/.90 = 0.87$ and $.10/.20 = 0.50$.

Class Proportions. It is possible, to a certain extent, to use the class proportion values themselves to assign meaning to the classes. Consider the case in which you have a population-based sample and one of the resultant classes has an estimated class proportion of greater than 0.50—that is, the class represents more than 50% of the overall population. Then part of your interpretation of this class may include an attribution of "normal," "regular," or "typical" in that the class represents the statistical majority of the overall population. Similarly, if you had a resultant class with a small estimated class proportion (e.g., 0.10) part of your interpretation of that class might include an attribution of "rare," "unusual," or "atypical," ever mindful that such attribution labels, depending on the context, could carry an unintended negative connotation, implying the presence of deviance or pathology in the subpopulation represent by that class. Also remember that the estimated class proportion reflects the distribution of the latent classes *in the sample*. Thus, if you have a nonrandom or nonrepresentative sample, exercise caution when using the estimated class proportions in the class interpretations. For example, a "normal" class in a clinical sample may still be present in a nonclinical sample but may have a much smaller "atypical" representation in the overall population.

Hypothetical Example. Continuing with the hypothetical example of a three-class LCA with five binary indicators, Table 25.1 provides hypothetical model-estimated item response probabilities for each class along with the item response odds ratios calculated following Equation 7. Classes 1, 2, and 3 all have high homogeneity with respect to items u_1, u_2, and u_4 because all class-specific item response probabilities are greater than 0.70 or less than 0.30. Class 1 also has high homogeneity with respect to item u_3, whereas Classes 2 and 3 do not. Thus, Classes 2 and 3 are not well characterized by item u_3—that is, there is not a response to item u_3 that typifies either Class 2 or 3. None of the classes are well characterized by item u_5, and this might be an item that is considered for revision or elimination in future studies.

Class 1 is well separated from Class 2 by all the items except the last, with $\hat{OR}_{m|1,2} > 5$. Class 1 is not well distinguished from Class 3 by items u_1 and u_2 but is well separated from Class 3 by items u_3 and u_4. Classes 2 and 3 are well separated by items u_1 and u_2 but not by items u_3 and u_4. Thus, as a result of Classes 2 and 3 not being well characterized by item u_3, they are consequently not distinguishable from each other with respect to item u_3. Because none of the classes have a high degree of homogeneity with respect to item u_5, none of the classes are well separated from each other by that item.

The class homogeneity and separation information contained in Table 25.1 is usually depicted graphically in what is often referred to as a "profile plot" in which the class-specific item probabilities (*y*-values) are plotted in a line graph for each of the items (*x*-values). Figure 25.3 depicts a profile plot using the hypothetical model results presented in Table 25.1. I have added horizontal lines to the profile plot at 0.70 and 0.30 to assist in the visual inspection with respect to both class homogeneity and class separation. Class 1 can be interpreted as a group of individuals with a high propensity for endorsing items $u_1 - u_4$; Class 2, a group of individuals with a low propensity for endorsing items u_1, u_2, and u_4; and Class 3, a group of individuals with a high propensity for endorsing item u_1 and u_2 with a low propensity for endorsing item u_4. Notice that I do not use items with low class homogeneity for the interpretation of that class nor do I use language in the class interpretation that would imply a class separation with respect to an item that isn't meaningful.

Table 25.1. Hypothetical Example: Model-Estimated, Class-Specific Item Response Probabilities and Odds Ratios Based on a Three-Class Unconditional Latent Class Analysis

Item	$\hat{\omega}_{m|k}$ Class 1 (70%)	Class 2 (20%)	Class 3 (10%)	$\hat{OR}_{m|jk}$ Class 1 vs. 2	Class 1 vs. 3	Class 2 vs. 3
u_1	**0.90***	**0.10**	**0.90**	**81.00****	1.00	**0.01**
u_2	**0.80**	**0.20**	**0.90**	**16.00**	0.44	**0.03**
u_3	**0.90**	0.40	0.50	**13.50**	**9.00**	0.67
u_4	**0.80**	**0.10**	**0.20**	**36.00**	**16.00**	0.44
u_5	0.60	0.50	0.40	1.50	2.25	1.50

*Item probabilities >0.7 or <0.3 are bolded to indicate a high degree of class homogeneity.
**Odds ratios >5 or <0.2 are bolded to indicate a high degree of class separation.

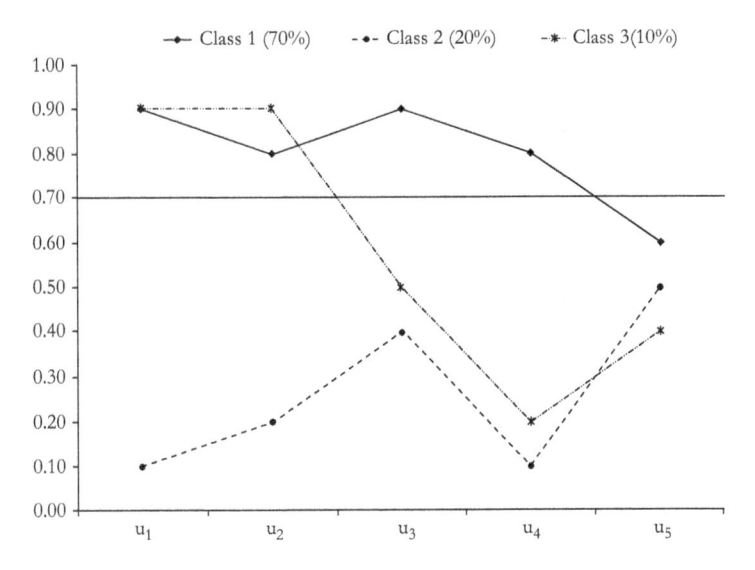

Figure 25.3 Hypothetical example: Class-specific item probability profile plot for a three-class unconditional LCA.

For example, both Classes 2 and 3 are interpreted as groups of individuals with low propensity for endorsing item u_4, but I do not, in the interpretation of Classes 2 and 3, imply that the two classes are somehow distinct with respect to u_4—only that they are both distinct form Class 1 with respect to u_4. I am also careful in my interpretation of the classes with categorical indicators to use explicit language regarding the probability or propensity of item endorsement rather than language that might incorrectly imply continuous indicators. For example, in this setting it would be incorrect to interpret Class 1 as a group of individuals with high levels of u_1 and u_2 with low levels of u_4, on average.

Based on the estimated class proportions, assuming a random and representative sample from the overall population, one might also apply a modifier label of "normal" or "typical" to Class 1 because its members make up an estimated 70% of the population.

The next three subsections present some of the technical details of LCA related to model estimation, model selection, and missing data. For the novice mixture modelers, I suggest that you may want to skip these subsections on your first reading of this chapter and go directly to the real data example that follows.

Model Estimation

As discussed in the mixture modeling historical overview, the most significant turning point for mixture modeling estimation was the development of the EM algorithm by Dempster, Laird, and Rubin (1977) for maximum likelihood (ML) estimation from incomplete data and the realization that if one reconceives of *latent* class membership as *missing* class membership, then the EM algorithm can be used to obtain maximum likelihood estimates (MLEs) of LCA parameters.

The first step in any ML estimation is specifying the likelihood function. The complete data likelihood function, put simply, is the probability density of all the data (the array of all values on all variables, latent and observed, in the model for all individuals in the sample) given a set of parameters values. Maximizing the likelihood function with respect to those parameters yields the maximum likelihood estimates (MLEs) of those parameters—that is, the MLEs are the values of the parameters that maximize the likelihood of the data. For a traditional LCA model, the complete data likelihood for a single individual i, with the missing latent class variable, c_i, is given by

$$l_i(\Theta) = \Pr(\mathbf{u}_i, c_i|\Theta) = \Pr(\mathbf{u}_i|c_i, \Theta) \cdot \Pr(c_i|\Theta), \quad (8)$$

where Θ is a vector of all the model parameters to be estimated. Typically, it is assumed that all cases are identically distributed such that the individual likelihood function, as expressed in Equation 8, is applicable for all cases. In the hypothetical LCA example with five binary indicators and three classes, Θ would include 18 separate parameters: all the class-specific item response probabilities along with the class proportions—that is, $\Theta = (\omega_{\cdot|1}, \omega_{\cdot|2}, \omega_{\cdot|3}, \pi_1, \pi_2, \pi_3)$, with $\omega_{\cdot|k} =$

($\omega_{1|k}, \omega_{2|k}, \omega_{3|k}, \omega_{4|k}, \omega_{5|k}$). The likelihood function, L, for the whole sample is just the product of the individual likelihoods when assuming that all individuals in the sample are independent observations—that is, $L(\Theta) = \prod l_i(\Theta)$. Usually, it is easier mathematically to maximize the natural log of the likelihood function, $\ln(L(\Theta)) = LL(\Theta)$. Because the natural log is a monotonically increasing function, the values for Θ that maximize the log likelihood function are the maximum likelihood estimates, $\hat{\Theta}_{ML}$.

For most mixture models, with all individuals missing values for c, it is not possible obtain the MLEs by just applying the rules of calculus and solving a system of equations based on partial derivatives of the log likelihood function with respect to each parameter—that is, there is not a closed-form solution. Rather, an iterative approach must be taken in which successive sets of parameters estimates are tried using a principled search algorithm with a pair of stopping rules: (1) a maximum number of iterations and (2) a convergence criterion. To understand the concept behind iterative maximum likelihood estimation, consider the following analogy: imagine that the log likelihood function is a mountain range and the estimation algorithm is a fearless mountain climber. The goal of the climber is to reach the highest peak (global maximum) in the range, but the climber can't see where the highest peak is from the base of the mountain range. So the climber chooses an informed starting point (the initial staring values for the parameter estimates), using what he can see (the observed data), and begins to climb. Each foothold is a new set of parameter estimates. After each step the climber stops and assesses which of the footholds within reach (nearby parameter estimates values) will give him the greatest gain in height in a single step and he then leaves his current position to move to this higher point. He repeats this stepping process until he reaches a peak such that a step in any direction either takes him lower or not noticeably higher. The climber then knows he is at the peak (the convergence criterion is met), and it is here that he plants his flag, at the maximum log likelihood function value. But the climber, even as skilled as he is, cannot climb forever. He has limited food and water and so even if he has not reached the peak, there is a point at which he must stop climbing (the maximum number of iterations). If he runs out of supplies before he reaches a peak (exceeds the maximum number of iterations before meeting the convergence criterion), then he does not plant his flag (fails to converge).

As previously noted, the most common estimation algorithm in use for mixture models is the EM algorithm (Dempster, Laird, & Rubin, 1977; Muthén & Shedden, 1999). Each iteration of the EM algorithm involves an expectation step (E-step) in which the estimated expected value for each missing data value is computed based on the current parameters estimates and observed data for the individual. In the case of LCA, the E-step estimates expected class membership for each individual. The E-step is followed by a maximization step (M-step) in which new parameter estimates, $\hat{\Theta}$, are obtained that maximize the log likelihood function using the complete data from the E-step. Those parameter estimates are then used in the E-step of the next iteration, and the algorithm iterates until one of the stopping rules applies.

Although it would seem to go without saying, for the EM algorithm "mountain climber" to have even the slightest possibility of success in reaching the global peak of the log likelihood function, such a peak must exist. In other words, the model for which the parameters are being estimated must be *identified*—that is, there must be a unique solution for the model's parameters. However, this necessary fact may not be as trivial to establish as it would initially appear. When there is not a closed-form solution for the MLEs available, you cannot *prove*, mathematically speaking, that there is a global maximum. In this case, you are also unable to determine, theoretically, whether the solution you obtain from the estimation procedure is a global or local maximum nor can you tell, when faced with multiple local maxima (a mountainous range with many peaks of varying heights), whether the highest local maxima is actually the global maximum (highest peak). If the estimation algorithm fails to converge, then it could be an indication that the model is not theoretically identified, but it is not solid proof. There is also a gray area of empirical underidentification and weak identification in the span between identified models and unidentified models (i.e., models with no proper solution for all the model's parameters—failure of even one parameter to be identified causes the model to be under- or unidentified). This predicament is made more troublesome by the reality that the log likelihood surfaces for most mixture models are notoriously difficult for estimation algorithms to navigate, tending to have multiple local maxima, saddle points, and regions that are virtually flat, confusing even the most expert "climbers." To better understand some of the challenging log likelihood functions that may present themselves, I discuss some exemplar log likelihood function plots for a unidimensional parameter space while providing some practical strategies to apply during the mixture model estimation process to help ensure the model you specify is well identified and the MLEs you obtain are stable and trustworthy solutions corresponding to a global maximum.

Figure 25.4 has six panels that represent a range of hypothetical log likelihood functions for a single parameter, θ. The unimodal log likelihood function in Figure 25.4.a has only one local maximum that is the global maximum. $\hat{\theta}_{(0)}$ is the MLE for θ because the $LL(\hat{\theta}_{(0)})$ is the maximum value achieved by $LL(\theta)$ across all values of θ. It is clear that no matter what starting position on the x-axis (starting value, $\hat{\theta}_{(s)}$, for the estimate of the parameter, θ) is selected, the mountain climber would easily find that global peak. This LL function reflects a well-identified model. There is one unique global maximum (MLE) that would be readily reached from any starting point. Now examine the multimodal likelihood function in Figure 25.4.b. There is still a single global maximum, $\hat{\theta}_{(0)}$, but there are three other local maxima, $\hat{\theta}_{(1)}, \hat{\theta}_{(2)}$, and $\hat{\theta}_{(3)}$. You can imagine that if you started your algorithm mountain climber at a point $\hat{\theta}_{(s)} < \hat{\theta}_{(2)}$, then he might conclude his climb, reaching the convergence criterion and planting his flag, on the peak of the log likelihood above $\hat{\theta}_{(2)}$, never realizing there were higher peaks down range. Similarly, if you started your climber at a point $\hat{\theta}_{(s)} > \hat{\theta}_{(1)}$, then he might conclude his climb on the peak of the log likelihood above $\hat{\theta}_{(1)}$, never reaching the global peak above $\hat{\theta}_{(0)}$.

With a log likelihood function like the one depicted in Figure 25.4.b, one could expect the estimation algorithm to converge on a local rather than global maximum. If you obtained only one solution, $\hat{\theta}$, using one starting value, $\hat{\theta}_{(s)}$, then you have no way of knowing whether $\hat{\theta}$ corresponds to the highest peak in the range or just a peak of the log likelihood in the range of θ. Because it isn't possible to resolve this ambiguity mathematically, it must be resolved empirically. In keeping with the analogy, if you want to find the highest peak in the range, then rather than retaining a single expert mountain climber, you could retain the services of a whole army of expert mountain climbers. You start each climber at a different point in the range. A few will "converge" to the lower local peaks, but most should reach the global peak. The more climbers from different starting points (random sets of starting values) that converge to the same peak (solution replication), the more confident you are in that particular peak being the global maximum. This strategy corresponds to using multiple sets of random starting values for the EM algorithm, iterating each set of starting values to convergence, and demanding a high frequency (in absolute and relative terms) of replication of the best log likelihood value.

I should note here that although replication of the maximum likelihood solution from different

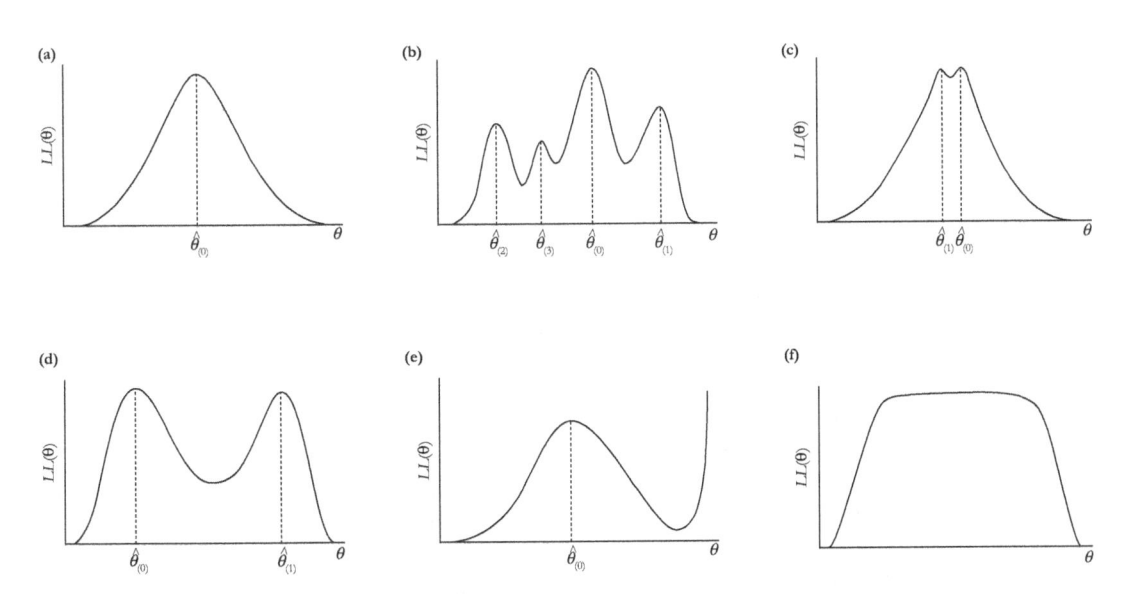

Figure 25.4 Hypothetical log likelihood (LL) functions for a single parameter, θ: (a) unimodal LL; (b) multimodal LL; (c) bimodal LL with proximate local maxima; (d) bimodal LL with distant local maxima; (e) unbounded LL; and (f) LL with flat region.

sets of starting values increases confidence in that solution as the global optimum, replication of the likelihood value is neither a necessary nor a sufficient requirement to ensure that a global (rather than a local) maximum has been reached (Lubke, 2010). Thus, failure to replicate the best log likelihood value does not mean that you must discard the model. However, further exploration should be done to inform your final model selection. Consider the cases depicted in Figures 25.4.c and 25.4.d for which there is a global maximum at $\hat{\theta}_{(0)}$ and a local maximum of nearly the same log likelihood value at $\hat{\theta}_{(1)}$. In cases such as these, the relative frequency of replication for each of the two solutions across a random set of start values may also be comparable. In Figure 25.4.c, not only are the two solution very close in terms of the log likelihood values, they are also close to each other in the range of θ such that $\hat{\theta}_{(0)} \approx \hat{\theta}_{(1)}$. In this case you can feel comforted by the fact that even if you had inadvertently missed the global maximum at $\hat{\theta}_{(0)}$ and incorrectly taken $\hat{\theta}_{(1)}$ as your MLE, your inferences and interpretations would be close to the mark. However, in the case depicted in Figure 25.4.d, $\hat{\theta}_{(1)}$ is quite distant on the scale of θ from $\hat{\theta}_{(0)}$ and you would not want to base conclusions on the $\hat{\theta}_{(1)}$ estimate. To get a sense of whether the highest local peaks in your log likelihood function are proximal or distal solutions in the parameter space, obtain the actual parameter estimates for the best log likelihood value across all the sets of random starting values and make a descriptive comparison to the parameter estimates corresponding to the "second-best" log likelihood value. (For more about comparing local maximum log likelihood solutions to determine model stability, see, for example, Hipp & Bauer, 2006.)

I pause here to make the reader aware of a nagging clerical issue that must be tended to whenever different maximum likelihood solutions for mixture models are being compared, whether for models with the same or differing numbers of classes: label switching (Chung, Loken, & Schafer, 2004). The ordering of the latent classes as they are outputted by an estimation algorithm are completely arbitrary—for example, "Class 1" for starting values Set 1 may correspond to "Class 3" for starting values Set 2. Even solutions identical in maximum likelihood values can have class labels switched. This phenomenon is not a problem statistically speaking—it merely poses a bookkeeping challenge. So be cognizant of label switching whenever you are comparing mixture model solutions.

Figures 46.4.e and 46.4.f depict log likelihood functions that would be likely to result in either some or all of the random sets of starting values failing to converge—that is, the estimation algorithm stops because the maximum number of iterations is exceeded before a peak is reached. In Figure 25.4.e, the log likelihood function is unbounded at the boundary of the range of θ (which is not an uncommon feature for the LL function of mixture models with more complex within-class variance–covariance structures) but also has a maximum in the interior of the range of $\theta \cdot \hat{\theta}_{(0)}$ represents the proper maximum likelihood solution, and that solution should replicate for the majority of random sets of stating values; however, some in the army of expert mountain climbers are likely to find themselves climbing the endless peak, running out of supplies and stopping before convergence is achieved. The log likelihood function in Figure 25.4.f corresponds to an unidentified model. The highest portion of the log likelihood function is flat and there are not singular peaks or unique solutions. No matter where the estimation algorithm starts, it is unlikely to converge. If it does converge, then that solution is unlikely to replicate because it will be a false optimum.

A model that is *weakly identified* or *empirically underidentified* is a model that, although theoretically identified, has a shape with particular sample data that is nearly flat and/or has many, many local maxima of approximately the same height (think: egg-crate) such that the estimation algorithm fails to converge for all or a considerable number of random sets of starting values. For a model to be identified, there must be enough "known" or observed information in the data to estimate the parameters that are not known. Ensuring positive degrees of freedom for the model is a necessary but not sufficient criterion for model identification. As the ratio of "known" to "unknown" decreases, the model can become weakly identified. One quantification of this ratio of information for MLE is known as the *condition number*. It is computed as the ratio of the smallest to largest eigenvalue of the information matrix estimate based on the maximum likelihood solution. A low condition number, less than 10^{-6}, may indicate singularity (or near singularity) of the information matrix and, hence, model non-identification (or empirical underidentification) (Muthén & Muthén, 1998–2011). A final indication that you may be "spreading" your data "too thin" is class collapsing, which can occur when you are attempting to extract more latent classes than your data will support. This collapsing usually presents as one or more estimated class proportions nearing zero but can also emerge as a nearly complete lack of separation between two or more of the latent classes.

Strategies to achieve identification all involve reducing the complexity of the model to increase the ratio of "known" to "unknown" information. The number of latent classes could be reduced. Alternatively, the response categories for one or more of the indicator variables in the measurement model could be collapsed. For response categories with low frequencies, this category aggregation will remove very little information about population heterogeneity while reducing the number of class-specific item parameters that must be estimated. Additionally, one or more items might be combined or eliminated from the model. This item-dropping must be done with extreme care, making sure that removal or aggregation does not negatively impact the model estimation (Collins & Lanza, 2010). Conventional univariate, bivariate, and multivariate data screening procedures should result in careful data recoding and reconfiguration that will protect against the most obvious threats to empirical identification.

In summary, MLE for mixture models can present statistical and numeric challenges that must be addressed during the application of mixture modeling. Without a closed-form solution for the maximization of the log likelihood function, an iterative estimation algorithm—typically the EM algorithm—is used. It is usually not possible to prove that the model specified is theoretically identified, and, even if it was, there could still be issues related to weak identification or empirical underidentification that causes problems with convergence in estimation. Furthermore, since the log likelihood surface for mixtures is often multimodal, if the estimation algorithm does converge on a solution, there is no way to know for sure that the point of convergence is at a global rather than local maximum. To address these challenges, it is recommended the following strategy be utilized during mixture model estimation. First and foremost, use multiple random sets of starting values with the estimation algorithm (it is recommended that a minimum of 50–100 sets of extensively, randomly varied starting values be used (Hipp & Bauer, 2006), but more may be necessary to observe satisfactory replication of the best maximum log likelihood value) and keep track of the information below:

1. the number and proportion of sets of random starting values that converge to proper solution (as failure to consistently converge can indicate weak identification);

2. the number and proportion of replicated maximum likelihood values for each local and the apparent global solution (as a high frequency of replication of the apparent global solution across the sets of random starting values increases confidence that the "best" solution found is the true maximum likelihood solution);

3. the condition number for the best model (as a small condition number can indicate weak or nonidentification); and

4. the smallest estimated class proportion and estimated class size among all the latent classes estimated in the model (as a class proportion near zero can be a sign of class collapsing and class overextraction).

This information, when examined collectively, will assist in tagging models that are nonidentified or not well identified and whose maximum likelihoods solutions, if obtained, are not likely to be stable or trustworthy. Any not well-identified model should be discarded from further consideration or mindfully modified in such a way that the empirical issues surrounding the estimation for that particular model are resolved without compromising the theoretical integrity and substantive foundations of the analytic model.

Model Building

Placing LCA in a broader latent variable modeling framework conveniently provides a ready-made general sequence to follow with respect to the model-building process. The first step is always to establish the measurement model for each of the latent variables that appear in the structural equations. For a traditional LCA, this step corresponds to establishing the measurement model for the latent class variable.

Arguably, the most fundamental and critical feature of the measurement model for a latent class variable is the *number of* latent classes. Thus far, in my discussion of model specification, interpretation, and estimation, the number of latent classes, K, has been treated as if it were a known quantity. However, in most all applications of LCA, the number of classes is not known. Even in direct applications, when one assumes *a priori* that the population is heterogeneous, you rarely have specific hypotheses regarding the exact number or nature of the subpopulations. You may have certain hunches about one or more subpopulations you expect to find, but rarely are these ideas so well formed that they translate into an exact total number of classes and constraints on the class-specific parameters that would inform a measurement model specification similar to the sort associated with CFA. And in indirect applications, as you are only interested in making sure you use enough mixture components (classes) to adequately describe the overall population distribution of the indicator variables, there is no preformed notion of class number. Thus, in either case (direct or indirect), you must begin with the model building with an exploratory class enumeration step.

Deciding on the number of classes is often the most arduous phase of the mixture modeling process. It is labor intensive because it requires consideration (and, therefore, estimation) of a set of models with a varying numbers of classes, and it is complicated in that the selection of a "final" model from the set of models under consideration requires the examination of a host of fit indices along with substantive scrutiny and practical reflection, as there is no single method for comparing models with differing numbers of latent classes that is widely accepted as best (Muthén & Asparouhov, 2006; Nylund, Asparouhov, & Muthén, 2007). This section first reviews the preferred tools available for the statistical evaluation of latent class models and then explains how these tools may be applied in concert with substantive evaluation and the parsimony principle in making the class enumeration determination. The tools are divided into three categories: (1) evaluations of absolute fit; (2) evaluations of relative fit; and (3) evaluations of classification.

Absolute Fit. In evaluating the absolute fit of a model, you are comparing the model's representation of the data to the actual data—that is, the overall model-data consistency. Recall that in traditional LCA, the observed data for individual responses on a set of categorical indicator variables can be summarized by a frequency table where each row represents one of the finite number of possible response patterns and the frequency column contains the number of individuals in the sample manifesting each particular pattern. The entire $n \times M$ data matrix can be identically represented by $R \times (M+1)$ frequency table where R is the number of total observed response patterns. For example, in the hypothetical LCA example with five binary indicator variables, there would be $2^5 = 32$ possible response patterns with $R \leq 32$. Assuming for the moment that $R = 32$, all the observed data on those five binary indicators could be represented in the following format:

u_1	u_2	u_3	u_4	u_5	f_r
1	1	1	1	1	f_1
1	1	1	1	0	f_2
1	1	1	0	1	f_3
⋮	⋮	⋮	⋮	⋮	⋮
0	0	0	0	0	f_{32}

where f_r is the number of individuals in the sample with response pattern r corresponding to specific responses to the us displayed in row r of the table and $\sum f_r = n$. Thus, when evaluating absolute fit for a latent class measurement model, comparing the model representation of the data to the actual data will mean comparing the model-estimated frequencies to the observed frequencies across all the response patterns.

The most common test of absolute fit for observed categorical data and the one preferred in the LCA setting is the likelihood ratio (LR) chi-square goodness-of-fit test (Agresti, 2002; Collins & Lanza, 2010; McCutcheon, 1987). The test statistic, X^2_{LR} (sometime denoted by G^2 or L^2), is calculated as follows:

$$X^2_{LR} = 2 \sum_{r=1}^{R} \left[f_r \log \left(\frac{f_r}{\hat{f}_r} \right) \right], \tag{9}$$

where R is the total number of observed data response patterns; f_r is the observed frequency count for the response pattern r; and $\hat{f}_r$ is the model-estimated frequency count for the response pattern r. Under the null hypothesis that the data are governed by the assumed distribution of the specified model, the test statistic given in Equation 9 is distributed chi-square with degrees of freedom given by

$$df_{X^2_{LR}} = R - d - 1, \tag{10}$$

where d is the number of parameters estimated in the model. When the model fits the sample data perfectly (i.e., $f_r = \hat{f}_r$, $\forall r$), the test statistic, X^2_{LR}, is equal to zero and the p-value is equal to 1. Failure to reject the null hypothesis implies adequate model-data consistency; rejection of the null implies the model does not adequately fit the data—the larger the test statistic, the larger the discrepancy and the poorer the fit between the model representation and the actual observed data.

Although it is very useful to have a way to statistical evaluate overall goodness-of-fit of a model to the data, the X^2_{LR} test statistic relies on large sample theory and may not work as intended (i.e., X^2_{LR} may not be well approximated by a chi-square distribution under the null hypothesis, marking the *p*-values based on that distribution of questionable validity) when the data set is small or the data are sparse, meaning there is a non-negligible number of response patterns with small frequencies (Agresti, 2002). There are some solutions, including parametric bootstrapping and posterior predictive checking, that are available to address this shortcoming (Collins & Lanza, 2010) but they are not widely implemented for this particular goodness-of-fit test in most mixture modeling software and are beyond the scope of this chapter.

Chi-square goodness-of-fit tests, in general, are also known to be sensitive to what would be considered negligible or inconsequential misfit in very large samples. In these cases, the null hypothesis may be rejected and the model determined to be statistically inadequate but, upon closer practical inspection, may be ruled to have a "close enough" fit. In factor analysis models, there is a wide array of closeness-of-fit indices for one to reference in addition to the exact-fit chi-square test, but this is not the case for mixture models. However, you can still inspect the closeness-of-fit for latent class models by examining the standardized residuals. Unlike residual diagnostics in the regression model, which compare each individual's predicted outcome to the observed values, or residual diagnostics in factor analysis, which compare the model-estimated means, variances, covariances, and correlations to the observed values, the LCA residuals are constructed using the same information that goes into the overall goodness-of-fit test statistic: the model-estimated response pattern frequencies and the observed frequencies. The raw residual for each response pattern is simply the difference between the observed and model-estimated frequency, $r\hat{e}s_r = f_r - \hat{f}_r$, and the standardized residual is calculated by

$$stdr\hat{e}s_r = \frac{f_r - \hat{f}_r}{\sqrt{\hat{f}_r \left(1 - \frac{\hat{f}_r}{n}\right)}}. \quad (11)$$

The values of the standardized residuals can be compared to a standard normal distribution (Haberman, 1973), with large values (e.g., $|stdr\hat{e}s_r| > 3$) indicating response patterns that were more poorly fit, contributing the most to the X^2_{LR} and the rejection of the model. Because the number of possible response patterns can become large very quickly with increasing numbers of indicators and/or response categories per indicator, it is common to have an overwhelmingly large number of response patterns, many with observed and expected frequencies that are very small—that is, approaching or equal to zero. However, there is usually a much smaller subset of response patterns with relatively high frequencies, and it can be helpful to focus your attention on the residuals of these patterns where the bulk of data reside (Muthén & Asparouhov, 2006). In addition to examining the particular response patterns with large standardized residuals, it is also relevant to examine the overall proportion of response patterns with large standardized residuals. For a well-fitting model, one would still expect, by chance, to have some small percentage of the response patterns to have significant residual values, so you would likely only take proportions in notable excess of, say, 1% to 5%, to be an indication of a poor-fitting model.

Relative Fit. In evaluating the relative fit of a model, you are comparing the model's representation of the data to another model's representation. Evaluations of relative fit do not tell you anything about the *absolute fit* so keep in mind even if one model is a far better fit to the data than another, *both* could be poor in overall goodness of fit.

There are two categories of relative fit comparisons: (1) inferential and (2) information-heuristic. The most common ML-based inferential comparison is the likelihood ratio test (LRT) for nested models. For a Model 0 (null model) to be nested within a Model 1 (alternative model), Model 0 must be a "special case" of Model 1—that is, Model 0 is Model 1 with certain parameter restrictions in place. The likelihood ratio test statistic (LRTS) is computed as

$$X^2_{diff} = -2(LL_0 - LL_1), \quad (12)$$

where LL_0 and LL_1 are the maximized log likelihood values to which the EM algorithm converges during the model estimation for Model 0 and Model 1, respectively. Under the null hypothesis that there is no difference between the two models (i.e., that the parameter restrictions placed on Model 1 to obtain Model 0 are restrictions that match the true population model) and with certain regularity conditions in place (e.g., the parameter restrictions do not fall on the boundary of the parameter space), X^2_{diff} has a chi-square distribution with degrees of freedom given by

$$df_{diff} = d_1 - d_0, \quad (13)$$

where d_1 and d_0 are the numbers of parameters estimated in Model 1 and Model 0, respectively. Failure to reject the null hypothesis implies there is not statistically significant difference in fit to the data between Model 0 and Model 1. Thus, Model 0 would be favored over Model 1 since it is a simpler model with comparable fit. Rejection of the null hypothesis would imply that the parameter restrictions placed on Model 1 to obtain Model 0 resulted in a statistically significant decrement of fit. In general, this result would lead you to favor Model 1, unless the absolute fit of Model 0 was already deemed adequately. Following the principle of parsimony, if Model 0 had adequate absolute fit, then it would likely be favored over any more complicated and parameter-laden model, even if the more complicated model fit significantly better, relatively speaking.

There are two primary limitations of the likelihood ratio test comparison of relative model fit: (1) it only allows the comparison of two models at a time, and (2) those two models must be nested under certain regularity conditions. Information-heuristic tools overcome those two limitations by allowing the comparison of relative fit across a set of models that may or may not be nested. The downside is the comparisons are descriptive—that is, you can use these tools to say one model is "better" than another according to a particular criterion but you can't test in a statistical sense, as you can with the X^2_{diff}, how much better. Most information-heuristic comparisons of relative fit are based on *information criteria* that weigh the fit of the model (as captured by the maximum log likelihood value) in consideration of the model complexity. These criteria recognize that although one can always improve the fit of a model by adding parameters, there is a cost for that improvement in fit to model parsimony. These information criteria can be expressed in the form

$$-2LL + penalty, \quad (14)$$

where LL is the maximized log likelihood function value to which the EM algorithm converges during the model estimation. The *penalty* term is some measure of the complexity of the model involving sample size and the number of parameters being estimated in the model. For model comparisons, a particular information criterion value is computed for each of the models under consideration, and the model with the minimum value for that criterion is judged as the (relative) best among that set of models. What follows is a cataloging of the three most common information criteria used in mixture model relative fit comparisons. These criteria differ only in the computation of the penalty term.

• Bayesian Information Criterion (BIC; Schwarz, 1978)

$$BIC = -2LL + d\log(n), \quad (15)$$

where d is the number of parameters estimated in the model; n is the number of subjects or cases, in the analysis sample.

• Consistent Akaike's Information Criterion (CAIC; Bozdogan, 1987)

$$CAIC = -2LL + d[\log(n) + 1]. \quad (16)$$

• Approximate Weight of Evidence Criterion (AWE; Banfield & Raftery, 1993)

$$AWE = -2LL + 2d[\log(n) + 1.5]. \quad (17)$$

Although the information-heuristic descriptive comparisons of model are usually ordinal in nature, there are a few descriptive quantifications of relative fit based on information criteria that, although still noninferential, do allow you to get a sense of "how much" better one model is relative to another model or relative to a whole set of models. The two quantifications presented here are based on rough approximations to comparisons available in a Bayesian estimation framework and have been popularized by Nagin (1999) in the latent class growth modeling literature.

The first, the approximate Bayes Factor (BF), is a pairwise comparison of relative fit between two models, Model A and Model B. It is calculated as

$$B\hat{F}_{A,B} = \exp[SIC_A - SIC_B], \quad (18)$$

where SIC is the Schwarz Information Criterion (Schwarz, 1978), given by

$$SIC = -0.5 BIC. \quad (19)$$

$BF_{A,B}$ represents the ratio of the probability of Model A being the correct model to Model B being the correct model when Models A and B are considered the competing models. According to Jeffrey's Scale of Evidence (Wasserman, 1997), $1 < BF_{A,B} < 3$ is weak evidence for Model A, $3 < BF_{A,B} < 10$ is moderate evidence for Model A, and $BF_{A,B} > 10$ is considered strong evidence for Model A. Schwarz (1978) and Kass and Wasserman (1995) showed that $B\hat{F}_{A,B}$ as defined in Equation 18 is a reasonable approximation of $BF_{A,B}$ when equal weight is placed on the prior probabilities of Models A and B (Nagin, 1999).

The second, the approximate correct model probability (cmP), allows relative comparisons of each of

J models to an entire set of J models under consideration. There is a cmP value for each of the models, Model A (A = 1, ..., J) computed as

$$cm\hat{P}_A = \frac{\exp(SIC_A - SIC_{\max})}{\sum_{j=1}^{J} \exp(SIC_j - SIC_{\max})}, \quad (20)$$

where $SIC_{\max}$ is the maximum SIC score of the J models under consideration. In comparison to the $\hat{BF}_{A,B}$, which compares only two models, the cmP is a metric for comparing a set of more than two models. The sum of the cmP values across the set of models under consideration is equal to 1.00—that is, the true model is assumed to be one of the models in the set. Schwarz (1978) and Kass and Wasserman (1995) showed that $cm\hat{P}_A$ as defined in Equation 20 is a reasonable approximation of the actual probability of Model A being the correct model relative to the other J models under consideration when equal weight is placed on the prior probabilities of all the model (Nagin, 1999). The ratio of $cm\hat{P}_A$ to $cm\hat{P}_B$ when the set of models under consideration is limited to only Models A and B reduces to $\hat{BF}_{A,B}$.

Classification Diagnostics. Evaluating the precision of the latent class assignment for individuals by a candidate model is another way of assessing the degree of class separation and is most useful in direct applications wherein one of the primary objectives is to extract from the full sample empirically well-separated, highly-differentiated groups whose members have a high degree of homogeneity in their responses on the class indicators. Indeed, if there is a plan to conduct latent class assignment for use in a subsequent analysis—that is, in a multistage classify–analyze approach, the within-class homogeneity and across-class separation and differentiation is of primary importance for assessing the quality of the model (Collins & Lanza, 2010). Quality of classification could, however, be completely irrelevant for indirect applications. Further, it is important to keep in mind that it is possible for a mixture model to have a good fit to the data but still have poor latent class assignment accuracy. In other words, model classification diagnostics can be used to evaluate the utility of the latent class analysis as a model-based clustering tool for a given set of indicators observed on a particular sample but should *not* be used to evaluate the model-data consistency in either absolute or relative terms.

All of the classification diagnostics presented here are based on estimated *posterior class probabilities*. Posterior class probabilities are the model-estimated values for each individual's probabilities of being in each of the latent classes based on the maximum likelihood parameter estimates and the individual's observed responses on the indicator variables. The posterior class probability for individual i corresponding to latent Class k, $\hat{p}_{ik}$, is given by

$$\hat{p}_{ik} = \hat{\Pr}(c_i = k | \mathbf{u}_i, \hat{\theta}) = \frac{\hat{\Pr}(\mathbf{u}_i | c_i = k, \hat{\theta}) \cdot \hat{\Pr}(c_i = k)}{\hat{\Pr}(\mathbf{u}_i)}, \quad (21)$$

where $\hat{\theta}$ is the set of parameter estimates for the class-specific item response probabilities and the class proportions. Standard *post hoc* model-based individual classification is done using *modal* class assignment such that each individual in the sample is assigned to the latent class for which he or she has the largest posterior class probability. In more formal terms, model-based modally assigned class membership for individual i, $\hat{c}_{\text{modal},i}$, is given by

$$\hat{c}_{\text{modal},i} = k : \max(\hat{p}_{i1}, \ldots, \hat{p}_{iK}) = \hat{p}_{ik}. \quad (22)$$

Table 25.2 provides examples of four individual sets of estimated posterior class probabilities and the corresponding modal class assignment for the hypothetical three-class LCA example. Although individuals 1 and 2 are both modally assigned to Class 1, individual 1 has a very high estimated posterior class probability for Class 1, whereas individual 2 is not well classified. If there were many cases like individual 2, then the overall classification accuracy would be low as the model would do almost no better than random guessing at predicting latent class membership. If there were many cases like individual 1, then the overall classification accuracy would be high. The first classification diagnostic, relative entropy, offers a systematic summary of the levels of posterior class probabilities across classes and individuals in the sample.

Relative entropy, E_K, is an index that summarizes the overall precision of classification for the whole sample across all the latent classes (Ramasway, DeSarbo, Reibstein, & Robinson, 1993). It is computed by

$$E_K = 1 - \frac{\sum_{i=1}^{n} \sum_{k=1}^{K} [-\hat{p}_{ik} \ln(\hat{p}_{ik})]}{n \log(K)}. \quad (23)$$

E_K measures the posterior classification uncertainty for a K-class model and is bounded between 0 and 1; $E_K = 0$ when posterior classification is no better than random guessing and $E_K = 1$ when there is perfect posterior classification for all individuals in the sample—that

Table 25.2. Hypothetical Example: Estimated Posterior Class Probabilities and Modal Class Assignment Based on Three-Class Unconditional Latent Class Analysis for Four Sample Participants

i	$\hat{p}_{ik1}$			$\hat{c}_{modal(i)}$
	$\hat{p}_{i1}$	$\hat{p}_{i2}$	$\hat{p}_{i3}$	
1	0.95	0.05	0.00	1
2	0.40	0.30	0.30	1
3	0.20	0.70	0.10	2
4	0.00	0.00	1.00	3

is, $\max(\hat{p}_{i1}, \hat{p}_{i2}, \ldots, \hat{p}_{iK}) = 1.00$, $\forall i$. Because even when E_K is close to 1.00 there can be a high degree of latent class assignment error for particular individuals, and because posterior classification uncertainty may increase simply by chance for models with more latent classes, E_K was never intended for, nor should it be used for, model selection during the class enumeration process. However, E_K values near 0 may indicate that the latent classes are not sufficiently well separated for the K classes that have been estimated (Ramaswamy et al., 1993). Thus, E_K may be used to identify problematic overextraction of latent classes and may also be used to judge the utility of the LCA directly applied to a particular set of indicators to produce highly-differentiated groups in the sample.

The next classification diagnostic, the average posterior class probability (AvePP), enables evaluation of the specific classification uncertainty for each of the latent classes. The AvePP for Class k, $AvePP_k$, is given by

$$AvePP_k = \text{Mean}\{\hat{p}_{ik}, \forall i : \hat{c}_{modal,i} = k\}. \quad (24)$$

That is, $AvePP_k$ is the mean of the Class k posterior class probabilities across all individuals whose maximum posterior class probability is for Class k. In contrast to E_K which provides an overall summary of latent class assignment error, the set of $AvePP_k$ quantities provide class-specific measures of how well the set of indicators predict class membership in the sample. Similarly to E_K, $AvePP_k$ is bounded between 0 and 1; $AvePP_k = 1$ when the Class k posteriori probability for every individual in the sample modally assigned to Class k is equal to 1. Nagin (2005) suggests a rule-of-thumb that

all AvePP values be above 0.70 (i.e., $AvePP_k > .70$, $\forall k$) to consider the classes well separated and the latent class assignment accuracy adequate.

The odds of correct classification ratio (OCC; Nagin, 2005) is based on the $AvePP_k$ and provides a similar class-specific summary of classification accuracy. The odds of correction classification ratio for Class k, OCC_k, is given by

$$OCC_k = \frac{AvePP_k/(1 - AvePP_k)}{\hat{\pi}_k/(1 - \hat{\pi}_k)}, \quad (25)$$

where $\hat{\pi}_k$ is the model-estimated proportion for Class k. The denominator is the odds of correct classification based on random assignment using the model-estimated marginal class proportions, $\hat{\pi}_k$. The numerator is the odds of correct classification based on the maximum posterior class probability assignment rule (i.e., modal class assignment). When the modal class assignment for Class k is no better than chance, then $OCC_k = 1.00$. As $AvePP_k$ gets close to the ideal value of 1.00, OCC_k gets larger. Thus, large values of OCC_k (i.e., values 5.00 or larger; Nagin, 2005) for all K classes indicate a latent class model with good latent class separation and high assignment accuracy.

The final classification diagnostic presented here is the modal class assignment proportion (mcaP). This diagnostic is also a class-specific index of classification certainly. The modal class assignment proportion for Class k, $mcaP_k$, is given by

$$mcaP_k = \frac{\sum_{i=1}^{n} \text{I}\{\hat{c}_{modal,i} = k\}}{n}, \quad (26)$$

Put simply, $mcaP_k$ is the proportion of individuals in the sample modally assigned to Class k. If individuals were assigned to Class k with perfect certainty, then $mcaP_k = \hat{\pi}_k$. Larger discrepancies between $mcaP_k$ and $\hat{\pi}_k$ are indicative of larger latent class assignment errors. To gage the discrepancy, each $mcaP_k$ can be compared to the to 95% confidence interval for the corresponding $\hat{\pi}_k$.

Class Enumeration. Now that you have a full set of tools for evaluating models in terms of absolute fit, relative fit, and classification accuracy, I can discuss how to apply them to the first critical step in the latent class modeling process: deciding on the number of latent classes. This process usually begins by specifying a one-class LCA model and then fitting additional models, incrementing the number of classes by one, until the models are no longer well identified (as defined in the subsection

"Model Estimation"). The fit of each of the models is evaluated in the absolute and relative terms. The parsimony principle is also applied such that the model with the fewest number of classes that is statistically and substantively adequate and useful is favored.

In terms of the relative fit comparisons, the standard likelihood ratio chi-square difference test presented earlier cannot be used in this setting, because the necessary regularity conditions of the test are violated when comparing a K-class model to a $(K - g)$-class model (McLachlan & Peel, 2000); in other words, although X^2_{diff} can be calculated, it does not have a chi-square sampling distribution under the null hypothesis. However, two alternatives, currently implemented in mainstream mixture modeling software, are available: (1) the adjusted Lo-Mendell-Rubin likelihood ratio test (adjusted LMR-LRT; Lo, Mendell, & Rubin, 2001), which analytically approximates the X^2_{diff} sampling distribution when comparing a K-class to a $(K - g)$-class finite mixture model for which the classes differ only in the mean structure; and (2) the parametric bootstrapped likelihood ratio test (BLRT), recommended by McLachlan and Peel (2000), which uses bootstrap samples (generated using parameter estimates from a $[K - g]$-class model) to empirically derive the sampling distribution of X^2_{diff} under the null model. Both of these tests and their performance across a range of finite mixture models has been explored in detail in the simulation study by Nylund, Asparouhov, and Muthén (2007). As executed in Mplus V6.1 (Muthén & Muthén, 1998–2011), these tests compare a $(K - 1)$-class model (the null model) with a K-class model (the alternative, less restrictive model), and a statistically significant p-value suggests the K-class model fits the data significantly better than a model with one less class.

As mentioned before, there is no single method for comparing models with differing numbers of latent classes that is widely accepted as best (Muthén & Asparouhov, 2006; Nylund et al., 2007). However, by careful and systematic consideration of a set of plausible models, and utilizing a combination of statistical and substantive model checking (Muthén, 2003), researchers can improve their confidence in the tenability of their decision regarding the number of latent classes. I recommend the follow sequence for class enumeration, which is illustrated in detail with the empirical example that follows after the next subsection.

1. Fit a one-class model, recording the log likelihood value (LL); number of parameters estimated ($npar$); the likelihood ratio chi-square goodness-of-fit statistic (X^2_{LR} with df and corresponding p-value); and the model BIC, CAIC, and AWE values.

2. Fit a two-class model, recording the same quantities as listed in Step 1, along with: the adjusted LMR-LRT p-value, testing the two-class model against the null one-class model; the BLRT p-value, testing the two-class model against the null one-class model; and the approximate Bayes factor ($B\hat{F}_{1,2}$), estimating the ratio of the probability of the one-class model being the correct model to the probability of the two-class being the correct model.

3. Repeat the following for $K \geq 3$, increasing K by 1 at each repetition until the K-class model is not well identified:

Fit a K-class model, recording the same quantities as listed in Step 1, along with the adjusted LMR-LRT p-value, testing the K-class model against the null $(K - 1)$-class model; the BLRT p-value, testing the K-class model against the null $(K - 1)$-class model; and the approximate Bayes factor ($B\hat{F}_{K-1,K}$), estimating the ratio of the probability of the $(K - 1)$-class model being the correct model to the probability of the K-class being the correct model.

4. Let K_{max} be the largest number of classes that could be extracted in a single model from Step 3. Compute the approximate correct model probability (cmP) across the one-class through K_{max}-class models fit in Steps 1–3.

5. From the K_{max} models fit in Steps 1 through 3, select a smaller subset of two to three candidate models based on the absolute and relative fit indices using the guidelines (a)-(e) that follow. I assume here, since it is almost always the case in practice, that there will be more than one "best" model identified across the different indices. Typically, the candidate models are adjacent to each other with respect to the number of classes (e.g., three-class and four-class candidate models).

a. For absolute fit, the "best" model should be the model with the fewest number of classes that has an adequate overall goodness of fit—that is, the most parsimonious model that is not rejected by the exact fit test.

b. For the BIC, CAIC, and AWE, the "best" model is the model with the smallest value. However, because none of the information criteria are guaranteed to arrive at a single lowest value corresponding to a K-class model with $K < K_{\max}$, these indices may have their smallest value at the $K_{\max}$-class model. In such cases, you can explore the diminishing gains in model fit according to these indices with the use of "elbow" plots, similar to the use of scree plots of Eigen values used in exploratory factor analysis (EFA). For example, if you graph the BIC values versus the number of classes, then the addition of the second and third class may add much more information, but as the number of classes increases, the marginal gain may drop, resulting in a (hopefully) pronounced angle in the plot. The number of classes at this point meets the "elbow criterion" for that index.

c. For the adjusted LMR-LRT and BLRT, the "best" model is the model with the smallest number of classes that is *not* significantly improved by the addition of another class—that is, the most parsimonious K-class model that is not rejected in favor of a $(K + 1)$-class model. Note that the adjusted LMR-LRT and BLRT may never yield a non-significant p-value, favoring a K-class model over a $(K + 1)$-class model, before the number of classes reaches $K_{\max}$. In these cases, you can examine a plot of the log likelihood values for an "elbow" as explained in Substep b.

d. For the approximate BF, the "best" model is the model with the smallest number of classes for which there is moderate to strong evidence compared to the next largest model—that is, the most parsimonious K-class model with a $B\hat{F} > 3$ when compared to a $(K + 1)$-class model.

e. For the approximate correct model probabilities, the "best" model is the model with the highest probability of being correct. Any model with $cm\hat{P}_K > .10$ could be considered a candidate model.

6. Examine the standardized residuals and the classification diagnostics (if germane for your application of mixture modeling) for the subset of candidate models selected in Step 5. Render an interpretation of each latent class in each of the candidate models and consider the collective substantive meaning of the resultant classes for each of the models. Ask yourself whether the resultant latent classes of one model help you to understand the phenomenon of interest (Magnusson, 1998) better than those of another. Weigh the simplicity and clarity of each of the candidate models (Bergman & Trost, 2006) and evaluate the utility of the additional classes for the less parsimonious of the candidate models. Compare the modal class assignments of individuals across the candidate models. Don't forget about label switching when you are making your model comparisons. And, beyond label switching, remember that if you estimate a K-class model and then a $(K + 1)$-class model, then there is no guarantee that any of the K classes from the K-class model match up in substance or in label to any of the classes in the $(K + 1)$-class model.

7. On the basis of all the comparisons made in Steps 5 and 6, select the final model in the class enumeration process.

If you have the good fortune of a very large sample, then the class enumeration process can be expanded and strengthened using a split-sample cross-validation procedure. In evaluating the "largeness" of your sample, keep in mind that sample size plays a critical role in the detection of what may be less prevalent classes in the population and in the selection between competing models with differing class structures (Lubke, 2010) and you don't want to split your sample for cross-validation if such a split compromises the quality and validity of the analyses within each of the subsamples because they are not of adequate size. For a split-sample cross-validation approach:

i. Randomly partition the full sample into two (approximately) equally sized subsamples: Subsample A (the "calibration" data set) and Subsample B (the "validation" data set).

ii. Conduct latent class enumeration Steps 1–7 on Subsample A.

iii. Retain all the model parameters estimates from the final K-class model selected in Step 7.

iv. Fit the K-class model to Subsample B, fixing all parameters to the estimated values retained in Step iii.

v. Evaluate the overall fit of the model. If the parameter estimates obtained from the K-class model fit to Subsample A, then provide an acceptable fit when used as fixed parameter values for a K-class model applied to Subsample B, then the model validates well and the selection of the

K-class model is supported (Collins, Graham, Long, & Hansen, 1994).

vi. Next fit a K-class model to Subsample B, allowing all parameters to be freely estimated.

vii. Using a nested-model likelihood ratio test, compare the fit of the K-class model applied to Subsample B using fixed parameter values based on the estimates from the Subsample A K-class model estimation to the fit of the K-class model applied to Subsample B with freely estimated parameters. If there is not a significant decrement in fit for the Subsample B K-class model when fixing parameter values to the Subsample A K-class model parameters estimates, then the model validates well, the nature and distribution of the K latent classes can be considered stable across the two subsamples, and the selection of the K-class model is supported.

There are variations on this cross-validation process that can be made. One variation is to carry out Steps iii through vii for all of the candidate models selected in Step 5 rather than just the final model selected in Step 7 and then integrate in Step 6 the additional information regarding which of the candidate models validated in Subsample B according to the results from both Steps v and vii. Another variation is to do a double (or twofold) cross-validation (Collins et al., 1994; Cudek & Browne, 1983) whereby Steps ii through vii are applied using Subsample A as the calibration data set and Subsample B as the validation data set and then are repeated using Subsample B as the calibration data set and Subsample A as the validation data set. Ideally, the same "best" model will emerge in both cross-validation iterations, although it is not guaranteed (Collins & Lanza, 2010). I illustrate the double cross-validation procedure in the empirical example that follows after the next subsection.

Missing Data

Because most mixture modeling software already utilizes a maximum likelihood estimation algorithm designed for ignorable missing data (primarily the EM algorithm), it is possible to accommodate missingness on the manifest indicators as well, as long as the missing data are either *missing completely at random* (MCAR) or *missing at random* (MAR). Assuming the data on the indicator variables are missing at random means the probability of a missing response for an individual on a given indicator is unrelated to the response that would have been observed, conditional on the individual's actual observed data for the other response variables. Estimation with the EM algorithm is a *full information maximum likelihood* (FIML) method in which individuals with complete data and partially complete data all contribute to the observed data likelihood function. The details of missing data analysis, including the multiple imputation alternative to FIML, is beyond the scope of this chapter. Interested readers are referred to Little and Rubin (2002), Schaefer (1997), and Enders (2010) for more information.

Of all the evaluations of model fit presented prior, the only one that is different in the presence of missing data is the likelihood ratio goodness-of-fit test. With partially complete data, the number of observed response patterns is increased to include observed response patterns with missingness. Returning to the five binary indicator hypothetical example, you might have some of the following incomplete response patterns:

u_1	u_2	u_3	u_4	u_5	f_r
1	1	1	1	1	f_1
1	1	1	1	0	f_2
1	1	1	1	•	f_3
⋮	⋮	⋮	⋮	⋮	⋮
1	0	0	0	0	f_{R^*-2}
0	0	0	0	0	f_{R^*-1}
•	0	0	0	0	f_{R^*}

where "•" indicates a missing response and R^* is the number of observed response patterns, *including* partially complete response patterns. The LR chi-square goodness-of-fit test statistic is now calculated as

$$X^2_{LR} = 2 \sum_{r^*=1}^{R^*} \left[f_{r^*} \log \left(\frac{f_{r^*}}{\hat{f}_{r^*}} \right) \right], \quad (27)$$

where f_{r^*} is the observed frequency count for the response pattern r^* and $\hat{f}_{r^*}$ is the model-estimated frequency count for the response pattern r^*. The degrees of freedom for the test is given by

$$df = R^* - d - 1. \quad (28)$$

This test statistic, because it includes contributions from both complete and partially complete response patterns using model-estimated frequencies from a model estimated under the MAR assumption, is actually a test of *both* the exact fit and the degree to which the data depart from MCAR against the MAR alternative (Collins & Lanza, 2010; Little & Rubin, 2002). Thus, the X^2_{LR} with missing data is inflated version of a simple test of only model goodness-of-fit. However, the X^2_{LR} is easily adjusted by subtracting the contribution to the chi-square from the MCAR component, and this adjusted X^2_{LR} can then be compared to the reference chi-square distribution (Collins & Lanza, 2010; Shafer, 1997). Note that the standardized residuals for partially complete response patterns are similarly inflated, and this should be considered when examining residuals for specific complete and partially complete response patterns.

The next subsection should be the most illuminating of all the subsections under Latent Class Analysis, as it is here that I fully illustrate the unconditional LCA modeling process with a real data example, show the use of all the fit indices, classification diagnostics, the double cross-validation procedures, and demonstrate the graphical presentation and substantive interpretation of a selected model.

Longitudinal Study of American Youth Example for Latent Class Analysis

The data used for the LCA example come from Cohort 2 of the Longitudinal Study of American Youth (LSAY), a national longitudinal study, funded by the National Science Foundation (NSF) (Miller, Kimmel, Hoffer, & Nelson, 2000). The LSAY was designed to investigate the development of student learning and achievement—particularly related to mathematics, science, and technology—and to examine the relationship of those student outcomes across middle and high school to post-secondary educational and early career choices. The students of Cohort 2 were first measured in the fall of 1988 when they were in eighth grade. Study participants were recruited through their schools, which were selected from a probability sample of U.S. public school districts (Kimmel & Miller, 2008). For simplicity's sake, I do not incorporate information related to the complex sampling design or the clustering of schools within districts and students within school for the modeling illustrations in this chapter; however, the analytic framework presented does extend to accommodate sampling weights and multilevel data. There were a total of $n = 3116$ students in the original LSAY Cohort 2 (48% female; 52% male).

For this example, nine items were selected from the eighth grade (Fall, 1998) student survey related to math attitudes for use as observed response indicators for an unconditional latent class variable that was intended to represent profiles of latent math dispositions. The nine self-report items were measured on a five-point, Likert-type scale (1 = strongly agree; 2 = agree; 3 = not sure; 4 = disagree; 5 = strongly disagree). For the analysis, I dichotomized the items to a 0/1 scale after reverse coding certain items so that all item endorsements (indicated by a value of 1) represented pro-mathematics responses. Table 25.3 presents the original language of the survey prompt for the set of math attitude items along with the full text of the each item statement and the response categories from the original scale that were recoded as a pro-math item endorsements. In examining the items, I determined that the items could be tentatively grouped into three separate aspects of math disposition: items 1–3 are indicators of positive math affect and efficacy; items 4–5 are indicators of math anxiety; and items 6–9 are indicators of the student assessment of the utility of mathematics knowledge. I anticipated that this conceptual three-part formation of the items might assist in the interpretation of the resultant latent classes from the LCA modeling.

Table 25.3 also displays the frequencies and relative frequencies of pro-math item endorsements for the full analysis sample of $n = 2,675$ (excluding 441 of the total participant sample who had missing responses on *all* nine of selected items). Note that all nine items have a reasonable degree of variability in responses and therefore contain information about individual differences in math dispositions. If there were items with relative frequencies very near 0 or 1, there would be very little information about individual differences to inform the formation of the latent classes.

With nine binary response items, there are $2^9 = 512$ possible response pattern, but only 362 of those were observed in the sample data. Of the total sample, 2,464 participants (92%) have complete data on all the items. There are 166 observed response patterns in the data with at least one missing response. Of the total sample, 211 participants (8%) have missing data on one of more of the items, with 135 (64%) of those participants missing on only one item. Upon closer inspection, there is not any single item that stands out with a high frequency of missingness that might indicate a systematic skip pattern of responding that would make one reconsider that item's

Table 25.3. LSAY Example: Pro-math Item Endorsement Frequencies (f) and Relative Frequencies (rf) for the Total Sample and the Two Random Cross-Validation Subsamples, A and B

Survey prompt: "Now we would like you to tell us how you feel about math and science. Please indicate for you feel about each of the following statements."	Pro-math response categories*	Total sample (n_T = 2675) f	rf	Subsample A (n_A = 1338) f	rf	Subsample B (n_B = 1337) f	rf
1) I enjoy math.	sa/a	1784	0.67	894	0.67	890	0.67
2) I am good at math.	sa/a	1850	0.69	912	0.68	938	0.70
3) I usually understand what we are doing in math.	sa/a	2020	0.76	1011	0.76	1009	0.76
4) Doing math often makes me nervous or upset.	d/sd	1546	0.59	765	0.59	781	0.59
5) I often get scared when I open my math book see a page of problems.	d/sd	1821	0.69	917	0.69	904	0.68
6) Math is useful in everyday problems.	sa/a	1835	0.70	908	0.69	927	0.70
7) Math helps a person think logically.	sa/a	1686	0.64	854	0.65	832	0.63
8) It is important to know math to get a good job.	sa/a	1947	0.74	975	0.74	972	0.74
9) I will use math in many ways as an adult.	sa/a	1858	0.70	932	0.70	926	0.70

*Original rating scale: 1 = strongly agree (sa); 2 = agree (a); 3 = nor sure (ns); 4 = disagree (d); 5 = strongly disagree (sd). Recoded to 0/1 with 1 indicating a pro-math response.

inclusion in the analysis. The three most frequent complete data response patterns with observed frequency counts are: $(1,1,1,1,1,1,1,1,1)$, $f = 502$; $(1,1,1,0,0,1,1,1,1)$, $f = 111$; and $(1,1,1,0,1,1,1,1,1)$, $f = 94$. More than 70% (258 of 362) of the complete data response patterns have $f < 5$. The three most frequent incomplete data response patterns with observed frequency counts are: $(1,1,1,?,1,1,1,1,1)$, $f = 9$; $(1,1,1,1,1,1,1,?,1)$, $f = 7$; and $(1,1,1,1,1,1,?,1,1)$, $f = 6$ (where "?" indicates a missing value).

Because this is a large sample, it is possible to utilize a double cross-validation procedure for establishing the unconditional latent class model for math dispositions. Beginning with Step i, the sample is randomly split into halves, Subsample A and Subsample B. Table 25.3 provides the item response frequencies and relative frequencies for both subsamples.

The class enumeration process begins by fitting 10 unconditional latent class models with $K = 1$ to $K = 10$ classes. After $K = 8$, the models ceased to be well identified (e.g., there was a high level of nonconvergence across the random sets of starting values; a low level of maximum log likelihood solution replication; a small condition number; and/or the smallest class proportion corresponded to less than 20 individuals). For $K = 1$ to $K = 8$, the models appeared well identified. For example, Figure 25.5 illustrates a high degree of replication of the "best" maximum likelihood value, -6250.94, for the five-class model, depicting the relative frequencies of the final stage log likelihood values at the local maxima across 1000 random sets of start values.

Table 25.4 summarizes the results from class enumeration Steps 1 through 5 for Subsample A. Bolded values indicate the value corresponding to the "best" model according to each fit index and the boxes indicate the candidate models based on each index (which include the "best" and the "second best" models). For the adjusted LR chi-square test of exact fit, the four-class model is marginally adequate and the five-class model has a high level of model-data consistency. Although the six-, seven-, and eight-class models also have a good fit to the data, the five-class model is the most parsimonious. The BIC has the smallest value for the five-class model but the six-class BIC value is very close. The same is true for the CAIC. The AWE has the smallest value for the four-class model, with the five-class value a close second. The four-class model is rejected in favor of the five-class model by the adjusted LMR-LRT, but the five-class model is not rejected in favor of the six-class model. All K-class model were rejected in favor of a $(K + 1)$-class model by the BLRT for all values of K considered so there was no "best" or even candidate models to be selected based on the BLRT, and those results are not presented in the summary table. According to the approximate BF, there was strong evidence for the five-class model over the four-class model, and there was strong evidence for the five-class model over the six-class model. Finally, based on the approximate correct model probabilities, of the eight models, the five-class model has the highest probability of being correct followed by the six-class model. Based on all these indices, I select the four-, five-, and six-class models for attempted cross-validation in Subsample B, noting that the five-class model is the one of the three candidate models most favored across all of the indices.

The first three rows of Table 25.5 summarize the cross-validation results for the Subsample A candidate models. For the first row, I took the four-class parameters estimates obtained by fitting a four-class model to Subsample A, used those estimates as fixed parameter values in Subsample B, and evaluated the overall fit of the model, following cross-validation Steps iv through v. The overall fit of the model, as determined by the LR chi-square goodness-of-fit test, was not adequate, and by this criterion, the estimated four-class model from Subsample A did not replicate in Subsample B. I next estimated a four-class model in Subsample B, allowing all parameters to be freely estimated, and compared the fit to the model with all the parameters fixed to the estimated values from Subsample A, following cross-validation Steps vi through vii. The likelihood ratio test of

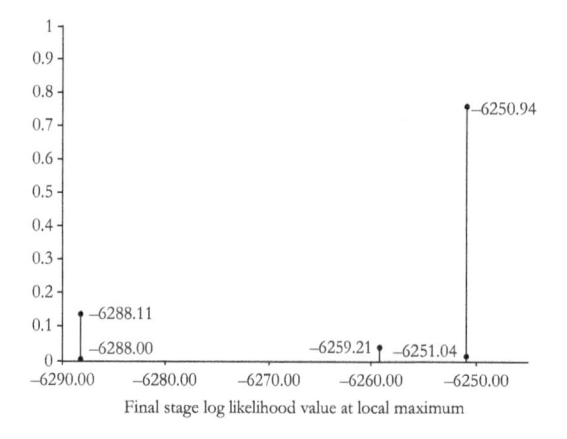

Figure 25.5 LSAY example: Relative frequency plot of final stage log likelihood values at local maxima across 1000 random sets of start values for the five-class unconditional LCA.

Table 25.4. LSAY Example: Model Fit Indices for Exploratory Latent Class Analysis Using Calibration Subsample A ($n_A = 1338$)

Model	LL	npar*	Adj. X^2_{LR} (df), p-value	BIC	CAIC	AWE	Adj. LMR-LRT p-value (H_0:K classes; H_1:K + 1 classes)	$\hat{BF}_{K,K+1}$	$cm\hat{P}_K$
one-class	−7328.10	9	1289.21 (368), <0.01	14,721.00	14,730.00	14,812.79	<0.01	<0.10	<0.01
two-class	−6612.88	19	943.97 (358), <0.01	13,362.55	13,381.55	13,556.33	<0.01	<0.10	<0.01
three-class	−6432.53	29	586.66 (348), <0.01	13,073.83	13,102.83	13,369.60	<0.01	<0.10	<0.01
four-class	−6331.81	39	382.14 (338), 0.05	12,944.38	12,983.38	13,342.13	<0.01	<0.10	<0.01
five-class	−6250.94	49	218.64 (328), >0.99	12,854.63	12,903.63	13,354.37	0.15	6.26	0.87
six-class	−6216.81	59	157.25 (318), >0.99	12,858.35	12,917.35	13,460.09	0.13	>10	0.13
seven-class	−6192.32	69	105.70 (308), >0.99	12,881.37	12,950.37	13,585.09	0.23	>10	<0.01
eight-class	−6171.11	79	69.55 (298), >0.99	12,910.93	12,989.93	13,716.64	—	—	<0.01
nine-class	Not well identified								
ten-class	Not well identified								

*number of parameters estimated

Table 25.5. LSAY Example: Double Cross-Validation Summary of Model Fit Using the Two Random Subsamples, A and B ($n_A = 1338$; $n_B = 1337$)

Model	Calibration	Validation	Adj. X^{2*}_{LR}	df	p-value	LRTS**	df***	p-value
four-class	Subsample A	Subsample B	501.975	363	<0.001	38.50	39	0.49
five-class			353.036	363	0.64	59.71	49	0.14
six-class			365.876	363	0.45	136.66	59	<0.001
four-class	Subsample B	Subsample A	425.04	377	0.04	43.67	39	0.28
five-class			282.63	377	1.00	64.21	49	0.07
six-class			260.37	377	1.00	101.85	59	<0.001

*Goodness-of-fit of the model to validation subsample with all parameter values fixed at the estimates obtained from the calibration subsample.
** $LRTS = -2(LL_0 - LL_1)$ where LL_0 is the maximized log likelihood value, -6250.94, for the K-class model fit to the validation subsample with all parameter values fixed at the estimates obtained from the calibration subsample and LL_1 is the maximized log likelihood value for the K-class model fit to the validation subsample with all parameters freely estimated.
*** df = number of parameters in the K-class model

these nested models was not significant, indicating that the parameter estimates for the four-class model using Subsample B data were not significantly different from the parameter estimates from Subsample A. Thus, by this criterion, the estimated four-class model from Subsample A did replicate in Subsample B (indicated by bolded text in the table). The five-class model from Subsample A was the only one of the three candidate models that validated by both criteria (indicated by the boxed text).

For a double cross-validation, the full process above is repeated for Subsample B. I estimated $K = 1$ to $K = 10$ class models; selected a subset of candidate models, which were the same four-, five-, and six-class models as I selected for Subsample A; favoring the five-class model; and then cross-validated using Subsample A. As shown in Table 25.5, the five-class model from Subsample B was the only one of the three candidate models that cross-validated by both criteria in Subsample A.

Before the five-class model is anointed as the "final" unconditional model, there are a few more evaluations necessary. Although the five-class model is not rejected in the LR chi-square exact fit test, it is still advisable to examine the standardized residuals. Only six of the response patterns with model-estimated frequencies above 1.0 have standardized residuals greater than 3.0, only slightly more than the 1% one would expect by chance, and only one of those standardized residuals is greater than 5.0. Thus, closer examination of the model residuals does not raise concern about the fit of the five-class model to the data. Table 25.6 provides a summary of the observed and model-estimated frequencies for all observed response patterns with frequencies greater than 10 along with the standardized residual values.

Because I have approached this analysis as a direct application of mixture modeling, in that I am assuming *a priori* that the population is heterogeneous with regards to math dispositions and that the items selected for the analysis are indicators of membership in one of an unknown number of subgroups with characteristically different math disposition profiles, it is also necessary to examine the classification diagnostics for the five-class model as well as evaluate the substantive meaning and utility of the resultant classes. Table 25.7 summarizes the classification diagnostic measures for the five-class model with relative entropy of $E_5 = .77$. The modal class assignment proportions (mcaP) are all very near the estimated class proportions and well within the corresponding 95% (bias-corrected bootstrap) confidence intervals for $\hat{\pi}_k$, the AvePP are all greater than 0.70, and the odds of correct classification ratios are all well above 5.0, collectively indicating that the five classes are well separated and there is high accuracy in the latent class assignment. This result further endorses the choice of the five-class model.

The interpretation of the resultant five classes is based primarily on the model-estimated, class-specific item response probabilities provided in Table 25.8 and depicted graphically in the profile plot

Table 25.6. LSAY Example: Observed Response Patterns ($f > 10$), Observed and Estimated Frequencies, and Standardized Residuals for Subsample A with Estimated Posterior Class Probabilities and Modal Class Assignments Based on the Five-Class Unconditional LCA

r^*	(1)	(2)	(3)	(4)	(5)	(6)	(7)	(8)	(9)	f_{r^*}	$\hat{f}_{r^*}$	$std\hat{r}es_{r^*}$	$\hat{p}_{i1}$	$\hat{p}_{i2}$	$\hat{p}_{i3}$	$\hat{p}_{i4}$	$\hat{p}_{i5}$	$\hat{c}_{modal(i)}$
1	1	1	1	1	1	1	1	1	1	254.00	234.24	1.44	0.99	0.01	0.01	0.00	0.00	1
2	1	1	1	0	0	1	1	1	1	53.00	47.91	0.75	0.00	0.99	0.00	0.01	0.00	2
3	1	1	1	0	1	1	1	1	1	46.00	44.80	0.18	0.86	0.12	0.01	0.01	0.00	1
4	0	0	0	0	0	0	0	0	0	36.00	23.90	2.50	0.00	0.00	0.00	0.00	1.00	5
5	1	1	1	1	1	0	1	1	1	31.00	39.62	−1.39	0.93	0.01	0.06	0.00	0.00	1
6	0	1	1	1	1	1	1	1	1	26.00	29.00	−0.56	0.95	0.00	0.02	0.03	0.00	1
7	1	1	1	1	0	1	1	1	1	22.00	22.24	−0.05	0.85	0.02	0.13	0.00	0.00	1
8	1	1	1	0	0	1	1	1	1	19.00	16.91	0.51	0.00	0.97	0.02	0.01	0.00	2
9	1	1	1	1	1	0	0	0	0	18.00	10.54	2.31	0.00	0.00	0.99	0.00	0.01	3
10	1	1	1	1	1	1	1	1	0	17.00	18.12	−0.27	0.84	0.01	0.15	0.00	0.00	1
11	0	0	0	0	0	1	1	1	1	17.00	9.51	2.44	0.00	0.00	0.00	1.00	0.00	4
12	1	1	1	1	1	0	0	1	1	15.00	8.07	2.45	0.37	0.01	0.61	0.00	0.00	3
13	0	0	0	1	1	0	0	0	0	15.00	4.75	4.72	0.00	0.00	0.02	0.01	0.98	5
14	1	0	1	1	1	1	1	1	1	14.00	19.63	−1.28	0.93	0.01	0.01	0.05	0.00	1
15	0	0	1	1	1	1	1	1	1	14.00	5.87	3.36	0.37	0.00	0.02	0.61	0.00	4
16	1	1	1	1	1	1	1	0	1	13.00	14.87	−0.49	0.88	0.02	0.11	0.00	0.00	1
17	1	1	1	1	1	0	1	1	0	11.00	6.74	1.65	0.19	0.01	0.81	0.00	0.00	3

[+] (1) I enjoy math; (2) I am good at math; (3) I usually understand what we are doing in math; (4) Doing math often makes me nervous or upset; (5) I often get scared when I open my math book see a page of problems; (6) Math is useful in everyday problems; (7) Math helps a person think logically; (8) It is important to know math to get a good job; (9) I will use math in many ways as an adult. (~Reverse coded.)

Table 25.7. LSAY Example: Model Classification Diagnostics for the Five-Class Unconditional Latent Class Analysis ($E_5 = .77$) for Subsample A ($n_A = 1338$)

Class k	$\hat{\pi}_k$	95% C.I.*	$mcaP_k$	$AvePP_k$	OCC_k
Class 1	0.392	(0.326, 0.470)	0.400	0.905	14.78
Class 2	0.130	(0.082, 0.194)	0.125	0.874	46.42
Class 3	0.182	(0.098, 0.255)	0.176	0.791	17.01
Class 4	0.190	(0.139, 0.248)	0.189	0.833	21.26
Class 5	0.105	(0.080, 0.136)	0.109	0.874	59.13

*Bias-corrected bootstrap 95% confidence intervals

Table 25.8. LSAY Example: Model-Estimated, Class-Specific Item Response Probabilities Based on the Five-Class Unconditional Latent Class Analysis Using Subsample A ($n_A = 1338$)

		$\hat{\omega}_{m|k}$				
Item aspects	Item statements	Class 1 (39%)	Class 2 (13%)	Class 3 (18%)	Class 4 (19%)	Class 5 (10%)
Math affect and math efficacy	I enjoy math.	0.89	0.99	0.72	0.21	0.18
	I am good at math.	0.93	0.91	0.84	0.17	0.14
	I usually understand what we are doing in math.	0.96	0.89	0.91	0.43	0.23
Math anxiety	~Doing math often makes me nervous or upset.	0.86	0.26	0.71	0.32	0.25
	~I often get scared when I open my math book see a page of problems.	1.00	0.10	0.82	0.52	0.37
Math utility	Math is useful in everyday problems.	0.92	0.85	0.33	0.77	0.09
	Math helps a person think logically.	0.86	0.83	0.37	0.67	0.06
	It is important to know math to get a good job.	0.95	0.89	0.47	0.83	0.11
	I will use math in many ways as an adult.	0.94	0.89	0.35	0.79	0.05

~ Reverse coded.

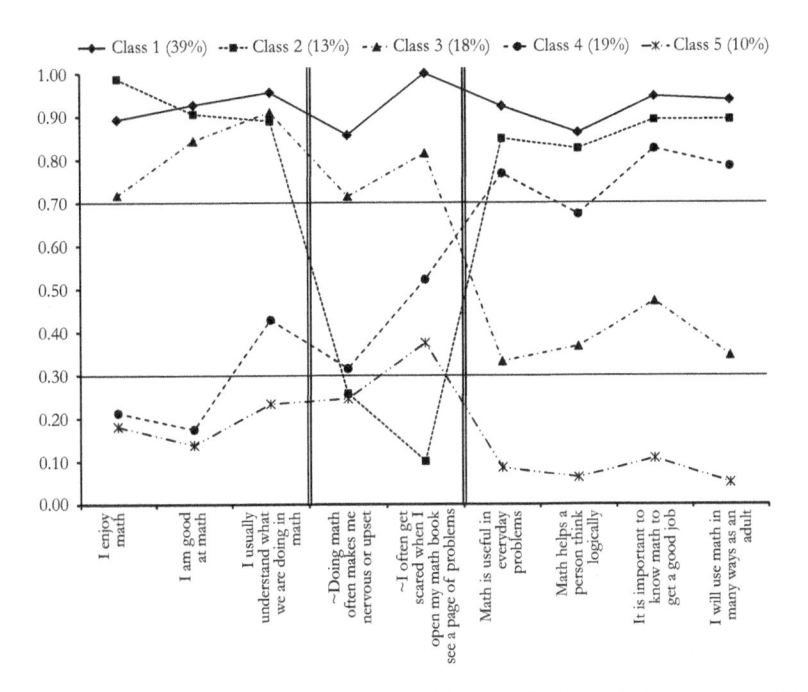

Figure 25.6 LSAY example: Model-estimated, class-specific item probability profile plot for the five-class unconditional LCA.

in Figure 25.6. Item response probabilities with a high degree of class homogeneity (i.e., estimated values greater than 0.7 or less than 0.3) are bolded in Table 25.8. All the items have high class homogeneity for at least three of the five classes, indicating that all nine items are useful for characterizing the latent classes. In Figure 25.6, the horizontal lines at the 0.7 and 0.3 endorsement probability levels help provide a visual guide for high levels of class homogeneity. These lines also help with the visual inspection of class separation with respect to each item—for example, two classes with item response probabilities above the 0.7 line for a given item are likely not well separated with respect to that item. Table 25.9 provides all the model-estimated item response odds ratios for each pairwise latent class comparison. Bolded values indicate the two classes being compared are well separated with respect to that set of items. The numbers in Table 25.9 correspond to visual impressions based on Figure 25.6; for example, Class 1 and Class 5 both have high homogeneity with respect to items 1 through 3 and appear to be well separated as confirmed with very large item response odds ratios (all in great excess of 5.0).

Tables 25.8 and 25.9 along with Figure 25.6 also distinguish the observed items by their affiliation with one of three substantive aspects of math disposition previously discussed. As can be seen in both the tables and figure, the class-specific item probabilities are similar in level of class homogeneity within each of these three aspects as are the pattern of class separation—that is, most pairs of classes are either well separated with respect to all or none of the items within an aspect group. Thus, as anticipated earlier, these three aspects can be used to refine the substantive interpretation of the five classes rather than characterizing the classes item by item. In attaching substantive meaning to the classes, I take into account both class homogeneity and class separation with respect to all the items. It is also useful to return to the actual observed response patterns in the data to identify *prototypical* response patterns for each the classes. Prototypical patterns should have reasonably sized observed frequencies, non-significant standardized residuals, and an estimated posterior probability near 1.0 for the class to which an individual with that response pattern would be modally assigned. I identify prototypical patterns for each of the five classes using the information provided in Table 25.6; some prototypical responses are boxed by solid lines in the table.

Class 1, with an estimated proportion of 39%, is characterized by an overall positive math disposition, with high probabilities of endorsing positive math affect and efficacy items, positive math anxiety items (indicating a low propensity for math anxiety), and positive math utility items. Class 1 has a high

Table 25.9. LSAY Example: Model-Estimated Item Response Odds Ratios for All Pairwise Latent Class Comparisons Based on the Five-Class Unconditional Latent Class Analysis Using Subsample A ($n_A = 1338$)

Item aspects	Item statements	Class 1 vs. 2	Class 1 vs. 3	Class 1 vs. 4	Class 1 vs. 5	Class 2 vs. 3	Class 2 vs. 4	Class 2 vs. 5	Class 3 vs. 4	Class 3 vs. 5	Class 4 vs. 5
Math affect and math efficacy	I enjoy math.	0.11	3.28	30.91	37.83	30.72	>100	>100	9.42	11.53	1.22
	I am good at math.	1.31	2.34	59.92	78.96	1.78	45.60	60.10	25.61	33.75	1.32
	I usually understand what we are doing in math.	2.70	2.15	28.99	71.52	0.80	10.75	26.52	13.49	33.28	2.47
Math anxiety	~Doing math often makes me nervous or upset.	17.32	2.39	13.03	18.47	0.14	0.75	1.07	5.45	7.72	1.42
	~I often get scared when I open my math book see a page of problems.	>100	>100	>100	>100	0.03	0.10	0.19	4.03	7.36	1.82
Math utility	Math is useful in everyday problems.	2.16	24.48	3.67	>100	11.36	1.70	60.04	0.15	5.29	35.30
	Math helps a person think logically.	1.32	10.85	3.05	>100	8.19	2.30	71.66	0.28	8.75	31.16
	It is important to know math to get a good job.	2.13	19.83	3.74	>100	9.29	1.75	68.99	0.19	7.43	39.33
	I will use math in many ways as an adult.	1.81	28.79	4.17	>100	15.91	2.30	>100	0.14	9.99	69.06

~Reverse coded.

level of homogeneity with respect to all the items. This class might be labeled the "Pro-math without anxiety" class, where "pro-math" implies both liking and valuing the utility of mathematics. Response pattern 1 in Table 25.6 is a prototypical response pattern for Class 1, with individuals endorsing all nine items.

Class 5, with an estimated proportion of 10%, is characterized by an overall negative math disposition, with low probabilities of endorsing positive math affect and efficacy items, positive math anxiety items (indicating a high propensity for math anxiety), and positive math utility items. Class 5 has a high level of homogeneity with respect to all the items and is extremely well separated from Class 1 with respect to all the items. This class might be labeled the "Anti-math with anxiety" class, where "anti-math" implies both disliking and undervaluing the utility of mathematics. Response pattern 4 in Table 25.6 is a prototypical response pattern for Class 5, with individuals endorsing none of the nine items.

Because Classes 1 and 5 represent clear profiles of positive and negative math dispositions across the entire set of items with high levels of class homogeneity across all the items (with the exception of item 5 in Class 5) and are well separated from each other with respect to all items (with item response odds ratios all well in excess of 5.0), the class separation of the remaining three classes will be evaluated primarily with respect to Classes 1 and 5.

Class 2, with an estimated proportion of 13%, is characterized by an overall positive math disposition like Class 1, with the exception that this class has very low probabilities of endorsing positive math anxiety items (indicating a high propensity for math anxiety). Class 2 has a high level of homogeneity with respect to all the items, is well separated from Class 1 with respect to the math anxiety items but not the math affect and efficacy or the math utility items (with the exception of item 1), and is well separated from Class 5 with respect to the math affect and efficacy and the math utility items. This class might be labeled the "Pro-math with anxiety" class. Response pattern 2 in Table 25.6 is a prototypical response pattern for Class 2, with individuals endorsing all but the two math anxiety items.

Class 3, with an estimated proportion of 18%, is characterized by high probabilities of endorsing positive math affect and efficacy items and positive math anxiety items (indicating a low propensity for math anxiety). Class 3 does not have a high level of homogeneity with respect to the math utility items which means that this class is *not* characterized by either high or low response propensities. However, Class 3 is well separated from Class 1 and Class 5 with respect to those items. Generally speaking, Class 3 is not well separated from Class 1 with respect to the math affect and efficacy and the math anxiety items but is well separated from Class 5 with respect to those same items. This class might be labeled the "Math lover" class, where "love" implies both a positive math affect and a low propensity for math anxiety. Response pattern 9 in Table 25.6 is a prototypical response pattern for Class 3, with individuals endorsing all but the math utility items.

Class 4, with an estimated proportion of 19%, is mostly characterized by low probabilities of endorsing positive math affect and efficacy items and high probabilities of endorsing positive math utility items. Class 4 does not have a high level of homogeneity with respect to the math anxiety items, which means that this class is not characterized by either high or low response probabilities. It is well separated from Class 1 with respect to the math anxiety items as well as the math affect and efficacy item but not well separated from Class 5 for those same items. Class 4 is well separated from Class 5 with respect to the math utility item but not well separated from Class 1. This class might be labeled the "I don't like math but I know it's good for me" class. Response pattern 11 in Table 25.6 is a prototypical response pattern for Class 4, with individuals endorsing only the math utility items.

None of the five resultant classes have an estimated class proportion corresponding to a majority share of the overall population nor are any of the classes distinguished from the rest by a relatively small proportion. Thus, although it is quite interesting that the "Pro-math without anxiety" class is the largest at 40%, and the "Anti-math with anxiety" class is the smallest at 10%, the estimated class proportions themselves, in this case, did not contribute directly to the interpretation of the classes.

As a final piece of the interpretation process, I also examine response patterns that are not well fit and/or not well classified by the selected model. These patterns could suggest additional population heterogeneity that does not have a strong "signal" in the present data and is not captured by the resultant latent classes. Noticing patterns that are not well fit or well classified by the model can deepen understanding of the latent classes that do emerge and may also suggest directions for future research, particularly regarding enhancing the item set. Enclosed by a dashed box in Table 25.6, response pattern 13 has a large standardized residual and is not well fit by the model. Although individuals with this response pattern have a high posterior probability for Class 5, their pattern of response, only endorsing the math anxiety items, is not prototypical of any of the classes. These cases are individuals who have a low propensity toward math anxiety but are inclined to dislike and undervalue mathematics. They don't like math but are "fearless." These individuals could represent just a few random outliers or they could be indicative of a smaller class that is not detected in this model but is one that might emerge in a future study with a larger sample and with an expanded item set. Individuals with response pattern 15 in Table 25.6 are also not well classified. Although individuals with this response pattern would be modally assigned to Class 4, the estimated posterior probability for Class 4 is only 0.61 while the estimated posterior probability for Class 1 is 0.37. These individuals, endorsing all but the first two math affect and efficacy items, although more consistent with the Class 4 profile, are very similar to individuals with response patterns such as pattern 14 in Table 25.6, that endorse all but one of the math affect and efficacy items and have a high estimated posterior probability for Class 1. Not surprisingly, it is harder to classify response patterns to classes without a high degree of homogeneity on the full set of items, such as Classes 3 and 4, as is evident from the relative lower AvePPs found in Table 25.7 for Classes 3 and 4 compared to Classes 1, 2, and 5.

Concluding now the full empirical illustration of latent class analysis, I switch gears to introduce traditional finite mixture modeling, also known as LPA (the moniker used herein) and LCCA.

Latent Profile Analysis

Essentially, a latent profile model is simply a latent class model with continuous—rather than categorical—indicators of the latent class variable. Almost everything learned in the previous section on LCA can be applied to LPA, but there are a few differences—conceptual, analytic, and practical—that must be remarked on before proceeding to the real data example of LPA. This section follows the same order of topics as the section on LCA, beginning with LPA model formulation.

Model Formulation

I begin the formal LPA model specification with an unconditional model in which the only observed variables are the continuous manifest variables of the latent class variable. This model is the unconditional measurement model for the latent class variable.

Suppose there are M continuous (interval scale) latent class indicators, $y_1, y_2, \ldots, y_M$, observed on n study participants, where y_{mi} is the observed response to item m for participant i. It is assumed for the unconditional LPA that there is an underlying unordered categorical latent class variable, denoted by c, with K classes, where $c_i = k$ if individual i belongs to Class k. As before, the proportion of individuals in Class k, $\Pr(c = k)$, is denoted by π_k. The K classes are exhaustive and mutually exclusive such that each individual in the population has membership in exactly one of the K latent classes and $\Sigma \pi_k = 1$. The relationship between the observed responses on the M items and the latent class variable, c, is expressed as

$$f(\mathbf{y}_i) = \sum_{k=1}^{K} \left[\pi_k \cdot f_k(\mathbf{y}_i) \right], \qquad (29)$$

where $\mathbf{y}_i = (y_{1i}, y_{1i}, \ldots, y_{Mi})$, $f(\mathbf{y}_i)$ is the multivariate probability density function for the overall population, and $f_k(\mathbf{y}_i) = f(\mathbf{y}_i | c_i = k)$ is the class-specific density function for Class k. Thus, the LPA measurement model specifies that the overall joint distribution of the M continuous indicators is the result of a mixing of K component distributions of the M indicators, with $f_k(\mathbf{y}_i)$ representing the component-specific joint distribution for $\mathbf{y}_i$.

As with the LCA model, the structural parameters are those related to the distribution of the latent class variable, which for the unconditional LPA model are simply the class proportions, π_k. The measurement parameters are all those related to the class-specific probability distributions. Usually, as was done in the very first finite mixture model applications, the within-class distribution of the continuous indicator variables is assumed to be multivariate normal. That is,

$$[\mathbf{y}_i | c_i = k] \sim \text{MVN}(\boldsymbol{\alpha}_k, \boldsymbol{\Sigma}_k), \qquad (30)$$

where $\boldsymbol{\alpha}_k$ is the vector of the Class k means for the ys (i.e., $E(\mathbf{y}_{i|k}) = \boldsymbol{\alpha}_k$) and $\boldsymbol{\Sigma}_k$ is the Class k variance–covariance matrix for the ys (i.e., $\text{Var}(\mathbf{y}_{i|k}) = \boldsymbol{\Sigma}_k$). Alternatively, the expression in Equation 30 can be written as

$$\mathbf{y}_{i|k} = \boldsymbol{\alpha}_k + \boldsymbol{\varepsilon}_{ik},$$
$$\boldsymbol{\varepsilon}_{ik} \sim \text{MVN}(\mathbf{0}, \boldsymbol{\Sigma}_k). \qquad (31)$$

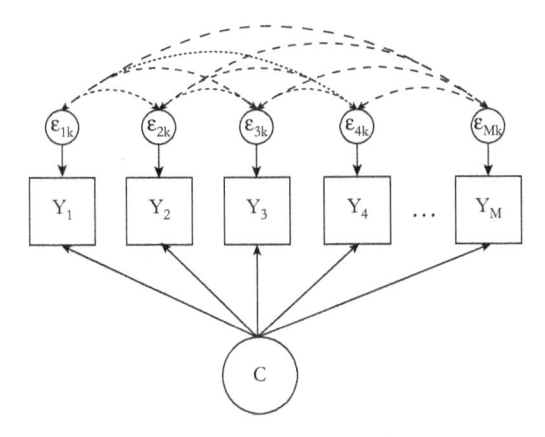

Figure 25.7 Generic path diagram for an unconditional latent profile model.

be specified to explain all of the covariation between the indicators in the overall population.

With increased flexibility in the within-class model specification comes additional complexity in the model-building process. But before getting into the details of model building for latent profiles models, let me formally summarize the main within-class variance–covariance structures that may be specified for Σ_k (presuming here that α_k will be left unconstrained within and across the classes in all cases). Starting from the least restrictive of variance–covariance structures, there is *class-varying, unrestricted* Σ_k of the form

$$\Sigma_k = \begin{bmatrix} \theta_{11k} & & & \\ \theta_{21k} & \theta_{22k} & & \\ \vdots & \vdots & \ddots & \\ \theta_{M1k} & \theta_{M2k} & \cdots & \theta_{MMk} \end{bmatrix}, \quad (32)$$

where θ_{mmk} is the variance of item m in Class k and θ_{mjk} is the covariance between items m and j in Class k. In this structure for Σ_k, all the indicator variables are allowed to covary within class, and the variances and covariances are allowed to be different across the latent classes. The *class-invariant, unrestricted* Σ_k has the form

$$\Sigma_k = \Sigma = \begin{bmatrix} \theta_{11} & & & \\ \theta_{21} & \theta_{22} & & \\ \vdots & \vdots & \ddots & \\ \theta_{M1} & \theta_{M2} & \cdots & \theta_{MM} \end{bmatrix},$$

$$\forall k \in (1, \ldots, K), \quad (33)$$

such that all the indicator variable are allowed to covary within class, and the variances and covariances are constrained to be equal across the latent classes (class-invariant). The *class-varying, diagonal* Σ_k has the form

$$\Sigma_k = \begin{bmatrix} \theta_{11k} & & & \\ 0 & \theta_{22k} & & \\ \vdots & \vdots & \ddots & \\ 0 & 0 & \cdots & \theta_{MMk} \end{bmatrix}, \quad (34)$$

such that conditional independence is imposed and the covariances between the indicators are fixed at zero within class while the variances are freely estimated and allowed to be different across the latent classes. The most constrained within-class variance–covariance structure is the *class-invariant, diagonal*

The measurement parameters *are* then the class-specific means, variances, and covariances of the indicator variables. Notice that although one necessarily assumes a particular parametric distribution *within* each class that is appropriate for the measurement scales of the variables, there are not any assumptions made about the joint distribution of the indicators in the overall population.

The model expressed in Equations 29 and 30 can be represented by a path diagram as shown in Figure 25.7. If you compare Figure 25.7 to Figure 25.2, along with replacing the u with y to represent continuous rather than categorical manifest variables, "residuals" terms have been added, represented by the ε indexed by k, to indicate that there is within-class variability on the continuous indicators that may differ across the classes in addition to the mean structure of the y that may vary across the classes as indicated by the arrows from c directly to the y. Unlike with categorical indicators, the class-specific estimated means and variances/covariances (assuming normality within class) and can be uniquely identified for each class.

Traditionally, the means of the y are automatically allowed to vary across the classes as part of the measurement model—that is, the mean structure is always class-varying. The within-class variances may be class-varying or constrained to be class-invariant (i.e., within-class variances held equal across the classes). And, as implied by Figure 25.7, the conditional independence assumption is not necessary for the within-class covariance structure. Unlike LCA, latent profile models do not require partial conditional independence for model identification—all indicators can covary with all other indicators within class. Hence, the latent class variable does not have to

Σ_k with the form

$$\Sigma_k = \Sigma = \begin{bmatrix} \theta_{11} & & & \\ 0 & \theta_{22} & & \\ \vdots & \vdots & \ddots & \\ 0 & 0 & \cdots & \theta_{MM} \end{bmatrix},$$

$$\forall k \in (1,\ldots,K), \qquad (35)$$

such that conditional independence is imposed and the covariances between the indicators are fixed at zero within class while the variances are constrained to be equal across the latent classes.

The determination of the number of latent classes as well as the estimates of the structural parameters (class proportions) and the measurement parameters (class-specific means, variances, and covariances) and interpretation of the resultant classes will very much depend on the specification of the within-class joint distribution of the latent class indicators. This dependence is analogous to the dependence of clustering on the selection of the attribute space and the resemblance coefficient in a cluster analysis. As it happens, specifying a class-invariant, diagonal Σ_k in a K-class LPA model will yield a solution that is the model-based equivalent to applying a K-means clustering algorithm to the latent profile indicators (Vermunt & Magidson, 2002).

To better understand how the number and nature of the latent classes can be influenced by the specification of Σ_k, let's consider a hypothetical data sample drawn from an unknown but distinctly non-normal bivariate population distribution. The scatter plot for the sample observations is displayed in Figure 25.8.a. Figure 25.8.b shows a path diagram for a three-class latent profile model with a class-invariant, diagonal Σ_k along with the empirical results of applying the three-class LPA model to the sample data depicted as a scatter plot with: individual observations marked with symbols corresponding to modal assignment into one of the three latent classes (circles, x, and triangles); diamonds representing the class centroids, $(\alpha_{1k}, \alpha_{2k})$—that is, the model-estimated, class-specific means for y_1 and y_2; trend lines representing the class-specific linear associations for y_2 versus y_1; and ellipses to provide a visual impression of the model-estimated, class-specific variances for y_1 and y_2, where the width of each ellipse is equal to three model-estimated, class-specific standard deviations for y_1 and the height is equal to three model-estimated, class-specific standard deviations for y_2. The model in Figure 25.8.b imposes the conditional independence assumption, and thus, y_1 and y_2 are uncorrelated within class, shown by the flat trend lines for each of the three classes. The model also constrains the within-class

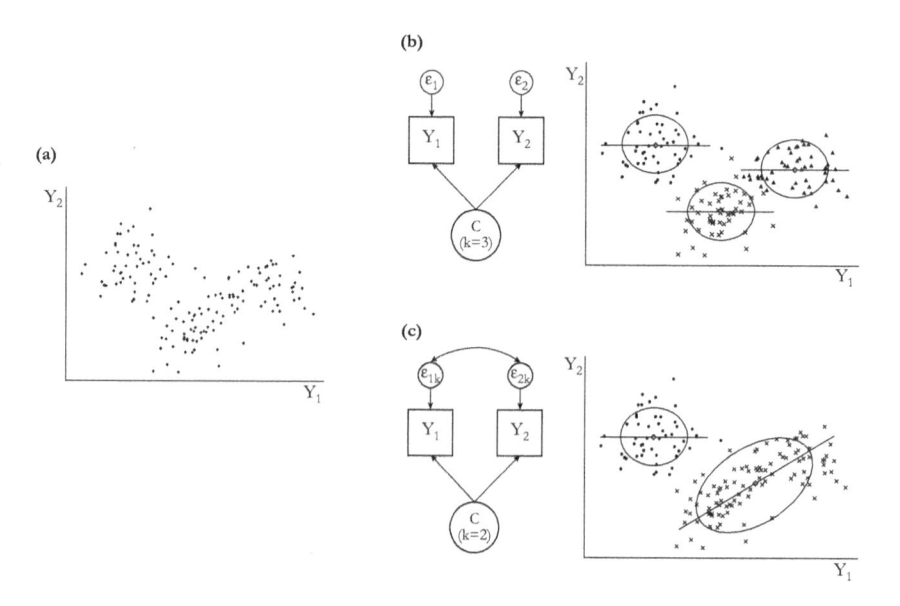

Figure 25.8 (a) Bivariate scatterplot based on a hypothetical sample from an overall bivariate non-normal population distribution; (b) Path diagram for a three-class model with class-invariant, diagonal Σ_k and the scatter plot of sample values marked by modal latent class assignment based on the three-class model; and (c) Path diagram for a two-class model with class-varying, unrestricted Σ_k and the scatter plot of sample values marked by modal latent class assignment based on the two-class model. In (b) and (c), diamonds represent the model-estimated class-specific bivariate mean values, trend lines depict the model-estimated within-class bivariate associations, and the ellipse heights and widths correspond to 3.0 model-estimated within-class standard deviations on y_2 and y_1, respectively.

variance–covariance structure to be the same across the class, shown by the same size ellipses for each of the three classes.

Figure 25.8.c displays a path diagram for a two-class latent profile model with a class-varying, unconstrained Σ_k along with the empirical results of applying the two-class LPA model to the sample data depicted as a scatter plot using the same conventions as Figure 25.8.b. The results of these two models, shown in Figures 25.8.b and 25.8.c, applied to the same sample data shown in Figure 25.8.a are different both in the number and nature of the latent classes. They provide alternative representations of the population heterogeneity with respect to the latent class continuous indicators, y_1 and y_2. And they would lead to quite different substantive interpretations. You could make comparisons of fit between the two models to determine whether one is more consistent with the observed data, but if they both provide adequate fit and/or are comparable in fit to each other, then you must rely on theoretical and practical considerations to choose one representation over the other. Because you don't ever know the "true" within-class variance–covariance structure just as you don't ever know the "correct" number of latent classes when you embark on a latent profile analysis, and now understanding how profoundly the specification of Σ_k could influence the formation of the latent classes, the LPA model-building process must compare models, statistically and substantively, across a full range of Σ_k specifications.

Model Interpretation

If you were engaged in an indirect application of finite mixture modeling to obtain a semi-parametric approximation for an overall non-normal homogeneous population, then you would focus on the "remixed" results for the overall population and would not be concerned with the distinctiveness or separation of the latent classes and would not interpret the separate mixture components. However, if you are using a latent profile analysis in a direct application, assuming *a priori* that the population is made up of two or more normal homogeneous subpopulations, then you would place high value on results that yield classes that are disparate enough from each other that it is reasonable to interpret each class as representative of a distinct subpopulation.

In some sense, the direct application of finite mixture modeling is a kind of stochastic model-based clustering method in which one endeavors to arrive at a latent class solution with the number and nature of latent classes (clusters) such that the individual variability with respect to the indicator variables within the classes is minimized and/or the between-class variability is maximized. (For more on mixture modeling as a clustering method and comparison to other clustering techniques, *see* Vermunt & Magidson, 2002, and the chapter on clustering within this handbook.) These clustering objectives can be restated in the terms used when presenting the interpretation of latent class models: For distinct and optimally interpretable latent classes, it is desirable to have a latent profile model with a high degree of class homogeneity (low within-class variability) along with a high degree of class separation (high between-class variability).

Just as was done with LCA, the concepts of latent class homogeneity and latent class separation and how they both relate to the parameters of the unconditional measurement model will be discussed as well as how they inform the interpretation of the latent classes resulting from a LPA. To assist this discussion, consider a hypothetical example with two continuous indicators ($M = 2$) measuring a two-class categorical latent variable ($K = 2$). And suppose that you decide to use a class-varying, unrestricted Σ_k specification for the LPA. The unconditional model is given by

$$f(y_{1i}, y_{2i}) = \sum_{k=1}^{2} \left[\pi_k \cdot f_k(y_{1i}, y_{2i}) \right], \quad (36)$$

where

$$[y_{1i}, y_{2i} | c_i = k] \sim \text{MVN} \left(\alpha_k = \begin{bmatrix} \alpha_{1k} & \alpha_{2k} \end{bmatrix}, \Sigma_k = \begin{bmatrix} \theta_{11k} & \\ \theta_{21} & \theta_{22k} \end{bmatrix} \right). \quad (37)$$

Class Homogeneity. The first and primary way that you can evaluate the degree of class homogeneity is by examining the model-estimated within-class variances, $\hat{\theta}_{mmk}$, for each indicator m across the K classes and comparing them to the total overall sample variance, $\hat{\theta}_{mm}$, for the continuous indicator. It is expected that all of the within-class variances will be notably smaller than the overall variance. Classes with smaller values of $\hat{\theta}_{mmk}$ are more homogeneous with respect to item m than classes with larger values of $\hat{\theta}_{mmk}$. You can equivalently compare within-class standard deviations, $\sqrt{\hat{\theta}_{mmk}}$, for each item m across the K classes, that approximate for each class the average distance of class members' individual values on item m to the corresponding model-estimated class mean, $\hat{\alpha}_{mk}$. You want classes for which class members are close, on average, to the class-specific mean because you want to be able to use the class mean values in your interpretation of the latent classes as values that "typify" the observed responses on the indicator variables for members of that class.

You cannot, of course, directly compare values of $\hat{\theta}_{mmk}$ across items because different items may have very different scales and the magnitude of the variance (and, hence, the standard deviation) is scale-dependent. Even for items with the same measurement scales, you cannot compare within-class variances across items unless the overall variances of those items are comparable. However, it is possible to summarize class homogeneity across items and classes by calculating the percent of the overall total variance in the indicator set explained by the latent class variable, similarly to the calculations done in a principal component analysis (Thorndike, 1953).

The phrase "class homogeneity" refers here to an expectation that the individuals belonging to the same class will be more similar to each other with respect to their values on the indicator variables than they are to individuals in other classes. However, you should still keep in mind that a LPA assumes *a priori* that the classes *are* homogeneous in the sense that all members of a given class are assumed to draw from a single, usually multivariate normal, population distribution. And, as such, any within-class correlation between continuous indicators, if estimated, is assumed to be an association between those variables that holds for all members of that class. Evaluating the statistical and practical significance of an estimated within-class indicator correlation, if not fixed at zero in the model specification, can assist in judging whether that correlation could be used in the characterization of the subpopulation represented by that particular latent class. Significant within-class correlations, when present, may be as much a part of what distinguishes the classes as the class-specific means and variances.

Class Separation. The first and primary way you can evaluate the degree of class separation is by assessing the actual distance between the class-specific means. It is not enough to simply calculate the raw differences in estimated means (i.e., $\hat{\alpha}_{mj} - \hat{\alpha}_{mk}$) because what is most relevant is the degree of overlap between the class-specific distributions. And the degree of overlap between two normal distributions depends not only on the distance between the means but the variances of the distributions as well. Consider, for example, the two scenarios shown in

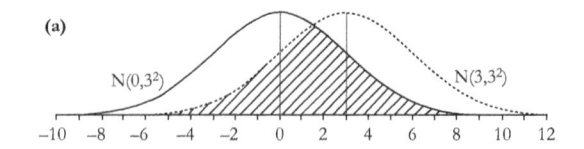

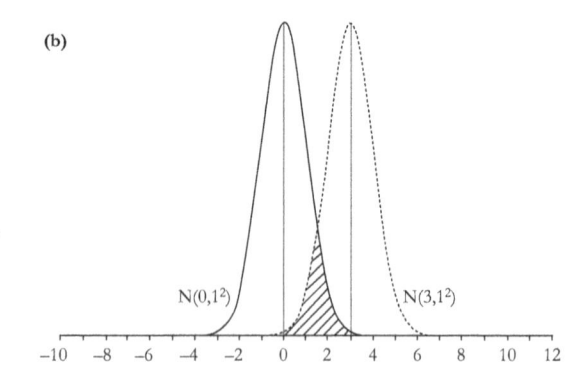

Figure 25.9 Hypothetical finite mixture distributions for a single continuous indicator variable with K = 2 underlying latent classes with class-specific means of 0 and 3, respectively, and with-class standard deviations of (a) 3, and (b) 1.

Figure 25.9. Figure 25.9.a depicts two hypothetical class-specific indicator distributions with means 3.0 units apart and class-specific standard deviations of 3, and Figure 25.9.b depicts two hypothetical class-specific indicator distributions with the same mean separation as in Figure 25.9.a with class-specific standard deviations of 1. There is considerable overlap of the distributions in Figure 25.9.a and very little overlap in Figure 25.9.b. The two classes in Figure 25.9.b are far better separated than the two classes in Figure 25.9.a with respect to the indicator, although the difference in means is the same. To quantify class separation between Class j and Class k with respect to a particular item m, compute a standardized mean difference, adapting the formula for Cohen's d (Cohen, 1988), as given below,

$$\hat{d}_{mjk} = \frac{\hat{\alpha}_{mj} - \hat{\alpha}_{mk}}{\hat{\sigma}_{mjk}}, \qquad (38)$$

where $\hat{\sigma}_{mjk}$ is a pooled standard deviation given by

$$\hat{\sigma}_{mjk} = \sqrt{\frac{(\hat{\pi}_j)(\hat{\theta}_{mmj}) + (\hat{\pi}_k)(\hat{\theta}_{mmk})}{(\hat{\pi}_j + \hat{\pi}_k)}}. \qquad (39)$$

A large $\left|\hat{d}_{mjk}\right| > 2.0$ corresponds to less than 20% overlap in the distributions, meaning that less than 20% of individuals belonging to either Class j or Class k have values on item m that fall in the range of y_m corresponding to the area of overlap between the two class-specific distributions of y_m. A large $\left|\hat{d}_{mjk}\right|$ indicates a high degree of separation between the Classes j and k with respect to item m. A small $\left|\hat{d}_{mjk}\right| < 0.85$ corresponds to more than 50% overlap and a low degree of separation between the Classes j and k with respect to item m.

If you are using a latent profile model specification that allows a class-varying variance–covariance structure for the classes, then you can also evaluate whether the classes are distinct from each other with respect to the item variances or covariances. To make a descriptive assessment of the separation of the classes in this regard, you can examine whether there is any overlap in the 95% confidence intervals for the estimates of the class-specific variances and covariances with non-overlap indicating good separation. An equivalent assessment can be made using the model-estimated class-specific item standard deviations and correlations.

Class Proportions. The guidelines and cautions provided in the section on LCA for the use of the estimated class proportions in the interpretation of the latent classes are all applicable for LPA as well.

Hypothetical Example. Continuing with the hypothetical example of a two-class LPA with two continuous indicators initially presented in Figure 25.8.c, Table 25.10 provides the overall sample means and standard deviations along with the model-estimated class-specific means, standard deviations, and correlations (with the standard deviations and correlation estimates calculated using the measurement parameter estimates for the class-specific item variances and covariances). The class-specific standard deviations for the items y_1 and y_2 are all noticeably smaller than the corresponding overall sample standard deviations, but Class 1 is more homogenous than Class 2 with respect to both indicators—particularly y_1. There is a small, non-significant correlation between y_1 and y_2 in Class 1 but a large and significant positive correlation between y_1 and y_2 in Class 2 that should therefore be considered in the interpretation of Class 2.

Applying Equations 38 and 39 to the class-specific mean and standard deviation estimates given in Table 25.10, the standardized differences in indicator means between Class 1 and Class 2 was calculated as $\hat{d}_1 = -2.67$, indicating a high degree of separation with respect to y_1, and $\hat{d}_2 = 1.70$, indicating a moderate degree of separation with respect to y_2. In terms of the class-specific variance–covariance structures, evaluate the separation between the classes

Table 25.10. Hypothetical Example: Overall Sample Means and Standard Deviations (SD); Model-Estimated, Class-Specific Means, Standard Deviations, and Correlations With Corresponding Bias-Corrected Bootstrap 95% Confidence Intervals Based on a Two-Class Latent Profile Analysis with Class-Varying, Unrestricted Σ_k

	Variable	Mean	SD	Correlations (1)	(2)
Overall sample	y_1	0.06	2.71	1.00	
	y_2	1.47	1.70	−.21	1.00

Class	Variable	Mean ($\hat{\alpha}_{mk}$)	SD ($\sqrt{\hat{\theta}_{mmk}}$)	Correlations (1)	(2)
Class 1 (33%)	y_1	−2.93 (−3.19, −2.58)	1.00 (0.80, 1.26)	1.00	
	y_2	2.97 (2.65, 3.35)	1.12 (0.95, 1.38)	0.04 (−0.25, 0.26)	1.00
Class 2 (77%)	y_1	1.55 (1.18, 1.93)	1.93 (1.77, 2.11)	1.00	
	y_2	0.73 (0.45, 0.99))	1.41 (1.26, 1.59)	0.68 (0.54, 0.76)	1.00

with respect to the within-class item standard deviations and correlations by examining the differences in the point estimates and also observing the presence of overlap in the 95% confidence intervals for the point estimates. Note that the 95% confidence intervals provided in Table 25.10 are estimated using a bias-corrected bootstrap technique because the sampling distributions for standard deviations are not symmetric and estimated correlations are nonlinear functions of three different maximum likelihood parameter estimates. The variability in Class 2 for y_1 is notably larger than Class 1, whereas the classes are not well separated with respect to the standard deviations for y_2. The correlation between y_1 and y_2 is very different for Classes 1 and 2 where there is virtually no correlation at all in Class 1 but there is a large and significant correlation within Class 2. Thus, there is a high degree of separation between Classes 1 and 2 with respect to the relationship between y_1 and y_2.

The class homogeneity and separation information contained in Table 25.10 is not always, but can be, depicted graphically in a series of bivariate scatter plots, particularly when the total number of latent class indicator variables is small. In this example, with only two items, a single bivariate plot is all that is needed. The estimated class-specific means are plotted and specially identified with data point markers different from the observed data points. All the observed data points are included in the plot and are marked according to their modal class assignment. A trend line is drawn through each class centroid derived from the model-estimated class-specific correlations between the two items. Ellipses are drawn, one centered around each class centroid, with the axis lengths of the ellipse corresponding to three standard deviations on the corresponding indicator variable. All of these plot features are displayed in Figure 25.8.c and help to provide a visual impression of all the aspects of the class-specific distributions that distinguish the classes (along with those aspects that don't) and the overall degree of class separation.

You can see visually in Figure 25.8.c what I have already remarked on using the information in Table 25.10: Class 1 (individual cases in the sample with modal class assignment to Class 1 have data points marked by circles) is more homogenous with respect to both y_1 and y_2—particularly y_1—than Class 2 (individual cases with modal class assignment to Class 2 have data points marked by x); there is a high degree of separation between Classes 1 and 2 with respect to values on y_1 and only moderate separation with respect to values on y_2; there is a strong positive association between y_1 and y_2 in Class 2 that is not present in Class 1. You could interpret Class 1 as a homogenous group of individuals with a low average level on y_1 ($\hat{\alpha}_{11} = -2.93$), relative to the overall sample mean, and a high average level of y_2 ($\hat{\alpha}_{21} = 2.97$). You could characterize Class 2 as a less homogeneous (relative to Class 1) group of individuals with a high average level on y_1 ($\hat{\alpha}_{12} = 1.55$), low average level of y_2 ($\hat{\alpha}_{22} = 0.73$), and a strong positive association between individual levels on y_1 and y_2 ($r_2 = .68$).

Based on the estimated class proportions, assuming a random and representative sample from the overall population, you might also apply a modifier label of "normal" or "typical" to Class 2 because its members make up an estimated 67% of the population.

Model Estimation

As with LCA, the most common approach for latent profile model estimation is FIML estimation using the EM algorithm under the MAR assumption. And, as with latent class models, the log likelihood surfaces for finite mixture models can be challenging for the estimation algorithms to navigate. Additionally, although the log likelihood function of a identified latent profile model with class-invariant Σ_k usually has a global maximum in the interior of the parameter space, the log likelihood functions for LPA models with class-varying Σ_k are unbounded (like Fig. 25.4.e), which means that the maximum likelihood estimate (MLE) as a global maximizer does not exist. But you may still proceed as the MLE may still exist as a local maximizer possessing the necessary properties of consistency, efficiency, and asymptotic normality (McLachlan & Peel, 2000). When estimating latent profile models, I recommend following the same strategy of using multiple random sets of starting values and keeping track of all the convergence, maximum likelihood replication, condition number, and class size information as with LCA model estimation, to single out models that are not well identified.

Model Building

Principled model building for LPA proceeds in the same manner described in the section on LCA, beginning with the establishment of the (unconditional) measurement model for the latent class variable, with the chief focus during that stage of model building on latent class enumeration. The following subsections highlight any differences in the evaluations of absolute fit, relative fit, classification accuracy, and the class enumeration process for LPA compared to what has already been advanced in this chapter for LCA.

Absolute Fit. At present, there are not widely accepted or implemented measures of absolute fit for latent profile models. Although it would be theoretically possible to modify exact tests of fit or closeness-of-fit indices available for factor analysis, most of these indices are limited to assessing the model-data consistency with respect to only the mean and variance–covariance structure, which would not be appropriate for evaluation of overall fit for finite mixture models. With finite mixture modeling, you are using an approach that requires individual level data because the formation of the latent class variable depends on all the high-order moments in the data (e.g., the skewness and kurtosis)—not just the first- and second-order moments. You would choose finite mixture modeling over a robust method for estimating just the mean and variance–covariance structure (robust to non-normality in the overall population), even for indirect applications, if you believed that those higher order moments in the observed data provide substantively important information about the overall population heterogeneity with respect to the item set. Because the separate individual observations are necessary for the model estimation, any overall goodness-of-fit index for LPA models would need to compare each observed and model-estimated individual value across all the indicator variables, similarly to techniques used in linear regression diagnostics.

Although you are without measures of absolute model fit, you are not without some absolute fit diagnostic tools. It is possible to compute the overall model-estimated means, variances, covariances, univariate skewness, and univariate kurtosis of the latent class indicator variables and compare them to the sample values, providing residuals for the first- and second-order multivariate moments and the univariate third- and fourth-order moments for the observed items. These limited residuals allow at least some determination to be made about how well the model is fitting the observed data beyond the first- and second-order moments and also allow some comparisons of relative overall fit across models.

In addition to these residuals, you can provide yourself with an absolute fit benchmark by estimating a fully-saturated mean and variance–covariance model that *is* an exact fit to the data with respect to the first- and second-order moments but assumes all higher-order moments have values of zero. This corresponds to fitting a one-class LPA with an unrestricted Σ specification. In the model-building process, you would want to arrive at a measurement model that fit the individual data *better* (as ascertained by various relative fit indices) than a model only informed by the sample means and covariances.

Relative Fit. All of the measures of relative fit presented and demonstrated for latent class models are calculated and applied in the same way for latent profile models.

Classification Diagnostics. It is possible to obtain estimated posterior class probabilities for all individuals in the sample using the maximum likelihood parameters estimates from the LPA and the individuals' observed values on the continuous indicator variables. Thus, all of the classification diagnostics previously described and illustrated for latent class models are calculable and may be used in the same manner for evaluating latent class separation and latent class assignment accuracy for latent profile models.

Class Enumeration. The class enumeration process for LPA is similar to the one for LCA but with the added complication that because the specification of Σ_k can influence the formation of the latent classes, you should consider a full range of Σ_k specifications. I recommend the following approach:

Stage I: Conduct a separate class enumeration sequence following Steps 1 through 7 as outlined in the LCA section of this chapter for each type of Σ_k specification: class-invariant, diagonal Σ_k; class-varying, diagonal Σ_k; class-invariant, unrestricted Σ_k; and class-varying, unrestricted Σ_k. Note that the one-class models for the class-invariant, diagonal Σ_k and class-varying, diagonal Σ_k specifications will be the same, as will the one-class models for class-invariant, unrestricted Σ_k and class-varying, unrestricted Σ_k specifications. The "benchmark" model mentioned in the subsection on absolute fit *is* the initial one-class model for class-invariant, unrestricted Σ_k specification.

Stage II: Take the four candidate models yielded by (I) and recalculate the approximate correct model probabilities using just those four models as the full set under consideration. Repeat Steps 5 through 7 with the four candidate models to arrive at your final model selection.

The only two modifications of class enumeration Steps 5 through 7 necessary for applying Stages I and II in LPA are in Steps 5a and 6. In regards to Step 5a:

Rather than relying on the exact test of fit for absolute fit, the "best" model should be the model with the fewest number of classes that has a better relative fit (in terms of the log likelihood value) than the "benchmark" model. Regarding Step 6: Rather than examining the standardized residuals and the classification diagnostics, you should examine the residuals for the means, variances, covariances, univariate skewness, and univariate kurtosis of the indicator variables along with the classification diagnostics. Cross-validation of the final measurement model can be done in the same fashion as described for latent class analysis.

I should note that in Step 7, for both Stages I and II, there may be occasions in the LPA setting for which the model favored by the parsimony principle it not the same the model favored by the interests of conceptual simplicity and clarity. Take the hypothetical example in Figure 25.8. Let's suppose that the two models depicted in Figures 25.8.b and 25.8.c are comparable on all relative fit measures as well as residuals and classification diagnostics. One might perceive the two-class model as more parsimonious than the three-class model (although the two-class model has one more freely estimated parameter than the three-class model), but to interpret and assign substantive labels to the latent classes, you have to account for not only the different means (locations) of the latent classes but also the differences between the classes with respect to the within-class variability and the within-class correlation, which could get decidedly unsimple and unclear in its presentation. However, for the three-class model, you only need to consider the different class-specific means (and the corresponding class separation) to interpret and assign substantive labels to the latent classes because the model imposes constraints such that the classes are identical with respect to within-class variability, and the class indicators are assumed to be unrelated within class for all the classes. There is not an obvious model choice in this scenario. In such a situation, and in cases where the models are agonizingly similar with respect to their fit indices, it is essential to apply substantive and theoretical reflections in the further scrutiny of the model usefulness, especially keeping in mind the intended conditional models to be specified once the measurement model is established.

In the next subsection, I fully illustrate the unconditional LPA modeling process with a real data example, with special attention to elements of the process that are distinct for LPA in comparison to what was previously demonstrated for LCA.

Diabetes Example for Latent Profile Analysis

The data used for the LPA example come from a study of the etiology of diabetes conducted by Reaven and Miller (1979). The data were first made publically available by Herzberg and Andrews (1985) and have become a "classic" example for illustrating multivariate clustering-type techniques (see, for example, Fraley & Raftery, 1998, and Vermunt & Magidson, 2002). The original study of 145 nonobese subjects measured participants' ages, relative weights, and collected experimental data on a set of four metabolic variables commonly used for diabetes diagnosis: fasting plasma glucose, area under the plasma glucose curve for the 3-hour oral glucose tolerance test (a measure of glucose intolerance), area under the plasma insulin curve for the oral glucose tolerance test (a measure of insulin response to oral glucose), and the steady state plasma glucose response (a measure of insulin resistance) (Reaven & Miller, 1979). The correlation between the fasting plasma glucose and area under the plasma glucose curve was 0.97 and so the original authors excluded the fasting plasma glucose measure in their analyses of the data. For this illustration, Table 25.11 lists the same three remaining metabolic measures utilized, by name and label, along with descriptive statistics for the study sample. Also included in the example data are the conventional clinical classifications of the subjects into one of the three diagnostic groups (non-diabetics, chemical diabetics, and overt diabetics) made by Reaven and Miller (1979) applying standard clinical criteria that each take into account only one aspect of a participant's carbohydrate metabolism. In their 1979 paper, Reaven and Miller were interested using their data to exploring the viability of a multivariate analytic technique that could classify subjects on the basis of *multiple* metabolic characteristics, independent of prior clinical assessments, as an alternative to the rigid clinical classification with arbitrary cut-off value criteria (e.g., individuals with fating plasma glucose levels in excess of 110 mg/mL are classified as *overt diabetics*). In this example, the original research aim is furthered by investigating the classification of subjects using LPA and comparing the results to the conventional clinical classifications.

In conducting the class enumeration process, knowledge of the existing clinical classification scheme is ignored so that is does not influence decisions with respect to either the number of classes or their interpretation. I begin Stage I of the class enumeration by fitting six models with $K = 1$

Table 25.11. Diabetes Example: Descriptive Statistics for Indicator Measures ($n = 145$)

Measure	Variable name	Mean	SD	Skewness	Kurtosis	[Min, Max]	Correlations (1)	(2)
(1) Glucose area (mg/10mL/hr)	Glucose	54.36	31.70	1.78	2.16	[26.90, 156.80]	1.00	
(2) Insulin area (μU/0.10mL/hr)	Insulin	18.61	12.09	1.80	4.45	[1.00, 74.80]	−0.34**	1.00
(3) Steady state plasma glucose (mg/10mL)	SSPG	18.42	10.60	0.69	−0.23	[2.90, 48.00]	0.77**	0.01

**$p < 0.01$

to $K = 6$ classes for each of four within-class variance–covariance specifications: class-invariant, diagonal Σ_k; class-varying, diagonal Σ_k; class-invariant, unrestricted Σ_k; and class-varying, unrestricted Σ_k. After $K = 5$, the models for the diagonal unrestricted Σ_k specifications ceased to be well identified, as was the case after $K = 4$ for the class-invariant, unrestricted Σ_k specification and after $K = 3$ for the class-varying, unrestricted Σ_k.

Table 25.12 summarizes the results from the set of class enumerations for each of the Σ_k specifications. Only the results from the well-identified models are presented. Recall that the one-class models for the class-invariant, diagonal Σ_k and class-varying, diagonal Σ_k specifications are the same, as are the $K = 1$ models for the class-invariant, unrestricted Σ_k and class-varying, unrestricted Σ_k specifications. Recall also that the one-class model for the unrestricted Σ_k specification is the minimum-goodness-of-fit benchmark model, and results from this model are enclosed by a bold dashed box for visual recognition. Bolded values in Columns 5 through 10 indicate the value corresponding to the "best" model within each set of enumerations according to each fit index. As was the case for the LCA example, all K-class model were rejected in favor of a ($K+1$)-class model by the BLRT for all values of K considered so there was no "best" or even candidate models to be selected based on the BLRT and those results are not presented in the summary table.

Figure 25.10 displays four panels with plots of the: (a) LL; (b) BIC; (c) CAIC and (d) AWE model values, all plotted on the y-axis versus the number of classes. Each panel has four plot lines, one for each of the Σ_k specifications. The double horizontal line corresponds to the index value of the minimum-goodness-of-fit benchmark of the one-class, unrestricted Σ_k specification. These plots clearly show that all of the models with $K \geq 2$ are improvements over the benchmark model. These plots also illustrate the concept of the "elbow" criteria mentioned in the initial description of the class enumeration process in the LCA section. Observe the BIC plot for the class-varying, diagonal Σ_k specification. Although the smallest BIC value out of the $K = 1$ to $K = 5$ class models corresponds to the four-class model, the BIC values for the three-, four-, and five-class models are nearly the same compared to the values for the one- and two-class models. There is evidence of an "elbow" in the BIC plot at $K = 3$. The bolded values in Column 2 of Table 25.12 indicate the pair of candidate models selected within each of the class enumeration for further scrutiny (following class enumeration Steps 5 and 6 in Stage I) and the boxed values indicates the "best" model selected within each of the class enumeration sets (Step 7 of Stage I). The selection of the four "best" models concluded Step I of the LPA class enumeration process.

For Stage II, I compared the four candidate models, one from each of the Σ_k specifications. Column 11 in Table 25.12 displays the results of recalculating the correct model probabilities using only those four models. This index strongly favors the three-class model with class-varying, unrestricted Σ_k, enclosed by a solid box in Table 25.12. The single horizontal line in all the panel plots of Figure 25.10 corresponds to the best indice values across all the models considered. It is clear from Figure 25.10 that the models with class-varying Σ_k specifications (either diagonal or unrestricted) offer consistently better fit over the models with class-invariant specifications, although the five-class models with class-invariant, diagonal Σ_k approaches the fit of the three- and four-class

Table 25.12. Diabetes Example: Model Fit Indices for Exploratory Latent Profile Analysis Using Four Different Within-Class Variance–Covariance Structure Specifications ($n = 145$)

1	2	3	4	5	6	7	8	9	10	11
Σ_k	# of classes ($K \rightarrow$)	LL	npar*	BIC	CAIC	AWE	Adj. LMR-LRT p-value (H_0:K classes; H_1:K⇓1 classes)	$\hat{BF}_{K,K \Downarrow 1}$	$cm\hat{P}_K$	$cm\hat{P}.$
Class-invariant, diagonal $\Sigma_k \mathcal{E} \Sigma$	1	−1820.68	6	3671.22	3677.22	3719.08	<0.01	<0.10	<0.01	–
	2	−1702.55	10	3454.88	3464.88	3534.64	<0.01	<0.10	<0.01	–
	3	−1653.24	14	3376.15	3390.15	3487.82	<0.01	<0.10	<0.01	–
	4	−1606.30	18	3302.18	3320.18	3445.76	0.29	<0.10	<0.01	–
	5	**−1578.21**	**22**	**3265.90**	**3287.90**	**3441.39**	–	–	**>0.99**	<0.01
Class-varying, diagonal Σ_k	1	−1820.68	6	3671.22	3677.22	3719.08	<0.01	<0.10	<0.01	–
	2	−1641.95	13	3348.60	3361.60	3452.30	<0.01	<0.10	<0.01	–
	3	−1562.48	20	3224.49	3244.49	3384.03	<0.01	0.38	0.25	–
	4	**−1544.10**	**27**	**3222.57**	**3249.57**	**3437.95**	**0.15**	**7.76**	**0.66**	0.08
	5	−1528.73	34	3226.67	3260.67	3497.88	–	–	0.09	–
Class-invariant, unrestricted $\Sigma_k \mathcal{E} \Sigma$	1	−1730.40	9	3505.60	3514.60	3577.39	<0.01	<0.10	<0.01	–
	2	−1666.63	13	3397.95	3410.95	3501.65	<0.01	<0.10	<0.01	–
	3	−1628.86	17	3342.33	3359.33	3477.93	0.19	<0.10	<0.01	–
	4	**−1591.84**	**21**	**3288.19**	**3309.19**	**3455.70**	–	–	**>0.99**	<0.01
Class-varying, unrestricted Σ_k	1	−1730.40	9	3505.60	3514.60	3577.39	<0.01	<0.10	<0.01	–
	2	−1590.57	19	3275.69	3294.69	3427.25	<0.01	<0.10	<0.01	–
	3	**−1536.64**	**29**	**3217.61**	**3246.61**	**3448.93**	–	–	**>0.99**	**0.92**

*number of parameters estimated

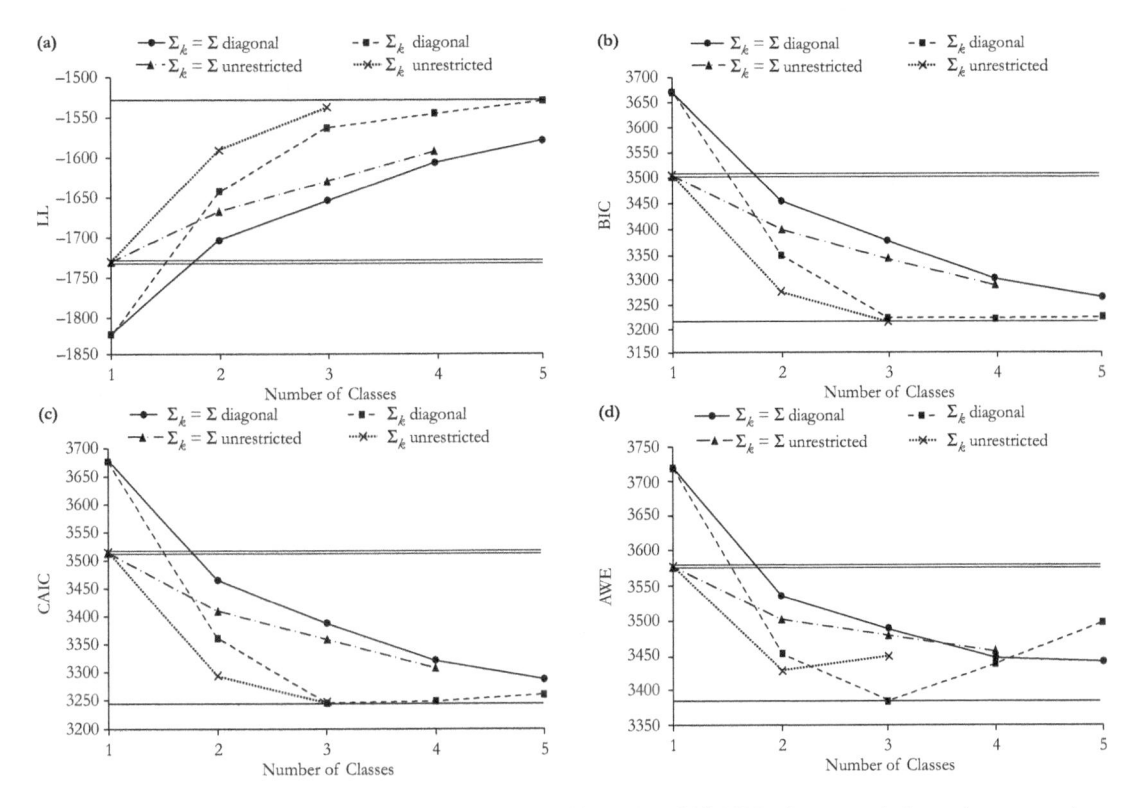

Figure 25.10 Diabetes example: Plots of model (a) LL, (b) BIC, (c) CAIC, and (d) AWE values versus the latent class enumeration ($K = 1, 2, 3, 4, 5$) across four different within-class variance–covariance structure specifications.

models with class-varying Σ_k. The three-class model with class-varying, unrestricted Σ_k and the four-class model with class-varying, diagonal Σ_k were the two candidate models selected for further inspection. Following Step 6 in Stage II, I closely examined the residuals and classification diagnostics of the final two candidate models. Table 25.13 displays the observed, model-estimated, and residuals for the means, variance, covariances, and univariate skewness and kurtosis values of the data for the three-class model with class-varying, unrestricted Σ_k showing a satisfactory fit across all these moments. The four-class model with class-varying, diagonal Σ_k had satisfactory fit in this regard as well, although the fit to the variance–covariance structure of the data was not quite as close. Table 25.14 summarizes the classification diagnostic measures for the three-class model with class-varying, unrestricted Σ_k. All the measures indicate that the three classes are very well separated and there is high accuracy in the latent class assignment. The four-class model with class-varying, diagonal Σ_k had comparably good values on the classification diagnostics. Considering all the information from Stage II, Steps 5 and 6, the three-class model with class-varying, unrestricted Σ_k was selected as the "final" unconditional latent profile model. I should remark here that this model was not in any way conspicuously better fitting than the other candidate model and another researcher examining the same results could ultimately select the other model by giving slightly less weight to model parsimony and giving less consideration that a match between the final class enumeration and the number of diagnostic groups greatly simplifies the planned comparison between subjects' latent class assignments and their conventional clinical classifications.

For the interpretation of the resultant three classes from the final model, it is necessary to examine the model-estimated, class-specific item means, standard deviations, and correlations, provided in Table 25.15 and depicted graphically by the three scatter plots in Figure 25.11. Inspecting the class-specific standard deviation estimates, Class 1 has a high level of homogeneity with respect to all three indicator variables, with notably less variability than in the overall sample and less than either of the other two classes. Class 3 is the least homogeneous with respect to *glucose* and *SSPG*, with variability in both actually greater than the overall sample. Class

Table 25.13. Diabetes Example: Observed, Mixed Model-Estimated, and Residual Values for Means, Variances, Covariances and Correlations, Univariate Skewness, and Univariate Kurtosis Based on the Three-Class Latent Profile Analysis with Class-Varying, Unrestricted Σ_k (n = 145)

Variable	Observed	Model-estimated	Residual
Mean(Glucose)	54.36	54.36	0.00
Mean(Insulin)	18.61	18.61	0.00
Mean(SSPG)	18.42	18.42	0.00
Var(Glucose)	1004.58	997.65	6.93
Var(Insulin)	146.25	145.24	1.01
Var(SSPG)	112.42	111.65	0.78
Cov(Glucose,Insulin) (Correlation)	−129.18 (−0.34)	−128.29 (−0.34)	−0.89 (0.00)
Cov(Glucose,SSPG) (Correlation)	259.09 (0.77)	257.30 (0.77)	1.79 (0.00)
Cov(Insulin,SSPG) (Correlation)	1.02 (0.01)	1.01 (0.01)	0.01 (0.00)
Skewness(Glucose)	1.78	1.75	0.03
Skewness(Insulin)	1.80	1.49	0.31
Skewness(SSPG)	0.69	0.72	−0.03
Kurtosis(Glucose)	2.16	2.49	−0.32
Kurtosis(Insulin)	4.45	2.96	1.49
Kurtosis(SSPG)	−0.23	0.19	−0.42

Table 25.14. Diabetes Example: Model Classification Diagnostics for the Three-Class Latent Profile Analysis With Class-Varying, Unrestricted Σ_k (E_3 = .88; n = 145)

Class k	$\hat{\pi}_k$	95% C.I.*	$mcaP_k$	$AvePP_k$	OCC_k
Class 1	0.512	(0.400, 0.620)	0.524	0.958	21.74
Class 2	0.211	(0.119, 0.307)	0.221	0.918	41.86
Class 3	0.277	(0.191, 0.386)	0.255	0.973	94.06

*Bias-corrected bootstrap 95% confidence intervals

2 is the least homogenous with respect to *insulin*, also having greater variability than the overall sample. The similarities and differences in the level of class homogeneity with respect to each of the three items can be judged visually in Figure 25.11 by length and width of the overlaid ellipses in the three plots.

In judging class separation for the two classes that do not have a high degree of homogeneity for at least one of the indicator variables, the distances

Table 25.15. Diabetes Example: Model-Estimated, Class-Specific Means, Standard Deviations (SDs), and Correlations with Corresponding Bias-Corrected Bootstrap 95% Confidence Intervals Based on the Three-Class Latent Profile Analysis With Class-Varying, Unrestricted Σ_k ($n = 145$)

Class	Variable	Mean ($\hat{\alpha}_{mk}$)	SD ($\sqrt{\hat{\theta}_{mmk}}$)	Correlations (1)	(2)
Class 1 (52%)	(1) *Glucose*	35.69 (34.09, 37.18)	4.39 (3.11, 5.50)	1.00	
	(2) *Insulin*	16.58 (15.31, 17.96)	5.17 (4.24, 6.11)	0.15 (−0.14, 0.42)	1.00
	(3) *SSPG*	10.50 (8.90, 12.43)	4.33 (3.48, 5.97)	0.29 (−0.05, 0.57)	0.36** (0.08, 0.57)
Class 2 (22%)	(1) *Glucose*	47.66 (43.93, 52.72)	7.29 (4.95, 10.73)	1.00	
	(2) *Insulin*	34.35 (27.38, 44.06)	15.12 (11.43, 19.40)	0.36 (−0.33, 0.77)	1.00
	(3) *SSPG*	24.41 (22.52, 25.99)	3.71 (2.15, 5.49)	0.03 (−0.40, 0.50)	−0.10 (−0.73, 0.54)
Class 3 (26%)	(1) *Glucose*	93.92 (78.13, 112.48)	35.76 (30.30, 41.51)	1.00	
	(2) *Insulin*	10.38 (7.97, 13.31)	6.03 (4.74, 8.34)	−0.76** (−0.87, −0.58)	1.00
	(3) *SSPG*	28.48 (24.42, 33.93)	10.65 (8.22, 12.80)	0.73** (0.41, 0.85)	−0.40** (−0.61, −0.08)

** $p < 0.01$

between the class means for those variables must be large for the overlap between the classes to still be small. Table 25.16 presents the distance estimates (i.e., standardized differences in means) for each pairwise class comparison on each of the three indicators variables. Large estimated absolute distance values greater than 2.0, corresponding to less than 20% overlap, are bolded for visual clarity. All classes are well separated with moderate to large estimated distances on at least two of the three items, and every item distinguishes between at least two of the three classes. The classes are all well separated with respect to their means on *glucose*, with the greatest distances between Class 1 and the other two classes. There is a similar pattern for the separation on *SSPG* with large distances between Class 1 and Classes 2 and 3. However, in the case of *SSPG*, there is a very small separation between Classes 2 and 3—meaning that there is a high degree of overlap in the distribution of individual values on *SSPG* across those two classes, rendering those two classes difficult to distinguish with respect to *SSPG*. In contrast, Classes 2 and 3 have a large distance between their means for *insulin*, whereas there is only a modest separation between Classes 1 and 3. Figure 25.11 provides a visual impression of these varying degrees of separation across the classes with respect to each of the three measures.

Because the final model selected had a class-varying, unrestricted Σ_k, the distinctness of the classes must also be evaluated with regards to the class-specific variance–covariance structure before a full substantive interpretation of the classes is rendered. I have already remarked, when assessing class homogeneity, that Class 3 was much more variable than the other two classes with respect to *glucose* and *SSPG* and that Class 2 was much more variable with respect to *insulin*. In terms of the covariance structure, presented as correlations in Table 25.15, Class 3 has a large and significant negative

Table 25.16. Diabetes Example: Estimated Standardized Differences in Class-Specific Indicator Means, $\hat{d}_{m\cdot\cdot}$, Based on Model-Estimated, Class-Specific Indicator Means and Variances from the Three-Class Latent Profile Analysis With Class-Varying, Unrestricted Σ_k ($n = 145$)

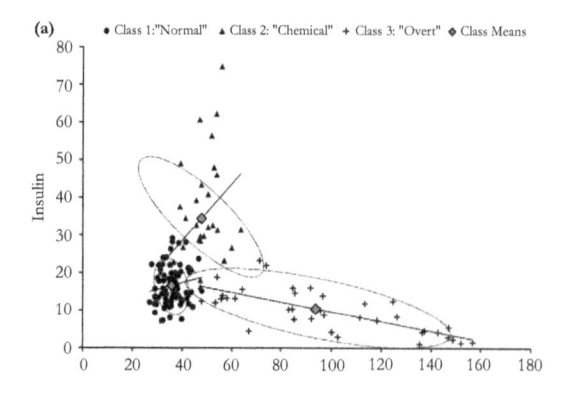

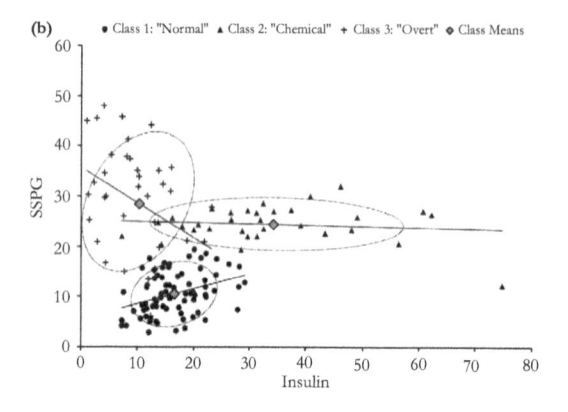

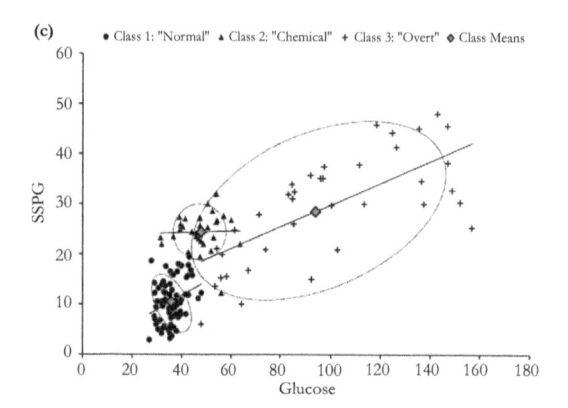

Variable	Class 1 vs. Class 2	Class 1 vs. Class 3	Class 2 vs. Class 3
(1) Glucose	−2.21	−2.78	−1.73
(2) Insulin	−1.91	1.13	−2.15
(3) SSPG	−3.34	−2.53	−0.49

Figure 25.11 Diabetes example: Scatter plots of observed sample values marked by modal latent class assignment based on the unconditional three-class LPA for (a) insulin versus glucose, (b) SSPG versus insulin, and (c) SSPG versus glucose. For (a)-(c), diamonds represent the model-estimated class-specific bivariate mean values, trend lines depict the model-estimated within-class bivariate associations, and the ellipse heights and widths correspond to 3.0 model-estimated within-class standard deviations for the indictors on the y- and x-axis, respectively.

correlation between *glucose* and *insulin*, whereas that correlation is positive and non-significant for both Classes 1 and 2. Class 3 has a large and significant positive correlation between *glucose* and

SSPG, whereas that correlation, although positive, is non-significant for both Classes 1 and 2. Class 3 has a moderate and significant negative correlation between *insulin* and *SSPG*, whereas Class 1 has a moderate and significant negative correlation and Class 2's correlation is negative and non-significant. Because the correlation between *insulin* and *SSPG* is the only significant correlation for Class 1 and none of the correlations were significant for Class 2, Classes 1 and 2 are not well separated by their covariance structure. Class 3 is the class with two quite large and all significant correlations, and these features are an important part of what distinguishes Class 3, and Class 3 is well separated from both Class 1 and Class 2 with respect to all covariance elements. However, because Class 3 only represents 26% of the population, it is not surprising that the results of the three-class model with a class-varying, diagonal Σ_k were so close to the results of this model, allowing the within-class correlations.

For the substantive class interpretation, I begin with the class most distinct in means and variance–covariance structure from the other classes, Class 3, with an estimated proportion of 26%. Class 3 consists of individuals with high values on *glucose*, on average, compared to the overall sample and Classes 1 and 2. Within this class, there is a strong negative association between *glucose* and *insulin* and strong positive association between *glucose* and *SSPG* such that the individuals in Class 3 with higher values on *glucose* have lower values on *insulin* and higher values on *SSPG*, on average. The high average value on *glucose* and *SSPG* with the lower average value on *insulin* along with the very strong associations across the three indicators, leads this class to be labeled the "overt" diabetic class.

Class 2, with an estimated proportion of 22%, consists of individuals with *insulin* and *SSPG* values, higher, on average, than the overall population means and notably higher than Class 1. Class 2 is not much different than Class 3 with respect to *SSPG* but has a much higher mean on *insulin*. Individuals in Class 2 have higher-than-average values for *glucose*, and Class 2 is nearly as different from Class 1 as Class 3 is in terms of average *glucose* values even though the mean in Class 2 is lower than Class 3. There are no significant associations between the three indicators in Class 2. The higher-than-average values on *glucose*, *insulin*, and *SSPG*, with a notably higher *insulin* mean but lower *glucose* mean than the "overt" diabetic class, suggests the label of the "chemical" diabetic for this class.

Class 1, with an estimated proportion of 52%, consists of individuals with *glucose* and *SSPG* values lower, on average, than the overall population mean and notably lower than either Class 2 or Class 3. The individuals in Class 1 have *insulin* values, on average, near the overall population mean, higher than the "chemical" diabetic class and lower than the "overt" diabetic class. For the Class 1 subpopulation, there is a moderate positive association between *glucose* and *SSPG* such that individuals with higher values on *glucose* in Class 1 have higher value, on average, for *SSPG*. This association is quite different from the moderate negative association in the "overt" diabetic group such that among those in Class 3, individuals with higher values on *glucose* have lower values on *SSPG*, on average. The lower *glucose* and *SSPG* average levels, the average *insulin* levels, the positive association between *glucose* and *SSPG*, and the estimated class proportion greater than 50% suggest the label of the "normal" (non-diabetic) for this class.

With the results from the unconditional LPA in-hand, I can compare individual model-estimated class membership for individuals in the sample to their clinical classifications. As it happens, a three-class model for the LPA was selected and the latent classes were interpreted in a way that matched, at the conceptual level, the three clinical classification categories. To make the descriptive, *post hoc* comparisons, I use the modal class assignment for each participant to compare to the clinical classification. Because the comparison is descriptive (rather than inferential) and there is a very high level of classification accuracy for all three classes (*see* Table 25.14), it is reasonable to use the modal class assignment to get a sense of the correspondence between "true" class membership and the clinical classifications. Table 25.17 displays a cross-tabulation comparison between latent class (modal) membership and the clinical classifications. Cells corresponding to "matches" between the modal class assignments and the clinical classifications are boxed in bold. In general, there is a strong concordance across all three latent classes, with only 22 (15%) of the participants having a mismatch between modal latent classification and clinical status. The highest correspondence is between the "normal" latent class and the non-diabetic clinical classification, with 91% of those modally assigned to the "normal" class also having a non-diabetic clinical status. The lowest correspondence is between the "chemical" latent class and the chemical clinical classification but was still reasonably high, with 72% of those modally assigned to the "chemical" diabetes class also having a chemical diabetic clinical status. It is also informative to examine the nature of the noncorrespondence. Of those individuals modally assigned to the "normal" class, none had an overt diabetic clinical status. Similarly, of those individuals modally assigned to the "overt" class, none had a non-diabetic clinical status. In both cases, the mismatch involved individuals with a chemical diabetic clinical status. Of the individuals modally assigned to the "chemical" diabetes class that did not have a chemical diabetic clinical status, most had a non-diabetic clinical status, but two did have an overt diabetic clinical status.

Because it was originally of interest whether a multivariate model-based classification could offer improvements over the univariate cut-off criteria used in the clinical classifications, I closely examined the 22 cases for which there is a mismatch. Table 25.18 summarizes the average posterior class probabilities stratified by both modal class assignments and clinical classifications. What can be seen in this table is that the average posterior class probabilities for the modally assigned classes, bolded and boxed in Table 25.18, are all reasonably high. In other words, even those groups of individuals with a mismatch between the modal latent class membership and clinical status are relatively well classified, on average, by the model. If one examines the raw data for these individuals, it can be seen that these individuals were *not* well classified by the clinical criteria. For example, most of the patients with a chemical diabetic clinical status and a "normal" modal class assignment were all borderline on clinical diagnosis criteria. Some of the patients with a non-diabetic clinical status that were hyperinsulinemic and insulin-resistant, but managed to maintain

Table 25.17. Diabetes Example: Modal Latent Class Assignment vs. Clinical Classification Frequencies and Row Percentages

Modal class assignment	Clinical classification			
	Non-diabetic	Chemical diabetic	Overt diabetic	Total
"Normal"	69 (91%)	7 (9%)	0 (0%)	76 (100%)
"Chemical"	7 (22%)	23 (72%)	2 (6%)	32 (100%)
"Overt"	0 (0%)	6 (16%)	31 (84%)	37 (100%)
Total	76	36	33	145

Table 25.18. Diabetes Example: Average Posterior Class Probabilities by Modal Latent Class Assignment and Clinical Classification

Modal class assignment	Clinical classification	f	Mean($\hat{p}_{normal}$)	Mean($\hat{p}_{chemical}$)	Mean($\hat{p}_{overt}$)
"Normal"	Non-diabetic	69	0.97	<0.01	0.02
	Chemical diabetic	7	0.79	0.05	0.15
	Overt diabetic	0	–	–	–
"Chemical"	Non-diabetic	7	0.06	0.85	0.09
	Chemical diabetic	23	0.02	0.93	0.04
	Overt diabetic	2	<0.01	>0.99	<0.01
"Overt"	Non-diabetic	0	–	–	–
	Chemical diabetic	6	0.07	0.08	0.85
	Overt diabetic	31	<0.01	<0.01	>0.99

normal glucose tolerance, were modally assigned by the model to the "chemical" diabetes class. These differences suggest that using a model that takes into account multiple metabolic characteristics may offer improved and more medically comprehensive classification over the rigid and arbitrary univariate clinical cut-off criteria.

Latent Class Regression

The primary focus, thus far, has been on the process for establishing the measurement model for latent class variables with either categorical indicators (LCA) or continuous indicators (LPA). However, that process is usually just the first step in a structural equation mixture analysis in which the latent class variable (with its measurement model) is placed in a larger system of variables that may include hypothesized predictors and outcomes of latent class membership. To provide readers with a sense of how these structural relationships can be specified, I present in this section a latent class regression (LCR) model for incorporating predictors of latent class membership. This presentation is applicable for both LCA and LPA models.

Covariates of latent class membership may serve different purposes depending on the particular aims of the study analysis. If attention is on developing and validating the measurement model for a given construct using a latent class variable, covariates can be used to assess criterion-related validity of the latent class measurement model. It may be possible, based on the conceptual framework for the latent class variable, to generate hypotheses about how the latent classes should relate to a select set of covariates. These hypotheses can then be evaluated using a LCR model (Dayton & Macready, 2002); support for the hypotheses equates to increased validation of the latent class variable. You may also gain a richer characterization and interpretation of the latent classes through their relationships with covariates.

Beyond construct validation, covariates can be used to test hypotheses related to a theoretical variable system in which the latent class variable operates. In such a variable system, you may have one or more theory-driven covariates that are hypothesized to explain individual variability in an outcome where the individual variability is captured by the latent class variable.

In the remainder of this section I describe the formulation of the LCR model and illustrate its use in the LSAY example.

Model Formulation

For a LCR model, the measurement model parameterization, describing the relationships between the latent class variable and its indicators, remains the same as for the unconditional models but the structural model changes in that the latent class proportions are now conditional on one or more covariates. For example, in the LCA specification, the conditional version of Equation 4 is given by

$$\Pr(u_{1i}, u_{2i}, \ldots, u_{Mi}, x_i)$$
$$= \sum_{k=1}^{K} \left[\Pr(c_i = k | x_i) \cdot \Pr(u_{1i}, u_{2i}, \ldots, u_{Mi} | c_i = k) \right]. \quad (40)$$

A multinomial regression is used to parameterize the relationship between the probability of latent class membership and a single covariate, x, such that

$$\Pr(c_i = k | x_i) = \frac{\exp(\gamma_{0k} + \gamma_{1k} x_i)}{\sum_{j=1}^{K} \exp(\gamma_{0j} + \gamma_{1j} x_i)}, \quad (41)$$

where Class K is the reference class and $\gamma_{0K} = \gamma_{1K} = 0$ and for identification. γ_{0k} is the log odds of membership in Class k versus the reference class, Class K, when $x = 0$ and γ_{1k} is the log odds ratio for membership in Class k (versus Class K) corresponding to a one unit difference on x. Equations 40 and 41 are represented in path diagram format as shown in Figure 25.12. Equation 41 can easily be expanded to include multiple covariates. (For more general information about multinomial regression, *see*, for example, Agresti, 2002.) It is also possible to examine latent class difference with respect to a grouping or concomitant variable using a multiple-group approach similar to multiple-group

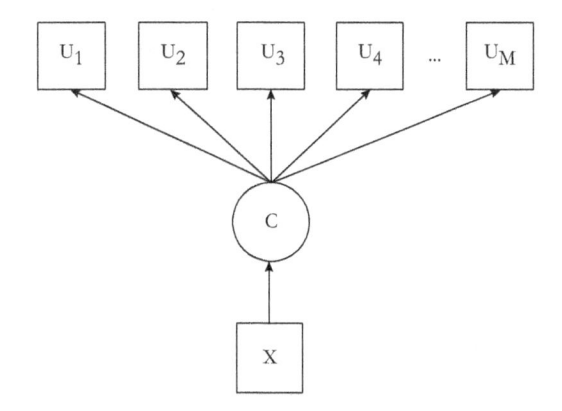

Figure 25.12 Generic path diagram for a latent class regression model.

factor analysis (Collins & Lanza, 2010; Dayton & Macready, 2002), but such models are beyond the scope of this chapter.

Model Building

As previously explained in the earlier model-building subsections, the first step in the model-building process—even if the ultimate aims of the analysis include testing hypotheses regarding the relationships between predicting covariates and latent class membership—is to establish the measurement model for the latent class variable. Based on simulation work (Nylund & Masyn, 2008), showing misspecification of covariate effects in a LCA can lead to bias in the class enumeration, it is strongly recommended that the building of the measurement model—particularly the class enumeration stage—is conducted with unconditional models, only adding covariates once the final measurement model has been selected. The selection and order of covariate inclusion should be theory-driven and follow the same process as with any regular regression model with respect to risk factors or predictors of interest, control of potential confounders, and so forth.

The specification provided in Equations 40 and 41 assumes that there is no direct effect of x on the latent class indicator variables (which would be represented in Figure 25.12 by a path from x to one or more the us). However, omission of direct covariate effects (if actually present) can lead to biased results (similarly to the omission of direct effects in a latent factor model). If direct effects are incorrectly omitted, then the measurement parameters for the latent class variable can be distorted, shifting from their unconditional model estimates and potentially misrepresenting the nature of the latent classes; in addition, the estimated latent class proportions and the effects of the covariate on latent class membership can be biased. In fact, if no direct effects are included and the latent classes in the LCR model change substantively in size or meaning relative to the final unconditional latent class model, then this can signal a misspecification of the covariate associations with the latent class indicators, recommending a more explicit test of direct effects. The presence of direct effects is analogous to the presence of measurement non-invariance in a factor model or differential item functioning in an item response theory model—a direct effect on an indicator variable means that individuals belonging to the *same* latent class but with *different* values of *x* have different expected outcomes for that observed indicator. Although elaborating on the process of testing for direct effects and measurement non-invariance with respect to covariates being incorporated into a LCR model is beyond the scope of this chapter, I do recommend that, in the absence of prior knowledge or strong theoretical justification, direct effect should be tested as part of the conditional model-building process and the addition of latent class covariates. (For more on covariate direct effects, measurement non-invariance, and violations of the conditional independence assumption resulting from direct covariate effects in LCRs, *see*, for example, Bandeen-Roche, Miglioretti, Zeger, Rathouz, & Paul, 1997; Hagenaars, 1988; and Reboussin, Ip, & Wolfson, 2008.)

I should remark here that a LCR analysis following the building of a latent class measurement model using a full latent class enumeration process without any *a priori* restrictions on the number and nature of the latent classes is a blend of confirmatory (LCR) and exploratory (latent class enumeration) elements. Although the establishment of the measurement model proceeds in a more exploratory way, the model that you carry forward to inferential structural models is not constrained in the same way it would be when conducting an EFA and then subsequent CFA in the same sample, and thus you do not face the same dangers of inflating Type I error rates and capitalizing on chance. However, it is preferable, if possible, to validate the measurement model with new data so that you can feel more confident that the measurement model might generalize to other samples and that your latent classes are not being driven by sampling variability and are not overfit to the particular sample data at hand. Otherwise, it is important to acknowledge in the interpretation of the results the exploratory and confirmatory character of the analysis (Lubke, 2010).

Longitudinal Study of American Youth Example for Latent Class Regression

To illustrate LCR, I return to the LSAY example used in the Latent Class Analysis section. In addition to the nine math disposition items, the example data set also included the variable of student sex (coded here as *female* = 1 for females students and *female* = 0 for male students). Beginning with the five-class unconditional model, I fit two models: Model 0, a five-class model with the latent class variable regressed on *female* but with all multinomial regression coefficients for *female* fixed at zero; Model 1, a five-class model with the latent class variable regressed on *female* with all multinomial regression coefficients for *female* freely estimated. I conducted parallel analyses for both Subsamples A and B and found similar results; only the results for Subsample A are presented here.

There is a significant overall association between student sex and math disposition class membership (Model 0 vs. Model 1: $X^2_{diff} = 27.76$, $df = 4$, $p < .001$). There was no significant shift in the measurement parameters between Model 0 and Model 1 that would have suggested the presence of one or more direct effects of *female* on the items themselves. This descriptive comparison of parameter estimates is not a concrete test of direct effects (that should normally be done), but because explicit testing for differential item functioning in latent class models is beyond the scope of this chapter, I will cautiously treat this model comparison as a satisfactory heuristic evaluation of measurement invariance that allows me to proceed with an interpretation of the LCR results without including direct effects.

Examining the results of the LCR presented in Table 25.19, the multinomial regression parameters represent the effects of student sex on class membership in each class relative to the reference class (selected here as Class 1: "Pro-math without anxiety"). Given membership in either Class 1 ("Pro-math without anxiety") or Class 2 ("Pro-math with anxiety"), females are significantly less likely to be in Class 2 than Class 1 ($\hat{OR} = 0.52$), whereas females are significantly more likely to be in Class 4 ("I don't like math but I know it's good for me") than Class 1 ($\hat{OR} = 1.72$). There is no significant difference in the likelihood of membership in Class 5 ("Anti-math with anxiety") among males

Table 25.19. LSAY Example: Five-Class Latent Class Regression Results for the Effects of Student Sex (female = 1 for female; female = 0 for male) on Latent Class Membership for Subsample A ($n_A = 1338$)

C regressed on female		$\hat{\gamma}_{1k}$	s.e.	p-value	$\hat{OR}$
Class 1 (ref)	"Pro-math without anxiety"	0.00	–	–	1.00
Class 2	"Pro-math with anxiety"	–0.66	0.21	<0.01	0.52
Class 3	"Math lover"	0.17	0.21	0.43	1.18
Class 4	"I don't like math but I know it's good for me"	0.55	0.19	<0.01	1.72
Class 5	"Anti-math with anxiety"	–0.32	0.22	0.14	0.73

and females in either Class 1 or 5. Rather than making all pairwise class comparisons for student sex by changing the reference class, a better impression of the sex differences in class membership can be given through a graphical presentation such as the one depicted in Figure 25.13, which shows the model-estimated class proportions for the total population and for the two values of the covariate—that is, for males and females. You can see in this figure that the sex differences are primarily in the distribution of individuals across Classes 2 ("Pro-Math With Anxiety") and 4 ("I Don't Like Math but I Know It's Good for Me") with females more likely than males, overall, to be in Class 4 and less likely to be in Class 2.

Post Hoc Class Comparisons

This section has presented a LCR model that simultaneously estimates the latent class measurement model and the structural relationships between the latent class variable and one or more covariates. The simultaneous estimation of the measurement and structural models is recommended whenever possible. However, there is a not-so-unusual practice in the applied literature of doing *post hoc* class comparisons, taking the modal class assignments based on the unconditional latent class measurement model and treating those values as observed values on a manifest multinomial variable in subsequent analyses. This is what I did for the diabetes example, comparing the modal class assignments to the clinical classifications, and such a *post hoc* comparison can be a very useful descriptive technique for further understanding and validation of the latent classes. The problem of this *post hoc* classification approach comes when modal class assignments are used in formal hypothesis testing, moving beyond the descriptive to inferential analyses.

Such a "classify-analyze" approach is problematic because it ignores the error rates in assigning subjects to classes. Because the error rates can vary from class to class, with smaller classes having higher prior probabilities of incorrect assignment, even with well-separated classes, there can be bias in the point estimates as well as the standard errors for parameters related to latent class membership. In addition, there is error introduced from the posterior class probabilities that are used for the modal class assignment because they are computed using parameter estimates and contain the uncertainty from those estimates. Studies have shown that assignment error rates can be considerable (Tueller, Drotar, & Lubke, 2011), posing serious threats to the validity of *post hoc* testing.

Advanced Mixture Modeling

Although a substantial amount of information has been covered in this chapter, I have only scratched the surface in terms of the many types of population heterogeneity that can be modeled using finite mixtures. However, what is provided here is the foundational understanding that will enable you to explore these more advanced models. Just as with factor analysis and traditional structural equation modeling, the basic principles of model specification, estimation, evaluation, and

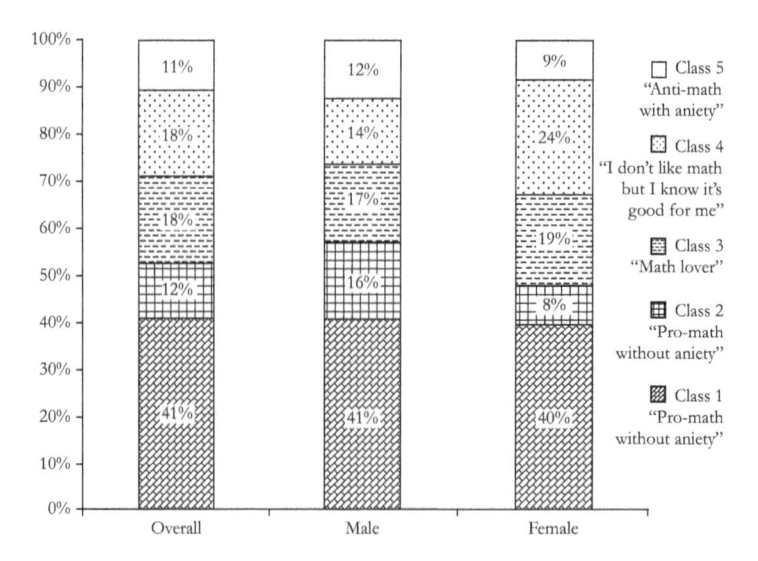

Figure 25.13 LSAY example: Model-estimated overall and sex-specific latent class proportions for the five-class LCR.

interpretation extend quite naturally into more complicated modeling scenarios.

This section provides a very brief overview of some of modeling extensions currently possible in a mixture modeling framework. The first extension relates to the latent class indicators and their within-class distributions. I presented two models—LCA and LPA—that had exclusively categorical or exclusively continuous indicator variables. However, recent advances in maximum likelihood estimation using complex algorithms in a general latent variable modeling framework (see, for example, Asparouhov & Muthén, 2004, and Skrondal & Rabe-Hesketh, 2004) have rendered the necessity of uniformity of measurement scales among the indicators obsolete, allowing indicators for a single latent class variable to be of mixed measurement modalities, while also expanding the permissible scales of measures and error distributions for the manifest variables. It is now possible to specify a latent class variable with indicators of mixed modalities or measurement scales including interval and ratio scales of measures, censored interval scales, count scales, ordinal or Likert scales, binary or multinomial responses, and so forth. It is also possible to specify a range of within-class distributions for those indicators—for example, Poisson, zero-inflated Poisson, or negative binomial for count scales; normal, censored normal, censored-inflated normal for interval scales, and so forth. Additionally, the class-specific distribution functions can be from different parametric families across the classes.

Another extension involves the scale of the latent class variable. In this presentation, I used the traditional formulation of the latent class variable as a latent multinomial variable. However, there are latent class models that bridge the gap between the latent multinomial variable models and the latent factor models, such as discretized latent trait models, located latent class models, and latent class scaling models (Croon, 1990, 2002; Dayton, 1998; Heinen, 1996)—all forms of *ordered* latent class models. In addition, recent advances have further blurred the lines of conventional classification schemes for latent variable models (Heinen, 1996) by allowing both latent factors *and* latent class variables to be included in the same analytic model. These so-called hybrid models, also termed *factor mixture models*, include both continuous and categorical latent variables as part of the same measurement model (Arminger, Stein, & Wittenburg, 1999; Dolan & van der Maas, 1998; Draney, Wilson, Gluck, & Spiel, 2008; Jedidi, Jagpal, & DeSarbo, 1997; Masyn, Henderson, & Greenbaum, 2010; Muthén, 2008; Vermunt & Magidson, 2002; von Davier & Yamamoto, 2006; Yung, 1997). These models combine features from both conventional factor analysis and LCA. Special cases of these hybrid models include mixture item response theory models and growth mixture models.

Extensions in mixture model specification and estimation include the accommodation of complex sampling weights (Patterson, Dayton, & Graubard, 2002); the use of Bayesian estimation

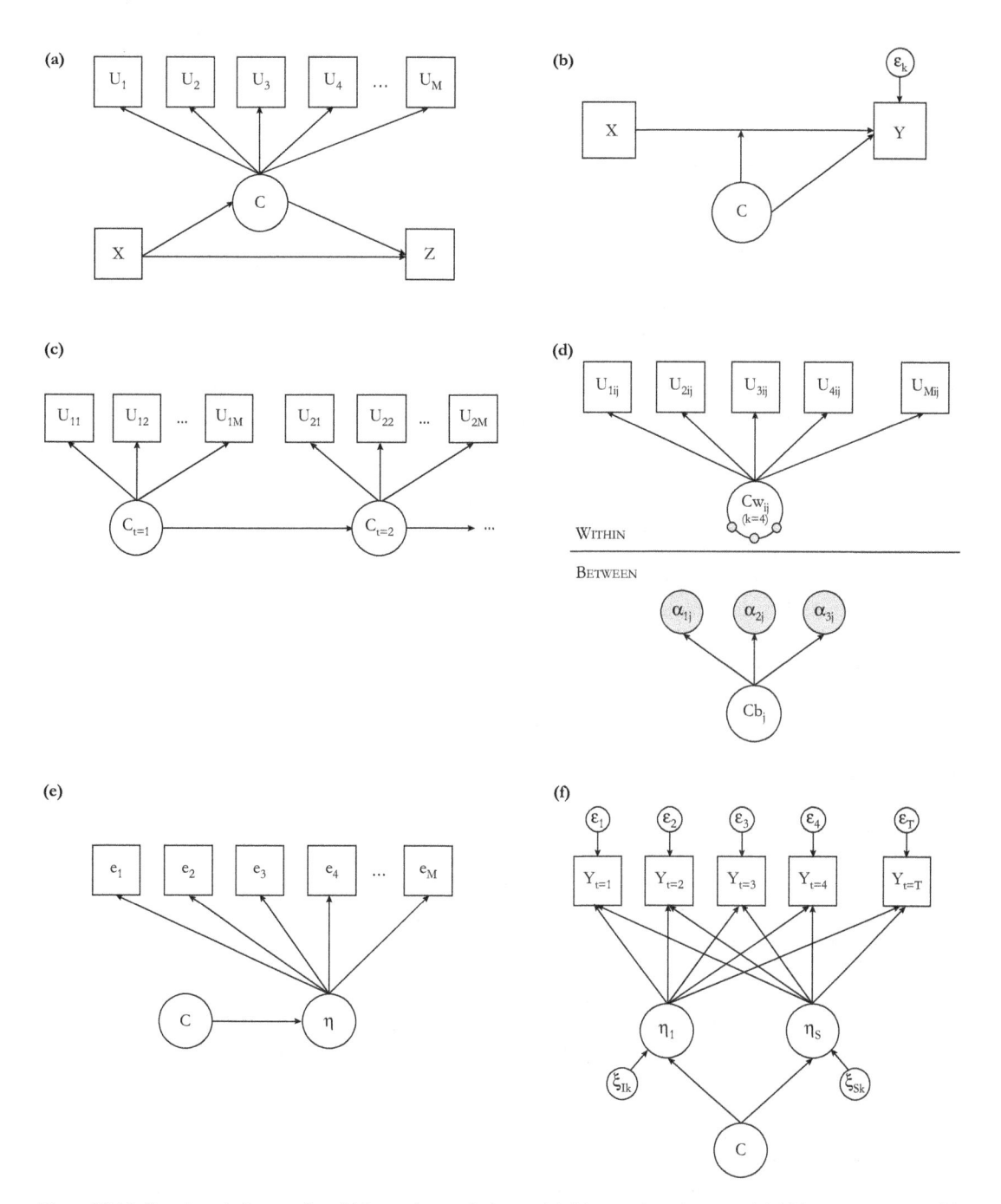

Figure 25.14 Generic path diagrams for a (a) latent class mediation model, (b) regression mixture model, (c) latent transition model, (d) multilevel latent class model, (e) discrete-time survival factor mixture model, and (f) growth mixture model.

techniques (Asparouhov & Muthén, 2010; Garrett & Zeger, 2000; Gelfand & Smith, 1990; Lanza, Collins, Schafer, & Flaherty, 2005) in place of full-information maximum likelihood; the adaptation of fuzzy clustering algorithms and allowing graded latent class membership (Asparouhov & Muthén, 2008; Yang & Yu, 2005); and the use of multiple imputation for missing data combined with MLE (Vermunt, Van Ginkel, Van der Ark, & Sijtsma, 2008).

The six panels of Figure 25.14 display path diagram representations of some of the many advanced mixture models available to researchers. Figure 25.14.a depicts is a latent class mediation model

(Petras, Masyn, & Ialongo, 2011), extending the LCR model to include an outcome of latent class membership that may also be influenced by the covariate. Figure 25.14.b depicts a regression mixture model (RMM; Desarbo, Jedidi, & Sinha, 2001; Van Horn, Jaki, Masyn, Ramey, Antaramian, & Lamanski, 2009) in which the latent class variable is measured by the conditional distribution of an outcome variable, y, regressed on x—that is, the latent class is specified to characterize differential effects of x on y present in the overall population. Figure 25.14.c displays the longitudinal extension of latent class analysis: latent transition analysis (LTA). In LTA (Collins & Lanza, 2010; Nylund, 2007), a special case of a broader class of mixture models called Markov chain models (Langeheine & van de Pol, 2002), there is a latent class variable at each time-point or wave, and the relationship between the classes across time describe individual transitions in class membership through time. Figure 25.14.d displays the multilevel extension of LCA. In MLCA (Asparouhov & Muthén, 2008; Henry & Muthén, 2010; Nylund-Gibson, Graham, & Juvonen, 2010), the class proportions within cluster (represented by shaded circles on the boundary of the *within*-cluster latent class variable, cw) vary across clusters. And the variability in class proportions across clusters is captured by a *between*-cluster latent class variable, cb. The classes of cb represent different groups of clusters characterized by their distributions of individuals across classes of cw. Figures 46.14.e and 46.14.f depict two special types of factor mixture models. The diagram in Figure 25.14.e represents a discrete-time survival factor mixture model (Masyn, 2009) in which there is an underlying factor that captures individual-level frailty in the discrete-time survival process measured by the event history indicator, e_m, and the latent class variable characterizes variability in the individual frailties. The diagram in Figure 25.14.f represents a growth mixture model (Feldman, Masyn, & Conger, 2009; Muthén & Asparouhov, 2009; Petras & Masyn, 2010) in which there are latent growth factors that capture the intra-individual growth process, defining individual growth trajectories, and a latent class variable that characterizes (part of) the interindividual variability in the growth trajectories. Examples of other advanced mixture models not depicted in Figure 25.14 include pattern-mixture and selection models for non-ignorable missing data (Muthén, Asparouhov, Hunter, & Leuchter, 2011) and complier average causal effect models (Jo, 2002). What I have provided here is by no means a fully comprehensive or exhaustive list of advanced mixture models but is intended to give the reader a flavor of what extensions are possible.

Conclusion

This chapter represents what I believe to be the current, prevailing "best practices" for basic mixture modeling, specifically LCA and LPA, in terms of model specification, estimation, evaluation, selection, and interpretation. I have also provided a very limited introduction to structural equation mixture modeling in the form of LCR. In addition, in the previous section, you have been given a partial survey of the many more advanced mixture models currently in use. It should be evident that mixture models offer a flexible and powerful way of modeling population heterogeneity. However, mixture modeling, like all statistical models, has limitations and is perhaps even more susceptible to misapplication that other more established techniques. Thus, I take the opportunity in closing to remind readers about some of the necessary (and untestable) assumptions of mixture modeling and caution against the most common misuses.

Most of this chapter has focused on *direct* applications of mixture modeling, for which one assumes *a priori* that the overall population consists of two or more homogeneous subpopulations. The direct application is far more common in social science applications than the indirect application. One assumes that there are, in truth, distinct types of groups of individuals that are in the population to be revealed. "This assumption is critical, because it is always possible to organize any set of data into classes, which then can be said to indicate types, but there is no real finding if an analysis merely indicates classifications in a particular sample. To be of scientific value, the classifications must represent lawful phenomena, must be replicable, and must be related to other variables within a network that defines construct validity." (Horn, 2000, p. 927) Because this assumption is an *a priori* assumption of a mixture model, utilizing a direct mixture modeling approach does *not* test a hypothesis about the existence of discrete groups or subtypes. (There are analytic approaches that are designed to explore the underlying latent structure of a given construct, e.g., whether the underlying construct is continuous or categorical in nature, and interested readers are referred to the chapter in this handbook on taxometric methods and also Masyn, Henderson, and

Greenbaum, 2010.) Nor does the fact that a K-class model is estimable with the sample data prove there are K classes in the population from which the sample was drawn.

Furthermore, the (subjective) selection of a final K-class model does not prove the existence of *exactly* K subgroups. Recall how the specification of Σ_k in a latent profile analysis can influence which class enumeration is "best." The number of latent classes that you settle on at the conclusion of the class enumeration process could very well not reflect the actual number of distinct groups in the population. Attention must also be paid, during the interpretation process, to the fact that the latent classes extracted from the data are inextricably linked to the items used to identify those classes because the psychometric properties of the items can influence the formation of the classes. You assume that you have at your disposal the necessary indicators to identify all the distinct subgroups in the population and can only increase confidence in this assumption through validation of the latent class structure.

I did not provide concrete guidelines about sample size requirements for mixture modeling because they depend very much on the model complexity; the number, nature, and separation of the "true" classes in the population; and the properties of the latent class indicators themselves (Lubke, 2010). "Analyses for a very simple latent class models may be carried out probably with as few as 30 subjects, whereas other analyses require thousands of subjects." (Lubke, 2010, p. 215) Thus, what is critical to be mindful of in your interpretation of findings from a mixture model is that mixture models can be sensitive to sampling fluctuation that may limit the generalizability of the class structure found in a given sample and that smaller samples may be underpowered to detect smaller and/or not well-separated classes (Lubke, 2010).

None of these limitations detracts from the usefulness of mixture modeling or the scientific value of the emergent latent class structure for characterizing the population heterogeneity of interest. However, any interpretation must be made with these limitations in mind and care must be taken not to reify the resultant latent classes or to make claims about proof of their existence.

Future Directions

In the historical overview of mixture modeling at the beginning of this chapter, I remarked on the rapid expansion in the statistical theory (model specification and estimation), software implementation, and applications of mixture modeling in the last 30 years. And the evolution of mixture modeling shows no signs of slowing. There are numerous areas of development in mixture modeling, and many investigations are currently underway. Among those areas of development are: measures of overall goodness-of-fit, individual fit indices, graphical residual diagnostics, and assumption-checking *post hoc* analyses—particularly for mixture models with continuous indicators and factor mixture models; Bayesian estimation and mixture model selection; class enumeration processes for multilevel mixture models with latent class variable on two or more levels; missing data analysis—particularly maximum likelihood approaches and multiple imputation approaches for non-ignorable missingness related to latent class membership; detection procedures for differential item functioning in latent class measurement models; multistage and simultaneous approaches for analyzing predictors and distal outcomes of latent class membership including multiple imputation of latent class membership by way of plausible values from Bayesian estimation techniques; integration of causal inference techniques such as propensity scores and principal stratification with mixture models; and informed study design, including sample size determination, power calculations, and item selection. In addition to these more specific areas of methods development, the striking trend of extending other statistical models by integrating or overlaying finite mixtures will surely continue and more hybrid models are likely to emerge. Furthermore, there will be advancing substantive areas, yielding new kinds of data, for which mixture modeling may prove invaluable—for example, genotypic profile analysis of single nucleotide polymorphisms. And although it is difficult to predict which area of development will prove most fruitful in the coming decades, it is certain that mixture modeling will continue to play an increasingly prominent role in ongoing empirical quests to describe and explain general patterns and individual variability in social science phenomena.

List of Abbreviations

ANOVA   Analysis of variance (ANCOVA—Analysis of covariance)
AvePP   Average posterior class probability

AWE	Approximate weight of evidence criterion
BF	Bayes factor
BIC	Bayesian information criterion
CACE	Complier average causal effect
CAIC	Consistent Akaike information criterion
CFA	Confirmatory factor analysis (EFA—Exploratory factor analysis)
cmP	Correct model probability
df	Degree(s) of freedom
DIF	Differential item functioning
E_K	Entropy
EM	Expectation-maximization algorithm
GMM	Growth mixture model
IRT	Item response theory
LCA	Latent class analysis
LCCA	Latent class cluster analysis
LCR	Latent class regression
LL	Log likelihood
LPA	Latent profile analysis
LR	Likelihood ratio (LRT—Likelihood ratio test; LRTS—LRT statistic; LMR-LRT—Lo, Mendell, & Rubin LRT; BLRT—bootstrapped LRT)
LSAY	Longitudinal Study of American Youth
LTA	Latent transition analysis
MAR	Missing at random (MCAR—missing completely at random)
mcaP	Modal class assignment proportion
ML	Maximum likelihood (MLE—Maximum likelihood estimate; FIML—Full information maximum likelihood)
MVN	Multivariate normal distribution
npar	Number of free parameters
OCC	Odds of correct classification ratio
OR	Odds ratio
RMM	Regression mixture model
SIC	Schwarz information criterion
SSPG	Steady state plasma glucose

Appendix

A technical appendix with Mplus syntax and supplementary Excel files for tabulating and constructing graphical summaries of modeling results is available by request from the chapter author.

Author Note

The author would like to thank Dr. Karen Nylund-Gibson and her graduate students, Amber Gonzalez and Christine Victorino, for research and editorial support. Correspondence concerning this chapter should be addressed to Katherine Masyn, Graduate School of Education, Harvard University, Cambridge, MA 02138. E-mail: katherine_masyn@gse.harvard.edu.

References

Agresti, A. (2002). *Categorical data analysis*. Hoboken, NJ: John Wiley & Sons.

Arminger, G., Stein, P., & Wittenburg, J. (1999). Mixtures of conditional and covariance structure models. *Psychometrika, 64*(4), 475–494.

Asparouhov, T., & Muthén, B. (2004). *Maximum-likelihood estimation in general latent variable modeling*. Unpublished manuscript.

Asparouhov, T., & Muthén, B. (2008). Multilevel mixture models. In G.R. Hancock & K.M. Samuelsen (Eds.), *Advances in latent variable mixture models* (pp. 27–51). Charlotte, NC: Information Age Publishing.

Bandeen-Roche, K., Miglioretti, D. L., Zeger, S. L., & Rathouz, P. J. (1997). Latent variable regression for multiple discrete outcomes. *Journal of the American Statistical Association, 92*(440), 1375–1386.

Banfield, J. D., & Raftery, A. E. (1993). Model-based Gaussian and non-Gaussian clustering. *Biometrics, 49*, 803–821.

BeLue, R., Francis, L. A., Rollins, B., & Colaco, B. (2009). One size does not fit all: Identifying risk profiles for overweight in adolescent population subsets. *The Journal of Adolescent Health, 45*(5), 517–524.

Bergman, L. R., & Trost, K. (2006). The person-oriented versus the variable-oriented approach: Are they complementary, opposites, or exploring different worlds? *Merrill-Palmer Quarterly, 52*(3), 601–632.

Bozdogan, H. (1987). Model selection and Akaike's information criterion (AIC): The general theory and its analytical extensions. *Psychometrika, 52*(3), 345–370.

Bray, B. C. (2007). *Examining gambling and substance use: Applications of advanced latent class modeling techniques for cross-sectional and longitudinal data*. Unpublished doctoral dissertation, The Pennsylvania State University, University Park.

Christie, C. A., & Masyn, K. E. (2010). Latent profiles of evaluators' self-reported practices. *The Canadian Journal of Program Evaluation, 23*(2), 225–254.

Chung, H., Flaherty, B. P., & Schafer, J. L. (2006). Latent class logistic regression: Application to marijuana use and attitudes among high school seniors. *Journal of the Royal Statistical Society: Series A, 169*(4), 723–743.

Chung, H., Loken, E., & Schafer, J. L. (2004). Difficulties in drawing inferences with finite-mixture models. *The American Statistician, 58*(2), 152–158.

Clogg, C. C. (1977). *Unrestricted and restricted maximum likelihood latent structure analysis: A manual for users*. University Park, PA: Population Issues Research Center, Pennsylvania State University.

Cohen, J. (1988). *Statistical power analysis for the behavioral sciences*. Hillsdale, NJ: Lawrence Erlbaum Associates.

Collins, L. M., Graham, J. W., Long, J. D., & Hansen, W. B. (1994). Crossvalidation of latent class models of early substance use onset. *Multivariate Behavioral Research, 29*(2), 165-183.

Collins, L. M., & Lanza, S. T. (2010). *Latent class and latent transition analysis with applications in the social, behavioral, and health sciences.* Hoboken, NJ: John Wiley & Sons.

Crissey S. R. (2005). Race/ethnic differences in the marital expectations of adolescents: The role of romantic relationships. *Journal of Marriage and the Family, 67*(3), 697-709.

Croon, M. (1990). Latent class analysis with ordered latent classes. *British Journal of Mathematical and Statistical Psychology, 43*, 171-192.

Croon, M. (2002). Ordering the classes. In J. A. Hagenaars & A. L. McCutcheon (Eds.), *Applied latent class analysis* (pp. 137-162). Cambridge: Cambridge University Press.

Cudeck, R., & Browne, M.W. (1983). Cross-validation of covariance structures. *Multivariate Behavioral Research, 18*, 147-167.

Dayton, C.M. (1998). *Latent class scaling analysis.* Thousand Oaks, CA: Sage.

Dayton, C.M. & Macready, G.B. (1988). Concomitant variable latent class models. *Journal of the American Statistical Association, 83*, 173-178.

DeCarlo, L. T. (2005). A model of rater behavior in essay grading based on signal detection theory. *Journal of Educational Measurement, 42*(1), 53-76.

Dempster, A. P., Laird, N. M., & Rubin, D. B. (1977). Maximum likelihood from incomplete data via the EM algorithm (with discussion). *Journal of the Royal Statistical Society, 39*, 1-38.

Desarbo, W. S., Jedidi, K., & Sinha, I. (2001). Customer value analysis in a heterogeneous market. *Strategic Management Journal, 22*(9), 845-857.

Dolan, C. V., & van der Maas, H. L. J. (1998). Fitting multivariate normal finite mixtures subject to structural equation modeling. *Psychometrika, 63*, 227-253.

Draney, K., Wilson, M., Gluck, J., & Spiel, C. (2008). Mixture models in a developmental context. In G. R. Hancock & K. M. Samuelson (Eds.), *Advances in latent variable mixture models* (pp. 199-216). Charlotte, NC: Information Age Publishing.

Eckart, C. & Young, G. (1936). The approximation of one matrix by another of lower rank. *Psychometrika, 1*, 211-218.

Enders, C. K. (2010). *Applied missing data analysis.* New York: Guilford Press.

Feldman, B., Masyn, K., & Conger, R. (2009). New approaches to studying problem behaviors: A comparison of methods for modeling longitudinal, categorical data. *Developmental Psychology, 45*(3), 652-676.

Formann, A. K. (1982). Linear logistic latent class analysis. *Biometrical Journal, 24*, 171-190.

Formann, A. K. (1992). Linear logistic latent class analysis for polytomous data. *Journal of the American Statistical Association, 87*, 476-486.

Fraley, C., and Raftery, A.E. (1998). *How many clusters? Which clustering method? Answers via model-based cluster analysis. The Computer Journal, 41*(8), 578-588.

Garrett, E. S., & Zeger, S. L. (2000). Latent class model diagnosis. *Biometrics, 56*, 1055-1067.

Gelfand, A. E. and Smith, A. F. M. (1990). Sampling-based approaches to calculating marginal densities. *Journal of the American Statistical Association,85*, 398-409.

Goodman, L. A. (1974). Exploratory latent structure analysis using both identifiable and unidentifiable models. *Biometrika, 61*, 215-231.

Goodman, L. A. (2002). Latent class analysis: The empirical study of latent types, latent variables, and latent structures. In J. A. Hagenaars & A. L. McCutcheon (Eds.), *Applied latent class analysis* (pp. 3-55). Cambridge: Cambridge University Press.

Haberman, S. J. (1973). The analysis of residuals in cross-classified tables. *Biometrics, 29*, 205-220.

Hagenaars, J.A. (1998). Categorical causal modeling: Latent class analysis and directed log-linear models with latent variables. *Sociological Methods & Research, 26*, 436-486.

Hagenaars, J. A., & McCutcheon, A. L. (2002). *Applied latent class analysis.* Cambridge; New York: Cambridge University Press.

Hamil-Luker, J. (2005). Trajectories of public assistance receipt among female high school dropouts. *Population Research and Policy Review, 24*(6), 673-694.

Hancock, G. R., & Samuelson, K. M. (Eds.). (2008). *Advances in latent variable mixture models.* Charlotte, NC: Information Age Publishing.

Heinen, D. (1996). *Latent class and discrete latent trait models: Similarities and differences.* Thousand Oaks, CA: Sage Publications.

Henry, K. & Muthén, B. (2010). Multilevel latent class analysis: An application of adolescent smoking typologies with individual and contextual predictors. *Structural Equation Modeling, 17*, 193-215.

Herzberg, A. M., & Andrews, D. F. (1985). *Data: A collection of problems from many fields for the student and research worker.* Brooklyn, NY: Springer.

Hipp, J. R., & Bauer, D. J. (2006). Local solutions in the estimation of growth mixture models. *Psychological Methods,*11(1), 36-53.

Horn, J. L. (2000) Comments on integrating person-centered and variable-centered research on problems associated with the use of alcohol. *Alcoholism: Clinical and Experimental Research, 24*(6) 924-930.

Huang, G. H., & Bandeen-Roche, K. (2004). Latent class regression with covariate effects on underlying and measured variables. *Psychometrika, 69*(1), 5-32.

Jedidi, K., Jagpal, H. S., & DeSarbo, W. S. (1997). Finite-mixture structural equation models for response-based segmentation and unobserved heterogeneity. *Marketing Science,* 16(1), 39-59.

Jo, B. (2002). Statistical power in randomized intervention studies with noncompliance. *Psychological Methods, 7*, 178-193.

Kass, R. E., & and Wasserman, L. (1995). A reference Bayesian test for nested hypotheses and its relationship to the Schwarz criterion. *Journal of the American Statistical Association,* 90(434), 928-934.

Kimmel, L. G., & Miller, J. D. (2008). The longitudinal study of American youth: Notes on the first 20 years of tracking and data collection. *Survey Practice,* December, 2008.

Langeheine, R., & van de Pol, F. (2002). Latent Markov chains. In J. A. Hagenaars & A. L. McCutcheon (Eds.), *Applied latent class analysis* (pp. 304-341). Cambridge, UK: Cambridge University Press.

Lanza, S. T., Collins, L. M., Schafer, J. L., & Flaherty, B. P. (2005). Using data augmentation to obtain standard errors and conduct hypothesis tests in latent class and latent transition analysis. *Psychological Methods, 10,* 84–100.

Lanza, S. T., Dziak, J. J., Huang, L., Xu, S., & Collins, L. M. (2011). *PROC LCA & PROC LTA User's Guide Version 1.2.6.* University Park: The Methodology Center, Penn State.

Laursen, B. & Hoff, E. (2006). Person-centered and variable-centered approaches to longitudinal data. *Merrill-Palmer Quarterly, 52,* 377–389.

Lazarsfeld, P., & Henry, N. (1968). *Latent structure analysis.* New York: Houghton Mifflin.

Little, R. J. & Rubin, D. B. (2002). *Statistical analysis with missing data* (2nd ed.). New York: John Wiley and Sons.

Lo, Y., Mendell, N., & Rubin, D. (2001). Testing the number of components in a normal mixture. *Biometrika, 88,* 767–778.

Lubke, G. H. (2010). Latent variable mixture modeling. In G. R. Hancock & R. O. Mueller (Eds.), *The reviewer's guide to quantitative methods in the social sciences.* New York, NY: Routledge.

Magnusson, D. (1998). The logic and implications of a person-oriented approach. In R. B. Cairns, L. R. Bergman, & J. Kagan (Eds.), *Methods and models for studying the individual* (pp. 33–64). Thousand Oaks, CA: Sage.

Markon, K. E, & Krueger, R. F. (2005). Categorical and continuous models of liability to externalizing disorders: A direct comparison in NESARC. *Archives of General Psychiatry, 62*(12), 1352–1359.

Marsh, H. W., Lüdtke, O., Trautwein, U., & Morin, A. J. S. (2009). Classical latent profile analysis of academic self-concept dimensions: Synergy of person- and variable-centered approaches to theoretical models of self-concept. *Structural Equation Modeling, 16*(2), 191–225.

Masyn, K., Henderson, C., & Greenbaum, P. (2010). Exploring the latent structures of psychological constructs in social development using the Dimensional-Categorical Spectrum. *Social Development, 19*(3), 470–493.

Masyn, K. E. (2009). Discrete-time survival factor mixture analysis for low-frequency recurrent event histories. *Research in Human Development, 6,* 165–194.

McCutcheon, A. C. (1987). *Latent class analysis.* Beverly Hills, CA: Sage.

McLachlan, G. & Peel, D. (2000). *Finite mixture models.* New York: John Wiley & Sons.

Miller, J. D., Kimmel, L., Hoffer, T. B., & Nelson, C. (2000). *Longitudinal study of American youth: User's manual.* Chicago, IL: Northwestern University, International Center for the Advancement of Scientific Literacy.

Muthén & Muthén. (September, 2010). *Bayesian analysis of latent variable models using Mplus.* (Technical Report, Version 4). Los Angeles, CA: Asparouhov, T., & Muthén, B. (2010).

Muthén, B. (2003). Statistical and substantive checking in growth mixture modeling. *Psychological Methods, 8,* 369–377.

Muthén, B. (2008). Latent variable hybrids: Overview of old and new models. In G. R. Hancock & K. M. Samuelsen (Eds.), *Advances in latent variable mixture models* (pp. 1–24). Charlotte, NC: Information Age Publishing.

Muthén, B. & Asparouhov, T. (2006). Item response mixture modeling: Application to tobacco dependence criteria. *Addictive Behaviors, 31,* 1050–1066.

Muthén, B. & Asparouhov, T. (2009). Growth mixture modeling: Analysis with non-Gaussian random effects. In G. Fitzmaurice, M. Davidian, G. Verbeke, & G. Molenberghs (Eds.), *Longitudinal data analysis* (pp. 143–165). Boca Raton: Chapman & Hall/CRC Press.

Muthén, B., Asparouhov, T., Hunter, A. & Leuchter, A. (2011). Growth modeling with non-ignorable dropout: Alternative analyses of the STAR*D antidepressant trial. *Psychological Methods, 16,* 17–33.

Muthén, B., & Muthén, L. K. (1998–2011). *Mplus* (Version 6.11) [Computer software]. Los Angeles, CA: Muthén & Muthén.

Muthén, B. & Shedden, K. (1999). Finite mixture modeling with mixture outcomes using the EM algorithm. *Biometrics, 55,* 463–469.

Nagin, D. S. (1999). Analyzing developmental trajectories: A semiparametric, group-based approach. *Psychological Methods, 4,* 139–157.

Nagin, D. S. (2005). *Group-based modeling of development.* Cambridge: Harvard University Press.

Nylund, K. (2007). *Latent transition analysis: Modeling extensions and an application to peer victimization.* Unpublished doctoral dissertation, University of California, Los Angeles.

Nylund, K., Asparouhov, T., & Muthén, B. (2007). Deciding on the number of classes in latent class analysis and growth mixture modeling: A Monte Carlo simulation study. *Structural Equation Modeling, 14,* 535–569.

Nylund, K. L., & Masyn, K. E. (May, 2008). *Covariates and latent class analysis: Results of a simulation study.* Paper presented at the meeting of the Society for Prevention Research, San Francisco, CA.

Nylund-Gibson, K., Graham, S., & Juvonen, J. (2010). An application of multilevel LCA to study peer victimization in middle school. *Advances and Applications in Statistical Sciences, 3*(2), 343–363.

Patterson, B., Dayton, C. M., & Graubard, B. (2002). Latent class analysis of complex survey data: application to dietary data. *Journal of the American Statistical Association, 97,* 721–729.

Pearson, K. (1894). Contributions to the mathematical theory of evolution. *Philosophical Transactions of the Royal Society of London (Series A), 185,* 71–110.

Petras, H. & Masyn, K. (2010). *General growth mixture analysis with antecedents and consequences of change.* In A. Piquero & D. Weisburd (Eds.), Handbook of Quantitative Criminology (pp. 69–100). New York: Springer.

Petras, H., Masyn, K., & Ialongo, N. (2011). The developmental impact of two first grade preventive interventions on aggressive/disruptive behavior in childhood and adolescence: An application of latent transition growth mixture modeling. *Prevention Science,* 12, 300–313.

Rabe-Hesketh, S., Skrondal, A., & Pickles, A. (2004). Generalized multilevel structural equation modelling. *Psychometrika, 69,* 167–190.

Ramaswamy, V., Desarbo, W. S., Reibstein, D. J., & Robinson, W. T. (1993). An empirical pooling approach for estimating marketing mix elasticities with PIMS data. *Marketing Science, 12*(1), 103–124.

Reaven. G. M., & Miller, R. G. (1979). An attempt to define the nature of chemical diabetes using a multidimensional analysis. *Diabetologia, 16*(1), 17–24.

Reboussin, B. A., Ip, E. H., & Wolfson, M. (2008), Locally dependent latent class models with covariates: an application to under-age drinking in the USA. *Journal of the Royal Statistical Society: Series A, 171,* 877–897.

Schafer, J. L. (1997). *Analysis of incomplete multivariate data.* London: Chapman & Hall.

Schwartz, G. (1978). Estimating the dimension of a model. *The Annals of Statistics, 6*, 461–464.

Skrondal, A. & Rabe-Hesketh, S. (2004). *Generalized latent variable modeling. Multilevel, longitudinal, and structural equation models.* London: Chapman Hall.

Soothill, K., Francis, B., Awwad, F., Morris, Thomas, & McIllmurray. (2004). Grouping cancer patients by psychosocial needs. *Journal of Psychosocial Oncology, 22*(2), 89–109.

Spearman, C. (1904). General intelligence, objectively determined and measured. *American Journal of Psychology, 15*, 201–293.

Tan, W. Y., & Chang, W. C. (1972). Some comparisons of the method of moments and the method of maximum likelihood in estimating parameters of a mixture of two normal densities. *Journal of the American Statistical Association, 67*(339), 702–708.

Thorndike, R. L. (1953). Who belong in the family? *Psychometrika, 18*(4), 267–276.

Titterington, D. M., Smith, A. F. M., & Makov, U. E. (1985). *Statistical analysis of finite mixture distributions.* Chichester, UK: John Wiley & Sons.

Tueller, S. J., Drotar, S. & Lubke, G. H. (2011). Addressing the problem of switched class labels in latent variable mixture model simulation studies. *Structural Equation Modeling, 18*, 110–131.

Van Horn, M. L., Jaki, T., Masyn, K., Ramey, S. L., Smith, J. A., & Antaramian, S. (2009). Assessing differential effects: Applying regression mixture models to identify variations in the influence of family resources on academic achievement. *Developmental Psychology, 45*(5), 1298–1313.

Vermunt, J. K. (1999). A general non parametric approach to the analysis of ordinal categorical data. *Sociological Methodology*,29, 197–221.

Vermunt, J. K., & Magidson, J. (2002). Latent class cluster analysis. In J. A. Hagenaars & A. L. McCutcheon (Eds.), *Applied latent class analysis* (pp. 89–106). Cambridge: Cambridge University Press.

Vermunt, J. K., & Magidson, J. (2005). *Latent GOLD 4.0 users's guide.* Belmont, MA: Statistical Innovations.

Vermunt, J. K., & McCutcheon, A. L. (2012). *An introduction to modern categorical data analysis.* Thousand Oaks, CA: Sage.

Vermunt, J.K., Van Ginkel, J. R., Van der Ark, and L. A., Sijtsma K. (2008). Multiple imputation of categorical data using latent class analysis. *Sociological Methodology, 33*, 369–297.

von Davier, M., & Yamamoto, K. (2006). Mixture distribution Rasch models and hybrid Rasch models. In M. von Davier & C. H. Carstensen (Eds.), *Multivariate and mixture distribution Rasch models* (pp. 99–115). New York: Springer-Verlag.

Weldon, W. F. R. (1893). On certain correlated variations in carcinus moenas. *Proceedings of the Royal Society of London*, 54, 318–329.

Yang, M. & Yu, N. (2005). Estimation of parameters in latent class models using fuzzy clustering algorithms. *European Journal of Operational Research, 160*, 515–531.

Yang, X. D., Shaftel, J., Glasnapp, D., & Poggio, J. (2005). Qualitative or quantitative differences? Latent class analysis of mathematical ability for special education students. *Journal of Special Education, 38*(4), 194–207.

Yung, Y. F. (1997). Finite mixtures in confirmatory factor analysis models. *Psychometrika, 62*, 297–330.

CHAPTER
26 Taxometrics

Theodore P. Beauchaine

Abstract

Taxometric methods were developed to ascertain which behavioral traits—particularly psychiatric syndromes—comprise discrete latent classes. Although individual differences in most forms of psychopathology are likely distributed along continua, knowing which are typolgal may have significant implications for diagnostic precision, treatment development, early identification of latent vulnerability to psychopathology, and improved understanding of etiology. In practice, however, distinguishing types from continua has proved difficult because most behavioral measures include several sources of error, which obscures true scores. Furthermore, conflicting results have often been reported by different research groups studying the same or similar traits. This has led some authors to question the utility of taxometrics. In this chapter, I (1) outline the conceptual bases of taxometrics, (2) provide descriptions of several taxometric procedures, (3) discuss strategies for selecting valid indicator variables, (4) provide brief example analyses, and (5) discuss common pitfalls of the taxometric approach. Despite certain limitations, careful attention to the types of variables subjected to taxometric analysis can produce valid and replicable results.

Key Words: Taxometrics, classification, MAMBAC, MAXCOV, MAXEIG, L-Mode

Behavioral scientists, particularly psychopathologists, have long debated the merits of categorical versus dimensional approaches to characterizing human behavior. At present, there is general consensus that many forms of psychopathology reflect extreme expressions of a limited number of continuously distributed individual differences (*see* Beauchaine, 2003, 2007; Beauchaine & Marsh, 2006; Cuthbert, 2005; Kendell, 1989; Krueger, Watson, & Barlow, 2005; Meehl, 1995a; Widiger, 2007; Widiger & Samuel, 2005). Nevertheless, the *Diagnostic and Statistical Manual of Mental Disorders* (DSM; American Psychiatric Association, 2000), usually the sole source of diagnostic criteria in applied settings, specifies categorical cutoffs when symptom thresholds are exceeded. Thus, one either has or does not have a disorder, which determines whether treatment is necessary, whether insurance can be billed, and whether an individual qualifies for special services under federal and state law. This has created a clear disconnect between current theories of psychopathology that emphasize individual differences in dimensional traits and the use of dichotomous diagnostic thresholds. Indeed, considerable dissatisfaction with the strictly categorical approach to diagnosis has been expressed in anticipation of the forthcoming *DSM-V* (e.g., Clark, 2005; First, 2005; Helzer et al., 2008; Kendall & Drabick, 2010; Krueger, Watson et al., 2005; Kupfer, 2005).

Dissatisfaction with the *DSM* has led some to question the validity of *all* categorical models of psychopathology, despite evidence that some psychiatric classes, such as schizophrenia, endogenous depression, and a limited number of others, are probably distributed as latent typologies (*see* Ambrosini, Bennett, Cleland, & Haslam, 2002; Beach & Amir, 2003; Beauchaine, Lenzenweger,

& Waller, 2008; Blanchard, Gangestad, Brown, & Horan, 2000; Fossati et al., 2005; Golden & Meehl, 1979; Grove et al., 1987; Haslam & Beck, 1994; Korfine & Lenzenweger, 1995; Lenzenweger, 1999, 2010; Lenzenweger & Korfine, 1995; Munson et al., 2008; Richey et al., 2009; Schmidt et al., 2007; Tyrka et al., 1995; Tyrka, Haslam, & Cannon, 1995). Accordingly, the proper question is probably not whether categorical or dimensional models of psychopathology are correct. Rather, we should seek to determine which psychiatric syndromes reflect categories and which reflect continua—even if the former are likely to be rare (*see also* Beauchaine & Marsh, 2006; Flanagan & Blashfield, 2002; Meehl, 1995a).

For psychiatric syndromes that are distributed typologically, ascertaining correct diagnostic boundaries may advance our understanding of etiology, improve treatment efficacy, and provide for prevention programs that target the most vulnerable members of high-risk populations (*see* Beauchaine, 2003, 2007; Beauchaine & Beach, 2006; Beauchaine & Marsh, 2006; Meehl, 1992; 1995a). For example, genetic risk for schizophrenia, expressed as schizotypy (Meehl, 1962), has emerged in numerous studies as a discretely distributed trait that affects about 5% of the population (*see* Beauchaine, Lenzenweger et al. 2008; Lenzenweger, 1999; Lenzenweger, McLachlan, & Rubin, 2007). Through taxometric analyses of carefully chosen behavioral, cognitive, and neuromotor variables, those who are genetically vulnerable can be identified *before* the expression of full-blown schizophrenia (Erlenmeyer-Kimling, Golden, & Cornblatt, 1989; Tyrka et al., 1995). These individuals can then be assigned to prevention programs that substantially reduce future risk of psychosis (*see* Beauchaine & Marsh, 2006).

Given space constraints, I will not discuss the practical advantages of identifying discrete psychiatric syndromes further. Interested readers are referred elsewhere for more thorough accounts (Beauchaine 2003, 2007; Beauchaine & Marsh, 2006; Meehl, 1995a; Ruscio, Haslam, & Ruscio, 2006; Ruscio & Ruscio, 2008; Waller & Meehl, 1998). In the remainder of this chapter, I present descriptions of a limited number of commonly used taxometric methods and provide examples of their execution. Before doing so, however, I discuss measurement imprecision, which is usually not considered adequately by those who conduct taxometric analyses but which limits the power of all inferential methods, including taxometrics.

The Problem With Imprecise Measures

Taxometric methods comprise a set of several procedures—some of which are closely related and others which are not—developed by Meehl and colleagues (*see* Meehl, 1995a) to search for disjunctions in the structure of data (e.g., means, covariances, eigenvalues). For reasons articulated below, these structural disjunctions may indicate discrete latent subgroups within a larger multivariate distribution (Grove & Meehl, 1993; Meehl, 1999, Meehl & Yonce, 1994; 1996; Waller & Meehl, 1998). In the nomenclature of taxometrics, when latent typologies are found, the smaller base rate group, which in psychopathology research is almost always the diagnostic group, is referred to as the *taxon*, and the larger base rate group is referred to as the *complement class* (*see* Fig. 26.1).

As articulated by Meehl (1973; 1995a), we usually cannot observe the causes of mental disorders directly. As a result, we must infer psychopathology from observed behavioral indicators (symptoms) and other markers (signs) of latent (unobserved) psychopathological traits. Collectively, these symptoms (e.g., anhedonia) and signs (e.g., eye tracking dysfunction) comprise the *phenotype* of a disorder (e.g., schizotypy). However, because symptoms and signs are far removed from the genetic, neural, and physiological substrates of psychopathology (*see* Beauchaine, 2009; Beauchaine & Marsh, 2006), they carry significant measurement error. Manifest indicators are therefore almost always imprecise markers of latent traits. This is especially so when symptoms are rated on Likert scales, which carry several systematic sources of measurement error, including response biases (e.g., Macmillan & Creelman, 1990; Rajendar, 1996) and halo effects (e.g., Saal, Downey, & Lahey, 1980) In fact, nearly half of the variance in Likert ratings may be attributable to measurement error (*see* Hoyt & Kerns, 1999).

Figure 26.2 illustrates the effects of error variance on a two-group latent typology. The top panel depicts a discrete dichotomous distribution that is measured without error (i.e., perfect precision), with 500 members in each class. Near-perfect measurement precision is expected when genotyping a single locus disorder such as Huntington's chorea (although the population proportion would not be 50:50). The middle panel depicts the same discrete variable when assessed using a *reliable* phenotypic indicator. Because phenotypes are almost always measured with error, observed scores are likely to overlap across groups. Note, however, that the middle distribution of scores is still

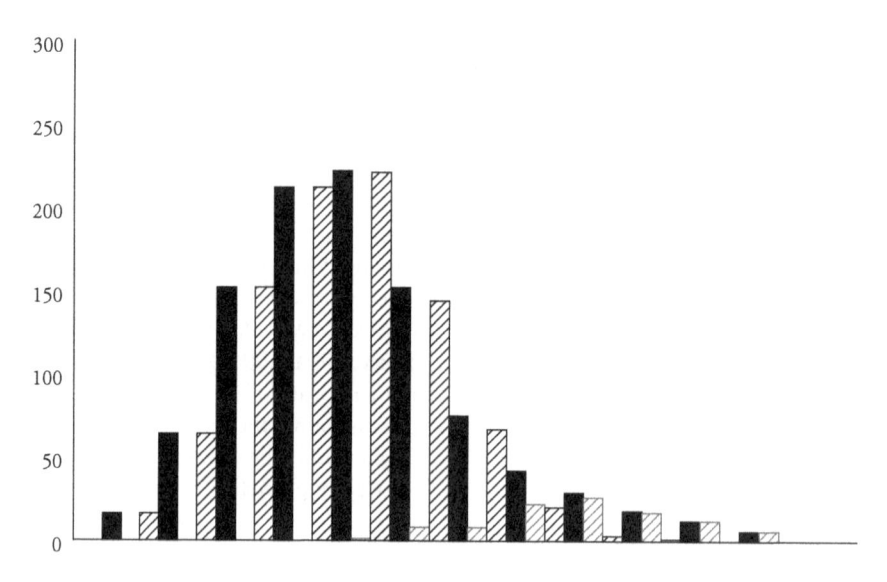

Figure 26.1 Mixture of two normally distributed groups of $n = 950$ and $n = 50$. The larger group (Dark hatched bars) comprises the complement class, and the smaller group (light hatching) comprises the taxon. Note that although these two distributions are separated by 3.0 *SD*, there is no evidence of bimodality in the combined sample, which is continuous yet skewed (solid bars). Thus, bimodality is an extremely weak criterion for inferring latent subgroups within a distribution.
Adapted with permission from Beauchaine and Marsh (2006), p. 938. Copyright 2006, Wiley.

bimodal, suggesting considerable measurement precision, despite some degree of normally distributed error around the mean of each group. Error in symptom expression is introduced at many levels of analysis between genes and behavior (*see*, e.g., Lenzenweger, 2004). In the middle panel of Figure 26.2, the effect size (Cohen's *d*) separating the distributions is 4.0, a very large effect for psychological research (Cohen, 1988). For variables measured on rating scales, additional error variance is introduced, resulting in much smaller effect sizes. In the bottom panel of Figure 26.2, an additional 50% error variance has been added, which is not uncommon for Likert-type data (Hoyt & Kerns, 1999). The mixed distribution appears normal, although it contains two discrete groups separated by $d = 1.6$. This example illustrates why detecting taxa can be so difficult (Ruscio & Ruscio, 2004a) and why bimodality is a poor criterion for inferring latent typologies (Beauchaine & Beauchaine, 2002; Waller & Meehl, 1998). It should also be mentioned that the opposite problem—inducing bimodality into a dimensional distribution of scores—can result from stereotypes and response biases of raters (Beauchaine & Waters, 2003).

Taxometric Methods

With problems imposed by imprecise measures in mind, I now describe several of the most commonly used taxometric procedures, and provide some example analyses. Although these analyses are conducted on simulated data for clarity of presentation, I use the example of schizotypy, which has emerged repeatedly as a discrete latent class in different labs, and with different although carefully chosen indicators (*see* Beauchaine, Lenzenweger et al., 2008; Blanchard et al., 2000; Erlenmeyer-Kimling et al., 1989; Golden & Meehl, 1979; Horan, Blanchard, Gangestad, & Kwapil, 2004; Korfine & Lenzenweger, 1995; Lenzenweger, 1999; Lenzenweger & Korfine, 1992, 1995; Lenzenweger et al., 2007; Tyrka, Cannon et al., 1995; Tyrka, Haslam et al., 1995).

Mean Above Minus Below a Cut

Mean above minus below a cut (MAMBAC; Meehl, 1995a; Meehl & Yonce, 1994), which operates on variable pairs, is among the most commonly used taxometric procedures (Haslam & Kim, 2002). As depicted in left panel of Figure 26.3, one variable (*x*) is first sorted, which partially sorts the other variable (*y*), provided that the variables are correlated, a necessary but insufficient condition for a latent taxon to be identified (*see* below; Meehl & Yonce, 1996). Next, a sliding "cut" is moved along *x* (neuromotor performance), step-by-step, and the mean of *y* (eye tracking dysfunction) is calculated both above and below this cut. At each increasing value

MAMBAC function. If there is no taxon, or if the effect size is inadequate for either or both variables, then the MAMBAC function is often dish-shaped. This is shown in the right panel of Figure 26.3, using low energy (x) and poor concentration (y) as indicators. Although both of these symptoms are common among those with schizophrenia and schizophrenia liability, they also characterize many other disorders and are therefore not good candidates for taxometric analysis. Typically, results from MAMBAC are compared with results from other taxometric procedures, which provide corroboration for any taxonic inferences (see Performing a Taxometric Analysis, below).

Maximum Covariance

Maximum covariance (MAXCOV; Meehl, 1973; Meehl & Yonce, 1996; Waller & Meehl, 1998), which operates on variable triplets, is among the most commonly used and thoroughly researched taxometric procedures (Haslam & Kim, 2002). Maximum covariance evaluates the covariance between two variables in successive windows of a third variable. For example, the top panel of Figure 26.4 depicts a MAXCOV plot of the same fictitious data used above (neuromotor performance and eye tracking dysfunction), with the addition of a third variable, sustained attention deficit (z). Here, the covariance of neuromotor performance (x) and eye tracking dysfunction (y) is computed across the range of sustained attention deficit (z), within 16 successive intervals. As shown in the top panel of Figure 26.4, given a latent taxon and adequate effects sizes separating the two groups on *all three* variables, a marked peak appears in the covariance function. The exact location of the peak indicates the value of sustained attention deficit (z) that best differentiates between the taxon and complement class. In performing MAXCOV, all trivariate combinations of variables are subjected to analysis, and the consistency of results is evaluated (see below). If there is no latent taxon, or if one or more indicators are of insufficient effect size, then the MAXCOV function yields no peak, as shown in the bottom panel of Figure 26.4.

Given a latent taxon, the location of the MAXCOV peak shifts with differing base rates. When the base rate is 0.50, the MAXCOV function peaks near the mode of the cut variable (z). With lower taxon base rates, as in the top panel of Figure 26.4, the peak shifts toward higher z-values. At very low taxon base rates, a steep rise in the covariance function (rather than a peak) is observed at the right end of the plot.

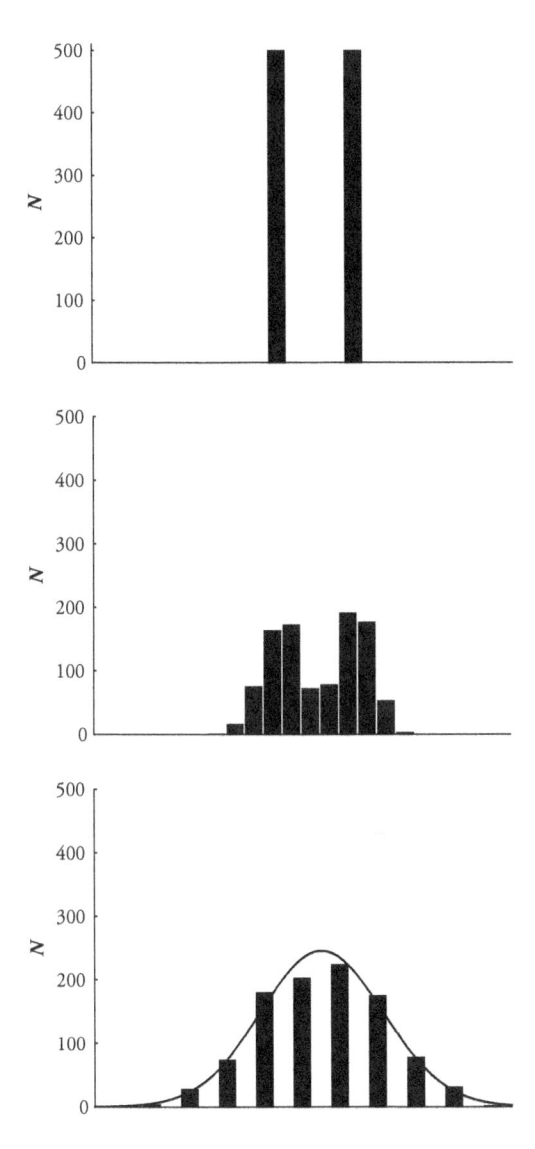

Figure 26.2 The effect of measurement error on observed scores of a discretely distributed latent variable. The top panel represents an evenly distributed dichotomous trait in a sample of 1000. This assumes near perfect measurement precision, such as that observed when genotyping a trait with a single locus. The middle panel depicts a distribution of the same trait when assessed by very precise phenotypes, or symptoms, which always carry at least some measurement error. The bottom panel includes an additional 50% error variance, which often characterizes imprecise Likert measurement. Despite containing two discrete groups, the bottom distribution is unimodal and near normal. All figures have equivalent x-axis scaling.
From Beauchaine (2007), p. 657. Copyright 2007, Erlbaum.

of neuromotor performance, the mean of eye tracking dysfunction above the cut is subtracted from the mean of eye tracking dysfunction below the cut, and all values are plotted. If a latent taxon exists *and* the effect size separating the group means is adequate for both variables, then a peak appears in the

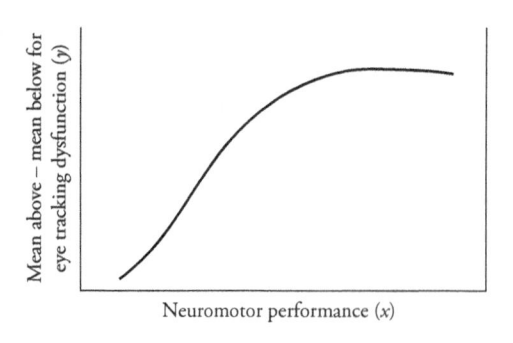

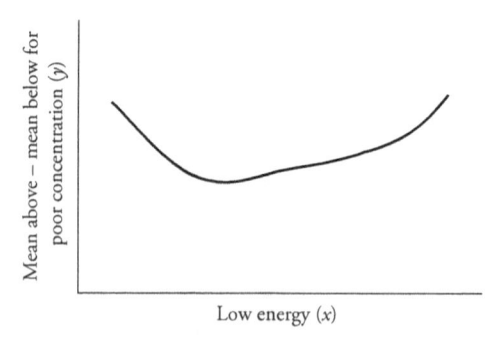

Figure 26.3 Examples of MAMBAC using taxonic data, such as that derived from markers of schizotypy (left panel) and dimensional data, derived from symptoms that are not specific to schizotypy (right panel). The left panel depicts a smoothed MAMBAC plot from data comprising two groups of $n = 100$ (schizotypy taxon) and $n = 900$ (complement class), with an effect size of $d = 2.0$. The right panel depicts a MAMBAC analysis of continuous normal distributions of $n = 1000$.

Under such circumstances, distinguishing between a taxon-induced rise to the right and an upward inflection caused by variable skew or some other type of measurement-induced nonlinearity can be difficult, which is why consistency tests, simulation techniques, and fit indices are important (see Assessing Fit, below).

Maximum covariance and several other taxometric procedures, including MAXEIG, L-Mode (Waller & Meehl, 1998; see below), and MAX-SLOPE (see Beauchaine, 2007), all capitalize on larger covariances between groups than within groups (i.e., local independence) toward detecting latent classes. Accordingly, further description of the mathematical underpinnings of MAXCOV is warranted. Given large enough effect sizes separating the taxon group and complement class, moderate within-groups correlations, and two valid indicators of taxon group membership, x and y, the between-groups indicator covariance [$cov(xy)$] will exceed the within-groups covariances [$(cov)_t(xy)$, $(cov)_c(xy)$], as outlined in the General Covariance Mixture Theorem (GCMT; Meehl, 1995a, p. 271; Meehl & Yonce, 1996, p. 1097):

$$cov(xy) = p(cov)_t(xy) + q(cov)_c(xy)$$
$$+ pq(\bar{x}_t - \bar{x}_c)(\bar{y}_t - \bar{y}_c), \quad (1)$$

where $cov(xy)$ represents the covariance of variables x and y, p represents the proportion of taxon group members in the mixed sample, q represents the proportion of non-taxon group members in the mixed sample, $\bar{x}_i$ represents the mean of variable x in group i, $\bar{y}_i$ represents the mean of variable y in group i, and t and c represent the taxon group and complement class, respectively.

The logic behind the GCMT is presented in Figure 26.5, which depicts a scatter plot of two variables, (x) and (y), both of which mark a latent taxon. As indicated by the upward slope of the regression line, the two variables are correlated. However, this correlation is imparted solely as a result of mixing two discrete groups, indicated by dots ($n = 500$) and open squares ($n = 500$). Within each group, the correlation between x and y is zero, as indicated by the smoothed regression line. Maximum covariance and other taxometric procedures provide estimates of several parameters describing the taxon and complement class distributions. These include the taxon base rate, the sample sizes of the taxon group and complement class, the hitmax value, and the false–positive and false–negative rates of group assignments (see Meehl & Yonce, 1996).

Maximum Eigenvalue

Maximum eigenvalue (MAXEIG) is a multivariate extension of MAXCOV that operates on any number of putative indicators greater than three[1]. One variable, designated the input indicator, is parsed into successive overlapping windows, and a variance–covariance matrix is computed within each. Variances (diagonals) of the variance–covariance matrix are replaced with zeros, and a principal components analysis (PCA) is computed. The first eigenvalue from each PCA is then extracted and plotted across windows. As with MAXCOV, a peak appears in the MAXEIG function if a taxon is present and the effect size is adequate for all indicators. This peak emerges because larger eigenvalues indicate higher correlations among variables. Once again, these correlations peak at the hitmax value—the point that best differentiates between groups (see Fig. 26.6).

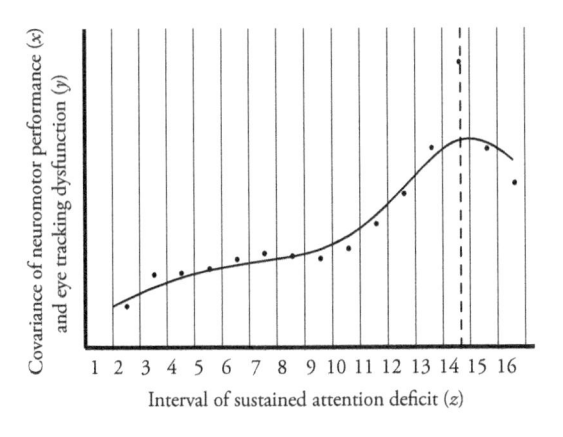

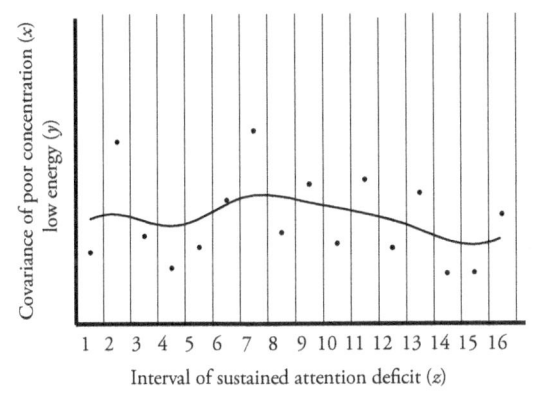

Figure 26.4 Examples of MAXCOV with taxonic data, such as that derived from markers of schizotypy (top panel) and dimensional data, derived from symptoms that are not specific to schizotypy (bottom panel). The top panel includes groups of $n = 100$ (schizotypy taxon) and $n = 900$ (complement class), with an effect size of $d = 2.0$. The bottom panel depicts a MAXCOV analysis of continuous normal data ($n = 1000$). In the case of schizotypy (top panel), the covariance between neuromotor performance (x) and eye tracking dysfunction (y), calculated within 16 adjacent intervals of sustained attention deficit (z), peaks at the value of sustained attention deficit (z) that best differentiates between groups. This is referred to as the hitmax value (dashed line). In the dimensional data (bottom panel), the covariances of poor concentration (x) and low energy (y) fluctuate unsystematically across levels of thought problems (z). These variables do not mark the schizotypy taxon.
Adapted from Beauchaine (2007), p. 659. Copyright 2007, Erlbaum.

In recent years, MAXEIG (Waller & Meehl, 1998) has become quite popular in taxometrics research, following suggestions by some that it become the preferred taxometric method (e.g., Ruscio & Ruscio, 2004a). However, we (Beauchaine, 2007; Beauchaine & Marsh, 2006; Beauchaine, Lenzenweger et al., 2008) suggest using multiple taxometric procedures in any analysis, and examining the convergence of several parameters (e.g., base rates, Bayesian-estimated probabilities of taxon group membership, taxon and complement class means, etc.) across procedures, a practice Meehl (1995) referred to as consistency testing (*see* Consistency Tests, below).

Latent Mode Factor Analysis

Latent mode factor analysis (L-Mode; Waller & Meehl, 1998), which has become popular only recently, requires three or more indicators. These are factor analyzed, and the first and therefore largest factor is extracted. Factor scores are then computed for all observations using the Bartlett (1937) method, and factor score densities are plotted. A unimodal distribution suggests dimensional latent structure, whereas bimodality suggests a latent taxon (*see* Fig. 26.7). Although factor analysis has been used traditionally to identify latent dimensions (traits), when covariance among indicators is imparted by mixing discrete groups (*see* above), a dichotomous latent factor emerges (Waller & Meehl, 1998). Locations of the modes can be used to estimate the taxon base rate, taxon and complement class means, and so forth. To date, the operating characteristics of L-Mode have not been evaluated to the extent of other taxometric methods. However, at least one recent Monte Carlo study has suggested that L-Mode can be effective in distinguishing between dimensional and categorical latent structure (Walters et al., 2010).

Performing a Taxometric Analysis
Selecting Suitable Indicators

An important initial step in conducting a taxometric analysis—although one that is often underappreciated—is selecting reliable and valid indicators that contain minimal measurement error. Ideally, this includes planning the taxometric analysis before data are collected. To date, many if not most taxometric analyses have been conducted on large data sets of convenience that were collected to address a different research question. This can be highly problematic because variables that are suited for other research purposes may not be precise enough for a taxometric analysis (*see* Beauchaine, 2007; Beauchaine, Lenzenweger et al., 2008). As emphasized above, Likert-type data may contain up to 50% measurement error, which is typically adequate for latent variable modeling, but obscures discrete latent structure in taxometric analyses. As a result, using such variables is likely to result in false–negative errors in which valid taxa go undetected (Meehl, 1995a)[2], or in false–positive errors

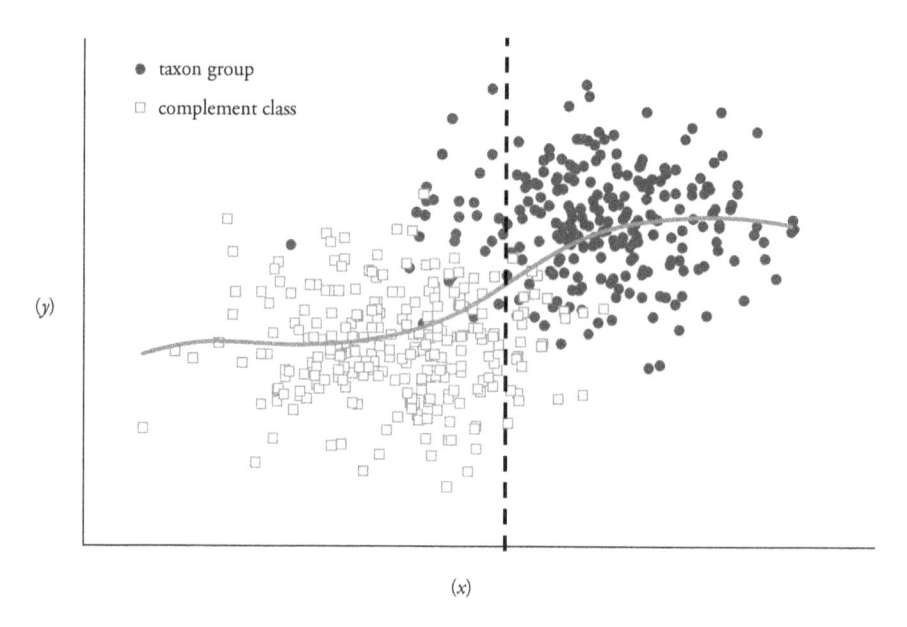

Figure 26.5 Scatterplot of two indicators (x, y) of a taxon group ($n = 500$), indicated by dots, and a complement class ($n = 500$), indicated by open squares. The groups are separated by effect sizes of $d = 2.0$ on both variables. Note that the slope of the smoothed regression line is flat within groups (local independence) but increases near the point along x that best differentiates between the taxon group and complement class. This point is referred to as the hitmax value, indicated by the vertical dashed line.

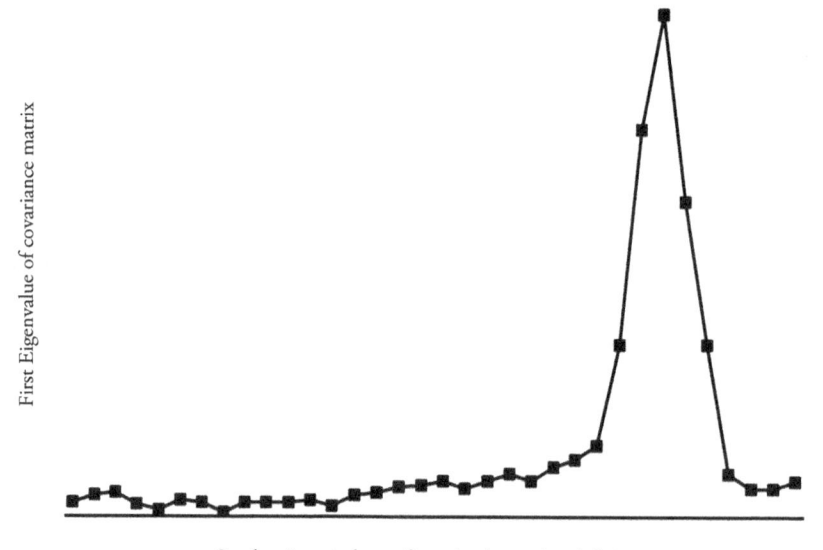

Figure 26.6 MAXEIG plot derived from fictitious distributions of neuromotor performance, eye tracking dysfunction, working memory impairment, and sustained attention deficit. Sustained attention deficit served as the input (x) variable, along the full range of which first Eigenvalues from the neuromotor performance, eye tracking dysfunction, working memory impairment variance-covariance matrix were plotted in successive moving windows. The Eigenvalue function is maximized at the value of sustained attention deficit that best discriminates between the taxon group ($n = 900$) and the taxon group ($n = 100$).

in which spurious taxa are detected (Beauchaine & Waters, 2003), depending on whether the source of measurement error is random or systematic. Although considerable attention has been paid to the possibility of false–positives in taxometrics research (e.g., Ruscio, 2007; Ruscio, Ruscio, & Keane, 2004; Widiger, 2001), false–negatives may be more likely if measures are imprecise (Beauchaine & Marsh,

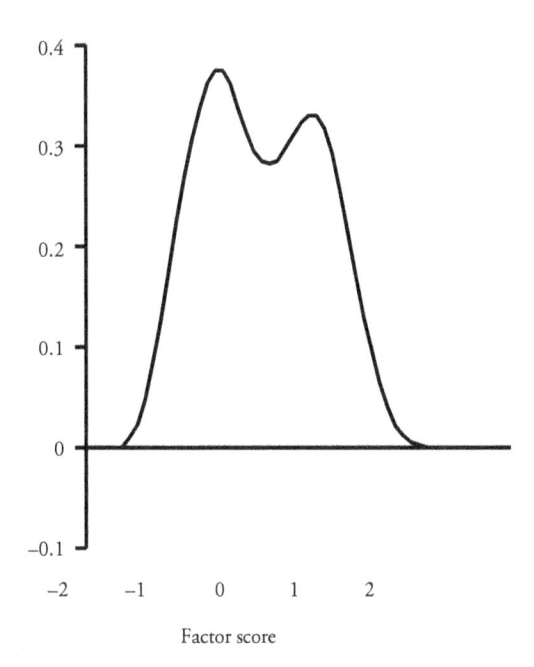

Figure 26.7 L-Mode factor score density plot computed from fictitious taxonic data. The two modes suggest a single taxon and complement class. Additional modes are observed when more latent classes are present (Walters, McGrath, & Knight, 2010). Dimensional data yield a single mode.

2006; Beauchaine, Lenzenweger et al., 2008). I address both types of error below.

False–Positives. Several authors have warned against identifying spurious latent classes in taxometrics studies (e.g., Ruscio, 2007; Ruscio & Ruscio, 2000; 2004a; Ruscio et al., 2004; Widiger, 2001). Sometimes referred to as pseudotaxonicity (Brown, 2001; Meehl, 1996), these errors may arise from either (1) inappropriate sampling (Grove, & Tellegen, 1991), or (2) biases in rating scale data (Beauchaine & Waters, 2003). Although nonrepresentative sampling is problematic for any inferential statistic, one practice in particular has resulted in identifying several spurious taxa. This involves recruitment of clinical samples, and mixing their psychopathology scores with those collected from normal controls. Based on positive results in taxometric analyses, evidence for typologies of psychopathology has been claimed. For example, at least two taxometric studies have appeared in which subtypes of eating disorders have been asserted. In both cases, symptoms of those anorexia, bulimia, and/or binge-eating disorder were mixed with symptoms of normal controls (Gleaves, Lowe, Green, Cororve, & Williams, 2000; Williamson et al., 2002). However, conducting taxometric analyses with bimodal samples is tautological. As long as the indicators are valid, such an analysis will identify a latent taxon *every time*. Testing taxonic hypotheses requires that participants be recruited *representatively* across all symptom levels. Taxometric analyses of eating disorder symptoms collected from representative samples yield no evidence for latent taxonic structure (Tylka & Subich, 2003).

Cognitive response biases can also induce spurious latent structure into a data set. For example, we (Beauchaine & Waters, 2003) manipulated raters' beliefs about a construct as dimensional versus categorical. Doing so imparted latent taxonic structure into observers' Likert ratings of that construct. This is consistent with a long line of research demonstrating that attitudes and beliefs are susceptible to categorical cognitive biases whereby humans implicitly dichotomize or otherwise group continua and classify their observations based on pre-existing opinions (Cantor & Genero, 1986; Cantor & Mischel, 1979, Malt, 1993; Rosch & Lloyd, 1978; Semin & Rosch, 1981; Simon, Pham, Le, & Holyoak, 2001). Such findings, combined with the problems noted above regarding measurement error in Likert scales, suggest that we should (1) be conservative about inferring latent taxonic structure from strictly rating scale data, and (2) plan which measures we will subject to taxometric analyses *before* we collect data. Our group has suggested that variables be selected from multiple levels of analysis, including biological markers/endophenotypes that are often measured with less error than Likert scales and are usually not subject to rater biases (Beauchaine, Lenzenweger et al., 2008). For example, the schizotypy taxon has been identified using objective measures, including eye-tracking dysfunction, sustained visual attention deficits, neuromotor performance abnormalities, and cognitive dysfunction (e.g., Erlenmeyer-Kimling et al., 1989; Lenzenweger et al., 2007). Therefore, the taxon cannot be attributed to any of several sources of error contained in rating scale measures. I am not suggesting that Likert data be off limits to those conducting taxometric analyses. Rather, such measures should be combined with other types of data. Although we first identified this issue nearly a decade ago (Beauchaine & Waters, 2003), most taxometric studies are still conducted exclusively with rating scales (*see* Beauchaine, Lenzenweger et al., 2008; Beauchaine & Marsh, 2006).

False–Positives. As noted above, many authors have warned against identifying spurious taxa (Beauchaine & Waters, 2003; Miller, 1996; Ruscio, 2007; Ruscio & Ruscio, 2002, 2004a; Widiger,

2001). Few, however, have considered false–negatives (Beauchaine, Lenzenweger et al., 2008). This is worrisome for a number of reasons. First, because most data collected by social scientists contains considerable measurement error (*see* above), obtaining indicators of sufficient effect size can be difficult. As a result, many taxometric analyses are underpowered (*see* Fig. 26.1). Large Monte Carlo studies conducted by Meehl and others have indicated consistently that taxometric methods, including MAMBAC, MAXCOV, and MAXEIG, cannot uncover latent taxa when effect sizes separating the taxon group mean from the complement mean is below about $d = 1.2$ (Beauchaine & Beauchaine, 2002; Meehl, 1995a; *see also* Ruscio, 2007). This is *double* the average effect size observed in psychological research (Cohen, 1988). Thus, if a latent taxon is separated from the complement class by $d = 1.0$ on all indicators, then the taxon will go undetected even though this is a large effect size (i.e., $d > 0.80$) by psychological standards. Yet to conclude that the analyzed construct is dimensional would be incorrect, amounting to a Type II error.

Although we have warned against this elsewhere (Beauchaine, 2003; Beauchaine & Marsh, 2006; Beauchaine, Lenzenweger et al., 2008; Waters & Beauchaine, 2003), few have considered the possibility of Type II errors in taxometrics research. However, taxometric methods search for discrete latent structure. When such structure is not found, there are many possible causes—including inadequate power, invalid indicators, and so forth—only one of which is dimensional latent structure (Beauchaine, 2007; Ruscio, 2007). Thus, the effective null hypothesis is one of dimensional latent structure, whereas the effective alternative hypothesis is one of discrete latent structure. This parallels null hypothesis significance testing almost perfectly: When the effect size separating the alternative distribution (taxon group) from the null distribution (complement class) is insufficient, real effects go undetected. Concluding that a negative result from a taxometric analysis suggests a continuous distribution is therefore equivalent to proving the null; it is always possible (even if unlikely) that more precise indicators would reveal a latent taxon. I am not suggesting that such interpretations are never warranted. Rather, those who conduct taxometric analyses should be exceedingly careful in selecting indicators that have enough precision to find a taxon, if one exists.

Indicator Correlations. For a variable to be considered a candidate indicator of a putative latent taxon, it must be correlated with all other indicators in the analysis, although not too strongly. The reason for this requirement is outlined above, where I describe the GCMT (Equation 1), and illustrated in Figure 26.5. Here, it is important to distinguish between within-group and between-groups correlations. Within-group correlation refers to the correlation of x and y within the taxon group and complement class. This was referred to by Meehl as *nuisance correlation*. In contrast, between-groups correlation is induced by mixing discrete groups, as described above. This is the correlation of primary interest when conducting a taxometric analysis. An assumption of both taxometrics and latent class analysis (LCA) is that nuisance correlations are zero (local independence) and that any observed correlation is imparted by mixing latent subgroups. Nevertheless, taxometric methods can be used effectively with nuisance correlations approaching .30, provided indicator correlations in the mixed sample exceed this value (Beauchaine & Beauchaine, 2002; Meehl, 1995b). Thus, although indicator variables can be correlated in the absence of discrete latent structure, taxa cannot be detected in the absence of at least moderate indicator correlations. To date, this requirement has been overlooked by many psychopathology researchers, who often subject all theoretically relevant symptoms to analysis, without examining variable correlations.

There is no specific minimum for the magnitude of indicator correlations when performing a taxometric analysis. Given a latent taxon, expected indicator correlations depend on the taxon base rate, the effect size separating the taxon group and complement class, and observed nuisance correlations. Meehl and Yonce (1996, p. 1147) have provided a table of expected indicator correlations in which these parameters are varied. This table should be examined when planning a taxometric analysis and when selecting putative indicators. Furthermore, correlation matrices should be presented in all taxometrics studies, so readers can determine whether indicators are correlated sufficiently.

Winnowing Indicators

As we have noted elsewhere (Beauchaine, 2007; Beauchaine & Marsh, 2006), even when a latent taxon is present and careful attention is paid to selecting valid and correlated indicators, some are usually more effective than others in distinguishing between the taxon and complement class. This occurs for two primary reasons. First, by its very nature, taxometrics is a bootstrapping procedure through which we seek to uncover discrete latent (unobserved) structure, if any, by examining interrelations among imprecise measures (Beauchaine, 2007; Beauchaine, Lenzenweger et al., 2008; Meehl, 1995a). There are no gold standards or litmus tests for confirming the validity of particular symptoms as markers of a discrete latent class. Thus, we do not know ahead of time which indicators will mark a taxon, if one is present, and which indicators will not. Because taxa cannot be observed directly, the validity of an indicator is only revealed based on its performance with other candidate variables. If a variable performs poorly vis-à-vis other variables in the analysis, then it should be eliminated from the indicator pool. As demonstrated below, retaining such indicators often results in false–negative outcomes (Beauchaine & Marsh, 2006).

Here, I provide an instructive example adapted from Beauchaine (2007). If I have eight indicators available for analysis, and six are characterized by large effect sizes ($d = 2.0$) yet two are characterized by small effect sizes by taxometrics standards ($d = 0.8$), a real taxon may go undetected. For illustrative purposes, I present taxometric analyses of an artificial data set containing 425 complement class and 75 taxon group members. Thus, the taxon base rate is $\frac{75}{425+75} = 0.15$. As proposed by Meehl (1995a, 1999) and implemented by others (Beauchaine & Waters, 2003; Waller, Putnam, & Carlson, 1996), the first step in winnowing indicators is to subject all pairwise combinations of variables to a series of MAMBAC analyses. The resulting MAMBAC plots can then be arranged by rows and columns and examined for evidence of discrete latent structure (see Beauchaine & Waters, 2003). The number of plots is given by $2\binom{k}{2} = 2\binom{6}{2} = 56$ combinations. These plots are presented for the fictitious data I created in Figure 26.8.

An even casual inspection reveals that most of the plots are peaked and of roughly the same shape, suggesting a latent taxon. However, the columns of plots for Variables 1 and 2 are more consistent with dimensional latent structure. These are the variables of smaller effect size ($d = 0.8$). Given that this effect size is too small for detecting latent taxa, the plots are not right-peaked as expected for a low base rate taxon. In contrast, each and every plot in which variables of large effect size ($d = 2.0$) are paired yields a right-end peak, corresponding with the low base rate taxon. For reasons that are not entirely clear, flat MAMBAC plots are observed when the smaller effect size indicators are used as output variables in computing the MAMBAC functions (Columns 1 and 2), yet not when they are used as the sort variable (Rows 1 and 2). Nonetheless, the matrix of MAMBAC plots indicate clearly which variables are valid indicators of the latent taxon. In this example, Variables 1 and 2 must be eliminated from further analysis, or the taxon may not be detected in subsequent analyses (see below). If, at this step, none of the indicators yields consistently peaked MAMBAC plots, further analyses should be abandoned.

Winnowing indicators is an extremely important step since further analyses using MAXCOV, MAXEIG, and/or L-Mode, which operate on more than two variables at a time (see above), will not detect a latent taxon if even one or two variables are of insufficient effect size (see Beauchaine, 2007; Beauchaine & Marsh, 2006, p. 948). Thus, if no winnowing procedure is used, the likelihood of a false–negative outcome is inflated considerably. Importantly, I am not advocating a process in which any and all available indicators are subjected to winnowing. Rather, the procedure should be applied to variables that are selected carefully based on theory.

It should be noted that some have criticized indicator winnowing, suggesting that it increases the likelihood of identifying spurious taxa (Widiger, 2001). In large part, these criticisms follow from concerns about cognitive biases in human thinking that produce artificially dichotomous judgments about observed events (see Beauchaine & Waters, 2003). When rating scale data reflect such biases, winnowing may indeed increase the likelihood of a false–positive finding. Yet when indicators are chosen from multiple levels of analysis, as suggested in this chapter, and when several taxometric procedures produce consistently similar latent parameter estimates (e.g., base rates, hitmax values, etc.), Type I error rates are exceedingly low. As noted elsewhere (e.g., Beauchaine, 2007; Beauchaine & Marsh, 2006; Jevons, 1958; Salmon, 1984; 1989; Meehl, 1995a; Whewell, 1966), the probability that several objective indicators from multiple levels of analysis will yield highly consistent base rate, hitmax, taxon group mean, and non-taxon group mean values using multiple taxometric methods is near zero if no taxon is present. Furthermore, winnowing is similar to procedures followed by psychometricians during scale construction. In this context, items are removed from the initial item pool if they yield low α coefficients and are therefore invalid (see Nunnally & Bernstein, 1994). Thus, invalid items are therefore not retained when constructing a scale to assess a

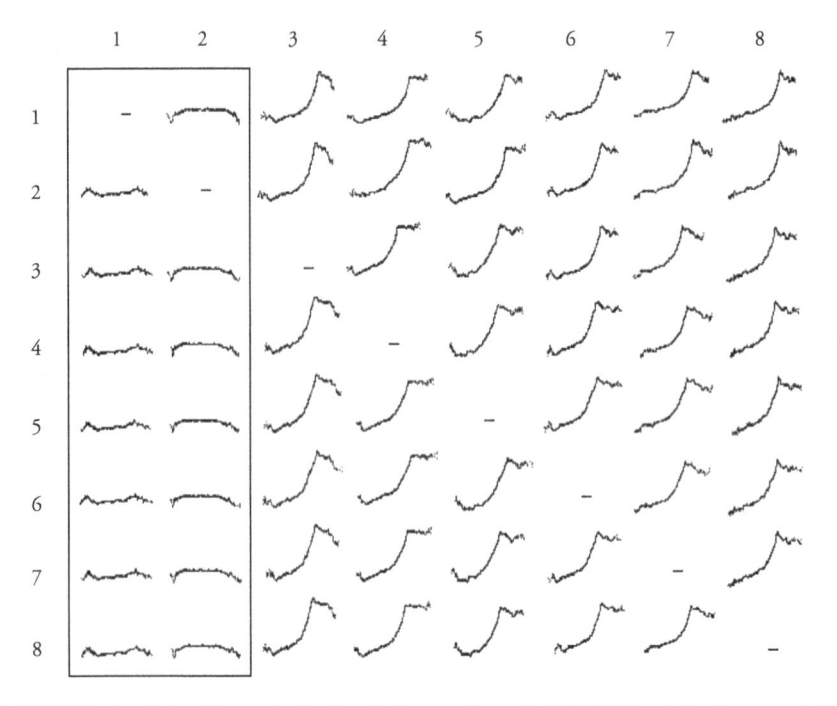

Figure 26.8 MAMBAC plots derived from eight fictitious indicators. For each MAMBAC analysis, the sort variable is represented across rows and the output variable is represented down columns. Variables 3 through 8 are characterized by and effect size $d = 2.0$. Plots for MAMBAC analyses using these variables show a consistent peak, suggesting a moderate base rate taxon (the true base rate is 0.15). In contrast, Variables 1 and 2 are characterized by an effect size of 0.8, which is not adequate for detecting latent taxa (*see* text). These variables should therefore not be included in further analyses.

continuously distributed trait. The integrity of a taxometric analysis is similarly sensitive to the validity of all indicators used.

The problem with subjecting all indicators to analysis without winnowing is exemplified in research on the latent structure of depression. In the mood disorder literature, there is a longstanding tradition of distinguishing between melancholic and non-melancholic subtypes of depression (e.g., Harrington, Rutter, & Fombonne, 1996). Melancholic (endogenous) depression is affected more by heritable biological predispositions (*see* e.g., Ruiz et al., 2001), whereas non-melancholic (exogenous) depression is more likely to be triggered by environmental events. Criteria for melancholia include vegetative symptoms such as psychomotor retardation, agitation, sleep disturbance, loss of weight, loss of appetite, and diminished libido. Such symptoms indicate disturbed homeostatic processes, whereas other symptoms of depression such as mood disturbance and feelings of hopelessness reflect distress, which is observed in both subtypes.

Taxometric analyses of melancholic symptoms consistently yield a latent taxon among both adolescents and adults (Ambrosini et al., 2002; Haslam & Beck, 1994; Beach & Amir, 2003; Grove et al., 1987). In contrast, taxometric analyses that include all symptoms of depression usually do not (Beach & Amir, 2003; Haslam & Beck, 1994; Ruscio & Ruscio, 2000; 2002; for an exception, *see* Solomon, Ruscio, & Lewinsohn, 2006). Thus, when all symptoms of depression are subjected to taxometric analysis without winnowing out non-melancholic symptoms, the melancholic depression taxon is not detected. Importantly, melancholia confers much higher risk for suicide than unipolar depression (*see* Coryell & Schlesser, 2001), so identifying members of the taxon may have important clinical implications (*see* Beauchaine & Marsh, 2006).

There are many other examples in which criterion lists for *DSM* disorders have been subjected to taxometric analysis, without any winnowing procedure. These studies have yielded exceedingly few latent typologies (Beauchaine, 2007). We have argued that discrete subtypes of psychopathology, although probably rare, are more likely to be identified by subsets of symptoms that specify more homogenous groups than most *DSM* disorders identify (Beauchaine, 2003, 2007; Beauchaine, Lenzenweger et al., 2008; Beauchaine & Marsh, 2006).

Identifying such symptom subsets will likely require an empirical approach to indicator selection that winnows out invalid indicators.

Assessing Fit

Consistency Tests. Meehl (1995a, 1999) and others who developed taxometric methods (e.g., Grove, 2006, Waller & Meehl, 1998) advocated strongly for the use of multiple consistency tests in assessing taxonic hypotheses (*see also* Ruscio, Walters, Marcus, & Kaczetow, 2010). Consistency tests, which protect against false–positive findings, refer to replication of latent distributional parameters (means, base rates, variances, etc.) both within and across alternative procedures. In performing consistency tests, we assume that a valid latent taxon should be detectable using multiple taxometric methods, and that agreement should be observed in estimates of distributional parameters. Below I evaluate the consistency of a subset of parameters from MAXCOV analyses of the data that were winnowed from eight indicators to six above.

Because MAXCOV operates on variable triplets, there are $i \times \frac{(i-1)!}{(i-3)!2!} = 6 \times \frac{120}{6 \times 2} = 60$ combinations available for analysis of six indicators. Maximum covariance plots from the winnowed data (Indicators 3–8) appear in Figure 26.9. Recall that each of these variables is characterized by an effect size of $d = 2.0$. Note that all of the MAXCOV plots rise steeply from left to right and that most exhibit a marked peak. This shape is prototypical for moderate base rate taxa (*see* Meehl, 1995a; Meehl & Yonce, 1996). Among all of the MAXCOV runs using the large effect size indicators, base rate estimates are highly consistent, with a mean of 0.17 and a *SD* of 0.04. Thus, across 60 runs, the MAXCOV-estimated base rate was very close to the actual base rate of 0.15. Furthermore, the small *SD* suggests that most base rate estimates were quite near the actual taxon base rate.

In the far left column of Figure 26.9, I have also included 10 MAXCOV plots derived from indicators of low effect size. The shapes of these plots are inconsistent, with some peaking to the left, some peaking to the right, and others appearing flat. The mean base rate estimate from these MAXCOV analyses was 0.57, far from the true taxon base rate of 0.15. Furthermore, the *SD* of base rate estimates was 0.30—almost eight times the value obtained when using variables of sufficient effect size. This illustrates the value of consistency tests in confirming taxonic inferences. The consistency of base rate estimates forms the basis of the fit index for taxonic structure (FITS; Beauchaine & Beauchaine, 2006), described under the heading Fit Indices, below.

Although agreement of taxon base rate estimates is probably the most commonly used consistency test, many others have been suggested and used. These include but are not limited to (1) the consistency of estimated taxon group means $(\mu_{t_x}, \mu_{t_y}, \mu_{t_z} \ldots \mu_{t_n})$ and complement class means $(\mu_{c_x}, \mu_{c_y}, \mu_{c_z} \ldots \mu_{c_n})$ across indicators and methods; (2) the consistency of estimated taxon group variances $(\sigma_{t_x}^2, \sigma_{t_y}^2, \sigma_{t_z}^2 \ldots \sigma_{t_n}^2)$ and complement class variances $(\sigma_{c_x}^2, \sigma_{c_y}^2, \sigma_{c_z}^2 \ldots \sigma_{c_n}^2)$ across indicators and methods; (2) the consistency of estimated taxon group nuisance correlations $(r_{t_{xy}}, r_{t_{xz}}, r_{t_{yz}} \ldots r_{t_{mn}})$ and complement class nuisance correlations $(r_{c_{xy}}, r_{c_{xz}}, r_{c_{yz}} \ldots r_{c_{mn}})$ across indicators and methods; (3) correlations among Bayesian-estimated probabilities of taxon group membership across different procedures (high correlations indicate agreement across methods); and (5) Grove's (2006) disattenuated kappa (κ) coefficient test, among others (*see*, e.g., Ruscio & Ruscio, 2004b). Grove's disattenuated κ is derived by estimating the sensitivity and specificity of Bayesian-estimated group assignments of observations to the taxon group and complement class and substituting these values into the disattenuation formula for Cohen's κ (1960). The disattenuated κ coefficient approaches 1.0 if the different procedures are identifying the same taxon.

It is worth repeating that consistency tests are a central component of the taxometric method, and that Meehl (1995a) and others (e.g., Beauchaine, 2007; Grove, 2006; Waller & Meehl, 1998) have advocated for the use of multiple consistency tests in any taxometric analysis. Recently, however, there have been trends toward (1) averaging MAMBAC, MAXCOV, MAXEIG, and L-Mode, curves rather than presenting all and examining each for consistency, and (2) relying on single fit indices in making judgments about discrete versus dimensional latent structure (see Fit Indices below). In our view, although the emergence of fit indices is a positive development in taxometrics research, such indices should augment rather than replace traditional approaches to consistency testing and never be reported in isolation. Rather, similarly to the case of structural equation modeling, several fit indices should be reported, as each has strengths and weaknesses. We describe key fit indices below.

Data Simulations. Variable skew has received considerable attention as a possible source of inducing

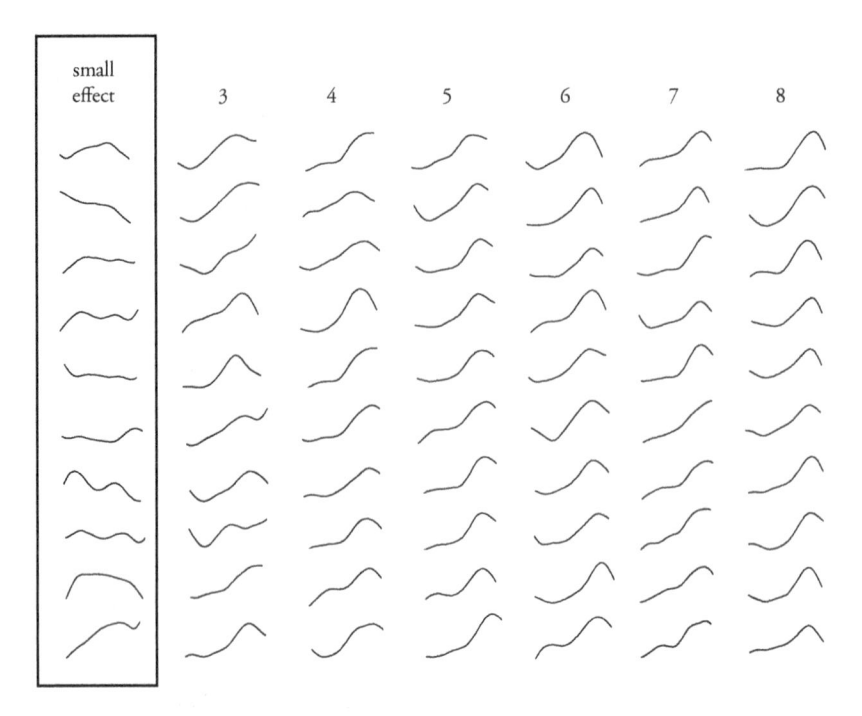

Figure 26.9 MAXCOV plots for all combinations of the six indicators winnowed previously using MAMBAC (Variables 3–8). Input variables are listed across the top, with plots for all output variable pairs appearing down columns. All winnowed indicators have effect sizes of $d = 2.0$. Each MAXCOV plot shows a marked peak, suggesting a moderate base rate taxon (the true base rate is 0.15). MAXCOV plots in the far left column, enclosed in the box, include small effect size indicators. These plots are shaped variably, with no consistently placed peak.

spurious taxa (e.g., Ruscio & Ruscio, 2002; Ruscio et al., 2004). In 2002, Ruscio and Ruscio noted that dimensionally distributed yet skewed indicators may produce right-end peaked MAMBAC, MAXCOV, and MAXEIG plots that falsely suggest low base rate taxa. Thus, taxometric analyses of skewed indicators can be difficult to disambiguate, which is especially problematic because skewed data are expected when a small base rate taxon is embedded in the tail of a larger complement class. In an effort to distinguish between skew-induced pseudotaxa and genuine low base rate taxa, Ruscio and Ruscio introduced a procedure in which both latent dimensional and latent taxonic data are simulated to match (as closely as possible) observed data parameters, including univariate means, SDs, and skew. Taxometric analyses are then conducted on the observed data, the simulated dimensional data, and the simulated taxonic data. Inferences regarding latent structure are drawn based on whether results from the observed data are more similar to results from the simulated dimensional or the simulated taxonic data. If analyses from the observed data are more similar to analyses of the simulated dimensional data than analyses of the simulated taxonic data, then it is assumed that variable skew produced a spurious result.

Since being introduced in 2002 to address variable skew, the Ruscio and Ruscio (2002) simulation technique has been refined (Ruscio, Ruscio, & Meron, 2007), and it is now used as a matter of course in almost all taxometric analyses. Although it is probably unnecessary when skew is below about 2.0 (*see* Beauchaine, Lenzenweger et al., 2008; Beauchaine & Beauchaine, 2002), data simulations are likely here to stay, and under certain conditions, aid considerably in making judgments about the underlying latent structure of data

Figure 26.10 depicts (1) observed data from the MAMBAC analyses performed above on Indicators 3 through 8, and plots of (2) simulated taxonic and (3) simulated dimensional data. In each case, 10 simulations of $n = 500$ are plotted. As indicated, the distribution of observed data is far more similar to the simulated taxonic data than the simulated dimensional data. This, of course, should be expected because the data were generated as taxonic. In a research context in which the latent structure of the observed data is unknown, inferences depend on which of the simulations the observed data match most closely. In a case such as this example, the choice is easy. In other cases, however, the observed data may fall somewhere in between the simulated

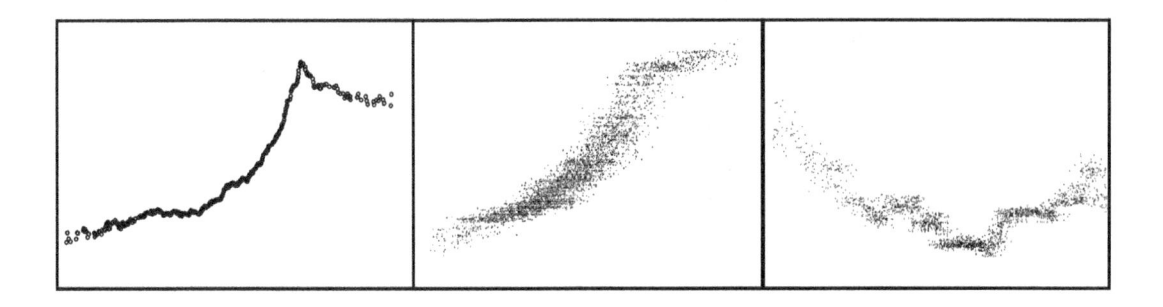

Figure 26.10 Observed data (left panel), simulated taxonic data (middle panel), and simulated dimensional data (right panel) for the MAMBAC analyses described previously, and depicted in Figure 26.8. The distribution of observed data is much more similar to the simulated taxonic data than the simulated dimensional data. In both the taxonic and dimensional cases, data points represent 10 simulations of $n = 500$.

taxonic and simulated dimensional prototypes, rendering a decision difficult. In such cases, fit indices can be especially helpful.

Fit Indices. Several fit indices have been proposed to evaluate whether a discrete latent structural model better captures observed data than a dimensional latent structural model. The first of these, introduced by Waller and Meehl (1998), was the goodness-of-fit index (GFI; Jöreskog & Sörbom, 1988). After estimating the taxon base rate and the within-groups variances of each indicator, a predicted variance–covariance matrix is calculated, which is then compared with the observed variance–covariance matrix. Thus, as when it is used to evaluate the fit of structural equation models, the GFI provides an objective index of similarity between the observed and predicted variance–covariance matrices. Waller and Meehl (1998) noted that taxonic data typically yield GFIs greater than .90. Although this has proved to be the case, dimensional data often produce GFIs greater than .90 as well, so discriminating power of the fit statistic is poor, as reported by several research groups (Beauchaine & Beauchaine, 2006; Cleland, Rothschild, & Haslam, 2000; Haslam & Cleland, 2002; Ruscio et al., 2007).

A fit statistic that is being used increasingly in taxometrics research is the comparison curve fit index (CCFI; Ruscio et al., 2006; Ruscio et al., 2007). The CCFI assesses the relative fit of observed data compared with simulated taxonic versus simulated dimensional data (*see* above). To compute the CCFI, one first calculates the root mean squared residual between all points on the observed curve (averaged across all MAMBAC, MAXCOV, MAXEIG, or L-Mode analyses) and all points on the simulated curves (both dimensional and taxonic):

$$Fit_{RMSR} = \sqrt{\frac{\sum (y_{res.data} - y_{sim.data})^2}{N}} \quad (2)$$

Next, the $Fit_{RMSR.taxonic}$ and $Fit_{RMSR.dimensional}$, values are used to compute the CCFI:

$$CCFI = \frac{Fit_{RMSR.dimensional}}{Fit_{RMSR.dimensional} + Fit_{RMSR.taxonic}} \quad (3)$$

Comparison curve fit index values approaching 1.0 indicate a close fit to the simulated taxonic data, whereas values near 0.0 indicate a close fit to the simulated dimensional data. Notably, values around .50 indicate equivalent fit to the simulated taxonic and simulated dimensional data.

As noted above, the CCFI has become increasingly popular in taxometrics work of late. Although the fit statistic has clear value in judging the fit of competing structural models, there is some danger in relying on a single fit statistic derived from all curves averaged together. As demonstrated above with both MAMBAC and MAXCOV, in any taxometric analysis there may be one or more invalid indicators. When working only with averaged curves, which has become increasingly common, such invalid indicators may go undetected, remaining in the analysis when they should have been removed. Therefore, we recommend that indicators be winnowed carefully, as described in sections above, before using the CCFI (or any other fit statistic). Relying solely on the CCFI to make judgments about the latent structure of data also ignores the importance of performing multiple consistency tests, as outlined above. Thus, I see the CCFI as one among other important indices of fit. Notably, efforts have been made toward combining the CCFI and consistency test approaches (Ruscio et al., 2010).

In effort to develop a fit index that is more compatible with traditional approaches to consistency testing, we (Beauchaine & Beauchaine, 2006) derived the FITS (*see also* Beauchaine, 2007). Following the consistency test logic (*see* above), the FITS evaluates the degree of homogeneity among parameter (e.g., base rate) estimates across multiple runs of any taxometric procedure (e.g., MAMBAC, MAXCOV, L-Mode, etc.). The FITS is given by:

$$\text{FITS} = 1 - 2 \times \sqrt{\sum_j (br_j - \overline{br})^2 / (N-1)}, \quad (4)$$

where br_j = the estimated base rate from variable combination j, $\overline{br}$ is the mean of base rate estimates across all variable combinations, and N = the number of variable combinations available for analysis. The radicand of this equation is simply the standard deviation of base rate (or other parameter) estimates. Fit index for taxonic structure values range from 0.0 to 1.0, with 1.0 indicating perfect agreement among base rate estimates. Values above .90 strongly suggest discrete latent structure. For the MAXCOV analyses performed above with Variables 3 through 8, all of which mark a latent taxon with an effect size of $d = 2.0$, the FITS value was .92, indicating a latent taxon. In contrast, the analyses including the small effect size indicators yielded a FITS value of .41, which does not suggest a taxon. In a large Monte Carlo study evaluating the effectiveness of the FITS across wide ranges of sample size, effect size, nuisance covariance, and other distributional parameters, values below .65 were never observed for taxonic data when valid indicators were used (Beauchaine & Beauchaine, 2006).

Although the FITS has appeared sparingly in taxometrics research to date, it will likely be of value in discriminating between discrete and dimensional latent structure—especially when used with other fit statistics. Importantly, the FITS can be calculated for any of several distributional parameters that are commonly used for consistency testing (e.g., *SD*s, means, etc.; *see* above). However, doing so will require additional simulation studies to determine relevant cut-points.

Assigning Cases to the Taxon Group and Complement Class

If a latent taxon is identified, then observations, cases, individuals, and so forth can be assigned to the taxon group and the complement class using Bayes' Theorem (Meehl, 1973, Waller & Meehl, 1998).

For example, with three variables using MAXCOV (the simplest case), Bayesian estimated probabilities of taxon group membership are given by the equation (Waller & Meehl, 1998, p. 29):

$$Pr(t|x^+ y^- z^+) = \frac{P p_{tx} q_{ty} p_{tz}}{P p_{tx} q_{ty} p_{tz} + Q p_{cx} q_{cy} p_{cz}}, \quad (5)$$

where $Pr(t|x^+ y^- z^+)$ represents the probability of taxon group membership given scores above the hitmax value on x and z, and below the hitmax value on y; P represents the taxon base rate; Q represents the non-taxon base rate; p_{tx} represents the true positive rate for variable x (*see* below); p_{cx} represents the false–positive rate for variable x as derived by MAXCOV; q_{tx} equals $1 - p_{tx}$; and q_{cx} equals $1 - p_{cx}$. Within each interval, true positives are estimated by taking the positive root of the quadratic equation, and true negatives are estimated by taking the negative root (Meehl & Yonce, 1996, pp. 1120–1121):

$$p_{xi} = \quad (6)$$
$$\frac{(\bar{y}_t - \bar{y}_c)(\bar{z}_t - \bar{z}_c) \pm \sqrt{((\bar{y}_t - \bar{y}_c)(\bar{z}_t - \bar{z}_c))^2 - 4(\bar{y}_t - \bar{y}_c)(\bar{z}_t - \bar{z}_c) cov_{yzi}}}{2(\bar{y}_t - \bar{y}_c)(\bar{z}_t - \bar{z}_c)},$$

where p_{xi} represents the true positive rate of taxon group members identified within interval i of variable x, and cov_{yzi} represents the covariance of variables y and z within the same interval of variable x. Estimates are summed to yield sample-wide true and false–positive rates.

These formulae yield a probability (0.0–1.0) that each observation belongs to the taxon group. Typically, observations with probabilities below .50 are assigned to the complement class, and observations with probabilities above .50 are assigned to the taxon. Because we are dealing with probabilities, assigning individuals to groups can never be accomplished with perfect accuracy, as the latent distributions almost always overlap. Nevertheless, specifying the most accurate cut-point (usually .50) is important because it minimizes misclassifications.

Interpreting Results

Positive Results. There are a number of possible implications for positive results from a taxometric analysis, depending on the nature of the data analyzed. As noted above (e.g., Beauchaine, Neuhaus, Brenner, & Gatzke-Kopp, 2008), taxometric analyses can and have been used to specify symptom thresholds for children who are vulnerable to psychopathology. For example, by performing taxometric analyses on sustained visual attention, neuromotor performance, and intelligence measures, Erlenmeyer-Kimling et al. (1989) identified a schizotypy taxon group of 7- to 12-year-old children who had at least one parent with schizophrenia. Although only about 5% of the general population suffers from schizotypy (Blanchard et al., 2000; Golden & Meehl, 1979; Korfine & Lenzenweger, 1995; Lenzenweger, 1999; Lenzenweger & Korfine, 1992; Lenzenweger et al., 2007), 47% of children with an afflicted parent were taxon group members, compared with the expected 4% of controls. Fifteen years later, 43% of the schizotypy taxon group had been either hospitalized or received significant treatment. Nearly identical results were reported by Tyrka et al. (1995), who found that 48% of 10- to 19-year-old offspring of mothers with schizophrenia belonged to a schizotypy taxon group. Among this group, 40% were diagnosed with a schizophrenia spectrum disorder 24 to 27 years later.

These findings are especially significant because they have direct implications for prevention. Enrolling every child of a parent with schizophrenia into a prevention/intervention program is woefully inefficient because only 10% to 15% eventually develop a schizophrenia spectrum disorder (see Cornblatt, Obuchowski, Roberts, Pollack, & Erlenmeyer-Kimling, 1999). Yet in the taxometric studies outlined above, taxon group members exhibited about four times this level of risk, making targeted prevention much more plausible (Cornblatt, 2001; Cornblatt, Lencz, & Kane, 2001). The importance of early identification is difficult to overstate given (1) increasing effectiveness of modern prevention programs in attenuating risk for future psychosis (e.g., McGorry et al., 2002), and (2) clear links between early intervention and improved long-term course (see Cornblatt, 2001; Cornblatt et al., 1999). This example demonstrates how taxometric analyses can be used to identify accurate clinical cutoffs for children at especially high risk for severe psychopathology

Null Results. I have already described the likely effect of including even one or two invalid indicators in a taxometric analysis. As the example analyses above demonstrate, taxa often go undetected if indicator validity is ignored. Although the probability of false–negatives is reduced by subjecting all putative indicators to the winnowing procedure outlined above, one should still be careful about interpreting null findings as strong evidence for dimensional latent structure. Taxometric methods search for disjunctions in means, covariances, eigenvalues, and so forth toward detecting latent taxa. When no taxon is found, dimensional latent structure is assumed based on the *absence* of disjunctions in the data. This renders the dimensional interpretation the effective null hypothesis. It bears repeating that it is always possible that more precise indicators (i.e., those with less measurement error) will reveal a latent taxon in future studies, especially if the null result derives from rating scale data, as in most taxometrics research conducted to date (*see* above). For this reason alone, researchers should be conservative when interpreting null findings (for an alternative interpretation, *see* Ruscio, 2007) and should offer recommendations for future research using indicators with greater measurement precision.

One way to improve measurement precision is to use indicators other than *DSM* symptoms, including putative biological markers of latent traits, which are by nature more precise than rating scale data (for a detailed discussion, *see* Beauchaine, 2003). Although behavioral indicators may be valid markers of a particular trait (e.g., anhedonia as a symptom of depression), they are difficult to measure without error, which reduces the power of taxometric procedures (*see* above). Although most taxometrics studies have been performed using strictly Likert-type measures, a few researchers—particularly those studying schizotypy—have identified and used biological markers and endophenotypes in taxometric analyses and other studies, with promising results (Erlenmeyer-Kimling et al., 1989; Grove, Clementz, Iacono, & Katsanis, 1992; Lenzenweger, & Maher, 2002; Lenzenweger et al., 2007; Tyrka et al., 1995).

Other Important Considerations

Those interested in the operating characteristics of taxometric procedures, including our group and others, have evaluated the performance of MAMBAC, MAXCOV, MAXEIG, and L-Mode under a wide range of data parameters that could adversely affect taxon detection and/or induce spurious taxonic structure into dimensionally distributed traits. These include situations in which (1) nuisance (within-group) correlations among indicators are high, violating the assumption of local independence (Beauchaine & Beauchaine, 2002; Meehl, 1995b); (2) indicators are skewed (Cleland & Haslam, 1996; Haslam & Clelend, 1996; Ruscio, 2007); (2) indicators are dichotomous (Golden, 1982, 1991); (3) effect sizes among indicators vary (Haslam & Cleland, 2002); (5) base rates are very low (Beauchaine & Beauchaine, 2002); (6) sample sizes are relatively small (Beauchaine & Beauchaine, 2002; Meehl, 1995); (6) the number of indicators is varied (Beauchaine & Beauchaine, 2002); (8) the number latent classes is varied (Walters et al., 2010); (9) items are summed to form indicators (Walters & Ruscio, 2009); and (10) indicator variances are unequal (Ruscio, 2007). Several issues stand out from these studies.

Sample Size

Monte Carlo studies conducted by independent research groups have indicated consistently that the minimum sample size for conducting MAMBAC and MAXCOV analyses is about 200 under ideal conditions with highly valid indicators (e.g., Beauchaine & Beauchaine, 2002; Meehl, 1995a; Meehl & Yonce, 1994). However, given the difficulties outlined above in ensuring precise measurement, which affects validity, sample sizes exceeding 300 are preferred (Meehl, 1995a). This eliminates many data sets from consideration for taxometric analysis. Although preliminary evidence suggests that MAXEIG may accommodate slightly smaller samples (Waller & Meehl, 1998), this remains to be evaluated in rigorous Monte Carlo studies.

Number of Indicators

Although taxometric procedures can be performed with as few as two indicators using MAMBAC, no studies have been published using less than three. Monte Carlo simulations suggest that even this is inadequate because power to detect latent taxa increases steadily with more indicators until asymptoting at 7 to 8 (Beauchaine & Beauchaine, 2002). We have therefore recommended that taxometric analyses be conducted with no fewer than 5 to 6 indicators (Beauchaine, 2007; Beauchaine & Marsh, 2006). Because some potential indicators will probably be winnowed out of most studies (*see* above), those planning a taxometric analysis should include as many putative indicators as possible. Furthermore, indicator redundancy, or the use of several variables that mark the same latent construct, is not only acceptable, it is necessary for a taxometric analysis (*see*, e.g., Meehl, 1995a). As is the case with scale construction, multiple redundant indicators should be sought, preferably across alternative levels of analysis spanning behavior ratings, observations, and biomarkers (Beauchaine & Marsh, 2006; Beauchaine, Lenzenweger et al., 2007).

Skew

Indicator skew has probably received more attention than any other data characteristic known to affect the performance of taxometric methods (e.g., Beach & Amir, 2003; Marcus, John, & Edens, 2004; Ruscio, 2007; Ruscio & Ruscio, 2004a, 2004b; Ruscio et al., 2004). Although early Monte Carlo studies indicated that both MAMBAC and MAXCOV are sensitive and specific when using moderately skewed indicators (Cleland & Haslam, 1996; Haslam & Clelend, 1996), more recent studies have indicated a tendency for these and other taxometric procedures to produce plots indicative of low base rate taxa when continuously distributed indicators are highly skewed (Ruscio & Ruscio, 2004a; Ruscio et al., 2004). As outlined above, Ruscio and Ruscio (2002; 2004a) advanced their simulation technique to deal with this problem. Shortly after their simulation technique was advanced, an extensive Monte Carlo simulation (Beach, Amir, & Bau, 2005) revealed that the method often yields false–negative findings when the taxon base rate is low and skew is high—precisely the conditions for which the technique was supposed to provide clarification. As noted above, however, the simulation technique has since been refined (Ruscio et al., 2007). This, coupled with the development and use of the CCFI (Ruscio et al., 2006; Ruscio et al., 2007) described previously, appears to have resolved the false–negative problem (Ruscio, 2007; Ruscio et al., 2010). It should be noted, however, that taxometric methods are capable of resolving latent taxonic structure without false–positives when skew values are as high as 2.0 (Beauchaine & Beauchaine, 2006). Thus, although Ruscio's simulation technique is now used in almost all taxometrics studies, there is justification for conducting analyses without simulations given certain conditions under which such simulations may complicate interpretation of results (*see* Beauchaine, Lenzenweger et al., 2007)

As alluded to above, it is important to note that skew is always imparted into indicator variables when a low base rate taxon is embedded in the tail of a normal distribution of complement class scores. One should therefore not remove potential indicators from a taxometric analysis solely because they are skewed. Doing so will eliminate valid indicators—especially if a low base rate taxon is suspected.

Replication

Within this chapter, I have outlined several strategies aimed at preserving the validity of a taxometric analysis. Nevertheless, firm conclusions about discrete versus dimensional latent structure of a clinical disorder, personality trait, and so forth can only be reached through replication (for an extended discussion, *see* Beauchaine, Lenzenweger et al., 2008). Single studies are always subject to sample-specific variation in symptom levels that may be attributable to chance and/or systematic error variance. Thus, confirmation of results should be sought across multiple studies before drawing inferences about the latent structure of a disorder or about appropriate diagnostic thresholds (Beauchaine & Marsh, 2006). As noted in the introduction of this chapter, psychiatric conditions for which multiple studies have yielded evidence of discrete latent structure include schizotypy (Blanchard et al., 2000; Erlenmeyer-Kimling et al., 1989; Golden & Meehl, 1979; Horan et al., 2004; Korfine & Lenzenweger, 1995; Lenzenweger, 1999; Lenzenweger & Korfine, 1992, 1995; Lenzenweger et al., 2007; Tyrka, Haslam, & Cannon, 1995; Tyrka et al., 1995; *see also* Lenzenweger, 2010) and certain forms of depression, especially the endogenous subtype (Ambrosini et al., 2002; Beach & Amir, 2003; Grove et al., 1987; Haslam & Beck, 1994; Richey et al., 2009; Schmidt et al., 2007; Solomon et al., 2006). Other disorders and high-risk traits for which some replicated evidence of discrete latent structure exists include anxiety (e.g., Kotov et al., 2005; Schmidt et al., 2007; Woodward et al., 2000) and severe antisocial behavior (e.g., Harris et al., 1994; Skilling et al., 2001). However, null findings regarding the latter have also been reported (Edens, Marcus, Lilienfeld, & Poythress, 2006).

We have also advocated for replication within studies using alternative classification methods such as LCA (Beauchaine & Marsh, 2006). Although this is not intended as a substitute for replicating across studies, confirming a result with both taxometric methods and LCA provides for increased confidence in one's inferences about the latent structure of psychopathology, personality, and so forth. For example, in a recent study, we found evidence for discrete subgroups of children with autism spectrum disorders based on cognitive performance measures (Munson et al., 2008). Using MAMBAC, MAXCOV, and LCA, we identified a discrete taxon group of high-functioning individuals. We await replication by other labs to determine whether our finding is valid.

Other Approaches

Taxometric methods represent only one of several approaches to evaluating the latent structure of behavioral traits. Other methods developed to address similar questions include LCA, latent profile analysis, finite mixture modeling, cluster analysis, growth mixture modeling, and information-theoretic models (*see* Aldenderfer & Blashfield, 1984; Blashfield & Aldenderfer, 1988; Everitt, 2001; Gibson, 1959; Krueger, Markon, et al., 2005; Lazarsfeld & Henry, 1968; McLachlan & Peel, 2000; Muthén, 2001; Muthén & Shedden, 1999; Nagin, 1999). Although these approaches cannot be described here, I provide a very brief description of their performance compared with taxometrics.

As we and others have noted (Beauchaine, 2003; Beauchaine & Beauchaine, 2002; Beauchaine & Marsh, 2006; Blashfield & Aldenderfer, 1988), cluster analysis is limited as a method of identifying discrete latent structure because most clustering algorithms always divide data sets into subgroups, whether or not latent classes exist. Furthermore, despite considerable effort by several research groups over the past 30 years, there are still no reliable methods for determining (1) the correct number of clusters (unless cluster overlap is minimal, an exceedingly rare situation in psychopathology research), or (2) whether a discrete model better captures the latent structure of a data set than a dimensional model (e.g., Tonidandel & Overall, 2004).

In contrast, LCA and mixture modeling offer much more effective means of choosing among competing multiple latent class solutions, including solutions with three or more groups. This is an advantage over taxometric methods, which were designed to be used in the two-group case (taxon, complement class). Nevertheless, when using LCA and mixture modeling, one cannot be certain whether the latent classes identified are truly discrete. These methods almost always converge on multiple group solutions, even when continuous variables serve as inputs (*see*, e.g., Bauer & Curran, 2003a, 2003b). As a result, a primary advantage of taxometrics over LCA and mixture modeling is a lower probability of false–positives (Beauchaine & Beauchaine, 2002). This lower probability of false–positives has nothing to do with differences in the statistical bases of the methods. As noted above, most taxometric methods share the same local independence assumption of LCA. However, selection of competing structural models (discrete vs. dimensional) are made quite differently. In taxometrics, one bases his or her decision largely on consistency tests (*see* above), which must converge for a discrete latent structure interpretation to be supported. Otherwise, latent dimensional structure is assumed. In contrast, when using LCA and other methods, fit statistics (e.g., Bayesian information criterion, entropy) are more likely to be used that compare models with different numbers of discrete groups. Using these statistics, one-class solutions are rarely compared to *n*-class solutions. Rather, researchers are usually looking for the best-fitting *n*-class solution.

Conclusion

As I hope to have demonstrated in the sections above, although difficult, discerning the latent structure of psychopathology has implications for our understanding of etiology, our ability to diagnose accurately, and in some cases our capacity to assign vulnerable individuals to prevention and early intervention programs. Although the large body of taxometrics research conducted to date indicates that discretely distributed psychiatric disorders are likely to be rare (*see* Beauchaine, 2007; Beauchaine, Lenzenweger et al., 2007), identifying conditions that are discrete is important if we wish to detect incipient vulnerability to psychopathology early in life, when behavior is more plastic and prevention is more likely to succeed (Beauchaine et al., 2008). I presented literature demonstrating that taxometrics have (1) advanced our understanding of the latent structure of endogenous depression, and (2) enabled premorbid identification of children who are at nearly 50% risk of developing schizophrenia. I also provided example analyses that should make taxometrics more accessible to readers. Those who seek more technical details about the procedures I described are referred to for the original sources provided in the reference list.

Author Note

Theodore P. Beauchaine, Professor of Psychology, Washington State University, PO Box 644820, Pullman, WA 99164–4820.

Notes

1. Given no nuisance (between groups) covariance, MAXEIG reduces to MAXCOV in the three variable case.

2. It is important to note that in this context, false–positives and false–negatives refer to the presence versus absence of discrete latent *distributions* (taxa) and not to the sorting of *individuals* into a taxon after it is identified.

References

Aldenderfer, M. S., & Blashfield, R. K. (1984). *Cluster analysis*. Newbury Park, CA: Sage.

Ambrosini, P. J., Bennett, D. S., Cleland, C. M., & Haslam, N. (2002). Taxonicity of adolescent melancholia: A categorical or dimensional construct? *Journal of Psychiatric Research, 36*, 247–256.

American Psychiatric Association (2000). *Diagnostic and Statistical Manual of Mental Disorders* (4th ed., text revision). Washington, DC: Author.

Bartlett, M. S. (1937). The statistical conception of mental factors. *British Journal of Psychology, 28*, 97–104.

Bauer, D. J., & Curran, P. J. (2003a). Distributional assumptions of growth mixture models: Implications for overextraction of latent trajectory classes. *Psychological Methods, 8*, 338–363.

Bauer, D. J., & Curran, P. J. (2003b). Overextraction of latent trajectory classes: Reply to Rindskopf (2003), Muthén (2003), and Cudek and Henly (2003). *Psychological Methods, 8*, 384–393.

Beach, S. R. H., & Amir, N. (2003). Is depression taxonic, dimensional, or both? *Journal of Abnormal Psychology, 112*, 228–236.

Beach, S. R. H., Amir, N., & Bau, J. (2005). Can Sample Specific Simulations Help Detect Low Base Rate Taxonicity? *Psychological Assessment, 17*, 446–461.

Beauchaine, T. P. (2003). Taxometrics and developmental psychopathology. *Development and Psychopathology, 15*, 501–527.

Beauchaine, T. P. (2007). A brief taxometrics primer. *Journal of Clinical Child and Adolescent Psychology, 36*, 654–676.

Beauchaine, T. P. (2009). The role of biomarkers and endophenotypes in prevention and treatment of psychopathological disorders. *Biomarkers in Medicine, 3*, 1–3.

Beauchaine, T. P., & Beach, S. R. H. (2006). Taxometrics and relational processes: Relevance, promises, and challenges for the next nosology of mental disorders. In S. R. H. Beach and R. E. Heyman (Eds.) *Relational processes and DSM-V: Neuroscience, assessment, prevention, and treatment* (pp. 123–137). American Psychiatric Press.

Beauchaine, T. P., & Beauchaine, R. J. III. (2002). A comparison of maximum covariance and *k*-means cluster analysis in classifying cases into known taxon groups. *Psychological Methods, 7*, 245–261.

Beauchaine, T. P., & Beauchaine, R. J. III. (2006). A Comparison of measures of fit for inferring taxonic structure from Maximum Covariance analyses. Unpublished manuscript.

Beauchaine, T. P., Lenzenweger, M. F., & Waller, N. (2008). Schizotypy, taxometrics, and disconfirming theories in soft science. *Personality and Individual Differences, 44*, 1652–1662.

Beauchaine, T. P., & Marsh, P. (2006). Taxometric methods: Enhancing early detection and prevention of psychopathology by identifying latent vulnerability traits. In D. Cicchetti & D. Cohen (Eds.), *Developmental Psychopathology*, 2nd Ed. (pp. 931–967). Hoboken, NJ: Wiley.

Beauchaine, T. P., Neuhaus, E., Brenner, S. L., & Gatzke-Kopp, L. (2008). Ten good reasons to consider biological processes in prevention and intervention research. *Development and Psychopathology, 20,* 745–774.

Beauchaine, T. P., & Waters, E. (2003). Pseudotaxonicity in MAMBAC and MAXCOV analyses of rating scale data: Turning continua into classes by manipulating observer's expectations. *Psychological Methods, 8,* 3–15.

Blanchard, J. J., Gangestad, S. W., Brown, S. A., & Horan, W. P. (2000). Hedonic capacity and Schizotypy revisited: A taxometric analysis of social anhedonia. *Journal of Abnormal Psychology, 109,* 87–95.

Blashfield, R. K., & Aldenderfer, M. S. (1988). The methods and problems of cluster analysis. In J. Nesselroade & R. B. Cattell (Eds.), *Handbook of multivariate experimental psychology* (2nd ed., pp. 447–474). New York: Plenum Press.

Brown, T. A. (2001). Taxometric methods and the classification and comorbidity of mental disorders: Methodological and conceptual considerations. *Clinical Psychology Science and Practice, 8,* 534–541.

Cantor, N., & Genero, N. (1986). Psychiatric diagnosis and natural categorization: A close analogy. In T. Milton & G. Klerman (Eds.), *Contemporary directions in psychopathology: Toward the DSM-IV* (pp. 233–256). New York: Guilford.

Cantor, N., & Mischel, W. (1979). Prototypes in person perception. In L. Berkowitz (Ed.), *Advances in experimental social psychology* (Vol. 12). Orlando, FL: Academic Press.

Clark, L. A. (2005). Temperament as a unifying basis for personality and psychopathology. *Journal of Abnormal Psychology, 114,* 505–521.

Cleland, C., & Haslam, N. (1996). Robustness of taxometric analyses with skewed indicators: I. A Monte Carlo study of the MAMBAC procedure. *Psychological Reports, 79,* 243–248.

Cleland, C., Rothschild, L., & Haslam, N. (2000). Detecting latent taxa: Monte Carlo compareison of taxometric, mixture, and clustering methods. *Psychological Reports, 87,* 37–47.

Cohen J. (1960). A coefficient of agreement for nominal scales. *Educational and Psychological Measurement, 20,* 37–46.

Cohen, J. (1988). *Statistical power analysis for the behavioral sciences* (2nd ed.). New York: Academic Press.

Cornblatt, B. A. (2001). Predictors of schizophrenia and preventive intervention. In A. Breier & P. Tran (Eds.), *Current issues in the psychopharmacology of schizophrenia* (pp. 389–406). Philadelphia, PA: Lippincott Williams & Wilkins.

Cornblatt, B. A., Lencz, T., & Kane, J. M. (2001). Treating the schizophrenia prodrome: Is it presently ethical? *Schizophrenia Research, 51,* 31–38.

Cornblatt, B. A., Obuchowski, M., Roberts, S., Pollack, S., & Erlenmeyer-Kimling, L. (1999). Cognitive and behavioral precursors of schizophrenia. *Developmental Psychopathology, 11,* 487–508.

Coryell, W., & Schlesser, M. (2001). The dexamethasone suppression test and suicide prediction. *American Journal of Psychiatry, 158,* 748–753.

Cuthbert, B. N. (2005). Dimensional models of psychopathology: Research agenda and clinical utility. *Journal of Abnormal Psychology, 114,* 565–569.

Edens, J. F., Marcus, D. K., Lilienfeld, S. O., & Poythress, N. G. (2006). Psychopathic, not psychopath: taxometric evidence for the dimensional structure of psychopathy. *Journal of Abnormal Psychology, 115,* 131–144.

Erlenmeyer-Kimling, L., Golden, R. R., & Cornblatt, B. A. (1989). A taxometric analysis of cognitive and neuromotor variables in children at risk for schizophrenia. *Journal of Abnormal Psychology, 98,* 203–208.

Everitt, B. (2001). *Cluster analysis.* New York: Oxford University Press.

First, M. B. (2005). Clinical utility: A prerequisite for the adoption of a dimensional approach to DSM. *Journal of Abnormal Psychology, 114,* 551–556.

Flanagan, E. H., & Blashfield, R. K. (2002). Psychiatric classification through the lens of ethnobiology. In L. E. Beutler & M. L. Malik (Eds.), *Rethinking the DSM* (pp. 121–145). Washington, DC: American Psychological Association.

Fossati, A., Beauchaine, T. P., Grazioli, F., Carretta, I., Cortinovis, F., & Maffei, C. (2005). A latent structure analysis of *Diagnostic and Statistical Manual of Mental Disorders, Fourth Edition,* narcissistic personality disorder criteria. *Comprehensive Psychiatry, 46,* 361–367.

Gibson, W. A. (1959). Three multivariate models: Factor analysis, latent structure analysis, and latent profile analysis. *Psychometrika, 24,* 229–252.

Gleaves, D. H., Lowe, M. R., Green, B. A., Cororve, M. B., & Williams, T. L. (2000). Do anorexia and bulimia nervosa occur on a continuum? A taxometric analysis. *Behavior Therapy, 31,* 195–219.

Golden, R. R. (1982). A taxometric model for the detection of a conjectured latent taxon. *Multivariate Behavioral Research, 17,* 389–416.

Golden, R. R. (1991). Bootstrapping taxometrics: On the development of a method for detection of a single major gene. In D. Cicchetti & W. M. Grove (Eds.), *Thinking clearly about psychology* (Vol. 2, pp. 259–294). Minneapolis, MN: University of Minnesota Press.

Golden, R. R., & Meehl, P. E. (1979). Detection of the schizoid taxon with MMPI indicators. *Journal of Abnormal Psychology, 88,* 212–233.

Grove, W. M. (2006). A disattenuated kappa coefficient for agreement between two latent taxa. *Research Reports of the Department of Psychology,* PR-06-02. University of Minnesota.

Grove, W. M., Andreasen, N. C., Young, M., Endicott, J., Keller, M. B., Hirschfeld, R. M., et al. (1987). Isolation and characterization of a nuclear depressive syndrome. *Psychological Medicine, 17,* 471–484.

Grove, W. M., Clementz, B. A., Iacono, W. G., & Katsanis, J. (1992). Smooth pursuit ocular motor dysfunction in schizophrenia: Evidence for a major gene. *American Journal of Psychiatry, 149,* 1362–1368.

Grove, W. M., & Meehl, P. E. (1993). Simple regression-based procedures for taxometric investigation. *Psychological Reports, 73,* 707–737.

Grove, W. M., & Tellegen, A. (1991). Problems in the classification of personality disorders. *Journal of Personality disorders, 5,* 31–41.

Harrington, R., Rutter, M., & Fombonne, E. (1996). Developmental pathways in depression: Multiple meanings, antecedents, and endpoints. *Development and Psychopathology, 8,* 601–616.

Harris, G. T., Rice, M. E., & Quinsey, V. L. (1994). Psychopathy as a taxon: Evidence that psychopaths are a discrete class. *Journal of Consulting and Clinical Psychology, 62,* 387–397.

Haslam, N., & Beck, A. T. (1994). Subtyping major depression: A taxometric analysis. *Journal of Abnormal Psychology, 103,* 686–692.

Haslam, N., & Cleland, C. (1996). Robustness of taxometric analysis with skewed indicators: II. A Monte Carlo study of the MAXCOV procedure. *Psychological Reports, 79,* 1035–1039.

Haslam, N., & Cleland, C. (2002). Taxometric analysis of fuzzy categories: A Monte Carlo study. *Psychological Reports, 90,* 401–404.

Haslam, N., & Kim, H. C. (2002). Categories and continua: A review of taxometric research. *Genetic, Social, and General Psychology Monographs, 128,* 271–320.

Helzer, J. E., Kraemer, H. C., Krueger, R. F., Wittchen, H-U., Sirovatka, P. J., & Regier, D. A. (Eds.). (2008). *Dimensional approaches in diagnostic classification: Refining the research agenda for DSM-V.* Washington, DC: American Psychiatric Association.

Horan, W. P., Blanchard, J. J., Gangestad, S. W., & Kwapil, T. R. (2004). The psychometric detection of schizotypy: Do putative schizotypy indicators identify the same latent class? *Journal of Abnormal Psychology, 113,* 339–357.

Hoyt, W. T., & Kerns, M. D. (1999). Magnitude and moderators of bias in observer ratings: A meta-analysis. *Psychological Methods, 4,* 403–424.

Jevons, W. S. (1958). *The principles of science.* New York: Dover. (Original work published in 1874).

Jöreskog, K. G., & Sörbom, D. (1988). *LISREL 7: A guide to the program and applications.* Chicago: SPSS.

Kendall, P. C., & Drabick, D. A. G. (2010). Problems for the book of problems? Diagnosing mental health disorders among youth. *Clinical Psychology Science & Practice, 17,* 265–271.

Kendell, R. E. (1989). Clinical validity. *Psychological Medicine, 19,* 45–55.

Korfine, L., & Lenzenweger, M. F. (1995). The taxonicity of schizotypy: A replication. *Journal of Abnormal Psychology, 104,* 26–31.

Kotov, R., Schmidt, N. B., Lerew, D. R., Joiner, T. E., & Ialongo, N. S. (2005). Latent structure of anxiety: Taxometric exploration. *Psychological Assessment, 17,* 369–374.

Krueger, R. F., Markon, K. E., Patrick, C. J., & Iacono, W. G. (2005). Externalizing psychopathology in adulthood: A dimensional-spectrum conceptualization and its implications for *DSM-IV. Journal of Abnormal Psychology, 114,* 537–550.

Krueger, R. F., Watson, D., & Barlow, D. H. (2005). Toward a dimensionally based taxonomy of psychopathology [Special section]. *Journal of Abnormal Psychology, 114* (3).

Kupfer, D. J. (2005). Dimensional models for research and diagnosis: A current dilemma. *Journal of Abnormal Psychology, 114,* 557–559.

Lazarsfeld, P. F., & Henry, N. W. (1968). *Latent structure analysis.* Boston, MA: Houghton Mifflin.

Lenzenweger, M. F. (1999). Deeper into the schizotypy taxon: On the robust nature of maximum covariance analysis. *Journal of Abnormal Psychology, 108,* 182–187.

Lenzenweger, M. F. (2004). Consideration of the challenges, complications, and pitfalls of taxometric analysis. *Journal of Abnormal Psychology, 113,* 10–23.

Lenzenweger, M. F. (2010). *Schizotypy and schizophrenia.* New York: Guilford.

Lenzenweger, M. F., & Korfine, L. (1992). Confirming the latent structure and base rate of schizotypy: A taxometric analysis. *Journal of Abnormal Psychology, 101,* 567–571.

Lenzenweger, M. F., & Korfine, L. (1995). Tracking the taxon: On the latent structure and baserate of schizotypy. In A. Raine, T. Lencz, & S. A. Mednick (Eds.) *Schizotypal personality disorder* (pp. 135–167). New York: Cambridge University Press.

Lenzenweger, M. F., & Maher, B. A. (2002). Psychometric schizotypy and motor performance. *Journal of Abnormal Psychology, 111,* 546–555.

Lenzenweger, M. F., McLachlan, G., & Rubin, D. B. (2007). Resolving the latent structure of schizophrenia endophenotypes using expectation-maximization-based finite mixture modeling. *Journal of Abnormal Psychology, 116,* 16–29.

Macmillan, N. A., & Creelman, C. D. (1990). Response bias: Characteristics of detection theory, threshold theory and "nonparametric" indices. *Psychological Bulletin, 107,* 401–413.

Malt, B. (1993). Concept structure and category boundaries. In G. V. Nakamura, D. L. Medin, & R. Taraban (Eds.), *Categorization by humans and machines. The psychology of learning and motivation: Advances in research and theory* (Vol. 29, pp. 363–390). San Diego, CA: Academic Press.

Marcus, D. K., John, S. L., & Edens, J. F. (2004). A taxometric analysis of psychopathic personality. *Journal of Abnormal Psychology, 113,* 626–635.

McGorry, P. D., Yung, A. R., Phillips, L. J., Yuen, H. P., Francey, S., Cosgrave, E. M., et al. (2002). Randomized controlled trial of interventions designed to reduce the risk of progression to first episode psychosis in a clinical sample with subthreshold symptoms. *Archives of General Psychiatry, 59,* 921–928.

McLachlan, G. J., & Peel, D. (2000). *Finite mixture models.* New York: Wiley.

Meehl, P. E. (1962). Schizotaxia, schizotypy, schizophrenia. *American Psychologist, 17,* 827–838.

Meehl, P. E. (1973). MAXCOV-HITMAX: A taxonomic search method for loose genetic syndromes. *Psychodiagnosis: Selected papers* (pp. 200–224). Minneapolis, MN: University of Minnesota Press.

Meehl, P. E. (1992). Factors and taxa, traits and types, differences of degree and differences in kind. *Journal of Personality, 60,* 117–174.

Meehl, P. E. (1995a). Bootstraps taxometrics: Solving the classification problem in psychopathology. *American Psychologist, 50,* 266–275.

Meehl, P. E. (1995b). Extension of the MAXCOV-HITMAX taxometric procedure to situations of sizable nuisance covariance. In D. Lubinski & R. V. Dawis (Eds.), *Assessing individual differences in human behavior: New concepts, methods, and findings* (pp. 81–92). Palo Alto, CA: Davies-Black.

Meehl, P. E. (1999). Clarifications about taxometric method. *Applied and Preventive Psychology, 8,* 165–174.

Meehl, P. E., & Yonce, L. J. (1994). Taxometric analysis: I. Detecting taxonicity with two quantitative indicators using means above and below a sliding cut (MAMBAC procedure). *Psychological Reports, 74,* 1059–1274.

Meehl, P. E., & Yonce, L. J. (1996). Taxometric analyses II. Detecting taxonicity using covariance of two quantitative indicators in successive intervals of a third indicator. *Psychological Reports, 78,* 1091–1227.

Miller, M. B. (1996). Limitations of Meehl's MAXCOV-HITMAX procedure. *American Psychologist, 51*, 554–556.

Munson, J., Dawson, G., Sterling, L., Beauchaine, T., Zhou, A., Koehler, E., et al. (2008). Evidence for latent classes of IQ in young children with autism spectrum disorder. *American Journal on Mental Retardation, 113*, 439–452.

Muthén, B. O. (2001). Second-generation structural equation modeling with a combination of categorical and continuous latent variables: New opportunities for latent class/latent growth modeling. In A. Sayer & L. Collins (Eds.), *New methods for analysis of change* (pp. 291–322). Washington, DC: American Psychological Association.

Muthén, B., & Shedden, K., (1999). Finite mixture modeling with mixture outcomes using the EM algorithm. *Biometrics, 55*, 463–469.

Nagin, D. S. (1999). Analyzing developmental trajectories: A semiparametric, group-based approach. *Psychological Methods, 4*, 139–157.

Nunnally, J. C., & Bernstein, I. H. (1994). *Psychometric theory* (3rd ed.). New York: McGraw-Hill.

Rajendar, G. K. (1996). The influence of positive and negative wording and issue involvement on responses to Likert scales in marketing research. *Journal of the Market Research Society, 38*, 235–246.

Richey, J. A., Schmidt, N. B., Lonigan, C. J., Phillips, B. M., Catanzaro, S. J., Lauren, J., et al. (2009). The latent structure of child depression: A taxometric analysis. *Journal of Child Psychology and Psychiatry, 50*, 1147–1155.

Rosch, E., & Lloyd, B. (1978). *Cognition and categorization*. New York: Wiley.

Ruiz, M., Lind, U., Gåfvels, M., Eggertsen, G., Carlstedt-Duke, J., Nilsson, L., et al. (2001). Characterization of two novel mutations in the glucocorticoid receptor gene in patients with primary cortisol resistance. *Clinical Endocrinology, 55*, 363–371.

Ruscio, A., & Ruscio, J. (2002). The latent structure of analogue depression: Should the Beck Depression Inventory be used to classify groups? *Psychological Assessment, 14*, 135–145.

Ruscio, J. (2007). Taxometric analysis: An empirically grounded approach to implementing the method. *Criminal Justice and Behavior, 34*, 1588–1622.

Ruscio J., Haslam, N., & Ruscio, A. M. (2006). *Introduction to the taxometric method: A practical guide*. Mahwah, NJ: Erlbaum.

Ruscio, J., & Ruscio, A. (2000). Informing the continuity controversy: A taxometric analysis of depression. *Journal of Abnormal Psychology, 109*, 473–487.

Ruscio, J., & Ruscio, A. M. (2004a). Clarifying boundary issues in psychopathology: The role of taxometrics in a comprehensive program of structural research. *Journal of Abnormal Psychology, 113*, 24–38.

Ruscio, J., & Ruscio, A. M. (2004b). A conceptual and methodological checklist for conducting a taxometric investigation. *Behavior Therapy, 35*, 403–447.

Ruscio, J., & Ruscio, A. M. (2008). Categories and dimensions: Advancing psychological science through the study of latent structure. *Current Directions in Psychological Science, 17*, 203–207.

Ruscio, J., Ruscio, A. M., & Keane, T. M. (2004). Using taxometric analysis to distinguish a small latent taxon from a latent dimension with positively skewed indicators: The case of involuntary defeat syndrome. *Journal of Abnormal Psychology, 113*, 145–154.

Ruscio, J., Ruscio, A. M., & Meron, M. (2007). Applying the bootstrap to taxometric analysis: Generating empirical sampling distributions to help interpret results. *Multivariate Behavioral Research, 42*, 349–386.

Ruscio, J., Walters, G. D., Marcus, D. K., & Kaczetow, W. (2010). Comparing the relative fit of categorical and dimensional latent variable models using consistency tests. *Psychological Assessment, 22*, 5–21.

Saal, F. E., Downey, R. G., & Lahey, M. A. (1980). Rating the ratings: Assessing the psychometric quality of rating data. *Psychological Bulletin, 88*, 413–428.

Salmon, W. C. (1984). Scientific explanation and the causal structure of the world. Princeton NJ: Princeton University Press.

Salmon, W. C. (1989). *Four decades of scientific explanation*. Minneapolis, MN: University of Minnesota Press.

Schmidt, N. B., Kotov, R., Bernstein, A., Zvolensky, M. J., Joiner, T. E., & Lewinsohn, P. M. (2007). Mixed anxiety and depression: Taxometric exploration of the validity of a diagnostic category in youth. *Journal of Affective Disorders, 98*, 83–89.

Semin, G. R., & Rosch, E. (1981). Activation of bipolar prototypes in attribute inferences. *Journal of Experimental Social Psychology, 17*, 472–484.

Shannon, K. E., Beauchaine, T. P., Brenner, S. L., Neuhaus, E., & Gatzke-Kopp, L. (2007). Familial and temperamental predictors of resilience in children at risk for conduct disorder and depression. *Development and Psychopathology, 19*, 701–727.

Simon, D., Pham, L. B., Le, Q. A., & Holyoak, K. J. (2001). The emergence of coherence over the course of decision making. *Journal of Experimental Psychology: Learning, Memory, and Cognition, 27*, 1250–1260.

Skilling, T. A., Quinsey, V. L., & Craig, W. M. (2001). Evidence of a taxon underlying serious antisocial behavior in boys. *Criminal Justice and Behavior, 28*, 450–470.

Solomon, A., Ruscio, J., Seeley, J. R., & Lewinsohn, P. R. (2006). A taxometric investigation of unipolar depression in a large community sample. *Psychological Medicine, 36*, 973–986.

Tonidandel, S., & Overall, J. E. (2004). Determining the number of clusters by sampling with replacement. *Psychological Methods, 9*, 238–249.

Tylka, T. L., & Subich, L. M. (2003). Revisiting the latent structure of eating disorders: Taxometric analyses with non-behavioral indicators. *Journal of Counseling Psychology, 50*, 276–286.

Tyrka, A., Haslam, N., & Cannon, T. D. (1995). Detection of a longitudinally-stable taxon of individuals at risk for schizophrenia spectrum disorders. In A. Raine, T. Lencz, & S. A. Mednick (Eds.) *Schizotypal personality disorder* (pp. 168–191). New York: Cambridge University Press.

Tyrka, A. R., Cannon, T. D., Haslam, N., Mednick, S. A., Schulsinger, F., Schulsinger, H., et al. (1995). The latent structure of schizotypy: I. Premorbid indicators of a taxon in individuals at risk for schizophrenia-spectrum disorders. *Journal of Abnormal Psychology, 104*, 173–183.

Waller, N. G., & Meehl, P. E. (1998). *Multivariate taxometric procedures: Distinguishing types from continua*. Newbury Park, CA: Sage.

Waller, N. G., Putnam, F. W., & Carlson, E. B. (1996). Types of dissociation and dissociative types: A taxometric analysis of dissociative experiences. *Psychological Methods, 1*, 300–321.

Walters, G. D., McGrath, R. E., & Knight, R. A. (2010). Taxometrics, polytomous constructs, and the comparison curve fit index: A Monte Carlo analysis. *Psychological Assessment, 22*, 149–156.

Walters, G. D., & Ruscio, J. (2009). To sum or not to sum: Taxometric analysis with ordered categorical assessment items. *Psychological Assessment, 21*, 99–111.

Whewell, W. (1966). *The philosophy of the inductive sciences, founded upon their history.* New York: Johnson Reprint. (Original work published 1847).

Widiger, T. A. (2001). What can be learned from taxometric analyses? *Clinical Psychology Science and Practice, 8*, 528–533.

Widiger, T. A. (2007). Plate tectonics in the classification of personality disorder: Shifting to a dimensional model. *American Psychologist, 62*, 71–83.

Widiger, T. A., & Samuel, D. B. (2005). Diagnostic categories or dimensions? A question for the *DSM-IV. Journal of Abnormal Psychology, 114*, 494–504.

Williamson, D. A., Womble, L. G., Smeets, M. A. M., Netemeyer, R. G., Thaw, J. M., Kutlesic, V., et al. (2002). Latent structure of eating disorders symptoms: A factor analytic and taxometric investigation. *American Journal of Psychiatry, 159*, 412–418.

Woodward, S. A., Lenzenweger, M. F., Kagan, J., Snidman, N., & Arcus, D. (2000). Taxonic structure of infant reactivity: Evidence from a taxometric perspective. *Psychological Science, 11*, 296–301.

CHAPTER
27 Missing Data Methods

Amanda N. Baraldi *and* Craig K. Enders

Abstract

This chapter introduces the missing data methods currently in use and identifies the strengths and weaknesses of each of these methods. We first describe Rubin's missing data theory and outline three missing data mechanisms: MCAR, MAR, and NMAR. Next, we describe a variety of missing data techniques and their requisite assumptions. These techniques included traditional missing data procedures such as deletion and single imputation as well as the modern missing data techniques of maximum likelihood and multiple imputation. We also discuss a few of the many options for an NMAR mechanism. In the final section, we discuss ways in which missing data may be purposefully incorporated into a research design to maximize available resources and minimize respondent burden.

Key Words: Missing data mechanisms, multiple imputation, maximum likelihood, planned missing data, missing at random, not missing at random

Missing data are an inevitable burden on research involving human subjects and a problem that plagues social, behavioral, and medical scientists. Accordingly, methodologists have been studying missing data problems for several decades. Researchers have traditionally relied on various *ad hoc* techniques that discard incomplete values or fill in missing values to make the data set whole. Although these techniques continue to receive widespread use in published research (Bodner, 2006; Peugh & Enders, 2004), they require a strict assumption regarding the reason for missingness and result in biased population estimates when this assumption is not met. In the 1970s, a major breakthrough in missing data analysis came with the advent of maximum likelihood estimation and multiple imputation (Beale & Little, 1975; Dempster, Laird, & Rubin, 1977; Rubin, 1978, 1987). At the time, these "modern" missing data techniques were difficult to implement because they were computationally intensive, but contemporary computers now make maximum likelihood and multiple imputation techniques quite feasible. Because they require a less stringent assumption about the cause of missingness, these methods produce accurate estimates under a wider range of situations.

The goal of this chapter is to provide an overview of the analysis issues that arise with missing data and to demonstrate how these techniques may be used in research. We begin by introducing Rubin's missing data theory (1976). Rubin outlined three so-called missing data mechanisms: missing completely at random (MCAR), missing at random (MAR), and not missing at random (NMAR). These missing data mechanisms are important because they essentially serve as assumptions for a missing data analysis. Next, we describe a variety of missing data techniques and discuss their requisite assumptions. These techniques include traditional missing data procedures such as deletion and single imputation as well as the modern missing data

Table 27.1. Complete-Data Descriptive Statistics From the Artificial Data Set

Wave	Male (n = 1000)				Female (n = 1000)			
	M	SD	Skew.	Kurt.	M	SD	Skew.	Kurt.
1	10.383	1.825	0.734	1.392	9.434	1.834	0.984	3.224
2	10.231	1.783	0.998	3.395	9.274	1.858	1.157	3.332
3	10.139	1.763	1.088	2.455	9.155	1.782	1.049	2.635
4	10.077	1.809	0.832	1.530	8.965	1.836	1.109	2.671
5	9.978	1.828	0.789	1.428	8.878	1.902	1.347	4.695
6	9.960	1.829	0.904	2.336	8.687	1.838	0.718	2.412

techniques: maximum likelihood, multiple imputation, and techniques for data that are NMAR. Next, we describe the benefits and shortcomings of various missing data techniques, and we use an artificial data analysis example to illustrate their performance. To conclude, we discuss ways in which missing data may be purposefully incorporated into research design to maximize available resources and minimize respondent burden.

Artificial Data Example

Throughout the chapter, we use an artificial data set that is loosely based on Odgers et al.'s (2009) longitudinal study of antisocial behavior. The data set mimics a scenario where researchers collect six yearly assessments of antisocial behavior from 2000 children. The sample is comprised of two equal subgroups that we henceforth treat as a gender variable (0 = male, 1 = female). Table 27.1 gives the complete-data descriptive statistics for each group. As seen in the table, males had higher antisocial behavior scores at the initial wave and declined at a slower rate than females. Finally, notice that the repeated measures variables are positively skewed and are leptokurtic. We incorporated this nuance to illustrate the impact of non-normal data on various missing data handling techniques. We made three copies of the complete data set and used a different causal mechanism to introduce missing values in each. We will elaborate on these mechanisms in the next section. Regardless of the reason for missingness, each data set had a monotone missing data pattern, such that a designated proportion of the sample permanently dropped out of the study beginning at the second wave. Table 27.2 shows the

Table 27.2. Missing Data Patterns From the Artificial Data Set

Pattern	Data collection wave						%of Sample
	1	2	3	4	5	6	
1	O	O	O	O	O	O	60%
2	O	O	O	O	O	M	15%
3	O	O	O	O	M	M	10%
4	O	O	O	M	M	M	5%
5	O	O	M	M	M	M	5%
6	O	M	M	M	M	M	5%

Note: O = observed, M = missing.

missing data patterns and the distribution of the sample across the patterns.

The subsequent analysis examples utilize a linear growth model (i.e., a mixed effects, multilevel latent growth curve model) with a binary predictor variable. We give a brief overview of the model here, and the Chapter 18 by Wu and colleagues in this Handbook provides additional details. The linear growth model expresses the outcome variable as a function of data collection wave and gender, as follows

$$Y_{ti} = \beta_0 + \beta_1(WAVE_t) + \beta_2(FEMALE_i) \\ + \beta_3(WAVE_t)(FEMALE_i) \\ + b_{0i} + b_{1i}(WAVE_t) + \varepsilon_{ti}, \quad (1)$$

where Y_{ti} is the outcome score for case i at wave t, $WAVE_t$ is the temporal predictor variable that indexes the data collection wave, and FEMALE is the binary grouping variable (0 = male, 1 = female). To facilitate the interpretation of the parameter estimates, we expressed *WAVE* relative to the initial assessment, such that the centered scores took on values of 0, 1, 2, 3, 4, and 5. Under this parameterization, β_0 (i.e., the intercept) represents the average baseline score for males, β_1 is the yearly growth rate for males, β_2 quantifies the gender difference at the initial assessment, and β_2 is the difference between male and female growth rates. Turning to the so-called random effects, b_{0i} and b_{1i} are residual terms that capture individual differences in the intercepts and slopes, respectively, and ε_{ti} is a time-specific residual. The growth curve model yields a variance estimate for each residual term as well as a covariance between the intercept and slope residuals. The variance of b_0 quantifies the true score variation in baseline scores that persists after accounting for gender, and the variance of b_1 captures residual variation in the individual growth rates. Finally, the variance of ε_t quantifies the average squared distance between a participant's observed data and his or her idealized linear growth trajectory (i.e., residual variation in the repeated measures variables, controlling for individual growth).

Growth models are estimable from either the multilevel or the structural equation modeling framework. We focus on the latter approach because structural equation modeling programs offer a variety of tools for dealing with missing data. Viewed as a structural equation model, the individual growth components (i.e., b_{0i} and b_{1i}) are latent variables, and β_0 and β_1 are latent means that define the average growth trajectory. To illustrate, Figure 27.1 shows a path diagram of the growth model from Equation 1. The unit factor loadings for the intercept latent variable reflect the fact that the intercept is a constant component of each individual's growth trajectory, and the loadings for the slope latent variable correspond to the centered values of the *WAVE* variable (i.e., the amount of elapsed time between each assessment).

Missing Data Mechanisms

The missing data theory developed by Rubin and colleagues (Rubin, 1976; Little & Rubin, 2002) has become standard in the methodological literature. Rubin's classification system uses three so-called missing data mechanisms to describe the relationship between measured variables and the propensity for missingness on a given variable: MCAR, MAR, and NMAR. From a practical standpoint, these

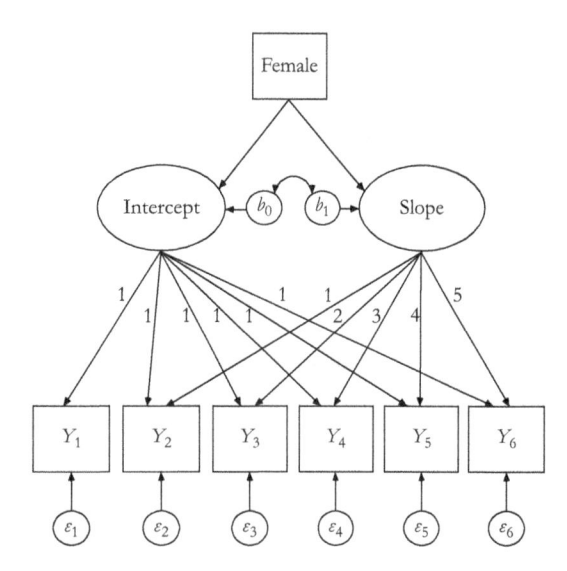

Figure 27.1 Path diagram of linear latent growth model from Equation 1. The individual growth components (i.e., b_{0i} and b_{1i}) are latent variables expressed in deviation form. The latent variable means define the average growth trajectory. The unit factor loadings for the intercept latent variable reflect the fact that the intercept is a constant component of each individual's growth trajectory, and the loadings for the slope latent variable correspond to the amount of elapsed time between each assessment.

missing data mechanisms may be viewed as assumptions underlying missing data techniques. As we discuss later, the most popular conventional missing data techniques, listwise and pairwise deletion, require the MCAR mechanism, whereas multiple imputation and maximum likelihood estimation assume a MAR mechanism.

The most basic missing data mechanism is MCAR. To satisfy the MCAR mechanism, the propensity for missing data on one variable must be completely unrelated to other variables in the data set (and, by extension, in the analysis). When this occurs, the observed data represent a random sample of the hypothetically complete data. In the longitudinal study of antisocial behavior that we described in the previous section, data may fulfill the MCAR mechanism for a variety of reasons. For example, if the study takes place within a particular school district, students may move to another school district for reasons unrelated to variables in the study (e.g., parental job relocation). There are myriad other benign reasons that a participant may miss a scheduled assessment unrelated to the variables of interest (e.g., a scheduling conflict or illness, an administrative blunder where some assessments were inadvertently lost or misplaced). Returning to the artificial data analysis example, we used a uniform random number to assign cases to the six missing patterns in Table 27.2. This produced a data set where the probability of attrition was unrelated to both gender and the repeated measures variables.

Despite the potentially confusing name, the MAR mechanism occurs when the propensity for missing data on a variable Y is related to other measured variables but not to the hypothetical value of Y itself. In other words, the MAR mechanism is satisfied when other variables in the analysis are associated with missingness, but after partialling out these variables, there is no longer a relationship between the Y scores and the propensity for missing data on Y. Despite its confusing moniker, the MAR mechanism differs from MCAR because there is a variable in the analysis that explains missingness. Returning to the hypothetical antisocial behavior study, the growth curve analysis would satisfy the MAR mechanism if the propensity for missingness at a particular wave is related to gender or to the observed scores at the previous wave. In the MAR data set for our data analysis examples, cases in the upper tail of the antisocial behavior distribution at wave t had the highest probability of attrition at the subsequent wave, and males had higher missing data rates than females. Consequently, after partialling out gender and previous antisocial behavior scores, there was no residual relationship between the propensity for missing data at wave t and the would-be scores at that wave.

Finally, the NMAR (also referred to as MNAR) mechanism occurs when the probability of missingness on Y is directly related to scores on the hypothetically complete Y variable, even after partialling out other variables in the analysis model. In other words, missingness depends on the would-be scores of the variable, had the data been complete. Returning to the antisocial behavior example, there are many theoretical reasons why the growth curve analysis could satisfy the NMAR mechanism. For example, participants who are in the juvenile correction system because of their antisocial behavior would miss one or more assessments. For the data analysis examples, we generated NMAR missingness by relating the probability of missing data at wave t to the antisocial behavior score at the same wave, such that cases with elevated antisocial behavior scores had the highest probability of missing data, even after controlling for gender and the preceding behavior scores. The NMAR mechanisms are particularly problematic for longitudinal studies, and a great deal of methodological research has focused on analytic approaches for dealing with this type of situation. We outline three classic NMAR approaches later in the chapter.

Based on recommendations from the methodological literature (e.g., Schafer & Graham, 2002), multiple imputation and maximum likelihood estimation have increased in popularity in recent years. These approaches require the MAR mechanism and can produce biased parameter estimates under an NMAR mechanism. It is important to emphasize that there is no way to empirically differentiate these two mechanisms because doing so would require knowledge of the missing scores. We used the antisocial behavior data to illustrate this point. In the MAR and NMAR data sets, we classified cases as complete or missing at the final wave and then compared the group means at the first five waves. Table 27.3 shows the means and standard deviations from these analyses. Notice that from the analyst's standpoint, MAR and NMAR produced a similar result—the cases with missing data at the final wave had higher means at the first five waves than the cases with complete data at wave 6. Because there is no way to empirically differentiate the two mechanisms, researchers must formulate logical arguments that support a particular missing data mechanism and choose an

Table 27.3. Means and Standard Deviations for Cases With Missing and Complete Data at Wave 6

Variable	Y_6 complete M	SD	Y_6 missing M	SD
MAR mechanism			
Y_1	9.26	1.56	10.88	1.93
Y_2	9.07	1.47	10.65	1.89
Y_3	8.94	1.37	10.43	1.70
Y_4	8.73	1.44	10.40	1.72
Y_5	8.51	1.42	10.73	1.36
MNAR mechanism			
Y_1	9.34	1.67	10.76	1.89
Y_2	9.15	1.60	10.28	1.66
Y_3	9.01	1.45	10.08	1.65
Y_4	8.83	1.55	9.94	1.74
Y_5	8.65	1.49	9.56	1.76

analysis method that is most defensible, given their assumptions about missingness.

Finally, it is important to point out Rubin's missing data mechanisms are not characteristics of a data set. Rather, the mechanisms are assumptions that apply to a specific analysis. Further, the variables in a particular analysis and the correlations among those variables determine the mechanism. As an example, reconsider our MAR data set where missingness was related to gender. Technically, MAR is only satisfied if gender is a variable in the growth curve analysis. Omitting a correlate of missingness (e.g., gender) can induce a spurious correlation between Y and the probability of missing data, thereby producing a NMAR mechanism. However, the impact of such an omission also depends on the correlations among the variables. For example, if gender is related to missingness but is unrelated to the analysis variables, then the mechanism is MCAR and no bias would result. In contrast, strong correlations between gender and the analysis variables could produce serious biases if the variable is not part of the analysis. Collins et al. (2001) have showed that omitting a correlate of missingness is generally not as problematic as an NMAR mechanism that occurs when the would-be value of Y directly influences missingness (e.g., a high antisocial behavior score at wave t tends to result in a missing value at that wave). Nevertheless, omitting a potential correlate of missingness can result in a NMAR mechanism. Therefore, methodologists generally recommend an inclusive strategy that incorporates auxiliary variables (i.e., potential correlates of missingness or correlates of the analysis variables) into an analysis (Collins et al., 2001). We return to this issue later in the chapter.

Atheoretical Missing Data Handling Methods

Having provided a brief overview of missing data theory, the next few sections describe several common missing data handling methods. To emphasize their underlying assumptions, we group the techniques by missing data mechanism. We begin with a group of atheoretical methods that do not rely on a particular mechanism. In our classification system, atheoretical methods for handling missing data include methods that (1) are known to produce bias regardless of the missing data mechanism or (2) do not have a theoretical foundation that predicts their performance. This class of methods is largely comprised of techniques that attempt to fill in the missing data with a single set of replacement values (i.e., single imputation). These methods include mean imputation, averaging the available items, last observation carried forward, and similar response pattern imputation. This list is not exhaustive, but it does include procedures that researchers are likely to see in published research articles or in popular software programs.

Mean Imputation

Mean imputation fills in the missing values with the arithmetic mean of the available cases. This approach is one of the earliest cited methods for handling missing data and dates back nearly 100 years (Wilks, 1932). Mean imputation is appealing because it produces a complete data set, thereby allowing the researcher to apply standard analysis procedures. The appeal of mean imputation, however, is counteracted by severe limitations. For one, this approach distorts parameter estimates, even when the data are MCAR. By imputing values at the arithmetic mean (i.e., the center) of the distribution, variability is reduced. This results in smaller standard deviations and variances, and the restriction in variability also attenuates covariances and correlations. Little and Rubin (2002, pp. 61–62) have outlined adjustment terms that produce consistent estimates of variances and covariances under an MCAR mechanism, but these corrections end up producing estimates that are identical to those of pairwise deletion (*see* the next section). A multitude of simulation studies have confirmed the biases associated with mean imputation (e.g., Brown, 1994; Enders, 2001; Wothke, 2000), and this approach is perhaps the worst technique that one could employ.

Averaging Available Items

Researchers in behavioral sciences frequently use multiple-item questionnaires to measure complex constructs such as depression, attitudes, or personality traits. Averaging or summing the responses to individual items yields a scale score that quantifies the construct. Often, respondents may not completely answer all items on a questionnaire. To handle missing data in this scenario, researchers often use a variation of mean imputation known as averaging the available items (test manuals often refer to this approach as a prorated scale score). For example, suppose that the antisocial behavior score from our previous example is defined as the sum of 20 Likert items. If a teen answered only 12 of the items, then his or her scale score would be the mean of the 12 items (multiplying the score by the number of items expresses the average as a sum). By averaging the available items, researchers can compute a scale score for every respondent that answered at least one item.

There is limited empirical research on this method, but Schafer and Graham (2002) have noted a number of potential problems with the approach and have speculated that averaging available items may produce biased parameter estimates in some situations. For example, it seems reasonable that there might be something unique about a particular item's content that causes a subject to skip the item (e.g., the content of the omitted item is more sensitive or in some way more extreme than other items). When this is true, computing a composite from disparate subsets of questions makes it difficult to interpret the resulting scores because the meaning of the scale varies across respondents. From a statistical perspective, averaging the available items may work best when inter-item correlations and the variable means are relatively uniform in magnitude (i.e., the items conform to a parallel factor structure; Graham, 2009; Schafer & Graham, 2002). Because there is limited empirical research on this method, researchers should be cautious about averaging the available items. The multiple imputation procedure that we describe in a later section is generally a better option for dealing with item-level missing data.

Last Observation Carried Forward Imputation

Last observation carried forward is a specialized imputation technique that researchers use in longitudinal designs. With last observation carried forward imputation, the missing repeated measure variables are filled in with the measurement that immediately precedes a subject's missing value (or values). To illustrate, Table 27.4 shows six waves of antisocial behavior data for a small subset of cases. Notice that the last complete observation for each case replaces subsequent data points; this is true for subjects who permanently withdraw from the study and for subjects with intermittent missing data. Although last observation carried forward is relatively uncommon in the behavioral and social sciences, researchers routinely employ this approach in medical research and clinical trials (Wood, White, & Thompson, 2004). Despite the frequency of its use in medical research and clinical trials, the methodological literature suggests that last observation carried forward is a subpar strategy for handling missing data in longitudinal research that is capable of producing bias, even under a MCAR mechanism

Table 27.4. Illustration of Last Observation Carried Forward Imputation

Case	1	2	3	4	5	6
			Observed data			
1	9.11	10.01			9.17	9.25
2	12.85	10.69				
3	10.88	10.93	10.32	10.27	9.39	
4	10.13	8.8	10.83			
5	8.24	8.61	8.48		9.5	8.03
			Imputed data			
1	9.11	10.01	**10.01**	**10.01**	9.17	9.25
2	12.85	10.69	**10.69**	**10.69**	**10.69**	**10.69**
3	10.88	10.93	10.32	10.27	9.39	**9.39**
4	10.13	8.8	10.83	**10.83**	**10.83**	**10.83**
5	8.24	8.61	8.48	**8.48**	9.5	8.03

Note: Bold typeface denotes imputed values.

(Cook, Zeng & Yi, 2004; Molenberghs et al., 2004; Shao & Zhong, 2004).

Similar Response Pattern Imputation

The final atheoretical approach we will discuss is similar response pattern imputation (in the survey sampling literature, this approach is referred to as nearest neighbor hot deck). Although similar response pattern imputation is not necessarily common in published articles, its availability in the popular structural equation modeling software package LISREL warrants a brief description (Jöreskog & Sörbom, 2006). The basic idea behind this procedure is to replace missing values with the data from another case that has similar scores on a set of matching variables. The user specifies the set of matching variables, and the software algorithm uses a standardized distance measure to identify a single donor individual with a comparable score profile on the matching variables. If a single donor exists, then that individual's score replaces the missing value. If multiple cases have profiles that match equally well, then the average donor score replaces the missing value. Computer simulations suggest that this approach may produce accurate estimates with a MCAR mechanism, but it can produce biases under MAR (Brown, 1994; Enders, 2001; Enders & Bandalos, 2001; Gold & Bentler, 2000). As such, similar response pattern imputation should be used with caution.

Methods That Assume Missing Completely At Random

A second set of missing data handling methods requires the MCAR mechanism. Recall that MCAR is satisfied when the probability of missing data on a variable Y is unrelated to other measured variables and to the value of Y itself (e.g., in a study of antisocial behavior, scores are missing because students relocated to a different school district, or because they missed an assessment because of scheduling conflicts or illness). We outline three MCAR-based analysis methods in this section: regression imputation, listwise deletion, and pairwise deletion. The latter two approaches have enjoyed widespread use in published research articles. As an aside, it is important to note that the MAR-based procedures in the next section generally outperform the methods in this section (e.g., because they maximize power), even when the mechanism is MCAR. Consequently, there is usually no reason to employ a technique that assumes MCAR.

Regression Imputation

Regression imputation is a procedure that has been around for approximately 50 years (Buck, 1960). The procedure begins with an estimate of the mean vector and the covariance matrix (e.g., obtained by deleting cases from the data). After sorting cases into groups that share the same missing data pattern, the procedure uses regression equations to predict the incomplete variables from the complete variables. The predicted scores from these regression equations replace the missing values and produce a complete data set. Regression imputation is conceptually attractive because it borrows information from the observed data to impute incomplete values. Although borrowing information is an excellent strategy (and one that is shared with multiple imputation and maximum likelihood), regression imputation has its limitations. Because a linear equation is used to generate missing values, the imputed values fall directly on a straight line. As such, the filled-in values lack variability that would have existed had the data been complete. The fact that the imputed values are a perfect linear function of the predictors also implies that, among the filled-in cases, there will be an artificially high level of collinearity between the incomplete variables and the complete variables (in a bivariate scenario where one variable is missing, the imputed values are perfectly correlated with the complete predictor variable). Not surprisingly, this collinearity biases measures of association. We classify regression imputation as a MCAR-based procedure because corrective adjustments are available that produce unbiased estimates of variances and covariances under a MCAR mechanism (Beale & Little, 1975; Buck, 1960). However, there is no reason to go through the additional effort of applying these corrections when more sophisticated missing data techniques are readily available.

Deletion Methods

Deletion methods are arguably the most common missing data techniques. Because they are the default routines in many statistical software packages, these methods are common in published research articles. Listwise deletion (also called complete-case analysis or casewise deletion) discards any case with missing values, such that the analyses are restricted to cases with complete data. Listwise deletion is alluring because it produces a complete data set, thereby allowing researchers to use standard analysis techniques. Despite this benefit, listwise deletion is ripe with disadvantages. The biggest disadvantage is that the MCAR requirement is a rather stringent assumption. When this assumption is violated—as often is the case in research studies—listwise deletion can produce severely biased estimates. Additionally, deleting incomplete cases dramatically reduces the total sample size, resulting in a loss of statistical power. Researchers typically put significant resources into data collection, so eliminating cases is obviously wasteful, even if MCAR is plausible.

Pairwise deletion (also known as available case analysis) is a less aggressive version of listwise deletion that discards cases on an analysis-by-analysis basis. As such, any given case may contribute to some analyses but not others. Using all of the available data is often an improvement over listwise deletion, but pairwise deletion is still subject to the stringent MCAR assumption. Consequently, this approach will produce biased estimates under a MAR or NMAR mechanism. Although pairwise deletion does not discard cases as aggressively as listwise deletion, the reduction of cases may still have a significant impact on statistical power. Further, estimation issues can arise because each element in a pairwise covariance matrix is based on a different subsample of cases (e.g., the elements in the covariance matrix could be mathematically impossible with complete data). Finally, the lack of a consistent sample base also leads to problems in computing standard errors because there is no single value of N that is applicable to entire analysis. As a general rule, the methodological literature has demonstrated that deletion methods are inferior to the approaches that rely on the MAR mechanism, so discarding data should be avoided unless the proportion of missing data is trivially small.

Methods That Assume Missing At Random

Recall that the MAR assumption is satisfied when the propensity for missing data on a variable Y is unrelated to the would-be values of Y after controlling for other variables in the analysis model (e.g., in a study of antisocial behavior, males are more likely to be missing than females, but the there is no relationship between antisocial behavior and missingness). This section outlines three MAR-based missing data handling methods: stochastic regression imputation, multiple imputation, and maximum likelihood estimation. Collectively, these techniques are advantageous because MAR is a less strict assumption than MCAR. From a practical perspective, this means that their estimates will be accurate under a wider variety of circumstances. We devote considerable attention to multiple imputation and maximum likelihood because methodologists have characterized these methods as the current "state of the art" (Schafer & Graham, 2002). Although multiple imputation and maximum likelihood are not yet the predominate methods in published research articles, there has been a noticeable shift to these MAR-based approaches in the last 10 years.

Stochastic Regression Imputation

Stochastic regression imputation is the one traditional missing data procedure that yields unbiased parameter estimates under the MAR mechanism. Like standard regression imputation, stochastic regression imputation uses regression equations to predict the incomplete variables from the complete variables. However, in stochastic regression imputation, each predicted score is augmented with a normally distributed residual term. Adding residuals to the imputed values restores variability to the data and effectively eliminates the biases associated with regression imputation. In this way, stochastic regression imputation preserves the variability of the data in a way that other single imputation techniques do not. Although stochastic regression imputation produces unbiased parameter estimates, the corresponding standard errors are always too small. Conceptually, filling in the missing values should increase standard errors because the imputations are just guesses about the real data values. However, software routines that treat the imputed values as actual data have no way of estimating an inflation factor for the standard errors. Consequently, stochastic regression imputation attenuates standard errors, leading to an increased risk of type I errors. Although multiple imputation uses an identical procedure to fill in the data, it provides a mechanism for correcting standard errors.

Multiple Imputation

Multiple imputation creates several copies of the original data set, each of which contains different estimates of the missing values. A multiple imputation analysis consists of three stages: an imputation phase, an analysis phase, and a pooling phase. In the imputation phase, each copy of the data set is filled in with a different set of plausible replacement values. Conceptually, this step is an iterative version of the stochastic regression procedure from the previous section. Next, in the analysis phase, the researcher performs a statistical analysis (e.g., a growth curve analysis) on each filled-in data set. Finally, the pooling phase combines the estimates and standard errors from the analysis phase into a single set of values. In this section, we briefly describe the three phases of multiple imputation. Although the analysis and pooling phases of multiple imputation may seem arduous, software packages typically automate these steps, making multiple imputation relatively painless.

The imputation phase is the first step in a multiple imputation analysis. In the imputation phase, each copy of the data set is filled in (or imputed) with plausible scores that replace the missing values. Although many algorithms have been proposed for the imputation phase (King, Honaker, Joseph, & Scheve, 2001; Lavori, Dawson, & Shera, 1995; Raghunathan, Lepkowski, Van Hoewyk, & Solenberger, 2001; Royston, 2005; Schafer, 1997, 2001; Van Buuren, 2007), the data augmentation algorithm is one of the commonly used algorithms for multivariate normal data. The data augmentation algorithm is a two-step iterative algorithm that repeatedly cycles through an imputation step (I-step) and a posterior step (P-step). During the I-step, regression equations impute missing values in a way that is identical to stochastic regression analysis. That is, regression equations predict the incomplete variables from the complete variables, and the sum of a predicted score and random residual term replaces each missing value. Next, the P-step randomly perturbs the imputation regression coefficients, resulting in a distinct set of regression coefficients for use in the next I-step. Although the technical details are complex and rely on Bayesian estimation principles, the perturbation process effectively adds a random residual term to each of the imputation regression coefficients from the preceding I-step. Having generated a new set of regressions, the algorithm proceeds to the next I-step and generates a new data set with different imputed values. These two steps repeat for a designated number of cycles.

In the analysis phase, the researcher analyzes each filled-in data set using the same procedures that would have been used had the data been complete. This analysis is based entirely on the research question of interest, and no special considerations need to be made to accommodate the missing data. For example, in a subsequent section, we generate 50 imputed data sets and estimate the growth model from Equation 1 on each data set. The analysis phase yields a separate set of parameter estimates and standard errors for each data set.

Finally, the pooling phase combines the estimates and standard errors from the analysis phase into a single set of values. Rubin (1987) outlined formulas for pooling parameter estimates and standard errors. Pooled parameter estimates are derived by taking the arithmetic mean of each parameter estimate from each data set. Pooling the standard errors is slightly more complicated because multiple imputation standard errors take into account both within-imputation (i.e., complete-data) sampling variance and between-imputation (i.e., missing-data) sampling variance. Specifically, the within-imputation variance is the arithmetic average of the squared standard errors from each complete data set

$$V_W = \frac{1}{m} \sum_{t=1}^{m} SE_t^2, \quad (2)$$

where t denotes a particular imputed data set and m is the total number of imputed data sets. The within-imputation variance quantifies the sampling error (i.e., squared standard error) that would have been obtained had the data been complete. Between-imputation variance quantifies the amount of additional sampling error in a particular parameter that results from the missing data. The extent to which the estimates vary across imputed data sets determines this value. More specifically, the formula for the between-imputation variance is

$$V_B = \frac{1}{m-1} \sum_{t=1}^{m} (\hat{\theta}_t - \bar{\theta})^2, \quad (3)$$

where $\hat{\theta}_t$ is the parameter estimate from filled-in data set t, and $\bar{\theta}$ is the average parameter estimate across all imputed data sets. The reader may notice that Equation 3 is actually the sample variance formula with parameter estimates serving as the data points. Conceptually, the only reason why estimates vary from one data set to the next is because each imputed data set contains different filled-in values. Consequently, this between-imputation variation represents the amount by which you have to inflate the squared standard error to account for missing data.

Finally, the pooled standard error combines the within- and the between-imputation variance (Equations 2 and 3, respectively), as:

$$SE = \sqrt{V_W + V_B + V_B/m}. \quad (4)$$

It is this pooling of different sources of sampling error that yields better standard error estimates than single imputation techniques such as stochastic regression. As previously mentioned, single imputation methods treat the imputed values as actual data. As a result, standard errors are effectively based only on the within-imputation component of Equation 4. By incorporating the between-imputation (i.e., missing data) sampling variance, multiple imputation standard errors explicitly account for the fact that imputed scores are merely guesses about the true data values. Including this extra source of sampling variation yields a better standard error estimate. Decomposing the sampling variance into two components also provides a mechanism for computing diagnostic measures that quantify the impact of missing data on a given standard error. For example, the fraction of missing information is a summary measure that quantifies the proportion of a parameter's total sampling variance that results from the missing data (i.e., FMI = $[V_B + V_B/m]/SE^2$). The relative increase in variance is a related measure. Additional details on these diagnostic statistics are available in Enders (2010) and Schafer (1997).

Practical Issues With Multiple Imputation. There are many practical considerations associated with a multiple imputation analysis. This section describes a few of these considerations, and additional information is available from other sources (Enders, 2010; Schafer, 1997; Schafer & Olsen, 1998).

The first consideration involves the selection of variables for the imputation phase. At a minimum, the imputation process should include all variables or effects that will appear in a subsequent analysis. For example, if the substantive question involves a moderating variable, then the researcher should either include a product term in the imputation process (if the moderator is continuous) or should impute the data separately by subgroup (if the moderator is categorical). In addition to including the analysis variables, the imputation phase should also incorporate additional variables that either predict the propensity for missing data or predict the incomplete analysis variables. Including these so-called auxiliary variables can reduce nonresponse bias and improve power. We discuss auxiliary variables in more detail later in the chapter. Finally, the imputation process must preserve any special features of the data. For example, multilevel data structures require specialized imputation algorithms that preserve any random intercepts and slopes that may be present in the data.

As described previously, the goal of multiple imputation is to generate a number of complete data sets. Deciding on the number of imputed data sets is a second practical consideration. Historically, statisticians have recommended using relatively few data sets (e.g., three to five is a common rule of thumb), but recent computer simulations show that using a larger number of data sets can substantially improve power (Graham, Olchowski & Gilreath, 2007). This research suggests that 20 data sets are often sufficient, although there is no harm in using an even larger number of imputations.

Third, when implementing multiple imputation, it is crucial that the imputed values in a given data set are independent from the imputed values in other data sets. Although it is not immediately obvious, the data augmentation algorithm produces serial dependencies that can linger for many computational cycles. Consequently, the data sets that are used in the analysis phase should not come from successive I-steps. To generate independent imputations, a number of data augmentation cycles should separate the data files that are used for the analyses (this separation interval is often referred to as the number of between-imputation iterations). For example, a researcher might decide to allow the data augmentation algorithm to cycle for thousands of iterations, saving a data set for analysis after every 300th I-step. In this way, the multiple imputed data sets mimic random samples from a distribution of plausible replacement scores. Choosing the correct interval is an important practical issue because, if the number of between-imputation iterations is too small, then the correlated imputations will shrink the between-imputation variance in Equation 4, resulting in negatively biased standard errors. Graphical diagnostics such as time-series plots and autocorrelation function plots can highlight these serial dependencies and help determine the number of between-imputation iterations (e.g., see Enders, 2010; Schafer, 1997; Schafer & Olsen, 1998).

Fourth, there are times when the data augmentation algorithm fails to converge. In this context, a convergence failure effectively means that the algorithm is unable to generate imputed values from a stable score distribution. Convergence failures can happen because the number of variables is too large (e.g., the number of variables approaches or exceeds the number of cases) or because of a peculiar missing data pattern (e.g., one of the subgroups in a set of categorical dummy codes has no data on a variable). When the data augmentation algorithm fails to converge, reducing the number of variables or eliminating problematic variables may alleviate the problem. An alternate strategy is to use a ridge prior distribution. The ridge prior is a Bayesian idea that stabilizes estimation by infusing the data with a small number of imaginary data points from a distribution where the variables are uncorrelated. Convergence failures are often easy to spot using the same graphical techniques that help determine the number of between-imputation cycles.

Finally, it is important to note that multiple imputation offers several significance testing options. Dividing the pooled parameter estimate by its standard error (i.e., Equation 4) and referencing this ratio to a z or t reference distribution is the most common way to test individual parameters. Multiparameter inferential procedures are also available for testing sets of parameters (e.g., a test statistic that mimics the omnibus F from a multiple regression analysis). Specifically, the D_1 statistic uses multivariate extensions of the previous pooling equations (Equations 2–4) to generate a test that closely resembles the Wald chi-square from a maximum likelihood analysis. In contrast, the D_2 statistic combines m Wald tests from the analysis phase, and the D_3 statistic similarly pools m likelihood ratio tests. Although the D_1 and D_3 statistics are asymptotically equivalent, D_1 is arguably easier to implement and it is widely available in popular software packages (e.g., SAS, NORM, Mplus). D_3 is also available in Mplus, but its implementation is limited to comparisons that involve a saturated model (e.g., the chi-square test of model fit from a structural equation model). Additional computational details are available in Enders (2010) and Schafer (1997).

Maximum Likelihood Estimation

Maximum likelihood estimation is a second MAR-based analysis approach that is becoming increasingly common in published research. When the variables in a maximum likelihood analysis are identical to the variables in the imputation phase of a multiple imputation analysis, the two procedures tend to yield comparable parameter estimates and standard errors (Collins et al., 2001; Schafer, 2003). All things being equal, the two procedures are asymptotically (i.e., in large samples) equivalent. However, unlike multiple imputation, maximum likelihood estimation does not impute missing values. Rather, the estimation routine uses all available data to identify the population parameter values that have the highest probability of producing the sample data. Our focus in this section will be on normally distributed outcome variables, but the mechanics and the logic of maximum likelihood estimation is similar for other measurement scales. We will introduce maximum likelihood estimation at a broad conceptual level; the mathematics behind the procedure should not deter you from using this approach when dealing with missing data. Software packages that implement maximum likelihood are user friendly and do not require an in-depth understanding of the mathematical nuances of estimation.

As previously mentioned, maximum likelihood estimation identifies the population parameter values that have the highest probability of producing the sample data. To do so, estimation uses a mathematical function called log likelihood to quantify the standardized distance between a participant's data points and the parameter of interest (e.g., the mean, the average growth trajectory). More specifically, the log likelihood value is the relative probability that a set of scores for a given individual come from a normally distributed population with a particular mean vector and covariance matrix. With multivariate normal population data, an individual's log likelihood value is

$$\log L_i = -\frac{k_i}{2}\log(2\pi) - \frac{1}{2}\log|\Sigma_i| \\ - \frac{1}{2}(Y_i - \mu_i)^T \Sigma_i^{-1}(Y_i - \mu_i), \quad (5)$$

where k_i is the number of observed variables for case i, Y_i is the score vector for that individual, and μ and Σ are the population mean vector and covariance matrix, respectively (in our growth model example, μ and Σ are model-implied matrices). Although Equation 5 may seem complex, notice that it contains the matrix formula for a squared z-score (also known as Mahalanobis distance):

$$(Y_i - \mu_i)^T \Sigma_i^{-1}(Y_i - \mu_i).$$

The value of the log likelihood in Equation 5 is largely driven by this term. Specifically, a small z-score (i.e., a small standardized distance between a set of scores and the parameter values) reflects better fit to μ and Σ, whereas a large z-score indicates worse fit. The sample log likelihood quantifies the fit of the entire sample by summing the individual log likelihood values.

The ultimate goal of estimation is to minimize the standardized distances between the sample data and the parameter estimates. Maximum likelihood uses the sample log likelihood to "audition" and choose among different plausible parameter values. Conceptually, the sample log likelihood is similar to the loss function in ordinary least squares (OLS) regression, where the goal is to minimize the sum of the squared residuals. Here, we want to maximize the sum of the individual log likelihoods (because log likelihood values quantify fit on a probability-like metric, a small squared z-score corresponds to a large log likelihood). The parameter estimates that maximize the sum of the log likelihood values (and thus minimize the z-scores) are the so-called maximum likelihood estimates.

A crucial aspect of maximum likelihood missing data handling is that it does not require complete information on all variables. Notice that the data and parameter matrices in Equation 5 (i.e., Y_i, μ_i, and Σ_i) have i subscripts. This allows the size and content of these matrices to vary across cases with different configurations of missing and complete data. To illustrate, consider an analysis that estimates the mean vector and covariance matrix for three variables: X, Y, and Z. The squared z-score for an individual with complete data would be based on all the parameters, and the individual log likelihood value for such an individual would be.

$$\log L_i = -\frac{3}{2}\log(2\pi) - \frac{1}{2}\log \begin{vmatrix} \hat{\sigma}_X^2 & \hat{\sigma}_{XY} & \hat{\sigma}_{XZ} \\ \hat{\sigma}_{YX} & \hat{\sigma}_Y^2 & \hat{\sigma}_{YZ} \\ \hat{\sigma}_{ZX} & \hat{\sigma}_{ZY} & \hat{\sigma}_Z^2 \end{vmatrix}$$
$$-\frac{1}{2}\left(\begin{bmatrix} X_i \\ Y_i \\ Z_i \end{bmatrix} - \begin{bmatrix} \hat{\mu}_X \\ \hat{\mu}_Y \\ \hat{\mu}_Z \end{bmatrix}\right)^T$$
$$\times \begin{vmatrix} \hat{\sigma}_X^2 & \hat{\sigma}_{XY} & \hat{\sigma}_{XZ} \\ \hat{\sigma}_{YX} & \hat{\sigma}_Y^2 & \hat{\sigma}_{YZ} \\ \hat{\sigma}_{ZX} & \hat{\sigma}_{ZY} & \hat{\sigma}_Z^2 \end{vmatrix}^{-1}$$
$$\times \left(\begin{bmatrix} X_i \\ Y_i \\ Z_i \end{bmatrix} - \begin{bmatrix} \hat{\mu}_X \\ \hat{\mu}_Y \\ \hat{\mu}_Z \end{bmatrix}\right)$$

For an individual with a missing Y-value, the squared z-score would be based only on the elements of $\boldsymbol{\mu}$ and $\boldsymbol{\Sigma}$ that depend on X and Z. The individual log likelihood equation in this case would be:

$$\log L_i = -\frac{2}{2}\log(2\pi) - \frac{1}{2}\log \begin{vmatrix} \hat{\sigma}_X^2 & \hat{\sigma}_{XZ} \\ \hat{\sigma}_{ZX} & \hat{\sigma}_Z^2 \end{vmatrix}$$
$$-\frac{1}{2}\left(\begin{bmatrix} X_i \\ Z_i \end{bmatrix} - \begin{bmatrix} \hat{\mu}_X \\ \hat{\mu}_Z \end{bmatrix}\right)^T \begin{bmatrix} \hat{\sigma}_X^2 & \hat{\sigma}_{XZ} \\ \hat{\sigma}_{ZX} & \hat{\sigma}_Z^2 \end{bmatrix}^{-1}$$
$$\left(\begin{bmatrix} X_i \\ Z_i \end{bmatrix} - \begin{bmatrix} \hat{\mu}_X \\ \hat{\mu}_Z \end{bmatrix}\right).$$

Finally, the log likelihood computation for an individual with complete data on X only would depend on the X parameters:

$$\log L_i = -\frac{1}{2}\log(2\pi) - \frac{1}{2}\log |\hat{\sigma}_X^2|$$
$$-\frac{1}{2}(X_i - \hat{\mu}_X)^T[\hat{\sigma}_X^2]^{-1}(X_i - \hat{\mu}_X).$$

In the context of the earlier longitudinal growth model example, X, Y, and Z could represent the repeated measures variables. The previous equations imply that the analysis would utilize the entire sample, including those individuals that prematurely dropped out of the study. The logic of estimation is identical in this more complicated scenario, with the exception that the model-implied mean vector and the model-implied covariance matrix from the growth model replace μ and Σ, respectively.

It may not be obvious from the previous equations, but including the partially complete cases steers estimation toward a more accurate set of estimates than would have been possible with the complete cases alone. Although the estimation process does not explicitly fill in the missing data, the observed scores for the incomplete cases do imply plausible replacement values. To illustrate, consider a bivariate analysis that involves the first two waves from the antisocial behavior data set; recall that that the data are complete at the first wave, but 5% of the sample dropped out at the second wave. At any given iteration of the estimation process, the log likelihood quantifies the relative probability of the data, given the parameter values at that cycle. The log likelihood function in Equation 5 is based on the normal distribution, and the top panel of Figure 27.2 shows the bivariate normal distribution for this scenario. Because the log likelihood function is the natural log of the equation that defines the shape of the multivariate normal distribution, the height of the curve effectively corresponds to the log likelihood value for a particular pair of scores (i.e., solving Equation 5 gives a value that denotes the corresponding height of the distribution where the two score values intersect).

To illustrate how estimation works with missing data, consider an individual with a baseline antisocial behavior score of 10 and a missing value at the second wave. The multivariate normal distribution effectively constrains the range of plausible values at the second wave, such that certain antisocial behavior scores are more probable than others. To demonstrate, the middle panel of Figure 27.2 shows the slice of the multivariate normal distribution that corresponds to a wave 1 score of $Y_1 = 10$ (i.e., the conditional distribution of Y_2 given Y_1). Because the normal curve slice is centered at 9.5, the most likely value for the missing antisocial behavior score is approximately $Y_2 = 9.5$. Next, consider an individual with a baseline score of 8 and a missing value at the second wave. The bottom panel of Figure 27.2 depicts the slice of the multivariate normal distribution that corresponds to this scenario (i.e., the conditional distribution of Y_2 given that $Y_1 = 8$). Now, the normal curve slice is centered at roughly 8.5, and the most plausible value for the missing wave 2 score is $Y_2 = 8.5$. Although maximum likelihood estimation does not literally fill in the missing scores, it uses integral calculus to implicitly replace the values. Conceptually, estimation replaces the wave 2 score for the first respondent with the weighted average of the Y_2 values from the middle panel of Figure 27.2, where the height of the normal curve slices determines the weights. Similarly, the weighted average of the Y_2 values from the bottom panel of Figure 27.2 replaces the missing value for the second respondent. It is the distributional assumption (here, bivariate normality) that constrains the missing scores to a certain range and allows the estimation algorithm to utilize

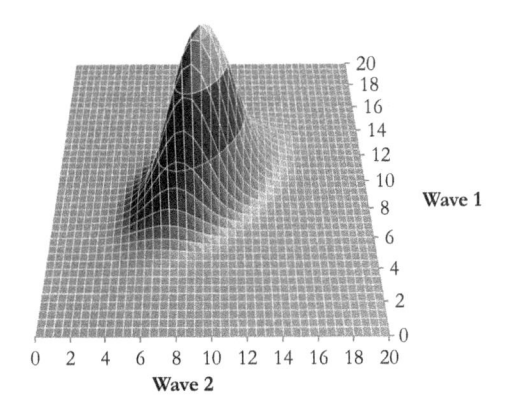

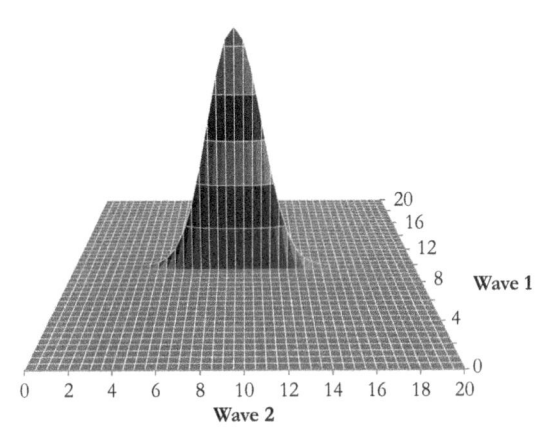

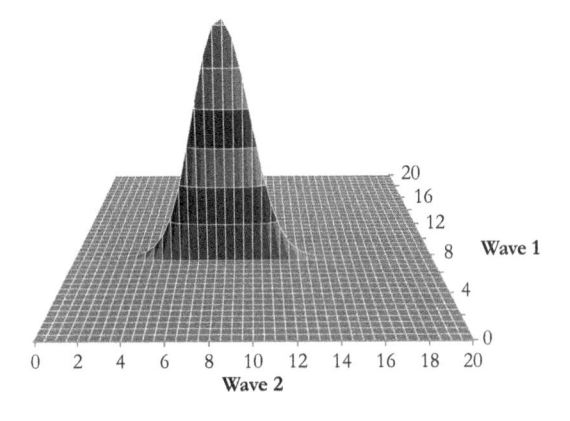

Figure 27.2 The top panel depicts the bivariate normal distribution for the first two waves of the antisocial behavior data set. The middle panel shows the slice of the bivariate normal distribution at wave 1 for $Y_i = 10$. The bottom panel shows the slice of the bivariate normal distribution at wave 1 for $Y_i = 8$.

the observed data to infer information about the parameters with missing data.

Practical Issues With Maximum Likelihood. Because maximum likelihood estimation is arguably easier to implement than multiple imputation, there are usually fewer practical nuances to worry about. We discuss two important issues to which researchers need to attend when implementing maximum likelihood estimation: incomplete explanatory variables and standard error computations.

Depending on the substantive analysis, software packages may or may not include cases with missing explanatory variables. To understand why, reconsider the log likelihood in Equation 5. In some analyses, explanatory variables do not appear in the Y vector but, rather, contribute to the definition of $\boldsymbol{\mu}$ (e.g., in a regression model, $\boldsymbol{\mu}$ is a conditional mean defined by $\beta_0 + \beta_1 X_1 + \ldots + \beta_p X_p$). For many analysis models, structural equation modeling programs are an ideal platform for dealing with incomplete explanatory variables. By specifying an incomplete predictor variable as the sole manifest indicator of a latent variable, the software program will interpret the incomplete predictor as a Y variable, while still maintaining its exogenous status in the model. Some software packages (e.g., Mplus) allow the user to convert an X variable to a Y variable with very little effort. However, when implementing this programming trick, it is important to explicitly specify the covariances among the explanatory variables because software packages tend to omit associations among the Ys. Finally, it is also important to note that converting an incomplete predictor to a Y variable impacts nested model testing with the likelihood ratio statistic. Readers who are interested in more details on this issue can consult Enders (2010, pp. 116–118).

The computation of standard errors is a second practical issue that arises with maximum likelihood estimation. Although missing data maximum likelihood estimation is largely the same as complete-data estimation, the missing values add an important nuance to standard error computations. The second derivatives of the log likelihood function largely determine maximum likelihood standard errors. Conceptually, these second derivatives capture the curvature or peakedness of the log likelihood function near the maximum, such that larger derivative values (i.e., a function that is steep near its maximum) translate into smaller standard errors. There are two approaches for computing missing data standard errors: expected information and observed information. The expected information replaces deviation scores (i.e., $\mathbf{Y}_i - \boldsymbol{\mu}_i$) in the second derivative formulas with zero (i.e., the expected value of a deviation score), whereas observed information uses the observed data to compute the deviation scores in the derivative equations. Interestingly, Kenward and Molenberghs (1998) have showed that the two computational approaches require different assumptions about the missing data mechanism.

To understand the differences between the expected and the observed information, consider what happens to a set of deviation scores under different missing data mechanisms. With an MCAR mechanism, the missing Y values should be haphazardly dispersed above and below the Y mean because the observed values are random sample of the hypothetically complete data. In this situation, the expected information and the observed information should produce the same standard error estimates, on average, because the deviation scores in the second derivative equations should sum to zero. That is, it makes no difference whether you use the data to compute the deviation scores or simply replace them with zeros. In contrast, under an MAR mechanism, the systematic selection mechanism tends to produce more missing values in one tail of the distribution than the other (e.g., if cases with high baseline antisocial scores have a higher propensity for missing data at the second wave, then there will be fewer Y_2 values observed above the mean than below the mean). In this situation, replacing the deviation scores with their expectations is incorrect because these values no longer sum to zero, but using the observed data to compute the deviation scores in second derivative equations is appropriate.

From a practical perspective, the computational differences can have a substantial impact on the accuracy of missing data standard errors. Simulation studies have shown that standard errors based on the expected information can be far too small under an MAR mechanism, whereas standard errors based on the observed information are accurate (Enders, 2010; Kenward & Molenberghs, 1998). This is an important point because software packages differ in their computations; some programs use observed information as the default, others use the expected information as the default, yet others do not offer the observed information as an option. Whenever possible, standard errors should be based on the observed information.

Methods That Assume Not Missing At Random

According to Rubin, an NMAR mechanism holds when the probability of missing data on Y depends on the values of Y, even after controlling for other variables in the model. From a practical perspective, this means that an NMAR-based analysis must include a set of parameters that describes the propensity for missing data. We describe three such approaches in this section: the selection model, the shared parameter model, and the pattern mixture model. Although these three models are quite different from one another, they all supplement the substantive model (e.g., the growth model from Equation 1) with a submodel that explains the probability of missingness. Space limitations preclude a thorough overview of NMAR methods, but a number of other sources provide detailed descriptions of these approaches (Albert & Follmann, 2009; Hedeker & Gibbons, 1997, 2006; Enders, 2010, 2011; Little, 2009).

Heckman (1976, 1979) outlined the selection model for regression analyses with NMAR data on the outcome variable. Heckman's basic idea was to augment the linear regression model with an additional regression equation that predicts a binary missing data indicator (e.g., $R = 0$ if the outcome variable is observed, $R = 1$ if the outcome is missing). When certain assumptions hold (e.g., normality), simultaneously estimating these two models corrects for NMAR nonresponse bias. Diggle and Kenward (1994) extended the selection model approach to longitudinal data analyses. Like the classic selection model, the Diggle-Kenward model combines a growth curve analysis with a set of regression equations that predict binary missing data indicators. To illustrate, Figure 27.3 applies their approach to a linear growth model that is similar to that in Equation 1 (to reduce visual clutter, we omitted gender from the diagram). The rectangles labeled R_2 through R_6 are binary variables that denote whether the outcome variable is observed or missing at each wave (e.g., $R_t = 0$ if the outcome is observed, $R_t = 1$ if the outcome is missing). The arrows pointing to the R variables represent logistic regression equations that relate the probability of missing data at wave t to the outcome variable at wave t as well as to the outcome variable from the preceding assessment (e.g., Y_1 and Y_2 predict R_2, Y_2 and Y_3 predict R_3, and so on). Although the diagram omits gender from the model, this variable can also predict the missing data indicators.

The shared parameter model (Wu & Carroll, 1988) is comparable to the selection model but uses individual growth trajectories (i.e., the latent variables, b_0 and b_1) rather than the repeated measures variables to predict the missing data indicators. To illustrate, Figure 27.4 applies the approach to a linear growth model. Consistent with the selection model diagram, the arrows that link the latent

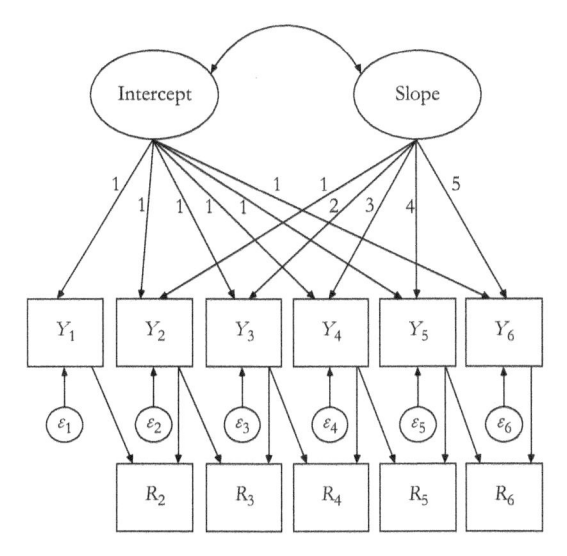

Figure 27.3 The Diggle-Kenward model applied to a linear growth curve analysis. The rectangles labeled R_2 through R_6 are binary variables that denote whether the outcome variable is observed or missing at each wave (e.g., $R_t = 0$ if the outcome is observed, $R_t = 1$ if the outcome is missing). The arrows pointing to the R variables represent logistic regression equations that relate the odds of missing data at wave t to the outcome variable at wave t as well as to the outcome variable from the preceding assessment.

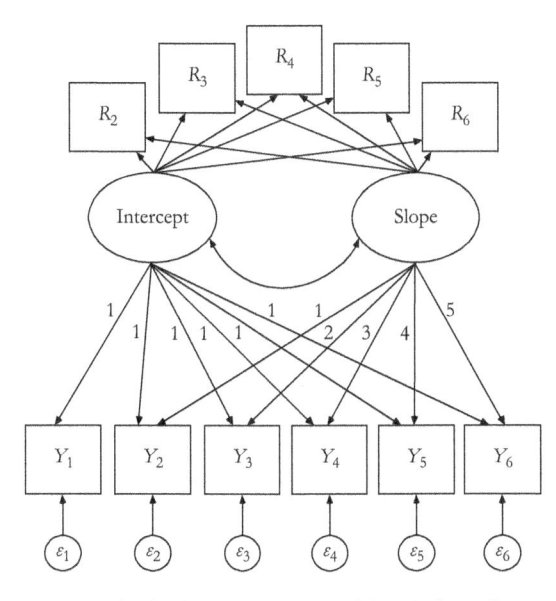

Figure 27.4 The shared parameter model applied to a linear growth curve analysis. The rectangles labeled R_2 through R_6 are binary variables that denote whether the outcome variable is observed or missing at each wave (e.g., $R_t = 0$ if the outcome is observed, $R_t = 1$ if the outcome is missing). The arrows pointing to the R variables represent logistic regression equations that relate the odds of missing data to the individual intercepts and slopes.

variables (i.e., the individual intercepts and slopes) to the binary missing data indicators represent logistic regression equations. Regressing the indicator variables on the intercepts and slopes effectively allows the probability of missing data to depend on an individual's overall developmental trajectory rather than a single error-prone realization of the outcome variable (Albert & Follmann, 2009; Little, 1995). Although the diagram omits the gender variable, it, too, can predict the missing data indicators.

Although it is not obvious, selection and shared parameter models are only estimable by invoking untestable distributional assumptions, typically multivariate normality. For example, reconsider the Diggle-Kenward selection model. The regression of R_t on the outcome variable at wave t is inestimable because the outcome is always missing whenever R equals one. By invoking the normality assumption, the estimation routine effectively fills in the values that would have resulted had the repeated measures variables originated from a multivariate normal distribution. In a similar vein, the shared parameter model requires distributional assumptions for the so-called random effects (i.e., the latent variables, b_0 and b_1). Because the distributional assumptions are fundamental to identification and estimation, the resulting parameter estimates can be quite sensitive to even modest departures from normality. In addition, the accuracy of the selection and shared parameter models depends on the correct specification of the missing data model. For example, omitting an important predictor of missingness or including an unnecessary predictor in the logistic regressions can produce substantial bias. We illustrate this point in one of the later analysis examples.

The pattern mixture model also integrates a model for the missing data into the analysis, but it does so in a different fashion than the selection model. Specifically, a pattern mixture analysis stratifies the sample into subgroups that share the same missing data pattern and estimates the substantive model (e.g., the growth model from Equation 1) separately within each pattern. Returning to the missing data patterns in Table 27.2, each of the six subgroups would yield unique estimates of the growth model parameters. The pattern-specific estimates may be informative, but the usual goal is to estimate the population parameters. Computing the weighted average of the group-specific estimates yields an estimate that averages over the missing data patterns. For example, the pattern mixture estimate of the male baseline mean from Equation 1 would be

$$\hat{\bar{\beta}}_0 = \hat{\pi}^{(1)}\hat{\beta}_0^{(1)} + \hat{\pi}^{(2)}\hat{\beta}_0^{(2)} + \hat{\pi}^{(3)}\hat{\beta}_0^{(3)} + \hat{\pi}^{(4)}\hat{\beta}_0^{(4)}$$
$$+ \hat{\pi}^{(5)}\hat{\beta}_0^{(5)} + \hat{\pi}^{(6)}\hat{\beta}_0^{(6)},$$

where the numeric superscript denotes the missing data pattern, and $\hat{\pi}^{(p)}$ is the proportion of cases in missing data pattern p.

Although it may not be immediately obvious, the pattern mixture model is not estimable without invoking one or more untestable assumptions. Returning to the missing data patterns in Table 27.2, notice that the cases in Pattern 6 have only one observation. As such, the male baseline mean and the baseline mean difference (i.e., β_0 and β_2, respectively) are estimable but the slope parameters (i.e., β_1 and β_3, respectively) are not. Similarly, the regression coefficients from Equation 1 are estimable for Pattern 5, but certain variance estimates are not. Estimating the pattern mixture model requires the user to supply values for the inestimable parameters. One way to specify these values is to borrow estimates from other patterns. For example, the inestimable linear parameters for Pattern 6 could be equated to the corresponding estimates from the group of cases with comparable dropout—in this case, Pattern 5. This is just one of several options, and the methodological literature describes several alternatives (Demirtas & Schafer, 2003; Hedeker & Gibbons, 1997, 2006; Enders, 2011; Molenberghs, Michiels, Kenward, & Diggle, 1998; Thijs, Molenberghs, Michiels, & Curran, 2002; Verbeke & Molenberghs, 2000).

Improving Missing At Random-Based Analyses

Because NMAR-based analysis methods tend to work well in a limited set of situations, some authors have argued that researchers are better off trying to implement the best possible MAR-based analysis (Demirtas & Schafer, 2003; Schafer & Graham, 2002; Enders & Gottschall, 2011). To this end, this section describes two strategies for improving the accuracy of multiple imputation and maximum likelihood estimation. We first introduce the idea of an inclusive analysis strategy that incorporates auxiliary variables. Auxiliary variables can reduce bias by making the MAR assumption more plausible, and they can also improve power. Next we describe procedures that correct for normality violations. Although multiple imputation and maximum likelihood both rely heavily on distributional assumptions, normality violations are not necessarily detrimental to missing data analysis because methodologists have developed procedures that counteract the problem.

The Role of Auxiliary Variables

The methodological literature generally recommends an inclusive analysis strategy that incorporates auxiliary variables into the analysis model or into the imputation phase (Collins et al., 2001; Graham, 2003; Rubin, 1996; Schafer & Graham, 2002). Auxiliary variables are peripheral to one's substantive research questions but are potentially related to a participant's propensity for missing data or to the incomplete analysis variables. Incorporating these additional variables into the missing data routine can reduce or eliminate bias and can improve power (Collins et al., 2001). Importantly, the auxiliary variables need not be complete and still provide these benefits, even if they are missing according to an NMAR mechanism (Enders, 2008).

As described previously, Rubin's missing data mechanisms are not a characteristic of a data set but, rather, a characteristic of the variables that are included in a particular analysis (or in a particular imputation process). For example, in the MAR example where missingness is related to gender, the MAR mechanism only holds if gender is included in the growth curve analysis. There may be times when the research question does not dictate the inclusion of certain auxiliary variables, yet these variables are crucial to satisfying the MAR assumption (e.g., because they are associated with the propensity for missing data on one of the analysis variables). Incorporating these correlates of missingness into the missing data handling procedure can reduce nonresponse bias by making the MAR assumption more plausible.

Bias aside, there may be situations where auxiliary variables, by virtue of their correlations with the analysis variables, carry information that can reduce the sampling error incurred from the missing data. For example, Baraldi and Enders (2010) have demonstrated an example from the Longitudinal Study of American Youth, where including a small set of auxiliary variables in a regression analysis reduced standard errors by a margin that was commensurate with a 12% to 18% increase in the sample size. The magnitude of the standard error reduction depends on the correlation between the auxiliary variable and the incomplete analysis variable, and methodologists generally recommend including variables with correlations that exceed ±0.40 (Collins et al., 2001).

No special procedures are required to incorporate auxiliary variables into a multiple imputation analysis—simply include the auxiliary variables in the imputation process. Incorporating an auxiliary variable as an additional predictor in the imputation regression equations infuses the predicted scores with the variable's information (note that the auxiliary variables themselves need not be complete), making it unnecessary to utilize the additional variable in any subsequent analysis. Adding auxiliary variables to a maximum likelihood analysis is not quite as straightforward. There are two structural equation modeling strategies for incorporating auxiliary variables into a maximum likelihood analysis: the extra dependent variable model and the saturated correlates model (Graham, 2003). We focus on the saturated correlates model because this approach is automated by some software packages (e.g., Mplus and EQS); readers interested in the extra dependent variable model can consult Graham (2003).

The saturated correlates model uses a series of correlations to incorporate the auxiliary variables into the analysis without altering the substantive interpretation of the parameter estimates. The exact pattern of correlations depends on whether the analysis involves latent variables. For models that include only manifest variables, auxiliary variables must correlate with (1) explanatory variables, (2) other auxiliary variables, and (3) the residual terms of all outcome variables. Returning to the antisocial data example, suppose that a researcher wants to examine gender differences at the final wave while controlling for baseline antisocial behavior. Figure 27.5 shows a path diagram of the regression model with two auxiliary variables.

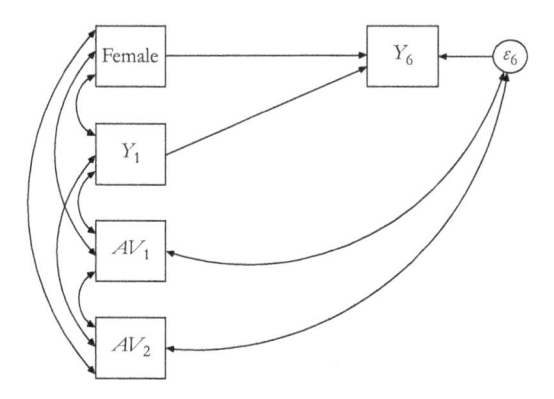

Figure 27.5 Path diagram of a regression model with two auxiliary variables, AV_1 and AV_2. The curved double-headed arrows denote correlations. Notice that the auxiliary variables are correlated with (a) the explanatory variables, (b) themselves, and (c) the residual term of the outcome variable.

The rules for incorporating auxiliary variables change slightly for analyses that include latent variables. In a latent variable model, auxiliary variables must correlate with (1) manifest explanatory variables, (2) other auxiliary variables, and (3) the residual terms of all manifest outcome variables (e.g., indicators of a latent variable). Importantly, the auxiliary variables never correlate with the latent variables themselves or with the latent disturbance terms. Returning to the growth model in Figure 27.1, auxiliary variables would need to correlate with the manifest gender variable and the six residuals terms, ε_1 to ε_6. Importantly, the auxiliary variables would not directly correlate with the intercept and slope latent variables.

From a substantive perspective, the saturated correlates model transfers information from the auxiliary variables to the analysis variables without impacting the interpretation of the parameter estimates. For example, in Figure 27.5, the auxiliary variables do not affect the interpretation of the gender coefficient because the extraneous variables are not partialled out of the outcome (i.e., the auxiliary variables correlate with the residual term rather than directly predict the outcome variable). Although the numeric estimate of the gender coefficient might change after adding the auxiliary variables (e.g., because bias is reduced), the meaning of the effect is the same with or without the peripheral variables. We do not use auxiliary variables in the subsequent analysis examples, but illustrative analyses are available elsewhere in the literature (Baraldi & Enders, 2010; Enders, 2006, 2010; Peugh & Enders, 2004).

Based on the relative ease of adding auxiliary variables to a missing data handling procedure, researchers should use an inclusive analysis strategy whenever possible. Further, researchers should be proactive about collecting information that might relate to a participant's propensity to drop out of a study. The idea of proactively measuring correlates of missingness is particularly relevant in longitudinal studies. For example, Schafer and Graham (2002) recommended including a survey question at each assessment that asks, "How likely are you to drop out of the study before the next session?" Similarly, researchers may consider asking questions that ask how likely respondents are to move before the next assessment or how far away the respondents live from the testing site. By including auxiliary variables such as these into the missing data handling procedure, researchers are more likely to satisfy the MAR mechanism, thereby maximizing the accuracy of maximum likelihood and multiple imputation.

Dealing with Non-Normal Data

Our previous descriptions of multiple imputation and maximum likelihood assumed a multivariate normal distribution (e.g., the I-step of multiple imputation used linear regression with normal residuals; the log likelihood function in Equation 5 described the shape of the multivariate normal distribution). This assumption may be rarely met in practice (Micceri, 1989). For example, even if the antisocial behavior scores from our earlier example approximate a continuous distribution, their distributions would likely be positively skewed. The methodological literature suggests that normality violations have relatively little impact on maximum likelihood parameter estimates but may bias standard errors and distort tests of model fit (for an overview, *see* Finney & DiStefano, 2006). Corrective procedures for non-normality have long been available for complete-data maximum likelihood estimation (Bentler, 1983; Bollen & Stine, 1992; Browne, 1984; Satorra & Bentler, 1988, 1994, 2001), and methodologists have extended these approaches to accommodate missing data (Arminger & Sobel, 1990; Enders, 2002; Savalei & Bentler, 2009; Yuan & Bentler, 2000). We briefly discuss two such options: rescaling and bootstrap resampling.

Normality violations can cause standard errors to be too high or too low, depending on the degree of kurtosis (Yuan, Bentler & Zhang, 2005). So-called robust (i.e., sandwich estimator) standard errors address this issue by incorporating a correction term based on individual deviations from the mean. With positive kurtosis (e.g., a preponderance of large deviation scores), this correction term attenuates standard errors, whereas with negative kurtosis (e.g., a preponderance of small deviation scores), the correction inflates standard error estimates. In contrast, bootstrap resampling uses Monte Carlo computer simulations to generate standard error estimates. The basic idea behind bootstrap resampling is to repeatedly draw samples of size N with replacement from the incomplete data set. Fitting the statistical model (e.g., the antisocial behavior growth model) to each bootstrap sample yields an empirical sampling distribution for each parameter, the standard deviation of which is an estimate of the standard error. The empirical sampling distribution makes no distributional assumptions and reflects the natural fluctuation of the parameter with non-normal data. Importantly, robust standard errors and the bootstrap resampling are applicable to both multiple imputation and maximum likelihood estimation. For example, a researcher could impute the missing values and subsequently employ robust standard errors in the analysis phase. Alternatively, the researcher could use maximum likelihood estimation with robust standard errors without filling in the missing values.

Kurtosis also impacts the accuracy of the likelihood ratio test. Again, the test statistic can be too large or too small, depending on exact departure from normality. Well-known rescaling procedures for complete-data analyses (e.g., the Satorra-Bentler chi-square; Satorra & Bentler, 1988, 1994) are also available for missing data (Yuan & Bentler, 2000). The idea behind the rescaling procedure is to multiply the normal theory likelihood ratio statistic by a constant, the value of which largely depends on multivariate kurtosis, so that the likelihood ratio more closely approximates the appropriate central chi-square distribution. Bootstrap resampling provides an alternate approach. Unlike rescaling, the bootstrap leaves the normal theory likelihood ratio test intact and attempts to generate an empirical sampling distribution for the test statistic. The basic bootstrap procedure is similar to that for standard errors (i.e., repeated draw samples from the data with replacement, perform the analysis on each bootstrap sample), but it is necessary to transform the data to have the same mean and covariance structure as the null hypothesis prior to drawing the samples. The corrective procedures for the likelihood ratio test are readily available for maximum likelihood analyses (e.g., the Mplus and EQS software packages) but not for multiple imputation.

Using normal theory approaches is often very reasonable (e.g., when variables are continuous but skewed), but many situations warrant a more flexible missing data handling procedure. For example, researchers in the social and behavioral sciences routinely perform analyses that include both continuous and categorical variables. Returning to the antisocial behavior analysis, suppose that a researcher wanted to estimate a structural equation model where a binary indicator of maternal depression history predicts the development of antisocial behavior and the developmental trajectories predict a distal measure of incarceration (also a binary variable). One option is to assume that all variables share a joint normal distribution and apply rescaling procedures or the bootstrap to counteract normality violations. However, this strategy may produce undesirable results. For example, applying a normality-based multiple imputation routine would generate fractional imputed values for the binary variables (e.g., a depression score of 0.36 rather than a discrete value of 0 or 1). The researcher could use the fractional scores in the subsequent analyses, or she could apply an *ad hoc* rounding scheme to convert the imputations to discrete values.

Fortunately, software options have evolved to the point where it is unnecessary to adopt a single joint distribution for all variables. Many software packages can incorporate incomplete categorical and continuous variables in the same model. In the context of multiple imputation, the sequential regression algorithm (also referred to as fully conditional specification or multiple imputation with chained equations) allows researchers to specify a different population distribution for each variable. For example, the algorithm could use a normal distribution to impute the continuous antisocial behavior scores and a logistic function to impute the incomplete binary variables. Depending on the software package, a number of other distribution choices may be available (e.g., Poisson imputation for count outcomes). Some software packages offer similar flexibility for maximum likelihood estimation. For example, the Mplus package allows researchers to incorporate different outcome distributions into a single analysis. Returning to the antisocial behavior example, the researcher could estimate a structural equation model that applies a multivariate normal distribution to the repeated measures variables and a logistic function to the binary incarceration variable.

Data Analysis Examples

Having outlined a number of common missing data handling techniques, we now apply a subset of these approaches to the antisocial behavior data. Specifically, we used Mplus 6 to fit the linear growth model from Equation 1 (or alternatively, Fig. 27.1) to the MCAR, MAR, and NMAR data sets. Because the repeated measures variables are not multivariate normal, we utilized robust (i.e., sandwich-estimator) standard errors for all analyses, including multiple imputation. To begin, we used SPSS to implement several atheoretical and MCAR-based approaches (i.e., arithmetic mean imputation, last observation carried forward, listwise deletion, and regression imputation). We implemented two MAR-based methods: multiple imputation and maximum likelihood. Maximum likelihood requires no data preparation because Mplus estimates the model directly from the incomplete raw data. For the multiple imputation analyses, we used Mplus to generate and analyze 50 imputed data sets. Finally, we implemented three NMAR analyses: the selection model, shared parameter model, and pattern

mixture model. The selection model and the shared parameter model were similar to the path diagrams in Figures 27.3 and 27.4, respectively, but additionally included a logistic regression coefficient that linked the binary missing data indicators to the gender variable. We estimated the pattern mixture model by equating the inestimable slope parameters for Pattern 6 (the cases that dropped out after the baseline assessment) to the estimates from Pattern 5 (the cases that dropped out after the second wave). Additionally, we assumed that the six patterns shared a common covariance matrix. These pattern mixture model specifications represent just one set of assumptions about the inestimable parameters, and many others are possible (e.g., Demirtas & Schafer, 2003; Enders, 2010, 2011; Hedeker & Gibbons, 1997, 2006). The Mplus syntax files and the raw data for all analyses are available at www.appliedmissingdata.com/papers.

Complete Data

To provide a basis for evaluating different missing data techniques, we started by fitting the growth curve model to the complete data. The top row of Table 27.5 gives the resulting parameter estimates. As seen in the tables, males had a baseline mean of 10.337 and an average yearly growth rate of –0.083 (i.e., β_0 and β_1, respectively). The female mean was approximately –0.906 lower at baseline (i.e., β_2), and the female growth rate was, on average, 0.063 lower than that for males (i.e., β_2). In developmental studies such as this, it is often interesting to examine group differences at the final data collection wave. Algebraically manipulating the growth model parameters gives the model-implied mean difference at the final assessment

$$\hat{\mu}_{Male} - \hat{\mu}_{Female} = \hat{\beta}_2 + 5 \cdot \hat{\beta}_3,$$

where the $\hat{\beta}$ terms are the regression coefficients that link the latent variables to the gender variable (i.e., the latent mean differences), and 5 is the value of the linear factor loading at the final wave. Substituting the appropriate estimates into this equation yields a model-predicted mean difference of –1.221 at wave 6 (i.e., females scored lower by roughly one and a quarter points, on average). Expressed relative to the baseline standard deviation, this mean difference corresponds to a standardized mean difference of $d = 0.667$, which is slightly greater than Cohen's (1988) threshold for a medium effect size (i.e., $d > 0.50$). The goal of a missing data analysis is to generate accurate estimates of the population parameters, not to reproduce that answer that would

Table 27.5. Performance of Selected Missing Data Handling Techniques Under an MCAR Mechanism

Analysis method	Male Baseline (β_0) Est.	SE	Male Growth (β_1) Est.	SE	Baseline Difference (β_2) Est.	SE	Growth Difference (β_3) Est.	SE	Wave 6 Difference Est.	d
Complete data	10.337	0.051	−0.083	0.011	−0.906	0.073	−0.063	0.016	1.221	0.666
Atheoretical methods										
Mean imputation	10.370	0.052	**−0.128**	0.011	**−0.995**	0.074	**0.038**	0.016	0.806	0.430
Last observation forward	10.334	0.051	**−0.067**	0.011	−0.926	0.073	−0.053	0.015	1.191	0.646
MCAR-based methods										
Listwise deletion	**10.392**	0.065	−0.085	0.014	−0.931	0.094	−0.062	0.020	1.243	0.667
Regression imputation	10.339	0.051	−0.078	0.009	−0.924	0.073	−0.063	0.013	1.241	0.675
MAR-based methods										
Maximum likelihood	10.353	0.052	−0.086	0.012	−0.929	0.074	−0.061	0.018	1.233	0.672
Multiple imputation	10.345	0.052	−0.081	0.013	−0.925	0.074	−0.063	0.018	1.239	0.674
MNAR-based methods										
Selection model	10.363	0.053	**−0.193**	0.014	−0.912	0.075	−0.059	0.019	1.210	0.659
Shared parameter model	10.350	0.050	−0.088	0.012	−0.920	0.069	−0.064	0.014	1.239	0.675
Pattern mixture model	10.353	0.052	−0.083	0.029	−0.924	0.075	−0.060	0.043	1.221	0.667

Note: Bold typeface denotes estimates that differ from complete-data values by more than one standard error unit.

have been obtained had the data been complete. Nevertheless, the relatively large sample size allows us to use the complete-data estimates as benchmarks, against which to compare the performance of different missing data handling techniques.

Missing Completely At Random Data

Having established benchmark parameter estimates, we applied a variety of missing data handling approaches to the MCAR data set. Table 27.5 gives selected parameter estimates and standard errors from the analyses. To facilitate interpretation, bold typeface denotes estimates that differ from the complete-data values by more than one standard error unit. As expected, the atheoretical methods (mean imputation, last observation carried forward) produced one or more parameter estimates that substantially deviated from the complete-data estimates. To better illustrate the nature of this bias, Figure 27.6 shows the model-implied growth trajectories for these approaches along with the corresponding complete-data growth curves. As expected, the MCAR- and MAR-based approaches accurately reproduced the growth trajectories. Although listwise deletion slightly overestimated the baseline mean for males, Figure 27.6 shows that the distortion in the growth curves was minimal. Finally, the performance of the NMAR models was mixed; the shared parameter model and the pattern mixture model produced accurate estimates, but the selection model yielded the largest discrepancies with the complete-data results. As seen in Figure 27.6, the selection model incorrectly suggested a rather steep decline in antisocial behavior for both gender groups.

Missing At Random Data

Next, we applied the same set of missing data handling approaches to the MAR data set. Table 27.6 gives selected parameter estimates and standard errors from the analysis. As before, bold typeface denotes estimates that differ from the complete-data values by more than one standard error unit. As expected, both the atheoretical and the

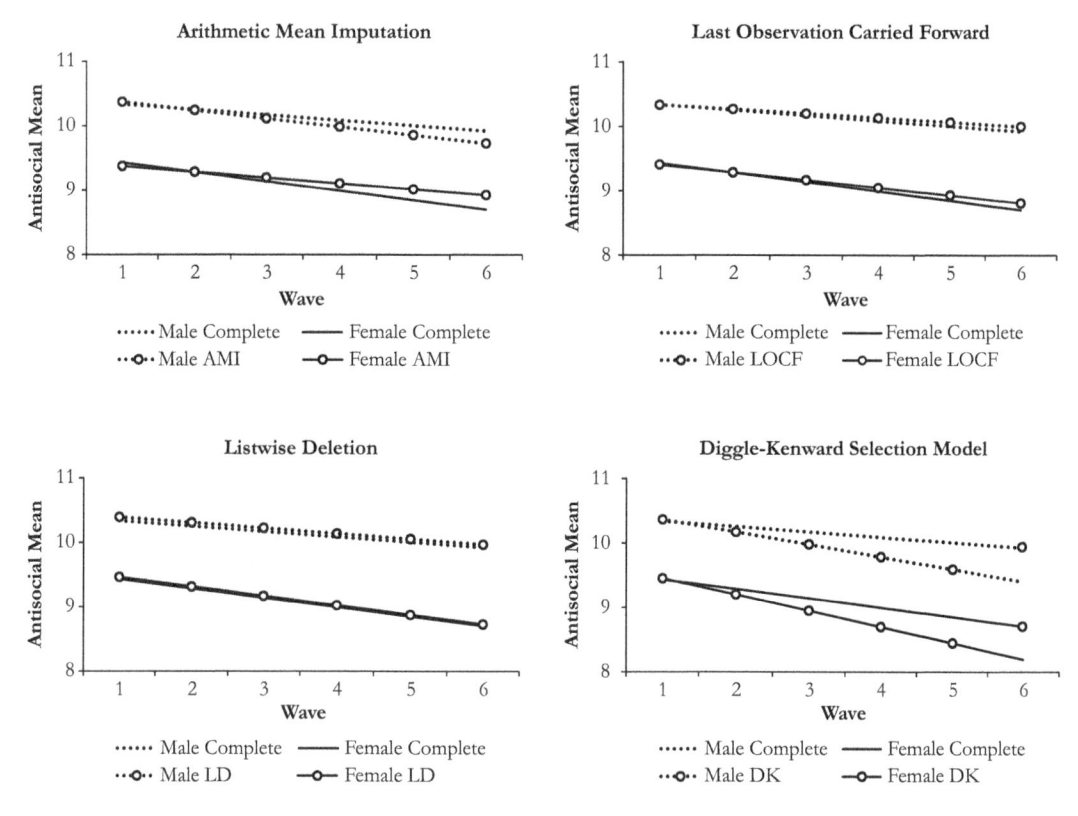

Figure 27.6 Model-implied growth curves from the MCAR data.

MCAR-based methods gave estimates that diverged from those of the complete data. To better illustrate the bias, Figure 27.7 gives the model-implied trajectories for these approaches. Although the nature of the bias varied across methods, the estimated growth curves are clearly inaccurate. In contrast, multiple imputation and maximum likelihood produced estimates that closely approximated the complete-data values. This finding is expected based on Rubin's (1976) missing data theory. Turning to the NMAR models, the results were again mixed, and the models performed differently than they did in the MCAR analyses. Specifically, the selection model estimates were quite accurate, whereas the pattern mixture model estimates were severely distorted. In fact, the pattern mixture model results suggested that antisocial behavior increased, rather than decreased, over time. The shared parameter model failed to converge.

Not Missing At Random Data

Finally, we applied the missing data handling approaches to the NMAR data set. Table 27.7 gives selected parameter estimates and standard errors from the analysis. As seen in the table, all of the approaches produced one or more biased estimates, with the exception of the last observation carried forward. The fact that this *ad hoc* approach gave accurate estimates almost certainly results from idiosyncratic nuances of this particular data set. No empirical research exists that supports the use of this technique under an MCAR mechanism, much less an NMAR mechanism. The growth curves for the atheoretical and MCAR-based approaches were quite similar to those in Figure 27.7, so no further graphical displays are needed to convey these results. Consistent with theoretical expectations, multiple imputation and maximum likelihood produced biased parameter estimates. To illustrate the bias, Figure 27.8 gives the model-implied trajectories for maximum likelihood (the multiple imputation slopes were virtually identical). Turning to the NMAR-based approaches, the selection model and the shared parameter model provided some improvement over MAR-based methods. Figure 27.8 shows the model-implied growth trajectories for these methods. As seen in the figure, the shared parameter model produced the most

Table 27.6. Performance of Selected Missing Data Handling Techniques Under an MAR Mechanism

	Male Baseline (β_0)		Male Growth (β_1)		Baseline Difference (β_2)		Growth Difference (β_3)		Wave 6 Difference	
Analysis method	Est.	SE	Est.	SE	Est.	SE	Est.	SE	Est.	d
Complete data	10.337	0.051	−0.083	0.011	−0.906	0.073	−0.063	0.016	1.221	0.666
				Atheoretical methods						
Mean imputation	10.412	0.048	**−0.289**	0.012	−0.960	0.070	**0.067**	0.016	0.623	0.335
Last observation forward	10.305	0.055	**0.061**	0.011	−0.901	0.077	**−0.104**	0.016	1.420	0.738
				MCAR-based methods						
Listwise deletion	9.604	0.053	−0.127	0.013	−0.676	0.073	−0.039	0.018	0.868	0.579
Regression imputation	10.417	0.051	−0.185	0.010	−0.938	0.073	**−0.022**	0.014	1.047	0.563
				MAR-based methods						
Maximum likelihood	10.346	0.052	−0.085	0.013	−0.910	0.074	−0.063	0.017	1.225	0.666
Multiple imputation	10.341	0.052	−0.082	0.014	−0.904	0.074	−0.065	0.017	1.231	0.669
				MNAR-based methods						
Selection model	10.340	0.052	−0.078	0.014	−0.907	0.073	−0.063	0.017	1.222	0.665
Shared parameter model	N/A	N/A	N/A	N/A	N/A	N/A	N/A	N/A	N/A	N/A
Pattern mixture model	10.126	0.046	**0.224**	0.029	−0.678	0.060	−0.002	0.050	0.686	0.458

Note: Bold typeface denotes estimates that differ from complete-data values by more than one standard error unit.

accurate estimates, whereas the pattern mixture model produced the least accurate estimates.

Not Missing At Random-Based Approaches Revisited

At first glance, the less-than-perfect performance of the NMAR analysis methods may be perplexing given that these approaches are designed for this type of data. Although it is not immediately obvious, these analyses are negatively affected by assumption violations and by model misspecifications. For example, recall that the selection model and the shared parameter model rely heavily on distributional assumptions—in this case, multivariate normality; in fact, the models are only estimable because of this assumption. However, the antisocial behavior scores are positively skewed and kurtotic (see Table 27.1). Although the degree of nonnormality is not necessarily excessive, it is enough to introduce substantial bias. This is in contrast to the MAR-based analysis methods, where normality violations tend to impact the standard errors but not the estimates themselves.

For the selection model and the shared parameter model, the specification of the logistic regressions is a second problem. To illustrate, consider the Diggle-Kenward model in Figure 27.3. Notice that the logistic model includes concurrent associations (e.g., the regression of R_t on Y_t) and lagged associations (e.g., the regression of R_t on Y_{t-1}). The model that we estimated also includes a regression coefficient that links the missing data indicators to the gender variable. In our NMAR data set, the probability of missing data at wave t solely results from the antisocial behavior score at that wave. Consequently, the logistic portion of the selection model is misspecified because it estimates additional associations not present in the data (i.e., the regression of R_t on Y_{t-1} and the regression of R_t on gender). Although you might not expect these unnecessary parameters to have an impact, they do.

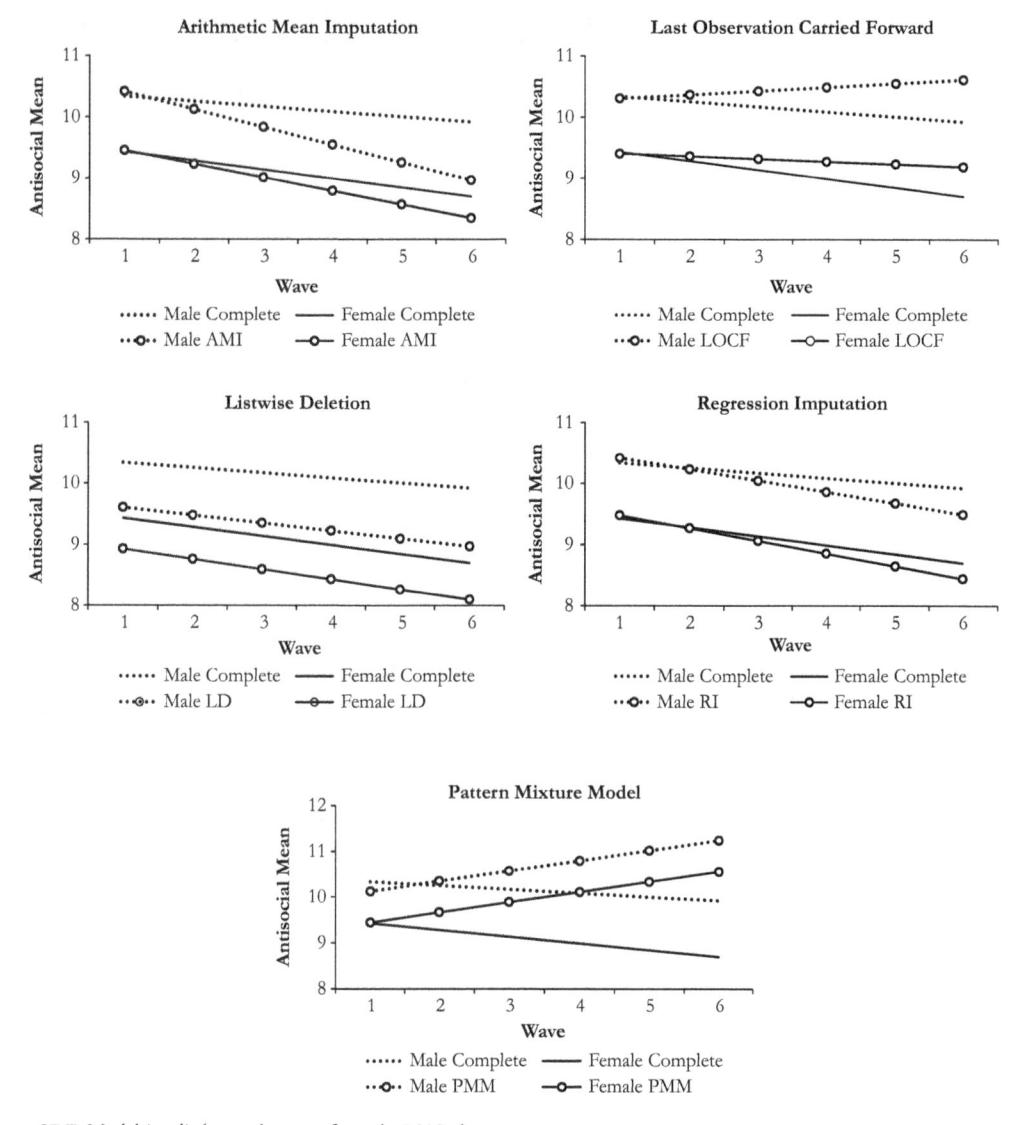

Figure 27.7 Model-implied growth curves from the MAR data.

To better illustrate the impact of assumption violations and model misspecification, we generated a second NMAR data set where the repeated measures variables were multivariate normal. We then estimated the Diggle-Kenward selection model under different combinations of conditions (e.g., a correctly specified model with normal data, a correctly specified model with nonnormal data, a misspecified model with normal data, etc.). Table 27.8 gives the resulting parameter estimates and standard errors. As seen in the row labeled Model 1, the selection model estimates were quite similar to those of the complete data when the normality assumption was satisfied and when the logistic portion of the model was correctly specified (i.e., the logistic model included only the concurrent regression of R_t on Y_t). In contrast, the estimates were biased when the logistic model was misspecified or when the normality assumption was violated. As seen in the row labeled Model 5, the combination of these two factors produced the largest distortions.

Planned Missing Data Designs

The ability to implement modern missing data techniques has led methodologists to develop research designs that produce intentional MCAR or MAR data. Planned missing data may seem counterintuitive because missing values are generally thought of as problematic in research. However, now

Table 27.7. Performance of Selected Missing Data Handling Techniques Under an MNAR Mechanism

	Male Baseline (β_0)		Male Growth (β_1)		Baseline Difference (β_2)		Growth Difference (β_3)		Wave 6 Difference	
Analysis method	Est.	SE	Est.	SE	Est.	SE	Est.	SE	Est.	d
Complete data	10.337	0.051	−0.083	0.011	−0.906	0.073	−0.063	0.016	1.221	0.666
Atheoretical methods										
Mean imputation	10.383	0.049	**−0.306**	0.011	−0.982	0.069	**0.077**	0.016	**0.596**	0.322
Last observation forward	10.294	0.048	−0.088	0.011	−0.923	0.069	−0.054	0.015	1.193	0.661
MCAR-based methods										
Listwise deletion	**9.774**	0.061	**−0.142**	0.014	**−0.749**	0.081	−0.036	0.019	**0.930**	0.578
Regression imputation	10.365	0.048	**−0.217**	0.009	−0.949	0.069	−0.007	0.014	**0.984**	0.542
MAR-based methods										
Maximum likelihood	10.327	0.050	**−0.171**	0.013	−0.934	0.070	−0.029	0.017	1.076	0.595
Multiple imputation	10.319	0.050	**−0.167**	0.013	−0.927	0.070	−0.031	0.017	1.083	0.601
MNAR-based methods										
Selection model	10.362	0.051	**−0.151**	0.013	−0.930	0.071	−0.040	0.017	1.131	0.625
Shared parameter model	**10.264**	0.045	−0.103	0.008	−0.858	0.064	−0.075	0.011	1.231	0.686
Pattern mixture model	**10.216**	0.048	−0.169	0.031	**−0.662**	0.068	−0.054	0.049	0.933	0.565

Note: Bold typeface denotes estimates that differ from complete-data values by more than one standard error unit.

that advanced missing data handling techniques are readily accessible, new opportunities exist to use missing data as an advantage in research design. These planned missing data designs can potentially maximize resources, reduce respondent burden and facilitate the logistics of large-scale data collection. Although often met with skepticism, we hope to demonstrate the potential value of planned missing data design. In this section, we discuss three applications of planned missing data design: two-method measurement, three-form design, and planned missing data in longitudinal studies. Additional information on these designs can be found in the work of Graham and colleagues (Graham, Taylor, & Cumsille, 2001; Graham, Taylor, Olchowski & Cumsille, 2006)

Two-Method Measurement

In many research scenarios, a construct may be prohibitively costly to administer to the entire sample. In these scenarios, Graham et al. (2006) have recommended the so-called two-method measurement design. For example, suppose that a researcher is interested in determining whether online dating impacts the likelihood of contracting genital herpes among college-aged women. The researcher may only have the resources to do a blood test for the herpes virus in a small subset of the sample. On the other hand, the researcher could easily collect self-reports of past symptoms from the entire sample. Although the self-reports are informative, they may not be as reliable as the blood tests. By collecting both types of information, the researcher now has the complete sample with the less reliable self-report measures and the smaller subsample that includes both the self-report measures and the more reliable blood test. By using multiple imputation or maximum likelihood estimation to deal with the missing data, the researcher can use the entire sample to estimate the relationship between online dating and herpes risk, although a subset of cases are missing the diagnostic blood test. In this scenario, the self-report measure effectively functions

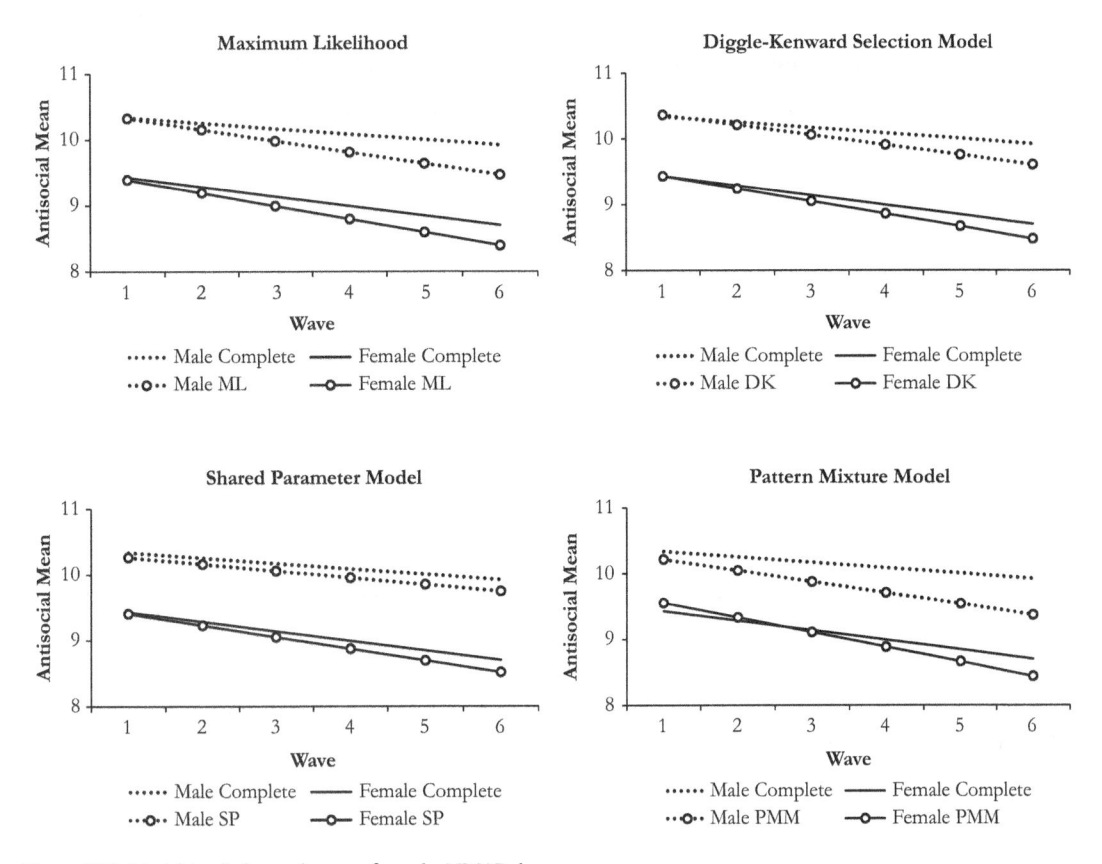

Figure 27.8 Model-implied growth curves from the NMAR data.

as an auxiliary variable that allows the researcher to recapture the missing blood test information.

As another example, consider the antisocial behavior research study used throughout this chapter. Suppose that researchers in the antisocial behavior study wanted to administer an additional distal outcome (e.g., behavioral problems during the senior year of high school) but only had the time and resources to track a subsample of the original participants. Again, a planned missing data design could be used to include an additional assessment when there are not enough resources to utilize the entire original sample. In these examples, the intuitive course of action may be to analyze only those cases that include the expensive measure (e.g., the herpes blood test, observational evaluation, and distal outcome). Again, maximum likelihood and multiple imputation allow the researcher to use the entire sample for the analyses.

Three-Form Design

A second situation where planned missing data designs are useful is in studies that use large survey batteries to collect data. Time constraints (e.g., a survey that must be administered during the first class period of the school day), subject willingness (e.g., an interviewer can only ask as many survey questions as the preschooler's attention span will allow), cost or other logistical constraints may limit the number of survey items that a researcher can administer. Rather than going through the task of determining which questions are expendable, researchers could consider the three-form design proposed by Graham and colleagues (Graham, Hofer, & Mackinnon, 1996; Graham et al., 2006) as a way to reduce the number of items that each participant answers.

To implement the three-form design, researchers create three test booklets, each of which is missing a different subset of items. Specifically, all of the available items or questionnaires are distributed across four subsets: X, A, B, and C. All respondents receive the items or questionnaires in subset X, but subset A, B, and C are missing from one of the three test forms (i.e., the three test forms are comprised of XAB, XAC, and XBC). To illustrate, suppose that a researcher is interested in administering a set of 80 questions from four questionnaires to teenagers in

Table 27.8. Impact of Misspecification on Diggle-Kenward Selection Model Under an MNAR Mechanism

Analysis method	Male Baseline (β_0) Est.	SE	Male Growth (β_1) Est.	SE	Baseline Difference (β_2) Est.	SE	Growth Difference (β_3) Est.	SE	Wave 6 Difference Est.	d
Complete data	10.342	0.051	−0.084	0.011	−0.923	0.073	−0.059	0.015	1.218	0.669
Diggle-Kenward selection models										
Model 1	10.330	0.052	−0.091	0.014	−0.933	0.073	−0.060	0.018	1.234	0.680
Model 2	10.317	0.051	−0.118	0.013	−0.923	0.072	−0.057	0.017	1.209	0.667
Model 3	10.336	0.052	−0.116	0.015	−0.934	0.072	−0.049	0.018	1.181	0.652
Model 4	10.337	0.051	−0.122	0.015	−0.935	0.072	−0.045	0.018	1.161	0.641
Model 5	10.362	0.051	−0.151	0.013	−0.930	0.071	−0.040	0.017	1.131	0.625

Model 1: Correctly specified with logistic regressions for R_t on Y_t, normally distributed data.
Model 2: Correctly specified with logistic regressions for R_t on Y_t, skewed data.
Model 3: Misspecified with logistic regressions for R_t on Y_t and on Y_{t-1}, normally distributed data.
Model 4: Misspecified with logistic regressions for gender, R_t on Y_t and on Y_{t-1}, normally distributed data.
Model 5: Misspecified with logistic regressions for gender, R_t on Y_t and on Y_{t-1}, skewed data.

Table 27.9. Missing Data Patterns From a Three-Form Design

	Item sets			
Form	X	A	B	C
1	O	M	O	O
2	O	O	M	O
3	O	O	O	M

Note: O = observed, M = missing.

the juvenile correction system. Perhaps past experience suggests that administering 80 questions to this particular population is too burdensome, but subjects could realistically answer 60 questions. Using the three-form design, the researcher can administer all 80 questions by assigning 20 items to each of the four subsets X, A, B, and C. Table 27.9 shows the configuration of missing and complete questionnaires from the three-form design. Note that each participant will only respond to 60 items, but the researcher can use maximum likelihood or multiple imputation to analyze the entire item pool.

Although there is much to be gained from the three-form design, there are a host of implementation issues to consider. A full discussion of these issues is beyond the scope of this chapter, but we highlight a few important considerations. Additional details on the design are available elsewhere in the literature (Enders, 2010; Graham et al., 2006). First, the sample size reduction in subsets A, B, or C can translate into a loss of statistical power (e.g., the association between an A-set variable and a B-set variable will have 33% complete data). Despite this potential pitfall, Graham's work has demonstrated that the power loss is generally not proportionate with the overall reduction in sample size. Furthermore, carefully assigning questionnaires to the four sets can mitigate the power loss. For example, pairs of variables that are expected to produce a small effect size could be assigned to the X set to maximize power. On the other hand, pairs of variables that are expected to yield a large effect size do not have as stringent sample size requirements and can be assigned to one of the missing item subsets. Second, although the three-form design increases the number of variables that may be included in a study, it potentially reduces the ability to explore higher order effects. For example, if the substantive analysis involves a moderated regression with a two-way interaction, at least one of the variables in the regression model must be in the X set (it makes no difference whether this variable is a predictor or the outcome). Similarly, a three-way interaction requires that the outcome and one of the predictors be assigned to the X set. Finally, the three-form design is flexible and does not require the same number of items in each of the four sets. Further, if multiple questionnaires are used, then it is possible to distribute individual questionnaire items or entire questionnaires across the item sets. Although the former strategy can produce higher power, Graham et al. (2006) have recommended the latter approach for logistical reasons.

Longitudinal Designs

Respondent burden can be even more acute in longitudinal studies. Graham et al. (2001) have outlined several planned missing data designs that apply the logic of the three-form design to longitudinal data. In these designs, participants are randomly assigned to subgroups, and each subgroup has one or more waves of intentionally missing data. Table 27.10 provides an illustration of such a design. This particular design assigns participants to one of six subgroups (i.e., missing data patterns), such that every subgroup has complete data at the first and last wave but has missing data at two other waves. Although the design in Table 27.10 equally distributes the sample across the six missing data patterns, this is not necessary. The design is very flexible, and researchers can modify it to fit their needs (e.g., by adding a subgroup of complete cases,

Table 27.10. Planned Missing Data Design for a Six-Wave Longitudinal Study

	Data collection wave						% of
Pattern	1	2	3	4	5	6	Sample
1	O	M	M	O	O	O	16.7%
2	O	M	O	M	O	O	16.7%
3	O	M	O	O	M	O	16.7%
4	O	O	M	M	O	O	16.7%
5	O	O	M	O	M	O	16.7%
6	O	O	O	M	M	O	16.7%

Note: O = observed, M = missing.

eliminating or adding missing data patterns, allocating different percentages of respondents across the patterns).

When planning longitudinal studies, researchers often find themselves in one of two situations: (1) because of budget constraints, the total number of assessments is fixed, but the total sample size is flexible, or (2) the total sample size is fixed, but the number of assessments per participant is flexible. Mistler and Enders (2011) investigated the power of the design in Table 27.10 under these two scenarios. In a scenario where the number of assessments is fixed, suppose that the research budget allows researchers to collect a total of 1500 assessments. The researchers could collect complete data from 250 participants (i.e., 250 participants × 6 waves = 1500 assessments), or they could collect incomplete data from 375 participants (i.e., 375 participants × 6 waves = 1500 assessments). Interestingly, Mistler and Enders showed that the planned missing data design actually produced higher power to detect linear growth than the complete-data design. The authors also examined power under the second scenario where the total sample size was fixed at 250. In this situation, the complete-data design (i.e., 250 participants × 6 waves = 1500 assessments) produced better power than the planned missingness design in Table 27.10 (i.e., 250 participants × 4 waves = 1000 assessments). However, the power difference was modest (e.g., 0.83 vs. 0.77, respectively), particularly given that the planned missing data design reduced the number of assessments by one-third.

The design in Table 27.10 is just one of many possibilities. Graham et al. (2001) have discussed several others. Consistent with the three-form design, longitudinal planned missing data designs require careful planning to maximize power. Fortunately, it is relatively straightforward to use Monte Carlo computer simulations to explore the power of various design configurations. Interested readers can consult Mistler and Enders (2011) for a tutorial on this topic.

Conclusion

As missing data are an inevitable component of research, understanding various missing data handling options has become increasingly important. The goal of this chapter was to introduce the missing data methods currently in use as well as identify the strengths and weaknesses of each of these methods. We first introduced Rubin's missing data theory (1976) and outlined three missing data mechanisms: MCAR, MAR, and NMAR. These missing data mechanisms essentially serve as assumptions for a missing data analysis. Next, we described a variety of missing data techniques and their requisite assumptions. These techniques included traditional missing data procedures such as deletion and single imputation as well as the modern missing data techniques, maximum likelihood and multiple imputation. We also discussed a few of the many options for an NMAR mechanism. An artificial data example from a longitudinal study on antisocial behavior was used to illustrate the performance of several common techniques across data that satisfied the three missing data mechanisms. In the final section, we discussed ways in which missing data may be purposefully incorporated into a research design to maximize available resources and minimize respondent burden.

Throughout the chapter, we organized missing data techniques by the assumptions that they require. Unfortunately, many of the missing data procedures that are in widespread use (e.g., deletion methods) require a strict assumption regarding the reason for missingness (i.e., MCAR), and violating this assumption may result in substantially biased estimates. Ultimately, the atheoretical and MCAR-based approaches tend to be flawed and/or limited in their ability to recapture missing information. Even when MCAR is plausible, traditional methods that assume this mechanism are worse than techniques that assume MAR (e.g., because they are less powerful). For this reason, we support the idea of abandoning atheoretical and MCAR techniques in favor of multiple imputation and maximum likelihood estimation. We also described three general approaches for dealing with an NMAR mechanism: the selection model, the shared parameter model, and the pattern mixture model. Although these methods differ in their approach, they all incorporate a submodel that describes the probability of missingness. Not missing at random analyses are intuitively appealing because they allow the probability of missing data on Y to relate to other variables as well as to Y itself. However, our analysis examples show that none of the NMAR methods are perfectly suited for all situations. These methods require strict assumptions that go beyond the missing data mechanism (e.g., multivariate normality), and violating these assumptions can result in estimates that are no better than those of an MAR-based analysis.

The field of missing data analysis has seen tremendous growth over the last several decades, and sophisticated missing data analyses are now readily available in statistical software packages. Ideally, researchers should choose a missing data handling technique that is appropriate for the mechanism that caused the missing data. After ruling out MCAR as a working assumption (e.g., because MAR-based analyses excel under an MCAR mechanism), researchers must choose between MAR- and NMAR-based analysis methods. Because there is no way to empirically differentiate these two conditions, a missing data analysis ultimately relies on one or more untestable assumptions. For multiple imputation and maximum likelihood estimation, MAR is the primary assumption; distributional assumptions are less important because corrective procedures are readily available in software packages. In contrast, NMAR analyses require strict assumptions that go beyond the missing data mechanism (e.g., multivariate normality), so these techniques tend to perform well in limited situations. In the end, researchers need to evaluate the plausibility of the MAR and NMAR missing data mechanisms and construct a logical argument that supports the use of a particular analytic technique.

Author Note

Craig K. Enders, PhD, Department of Psychology, Arizona State University. Amanda N. Baraldi, MA, Department of Psychology, Arizona State University, 950 S. McAllister, Room 237, P.O. Box 871104, Tempe, AZ 85287–1104.

References

Albert, P.S., & Follmann, D.A. (2009). Shared-parameter models. In G. Fitzmaurice, M. Davidian, G. Verbeke, & G. Molenberghs (Eds.), *Longitudinal data analysis* (pp. 433–452). Boca Raton, FL: Chapman & Hall.

Arminger, G., & Sobel, M.E. (1990). Pseudo-maximum likelihood estimation of mean and covariance structures with missing data. *Journal of the American Statistical Association, 85*, 195–203.

Baraldi, A.N., & Enders, C.K. (2010). An introduction to modern missing data analyses. *Journal of School of Psychology, 48*, 5–37.

Beale, E.M.L., & Little, R.J.A. (1975). Missing values in multivariate analysis. *Journal of the Royal Statistical Society, Ser. B, 37*, 129–145.

Bentler, P.M. (1983). Some contributions to efficient statistics in structural models: Specification and estimation of moment structures. *Psychometrika, 48*, 493–517.

Bodner, T.E. (2006). Missing data: Prevalence and reporting practices. *Psychological Reports, 99*, 675–680.

Bollen, K.A. & Stine, R.A. (1992). Bootstrapping goodness-of-fit measures in structural equation models. *Sociological Methods and Research, 21*, 205–229.

Brown, R.L. (1994). Efficacy of the indirect approach for estimating structural equation models with missing data: A comparison of five methods. *Structural Equation Modeling: A Multidisciplinary Journal, 1*, 287–316.

Browne, M.W. (1984). Asymptotic distribution-free methods for the analysis of covariance structures. *British Journal of Mathematical and Statistical Psychology, 37*, 62–83.

Buck, S.F. (1960). A method of estimation of missing values in multivariate data suitable for use with an electronic computer. *Journal of the Royal Statistical Society, Ser. B, 22*, 302–306.

Cohen, J. (1988). *Statistical power analysis for the behavioral sciences* (2nd edn.). Hillsdale, NJ: Erlbaum.Collins, L.M., Schafer, J.L., & Kam, C-M. (2001). A comparison of inclusive and restrictive strategies in modern missing data procedures. *Psychological Methods, 6*, 330–351.

Cook, R.J., Zeng, L., & Yi, G.Y. (2004). Marginal analysis of incomplete longitudinal binary data: A cautionary note on LOCF imputation. *Biometrics, 60*, 820–828.

Demirtas, H., & Schafer, J.L. (2003). On the performance of random-coefficient pattern-mixture models for non-ignorable drop-out. *Statistics in Medicine, 22*, 2553–2575.

Dempster, A.P., Laird, N.M., & Rubin, D.B. (1977). Maximum likelihood from incomplete data via the EM algorithm. *Journal of the Royal Statistical Society, Ser. B, 39*, 1–38.

Diggle, P., & Kenward, M.G. (1994). Informative dropout in longitudinal data analysis. *Applied Statistics, 43*, 49–94.

Enders, C.K. (2001). The impact of nonnormality on full information maximum likelihood estimation for structural equation models with missing data. *Psychological Methods, 6*, 352–370.

Enders, C.K. (2002). Applying the Bollen-Stine bootstrap for goodness-of-fit measures to structural equation models with missing data. *Multivariate Behavioral Research, 37*, 359–377.

Enders, C.K. (2006). A primer on the use of modern missing-data methods in psychosomatic medicine research. *Psychosomatic Medicine, 68*, 427–436.

Enders, C.K. (2008). A note on the use of missing auxiliary variables in full information maximum likelihood-based structural equation models. *Structural Equation Modeling: A Multidisciplinary Journal, 15*, 434–448.

Enders, C.K. (2010). *Applied missing data analysis.* New York: Guilford.

Enders, C.K. (2011). Missing not at random models for latent growth curve analyses. *Psychological Methods, 16*, 1–16.

Enders, C.K., & Bandalos, D.L. (2001). The relative performance of full information maximum likelihood estimation for missing data in structural equation models. *Structural Equation Modeling: A Multidisciplinary Journal, 8*, 430–457.

Enders, C.K., & Gottschall, A.C. (2011). The impact of missing data on the ethical quality of a research study. In A.T. Panter and S.K. Sterba (Eds.), *Handbook of ethics in quantitative methodology* (pp. 357–381). New York: Routledge.

Finney, S. J., & DiStefano, C. (2006). Nonnormal and categorical data in structural equation models. In G.R. Hancock & R.O. Mueller (Eds.). *A second course in structural equation modeling* (pp. 269–314). Greenwich, CT: Information Age.

Gold, M.S., & Bentler, P.M. (2000). Treatments of missing data: A Monte Carlo comparison of RBHDI, iterative stochastic regression imputation, and expectation-maximization. *Structural Equation Modeling: A Multidisciplinary Journal, 7*, 319–355.

Graham, J.W. (2003). Adding missing-data relevant variables to FIML-based structural equation models. *Structural Equation Modeling: A Multidisciplinary Journal, 10*, 80–100.

Graham, J.W. (2009). Missing data analysis: Making it work in the real world. *Annual Review of Psychology, 60*, 549–576.

Graham, J.W., Hofer, S.M., & MacKinnon, D.P. (1996). Maximizing the usefulness of data obtained with planned missing value patterns: An application of maximum likelihood procedures. *Multivariate Behavioral Research, 31*, 197–218.

Graham, J.W., Olchowski, A.E., & Gilreath, T.D. (2007). How many imputations are really needed? Some practical clarifications of multiple imputation theory. *Prevention Science, 8*, 206–213.

Graham, J.W., Taylor, B.J., & Cumsille, P.E. (2001). Planned missing data designs in the analysis of change. In L.M. Collins & A.G. Sayer (Eds.), *New methods for the analysis of change* (pp. 335–353). Washington, DC: American Psychological Association.

Graham, J.W., Taylor, B.J., Olchowski, A.E., & Cumsille, P.E. (2006). Planned missing data designs in psychological research. *Psychological Methods, 11*, 323–343.

Heckman, J.T. (1976). The common structure of statistical models of truncation, sample selection and limited dependent variables and a simple estimator for such models. *The Annals of Economic and Social Measurement, 5*, 475–492.

Heckman, J.T. (1979). Sample selection bias as a specification error. *Econometrica, 47*, 153–161.

Hedeker, D., & Gibbons, R.D. (1997). Application of random-effects pattern-mixture models for missing data in longitudinal studies. *Psychological Methods, 2*, 64–78.

Hedeker, D., & Gibbons, R. D. (2006). *Longitudinal Data Analysis.* New York: Wiley.

Jöreskog, K.G., & Sörbom, D. (2006). *LISREL 8.8 for Windows* [Computer software and manual]. Lincolnwood, IL: Scientific Software International, Inc.

Kenward, M.G., & Molenberghs, G. (1998). Likelihood based frequentist inference when data are missing at random. *Statistical Science, 13*, 236–247.

King, G., Honaker, J., Joseph, A., & Scheve, K. (2001). Analyzing incomplete political science data: An alternative algorithm for multiple imputation. *American Political Science Review, 95*, 49–69.

Lavori, P.W., Dawson, R., & Shera, D. (1995). A multiple imputation strategy for clinical trials with truncation of patient data. *Statistics in Medicine, 14*, 1913–1925.

Little, R.J.A. (1995). Modeling the drop-out mechanism in repeated-measures studies. *Journal of the American Statistical Association, 90*, 1112–1121.

Little, R. J. A. (2009). Selection and pattern mixture models. In G. Fitzmaurice, M. Davidian, G. Verbeke, & G. Molenberghs (Eds.), *Longitudinal data analysis* (pp. 409–431). Boca Raton, FL: Chapman & Hall.

Little, R.J.A., & Rubin, D.B. (2002). *Statistical analysis with missing data* (2nd Ed.). Hoboken, NJ: Wiley.

Micceri, T. (1989). The unicorn, the normal curve, and other improbable creatures. *Psychological Bulletin, 105*, 156–166.

Mistler, S.A., & Enders, C.K. (2011). An introduction to planned missing data designs for developmental research. In B. Laursen, T. Little & N. Card (Eds.), *Handbook of Developmental Research Methods* (pp. 742–754). New York: Guilford.

Molenberghs, G., Michiels, B., Kenward, M.G., & Diggle, P.J. (1998). Monotone missing data and pattern-mixture models. *Statistica Neerlandica, 52*, 153–161.

Molenberghs, G., Thijs, H., Jansen, I., & Beunckens, C., Kenward, M.G., Mallinckrodt, C., et al. (2004). Analyzing incomplete longitudinal clinical trial data. *Biostatistics, 5,* 445–464.

Odgers, C.L., Moffitt, T.E., Tach, L.M., Sampson, R.J., Taylor, A., Mathews, C.L., et al. (2009). The protective effects of neighborhood collective efficacy on British children growing up in deprivation: A developmental analysis. *Developmental Psychology, 45,* 942–957.

Peugh, J.L., & Enders, C.K. (2004). Missing data in educational research: A review of reporting practices and suggestions for improvement. *Review of Educational Research, 74,* 525–556.

Raghunathan, T.E., Lepkowski, Van Hoewyk, J., & Solenberger, P. (2001). A multivariate technique for multiply imputing missing values using a sequence of regression models. *Survey Methodology, 27,* 85–95.

Royston, P. (2005). Multiple imputation of missing values: Update. *The Stata Journal, 5,* 1–14.

Rubin, D. B. (1976). Inference and missing data. *Biometrika, 63,* 581–592.

Rubin, D.B. (1978). Multiple imputations in sample surveys—a phenomenological Bayesian approach to nonresponse. *Proceedings of the Survey Research Methods Section of the American Statistical Association,* Washington, DC, 20–34.

Rubin, D.B. (1987). *Multiple imputation for nonresponse in surveys.* Hoboken, NJ: Wiley.

Rubin, D.B. (1996). Multiple imputation after 18+ years. *Journal of the American Statistical Association, 91,* 473–489.

Satorra, A., & Bentler, P.M. (1988). Scaling corrections for chi-square statistics in covariance structure analysis. *Proceedings of Business and Economics Sections* (pp. 308–313). Alexandria, VA: American Statistical Association.

Satorra, A., & Bentler, P.M. (1994). Corrections to test statistics and standard errors in covariance structure analysis. In A. Von Eye & C.C. Clogg (Eds.), Latent variables analysis: *Applications for developmental research* (pp. 399–419). Newbury Park, CA: Sage.

Satorra, A., & Bentler, P.M. (2001). A scaled difference chi-square test statistic for moment structure analysis. *Psychometrika, 66,* 507–514.

Savalei, V., & Bentler, P.M. (2009). *A two-stage approach to missing data: Theory and application to auxiliary variables. Structural Equation Modeling, 16,* 477–497.

Schafer, J.L. (1997). *Analysis of incomplete multivariate data.* Boca Raton, FL: Chapman & Hall.

Schafer, J.L. (2001). Multiple imputation with PAN. In A.G. Sayer & L.M. Collins (Eds.), *New methods for the analysis of change* (pp. 355–377). Washington, DC: American Psychological Association.

Schafer, J.L. (2003). Multiple imputation in multivariate problems when the imputation and analysis models differ. *Statistica Neerlandica, 57,* 19–35.

Schafer, J.L., & Graham, J.W. (2002). Missing data: Our view of the state of the art. *Psychological Methods, 7,* 147–177.

Schafer, J.L., & Olsen, M.K. (1998). Multiple imputation for multivariate missing-data problems: A data analyst's perspective. *Multivariate Behavioral Research, 33,* 545–571.

Shao, J., & Zhong, B. (2004). Last observation carry-forward and last observation analysis. *Statistics in Medicine, 22,* 2429–2441.

Thijs, H., Molenberghs, G., Michiels, B., & Curran, D. (2002). Strategies to fit pattern-mixture models. *Biostatistics, 3,* 245–265.

Van Buuren, S. (2007). Multiple imputation of discrete and continuous data by fully conditional specification. *Statistical Methods in Medical Research, 16,* 219–242.

Verbeke, G., & Molenberghs, G. (2000). *Linear mixed models for longitudinal data.* New York: Springer-Verlag.

Wilks, S.S. (1932). Moments and distributions of estimates of population parameters from fragmentary samples. *The Annals of Mathematical Statistics, 3,* 163–195.

Wood, A.M., White, I.R., & Thompson, S.G. (2004). Are missing outcome data adequately handled? A review of published randomized controlled trials in major medical journals. *Clinical Trials, 1,* 368–376.

Wothke, W. (2000). Longitudinal and multi-group modeling with missing data. In T.D. Little, K.U. Schnabel, & J. Baumert (Eds.), *Modeling longitudinal and multiple group data: Practical issues, applied approaches and specific examples* (pp. 219–240). Mahwah, NJ: Erlbaum.

Wu, M.C., & Carroll, R.J. (1988). Estimation and comparison of changes in the presence of informative right censoring by modeling the censoring process. *Biometrics, 44,* 175–188.

Yuan, K-H., & Bentler, P.M. (2000). Three likelihood-based methods for mean and covariance structure analysis with nonnormal missing data. *Sociological Methodology, 30,* 165–200.

Yuan, K-H., Bentler, P.M., & Zhang, W. (2005). The effect of skewness and kurtosis on mean and covariance structure analysis: The univariate case and its multivariate implication. *Sociological Methods and Research, 24,* 240–258.

CHAPTER 28

Secondary Data Analysis

M. Brent Donnellan *and* Richard E. Lucas

Abstract

Secondary data analysis refers to the analysis of existing data collected by others. Secondary analysis affords researchers the opportunity to investigate research questions using large-scale data sets that are often inclusive of under-represented groups, while saving time and resources. Despite the immense potential for secondary analysis as a tool for researchers in the social sciences, it is not widely used by psychologists and is sometimes met with sharp criticism among those who favor primary research. The goal of this chapter is to summarize the promises and pitfalls associated with secondary data analysis and to highlight the importance of archival resources for advancing psychological science. In addition to describing areas of convergence and divergence between primary and secondary data analysis, we outline basic steps for getting started and finding data sets. We also provide general guidance on issues related to measurement, handling missing data, and the use of survey weights.

Key Words: Classical Test Theory, correlational research, missing data techniques, psychological science, reliability, survey research, survey weighting, validity

The goal of research in the social science is to gain a better understanding of the world and how well theoretical predictions match empirical realities. Secondary data analysis contributes to these objectives through the application of "creative analytical techniques to data that have been amassed by others" (Kiecolt & Nathan, 1985, p. 10). Primary researchers *design* new studies to answer research questions, whereas the secondary data analyst *uses* existing resources. There is a deliberate coupling of research design and data analysis in primary research; however, the secondary data analyst rarely has had input into the design of the original studies in terms of the sampling strategy and measures selected for the investigation. For better or worse, the secondary data analyst simply has access to the final products of the data collection process in the form of a codebook or set of codebooks and a cleaned data set.

The analysis of existing data sets is routine in disciplines such as economics, political science, and sociology, but it is less well established in psychology (*but see* Brooks-Gunn & Chase-Lansdale, 1991; Brooks-Gunn, Berlin, Leventhal, & Fuligini, 2000). Moreover, biases against secondary data analysis in favor of primary research may be present in psychology (*see* McCall & Appelbaum, 1991). One possible explanation for this bias is that psychology has a rich and vibrant experimental tradition, and the training of many psychologists has likely emphasized this approach as the "gold standard" for addressing research questions and establishing causality (*see*, e.g., Cronbach, 1957). As a result, the nonexperimental methods that are typically used in secondary analyses may be viewed by some as inferior. Psychological scientists trained in the experimental tradition may not fully appreciate the unique strengths that nonexperimental techniques

665

have to offer and may underestimate the time, effort, and skills required for conducting secondary data analyses in a competent and professional manner. Finally, biases against secondary data analysis might stem from lingering concerns over the validity of the self-report methods that are typically used in secondary data analysis. These can include concerns about the possibility that placement of items in a survey can influence responses (e.g., differences in the average levels of reported marital and life satisfaction when questions occur back to back as opposed to having the questions separated in the survey; *see* Schwarz, 1999; Schwarz & Strack, 1999) and concerns with biased reporting of sensitive behaviors (*but see* Akers, Massey, & Clarke, 1983).

Despite the initial reluctance to widely embrace secondary data analysis as a tool for psychological research, there are promising signs that the skepticism toward secondary analyses will diminish as psychology seeks to position itself as a hub science that plays a key role in interdisciplinary inquiry (*see* Mroczek, Pitzer, Miller, Turiano, & Fingerman, 2011). Accordingly, there is a compelling argument for including secondary data analysis into the suite of methodological approaches used by psychologists (*see* Trzesniewski, Donnellan, & Lucas, 2011).

The goal of this chapter is to summarize the promises and pitfalls associated with secondary data analysis and to highlight the importance of archival resources for advancing psychological science. We limit our discussion to analyses based on large-scale and often longitudinal national data sets such as the National Longitudinal Study of Adolescent Health (Add Health), the British Household Panel Study (BHPS), the German Socioeconomic Panel Study (GSOEP), and the National Institute of Child Health and Human Development (NICHD) Study of Early Child Care and Youth Development (SEC-CYD). However, much of our discussion applies to all secondary analyses. The perspective and specific recommendations found in this chapter draw on the edited volume by Trzesniewski et al. (2011). Following a general introduction to secondary data analysis, we will outline the necessary steps for getting started and finding data sets. Finally, we provide some general guidance on issues related to measurement, approaches to handling missing data, and survey weighting. Our treatment of these important topics is intended to draw attention to the relevant issues rather than to provide extensive coverage. Throughout, we take a practical approach to the issues and offer tips and guidance rooted in our experiences as data analysts and researchers with substantive interests in personality and life span developmental psychology.

Comparing Primary Research and Secondary Research

As noted in the opening section, it is possible that biases against secondary data analysis exist in the minds of some psychological scientists. To address these concerns, we have found it can be helpful to explicitly compare the processes of secondary analyses with primary research (*see also* McCall & Appelbaum, 1991). An idealized and simplified list of steps is provided in Table 28.1. As is evident from this table, both techniques start with a research question that is ideally rooted in existing theory and previous empirical results. The areas of biggest divergence between primary and secondary approaches occur after researchers have identified their questions (i.e., Steps 2 through 5 in Table 28.1). At this point, the primary researcher develops a set of procedures and then engages in pilot testing to refine procedures and methods, whereas the secondary analyst searches for data sets and evaluates codebooks. The primary researcher attempts to refine her or his procedures, whereas the secondary analyst determines whether a particular resource is appropriate for addressing the question at hand. In the next stages, the primary researcher collects new data, whereas the secondary data analyst constructs a working data set from a much larger data archive. At these stages, both types of researchers must grapple with the practical considerations imposed by real world constraints. There is no such thing as a perfect single study (*see* Hunter & Schmidt, 2004), as all data sets are subject to limitations stemming from design and implementation. For example, the primary researcher may not have enough subjects to generate adequate levels of statistical power (because of a failure to take power calculations into account during the design phase, time or other resource constraints during the data collection phase, or because of problems with sample retention), whereas the secondary data analyst may have to cope with impoverished measurement of core constructs. Both sets of considerations will affect the ability of a given study to detect effects and provide unbiased estimates of effect sizes.

Table 28.1 also illustrates the fact that there are considerable areas of overlap between the two techniques. Researchers stemming from both traditions

Table 28.1. Comparisons of Primary Research and Secondary Data Analysis

Step	Primary research	Secondary data analysis
1.	Formulate research questions and specify tentative hypotheses.	Formulate research questions and specify tentative hypotheses.
2.	Design study. Decide on sample and sample size. Select measures and manipulations.	Search for potential data sets to address research questions. Conduct literature review to avoid duplicating existing work.
3.	Conduct pilot tests. Make design adjustments. Finalize research questions	Obtain data sets and supporting materials. Gain familiarity with codebooks and data structure. Finalize research questions.
4.	Collect data.	Construct and evaluate measures.
5.	Prepare data for analysis.	Create final data set for analyses.
6.	Conduct analyses.	Conduct analyses.
7.	Interpret results	Interpret results
8.	Attend to limitations and unanswered questions	Attend to limitations and unanswered questions
9.	Write report	Write report

Note: Steps modified and expanded from McCall and Appelbaum (1991).

analyze data, interpret results, and write reports for dissemination to the wider scientific community. Both kinds of research require a significant investment of time and intellectual resources. Many skills required in conducting high-quality primary research are also required in conducting high-quality secondary data analysis including sound scientific judgment, attention to detail, and a firm grasp of statistical methodology.

We argue that both primary research and secondary data analysis have the potential to provide meaningful and scientifically valid research findings for psychology. Both approaches can generate new knowledge and are therefore reasonable ways of evaluating research questions. Blanket pronouncements that one approach is inherently superior to the other are usually difficult to justify. Many of the concerns about secondary data analysis are raised in the context of an unfair comparison—a contrast between the idealized conceptualization of primary research with the actual process of a secondary data analysis. Our point is that both approaches can be conducted in a thoughtful and rigorous manner, yet both approaches involve concessions to real-world constraints. Accordingly, we encourage all researchers and reviewers of papers to keep an open mind about the importance of both types of research.

Advantages and Disadvantages of Secondary Data Analysis

The foremost reason why psychologists should learn about secondary data analysis is that there are many existing data sets that can be used to answer interesting and important questions. Individuals who are unaware of these resources are likely to miss crucial opportunities to contribute new knowledge to the discipline and even risk reinventing the proverbial wheel by collecting new data. Regrettably, new data collection efforts may occur on a smaller scale than what is available in large national datasets. Researchers who are unaware of the potential treasure trove of variables in existing data sets risk unnecessarily duplicating considerable amounts of time and effort. At the very least, researchers may wish to familiarize themselves with publicly available data to truly address gaps in the literature when they undertake projects that involve new data collection.

The biggest advantage of secondary analyses is that the data have already been collected and are ready to be analyzed (*see* Hofferth, 2005), thus conserving time and resources. Existing data sources are often of much larger and higher quality than could be feasibly collected by a single investigator. This advantage is especially pronounced when considering the investments of time and money necessary to collect longitudinal data. Some data sets were collected with scientific sampling plans (such as the GSOEP), which make it possible to generalize the findings to a specific population. Further, many publicly available data sets are quite large, and therefore provide adequate statistical power for conducting many analyses, including hypotheses about statistical interactions. Investigations of interactions often require a surprisingly high number of participants to achieve respectable levels of statistical power in the face of measurement error (*see* Aiken & West, 1991).[1] Large-scale data sets are also well suited for subgroup analyses of populations that are often under-represented in smaller research studies.

Another advantage of secondary data analysis is that it forces researchers to adopt an open and transparent approach to their craft. Because data are publicly available, other investigators may attempt to replicate findings and specify alternative models for a given research question. This reality encourages transparency and detailed record keeping on the part of the researcher, including careful reporting of analysis and a reasoned justification for all analytic decisions. Freese (2007) has provided a useful discussion about policies for archiving material necessary for replicating results, and his treatment of the issues provides guidance to researchers interested in maintaining good records.

Despite the many advantages of secondary data analysis, it is not without its disadvantages. The most significant challenge is simply the flipside of the primary advantage—the data have already been collected *by somebody else!* Analysts must take advantage of what has been collected without input into design and measurement issues. In some cases, an existing data set may not be available to address the particular research questions of a given investigator without some limitations in terms of sampling, measurement, or other design feature. For example, data sets commonly used for secondary analysis often have a great deal of breadth in terms of the range of constructs assessed (e.g., finances, attitudes, personality, life satisfaction, physical health), but these constructs are often measured with a limited number of survey items. Issues of measurement reliability and validity are usually a major concern. Therefore, a strong grounding in basic and advanced psychometrics is extremely helpful for responding to criticisms and concerns about measurement issues that arise during the peer-review process.

A second consequence of the fact that the data have been collected by somebody else is that analysts may not have access to all of the information about data collection procedures and issues. The analyst simply receives a cleaned data set to use for subsequent analyses. Perhaps not obvious to the user is the amount of actual cleaning that occurred behind the scenes. Similarly, the complicated sampling procedures used in a given study may not be readily apparent to users, and this issue can prevent the appropriate use of survey weights (Shrout & Napier, 2011).

Another significant disadvantage for secondary data analysis is the large amount of time and energy initially required to review data documentation. It can take hours and even weeks to become familiar with the codebooks and to discover which research questions have already been addressed by investigators using the existing data sets. It is very easy to underestimate how long it will take to move from an initial research idea to a competent final analysis. There is a risk that, unbeknownst to one another, researchers in different locations will pursue answers to the same research questions. On the other hand, once a researcher has become familiar with a data set and developed skills to work with the resource, they are able to pursue additional research questions resulting in multiple publications from the same data set. It is our experience that the process of learning about a data set can help generate new research ideas as it becomes clearer how the resource can be used to contribute to psychological science. Thus, the initial time and energy expended to learn about a resource can be viewed as initial investment that holds the potential to pay larger dividends over time.

Finally, a possible disadvantage concerns how secondary data analyses are viewed within particular subdisciplines of psychology and by referees during the peer-review process. Some journals and some academic departments may not value secondary data analyses as highly as primary research. Such preferences might break along Cronbach's two disciplines or two streams of psychology—correlational versus experimental (Cronbach, 1957; Tracy, Robins, & Sherman, 2009). The reality is that if original data collection is more highly valued in a given setting, then new investigators looking to build a strong case for getting hired or getting promoted might face obstacles if they base a career exclusively on secondary data analysis. Similarly, if experimental methods are highly valued and correlational methods are denigrated in a particular subfield, then results of secondary data analyses will face difficulties getting attention (and even getting published). The best advice is to be aware of local norms and to act accordingly.

Steps for Beginning a Secondary Data Analysis

Step 1: Find Existing Data Sets. After generating a substantive question, the first task is to find relevant data sets (*see* Pienta, O'Rouke, & Franks, 2011). In some cases researchers will be aware of existing data sets through familiarity with the literature given that many well-cited papers have used such resources. For example, the GSOEP has now been widely used to address questions about correlates and developmental course of subjective well-being (e.g., Baird, Lucas, & Donnellan, 2010; Gerstorf, Ram, Estabrook, Schupp, Wagner, & Lindenberger, 2008; Gerstorf, Ram, Goebel, Schupp, Lindenberger, & Wagner, 2010; Lucas, 2005; 2007), and thus, researchers in this area know to turn to this resource if a new question arises. In other cases, however, researchers will attempt to find data sets using established archives such as the University of Michigan's Interuniversity Consortium for Political and Social Research (ICPSR; http://www.icpsr.umich.edu/icpsrweb/ICPSR/). In addition to ICPSR, there are a number of other major archives (*see* Pienta et al., 2011) that house potentially relevant data sets. Here are just a few starting points:

- The Henry A. Murray Research Archive (http://www.murray.harvard.edu/)
- The Howard W. Odum Institute for Research in Social Science (http://www.irss.unc.edu/odum/jsp/home2.jsp)
- The National Opinion Research Center (http://norc.org/homepage.htm)
- The Roper Center of Public Opinion Research (http://ropercenter.uconn.edu/)
- The United Kingdom Data Archive (http://www.data-archive.ac.uk/)

Individuals in charge of these archives and data depositories often catalog metadata, which is the technical term for information about the constituent data sets. Typical kinds of metadata include information about the original investigators, a description of the design and process of data collection, a list of the variables assessed, and notes about sampling weights and missing data. Searching through this information is an efficient way of gaining familiarity with data sets. In particular, the ICPSR has an impressive infrastructure for allowing researchers to search for data sets through a cataloguing of study metadata. The ICPSR is thus a useful starting point for finding the raw material for a secondary data analysis. The ICPSR also provides a new user tutorial for searching their holdings (http://www.icpsr.umich.edu/icpsrweb/ICPSR/help/newuser.jsp). We recommend that researchers search through their holdings to make a list of potential data sets. At that point, the next task is to obtain relevant codebooks to learn more about each resource..

Step 2: Read Codebooks. Researchers interesting in using an existing data set are strongly advised to thoroughly read the accompanying codebook (Pienta et al., 2011). There are several reasons why a comprehensive understanding of the codebook is a critical first step when conducting a secondary data analysis. First, the codebook will detail the procedures and methods used to acquire the data and provide a list of all of the questions and assessments collected. A thorough reading of the codebook can provide insights into important covariates that can be included in subsequent models, and a careful reading will draw the analyst's attention to key variables that will be missing because no such information was collected. Reading through a codebook can also help to generate new research questions.

Second, high-quality codebooks often report basic descriptive information for each variable such as raw frequency distributions and information about the extent of missing values. The descriptive information in the codebook can give investigators a baseline expectation for variables under consideration, including the expected distributions of the variables and the frequencies of underrepresented groups (such as ethnic minority participants). Because it is important to verify that the descriptive statistics in the published codebook match those in the file analyzed by the secondary analyst, a familiarity with the codebook is essential. In addition to codebooks, many existing resources provide copies of the actual surveys completed by participants (Pienta et al., 2011). However, the use of actual pencil-and-paper surveys is becoming less common with the advent of computer assisted interview techniques and Internet surveys. It is often the case that survey methods involve skip patterns (e.g., a participant is not asked about the consequences of her drinking if she responds that she doesn't drink alcohol) that make it more difficult to assume the perspective of the "typical" respondent in a given study (Pienta et al., 2011). Nonetheless, we recommend that analysts try to develop an understanding for the experiences of the participant in a given study. This perspective can help secondary analysts develop an intuitive understanding of certain patterns of missing data and anticipate concerns about question ordering effects (*see*, e.g., Schwarz, 1999).

Step 3: Acquire Datasets and Construct a Working Datafile. Although there is a growing availability of Web-based resources for conducting basic analyses using selected data sets (e.g., the Survey Documentation Analysis software used by ICPSR), we are convinced that there is no substitute for the analysis of the raw data using the software packages of preference for a given investigator. This means that the analysts will need to acquire the data sets that they consider most relevant. This is typically a very straightforward process that involves acknowledging researcher responsibilities before downloading the entire data set from a website. In some cases, data are classified as restricted-use, and there are more extensive procedures for obtaining access that may involve submitting a detailed security plan and accompanying legal paperwork before becoming an authorized data user. When data involve children and other sensitive groups, Institutional Review Board approval is often required.

Each data set has different usage requirements, so it is difficult to provide blanket guidance. Researchers should be aware of the policies for using each data set and recognize their ethical responsibility for adhering to those regulations. A central issue is that the researcher must avoid deductive disclosure whereby otherwise anonymous participants are identified because of prior knowledge in conjunction with the personal characteristics coded in the dataset (e.g., gender, racial/ethnic group, geographic location, birth date). Such a practice violates the major ethical principles followed by responsible social scientists and has the potential to harm research participants.

Once the entire set of raw data is acquired, it is usually straightforward to import the files into the kinds of statistical packages used by researchers (e.g., R, SAS, SPSS, and STATA). At this point, it is likely that researchers will want to create smaller "working" file by pulling only relevant variables from the larger master files. It is often too cumbersome to work with a computer file that may have more than a thousand columns of information. The solution is to construct a working data file that has all of the needed variables tied to a particular research project. Researchers may also need to link multiple files by matching longitudinal data sets and linking to contextual variables such as information about schools or neighborhoods for data sets with a multilevel structure (e.g., individuals nested in schools or neighborhoods).

Explicit guidance about managing a working data file can be found in Willms (2011). Here, we simply highlight some particularly useful advice: (1) keep exquisite notes about what variables were selected and why; (2) keep detailed notes regarding changes to each variable and reasons why; and (3) keep track of sample sizes throughout this entire process. The guiding philosophy is to create documentation that is clear enough for an outside user to follow the logic and procedures used by the researcher. It is far too easy to overestimate the power of memory only to be disappointed when it comes time to revisit a particular analysis. Careful documentation can save time and prevent frustration. Willms (2011) noted that "keeping good notes is the sine qua non of the trade" (p. 33).

Step 4: Conduct Analyses. After assembling the working data file, the researcher will likely construct major study variables by creating scale composites (e.g., the mean of the responses to the items assessing the same construct) and conduct initial analyses. As previously noted, a comparison of the distributions and sample sizes with those in the study codebook is essential at this stage. Any deviations for the variables in the working data file and the codebook should be understood and documented. It is particularly useful to keep track of missing values to make sure that they have been properly coded. It should go without saying that an observed value of −9999 will typically require recoding to a missing value in the working file. Similarly, errors in reverse scoring items can be particularly common (and troubling) so researchers are well advised to conduct through item-level and scale analyses and check to make sure that reverse scoring was done correctly (e.g., examine the inter-item correlation matrix when calculating internal consistency estimates to screen for negative correlations). Willms (2011) provides some very savvy advice for the initial stages of actual data analysis: "Be wary of surprise findings" (p. 35). He noted that "too many times I have been excited by results only to find that I have made some mistake" (p. 35). Caution, skepticism, and a good sense of the underlying data set are essential for detecting mistakes.

An important comment about the nature of secondary data analysis is again worth emphasizing: These data sets are available to others in the scholarly community. This means that others should be able to replicate your results! It is also very useful to adopt a self-critical perspective because others will be able to subject findings to their own empirical scrutiny. Contemplate alternative explanations and attempt to conduct analyses to evaluate the plausibility of these explanations. Accordingly, we recommend that researchers strive to think of theoretically relevant control variables and include them in the analytic models when appropriate. Such an approach is useful both from the perspective of scientific progress (i.e., attempting to curb confirmation biases) and in terms of surviving the peer-review process.

Special Issue: Measurement Concerns in Existing Datasets

One issue with secondary data analyses that is likely to perplex psychologists are concerns regarding the measurement of core constructs. The reality is that many of the measures available in large-scale data sets consist of a subset of items derived from instruments commonly used by psychologists (*see* Russell & Matthews, 2011). For example, the 10-item Rosenberg Self-Esteem scale (Rosenberg, 1965) is the most commonly used measure of global self-esteem in the literature (Donnellan, Trzesniewski, & Robins, 2011). Measures of self-esteem are available in many data sets like Monitoring the Future (*see* Trzesniewski & Donnellan, 2010) but these measures are typically shorter than the original Rosenberg scale. Similarly, the GSOEP has a single-item rating of subjective well-being in the form of happiness, whereas psychologists might be more accustomed to measuring this construct with at least five items (e.g., Diener, Emmons, Larsen, & Griffin, 1985). Researchers using existing data sets will have to grapple with the consequences of having relatively short assessments in terms of the impact on reliability and validity.

For purposes of this chapter, we will make use of a conventional distinction between reliability and validity. Reliability will refer to the degree of measurement error present in a given set of scores (or alternatively the degree of consistency or precision in scores), whereas validity will refer to the degree to which measures capture the construct of interest and predict other variables in ways that are consistent with theory. More detailed but accessible discussions of reliability and validity can be found in Briggs and Cheek (1986), Clark and Watson (1995), John and Soto (2007), Messick (1995), Simms (2008), and Simms and Watson (2007). Widaman, Little, Preacher, and Sawalani (2011) have provided a discussion of these issues in the context of the shortened assessments available in existing data sets.

Short Measures and Reliability. Classical Test Theory (e.g., Lord & Novick, 1968) is the measurement perspective most commonly used among psychologists. According to this measurement philosophy, any observed score is a function of the underlying attribute (the so-called "true score") and measurement error. Reliability is conceptualized as any deviation or inconsistency in observed scores for the same attribute across multiple assessments of that attribute. A thought experiment may help crystallize insights about reliability (e.g., Lord & Novick, 1968): Imagine a thousand identical clones each completing the same self-esteem instrument simultaneously. The underlying self-esteem attribute (i.e., the true scores) should be the same for each clone (by definition), whereas the observed scores may fluctuate across clones because of random measurement errors (e.g., a single clone misreading an item vs. another clone being frustrated by an extremely hot testing room). The extent of the observed fluctuations in reported scores across clones offers insight into how much measurement error is present in this instrument. If scores are tightly clustered around a single value, then measurement error is minimal; however, if scores are dramatically different across clones, then there is a clear indication of problems with reliability. The measure is imprecise because it yields inconsistent values across the same true scores.

These ideas about reliability can be applied to observed samples of scores such that the total observed variance is attributable to true score variance (i.e., true individual differences in underlying attributes) and variance stemming from random measurement errors. The assumption that measurement error is random means that it has an expected value of zero across observations. Using this framework, reliability can then be defined as the ratio of true score variance to the total observed variance. An assessment that is perfectly reliable (i.e., has no measurement error) will have a ratio of 1.0, whereas an assessment that is completely unreliable will yield a ratio of 0.0 (*see* John & Soto, 2007, for an expanded discussion). This perspective provides a formal definition of a reliability coefficient.

Psychologists have developed several tools to estimate the reliability of their measures, but the approach that is most commonly used is coefficient α (Cronbach, 1951; *see* Schmitt, 1996, for an accessible review). This approach considers reliability from the perspective of internal consistency. The basic idea is that fluctuations across items assessing the same construct reflect the presence of measurement error. The formula for the standardized α is a fairly simple function of the average inter-item correlation (a measure of inter-item homogeneity) and the total number of items in a scale. The α coefficient is typically judged acceptable if it is above 0.70, but the justification for this particular cutoff is somewhat arbitrary (*see* Lance, Butts, & Michels, 2006). Researchers are therefore advised to take a more critical perspective on this statistic. A relevant concern is that α is negatively impacted when the measure is short.

Given concerns with scale length and α, many methodologically oriented researchers recommend evaluating and reporting the average inter-item correlation because it can be interpreted independently of length and thus represents a "more straightforward indicator of internal consistency" (Clark & Watson, 1995, p. 316). Consider that it is common to observe an average inter-item correlation for the 10-item Rosenberg Self-Esteem (Rosenberg, 1965) scale around 0.40 (this is based on typically reported α coefficients; *see* Donnellan et al., 2011). This same level of internal homogeneity (i.e., an inter-item correlation of 0.40) yields an α of around 0.67 with a 3-item scale but an α of around 0.87 with 10 items. A measure of a broader construct like Extraversion may generate an average inter-item correlation of 0.20 (Clark & Watson, 1995, p. 316), which would translate to an α of 0.43 for a 3-item scale and 0.71 for a 10-item scale. The point is that α coefficients will fluctuate with scale length and the breadth of the construct. Because most scales in existing resources are short, the α coefficients might fall below the 0.70 convention despite having a respectable level of inter-item correlation.

Given these considerations, we recommend that researchers consider the average inter-item correlation more explicitly when working with secondary data sets. It is also important to consider the breadth of the underlying construct to generate expectations for reasonable levels of item homogeneity as indexed by the average inter-item correlation. Clark and Watson (1995; *see also* Briggs & Cheek, 1986) recommend values of around 0.40 to 0.50 for measures of fairly narrow constructs (e.g., self-esteem) and values of around 0.15 to 0.20 for measures of broader constructs (e.g., neuroticism). It is our experience that considerations about internal consistency often need to be made explicit in manuscripts so that reviewers will not take an unnecessarily harsh perspective on α's that fall below their expectations. Finally, we want to emphasize that internal consistency is but one kind of reliability. In some cases, it might be that test–retest reliability is more informative and diagnostic of the quality of a measure (McCrae, Kurtz, Yamagata, & Terracciano, 2011). Fortunately, many secondary data sets are longitudinal so it possible to get an estimate of longer term test–retest reliability from the existing data.

Beyond simply reporting estimates of reliability, it is worth considering why measurement reliability is such an important issue in the first place. One consequence of reliability for substantive research is that measurement imprecision tends to depress observed correlations with other variables. This notion of attenuation resulting from measurement error and a solution were discussed by Spearman as far back as 1904 (*see*, e.g., pp. 88–94). Unreliable measures can affect the conclusions drawn from substantive research by imposing a downward bias on effect size estimation. This is perhaps why Widaman et al. (2011) advocate using latent variable structural modeling methods to combat this important consequence of measurement error. Their recommendation is well worth considering for those with experience with this technique (*see* Kline, 2011, for an introduction). Regardless of whether researchers use observed variables or latent variables for their analyses, it is important to recognize and appreciate the consequences of reliability.

Short Measures and Validity. Validity, for our purposes, reflects how well a measure captures the underlying conceptual attribute of interest. All discussions of validity are based, in part, on agreement in a field as to how to understand the construct in question. Validity, like reliability, is assessed as a matter of degree rather than a categorical distinction between valid or invalid measures. Cronbach and Meehl (1955) have provided a classic discussion of construct validity, perhaps the most overarching and fundamental form of validity considered in psychological research (*see also* Smith, 2005). However, we restrict our discussion to content validity and criterion-related validity because these two types of validity are particularly relevant for secondary data analysis and they are more immediately addressable.

Content validity describes how well a measure captures the entire domain of the construct in question. Judgments regarding content validity are ideally made by panels of experts familiar with the focal construct. A measure is considered *construct deficient* if it fails to assess important elements of the construct. For example, if thoughts of suicide are an integral aspect of the concept depression and a given self-report measure is missing items that tap this content, then the measure would be deemed construct-deficient. A measure can also suffer from *construct contamination* if it includes extraneous items that are irrelevant to the focal construct. For example, if somatic symptoms like a rapid heartbeat are considered to reflect the construct of anxiety and not part of depression, then a depression inventory that has such an item would suffer from construct contamination. Given the reduced length of many assessments, concerns over construct deficiency are likely to be especially pressing. A short assessment may not include enough items to capture the full breadth of a broad construct. This limitation is not readily addressed and should be acknowledged (*see* Widaman et al., 2011). In particular, researchers may need to clearly specify that their findings are based on a narrower content domain than is normally associated with the focal construct of interest.

A subtle but important point can arise when considering the content of measures with particularly narrow content. Internal consistency will increase when there is redundancy among items in the scale; however, the presence of similar items may decrease predictive power. This is known as the attenuation paradox in psychometrics (*see* Clark & Watson, 1995). When items are nearly identical, they contribute redundant information about a very specific aspect of the construct. However, the very specific attribute may not have predictive power. In essence, reliability can be maximized at the expense of creating a measure that is not very useful from the point of view of prediction (and likely explanation). Indeed, Clark and Watson (1995) have argued that the "goal of scale construction is to maximize validity rather than reliability" (p. 316). In short, an evaluation of content validity is also important when considering the predictive power of a given measure.

Whereas content validity is focused on the internal attributes of a measure, criterion-related validity is based on the empirical relations between measures and other variables. Using previous research and theory surrounding the focal construct, the researcher should develop an expectation regarding the magnitude and direction of observed associations (i.e., correlations) with other variables. A good supporting theory of a construct should stipulate a pattern of association, or nomological network, concerning those other variables that should be related and unrelated to the focal construct. This latter requirement is often more difficult to specify from existing theories, which tend to provide a more elaborate discussion of convergent associations rather than discriminant validity (Widaman et al., 2011). For example, consider a very truncated nomological network for Agreeableness (dispositional kindness and empathy). Measures of this construct should be positively associated with romantic relationship quality, negatively related to crime (especially violent crime), and distinct from measures of cognitive ability such as tests of general intelligence.

Evaluations of criterion-related validity can be conducted within a data set as researchers document that a measure has an expected pattern of associations with existing criterion-related variables. Investigators using secondary data sets may want to conduct additional research to document the criterion-related validity of short measures with additional convenience samples (e.g., the ubiquitous college student samples used by many psychologists; Sears, 1986). For example, there are six items in the Add Health data set that appear to measure self-esteem (e.g., "I have a lot of good qualities" and "I like myself just the way I am") (*see* Russell, Crockett, Shen, & Lee, 2008). Although many of the items bear a strong resemblance to the items on the Rosenberg Self-Esteem scale (Rosenberg, 1965), they are not exactly the same items. To obtain some additional data on the usefulness of this measure, we administered the Add Health items to a sample of 387 college students at our university along with the Rosenberg Self-Esteem scale and an omnibus measure of personality based on the Five-Factor model (Goldberg, 1999). The six Add Health items were strongly correlated with the Rosenberg ($r = 0.79$), and both self-esteem measures had a similar pattern of convergent and divergent associations with the facets of the Five-Factor model (the two profiles were very strongly associated: $r > 0.95$). This additional information can help bolster the case for the validity of the short Add Health self-esteem measure.

Special Issue: Missing Data in Existing Data Sets

Missing data is a fact of life in research—individuals may drop out of longitudinal studies or refuse to answer particular questions. These behaviors can affect the generalizability of findings because results may only apply to those individuals who choose to complete a study or a measure. Missing data can also diminish statistical power when common techniques like listwise deletion are used (e.g., only using cases with complete information, thereby reducing the sample size) and even lead to biased effect size estimates (e.g., McKnight & McKnight, 2011; McKnight, McKnight, Sidani, & Figuredo, 2007; Widaman, 2006). Thus, concerns about missing data are important for all aspects of research, including secondary data analysis. The development of specific techniques for appropriately handling missing data is an active area of research in quantitative methods (Schafer & Graham, 2002).

Unfortunately, the literature surrounding missing data techniques is often technical and steeped in jargon, as noted by McKnight et al. (2007). The reality is that researchers attempting to understand issues of missing data need to pay careful attention to terminology. For example, a novice researcher may not immediately grasp the classification of missing data used in the literature (*see* Schafer & Graham, 2002, for a clear description). Consider the confusion that may stem from learning that data are missing at random (MAR) versus data are missing completely at random (MCAR). The term MAR does not mean that missing values only occurred because of chance factors. This is the case when data are missing completely at random (MCAR). Data that are MCAR are absent because of truly random factors. Data that are MAR refers to the situation in which the probability that the observations are missing depends only on other available information in the data set. Data that are MAR can be essentially "ignored" when the other factors are included in a statistical model. The last type of missing data, data missing not at random (MNAR), is likely to characterize the variables in many real-life data sets. As it stands, methods for handing data that are MAR and MCAR are better developed and more easily implemented than methods for handling data MNAR. Thus, many applied researchers will assume data are MAR for purposes of statistical modeling (and the ability to sleep comfortably at night). Fortunately, such an assumption might not create major problems for many analyses and may in fact represent the "practical state of the art" (Schafer & Graham, 2002, p. 173).

The literature on missing data techniques is growing, so we simply recommend that researchers keep current on developments in this area. McKnight et al. (2007) and Widaman (2006) both provide an accessible primer on missing data techniques. In keeping with the largely practical bent to the chapter, we suggest that researchers keep careful track of the amount of missing data present in their analyses and report such information clearly in research papers (*see* McKnight & McKnight, 2011). Similarly, we recommend that researchers thoroughly screen their data sets for evidence that missing values depend on other measured variables (e.g., scores at Time 1 might be associated with Time 2 dropout). In general, we suggest that researchers avoid listwise and pairwise deletion methods because there is very little evidence that these are good practices (*see* Jeličić, Phelps, & Lerner, 2009; Widaman, 2006). Rather, it might be easiest to use direct fitting methods such as the estimation procedures used in conventional structural equation modeling packages (e.g., Full Information Maximum Likelihood; *see* Allison, 2003). At the very least, it is usually instructive to compare results using listwise deletion with results obtained with direct model fitting in terms of the effect size estimates and basic conclusions regarding the statistical significance of focal coefficients.

Special Issue: Sample Weighting in Existing Data Sets

One of the advantages of many existing data sets is that they were collected using probabilistic sampling methods so that researchers can obtain unbiased population estimates. Such estimates, however, are only obtained when complex survey weights are formally incorporated into the statistical modeling procedures. Such weighting schemes can affect the correlations between variables, and therefore all users of secondary data sets should become familiar with sampling design when they begin working with a new data set. A considerable amount of time and effort is dedicated toward generating complex weighting schemes that account for the precise sampling strategies used in the given study, and users of secondary data sets should give careful consideration to using these weights appropriately.

In some cases, the addition of sampling weights will have little substantive implication on findings, so extensive concern over weighting might be overstated. On the other hand, any potential difference is ultimately an empirical question, so researchers are well advised to consider the importance of sampling weights (Shrout & Napier, 2011). The problem is that many psychologists are not well versed in the use of sampling weights (Shrout & Napier, 2011). Thus, psychologists may not be in a strong position to evaluate whether sample weighting concerns are relevant. In addition, it is sometimes necessary to use specialized software packages or add-ons to adjust analytic models appropriately for sampling weights. Programs such as STATA and SAS have such capabilities in the base package, whereas packages like SPSS sometimes require a complex survey model add-on that integrates with its existing capabilities. Whereas the graduate training of the modal sociologist or demographer is likely to emphasize survey research and thus presumably cover sampling, this is not the case with the methodological training of many psychologists (Aiken, West, & Millsap, 2008). Psychologists who are unfamiliar with sample weighting procedures are well advised to seek the counsel of a survey methodologist before undertaking data analysis.

In terms of practical recommendations, it is important for the user of the secondary data set to develop a clear understanding of how the data were collected by reading documentation about the design and sampling procedure (Shrout & Napier, 2011). This insight will provide a conceptual framework for understanding weighting schemes and for deciding how to appropriately weight the data. Once researchers have a clear idea of the sampling scheme and potential weights, actually incorporating available weights into analyses is not terribly difficult, provided researchers have the appropriate software (Shrout & Napier, 2011). Weighting tutorials are often available for specific data sets. For example, the Add Health project has a document describing weighting (http://www.cpc.unc.edu/projects/addhealth/faqs/aboutdata/weight1.pdf) as does the Centers for Disease Control and Prevention for use with their Youth Risk Behavior Surveys (http://www.cdc.gov/HealthyYouth/yrbs/pdf/YRBS_analysis_software.pdf). These free documents may also provide useful and accessible background even for those who may not use the data from these projects.

Conclusion

Secondary data analysis refers to the analysis of existing data that may not have been explicitly collected to address a particular research question. Many of the quantitative techniques described in this volume can be applied using existing resources. To be sure, strong data analytic skills are important for fully realizing the potential benefits of secondary data sets, and such skills can help researchers recognize the limits of a data set for any given analysis.

In particular, measurement issues are likely to create the biggest hurdles for psychologists conducting secondary analyses in terms of the challenges associated with offering a reasonable interpretation of the results and in surviving the peer-review process. Accordingly, a familiarity with basic issues in psychometrics is very helpful. Beyond such skills, the effective use of these existing resources requires patience and strong attention to detail. Effective secondary data analysis also requires a fair bit of curiosity to seek out those resources that might be used to make important contribution to psychological science.

Ultimately, we hope that the field of psychology becomes more and more accepting of secondary data analysis. As psychologists use this approach with increasing frequency, it is likely that the organizers of major ongoing data collection efforts will be increasingly open to including measures of prime interest to psychologists. The individuals in charge of projects like the BHPS, the GSOEP, and the National Center for Education Statistics (http://nces.ed.gov/) want their data to be used by the widest possible audiences and will respond to researcher demands. We believe that it is time that psychologists join their colleagues in economics, sociology, and political science in taking advantage of these existing resources. It is also time to move beyond divisive discussions surrounding the presumed superiority of primary data collection over secondary analysis. There is no reason to choose one over the other when the field of psychology can profit from both. We believe that the relevant topics of debate are not about the method of initial data collection but, rather, about the importance and intrinsic interest of the underlying research questions. If the question is important and the research design and measures are suitable, then there is little doubt in our minds that secondary data analysis can make a contribution to psychological science.

Author Note

1. M. Brent Donnellan, Department of Psychology, Michigan State University, East Lansing, MI 48824.

2. Richard E. Lucas, Department of Psychology, Michigan State University, East Lansing, MI 48824.

Note

1. One consequence of large sample sizes, however, is that issues of effect size interpretation become paramount given that very small correlations or very small mean differences between groups are likely to be statistically significant using conventional

null hypothesis significance tests (e.g., Trzesniewski & Donnellan, 2009). Researchers will therefore need to grapple with issues related to null hypothesis significance testing (*see* Kline, 2004).

References

Aiken, L. S., & West, S. G. (1991). *Multiple regression: Testing and interpreting interactions.* Newbury Park, CA: Sage.

Aiken, L. S., West, S. G., & Millsap, R. E. (2008). Doctoral training in statistics, measurement, and methodology in psychology: Replication and extension of Aiken, West, Sechrest, and Reno's (1990) survey of Ph.D. programs in North America. *American Psychologist, 63,* 32–50.

Akers, R. L., Massey, J., & Clarke, W. (1983). Are self-reports of adolescent deviance valid? Biochemical measures, randomized response, and the bogus pipeline in smoking behavior. *Social Forces, 62,* 234–251.

Allison, P. D. (2003). Missing data techniques for structural equation modeling. *Journal of Abnormal Psychology, 112,* 545–557.

Baird, B. M., Lucas, R. E., & Donnellan, M. B. (2010). Life Satisfaction across the lifespan: Findings from two nationally representative panel studies. *Social Indicators Research, 99,* 183–203.

Briggs, S. R., & Cheek, J. M. (1986). The role of factor analysis in the development and evaluation of personality scales. *Journal of Personality, 54,* 106–148.

Brooks-Gunn, J., Berlin, L. J., Leventhal, T., & Fuligini, A. S. (2000). Depending on the kindness of strangers: Current national data initiatives and developmental research. *Child Development, 71,* 257–268.

Brooks-Gunn, J., & Chase-Lansdale, P. L. (1991) (Eds.). Secondary data analyses in developmental psychology [Special section]. *Developmental Psychology, 27,* 899–951.

Clark, L. A., & Watson, D. (1995). Constructing validity: Basic issues in objective scale development. *Psychological Assessment, 7,* 309–319.

Cronbach, L. J. (1951). Coefficient alpha and the internal structure of tests. *Psychometrika, 16,* 297–234.

Cronbach, L. J. (1957). The two disciplines of scientific psychology. *American Psychologist, 12,* 671–684.

Cronbach, L. J., & Meehl, P. (1955). Construct validity in psychological tests. *Psychological Bulletin, 52,* 281–302.

Diener, E., Emmons, R. A., Larsen, R. J., & Griffin, S. (1985). The Satisfaction with Life Scale. *Journal of Personality Assessment, 49,* 71–75.

Donnellan, M. B., Trzesniewski, K. H., & Robins, R. W. (2011). Self-esteem: Enduring issues and controversies. In T. Chamorro-Premuzic, S. von Stumm, and A. Furnham (Eds). *The Wiley-Blackwell Handbook of Individual Differences* (pp. 710–746). New York: Wiley-Blackwell.

Freese, J. (2007). Replication standards for quantitative social science: Why not sociology? *Sociological Methods & Research, 36,* 153–172.

Gerstorf, D., Ram, N., Estabrook, R., Schupp, J., Wagner, G. G., & Lindenberger, U. (2008). Life satisfaction shows terminal decline in old age: Longitudinal evidence from the German Socio-Economic Panel Study (SOEP). *Developmental Psychology, 44,* 1148–1159.

Gerstorf, D., Ram, N., Goebel, J., Schupp, J., Lindenberger, U., & Wagner, G. G. (2010). Where people live and die makes a difference: Individual and geographic disparities in well-being progression at the end of life. *Psychology and Aging, 25,* 661–676.

Goldberg, L. R. (1999). A broad-bandwidth, public domain, personality inventory measuring the lower-level facets of several five-factor models. In I Mervielde, I. Deary, F. De Fruyt, & F. Ostendorf (Eds.), *Personality psychology in Europe* (Vol. 7, pp. 7–28). Tilburg, The Netherlands: Tilburg University Press.

Hofferth, S. L., (2005). Secondary data analysis in family research. *Journal of Marriage and the Family, 67,* 891–907.

Hunter, J. E., & Schmidt, F. L. (2004). *Methods of meta-analysis: Correcting error and bias in research findings* (2nd ed.). Newbury Park, CA: Sage.

Jeličić, H., Phelps, E., & Lerner, R. M. (2009). Use of missing data methods in longitudinal studies: The persistence of bad practices in developmental psychology. *Developmental Psychology, 45,* 1195–1199.

John, O. P., & Soto, C. J. (2007). The importance of being valid. In R. W. Robins, R. C. Fraley, and R. F. Krueger (Eds). *Handbook of Research Methods in Personality Psychology* (pp. 461–494). New York: Guilford Press.

Kiecolt, K. J. & Nathan, L. E. (1985). *Secondary analysis of survey data.* Sage University Paper series on Quantitative Applications in the Social Sciences, No. 53). Newbury Park, CA: Sage.

Kline, R. B. (2004). *Beyond significance testing: Reforming data analysis methods in behavioral research.* Washington, DC: American Psychological Association.

Kline, R. B. (2011). *Principles and practice of structural equation modeling* (3rd ed.). New York: Guilford Press.

Lance, C. E., Butts, M. M., & Michels, L. C. (2006). The sources of four commonly reported cutoff criteria: What did they really say? *Organizational Research Methods, 9,* 202–220.

Lord, F., & Novick, M. R. (1968). *Statistical theories of mental test scores.* Reading, MA: Addison-Wesley.

Lucas, R. E. (2005). Time does not heal all wounds. *Psychological Science, 16,* 945–950.

Lucas, R. E. (2007). Adaptation and the set-point model of subjective well-being: Does happiness change after major life events? *Current Directions in Psychological Science, 16,* 75–79.

McCall R, B., & Appelbaum, M. I. (1991). Some issues of conducting secondary analyses. *Developmental Psychology, 27,* 911–917.

McCrae, R. R., Kurtz, J. E., Yamagata, S., & Terracciano, A. (2011). Internal consistency, retest reliability, and their implications for personality scale validity. *Personality and Social Psychology Review, 15,* 28–50.

Messick, S. (1995). Validity of psychological assessment: Validation of inferences from persons' responses and performances as scientific inquiry into score meaning. *American Psychologist, 50,* 741–749.

McKnight, P. E., & McKnight, K. M. (2011). Missing data in secondary data analysis. In K. H. Trzesniewski, M. B. Donnellan, & R. E. Lucas (Eds). *Secondary data analysis: An introduction for psychologists* (pp. 83–101). Washington, DC: American Psychological Association.

McKnight, P. E., McKnight, K. M., Sidani, S., & Figuredo, A. (2007). *Missing data: A gentle introduction.* New York: Guilford Press.

Mroczek, D. K., Pitzer, L., Miller, L., Turiano, N., & Fingerman, K. (2011). The use of secondary data in adult development and aging research. In K. H. Trzesniewski, M. B. Donnellan, and R. E. Lucas (Eds). *Secondary data analysis: An introduction for psychologists* (pp. 121–132). Washington, DC: American Psychological Association.

Pienta, A. M., O'Rourke, J. M., & Franks, M. M. (2011). Getting started: Working with secondary data. In K. H. Trzesniewski, M. B. Donnellan, and R. E. Lucas (Eds). *Secondary data analysis: An introduction for psychologists* (pp. 13–25). Washington, DC: American Psychological Association.

Rosenberg, M. (1965). *Society and adolescent self-image*, Princeton, NJ: Princeton University.

Russell, S. T., Crockett, L. J., Shen, Y-L, & Lee, S-A. (2008). Cross-ethnic invariance of self-esteem and depression measures for Chinese, Filipino, and European American adolescents. *Journal of Youth and Adolescence, 37,* 50–61.

Russell, S. T., & Matthews, E. (2011). Using secondary data to study adolescence and adolescent development. In K. H. Trzesniewski, M. B. Donnellan, & R. E. Lucas (Eds). *Secondary data analysis: An introduction for psychologists* (pp. 163–176). Washington, DC: American Psychological Association.

Schafer, J. L. & Graham, J. W. (2002). Missing data: Our view of the state of the art. *Psychological Methods, 7,* 147–177.

Schmitt, N. (1996). Uses and abuses of coefficient alpha. *Psychological Assessment, 8,* 350–353.

Schwarz, N. (1999). Self-reports: How the questions shape the answers. *American Psychologist, 54,* 93–105.

Schwarz, N. & Strack, F. (1999). Reports of subjective well-being: Judgmental processes and their methodological implications. In D. Kahneman, E. Diener, & N. Schwarz (Eds.). *Well-being: The foundations of hedonic psychology* (pp.61–84). New York: Russell Sage Foundation.

Sears, D. O. (1986). College sophomores in the lab: Influences of a narrow data base on social psychology's view of human nature. *Journal of Personality and Social Psychology, 51,* 515–530.

Shrout, P. E., & Napier, J. L. (2011). Analyzing survey data with complex sampling designs. In K. H. Trzesniewski, M. B. Donnellan, & R. E. Lucas (Eds). *Secondary data analysis: An introduction for psychologists* (pp. 63–81). Washington, DC: American Psychological Association.

Simms, L. J. (2008). Classical and modern methods of psychological scale construction. *Social and Personality Psychology Compass, 2/1,* 414–433.

Simms, L. J., & Watson, D. (2007). The construct validation approach to personality scale creation. In R. W. Robins, R. C. Fraley, & R. F. Krueger (Eds). *Handbook of Research Methods in Personality Psychology* (pp. 240–258). New York: Guilford Press.

Smith, G. T. (2005). On construct validity: Issues of method and measurement. *Psychological Assessment, 17,* 396–408.

Tracy, J. L., Robins, R. W., & Sherman, J. W. (2009). The practice of psychological science: Searching for Cronbach's two streams in social-personality psychology. *Journal of Personality and Social Psychology, 96,* 1206–1225.

Trzesniewski, K.H. & Donnellan, M. B. (2009). Re-evaluating the evidence for increasing self-views among high school students: More evidence for consistency across generations (1976–2006). *Psychological Science, 20,* 920–922.

Trzesniewski, K. H. & Donnellan, M. B. (2010). Rethinking "Generation Me": A study of cohort effects from 1976–2006. *Perspectives in Psychological Science, 5,* 58–75.

Trzesniewski, K. H., Donnellan, M. B., & Lucas, R. E. (2011) (Eds). *Secondary data analysis: An introduction for psychologists.* Washington, DC: American Psychological Association.

Widaman, K. F. (2006). Missing data: What to do with or without them. *Monographs of the Society for Research in Child Development, 71,* 42–64.

Widaman, K. F., Little, T. D., Preacher, K. K., & Sawalani, G. M. (2011). On creating and using short forms of scales in secondary research. In K. H. Trzesniewski, M. B. Donnellan, & R. E. Lucas (Eds). *Secondary data analysis: An introduction for psychologists* (pp. 39–61). Washington, DC: American Psychological Association.

Willms, J. D. (2011). Managing and using secondary data sets with multidisciplinary research teams. In K. H. Trzesniewski, M. B. Donnellan, & R. E. Lucas (Eds). *Secondary data analysis: An introduction for psychologists* (pp. 27–38). Washington, DC: American Psychological Association.

CHAPTER 29

Data Mining

Carolin Strobl

Abstract

The term data mining refers to a variety of exploratory data analysis techniques developed in computer sciences and computational statistics. This chapter points out the commonalities and differences between data mining and classical statistical modeling. Common features of data mining techniques are then illustrated by means of one particular class of data mining techniques: the recursive partitioning methods classification and regression trees, bagging and random forests. In the end of the chapter an outlook on other popular data mining techniques as well as a short literature and software guide are given.

Key Words: Classification and regression trees, CART, Bagging, Random forests, Bootstrap sampling, Subsampling, Prediction, Variable importance

Introduction

Data mining is an umbrella term for a variety of techniques that were developed in statistics and computer sciences for analyzing large amounts of data. Tantamount terms are *pattern recognition*, *statistcal learning*, and *machine learning*.

Techniques referred to with the term *data mining* have certain characteristics in common that distinguish them from classical statistical approaches. Throughout this chapter, we will first review some of the properties of classical statistical models before we contrast them with common properties of data mining techniques.

These common properties will later be illustrated by means of one particular class of data mining techniques—namely, the recursive partitioning methods termed classification and regression trees, bagging, and random forests. In the end of the chapter, an outlook on other popular data mining techniques as well as a short literature and software guide are given.

Classical Statistics: Parametric Models

Classical statistical models assume a certain functional form to describe the association between the predictor variables and the response. The best example for this is a linear regression model (described in detail in Chapter ???).

In a linear regression model, the functional form of the association between the predictor variable X and the response variable Y is assumed to be linear. Because of this assumption, the association can be described in a very simple way by means of two values, which are the two parameters of the linear regression model: the intercept β_0 and the slope β_1.

This is why classical statistical models are termed parametric: To describe the given function, only a small number of parameters is necessary. These parameters are later estimated from the data. The main advantage of this approach is that the complexity of the association is reduced to a small number of model parameters. However, this approach crucially relies on the assumption that the postulated functional form actually holds—whereas in many situations, a linear relationship may be too simple to describe the true association between the variables.

Another important assumption of the linear regression model is how empirical observations vary from the linear function: It is assumed that the observed values are scattered randomly around the line—some above, some below—but on average the linear function is supposed to hold. Moreover, the variability around the line is supposed to be the same over the entire range of the predictor variable. This assumption is important for the optimality of the rule used for estimating the intercept and slope parameters from the data, the least squares estimator. When in addition a normal distribution is assumed for the random deviations from the line, the ever greater toolbox of likelihood inference is available for estimating the model parameters and deriving statistical tests for them.

It is important to note here for our later reasoning that model assumptions such as the linearity of the function and equal variance or even equal distributions of all errors are important mainly for technical reasons. For example, the assumptions make the parameter estimation comparatively easy. The estimation problem can be written as a closed formula, so, at least for small data sets, one can compute the estimates by hand. (All you would have to do is find the minimum of the sum of squares—or the maximum of the likelihood—by computing the derivative). Yet, the assumptions may be very unrealistic.

Therefore, when a parametric model is applied in practice, the model assumptions should always be tested, and if they do not hold, then a model with less stringent assumptions, like a classical nonparametric method or one of those discussed in this chapter, should be used.

Non-Classical Statistics: Data Mining Techniques

As opposed to parametric models, most data mining techniques make many fewer—if any—assumptions about the functional form and distribution of the data. Accordingly, they are more flexible and often more realistic, but it is usually not possible to write down the model as a simple formula or estimate it by hand in a closed form. Rather, the methods are algorithmic in the sense that they rely on computer programs to determine the functional form in an exhaustive search manner.

Common properties of data mining techniques are:

- Automated data processing

The term *data mining* is inspired by the idea that there are large amounts of data—for example, access statistics from websites that are collected automatically in large amounts—that need to be "mined" automatically. The algorithmic nature of the methods does not require much human interaction. In particular, it need not be stated in advance by the researcher which variables should be included in the model in which particular functional form, but the entire data set is blindly handed over to the algorithms that then makes all decisions.

This may sound like science fiction—and, of course, the rules by which the algorithm goes have been implemented by a human researcher in the first place—but when you think about it, this automatic and purely data driven character of data mining is a property that nicely meets the high scientific standard of objectivity: An analysis should give the same results, regardless of who "pushed the buttons." On the other hand, this kind of usage implies that the methods are used in an exploratory fashion only, as discussed below.

- Large numbers of variables at a time, often automatic variable selection

Besides situations where large amounts of data refer to a large number of observations, data mining techniques are also very important in situations with a large number of predictor variables. For example, one area where data mining techniques have been accepted very quickly was genetics, where after the genotyping of the human and other genomes was possible but still expensive, data sets contained information about the expression of tens of thousands of genes, but only a few dozen or a hundred individuals.

Classical statistical methods, such as linear or logistic regression, cannot deal with problems where the numbers of variables is greater than the number of observations, simply because the formulas used to compute the parameter estimates are not suitable for this case. Data mining techniques, on the other hand, can deal with this situation very well. Many of them include some sort of variable selction step, as outlined below, so that not all variables are processed at the same time (as they would be in a regression estimate).

But even if we are not talking about thousands of genes, in parametric regression models you soon come to the point where the number of observations is too small to estimate all parameters of interest—namely, when you want to include interaction terms. In many real-world applications, interaction effects are crucial for representing the complexity of the underlying biological or social mechanism but are not accounted for because the model used to describe reality is too simple—or has to be too simple to be estimable. In this sense, again, data mining techniques may be able to more realistically grasp the true functional form of the association between the predictor and response variables. However, the form may be so complicated that we, as humans, cannot interpret it anymore. This leads us directly to the next property of many data mining approaches:

- Black–boxes

Because the functional form detected by a data mining algorithm may be too complicated to interpret, data mining techniques are often used only as "black boxes": you "plug in" the data, and out comes a prediction.

For example, imagine we were trying to diagnose a certain disease that we suspect has a genetic component (because we find it often appears in more than one family member), but the biologists have no specific hypothesis yet about which genes cause the disease. What we need now is a learning sample. For this sample of persons, we need to have both their values on all suspected predictor variables (their genotyping plus some environmental variables like nutrition intake, smoking, and drinking habits) and their value of the response variable (the diagnosis whether the person has the disease, so here we are thinking of a case–control study with patients and healthy controls).

From the learning sample we can derive the rule that relates the predictor variables to the response. If it was an easy rule, then it might be something like: Individuals who have an anomaly on gene XY and eat too much sugar are more likely to develop the disease.

More likely, however (especially for diseases where no single genetic risk factor has been found yet), the disease will be caused by a variety of genetic and environmental risk factors, so that the rule is much more complicated. The data mining method can still derive even this complicated rule from the learning data (in a way that will become more clear in the section on Exemplary Techniques), and even if the rule is so complicated that no doctor could even memorize it, we can then use it for a very important purpose—the prediction of future observations.

Because now that we have learned the rule, once a new person comes to us and wants to know if he or she is at risk for developing the disease, we can pass his or her values of the predictor variables (the gene profile, eating habits, etc.) to the algorithm, and it will "spit out" a prediction: whether the person is likely to develop the disease. In this sense, it is not necessary to "look into the black box" and know the exact functional form of the complicated relationship between predictors and response to make valuable predictions from it.

Still, because humans are curious creatures, many data mining techniques also offer some means of interpretation or visualization that can help understand the functional form. This functional form will often be much more complicated than what we are used to from parametric models (but this may only mean that parametric models are far too simple for many of the research questions of a complicated world).

- Exploratory as opposed to hypothesis-driven

In the social sciences, the term *data mining* is often used in a derogatory sense for what is also known as "fishing for effects"—as opposed to stating a clear research hypothesis, that is then statistically tested. To understand (and question) this point of view, let us review the general rationale behind the hypothesis-driven approach to research. Figure 29.1 displays a simplified version of common illustrations of the scientific process as it is displayed in many textbooks on empirical social research, such as Schnell et al. (1999, p. 8). The central steps of the scientific process are (1) the generation of the research hypothesis, (2) the design of a study plan and the collection of data appropriate for testing the hypothesis, and (3) the analysis of the data that may lead to a rejection of the hypothesis. Usually illustrations of this scientific process also include a feedback loop from the last step, the data analysis and interpretation of the results, back to the first step, a modification of existing or generation of new hypotheses.

This view of the scientific process is usually considered appropriate in the social sciences. One point that should be emphasized, however, is that the feedback loop—that after you have seen first results you go back to modify your hypothesis—is only legitimate if <u>new</u> data are then collected to test this modified hypothesis. As opposed to that, it is not

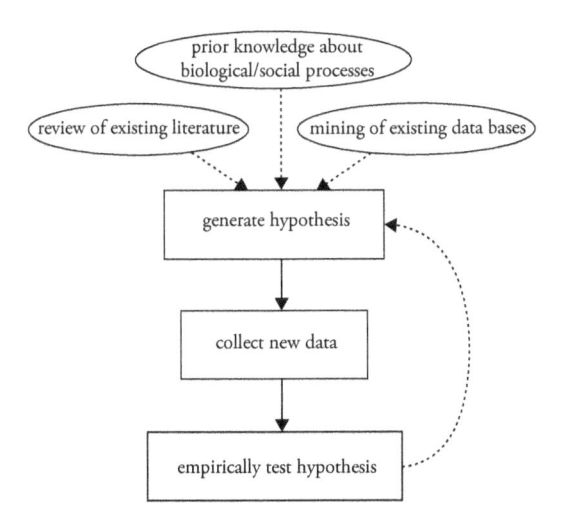

Figure 29.1 Simplified illustration of the scientific research process.

legitimate to look at a given data set first and then claim that whatever you have found in it was exactly what you thought would happen (i.e., to use the same data to generate and test the hypothesis).

When people refer to data mining in a negative way, they often assume that it is used in this latter, circular fashion. However, there is a sensible and legitimate way to employ data mining techniques in an exploratory way that does not interfere with the strict scientific standards that we keep up in the social sciences: Data mining on existing data bases can be one out of many valuable sources for generating hypothesis—especially in research areas where no other prior information is available.

Think again, for example, about research on genetic determinants of diseases: Ideally, if we know from previous biological research that a certain protein affects the human system and causes a disease, then we can go looking for the gene responsible for producing this protein, and sometimes (usually in an animal model) even experimentally turn the gene on and off to test its effect on the disease. This would be a purely hypothesis-driven approach, but unfortunately it is only possible when we have prior information.

However, there may be situations where we know so little about the underlying biological or social mechanisms that we have no starting point for this procedure. In these situations, the only thing we can do is search over all possible genes. Moreover, it may not be a single gene but an interaction of several genes or of genes and environmental factors that cause a disease, as already discussed above. In this situation, research would "get stuck" if it was not allowed to search for possible causes. And here data mining techniques come into play as a means of searching through large data-bases to extract possible associations between certain patterns of gene expression and environmental risk factors and the disease.

What is important to note, however, is that this exploratory approach can only be the first step, that helps generate hypotheses. Later, of course, we should go back to the biologist and check whether there is a plausible biological explanation for the association and, most importantly, test whether the association can still be found in fresh data (or ideally tested in a randomized experiment, if it is possible to switch the gene off).

The importance of new data is the following: Imagine that 100 scientists search for interesting effects within the same data-base, and imagine they all performed significance tests with 5% error probability. Of course, we would expect about five of them to find significant effects just by chance even if there was only random noise in the data. In this sense, mining data-bases is like fishing for effects, whereas testing only a small number of previously stated hypotheses keeps down the probability of falsely detecting a nonexistent effect. This is why it is so important that data mining be considered as a first—but not the final—step of a research process.

When hypotheses generated by means of data mining—just like those generated from other sources—are later tested on fresh data, this is fully in accordance with the high scientific standards kept up in the social sciences.

Exemplary Techniques

After we have considered some of the general properties of data mining techniques, we will now illustrate these properties by means of one particular class of data mining techniques, namely the recursive partitioning methods termed *classification* and *regression trees*, *bagging*, and *random forests*. These techniques have in common that the are based on a simple algorithm for finding patterns in the data. These patterns can be visualized by means of diagrams that look like upside-down

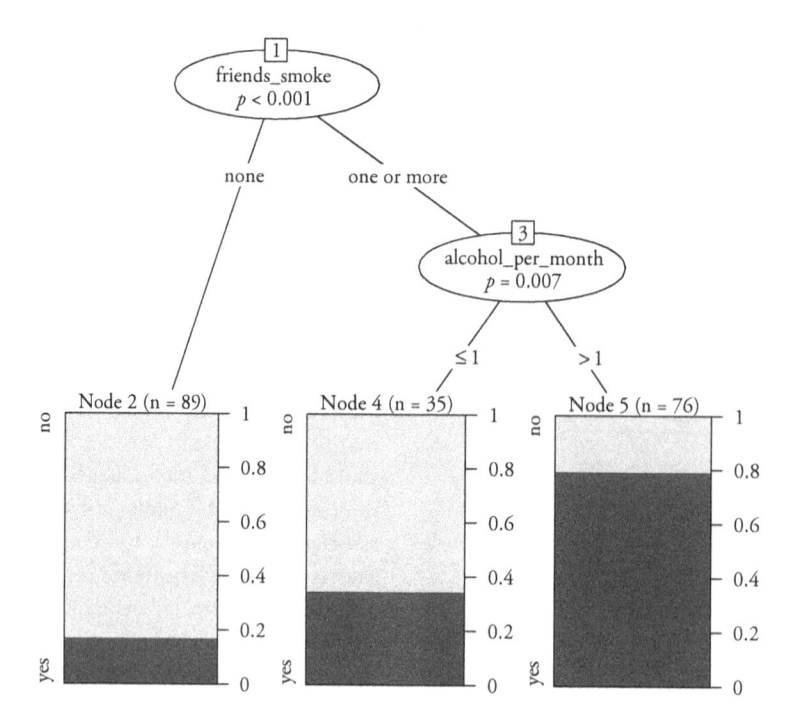

Figure 29.2 Binary classification tree.

trees, as illustrated in Figure 29.2. Accordingly, the terminology for describing the underlying model is often borrowed from real trees, too, including terms like "root node" (the first node, actually at the top of the the upside down tree) and "leafs" (the final nodes at the bottom, where the tree is widest).

Illustrated in Figure 29.2 is the instructive example from Strobl et al. (2009), that is well suited for illustrating the principle of recursive partitioning. Inspired by the study of Kitsantas et al. (2007) on determinants of adolescent smoking habits, an artificial data set was generated that resembles the original findings of the study. The response variable is the binary variable intention_to_smoke, describing the adolescents' intention to smoke a cigarette within the next year. Moreover, the data set contains four possible risk factors: the binary predictor variables lied_to_parents, indicating whether the subject has ever lied to the parents about doing something they would not approve of; friends_smoke, indicating peer smoking of one or more among the four best friends; the numeric predictor variables age, indicating the age in years; and alcohol_per_month, indicating how many times the subject drank alcohol in the past month.

The data were generated as to resemble the key results of Kitsantas et al. (2007). Only the variables age and alcohol_per_month (that are used only in a discretized form by Kitsantas, Moore, & Sly, 2007) were generated as numeric variables to later illustrate the selection of optimal cut-points in recursive partitioning.

Figure 29.2 displays the classification tree derived from these smoking data. From the tree, we can see the following: From the entire sample of 200 adolescents, a group of 89 adolescents is separated from the rest in the first split. This group (represented by node 2, where the node numbers are mere labels assigned sequentially from left to right starting from the top node) is characterized by the fact that "none" of their four best friends smoke and that within this group only few subjects intend to smoke within the next year. The remaining 111 subjects are further split into two groups (nodes 4 and 5) according to whether they drank alcohol in one or less or more than one occasions in the past month. These two groups again vary in the percentage of subjects who intend to smoke.

This example already illustrates that classification trees use the predictor variables to find groups of persons with the same or similar responses. Some of the predictor variables that were available in the data set are actually used for splitting up the groups, whereas others are not. The rules and rationale behind this is explained in the following sections, where we will also refer back to this example.

Classification and Regression Trees

Classification and regression trees belong to the nonparametric regression methods. The aim is the same as in classical parametric regression—the value of a response variable Y is predicted by means of one or more predictor variables $X_1, \ldots, X_p$. In classical statistics, logistic or linear regression would be used in the cases where we will introduce classification and regression trees. However, because in classification and regression trees the functional form is not explicitly stated and no distribution assumptions are made, they are summarized under the nonparametric rather than parametric regression methods.

The name classification and regression trees was termed by Breiman et al. (1984) and is really a summary for two cases. When the response variable Y is categorical, we speak of classification trees; if it is continuous, we speak of regression trees. Another summary term for classification and regression trees, as well as the so-called ensemble methods bagging and random forests, which combine the predictions of several trees as explained below, is recursive partitioning. The term recursive partitioning refers to the fact that the sample is split along a predictor variable into separate groups, that are then again split into groups and so forth, as represented by the tree structure.

The idea behind recursive partitioning methods was first introduced by Morgan and Sonquist (1963) in their seminal work on what they called automated interaction detection (later it will also become clear why interactions are such an important issue in recursive partitioning). Then in the 1980s, the two most popular algorithms for classification and regression trees, CART and C4.5, were introduced by Breiman et al. (1984) and independently by Quinlan (1986, 1993).

These two early algorithms are still the most widely known, and variants of them are available in many software packages. However, it was found later that these early algorithms have some problems that can be overcome by means of more advanced statistical methodology. In the following section, we will outline the general functioning that all recursive partitioning algorithms have in common and then shortly outline the problems of the early algorithms.

Another distinction between different recursive partitioning algorithms is by the number of nodes they produce in each split. Both the CART algorithm of Breiman et al. (1984) and the C4.5 algorithm (and its predecessor ID3) of Quinlan (1986, 1993) conduct binary splits in numeric predictor variables, as depicted in Figure 29.2. In categorical predictor variables (of nominal or ordinal scale of measurement), however, C4.5 produces as many nodes as there are categories (often referred to as "k-ary" or "multiple" splitting), whereas CART again creates binary splits between the ordered or unordered categories. We concentrate on binary splitting trees in the following and refer to Quinlan (1993) for k-ary splitting.

RECURSIVE PARTITIONING

The main characteristic of classification and regression trees is that the feature space—that is, the space spanned by all predictor variables—is recursively partitioned (i.e., split repeatedly in the predictor variables). By this the observations are split into different groups, such as the adolescents that have one or more friends that smoke and drink alcohol more than once per month.

In Figure 29.2 these successive splits are illustrated as a tree, that is easy to understand, but it is also possible to illustrate the same groups as a set of rectangular areas, as illustrated in Figure 29.3. You can follow the splits in the tree, and will find that each split corresponds to a split in the feature space. The first split in the variable `friends_smoke` divides the sample into two groups in the tree and entirely bisects the feature space. The next split in the variable `alcohol_per_month`, on the other hand, affects only the group of adolescents who have one or more friends that smoke and corresponds to a bisection of the rectangle for this particular sub-sample only. The partition representation in Figure 29.3 is even better suited than the tree representation to illustrate that recursive partitioning creates nested rectangular prediction areas corresponding to the terminal nodes of the classification tree.

The resulting partition is one of the main differences between classification trees and, for example, linear regression models. Whereas in linear regression, the information from different predictor variables is combined linearly, here the range of possible combinations includes all rectangular partitions that can be derived by means of recursive splitting, including multiple splits in the same variable. In particular, this includes nonlinear and even non-monotone association rules (such as a u-shaped

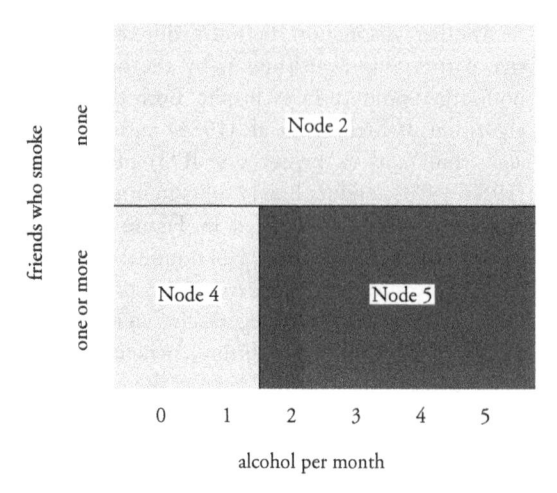

Figure 29.3 Partition of the smoking data by means of a binary classification tree. The tree representation displayed in Figure 29.2 corresponds to a rectangular recursive partition of the feature space.

association, where, e.g., very young and very old persons are more likely to show a certain response than those of middle ages, or even more complex shapes).

The advantage of classification and regression trees is that the functional form need not be known or specified in advance, but is automatically detected by the algorithm in a data-driven way. However, the rectangular splits can only give a rough approximation of any smooth function. So if the relationship was truly linear, then a classification or regression tree would not give a very good approximation of this function (it could only approximate it with many rectangular steps), whereas a linear model would be able to describe the linear relationship perfectly well. On the other hand, if the true relationship was, say, cubic, then one would have to explicitly include the cubic term x^3 in the model, and if this is not done, then the linear model will fail to detect the association, whereas a recursive partitioning algorithm can at least approximate it, as illustrated in Figure 29.4.

SPLIT SELECTION CRITERIA

To create a classification or regression tree, statistical criteria are neccessary to determine (1) what variables should be used for splitting up the groups, and (2) at what cut-points within the range of the variables the splits should best be made. Different criteria are available in the different algorithms for making these decisions, but it is easy to summarize their idea.

The aim is to find those variables and cut-points that best predict the response values of the persons. In our example, it is both intuitive and supported by the data that, for example, whether an adolescent's friends smoke can help us predict whether he or she will start smoking as well. In this sense, the variable `friends_smoke` is a good predictor. It is associated with the response variable such that those adolescents whose friends smoke are also more likely to smoke.

With this in mind, it is straighforward that any statistical measure of association can be used as a criterion for selecting those variables that are worthwhile for splitting. This rationale is followed in most modern recursive partitioning algorithms.

The first suggested classification tree algorithms, CART and C4.5, however, follow an approach that at first sight seems to have little in common with association tests as you may know them from statistics classes. We will shortly outline this approach anyway, because you may come across it in the literature on classification and regression trees.

The algorithms CART and C4.5, which were the first widely known recursive partitioning algorithms, follow an approach termed *impurity reduction* for selecting the splitting variable and cut-point in classification problems. (In regression, they use the deviance, see, e.g., Hastie, Tibshirani, & Friedman, 2001, but the case of classification is easier to illustrate.) This approach is inspired by entropy measures, and we will illustrate it by means of our smoking data example. In Figure 29.5 the relative frequencies of both response classes are displayed not only for the terminal nodes but also for the inner nodes of the tree previously presented in Figure 29.2. Starting from the "root node" at the top, we find that the relative frequency of "yes" answers in the entire sample of 200 adolescents is about 40%. By means of the first split, the group of 89 adolescents with the lowest frequency of "yes" answers (below 20%, node 2) can be isolated from the rest, who have a higher frequency of "yes" answers (about 60%, node 3). These 111 subjects are then further split to form two groups: one smaller group with a medium (below 40%, node 4) and one larger group with a high (about 80%, node 5) frequency of "yes" answers to the intention to smoke question.

From this example we can see that, following the principle of impurity reduction, each split in the tree-building process results in daughter nodes that are more "pure" than the parent node in the sense that groups of subjects with a majority for either response class are isolated. The impurity

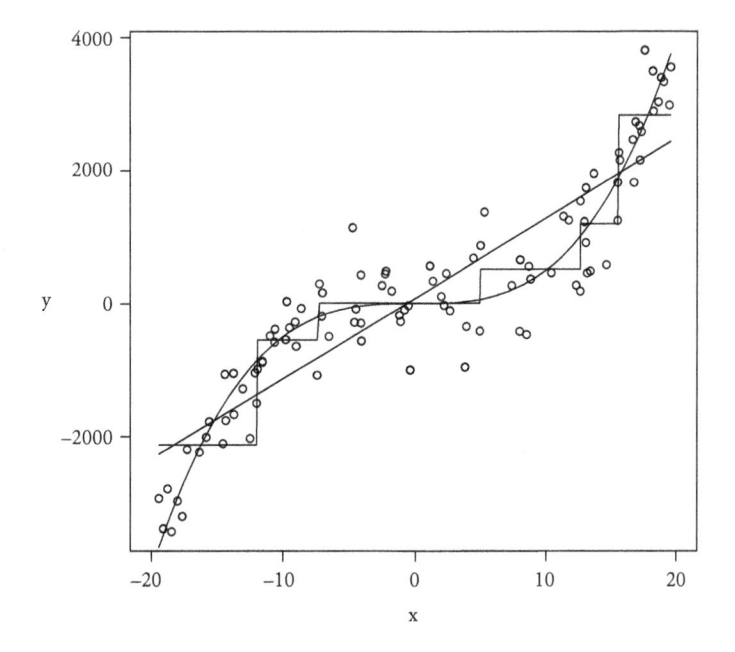

Figure 29.4 Simulated data with the true, cubic association, a linear model regression line and the prediction function from a regression tree.

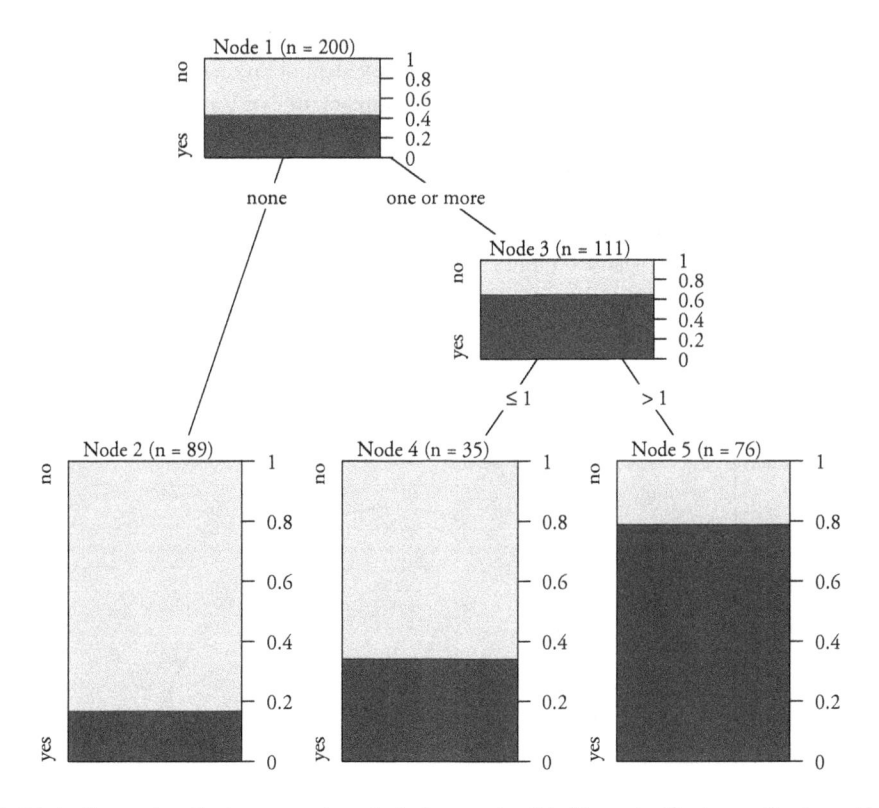

Figure 29.5 Relative frequencies of both response classes in the inner nodes of the binary classification tree for the smoking data. The dark and light grey shaded areas again represent the relative frequencies of "yes" and "no" answers to the intention to smoke question in each group, respectively.

reduction achieved by a split is measured by the difference between the impurity in the parent node and the average impurity in the two daughter nodes. Entropy measures, such as the Gini Index or the Shannon Entropy (you may be familiar with this entropy measure from physics class), are used to quantify the impurity in each node. These entropy measures have in common that they reach their minimum for perfectly pure nodes with the relative frequency of one response class being zero and their maximum for an equal mixture with the same relative frequencies for both response classes, as illustrated in Figure 29.6.

Although the principle of impurity reduction may be more intuitive for readers with a natural or computer sciences background and has added much to the popularity of classification trees in their beginning, for people with a social sciences background and some statistics training, it may be more helpful to think of impurity reduction as merely one of many possible means of measuring the strength of the association between the splitting variable and the response. Most recent classification tree algorithms (see section on Other Data Mining Techniques, Literature, and Software) rely on this strategy and employ the p-values of association tests for variable and cut-point selection.

There is, however, one more technical issue to keep in mind—the cut-point selection, which makes it a little bit more complicated to measure the association between predictor and response in a statistically sound way, as explained in the next section.

CUT-POINT SELECTION AND VARIABLE SELECTION BIAS

We have argued before that the impurity measure used in the early classification tree algorithms can be considered as measures of the association between a candidate predictor variable and the response. Accordingly, one can also use association measures, such as the χ^2-statistic, as splitting criteria.

However, there is one aspect of the split selection that we have not considered so far: In addition to deciding which variable is most informative, we also need to select the best cut-point within this variable. For binary variables, this is easy because they offer only one cut-point, but for variables with more categories as well as continuous variables, we want to split up the groups along the best cut-point—the one that best distinguishes between the groups. For example, the optimal cut-point identified in the range of the numeric predictor variable `alcohol_per_month` in our example is between the values 1 and 2, because adolescents who drank alcohol on one or less occasions have a lower frequency of "yes" answers than those who drank alcohol in two or more occasions.

In the early classification tree algorithms, the best splitting variable and cut-point were selected at the same time. For each variable, the impurity reduction (or association measure) was computed for each

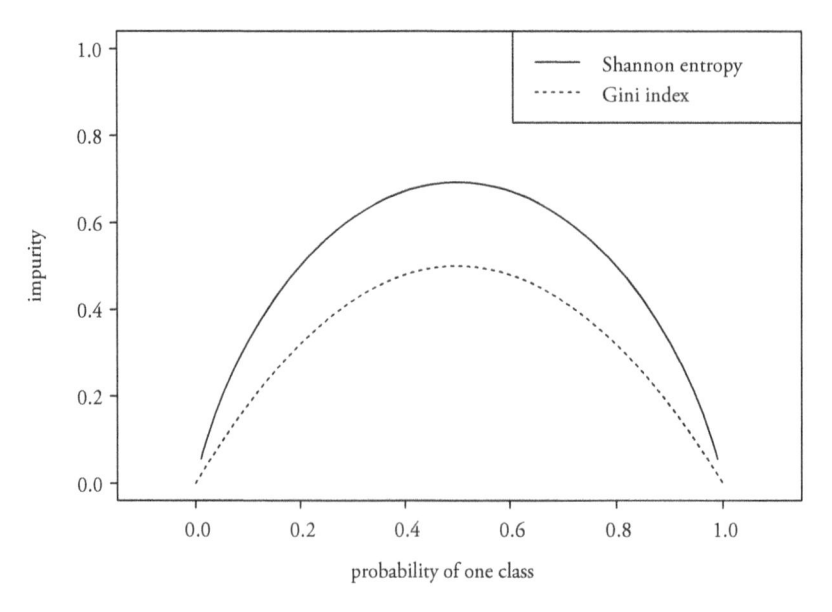

Figure 29.6 Gini index and Shannon entropy as functions of the relative frequency of one response class. Pure nodes containing only observations of one class receive an impurity value of 0, whereas mixed nodes receive higher impurity values.

possible cut-point, and the variable with the highest value in its best cut-point was selected for the next split. The problem with this approach is that variables that offer many cut-points (i.e., variables with many categories and continuous variables) get more chances and thus have a higher probability to produce a good value by chance, even if they are not informative.

This effect, that variables offering many possible cut-points are selected more often than variables with less cut-points (even if none of the variables is informative) is termed *variable selection bias*. It affects the early classification tree algorithms CART and C4.5 (as well as implementations with different names that rely on the same principles, see section on Other Data Mining Techniques, Literature, and Software).

However, today there are more advanced algorithms (also see section on Other Data Mining Techniques, Literature, and Software) that have eliminated this problem either by means of separating the issues of variable and cut-point selection, or by accounting for the optimal selection of the cut-point when computing the p-value of the association measure (see, e.g., Kass, 1980; White & Liu, 1994; Loh and Shih, 1997; Kim and Loh, 2001; Dobra and Gehrke, 2001; Lausen et al., 2004; Hothorn et al., 2006; Strobl et al., 2007).

STOPPING AND PRUNING

After a split is conducted, the observations in the learning sample are divided into the different nodes defined by the respective splitting variable and cut-point, and in each node splitting continues recursively until some stop condition is reached. Common stop criteria are: split until a given threshold for the minimum number of observations left in a node is reached or a given threshold for the minimum change in the impurity measure is not met anymore by any variable. Recent classification tree algorithms also provide statistical stopping criteria that incorporate the distribution of the splitting criterion (e.g., Hothorn et al., 2006), whereas early algorithms relied on pruning the complete tree to avoid overfitting.

The term *overfitting* refers to the fact that a classifier that adapts too closely to the learning sample will not only discover the systematic components of the structure that is present in the population, but also the random variation from this structure that is present in the learning data due to random sampling. When such an overfitted model is later applied to a new test sample from the same population, its performance will be poor because it does not generalize well. However, it should be noted that overfitting is an equally relevant issue in parametric models. With every variable, and thus every parameter, that is added to the regression model, its fit to the learning data improves, because the model becomes more flexible.

This is evident, for example, in the R^2 statistic reflecting the portion of variance explained by the model, which increases with every parameter added to the model. For example, in the extreme case where as many parameters as observations are available, any parametric model will show a perfect fit on the learning data, yielding a value of $R^2 = 1$, but will perform poorly in future samples.

In parametric models, a common strategy to deal with this problem is to use significance tests for variable selection in regression models. However, one should be aware that in this case, significance tests do not work in the same way as in a designed study, where a limited number of hypotheses to be tested are specified in advance. In common forward and/or backward stepwise regression, it is not known beforehand how many significance tests will have to be conducted. Therefore, it is hard to control the overall significance level, which controls the probability of falsely declaring at least one of the coefficients as significant.

Alternative variable selection strategies that have been developed for parametric models employ model selection criteria such as the Akaike information criterion (AIC) and Bayesian information criterion (BIC), which include a penalization term for the number of parameters in the model. For a detailed discussion of approaches that account for the complexity of parametric models, see Burnham and Anderson (2002) or Burnham and Anderson (2004).

Because information criteria such as the AIC and BIC are, however, not applicable to nonparametric models (see, e.g., Claeskens & Hjort, 2008), in recursive partitioning the classic strategy to cope with overfitting is to "prune" the trees after growing them, which means that branches that do not add to the prediction accuracy in cross-validation are eliminated. Pruning is not discussed in detail here, because many modern classification and regression tree algorithms employ *p*-values both for variable selection and as a stopping criterion and, therefore, do not rely on pruning. Moreover, ensemble methods, which we will address in the later sections, usually employ unpruned trees.

PREDICTION AND INTERPRETATION

Once the tree building is completed, a response class is predicted in each terminal node of the tree (or each rectangular section in the partition, respectively) by means of deriving from all observations in this node either the average response value in regression or the most frequent response class in classification trees. Note that this means that a regression tree creates a piecewise (or rectangle-wise for two dimensions and cuboid-wise in higher dimensions) constant prediction function, as was illustrated in Figure 29.4. We will see later that ensemble methods, by combining the predictions of many single trees, can approximate functions more smoothly, too.

The predicted response classes in our example are the majority class in each node in Figure 29.2, as also indicated by the shading in Figure 29.3: Subjects who have no friends that smoke as well as those who have one or more friends that smoke but drank alcohol in one or less occasions are not very likely to intend to smoke, whereas those who have one or more friends that smoke and drank alcohol on two or more occasions are likely to intend to smoke within the next year.

For classification problems, it is also possible to predict an estimate of the class probabilities from the relative frequencies of each class in the terminal nodes. In our example, the predicted probabilities for answering "yes" to the intention to smoke question would thus be approximately 17%, 34%, and 79% in the three groups, respectively, which may preserve more information than the majority vote that merely assigns the class with the highest relative frequency as the prediction.

Reporting the predicted class probabilities also more closely resembles the output of logistic regression models and can be employed, for example, in estimating treatment probabilities or propensity scores. Note, however, that no confidence intervals are available for the estimates, unless, for example, bootstrapping is used in combination with refitting to assess the variability of the prediction.

INTERPRETATION

The easy interpretability of the visual representation of classification and regression trees that we have illustrated above has added much to the popularity of this method. However, the downside of this apparently straightforward interpretability is that the visual representation may be misleading, because the actual statistical interpretation of a tree model is not trivial: First, no information of confidence is available for the tree structure (see also the section on Instability of Trees). Second, the interpretaion of the tree structure itself is often not clear.

Especially for readers who are familiar with parametric regression models, it is important to understand how main effects and interactions are represented in classification and regression trees. This understanding is crucial for seeing the benefits of this method as well as its most common ground for criticism.

In the literature on classification and regression trees, the notions of main effects and interactions are often confused or used incautiously, as seems to be the casein, for example, Berk (2006, p. 272), where it is stated that a branch that is not split any further indicate a main effect. However, when splitting continues in the other branch created by the same variable splitting continues, as is the case in the example of Berk (2006), this statement is not correct. Indeed there are different representations of interaction effects in classification and regression trees, which are outlined in the following.

The statistical term "interaction" describes the fact that the effect of one predictor variable, (in our example, `alcohol_per_month` on the response depends on the value of another predictor variables (in our example, `friends_smoke`). For classification trees, this means that, if in one branch created by `friends_smoke` it is not necessary to split in `alcohol_per_month`, whereas in the other branch created by `friends_smoke` it is necessary, as in Figure 29.2, an interaction between `friends_smoke` and `alcohol_per_month` is present.

We will further illustrate this important issue and source of misinterpretations by means of varying the effects in our artificial data set. The resulting classification trees are given in Figure 29.7. Only the left plot in Figure 29.7, where the effect of `alcohol_per_month` is the same in both branches created by `friends_smoke`, represents two main effects of `alcohol_per_month` and `friends_smoke` without an interaction: The main effect of `friends_smoke` shows in the higher relative frequencies of "yes" answers in nodes 6 and 7 as compared to nodes 3 and 4. The main effect of `alcohol_per_month` shows in the higher relative frequencies of "yes" answers in nodes 4 and 7 as compared to nodes 3 and 6, respectively.

As opposed to that, both the right plot in Figure 29.7 and the original plot in Figure 29.3 represent interactions, because the effect of `alcohol_per_month` is different in both

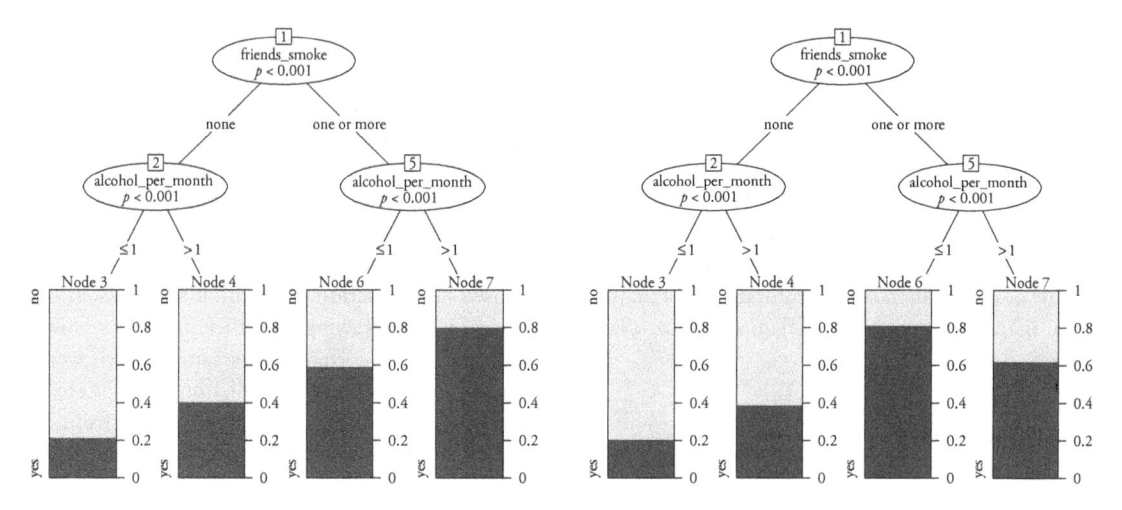

Figure 29.7 Classification trees based on variations of the smoking data with two main effects (left) and interactions (right). The tree depicted in Figure 29.2 based on the original data also represents an interaction.

branches created by friends_smoke. In the right plot in Figure 29.7 the same split in alcohol_per_month is conducted in every branch created by friends_smoke, but the effect on the relative frequencies of the response classes is different. For those subjects who have no friends who smoke, the relative frequency of a "yes" answer is higher if they drank alcohol on two or more occasions (node 4 as compared to node 3), whereas for those who have one or more friends who smoke, the frequency of a "yes" answer is lower if they drank alcohol on two or more occasions (node 7 as compared to node 6). This example represents a typical interaction effect as known from standard statistical models, where the effect of alcohol_per_month depends on the value of friends_smoke.

In the original plot in Figure 29.2 on the other hand, the effect of alcohol_per_month is also different in both branches created by friends_smoke, because alcohol_per_month has an effect only in the right branch, but not in the left branch.

Although this kind of "asymmetric" interaction is very common in classification trees, they are unlikely to discover a symmetric interaction pattern as that in Figure 29.7 (right) or even a main effect pattern as that in Figure 29.7 (left) in real data.

The reason for this is that even if the true distribution of the data in both branches was very similar, because of random variations in the sample and the deterministic variable and cut-point selection strategy of classification trees, it is extremely unlikely that the same splitting variable—and also the exact same cut-point—would be selected in both branches. However, even a slightly different cut-point in the same variable would, strictly speaking, represent an interaction. Thus, only if the two main effects and their respective cut-points are very clear—and no other competitor variable is strong enough to outperform the two original variables in either node—will the main effects pattern be identified by a tree.

Therefore it is stated in the literature that classification trees cannot (or, rather, are extremely unlikely to) represent additive functions that consist only of main effects, whereas they are perfectly well suited for representing complex interactions. As opposed to that, standard regression models are, by definition, perfectly well suited for representing strictly additive functions but may not be able to represent complex interaction patterns and nonlinear effects.

In this sense, each statistical model imposes different limitations on the range of functions that can be represented by it and may thus be more or less well suited to describe the (unknown) true structure of the data set at hand, which will hardly ever follow either a strict linear additive or a strict stepwise recursive pattern (but we will find later that the ensemble methods bagging and random forests can serve as a more flexible means for approximating different functional forms.)

Accordingly, what is easy for one class of statistical models may prove very hard for another class. Although it may seem surprising that classification trees cannot deal with such an easy problem as that of two main effects, one should note, for example, that logistic regression cannot deal with the (maybe even easier) problem of perfectly separable response classes (in which case, the coefficient estimates become infinite, so that there is no unique Maximum-Likelihood solution unless, e.g., a penalty term is employed).

For exploratory data analysis, further means for illustrating the effects of particular variables in classification trees are provided by the partial dependence plots described in Hastie, Tibshirani, and Friedman (2001b, 2009) and the CARTscans toolbox (Nason et al., 2004).

INSTABILITY OF TREES

Besides the notions of main effects and interactions, another caveat in the interpretation of classification and regression trees is their instability to small changes in the learning data. In recursive partitioning, the exact position of each cut-point in the partition, as well as the decision, which variable to split in, determines how the observations are split up in new nodes, in which splitting continues recursively. However, the exact position of the cut-point, as well as the selection of the splitting variable, strongly depend on the particular distribution of observations in the learning sample.

Thus, as an undesired side effect of the recursive partitioning approach, the entire tree structure could be altered if the first splitting variable, or only the first cut-point, was chosen differently because of a small change in the learning data. Because of this instability, the predictions of single trees show a high variability, as illustrated below. Moreover, the exact configuration of the tree—particularly the ordering of the variables – should not be overinterpreted, as illustrated by Malley, Malley, and Pajevic (2011).

The high variability of single trees can be illustrated, for example, by drawing bootstrap samples from the original data set and investigating whether the trees built on the different samples have a different structure. The rationale of bootstrap samples, where a sample of the same size as the original sample is drawn with replacement (so that some observations are left out, whereas others may appear more than once in the bootstrap sample), is to reflect the variability inherent in any sampling process. Random sampling preserves the systematic effects present in the original sample or population, but in addition to this it induces random variability. Thus, if classification trees built on different bootstrap samples vary too strongly in their structure, then this proves that their interpretability can be severely affected by the random variability present in any data set.

Classification trees built on four bootstrap samples drawn from our original smoking data are displayed in Figure 29.8. Apparently, the effect of the variable friends_smoke is strong enough to remain present in all four trees, whereas the further splits vary strongly with the sample.

As a solution to the problem of instability, the average over a set of trees, rather than a single tree, is used for prediction in ensemble methods, as outlined in the following. Another problem of single trees, which is solved by the same model averaging approach, is that the prediction of single trees is piecewise constant and thus may "jump" from one value to the next even for small changes of the predictor values, as illustrated in Figure 29.4. As described in the next section, ensemble methods have the additional advantage that their decision boundaries are more smooth than those of single trees.

Ensemble Methods

The rationale behind ensemble methods is to base the prediction on a whole set of classification or regression trees, rather than a single tree. The related methods bagging and random forests vary only in the way this diverse set of trees is constructed. In both bagging and random forests, a set of trees is built on random samples drawn from the learning sample. The only difference between bagging, and random forests is that in bagging variable selection follows the same principle as in single classification trees, whereas in random forests, variable selection is also randomized by means of random sampling from the set of all predictor variables to make the resulting set of trees even more diverse.

Thus, the first section of this part explains the bagging procedure, which is based solely on random sampling from the learning data, whereas the second section explains in more detail the random sampling from the predictor variables that distinguishes random forests from bagging.

BAGGING

In each step of the algorithms for bagging and random forests, either a bootstrap sample (of the same size, drawn with replacement) or a subsample (of smaller size, drawn without replacement) of the learning sample is drawn randomly, and an individual tree is grown on each sample.

As we have seen above, each random sample reflects the same data-generating process but differs slightly from the original learning sample because of random variation. Keeping in mind that each individual classification tree depends highly on the

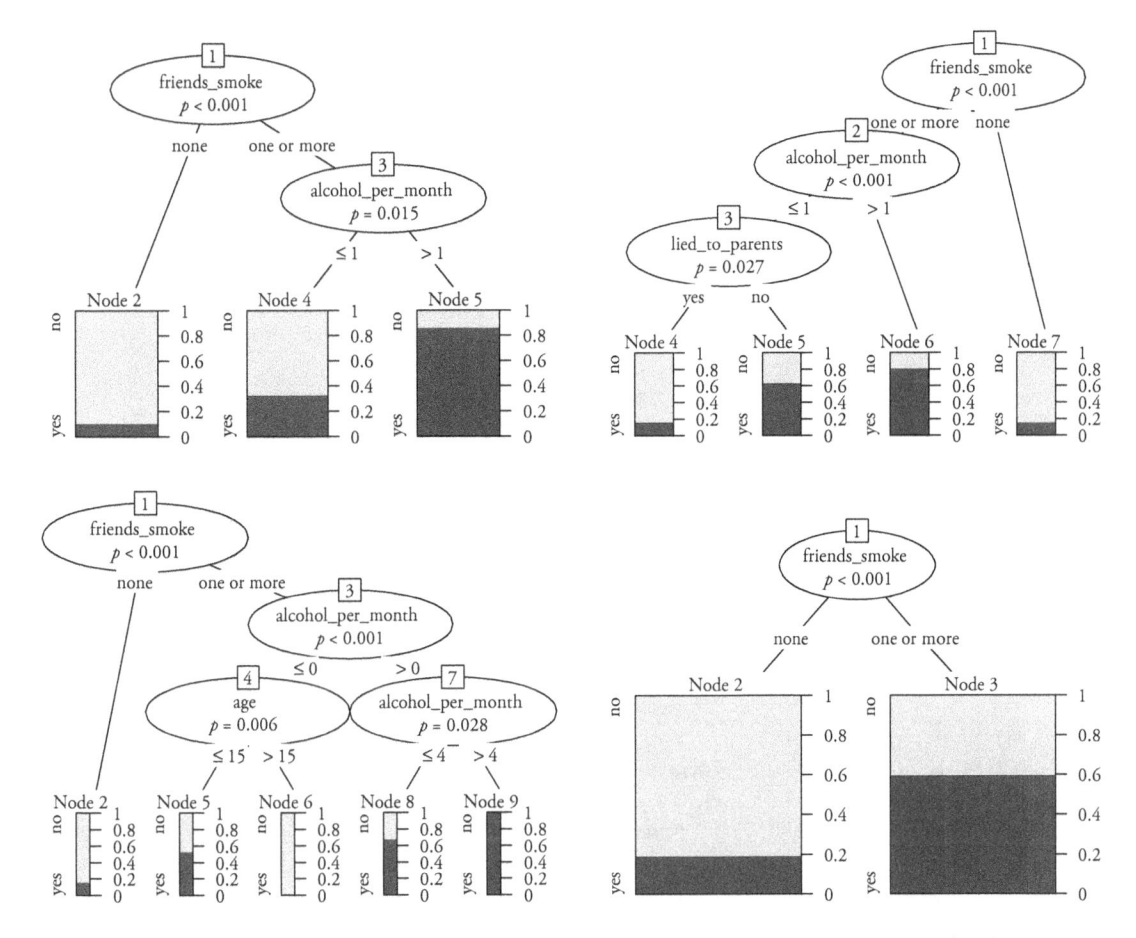

Figure 29.8 Classification trees based on four bootstrap samples of the smoking data, illustrating the instability of single trees.

learning sample as outlined above, the resulting trees can differ substantially.

Another feature of the ensemble methods bagging and random forests is that usually trees are grown very large, without any stopping or pruning involved (although recent research indicates that in some situations, shorter trees are more appropriate; Lin & Jeon, 2006). As illustrated again for four bootstrap samples from the smoking data in Figure 29.9, large trees can become even more diverse and include a large variety of combinations of predictor variables.

By combining the prediction of such a diverse set of trees, ensemble methods utilize the fact that classification trees are instable but on average produce the right prediction (i.e. trees are unbiased predictors), which has been supported by several empirical as well as simulation studies (cf., e.g., Bauer & Kohavi, 1999; Breiman, 1996a, 1998; Dietterich, 2000) and especially the theoretical results of Bühlmann and Yu (2002), which show the superiority in prediction accuracy of bagging over single classification or regression trees. Bühlmann and Yu (2002) were able to show by means of asymptotic methods that the improvement in the prediction is achieved by means of smoothing the hard cut decision boundaries created by splitting in single classification trees, which in return reduces the variance of the prediction (see also Biau et al., 2008). The smoothing of hard decision boundaries also makes ensembles more flexible than single trees in approximating functional forms that are smooth rather than piecewise constant.

RANDOM FORESTS

In random forests, an extra source of diversity is introduced when the set of predictor variables to select from is randomly restricted in each split, producing even more diverse trees. The number of randomly preselected splitting variables, termed `mtry` in most algorithms, as well as the overall number of trees, usually termed `ntree`, are parameters of random forests that affect the stability of the results (see Stretal et al., 2009, for details). Obviously random forests include bagging as the special

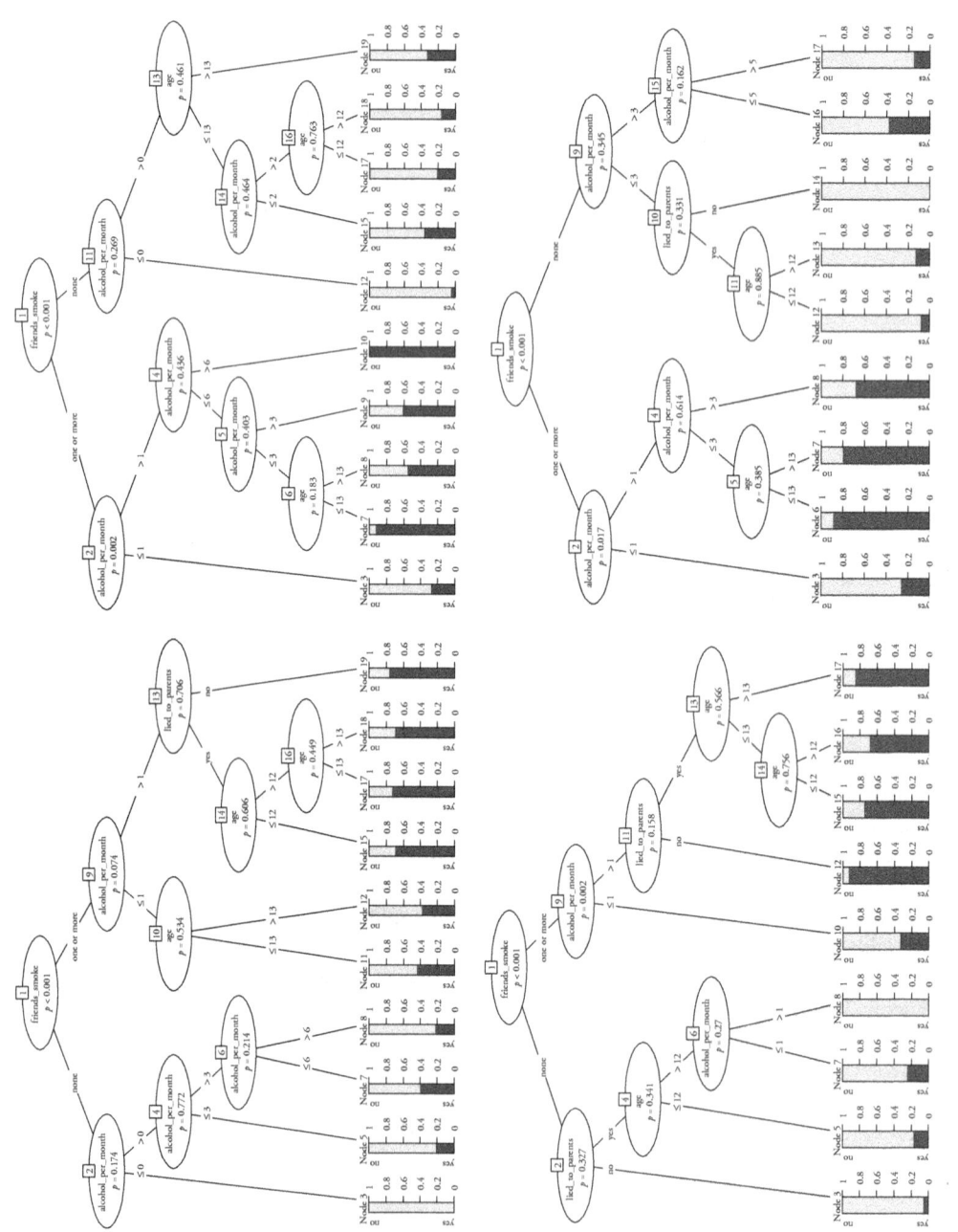

Figure 29.9 Classification trees (grown without stopping or pruning) based on four bootstrap samples of the smoking data, illustrating the principle of bagging.

case where the number of randomly preselected splitting variables is equal to the overall number of variables.

Intuitively speaking, random forests can improve the predictive performance even further as compared to bagging, because the single trees involved in averaging are even more diverse. From a statistical point of view, this can be explained by the theoretical results presented by Breiman (2001a) that the upper bound for the generalization error of an ensemble depends on the correlation between the individual trees, such that a low correlation between the individual trees results in a low upper bound for the error.

In addition to the smoothing of hard decision boundaries, the random selection of splitting variables in random forests allows predictor variables, which were otherwise outplayed by a stronger competitor, to enter the ensemble. If the stronger competitor cannot be selected then a new variable has a chance to be included in the model and may reveal interaction effects with other variables that otherwise would have been missed.

The effect of randomly restricting the splitting variables is again illustrated by means of four bootstrap samples drawn from the smoking data. In addition to growing a large tree on each bootstrap sample, as in bagging, now the variable selection is limited to `mtry=2` randomly preselected candidates in each split. Figure 29.10 displays the resulting trees. We find that because of the random restriction, the trees have become even more diverse; for example, the strong predictor variable `friends_smoke` is no longer chosen for the first split in every single tree.

The reason why even suboptimal splits in weaker predictor variables can often improve the prediction accuracy of an ensemble is that the split selection process in regular classification trees is only locally optimal in each node. A variable and cut-point are chosen with respect to the impurity reduction they can achieve in a given node defined by all previous splits, but regardless of all splits yet to come.

Thus, variable selection in a single tree is affected by order effects similar to those present in stepwise variable selection approaches for parametric regression (that is also instable against random variation of the learning data, as pointed out by Austin & Tu, 2004). In both recursive partitioning and stepwise regression, the approach of adding one locally optimal variable at a time does not necessarily (or rather hardly ever) lead to the globally best model over all possible combinations of variables.

Because, however, searching for a single globally best tree is computationally infeasible (a first approach involving dynamic programming was introduced by van Os & Meulman, 2005), the random restriction of the splitting variables provides an easy and efficient way to generate locally suboptimal splits that can improve the global performance of an ensemble of trees.

Besides intuitive explanations for "how ensemble methods work," recent publications have contributed to a deeper understanding of the statistical background behind many machine learning methods. The work of Bühlmann and Yu (2002) provided the statistical framework for bagging, Friedman, Hastie, and Tibshirani (2000) and Bühlmann and Yu (2003) for the related method of boosting, and, most recently, Lin & Jeon (2006) and Biau et al. (2008) for random forests. In their work, Lin & Jeon (2006) have explored the statistical properties of random forests by means of placing them in a k-nearest neighbor (k-NN) framework, where random forests can be viewed as adaptively weighted k-NN with the terminal node size determining the size of neighborhood. However, to be able to mathematically grasp a computationally complex method like random forests that involves several steps of random sampling, simplifying assumptions are often necessary. Therefore well-planned simulation studies still offer valuable assistance for evaluating statistical aspects of the method in its original form.

Variable selection bias, which was pointed out as a problem of classification and regression trees above, is also carried forward to ensembles of trees. Especially the variable importance can be biased when a data set contains predictor variables of different types (Strobl et al., 2007). The bias is particularly pronounced for the Gini importance, which is based on the biased Gini gain split selection criterion (Strobl et al., 2007) but can also affect the permutation importance. Only when subsamples drawn without replacement, rather than bootstrap samples, in combination with unbiased split selection criteria, are used in constructing the forest, can the resulting permutation importance be interpreted reliably (see also section on Other Data Mining Techniques, Literature, and Software).

PREDICTIONS FROM ENSEMBLES

In an ensemble of trees, the predictions of all individual trees need to be combined. This is usually accomplished by means of (weighted or unweighted) averaging in regression or voting in classification.

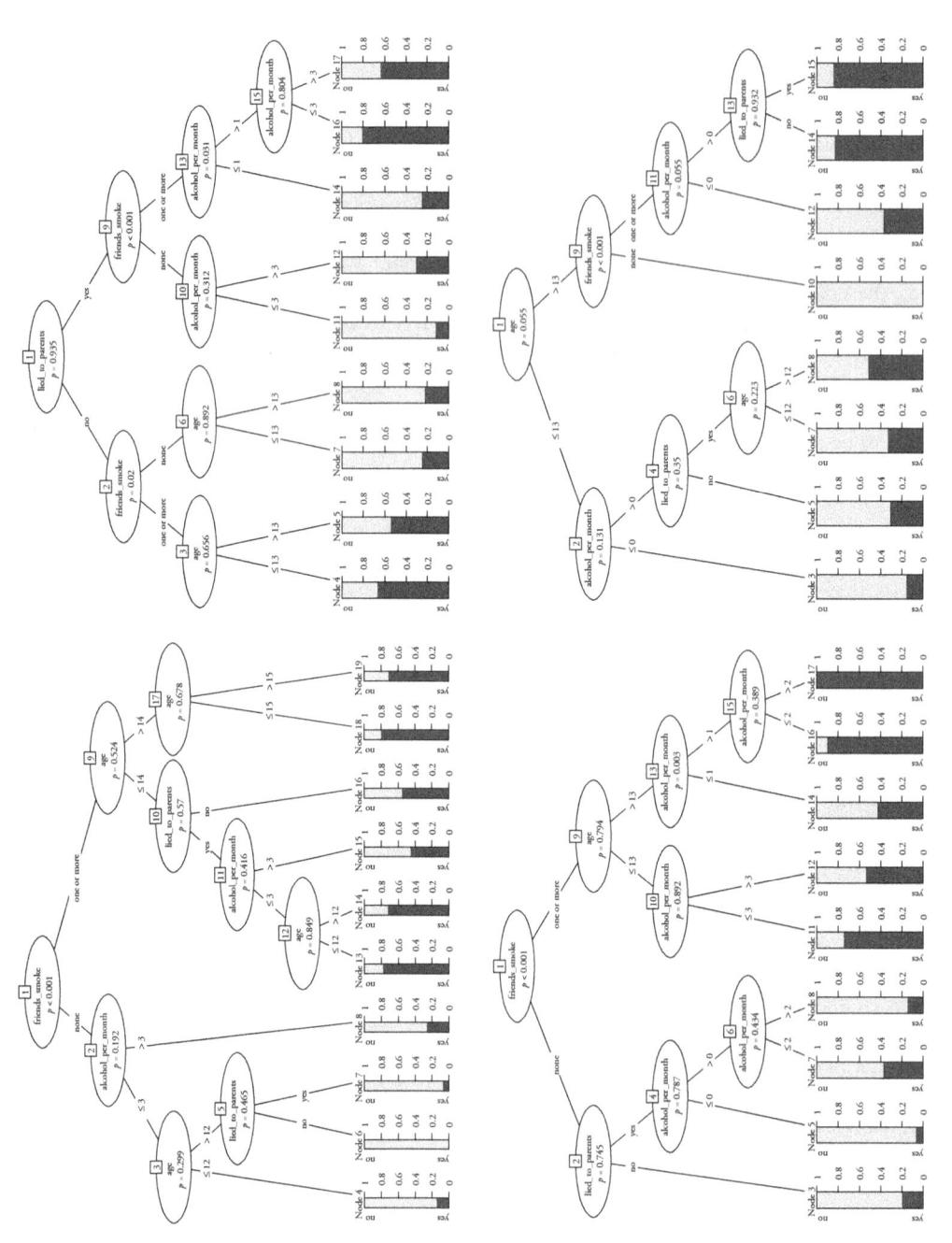

Figure 29.10 Classification trees (grown without stopping or pruning and with a random preselection of two variables in each split) based on four bootstrap samples of the smoking data, illustrating the principle of random forests

The term "voting" can be taken literally here. Each subject with given values of the predictor variables is "dropped through" every tree in the ensemble, so that each single tree returns a predicted class for the subject. The class for which most trees "vote" is returned as the prediction of the ensemble. This democratic voting process is the reason ensemble methods are also called "committee" methods. Note, however, that there is no diagnostic for the unanimity of the vote. For regression and for predicting probabilities—that is, relative class frequencies—the results of the single trees are averaged; some algorithms also employ weighted averages. A summary over several aggregation schemes is given in Gatnar (2007). However, even with the simple aggregation schemes used in the standard algorithms, ensemble methods reliably outperform single trees and many other advanced methods. In some comparison studies, random forests clearly outperform their competitors (cf., e.g., Wu et al., 2003), whereas in others they are slightly outperformed (cf., e.g., König et al., 2008, for a comparison of several statistical learning methods in a medical example of moderate size, where logistic regression was also applicable).

Aside from the issue of aggregation, for bagging and random forests, there are two different prediction modes: ordinary prediction and the so called out-of-bag prediction. Although in ordinary prediction, each observation of the original data set—or a new test data set—is predicted by the entire ensemble, out-of-bag prediction follows a different rationale. Remember that each tree is built on a bootstrap sample, which serves as a learning sample for this particular tree. However, some observations—namely, the out-of-bag observations—were not included in the learning sample for this tree. Therefore, they can serve as a "built-in" test sample for computing the prediction accuracy of that tree.

The advantage of the out-of-bag error is that it is a more realistic estimate of the error rate that is to be expected in a new test sample, than the naive and over-optimistic estimate of the error rate resulting from the prediction of the entire learning sample (Breiman, 1996b; see also Boulesteix et al., 2007, for a review on resampling-based error estimation). For example, the standard and out-of-bag prediction accuracy for bagging in our smoking data example is 78% and 76.5%, respectively, where the out-of-bag prediction accuracy is a little more conservative.

However, in this very simple artificial example, random forests and even a single tree would perform equally well as bagging, because the interaction of `friends_smoke` and `alcohol_per_month`, which was already correctly identified by the single tree, is the only effect that was induced in the data, whereas in most real data applications—especially in cases where many predictor variables work in complex interactions—the prediction accuracy of random forests is found to be higher than for bagging, and both ensemble methods usually highly outperform single trees.

VARIABLE IMPORTANCE

As described in the previous sections, single classification trees are easily interpretable, both intuitively at first glance and descriptively when looking in detail at the tree structure. In particular, variables that are not included in the tree did not contribute to the model—at least not in the context of the previously chosen splitting variables.

As opposed to that, ensembles of trees are not easy to interpret at all, because the individual trees in them are not nested in any way. Each variable may appear at different positions, if at all, in different trees, as depicted in Figures 29.9 and 29.10, so that there is no such thing as an "average tree" with a simple structure, that could be visualized for interpretation.

In this sense, an ensemble of trees is a "black box": The underlying functional form is so complex that it cannot be written down as a simple formula, and we cannot grasp it at one glance.

On the other hand, an ensemble of trees has the advantage that it gives each variable the chance to appear in different contexts with different covariates, and can thus better reflect its potentially complex effect on the response. Moreover, order effects induced by the recursive variable selection scheme employed in constructing the single trees are eliminated by averaging over the entire ensemble. Therefore, in bagging and random forests, variable importance measures are computed to assess the relevance of each variable over all trees of the ensemble.

Variable importance measures can incorporate a (weighted) mean of the individual trees' improvement in the splitting criterion produced by each variable (Friedman, 2001). An example for such a measure in classification is the "Gini importance" available in many random forest implementations. It describes the average improvement in the "Gini gain" splitting criterion (from the impurity reduction framework outlined in the section on Split Selection Criteria) that a variable has achieved in all of its positions in the forest. However, in many applications involving predictor variables of different types, this measure is biased in favor of variables offering many cutpoints, as outlined in the section on Cut-Point Selection and Variable Selection Bias.

The most advanced variable importance measure available in random forests is the permutation importance. Its rationale is that by randomly permuting the values of a predictor variable, its original association with the response is broken. For example, in the original smoking data, those adolescents who drank alcohol on more occasions are more likely to intend to smoke. Randomly permuting the values of alcohol_per_month over all subjects, however, destroys this association. Accordingly, when the permuted variable, together with the remaining unpermuted predictor variables, is now used to predict the response, the prediction accuracy decreases substantially.

Thus, a reasonable measure for variable importance is the difference in prediction accuracy (i.e., the number of observations classified correctly; usually the out-of-bag prediction accuracy is used) before and after permuting a variable, averaged over all trees.

If, on the other hand, the original variable was not associated with the response, it is either not included in the tree (and its importance for this tree is zero by definition), or it is included in the tree by chance. In the latter case, permuting the variable results only in a small random decrease in prediction accuracy, or the permutation of an irrelevant variable can even lead to a small increase in the prediction accuracy (if, by chance, the permutated variable happens to be slightly better suited than the original one). Thus the permutation importance can even show (small) negative values for irrelevant predictor variables, as illustrated for the irrelevant predictor variable age in Figure 29.11 (right).

Note that in our simple example the two relevant predictor variables friends_smoke and alcohol_per_month are correctly identified by the permutation variable importance of both bagging and random forests, although the positions of the variables vary more strongly in random forests (cf. again Figures 29.9 and 29.10). In real data applications, however, the random forest variable importance may reveal higher importance scores for variables working in complex interactions, which may have gone unnoticed in single trees and bagging (as well as in parametric regression models, where modeling high-order interactions is usually not possible at all).

Another important thing to note in the permutation importance scores for bagging and random forests displayed in Figure 29.11 is that although the two relevant predictor variables are correctly identified in both cases, the absolute values of the importance scores are not identical; they depend on characteristics of the data set and the values of tuning parameters. Thus, the absolute values of the importance scores should not be interpreted or compared over different studies, and only a ranking of the most important variables should be reported.

As already mentioned, the main advantage of the random forest permutation accuracy importance, as compared to univariate screening methods, is that it covers the impact of each predictor variable individually as well as in multivariate interactions with other predictor variables. For example, Lunetta et al. (2004) have found that genetic markers relevant in interactions with other markers or environmental variables can be detected more efficiently by means of random forests than by means of univariate screening methods like Fisher's exact test.

In addition to the descriptive use of the variable importance measures suggested here, a variety of statistical significance tests for random forest variable importance measures have been suggested. However, many of the approaches suggested so far produce misleading results, as summarized in Strobl, Malley, and Tutz (2009).

RANDOMNESS

One special characteristic of random forests and bagging, of which new users are often not entirely aware, is that they are truly "random" models in the sense that for the same data set, the results may differ between two computation runs.

The two sources of randomness that are responsible for these possible differences are (1) the bootstrap samples (or subsamples) that are randomly drawn in bagging and random forests and (2) the random preselection of predictor variables in random forests. When the permutation importance is computed, another source of variability is the random permutation of the predictor vectors.

Because of these random processes, a random forest is only exactly reproducible when the random seed, a number that can be set by the user and determines the internal random number generation of the computer, is fixed. Otherwise, the results may vary between two runs of the same model.

However, the differences between two runs will be negligible as long as the tuning parameters have been chosen such as to guarantee stable results.

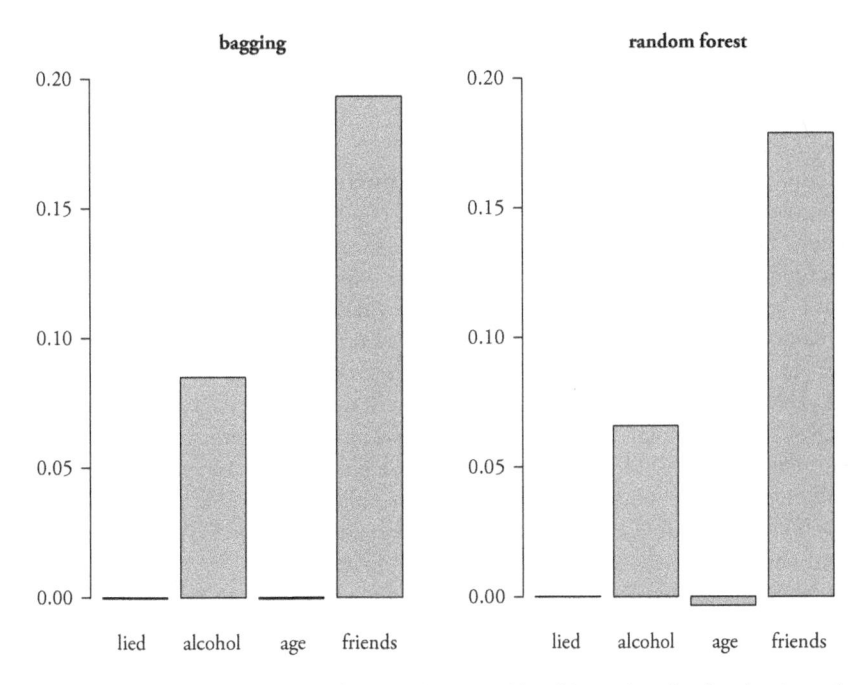

Figure 29.11 Permutation variable importance scores for the predictor variables of the smoking data from bagging and random forests.

Most importantly, the number of trees `ntree` should be much larger than the number of variables to produce stable results. The effect of the other tuning parameters (the depth of the trees and the number of preselected predictor variables `mtry`) is still under research (cf. Strobl et al., 2009, for an overview). Still, as compared to many other data mining methods, the empirical comparisons conducted, for example, by Caruana and Niculescu-Mizil (2006) and Svetnik et al. (2004) have indicated that random forests are among the best performing methods even without extra tuning. Therefore, random forests can be considered as a valuable "off- the shelf" tool for exploring complex data sets.

Other Data Mining Techniques, Literature, and Software

In this chapter, recursive partitioning methods were highlighted as one very popular example of data mining techniques. However, there are many other techniques commonly associated with data mining, including neural networks (see, e.g., Kriesel, 2007, for a comprehensible introduction including the original references), support vector machines (Vapnik, 1998), and boosting (Freund & Schapire, 1997; Friedman et al., 2000). These supervised learning techniques function in different ways but share the general characteristics discussed in the starting section of this chapter. Their aim is to predict the value of a response variable by means of a potentially very complex combination of the predictor variables, but their exact statistical and computational approaches vary. Moreover, unsupervised learning techniques, such as clustering and dimensionality reduction, where the aim is to condense information from different variables rather than to predict the value of a specific response variable, are often also referred to as data mining.

If you want to read more about data mining techniques, look for textbooks that have *data mining, pattern recognition, machine learning,* or *statistical learning* in their title. The literature on these techniques is somewhat divided between the statistical and computer science communities. Depending on your own background and statistical training, you may find textbooks and articles coming from statistics more intuitive. On recursive partitioning methods, the original works of Breiman (1996a,b, 1998, 2001a,b), to name a few, are also well suited and not too technical for further reading. Textbooks that include a broader range of topics and are suited for readers with some statistical background include Hastie, Tibshirani, and Friedman (2009) and Ripley (1996). The textbook of Malley, Malley, Pajevic (2011) and is focused on verbal explanations and can offer a good starting point for understanding the main ideas of several key data mining techniques. Other textbooks, such as Vapnik (1995), are better suited for readers with a stronger mathematical background. However, because data mining is a fast evolving field, you will hardly find a textbook that contains all approaches ever referred to as data mining techniques.

For practical applications of data mining techniques, many tools for data analysis are freely available in the R system for statistical computing (R Development Core Team, 2011) and the WEKA data mining software (Hall et al., 2009). For R, a list of available data mining techniques is listed under http://cran.r-project.org/web/views/MachineLearning.html. For WEKA, a list of respective functions is available at http://wiki.pentaho.com/display/DATAMINING/Classifiers.

Although some of the most popular data mining techniques are also available in commercial software packages like SPSS, the open source software packages are usually more up-to-date and contain a larger variety of techniques. Besides the software documentations, an increasing number of textbooks is also available that introduces a selection of techniques together with their software applications, such as Everitt and Hothorn (2006), Torgo (2010), and Witten, Frank, and Hall (2011).

Because we also discussed the issue of variable selection bias, note that both the original CART and C4.5 algorithms as well as many more recent implementations that rely on the same split selection principles are affected—for example, the functions tree (Ripley, 2007) and rpart (Therneau & Atkinson, 2006) for trees and randomForest (Breiman et al., 2006; Liaw & Wiener, 2002) for bagging and random forests in R, as well as the respective functions J48 (a cousin of Quinlan's C4.5 algorithm) and RandomForest from package weka.classifiers.trees in WEKA. These algorithms are not suggested when your data set contains predictor variables of different types (such as factors with different numbers of categories or factors and numeric variables).

Unbiased recursive partitioning algorithms that can be safely used for comparing even predictor variables of different types are the functions ctree for classification and regression trees and cforest for bagging and random forests (both freely available in the add-on package party; Hothorn et al., 2006, 2011) in R as well as the CHAID algorithm (Kass, 1980) availabe in SPSS.

Conclusion

We have seen that data mining techniques can be used for the same kind of regression problems for which classical statistical models can be used. Yet, data mining methods approach the problems in a rather different way than parametric models: They are more flexible because the functional form need not be specified in advance, but they may also produce too rough of an approximation or a rule too complex to interpret. In this sense, they are "black boxes" that are much less interpretable than the simple models we are used to from classical statistics.

Accordingly, one way of utilizing data mining techniques is as a "black box" for prediction only. But, together with visualization techniques and variable importance measures, they can also become a means of generating hypotheses—especially in complex settings such as genetics, where little prior knowledge is available, but large data bases can be searched in an exploratory manner.

This has led to a wide-spread of data mining techniques (including the recursive partitioning methods highlighted here) in genetics and related disciplines for the analysis of microarray data, DNA sequencing, and many other large-scale applications (cf.,e.g., Gunther et al., 2003; Lunetta et al., 2004; Segal et al., 2004; Bureau et al., 2005; Huang et al., 2005; Shih, 2005; Diaz-Uriarte & de Andrés, 2006; Qi et al., 2006; Ward et al., 2006), but first applications in the social sciences (e.g., Rossi et al., 2005; Baca-Garcia et al., 2007; Marinic et al., 2007) show that random forests can be of use in a wide variety of applications in this field as well.

The decision whether to apply a classical or data mining approach depends most of all on the question how much previous knowledge you have on the subject matter—particularly the questions of which variables should be included and which functional form will best describe the true association between predictor variables and response, but also on the credibility of distribution assumptions, which are necessary for most classical but not for data mining approaches. In any case, the rich variety of methods summarized under the term *data mining* deserves to be considered as one of many possible ways to learn about our complex world. And as long as we stick to the high scientific principles we have—especially in the social sciences—we can only profit from that.

Acknowledgment

Portions of this chapter are adapted from C. Strobl, J. Malley und G. Tutz (2009): An Introduction to Recursive Partitioning: Rationale, Application and Characteristics of Classification and Regression Trees, Bagging and Random Forests. *Psychological Methods* 14(4), 323–348.

Author Note

Carolin Strobl, Chair for Psychological Methods, Evaluation and Statistics, University of Zurich, Department of Psychology, Binzmuehlestrasse 14, 8050 Zurich, Switzerland.

References

Austin, P. & Tu, J. (2004). Automated variable selection methods for logistic regression produced unstable models for predicting acute myocardial infarction mortality. *Journal of Clinical Epidemiology* 57(11), 1138–1146.

Baca-Garcia, E., Perez-Rodriguez, M. M., Saiz-Gonzalez, D., Basurte-Villamor, I., Saiz-Ruiz, J., Leiva-Murillo, J. M. de Prado-Cumplido, M. et al. (2007). Variables associated with familial suicide attempts in a sample of suicide attempters. *Progress in Neuro-Psychopharmacology & Biological Psychiatry* 31, 1312–1316.

Bauer, E. & Kohavi, R. (1999). An empirical comparison of voting classification algorithms: Bagging, boosting, and variants. *Machine Learning* 36(1-2), 105–139.

Berk, R. A. (2006). An introduction to ensemble methods for data analysis. *Sociological Methods & Research* 34(3), 263–295.

Biau, G., Devroye, L., & Lugosi, G. (2008). Consistency of random forests and other averaging classifiers. *Journal of Machine Learning Research* 9, 2015–2033.

Boulesteix, A.-L., Strobl, C., Augustin, T., & Daumer, M. (2008). Evaluating microarray-based classifiers: An overview. *Cancer Informatics* 6, 77–97.

Breiman, L. (1996a). Bagging predictors. *Machine Learning* 24(2), 123–140.

Breiman, L. (1996b). Out-of-bag estimation. *Unpublished Technical Report, Statistics Department, University of California at Berkeley, CA, USA*.

Breiman, L. (1998). Arcing classifiers. *The Annals of Statistics* 26(3), 801–849.

Breiman, L. (2001a). Random forests. *Machine Learning* 45(1), 5–32.

Breiman, L. (2001b). Statistical modeling: The two cultures. *Statistical Science* 16(3), 199–231.

Breiman, L., Cutler, A., Liaw, A., & Wiener, M. (2006). *Breiman and Cutler's Random Forests for Classification and Regression*. R package version 4.5-16.

Breiman, L., Friedman, J. H., Olshen, R. A., & Stone, C. J. (1984). *Classification and Regression Trees*. New York: Chapman and Hall.

Bühlmann, P. & Yu, B. (2002). Analyzing bagging. *The Annals of Statistics* 30, 927–961.

Bühlmann, P. & Yu, B. (2003). Boosting with the L2 loss: Regression and classification. *Journal of the American Statistical Association* 98, 324–339.

Bureau, A., Dupuis, J., Falls, K., Lunetta, K. L., Hayward, B., Keith, T. P., & Eerdewegh, P. V. (2005). Identifying SNPs predictive of phenotype using random forests. *Genetic Epidemiology* 28(2), 171–182.

Burnham, K. & Anderson, D. (2002). *Model Selection and Multimodel Inference*. New York: Springer.

Burnham, K. & Anderson, D. (2004). Multimodel inference. *Sociological Methods & Research* 33(2), 261–304.

Caruana, R. & Niculescu-Mizil, A. (2006). An empirical comparison of supervised learning algorithms. In W. Cohen and A. Moore (Eds.), *Proceedings of the 23rd International Conference on Machine Learning (ICML 2006)*, (pp. 161–168). New York, ACM Press.

Claeskens, G. & Hjort, N. (2008). *Model Selection and Model Averaging*. Cambridge: Cambridge University Press.

Diaz-Uriarte, R. & de Andrés, S. A. (2006). Gene selection and classification of microarray data using random forest. *BMC Bioinformatics* 7, 3.

Dietterich, T. G. (2000). An experimental comparison of three methods for constructing ensembles of decision trees: Bagging, boosting, and randomization. *Machine Learning* 40(2), 139–157.

Dobra, A. & Gehrke, J. (2001). Bias correction in classification tree construction. In Brodley, C. E. and Danyluk, A. P. (Eds.), *Proceedings of the Eighteenth International Conference on Machine Learning (ICML 2001), Williams College, Williamstown, MA, USA*, (pp. 90–97). Morgan Kaufmann.

Everitt, B. & Hothorn, T. (2006). *A Handbook of Statistical Analyses Using R*. Boca Raton, FL: Chapman & Hall/CRC.

Freund, Y. & Schapire, R. E. (1997). A decision-theoretic generalization of on-line learning and an application to boosting. *Journal of Computer and System Sciences* 55, 119–139.

Friedman, J. (2001). Greedy function approximation: A gradient boosting machine. *The Annals of Statistics* 29(5), 1189–1232.

Friedman, J., Hastie, T., & Tibshirani, R. (2000). Additive logistic regression: a statistical view of boosting. *The Annals of Statistics* 28(2), 337–407.

Gatnar, E. (2007). Fusion of multiple statistical classifiers. In H. H. Bock, W. Gaul, and M. Vichi, (Eds.), *Proceedings of the 31st Annual Conference of the German Classification Society (GfKl), Freiburg i. Br., Germany*. (pp. 19–27).

Gunther, E. C., Stone, D. J., Gerwien, R. W., Bento, P., & Heyes, M. P. (2003). Prediction of clinical drug efficacy by classification of drug-induced genomic expression profiles *in vitro*. *Proceedings of the National Academy of Sciences* 100(16), 9608–9613.

Hall, M., Frank, E., Holmes, G., Pfahringer, B., Reutemann, P., & Witten, I. (2009). The WEKA Data Mining Software: An Update.

Hastie, T., Tibshirani, R., & Friedman, J. H. (2001a). *The elements of statistical learning*. New York: Springer-Verlag.

Hastie, T., Tibshirani, R., & Friedman, J. H. (2001b). *The Elements of Statistical Learning*. New York: Springer.

Hastie, T., Tibshirani, R., & Friedman, J. H. (2009). *The Elements of Statistical Learning, 2nd Edition*. New York: Springer.

Hothorn, T., Hornik, K., Strobl, C., & Zeileis, A. (2011). party: A laboratory for recursive part(y)itioning. R package version 0.9-995.

Hothorn, T., Hornik, K., & Zeileis, A. (2006). Unbiased recursive partitioning: A conditional inference framework.

Journal of Computational and Graphical Statistics 15(3), 651–674.

Huang, X., Pan, W., Grindle, S., Han, X., Chen, Y., Park, S. J., Miller, L. W., & Hall, J. (2005). A comparative study of discriminating human heart failure etiology using gene expression profiles. *BMC Bioinformatics 6*, 205.

Kass, G. (1980). An exploratory technique for investigating large quantities of categorical data. *Applied Statistics 29*(2), 119–127.

Kim, H. & Loh, W. (2001). Classification trees with unbiased multiway splits. *Journal of the American Statistical Association 96*, 589–604.

Kitsantas, P., Moore, T., & Sly, D. (2007). Using classification trees to profile adolescent smoking behaviors. *Addictive Behaviors 32*(1), 9–23.

König, I., Malley, J. D., Pajevic, S., Weimar, C., Diener, H.-C. & Ziegler, A. (2008). Patient-centered yes/no prognosis using learning machines. *International Journal of Data Minig and Bioinformatics*, 2(4), 289–391.

Kriesel, D. (2007). *A Brief Introduction to Neural Networks*. Manuscript available at www.dkriesel.com

Lausen, B., Hothorn, T., Bretz, F., & Schumacher, M. (2004). Assessment of optimal selected prognostic factors. *Biometrical Journal 46*(3), 364–374.

Liaw, A. & Wiener, M. (2002). Classification and regression by randomForest. *R News 2*(3), 18–22.

Lin, Y. & Jeon, Y. (2006). Random forests and adaptive nearest neighbors. *Journal of the American Statistical Association 101*(474), 578–590.

Loh, W. & Shih, Y. (1997). Split selection methods for classification trees. *Statistica Sinica 7*, 815–840.

Lunetta, K. L., Hayward, L. B., Segal, J., & Eerdewegh, P. V. (2004). Screening large-scale association study data: Exploiting interactions using random forests. *BMC Genetics 5*, 32.

Malley, J., Malley, K., & Pajevic, S. (2011). *Statistical Learning for Biomedical Data*. Cambridge: Cambridge University Press.

Marinic, I., Supek, F., Kovacic, Z., Rukavina, L., Jendricko, T., & D. Kozaric-Kovacic (2007). Posttraumatic stress disorder: Diagnostic data analysis by data mining methodology. *Croatian Medical Journal 48*(2), 185–197.

Morgan, J. N. & Sonquist, J. A. (1963). Problems in the analysis of survey data, and a proposal. *Journal of the American Statistical Association 58*(302), 415–434.

Nason, M., Emerson, S., & Leblanc, M. (2004). CARTscans: A tool for visualizing complex models. *Journal of Computational and Graphical Statistics 13*(4), 1–19.

van Os, B. J., and Meulman, J. (2005). Globally optimal tree models. In Azen, S., Kontoghiorghes, E., and Lee, J. C. (Eds.), *Abstract Book of the 3rd World Conference on Computational Statistics & Data Analysis of the International Association for Statistical Computing*, p. 79). Cyprus, Greece: Matrix Computations and Statistics Group.

Qi, Y., Bar-Joseph, Z., & Klein-Seetharaman, J. (2006). Evaluation of different biological data and computational classification methods for use in protein interaction prediction. *Proteins 63*(3), 490–500.

Quinlan, J. R. (1986). Induction of decision trees. *Machine Learning 1*(1), 81–106.

Quinlan, J. R. (1993). *C4.5: Programs for Machine Learning*. San Francisco, CA: Morgan Kaufmann Publishers.

R Development Core Team (2011). R: *A Language and Environment for Statistical Computing*. Vienna, Austria: R Foundation for Statistical Computing. ISBN 3-900051-07-0.

Ripley, B. (2007). tree: *Classification and Regression Trees*. R package version 1.0-26.

Ripley, B. D. (1996). *Pattern Recognition and Neural Networks*. Cambridge, UK: Cambridge University Press.

Rossi, A., Amaddeo, F., Sandri, M., & Tansella, M. (2005). Determinants of once-only contact in a community-based psychiatric service. *Social Psychiatry and Psychiatric Epidemiology 40*(1), 50–56.

Schnell, R., Hill, P., & Esser, E. (1999). *Methoden der empirischen Sozialforschung*. München: Oldenbourg.

Segal, M. R., Barbour, J. D., & Grant, R. M. (2004). Relating HIV-1 sequence variation to replication capacity via trees and forests. *Statistical Applications in Genetics and Molecular Biology 3*(1), 2.

Shih, Y.-S. (2005). Tumor classification by tissue microarray profiling: Random forest clustering applied to renal cell carcinoma. *Modern Pathology 18*, 547–557.

Strobl, C., Boulesteix, A.-L., & Augustin, T. (2007). Unbiased split selection for classification trees based on the Gini Index. *Computational Statistics & Data Analysis 52*(1), 483–501.

Strobl, C., Boulesteix, A.-L., Zeileis, A., & Hothorn, T. (2007). Bias in random forest variable importance measures: Illustrations, sources and a solution. *BMC Bioinformatics 8*, 25.

Strobl, C., Malley, J., & Tutz, G. (2009). An introduction to recursive partitioning: Rationale, application and characteristics of classification and regression trees, bagging and random forests. *Psychological Methods 14*(4), 323–348.

Svetnik, V., Liaw, A., Tong, C., & Wang, T. (2004). Application of breimanan's random forest to modeling structure-activity relationships of pharmaceutical molecules. In Roli, F., Kittler, J., and Windeatt, T. (Eds.), *Lecture Notes in Computer Science: Multiple Classifier Systems* (pp. 334–343). Berlin/Heidelberg: Springer.

Therneau, T. & Atkinson, B. (2006). rpart: Recursive partitioning. R package version 3.1–30.

Torgo, L. (2010). *Data Mining with R: Learning with Case Studies*. Chapman & Hall/CRC Data Mining and Knowledge Discovery Series. Boca Raton, Florida: CRC Press.

Vapnik, V. N. (1995). *The Nature of Statistical Learning Theory*. New York: Springer.

Vapnik, V. N. (1998). *Statistical Learning Theory*. New York: John Wiley & Sons.

Ward, M. M., Pajevic, S., Dreyfuss, J., & Malley, J. D. (2006). Short-term prediction of mortality in patients with systemic lupus erythematosus: Classification of outcomes using random forests. *Arthritis and Rheumatism 55*(1), 74–80.

White, A. & Liu, W. (1994). Bias in information based measures in decision tree induction. *Machine Learning 15*(3), 321–329.

Witten, I., Frank, E., & Hall, M. (2011). *Data Mining: Practical Machine Learning Tools and Techniques*. Massachusetts: Morgan Kaufman.

Wu, B., Abbott, T., Fishman, D., McMurray, W., Mor, G., Stone, K., Ward, D., et al. (2003). Comparison of statistical methods for classification of ovarian cancer using mass spectrometry data. *Bioinformatics 19*(13), 1636–1643.

CHAPTER 30

Meta-Analysis and Quantitative Research Synthesis

Noel A. Card *and* Deborah M. Casper

Abstract

Meta-analysis is an increasingly common method of quantitatively synthesizing research results, with substantial advantages over traditional (i.e., qualitative or narrative) methods of literature review. This chapter is an overview of meta-analysis that provides the foundational knowledge necessary to understand the goals of meta-analysis and the process of conducting a meta-analysis, from the initial formulation of research questions through the interpretation of results. The chapter provides insights into the types of research questions that can and cannot be answered through meta-analysis as well as more practical information on the practices of meta-analysis. Finally, the chapter concludes with some advanced topics intended to alert readers to further possibilities available through meta-analysis.

Key Words: Artifacts/Artifact correction, effect size(s), fixed effects, heterogeneity, literature review, meta-analysis, multivariate statistics, research synthesis, random effects

Introduction to Meta-analysis

Meta-analysis, also referred to as quantitative research synthesis, is a systematic approach to quantitatively synthesizing empirical literature. By combining and comparing research results, meta-analysis is used to advance theory, resolve conflicts within a discipline, and identify directions for future research (Cooper & Hedges, 2009). We begin by describing what meta-analysis is and what it is not.

Basic Terminology

It is important to provide a foundation of basic terminology on which to build a more technical and advanced understanding of meta-analysis. First, we draw the distinction between meta-analysis and primary and secondary analysis. The second distinction we draw is between quantitative research synthesis and qualitative literature review.

Glass (1976) defined primary-, secondary-, and meta-analysis as the analysis of data in an original study, the re-analysis of data previously explored in an effort to answer new questions or existing questions in a new way, and the quantitative analysis of results from multiple studies, respectively. A notable distinction between meta-analysis as compared to primary and secondary analysis involves the unit of analysis. In primary and secondary analyses, the units of analysis are most often the individual participants. In contrast, the units of analysis in a meta-analysis are the studies themselves or, more accurately, the effect sizes (defined below) of these studies.

A second foundational feature to consider is the distinction between quantitative research synthesis and qualitative literature review. Although both approaches are valuable to the advancement of knowledge, they differ with regard to focus and methodology. The focus of meta-analysis is on the integration of research outcomes, specifically in terms of effect sizes. In contrast, the focus of a qualitative literature review can be on research outcomes (although typically not focusing on effect sizes) but can also be on theoretical perspectives or typical practices in research. In terms of methods, scientists utilizing meta-analytic methodologies quantitatively synthesize findings to draw conclusions based on statistical principle. In contrast, scholars who conduct a qualitative literature review subjectively interpret and integrate research. Not considered in this chapter are other methodologies that fall between these two approaches on the taxonomy of literature review (for a more comprehensive review, *see* Card, 2012; Cooper 1988).

As previously acknowledged, both quantitative research synthesis and qualitative literature review merit recognition for their respective contributions to the advancement of scientific knowledge. Quantitative literature reviews were developed to overcome many of the limitations of qualitative literature reviews, and we will highlight the advantages of quantitative literature reviews below. However, it is worth noting that quantitative research synthesis has also faced criticisms (Chalmers, Hedges, & Cooper, 2002). Following are some highlights in the history of meta-analysis (for more thorough historical account, *see* Chalmers, Hedges, & Cooper, 2002; Hedges, 1992; Hunt, 1997; Olkin, 1990).

A Brief History

Research synthesis methodology can be traced as far back as 1904 when Karl Pearson integrated five studies looking at the association between inoculation for typhoid fever and morality (*see* Olkin, 1990). By the 1970s, at least three independent groups had started to combine results from multiple studies (Glass, 1976; Rosenthal & Rubin, 1978; Schmidt & Hunter, 1977), but the most influential work was Mary Smith and Gene Glass' (1977) "meta-analysis" of psychotherapy, which was both ground-breaking and controversial. Smith and Glass's (1977) meta-analysis sparked considerable controversy and debate as to the legitimacy of not only the findings but of the methodology itself (Eysenck, 1978). It is worth noting, however, that some have suggested the controversy surrounding Smith and Glass' (1977) meta-analysis had much more to do with the results than the methodology (Card, 2012).

Following the somewhat turbulent introduction of meta-analysis into the social sciences, the 1980s offered significant contributions. These contributions came from both the advancement and dissemination of knowledge of meta-analytic techniques by way of published books describing the approach, as well as through the publication of research utilizing the methods (Glass, McGaw, & Smith, 1981; Hedges & Olkin, 1985; Hunter, Schmidt, & Jackson, 1982; Rosenthal, 1984). Since its introduction into the social sciences in the 1970s, meta-analysis has become increasingly visible and has made considerable contributions to numerous bodies of scholarly research (*see* Cochran, 1937; Hunter, Schmidt, & Hunter, 1979; Pearsons, 1904; Rosenthal & Rubin, 1978; Glass & Smith, 1979; Smith & Glass, 1977).

Research Synthesis in the Social Sciences

Glass (1976) brought the need for meta-analysis to the forefront in a presidential address. It is not uncommon to observe conflicting findings across studies (Cooper & Hedges, 2009). These inconsistencies lead to confusion and impede progress in social science (as well as in the so-called hard sciences; Hedges, 1987). Quantitative research synthesis is a powerful approach that addresses this problem through the systematic integration of results from multiple studies that often individually report conflicting results.

Chapter Overview

The following chapter is an overview of meta-analysis that provides the foundational knowledge necessary to understand the goals of meta-analysis and the process of conducting a meta-analysis, from the initial formulation of research questions through the interpretation of results. The chapter provides insights into the types of research questions that can and cannot be answered through meta-analysis as well as more practical information on the practices of meta-analysis. Finally, we conclude the chapter with some advanced topics intended to alert readers to further possibilities available through meta-analysis. To begin, we consider the types of questions that can and cannot be answered through meta-analysis.

Problem Formulation
Questions That Can and Cannot be Answered Through Meta-Analysis

One of the first things to consider when conducting scientific research is the question for which you seek an answer; meta-analysis is no exception. A primary purpose for conducting a meta-analytic review is to integrate findings across multiple studies; however, not all questions are suitable for this type of synthesis. Hundreds, or sometimes thousands, of individual research reports potentially exist on any given topic; therefore, after an initial search of the literature, it is important to narrow the focus, identify goals, and articulate concise research questions that can be answered by conducting a tractable meta-analysis. A common misconception by those unfamiliar with meta-analysis is that an entire discipline or phenomenon can be "meta-analyzed" (Card, 2012). Because of the infinite number of questions that could be asked—many of which could be answered using meta-analysis—this sort of goal is too aspecific. Rather, a more appropriate approach to quantitative research synthesis is to identify a narrowly focused goal or set of goals and corresponding research questions.

Identifying Goals and Research Questions

Cooper's (1988) taxonomy of literature reviews identified multiple goals for meta-analysis. These include integration, theory development, and the identification of central issues within a discipline. We consider each of these goals in turn.

Integration. There are two general approaches to integrating research findings in meta-analysis: combining and comparing studies. The approach of combining studies is used to integrate effect sizes from multiple primary studies in an effort to estimate an overall, typical effect size. It would then be expectable to make inferences about this mean effect size by way of significance testing and/or confidence intervals. A second approach commonly used to integrate findings involves comparing studies. Also known as *moderator analyses* (addressed in more detail below), comparisons can be made across studies when a particular effect size is hypothesized to systematically vary on one or more of the coded study characteristics. Analyses to address each of these two approaches to integration will be described below.

Theory Development. A second goal of meta-analysis involves the development of theory. Meta-analysis can be used quite effectively and efficiently toward this end. If associations between variables that have been meta-analytically combined are weak, then this might indicate that a theory positing stronger relations of the constructs in question should be abandoned or modified (Schmidt, 1992). If, on the other hand, associations are strong, then this may be an indication that the phenomenon under investigation is moving toward a more integrated theory. Ideally, meta-analyses can be used to evaluate competing theories that make different predictions about the associations studied. Either way, meta-analysis is a powerful tool that can be used toward the advancement of theory within the social sciences.

Integration of Central Issues. A final goal has to do with identifying central issues within a discipline or phenomenon. The exhaustive review of empirical findings can aid in the process of identifying key issues within a discipline, such as whether there is inadequate study of certain types of samples or methodologies. The statistical techniques of meta-analysis can address inconsistencies in the findings, attempting to predict these inconsistencies with coded study characteristics (i.e., moderator analyses). Both of these contributions are important to the process of identifying directions for future research and the advancement of knowledge.

Critiques of Meta-Analysis

Earlier, we described how the controversial nature of one of the earliest meta-analyses (Smith & Glass, 1977) drew criticism not only of their findings but also of the technique of meta-analysis itself. Although these critiques have largely been rebuffed, they are still occasionally applied. Among the most common criticisms of meta-analysis are: (1) the "file drawer" problem; (2) the apples and oranges problem; (3) garbage in and garbage out; (4) the level of expertise required of the meta-analyst; and (5) the potential lack of qualitative finesse.

The "file drawer" problem. The "file drawer" problem, also known as the threat of publication bias, is based on the notion that significant results get published and nonsignificant findings get relegated to the "file drawer," resulting in the potential for a publication bias in meta-analysis (Rosenthal, 1979). To answer this criticism, however, meta-analysts typically employ both systematic and exhaustive search strategies to obtain published and unpublished reports in an effort to minimize this threat. In addition, there is an extensive collection of statistical procedures in meta-analysis that can be used to probe the existence, extent, and likely impact of publication bias (Rothstein, Sutton, & Borenstein, 2005).

The apples and oranges problem. The apples and oranges problem describes the potential process of combing such a diverse range of studies that the aggregated results are meaningless. For example, if a meta-analyst attempted to investigate the predictors of childhood internalizing problems by including studies focusing on depression, anxiety, and social withdrawal, then it could be argued that the aggregation of results across this diverse range of problems is meaningless. This critique, in our opinion, is conceptual rather than methodological: Did the scientist using meta-analytic techniques define a sampling frame of studies within which it is useful to combine results? Fortunately, meta-analytic reviews can use both (1) combination to estimate mean results and (2) comparison to evaluate whether studies with certain features differ. Put differently, meta-analysis allows for both general and specific results. Returning to the example of a meta-analyst investigating the predictors of child psychopathology, it might be useful to present results of both (1) predictors of general internalizing problems, and (2) comparisons of the distinct predictors of depression, anxiety, and social withdrawal.

Garbage in and garbage out. Garbage in, garbage out describes the practice of including poor-quality research reports in a meta-analysis, which result in only poor-quality conclusions. Although this critique is valid in some situations, we believe a more nuanced consideration of "garbage" is needed before being used as a critique of a particular meta-analysis. In the next section, we will provide this consideration by discussing how the limits of primary research place limits on the conclusions that can be drawn from meta-analysis of that research.

The level of expertise required of the meta-analyst. A common misconception is that meta-analysis requires advanced statistical expertise. We would argue that with basic methodological and quantitative training, such as usually obtained in the first year of graduate school, many scientists could readily learn the basic techniques (through an introductory course or book on meta-analysis) to conduct a sound meta-analytic review.

The potential lack of qualitative finesse. A final criticism that has been raised is that meta-analysis lacks the "qualitative finesse" of a qualitative review. Perhaps tellingly, a definition of qualitative finesse is generally lacking when this critique is made, but it seems that this critique implies that a meta-analyst has not thought carefully and critically about the nuances of the studies and collection of studies. There certainly exist meta-analyses where this critique seems relevant—just as there exist primary quantitative studies in which careful thought seems lacking. The solution to this critique is not to abandon meta-analytic techniques, however, just as the solution to thoughtless primary studies is not to abandon statistical analyses of these data. Rather, this critique makes clear that meta-analysis—like any other methodological approach—is a tool to aid careful thinking, rather than a replacement for it.

Limits of Primary Research and Meta-Analysis

It is also important to recognize that the conclusions of a meta-analytic review must be tempered by the quality of the empirical research comprising this review. Many of the threats to drawing conclusions in primary research are likely to translate to meta-analysis as well. Perhaps the most salient threats involve flaws in the study design, sampling procedures, methodological artifacts, and statistical power.

Study design. The design of primary studies guides the types of conclusions that can be drawn from them; similarly, the design of studies included in a meta-analysis guides the types of conclusions that can be drawn. Experimental designs, although powerful in their ability to permit inferences of causality, often do not share the same ecological validity as correlational designs. Conversely, correlational designs cannot make inferences of causality. It would follow that any limitation existing within primary studies also exists within the meta-analyses that encompass these studies.

Sampling. Another limitation of primary studies is that it is difficult to support inferences generalizable beyond the sampling frame. When a sample is drawn from a homogeneous population, inferences can be made only for a limited set of individuals. Similarly, findings from a meta-analysis can only be generalized to populations within the sampling frame of the included studies; however, the collection of primary studies within a meta-analysis is likely to be more heterogeneous than one single primary study if it includes studies that are collectively diverse in their samples, even if each study sample is homogeneous.

Methodological artifacts. Both primary research and meta-analysis involve methodological shortcomings. Although it is difficult to describe all of the characteristics that make up a high-quality study, it is possible to identify those artifacts that likely lower the quality of the design. In primary studies, methodological issues need to be addressed prior to data collection. In contrast, meta-analysis can address these methodological artifacts in either one of two ways. The first way is to compare (through moderator analyses) whether studies with different methodological features actually yield different findings. Second, for some artifacts (e.g., measurement unreliability) described near the end of this chapter, corrections can be made that allow for the analysis of effect sizes free of these artifacts. Artifact correction is rarely performed in primary research (with the exception of latent variable modeling to correct for unreliability) but more commonly considered in meta-analyses.

Statistical power. Another limitation of much primary research is low statistical power (Maxwell, 2004). Statistical power is the probability of detecting an effect that truly does exist but is often unacceptably low in many primary research studies. This low power results in incorrect conclusions in primary studies that an effect does not exist (despite cautions against "accepting" the null hypothesis). Fortunately, meta-analysis is usually less affected by inadequate power of primary studies because it combines a potentially large number of studies, thus resulting in greater statistical power.

Strengths of Meta-Analysis

As outlined above, there are limits to meta-analysis; however, meta-analysis should be recognized for its considerable strengths. We next briefly describe three of the most important of these: (1) a systematic and disciplined review process; (2) sophisticated reporting of findings; and (3) a way of combining and comparing large amounts of data (Lipsey & Wilson, 2001).

Systematic and disciplined review process. First, systematic procedures must be followed to conduct a comprehensive literature search, consistently code comparable characteristics and effect sizes from studies, and to ensure the accuracy of combining results from multiple reports into one effect size. The processes of searching the literature, identifying studies, coding, and analyzing results have received tremendous attention in the literature on meta-analysis methodology, in contrast to most other forms of literature review. Although this work requires discipline, diligent attention to detail, and meticulous documentation on the part of the meta-analyst, when these procedures are followed, a large amount of data can be combined and compared and the outcome is likely to be a significant contribution to the field.

Combining and comparing large amounts of data. Perhaps one of the greatest strengths of meta-analytic techniques is the ability to combine and compare large amounts of data that would otherwise be impossible to integrate in a meaningful way. It would assuredly exceed the capacity of almost any scholar to combine the large amounts of data and draw meaningful conclusions without quantitative literature review techniques. Following the strength of combining and comparing large amounts of data is the strength in the way in which the findings are reported.

Sophisticated reporting of findings. Meta-analysis offers a level of sophistication in the way in which the findings are reported. Unlike qualitative literature reviews that derive and report conclusions and interpretations in a narrative format, meta-analysis uses statistical techniques to yield quantified conclusions. Meta-analysts commonly take advantage of visual tools such as stem-and-leaf plots, funnel plots, and tables of effect sizes to add a level of sophistication to the reporting of findings.

Searching the Literature
Defining a Sampling Frame

Similarly to primary research, a sampling frame must be considered in meta-analysis. However, the unit of analysis in a meta-analysis is the study itself, as compared to the individuals in most primary studies. If we are to make inferences about the population of studies of interest, it is necessary to define the population *a priori* by articulating a set of criteria of the type of studies included versus excluded from this sampling frame.

Identifying Inclusion and Exclusion Criteria

As mentioned, the inclusion and exclusion criteria define the sampling frame of a meta-analysis. Establishing clear and explicit criteria will help guide the search process, a consideration particularly important if multiple individuals are working on the project. A second reason for identifying clear criteria is that it will help define the population of interest to which generalizations can be made. A final reason that clear criteria are necessary has to do with the ideas of transparency and replication. As with the sampling in well-conducted and well-reported primary studies, each decision and subsequent procedure utilized in the literature search of a meta-analysis must be transparent and replicable. Some of the more common search techniques and sources of information are described next.

Search Techniques and Identifying Resources

Many techniques have been used quite successfully toward the goal of searching the literature and identifying relevant resources. Two important concepts related to the literature search are recall and precision (see White, 2009). Recall is the percentage of studies retrieved that meet your inclusion criteria from all of those that actually exist. Precision is the percentage of studies retrieved that meet the inclusion criteria for the meta-analysis. The ideal literature search strategy provides both high recall and precision, although the reality is that decisions that affect efforts to improve recall often lower precision and vice versa.

By using multiple methods of searching for literature, meta-analysts strive to maximize recall without imposing impractical detriments on precision. The use of multiple search techniques helps this effort. The techniques most commonly used include searching: electronic databases using keywords, bibliographical reference volumes, unpublished works and other outlets (described below), conference presentations, funding agency lists, research registries, backward searches, forward searches, and personal communications with colleagues.

Electronic databases. Electronic databases are probably one of the most helpful tools for conducting literature searches developed in the past decades. Now, electronic database searches can identify as much of the relevant literature in a matter of hours or days, as would have taken weeks or months a few decades earlier (not to mention that these searches can be done from the comfort of one's office rather than within the confines of a library). Most disciplines have electronic databases that serve primarily that particular discipline (e.g., PsychINFO for psychology, Medline for medicine, ERIC for education, etc.). With these and similar databases, the meta-analyst identifies the most relevant combination of keywords, wildcard marks (e.g.,*), and logical statements (e.g., and, or, not), and voluminous amounts of literature is quickly searched for matches. The electronic database is perhaps the most fruitful place to begin and is currently the primary tool used to search the literature.

Despite their advantages, it is worth mentioning a few cautions regarding electronic databases. First, an electronic search must not be used exclusively because of that which is not included in these databases. For example, many unpublished works might not be retrieved through electronic databases. Second, as mentioned previously, each discipline relies on one primary electronic database; therefore, multiple databases must be considered in your search. Third, electronic databases produce studies that match the keyword searches, but it is not possible to know what has been excluded. Using other search strategies and investigating why studies found by these strategies were not identified in the electronic database search is necessary to avoid unnecessary (and potentially embarrassing) omission of studies from a meta-analysis.

Bibliographical reference volumes. A method of locating relevant literature that was common as little as a decade ago is to search biographical reference volumes. These volumes are printed collections containing essentially the same information as electronic databases. Although these reference volumes are being phased out of circulation, you may find them useful if relevant literature was published some time ago (especially if the electronic databases have not yet incorporated this older literature).

Unpublished works. One of the challenges of meta-analysis has to do with publication bias (see Rothstein et al., 2005). If there is a tendency for significant findings to be more likely published than nonsignificant (presumably with smaller effect sizes) studies, then the exclusion of unpublished studies in a meta-analysis can be problematic. To balance this potential problem, the meta-analyst should make deliberate efforts to find and obtain unpublished studies. Some possible places to find such studies include conference program books, funding agency lists, and research registries.

Backward searches. Another technique commonly used in meta-analysis is the backward search. Once relevant reports are retrieved, it is recommended that the researcher thoroughly read each report and identify additional articles cited within these reports. This strategy is called a "backward" search because it proceeds backward in time from obtained studies toward previous studies.

Forward searches. A complimentary procedure, known as the forward search, involves searching for additional studies that have cited the relevant studies included in your meta-analysis ("forward" because the search proceeds from older studies to newer studies citing these previous works). To conduct this type of search, special databases (e.g., Social Science Citation Index) are used.

Personal communication with researchers in the field. A final search technique involves personal communication with the researchers in the field. It will be especially helpful to communicate with researchers in your field (those who will likely read your work) in an effort to locate resources that somehow escaped your comprehensive search efforts. An effective yet efficient way to do this is to simply e-mail researchers in your field, let them know what type of meta-analysis you are conducting, and ask if they would be willing to peruse your reference list to see if there are any glaring oversights.

Coding Study Characteristics

In a meta-analysis, study characteristics are systematically coded for two reasons. First, this coded information is presented to describe the collective field being reviewed. For example, do studies primarily rely on White college students, or are the samples more diverse (either within or across studies)? Do studies rely on the same measures or types of measures, or has the phenomenon been studied using multiple measures?

A second reason for systematically coding study characteristics is for use as potential predictors of variation in effect sizes across studies (i.e., moderators, as described below in section titled Moderator Analyses). In other words, does variation across studies in the coded study characteristics co-occur with differences in results (i.e., effect sizes) from these studies? Ultimately, the decision of what study characteristics should be coded derives from the meta-analysts' substantive understanding of the field. There are at least three general types of study features that are commonly considered: characteristics of the sample, the methodology, and the source.

Coding Sample Characteristics

Sample characteristics include any descriptions of the study samples that might systematically covary with study results (i.e., effect sizes). Some meta-analyses will include codes for the sampling procedures, such as whether the study used a representative sample or a convenience sample (e.g., college students), or whether the sample was selected from some specific setting, such as clinical treatment settings, schools, or prisons. Nearly all meta-analyses code various demographic features of the sample, such as the ethnic composition, proportion of the sample that is male or female, and the average age of participants in the sample.

Coding Methodological Characteristics

Potential methodological characteristics for coding include both design and measurement features. At a broad level, a meta-analyst might code broad types of designs, such as experimental, quasi-experimental, and single-subject ABAB studies. It might also be useful to code at more narrow levels, such as the type of control group used within experimental treatment studies (e.g., no contact, attention only, treatment as usual). Similarly, the types of measures used could be coded as either broad (e.g., parent vs. child reports) or narrow (CBCL vs. BASC parent reports). In practice, most meta-analysts will code methodological features at both broad and narrow levels, first considering broad-level features as predictors of variability in effect sizes, and then using more narrow-level feature if there exists unexplained variation in results within these broad features.

Coding Source Characteristics

Source characteristics include features of the report or author that might plausibly be related to study findings. The most commonly coded source characteristic is whether the study was published, which is often used to evaluate potential publication bias. The year of publication (or presentation, for unpublished works) is often used as a proxy for the historic time in which the study was conducted. If the year predicts differences in effect sizes, then this may be evidence for historic change in the phenomenon over time. Other source characteristics, such as characteristics of the researcher (e.g., gender, ethnicity, discipline), are less commonly coded but are possibilities. For example, some meta-analyses of gender differences have coded the gender of the first author to evaluate the possibility that the researchers' presumed biases may somehow impact the results found (e.g., Card, Stucky, Sawalani, & Little, 2008).

Coding Effect Sizes

As mentioned, study results in meta-analysis are represented as effect sizes. To be useful in meta-analysis, a potential effect size needs to meet four criteria. First, it needs to quantify the direction and magnitude of a phenomenon of interest. Second, it needs to be comparable across studies that use different sample sizes and scales of measurement. Third, it needs to be either consistently reported in studies included in the meta-analysis or else it can be computed from commonly reported results. Fourth, it is necessary that the meta-analyst can compute its standard error, which is used for weighting of studies in subsequent meta-analytic combination and comparison.

The three effect sizes most commonly used in meta-analyses all index associations between two variables. The correlation coefficient (typically denoted as r) quantifies associations between two continuous variables. The standardized mean differences are a family of effect sizes (we will focus on Hedges' g) that quantify associations between a dichotomous (group) variable and a continuous variable. The odds ratio (denoted as either o or OR) is a useful and commonly used index for associations between two dichotomous variables (Fleiss, 1994).

We next describe these three indexes of effect size, the correlation coefficient, the standardized mean difference, and the OR. After describing each of these effect sizes indexes, we will describe how these are computed from results commonly reported in empirical reports.

Correlation Coefficient

Correlation coefficients represent associations between two variables on a standardized scale from -1 to $+1$. Correlations near 0 denote the absence of association between two variables, whereas positive values indicate that scores on one variable tend to be similar to scores on another (relatively high scores on one variable tend to occur with relatively high scores on the other, as do low scores tend to occur with low scores), whereas negative scores indicate the opposite (high scores with low scores). The correlation coefficient has the advantage of being widely recognized by scientists in diverse fields. A commonly applied suggestion is that $r \approx \pm 0.10$ is considered small, $r \approx \pm 0.30$ is considered medium, and $r \approx \pm 0.50$ is considered large; however, disciplines and fields differ in their evaluations of what constitutes small or large correlations, and researchers should not be dogmatic in its application.

Although r has many advantages as an effect size, it has the undesirable property for meta-analysis of having sample estimates that are skewed around the population mean. For this reason, meta-analysts should transform r to Fisher's Z_r prior to analysis using the following equation:

$$Z_r = \frac{1}{2} \ln\left(\frac{1+r}{1-r}\right). \quad (1)$$

Although Z_r has desirable properties for meta-analytic combination and comparison, it is not very interpretable by most readers. Therefore, meta-analysts back-transform results in Z_r metric (e.g., mean effect size) to r for reporting using the following equation:

$$r = \frac{e^{2Z_r} - 1}{e^{2Z_r} + 1}. \quad (2)$$

As mentioned earlier, and will be described in greater detail below, it is necessary to compute the standard error of the estimation of the effect size (Z_r) for use in weighting studies in meta-analysis. The equation for the standard error of Z_r (SE_{Z_r}) is a simple function of the study sample size:

$$SE_{Z_r} = \frac{1}{\sqrt{N-3}}. \quad (3)$$

Standardized Mean Differences

There exist several standardized mean differences, which index associations between a dichotomous "group" variable and a continuous variable. Each of these standardized mean differences indexes the direction and magnitude of differences between two groups in standard deviation units. We begin with one of the more common of these indices, Hedges' g, which is defined as:

$$g = \frac{M_1 - M_2}{s_{pooled}}. \quad (4)$$

The numerator of this equation contains the difference between the means of two groups (groups 1 and 2) and will yield a positive value if group 1 has a higher mean than group 2 or a negative value if group 2 has a higher mean than group 1. Although it is arbitrary which group is designated 1 or 2, this designation must be consistent across all studies coded for a meta-analysis.

If all studies in a meta-analysis use the same measure, or else different measures with the same scale, then the numerator of this equation alone would suffice as an effect size for meta-analysis (this is the unstandardized mean difference). However, the more common situation is that different scales are used across different studies, and in this situation it would make no sense to attempt to combine these unstandardized mean differences across studies. To illustrate, if one study comparing treatment to control groups measured an outcome on a 1 to 100 scale and found a 10-point difference, whereas another study measured the outcome on a 0 to 5 scale and found a 2-point difference, then there would be no way of knowing which—if either—study had a larger effect. To make these differences comparable across studies, it is necessary to standardize them in some way, typically by dividing the mean difference by a standard deviation.

As seen in equation (4) above, this standard deviation in the divisor for g is the pooled (i.e., combined across the two groups) estimate of the population standard deviation. Other variants within the standardized mean difference family of effect sizes use different divisors. For example, the index d uses the pooled sample standard deviation and a less commonly used index, g_{Glass} (also denoted as Glass' Δ), uses the estimated population standard deviation for one group (the group that you believe is a more accurate estimate of population standard deviation, such as the control group if you believe that treatment impacts the standard deviation). The latter index (g_{Glass}) is less preferred because it cannot be computed from some commonly reported statistics (e.g., t tests), and it is a poorer estimate if the standard deviations are, in fact, comparable across groups (Hedges & Olkin, 1985).

In this chapter, we focus our attention primarily on g, and we will describe the computation of g from commonly reported results below. Like other standardized mean differences, g has a value of 0 when the groups do not differ (i.e., no association between the dichotomous group variable and the continuous variable), and positive or negative values depending on which group has a higher mean. Unlike r, g is not bounded at 1, but can have values greater than ±1.0 if the groups differ by more than one standard deviation.

Although g is a preferred index of standardized mean differences, it exhibits a slight bias when estimated from small samples (e.g., sample sizes less than 20). To correct for this bias, it is common to apply the following correction:

$$g_{adjusted} = 1 - \left(\frac{3}{4df - 1} \right). \quad (5)$$

As with any effect size used in meta-analysis, it is necessary to compute the standard error of estimates of g for weighting during meta-analytic combination. The standard error of g is more precisely estimated using the sample sizes from both groups under consideration (i.e., n_1 and n_1 for groups 1 and 2, respectively) using the left portion of Equation 6 but can be reasonably estimated using overall sample size (N_{Total}; right portion of Equation 6) when exact group sizes are unknown but approximately equal (no more than a 3-to-1 discrepancy in group sizes; Card, 2012; Rosenthal, 1991):

$$SE_g = \sqrt{\frac{n_1 + n_2}{n_1 n_2} + \frac{g^2}{2(n_1 + n_2)}} \approx \frac{4 + g^2}{N_{Total}}. \quad (6)$$

Odds Ratios

The odds ratio, denoted as either o or OR, is a useful index of associations between two dichotomous variables. Although readers might be familiar with other indices of two variable associations, such as the rate (also known as risk) ratio or the phi coefficient, the OR is advantageous because it is not affected by differences in the base rates of dichotomous variables across studies and is computed from a wider range of study designs (see Fleiss, 1994). The OR is estimated from 2 × 2 contingency tables by dividing the product of cell frequencies in the major diagonal (i.e., frequencies in the cells where values of the two variables are both 0 {n_{00}} or both 1 {n_{11}}) by the product of cell frequencies off the diagonal (i.e., frequencies in the cells where the two variables have different values, n_{10} and n_{01}):

$$o = \frac{n_{00} n_{11}}{n_{01} n_{10}}. \quad (7)$$

The OR has a rather different scale than either r or g. Values of 1.0 represent no association between the dichotomous variables, values from 1 down to 0 represent negative association, and values from 1 to infinity represent positive associations. Given this scale, o is obviously skewed; therefore, a log transformation is applied to o when included in a meta-analysis: $ln(o)$. The standard error of this log-transformed odds ratio is a function of number of participants in each cell of the 2 × 2 contingency table:

$$SE_{ln(o)} = \sqrt{\frac{1}{n_{00}} + \frac{1}{n_{01}} + \frac{1}{n_{10}} + \frac{1}{n_{11}}}. \quad (8)$$

Computing Effect Sizes From Commonly Reported Data

Ideally, all studies that you want to include in a meta-analysis will have effect sizes reported, and it is a fairly straightforward matter to simply record these. Unfortunately, many studies do not report effect sizes (despite many calls for this reporting; e.g., Wilkinson et al., 1999), and it is necessary to compute effect sizes from a wide variety of information reported in studies. Although it is not possible to consider all possibilities here, we next describe a few of the more common situations. Table 30.1 summarizes equations for computing r and g in these situations (note that it is typically necessary to reconstruct contingency tables from reported data to compute the odds ratio; see Fleiss, 1994).

It is common for studies to report group comparisons in the form of either the (independent samples) t-test or as the results of a two-group (i.e., 1 df) analysis of variance (ANOVA). This occurs either because the study focused on a truly dichotomous grouping variable (in which case, the desired effect size is a standardized mean difference such as g) or because the study authors artificially dichotomized one of the continuous variables (in which case the

Table 30.1. Summary of Equations Used for Computing r and g From Commonly Reported Information

	Pearson's r	Hedges' g
Independent t-test	$\sqrt{\dfrac{t^2}{t^2+df}}$	$\dfrac{t\sqrt{n_1+n_2}}{\sqrt{n_1 n_2}} \approx \dfrac{2t}{\sqrt{N}}$
Independent 1 df F-ratio	$\sqrt{\dfrac{F_{(1,df)}}{F_{(1,df)}+df}}$	$\sqrt{\dfrac{F_{(1,df)}(n_1+n_2)}{n_1 n_2}} \approx 2\sqrt{\dfrac{F_{(1,df)}}{N}}$
Dependent (repeated-measures) t-test	$\sqrt{\dfrac{t^2}{t^2+df}}$	$\dfrac{t_{dependent}}{\sqrt{N}}$
Dependent (repeated-measures) F-ratio	$\sqrt{\dfrac{F_{(1,df)}}{F_{(1,df)}+df}}$	$\sqrt{\dfrac{F_{repeated(1,df)}}{N}}$
2×2 (i.e., 1 df) contingency χ^2	$\sqrt{\dfrac{\chi^2_{(1)}}{N}}$	$2\sqrt{\dfrac{\chi^2_{(1)}}{N-\chi^2_{(1)}}}$
Probability levels from significance tests	$\dfrac{Z}{\sqrt{N}}$	$\dfrac{2Z}{\sqrt{N}}$

desired effect size is r). In these cases, either r or g can be computed from the t statistic of F ratio in Table 30.1. For the F ratio, it is critical that the result is from a two-group (i.e., 1 df) comparison (for discussion of computing effect sizes from > 1 df F ratios, see Rosenthal, Rosnow, & Rubin, 2000). When computing g (but not r), a more precise estimate can be made if the two group sizes are known; otherwise, it is necessary to use the approximations shown to the right of Table 30.1 (e.g., in the first row for g, the exact formula is on the left and the approximation is on the right).

An alternate situation is that the study has performed repeated-measures comparisons (e.g., pretreatment vs. posttreatment) and reported results of dependent, or repeated-measures, t-tests, or F ratios. The equations for computing r from these results are identical to those for computing from independent samples tests; however, for g, the equations differ for independent versus dependent sample statistics, as seen in Table 30.1.

A third possibility is that the study authors represent both variables that constitute your effect size of interest as dichotomous variables. The study might report the 1 df χ^2 of this contingency or the data that can be used to construct the contingency table and the subsequent value. In this situation, r and g are computed from this χ^2 value and sample size (N). As with the F ratio, it is important to keep in mind that this equation only applied to 1 df χ^2 values (i.e., 2×2 contingency tables).

The last situation we will discuss is when the authors report none of the above statistics but do report a significance level (i.e., p). Here, you can compute the one-tail standard normal deviate, Z, associated with this significance level (e.g., $Z = 1.645$ for $p = 0.05$) and then use the equations of Table 30.1 to compute r or g. These formulas are used when an exact significance level is reported (e.g., $p = 0.027$); if they are applied to ranges (e.g., $p < 0.05$), then they provide only a lower-bound estimate of the actual effect size.

Although we have certainly not covered all possible situations, these represent some of the most common situations you are likely to encounter when coding effect sizes for a meta-analysis. For details of these and other situations in which you might code effect sizes, see Card (2012) or Lipsey and Wilson (2001).

Analysis of Mean Effect Sizes and Heterogeneity

After coding study characteristics and effect sizes from all studies included in a meta-analysis, it is possible to statistically combine and compare results across studies. In this section, we describe a method (fixed effects) of computing a mean effect size and making inferences about this mean. We then describe a test of heterogeneity that informs whether the between-study variability in effect sizes is greater than expectable by sampling fluctuation alone. Finally, we describe an alternative approach to computing mean effect sizes (random effects) that accounts for between-study variability.

Fixed-Effects Means

One of the primary goals of meta-analytic combination of effect sizes from multiple studies is to estimate an average effect size that exists in the literature and then to make inferences about this average effect size in the form of statistical significance and/or confidence intervals. Before describing how to estimate and make inferences about a mean effect size, we briefly describe the concept of weighting.

Weighting in Meta-Analysis. Nearly all (and all that we describe here) analyses of effect sizes in meta-analysis apply weights to studies. These weights are meant to index the degree of precision in each study's estimate of the population effect size, such that studies with more precise estimates receive greater weight in the analyses than studies with less precise estimates. The most straightforward weight is the inverse of the variance of a study's estimate of the population effect size. In other words, the weight of study i is the inverse of the squared standard error from that study:

$$w_i = \frac{1}{SE_i^2}. \qquad (9)$$

As described above, the standard error of a study largely depends on the sample size (and for g, the effect size itself), such that studies with large samples have smaller standard errors than studies with small samples. Therefore, studies with large samples have larger weights than studies with smaller samples.

Fixed-Effects Mean Effect Sizes. After computing weights for each study using the equation above, estimating the mean effect size ($\bar{ES}$) across studies is a relatively simple matter of computing the weighted mean of effect sizes across all studies:

$$\bar{ES} = \frac{\sum(w_i ES_i)}{\sum w_i}. \qquad (10)$$

This value represents the estimate of a single effect size in the population based on information combined from all studies included in the meta-analysis. Because it is often useful to draw inferential conclusions, the standard error of this estimate is computed using the equation:

$$SE_{\bar{ES}} = \sqrt{\frac{1}{\sum w_i}}. \qquad (11)$$

This standard error can then be used to compute either statistical significance or confidence intervals. For determining statistical significance, the mean effect size is divided by the standard error, and the resulting ratio is evaluated as a standard normal deviate (i.e., Z-test, with, e.g., values larger than ± 1.96 having $p < 0.05$). For computing confidence intervals, the standard error is multiplied by the standard normal deviate associated with the desired confidence interval (e.g., $Z = 1.96$ for a 95% confidence interval), and this product is then subtracted from and added to the mean effect size to identify the lower- and upper-bounds of the confidence interval.

If the effect size chosen for the meta-analysis (i.e., r, g, or o) was transformed prior to analyses (e.g., r to Z_r), then the mean effect size and boundaries of its confidence interval will be in this transformed metric. It is usually more meaningful to back-transform these values to their original metrics for reporting.

Heterogeneity

In addition to estimating a mean effect size, meta-analysts evaluate the variability of effect sizes across studies. Some degree of variability in effect sizes across studies is always expectable; the fact that different studies relied on different samples results in somewhat different estimates of effect sizes because of sampling variability. In situations where effect sizes differ by an amount expectable due to sampling variability, the studies are considered *homogeneous* with respect to their population effect sizes. However, if effect sizes vary across studies more than expected by sampling fluctuation alone, then they are considered *heterogeneous* (or varying) with respect to their population effect sizes.

It is common to perform a statistical test to evaluate heterogeneity. In this test, the null hypothesis is of homogeneity, or no variability, in population effect sizes across studies (i.e., any variability in sample effect sizes is caused by sampling variability), whereas the alternative hypothesis is of heterogeneity, or variability, in population effect sizes across studies (i.e., variability in sample effect sizes that is not accounted for by sampling variability alone).

The result of this test is denoted by Q:

$$Q = \sum \left(w_i \left(ES_i - \bar{ES} \right)^2 \right)$$
$$= \sum \left(w_i ES_i^2 \right) - \frac{\left(\sum (w_i ES_i) \right)^2}{\sum w_i}. \quad (12)$$

The statistical significance of this Q is evaluated as a χ^2 distribution with df = number of studies − 1. You will note that this equation has two forms. The left portion of Equation 12 is the definitional equation, which makes clear that the squared deviation of the effect size from each study i from the overall mean effect size is being weighted and summed across studies. Therefore, small deviations from the mean will contribute to small values of Q (homogeneity), whereas large deviations from the mean will contribute to large values of Q (heterogeneity). The right portion of Equation 12 is an algebraic rearrangement that simplifies computation (i.e., a computational formula).

Results of this test have implications for subsequent analyses. Specifically, a conclusion of homogeneity (more properly, failure to conclude heterogeneity) suggests that the fixed-effects mean described above is an acceptable way to summarize effect sizes, and this conclusion may contraindicate moderator analyses (described below). In contrast, a conclusion of heterogeneity implies that the fixed-effects mean is not an appropriate way to summarize effect sizes, but, rather, a random-effects model (described in the next section) should be used. Further, a conclusion of heterogeneity indicates that moderator analyses (described below) may help explain this between-study variance (i.e., heterogeneity). It is worth noting that the result of this heterogeneity test is not the sole basis of deciding to use random-effects models or to conduct moderator analyses, and meta-analysts often base these decisions on conceptual rather than empirical grounds (see Card, 2012; Hedges & Vevea, 1998).

Random-Effects Means

Estimation of means via a random-effects model relies on a different conceptual model and analytic approach than estimation via a fixed-effects model. We describe this conceptual model and estimation procedures next.

Conceptualization of Random-Effects Means. Previously, when we described estimation of a fixed-effects mean, we describe a single population effect size. In contrast, a random-effects model assumes that there is a normal distribution of population effect sizes. This distribution of population effect sizes has a mean, which we estimate as described next. However, it also has a degree of spread, which can be indexed by the standard deviation (or variance) of effect sizes at the population level. To explicate the assumptions in equation form, the fixed- and random-effects models assume that the effect sizes observed in study i (ES_i) are a function of the following, respectively:

$$ES_i = \theta + \varepsilon_i \quad (13)$$
$$ES_i = \mu + \xi_i + \varepsilon_i. \quad (14)$$

In both Equation 13 (fixed effects) and Equation 14 (random effects), effect sizes in a study partly result from the sampling fluctuation of that study (ε_i). In the fixed-effects model, this sampling fluctuation is around a single population effect size (θ). In contrast, the random-effects model specifies that the population effect size is a function of both a mean population effect size (μ) as well as the deviation of the population effect size of study i from this mean (ξ_i). Although it is impossible to know the sampling fluctuation and the population deviation from a single study, it is possible to estimate the respective variances of each across studies.

Estimating Between-Study Population Variance. We described above the heterogeneity test, indexed by Q, which is a statistical test of whether variability in observed effect sizes across studies could be accounted for by sampling variability alone (i.e., the null hypothesis of homogeneity) or was greater than expected by sampling variability (i.e., the alternate hypothesis of heterogeneity). To estimate between-study population variance τ^2 in effect sizes, we evaluate how much greater Q is than that expected under the null hypothesis of homogeneity (i.e., sampling variance alone):

$$\tau^2 = \frac{Q - (k-1)}{\left(\sum w_i \right) - \frac{\left(\sum w_i^2 \right)}{\left(\sum w_i \right)}}. \quad (15)$$

Note that this equation is used only if $Q \geq k - 1$ to avoid negative variance estimates (if $Q < k - 1$, $\tau^2 = 0$). Although this equation is not intuitively obvious, consideration of the numerator helps clarify. Recall that large values of Q result when studies have effect sizes with large deviations from the mean effect size and that under the null hypothesis of homogeneity, Q is expected to equal the number of studies (k) minus 1. To the extent that Q is much larger than this expected value, the numerator of this equation will be large, implying large population between-study variability. In contrast, if Q

is not much higher than the expected value under homogeneity, then the population between-study variability will be near zero.

Estimating Random-Effects Means. If studies have a sizable amount of randomly distributed between-study variance in their population effect sizes, then this implies that each is a less precise estimate of mean population effect size. In other words, each contains more uncertainty as information for estimating this value. To capture this uncertainty, or lower precision, analyses under the random-effects model use a different weight than those of the fixed-effects model. Specifically, the random-effects weight, denoted as w^* (or sometimes w^{RE}), for study i is the inverse of the sum of this between-study variance (τ^2) and the sampling variance for that study (i.e., squared standard error, SE_i^2):

$$w_i^* = \frac{1}{\tau^2 + SE_i^2}. \quad (16)$$

This random-effects weight will be smaller than the comparable fixed-effects weight, with the discrepancy increasing with greater between-study variance. These random-effects weights are simply used in the equations above to estimate a random-effects mean effect size (Equation 10), as well as a standard error for this mean (Equation 9) for inferential tests.

Moderator Analyses

Moderator analyses are another approach to managing heterogeneity in effect sizes (Hedges & Pigott, 2004), but here the focus is on explaining (versus simply modeling as random) this between-study variance. These analyses use coded study characteristics to predict effect sizes; the reason these analyses are called "moderator" analyses is because they evaluate whether the effect size—a two-variable association—differs depending on the level of the third, moderator, variable—the study characteristic. It is often of primary interest to understand whether the association between two variables differs based on the level of a third variable (the moderator). Therefore, moderator analyses identifying those characteristics of the study that lead to higher or lower effects sizes are very commonly performed in meta-analyses. In this section, we briefly consider two types of moderators (i.e., categorical and continuous) along with the procedures used to investigate these two types of moderators in meta-analysis (i.e., an adapted ANOVA procedure and a multiple regression procedure, respectively).

Single Categorical Moderator

A categorical variable is any variable on which a participants, observations or, in the case of meta-analysis, studies can be distinctly classified. Testing categorical moderators in meta-analysis involves comparing the mean effects of groups of studies classified by their status on some categorical variable.

Evaluating the Significance of a Categorical Moderator. Categorical moderator analysis in meta-analysis is similar to ANOVA in primary research. In the context of primary research, ANOVA partitions variability between groups of individuals into variability between and within these groups. Similarly, in meta-analysis, the ANOVA procedure is used to partition between-study heterogeneity into heterogeneity that exists between and within groups of studies. Earlier (Equation 12), we provided equations for quantifying the heterogeneity as Q; we now provide this equation again, but now specifying that this is the total heterogeneity among studies:

$$Q_{Total} = \sum \left(w_i \left(ES_i - \bar{E}\bar{S} \right)^2 \right)$$
$$= \sum \left(w_i ES_i^2 \right) - \frac{\left(\sum (w_i ES_i) \right)^2}{\sum w_i}. \quad (17)$$

This Q_{Total} refers to the heterogeneity that exists across all studies. It can be partitioned into between-group ($Q_{Between}$) and within-group (Q_{Within}) components by the fact that $Q_{Total} = Q_{Between} + Q_{Within}$. It is simpler to compute Q_{Within} than $Q_{Between}$, so it is common to subtract this from the total heterogeneity to obtain the between group variance. Within each group of studies, g, the heterogeneity can be estimated among just the studies in this group:

$$Q_g = \sum \left(w_i \left(ES_i - \bar{E}\bar{S} \right)^2 \right)$$
$$= \sum \left(w_i ES_i^2 \right) - \frac{\left(\sum (w_i ES_i) \right)^2}{\sum w_i}. \quad (18)$$

Then, these estimates of heterogeneity within each group can be summed across groups to yield the within study heterogeneity:

$$Q_{Within} = \sum_{g=1}^{G} Q_g. \quad (19)$$

As stated above, testing categorical moderators within an ANOVA framework is done by separating the total heterogeneity (Q_{Total}) into between-group ($Q_{Between}$) and within-group (Q_{Within}) heterogeneity. Therefore, after computing the total heterogeneity (Q_{Total}) and the within-group heterogeneity (Q_{Within}), you simply subtract the within-group heterogeneity from the total heterogeneity to find $Q_{Between}$. This value is evaluated as a χ^2 distribution with df = number of groups − 1. If this value is statistically significant, then this is evidence that the level of the categorical moderator predicts variability in effect sizes—moderation.

Single Continuous Moderator

A continuous study characteristic is one that is measured on a scale that can potentially take on an infinite, or at least large number of values. In meta-analysis, a continuous moderator is a coded study characteristic (e.g., sample age, SES) that varies along a continuum of values and is hypothesizes to predict effect sizes.

Similarly to the use of an adapted ANOVA procedure in the evaluation of categorical moderators in meta-analysis, we use an adapted multiple regression procedure for the evaluation of continuous moderators in meta-analysis (Hedges & Pigott, 2004). This adaptation to the evaluation of a continuous moderator involves a weighted regression of the effect sizes (dependent variable) onto the continuous moderator.

To evaluate potential moderation of a continuous moderator within a multiple regression framework, we regress the effect sizes onto the hypothesized continuous moderator using a standard regression equation: $Z_{ES} = B_0 + B_1$ (Study Characeistic) $+ e$, using w as the (weighted least squares) weight. From the results, we are interested in the sum of squares of the regression model (which is the heterogeneity accounted for by the linear regression model, $Q_{Regression}$, and evaluated on a chi-square distribution with df = number of predictors), and sometimes the residual sum of squares (which is $Q_{Residual}$, or heterogeneity not explained by the study characteristic). The unstandardized regression coefficient indicates how the effect size changes per unit change in the continuous moderator. The standard error of this coefficient is inaccurate in the regression output and must be adjusted by dividing it by the square root of the $MS_{Residual}$.

The statistical significance of the predictor can also be evaluated by dividing the regression coefficient (B_1) by the adjusted standard error, evaluated on the standard two-tail Z distribution. Interpretation of moderation with continuous variables is not as straightforward as with categorical moderators; it is necessary to compute implied effect sizes at different levels of the continuous moderator.

Multiple Regression to Analyze Categorical Moderators

Thus far we have considered moderation by a single categorical variable within an ANOVA framework and by a continuous variable within a regression framework. Next, we address categorical moderators within a multiple regression framework. Before doing so, it is useful to consider how the analyses we have described to this point fit within this general multiple regression framework.

The Empty Model. By empty model, we are referring to a model that includes only an intercept (a constant value of 1 for all cases) as a predictor. A weighted regression of effect sizes predicted only by a constant is often useful for an initial analysis of the mean effect size and to evaluate heterogeneity of these effect sizes across studies. The following equation accomplishes this:

$$ES_i = B_O(1) + e_i. \quad (20)$$

In this empty model, the intercept regression coefficient is the mean effect size, and the sum of squares of the residual is the heterogeneity.

Use of Dummy Variables to Analyze Categorical Moderators. To evaluate the categorical moderators in this meta-regression framework, dummy variables can be used to represent group membership. Here, we select a reference group to which we would assign the value 0 for all the dummy codes for studies using that particular reference group, and each dummy variable represents the difference of another group relative to this reference group. The effect size is regressed onto the dummy variables, weighted by the inverse variance weight w, with the following equation:

$$ES_i = B_O + B_1(DV1) + B_2(DV2) + B_3(DV3) + e_i. \quad (21)$$

The results of this regression are interpreted as above. The $Q_{Regression}$ is equivalent to the $Q_{Between}$ of the ANOVA framework and is used to determine whether there is categorical moderation. To identify the particular groups that differ from the reference group, the regression coefficients for the dummy variables are considered. Again, the standard errors of these coefficients are inaccurate and need to be adjusted as described above.

Multiple Moderators. A multiple regression framework can also be used to evaluate multiple categorical and/or continuous predictors in meta-analysis. Here, it is likely of interest to consider both the overall regression model ($Q_{Regression}$) as well as the results of particular predictors. The former is evaluated by interpreting the model sum of squares as a

χ^2 distribution with df = number of predictors − 1. The latter is evaluated by dividing the regression coefficients by their adjusted standard errors.

Limitations to Interpretation of Moderators

Clearly, moderation analyses can enhance the conclusions drawn from meta-analysis, but there are some limitations that need also be considered. The first consideration is that of multicolinearity in meta-analytic moderator analyses. It is likely that some moderator variables will be correlated, but this can be assessed by regressing each moderator onto the set of other moderators using the weights you used in the moderator analyses. The second limitation is the possibility that uncoded variables are confounding the association and moderation of the variables that are coded. The best approach to avoid confounding variables is to code as many variables as possible. Finally, it will be important to feel confident that the literature included in your synthesis adequately covers the range of potential moderator values. This can best be analyzed by plotting the included studies at the various levels of the moderator.

Advanced Topics

Given the existence of meta-analytic techniques over several decades, and their widespread use during this time, it is not surprising that there exists a rich literature on meta-analytic techniques. Although space has precluded us from discussing all of these topics, we next briefly describe a few of the more advanced topics important in this field.

Alternative Effect Sizes

The three effect sizes described in this chapter (i.e., r, g, and o) quantify two-variable associations and are the most commonly used effect sizes for meta-analysis. However, there exist many other possibilities that might be considered.

Single Variable Effect Sizes. In some cases, it may be valuable to meta-analytically combine and/or compare information about single variables rather than two-variable associations. Central tendency can be indexed by the mean for continuous data or by the proportion for dichotomous variables; both of these effect sizes can be used in meta-analyses (*see* Lipsey & Wilson, 2001). It is also possible to use standard deviations or variances as effect sizes for meta-analysis to draw conclusions about interindividual differences. Meta-analytic combination of means and variances require that the same measure, or else different measures on the same scale, be used for all studies.

Meaningful Metric. The effect sizes we have described are all in some standardized metric. However, there may be instances when the scales of variables comprising the effect size are meaningful, and therefore it is useful to use unstandardized effect sizes. Meta-analysis of such effect sizes were described in a special section of the journal *Psychological Methods* (*see* Becker, 2003).

Multivariate Effect Sizes. Many research questions go beyond two-variable associations to consider multivariate effect sizes, such as whether X uniquely predicts Y above and beyond Z. It is statistically possible to meta-analytically combine and compare multivariate effects sizes, such as regression coefficients or partial/semipartial correlation to address the example associations among X, Y, and Z. However, it is typically not possible in practice to use multivariate effect sizes for meta-analyses. The primary reason is that their use would require that the same multivariate analyses are performed and reported across studies in the meta-analysis. For example, it would be necessary for all studies included to report the regression of Y on X controlling for Z; studies that failed to control for Z, that instead controlled for W, or that controlled for both Z and W could not be included. A more tractable alternative to the meta-analysis of multivariate effect sizes is to perform multivariate meta-analysis of bivariate effect sizes, which we briefly describe below.

Artifact Corrections

Artifacts are study imperfections that lead to biases—typically underestimations—of effect sizes. For example, it is well known that unreliability of a measure attenuates (i.e., reduces) the magnitude of observed associations that this variable has with others relative to what would have been found with a perfectly measured variable. In addition to measurement unreliability, other artifacts include imperfect validity of measures, artificial dichotomization of continuous variables, and range restriction of the sample on a variable included in the effect size (direct range restriction) or another variable closely related to a variable in the effect size (indirect range restriction).

The general approach to correcting for artifacts is to compute a correction factor for each artifact using one of a variety of equations (*see* Hunter & Schmidt, 2004). For example, one of the more straightforward corrections is for unreliability of a measure of X

(where r_{xx} is the reliability of X):

$$a_{unreliability} = \sqrt{r_{xx}}. \quad (22)$$

Each of the artifact corrections may yield a correction factor, which are then multiplied together to yield an overall artifact multiplier (a). This artifact multiplier is then used to estimate an adjusted effect size from the observed effect size to index what the effect size would likely have been if the artifacts (study imperfections) had not existed:

$$ES_{adjusted} = \frac{ES_{observed}}{a}. \quad (23)$$

This estimation of artifact-free effect sizes from observed effect sizes is unbiased (i.e., it will not consistently over- or underestimate the true effect size), but it is also not entirely precise. In other words, the artifact correction introduces additional uncertainty in the effect size estimate that must be considered in the meta-analysis. Specifically, the standard error of the effect size, which can be thought of as representing imprecision in the estimate of the effect size, is also adjusted by this artifact multiplier to account for this additional uncertainty introduced by artifact correction:

$$SE_{adjusted} = \frac{SE_{observed}}{a}. \quad (24)$$

Multivariate Meta-Analysis

Multivariate meta-analysis is a relatively new and underdeveloped approach, but one that has great potential for use. Because the approach is fairly complex, and there is not general agreement on what techniques are best in different situations, we describe this approach in fairly general terms, referring interested readers to Becker (2009) or Cheung and Chan (2005).

The key idea of multivariate meta-analysis is to meta-analytically combine multiple bivariate effect sizes, which are then used as sufficient statistics for multivariate analyses. For example, to fit a model in which variable X is regressed on variables Y and Z, you would perform three meta-analyses of the three correlations (r_{XY}, r_{XZ}, and r_{YZ}), and this matrix of meta-analytically combined correlations would then be used to estimate the multiple regression parameters.

Although the logic of this approach is reasonably simple, the application is much more complex. Challenges include how one handles the likely possibility that different studies provide different effect sizes, what the effective sample size is for the multivariate model when different studies inform different correlations, how (or even whether) to test for and potentially model between-study heterogeneity, and how to perform moderator analyses. Answers to these challenges have not been entirely agreed upon even by quantitative experts, making it difficult for those wishing to apply these models to answer substantive research questions. However, these models offer an extremely valuable potential for extending meta-analytic techniques to answer richer research questions than two-variable associations that are the typical focus of meta-analyses.

Conclusion

Although we have been able to provide only a brief overview of meta-analysis in this chapter, we hope that the opportunities of this methodology are clear. Given the overwhelming and increasing quantity of empirical research in most fields, techniques for best synthesizing the existing research are a critical tool in advancing our understanding.

References

Becker, B. J. (2003). Introduction to the special section on metric in meta-analysis. *Psychological Methods, 8*, 403–405.

Becker, B. J. (2009). Model-based meta-analysis. In H. Cooper, L. V. Hedges, & J. C. Valentine (Eds.), *The handbook of research synthesis and meta-analysis* (2nd ed.) (pp. 377–395). New York: Russell Sage Foundation

Card, N. A. (2012). *Meta-analysis: Quantitative synthesis of social science research*. New York: Guilford.

Card, N. A., Stucky, B. D., Sawalani, G. M., & Little, T. D. (2008). Direct and indirect aggression during childhood and adolescence: A meta-analytic review of gender differences, intercorrelations, and relations to maladjustment. *Child Development, 79*, 1185–1229.

Chalmers, I., Hedges, L. V., & Cooper, H. (2002). A brief history of research synthesis. *Evaluation and Health Professions, 25*, 12–37.

Cheung, M. W. L., & Chan, W. (2005). Meta-analytic structural equation modeling: A two-stage approach. *Psychological Methods, 10*, 40–64.

Cochran, W. G. (1937). Problems arising in the analysis of a series of similar experiments. *Journal of the Royal Statistical Society, 4*(Suppl.), 102–118.

Cooper, H. M. (1988). Organizing knowledge syntheses: A taxonomy of literature reviews. *Knowledge in Society, 1*, 104–126.

Cooper, H. M., & Hedges, L. V. (2009). Research synthesis as a scientificprocess. In H. Cooper, L. V. Hedges, & J. C. Valentine (Eds.), *The handbook of research synthesis and meta-analysis* (2nd ed.) (pp. 3–16). New York: Russell Sage Foundation.

Eysenck, H. J. (1978). An exercise in mega-silliness. *American Psychologist, 33*, 517.

Fleiss, J. H. (1994). Measures of effect size for categorical data. In H. Cooper & L. V. Hedges (Eds.), *The handbook of research synthesis* (pp. 245–260). New York: Russell Sage Foundation.

Glass, G. V. (1976). The critical state of the critical review article. *Quarterly Review of Biology*, 50th Anniversary Special Issue (1926–1976), 415–418.

Glass, G. V., McGraw, B., & Smith, M. L. (1981). *Meta-analysis in social research*. Thousand Oaks, CA: Sage.

Glass, G. V. & Smith, M. (1979). Meta-analysis of the relationship between class size and achievement. *Educational Evaluation and Policy Analysis, 1,* 2–16.

Hedges, L. V. (1987). How hard is hard science, how soft is soft science? The empirical cumulativeness of research. *American Psychologist, 42,* 443–455.

Hedges, L. V. (1992). Meta-analysis. *Journal of Educational Statistics, 17,* 279–296.

Hedges, L. V., & Olkin, I. (1985). *Statistical methods for meta-analysis*. San Diego, CA: Academic Press.

Hedges, L. V. & Pigott, T. D. (2004). The power of statistical tests for moderators in meta analysis. *Psychological Methods, 9.* 426–445.

Hedges, L. V., & Vevea, J. L. (1998). Fixed- and random-effects models in meta-analysis. *Psychological Methods, 3,* 486–504.

Hunt, M. (1997). *How science takes stock: The story of meta-analysis*. New York: Russell Sage Foundation.

Hunter, J. E., & Schmidt, F. L. (2004). *Methods of meta-analysis: Correcting error and bias in research findings* (2nd ed.). Thousand Oaks, CA: Sage.

Hunter, J. E., Schmidt, F. L., & Hunter, R. (1979). Differential validity of employment tests by race: A comprehensive review and analysis. *Psychological Bulletin, 86,* 721–735.

Hunter, J. E., Schmidt, F. L., & Jackson, G. B. (1982*). Meta-analysis: Cumulating research findings across studies*. Beverly Hills, CA: Sage.

Lipsey, M. W., & Wilson, D. B. (2001). *Practical meta-analysis*. Thousand Oaks, CA: Sage.

Maxwell, S. E. (2004). The persistence of underpowered studies in psychological research: Causes, consequences, and remedies. *Psychological Methods, 9,* 147–163.

Olkin, (1990). History and goals. In K. W. Wachter & M. L. Straf (Eds.), *The future of meta analysis* (pp. 3–10). New York: Russell Sage Foundation.

Pearsons, K. (1904). Report on certain enteric fever inoculation statistics. *British Medical Journal, 3,* 1243–1246.

Rosenthal, R. (1979). The "file drawer problem" and tolerance for null results. *Psychological Bulletin, 86,* 638–641.

Rosenthal, R. (1984). *Meta-analytic procedures for social research*. Beverly Hills, CA: Sage.

Rosenthal, R. (1991). *Meta-analytic procedures for social research* (revised edition). Newbury Park, CA: Sage.

Rosenthal, R., Rosnow, R. L., & Rubin, D. B. (2000). *Contrasts and effect sizes in behavioral research: A correlational approach*. New York: Cambridge University Press.

Rosenthal, R. & Rubin, D. (1978). Interpersonal expectancy effects: The first 345 studies. *Behavioral and Brain Sciences, 3,* 377–415.

Rothstein, H. R., Sutton, A. J., & Borenstein, M. (Eds.) (2005). *Publication bias in meta analysis: Prevention, assessment and adjustments*. Hoboken, NJ: Wiley.

Schmidt, F. L. (1992). What do data really mean? Research findings, meta-analysis, and cumulative knowledge in psychology. *American Psychologist, 47,* 1173–1181.

Schmidt, F. L., & Hunter, J. E. (1977). Development of a general solution to the problem of validity generalization. *Journal of Applied Psychology, 62,* 529–540.

Smith, M. L. & Glass, G. V. (1977). Meta-analysis of psychotherapy outcome studies. *American Psychologist, 32,* 752–760.

White, H. D. (2009). Scientific communication and literature retrieval. In H. Cooper, L. V. Hedges, & J. C. Valentine (Eds.), *The handbook of research synthesis and meta-analysis* (2nd ed.) (pp. 51–71). New York: Russell Sage Foundation.

Wilkinson, L., & The Task Force on Statistical Significance (1999). Statistical methods in psychology journals: Guidelines and explanations. *American Psychologist, 54,* 594–604.

CHAPTER 31

Common Fallacies in Quantitative Research Methodology

Lihshing Leigh Wang, Amber S. Watts, Rawni A. Anderson, *and* Todd D. Little

Abstract

Since the inception of scientific revolutions, quantitative research methodology has dominated the research literatures in many disciplines. Despite its long tradition in evidence-based research and practice, many fallacies and misconceptions continue to infiltrate the ways quantitative researchers conceive, collect, analyze, and interpret data. This chapter outlines 16 common fallacies and examines in depth 6 of those that are most consequential and prevalent in published quantitative research. The six major fallacies include Contextual Variable Fallacies, Measurement Error Fallacies, Missing Data Fallacies, Significance Testing Fallacies, Statistical Power Fallacies, and Factor Analysis Fallacies. These fallacies span the entire quantitative research process—from research design, sampling, and instrumentation to statistical analysis and interpretation. By drawing implications from recent advances in quantitative methodological research, this chapter examines the theoretical frameworks of those fallacies, traces their origins and developments in applied research, and provides recommendations to address the challenge of alternative solutions. We conclude with a checklist for quantitative researchers to guard against committing those and other common fallacies. Directions for future research in advancing quantitative methodology and recommendations for strategies to correct fallacious practices are also discussed.

Key Words: Quantitative research methodology, contextual variable, measurement error, missing data, significance testing, statistical power, factor analysis

Introduction

Quantitative research methodology in the educational, social, and behavioral sciences is characterized by the epistemological paradigm of classical and logical positivism, measurement of human attributes or social phenomena, and statistic analysis of quantitative data (Klee, 1999; Michell, 1997; Yu, 2006). With its appeal to drawing probabilistic inferences about the population beyond the sample at hand, quantitative methods provide powerful tools for establishing truths about the objective reality at an estimated level of precision and with a specified level of confidence. In the era of evidence-based research and practice, quantitative methods continue to permeate the scientific literatures across disciplinary boundaries, including medicine, psychology, education, and business (e.g., Donaldson, Christie, & Mark, 2009; Slavin, 2002).

During the past few decades, quantitative methods have undergone many scientific breakthroughs, including propensity score matching (Guo & Fraser, 2010; Steiner, Cook, & Shadish, 2011), power analysis (Maxwell, Kelley, & Rausch, 2008; Murphy, Myors, & Wolach, 2009), latent trait scaling (Nering & Ostini, 2010; Reckase, 2009; van der

Linden & Hambleton, 1997), missing data analysis (Enders, 2010; Baraldi & Enders, Chapter 27, this volume), structural equation modeling (Brown, Chapter 13, this volume; Kline, 2010; McArdle & Kadlec, Chapter 15, this volume), multilevel modeling (Hox, Chapter 14, this volume; Raudenbush & Bryk, 2002), longitudinal and contextual modeling (Little, Bovaird, & Card, 2007; Little, Schnabel & Baumert, 2000; Wu, Selig, & Little, Chapter 18, this volume), mixture modeling (Hancock & Samuelsen, 2008; Maysn, Chapter 25, this volume), and meta-analysis (Card & Casper, Chapter 30, this volume). Even the long-standing tradition of Null Hypothesis Significance Testing (NHST) has undergone a paradigmatic shift (Fidler & Cumming, 2008; Harlow, Mulaik, & Steiger, 1997; Thompson, Chapter 2, this volume), resulting in new reporting standards that require or recommend effect sizes, confidence intervals (CIs), and power estimation (e.g., AERA, 2006; APA, 2010b).

Alarmingly, surveys of doctoral methodology curricula in psychology (Aiken, West, & Millsap, 2008) and education (Leech & Goodwin, 2008) have shown a decline or stagnation in the breadth and depth of quantitative training in North America. As a direct result of the lack of rigorous quantitative course work, many fallacies and misconceptions continue to infiltrate the ways quantitative researchers conceive, collect, and analyze data (Andersen, 1990; Henson, Hull, & Williams, 2010; Huck, 2009; Good & Hardin, 2003; Lance & Vandenberg, 2009). Misapplication of quantitative methods is all the more dangerous than nonapplication because they create an illusion of scientific certainty and a false sense of objectivity (Berger & Berry, 1988). Bad science in its best disguise can bring more damage than good to evidence-based research, practice, and policy.

The purpose of this chapter is to (1) compile a comprehensive checklist of common fallacies in quantitative research methodology, (2) highlight some of the major fallacies in published research, and (3) provide recommendations for alternative solutions to persistent misguided thinking and practice. The six major fallacies include Contextual Variable Fallacies, Measurement Error Fallacies, Missing Data Fallacies, Significance Testing Fallacies, Statistical Power Fallacies, and Factor Analysis Fallacies. For further treatment of these and other topics that are not included here as major fallacies, we include additional readings (e.g., Dedrick et al., 2009; McDonald & Ho, 2002). The scope of the major fallacies spans the entire spectrum of the research process, from research design and data collection to data analysis (Black, 1999; Panter & Sterba, 2011). These fallacies also exist in a diverse array of disciplines involving human research, from neuroscience (Wang, 2009) and ophthalmology (Smith, 2008) to marketing (Zuccaro, 2010). This broad perspective helps to debunk the common misconceptions that quantitative methods are concerned exclusively with statistics and that researchers should be trained solely within their disciplinary boundaries.

We have included misconceptions, pitfalls, myths, and controversies under the general term of "fallacies" to emphasize the tendency to fall prey to the faulty logic underlying them. Wherever possible, evidence of the existence and persistence of each fallacy is provided by citing studies that have either committed the fallacy or have examined the prevalence of the fallacy. We have chosen fallacies that are likely to be committed by even seasoned researchers. Readers who are interested in a more elementary treatment of common misconceptions among novice researchers are referred to Huck's *Statistical Misconceptions* (2009). Independently, we have chosen three major fallacies—contextual variable fallacies, missing data fallacies, and factor analysis fallacies—that are also included in Lance and Vandenberg's (2009) *Statistical and Methodological Myths and Urban Legends*. This partial overlap lends support to the commonness of these fallacies. In contrast to Lance and Vandenberg's edited volume, our exclusive quantitative lens and comprehensive coverage make this chapter an ideal reference for quantitative researchers and methodologists alike.

We believe that using sound methodology in a research endeavor is not only an intellectual pursuit but also an ethical imperative (Evans, 1997). As Osborne (2008a) elegantly put it, researchers are "romantic fools" who believe in the magic of knowledge creation and "intrepid explorers" who go where no other human has gone before (p. ix). The challenge to identify and apply "the best practices" in quantitative research may sometimes seem insurmountable because of the intricacies embedded in the perplexing arrays of mathematical symbols and statistical formulas. Without recognizing the "unfounded lore" that permeates the literatures, quantitative researchers will continue to live in their fantasy world of "statistical and methodological myths and urban legends" (Lance & Vandenberg, 2009, p. xv). As Huck (2009) contends, we need to "undo" (p. xiii) the misconceptions so deeply ingrained in our human intuition and research training (p. xv). Without this conscientious effort, much of our research literatures will continue to be infiltrated with unsubstantiated findings and pseudo-science myths.

Contextual Variable Fallacies

Social and behavioral science researchers are fundamentally concerned about measurable processes involving contextual variables that may underlie the relation between a predictor variable and an outcome variable. Attention to causal mechanisms and processes by which biopsychosocial or other factors influence behavior is increasing with the maturity of social science disciplines and statistical analytic methods and computation. Questions that ask *how*, *when*, *for whom*, *which*, and *under what conditions* require investigations of possible contextual or so-called "third" variables that may explicate the relation between a predictor and outcome (Little, Bovaird, & Card, 2007; MacKinnon & Luecken, 2008). Such detailed examination of relations between variables can be categorized by three distinct contextual variable functions: mediation, moderation, and hierarchical influences. We address some of the fallacies related to contextual influences from *mediating variables*, *moderating variables*, and *nested variables*.

Fallacy 1: Mistaking Mediation for Moderation and Vice Versa

Despite the frequent occurrence of mediation and moderation hypotheses in published articles, as well as numerous useful discussions of these effects and the distinctions between them (e.g., Baron & Kenny, 1986; Holmbeck, 1997; Wu & Zumbo, 2008), a lack of terminological, conceptual, and statistical clarity in the study of contextual variable functions largely characterizes the social and behavioral science literature. Demonstrating cause-and-effect relationships has long been the pursuit of scholars in fields of evidence-based scientific research. Relations among variables, or constructs, however, are very often more complex than simple bivariate associations between a predictor and criterion; rather, relations are frequently informed and/or influenced by third variables. Baron and Kenny's (1986) landmark article helped distinguish "two often-confused functions of third variables" and presented a systematized statistical approach to investigating mediation and moderation. Since then, examples of hypotheses and models involving third variables in social and psychological literatures abound. Notwithstanding several subsequent presentations clarifying mediated and moderated effects (e.g., Frazier, Tix, & Barron, 2004; Holmbeck, 1997; MacKinnon & Luecken, 2008; Rose, Holmbeck, Coakley, & Franks, 2004; Wu & Zumbo, 2008), there continue to be inconsistencies in the use of the terms as well as confusion with respect to the meaning of and differences between them.

A mediator is a third variable that accounts for some or all of the relation between a predictor and an outcome. The nature of the mediated relationship is such that a predictor variable (X) has a causal influence on a third variable, called a mediator (M), which in turn has a causal influence on an outcome (Y; Baron & Kenny, 1986). In other words, mediating variables transmit the effect of one variable to another. By hypothesizing mediational models, researchers seek to understand the mechanisms directly influencing behavior and the chains of influence through which those mechanisms affect some criterion.

A moderator is a third variable that qualifies the association between a predictor and an outcome. *Moderation* refers to the case in which the nature of the influence of a predictor variable on an outcome varies as a function of the level or value of a third variable—this third variable is called a moderator. A moderator specifies the conditions under which a hypothesized effect occurs, as well as the conditions under which the direction and/or strength of the effect vary (Holmbeck, 1997). By analyzing moderators, researchers seek to understand ways in which some variables strengthen, attenuate, or qualitatively alter the influences of others.

Mediation and moderation are distinct, competing theories about the mechanism through which a third variable operates to influence cause and effect. Third variables are often hypothesized to function either as a mediator or a moderator to elucidate a causal relationship. Baron and Kenny's (1986) seminal article introduced a theoretical foundation to explain the distinction between mediation and moderation.

The process of articulating causal hypotheses linking constructs is instrumental to the accumulation of social and behavioral scientific knowledge. Questions about mechanisms or processes underlying the relation between antecedents and their consequences appeal to the concept of mediation. Mediation implies a causal chain of relations wherein the predictor (X) is causally antecedent

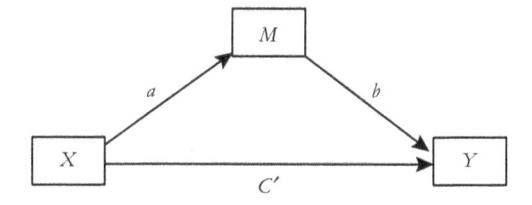

Figure 31.1 Simple mediation model with one predictor (X), one criterion (Y), and one mediator (M).

to the mediator (M), which in turn is causally antecedent to the outcome (Y). The most basic mediation model one can test takes the form in Figure 31.1. Many such models can be hypothesized by linking variables together in a sequence of causal associations.

Despite other sources on the topic—most notably James and Brett (1984), published earlier, and several more recent considerations (e.g., Hayes, 2009; MacKinnon, Lockwood, Hoffman, West, & Sheets, 2002)—the Baron and Kenny (1986) approach to testing mediation dominates the literature addressing mediated effects. Indeed, theirs is the most cited article published in the *Journal of Social and Personality Psychology* (Quinones-Vidal, Lopez-García, Penaranda-Ortega, & Tortosa-Gil, 2004); according to the *Social Science Citation Index*, Baron and Kenny (1986) had been referenced 14,407 times as of November 10, 2010.

Kenny (2008) conjectures two qualities of the 1986 paper that may inform its popularity and the widespread adoption of methods proposed within: (1) it provides clear definitions of terms, and (2) it offers clear and explicit guidelines for conducting mediational analyses. However, the causal steps approach has been soundly criticized on multiple grounds. Logical flaws have been established in the technical literature; however, a perusal of the broader social and behavioral science literature suggests that conventional wisdom and more recent developments on the topic have been ignored by many applied researchers, resulting in misconceptions about the quantification of indirect effects and the necessary conditions for establishing their presence among and across various disciplines.

of partial association and differences between groups or experimental conditions by quantifying these effects (r^2, t) and testing hypotheses about or constructing CI estimates for their size (Hayes, Preacher, & Myers, 2009). Accordingly, Hayes (2009) has asked: "Given that an indirect effect is quantified as the product of its constituent paths, should we not base inferences about indirect effects on tests of the product?"

The causal steps approach does not rely on any estimate of the indirect effect; rather, it tests the constituent paths respectively. As such, this approach does not facilitate conclusions regarding effect size, and it does not allow for the construction of a CI for the indirect effect to acknowledge the uncertainty in the estimation process. More important, however, the causal steps approach requires the investigator to think in categorical terms about each step in the model. Hypothesis tests are fallible. Each carries with it a possibility of decision error. If any of the conditions required to infer mediation according to the causal steps approach are not met, then a researcher is left with little to no information regarding the process studied—the only conclusion to be made is that the effect does not exist. There is nothing inherently wrong with this, if the causal steps approach yields the correct conclusion given the data available. Unfortunately, according to simulation studies (Fritz & MacKinnon, 2007; MacKinnon, Lockwood, Hoffman, West, & Sheets, 2002), the causal steps approach lacks statistical power (i.e., high Type II error rate); among methods for testing mediational hypotheses, if the influence of X on Y is carried—at least in part—indirectly through M, then the causal steps approach is least likely to detect the effect (Hayes, Preacher, & Myers, 2009).

The high Type II error rate observed for the causal steps approach to testing mediation reflects the requirement that the predictor (X) be significantly associated with the outcome (Y) before controlling for the mediator (M; Dearing & Hamilton, 2006). This requirement is another source of criticisms and misconception pointed out by Baron and Kenny (1986), which we now turn to in Fallacy 3 below.

Fallacy 2: Mediation is Tested With the Constituent Paths Rather Than the Product of the Paths

Social and behavioral scientists traditionally base claims, or inference, on tests of quantities pertinent to those claims. For example, they infer the existence

Fallacy 3: Presence of Direct Effect Should be Tested as Prerequisite Evidence of Mediation

Although mediational models are pervasive in applied research, a debate exists concerning the requisite statistical evidence for making inferences about mediation. Specifically, controversy surrounds the precondition for tests of mediation that the antecedent must demonstrate a significant total association with a criterion when considered alone (e.g., $X \rightarrow Y$; see Baron & Kenny, 1986; Preacher & Hayes, 2008). It seems intuitive that, without an effect to be mediated, there is no purpose in further evaluating the possibility of an indirect effect of X on Y through one or more intervening variables; however, this intuition is wrong. Investigators should not condition their search for indirect effects on a significant total effect, because it is possible for X to indirectly affect Y in the absence of evidence of an association between X and Y. Indeed, the literature contains examples of significant effects of predictor on mediator and of mediator on outcome variables, with no significant simple association between the predictor and outcome (e.g., inconsistent mediation; MacKinnon, Krull, & Lockwood, 2000). Two explanations why mediation may be found in the absence of a statistically significant total effect of X on Y—suppression and dilution—must be considered (Shrout & Bolger, 2002).

The most commonly used method for testing mediational hypotheses (i.e., causal steps approach) assumes consistent mediation, thus precluding identification of suppression or inconsistent mediation, in which the direct and indirect (i.e., mediated) effects of a predictor on an outcome have opposite signs (see MacKinnon et al., 2000). Situations in which direct and indirect effects demonstrate fairly similar magnitudes and opposite signs result in a non-zero but nonsignificant total relationship.

A lack of relationship between X and Y may also occur when Y is distal from X. The magnitude of the direct effect may be moderate or large when the causal process is temporally proximal; however, the effect often becomes diluted as the proposed causal chain takes longer to unfold when there are multiple intervening variables between the antecedent and consequent. The requirement that the predictor be significantly associated with the outcome before controlling for the mediator is unrealistic for developmental processes—for example, where distal influences demonstrate subtle effects over time if more proximal mediators are not considered (Shrout & Bolger, 2002).

Among the earliest contributors to the topic of mediation, Judd and Kenny (1981, p. 207) acknowledged the possibility of mediation in the absence of a significant association between predictor and outcome variables; however, this possibility simply is not considered in most applications of mediational analyses, especially those adhering to the causal steps approach. We emphasize that this approach is a common fallacious practice.

Fallacy 4: Cross-Sectional Models Can Be Used to Test Mediation

Questions about mediation are ultimately inquiries of causality. Meditational designs implicitly depict a causal $X \rightarrow M \rightarrow Y$ chain of relations. Substantial development regarding statistical tests of mediated relationships has been observed in the past few decades; far less attention has been devoted to conditions for strong causal inference in such designs. Although Baron and Kenny (1986) have explicitly stated the causal assumptions underlying mediational analyses, most published studies do not acknowledge these assumptions; "all too often persons conducting mediatio[n] either do not realize that they are conducting causal analyses or they fail to justify the assumptions that they have made in their causal model" (Kenny, 2008, p. 4). Importantly, if the mediational model is misspecified, then results from mediational analyses are misleading.

Fundamentally, mediational hypotheses hinge on the validity of the assertion that the $X \rightarrow M \rightarrow Y$ relations unfold in that sequence. As with structural equation modeling (SEM) techniques, multiple qualitatively different models can be fit equally well to the same covariance matrix (Mathieu & Taylor, 2006); no statistical test can equivocally differentiate one causal sequence from another. Analyses can be used to support tentative inferences about mediation; statistical evidence enables inferences regarding the extent to which study results are consistent with the assumed mediation model. Thus, statistical evidence alone provides a necessary but insufficient basis for inferring causal associations. Like Mathieu and Taylor (2006), we submit that *"inferences of mediation are founded first and foremost in terms of theory, research design, and the construct validity of measures employed, and second in terms of statistical evidence of relationships"* (p. 1032). The most valuable bases from which to advance inferences concerning mediational hypotheses include strong theory, experimental design features, and establishment of temporal precedence.

Despite appeals for longitudinal approaches to testing indirect causal effects (e.g., mediation; e.g., Cole & Maxwell, 2003; Gollob & Reichardt, 1985,

1987), the modal methodology for studying such processes continues to be cross-sectional (Maxwell & Cole, 2007). Maxwell and Cole (2007) searched the literature and identified the five APA journals most likely to have published studies evaluating mediational hypotheses. In 2005, the five identified journals published 68 articles containing 72 total studies that described tests of mediation in their titles or abstracts. Of these, 28 (39%) were based on cross-sectional designs, and 10 (14%) ignored or misused a longitudinal data structure (e.g., by averaging effects across multiple waves of data). These studies ($n = 38$; 53%) applied methods that did not allow time for their predictors to exert influence on the outcomes of interest. An additional 27 (38%) longitudinal studies applied "half-longitudinal designs" to mediational analyses, in which time elapsed either between the measurements of X and M or between M and Y, but not both (Cole & Maxwell, 2003). Among the remaining seven studies, only one controlled for prior levels of M when testing the association of X at time 1 and M at time 2, and prior levels of Y when testing the association between M at time 2 and Y at time 3. Unfortunately, cross-sectional models of mediation represent the norm in premier journals spanning diverse psychological disciplines.

Cross-sectional data describe relationships among variables at a single point in time. Such data do not provide information about how values of variables are related to prior values of the same or other variables, and they do not indicate the length of the causal interval of study. Omission of this information can result in severely biased estimates of the size of casual effects, such as mediation. This conclusion is derived from three principles defined by Gollob and Reichardt (1987) describing causal effects and causal intervals (i.e., time lags).

First, causes *always* take time to exert their effects—even when the time lag is extremely brief, as in apparent simultaneity of cause and effect. Values of a variable for a given case can be informed only by values of antecedent variables. Second, values of a variable for a given case can be informed by prior values of the same variable for that case (i.e., a variable can have an effect on itself). Such effects are called autoregressive effects. A model that omits an autoregressive effect assumes that the effect of prior values of a variable on itself is zero. Third, differing lengths of time lag typically suggest different effect sizes. It follows that interpretation and practical significance of an effect size depend on knowledge of the time lag. Consider the implications of a 1-unit increase in maternal IQ at time 1 predicting a 0.23-unit increase in child IQ at time 2, given varying time lags (e.g., 1 month, 1 year, 3 years; Gollob & Reichardt, 1987). The probable importance of the effect size clearly differs, and considerably, as a function of the length of time between the cause (maternal IQ) and the time for which its effect (child IQ) is assessed. Accordingly, many different time lags must be studied to achieve complete understanding of a variable's effects. The three principles regarding causal effects and intervals are seemingly intuitive; however, each of them is ignored when cross-sectional data are analyzed.

Available procedures for evaluating indirect effects—including both cross-sectional and longitudinal methods—differ in the extent to which they simply test whether the data are consistent with a hypothesized intervening variable model (e.g., as in the case of cross-sectional mediation) or establish other logical features that support causal inference. Assumptions of the correct specification of causal ordering and causal direction are especially important when cross-sectional data are analyzed but are very difficult to defend. Additionally, the assumption that both the effect of the predictor on the mediator and, in turn, the effect of the mediator on the outcome have occurred prior to the single time-point at which these variables are observed is of particular consequence. For example, in cases in which the predictor is distal to the outcome, cross-sectional data will not detect the direct effect. Failure to account for the time lag required for each antecedent variable to exert its effect on its consequent may inform inconsistent findings in some areas of research. For example, very many studies of childhood overweight assess self-esteem as a theoretical consequent of body composition (the results of which are inconsistent) and evaluate potential mechanisms of this hypothesized effect. Reviews of the literature suggest that longitudinal studies are generally likely to observe the predictor-outcome relation, whereas results of cross-sectional analyses are more varied (French, Story, & Perry, 1995; Miller & Downey, 1999; Strauss, 2000). Variability in the presence of the direct effect across single time-point studies may likely be a function of the ages of the children studied, such that the effect is significant among samples of older children for whom adequate time has elapsed for body weight to exert its influence on self-esteem. Clearly, study results are informed by the causal interval of the hypothesized effect(s), and this fact is not limited to the analysis of cross-sectional data or to the study of indirect effects. For a more complete discussion of time or lag moderated effects, *see* Selig (2010).

Causal theories, including those of mediation, cannot be definitively supported empirically unless the conditions of causality have been established by good research design (Hayes, Preacher, & Myers, 2009). In many studies in the published literature that include tests of mediation, the correct temporal sequencing of cause and effect cannot be established except through theoretical or logical argument. "[I]n the absence of a research design that affords a causal conclusion, confidence in one's causal inferences must necessarily be tempered" (Hayes, Preacher, & Myers, 2009). Specifically, confidence in the causal sequence of variables in a particular model depends on the extent to which the research is grounded in strong theory, utilizes true or quasi-experimental designs, and assesses variables over time in the proper sequence and intervals.

Fallacy 5: Moderation Is Confused With Additive Effects of a Multiple Regression Equation

Moderation addresses the "it depends" answers that can arise. For example, the question, "What is the relation between agency for ability and school performance?" is answered with, "It depends! It depends on whether you are a female or a male, as the strength of the relationship is different for males and females." Researchers often confuse, however, questions of multivariate prediction and the additive effects of multiple predictors with a true expectation of moderation. When the question is about one's standing on an outcome variable, it generally will be related to an answer relating to one's profile standing on a set of predictors. For example, math performance in school depends on one's standing on a set of important predictors of math performance, including ability, motivation, past performance, and gender. This type of question and answer is not a question of moderation. A moderator reflects the context that will change the ability of one variable to predict another. Additive effects are the set of variables that all uniquely contribute to determining one's level or standing on an outcome variable. Non-additive effects, on the other hand, inform us how interactions between the main predictor of interest and the auxiliary predictors that moderate the main predictor function together to exert impact on the criterion variable (Ho, 2008; Wiedemann, Lippke, Reuter, Ziegelmann, & Schwarzer, 2011).

Fallacy 6: Hierarchically Nested Data Structures Can Be Ignored or Should Be Avoided

In the edu-psycho-social sciences, data structures that yield interdependencies are common. In fact, the standard assumption in statistics—that observations are independent—is more likely to be the exception rather than the rule for most data collection activities—particularly in quasi-experimental studies. Examples of dependent data structures include repeated observations of individuals (e.g., repeated measures experiment or a long-term longitudinal investigation), measurements of individuals who are nested in similar context (e.g., students nested in classrooms, respondents nested in neighborhoods), assessments of couples (e.g., mutual best friends, romantic partners, twins), and collecting data on families or larger social networks—all of these data structures contain interdependent observations. That is, the information from one level (e.g., classroom climate) impacts or influences the information contained at another level (e.g., student performance).

Dependencies in the data will bias the results of an analysis if not properly modeled or controlled. Until recently, most applied researchers attempted to "remedy" this issue in one of two ways. They ignored the dependency and treated the observations as independent and suffered the consequences of invalid effect size estimates as well as inappropriate tests of significance. Fearful of such bad outcomes, the other alternative approach was to manipulate the collected data in an effort to eliminate the source of the dependency (e.g., analyze only one friends' data, average across units, etc.). Such attempts to "fix" the dependency problems are less than satisfying: Critical assumptions are knowingly ignored, or data is either removed or collapsed under dubious assumptions in an effort to conform to the independence requirement of standard statistical models. The reasons for these approaches to handling dependent data are not obvious. Perhaps because the growth in the nature of statistical models that can readily accommodate and even model the dependency in the data has been slow, researchers are also slow to adopt these methods for appropriately handling the dependency. Perhaps because the educational opportunities to master the available techniques are not sufficient, researchers do not know better. Regardless of the past reasons for attempting the suboptimal fixes, modern statistical estimation procedures that make these "fixes" are not only unnecessary but, in fact, unwarranted. Modern tools are now widely accessible and sufficiently user-friendly to be adopted readily by researchers. As a result, the dependency in data structures becomes a source of information that represents the context of the research project. When treated properly, the context becomes a key variable in the statistical model that can and should be included.

Modern statistical estimation procedures make it very easy to model any dependencies in one's data. For example, the class of statistical technique referred to as random coefficients modeling of multilevel modeling provides the statistical capabilities to estimate both the nature and degree of dependency that emerges from dependent data structures (*see* Bickle, 2007; Hox, Chapter 14, this volume). The multilevel capability of these modern modeling techniques allows researchers to statistically control for the influences and associations across levels of analysis. These general statistical techniques also have the tremendous capability of allowing researchers to include variables that can be used to predict the sources of influence at various levels. Treating dependent data with the respect it deserves opens up a whole world of potential research questions about the layered influences that give rise to many phenomena in the social and behavior sciences.

As mentioned in the introduction to this handbook, the interplay between theory and statistical analysis tool is often a synergistic dance. Sometimes theory pushes developments in statistical tools, and sometimes the increased capability of the statistical tools pushes theoreticians to consider sources of variance and influence that were previously ignored or had never entered the realm of theoretical consideration. The recent advances in multilevel modeling have opened up a tremendous amount of statistical grist for consideration, including questions of cross-level mediation and moderation.

The techniques for handling various types of dependencies in one's data are varied and they are steadily improving. Card, Selig, and Little (2008) have presented an entire volume dedicated to "*modeling dyadic and interdependent data in the developmental and behavioral sciences.*" Their volume contains 17 chapters that cover dozens of techniques and recent advances in the statistical models for different kinds of dependent data structures particularly found in the developmental sciences. The most advantageous outcome of these recent developments is the degree to which researchers' questions can move away from simple individual differences types of questions to more nuanced and possibly more enlightening types of questions such as predictors of selection and socialization effects in the longitudinal changes of adolescent social networks (Ojanen et al., 2010).

In this *Handbook of Quantitative Methods* and elsewhere, we have contributions on statistical techniques for modeling dyadic data (Kenny & Kashy, 2006), longitudinal data structures of varying complexity (Wu, Selig, & Little, Chapter 18, this volume), dynamical systems models (Deboeck, Chapter 19, this volume), social network models (Carrington, Scott, & Wasserman, 2005), as well as multilevel regression and multilevel SEM (Hox, Chapter 14, this volume). Many other topics also present techniques for modeling dependent data that have been around for some time, such as time series modeling (Wei, Chapter 22, this volume), event-history modeling (Peterson, Chapter 23, this volume), as well as twin studies and behavior genetics models (Neale & Cardon, 1992). Although the gamut of statistical models that have emerged for addressing dependencies in various kinds of data structures is now broad, there are still significant advances being made, particularly in the area of multilevel SEM models (Hox, Chapter 14, this volume; Bovaird, 2007).

The bottom line here is that dependency in one's data should not be ignored or fixed; rather, it should be embraced. Once embraced, we can then elevate the information to the point of theorizing about its origin and its impact in a given study design!

Measurement Error Fallacies
The Myth about Numbers

Quantitative researchers rely on numbers to tell stories about the phenomenon under investigation. Quantification of observed events provides "hard (or hard*er*) evidence" for the empirical claim and is generally considered more objective and scientific than anecdotal accounts (Johnson & Onwuegbuzie, 2004; Meadows & Morse, 2001). According to Michell (1997), measurement is "the logical basis of quantitative science with all its mathematical beauty, conceptual scope, empirical power and practical utility" (p. 358).

A unique challenge to social and behavioral researchers is that many constructs that are of interest in their scientific inquiries are not directly observable. Mental measurement of human latent traits is known to be prone to error (Fuller, 1987; Kane, 2010). As "constructed representation of the reality," mental measurement often invites criticisms from post-positivists about the construct validity of such attempts (Shadish, 1995, p. 67). In fact, the science of mental measurement is predicated on the identification of error sources, the mitigation of error variance, and the estimation of error magnitude (DeVellis, 2003; Furr & Bacharach, 2008). No measurement of human attributes, after all, is error-free.

In contrast to the keen awareness of sampling error among quantitative researchers, very little attention is paid to measurement error (Koretz, 2008). Aiken, West, and Millsap (2008), for example, have reported a median of 4.5 weeks of measurement training in the overall doctoral curriculum in psychology. This finding is consistent with another study by Leech and Goodwin (2008), which reported less than one measurement course, on average, across all doctoral programs in education. In a review of 174 published quantitative articles in education, Zientek Capraro, and Capraro (2008) have found that only 13% reported score reliability for their data. In another review of 91 correlational studies in various disciplines, Wang, Profitt, Suess, and Sun (2010) found only 31% reported local evidence of score reliability using the study sample. Although the AERA (2006) *Standards for Reporting on Empirical Social Science Research* suggests that, "[w]hen a previously developed measurement instrument or classification scheme is used, reference to a publication where these descriptions are provided may be sufficient" (4.1), study sample reliability should still be reported "if local scorers are employed to apply general scoring rules and principles specified by the test developer" (AERA, APA, NCME, 1999, Standard 2.13, p. 34).

Neglecting instrument quality can have detrimental consequences for the substantive conclusions drawn from the data. One heavily-researched consequence is the attenuation of effect sizes caused by random measurement error, resulting in less than optimal power to detect potentially meaningful effects (Archer et al., 2008; Carroll, Ruppert, Stefanski, & Crainiceanu, 2006; Schmidt & Hunter, 1999; Wang, 2010a). Another commonly recognized consequence is making invalid group inferences based on data that have been confounded by systematic measurement error, such as cultural (Reynolds, 2000), linguistic (Flynn, 2007), or rater (Linacre & Wright, 2002) bias.

Discussed below are four fallacies that are commonly associated with data collection in quantitative research. These fallacies broadly span all aspects of instrumentation, from coding, scaling, reliability, and validity to modeling individual and group differences. Without due regard for the extent and impact of measurement error, no sophisticated statistical procedures can be expected to yield valid results about the theory being tested or policy being scrutinized (Bond & Fox, 2007; Kane, 2010).

Fallacy 1: Summing Across Individual Items to Derive Composite Scores

When a scale is developed to measure the degree of a quantitative variable, it usually consists of multiple items measured on an ordinal scale (Cliff & Keats, 2003). The item scores are then typically summed to derive a composite index of the variable of interest. This seemingly straightforward practice, however, can be flawed if care is not taken to avoid some common errors in this operation.

Item Non-Response Bias. When non-response is present in one or more items, then summing across the items to derive a total score can result in underestimation of the measured variable because non-response is in effect treated as nonexistence of the trait value. When the variable measures a cognitive ability, such treatment is less problematic because unanswered items can usually be assumed to result from inability to respond. However, a host of other confounding factors can also contribute to item non-response, such as processing speed (unless, of course, speed is considered an integral part of the cognitive processing) or personality trait. When the variable measures an affective domain, such treatment is more problematic because item non-response usually results from neutrality, irrelevance, indifference, sensitivity, or burden rather than nonendorsement (Groves, Dillman, Eltinge, & Little, 2002).

When item non-response is non-ignorable, a simple solution is to use the average score rather than the sum score, which has the effect of coding the non-responded item as missing and deleting it from subsequent data analysis. However, averaging assumes homogeneity of items and equal contribution of items to the measurement of the latent construct (Enders, 2010). When this assumption is violated, differential weighting of items as described below should be sought. An alternative solution is to impute estimated values for the non-response items (Bernaards & Sijtsma, 2000). See the following section on Missing Data Fallacies for a detailed treatment on modern missing data imputation methods.

Mixed Item Orientation and Reverse Coding. When a scale consists of both positively and negatively phrased items, the negatively phrased items are typically reverse-coded such that the item score is consistent for all items. However, several studies have warned that reverse-coded items behave inconsistently with non-reverse-coded items. For example, Weems and Onwuegbuzie (2001) found "extremely large" effect sizes between positively and negatively phrased items on score estimation. Barnette (2000) found score reliability to be 0.1 lower when mixed items were used than when all positive or all negative items were used. Additionally, Bai, Wang, Pan, and Frey (2009) found item orientation potentially confounds the factor structure, creating different dimensions of the target construct. This finding is consistent with an earlier study that found reverse-coded items to load on a unique factor separate from the other substantive factors (Magazine, Williams, & Williams, 1996).

Our recommendation is to use mixed item orientation only when its purpose is justified (e.g., for reducing the response set or social desirability; de Jonge & Slaets, 2005) and even in such cases should be used only sparingly, perhaps no more than 5% of the total test (Barnette, 1999). Negatively phrased items should be removed from subsequent analysis if they do not load on the same dimension as the main scale or do not add value to the scale reliability.

Weighting of Items and Response Categories. When we sum across items of equal value to derive a composite score, we are making the implicit assumption that each item contributes equally to the individual's trait being measured (Rust & Golombok, 2009). In a Likert-type questionnaire with each item coded on a 1-to-5 scale, for example, a *Strongly Agree* response on one item would add the same amount of value (i.e., 5) to the total score as a *Strongly Agree* response on another item. Another implicit assumption is that the response categories in each item are measured on an equal-distance interval scale such that the same score increment anywhere in the item scale would contribute equally to the measurement of the construct. For example, the equal-distance coding of *Strongly Disagree* = 1, *Disagree* = 2, *Neutral* = 3, *Agree* = 4, and *Strongly Agree* = 5 would mean that the distance between *Agree* and *Strongly Agree* represents the same amount of the latent trait as the distance between *Neutral* and *Agree*.

Both of the above implicit assumptions of additivity have been rigorously contested, and a wealth of research has accumulated against such naïve equal-weighting practices (Furr & Bacharach, 2008; Wright, 1997). On the issue of item weighting, factor analytic procedures produce estimates of the best linear combination of items that maximizes the shared variance between the items and the construct they measure (Beauducel & Rabe, 2009; Floyd & Widaman, 1995). Latent trait modeling procedures produce estimates of nonlinear response models in a conjoint measurement framework (Luce & Tukey, 1964) that places item and trait parameters on the same scale (Karabatsos, 2001; Wright & Stone, 1979). These two approaches have been found to be conceptually and mathematically connected under a unified multidimensional framework (Finch, 2010; McDonald, 1999; Raykov & Marcoulides, 2011). Most notably, both procedures assign more weights to items that carry more information about the latent construct and discount the ones that carry less. On the issue of response category weighting, psychometricians have long recognized the unequal mental distance between response categories and developed sophisticated methods to gauge such variation. Many latent trait models have been developed to parameterize the step values of ordered or unordered response categories (Bond & Fox, 2007; Nering & Ostini, 2010; van der Linden & Hambleton, 1997).

Our recommendation is to apply differential weighting of both items and response categories whenever possible rather than assuming that measured responses are all equally spaced and weighted (Eaves, Erkanli, Silberg, Angold, Maes, & Foley, 2005; Ruscio & Walters, 2009). Such differential weighting yields measurement data that are interval in nature, which is required of many statistical tests. The particular choice of weighting method, however, may have significant impact on trait estimates and substantive conclusions (Grice, 2001; Kolen & Tong, 2010), so it must be approached cautiously. In general, the latent trait approach is preferred over the traditional factor analytic approach because of its modeling versatility, but recent developments in the parameterization of factor models (e.g., full-information estimation method, nonlinear item factor analysis, and latent variable modeling) have gradually closed the gap between the two approaches (Kamata & Bauer, 2008; Moustaki, Jöreskog, & Mavridis, 2004; Wirth & Edwards, 2007). When circumstances are less than ideal (e.g., sample size too small to reliably estimate differential weights) for interval scaling mechanisms to apply, summation scores can be used if there are sufficient items to substantiate an intervalist claim (Carifio & Perla, 2008).

Fallacy 2: Reliability as an Increasing Function of Test Length

Since Gulliksen's (1950) early work that found reliability as an asymptotically increasing nonlinear function of test length, psychometricians have recommended increasing the number of items as a quick fix for improving test reliability (Fitzpatrick & Yen, 2001). However, the reliability function can be easily misinterpreted or misapplied. Discussed below are some cautionary notes on reliability and test length.

Log-Concavity of Reliability Function. The monotonically positive relation between reliability and test length holds only if certain strong assumptions, such as parallel items and positive item-total correlations, are satisfied (Niemi, 1986; Yousfi, 2005). Item analysis that identifies weak items (i.e., low or negative item-total correlation) for deletion or revision is now available in many major statistical packages such as SAS and SPSS. The log-concavity of the reliability function also means that test reliability increases in a negatively accelerated manner after the test length reaches the inflection point (Cronbach, 1960). In other words, after the test reaches an optimal length, additional items bring lesser marginal returns in increasing reliability and the function asymptotically approaches zero at the upper end (Bagnoli & Bergstrom, 2005).

Reliability of Single-Item Measures and Short Forms. Many studies have tested the intuitive assumption that single-item measures have too much measurement error to have acceptable reliability. Depending on the nature and complexity of the latent construct being measured, some studies have found higher-than-expected reliability for single-item global measures (Dollinger, 2009), even for self-report questionnaires (Dolbier, 2005; Zimmerman, 2006). Similarly, short forms of many psychological tests have been developed with satisfactory psychometric properties (e.g., Crawford, Anderson, Rankin, & MacDonald, 2010). These brief tools provide quick preliminary screening but should be supplemented with full-length measures and/or a larger sample if high precision is desired for research or high-stake purposes (Ginns & Barrie, 2004). Computerized adaptive testing maximizes the efficacy of short forms by using sophisticated item-selection algorithms to select most informative items tailored to the individual's trait estimate (Cella, Gershon, Lai, & Choi, 2007; Davey & Parshall, 1997; van der Linden & Pashley, 2010).

Subscale Reliability and Diagnostic Profiling. When a measure is composed of several distinct but correlated subskills or categories, subscale scores are often reported in a diagnostic profile for the comparison of the relative strengths and weaknesses within an individual. Diagnostic use of subscales is important because it provides targeted information for remediation or treatment. Being more homogeneous in content, subscales may have higher reliabilities than the total scale. However, subscale scores sometimes suffer from low reliabilities because of their shortened length (Abdel-Khalek & Lester, 2002). It has therefore been recommended that subscale scores be based on a sufficient number of items to demonstrate reasonable reliabilities (Sinharay, Puhan, & Haberman, 2010). When the subscales are distinct but correlated, a multidimensional measurement model provides more accurate ability estimates and higher reliability estimates (Wang, Yao, Tsai, Wang, & Hsieh, 2006).

Fallacy 3: Ignorance of Latent Mixture and Multilevel Structure

In contrast to subscales that are developed to measure meaningful domains of a complex construct, latent dimensions sometimes exist as unintended systematic errors in observed scores. Some of these latent dimensions are nuisance variables that researchers would like to control (such as rater bias, response aberrancy, differential item functioning); others are meaningful variables that may be of theoretical interest in score interpretation (such as problem-solving strategies, response latency, group membership). A single global standard error of measurement under the classical test theory (Feldt & Qualls, 1999) no longer tells the whole story about an individual's test score. A conditional standard error of measurement estimated for each individual under the item response theory and other modeling frameworks (Lee, Brennan, & Kolen, 2000) also falls short in parsing the complex latent structure underlying an observed score. As the old saying goes, there is much we can learn from errors, as long as we know where to look (Kuhn, 1970; Popper, 1959).

One line of modeling techniques for uncovering underlying group membership is mixture modeling, in which latent classes are identified and within-class parameters are estimated (Mislevy & Verhelst, 1990;

Rijmen & De Boeck, 2005; Rost, 1991; von Davier & Carstensen, 2007). In contrast to latent class analysis, mixture modeling still assumes and estimates a real-valued continuous latent variable underlying the mixture distribution (von Davier, 2010). Mixture models improve measurement precision and validity by adjusting for effects of contingent variables on population invariance. For example, in examining the impact of response sets on personality assessment, Austin, Deary, and Egan (2006) have found evidence of two classes of responders—those who have the tendency to endorse extreme responses and those who tend to use the range of categories. As another example, Holden and Book (2009) used a mixture distribution Rasch model to improve the detection of social desirability (e.g., faking good) on a personality inventory. Some have taken mixture modeling even further to the individual level to explain idiosyncratic differences in cognitive processing (Smith & Batchelder, 2008).

Another line of modeling techniques for explaining residual errors in observed scores is multilevel modeling, in which a nested data structure is acknowledged and cross-level as well as within-level variation is estimated (De Boeck & Wilson, 2005; Fox & Glas, 2001). For example, Reise (2000) proposed using the multilevel modeling approach to studying person misfit in response aberrancy data. Wang, Pan, and Bai (2009) compared this approach to traditional person misfit indices and found equal or superior performance in recovering misfitting simulees.

When latent mixture and multilevel modeling approaches are combined, multilevel mixture modeling provides a powerful tool for testing complex hypotheses about measurement error (Cho & Cohen, 2010; DeJong & Steenkamp, 2010). Extensions of these modeling techniques can successfully recover missing parameters from a sparse data matrix (von Davier & Yamamoto, 2004). In choosing among competing models, researchers need to make thoughtful selection of the model-fit index (Li, Cohen, Kim, & Cho, 2009).

An exciting line of research has emerged in recent years that represents perfect synergy between substantive theory and measurement methodology—cognitive diagnostic assessment (Leighton & Gierl, 2007; Rupp, Templin, & Henson, 2010). By building systematic response patterns into a design matrix—each representing a theoretical approach to cognitive processing—a test developer can create an instrument that provides diagnostic profiling information of not only domain mastery but also processing strategies (Gierl, Alves, & Majeau, 2010; Mislevy, 1994). This exciting development opens up a whole new horizon in modeling item responses and redefines measurement error as a rich source for revealing human complexity.

Fallacy 4: Unreliability and Attenuated Effects

When measurement error is present but unaccounted for, the data provide unreliable information about the variable or construct we wish to measure. Data unreliability results in downward bias in effect size estimation and inflates the error variance in the power function, thereby yielding an underpowered test and obscuring potentially significant findings (Carroll, Ruppert, Stefanski, & Crainiceanu, 2006; Chesher, 1991; Hunter & Schmidt, 2004).

An intuitive understanding of the attenuating effect of measurement error can be gained from the bivariate graph reported in Dear, Puterman, and Dobson (1997) (Figure 31.2). When errors in measuring change in smoking prevalence (the horizontal band surrounding each data point) and change in coronary death rate (the vertical band surround each data point) are uncorrected, the scatter plot suggests little association between the two variables ($r = 0.04$), as is evident in the wide spread of the data points on both axes. However, once the measurement errors are accounted for, the correlation

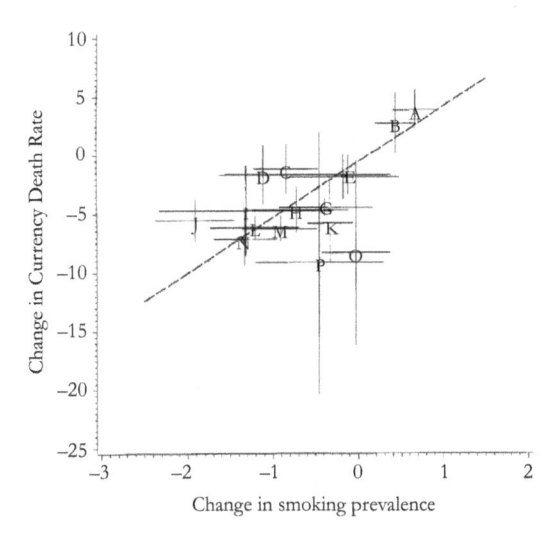

Figure 31.2 Scatter plot illustrating the attenuating effect of measurement error on correlation.
Note: Symbols indicate means for each subpopulation; lines indicate the mean plus or minus one standard error, and the dashed line represents the fitted regression line. (Dear, Puterman, & Dobson, 1997, p. 2185. Reprinted with permission.).

increases to 0.53, which is more realistic in depicting the true relationship between smoking and death rate.

Because of the theoretical interest in true-score population parameters, psychometricians and statisticians have long recognized the need to correct observed effects that are confounded by fallible measurement (Bobko, Roth, & Bobko, 2001; Johnson, 1950; Kristof, 1973). In the simple bivariate case, the conception of disattenuating Pearson's product-moment correlation was introduced more than a century ago (Spearman, 1904) and many methodological advances in the inferential properties of disattenuated effects have been proposed in the literature (Charles, 2005; Hakstian, Schroeder, & Rogers, 1988). In the more complex multivariate case, corrections for attenuated multiple regression coefficents have been extensively studied (Bohrnstedt, 1983; Osborne, 2008b), and SEM techniques exist to partial out measurement error from the parameter estimates (Hancock, 1997; Woodward & Hunter, 1999).

Unfortunately, the impact of unreliable instrumentation on effect size estimation has received little attention in applied research. It has been shown that the reported correlation, on average, underestimates the population correlation by 0.08 in the educational psychology literature (Osborne, 2008b, p. 244) and by 0.067 in genetic research (Archer et al., 2008, p. 1033). A content analysis of published articles between 2000 and 2010 indicates a persistent trend of lack of due concern for the impact of data unreliability on observed effect sizes (Wang, Profitt, Suess, & Sun, 2010). As a result, applied researchers have largely been ignorant of the attenuation issue and have interpreted their findings as if they were error-free.

Using Monte Carlo simulation, Wang, Profitt, Suess, and Sun (2010) showed that the mean observed correlations were attenuated across all simulated conditions. The lower the reliability and the larger the population correlation, the greater the extent of attenuation. Disattenuation successfully recovered the population parameters when reliability was 0.7 or higher but resulted in a positive bias (i.e., overcorrection) when reliability was low. The mean standard error of disattenuated correlation was greater than that of the observed correlation and the statistical power of disattenuated correlation was lower than that of the observed correlation across all conditions. The above simulation analysis supports previous research that the combined effect of small sample size and low reliability may limit the utility and interpretability of disattenuated correlations (Charles, 2005; Zimmerman & Williams, 1997).

Consistent with the *Standards for Educational and Psychological Testing* (AERA, APA, NCME, 1999, Standard 2.6, p. 32), we recommend reporting both the observed and disattenuated effect sizes and interpreting both with caution. When reliability is low, the researcher should either attempt to adjust the disattenuated effect (Wetcher-Hendricks, 2006; Zimmerman & Williams, 1977) or acknowledge the limitation and interpret the findings with caution (Muchinsky, 1996; Winne & Belfry, 1982). When sample size is adequate, advanced statistical procedures such as SEM and latent trait modeling that estimate effect sizes adjusted for measurement error should be considered (Bedeian, Day, & Kelloway, 1997; Hancock, 1997; Wang, 2004; Woodward & Hunter, 1999). No statistical procedures, however, can compensate for poor sampling or bad instrumentation because under such conditions error estimation itself will be very unstable (Cohen, Cohen, Teresi, Marchi, & Velez, 1990; DeShon, 1998; Wang & Jin, 2010).

Missing Data Fallacies

Persistently, scientists across the social and behavioral sciences think that missing data imputation is somehow cheating and "getting something for nothing." Modern approaches to handling missing data are not cheating nor is there a dubious quality to the procedures. Modern approaches to imputation include the full information maximum likelihood (FIML) estimation method and the multiply imputed (MI), data-based expectation-maximization (EM), and/or Markov-Chain Monte Carlo (MCMC) algorithms (*see* Enders, 2010; Baraldi & Enders, Chapter 27, this volume; Little & Rubin, 2002, for detailed explications of these algorithms).

Fallacy 1: Modern Missing-Data Treatments Are "Cheating"

The modern missing-data approaches are not only acceptable but, in fact, will enhance generalizability and statistical power. These modern approaches to handling missing data entered the scene in the late 1970s and emerged in a more widespread manner in the late 1990s, particularly when computing power made using the techniques feasible. In some disciplines, the modern approaches have become standard practice; in many other disciplines, however, they are still viewed with unfounded skepticism.

With a model-based FIML approach, the parameters of a statistical model are estimated in the presence of missing data, where all information is used to inform the parameters' values and standard errors. With a data-based MI approach, missing data points are filled in multiple times and then used to allow unbiased estimation of the parameters and standard errors of a statistical model. As long as missing data are handled using one of these two modern algorithms, the results will be essentially identical with FIML or MI and the parameter estimates of a statistical model will be as accurate as possible given that you have missing data in the first place.

Missing data can arise from three basic mechanisms: a truly random process, a measured/predictable process, and an unmeasured/unpredictable (but not random) process. In the missing data literature, these three processes or mechanisms are respectively labeled *missing completely at random* (MCAR), *missing at random* (MAR), and *missing not at random* (MNAR; see Fig. 31.3).

Missing data are often classified as related to attrition or to non-response. These classifications are not the mechanisms that give rise to missingness; they are more descriptive of where the data are missing rather than why the data are missing. These kinds of missing data are typically caused by a MAR or MCAR process. Both of these two mechanisms for missing data are easily handled by modern missing data procedures.

Model-based approaches started out with multiple-group estimation and later developed into FIML estimation. Both of these approaches have been very instrumental in helping skeptical scholars get comfortable with the idea that we can "use all the data available"—that we don't need to analyze complete cases only (listwise deletion) or resort to pairwise deletion. These latter approaches are akin to surgery to remove the infected parts of our data. The modern approaches, on the other hand, restore the infected area; that is, modern imputation is not plastic surgery to change or disguise the look of something—it is a restorative and reconstructive procedure.

In any study, all three mechanisms of missing data have the potential to be involved, although the degree to which any of mechanisms are actually involved is difficult to verify. For the data points that are MCAR (missing truly at random), the modern missing data procedures easily provide perfectly accurate estimates that recover the missing data information with no bias (and increased power). For the data points that are MAR (missing for a potentially knowable and therefore predictable reason), the modern missing data approaches perform extremely well. The degree to which modern approaches are able to recover the missing data process depends on (1) whether correlates of the missing data mechanism are measured and included on the data set and (2) the strength of the relationship of this known process and the missing data.

The estimates of a statistical model fitted to the data will be more accurate than estimates based on complete-case approaches or other classical treatments. Even when only a small amount of the missingness is systematically recovered, the estimated parameters still resemble the true population parameters more so than estimates derived from unimputed data. In such cases, the accuracy is not perfect but it is always in the direction of better generalizations. If we assume that the data are missing because of a combination of MCAR and MAR processes and if we take care to measure known predictors of missingness, then the quality of generalizations from a study will be superior to any of the classical approaches to handling missing data.

For the data points that are MNAR (missing for an unknown reason that is not random), the missing data imputation procedures may or may not recover any of the missing data mechanism. Here, the key to any potential recovery is what the unknown reason

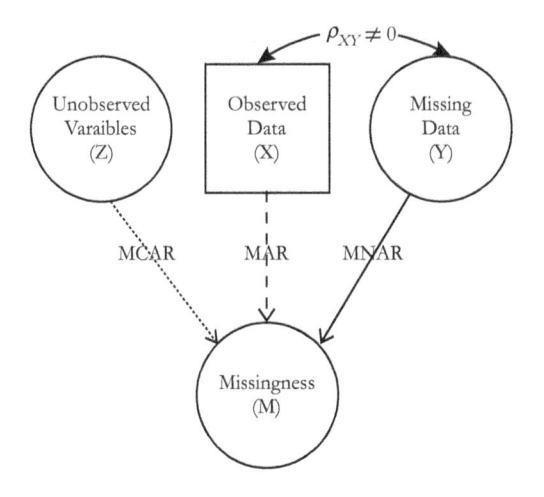

Figure 31.3 Missing data mechanisms.
Note: The key distinction between MCAR, MAR, and MNAR is whether the reason for missingness is related to the missing data themselves (MNAR), related to other observed data (MAR), or unrelated to both (MCAR). As ρ_{xy} increases, more of the missingness can be predicted by X, and MNAR becomes MAR.

is and whether the data set contains proxies or distal covariates of the unknown reasons. For example, if social economic status (SES) is the process leading to missing data and a measure of SES is not on the data set, the missing data process would be classified as MNAR. Other variables on the data set may exist that are correlated with SES such as being in a single-parent household and receiving free or reduced lunch. If these latter two variables are on the data set, then they would predict the missingness to some degree because they are correlated with SES—the true reason for missingness. In this case, even the MNAR missing data mechanism is partly recoverable.

If the variables associated with MAR are not included in the model, then the information that they can convey about the missing data process is not available and the estimation procedure would inappropriately treat all the missing data as if it where MCAR (truly random) when some of it is, in fact, MAR (a knowable reason but it is not included in the imputation process). In this unfortunate situation, the resulting model estimates would not be corrected for the missing data process and the generalizations would be weakened. Using FIML estimation, you can include the variables that you think are associated with missingness as auxiliary variables to inform the estimation of the parameters of the model. Both model- and data-based approaches are effective and provide the same degree of recoverability and same degree of (un)bias when the same variables are used.

Fallacy 2: Missing Data Is Not Something for Which You Can Prepare

A number of factors can be used to your advantage to ensure high-quality estimation in the presence of missing data. First, try to avoid unplanned missingness. Designing efficient protocols that do not burden participants, providing adequate incentives for participation, taking proactive steps to maintain contact with participants, and making them feel like a valued cog in the study—each will minimize attrition and non-response. Second, be sure to measure variables that are likely to be associated with any potential missing data. Carefully crafting a protocol to capture any missing data mechanisms will significantly enhance your ability to generalize back to the original population from which your sample was drawn.

Modern missing data treatment is an agnostic affair when it comes to designating some variables as independent and others as dependent, for example. The goal of modern approaches is to estimate a covariance matrix and mean vector or derive model parameter estimates that resemble the population from which the original sample was drawn. With data-based approaches, implied data points are inserted into locations where data are missing. These inserted data points are like pillars that support the bridge across the missing data divide. The bridge allows a full estimation of the variance, covariance, and mean that connects the observed data in the presence of the missing data.

Unplanned missingness can be the bane of research generalizations. Planned missingness, on the other hand, has tremendous (and for the most part unrealized) potential. More specifically, Graham and colleagues (Graham, Hofer, & MacKinnon, 1996; Graham, Taylor, Olchowski, & Cumsille, 2006) have described the merits of planned missing data designs (see also Enders, 2010). Planned missingness yields incomplete data that are MCAR because the missingness is planned and controlled by the investigator. As such, the data necessarily meet the MCAR assumptions. The various modern missing data approaches easily accommodate and accurately recover the missing data mechanism when it is MCAR. An important consequence of this accurate recovery is that a study can incorporate missing data patterns that result from the MCAR mechanism and, thus, recover the information (Rhemtulla, 2010)!

A number of planned missing designs are possible, including the three-form design (Graham et al., 1996; Graham et al., 2006), the two-method design (Graham et al., 2006), the multitrait/multimethod design (Bunting, Adamson, & Mulhall, 2002) as well as controlled entry in to longitudinal studies (McArdle & Hamagami, 1991). Planned missing data designs provide efficient ways to, for example, manage cost, improve data quality, reduce participant fatigue, increase statistical power to detect effects of interest, and reduce retest or practice effects that arise from repeated testing. Although planned missing data designs has been around for a long time, they have only recently become practical with the emergence of the modern missing data techniques (i.e., MI & FIML; Graham et al., 1996; Rhemtulla, 2010).

Statistical Significance Fallacies

Perhaps the most exciting part of conducting research is determining whether our hypotheses are supported by our data. Depending on the type of study design, our research hypothesis may be that an experimental group differs from a control group or that two variables are correlated with one another. The null hypotheses in these two cases would be that the groups do not differ from one another or that there is no correlation between the variables. Null hypothesis significance testing (NHST) is a method of making probabilistic decisions regarding the meaning of a statistical outcome. A researcher calculates a test statistic and compares it to the critical value corresponding to a predetermined error tolerance level (α). If the test statistic is greater than the critical value or, equivalently, if the probability corresponding to the test statistic is less than the predetermined α value, then the researcher concludes that the observed difference or relationship is unlikely if the null is true and declares the result to be "statistically significant."

The use of NHST has been widely debated for decades (e.g., Cohen, 1994; Fraley & Marks, 2007; Harlow, Mulaik, & Steiger, 1997; Kline, 2004; Meehl, 1978; Nickerson, 2000; Oakes, 1986; Rozeboom, 1960). The debate ranges from severe criticism of its lack of logical integrity (Cohen, 1994), calling for total abandonment of NHST (Fidler & Cumming, 2008), to positive endorsement of its "elegance and usefulness," citing misuse by researchers as the primary source of the problem (Hagen, 1997, p. 15). However, the debate continues largely unnoticed by the field of social and behavioral sciences. One review demonstrated that nearly all textbooks fail to acknowledge that the controversy exists and fail to provide alternative approaches (Gliner, Leech, & Morgan, 2002). The inevitable result, as Fidler and Cumming (2008) put it, is "uncritical statistical inertia and stagnation" in many disciplines (p. 8).

Many misconceptions are widely held about the meaning and interpretation of NHST. Zuckerman, Hodgins, Zuckerman, and Rosenthal (1993) surveyed 551 research psychologists and observed an accuracy rate of 59% regarding the interpretation of NHST and other methodological issues. Mittag and Thompson (2000) surveyed 225 AERA members and found that roughly half of the common misconceptions about NHST persisted. More recently, Saw, Berger, Mary, and Sosa (2009) reported that 109 individuals who took a quiz evaluating the knowledge of NHST—mostly students and faculty with a moderate to high statistics background—endorsed half of the false interpretations. Most of the misconceptions about NHST surround the meaning of p-values.

A p-value is the probability of obtaining a test statistic at least as extreme as the one that was observed, assuming the null hypothesis is true. Standard practice dictates rejecting the null hypothesis when p is less than 0.05 or 0.01, corresponding to a 5% or 1% chance, respectively, of rejecting the null hypothesis when it is true, also known as a Type I error. p-values are influenced by sample size, response distributions, and the size of the effect under investigation. Following is a list of false statements about p-values that are often thought to be true and brief explanations of why they are false.

Fallacy 1: A Significant p-Value Means the Research Hypothesis Is True

As researchers, we may assume that we use statistics to test our research hypothesis. In fact, what we test is the null hypothesis. We cannot actually test our research hypothesis; rather, we can only determine whether there is evidence to refute the null hypothesis. Researchers are sometimes confused by this asymmetry (Fraley & Marks, 2007; Rozeboom, 1960). A significant p-value does not confirm the research hypothesis or indicate that it is true. Rather, it indicates that the null hypothesis is unlikely to be true.

Fallacy 2: Smaller p-Values Indicate a Stronger Effect

Smaller p-values do not indicate a stronger effect or relationship. They are dependent on sample size, and thus, they do not accurately reflect the magnitude of the difference or the strength of the relationship being tested. They only tell us whether or not there is a significant effect in the data that is inconsistent with the null hypothesized effect. Two samples with the same effect strength but different sample sizes would have differing p-values. Larger samples reduce the amount of sampling error, making the estimated effect more precise and the p-value smaller, thus making it easier to reject the null hypothesis. Larger samples, however, do not make the observed effect larger or the p-value more meaningful.

Fallacy 3: Statistical Significance Indicates Practical Importance

p-values are not informative about the theoretical or real-world importance of a result. There are times when a statistically significant result means very little in the real world (Jacobson & Truax, 1991) and when a truly important difference does not attain statistical significance (Kirk, 1996). Although statistical tests are objective, sometimes subjective judgments are needed to determine the practical significance of a finding. This is particularly concerning in clinical and medical research. Jacobson and Truax (1991) have cited an example in which a treatment for weight loss is being tested. If the control group averages zero weight loss and the treatment group averages 2 pounds of weight loss, then the effect might be statistically significant. However, the loss of 2 pounds will not result in any improvements in health profile such as risk for cardiovascular events or diabetes. Effect sizes, described below, may give more information than p-values regarding practical significance.

Fallacy 4: p-Values Reflect Replicability

Interpreting a small p-value as a high chance ($1 - p$) of replicating the statistically significant finding is a persistent misconception that dies hard (Mittag & Thompson, 2000; Oakes, 1986; Sohn, 1998). p-values, in fact, vary quite dramatically over repeated replications and do not allow inferences to be drawn (Cumming, 2008; Miller, 2009). p-intervals, the range with a specified chance of including p given by replication, are quite wide regardless of sample size (Cumming, 2008). Repeated study is the most trustworthy way to convincingly demonstrate replicability of findings. Significant p-values cannot be substituted for the replication of results.

Fallacy 5: Lack of Significant Findings Means a Failed Study

Practice of NHST places emphasis on the attainment of $p < \alpha$ as the way to evaluate the results of research studies. This leads to the belief that failure to find a statistically significant result means the study failed or that the hypothesis was not worth studying. Researchers may fail to submit studies without significant findings for publication, journals may refuse to publish them, or there may be a long lag time before a study is published (Greenwald, 1975; Ioannidis, 1998; Sterne & Smith, 2001). Ultimately, this can bias interpretation of research literature because of "multiple repetitions of studies with false hypotheses" and "failure to publish smaller and less significant outcomes of tests of a true hypothesis" (Sterling, Rosenbaum, & Weinkam, 1995, p. 108). A biased literature perpetuates misguided and distorted theorizing in future research (*see also* Meehl, 1990).

Alternatives and Solutions

Several alternatives and solutions to misinterpreting NHST have been offered (e.g., Cohen, 1994; Denis, 2003; Fraley & Marks, 2007; Kileen, 2005; Kline, 2004). These range from simply adding CIs when reporting results to revolutionizing the state of academic publishing to reduce publication bias. The first and most important solution is to realize that there is no shortcut solution to the problem. No statistical method can substitute for thinking carefully about the meaning of the results and placing them in the context of previous and future research. Answers to research questions are discovered over a period of time across multiple studies—not in a single study. Some approaches to help put findings into a broader context are replication of results, resampling, and meta-analysis (Cohen, 1994; Kline, 2004). All of these redirect focus away from individual studies to more solid and reliable results within a larger framework, an important part of modifying this entrenched fallacy surrounding NHST.

Effect Size. Effect size is an indicator of the strength of the association between the independent and dependent variables of interest. In other words, it tells us how much variance in one variable is accounted for by knowledge of the other variable. Two common effect size statistics are ω^2 and η^2. Cohen's d is an estimate of the distance between two means. Use of effect size estimates is advantageous because it is more reliable than p and less dependent on sample size. Although effects sizes from small samples are less reliable than from larger samples, they are not a function of sample size as p-values are (Denis, 2003).

There is debate regarding whether effect sizes can replace significance testing or should be used as a complement (Chow, 1996). Additionally, the use of effect sizes also has limitations. Identification of small, medium, or large effect sizes is somewhat arbitrary and effect size estimates depend on how the dependent variable is operationalized (Favreau, 1997). Thus, it is suggested that both p-values and effect sizes be interpreted together (Chow, 1996; Denis, 2003). This allows us to understand whether the observed results are caused by chance *and* determine the size of the effect in the sample. Both pieces are helpful tools in understanding as much about the data as possible.

Confidence Interval. Confidence intervals provide an estimated range of values calculated from a sample that is likely to include the unknown population parameter. As such, CIs are more appropriate than effect sizes as a replacement for p-values (Meehl, 1997). The frequency with which the interval contains the parameter is determined by the confidence level. A CI indicates the reliability of an estimate. A smaller interval indicates a smaller margin of error. Confidence intervals contain all the same information contained in a NHST, plus additional information about the range of values within which the result lies. They provide both a hypothesis test and produce an estimate of the parameter (Becker, 1991). It is useful to report CIs in the unit of measurement to simplify interpretation of the practical significance (Cumming & Finch, 2005).

There are also a few common pitfalls and misconceptions when using and interpreting CIs (Cumming & Finch, 2005; Fidler, 2005). First, CIs are estimates of ranges of plausible population parameters, not sample parameters as sometimes misinterpreted (Fidler, 2005). Second, a 95% CI does not have a 95% chance of capturing the sample mean in a repeated study unless the initial sample mean was exactly equal to the population mean. It actually has an average probability of 83% of capturing the sample mean in a repeated study (Cumming, Williams, & Fidler, 2004). Third, when looking at figures of CI around sample means, most overestimate the difference necessary between the means to reach statistical significance (Belia, Fidler, Williams, & Cumming, 2005). When the p-value is about $p = 0.05$, the CIs overlap by about one-fourth the distance of the width (Cumming & Finch, 2005). Fourth, in a repeated measures design, the CI around the mean difference should be used.

Statistical Power. Calculating power is another important way to avoid misinterpretation of hypothesis testing. In most research, we test a sample and not the entire population. This leaves the possibility of sampling error that may cause our data to differ from what is present in the population. Sampling error is most problematic with small sample size and, therefore, low statistical power. Low statistical power results in a low probability of detecting significant differences or relationships even if they are present. Low power is directly related to small sample size and small effect size. Power calculations are a critical and largely ignored component of research conduct (Cohen, 1962, 1992; Hoenig & Heisey, 2001; Kline, 2004). Underpowered studies often provide biased estimates of the size of the effect. Studies with inadequate power do not lend confidence in drawing conclusions about the relationships we are hoping to explicate. Adequately powered studies reduce the likelihood of false or misleading interpretations of study results. For a more detailed description of power calculation and associated fallacies, *see* the section below entitled Statistical Power Fallacies.

In published work, researchers should report enough information to enable readers to draw conclusions from the results. The APA publication manual (APA, 2010b) now advocates the use and reporting of effect size, CIs, and power. These additional pieces of information should not merely be reported, they should also be discussed with regard to the value they add to interpreting the results. For example, a study by Fidler, Thomason, Cumming, Finch, and Leeman (2004) reports that despite increases in reporting CIs, published manuscripts still fail to interpret results with regard to the meaning of the CIs and recommend that researchers further educate themselves about the ways in which CIs can add meaning.

Alternative Paradigms Beyond Null Hypothesis Significance Testing

There are alternative philosophies of statistical methodology that do not rely on NHST but do require more careful thought and *a priori* specification of hypotheses—for example, comparing the fit of multiple models (Dixon, 2003; Dixon & O'Reilly, 1999; Edwards, 1965; Wilson, Miller, & Lower, 1967) or using a Bayesian estimation approach (e.g., Pereira, Stern, & Wechsler, 2008; Rouder, Speckman, Sun, Morey, & Iverson, 2009). When comparing multiple models, we can specify alternative models and compare which best describes the observed data rather than testing a model merely in opposition to the null hypothesis. Although it requires more prerequisite thought and planning, determining which of two or three models provides the better fit may tell us more about our data and research questions. A Bayesian approach allows the incorporation of previous knowledge into the process of determining probability. Decisions about hypotheses are made using deductive methods and with regard to the posterior probability rather than comparing a research hypothesis to a null hypothesis. Baio and Blangiardo (2008) offers a succinct treatment of Bayesian methods.

We conclude here by echoing Howard, Maxwell, and Fleming's (2000) recommendation that different approaches (NHST, meta-analysis, Bayesian analysis) to theory testing are not mutually exclusive but, rather, complement one another. Rather than condemning and discarding NHST, perhaps we can improve our scientific pursuits by avoiding the fallacies and following the best practices as described above (Balluerka, Gmez, & Hidalgo, 2005; Nickerson, 2000).

Statistical Power Fallacies

Despite the looming criticisms against NHST (Fidler & Cumming, 2008; Kline, 2004), this frequentist inferential framework remains the dominant (Cumming et al., 2007; Levine, Weber, Hullett, Park, & Lindsey, 2008) and viable practice among quantitative researchers in the foreseeable future (AERA, 2006; APA, 2010b; Balluerka, Gmez, & Hidalgo, 2005; Mulaik, Raju, & Harshman, 1997; Wainer & Robinson, 2003). Since Cohen's seminal work on effect size and power analysis (1988), applied quantitative researchers have come to recognize the importance of power associated with the statistical test they use. Whereas too much power may be cost-inefficient, underpowered studies may fail to unravel substantively meaningful effects (Maxwell, 2004). Major statistical packages such as SAS (Bauer & Lavery, 2004) and standalone software such as G*Power (Faul, Erdfelder, Lang, & Buchner, 2007) are now readily available for conducting power analysis.

Estimating the prospective (or *a priori*) power of a statistical test before the commencement of a study is generally considered a "universally accepted" practice (Thomas, 1997, p. 276). Prospective power analysis is useful for estimating the minimum sample size needed to achieve an optimal level of power for detecting a hypothesized effect size under a specified statistical significance level (Wilcox, 2008). However, reporting the retrospective power after the conclusion of a study remains a highly contested practice (Onwuegbuzie & Leech, 2004; Wang, 2010b). Retrospective power, also called *post hoc* power (Gillett, 1994; Yuan & Maxwell, 2005) or *observed* power (Hoenig & Heisey, 2001; Thomas & Krebs, 1997), is an area of controversy because its misuse and abuse has been highly prevalent in applied research (Goodman & Berlin, 1994; Hoenig & Heisey, 2001; O'Keefe, 2007; Sun, Pan, & Wang, 2011). We have identified below four common fallacies surrounding statistical power analysis, with a focus on retrospective power.

Fallacy 1: Statistical Power is a Single, Unified Concept

Despite (or perhaps resulting from) the heated debate over retrospective power, professional organizations continue to take a silent (AERA, 2006) or vague (APA, 2010b) stance on this topic. The most recent edition of the APA Publication Manual (2010b) states:

> When applying inferential statistics, take seriously the statistical power considerations associated with the test of hypotheses. Such considerations relate to the likelihood of correctly rejecting the tested hypotheses, given a particular alpha level, effect size, and sample size. In that regard, routinely provide evidence that the study has sufficient power to detect effects of substantive interest. (p. 30)

This recommendation blurs the great divide between prospective and retrospective power, fueling the misconceptions and fallacies associated with their use.

By applying the Bayes Theorem in probability, Zumbo and Hubley (1998) have showed that the retrospective power can be expressed as

$$P[H_0 \text{ is false}|\text{reject } H_0]$$
$$= P[\text{reject } H_0|H_0 \text{ is false}]\frac{P(H_0 \text{ is false})}{P(\text{reject } H_0)},$$

where $P[H_0 \text{ is false}|\text{reject } H_0]$ on the left is the retrospective power and $P[\text{reject } H_0|H_0 \text{ is false}])$ on the right is the prospective power. As such, retrospective power equals prospective power only under the highly unlikely circumstance that the unconditional probability that H_0 is false (i.e., $P[H_0$ is false]) equals the unconditional probability that we would reject H_0 (i.e., $P[\text{reject } H_0]$). With a large enough number of replications, these two unconditional probabilities will converge to the same truth, so retrospective power can be shown to approximate and ultimately equal prospective power (Sun, Pan, & Wang, 2011). In reality, however, this convergence does not happen in a single or even multiple studies.

Fallacy 2: Statistical Nonsignificance is Evidence for Null Hypothesis Being True

The danger of equating statistical nonsignificance with the null hypothesis being true has long been widely recognized in introductory statistics textbooks (e.g., Thompson, 2006). Failure to reject the null hypothesis is inconclusive as to whether the true effect does not exist or whether the sampling error is too large to detect such an effect. The most damaging case of misinterpretation is when the researcher's intent is to "prove" no effect, such as a less expensive product works equally well as a more expensive product or the posited statistical model fits the data well (*see* APA, 2010b, p. 30). This danger parallels Kline's (2004) warning about statistical significance: "If you increase the sample size enough, any result will be statistically significant. This is scary" (p. 16). The reverse logic applies: If you *decrease* the sample size enough, then any result will be statistically nonsignificant—thus supporting the theory that no effect exists. This is even scarier because a researcher could claim the posited theory of no effect by simply doing a small sample study!

Unfortunately, misinterpreting statistical nonsignificance as evidence of the null hypothesis being true continues to permeate the applied research fields (Finch, Cumming, & Thomason, 2001). Without power information or other supporting evidence, statistically nonsignificant results remain inconclusive and should be interpreted as such.

Fallacy 3: Statistical Nonsignificance Combined With High Retrospective Power Is Evidence for Null Hypothesis Being True

A common fallacy exists that a statistically nonsignificant result accompanied by high retrospective power lends strong support to the null hypothesis being true. Unfortunately, simulation studies have demonstrated that retrospective power, being a 1:1 inverse function of the p-value, can never be expected to reach a high level when the p-value is large (Hoenig & Heisey, 2001; Sun, Pan, & Wang, 2011). In fact, the maximum retrospective power associated with a statistically nonsignificant result has been shown to be capped at <0.5, regardless of the sample size (Gerard, Smith, & Weerakkody, 1998; *see* Figure 31.4).

As cautioned by Goodman & Berlin (1994), "[retrospective power] will *always* show that there is low power (<50%) with respect to a nonsignificant difference, making tautological and uninformative the claim that a study is 'underpowered' with respect to an observed nonsignificant result" (p. 202).

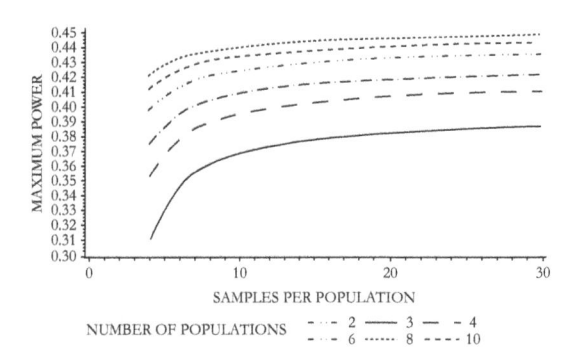

Figure 31.4 Maximum retrospective power at different numbers of populations and sample sizes.
(Reprinted with permission Gerard, Smith, & Weerakkody, 1998, p. 805.)

Fallacy 4: Lack of Retrospective Power in Rejecting a Null Hypothesis Is Evidence for a True Effect

Studies with statistically nonsignificant findings that contradict with the posited theory sometimes find their way into publication by claiming that low retrospective power is to blame (Sun, Pan, & Wang, 2011). Their reasoning is often based on advice like: "[A statistically nonsignificant result] may mean that (a) the treatment program had no effect or (b) there was insufficient power to detect the relationship that does in fact exist" (Oakes & Feldman, 2001, p. 3). Interpreted unthoughtfully, such advice could be mistaken to mean that low retrospective power means the effect is true. If only a larger sample had been used, as the reasoning goes, then the result would have reached statistical significance.

The rationale of using low retrospective power as evidence of true effect, as Goodman and Berlin (1994) aptly put it, "has an Alice-in-Wonderland feel, and any attempt to sort it out is guaranteed to confuse" (p. 202). In another sobering message, Kline (2004) wrote, "a post hoc analysis that shows low power is more like an autopsy than a diagnostic procedure" (p. 43). Because nil nulls are always implausible and guaranteed to be falsified with sufficient power (Meehl, 1978), the reverse logic of lack of power as evidence for true effect cannot hold on theoretical or empirical grounds.

Summary and Recommendations

Figure 31.5 summarizes the above four statistical power fallacies imbedded in the statistical inference process of NHST. The misuse and abuse of retrospective power can lead to unscientific discoveries of effects or non-effects that are not substantiated by the sample data at hand. When operating within the NHST framework, researchers must exercise caution against overinterpreting the statistical evidence obtained from the data.

The prospective power estimated from a hypothesized population effect and a planned sample size does not always accurately reflect the observed data at the conclusion of a study, so a retrospective look at the ensuing implementation of a planned study can still be worthwhile (Hancock, 2001; Onwuegbuzie & Leech, 2004). In other words, we must deal with "the posterior distribution of probable effect sizes conditional upon the estimate of effect size obtained in an experiment" (Gillett, 1994, p. 783). Although retrospective power provides limited diagnostic information, its judicious use can still

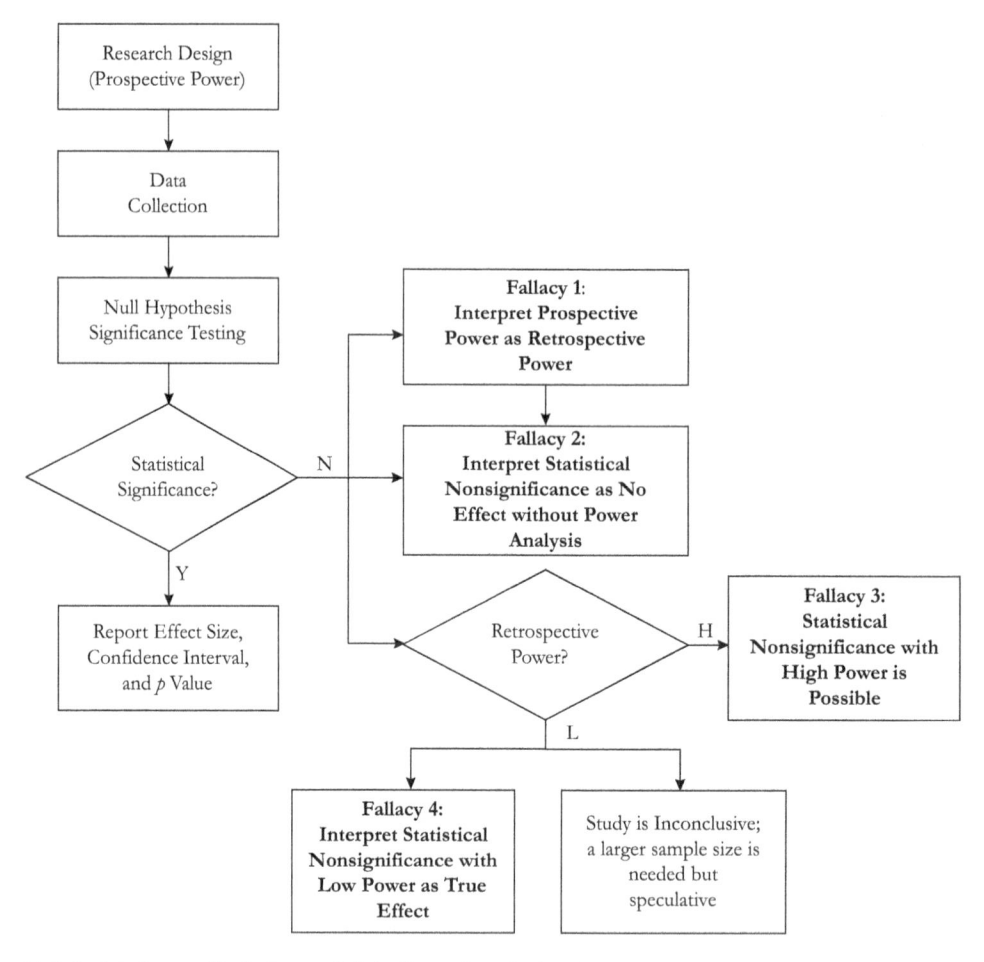

Figure 31.5 Statistical power fallacies in statistical significance hypothesis testing.

shed some light on the truthfulness of the hypothesized effect. Rather than discarding retrospective power entirely, as suggested by some (Levine & Ensom, 2001; Matcham, McDermott, & Lang, 2007), our recommendation is to guard against the fallacies, misconceptions, and misinterpretations associated with retrospective power (Hogarty & Kromrey, 2003).

Just because retrospective power is a perfect nonlinear function of the *p*-value, it does not necessarily imply that they are literally redundant of one another (Yuan & Maxwell, 2005). As a result of the maximum attainable power associated with a statistically nonsinificant result being capped at 0.50, however, researchers can only interpret the relative strength of the retrospective power within this 0 to 0.5 reference framework rather than the usual 0 to 1.0 power scale. Although it may be justifiable to use low retrospective power to suggest the need for a larger future sample, it should never be used as evidence that true effect exists in the present sample. When retrospective power is low, recommendation for a larger sample in a future study is only speculative with regard to a better chance of detecting a meaningful true effect, if indeed it exists in the population.

Perhaps the most important message for applied researchers is that retrospective power associated with a nonsignificant result is highly unstable (Froman & Shneyderman, 2004; Gillett, 1994). In fact, Yuan and Maxwell (2005) mathematically proved that observed power is "almost always a biased estimator of the true power. The bias can be negative or positive" (p. 141). As a result, retrospective power based on the observed effect size should never be calculated as a point estimate. Rather, the upper and lower limits of the CI about the observed effect size should be used (Hedges, 1983; Thompson, 2007; Wilkinson & the Task Force on Statistical Inference, APA Board of Scientific Affairs, 1999).

Unless we make the paradigm shift of rising above the NHST framework (Fidler & Cumming, 2008; Overall, 1969; Zumbo & Hubley, 1998), retrospective power expressed as a range of probability values corresponding to the CI about the observed effect size appears to be the most sensible solution (Smith, 2008; Steiger & Fouladi, 1997; Taylor & Muller, 1995; Thomas, 1997).

Factor Analysis Fallacies

Factor analysis is a statistical method often used to develop and evaluate measures of phenomena being studied. This technique identifies common underlying properties (factors) of multiple measured items by evaluating the pattern of covariance between them. As an example, it can be used to determine how well several questions on a test indicate a student's knowledge of a subject such as arithmetic, or how a person's responses to questionnaire items indicate the dimensions of his or her personality. It produces factor loadings that indicate how strongly each item relates to the factor that is common between all the items of a scale or measure.

After the advent of SEM, researchers began to distinguish traditional exploratory factor analysis (EFA) from modern confirmatory factor analysis (CFA). EFA is typically used when a researcher does not have a hypothesis about the factor structure of the data and consequently must make choices about number of factors, extraction methods, and rotation methods. By contrast, in CFA the researcher has a theory-driven hypothesis about the structure of the underlying factors and, accordingly, estimates the fit of a hypothesized factor structure to the observed data. In EFA the researcher does not specify the number of factors *a priori* but instead "explores" the data for how many factors to retain, whereas in CFA the number of factors is specified *a priori* and the relationship between the factors (orthogonal or oblique) is specified and tested. In EFA, the loading for each item is estimated on all factors, whereas in CFA the hypothesis specifies which items load on which factors.

The use of factor analysis has undergone rigorous criticism in recent years. Fabrigar, Wegener, MacCallum, and Strahan (1999) reviewed 217 research articles published in two prominent psychology journals and described the state of the art as "often far from optimal" (p. 295). Preacher and MacCallum (2003) have described the problems with using what is known as the "little jiffy" approach to factor analysis—using the default options in most of the popular statistical packages.

We describe below some common errors associated with factor analysis, discuss the various choices that must be made, and offer suggestions for how to avoid those errors. Preacher and MacCallum (2003) have provided a detailed illustration of how committing these common errors results in a very different solution than the application of appropriate techniques. Henson and Roberts (2006) independently came to the same conclusions and urged more complete reporting of the procedural details for external verification. As a subjective and exploratory quantitative method, such details in EFA must always be transparent.

Fallacy 1: Misuse of Principal Components when Common Factors Is More Appropriate for Factor Extraction in Exploratory Factor Analysis

Two techniques for factor extraction in EFA are principal components analysis (PCA) and common factors analysis. It is common to assume that PCA and common factors analysis are the same, but conceptually, mathematically, and procedurally they are very different (Velicer & Jackson, 1990). PCA is most useful for data reduction. It is appropriate for large sets of highly related variables with the goal of reducing them down to a general summary score with maximal variability and reliability (Floyd & Widaman, 1995). PCA is economical in that it reduces the number of observed variables to a small number of "principal components" that account for most of the variance. The first principal component accounts for most of the variance in the data. The second component accounts for the second largest amount of variance and is uncorrelated with the first component. Eigenvalues indicate how much variance is explained by each component.

Common factors analysis belongs to a class of techniques, called latent variable modeling, that hypothesize that variables we observe are made up of two components: the true score and random error. The variable of interest (a latent factor) can only be estimated imperfectly (by a measured variable). Thus, there is always measurement error, and this is accounted for in the factor analytic model. When we measure multiple related variables, we hope to more accurately describe the latent factor and thereby reduce the amount of measurement error in a sample. Common factors analysis is used to identify common latent factors that are indicated by measured variables. It partitions the variance into that which is common or shared among all the measured variables and that which is unique to each variable. The unique variance is further partitioned into specific and error variance. Common factors are latent variables that account for common variance and covariances among measured variables. Common factors analysis identifies latent constructs and the underlying factor structure. It estimates which measured items are indicators of which latent factors. Unlike PCA, common factors analysis is not intended to explain the most variance or summarize the items into one score. Rather, its goal is to help the researcher understand sources of common variance in the observed data. In EFA, model fit can be tested using chi-square and several other fit indices, whereas in PCA, percent of variance accounted for is used to assess model fit. For more information on components versus factors, the reader is referred to a special issue in the journal *Multivariate Behavioral Research* (Mulaik, 1990), in which 12 papers discuss the issues in selecting between the two.

Once the differences between PCA and common factors are clear, it easy to see why each might be selected depending on the researcher's goals. If the researcher's goal is to create a linear composite of variables that retains as much of the variance as possible, then it is best to use PCA. If the researcher's goal is to explain correlations among the measured variables that result in interpretable constructs, then it is best to use common factors analysis. Results of PCA and EFA are often similar when there are high loadings and a large number of indicators on each factor. However, this is not always the case. In data with low communalities, common factor analysis yields more accurate estimates, whereas PCA leads to positive bias in estimates and negative bias in correlation among factors (Floyd & Widaman, 1995).

Fallacy 2: Careless Selection of Number of Factors to Retain in EFA

There are several common ways to determine the number of factors to retain: the Kaiser-Guttman criterion (Eigenvalues >1.0), scree tests, and statistical tests. Each is discussed.

Kaiser-Guttman Criterion. The Kaiser-Guttman criterion suggests retention of factors with eigenvalues greater than or equal to 1.0. Guttman (1954) developed the criterion as a weakest lower bound for the number of factors to retain. Factors with eigenvalues greater than 1.0 account for at least as much variability as an individual measured variable if that variable is standardized to have unit variance.

Kaiser-Guttman criterion is the default in popular statistical software packages. There are several problems with relying on this approach without confirmation from other approaches. For example, it has been demonstrated to frequently over- or underestimate the number of factors (e.g., Cattell & Vogelmann, 1977; Cliff, 1988; Zwick & Velicer, 1986). Furthermore, it may depend on the number of variables (Gorsuch, 1983; Zwick & Velicer, 1986), the reliability of the factors (Cliff, 1988), the number of observed variables per factor and the range of communalities (Tucker, Koopman, & Linn, 1969). A third issue relates to the use of reduced versus unreduced correlation matrices. An unreduced correlation matrix has 1.0s on the diagonal (a variable's correlation with itself is 1.0). A reduced correlation matrix has communalities rather than 1.0s in the diagonal. Communalities represent the proportion of a variable's total variance that is explained by common factors. Sometimes the eigenvalues are misapplied to the reduced correlation matrix rather than the unreduced correlation matrix (Fabrigar, Wegener, MacCallum, & Strahan, 1999). Popular statistical packages provide both reduced and unreduced matrices in the output and users may confuse one type for the other.

Scree Tests. There are two types of scree test: subjective and Cattell-Nelson-Gorsuch (CNG) scree tests. The subjective scree test is conducted by "eyeballing" a plot of the drop in eigenvalues. The point at which the eigenvalues appear to drop off most rapidly determines the number of factors retained. Because subjective methods are prone to errors (Kaiser, 1970), a more objective option is the CNG scree test, which is based on regression slopes for clusters of eigenvalues. These may be used with either the reduced or unreduced correlation matrix. They are generally accurate in determining the number of factors (Cattell & Vogelmann, 1977), although they are best used in conjunction with other approaches including parallel analysis (Preacher & MacCallum, 2003). In parallel analysis, the scree plot from the observed data is compared to a scree plot from a set of random data. The intersection between the two plots is determined and the number of factors with eigenvalues above the intersection is retained. The CNG shows good accuracy in identifying the number of factors (Humphreys & Montanelli, 1975).

Statistical Tests. Some statistical tests for deciding the number of factors to retain include maximum likelihood estimation, generalized least squares estimation, and asymptotically distribution free estimation. These approaches involve obtaining solutions for a range of number of factors—for example, comparing a one-factor model to a two- or three- factor model. The more saturated model with nonsignificant fit improvement is discarded in favor of the more restricted model. Fit can be determined using SEM-like fit indices (e.g., root mean square error of approximation, RMSEA). One problem with these types of tests is that they depend on sample size. Larger sample sizes tend to result in retention of a larger number of factors, and smaller sample size may underestimate the number of factors that should be retained.

Suggestions for Selection the Number of Factors to Retain. Rather than relying solely on rules of thumb, careful thought about the meaning and interpretability of the factors should be used. Understanding the theory behind the constructs being measured and having knowledge of previous research in a research domain should help to confirm the number of factors that is reasonable given the data. With regard to the three approaches described, it is best to use multiple approaches and seek agreement between them. If the results are inconsistent, then it is advisable to consider rotated solutions with different numbers of factors to help judge the interpretability of the solution without overfitting the data (Preacher & MacCallum, 2003).

Fallacy 3: Default Use of Orthogonal Rotation in EFA

After the factors are extracted, they are rotated to give them a simple structure that allows for interpretability (Thurstone 1935, 1947). Simple structure exists when each variable loads strongly on one factor and weakly on the others. It is also easier to interpret when all have positive loadings. Orthogonal rotations such as varimax, used in the "little jiffy" approach, assumes that factors are uncorrelated with one another. In reality, factors rarely have a correlation of zero with one another because all items comprising factors typically originate from representation of a single but complex latent construct. In contrast, oblique rotation (e.g., quartimin, oblimin) allows the factors to correlate with one another and estimates the degree of correlation. Using an oblique rotation on uncorrelated factors will simply reveal them to be uncorrelated (Comrey & Lee, 1992; Nunnally & Bernstein, 1994). Although it requires the estimation of one additional parameter, there is little disadvantage to estimating the correlation when there is none, but not allowing it when it does exist could result in misleading outcomes.

See Browne (2001) for a thorough description of rotation types.

Fallacy 4: Using Confirmatory Factor Analysis to Confirm Analysis Performed with Exploratory Factor Analysis

Results obtained in EFA depend on the sample in which it is conducted and require subjective decision making. For these reasons, more confidence can be gained if the factor structure is validated by CFA (Jöreskog & Sorbom, 1989). In CFA, the factor structure can be subjected to more rigorous evaluation to determine how well it matches what was found in the initial exploratory analysis. Results of EFA often fit poorly when subsequently tested in CFA (McCrae, Zonderman, Costa, Bond, & Paunonen, 1996; van der Gaag et al., 2006). There are several potential explanations for this (van Prooijen & van der Kloot, 2001). As EFA results are sample-dependent, the factor structure found in one sample may not apply to a new sample with different characteristics such as age or culture. However, often the lack of fit in confirmation studies results from methodological issues. Inappropriate use of EFA, as described in the fallacies above, could result in inability to confirm factor structure using CFA. Inadequate selection of number of factors, rotation method, or use of PCA when common factor analysis is more appropriate could all lead to poor fit in CFA (Fabrigar, Wegener, MacCallum, & Strahan, 1999). Poor application of CFA can also be the cause of the misfit between the two approaches. Confirmatory factor analysis models are often adjusted to create better fit without regard to whether the modifications are consistent with the theory behind the model.

Another possible reason for lack of agreement between the two methods is that CFA is more restrictive than EFA. In EFA, loadings are estimated for all variables on all factors, even if they are very weak loadings, whereas in CFA each variable only fits on one factor, unless driven by hypothesis to the contrary. CFA validation results are especially poor fitting when coefficients that are low in EFA are fixed to zero in CFA (van Prooijen & van der Kloot, 2001).

It is a stronger validation to confirm a factor structure in a new sample rather than the same sample used for exploratory purposes. However, to be certain of the explanations for the differences found between EFA and CFA, results would have to be tested in the same sample, preferably by splitting the sample into halves and performing EFA in one half and CFA in the other. The choice between single-sample and two-sample analysis for cross-validation depends in part on the sample size (Browne, 2000). If agreement cannot be found between the two approaches in the same sample, then it is very unlikely that confirmation would be found in a new sample (van Prooijen & van der Kloot, 2001).

Other Issues in Factor Analysis

Several other issues contributing to appropriate conduct of factor analysis include data scale and distribution, ratio of variables to factors, sample size, and reporting results.

Data Scale and Distribution. Factor analysis is intended for use with interval or quasi-interval data with a multivariate normal distribution. If data do not meet these criteria, then statistical assumptions may be violated and results may be biased and difficult to replicate. Several options are available when data do not meet these criteria. For example, dichotomous data may be approached by creating parcels (Kishton & Widaman, 1994; Little, Cunningham, Shahar, & Widaman, 2002). Alternative analytic programs (such as TESTFACT by Wilson, Wood, & Gibbons, 1991 and NOVAX by Waller, 1994) that are more robust to distributional violations should be used. The common factor model assumes that variables are linearly related to the latent variables, but nonlinear factor analysis techniques are also well established (cf. McDonald, 1967). For CFA, data with non-normal distributions violate assumptions used in maximum likelihood estimation, but may be less problematic when using an unweighted least squares approach (Jöreskog & Sorbom, 1989). Regardless of which approach is used, careful consideration and thought should be used when analyzing non-normally distributed data.

Ratio of Variables to Factors. Factors with only one observed variable merely account for a portion of the unique variance (the variability that is not accounted for by common factors). A minimum of three variables per factor is recommended for the factor model to be identified (Anderson & Rubin, 1956; Comrey, 1988). More observed variables per factor increases the likelihood of a proper solution; however, adding more observed variables is not always better (Marsh, Hau, Balla, & Grayson, 1998).

Sample Size. Adequate sample size is another important issue that confuses many researchers because guidelines and rules of thumb for appropriate sample size in factor analysis vary. A rule of 4:1 or 5:1 ratio of participants to variables has traditionally been followed; however, studies suggest that total sample size (Gorsuch, 1983; Streiner, 1994), strength of item loadings, and number of items per factor (Guadagnoli & Velicer, 1988) are all critical to the stability of model estimation. Specifying models with care and avoiding estimation of extraneous parameters is advisable (Floyd & Widaman, 1995).

Reporting Results. Floyd and Widaman (1995) have suggested that many of the factor analyses in published articles fail to report sufficient detail to allow readers to properly evaluate or draw conclusions about the models—for example, reporting all factor loadings rather than only those that exceed an arbitrary threshold. For CFA, the initial proposed model and modifications made to improve model fit should also be reported. Floyd and Widaman offer a detailed list of information that should be reported for EFA and CFA.

Summary

As is true of all sound research conduct, it is best to carefully consider the research question to determine which techniques and decisions best answer that question. If the goal is to find an economical summary of a large number of highly correlated variables that retain as much of the variance as possible, or find components that explain as much variance as possible, then PCA is the best choice. If the goal is to explain covariances among observed variables, explore underlying latent constructs, or account for measurement error, then the best choice is common factor analysis. When in doubt, compare numerical results among principal component and common factor techniques. If results differ, then choose common factor analysis (McArdle, 1990).

When determining how many factors to retain, it is best to use multiple approaches and seek agreement between them. If the approaches do not agree, then test rotated solutions with different numbers of factors and choose the one that is most easily interpretable. Use an oblique rotation to allow for the possibility of factor correlation. Ensure that your data are scaled and distributed in accordance with the assumptions of the approach you are using. Ensure adequate sample size and include at least three variables for each factor. When using CFA to confirm EFA, consider how the fallacies associated with both methods and the differences between the two may result in poor fit between the two sets of results. Rely on theory to guide model modifications rather than solely seeking improved fit indices.

Finally, report the results in as much detail as possible to allow readers to understand and evaluate the results. Factor analysis is a very useful technique with a large variety of applications. Understanding the common fallacies associated with its use can result in more sound results and better scientific understanding.

Concluding Remarks and Summary Checklist

When applied judiciously, quantitative research methodology provides powerful tools for testing complex hypotheses about the phenomena at play. From research design to data collection and statistical analysis, many potential pitfalls may compromise the validity of a study. It is only with careful planning and thoughtful execution that we can build a scientifically rigorous knowledge base about the theory of interest.

In this chapter, we have examined in depth six common fallacies in quantitative research methodology: Contextual Variable Fallacies, Measurement Error Fallacies, Missing Data Fallacies, Statistical Significance Fallacies, Statistical Power Fallacies, and Factor Analysis Fallacies. Additional fallacies are included in the Checklist of Common Fallacies in Quantitative Research Methodology (Table 31.1). The additional fallacies are Quantitative Epistemology Fallacies, Research Ethics Fallacies, Design Compatibility Fallacies, Sampling Error Fallacies, Implementation Procedure Fallacies, Data Categorization Fallacies, Distributional Assumption Fallacies, Multiple Testing Fallacies, ANOVA/ANCOVA Fallacies, and Multilevel Modeling Fallacies. In all, 16 major fallacies and 65 sub-fallacies are included in the checklist. Although an exhaustive treatment is not possible in

Table 31.1. Summary Checklist of Common Fallacies in Quantitative Research Methodology (Y = *Fallacy Committed*, N = *Fallacy Not Committed*, NA = *Not Applicable*)

Fallacy	Y	N	NA
Research design fallacies			
1. Quantitative epistemology fallacies:			
1.1 Reductionism—complex phenomena are reduced to variables and numbers, overlooking contextual factors and process variables (e.g., studying treatment impact without due regard for moderators) (Brattico, 2008; Little, Bovaird, & Card, 2007; Melnyk, 2007)			
1.2 Deductionism—theory building focused on average and overall trend, overlooking residuals, uncertainty, and underlying structure (e.g., computing average growth and ignoring individual growth curves) (Duncan, Duncan, & Strycker, 2006; Mislevy, 1994; Rao, 1992)			
1.3 Objectivism—ontology of one objective reality, "numbers don't lie" thinking, and statistical testing without rationalization (e.g., $\alpha = 0.05$ or power $= 0.80$) (Cohen, 1990; Phillips & Burbules, 2000; Shadish, 1995)			
2. Research ethics fallacies:			
2.1 Lack of informed consent (e.g., random assignment into control group without treatment or standard practice) (Levine, 1988; Lynöe & Hoeyer, 2005; Shadish, Cook, & Campbell, 2002)			
2.2 Deception of research purpose and procedure (e.g., placebo treatment and blinding of group assignment without pre-warning or post-study debriefing) (APA, 2010a, Standard 8.07-8.08; Bensing & Verheul, 2010; Schenker, Fernandez, & Lo, 2009)			
2.3 Coercion and undue influence (e.g., studying disadvantaged or vulnerable populations under demand characteristics) (Liégeois & Eneman, 2008; Wynn, 2006)			

(continued)

Table 31.1. (*Continued*)

2.4 Fabrication and falsification of data (e.g., eliminating outliers without due cause) (Barnett & Lewis, 1994; Wells & Farthing, 2008)			
2.5 Confidentiality vs. anonymity (e.g., assuring anonymity but collecting IP addresses in online longitudinal survey for connectivity) (Bjarnason & Adalbjarnardottir, 2000; Strike, Anderson, Curren, Geel, Pritchard, & Robertson, 2002, Standard II.10)			
3. Design compatibility fallacies:			
3.1 Misalignment between purpose and design (e.g., using simple correlational design to study causation) (Maxwell, 2010; West & Thoemmes, 2010)			
3.2 Misuse of cross-sectional data for longitudinal inferences (e.g., comparing different cohorts across years instead of tracking the same cohorts over time) (Givens, Lu, Bartell, & Pearson, 2007; Lee, Bartolic, & Vandewater, 2009)			
3.3 Selection of time-points for trend analysis (e.g., studying pre- and post-test difference without delayed effect) (Ghosh, Ghosh, & Tiwari, 2011; Wiens & Palmer, 2001)			
4. Contextual variable fallacies:			
4.1 Mistaking mediation for moderation and vice versa (e.g., making a mediational claim with a moderational design) (Baron & Kenny, 1986; Wu & Zumbo, 2008)			
4.2 Mediation is tested with the constituent paths rather than the product of the paths (e.g., testing the direct effect from the predictor to the mediator and from the mediator to the criterion) (e.g., Fritz & MacKinnon, 2007; Hayes, Preacher, & Myers, 2009)			
4.3 Presence of direct effect should be tested as prerequisite evidence of mediation (e.g., testing mediation effect only after a significant direct effect between the predictor and criterion is found) (MacKinnon, Krull, & Lockwood, 2000; Shrout & Bolger, 2002)			
4.4 Using cross-sectional data for testing mediation hypotheses (e.g., studying the mediational effect of motivation on achievement without time lag for motivation to impact achievement)			
4.5 Moderation is confused with additive effects of a multiple regression equation (e.g., interpreting the regression coefficients of moderators as moderating effects) (Ho, 2008; Wiedemann, Lippke, Reuter, Ziegelmann, & Schwarzer, 2011)			
4.6 Hierarchically nested data structures can be ignored or should be avoided (e.g., collapsing across classrooms to obtain a school-level mean value) (Bickle, 2007; Card, Selig, & Little, 2008)			
Data collection fallacies			
5. Sampling error fallacies:			
5.1 Confusion of target population, accessible population, and target sample, and final sample (e.g., sampling from an undergraduate population but making inference about a clinical population) (Evans, Ashworth, & Peters, 2010; Williams & Kores, 2011)			
5.2 Underreporting of sampling method and representativeness of sample to population (e.g., describing participants and setting without commenting on how sample is selected or what population characteristics are) (AERA, 2006, Standard 3.1; Zientek, Capraro, & Capraro, 2008)			
5.3 Determination of sample size (e.g., no rationale for how sample size is determined, sample size too small for optimal power or too large for economic efficacy) (Kikuchi, Pezeshk, & Gittins, J., 2008; Kwong, Cheung, & Wen, 2010)			

(*continued*)

Table 31.1. (*Continued*)

6. Measurement error fallacies:			
6.1 Summing across individual items to derive composite scores without due regard for weighting or reverse coding (e.g., assigning 1 to *Agree* and 0 to *Disagree* when an item is negatively related to the total scale) (Barnette, 2000; Kolen & Tong, 2010; Weems & Onwuegbuzie, 2001)			
6.2 Increasing test length to improve reliability without due regard for item quality (e.g., adding items that are negatively related to the total score) (Bagnoli & Bergstrom, 2005; Yousfi, 2005)			
6.3 Reporting subscale scores without subscale reliabilities (e.g., prescribing remedial work in a subdomain when it is not significantly deficient than other skill areas) (Sinharay, Puhan, & Haberman, 2010; Wang, Yao, Tsai, Wang, & Hsieh, 2006)			
6.4 Ignoring mixture or multilevel structure in measurement error (e.g., central tendency vs. extremity response set) (De Boeck & Wilson, 2005; De Jong & Steenkamp, 2010; von Davier & Carstensen, 2007)			
6.5 Reporting attenuated effect sizes as if they were free from measurement error (e.g., estimating correlation without correction for unreliability) (Charles, 2005; Hunter & Schmidt, 2004; Wang, 2004)			
6.6 Inflated reliability due to bloated specifics and shared method variance (e.g., using repetitive recalls to retrospectively self-report diet and activity level) (Boyle, 1991; Reise, Morizot, & Hays, 2007)			
6.7 Using a published or locally developed instrument without evidence of psychometric quality (e.g., administering a standardized observational checklist without training observers for inter-rater consistency) (Wang, Profitt, Suess, & Sun, 2010; Zientek, Capraro, & Capraro, 2008)			
6.8 Lack of validity evidence for self-report data (e.g., taking self-report data on face value without triangulation) (Chan, 2009; Podsakoff, MacKenzie, Lee, & Podsakoff, 2003)			
7. Implementation procedure fallacies:			
7.1 Implementation infidelity (e.g., treatment group fails to follow the prescribed intervention regiment) (Century, Rudnick, & Freeman, 2010; Gearing, El-Bassel, Ghesquiere, Baldwin, Gillies, & Ngeow, 2011)			
7.2 Circumstantial threats to data quality (e.g., collecting sensitive data without providing a secure and private environment) (Galesic, Tourangeau, & Couper, 2006; Karanicolas, Farrokhyar, & Bhandari, 2010).			
7.3 Data entry and processing errors (e.g., data entry without a flagging mechanism, overlooking outlier effects) (Osborne & Overbay, 2008; Riera-Ledesma & Salazar-González, 2007)			
7.4 Lack of sufficient detail on who, when, where, and how the instrument is used for judging procedural appropriateness (AERA, 2006, Standard 3.2)			
8. Missing data fallacies:			
8.1 Missing data imputation is cheating or "getting something for nothing" (e.g., deleting all cases with missing data to avoid imputation or limiting the number of imputed values in multiple imputation) (Bodner, 2008; Buyse et al., 1999)			
8.2 Using outdated or unjustified methods for imputation (e.g., using mean substitution or regression imputation) (Enders, 2010; Little & Rubin, 2002)			

(*continued*)

Table 31.1. (*Continued*)

8.3 Confusion over different missing mechanisms and performing data imputation when unwarranted by the missing mechanism (e.g., perform an EM imputation without taking into consideration of auxiliary variables that are correlated with missingness) (Enders, 2010; Graham, 2009)			
8.4 Confusion over planned versus unplanned missingness (e.g., not utilizing planned missing data designs to increase validity and generalizability)(Bunting, Adamson, & Mulhall, 2002; Graham et al., 2006)			
9. Data categorization fallacies:			
9.1 Turning continuous variables into discrete variables by creating artificial categories (e.g., categorizing technology use into low, medium, and high exposure) (Cohen, 1983; MacCallum, Zhang, Preacher, & Rucker, 2002)			
9.2 Choosing arbitrary or sample-dependent cutoff points without theoretical justification (e.g., using median split to separate the total group into two high and low groups) (Maxwell & Delaney, 1993; Preacher, Rucker, MacCallum, & Nicewander, 2005)			
9.3 Confusing group comparison with experimental causation (e.g., assuming that by comparing group differences causal inferences can be made) (Lagakos, 1988; Royston, Altman, & Sauerbrei, 2006)			
Statistical analysis fallacies			
10. Statistical significance fallacies:			
10.1 Interpreting statistical significance as the theoretical hypothesis being true (e.g., claiming proof for the alternative hypothesis after the null hypothesis is rejected) (Fraley & Marks, 2007; Rozeboom, 1960)			
10.2 Confusing statistical significance with practical significance (e.g., interpreting a correlation with $p < 0.05$ as a strong relationship) (Kirk, 1996; Nickerson, 2000)			
10.3 Confusing statistical significance with replicability (e.g., interpreting $p < 0.05$ as greater than 95% chance of replicating the result in a different study) (Cumming, 2008; Miller, 2009)			
10.4 Interpreting statistical nonsignificance as study failure (e.g., rejecting a manuscript for publication unless statistical significance is found) (Sterne & Smith, 2001; Sterling, Rosenbaum, & Weinkam, 1995)			
10.5 Making dichotomous decision about theoretical hypothesis based on an arbitrary or conventional error tolerance level (e.g., rejecting the null hypothesis if $p < 0.05$) (Cohen, 1990; Kline, 2004)			
11. Distributional assumption fallacies:			
11.1 Applying non-robust statistical tests when distributional assumptions are violated (e.g., using Scheffé's multiple comparison test when variances are heterogeneous) (Erceg-Hurn & Mirosevich, 2008; Wells & Hintze, 2007; Zimmerman, 2004)			
11.2 Transforming data to fit distributional assumptions when population distribution unjustified or transformation method inappropriate (e.g., applying square-root transformation when logarithmic transformation is called for) (Osborne, 2008c; Rasmussen, 1989)			
11.3 Fitting a lower-order function to higher-order data (e.g., calculating a linear correlation when a curvilinear relation is present) (Cohen, Cohen, West, & Aiken, 2003; Ghosh, Ghosh, & Tiwari, 2011)			

(*continued*)

Table 31.1. (*Continued*)

12. Multiple testing fallacies:			
12.1 Applying nonparametric tests to individual items measured on an ordinal scale when inference is made at the interval scale level (e.g., performing the Mann-Whitney U test on individual items when the parametric t- or F-test is more appropriate and powerful) (Carifio & Perla, 2007; Pell, 2005)			
12.2 Performing multiple univariate tests at item or subscale level when the research hypothesis involves multivariate structure (e.g., the research hypothesis is whether there is a group difference in motivation, operationally defined as extrinsic and intrinsic motivation, but two separate univariate tests are performed on each individually) (Huberty & Morris, 1989; Keselman et al., 1998)			
12.3 Performing *post hoc* multiple comparison tests when *a priori* tests are called for (e.g., performing all pairwise contrasts when the experimenter is only interested in comparing various treatments to the control) (Keselman, Cribbie, & Holland, 2004; Kirk, 1995)			
13. Statistical power fallacies:			
13.1 Confusing prospective power with retrospective power (e.g., determining an appropriate sample size during the planning stage but failing to recognize the attrition and non-response rate after the study has been concluded) (Onwuegbuzie & Leech, 2004; Zumbo & Hubley, 1998)			
13.2 Interpreting statistical nonsignificance as no effect without discussion of power (e.g., concluding no effect without considering small sample size) (Finch, Cumming, & Thomason, 2001; Thompson, 2006)			
13.3 Interpreting statistical nonsignificance in the (expected) presence of high retrospective power as evidence for null being true; conversely, interpreting statistical nonsignificance in the presence of low retrospective power as evidence for true effect (Goodman & Berlin, 1994; Hoenig & Heisey, 2001; Wang, 2010b)			
13.4 Calculating retrospective power using observed effect size without confidence interval (e.g., calculating a point estimate for power without taking into consideration the standard error of the observed effect size) (Taylor & Muller, 1995; Yuan & Maxwell, 2005)			
14. ANOVA/ANCOVA fallacies:			
14.1 Ignoring sample dependency in repeated-measures ANOVA (e.g., failure to specify dependent samples in a pretest-posttest design as a within-subjects effect) (Keselman et al., 1998; Maxwell & Delaney, 2004)			
14.2 Using an incorrect error term in the F-test for analysis of variance (e.g., assuming a fixed effect of the independent variable when in fact random or treating a nested factor as random) (Fidler & Thompson, 2001; Siemer & Joormann, 2003; Wampold & Serlin, 2000)			
14.3 Ignoring interaction and simple effects in factorial ANOVA (e.g., testing only main effects when interaction may be present or of theoretical interest; after a significant interaction is found no follow-up tests of simple effects) (Embretson, 1996; Huopaniemi, Suvitaival, Nikkila, Oresic, & Kaski, 2010)			
14.4 Using ANCOVA to adjust for pretest differences in non-random cluster designs (e.g., assuming that by specifying the pretest as covariate group equivalency would be established) (Davison & Sharma, 1994; Wright, 2006)			

(*continued*)

Table 31.1. (*Continued*)

15. *Factor analysis fallacies:*
15.1 Confusing principal components with common factors (e.g., using the default principal component extraction method in exploratory factor analysis) (Floyd & Widaman, 1995; Velicer & Jackson, 1990)
15.2 Determining the number of factors to retain (e.g., relying on graphical methods or eyeballing to determine the break point in a scree plot) (Fabrigar, Wegener, MacCallum, & Strahan, 1999; Preacher & MacCallum, 2003)
15.3 Determining the factor rotation method (e.g., requesting orthogonal rotation when oblique rotation is more appropriate) (Browne, 2001; Nunnally & Bernstein, 1994)
15.4 Using confirmatory factor analysis to confirm an exploratory factor analysis model (e.g., conducting an EFA to find the factor structure and subsequently fit the same data to the resultant EFA model in a CFA) (Fabrigar, Wegener, MacCallum, & Straham, 1999; van Prooijen & van der Kloot, 2001)
16. *Multilevel modeling fallacies:*
16.1 Lack of rationale for modeling multilevel structure (e.g., no intra-class correlation or explained variance reported) (Gueorguieva & Krystal, 2004; Singer, 1998)
16.2 Under-reporting of choice of covariance structure, metric centering, and estimation method (e.g., using the default option to estimate a free covariance matrix when an autoregressive covariance structure is more efficient) (e.g., (Dedrick et al., 2009; Vallejo, Ato, & Valdés, 2008)
16.3 Ignorance of cross-classification, multiple membership, and/or multiple classification structure in the multilevel structure (e.g., treating each lower-level data unit as belonging to one and only one higher-level group) (Browne, Goldstein, & Rasbash, 2001; Grady & Beretvas, 2010)

this chapter, this list provides a starting point for quantitative researchers to critically reflect on their research methodology before drawing substantive conclusions. It also serves as a frame of reference for training quantitative researchers to critique published studies or unpublished manuscripts.

Many of the fallacies remain active research areas among quantitative methodologists. It is our hope that the checklist points to future directions for quantitative methodologists to continue their quest for further advancement in quantitative research methodology.

Author Note

Partial support for this project was provided by grant NSF 1053160 (Wei Wu & Todd D. Little, co-PIs) and by the Center for Research Methods and Data Analysis at the University of Kansas (Todd D. Little, director). Correspondence: Leigh Wang, University of Cincinnati (wanglh@ucmail.uc.edu); Amber Watts, University of Kansas (amberwatts@ku.edu); Rawni Anderson, University of Kansas (rawni@ku.edu); and Todd D. Little, University of Kansas (yhat@ku.edu). Web support: crmda.ku.edu.

References

Abdel-Khalek, A., & Lester, D. (2002). Using the short subscales of a questionnaire to assess subcomponents with low reliabilities: A cautionary note. *Psychological Reports, 90*(3), 1255–1256.

Aiken, L. S., West, S. G., & Millsap, R. E. (2008). Doctoral training in statistics, measurement, and methodology in psychology: Replication and extension of Aiken, West, Sechrest, and Reno's (1990) survey of PhD programs in North America. *American Psychologist, 63,* 32–50.

American Educational Research Association (2006). Standards for reporting on empirical social science research in AERA publications. *Educational Researcher, 35*(6), 33–40.

American Educational Research Association, American Psychological Association, & National Council on Measurement in Education (1999). *Standards for educational and psychological testing*. Washington, DC: Authors.

American Psychological Association (2010a). *Ethical standards of psychologists and code of conduct*. Washington, DC: Author.

American Psychological Association (2010b). *Publication manual of the American Psychological Association* (6th ed.). Washington, DC: Author.

Andersen, B. (1990). *Methodological errors in medical research*. London: Blackwell.

Anderson, T. W., & Rubin, H. (1956). Statistical inference in factor analysis. *Proceedings of the third Berkley Symposium on Mathematical Statistics and Probability, V*, 111–150.

Archer, K. J., Dumur, C. I., Taylor, G. S., Chaplin, M. D., Guiseppi-Elie, A., Buck, G. A, & Garett, C. T. (2008). A disattenuated correlation estimate when variables are measured with error: Illustration estimating cross-platform correlations. *Statistics in Medicine, 27*, 1026–1039.

Austin E. J., Deary I. J., & Egan, V. (2006). Individual differences in response scale use: Mixed Rasch modeling of responses to NEO-FFI items. *Personality and Individual Differences, 40*(6), 1235–1245.

Bagnoli, M., & Bergstrom, T. (2005). Log-concave probability and its applications. *Economic Theory, 26*(2), 445–469.

Bai, H., Wang, L., Pan, W., & Frey, M. (2009). Measuring mathematics anxiety: Psychometric analysis of a bidimensional affective scale. *Journal of Instructional Psychology, 36*(4), 185–193.

Balluerka, N., Gmez, J., & Hidalgo, D. (2005). The controversy over Null Hypothesis Significance Testing Revisited. *Methodology: European Journal of Research Methods for the Behavioral and Social Sciences, 1*(2), 55–85.

Baio, G., & Blangiardo, M. (2008). Introduction to Bayesian modeling for the social sciences. In J. W. Osborne (Ed.), *Best practices in quantitative methods* (pp. 509–534). Thousand Oaks, CA: Sage.

Barnett V., & Lewis, T. (1994). *Outliers in statistical data*. New York: Wiley.

Barnette, J. J. (1999). Nonattending response effects on internal consistency of self-administered surveys: A Monte Carlo simulation study. *Educational and Psychological Measurement, 59*(1), 38–46.

Barnette, J. J. (2000). Effects of stem and Likert response option reversals on survey internal consistency: If you feel the need, there is a better alternative to using those negatively worded stems. *Educational and Psychological Measurement, 60*(3), 361–370.

Baron, R. M., & Kenny, D. A. (1986). The moderator–mediator variable distinction in social psychological research: Conceptual, strategic, and statistical considerations. *Journal of Personality and Social Psychology, 51*(6), 1173–1182.

Bauer, D., & Lavery, R. (2004). *Proc Power in SAS 9.1*. Retrieved from http://www2.sas.com/proceedings/sugi29/195-29.pdf

Beauducel, A., & Rabe, S. (2009). Model-related factor score predictors for confirmatory factory analysis. *British Journal of Mathematical and Statistical Psychology, 62*, 489–506.

Becker, G. (1991). Alternative methods of reporting research results. *American Psychologist, 46*, 654–655.

Bedeian, A. G., Day, D. V., & Kelloway, E. K. (1997). Correcting for measurement error attenuation in structural equation models: Some important reminders. *Educational and Psychological Measurement, 57*(5), 785–799.

Belia, S., Fidler, F., Williams, J., & Cumming, G. (2005). Researchers misunderstand confidence intervals and standard error bars. *Psychological Methods, 10*, 389–396.

Bensing, J. M., & Verheul, W. (2010). The silent healer: The role of communication in placebo effects. *Patient Education & Counseling, 80*(3), 293–299.

Bernaards, C. A., & Sijtsma, K. (2000). Influence of imputation and EM methods on factor analysis when item nonresponse in questionnaire data is nonignorable. *Multivariate Behavioral Research, 35*(3), 321–364.

Berger, J. O., & Berry, D. A. (1988). Statistical analysis and the illusion of objectivity. *American Science, 76*, 159–165.

Bickle, R. (2007) Multilevel analysis for applied research: It's just regression. New York: Guilford.

Bjarnason, T., & Adalbjarnardottir, S. (2000). Anonymity and confidentiality in school surveys on alcohol, tobacco, and cannabis use. *Journal of Drug Issues, 30*(2), 335–344.

Black, T. R. (1999). *Doing quantitative research in the social sciences: An integrated approach to research design, measurement and statistics*. Thousand Oaks, CA: Sage.

Bobko, P., Roth, P. L., & Bobko, C. (2001). Correcting the effect size of d for range restriction and unreliability. *Organizational Research Methods, 4*(1), 46–61.

Bodner, T. E. (2008). What improves with increased missing data imputations? *Structural Equation Modeling, 15*(4), 651–675.

Bohrnstedt, G. W. (1983). Measurement. In P. H. Rossi, J. D. Wright, & A. B. Anderson (Eds.), *Handbook of survey research* (pp. 70–114). San Diego, CA: Academic Press.

Bond, T. G., & Fox, C. M. (2007). *Applying the Rasch model: Fundamental measurement in the human sciences* (2nd ed.). Mahwah, NJ: Lawrence Erlbaum.

Bovaird, J. A. (2007). Multilevel structural equation model for contextual factors. In T. D. Little, J. A. Bovaird, & N. A. Card (Eds.),. *Modeling contextual effects in longitudinal studies* (pp. 149–182). Mahwah, NJ: Lawrence Erlbaum.

Boyle, G. J. (1991). Does item homogeneity indicate internal consistency or item redundancy in psychometric scales? *Personality and Individual Differences, 12*(3), 291–294.

Brattico, P. (2008). Shallow reductionism and the problem of complexity in psychology. *Theory & Psychology, 18*(4), 483–504.

Browne, M. W. (2000). Cross-validation methods. *Journal of Mathematical Psychology, 44*(1), 108–132.

Browne, M. W. (2001). An overview of analytic rotation in exploratory factor analysis. *Multivariate Behavioral research, 36*, 111–150.

Browne, W. J., Goldstein, H., & Rasbash, J. (2001). Multiple membership multiple classification (MMMC) models. *Statistical Modelling, 1*, 103–124.

Bunting, B. P., Adamson, G., & Mulhall, P. K. (2002). A Monte Carlo examination of an MTMM model with planned incomplete data structures. *Structural Equation Modeling, 9*, 369–389.

Buyse, M., George, S. L., Evans, S., Geller, N. L., Ranstam, J., Scherrer, B et al. (1999). The role of biostatistics in the prevention, detection and treatment of fraud in clinical trials. *Statistics in Medicine, 18*(24), 3435–3451.

Card, N. A., Selig, J. P., & Little, T. D. (2008). *Modeling dyadic and interdependent data in the developmental and behavioral sciences*. New York: Routledge.

Carifio, J., & Perla, R. (2007). Ten common misunderstandings, misconceptions, persistent myths and urban legends about Likert scales and Likert response formats and their antidotes. *Journal of the Social Sciences, 3*(3), 106–116.

Carifio, J., & Perla, R. (2008). Resolving the 50-year debate around using and misusing Likert scales. *Medical Education, 42*(2), 1150–1152.

Carrington, P. J., Scott, J., & Wasserman, S. (Eds.). (2005). *Models and methods in social network analysis*. New York: Cambridge University Press.

Carroll, R. J., Ruppert, D., Stefanski, L. A., & Crainiceanu, C. M. (2006). *Measurement error in nonlinear models: A modern perspective*. New York: Chapman & Hall.

Cattell, R. B., & Vogelmann, S. (1977). A comprehensive trial of the scree and KG criteria for determining the number of factors. *Journal of Education Measurement, 14*, 289–325.

Cella, D., Gershon, R., Lai, J.-S., & Choi, S. (2007) The future of outcomes measurement: Item banking, tailored short-forms, and computerized adaptive assessment. *Quality of Life Research, 16*(Suppl. 1), 133–141.

Century, J., Rudnick, M., & Freeman, C. (2010). A framework for measuring fidelity of implementation: A foundation for shared language and accumulation of knowledge. *American Journal of Evaluation, 31*(2), 199–218.

Chan, D. (2009). So why ask me? Are self-report data really that bad? In C. E. Lance & R. J. Vandenberg (Eds.), *Statistical and methodological myths and urban legends* (pp. 309–335). New York: Routledge.

Charles, E. P. (2005). The correction for attenuation due to measurement error: Clarifying concepts and creating confidence sets. *Psychological Methods, 10*(2), 206–226.

Chesher, A. (1991). The effect of measurement error. *Biometrika, 78*(3), 451–462.

Cho, S. J., & Cohen, A. S. (2010). A multilevel mixture IRT model with an application to DIF. *Journal of Educational and Behavioral Statistics, 35*(3), 336–370.

Chow, S. L. (1996). *Statistical significance: Rationale, validity and utility*. London: Sage.

Cliff, N. (1988). The eigenvalues-greater-than-one rule and the reliability of components. *Psychological Bulletin, 103*, 276–279.

Cliff, N., & Keats, J. A. (2003). *Ordinal measurement in the behavioral sciences*. Mahwah, NJ: Lawrence Erlbaum.

Cohen, J. (1962). The statistical power of abnormal-social psychological research: A review. *Journal of Abnormal and Social Psychology, 65*, 145–153.

Cohen, J. (1983). The cost of dichotomization. *Applied Psychological Measurement, 7*, 249–253.

Cohen, J. (1988). *Statistical power analysis for the behavioral sciences*. New York: Academic.

Cohen, J. (1990). Things I have learned (so far). *American Psychologist, 45*(12), 1304–1312.

Cohen, J. (1992). A power primer. *Psychological Bulletin, 112*(1), 155–159.

Cohen, J. (1994). The earth is round (p < .05). *American Psychologist, 49*(12), 997–1003.

Cohen, J., Cohen, P., West, S., & Aiken, L. S. (2003). *Applied multiple regression/correlation analysis for the behavioral sciences*. Mahwah, NJ: Lawrence Erlbaum.

Cohen, P., Cohen, J., Teresi, J., Marchi, M., & Velez, C. N. (1990). Problems in the measurement of latent variables in structural equation causal models. *Applied Psychological Measurement, 14*(2), 183–196.

Cole, D. A., & Maxwell, S. E. (2003). Testing mediational models with longitudinal data: Questions and tips in the use of structural equation modeling. *Journal of Abnormal Psychology, 112*(4), 558–577.

Comrey, A. L. (1988). Factor-analytic methods of scale development in personality and clinical psychology. *Journal of Consulting and Clinical Psychology, 56*, 754–761.

Comrey, A. L., & Lee, H. B. (1992). *First course in factor analysis* (2nd ed.). Hillsdale, NJ: Lawrence Erlbaum.

Crawford, J. R., Anderson, V., Rankin, P. M., & MacDonald, J. (2010). An index-based short-form of the WISC-IV with accompanying analysis of the reliability and abnormality of differences. *British Journal of Clinical Psychology, 49*(2), 235–258.

Cronbach, L. J. (1960). *Essentials of psychological testing* (2nd ed.). New York: Harper and Row.

Cumming, G. (2008). Replication and *p* Intervals: *p* values predict the future only vaguely, but confidence intervals do much better. *Perspectives on Psychological Science, 3*, 286–300.

Cumming, G., Fidler, F., Leonard, M., Kalinowski, P., Christiansen, A., Kleinig, A., & Wilson, S. (2007). Statistical reform in psychology: Is anything changing? *Psychological Science, 18*, 230–232.

Cumming, G., & Finch, S. (2005). Inference by eye: Confidence intervals, and how to read pictures of data. *American Psychologist, 60*, 170–180.

Cumming, G., Williams, J., & Fidler, F. (2004). Replication, and researchers' understanding of confidence intervals and standard error bars. *Understanding Statistics, 3*, 299–311.

Davey, T., & Parshall, C. G. (1997). New algorithms for item selection and exposure control with computerized adaptive testing. *Journal of Educational and Behavioral Statistics, 22*(2), 203–226.

Davison, M. L., & Sharma, A. R. (1994). ANOVA and ANCOVA of Pre- and Post-test Ordinal data. *Psychometrika, 59*(4), 593–600.

Dear, K. G., Puterman, M. L., & Dobson, A. J. (1997). Estimating correlations from epidemiological data in the presence of measurement error. *Statistics in Medicine, 16*, 2177–2189.

Dearing, E., & Hamilton, L. C. (2006). Best practices in quantitative methods for developmentalists: V. contemporary advances and classic advice for analyzing mediating and moderating variables. *Monographs of the Society for Research in Child Development, 71*(3), 88–104.

Deboeck, P. R., & Wilson, M. (2005). *Explanatory item response models: A generalized linear and nonlinear approach*. New York: Springer-Verlag.

Dedrick, R. F., Ferron, J. M., Hess, M. R., Hogarty, K. Y., Kromrey, J. D., Lang, T. R., Niles, J. D., & Lee, R. S. (2009). Multilevel modeling: A review of methodological issues and applications. *Review of Educational Research, 79*(1), 69–102.

De Jong, M. G., & Steenkamp, J.-B. E. M. (2010). Finite mixture multilevel multidimensional ordinal IRT models for large scale cross-cultural research. *Psychometrika, 75*(1), 3–32.

De Jonge, P., & Slaets, J. P. J. (2005). Response sets in self-report data and their associations with personality traits. *The European Journal of Psychitry, 19*(4), 209–214.

Denis, D. J. (2003). Alternatives to null hypothesis statistical testing. *Theory & Science, 4*(1), [online]. Retrieved December 15, 2010 from http://theoryandscience.icaap.org/content/vol4.1/02_denis.html

DeShon, R. P. (1998). A cautionary note on measurement error corrections in structural equation models. *Psychological Methods, 3*(4), 412–423.

DeVellis, R. F. (2003). *Scale development: Theory and applications* (2nd ed.). Thousand Oaks, CA: Sage.

Dixon, P. (2003). The p-value fallacy and how to avoid it. *Canadian Journal of Experimental Psychology, 57*(3), 189–202.

Dixon, P., & O'Reilly, T. (1999). Scientific versus statistical inference. *Canadian Journal of Experimental Psychology, 53*, 133–149.

Dolbier, C. L. (2005). Reliability and validity of a single-item measure of job satisfaction. *American Journal of Health Promotion, 19*(3), 194–198.

Dollinger, S. J. (2009). Reliability and validity of single-item self-reports: With special relevance to college students' alcohol use, religiosity, study, and social life. *Journal of General Psychology, 136*(3), 231–241.

Donaldson, S. I., Christie, C. A., & Mark, M. M. (2009). (Eds.). *What counts as credible evidence in applied research and evaluation practice?* Thousand Oaks, CA: Sage.

Duncan, T. E., Duncan, S. E., & Strycker, L. A. (2006). *An introduction to latent variable growth curve modeling: Concepts, issues, and applications* (2nd ed.). Mahwah, NJ: Lawrence Erlbaum.

Eaves, L., Erkanli, A., Silberg, J., Angold, A., Maes, H. H., & Foley, D. (2005). Application of Bayesian inference using Gibbs sampling to item-response theory modeling of multi-symptom genetic data. *Behavior Genetics, 35*(6), 765–780.

Edwards, W. (1965). Tactical note on the relation between scientific and statistical hypotheses. *Psychological Bulletin, 63*, 400–402.

Embretson, S. E. (1996). Item response theory models and spurious interaction effects in factorial ANOVA designs. *Applied Psychological Measurement, 20*(3), 201–212.

Enders, C. K. (2010). *Applied missing data analysis*. New York: Guilford.

Erceg-Hurn, D. M., & Mirosevich, V. M. (2008). Modern robust statistical methods: An easy way to maximize the accuracy and power of your research. *American Psychologist, 63*, 591–601.

Evans, C., Ashworth, M., & Peters, M. (2010). Are problems prevalent in non-clinical populations? Problems and test-retest stability of a patient-generated measure, PSYCHLOPS. *British Journal of Guidance and Counselling, 38*(4), 431–439.

Evans, J. G. (1997). Ethical problems of futile research. *Journal of Medical Ethics, 23*(1), 5–6.

Fabrigar, L. R., Wegener, D. T., MacCallum, R. C., & Strahan, E. J. (1999). Evaluating the use of exploratory factor analysis in psychological research. *Psychological Methods, 4*(3), 272–299.

Faul, F., & Erdfelder, E., Lang, A.-G., & Buchner, A. (2007). G*Power 3: A flexible statistical power analysis program for the social, behavioral, and medical sciences. *Behavior Research Methods, 39*, 175–191.

Favreau, O. E. (1997). Sex and gender comparisons: Does null hypothesis testing create a false dichotomy? *Feminism & Psychology, 7*, 63–81.

Feldt, L. S., & Qualls, A. L. (1999). Variability in reliability coefficients and the standard error of measurement from school district to district. *Applied Measurement in Education, 12*, 367–381.

Fidler, F. (2005). From statistical significance to effect estimation: Statistical reform in psychology, medicine, and ecology. Department of History and Philosophy of Science, University of Melbourne. Retrieved December 23, 2010 from http://www.botany.unimelb.edu.au/envisci/docs/fidler/fidlerphd_aug06.pdf

Fidler, F., & Cumming, G. (2008). The new stats: Attitudes for the 21st century. In J. W. Osborne (Ed.), *Best practices in quantitative methods* (pp. 1–12). Thousand Oaks, CA: Sage.

Fidler, F., &Thompson, B. (2001). Computing correct confidence intervals for ANOVA fixed-and random-effects effect sizes. *Educational and Psychological Measurement, 61*, 575–604.

Fidler, F., Thomason, N. Cumming, G., Finch, S. & Leeman, J. (2004). Editors can lead researchers to confidence intervals, but can't make them think: Statistical reform lessons from medicine. *Psychological Science, 15*, 119–126.

Finch, H. (2010). Item parameter estimation for the MIRT model: Bias and precision of confirmatory factor analysis-based models. *Applied Psychological Measurement, 34*, 10–26.

Finch, S., Cumming, G., & Thomason, N. (2001). Reporting of statistical inference in the Journal of Applied Psychology: Little evidence of reform. *Educational and Psychological Measurement, 61*, 181–210.

Fitzpatrick, A. R., & Yen, W. M. (2001). The effects of test length and sample size on the reliability and equating of tests composed of constructed-response items. *Applied Measurement in Education, 14*(1), 31–57.

Floyd, F. J., & Widaman, K. F. (1995). Factor analysis in the development and refinement of clinical assessment instruments. *Psychological Assessment, 7*(3), 286–299.

Flynn, J. R. (2007). *What is intelligence? Beyond the Flynn Effect*. Cambridge, UK: Cambridge University Press.

Fox, J.-P., & Glas, C. A. W. (2001). Bayesian estimation of a multilevel IRT model using Gibbs sampling. *Psychometrika, 66*(2), 271–288.

Fraley, R. C., & Marks, M. J. (2007). The null hypothesis significance testing debate and its implications for personality research. In R. Robins, R. C. Fraley & R. Krueger (Eds.), *Handbook of research methods in personality psychology* (pp. 149–169). New York: Guilford.

Frazier, P. A., Tix, A. P., & Barron, K. E. (2004). Testing moderator and mediator effects in counseling psychology research. *Journal of Counseling Psychology, 51*(1), 115–134.

French, S. A., Story, M., & Perry, C. L. (1995). Self-esteem and obesity in children and adolescents: A literature review. *Obesity Research, 3*, 479–490.

Fritz, M. S., & MacKinnon, D. P. (2007). Required sample size to detect the mediated effect. *Psychological Science, 18*(3), 233–239.

Froman, T., & Shneyderman, A. (2004). Replicability reconsidered: An excessive range of possibilities. *Understanding Statistics, 3*, 365–373.

Fuller, W. A. (1987). *Measurement error models*. New York: Wiley.

Furr, R. M., & Bacharach, V. R. (2008). *Psychometrics: An introduction*. Thousand Oaks, CA: Sage.

Galesic, M., Tourangeau, R., & Couper, M. P. (2006). Complementing random-digit-dial telephone surveys with other approaches to collecting sensitive data. *American Journal of Preventive Medicine, 31*(5), 437–443.

Gearing, R. E., El-Bassel, N., Ghesquiere, A., Baldwin, S., Gillies, J., & Ngeow, E. (2011). Major ingredients of fidelity: A review and scientific guide to improving quality of intervention research implementation. *Clinical Psychological Review, 31*(1), 79–88.

Gerard, P. D., Smith, D. R., & Weerakkody, G. (1998). Limits of retrospective power analysis. *Journal of Wildlife Management, 62*(2), 801–807.

Ghosh, P., Ghosh, K., & Tiwari, R. C. (2011). Bayesian approach to cancer-trend analysis using age-stratified Poisson regression models. *Statistics in Medicine, 30*(2), 127–139.

Gierl, M. J., Alves, C., & Majeau, R. T. (2010). Using the attribute hierarchy method to make diagnostic inferences about examinees' knowledge and skills in mathematics: An operational implementation of cognitive diagnostic assessment. *Journal of International Testing, 10*(4), 318–341.

Gillett, R. (1994). Post hoc power analysis. *Journal of Applied Psychology, 79*(5), 783–785.

Ginns, P., & Barrie, S. (2004). Reliability of single-item ratings of quality in higher education: A replication. *Psychological Reports, 95*(3), 1023–1030.

Givens, M. L., Lu, C., Bartell, S. M., & Pearson, M. A. (2007). Estimating dietary consumption patterns among children: A comparison between cross-sectional and longitudinal study designs. *Environmental Research, 103*(3), 325–330.

Gliner, J. A., Leech, N. L., & Morgan, G. A. (2002).Problems with Null Hypothesis Significance Testing (NHST): What do the textbooks say? *The Journal of Experimental Education, 71*(1), 83–92.

Gollob, H. F., & Reichardt, C. S. (1985). Building time lags into causal models of cross-sectional data. *Proceedings of the Social Statistics Section of the American Statistical Association* (pp. 165–170). Washington, DC: American Statistical Association.

Gollob, H. F., & Reichardt, C. S. (1987). Taking account of time lags in causal models. *Child Development, 58*(1), 80–92.

Good, P. I., & Hardin, J. M. (2003). *Common errors in statistics (and how to avoid them)*. Hoboken, NJ: Wiley.

Goodman, S. N., & Berlin, J. A. (1994). The use of predicted confidence intervals when planning experiments and the misuse of power when interpreting results. *Annals of Internal Medicine, 121*(3), 200–206.

Gorsuch, R. L., (1983). *Factor analysis*. (2nd ed.) Hillsdale, NJ: Lawrence Erlbaum.

Grady, M. W., & Beretvas, S. N. (2010). Incorporating student mobility in achievement growth modeling: A cross-classified multiple membership growth curve model. *Multivariate Behavioral Research, 45*(3), 393–419.

Graham, J. (2009). Missing data analysis: Making it work in the real world. *Annual Review of Psychology, 60*, 549–576.

Graham, J. W., Hofer, S. M., & MacKinnon, D. P. (1996). Maximizing the usefulness of data obtained with planned missing value patterns: An application of maximum likelihood procedures. *Multivariate Behavioral Research, 31*, 197–218.

Graham, J. W., Taylor, B. J., Olchowski, A. E., & Cumsille, P. E. (2006). Planned missing data designs in psychological research. *Psychological Methods, 11*, 323–343.

Greenwald, A. G. (1975). Consequences of prejudice against the null hypothesis. *Psychological Bulletin, 82*(1), 1–20.

Grice, J. W. (2001). Computing and evaluating factor scores. *Psychological Methods, 11*, 430–450.

Groves, R. M., Dillman, D. A., Eltinge, J. L., & Little, R. J. A. (2002). (Eds.). *Survey nonresponse*. New York: Wiley.

Guadagnoli, E., & Velicer, W. F. (1988). The relationship of sample size to the stability of component patterns: A simulation study. *Psychological Bulletin, 103*, 265–275.

Gueorguieva, R., & Krystal, J. H. (2004). Move over ANOVA: Progress in analyzing repeated-measures data and its reflection in papers published in the Archives of General Psychiatry. *Archives of General Psychiatry, 61*(3), 310–317.

Gulliksen, H. (1950). *Theory of mental tests*. New York: Wiley.

Guo, S., & Fraser, M. W. (2010). *Propensity score analysis: Statistical methods and applications*. Thousand Oaks, CA: Sage.

Guttman, L. (1954). Some necessary conditions for common factor analysis. *Psychometrika, 19*, 149–161.

Hagen, R. L. (1997). In praise of the null hypothesis statistical test. *American Psychologist, 52*, 15–24.

Hakstian, A. R., Schroeder, M. L., & Rogers, W. T. (1988). Inferential procedures for correlation coefficients corrected for attenuation. *Psychometrika, 53*(1), 27–43.

Hancock, G. R. (1997). Correlation/validity coefficients disattenuated for score reliability: A structural equation modeling approach. *Educational and Psychological Measurement, 57*(4), 598–606.

Hancock, G. R. (2001). Effecct size, power, and sample size determination for structured means modeling and mimic approaches between-group hypothesis testing of means on a single latent construct. *Psychometrika, 66*(3), 373–388.

Hancock, G. R., & Samuelsen, K. M. (2008). (Eds.). *Latent variable mixture models*. Charlotte, NC: Information Age.

Harlow, L. L., Mulaik, S. A., & Steiger, J. H. (1997). (Eds.). *What if there were no significance tests?* Mahwah, NJ: Lawrence Erlbaum.

Hayes, A. F. (2009). Beyond Baron and Kenny: Statistical mediation analysis in the new millennium. *Communication Monographs, 76*(4), 408–420.

Hayes, A. F., Preacher, K. J., & Myers, T. A. (2009). Mediation and the estimation of indirect effects in political communication research. In E. P. Bucy, & R. L. Holbert (Eds.), *Sourcebook for political communication research: Methods, measures, and analytical techniques* (pp. 434–465). New York: Routledge.

Hedges, L. V. (1983). A random effects model for effect sizes. *Psychological Bulletin, 93*, 388–395.

Henson, R. K., Hull, D. M., & Williams, C. S. (2010). Methodology in our education research culture: Toward a stronger collective quantitative proficiency. *Educational Researcher, 39*(3), 229–240.

Henson, R. K., & Roberts, J. K. (2006). Use of exploratory factor analysis in published research: Common errors and some comment on improved practice. *Educational and Psychological Measurement, 66*(3), 393–416.

Ho, J. (2008). Community violence exposure of Southeast Asian American adolescents. *Journal of interpersonal violence, 23*(1), 136–146.

Hoenig, J. M., & Heisey, D. M. (2001). The abuse of power: The pervasive fallacy of power calculations for data analysis. *The American Statistician 55*, 19–24.

Hogarty, K. Y., & Kromrey, J. D. (2003). RETR_PWR: An SAS macro for retrospective statistical power analysis. *Behavioral Research Methods, Instruments, & Computers, 35*(4), 585–589.

Holden, R. R., & Book, A. S. (2009). Using hybrid Rasch-latent class modeling to improve the detection of fakers on a personality inventory. *Personality and Individual Differences, 47*(3), 185–190.

Holmbeck, G. N. (1997). Toward terminological, conceptual, and statistical clarity in the study of mediators and moderators: Examples from the child-clinical and pediatric psychology literatures. *Journal of Consulting and Clinical Psychology, 65*(4), 599–610.

Howard, G. S., Maxwell, S. E., & Fleming, K. J. (2000). The proof of the pudding: An illustration of the relative strengths of null hypothesis, meta-analysis, and Bayesian analysis. *Psychological Methods, 5*(3), 315–332.

Huberty, C. J., & Morris, J. D. (1989). Multivariate analysis versus multiple univariate analyses. *Psychological Bulletin, 105*(2), 302–308.

Huck, S. W. (2009). *Statistical misconceptions.* New York: Routledge.

Humphreys, L. G., & Montanelli, R. G. (1975). An investigation of the parallel analysis criterion for determining the number of common factors. *Multivariate Behavioral Research, 10,* 193–205.

Hunter, J. E., & Schmidt, F. L. (2004). *Methods of meta-analysis: Correcting error and bias in research findings.* Thousand Oaks, CA: Sage.

Huopaniemi, I., Suvitaival, T., Nikkila, J., Oresic, M., & Kaski, S. (2010). Multivariate multi-way analysis of multi-source data. *Bioinformatics, 26*(12), 391–398.

Ioannidis, J. P. A. (1998). Effect of the statistical significance of results on the time to completion and publication of randomized efficacy trials. *Journal of the American Medical Association, 279*(4), 281–286.

Jacobson, N. S. & Truax, P. (1991). Clinical significance: A statistical approach to defining meaningful change in psychotherapy research. *Journal of Consulting and Clinical Psychology, 59*(1), 12–19.

James, L. R., & Brett, J. M. (1984). Mediators, moderators and tests for mediation. *Journal of Applied Psychology, 69,* 307–321.

Johnson, H. G. (1950). Test reliability and correction for attenuation. *Psychometrika, 15,* 115–119.

Johnson, R. B., & Onwuegbuzie, A. J. (2004). Mixed-methods research: A research paradigm whose time has come. *Educational Researcher, 33*(7), 14–26.

Jöreskog, K. G., & Sorbom, D. (1989). *LISREL 7: User's reference guide.* Mooresville, IN: SSI.

Judd, C. M., & Kenny, D. A. (1981). Process analysis: Estimating mediation in treatment evaluations. *Evaluation Review, 5*(5), 602–619.

Kaiser, H. F. (1970). A second generation Little-Jiffy. *Psychometrika, 35,* 401–415.

Kamata, A., & Bauer, D. J. (2008). A note on the relation between factor analytic and item response theory models. *Structural Equation Modeling, 15,* 136–153.

Kane, M. (2010). *Errors of measurement, theory, and public policy.* Princeton, NJ: ETS.

Karabatsos, G. (2001). The Rasch model, additive conjoint measurement and new models of probabilistic measurement theory. *Journal of Applied Measurement, 2*(4), 389–423.

Kenny, D. A. (2008). Reflections on mediation. *Organizational Research Methods, 11*(2), 353–358.

Kenny, D. A., & Kashy, D. A. (2006). *Dyadic data analysis.* New York: Guilford.

Keselman, H. J., Cribbie, R. A., & Holland, B. (2004). Pairwise multiple comparison test procedures: An update for clinical child and adolescent psychologists. *Journal of Clinical Child & Adolescent Psychology, 33*(3), 623–645.

Keselman, H. J., Huberty, C. J., Lix, L. M., Olejnik, S., Cribbie, R. A., Donahue, B., & Keselman, J. C. (1998). Statistical practices of educational researchers: An analysis of their ANOVA, MANOVA, and ANCOVA analyses. *Review of Educational Research, 68*(3), 350–386.

Kikuchi, T., Pezeshk, H., & Gittins, J. (2008). A Bayesian cost–benefit approach to the determination of sample size in clinical trials. *Statistics in Medicine, 27*(1), 68–82.

Kileen, P. R. (2005). An alternative to null-hypothesis significance tests. *Psychological Science, 16*(5), 345–353.

Kirk, R. E. (1995). *Experimental design: Procedures for the behavioral sciences.* Pacific Grove, CA: Brooks/Cole.

Kirk, R. E. (1996). Practical significance: A concept whose time has come. *Educational and Psychological Measurement, 56,* 746–759.

Kishton, J. M., & Widaman, K. F. (1994). Unidimensional versus domain representative parceling of questionnaire items: An empirical example. *Educational and Psychological Measurement, 54,* 757–765.

Klee, R. (1999). (Ed.). *Scientific inquiry: Readings in the philosophy of science.* New York: Oxford University Press.

Kline, R. B. (2004). *Beyond significance testing: Reforming data analysis methods in behavioral research.* Washington, DC: American Psychological Association.

Kline, R. B. (2010). *Principles and practice of structural equation modeling* (3rd ed.). New York: Guilford.

Kolen, M. J., & Tong, Y. (2010). Psychometric properties of IRT proficiency estimates, *Educaitonal Measurement: Issues and Practice, 29*(3), 8–14.

Koretz, D. (2008). Further steps toward the development of an accountability-oriented science of measurement. In K. E. Ryan & L. A. Shepard (Eds.), *The future of test-based educational accountability* (pp.71–92). New York: Routledge.

Kristof, W. (1973). Testing a linear relation between true scores of two measures. *Psychometrika, 38*(1), 101–111.

Kuhn, T. S. (1970). *The structure of scientific revolutions* (2nd ed.). Chicago, IL: The University of Chicago Press.

Kwong, K. S., Cheung, S. H., & Wen, M.-J. (2010). Sample size determination in step-up testing procedures for multiple comparisons with a control. *Statistics in Medicine, 29*(26), 2743–2756.

Lagakos, S. W. (1988). Effects of mismodelling and mismeasuring explanatory variables on tests of their association with a response variable. *Statistics in Medicine, 7*(1–2), 257–274.

Lance, C. E., & Vandenberg, R. J. (2009). (Ed.). *Statistical and methodological myths and urban legends.* New York: Routledge.

Lee, S.-J., Bartolic, S., & Vandewater, E. A. (2009). Predicting children's media use in the USA: Differences in cross-sectional and longitudinal analysis. *British Journal of Developmental Psychology, 27*(1), 123–143.

Lee, W.-C., Brennan, R. L., & Kolen, M. J. (2000). Estimators of conditional scale-score standard errors of measurement: A simulation study. *Journal of Educational Measurement, 37*(1), 1–20.

Leech, N. L., & Goodwin, L. D. (2008). Building a methodological foundation: Doctoral-level methods courses in colleges of education. *Research in the Schools, 15*(1), 1–8.

Leighton, J. P., & Gierl, M. J. (2007). (Eds.). *Cognitive diagnostic assessment for education: Theory and practices.* Cambridge, UK: Cambridge University Press.

Levine, M., & Ensom, M. H. H. (2001). Post hoc power analysis: An idea whose time has passed? *Pharmacotherapy, 21*(4), 405–409.

Levine, R. J. (1988). *Ethics and regulation of clinical research.* New Haven, CT: Yale University Press.

Levine, T. R., Weber, R., Hullett, C., Park, H. S., & Lindsey, L. L. M. (2008). A critical assessment of null hypothesis significance testing in quantitative communication research. *Human Communication Research, 34*(2), 171–187.

Li, F., Cohen, A. S., Kim, S.-H., & Cho, S.-J. (2009). Model selection methods for mixture dichotomous IRT models. *Applied Psychological Measurement, 33*(5), 353–373.

Liégeois, A., & Eneman, M. (2008). Ethics of deliberation, consent and coercion in psychiatry. *Journal of Medical Ethics, 34*(2), 73–76.

Linacre, J. M., & Wright, B. D. (2002). Construction of measures from many-facet data. *Journal of Applied Measurement, 3*(4), 486–512.

Little, R. J. A., & Rubin, D. B. (2002). *Statistical analysis with missing data* (2nd Ed.). Hoboken, NJ: Wiley.

Little, T. D., Cunningham, W. A., Shahar, G., & Widaman, K. F. (2002). To parcel or not to parcel: Exploring the question, weighing the merits. *Structural Equation Modeling, 9*, 151–173.

Little, T. D., Bovaird, J. A., & Card, N. A. (2007). (Eds.). *Modeling contextual effects in longitudinal studies*. Mahwah, New Jersey: Lawrence Erlbaum.

Little, T. D., Schnabel, K. U., & Baumert, J. (2000). (Eds.). *Modeling longitudinal and multilevel data*. Mahwah, NJ: Lawrence Erlbaum.

Luce, R. D., & Tukey, J. W. (1964). Simultaneous conjoint measurement: A new type of fundamental measurement. *Journal of Mathematical Psychology, 1*, 1–27.

Lynöe, N., & Hoeyer, K. (2005). Quantitative aspects of informed consent: Considering the dose response curve when estimating quantity of information. *Journal of Medical Ethics, 31*(12), 736–738.

MacCallum R. C., Zhang, S., Preacher, K.J., & Rucker, D.D. (2002). On the practice of dichotomization of quantitative variables. *Psychological Methods, 7*(1), 19–40.

MacKinnon, D. P., Krull, J. L., & Lockwood, C. M. (2000). Equivalence of the mediation, confounding and suppression effect. *Prevention Science, 1*(4), 173–181.

MacKinnon, D. P., Lockwood, C. M., Hoffman, J. M., West, S. G., & Sheets, V. (2002). A comparison of methods to test mediation and other intervening variable effects. *Psychological Methods, 7*(1), 83–104.

MacKinnon, D. P., & Luecken, L. J. (2008). How and for whom? Mediation and moderation in health psychology. *Health Psychology, 27*(2, Suppl), S99–S100.

Magazine, S. L., Williams, L. J., & Williams, M. L. (1996). A confirmatory factor analysis examination of reverse coding effects in Meyer and Allen's Affective and Continuance Commitment Scales. *Educational and Psychological Measurement, 56*(2), 241–250.

Marsh, H. W., Hau, K. T., Balla, J. R., & Grayson, D. (1998). Is more ever too much? The number of indicators per factor in confirmatory factor analysis. *Multivariate Behavioral Research, 33*(2), 181–220.

Matcham, J., McDermott, M. P., & Lang, A. E. (2007). GDNF in Parkinson's disease: The perils of post-hoc power. *Journal of Neuroscience Methods, 163*, 193–196.

Mathieu, J. E., & Taylor, S. R. (2006). Clarifying conditions and decision points for mediational type inferences in organizational behavior. *Journal of Organizational Behavior, 27*(8), 1031–1056.

Maxwell, S. E. (2004). The persistence of underpowered studies in psychological research: Causes, consequences, and remedies. *Psychological Methods, 9*(2), 147–163.

Maxwell, S. E. (2010). Introduction to the special issue on Campbell's and Rubin's conceptualizations of causality. *Psychological Methods, 15*(1), 1–2.

Maxwell, S. E., & Cole, D. A. (2007). Bias in cross-sectional analyses of longitudinal mediation. *Psychological Methods, 12*(1), 23–44.

Maxwell, S. E., & Delaney, H. D. (1993). Bivariate median splits and spurious statistical significance. *Psychological Bulletin, 113*(1), 181–190.

Maxwell, S. E., & Delaney, H. D. (2004). *Designing experiments and analyzing data: A model comparison perspective*. Belmont, CA: Wadsworth.

Maxwell, S. E., Kelley, K., & Rausch, J. R. (2008). Sample size planning for statistical power and accuracy in parameter estimation. *Annual Review of Psychology, 59*, 537–563.

McArdle, J. J. (1990). Principles versus principles of structural factor analysis. *Multivariate Behavioral Research, 25*(1), 81–87.

McArdle, J. J., & Hamagami, F. (1991). *Modeling incomplete longitudinal and cross-sectional data using latent growth structural models*. Washington, DC: American Psychological Association.

McDonald, P. J., Kulkarni, A. V., Farrokhyar, F., & Bhandari, M. (2010). Practical tips for surgical research: Ethical issues in surgical research. *Canadian Journal of Surgery, 53*(2), 133–136.

McCrae, R. R., Zonderman, A. B., Costa, P. T., Bond, M. H., & Paunonen, S. V. (1996). Evaluating replicability of factors in the revised NEO Personality Inventory: Confirmatory factor analysis versus procrustes rotation. *Journal of Personality and Social Psychology, 70*, 552–566.

McDonald, R. P. (1967). Numerical methods for polynomial models in nonlinear factor analysis. *Psychometrika, 32*(1), 77–112.

McDonald, R. P. (1999). *Test theory: A unified treatment*. Mahwah, NJ: Lawrence Erlbaum.

McDonald, R. P., & Ho, M.-H. R. (2002). Principles and practice in reporting structural equation analyses. *Psychological Methods, 7*(1), 64–82.

Meadows, L. M., & Morse, J. M. (2001). Constructing evidence within the qualitative project. In J. M. Morse, J. M. Swanson, & A. J. Kuzel (Eds.), *The nature of qualitative evidence* (pp. 187–202). Thousand Oaks, CA: Sage.

Meehl, P. E. (1978). Theoretical risks and tabular asterisks: Sir Karl, Sir Ronald, and the slow progress of soft psychology. *Journal of Consulting and Clinical Psychology, 46*, 806–834.

Meehl, P. E. (1990). Why summaries of research on psychological theories are often uninterpretable. *Psychological Reports, 66*, 195–244.

Meehl, P. E. (1997). The problem is epistemology, not statistics: Replace significance tests by confidence intervals and quantify accuracy of risk numerical predictions. In L. L. Harlow, S. A. Mulaik, & J. H. Steiger (Eds.), *What if there were no significance tests?* (pp. 395–425). Mahwah, NJ: Lawrence Erlbaum.

Melnyk, A. (2007). Functionalism and psychological reductionism: Friends, not foes. In M. Schouten & H. L. de Long (Eds.), *The matter of the mind: Philosophical essays of psychology, neuroscience, and reduction* (pp. 31–50). Malden, MA: Blackwell.

Michell, J. (1997). Quantitative science and the definition of measurement in psychology. *British Journal of Psychology, 88*, 355–386.

Miller, J. (2009). What is the probability of replicating a statistically significant effect? *Psychonomic Bulletin & Review, 16*(4), 617–640.

Miller, C. T., & Downey, K. T. (1999). A meta-analysis of heavyweight and self-esteem. *Personality and Social Psychology Review, 3*, 68–84.

Mislevy, R. J. (1994). Evidence and inference in educational assessment. *Psychometrika, 59*(4), 439–483.

Mislevy, R. J., & Verhelst, N. (1990). Modeling item responses when subjects employ different solution strategies. *Psychometrika, 55*(2), 195–215.

Mittag, K. C., & Thompson, B. (2000). A national survey of AERA members' perceptions of statistical significance tests and other statistical issues. *Educational Researcher, 29*, 14–20.

Moustaki, I., Jöreskog, K., & Mavridis, D. (2004). Factor models for ordinal variables with covariate effects on the manifest and latent variables: A comparison of LISREL and IRT approaches. *Structural Equation Modeling Journal, 11*(4), 487–513.

Muchinsky, P. M. (1996). The correction for attenuation. *Educational and Psychological Measurement, 56*(1), 63–75.

Mulaik, S. (1990). (Ed.) *Multivariate Behavioral Research, 25*(1).

Mulaik, S. A., Raju, N. S., & Harshman, R. A. (1997). There is a time and a place for significance testing. In L. L. Harlow, S. A., Mulaik, & J. H. Steiger (Eds.), *What if there were no significance tests?* (pp. 65–115). Mahwah, NJ: Lawrence Erlbaum.

Murphy, K. R., & Myors, B., & Wolach, A. (2009). *Statistical power analysis: A simple and general model for traditional and modern hypothesis tests* (3rd ed.). Hillsdale, NJ: Lawrence Erlbaum.

Neale, M. C., & Cardon, L. R. (1992). *Methodology for genetic studies of twins and families*. Dordrecht, the Netherlands: Kluwer.

Nering, M., & Ostini, R. (2010). (Eds.). *Handbook of polytomous item response theory models*. New York: Routledge.

Nickerson, R. S. (2000). Null hypothesis significance testing: A review of an old and continuing controversy. *Psychological Methods, 5*(2), 241–301.

Niemi, R. G. (1986). The impact of scale length on reliability and validity: A clarification of some misconceptions. *Quality & Quantity, 20*(4), 371–376.

Nunnally, J. C., & Bernstein, I. H. (1994). *Psychometric theory* (3rd ed.). New York: McGraw-Hill.

Oakes, J. M., & Feldman, H. A. (2001). Statistical power for nonequivalent pretest-posttest designs. *Evaluation Review, 25*(1), 3–28.

Oakes, M. W. (1986). *Statistical inference: A commentary for the social and behavioral sciences*. New York: Wiley.

Ojanen, T., Sijtsema, J. J., Hawley, P. H., & Little, T. D. (2010). Intrinsic and extrinsic motivation in early adolescents' friendship development: Friendship selection, influence, and prospective friendship quality. *Journal of Adolescence, 33*(6), 837–851.

O'Keefe, K. J. (2007). Post hoc power, observed power, a priori power, retrospective power, prospective power, achieved power: Sorting out appropriate uses of statistical power analyses. *Communication Methods and Measures, 1*, 291–299.

Onwuegbuzie, A. J., & Leech, N. L. (2004). Post hoc power: A concept whose time has come. *Understanding Statistics, 3*(4), 201–230.

Osborne, J. W. (2008a). Using best practices is a moral and ethical obligation. In J. W. Osborne (Ed.), *Best practices in quantitative methods* (pp. ix–xii). Thousand Oaks, CA: Sage.

Osborne, J. W. (2008b). Is disattenuation of effects a best practice? In J. W. Osborne (Ed.), *Best practices in quantitatve methods* (pp. 239–245). Thousand Oaks, CA: Sage.

Osborne, J. W. (2008c). Best practices in data transformation: The overall effect of minimum values. In J. W. Osborne (Ed.), *Best practices in quantitatve methods* (pp. 197–204). Thousand Oaks, CA: Sage.

Osborne, J. W., & Overbay, A. (2008). Best practices in data cleaning: How outliers and "fringeliers" can increase error rates and decrease the quality and precision of your results. In In J. W. Osborne (Ed.), *Best practices in quantitative methods* (pp. 205–213). Thousand Oaks, CA: Sage.

Overall, J. E. (1969). Classical statistical hypotheses within the context of Bayesian theory. *Psychological Bulletin, 71*, 285–292.

Panter, A. T., & Sterba, S. K. (2011). (Eds.). *Handbook of ethics in quantitative methodology*. New York: Routledge.

Pell, G. (2005). Uses and misuses of Likert scales. *Medical Education, 39*(9), 970.

Pereira, C. A. B, Stern, J. M., & Wechsler, S. (2008). Can a significance test be genuinely Bayesian? *Bayesian Analysis, 3*(1), 79–100.

Phillips, D. C., & Burbules, N. C. (2000). *Postpositivism and educational research*. New York: Rowan and Littlefield.

Podsakoff, P. M., MacKenzie, S. B., Lee, J.-Y., & Podsakoff, N. P. (2003). Common method biases in behavioral research: A critical review of the literature and recommended remedies. *Journal of Applied Psychology, 88*(5), 879–903.

Popper, K. R. (1959). *The logic of scientific discovery*. London, UK: Hutchinson.

Preacher, K. J., & Hayes, A. F. (2008). Contemporary approaches to assessing mediation in communication research. In A. F. Hayes, M. D. Slater, & L. B. Snyder (Eds.), *The Sage sourcebook of advanced data analysis methods for communication research* (pp. 13–54). Thousand Oaks, CA: Sage.

Preacher, K. J., & MacCallum, R. C. (2003). Repairing Tom Swift's electric factor analysis machine. *Understanding Statistics, 2*(1), 13–43.

Preacher, K. J., Rucker, D. D., MacCallum, R. C., & Nicewander, W. A. (2005). Use of the extreme groups approach: A critical reexamination and new recommendations. *Psychological Methods, 10*(2), 178–192.

Quiñones-Vidal, E., Loźpez-García, Juan José, Peñarañda-Ortega, M., & Tortosa-Gil, F. (2004). The nature of social and personality psychology as reflected in *JPSP*, 1965–2000. *Journal of Personality and Social Psychology, 86*(3), 435–452.

Rao, C. R. (1992). R. A. Fisher: The founder of modern statistics. *Statistical Science, 7*(1), 34–48.

Rasmussen, J. L. (1989). Data transformation, Type I error rate and power. *British Journal of Mathematical and Statistical Psychology, 42*(2), 203–213.

Raudenbush, S. W., & Bryk, A. S. (2002). *Hierarchical linear models: Applications and data analysis methods* (2nd ed.). Thousand Oaks, CA: Sage.

Raykov, T., & Marcoulides, G. A. (2011). *Introduction to psychometric theory*. New York: Routledge.

Reckase, M. D. (2009). *Multidimensional item response theory*. New York: Springer.

Reise, S. P. (2000). Using multilevel logistic regression to evaluate person fit in IRT models. *Multivariate Behavioral Research, 35*(4), 543–568.

Reise, S. P., Morizot, J., & Hays, R. D. (2007). The role of the bifactor model in resolving dimensionality issues in health outcomes measures. *Qualify of Life Research, 16*(1), 19–31.

Reynolds, C. R. (2000). Methods for detecting and evaluating cultural bias in neuropsychological tests. In E.

Fletcher-Janzen, T. L. Strickland, & C. R. Reynolds (Eds.), *Handbook of cross-cultrual neuropsychology* (pp. 249–286). New York: Springer-Verlag.

Rhemtulla, M. (2010). Planned missing data designs for developmental research. Banting Fellowship Application: Canadian Government Research Agencies.

Riera-Ledesma, J., & Salazar-González, J.-J. (2007). A heuristic approach for the continuous error localization problem in data cleaning. *Computers and Operations Research, 34*(8), 2370–2383.

Rijmen, F., & De Boeck, P. (2005). Relation between a between-item multidimensional IRT model and the mixture Rasch model. *Psychometrika, 70*(3), 481–496.

Rose, B. M., Holmbeck, G. N., Coakley, R. M., & Franks, E. A. (2004). Mediator and moderator effects in developmental and behavioral pediatric research. *Journal of Developmental and Behavioral Pediatrics, 25*(1), 58–67.

Rost, J. (1991). A logistic mixture distribution model for polychotomous item responses. *British Journal of Mathematical and Statistical Psychology, 44*(1), 75–92.

Rouder, J. N., Speckman, P. L., Sun, D., Morey, R. D., & Iverson, G. (2009). Bayesian t tests for accepting and rejecting the null hypothesis. *Psychonomic Bulletin and Review, 16*, 225–237.

Rozeboom, W. W. (1960). The fallacy of the null hypothesis significance test. *Psychological Bulletin, 57*, 416–428.

Royston, P., Altman, D. G., & Sauerbrei, W. (2006). Dichotomizing continuous predictors in multiple regression: A bad idea. *Statistics in Medicine, 25*(1), 127–141.

Rupp, A. A., Templin, J., & Henson, R. A. (2010). *Diagnostic measurement: Theory, methods, and applications*. New York: Guilford.

Ruscio, J., & Walters, G. D. (2009). Using comparison data to differentiate categorical and dimensional data by examining factor score distributions: Resolving the mode problem. *Psychological Assessment, 21*(4), 578–594.

Rust, J., & Golombok, S. (2009). *Modern psychometrics: The science of psychological assessment* (3rd ed.). London: Routledge.

Saw, A.T., Berger, D.E., Mary, J.C., & Sosa, G. (April, 2009). *Misconceptions of hypothesis testing and p-values*. Paper presented at the meeting of the Western Psychological Association, Portland, Oregon.

Schenker, Y., Fernandez, A., & Lo, B. (2009). Placebo prescriptions are missed opportunities for doctor-patient communication. *American Journal of Bioethics, 9*(12), 48–54.

Schmidt, F. L., & Hunter, J. E. (1999). Theory testing and measurement error. *Intelligence, 27*(3), 183–198.

Selig, J. P. (2010). Where has the time gone? The role of time lags in models for longitudinal data. *Dissertation Abstracts International: Section B: The Sciences and Engineering, 70*(8-B), 5143–5259.

Shadish, W. R. (1995). Philosophy of science and the quantitative-qualitative debates: Thirteen common errors. *Evaluation and Program Planning, 18*(1), 63–75.

Shadish, W. R., Cook, T. D., & Campbell, D. T. (2002). *Experimental and quasi-experimental designs for generalized causal inference*. Boston, MA: Houghton Mifflin.

Shrout, P. E., & Bolger, N. (2002). Mediation in experimental and nonexperimental studies: New procedures and recommendations. *Psychological Methods, 7*(4), 422–445.

Siemer, M., & Joormann, J. (2003). Power and measures of effect size in analysis of variance with fixed versus random nested factors. *Psychological Methods, 8*(4), 497–517.

Singer, J. D. (1998). Using SAS PROC MIXED to fit multilevel models, hierarchical models, and individual growth models. *Journal of Educational and Behavioral Statistics, 23*(4), 323–355.

Sinharay, S., Puhan, G., & Haberman, S. J. (2010). Reporting diagnostic scores in educational testing: Temptations, pitfalls, and some solutions. *Multivariate Behavioral Research, 45*(3), 553–573.

Slavin, R. E. (2002). Evidence-based education policies: Transforming educational practice and research. *Educational Researcher, 31*(7), 15–21.

Smith, J. B., & Batchelder, W. H. (2008). Assessing individual differences in categorical data. *Psychonomic Bulletin & Review, 15*(4), 713–731.

Smith, S. D. (2008). Statistical tools in the quest for truth: Hypothesis testing, confidence intervals, and the power of clinical studies. *Ophthalmology, 115*(3), 423–424.

Sohn, D. (1998). Statistical significance and replicability: Why the former does not presage the latter. *Theory and Psychology, 8*, 291–311.

Spearman, C. (1904). The proof and measurement of association between two things. *American Journal of Psychology, 15*, 72–101.

Steiger, J. H., & Fouladi, R. T. (1997). Noncentrality interval estimation and the evaluation of statistical models. In L. L. Harlow, S. A., Mulaik, & J.H. Steiger (Eds.),*What if there were no significance tests?* (pp. 221–257). Mahwah, NJ: Erlbaum.

Steiner, P. M., Cook, T. D., & Shadish, W. R. (2011). On the importance of reliable covariate measurement in selection bias adjustments using propensity scores. *Psychological Methods, 36*(2), 213–236.

Sterling, T.D., Rosenbaum, W. L, & Weinkam, J. J. (1995). Publication decisions revisited: The effect of the outcome of statistical tests on the decision to publish and vice versa. *The American Statistician, 49*(1), 108–112.

Sterne, J. A. C., & Smith, G. D. (2001). Sifting the evidence—what's wrong with significance tests? *British Medical Journal, 322*, 226–231.

Strauss, R. S. (2000). Childhood obesity and self-esteem. *Pediatrics, 105*, 1–5.

Streiner, D. L. (1994). Figuring out factors: The use and misuse of factor analysis. *Canadian Journal of Psychiatry, 39*, 135–140.

Strike, K. A., Anderson, M. S., Curren, R., van Geel, T., Pritchard, I., & Robertson, E. (2002). *Ethical standards of the American Educational Research Association: Cases and commentary*. Washington, DC: American Educational Research Association.

Sun, S., Pan, W., & Wang, L. (2011). Rethinking observed power: Concept, practice, and implications. *Methodology: European Journal of Research Methods for the Behavioral and Social Sciences, 7*(3), 81–87.

Taylor, D. J., & Muller, K. E. (1995). Computing confidence bounds for power and sample size of the general linear univariate model. *The American Statistician, 49*, 43–47.

Thomas, L. (1997). Retrospective power analysis. *Conservation Biology, 11*(1), 276–280.

Thomas, L., & Krebs, C. J. (1997). A review of statistical power analysis software. *Bulletin of the Ecological Society of America, 78*, 126–139.

Thompson, B. (2006). *Foundations of behavioral statistics: An insight-based approach*. New York: Guilford.

Thompson, B. (2007). Effect sizes, confidence intervals, and confidence intervals for effect sizes. *Psychology in the Schools, 44*(5), 423–432.

Thurstone, L. L. (1935). *The vectors of mind*. Chicago, IL: University of Chicago Press.

Thurstone, L. L. (1947). *Multiple-factor analysis: A development and expansion of the vectors of mind*. Chicago, IL: University of Chicago Press.

Tucker, L. R., Koopman, R. F., & Linn, R. L. (1969). Evaluation of factor analytic research procedures by means of simulated correlation matrices. *Psychometrika, 34*, 421–459.

Vallejo, G., Ato, M., & Valdés, T. (2008). Consequences of misspecifying the error covariance structure in linear mixed models for longitudinal data. *Methodology: European Journal of Research Methods for the Behavioral and Social Sciences, 4*(1), 10–21.

Van der Gaag, M., Cuijpers, A., Hoffman, T., Remijsen, M., Hijman, R., de Haan, L., & Wiersma, D. (2006). The five-factor model of the positive and negative syndrome scale I: Confirmatory factor analysis fails to confirm 25 published five-factor solutions. *Schizophrenia Research, 85*(1–3), 273–279.

Van der Linden, W. J., & Hambleton, R. K. (1997). (Eds.). *Handbook of modern item response theory*. New York: Springer-Verlag.

Van der Linden, W. J., & Pashley, P. J. (2010). Item estimation and ability estimation in adaptive testing. In W. J. van der Linden & G. A. W. Glas (Eds.), *Elements of adaptive testing* (pp. 3–30). New York: Springer-Verlag.

Van Prooijen, J., & van der Kloot, W. A. (2001). Confirmatory analysis of exploratively obtained factor structures. *Educational and Psychological Measurement, 61*(5), 777–792.

Velicer, W. F., & Jackson, D. N. (1990). Component analysis versus common factor analysis: Some issues in selecting an appropriate procedure. *Multivariate Behavioral Research, 25*(1), 1–28.

Von Davier, M. (2010). Mixture distribution item response theory, latent class analysis, and diagnostic mixture models. In S. E. Embretson (Ed.), *Measuring psychological constructs: Advances in model-based approaches* (pp. 11–34). Washington, DC: APA.

Von Davier, M., & Carstensen, C. H. (2007). (Eds.) *Multivariate and mixture distribution Rasch models: Extensions and applications*. New York: Springer.

Von Davier, M., & Yamamoto, K. (2004). Partially observed mixtures of IRT models: An extension of the Generalized Partial-Credit Model. *Applied Psychological Measurement, 28*(6), 389–406.

Wainer, H., & Robinson, D. H. (2003). Shaping up the practice of null hypothesis significance testing. *Educational Researcher, 32*(7), 22–30.

Waller, N. G. (1994). NOVAX 1.3: A PC-DOS factor analysis program for ordered polytomous data and mainframe-size problems. *Applied Psychological Measurement, 18*(2), 195–196.

Wampold, B. E., & Serlin, R. C. (2000). The consequence of ignoring a nested factor on measures of effect size in analysis of variance. *Psychological Methods, 5*(4), 425–433.

Wang, L. (July, 2009). *Disattenuation of correlations due to fallible measurement in meta-analysis: A critique on the debate over "voodoo" correlations in social neuroscience*. Paper presented at the International Meeting of Psychometric Society, University of Cambridge, Great Britain.

Wang, L. (2010a). Disattenuation of correlations due to fallible measurement. *Special Issue on Quantitative Research Methodology. Journal of Newborn and Infant Nursing Reviews, 10*(1), 60–65.

Wang, L. (2010b). Retrospective statistical power: Fallacies and recommendations. *Special Issue in Quantitative Research Methodology. Journal of Newborn and Infant Nursing Reviews, 10*(1), 55–59.

Wang, L., Pan, W., & Bai, H. (2009). Detection efficacy of multilevel latent trait approach to differential person functioning: A Monte Carlo comparison with conventional person misfit statistics. In K. Shigemasu, Okada, A., Imaizumi, T., & Hoshino, T. (Ed.), *New trends in psychometrics* (pp. 535–542). Tokyo, Japan: Universal Academy Press.

Wang, L., Profitt, A., Suess, R., & Sun, S. (April, 2010). *Impact of measurement unreliability on effect size estimation and power: New evidence from recent published research and Monte Carlo simulations*. Paper presented at the 2010 National Council on Measurement in Education, Denver, Colorado.

Wang, W.-C. (2004). Direct estimation of correlation as a measure of association strength using multidimensional item response models. *Educational and Psychological Measurement, 64*(6), 937–955.

Wang, W.-C., & Jin, K.-Y. (2010). A generalized model with internal restrictions on item difficulty for polytomous items. *Educational and Psychological Measurement, 70*, 181–198.

Wang, W.-C., Yao, G., Tsai, Y.-J., Wang, J.-D., & Hsieh, C.-L. (2006). Validating, improving reliability and estimating correlation of the four subscales in the WHOQOL-BREF using multidimensional Rasch analysis. *Quality of Life Research, 15*, 607–620.

Weems, G. H., & Onwuegbuzie, A. J. (2001). The impact of midpoint responses and reverse coding in survey data. *Measurement and Evaluation in Counseling and Development, 34*, 166–216.

Wells, C. S., & Hintze, J. M. (2007). Dealing with assumptions underlying statistical tests. *Psychology in the Schools, 44*(5), 495–502.

Wells, F., & Farthing, M. (2008). (Eds.). *Fraud and misconduct in biomedical research* (4th ed.). London: Royal Society of Medicine Press.

West, S. G., & Thoemmes, F. (2010). Campbell and Rubin's perspectives on causal inference. *Psychological Methods, 15*(1), 18–37.

Wetcher-Hendricks, D. (2006). Adjustments to the correction for attenuation. *Psychological Methods, 11*(2), 207–215.

Wiedemann, A. U., Lippke, S., Reuter, T., Ziegelmann, J. P., & Schwarzer, R. (2011). How planning facilitates behavior change: Additive and interactive effects of a randomized controlled trial. *European Journal of Social Psychology, 41*(1), 42–51.

Wiens, S., & Palmer, S. N. (2001). Quadratic trend analysis and heartbeat detection. *Biological Psychology, 58*(2), 159–175.

Wilcox, R. R. (2008). Sample size and statistical power. In A. M. Nezu & C. M. Nezu (Eds.), *Evidence-based outcome research: A practical guide to conducting randomized controlled trials for psychosocial interventions* (pp. 123–134). New York: Oxford University Press.

Wilkinson, L., and the Task Force on Statistical Inference, APA Board of Scientific Affairs (1999). Statistical methods in psychology journals: Guidelines and explanations. *American Psychologist, 54*(8), 594–604.

Williams, S. T., & Kores, R. C. (2011). Psychogenic polydipsia: Comparison of a community sample with an institutionalized population. *Psychiatry Research, 187*(1), 310–311.

Wilson, D. T., Wood, R., & Gibbons, R. (1991). *TESTFACT: Test scoring, item statistics, and item factor analysis.* Chicago: Scientific Software.

Wilson, W., Miller, H. L., & Lower, J. S. (1967). Much ado about the null hypothesis. *Psychological Bulletin, 67,* 188–196.

Winne, P. H., & Belfry, M. J. (1982). Interpretive problems when correcting for attenuation. *Journal of Educational Measurement, 19*(2), 125–134.

Wirth, R. J., & Edwards, M. C. (2007). Item factor analysis: Current approaches and future directions. *Psychological Methods, 12*(1), 58–79.

Woodward, T. S., & Hunter, M. A. (1999). Estimation of unattenuated factor loadings. *Journal of Educational and Behavioral Statistics, 24*(4), 384–397.

Wright, B. D., & Stone, M. H. (1979). *Best test design: Rasch measurement.* Chicago, IL: MESA Press.

Wright, B. D. (1997). A history of social science measurement. *Educational Measurement: Issues and Practice, 16,* 33–45.

Wright, D. B. (2006). Comparing groups in a before-after design: When t test and ANCOVA produce different results. *British Journal of Educational Psychology, 76,* 663–675.

Wu, A. D., & Zumbo, B. D. (2008). Understanding and using mediators and moderators. *Social Indicators Research, 87,* 367–392.

Wynn, R. (2006). Coercion in psychiatric care: Clinical, legal, and ethical controversies. *International Journal of Psychiatry in Clinical Practice, 10*(4), 247–251.

Yousfi, S. (2005). Myths and paradoxes of classical test theory: About test length, reliability, and validity. *Diagnostica, 51*(1), 1–11.

Yu, C. H. (2006). *Philosophical foundations of quantitative research methodology.* Lanham, MD: Rowman and Littlefield.

Yuan, K.-H., & Maxwell, S. (2005). On the post hoc power in testing mean differences. *Journal of Educational and Behavioral Statistics, 30*(2), 141–167.

Zientek, L. R., Capraro, M. M., & Capraro, R. M. (2008). Reporting practices in quantitative teacher education research: One look at the evidence cited in the AERA panel report. *Educational Researcher, 37*(4), 208–216.

Zimmerman, D. W. (2004). Inflation of Type I error rates by unequal variances associated with parametric, nonparametric, and rank-transformation tests. *Psicologica: International Journal of Methodology and Experimental Psychology, 25*(1), 103–133.

Zimmerman, D. W., & Williams, R. H. (1977). The theory of test validity and correlated errors of measurement. *Journal of Mathematical Psychology, 16,* 135–152.

Zimmerman, D. W., & Williams, R. H. (1997). Properties of the Spearman correction for attenuation for normal and realistic non-normal distributions. *Applied Psychological Measurement, 21*(3), 253–270.

Zimmerman, M. (2006). Developing brief scales for use in clinical practice: The reliability and validity of single-item self-report measures of depression symptom severity, psychosocial impairment due to depression, and quality of life. *Journal of Clinical Psychiatry, 67,* 1536–1541.

Zuccaro, C. (2010). Statistical alchemy: The misuse of factor scores in linear regression. *International Journal of Market Research, 52*(4), 511–531.

Zuckerman, M., Hodgins, H. S., Zuckerman, A., & Rosenthal, R. (1993). Contemporary issues in the analysis of data: A survey of 551 psychologists. *Psychological Science, 4*(1), 49–53.

Zumbo, B. D., & Hubley, A. M. (1998). A note on misconceptions concerning prospective and retrospective power. *The Statistician, 47*(Part 2), 385–388.

Zwick, W. R., & Velicer, W. F. (1986). Comparison of five rules for determining the number of components to retain. *Psychological Bulletin, 99,* 432–442.

INDEX

A
Advanced mixture modeling, 603–606
Aiken, Leona S., 26–51
Alternating least squares scaling (ALSCAL), 238
Alternative models for binary outcomes, 35–36
Analysis of variance (ANOVA)
    computations, 12–13
    introduction of concept, 8
Anderson, Rawni A., 718–758
Anselin, Luc, 154–174
Approximate discrete model, 427–428
Assumptions, violations of, 28–29
Autocorrelation, 459–460
    global, 156–158
    local, 158–159

B
Baraldi, Amanda N., 635–664
Bayesian configural frequency analysis, 86–87
Bayesian hierarchical models
    hierarchical spatial models, 167–168
    and imaging analytics, 188–189
Bayesian methods of analysis
    and mediation analysis, 343
    probability and inference, 186–187
Bayesian models for fMRI, 189–191
Beauchaine, Theodore P., 612–634
Binary classification tree, 682
Binary logistic regression, 33–37
Binary variables, 58–59
Binomial test, 108–109
Blokland, Gabriëlla A. M., 198–218
Bootstrap methods, 126–131
Brose, Annette, 441–457
Brown, Timothy A., 257–280
Buskirk, Trent D., 106–141

C
Card, Noel A., 701–717
Case diagnostics, 47–49
Casper, Deborah M., 701–717
Categorical methods, 52–73
    categorical variables, 52–61
        measuring strength of association between, 58–61
        testing for significant association between, 52–58
    conclusions and future directions, 71–72
    effect sizes, 64–66
    key terms, 55
    logistic regression, 66–71
        binary response, 66–69
        proportional odds model, 69–71
    symbols used, 53–55
Categorical variables
    measuring strength of association between, 58–61
    testing for significant association between, 52–58
Cell frequencies, and configural frequency analysis, 87
Chi-Square test, 119–122
Classical statistical approaches, overview of, 7–25
Classification and regression trees, 683–690
    cut-point and variable selection bias, 686–687
    examples of, 691, 692
    instability of trees, 690
    interpretation, 688–690
    prediction and interpretation, 688
    recursive partitioning, 683–684
    split selection criteria, 684–686
    stopping and pruning, 687
Classification techniques
    See Clustering and classification techniques
Cluster analysis and MDS, 239–240
Clustering and classification techniques, 517–550
    chapter notation, 522
    concluding remarks, 543
    finite mixture and latent class models, 530–543
        absolute fit assessment, 542
        class-specific item response probabilities, 533
        constrained latent class models, 535–537, 539–540
        diagnostic classification models, 535, 536–537, 539
        instrument calibration *vs.* respondent scaling, 533
        investigating relative performance, 540
        item-fit assessment, 542–543
        item response probabilities for five assessment items, 539
        latent classes as attribute profiles, 535
        local/conditional independence assumption, 533
        model-data fit at different levels, 540–541
        for multiple quantitative response variables, 532–533
        parameter constraints via the Q-matrix, 535–536
        parameter values for five assessment items, 538
        person-fit assessment, 543
        relative fit assessment, 541
        for single quantitative response variables, 531–532
        software packages for, 540
        statistical structure of unrestricted latent class model, 534–535
        unconstrained latent class models, 533–535
    foundational terminology, 519–522
        exploratory *vs.* confirmatory techniques, 520–521
        nonparametric *vs.* parametric model-based techniques, 520
        observations *vs.* variables, 519
        variable types *vs.* measurement scales, 519–520
    glossary of key terms, 544–546
    introduction to, 517–518
    nonparametric techniques, 522–530
        additional example, 530
        agglomerative *vs.* divisive approaches, 522
        basic concepts, 522
        distance measures for multivariate space, 525–526
        graphical representation, 523
        K-means clustering, 527–529
        measures of intercluster distance, 526–527
        numerical representation, 522–523
        partitioning cluster methods, 527–529
        pre-processing choices for hierarchical techniques, 523–527
        software for, 529–530
    range of applications, 518
    standardization formulas for cluster analysis, 524
    suggested readings, 521–522
        books, 521
        peer-reviewed publications, 521–522
        professional associations, 522

Cochran's Q, 115–117
Coefficient interpretation, 37–38, 41
The column problem, 145–146
Configural frequency analysis (CFA), 74–105
  appropriate questions for, 75–76
  base models, 78–80
  future directions, 102
  null hypothesis, 80–81
  sample models and applications, 89–102
    longitudinal CFA, 93–97
    mediation configural frequency analysis, 97–102
    prediction configural frequency analysis, 89–91
    two-group CFA, 91–93
  significance tests for, 81–86
    protecting ∀, 81–82
    sampling schemes, 82–86
  six steps of, 86–89
  symbols and definitions, 103
  technical elements of, 76–81
Contextual variable fallacies, 720–725
  avoiding hierarchically nested data structures, 724–725
  confusing moderation with additive effects, 724
  direct effect and evidence of mediation, 721–722
  mistaking mediation for moderation, 720–721
  testing mediation with constituent paths, 721
  using cross-sectional models to test mediation, 722–724
Continuous time, models of, 416–426
  conclusions and future directions, 426–427
  first-order differential equation model, 420–423
  second-order differential equation model, 423–426
Control variables, associations with, 61–64
Coombs' contribution to MDS, 238
Correspondence analysis, 142–153
  application to other data types, 151
  canonical correspondence analysis, 151–152
  correspondence analysis displays, 146–147
  introductory example, 143
  measure of fit, 150–151
  multiple correspondence analysis, 147–150
  principal component analysis and multidimensional scaling, 143–147
  statistical inference, 152
Coxe, Stefany, 26–51
Curve estimation methods, 131–137

D
Data mining, 678–700
  binary classification tree, 682
  conclusion, 698
  exemplary techniques, 681–697
    classification and regression trees, 683–690, 691, 692
    ensemble methods, 690–697
  introduction to, 678–681

  classical statistics, 678–679
  neo-classical statistics, 679–681
  other techniques, literature, and software, 697–698
Deboeck, Pascal R., 411–431
Dellinger, Anne, 4
Density estimation, nonparametric, 131–135
Deviation, concepts of, 87–88
Diagnostics, model and case, 47–49
Differential item functioning, 65–66
Diggle-Kenward selection model, 649, 660
Ding, Cody S., 235–256
Discrete-time survival factor mixture model, diagram, 605
Distance measures, 48–49
Donnellan, M. Brent, 665–677
Dowsett, Chantelle, 4
Dynamic causal models, 192
Dynamic factor analysis, 441–457
  background, 442–444
  five steps for conducting
    between-person differences, 449, 451
    empirical illustration, 446, 447, 448, 449, 451
    person-specific models, 448–449
    research questions, 446
    study design and data collection, 446–447
    variable selection and data preprocessing, 447–448
  future directions, 451–454
    adaptive guidance, 453–454
    idiographic filters, 454
    non-stationarity, 452–453
  glossary, 455
  synopsis, 454–455
  technical background, 444–445
Dynamical systems, 411–431
  approximate discrete model, 427–428
  attractors and self-regulation, 414–416
  concept of, 412–413
  conclusions and future directions, 426–427
  language of, 413–414
  latent differential equation modeling, 428–430
  models of continuous time, 416–419
    first-order differential equation model, 420–423
    second-order differential equation model, 423–426

E
Edgeworth, Francis Y., 8
Edwards, Michael, 4
Effect sizes
  and categorical methods, 64–66
  introduction of concept, 9
  recommendations for best practice, 23–24
Eigenvalues, 21–22
Electroencephalography, and statistical parametric mapping, 177
Enders, Craig K., 635–664
Ensemble methods, of data mining, 690–697
  bagging, 690–691
  predictions from ensembles, 693–695
  random forests, 691–693

  randomness, 696–697
  variable importance, 695–696
Error covariance matrix, 184–185
Estimation theory, 12–13
Event history data analysis, 486–516
  conclusion, 514
  continuous state space, 511–514
  continuous time formulation, 493–499
    basic concepts, 493–494
    examples, 497–498
    rate and probability, 499
    specifications and estimation, 496–497
  discrete state space, 509–511
  discrete time formulation, 492–493
  hazard-rate framework, 492–493
  motivation, 488, 490–492
    censoring and time-varying covariates, 488
    illustration of the censoring problem, 488, 490–491
    initial statement of the solution, 491–492
  observability of the dependent variable, 506–507
  problems created for standard techniques, 489
  repeated events, 507–509
  time-dependent covariates, 502–506
    basic ideas, 502–504
    data management, 505–506
    exogeneity of covariates, 504
    illustration, 506
    survivor function, 504–505
  time-independent covariates, 499–502
    coefficients, 500–502
    illustration, 502
Excess zeros, concept of, 43–44
Extensions to space-time, 160–162

F
Factor analysis
  fallacies, 739–743
    default use of orthogonal rotation, 741
    misuse of principal components, 739–740
    number of factors retained in EFA, 740–741
    other issues in factor analysis, 742
    summary, 742–743
    using CFA analysis to confirm EFA analysis, 741–742
  and MDS, 239
Finite mixture modeling, 551–611
  advanced mixture modeling, 603–606
  conclusion, 606–607
  future directions, 607
  history of mixture modeling, 554–557
    finite mixture modeling, 554–555
    latent class analysis, 555–556
    the more recent past, 556–557
  as latent variable models, 552
  list of abbreviations, 607–608
  as a person-centered approach, 552–554
Fisher, Ronald A., 8
Fisherian school of statistics, 8
Fisher's exact test, 119–122
Frequentist configural frequency analysis, 86–87
Friedman's test, 115–117
Functional magnetic resonance imaging

and analytic models and designs, 183–184
and statistical parametric mapping, 177
Functional magnetic resonance imaging (fMRI)
Bayesian models for, 189–191

G

Gaussian processes, 460
General linear model (GLM)
 overview of, 9
 three classes of, 13–20
 times series model at the voxel level, 185
Generalized linear models (GLiM), 26–51
 common examples, 31, 33–46
  binary logistic regression, 33–37
  multinomial logistic regression, 31, 37–38
  ordinal logistic regression, 31, 38–39
  other GLiMs, 46
  Poisson regression, 31, 39–44
  two-part models, 44–46
 diagnostics, 47–49
 introduction to, 26–27
 maximum likelihood estimation, 30–33
 multiple regression, 27–29
 pseudo-R-squared measures of fit, 46–47
 summary and conclusions, 49–50
 three components of a GLiM, 29–30
Genes, quantitative analysis of, 219–234
 association analysis, 227–233
  case-control association tests, 227–229
  family-based association tests, 230–232
  genome-wide association studies, 232–233
  population stratification, 229
  quality control and prior data cleaning, 227
 linkage analysis, 221–226
  background, 221–222
  types of, 222–226
 overview of genetic data, 219–221
  DNA variation, 220–221
  obtaining genotypic data, 220
 significance of linkage, 226–227
 summary, 233
Genetics, twin studies, 198–218
 classical twin model, 202–215
  assumptions of the model, 205–208
  extensions to the model, 208–211
  multivariate modeling, 211–215
  structural equation modeling, 203–205
 introduction and overview, 198–202
 twin studies and beyond, 215
Global autocorrelation, 156–158
Global configural frequency analysis, 79
Gossett, William S., 8
Gottschall, Amanda C., 338–360
Greenacre, Michael J., 142–153
Growth mixture model, diagram, 605

H

Harshman, R.A., 8
Hau, Kit-Tai, 361–386
Heteroscedasticity, 28

Hierarchical linear model, 185–186
History of traditional statistics, 8–9
Hox, Joop J., 281–294
Hurdle regression models, 44–45

I

Imaging data, analysis of
 analytic methods, 180–182
  foundational issues in neuroimaging, 181
  model basics, 181–182
 analytic models and designs
  functional magnetic imaging models, 183–184
  positron emission tomography, 182
 Bayesian methods of analysis, 186–187
 Bayesian models for fMRI, 189–191
 classic frequentist probability, 187–189
 conclusion and future directions, 195
 dynamic causal models, 192
 early approaches based on general linear method, 176–177
 functional connectivity, 191–192, 193–195
 history of imaging methods and analyses, 176
 modeling serial correlation, 184–185
  time series general linear model at the voxel level, 185
 multilevel models, 185–186
  expectation maximization, 185–186
 multivariate autoregressive models, 192–193
 parameter estimation, 182
 spatial normalization and topological influence, 177–182
  statistical parametric mapping, 179–180
  steps from image acquisition to analysis, 180
 statistical parametric mapping, 177
 structural equation modeling, 193–195
Imaging data, analysis of, 175–197
Individual differences MDS models, 238
Individual differences scaling (INDSCAL), 238, 246–247
Influence measures, 49
Intensive longitudinal data
 See longitudinal data, intensive
Interaction
 See Moderation
Interpretation, recommendations for best practice, 23–24
Introduction, 1–6

J

Johnson, David, 4

K

K-means clustering, 527–529
Kadlec, Kelly M., 295–337
Kendall's t, 117–119
Kisbu-Sakarya, Yasemin, 338–360
Kruskal-Wallis test, 113–115
Kruskal's contribution to MDS, 237–238

L

Land use planning models, 170–171
Latent class analysis, 557–584
 a brief history of, 555–556
 mediation model, 605
 missing data, 573–584
 model building, 565–573
 model estimation, 561–565
 model formulation, 557–558
 model interpretation, 558–561
Latent differential equation modeling, 428–430
Latent mixture modeling, diagram, 605
Latent profile analysis, 584–606
 example of, 592–600
 example of latent class regression, 602–603
 latent class regression, 600–601
 model building, 590–592, 601–602
 model estimation, 590
 model formulation, 584–587, 601
 model interpretation, 587–590
 post hoc class comparisons, 603
Latent transition model, diagram, 605
Latent variable interpretation, 35
Latent variable measurement models, 257–280
 conclusion, 276–277
 confirmatory factor analysis, 260–266
 exploratory factor analysis, 258–260
 extensions of confirmatory factor analysis, 269–273
 future directions, 277–279
 higher-order models, 273–276
 hybrid latent variable measurement models, 266–269
 selected output for confirmatory factor analysis, 263
 selected output for exploratory structural equation modeling, 268–269
Lee, Jason and Steve, 4
Leverage measures, 48
Limited dependent variables, 28–29
Linear regression model, 163–165
Linearity, 28–29
Linkage analysis
 model-based linkage, 222–223
 model-free linkage, 223–226
Little, Todd D., 1–16, 387–410, 718–758
Local autocorrelation, 158–159
Location models, 169–170
Logistic regression, 66–71
 binary response, 66–69
  model fit, 66–67
  parameter interpretation, 68–69
 proportional odds model, 69–71
Longitudinal configural frequency analysis, 93–97
Longitudinal data, intensive, 432–440
 challenges and opportunities, 438–439
 idiographic-nomothetic continuum, 434–437
 reactivity, 436–437
 review of, 433
 recurring themes, 433–434
 sources of data, 433
 statistical models, 437–438
Longitudinal data analysis, 387–410
 advances in modeling, 406–407
 conclusion and discussion, 406–407

INDEX | 761

importance of, 387–389
multilevel modeling approach, 389–397
   curvilinear growth curve model, 392–393
   error structures, 396
   linear growth curve model, 389–392
   nonlinear growth curve model, 393–394
   spline curve models, 395
   time-constant covariates, 396–397
   time-varying covariates, 397
structural equation modeling approaches, 397–406
   autoregressive cross-lagged models, 401–402
   curvilinear latent curve model, 398–399
   general assumptions, 405–406
   latent difference score models, 403
   linear latent curve model, 397–398
   nonlinear latent curve model, 399–401
   parallel process latent curve model, 403–404
   second-order latent curve model, 404–405
Longitudinal mediation, 351–353
Lucas, Richard E., 665–677

M

MacKinnon, David P., 338–360
Magnetic resonance imaging
   and analytic models and designs, 183–184
   Bayesian models for, 189–191
   and statistical parametric mapping, 177
Mair, Patrick, 74–105
Marsh, Herbert W., 361–386
Masyn, Katherine E., 551–611
Maximum likelihood
   estimation, 30–33
   and MDS, 238–239, 250–251
McArdle, John J., 295–337
McNemar's test, 110–113
Mean, estimation of, 460
Measure of fit, 150–151
Measurement error fallacies, 725–730
   ignorance of latent mixture and multilevel structure, 728–729
   individual items and composite scores, 726–728
   the myth about numbers, 725–726
   reliability and test length, 728
   unreliability and attenuated effects, 729–730
Mediation analysis, 338–360
   causal inference in, 348–351
      experimental designs, 350–351
      principal stratification, 350
      sequential ignorability assumption, 348–350
   estimating the mediated effect, 340–342
      assumptions, 341
      coefficients approach, 340–341
      covariates, 341
      multiple mediators, 341–342
      point estimation, 340–342
      standard error, 342
   history, 339
   longitudinal mediation, 351–353
      autoregressive models, 352
      latent change score models, 352–353
      latent growth curve models, 352
      person-centered approaches, 353
      three (or more)-wave models, 351–353
      two-wave models, 351
   mediation analysis in groups, 345–348
      moderation and mediation, 346–347
      multilevel mediation, 347–348
   modern appeal, 339–340
   significance testing and confidence interval estimation, 342–345
      Bayesian methods, 343
      categorical and count outcomes, 343–344
      effect size measures, 343
      non-normality, 344
      small samples, 344–345
   summary and future directions, 353–354
Mediation configural frequency analysis, 97–102
   decisions concerning type, 98–102
   four base models for, 97–98
Medical imaging
   Bayesian models for fMRI, 189–191
   connectivity of brain regions, 191–192
   issues in neuroimaging, 181
   and statistical parametric mapping, 177
Medland, Sarah E., 198–218, 219–234
Meta-analysis, 701–717
   advanced topics, 715–716
      alternative effect sizes, 715
      artifact corrections, 715–716
      multivariate meta-analysis, 716
   analysis of mean effect sizes, 710–713
      fixed-effects means, 711
      heterogeneity, 711–712
      random-effects means, 712–713
   coding effect sizes, 707–710
      computing effect sizes, 709–710
      correlation coefficient, 708
      odds ratios, 709
      standardized mean differences, 708–709
   coding study characteristics, 707
   introduction to, 701–702
   moderator analyses, 713–715
      categorical moderators, 714–715
      limitations to, 715
      single categorical moderator, 713–714
      single continuous moderator, 714
   problem formulation, 702–705
      appropriate questions for meta-analysis, 702–703
      critiques of meta-analysis, 703–704
      identifying goals and research questions, 703
      limits of, 704–705
      strengths of, 705
   searching the literature, 705–707
      defining a sampling frame, 705
      identifying criteria, 705
      search techniques and resource identification, 705–707
Metric MDS model, 237
MIMIC data, 323–334
Missing data fallacies, 730–732
   attempting to prepare for missing data, 732
   missing-data treatments and notion of "cheating," 730–732
Missing data methods, 635–664
   artificial data example, 636–637
   atheoretical missing data handling methods, 639–641
      averaging available items, 639–640
      last observation carried forward imputation, 640
      mean imputation, 639
      similar response pattern imputation, 640–641
   conclusion, 661–662
   data analysis examples, 653–657
      complete data, 653–654
      missing at random data, 654–655, 656
      missing completely at random data, 654, 655
      not missing at random-based approaches revisited, 656–657
      not missing at random data, 655–656
   improving missing at random-based analyses, 650–653
      dealing with non-normal data, 652–653
      role of auxiliary variables, 650–651
   missing at random (MAR), 642–648
      maximum likelihood estimation, 645–648
      multiple imputation, 642–645
      stochastic regression imputation, 642
   missing completely at random (MCAR), 641–642, 654
      deletion methods, 641–642
      regression imputation, 641
   missing data mechanisms, 637–639
   not missing at random, 648–650
   planned missing data designs, 657–661
      longitudinal designs, 661
      three-form design, 659–661
      two-method measurement, 658–659
Model diagnostics, 47
Modeling
   See individual types of modeling
Models
   See individual model types
Moderation, 361–386
   analysis of variance, 364–365
   classic definition of, 362–363
   confounding nonlinear and interaction effects, 379–380
   distribution-analytic approaches, 377–378
   further research, 379
   graphs of interaction effects, 363–364
   interactions with more than two continuous variables, 381–382
   latent variable approaches, 374–375, 378
   and mediation, 346–347, 380–381
   moderated multiple regression approaches, 365–373
      disordinal interactions, 371–372
      interactions with continuous observed variables, 369–371
      multicollinearity involved with product terms, 372–373
      power in detecting interactions, 372
      standardized solutions for models with interactions terms, 368
      tests of statistical significance of interaction effects, 368–369

multilevel designs and clustered samples, 383
multiple group SEM approach to interaction, 375
non-latent approaches
  for observed variables, 364
  traditional approaches to interaction effects, 373–374
SEMs with product indicators, 375–377
  latent interaction, 376–377
separate group multiple regression, 365
summary, 378–379
tests of measurement invariance, 382–383
vs. causal ordering, 380–381
Molenaar, Peter C. M., 441–457
Morin, Alexandre J. S., 361–386
Mosing, Miriam A., 198–218
Mulaik, S. A., 8
Multidimensional scaling (MDS), 235–256
basics and applications of MDS models, 240–254
  computer programs for MDS analysis, 251–252
  individual differences models, 246–250
  metric model, 242–243
  new applications, 252–254
  nonmetric model, 243–246
  using maximum likelihood estimation, 250–251
  variety of data, 240–242
a brief description of MDS(X) programs, 253
and cluster analysis, 239–240
conclusion, 254
future directions, 254–255
historical review, 237–240
  four stages of MDS development, 237–239
and principal component analysis, 143–147
terminology and symbols, 236
Multilevel models
diagram of latent class model, 605
the hierarchical linear model, 185–186
Multilevel regression modeling
conclusion, 291
future directions, 291, 293
introduction, 281–282
key terms and symbols, 292
methodological and statistical issues, 289–291
  assumptions, 289–290
  further important issues, 290–291
  sample size, 290
typical applications, 282–286
  individuals within groups, 282–283
  measurement occasions within individuals, 283–286
Multilevel structural equation modeling
conclusion, 291
future directions, 291, 293
introduction, 281–282
key terms and symbols, 292
methodological and statistical issues, 289–291
  assumptions, 289–290
  further important issues, 290–291
  sample size, 290
typical applications, 286–289
  latent curve modeling, 286–287
Multinomial logistic regression, 31, 37–38
Multiple regression
assumptions, 27–28
limited dependent variables, 28–29
Multivariate statistics, 20–23
Mun, Eun-Young, 74–105
Murray, Alan T., 154–174

N

Nagengast, Benjamin, 361–386
Negative binomial regression, 31, 42–43
Neyman, Jerzy, 8
Neyman-Pearson school of statistics, 8
Non-normality, 28, 344
Nonmetric MDS model, 237–238
Nonparametric statistical techniques, 106–141
classical nonparametric methods, 108–122
  comparing more than two samples, 113–117
  comparing two dependent samples, 110–113
  comparing two independent samples, 109–110
  methods based on a single sample, 108–109
  nonparametric analysis of nominal data, 119–122
  nonparametric correlation coefficients, 117–119
curve estimation methods, 131–137
  density estimation, 131–135
  extensions to multiple regression, 137
  simple nonparametric regression, 135–137
future directions, 138–139
glossary of terms, 139–140
modern resampling-based methods, 122–131
  applying permutation tests to one sample, 122–
  bootstrap confidence interval methods, 129–130
  bootstrap methods, 126–129
  bootstrap methods and permutation tests, 131
  general permutation tests, 122
  other applications of bootstrap methods, 130–131
  statistical software for conducting, 137
vs. parametric methods, 137–138
Null hypothesis
  in configural frequency analysis (CFA), 80–81

O

Optimization modeling, 168–171
Ordinal logistic regression, 31, 38–39
Ordinal variables, 59–61
Organization of *Handbook of Quantitative Methods*, 2–4
Orthogonal rotation, 741

Overdispersed Poisson regression, 42–43
Overdispersion, 36–37, 41–42

P

P calculated values
  introduction of, 8
Parameter estimates and fit statistics, 450
Pearson, Karl and Egon S., 8
Pearson's computations, 10–11
Permutation tests, 122–126
  applying to one sample, 122–123
  applying to two samples, 123, 125–126
  full enumeration of eight samples, 124
Person-specific process, 443, 448–449, 450, 451, 455
Petersen, Trond, 486–516
Poisson regression, 31, 39–44
Population stratification, 229
Positron emission tomography
  and analytic models and designs, 182–183
  and statistical parametric mapping, 177
Practical significance effect sizes, 9, 13–15
Preacher, Kris, 4
Prediction configural frequency analysis, 89–91
Preference MDS models, 247
Price, Larry R., 175–197
Principal component analysis, 143–147
Proportional odds model, 69–71
Pseudo-R-squared measures of fit, 46–47

Q

Q-matrix, 535–536, 537
Quantitative research methodology, common fallacies in, 718–758
  concluding remarks, 743, 748
  contextual variable fallacies, 720–725
    avoiding hierarchically nested data structures, 724–725
    confusing moderation with additive effects, 724
    direct effect and evidence of mediation, 721–722
    mistaking mediation for moderation, 720–721
    testing mediation with constituent paths, 721
    using cross-sectional models to test mediation, 722–724
  factor analysis fallacies, 739–743
    default use of orthogonal rotation, 741
    misuse of principal components, 739–740
    number of factors retained in EFA, 740–741
    other issues in factor analysis, 742
    summary, 742–743
    using CFA analysis to confirm EFA analysis, 741–742
  introduction to, 718–720
  measurement error fallacies, 725–730
    ignorance of latent mixture and multilevel structure, 728–729
    individual items and composite scores, 726–728
    the myth about numbers, 725–726
    reliability and test length, 728
    unreliability and attenuated effects, 729–730

missing data fallacies, 730–732
   attempting to prepare for missing data, 732
   missing-data treatments and notion of "cheating," 730–732
statistical power fallacies, 736–739
   lack of retrospective power and null hypothesis, 737
   nonsignificance and null hypothesis, 736–737
   statistical power as a single, unified concept, 736
   summary and recommendations, 737–739
statistical significance fallacies, 732–735
   alternative paradigms, 735
   alternatives and solutions, 734–735
   p-values and strength of effect, 733
   p-values reflect replicability, 734
   relationship between significant findings and study success, 734
   significance of p-value and research hypothesis, 733
   statistical significance and practical importance, 733–734
summary checklist, 743–748

R

R Code, 332–334
Raju, N.S., 8
Ram, Nilam, 441–457
Regional configural frequency analysis, 79–80
Regression analysis, spatial, 162–168
Regression mixture model, diagram, 605
Regression specification, 163
Regression time series models, 475–478
Replicability, 18–20, 24
Rey, Sergio J., 154–174
Rhemtulla, Mijke, 4
The row problem, 145
Rupp, André A., 517–550

S

Scatterplot smoothing, 135–137
Secondary data analysis, 665–677
   advantages and disadvantages, 667–668
   conclusion, 675
   measurement concerns in existing data sets, 671–673
   missing data in existing data sets, 673–674
   primary research vs. secondary research, 666–667
   sample weighting in existing data sets, 674–675
   steps for beginning, 669–671
Selig, James P., 387–410
SEM-CALIS, 325–329
SEM-Mplus, 329–332
Serial correlation, modeling, 184–185
Sign test, 110–113
Significance testing
   in configural frequency analysis, 88–89
   and control variables, 61–64
Significant association, testing for, 52–58
Significant difference, introduction of term, 8

Snedecor, George W., 8
Software, statistical
   development of, 2
   for finite mixture and latent class models, 540
   for nonparametric techniques, 137, 529–530
Space-time, extensions to, 160–162
Spatial analysis, 154–174
   autocorrelation analysis, 156–162
   conclusion, 171–172
   exploratory spatial data analysis, 155–162
      spatial autocorrelation analysis, 156–159
      spatial clustering, 160–162
      spatial data, 155–156
   spatial optimization modeling, 168–169, 168–171
   spatial regression analysis, 162–168
      other spatial models, 166–168
      spatial dependence in the linear regression model, 163–165
      spatial effects in regression specifications, 163
      specification of spatial heterogeneity, 165–166
Spatial data, 155–156
Spearman's p, 117–119
Statistical approaches, overview of traditional methods, 7–25
   ANOVA computations, 12–13
   brief history of traditional statistics, 8–9
   general linear model, 9, 13–20
   variance partitions, 9–12
Statistical estimation theory, 12–13
Statistical inference, 152
Statistical parametric mapping, and medical imaging, 177
Statistical power fallacies, 736–739
   lack of retrospective power and null hypothesis, 737
   nonsignificance and null hypothesis, 736–737
   statistical power as a single, unified concept, 736
   summary and recommendations, 737–739
Statistical significance, 15–18
   fallacies, 732–735
      alternative paradigms, 735
      alternatives and solutions, 734–735
      p-values and strength of effect, 733
      p-values reflect replicability, 734
      relationship between significant findings and study success, 734
      significance of p-value and research hypothesis, 733
      statistical significance and practical importance, 733–734
   p calculated values, 8
   recommendations for best practice, 23
   vs. practical significance, 9
Strobl, Carolin, 678–700
Structural equation modeling, 193–195
   common factors and latent variables
      benefits and limitations of including common factors, 315
      common factors with cross-sectional observations, 315–316

common factors with longitudinal observations, 316–317
common factors with multiple longitudinal observations, 317–319
the future of, 319–321
and longitudinal data analysis, 397–406
as a tool, 311–315
   creating expectations, 312
   estimating linear multiple regression, 313–315
   as general data analysis technique, 311–312
   statistical indicators, 312–313
See also Structural equation models
Structural equation models, 295–337
   appendix: notes and computer programs, 321–334
      example of structural equation model fitting, 322–334
      fitting simulated MIMIC data with R Code, 332–334
      fitting simulated MIMIC data with SEM-CALIS, 325–329
      fitting simulated MIMIC data with SEM-Mplus, 329–332
      fitting simulated MIMIC data with standard modeling software, 323–325
      reconsidering simple linear regression, 321–322
   common factors and latent variables, 302–311
      benefits and limitations of including common factors, 315
      common factor models, 303–304
      common factor models within latent path regression, 305
      common factors with cross-sectional observations, 315–316
      common factors with longitudinal observations, 316–317
      common factors with multiple longitudinal observations, 317–319
      invariant common factors, 305–307
      multiple repeated measures, 307–311
   concept of, 298–302
      issues with means and covariances, 302
      missing predictors, 300
      path analysis diagrams, 299–300
      true feedback loops, 302
      unreliability of both predictors and outcomes, 301–302
      unreliable outcomes, 301
      unreliable predictors, 300–301
   confirmatory factor analysis, 296–297
   current state of research, 298
   currently available SEM programs, 311
   definition of, 295–296
   the future of, 319–321
   linear structural equation model (LISREL), 297
   with product indicators, 375–377
   as a tool, 311–315
      creating expectations, 312
      estimating linear multiple regression, 313–315
      and general data analysis, 311–312
      statistical indicators, 312–313
See also Structural equation modeling

T

T-test, introduction of, 8
Taxometrics, 612–634
  conclusion, 630
  other important considerations, 627–630
    number of indicators, 628
    other approaches, 629–630
    replication, 628–629
    sample size, 628
    skew, 628
  performing a taxometric analysis, 617–627
    assessing fit, 623–626
    interpreting results, 626–627
    selecting suitable indicators, 617–620
    taxon group and complement class, 618, 626
    winnowing indicators, 620–623
  problems with imprecise measures, 613–614
  taxometric methods, 614–617
    latent mode factor analysis, 617
    maximum covariance, 615–616
    maximum eigenvalue (MAXEIG), 616–617, 618
    mean above minus below a cut (MAMBAC), 614–615, 616, 622, 625
Testing for significant association, 52–58
Thompson, Bruce, 7–25
Time series analysis, 458–485
  commonly used terms, notations, and equations, 483–484
  concluding remarks and future directions, 482–484
  fundamental concepts, 459–461
    autocorrelation, 459
    estimating mean, variance, and autocorrelation, 460
    moving average and autoregressive representations, 460–461
    partial autocorrelation, 459–460
    strictly and weakly stationary processes, 459
    white noise and Gaussian processes, 460
  intervention and outlier analysis, 471–473
  regression time series models, 475–478
    regression with autocorrelated errors, 476
    regression with heteroscedasticity, 477–478
  time series forecasting, 469–471
    forecasting example, 471
    updating forecasts, 470–471
  time series model building, 464–469
    diagnostic checking, 466
    illustrative example of, 467–469
    model identification, 464–465
    model selection, 466–467
    parameter estimation, 466
  transfer function models, 473–475
  univariate time series models, 461–464
    nonstationary time series models, 462–463
    seasonal time series models, 462–463, 463–464
    stationary time series models, 461–462
  vector time series models, 478–482
    cointegrated processes, 480–481
    correlation and partial correlation matrix functions, 478–479
    identification of, 481–482
    nonstationary vector time series models, 480–481
    stationary vector time series models, 479–480, 482
Tomazic, Terry J., 106–141
Traditional statistical approaches, overview of, 7–25
Transfer function models, 473–475
Trees
  See Classification and regression trees
Truncated zeros, 44
Twin model, classical, 202–215
  assumptions of the model, 205–208
    degrees of genetic similarity, 206
    equal environments, 206–207
    generalizability, 205
    genotype-environment correlation, 207–208
    genotype-environment interaction, 207
    random mating, 205–206
  extensions to the model
    data from additional family members, 210–211
    liability threshold model, 209–210
    sex limitation, 208–209
  multivariate modeling
    causal model, 214
    common pathway model, 211–213
    cross-sectional cohort and longitudinal designs, 213–214
    independent pathway model, 213
    latent class analysis, 214–215
    structural equation modeling, 203–205
  See also Genetics, twin studies
Two-group configural frequency analysis, 91–93
Two-part models, 44–46

U

Univariate statistics, 9–12, 22–23

V

Variables
  See individual variable types
Variance, estimation of, 460
Variance partitions, 9–12, 20–23
Vector time series models, 478–482
Verweij, Karin J. H., 198–218
Von Eye, Alexander, 74–105
Von Weber, Stefan, 74–105

W

Walls, Theodore A., 432–440
Wang, Lihshing Leigh, 718–758
Watts, Amber S., 718–758
Wei, William W. S., 458–485
Weighted Euclidean Model, 238, 246–247
Wen, Zhonglin, 361–386
West, Stephen G., 26–51
What if There Were No Significance Tests (Mulaik, Raju, Harshman), 8
White noise process, 460
Wilcoxon Mann Whitney test, 109–110
Wilcoxon signed rank test, 110–113
Willoughby, Lisa M., 106–141
Woods, Carol M., 52–73
Wu, Wei, 387–410

Z

Zero-inflated regression models, 45–46
Zimmerman, Chad, 4